The Burgeoning European Print Trade

To Ger Luijten (1956–2022),
for his engaging enthusiasm, curiosity, and generous, open spirit,
from which so many have benefited.

THE BURGEONING EUROPEAN PRINT TRADE

The Distribution of Prints via the Plantin-Moretus Press of Antwerp

KAREN L. BOWEN AND DIRK IMHOF

HARVEY MILLER PUBLISHERS

HARVEY MILLER PUBLISHERS
An imprint of Brepols Publishers
London / Turnhout

www.harveymillerpublishers.com

British Library Cataloguing in Publication Data
A catalogue record of this book is available from
the British Library.

ISBN 978-1-915487-07-0
D/2025/0095/193

Designed by Paul van Calster

Printed and bound in the EU on acid-free paper.

TABLE OF CONTENTS

ACKNOWLEDGEMENTS

We are indebted to several institutions and individuals for their assistance with the completion of this project. We were honored to receive grants to facilitate the production of this book from both the Association of Print Scholars and the Frits and To Lugt Study Fund of the Fondation Custodia. Additionally, the beneficent, open-access policies of numerous repositories of printed matter have made it possible to provide numerous, edifying illustrations. Furthermore, we are indebted, in particular, to the following individuals for their exceptional help in locating and obtaining reproductions of specific images: Daan van Heesch of the Prints and Drawings Department of the Royal Library of Belgium, Brussels; Bernd W. Mayer of the Sammlung der Fürsten zu Waldburg-Wolfegg, Wolfegg; Nadine Orenstein of the Metropolitan Museum of Art, New York City; Stanislaw Rusch of the Wallraf-Richartz-Museum & Fondation Corboud, Graphische Sammlung, Cologne; and last, but far from least, Nico de Brabander and Denis van Velthoven from the Plantin-Moretus Museum of Antwerp. Above all, however, we are grateful for the enduring support and interest in our research, as well as for the helpful criticism kindly offered throughout our work on this project, from Marjolein Leesberg, the compiler of numerous Hollstein volumes, and David John McKitterick, of Trinity College, Cambridge: both are eminent colleagues and valued friends.

NOTE TO THE READER

The following conventions are used in this book:

Spelling
The spelling of words in transcriptions and titles has been normalized as follows:

- The use of *u* and *v*, as well as *i* and *j* have been normalized according to modern norms.
- Standard abbreviations, such as *q'* (for "que") and *ū* or *ā* (for "um" or "am", for example) have been written out in full.

Place Names
In this book, when we mention the Low Countries generally (or subdivided into the Northern and Southern Netherlands, when appropriate), we are referring to how they existed in the sixteenth and early seventeenth centuries. Places such as Douai and St. Omer, which were then part of the Low Countries but are now part of France, will be discussed as part of the Southern Netherlands. Cities that were then associated with the Holy Roman Empire, for instance Vienna and Prague, will be included in the discussions of the (German) empire (or will simply be referred to as German cities).

Measurements
All measurements are given in millimeters, with height preceding width.

Weights
One pound (lb.) in Antwerp in the sixteenth and seventeenth centuries was slightly less than half a kilo (0.470 kilo).[1] In 1614, one Antwerp pound was slightly heavier than one German pound.[2]

Currency
Unless noted otherwise, all of the sums of money in the cited records from the Plantin-Moretus Press were noted in florins (= fl.), which is another name for Carolus or Brabant guilders. The following equivalencies are relevant here:

1 florin (fl.) or Carolus or Brabant guilder = 20 stuivers (or patards) (st.); where:
  1 stuiver = 4 oorden (or: 1 "oortje" = 1/4 st.)
  1 stuiver = 3 Brabant denier (d.) (or 1 denier = 1/3 st.)
  3 stuivers = 4 "blank" (or: 1 "blank" = 3/4 st.)
  1 "blank" = 3 oorden

1 florin = 2 Parisian pounds, or livre de Paris
2 florins = 1 Spanish "escus", or escudos
6 florins = 1 Flemish pound, or groten Vlaams (£)
  = 20 Flemish schellingen (sh.), or sou = 240 Flemish deniers (d.); where: 1 schelling = 6 stuivers

Because payments made at the Frankfurt fairs often involved a variety of currencies, each of which may have been subject to its own local variations, we will be discussing any such values in terms of their equivalents in Brabant guilders as they were given in the accounts of the Plantin-Moretus Press.

Owing to ever fluctuating rates of currency, it is difficult to give a current (modern) value for the currencies used. Rather, often the most effective means of putting these values in some sort of perspective is by comparing them with contemporary wages, the purchasing power of certain groups of people, or the price of other contemporary products. A full range of print prices is given in the Appendix. Comparison can be made with the values of wages of Antwerp masons and a sampling of prices for books of hours and missals produced by the Plantin-Moretus Press, both of which are given in the table below. For a more detailed list of monetary values, as well as weights and measures, in different regions in Flanders, see Wyffels 1959 and Vandewalle 1984.

Sample Wages and Book Prices in Antwerp, ca. 1570–ca. 1640
See Scholliers 1976 and Scholliers 1989 for examples of the daily summer wages paid to masons working in Antwerp during the sixteenth and seventeenth centuries and their value relative to the prices of other commodities. See Voet, PP for the prices and numbers of sheets of the books of hours and missals from the 1570s and 1580s cited below. See MPM Arch. M 39, under the given year, for the prices and numbers of sheets of each of the cited books of hours and missals published between 1600 and 1642. Finally, see Imhof 2014a, cat. O-15, for the price and size of the book of hours from 1591. This sampling is offered as a general point of reference for the various specific prices noted in the course of the text. However, as is discussed in the introductory remarks to Appendix 1, changes in the prices of individual prints and print series (or the lack thereof) do not appear to have reflected any broader financial trends. For an example of the challenges in comparing prices in different commodities and books in particular, see Booton, Nuovo, and Proot 2022.

Year	*Assistant mason*	*Master mason*	*Book of hours in 24 with woodcut illustrations*	*Missal in large folio with engraved illustrations*
ca. 1570	7 st.	12 st.	1565 ed. (PP 1353) with 9 sheets: 3 st. 1572 ed. (PP 1767) possibly with 14 sheets:[3] 4½ st.	1574 ed. (PP 1685) possibly with 194 sheets: 7 fl. 5 st. (= 145 st.)[4]
ca. 1580	10 st.	18 st.	1575 ed. (PP 1778) with 12 sheets: 5 st.	(none known)
ca. 1590	12 st.	18 st.	1591 ed. with 11½ sheets: 6 st.	1587 ed. (PP 1700) with 168 sheets: 7 fl. 10 st. (= 150 st.)
ca. 1600	14 st.	22-24? st.	1601 ed. with 11½ sheets: 6 st.	1599 ed. with 167 sheets: 10 fl. (= 200 st.)
ca. 1610	14 st.	24 st.	1609 ed. with 12½ sheets: 8 st.	1610 ed. with 176 sheets: 10 fl. 10 st. (= 210 st.)
ca. 1620	14 st.	24 st.	1619 ed. with 12 sheets: 8 st.	1620 ed. with 197 sheets: 13 fl. (= 260 st.)
ca. 1630	14 st.	24 st.	1629 ed. with 13 sheets: 9 st.	1630 ed. with 202 sheets: 13 fl. 10 st. (=270 st.)
ca. 1640	14 st.	24 st.	1638 ed. with 14 sheets: 14 st.	1642 ed. with 207 sheets: 14 fl. (= 280 st.)

Book Formats

Although the focus here is on prints, some archival records indicate the relative size of either the prints or the individual leaves of paper on which certain images were printed. These indications of size were derived from the standard subdivisions of book formats, which was the intuitive point of reference for booksellers and their record keepers. Hence, the following information is provided as a context for such citations. The format of a book is determined by the number of times the original sheet of paper has been folded (and possibly cut) in order to form the individual leaves of paper making up the book. Consequently, a book's format provides an indication of the relative size of these leaves, although the size of the original sheets of paper used to print the book could vary.[5] The standard book formats mentioned in this volume are:

- folio (f°) = two leaves per full sheet of paper (on which as many as four pages could be printed);
- quarto (4°) = four leaves per full sheet of paper;
- octavo (8°) = eight leaves per full sheet of paper;
- duodecimo (12°) = twelve leaves per full sheet of paper;
- vigesimoquarto (24°) = twenty-four leaves per full sheet of paper;
- trigesimosecundo (32°) = thirty-two leaves per full sheet of paper.

During the sixteenth and seventeenth centuries, paper was typically sold in reams (usually called "riemen" or "rames" in the Plantin archives) or quires (usually called "boeken" or "mains" in the Plantin archives); one ream of paper comprised 500 whole sheets, or twenty quires of twenty-five sheets each.[6]

Print Formats and Units for Sale

Prints were sold individually, in series (or suites) of prints, and as print books (or books of prints, a phrase that Antony

Griffiths notes is often used in a broader sense. Griffiths defines print series as "sequences of prints that belonged to a single publisher and were sold together as a unit without letterpress text".[7] Print books, by contrast, typically contained a relatively large number of plates along with some form of a title page, which was usually engraved, and a brief introductory text (engraved or printed in letterpress). The latter may be a dedication or an explanation of the origin, content, or significance of the images. Among the transactions of the Plantin-Moretus Press in the sixteenth and early seventeenth centuries, print books (like ordinary printed books) were usually sold as self-contained units, without bindings and at a standard price per book. Single prints and print series, however, were sold either individually or together in bulk, as part of a larger group of leaves of paper with a variable number of images printed on them.[8]

Sometimes, it is possible to glean information about the actual dimensions of images associated with certain book formats. For example, in 1602, a selection of prints sold by Anton Wierix II were distinguished by a specific format. Occasionally, the identification indicates that an 8° or 16° format corresponded roughly to a print with a ca. 98 × 64 mm or 81 × 59 mm plate mark, respectively.[9] There are also several examples of images identified as being in 4°. While most of these prints have plate marks of ca. 150 × 100 mm, a few are inexplicably large (ca. 240 × 325 mm), suggesting that either some error was made by the record keeper or else that the image was printed on an exceptionally large sheet of paper.[10]

In other cases, the amount or type of paper used to print the images was cited to indicate their general size. For example, on 12 February 1580, Diericx sold Plantin "6 vander jacht groot Jo: Stradani in f° real met compartimenten van 6 bladeren" (6 of the large hunts by Johannes Stradanus in royal folio [paper] with compartments (or frames) with 6 leaves [each]).[11] On 15 February 1581, when she supplied him with additional sets of the same print series, they were identified as: "12 dobbel bladeren 2 cachie gra[nd] stradanj" (12 double leaves, 2 large hunts [by] Stradanus).[12] The combination of these records and the known dimensions of the prints in this series (ca. 327 × 448 mm) indicate that what was then referred to as a "double leaf" of royal folio paper is roughly the same as an A3 leaf of paper today, which is twice the size of a standard A4 leaf of paper.

The use of the term "double leaf" for these larger prints is also consistent with the use of the term "enkel bladeren" (single leaves) for images that, like Stradanus's smaller hunts, are roughly the size of an A4 leaf of paper.[13] Other records of Diericx's supply of exceptionally large prints confirm these general size relationships. For example, on 16 December 1573, she sold Plantin several of her husband's large engravings from the 1550s, including Giorgio Ghisi's *Adoration of the Shepherds* after Agnolo Bronzino (ca. 662 × 452 mm) and Joannes and Lucas van Doetecum's *Resurrection of Christ* after Frans Floris (ca. 638 × 445 mm), both of which were printed from two plates. In both cases, the size of the print is described as "2 bladeren dobbel" (2 double leaves), and the dimensions of the prints are, in fact, roughly twice the size of Stradanus's large hunts with frames.[14]

Together, these records document the following general progression of sizes for prints published in Antwerp over the later sixteenth and early seventeenth centuries; the measurements suggested below are based on the preceding examples:

- 2 double leaves (ca. 650 × 450 mm)
- double leaves (ca. 330 × 450 mm) (comparable to an A3 format today)
- single leaves (ca. 220 × 300 mm) (comparable to an A4 format today), which was the standard size for leaves of paper when prints were sold in bulk in quires of twenty-five leaves;
- smaller sizes identified in the book formats of 4°, 8°, 16°, 24°, and 32°, a few of which can be linked with the following general dimensions:
  - 4°: ca. 150 × 100 mm
  - 8°: ca. 98 × 64 mm
  - 16°: ca. 81 × 59 mm

Archival References

The vast majority of the archival documents and other primary sources cited here are preserved in the Plantin-Moretus Museum in Antwerp.[15] References to these items typically consist of the following: the abbreviations "MPM" (for the Plantin-Moretus Museum) and "Arch." (for archive) or "M" (for manuscript), followed by a number. The full title of each archival document or manuscript is given in the bibliography.

Usually, one of three basic systems was used to identify the pages in these record books:

1. Conventional (modern) page numbers (reflected in the notes here by the abbreviations "p." or "pp.");
2. A standard folio system, whereby a number (e.g., 30) was noted only in the upper right corner of the right-hand page and that page is then identified as "fol. 30 recto" (or abbreviated as "fol. 30r") and the subsequent page (on the back) as "fol. 30 verso" (or abbreviated as "fol. 30v");

3 An accounting system, whereby one number (e.g., 50) was written in the upper corners of both pages in a single opening of a "debit-credit" balance, which consists of the recto of the right-hand leaf and the verso of the preceding leaf. In this case, we refer to the right and left sides of the single opening, with the following abbreviations: e.g., "fol. 50 rht" (for the right side) and "fol. 50 lft" (for the left side).

The primary types of account books that we will be citing are:

1 *Journals*: chronological records of purchases and sales. Following initial years of experimentation (and haphazard bookkeeping) – the records of which are, moreover, incompletely preserved – Plantin began to keep a Journal for each year; it served as his primary record of all shipments of books and other miscellaneous items that were occasionally included in these shipments, like prints, paper or pens. His successors, the Moretuses, maintained this system of notation. Preserved for the years 1566 through ca. 1750, these Journals tend to offer the most detailed accounts of individual transactions.

2 *Grands livres*, or *Grootboeken*: summaries by name or institution (e.g., a monastery) of all the dealings with that individual or organization, usually drawn from the Journals. Plantin and his successors kept multiple types of *Grands livres*: for example, one for local booksellers and another for booksellers whom they usually met at the Frankfurt fairs. The main purpose of such account books was to provide an overview of the transactions of the Officina Plantiniana with other parties; this overview could then be used to settle the Moretuses' accounts via a debit-credit accounting system. Consequently, not all of the individual prices noted in a Journal consistently appear here. Rather, often only the total value of a transaction is recorded. In addition, discounts might be applied at certain times (usually without any clarification) when the accounts needed to be balanced. For this reason, we have tried to cite values from the Journals whenever possible, as they offer the most consistently kept and detailed records of such information. If prices for prints are given in both the Journals and the *Grands livres* (as is the case for many of Plantin's transactions with the important print publishers of his day: Cock, Diericx, Galle, and De Jode), the prices are almost always the same, indicating that generally no discount was applied to such sales. When the price in a *Grand livre* was reduced below the corresponding price in a Journal, this was an exception that most likely indicates that a special agreement had been struck during the balancing of the accounts, or possibly that a simple clerical error was made in one of the two record books.[16] Moreover, for individuals who were not regular, important clients or personal relatives, the (limited) transactions were listed only in the Journals. However, other types of notes, in particular, more detailed identifications of customers, are more common in the *Grands livres*. Consequently, while the Journals are usually more complete in terms of sales records, it is often best to use them in conjunction with *Grands livres* for the fullest understanding of a given transaction.

3 *Cahier de Francfort*: records of all of the transactions that occurred at a given Frankfurt fair.
Of all the record books in the Plantin-Moretus archives, the *Cahiers* provide the best overview of what was shipped, purchased, and left in stock at Frankfurt. These account books also contain records of various, additional financial transactions, from living costs for the duration of the fair to payments received for others, in addition to lists of the currencies used for payments at the fairs. As with the Journals, it is often useful to compare these entries with the corresponding ones in the *Grands livres*.

4 *Correspondence*: incoming letters and copies of outgoing letters.
While copies of outgoing correspondence are rare for the first decade of Plantin's activities as a printer-publisher (ca. 1555–1565), the majority of these documents for the following years appear to have been preserved. Nevertheless, some notable lacunae remain. For example, there are hardly any copies of Jan Moretus I's letters to other family members. The reverse is true of the incoming letters, as most do not survive, and what remains is highly irregular in terms of both the number of letters and who is represented by them. For example, while the outgoing correspondence documents how Balthasar Moretus I wrote regularly to the merchant-bookseller Paulus Claessens of Danzig (Gdańsk), only one letter written in return is known. By contrast, numerous letters from the French merchant-bookseller Théodore Rinsart are preserved.

1 Vandewalle 1984, pp. 5 (for remarks regarding the relative stability of the pound in this period) and 53.

2 See MPM Arch. 221, fol. 158v, where two tons were weighed both according to the local Frankfurt pounds and according to Antwerp pounds, where 1175 lb. Antwerp = 1080 lb. Frankfurt (or 1 lb. Antwerp = .919 lb. Frankfurt).

3 This estimate is based on the signature of the book (*-***8, A-Z8, Aa-Gg8, aa-ii8), as discussed in Bowen 1997, p. 233.

4 The number of sheets is based on a copy of this missal in Trinity College Library, Cambridge, E.3.56. See MPM Arch. 19, fol. 75 lft, for this price.

5 Gaskell 1972 (and 1995 reprint), pp. 80-107, provides a detailed discussion of book formats, for example.

6 See Verlinden, vol. I (1959), p. 14, for these equivalencies, as well as the observation that in Antwerp, writing paper was sold in quires of twenty-four leaves each.

7 Griffiths 2016, pp. 169-73 (print series) and 175-76 (print books).

8 See Chapter 2 on the sale of prints in bulk.

9 Appendix 1, WX-11 and WX-17 (for 8° formats), and WX-15 and WX-18 (for 16° formats).

10 See Appendix 1, PG-16, TG-6, TG-8, WX-4, and WX-20 for consistent examples of references to a 4° format, and GJ-37 for an example of exceptionally large prints identified as 4°. In Filedt Kok, Hinterding, and Van der Waals 1994, p. 370, there are examples of the range of sizes for certain formats of images printed in the northern Netherlands during the early seventeenth century, including images printed on exceptionally large sheets of paper. Our thanks to Marjolein Leesberg for bringing this article to our attention.

11 For this series, see MPM Arch. 58, fol. 19r; and Appendix 1, CD-11.

12 MPM Arch. 59, fol. 19r.

13 For this series, the sale of which is also discussed in Chapter 2, see MPM Arch. 59, fol. 19r; and Appendix 1, CD-12.

14 For these prints, see MPM Arch. 51, fol. 200r; and Appendix 1, CD-1 and CD-22, respectively. These records are also transcribed in Delen 1932, p. 7.

15 See also Voet, GC, vol. II, pp. 3-7, for an overview of these business records.

16 For example, in the Journal for 1573 (MPM Arch. 51, fol. 132r), six series of the Passion supplied by Philips Galle were valued at 1 fl. 16 st. (or 6 st. per set), while the price for these prints noted in the corresponding entry in Plantin's Grand livre (MPM Arch. 16, fol. 172 rht) was just 1 fl. 10 st. (or 5 st. per set). The prices for the other items sold with the Passion series were the same in both books. Consequently, while this one small reduction in price may reflect an exceptional discount, it may also be a clerical error or a misunderstanding as to exactly which Passion series was provided.

Detail of fig. 3.7: Frans Huys after Pieter Bruegel I, Naval Battle in the Strait of Messina, 1561.

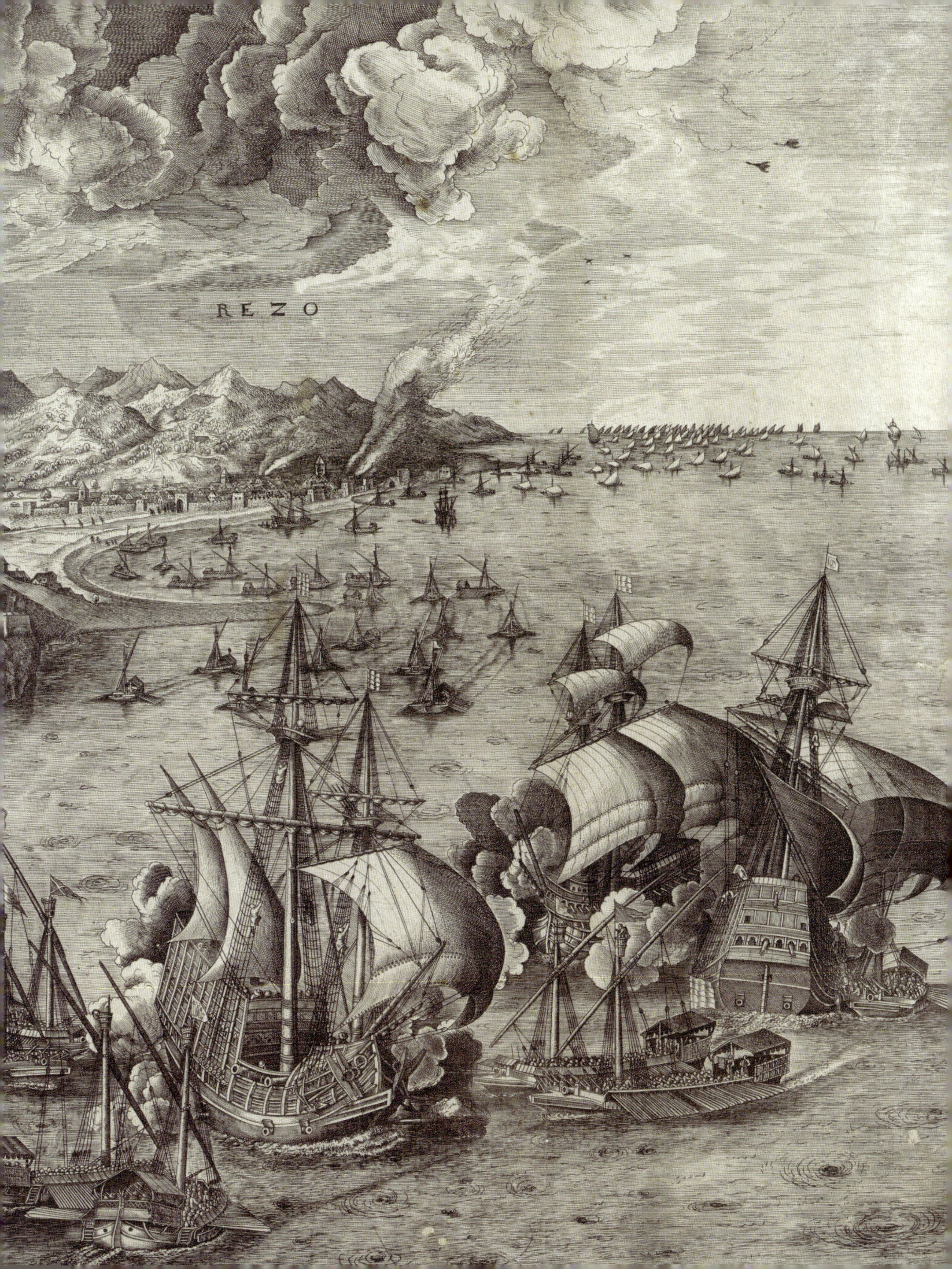
REZO

1.1 Binding with the "PEF" initials of Philips Eduard Fugger within the Fugger coat of arms, for a volume containing, among other print series, a 1590 edition of Bernardo Giunti's publication: *Cronica breve de i fatti illustri de' re di Francia, con le loro effigie dal naturale, cominciando da Faramondo primo re di Francia, che regno l'anno della nostra salute CCCXX, sino a Henrico III, che regna hora del 1588* (Venice). Wolfegg, Fürstlich zu Waldburg-Wolfegg'sche Kunstsammlungen: vol. KuKa 72.

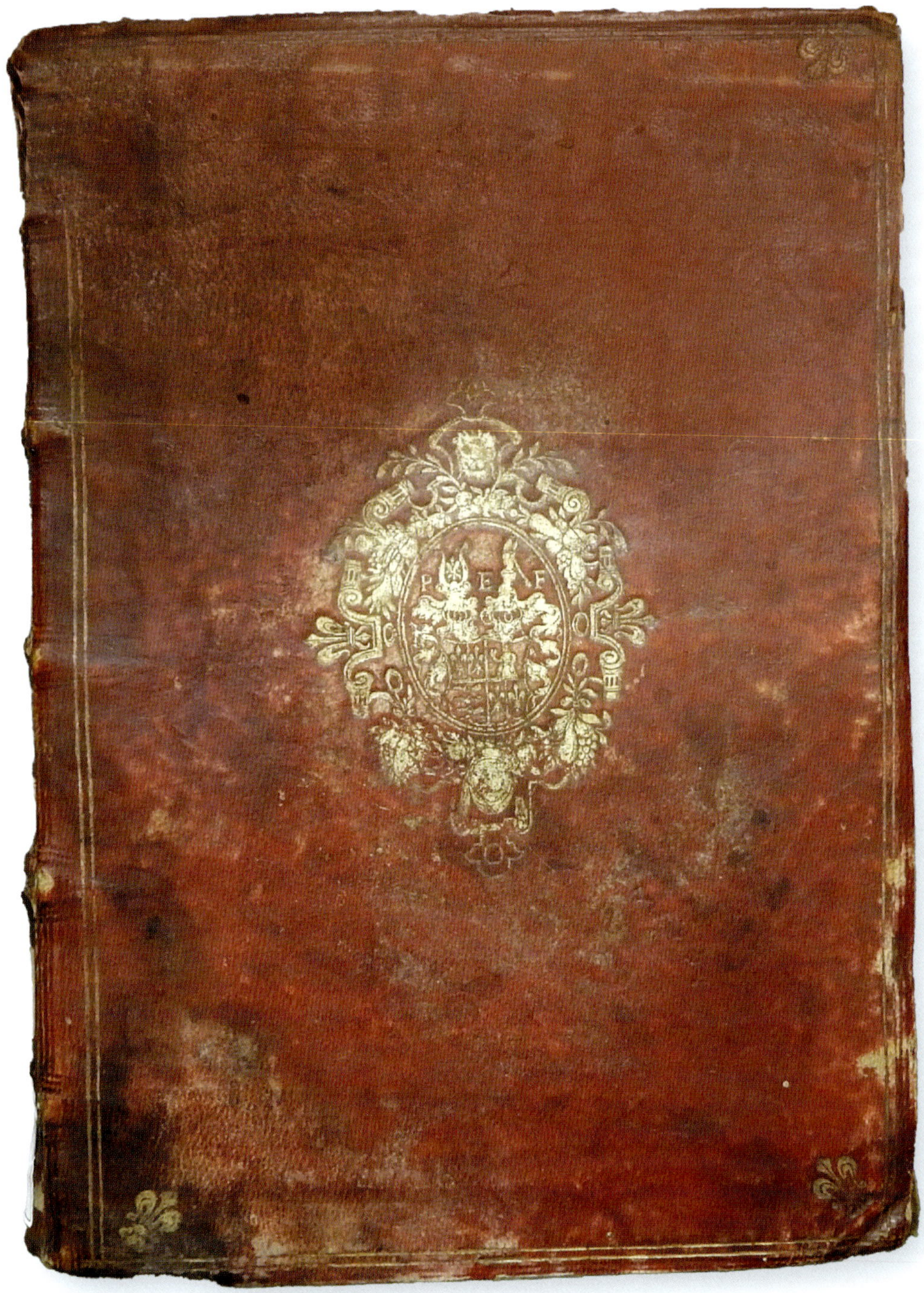

CHAPTER 1

INTRODUCTION

> His Excellency [Count Maximilian Willibald von Waldburg-Wolfegg] has purchased from the library of the deceased Count [Friedrich] Fugger at Augsburg bound albums comprising 34,000 items, Italian and Netherlandish prints, very beautiful in both large and small prints, and very rare.[1]

This report was part of a letter dated 9 June 1654 and written by the Antwerp painter and print dealer Joannes Meyssens to Charles Van den Bosch, then Bishop of Bruges, who, in addition to amassing a remarkable collection of books, was also an avid print collector.[2] The easily overlooked connection between collecting prints and collecting books evident here is essential for understanding why booksellers' records could shed novel, fundamental insights into the early modern European print trade. The following exploration of the extent to which ensembles of prints and those of books were linked intuitively, if not physically, highlights what is perpetually evident from the archives of the Plantin-Moretus Press: the fact that prints and books were routinely traded and treasured alongside one another. Providing a uniquely well-documented view of the surprisingly numerous, significant ways in which booksellers supported the burgeoning market for prints in the sixteenth and seventeenth centuries, the Press's records simultaneously offer new perspectives on the evolution of the international market for prints and how it functioned.

When Meyssens wrote the letter cited above, the intermingling of prints and books was commonplace. The comment was inspired, rather, by one collector's curiosity about another's collection that can be traced back to the previous summer when Meyssens met Count Willibald's secretary and had mentioned the bishop's collection. Since then, Max Willibald had asked to be introduced to Van den Bosch and had inquired whether he had a similar number of prints. To determine this, he had sent a list estimating the quantity of prints in his collection, which contained some 157,000 items, including the 34,000 prints he had recently acquired from the Fugger family. Some albums in the Fürstlich zu Waldburg-Wolfegg'sche Kunstsammlungen that bear the "PEF" monogram of Friedrich Fugger's father, Philipp Eduard, may have been among this last group (fig. 1.1).[3] Prior to his death, Philipp Eduard had stipulated that his entire library and everything associated with it – mathematical instruments, maps, portraits, and other works of art – should be inherited by his son Friedrich.[4]

Meyssens's letter is often cited for the information it conveys concerning Max Willibald's collection – now one of the best preserved from the seventeenth century – in addition to the details it offers of how print dealers and collectors interacted in this period.[5] It is also valuable for the evidence it provides of the intrinsic association between libraries and print collections. In the case of Max Willibald, both a will that he composed in 1667 shortly before his death and an inventory of the contents of his library, or "Bibliothec Zimmer," compiled soon thereafter, demonstrate that the collections in this room, which are described as belonging to his library, comprised not only books and manuscripts, but also bound and unbound collections of prints, drawings, paintings, and other special objects.[6]

The affinity between prints and books in the later seventeenth century is similarly evident from accounts of one of the most famous print collections amassed in this period, namely the immense, encyclopedic collection formed by Michel de Marolles, abbé de Villeloin, who has been described as a fanatical collector with an unbounded addiction to images.[7] Louis XIV's First Minister of State, Jean-Baptiste Colbert, purchased Marolles's collection in 1667, at a time when he was buying parts of other great French collections for Louis XIV, such as objects previously owned by Cardinal Mazarin and Armand-Jean de Vignerot du Plessis, the second Duke of Richelieu.[8] In a catalogue of his print collection that Marolles published in 1666 to facilitate its sale, he remarked that his albums of prints would be one of the most attractive ornaments that one could use to embellish and augment a large and impressive library at relatively little cost.[9] While clearly a sales pitch, Marolles's assertion would certainly have resonated with many of his contemporaries, whose libraries contained sizable print collections. In France, such figures included Jean Nicolas de Tralage, a politician and geographer, Claude-Nicolas Boucot, a lawyer, employed in the royal chancellery, Nicolas Clément, keeper of the royal library, and Pierre Fevret, an ecclesiastical representative to the Parliament in Dijon.[10] Collectors elsewhere in Europe were similarly minded. One well-known example is Samuel Pepys, one-time Secretary to the Admiralty and President of the Royal Society in London. At least up until 1700, both subject and author catalogues of his extensive library, in addition to a uniform binding style for some of his books and print albums, indicate that he regarded his print and book collections as a single entity.[11] Auctions of libraries held in London, Paris, and Delft in the late 1680s and 1690s similarly allude to the coexistence of prints and books within a single library.[12]

However, the intuitive connection between prints and libraries dates back to the late fifteenth century – when the production of intaglio prints and the printing of texts with movable type had begun in earnest – and flourished alongside improvements in these arts. Intermittently combined in one volume by printers from the incunabula period onwards, prints and books were natural bedfellows for many collectors, to be kept together, and periodically procured at the same time from booksellers and printmakers alike.

Consider three different collections: those of Hernando Colon (Ferdinand Columbus), a geographer and bibliophile who was part of the entourage of the Spanish royal family, King Philip II of Spain, and his cousin Archduke Ferdinand II of Tyrol.[13] While Colon was forming his collection by the 1520s–1530s, the other two date from the third quarter of the sixteenth century. These were among the largest collections of their time and included thousands of prints. In particular, Colon's inventories record as many as 3,204 prints in his possession, whereas Philip II amassed nearly 7,000 prints in thirty-six albums and Ferdinand had assembled approximately 6,500 prints in some thirty to forty albums. Each collection was also housed in a library. Specifically, the lists that Colon made of his print collection indicate that his prints were stored in chests kept in his remarkable library: boasting some 15,000–20,000 volumes, it may well have been the largest private collection of books in all of Europe at that time.[14] Philip II's print collection was formed largely by his librarian and chaplain, the Spanish theologian Benito Arias Montano, for inclusion in El Escorial, an impressive monastery and royal palace that Philip II commissioned in 1557. As part of a monastery (like other institutions run by religious orders), the library often contained a print collection.[15] In Ferdinand II's case, a 1596 inventory of his "biblioteca oder püecherkunstkammer" (library or book art room) reveals that albums with prints were shelved among books in rooms that also housed cases where selections from his extensive collection of rare and exotic objects were displayed.[16]

A similarly "multimedia" display of books, prints, and other precious items is evident from a 1598 inventory of the collection of the Dukes of Bavaria in Munich; the inventory was compiled when Wilhelm V, Ferdinand II's brother-in-law, abdicated and gave his title to his son Maximilian. Here, a case holding an assortment of special illustrated books and albums with drawings or printed images, along with a chest containing seventy-four drawers housing a variety of other graphic items, such as maps, were displayed during the standard tour of the art collection. Nevertheless, the works on paper continued to be associated with the library (though physically separated from it) and were often described as a subdivision of it.[17] The majority of these items most likely came from Wilhelm V's father, Duke Albrecht V, whose collection featured numerous works that he had purchased in 1565 from the bankrupt Hans Jakob Fugger, a member of the famous Fugger family of merchants and an uncle of Philipp Eduard Fugger, who was discussed above.[18]

One prominent example of the intricate lineages of the objects in the ducal collection is the library of Hartmann Schedel, the author of the so-called *Nuremberg Chronicle*, who was also an early and avid collector of prints and books with a penchant for pasting prints into his books and manuscripts. Hans Jakob Fugger purchased Schedel's library in 1552, and it subsequently became part of Albrecht V's collection.[19] A 1577 inventory of the maps in the ducal library likewise demonstrates the connection between objects that might have been displayed in the ducal art collection by 1598 and works that, under Albrecht V, were clearly associated with the library and most likely had come from the Fugger family. Of the forty maps listed, the majority date from the 1530s–1550s, when they would have been logical additions to an international merchant family's collection.[20] Indeed, when Samuel Quiccheberg, who was Hans Jakob Fugger's librarian and collections manager and who subsequently performed the same roles for Albrecht V, published his advice on forming an ideal, encyclopedic, and educative collection in his 1565 *Inscriptiones vel tituli theatri amplissimi*, he featured examples of worthy collectors, including the Fuggers.[21] While he would have been foolish not to mention his own employer in his publication, his description of the Fuggers' acquisition activities remains noteworthy for the link he creates between them, as model merchant-collectors, and the purchase of engraved images: "the Fuggers, who, for the sake of art, occupy themselves with collecting for specific museums everything that has ever existed. Antwerp, Venice, and Rome, trading ports that produce a good many artists and painters engraving images in copper, ought to take pride in patrons of this kind".[22] This was no idle remark, for just four years earlier, on 18 November 1561, a representative of the Fugger family, a certain Antoine van Augsburg, bought 19 florins worth of prints and print books from Christopher Plantin in Antwerp. His purchase included eight copies of the funeral procession honoring Charles V *(La magnifique et sumptueuse pompe funèbre)* (two were hand colored), four books with calligraphy by Pierre Hamon, sixty-eight sheets with unspecified images, and a series of round perspective prints published by Jacques Androuet du Cerceau.[23]

It is not surprising that the best-documented examples of significant sixteenth-century print collections associated with libraries were frequently owned by Europe's ruling elite. Nevertheless, since much of Albrecht V's collection, including important components of his library, was originally acquired by the Fugger family, other ranks of collectors evidently also formed impressive libraries containing printed images and other works of art. The striking socioeconomic diversity of these individuals is reflected in Quiccheberg's list of exemplary collectors of antiquities and printed images and of those who created libraries or cabinets of curiosities.[24] Extending from the nobility and high church officials to scholars and craftsmen, his list demonstrates that similar habits of collecting, albeit on potentially differing scales and for disparate motives, pervaded a variety of classes throughout Europe.

The intermingling of collections of books and images by learned collectors is evident, for example, in sixteenth- and seventeenth-century Italy. Cassiano dal Pozzo, a lawyer by training who was appointed to the household of Cardinal Francesco Barberini, became actively involved in cultural and learned societies in Rome during the first half of the seventeenth century. While his collections ranged from ancient cameos to contemporary paintings, he appears to have been interested above all in his library, which had some 4,500–5,000 volumes in addition to his "museo cartaceo" (paper museum).[25] By far, the best-recorded and most well-known components of Dal Pozzo's paper museum are numerous albums with drawings that he commissioned to serve as the basis for an illustrated encyclopedia, which was never realized. It appears that these albums were arranged thematically among the books in his library. While it is logical that his albums of prints would have been similarly shelved in his library, this has yet to be verified.[26]

The library and collections of the natural philosopher and scholar Ulisse Aldrovandi are, in this regard, better documented. Aldrovandi's library and museum, boasting extensive collections of specimens of animals, fruits, plants, and minerals, in addition to thousands of drawings, were internationally renowned during his lifetime and have been extensively studied since then.[27] Of importance here is the fact that Aldrovandi's own notes from 1599 on the arrangement of his *studio* reveal how this area contained not only a room for his museum of specimens, but also four adjacent rooms: two for his library and two for his collections of unbound drawings and prints, as well as some extra books and other "overflow". Aldrovandi stored his most precious notes, bound drawings, and other working materials in his second library, the room furthest removed from the main entrance to his *studio* and, hence, most likely his private workspace.[28] Consequently, books, drawings, and prints were intermingled and distributed according to need and convenience across several closely related spaces within Aldrovandi's *studio*. Among these sundry items were albums containing prints. These housed impressions of the woodcuts he had made for his own publications, as well as prints that, today, would be regarded as fine art and not simply useful comparative scholarly material. For example, one album holds Hendrick Goltzius's engraving after Johannes Stradanus's portrayal of a free and untamed horse (the "Equus liber et incompositus") (fig. 1.2), which was part of Stradanus's famous print series, *The Stable of Don Juan of Austria*, published by Philips Galle in Antwerp around 1580–1585.[29]

Similarly, some sixteenth- and seventeenth-century scholars in the Low Countries kept prints in their libraries. This practice is occasionally reflected in auction catalogues of individual collections. For instance, when the library of the Flemish humanist Bonaventura Vulcanius was sold in 1610, the inclusion of maps, portrayals of sieges during the wars in the Low Countries, and various portraits of famous men engraved in copper ("Variae Effigies Virorum insignium aeri incisae") in his collection was highlighted on the title page of the auction catalogue.[30] Peter Parshall takes the overlapping interest in books and printed images among the learned classes several steps further. In particular, he argues that scholars "bound themselves together not only by literary means but also through traffic in printed images" and that several sixteenth-century print publishers in Antwerp and Haarlem produced print series designed specifically to appeal to "a literate – though not necessarily Latinate – class of patrons" and thereby encouraged them to form print collections.[31]

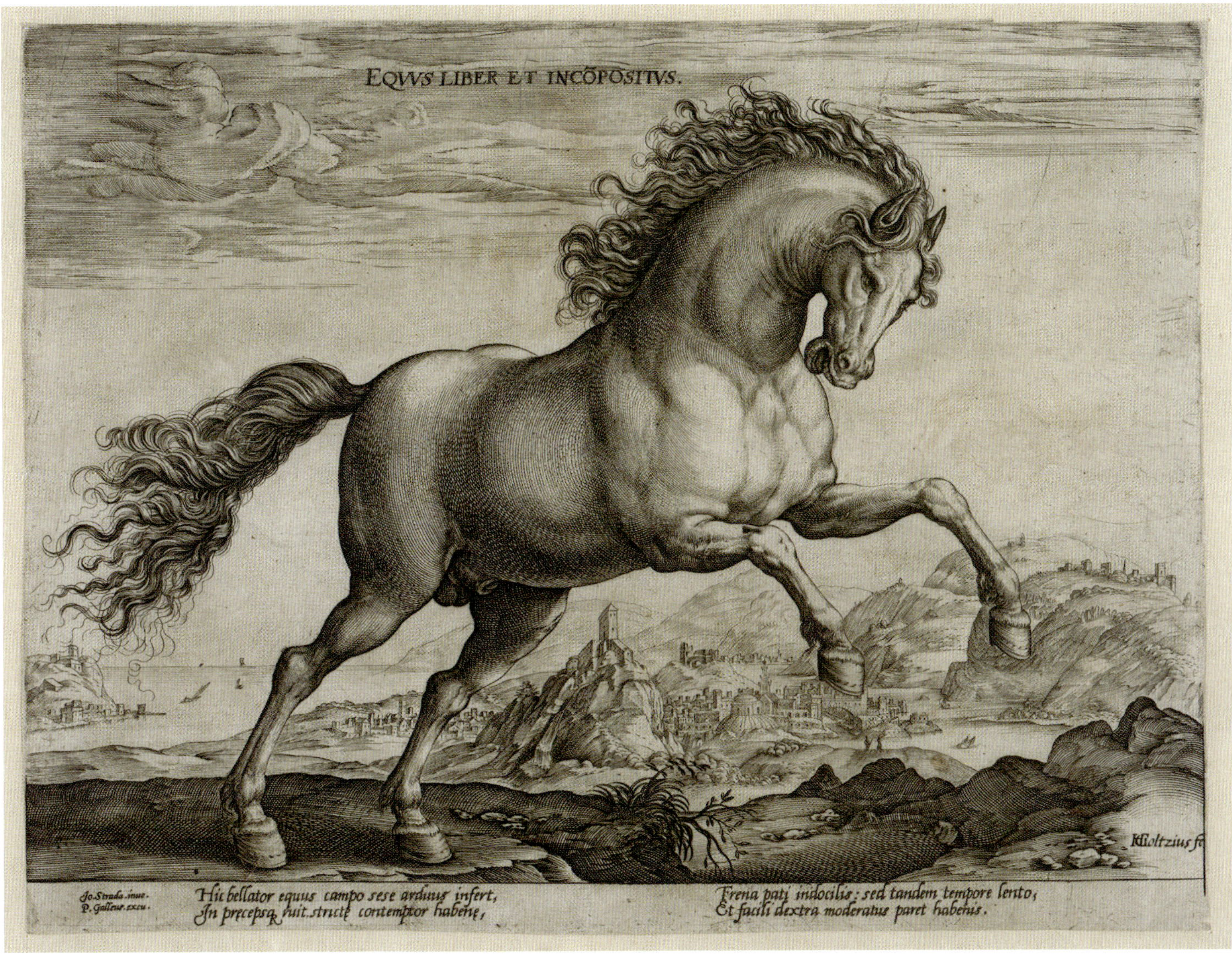

1.2 Hendrick Goltzius after Johannes Stradanus, *Free and Untamed Horse*, 1578–1582, engraving, 205 × 270 mm. Amsterdam, Rijksmuseum: RP-P-1998-609. Appendix 1: PG-106.

One prominent example of a scholar from the Low Countries who was actively involved in the worlds of both printed books and images is the Flemish cartographer Abraham Ortelius. Originally trained as a colorer of printed images and perpetually dabbling in the trade of works of art, Ortelius is best known for devising the first atlases by collecting the best maps, having them re-engraved at the same size, and publishing them in book form with commentary.[32] His *album amicorum* attests to the remarkable range of his personal contacts. It boasts successful scholars from a variety of fields – Justus Lipsius, Hubertus Goltzius, and Carolus Clusius, for example – as well as leading artists and publishers of books and prints – Otto van Veen, Arnold Mylius, Christopher Plantin, and Philips Galle, among others.[33] Hence, it is not surprising that Ortelius's personal interests and activities routinely involved a mix of books and prints. In particular, alongside his work as a publisher of atlases, Ortelius purchased copies of more than 800 publications from Plantin and his successor Jan Moretus I alone.[34] Though he routinely bought numerous copies of some editions, most likely for further distribution, the majority of his acquisitions were solitary copies of texts probably intended for his or someone else's personal library. Similarly, Ortelius obtained and exchanged engravings among his widespread circle of friends and acquaintances.[35] He was even occasionally involved in the production and publication of engraved images. In 1574, his friend Philips Galle completed an engraving of the *Death of the Virgin* after a sketch by Pieter Bruegel I, which Ortelius then distributed among his acquaintances (fig. 1.3). Galle simultaneously published images of ancient coins from Ortelius's own collection with an accompanying commentary in the *Deorum dearumque capita … ex musaeo Abrahami Ortelii*, in 1573 and 1582.[36] The extent to which Ortelius owned many prints aside from the maps essential to his own publications is not known, nor is it possible to determine the manner in which he organized his sundry collections. Nevertheless, his personal endeavors make it clear that scholars like those in his circle appreciated the frequently intertwined realms of prints and books.

The preceding sampling of collectors demonstrates that the intermingling of collections of prints and books was natural for diverse classes of collectors, from the ruling elite to merchants and scholars, throughout sixteenth- and seventeenth-century Europe. Whether albums of prints were placed alongside books in a library or kept separately in their own cases would have been determined by a variety of factors, such as the function of the collections, the timing of their formation, and the constraints of the available space. Regardless of these details, the underlying, intimate relationship between books and prints was intuitive, for the consultation of various combinations and permutations of printed images and texts was common; they were visual and verbal forms of communication and knowledge as well as aesthetically pleasing objects, and, consequently, were gathered both to satisfy individual needs and to provide personal enrichment.

The close ties between prints and books forged by collectors naturally begs the equally important, complementary question of the degree to which the trade in them also overlapped. Such a query is especially pertinent for the sixteenth and seventeenth centuries, prior to the rise of the "passion for prints" during the later seventeenth century, which supported the proliferation of "professional" print sellers in the years to come.[37] Since booksellers often lived in the same part of a city as printmakers and interacted with them in professional and personal circles, it is not surprising that they also traded in prints.[38] Examples of this practice date back to the early years of printing texts in the fifteenth century, when, for example, prints by Andrea Mantegna were purchased at a bookshop in 1471. Samuel Pepys's accounts reflect the continuation of such transactions at least through the seventeenth century.[39] In between, sporadic records reveal that disparate successful tradesmen engaged in this practice. Such tradesmen include the Florentine branch of the Giunti family of booksellers, who sold prints to the Benedictine monk and artistic advisor to the Medici family, Vincenzio Borghini, on several occasions between 1553 and 1572. Similarly, in 1609, the Amsterdam bookseller Cornelis Claesz published a list in Dutch (and, hence, most likely for a local clientele) of the prints and maps he had for sale.[40]

Nevertheless, however informative and valuable each of these isolated examples is, they cannot compare to the thousands of interrelated records of prints sold via the Plantin-Moretus Press of Antwerp, which document an astoundingly extensive trade in prints and an international array of customers from the mid-sixteenth century onwards. A. J. J. Delen provided a taste of what can be learned from these accounts in his frequently cited 1932 publication on Plantin's activities as a print seller.[41] Nevertheless, Delen's account is incomplete. Limited chronologically because of his focus on Plantin's management of his business, Delen analyzed a selection of potentially identifiable prints sold by major figures in the print world. Furthermore, he did not take full advantage of the uncommonly rich resources of the Plantin-Moretus archives to delve into the subsequent distribution of these prints. For this period, there are no comparable archival resources documenting either the activities of a European printing and publishing business or the activities of a printmaker and publisher. Only with the Plantin-Moretus Press can one consult and compare a broad range of records, which together provide three hundred years of continuous, complementary data, extending from the mid-sixteenth into the eighteenth century. Essential here are the day books (or "Journals"), where purchases and shipments were recorded on a daily basis, ledgers with small financial outlays (including purchases of prints), accounts of sales via the Press's own local bookshop, and records of the diverse and abundant transactions that took place at the biannual Frankfurt fairs. Additional insights into these documents are provided by incoming and outgoing correspondence, in addition to the "Grands livres", in which overviews of many of the individual entries in different account books were grouped together by customer.[42] The immense value of these sources for studying the international print trade is enhanced by the fact that the Plantin-Moretus Press was a major player in the European book trade during the sixteenth and seventeenth centuries and so had a wide assortment of

1.3 Philips Galle after Pieter Bruegel I, *Death of the Virgin*, ca. 1574, engraving, 330 × 435 mm. Antwerp, Museum Plantin-Moretus: PK.OP.18562.

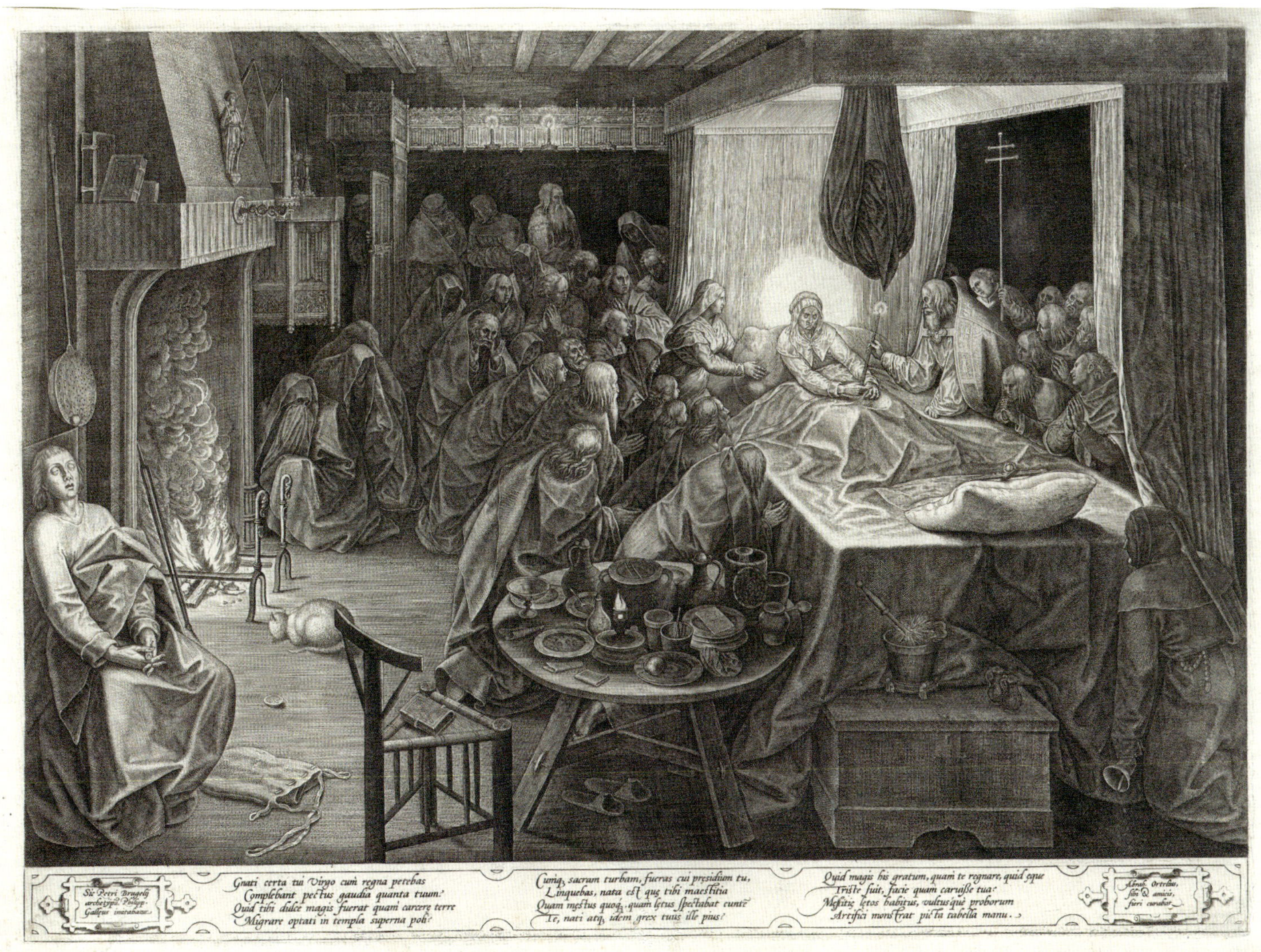

contacts. From 1556 to 1641 alone, there are more than 2,800 transactions concerning printmakers active in Antwerp and the international traffic in prints linked to them. Of these, more than 500 were noted in conjunction with Plantin's or the Moretuses' dealings at the Frankfurt fairs, while the rest appear among the records of their Antwerp business. Of the more than 800 individuals involved, many of whom are discussed in greater detail in the following chapters, approximately ninety percent can be identified in terms of their profession, social class, or place of residence. These data, in turn, provide a wealth of new information on the full range of people engaged in the print trade – from booksellers and printmakers to members of the clergy, merchants, and nobles – and the extent of their participation, in terms of both the nature and the volume of their transactions.

Hence, one can not only read what was offered for sale and at what price, as in Claesz's stock list, but also determine who purchased which items, in what quantities, and how they were then conveyed via an international transport network that stretched as far south as Spain and Italy, as far north as Scandinavia, and extended from England to central Europe and beyond. Similarly, the correspondence between the managers of the Plantin-Moretus Press and their clients, like the extant letters involving of the Giunti family, reveals how orders were placed and completed. But with the Plantin-Moretus accounts, one can delve deeper and consider who provided the prints in question, as well as the subtle distinctions and areas of specialization among the suppliers. The systematic documentation of the spectrum of prices charged (and paid) for these images simultaneously attests to common, standard prices for certain allotments of prints, while also revealing Plantin's and the Moretuses' own ambiguous stance concerning the incorporation of profit margins for themselves in their role of middlemen.

The Plantin-Moretus archives, moreover, are clearly an exceptional resource when compared with what is usually preserved from print sellers' businesses of the sixteenth and seventeenth centuries. Most often, surviving documents include individual stock lists (like those published by Antonio Lafreri around 1573 and by Jan Galle in the mid-seventeenth century), concern lawsuits and notarial acts, or are estate inventories, such as those of Volcxken Diericx, the widow of Hieronymus Cock, or Catharina Moerentorf, the widow of Theodore Galle.[43] For print prices in particular, aside from Claesz's 1609 stock list, one is frequently limited to post-mortem valuations of print publishers' wares or posthumously held auctions of their prints.[44] The opportunity not only to determine what individual print publishers charged for their prints during their lifetime, but also to compare numerous sales of the same images to different customers over time is unprecedented. However, the Plantin-Moretus archives make such a study possible for a variety of print sellers from Antwerp, one of the leading European centers of print production during the sixteenth and seventeenth centuries.

Consequently, although the Plantin-Moretus Press was not itself a print-publishing house, its business records comprise a unique wealth of data on the trade in hundreds of thousands of prints from Antwerp. In addition, these documents provide exceptional opportunities to make effective comparisons: not only over the course of time, but between various suppliers of prints and a disparate, international array of clients that features a similarly wide range of individuals – nobles, merchants, members of the clergy, and scholars.

Indeed, the very plethora of information pertaining to the trade in texts and printed images that can be derived from the Plantin-Moretus archives requires that some selection be made for the time period considered here, for instance, as well as among the topics and types of images to be traced. The earliest of Christopher Plantin's dealings in prints dates back to 1553, two years before he established himself as a printer and publisher of books. By extending our period of study to 1641, the year when Plantin's grandson and longtime manager of the Press, Balthasar Moretus I, died, we can examine the progress of this burgeoning traffic in prints over nearly one hundred years and across several generations of both print sellers and collectors. Throughout this volume, our focus remains on the trade in individual printed images, print series, and print books (that is, a unified group of prints to which a brief introductory or explanatory text might be appended, printed either in letterpress or from an additional copper plate).[45] Plantin's and the Moretuses' distribution of illustrated books will not be considered. A similar restriction applies to series of illustrations that were routinely sold in conjunction with independent, self-sufficient texts. Obvious examples of this practice include several of Joannes David's and Theodore Galle's related emblematic publications, Hieronymus Natalis's trend-setting *Evangelicae historiae imagines* and *Adnotationes et meditationes in evangelia*, and Jean Bourgeois's *Vitae passionis et mortis Jesu Christi mysteria*, each of which has already been the subject of many studies. Finally, Plantin's and the Moretuses' simultaneous involvement in the trade in maps, diverse aspects of which have already been examined elsewhere, will likewise not be explored here.

This volume will offer novel, exceptionally well-grounded perspectives on Antwerp print publishers and their active involvement in an extensive, flourishing European market for prints. Beginning with such renowned figures as Hans Liefrinck I, Hieronymus Cock, and Philips Galle, it traces how the trade in prints evolved and prospered in the seventeenth century under the supervision of new print sellers. Particularly noteworthy is the speed with which sundry entrepreneurs expanded what was on offer to satisfy the growing demand for a variety of prints, from small devotional images to grand works after Rubens, as well as costly images with a variety of special finishings. Similarly, numerous records of print orders placed by a variety of clients, encompassing the ruling elite, members of the clergy, and individual scholars, reveal how collectors chose to express their preferences when buying prints and so reflect underlying differences in taste and needs. At the same time, the astounding number of sales to booksellers and merchants throughout Europe attests to their often overlooked significance as middlemen in the international print trade of the sixteenth and seventeenth centuries. Furthermore, detailed shipping and payment records provide an unprecedented view of the logistical arrangements that made this extensive international traffic in hundreds of thousands of prints possible. Of primary importance here are connections among expatriates, in addition to intertwined professional networks. Throughout our study, the extensive, systematically kept, and interrelated accounts of the Plantin-Moretus Press will provide an invaluable, underlying, interwoven structure that will lend exceptional strength and depth to specific observations and comparisons. The result will be a richly informed, multifaceted, and novel account in which the distribution of prints from Antwerp will be portrayed as it contributed to the vibrant, early modern European print trade.

1 Vanden Bussche 1880, p. 360: "dat syn Excelencie nu eenen coop gedaen heeft tot Ausborch, de bibeloteck vanden verstorven graef Fugger, daer alle italiansche ende nederlantsche printen altemael jngebonden syn, seer schoon in groote en clyn printen, seer raer, tot 34,000 stucken".

2 Ibid, pp. 345–48. MPM Arch. 134, fol. 109, provides an overview of Van den Bosch's numerous and varied purchases of books from the Moretuses between 1630 and 1650.

3 The Fugger albums are now dispersed between the current print room and the adjacent library of the Fürstlich zu Waldburg-Wolfegg'sche Kunstsammlungen at Wolfegg. As is evident in fig. 1.1, they are distinguished by an old and often worn red leather binding with some combination of gold, stamped "PEF" initials or a Fugger family coat of arms.

4 Hartig 1917, p. 39 and n. 4: "Zum fünften thue ich Meinem Sohne Friderichen in Crafft diss mein ganze Bibliothec vnd wass in und bey dersselben an Contrafetten, Mappen vnd instrumenta mathematica, Kunst Stuckchen, vnd anderen zuefinden praelegieren".

5 See, for example, Mayer and Falk 2003, p. 10, on Max Willibald's collection, and Griffiths 2016, pp. 344, 350, and 438 on Meyssens and Van den Bosch.

6 Brakensiek 2003, pp. 215–16; and Eitel 1996, p. 26.

7 Griffiths 2016, pp. 428 and 447. See Brakensiek 2003, pp. 17–39, 82–121, 242–56, and 549–53, for a detailed discussion of Marolles's collection.

8 Schnapper 1986, pp. 194–95.

9 Marolles 1666, p. 6: "Aussi faut-il avouër que les Livres d'Estampes, quand elles sont exquises & bien choisies, font l'un des plus beaux ornemens qui se puissent apporter dans les grandes Biblioteques [sic]", and p. 18: "Il est certain aussi que de toutes les choses qu'on estime pour servir à l'embellissement & à l'augmentation d'une grande Bibliotheque [sic], il n'en est point de plus belle ny que puisse moins coûtre".

10 Fuhring 2010 for the first and Meyer 2015, pp. 37–38 and 42, for the other examples.

11 Van der Waals 1984, especially p. 240. For a detailed catalogue of this collection, with a useful introduction, see Aspital 1980.

12 Robinson 1981, pp. xxxi and xxxv.

13 On Colon, see McDonald 2004; and Pérez Fernández and Wilson-Lee 2021. On Philip II, see McDonald 1998; and Brakensiek 2003, pp. 122–38. For this assessment of Ferdinand's collection see Robinson 1981, p. xxxiii, while Parshall 1982, pp. 146–77, provides a detailed account of these albums.

14 McDonald 2004, pp. 15–16 and 120; and Pérez Fernández and Wilson-Lee 2021, pp. 39 and 42.

15 Griffiths 2016, p. 439. Numerous other examples of the clergy's participation in the print trade will be discussed in the following chapters, including Arias Montano's purchases of prints from Plantin.

16 Parshall 1994, p. 16; and Boeheim 1888–89 for the 1596 inventory, which was part of a much larger inventory of Ferdinand's possessions compiled following his death. According to Scheicher 1985, pp. 29 and 34, possibly on the basis of a 1621 inventory, Ferdinand's library was housed in a separate building connected to others comprising his collection of exotic objects.

17 Seelig 1985, p. 79; and Parshall 1982, p. 142, on these works on paper. See Hartig 1917, pp. 93–96, on their association with the library.

18 See Meadow 2002 on Hans Jakob Fugger, especially p. 191 on the sale of his collection; and Seelig 1985, pp. 76–78, on the formation of Albrecht's collection.

19 On Schedel's print collection, see, for example, Hernad 1990. See Parshall 1982, p. 140, on its subsequent sale.

20 Hartig 1917, pp. 352–56.

21 On Quiccheberg and his relations with the Fugger family, Albrecht V, and the content of his Inscriptiones, see Meadow and Robertson 2013.

22 Samuel Quiccheberg, Inscriptiones vel tituli theatri amplissimi (Munich: Adam Berg, 1565), fol. G4r, for the original text; and Meadow and Robertson 2013, p. 100, for this translation.

23 See MPM Arch. 36, fol. 16v, for this sale, and the introductory index to this record book for the identification of the buyer. Only a few items are mentioned in Delen 1932, p. 4. On the Pompe funèbre, see Appendix 1, CD-10; Hamon's publication may have been his *Alphabet de l'invention et utilité des lettres et karactères en diverses écritures* (Paris: Jean Le Royer, 1561). On Androuet du Cerceau, see Du Cerceau 2010.

24 Meadow and Robertson 2013, p. 32.

25 Haskell and Griffiths 1983, pp. 1–10; and Griffiths 1989, p. 3.

26 Haskell and Griffiths 1983, p. 8, on the drawing albums; Jansen 1997, p. 181, on the print albums; and Haskell and Griffiths 1983, p. 246, on the lack of evidence concerning the original location of the print albums.

27 Duroselle-Melish and Lines 2015, pp. 133–34 and notes 1–6 for recent literature on these topics. Our thanks to Lia Markey for bringing this article to our attention.

28 Duroselle-Melish and Lines 2015, pp. 135–38, including a diagram of his studio on p. 136.

29 Our warm thanks to Caroline Duroselle-Melish for providing us with examples of prints in Aldrovandi's albums. See New Holl. Stradanus, no. 543, state I, for this specific print; and Appendix 1, PG-106 for this print series and Plantin's possible distribution of it.

30 Van Selm 1987, fig. 14 on p. 96 and cat. no. 29 on pp. 162–63. Van der Waals states that such references appear regularly in seventeenth-century Dutch auction catalogues, but gives no examples (Van der Waals 1984, pp. 237 and 240, for example).

31 Parshall 1994, pp. 9 and 12–13.

32 Van den Broecke, Van der Krogt, and Meurer 1998; and Meganck 2017.

33 Ortelius's album amicorum is preserved in Pembroke College, Cambridge, inv. no. MS LC.2.113, and can be viewed online (https://cudl.lib.cam.ac.uk/view/MS-LC-00002-00113/1). For discussions of the significance of alba amicorum generally and that of Ortelius's in particular, see Parshall 1994, pp. 14–15; and Meganck 2017, pp. 207–13, respectively.

34 Dirk Imhof is preparing a study of Ortelius's book purchases from the Plantin-Moretus Press.

35 Consider, for example, a sampling of examples discussed in Ortelius's correspondence: Hessels 1887, nos. 141 (Francesco Soranzo, letter of 7 November 1584), 154 (Dominicus Lampsonius, letter of 2 November 1587), and no. 170 (Philips van Winghe, letter of 24 December 1589). Meganck 2017, pp. 33–34, discusses Van Winghe's help as an agent for Ortelius in Rome for the acquisition of various works of art and books.

36 See, for example, Meganck 2017, pp. 163–71; and New Holl. Galle, no. 229, for the former; and Bowen and Imhof 2008, pp. 257, 263, and 407, for the latter.

37 Robinson 1981, p. xxvii, citing Florent Le Comte's Cabinet des singularitez (Paris: 1699–1700), 3 vols., vol. I, p. 158; and Griffiths 2016, pp. 334–49, on print sellers.

38 Consider, for example, the situation in Antwerp and Paris, as discussed in Van der Stock 1998, pp. 60–69; and Grivel 1986, pp. 59–63, respectively.

39 See Carrara and Gregory 2000, p. 3, for the former; and Landau and Parshall 1994, pp. 347–49, for a range of references to similar dealings in northern Europe during the fifteenth century. See Van der Waals 1984, p. 238, for the latter, although he does not give a specific example.

40 Carrara and Gregory 2000 for the former; and Van Selm 1987, pp. 217–25, for the latter.

41 Delen 1932.

42 The primary sources used here are described in greater detail in the Note to the Reader.

43 Bury 2001, p. 121 and n. 11, for Lafreri's stock list; and Fuhring 2017 on Jan Galle's list. See Van der Stock 1998, Appendix III, pp. 301–413, for a sampling of legal documents and contracts involving printmakers (1417–1585); and Duverger 1984–2009, vol. I (1984), pp. 17–37, for Diericx's inventory, and vol. IV (1989), pp. 18–24, for Moerentorf's, both of which are selective transcriptions.

44 Consider, for example, Wuestman 1998 on prices paid for Rubens's prints.

45 See Griffiths 2016, pp. 164–76, for a more extensive discussion of these various options for grouping and selling prints.

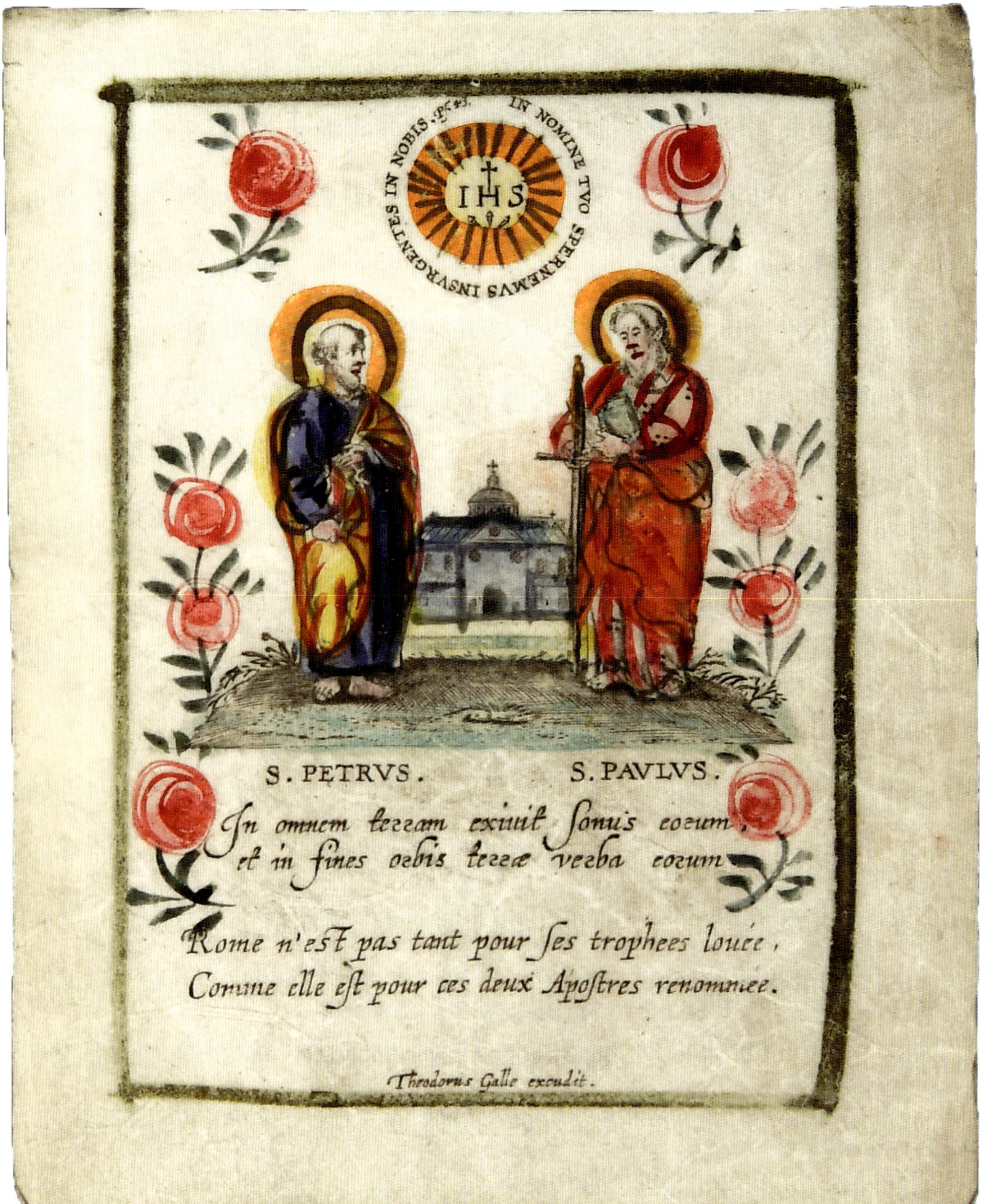
IN NOMINE TVO SPERNEMVS INSVRGENTES IN NOBIS. Ps. 43.
IHS
S. PETRVS.
S. PAVLVS.
In omnem terram exiuit sonus eorum,
et in fines orbis terræ verba eorum.
Rome n'est pas tant pour ses trophees louée,
Comme elle est pour ces deux Apostres renommee.
Theodorus Galle excudit.

CHAPTER 2

PRICES AND PRESENTATION

A CONSIDERATION OF COLORING, SUPPORTS, AND SALES OF PRINTS IN BULK

> From the unmarried woman Constantia van Merlen in the Grave chapel
> 200 images on parchment, large and illuminated at 10 fl. per hundred
> 200 [images] on parchment, small and illuminated at 5 fl. per hundred
> 200 [images] on parchment, small and illuminated … at 6 st. [per piece], one of which is included in this letter
> 40 [images] on parchment, large with stones at 5 ½ st. [per piece]
> 15 [images] on parchment, of the Virgin with many stones, of any sort at 12 st. [per piece]
> 30 [images] on parchment, colored by hand, in any way, at 24 st. [per piece]
> 200 [images] on parchment, small, with stones, of any sort at 3 st. [per piece], one of which is included in this letter[1]

2.5 Anonymous, *Saints Peter and Paul*, s.a., hand-colored engraving, ca. 100 × 74 mm, published by Theodore Galle. Antwerp, Ruusbroecgenootschap: RG-PC Randversieringen 61.

This series of nearly 900 prints was part of a commission for hundreds of books and thousands of other images that was sent to Balthasar Moretus II by the Gdańsk bookseller Georgius (or Georg) Förster in August 1644. Reflecting Förster's personal knowledge of the art market in Antwerp at the time, this part of his order, along with his request for 100 exceptionally large, gilded images from one specific shop, in addition to ten or fifteen attractive images (possibly miniatures, not prints) on parchment for his patron, indicates that he was catering to an upper-class market.[2] Nevertheless, the thousands of prints that he sought from the widow of Joannes Huberti may also have satisfied the wishes of those with different standards and less to spend. While these similarly comprised some 3,000 large and small illuminated images on parchment, offered at the same rates charged by Constantia van Merlen, Förster also requested an additional 200 images on parchment that were not colored, as well as 2,000 images in 4° that were printed on paper and sold at the notably low rate of just 18 st. per hundred (figs. 2.1 and 2.2).[3]

The managers of the Officina Plantiniana rarely received such specific requests for images with this range of special visual embellishments, much less what may have been miniatures (in contrast to hand-colored prints). Nonetheless, sales of thousands of printed images, often combined with the sale or shipment of an assortment of books, had been a part of their regular business dealings throughout the ninety-some years that followed Christopher Plantin's initial dabbling in the trade of prints during the mid-1550s. However, before we embark on a detailed consideration of the diverse facets of the involvement of the Officina Plantiniana in the European print trade and the range of images concerned, it would be useful to delineate some common, fundamental aspects of the traffic in Antwerp prints. In particular:

when did the sale of prints in bulk – namely, the trade in multiple impressions of unspecified images at a common unit price – begin in earnest? What were the base prices for prints sold in this fashion? How might these images have been printed and packaged? And, when did the practice of preparing hand-colored prints increase in popularity and become a burgeoning industry? Essential to understanding the full significance of the astounding range of sales of prints in which Plantin and the Moretuses were engaged, this information will also serve as a vital framework for contextualizing and understanding more fully other records of print sales elsewhere in Europe.

COLORING PRINTS

Nearly two-thirds of the prints Förster ordered in the summer of 1644 were colored or otherwise embellished with stones or minerals. Amounting to approximately 4,395 images in total, 100 of these were also gilded and eleven may have been pure miniatures – that is, without any

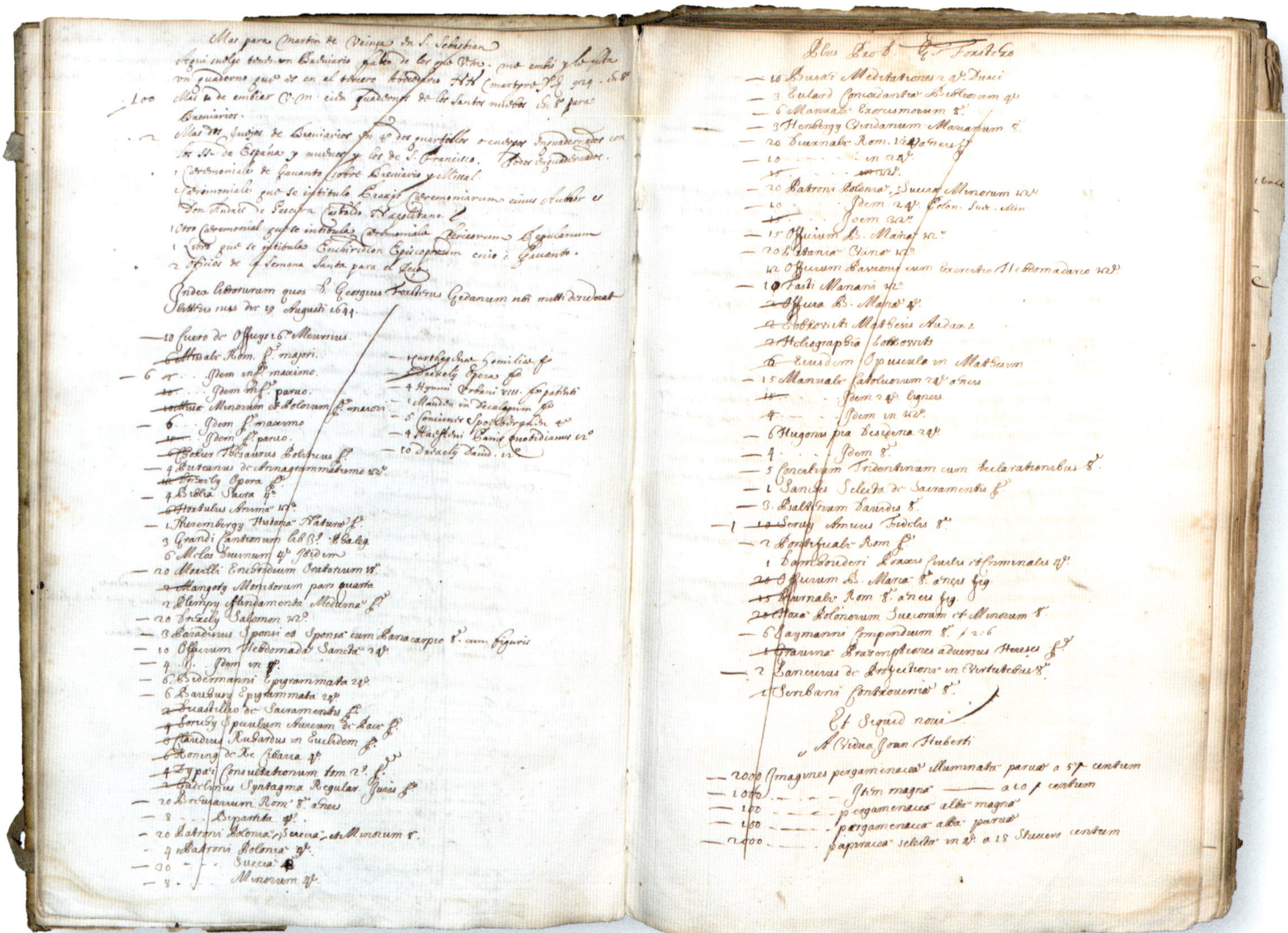

2.1 Order of books and prints for Georg Förster from 19 August 1644. Antwerp, Museum Plantin-Moretus: Arch. 364, *Comptes d'Espagne 1644–1665*, fols. 12v–13r.

printed, base image – as they alone were described as "mineaturae" in Balthasar's transcription of Förster's order and large- or medium-sized "images … miniées" in the record of what Förster was ultimately sent on 17 September 1644 (see figs. 2.2 and 2.4).[4] The main terms used in these records to refer to the other colored images for Förster were "illuminatae" (in his wish list) and "illum.[inées]" (in the sales record). The far more common term used in the records of the Officina Plantiniana to indicate the coloring of maps, books, and individual prints was "afgeset". The same word was also deployed for colored images on parchment that were sold at the identical, high price of 10 fl. per hundred – the sum that both Constantia van Merlen and the widow of Joannes Huberti charged for the "illuminated" images they sent to Förster in 1644.[5] Although these and other, related terms may be associated with distinct techniques and materials used for coloring images, as well as to the relative status of those responsible for the coloring, there is no indication of such a differentiation in any of the records of the Plantin-Moretus Press. Moreover, it is not possible to link any one record to a single, extant image that could, for example, be analyzed technically. What is consistent among these records is the implication that these items were all examples of color being added by hand after the image was printed, in contrast to images that were printed with colored inks from the start.[6]

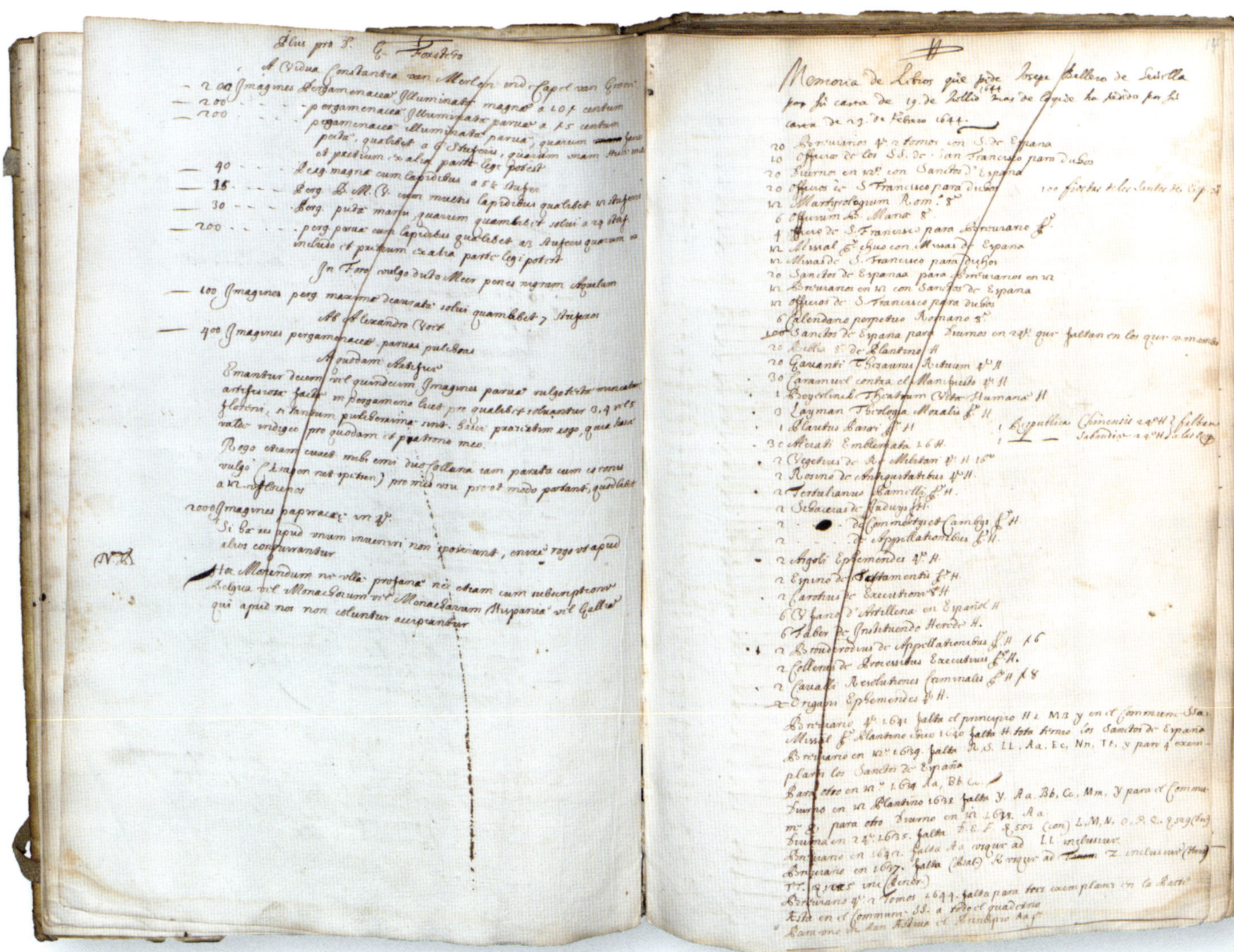

2.2 Order of books and prints for Georg Förster from 19 August 1644. Antwerp, Museum Plantin-Moretus: Arch. 364, *Comptes d'Espagne 1644–1665*, fol. 13v.

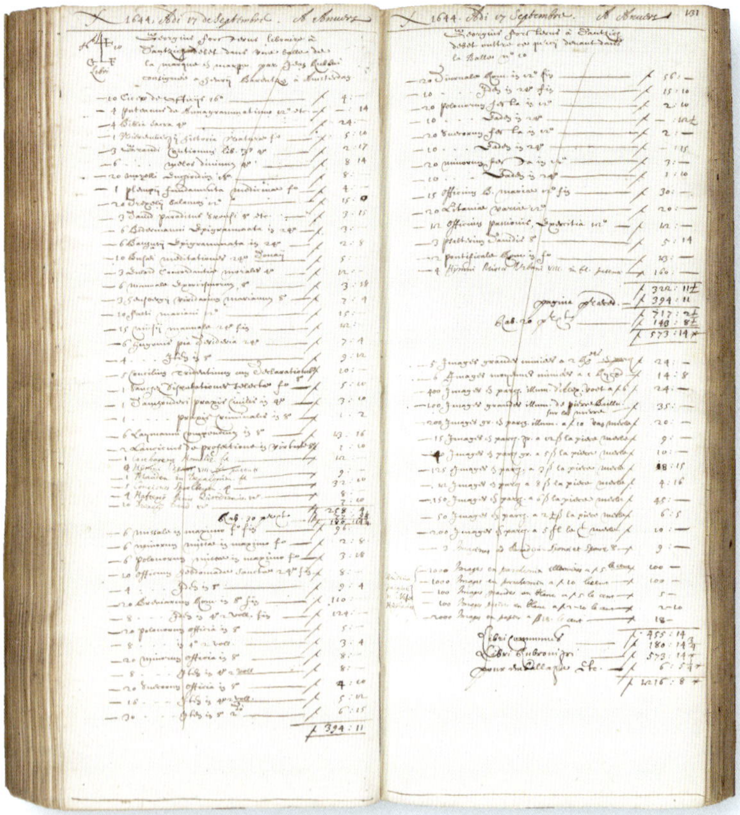

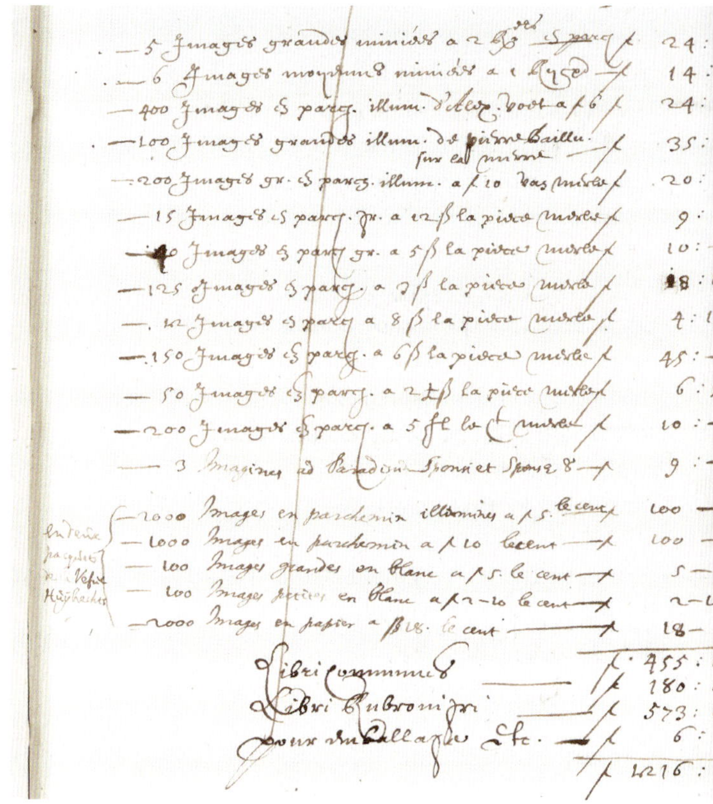

2.3 Record of shipment of books and prints to Georg Förster on 17 September 1644. Antwerp, Museum Plantin-Moretus: Arch. 252, *Journal 1644*, fols. 130v-131r.

2.4 Detail of the list of prints sent to Georg Förster on 17 September 1644. Antwerp, Museum Plantin-Moretus: Arch. 252, *Journal 1644*, fol. 131r.

In the records of Antwerp's Guild of St Luke, the individual who performed the hand-coloring was referred to as a "verlichter" or "verluchter" (illuminator) from the fifteenth century until the mid-sixteenth century. The one famous exception to this pattern is the citation of Abraham Ortelius (Ortels) as an "afsetter van carten" (colorer of maps) in 1547.[7] Hereafter – as of 1584 and with only an occasional exception in a few guild years, such as 1617–1618, 1639–1640, and 1640–1641 – the term "afsetter" (colorer) is clearly preferred and is what is also commonly used in the records of the Officina Plantiniana.[8] Among the various *afsetters* cited in the guild records are several women who are either identified as taking on apprentices to learn this trade or as *afsetters* themselves. The first such clear reference dates to 1624–1625, when a certain Maria Bauhuysen paid 10 fl. "voor heuren vrydom in t'afsetten" (for her freedom to work, coloring by hand).[9] However, women (in addition to men) had already been engaged in this field for decades, as is evident from the activities of (among others) Mynken Liefrinck, to whom Plantin regularly turned for commissions to color cartographic works.[10] The number of women mentioned in this context increases dramatically in the guild years of 1632–1637 and includes a reference to Constantia van Merlen as an *afsetterse* in 1634–1635, a mention of the widow of Pauwels Huybrechts taking on an apprentice *afsetter* in the year 1635–1636, and other, more general citations of a "widow Huybrechts" taking on two apprentice *verlichters* in 1640–1641.[11]

This trend is significant because the widow of Joannes Huberti and Constantia van Merlen were the individuals Förster singled out for the supply of the vast majority of the images he ordered – some 6,600, of which nearly 4,400 were specially decorated – while two other local dealers, Pierre Baillu and Alexander Voet I, provided the remaining 100 large, gilded images on parchment and an additional 400 "attractive" illuminated images, respectively.[12] As the records of the Officina Plantiniana demonstrate, it was not uncommon to have a woman manage a business that dealt in printed images: consider the transactions with Volcxken Diericx, Passchijnke van Gelre, and Marie de Man, for example. The Huberti (Huybrechts) family was well known in Antwerp for coloring printed images. Although the family patriarch, Adriaen Huberti, was the first to supply the Moretuses with colored prints for resale in bulk (in 1597), his son, Adriaen II, was the first in the family to be registered officially in the Guild of St Luke as an *afsetter* (in the guild year of 1611–1612) and was followed soon thereafter (in 1615–1616) by his brother Pauwels I.[13] In 1635, when he was fifty-two years old, Adriaen II signed a statement, together with his son Maarten (then twenty-two), that they had taken in a boy from Wallonia, Jacques Buriau, and instructed him as an apprentice in the art of coloring prints some four or five years earlier (although they do not appear to have registered him with the guild).[14] Consequently, references to widows among the Huybrechts taking on apprentices would have fit within established family business practices.

Constantia van Merlen, by contrast, had been active as an *afsetterse* herself. When she was registered as such in the Guild of St Luke for the guild year of 1634–1635, she would have been approximately twenty-five years old. Since she was the sister of Theodore van Merlen, and the print publisher Abraham van Merlen was her guardian, she had connections to a well-established family of print publishers in Antwerp. Never married, she was registered as a "geestelijke dochter" (spiritual daughter) in 1645, thereby declaring that she would devote her life to God, despite not entering a convent. Nevertheless, she evidently maintained her shop from which she sold prints until her death in 1655.[15]

Though not comprising a complete overview of everyone who was training or employed in the art of coloring printed images, the registration of *afsetters* in the Guild of St Luke reflects the general flux in demand for practitioners of this craft. Specifically, until the mid-1620s, isolated references to a *verlichter* or *afsetter* appeared sporadically, usually with gaps of several years between them. But from the guild year of 1624–1625, such references often appeared annually through the second quarter of the seventeenth century; two or more individuals were frequently noted per year, and as many as nine were recorded in 1640–1641 alone. Their numbers continued to increase dramatically across the second half of the seventeenth century.[16] This pattern coincides with trends in the Moretuses' traffic in hand-colored prints. Between 1587 and 1625, their sales of colored prints were dominated by occasional requests for illuminated altar cards (referred to as *canon missae* (or just canons) in their records), and exceptional sales of colored images in bulk occurred in 1592, 1597, and 1620.[17] When the suppliers of colored images are noted, the names that recur are Mynken Liefrinck (who assisted Plantin with the production and occasional coloring of canons), Adriaen Huberti (who was paid for both coloring canons and providing colored prints in bulk), and Michael Snijders (who supplied the Moretuses with specially finished altar cards in this period).[18] However, as of 1628, the Moretuses were engaged annually in satisfying the growing international demand for hand-colored prints from Antwerp in diverse formats and price categories. While the Huberti family may have been the most prominent practitioners of this art initially, assorted print publishers were also participating simultaneously in this new, burgeoning market by the late 1620s. Those who took the lead in the Moretuses' accounts in this regard were: Jan Cnobbaert and subsequently his widow, Marie de Man; Theodore Galle (fig. 2.5), followed by his widow, Catharina Moerentorf, and ultimately their son Jan Galle; and Michael Snijders. Notably, each began to provide the Moretuses with diverse sorts of hand-colored prints on parchment between 1628 and 1629.[19]

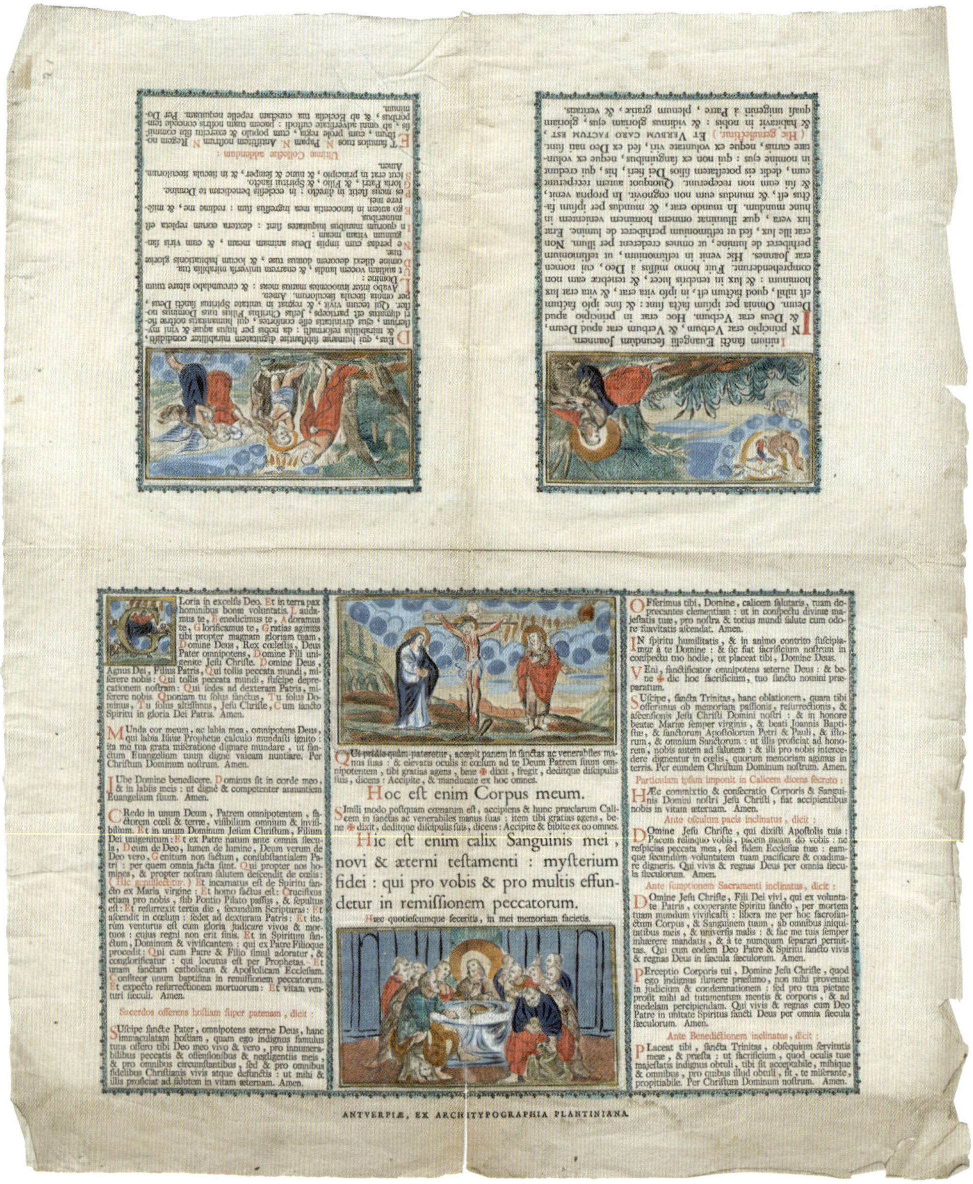

2.6 Anonymous, *Canon missae*, s.a., engraving and letterpress with hand coloring, 535 × 445 mm (sheet), published by the Moretuses. Antwerp, Museum Plantin-Moretus: 2–166.

The intensity of both the general demand for hand-colored prints and the need to engage individuals on an official basis who could prepare the requisite images in the mid-1620s is also reflected in contracts between two of these suppliers – Snijders and Cnobbaert – and individuals they sought to color prints for them.[20] In Snijders's case, the couple he wished to employ in December 1625, the *afsetter* Bartholomeus van Ginderdeuren and his wife, Magdalena de Swert, had already worked for him prior to the signing of the contract; there is a reference to Snijders agreeing to provide them with the prints that were to be colored in a more timely fashion than before. Whether the earlier employment had been a brief trial period or work of longer duration is not clear. The 1625 contract, which was to remain in effect for the rest of Van Ginderdeuren's and and De Swert's lives ("soo lange sy respective leven"), stipulated a detailed series of rates that Snijders was to pay for the coloring and gilding of images on paper and parchment. These ranged from 3 st. per piece for images on large half-leaves of parchment to 13 st. per dozen small images on parchment to 18 st. per dozen images in 4° and printed on paper. They also agreed to prices for illuminating canons: 4.5 st. per piece for large canons, 3.5 st. per piece for small ones, and 3 st. per piece for the usual accompanying image of St John the Evangelist or a "lavabor", a portrayal of a baptism, as in the canon published by the Moretuses (fig. 2.6). Aside from this lifetime provision, a promise by Snijders to give Van Ginderdeuren and his wife an annual New Year's bonus of 6 fl. per year, and the condition that Snijders furnish the prints on time, the other essential, mutually binding condition was that Snijders promised never to leave Van Ginderdeuren and De Swert without work and they agreed never to work for someone else.

Although the detailed list of charges per size and type of object in Snijders's agreement may have been exceptional, other aspects recur in the contract Cnobbaert signed some two years later with Jaspar van Lanckvelt; this contract described the conditions of employment for Van Lanckvelt's daughter Catharina, who was then approximately twenty years old. Since other members of the Lanckvelt family were subsequently registered as *verlichters*, they appear to have specialized in this craft like the Huberti/Huybrechts family before them.[21] In particular, even though the contract covered only an initial period of just two years, Cnobbaert similarly promised to provide Catharina with work continually, not even missing a day, and to pay her a daily wage of 2 fl. per day if he did not have work. For her part, Catharina agreed to work faithfully for him and to the best of her abilities; she was to embellish prints with not only the appropriate paints, but also gold and silver.[22] Thus, once again, a reciprocal, exclusive commitment between the print publisher and the individual employed to color prints was an essential component of the agreement. While the payment and work stipulations were essential for the *afsetters*, guaranteeing them a regular income, the description of the quality and materials to be used may indicate the intensity of the demand for illuminated prints and the competition to produce them at this time.

Given the existence of strict agreements for the execution of colored prints, is it possible to link them to a price breakdown of what these and other publishers of colored prints charged for their wares? Regrettably, the general lack of information on the relative size of the colored images supplied to the Moretuses for resale impedes such an analysis. Additionally, there is the complication of potentially significant variations in the costs of the materials used, from paints and precious metals to the quality of the parchment. Nevertheless, if one reduces the various rates charged by the Moretuses' three primary suppliers of colored prints on parchment to a price per print, some common patterns emerge (see Table 8). Remarkably, there is a striking concentration of prices between 2 and 3 st. per print; both the Galle and Cnobbaert families clearly offered a variety of options at regular price intervals of 2, 2.5, and 3 st. per print. A few exceptional rates at either end were also occasionally supplemented with additional options, such as plain prints on parchment, colored prints on paper, or even, on one occasion, colored prints on satin.[23] This information also indicates that the vast majority of the work provided by the suppliers whom Förster favored also fell within this range of prices. A comparison of the significantly greater cost of the images that were most likely pure miniatures – 2 fl. 8 st. and 4 fl. 16 st. (or 48 st. and 76 st.) per piece – with the most expensive items in Table 8, (prints sold at 10 st., or ½ florin, per piece) underscores their distinctive qualities.[24] Similarly, the prices Snijders agreed to pay to Van Ginderdeuren and De Swert could, generally, be covered by the selling prices commonly found among the items sold via the Moretuses. Notably, in one rare instance, the formats of some of the colored prints Snijders sold the Moretuses are given, namely, a group of 400 images in 4° that were printed two to a leaf of paper and sold for 2 st. per print in 1629. This indicates that the cost of having such prints colored (18 st. per dozen, or 1.5 st. per print for coloring and gilding) would have constituted approximately three-quarters of the total selling price (if the prints in questions were both colored and gilded). However, the price ratio for coloring images printed on the more costly support of parchment would most likely have differed. Since the Van Ginderdeurens charged 1.5 st. per piece for coloring images in 4° on both paper and parchment, their rates were not based on the support on which the image was printed, but its size (and, presumably, the materials used). Consequently, when the extra cost of the parchment support would have been added to the total selling price, the relative cost of the coloring would have been less.[25]

While such comparisons clearly provide valuable insight into the sale of colored prints, which became increasingly popular in the mid-seventeenth century, Antwerp prints had already been traded on the European market for decades and had been judged by criteria other than their colorful embellishment or printing on costly supports such as parchment and satin. Constituting the bulk of Plantin's and the Moretuses' trade in printed images, the sale of plain prints on paper offers a more extensive, informative view of the relative quantities and range of prices at which diverse Antwerp print publishers sold their wares.

PRINTS ON PAPER SOLD IN BULK

By 1558 – just a few years after he had begun work as a printer and publisher in Antwerp and five years following his first known transaction as a print dealer – Plantin began to sell unspecified prints on paper by the hundreds.[26] Continuing this practice in the decades to come, Plantin's successors expanded their sale of such images in response to an ever-growing demand for not simply hundreds of prints, but thousands upon thousands. As is documented in Table 7, the prices at which unspecified prints were sold in bulk to the managers of the Officina Plantiniana ranged from 4 st. per image (or leaf of paper) to 18 st. per 100 images (or just .18 st. per print). Both of these rates were used only occasionally by a few print sellers. While Hieronymus Cock, Philips Galle, and Theodore Galle offered prints for sale at 4 st. in

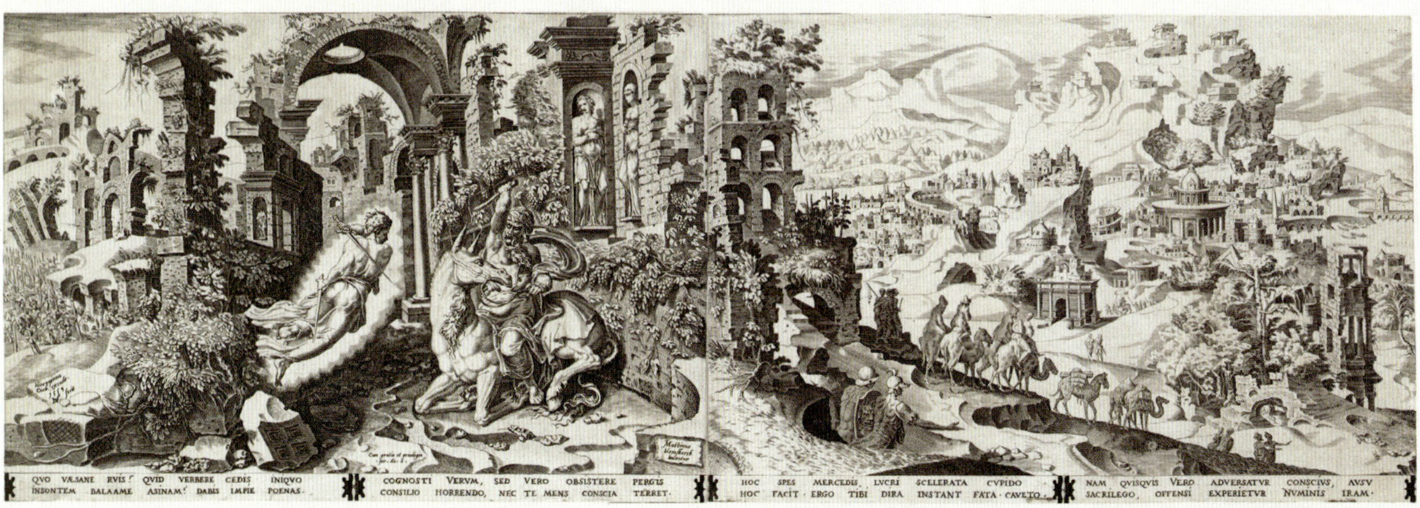

2.7 Dirck Volckertsz. Coornhert after Maarten van Heemskerck, *Landscape with Balaam and an Angel*, 1554, engraving, 295 × 850 mm. New York, The Metropolitan Museum of Art: Purchase, Marjorie Phelps Starr Bequest, 2023 (2023.382). Image courtesy of the Metropolitan Museum of Art. Appendix 1: CD-13.

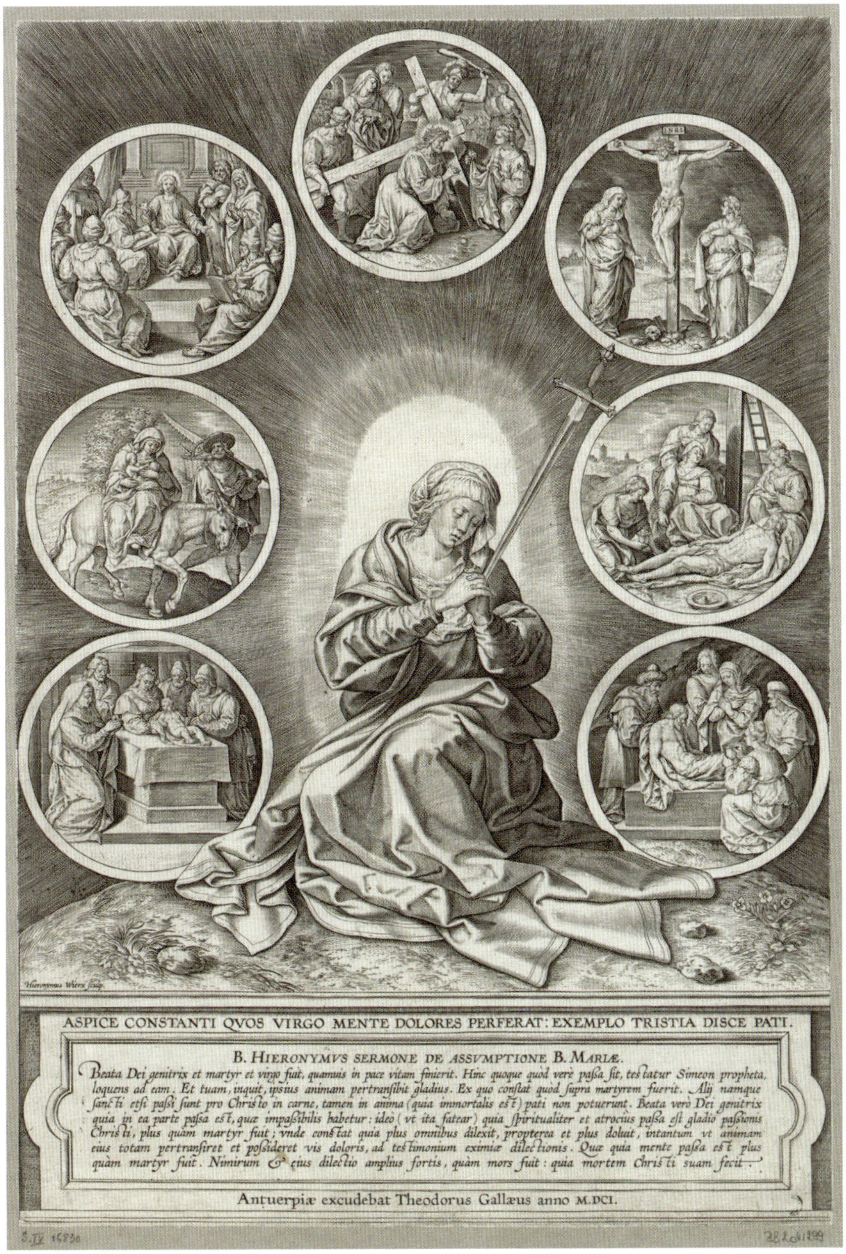

2.8 Hieronymus Wierix after Crispijn van den Broeck, *Seven Sorrows of the Virgin*, 1587 and reissued by Theodore Galle in 1601, engraving, 446 × 300 mm. Brussels, The Royal Library, Print Department: S.IV 16830. Appendix 1: TG-25.

1568, 1601, 1618, and 1625, Theodore Galle was the only one to sell images at just 18 st. per 100 (in 1615 and 1630). However, both Adriaen Collaert and Jan Cnobbaert offered prints at a similarly low rate (20 st. per 100 images) in 1608 and 1628, respectively.[27] Although it is not known specifically which prints were distributed at these two price extremes, a consideration of Plantin's and the Moretuses' trade in specific images provided by these same print sellers offers a few concrete examples of what they did sell at such prices. Specifically, in 1568, Cock sold Plantin an impression of his 1554 publication, *Landscape with Balaam and an Angel* (fig. 2.7) at 4 st., while, in 1602, Theodore Galle sold Jan Moretus I two impressions of an image of the *Seven Sorrows of the Virgin* at 4 st. per print. The latter was most likely an image that was commissioned from Hieronymus Wierix in 1587 (fig. 2.8) and that Galle subsequently acquired.[28]

Despite their common, high-end selling price, Galle's *Seven Sorrows of the Virgin* is roughly half the size of Cock's *Landscape with Balaam* (446 × 300 mm vs. 295 × 850 mm). Both of these works are, in turn, significantly larger than Hieronymus Wierix's *Death of Saint Cecilia* (152 × 117 mm), which he engraved after a composition by Francesco Vanni (fig. 6.7); 100 impressions of this print were sold to the Jesuit Thomas Sailly in 1606, also at 4 st. per print.[29] The remarkable range of images sold at this high price – two within four years of one another – reveals that what a print publisher could charge for the works in his or her stock was influenced by many.

That each print publisher had his or her own preferred range of prices for selling their stock is not surprising and is confirmed by both the bulk and individual print prices noted in the accounts of the Officina Plantiniana. As indicated above, Theodore Galle offered prints for sale in bulk at the widest range of prices; 2.5 st. per image was the most common rate charged at the upper end of this spectrum, while 36 st. per 100 (or just .36 st. per print) was the most common rate at the lower end. In between, Galle's prices varied incrementally, often with a potentially systematic .5 or .25 st. differential. This range was comparable to that of his father, Philips, although the vast majority of Philips's sales of prints in bulk were concentrated at the rate of 18 st. per quire of twenty-five leaves of prints, which typically amounted to .72 st. per engraving.[30] Whereas Theodore Galle was clearly endeavoring to serve a broad market of potential clients with his diverse offerings, his brother-in-law Charles de Mallery did the opposite by focusing on a limited niche in the general market for prints sold in bulk. When De Mallery provided the Moretuses with prints for resale in bulk, he almost invariably charged 50 st. per 100 images, or .5 st. per print. In the few instances when he sold a single image (rather than a series of prints) via the Moretuses, the same rate was applied.[31] If we compare Galle's and De Mallery's divergent approaches with the bulk rates favored by Adriaen Collaert, another brother-in-law of Galle's and De Mallery's, and with those used by Hieronymus Wierix, the personal nature of decisions about sale prices becomes evident. Collaert supplied the Moretuses with prints in bulk less frequently than did Galle, De Mallery, and Wierix, but when he did so, his works routinely fell in the lower end of the price spectrum, between .75 st. and .2 st. per print. Wierix, by contrast, regularly sold prints in bulk at notably higher rates of 2, 1.5, and 1 st. per print; only once did he use the price of .75 st. In order to contextualize these distinct price ranges properly, we need to know more about the individual works to which the price ranges were applied by each print seller. Though such data is not available for most sales, an examination of which specific prints each publisher sold at rates ranging from 1 to .72 st. is highly revealing. Above all, we learn that the basic size of the prints sold by Collaert, Theodore Galle, and Philips Galle (in addition to Gerard de Jode, Hieronymus Cock, and Volcxken Diericx) at these rates was remarkably similar. Most prints were approxiately 250 × 190 mm – more than twice the size of the engravings (ca. 100 × 70 mm) Wierix sold within this price range. Indeed, Wierix even sold prints of the former size at 2 st. per image: more than twice what the other print publishers charged for their significantly larger engravings. Similarly, the works De Mallery sold at his usual .5 st. per print were also notably smaller than what Philips Galle sold at .72 st. per image and what Theodore may have sold at .375 st. [32] Consequently, while the range of prices at which prints were sold may have been determined largely by the general size of the images, other factors, including the artists and print publishers involved, the subject matter, and the way in which the prints were executed, also affected the final selling price and, simultaneously, the demand for the various works.[33]

These observations notwithstanding, different print publishers also used some of the same rates for bulk sales of prints. By far the most common price applied to plain, unspecified prints sold in bulk via the Officina Plantiniana was 36 st. per 100 images (or .36 st. per print). Theodore Galle routinely sold prints to the Moretuses at this rate throughout his dealings with them from 1608 – several years after the establishment of his own print-publishing business – until his death in 1633. While his son Jan continued this practice in 1637, three other independent print publishers with whom the Moretuses traded – Abraham van Merlen, Michael Snijders, and Jan Boel – also periodically sold them prints at 36 st. per 100 images between 1615 and 1626.[34] Charles de Mallery and the Wierixes, notably, did not. The pervasiveness of this rate for selling prints in bulk is also demonstrated by a document from 26 June 1632 that was signed by several Antwerp print sellers, including Jan Boel, Peeter de Jode (I or II), Carel Collaert, Philips de Mallery, and Theodore van Merlen, each of whom either dealt directly with the Moretuses or was related to print publishers who did so on a regular basis. At the request of the engraver Cornelis van Tienen, this group, along with the art dealer Peeter van Lanckvelt I, agreed that the following were standard selling prices for plain prints on paper paid for in cash:

> 36 st. per 100 images in 4° and folio
> 18 st. per 100 images in "half quarto" ("halff quarten" = 8°)
> 3 fl. 12 st. (= 72 st.) per 100 images in whole folio ("heel foliën").[35]

In this case, the differences in price correspond to the relative sizes of the images; the lowest bulk rate found in the Moretuses' sales (18 st. per 100) is associated here with smaller, "half quarto" (or 8°) images, and prints sold for twice the price were at least twice as large (4° or folio). The next doubling in price and size occurs when we move from 4° or folio prints to "whole folio" prints sold at 72 st. per 100, or .72 st. per print. This rate was used only once by Theodore Galle (in 1633) for a bulk print sale, although he and a handful of other print publishers – Adriaen Collaert, Charles de Mallery, Hieronymus Wierix, and his father Philips – occasionally sold prints at a slightly higher rate of .75 st. per print between 1596 and 1624. A far more likely parallel with the 72 st.-per-100-prints price category is the rate favored for sales of prints in bulk by leading Antwerp print publishers active in the last third of the sixteenth century: 18 st. per quire of twenty-five leaves of prints, or .72 st. per leaf. Used primarily by Gerard de Jode, Volcxken Diericx, Philips Galle, and Adriaen Huberti in their transactions with Plantin and Jan Moretus I between 1570 and 1597, this rate was also periodically employed by a variety of other publishers, ranging from Hans Liefrinck in 1558 to Adriaen Collaert, Peeter de Jode I, and Theodore Galle in 1608, to Abraham van Merlen as late as 1619.[36] A rate of 18 st. per quire of twenty-five leaves of prints was, moreover, a standard for selling prints that was also recognized beyond Antwerp in this period. When the Amsterdam print, map, and bookseller Cornelis Claesz compiled his stock list of the maps and other works of art he had for sale in 1609, he listed numerous "historien" (narrative) and "enckelde folien" (single folios) of prints by diverse artists at the rate of 18 st. per "boeck" (quire), where two half leaves were reckoned as the same as one whole leaf (meaning, as is indicated in the stock list, that some leaves had two images printed together on one leaf).[37]

The essential question is what the relationship might have been between the "whole folio" images cited in the 1632 list of prices that was discussed above and the folios (referred to simply with the abbreviation "f°" or as "folien" or "folia") or leaves (most often described either as "fueilles" or "bladers") that in both Claessens's 1609 stock list and numerous records of the Plantin-Moretus Press are associated with sales of prints by the "boek" or "main" (for quire) of twenty-five units each.[38] A list of prints that Diericx sold Plantin on 12 February 1580 indicates how large a single leaf sold in bulk at 18 st. per quire might have been. Specifically, the total number of prints in this record (ninety-six) – six sets of Pieter van der Heyden's series of the *Seven Deadly Sins* after Pieter Bruegel I (with eight engravings per series) and four sets each of two different series of Johannes Stradanus's hunts without borders (with six engravings per series) – was noted as forty-eight folios (f°) for the *Seven Deadly Sins* and two groups of twenty-four folios (f°) for the hunts.[39] The price for all of these images was then calculated at the rate of 18 st. (per quire) and resulted in a total charge of 3 fl. 9.25 st. (or 69.25 st.). If one divides this total by the unit rate of 18 st., this results in 3.84 quires, which, when multiplied by twenty-five leaves per quire, gives us ninety-six, the total number of prints sold at this rate. Thus, each image was counted as a single leaf. Because these images are of a similar size, approximately 210–220 × 300 mm, the single leaf unit used in these calculations was roughly equivalent to an ordinary (A4) sheet of paper today and not the full sheet of paper used to print books. Similar conclusions can be drawn for sales of prints supplied by Gerard de Jode, Philips Galle, and Theodore Galle between 1580 and 1608. The only difference is that these prints were often slightly smaller (ca. 200–220 × 250–280 mm).[40] Consequently, the term "quire" was used to indicate the *number* of leaves of paper concerned, rather than the full sheet of paper that is implied when quires are cited in connection with reams of paper for printing books. Rather, the "whole folio" noted in the 1632 price list most likely was a leaf of paper comparable to an A4 format.[41]

As the cheaper rates of 36 st. and 18 st. per 100 images cited in the 1632 document indicate, smaller images were also sold in bulk. In the Plantin-Moretus accounts, prints were not sold at such prices until the first decades of the seventeenth century. During the late sixteenth century, however, the 18 st.-per-quire rate was applied to smaller images; in this instance, multiple images were printed on a single leaf of paper, in contrast to the individual "whole folio" engravings. For example, in 1588, Plantin sent the Jesuit Thomas Sailly 100 small figures on thirteen leaves, while, in 1587, he sent the bookseller François Boulet three quires of images in 8°, 16°, 24°, and 32°, implying that some quires must have comprised leaves with prints in different sizes.[42] Such references are most common among the quires of prints supplied by Adriaen Huberti in the 1590s. These make it clear that what counted in terms of pricing was the number of leaves of paper involved rather than the number of images printed on them. Consider when Huberti provided Jan Moretus I with two quires of prints for the bookseller Joos van der Straeten; each quire was valued at 18 st. per quire, but one was described as consisting of "small" images, eight to a leaf, while the other comprised "large" images, four to a leaf.[43]

Although one might assume that these were all cases of eight or four images printed on a single leaf of paper from eight or four discrete copper plates, some print publishers also had larger copper plates engraved with multiple smaller images per plate. The best documented example of this practice are the publications of the Altzenbach family of print publishers, who were active in Cologne from the early 1600s to around 1680. Like their local competitor, Peter Overadt and his heirs, they produced numerous large sheets with multiple images – most of which were devotional; there could be four to forty-eight distinct compositions, in addition to occasionally complete series of four, six, eight, or twelve subjects engraved per plate.[44] However, a number of Antwerp print publishers, including several who dealt with the Moretuses, also engaged in this practice. Examples range from smaller groups of thematically related images and decorative designs published by Theodore Galle, Anton Wierix (III?), Jan-Baptist Barbé, and Michael Snijders to larger leaves with multiple subjects, for instance the works published by Adriaen Collaert and Maarten van den Enden (figs. 2.9–2.14). The numbering of Van den Enden's plate containing the *Seven Sorrows of the Virgin* suggests that he (or a subsequent publisher) published so many prints in this fashion that it was simpler to refer to the plates by number instead of subject, as was done with many of the broadsides with multiple images published by the Altzenbach family.[45] Collaert's plate with eight images from the *Passion* and *Life of the Virgin* (fig. 2.13) is of particular interest when it is juxtaposed with a sales record from 1602, which states that he provided more than 5,000 small prints in various formats, including 400 leaves with eight images per leaf, for resale to the merchant Rocho di Gabrielli for export to Gdańsk.[46] Even if this particular plate was not in use by 1602, it indicates that Collaert, at least, had such group plates made prior to his death in 1618.

Print series were also occasionally sold with multiple images printed individually on a single leaf and not already cut into individual prints. This was evidently the case when, on 18 February 1580, Diericx supplied Plantin with two sets of Hans Vredeman de Vries's series of twenty architectural perspective views in oval frames (together with an engraved title page). The work was dedicated to Peter Ernst von Mansfeld and was in the form of eleven leaves with two figures per leaf.[47]

The above examples provide concrete reminders of two fundamental aspects of the trade in prints in the late sixteenth and early seventeenth centuries. First, while one may know how many *leaves* of paper with prints were sold, this total was not necessarily equivalent to the number of *prints* sold. At best, the number of leaves provides a minimum estimate of the number of prints. Second, although many of the sales recorded in the accounts of the Officina Plantiniana may present the works concerned as generic, unspecified bundles of prints, the actual images sold were not necessarily all nondescript, anonymous workshop productions. As the numerous works listed in Tables 1–6 and described in Appendix 1 make clear, the prints sold en masse via the Plantin-Moretus Press could also be remarkable images by leading sixteenth- and seventeenth-century artists. The Press sold works designed by renowned artists like Pieter Bruegel I, Hans Vredeman de Vries, Maarten van Heemskerck, Maarten de Vos, Johannes Stradanus, and Francesco Vanni. Additionally there were numerous images by respected printmakers like the Van Doetecum brothers, the Galle family, Hendrick Goltzius, Jan II and Adriaen Collaert, Charles de Mallery, and the Wierix brothers, whose work was so highly prized that they were able to ask more for it than the average print publisher, even when selling their engravings in bulk. However, in order to appreciate the full significance of the multitude of prints from Antwerp that were traded on the European market under the auspices of the managers of the Plantin-Moretus Press, one must also consider the individuals involved in all stages of the process – from the suppliers to the middlemen who facilitated the transactions to the clients who sought the images – as well as the underlying networks and disparate destinations to which the prints were sent. The vibrancy and immense potential of the print trade is suggested by the relative speed with which Plantin entered the fray in the mid-sixteenth century, just a few years after his arrival in Antwerp and before he had established his future livelihood in the city as a bookseller and printer. The following consideration of his evolving participation in the print trade not only introduces the major players in the print world of sixteenth-century Antwerp, but also sets the stage for how his successors, the Moretuses, would interact with subsequent generations of Antwerp print publishers and contribute to the European traffic in prints.

2.9 Anonymous, *Nativity*, *Crucifixion*, *Resurrection*, and *Lamb of God*, s.a., engraved together on one plate, 86 × 70 mm, published by Theodore Galle. Wolfegg, Fürstlich zu Waldburg-Wolfegg'sche Kunstsammlungen: vol. 221, print 316.

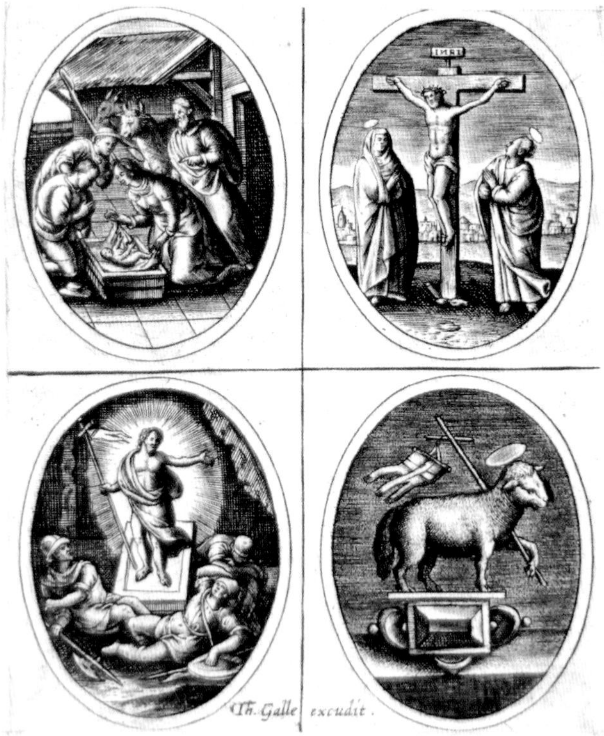

2.10 Anton Wierix III (attributed to), *Saint Teresa of Avila* and *Father John of the Cross*, s.a., engraved together on one plate, ca. 75 × 55 mm. Wolfegg, Fürstlich zu Waldburg-Wolfegg'sche Kunstsammlungen: vol. 205, print 879bis.

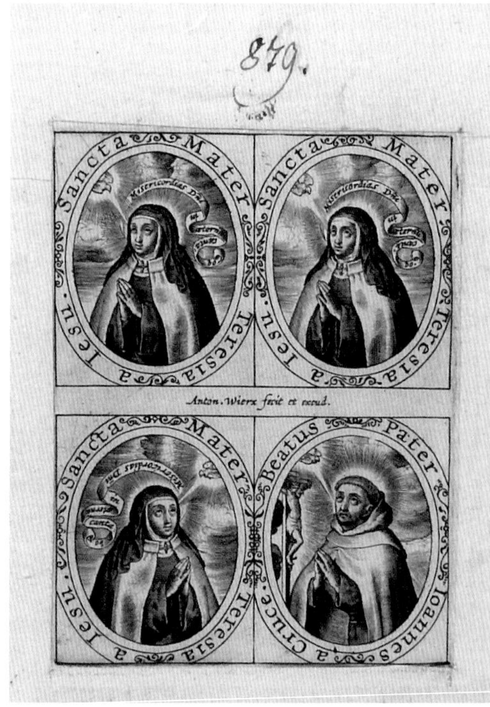

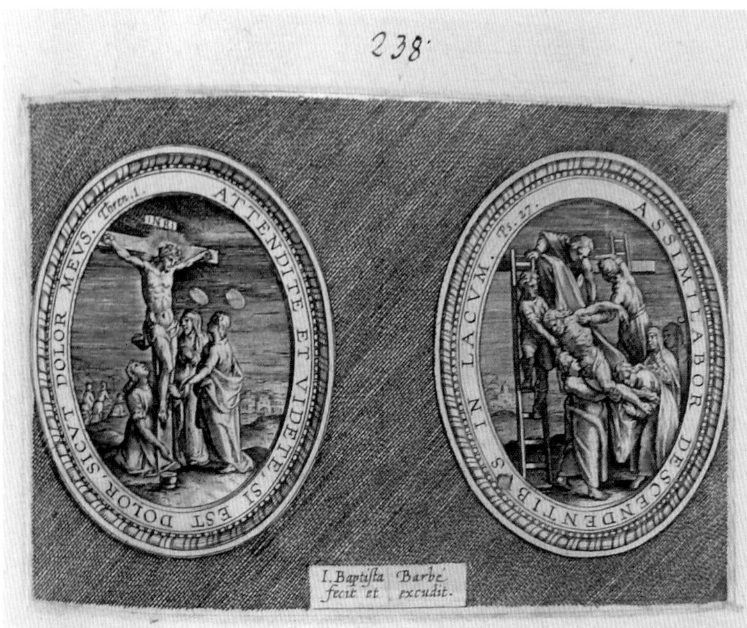

2.11 Jan-Baptist Barbé, *The Crucifixion* and the *Descent from the Cross*, s.a., engraved together on one plate, 71 × 105 mm. Wolfegg, Fürstlich zu Waldburg-Wolfegg'sche Kunstsammlungen: vol. 58, print 238.

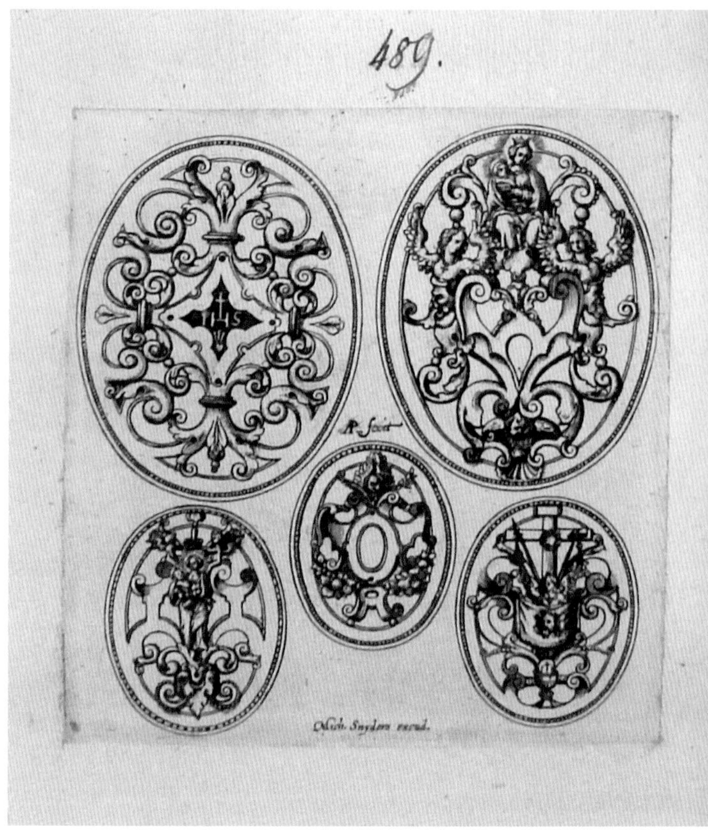

2.12 A.P., Five decorative ovals engraved together on one plate, s.a., 91 × 84 mm, published by Michael Snijders. Wolfegg, Fürstlich zu Waldburg-Wolfegg'sche Kunstsammlungen: vol. 221, print 489.

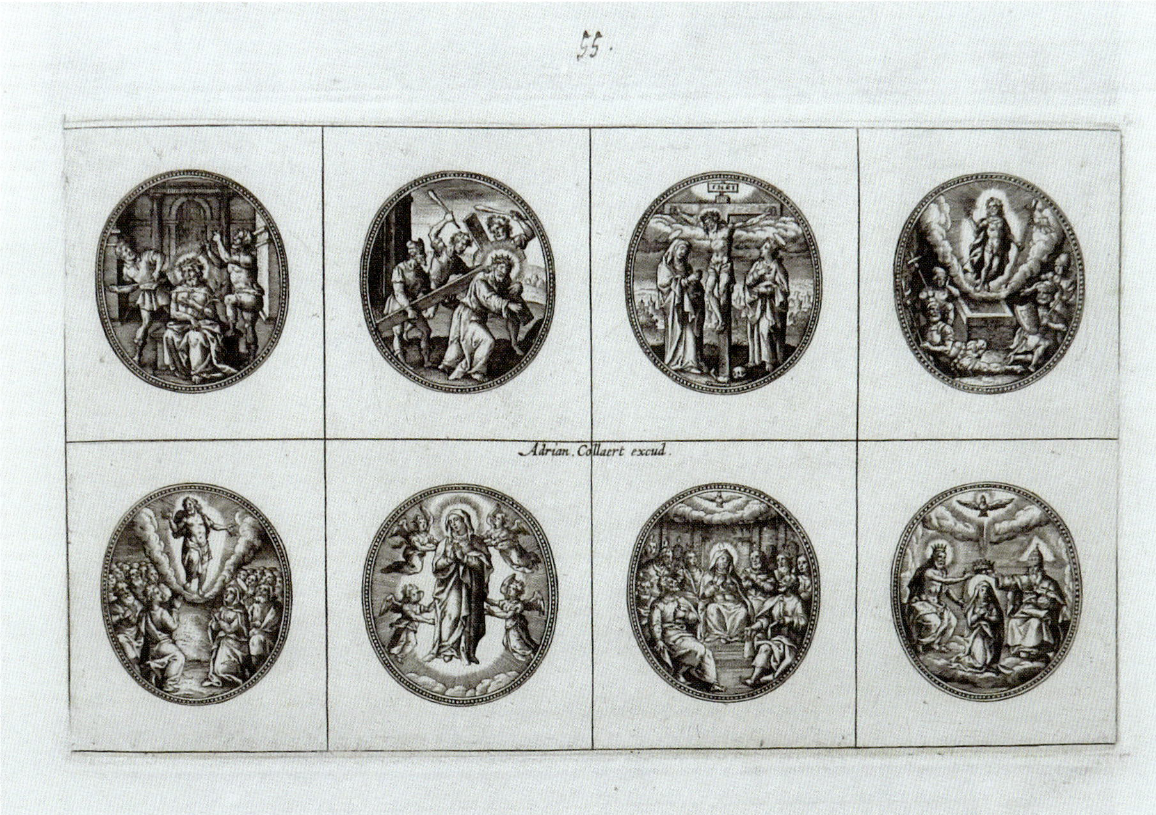

2.13 Anonymous, selected images from the *Passion* and the *Life of the Virgin*, s.a., eight ovals engraved together on one plate, 110 × 181 mm, published by Adriaen Collaert. Wolfegg, Fürstlich zu Waldburg-Wolfegg'sche Kunstsammlungen: vol. 193, print 355.

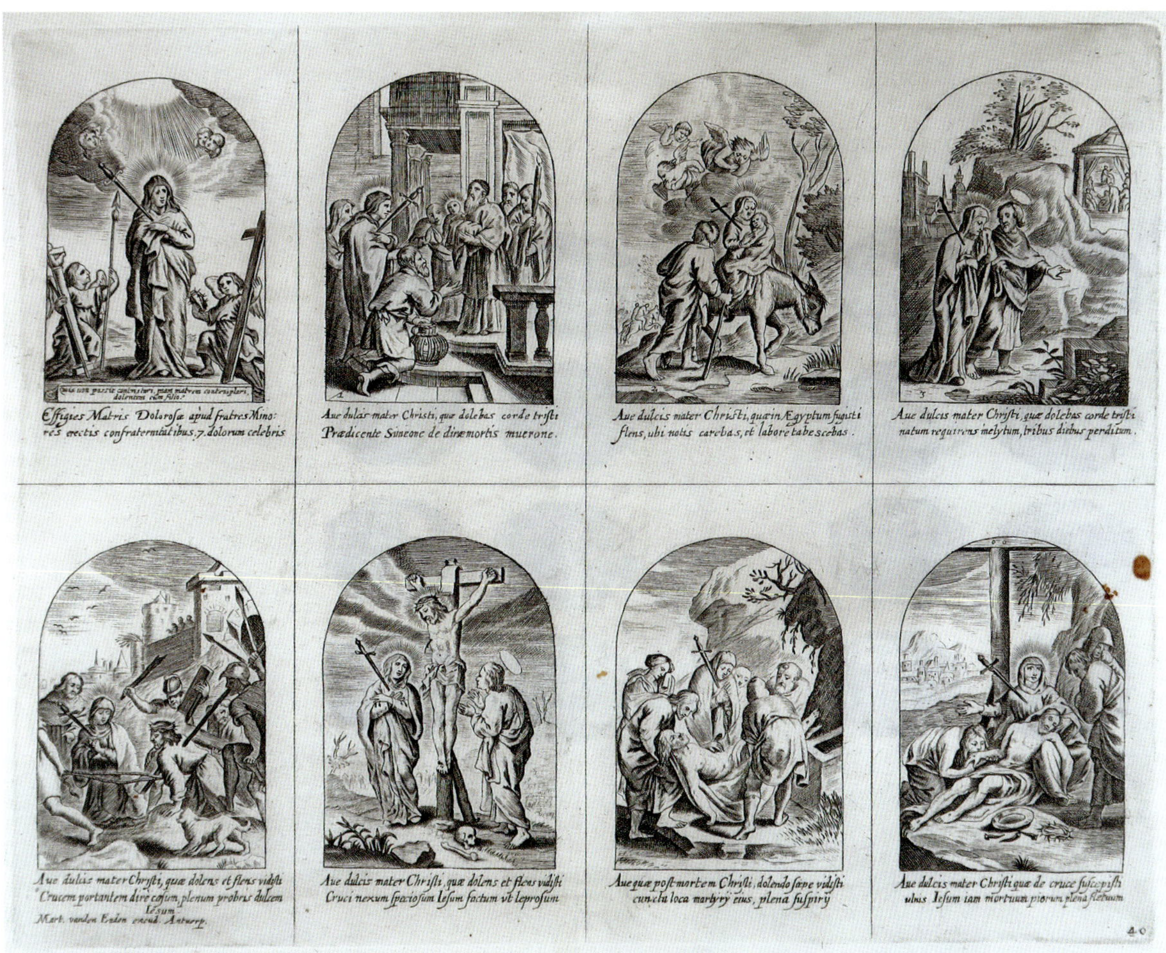

2.14 Anonymous, *Seven Sorrows of the Virgin*, s.a,, eight images engraved together on one plate, 291 × 234 mm, published by Maarten van den Enden. Wolfegg, Fürstlich zu Waldburg-Wolfegg'sche Kunstsammlungen: vol. 221, print 226.

1 MPM Arch. 364, fol. 13v:

"A vidua Constantia van Merlen inde Capel van Graeve
200 imagines pergamenaceae illuminatae magnae a 10 fl. centum
200 – pergamenaceae illuminatae parvae a fl. 5 centum
200 – pergamenaceae illuminatae parvae quarum facies pectae, qualibet a 6 stuferis, quarum unam hisce includo
40 – perg. magnae cum lapidibus a 5½ stufer
15 – perg. B.M.V. cum multis lapidibus qualibet 12 stuferis
30 – perg. pictae manu quarum quamlibet solvi a 24 stuf.
200 – perg. parvae cum lapidibus quaelibet a 3 stufferis quarum ex includo et pretium ex alia parte legi potest".

2 Ibid., fol. 13v: "In foro vulgo dicto Meer penes nigram Aquilam[:] 100 Imagines perg. maximae deauratae solvi quamlibet 7 stuferos", and "Emantur decem vel quindecim imagines parvae vulgo tectae mineaturae artificiosae factae in pergameno licet pro qualibet solvantur 3, 4 vel 5 floreni, si tantum pulcherrimae sunt. Hasce praesertim rogo, quia hasce valde indigeo pro quodam et patrono meo".

3 Ibid., fol. 13r:

"A Vidua Joan. Huberti
2,000 imagines pergamenaceae illuminatae parvae a 5 fl. centum
1,000 - item magnae – a 10 fl. centum
100 – pergamenaceae albae magnae
100 – pergamenaceae albae parvae
2,000 – papiraceae selectae in 4° a 18 stuvers centum".

4 Compare MPM Arch. 364, fol. 13v; and MPM Arch. 252, fol. 131r, respectively.

5 Compare Förster's records with the following examples of the supply of colored images on parchment: MPM Arch. 238, fol. 27r (1630: by Theodore Galle); MPM Arch. 1107, fol. 94r (1638: by Carel Collaert); and MPM Arch. 248, fol. 33v (1640: by Marie de Man, the widow of Jan Cnobbaert).

6 For examples of studies of the hand-coloring of prints in different periods, see: Fletcher, Glinsman, and Oltrogge 2009; Oltrogge 2009, from Parshall 2009, for coloring prints in the fifteenth century; Primeau 2002, who also considers works from the sixteenth century; and Thijs 1993, pp. 141–48, for an overview of coloring prints in Antwerp, in particular between 1630 and 1750, during which period Thijs asserts that stencils were not used (p. 143, n. 197). On printing images in color, see, for example, Savage and Stijnman 2015.

7 Rombouts and Van Lerius 1872, vol. I, pp. 4, 15, 19–21, 23, 53–55, 58, 69, 115, 156, 226 (for examples of "verlichters" between 1453 and 1561), and p. 159, for the reference to Ortelius.

8 Ibid, vol. I, p. 285 (1584), and pp. 543–44 (1617–1618); and vol. II, pp. 111, 115, 116, 118, 122, 123, and 125 (1639–1641).

9 Ibid., vol. I, p. 610.

10 Imhof 2020a.

11 Rombouts and Van Lerius 1872, vol. II, pp. 35, 42, 46, 59 (Van Merlen), 68 (Van Merlen and two others), 73 (apprentice to the widow of Pauwels Huybrechts), 80, and 123 (apprentices to a widow Huybrechts in the year 1640–1641).

12 While Voet is named in Förster's order (MPM Arch. 364, fol. 13v), Baillu's name and link with the shop at the sign of the Black Eagle on the Meir (as cited in Förster's order) are derived from the record of shipment of these images to Förster in September 1644 (MPM Arch. 252, fol. 131r). Förster did not specify the supplier of the possible miniatures, nor is that person identified in the record of shipment.

13 MPM Arch. 74, fol. 9v (payment to Huberti for supplying one quire of colored images in 4° and 8° for 2 fl. 10 st.); and Rombouts and Van Lerius 1872, vol. I, pp. 476 and 515, for the registration of Adriaen II and Pauwels I, respectively.

14 Antwerp, Felix Archives, N 4053 (Notaris van Ham), fol. 21r, 10 September 1635.

15 Lemmens and Thijs, pp. 105–06.

16 Rombouts and Van Lerius 1872, vol. I, pp. 543, 544, and 555, for the exceptional listing of three individuals as "verlichters"/"afsetters" between 1617 and 1619; Ibid., p. 610, for the start of the marked increase in references in 1624–1625; and vol. II, pp. 115–16, 118, and 122–23, for the exceptional concentration of references in 1640–1641. See Thijs 1993, p. 44, for the second half of the seventeenth century.

17 MPM Arch. 69, fol. 153v; MPM Arch. 74, fol. 9v; and MPM Arch. 227, fol. 205v, respectively.

18 See Chapter 3 in this volume on Liefrinck's involvement with Plantin's supply of illustrated canons; and MPM Arch. 20, fol. 255 rht, for an example of her being paid to color canons in 1587. See MPM Arch. 74, fol. 9v; and MPM Arch. 70, fol. 14r (5 February 1593), for examples of payments to Huberti in this regard; and MPM Arch. 232, fols. 97v and 104r, for examples of Snijders supplying the Moretuses with illuminated canons in 1625.

19 MPM Arch. 235, fols. 26r and 89r (Cnobbaert); and MPM Arch, 237, fol. 91v (T. Galle), and fols. 26r and 109v (Snijders).

20 Antwerp, Felix Archives, N 3840 (Notaris Van der Herstraeten, 1624–1628), contract dated 17 December 1625, and N 3462 (Notaris Van den Berghe 1628), contract dated 10 February 1628, respectively. The contract involving Snijders is also discussed in Duverger 1990–1991, pp. 106–07.

21 Rombouts and Van Lerius 1872, vol. II, pp. 36 (1632–1633: Peeter van Lanckvelt) and 122 (1640–1641: Francus Lancvelt [sic]).

22 In this part of the contract, the term "afsettinge" may be construed as referring only to the painted elements and "verlichtingen" to the application of gold and silver: "der affsettinge oft verlichtinge doen naer heur wterste best ende soo dat behoort ende daertoe te gebruycken alle goede ende bequame verven ende goud ende silver voor welcke verluchtinge" (to do her utmost best in coloring or illumination, including the use of all good and appropriate paints and gold and silver for such illumination).

23 Although Theodore Galle was the only one to provide (via the Moretuses) colored prints on silk, the other print publishers cited here also offered some assortment of these other alternatives, in addition to plain prints on paper, which are discussed below. All of the options provided by each print publisher are listed in Appendix 1. See also the Note to the Reader for a sampling of comparative prices for the period of this study.

24 See MPM Arch. 252, fol. 131r, for the prices of all the images that were ultimately sent to Förster, including the exceptionally costly "images … miniées".

25 See MPM Arch. 237, fol. 109v: "400 verlichte pampiren twee op een blat in 4to a st. 2 [per image]" (for the sale to Bernhard Raesfeld), and MPM Arch. 1047, fol. [115] lft, for reference to the shipment of the same to Raesfeld, with the note that the prints sent were of high quality from Snijders: "400 [beelden] op pampier afgeset … Snyders van de beste". Compare with Antwerp, Felix Archives, N 3840 (Notaris Van der Herstraeten, 1624–28), contract dated 17 December 1625: "voor daffsetten ende vergulden vande pampieren beeldekens in quarto a achthien strs. elck dosyn" (for coloring and gilding paper images in 4° at eighteen st. per dozen [=1.5 st. per piece]); and "de quartkens op parckement tot een stuyver den halven stuck" (the 4°s on parchment at one stuiver and a half [per] piece).

26 MPM Arch. 38, fol. 100r, for Hans Liefrinck's supply of some 2,458 leaves of paper with images in 1558 (see below for the discussion of the number of leaves in a "main" or quire of images). See Chapter 3 on Plantin's early career as a bookseller and print dealer.

27 These and all subsequent examples are listed in Table 8 and documented in Appendix 1 under the respective print publisher's name, under "Unspecified prints sold in bulk".

28 See Appendix 1, CD-13 and TG-25, for these images and the cited examples of their sale at 4 st. per print. The latter is also discussed in Chapter 4.

29 See Chapter 6 and Appendix 1, WX-2, for this sale.

30 See below.

31 See Appendix 1, CM-2, CM-3, and CM-5.

32 Compare Tables 1–6 and Appendix 1, CM-2, CM-3, and CM-5.

33 See also Bowen 2017 for a more extensive discussion of this topic on the basis of prints after Rubens and his contemporaries.

34 See Table 7 for examples from Jan Boel and Appendix 1, under each of the cited print sellers' names for examples of their sales.

35 Duverger 1984–2009, vol. III, pp. 308–09.

36 These examples are listed in Table 8 and are documented in Appendix 1 under the respective print publisher's name, under "Unspecified prints sold in bulk".

37 Wolfenbüttel, Herzog August Bibliothek, M: Bc Sammelbd. 10 (2), signatures: A3v-A4r, for the images sold at "18 stuyvers den boeck, twee halve bladen voor een heel".

38 For examples of the use of these terms by the recordkeepers of the Plantin-Moretus Press (beyond those listed in Appendix 1 under "Unspecified prints sold in bulk"), in which the number of leaves or folios per quire is consistently twenty-five, see MPM Arch. 48, fol. 139v (sale by H. Cock in 1568), MPM Arch. 58, fol. 25v (sale by P. Galle in 1580), and MPM Arch. 180, fols. 152r, 155r, and 155v (sales by P. de Jode I, A. Collaert, P. Galle, and T. Galle in 1608). We have yet to find a single example of prints being sold in groups of twenty-four leaves per quire, as postulated by J. van Grieken (Cock 2013, p. 23), in the Plantin-Moretus accounts.

39 See MPM Arch. 58, fol. 19r, for this sales record and Appendix 1, CD-30 and CD-12, respectively, for the cited series.

40 MPM Arch. 58, fols. 19r-v and 25v (P. Galle in 1580), 39v (De Jode in 1580), and MPM Arch. 180, fols. 155r-155v (P. and T. Galle in 1608). For examples of prints sold in this way, see Appendix 1, GJ-2, GJ-3, GJ-7, GJ-13, GJ-15-GJ-19, GJ-48, PG-34, PG-68, PG-93, PG-109, PG-110, PG-117, as well as the numerous prints listed in Table 3 under .72 st., and TG-15.

41 See the Note to the Reader for an overview of terms used to indicate the range of paper sizes in terms of this single leaf unit that were used in sixteenth-century Antwerp, in addition to more examples of the actual size of images printed on them.

42 MPM Arch. 65, fol. 102r: "1 c[ent] figures petites en 13 fueilles fl. __ st. 12"; and MPM Arch. 64, fol. 105v: "3 mains dImages in 16°, 24°, 8° et 32 acheptez de Adriaen [Huberti?] fl. 3 st. __".

43 MPM Arch. 71, fols. 127r-v.

44 Paas 2020 on the Altzenbachs; and Wolfegg, Fürstlich zu Waldburg-Wolfegg'sche Kunstsammlungen, vol. 221, print nos. 216–17, 220, 242–43, and 245–46, for example. See also Verheggen 2024 on these prints. Our thanks to Marjolein Leesberg for bringing this article to our attention.

45 Wolfegg, Fürstlich zu Waldburg-Wolfegg'sche Kunstsammlungen, vol. 221, print 226, with no. 40 in the lower right corner, for Van den Enden's plate; and Paas 2020, pp. XVI, n. 17, and 1041, for the Altzenbachs' numbered plates.

46 MPM Arch. 174, fol. 14r.

47 MPM Arch. 58, fol. 25v: "2 Perspective di Vrise dedicate comiti di Mansvelt f° 11 a 2 figures sur chaque fueille st. 8½ [per set, amounts to] - st. 17"; and MPM M 296 (= MPM Arch. 1227), fol. 388v: "Perspectives de Vries Corn. Mansvelt a 2 fig. sur fueille st. 8 ½". See Appendix 1, CD-2 for this series.

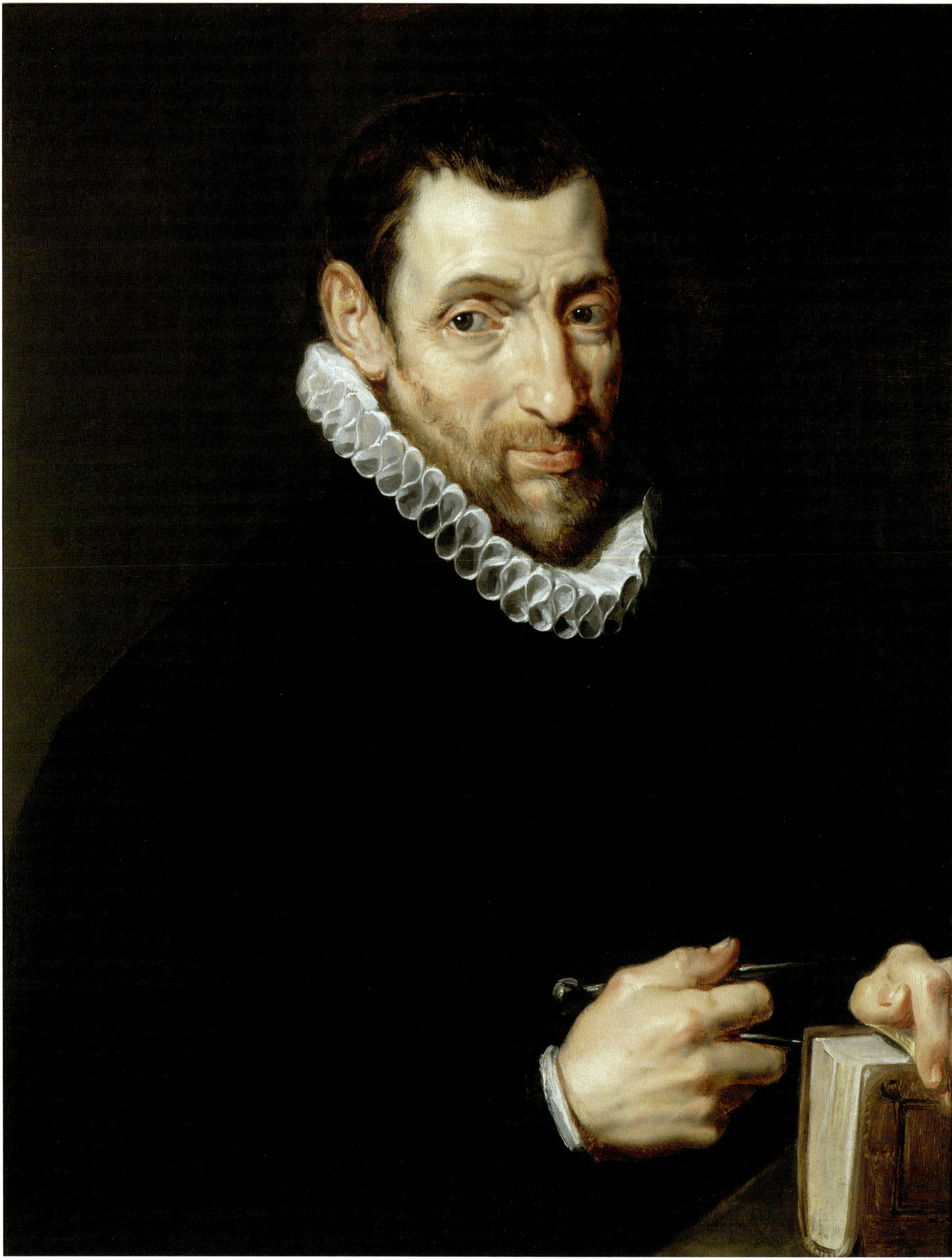

CHAPTER 3

CHRISTOPHER PLANTIN

FROM PRINT DEALER TO MIDDLEMAN

AND COURIER SERVICE

> In order to satisfy your request, I searched through all of the stores in this city where they sold images, which I found noted on the other page of your letter … I can present you with three sheets by Albrecht Dürer.[1]

3.1 Workshop of Peter Paul Rubens, *Christopher Plantin*, 1612–1616, painting, 659 × 507 mm. Antwerp, Museum Plantin-Moretus: V.IV.047.

Thus begins perhaps the single best known account of the bookseller Christopher Plantin's dealings in prints; it concerns his purchases of several images by Albrecht Dürer for the Gentile family in 1567 and 1568.[2] These sales are often cited because they provide examples of how prints by Dürer were sought long after they were first published and because Plantin (fig. 3.1) acknowledges in this same letter how prices for prints could be subjective and a matter of individual judgment and personal preference.[3] Specifically, he states:

> It happens that, due to the judgment or preference of painters or connoisseurs of such images, they value one print two, three, or four times as much as another, even if they were from the same hand and plate and were printed at the same time on the same day ….[4]

Plantin's purchases of prints after Dürer for the Gentiles support this observation. For example, while Plantin charged Stephano Gentile 30 st. for an impression of a print of St Hubert in 1567, he asked more than twice that amount (70 st., or 3 fl. 10 st.) in 1568 (fig. 3.2).[5] Similarly, for impressions of Dürer's *Three Peasants*, Plantin charged Gentile just 3 st. in 1567 and then 8 st. in 1568, while the price of Dürer's *Melancholia* stayed the same at 15 st. However, in the case of the 1568 sale, we can also see that Plantin actually paid less for these prints when he bought them from the cartographer Abraham Ortelius. The prices of Dürer prints were, evidently, not simply a matter of quality and taste, but might also include a markup by those who managed to procure them for distant clients eager to possess their own selection of famous prints.

But, to what extent were these transactions representative of Plantin's dealings in prints generally? There is no doubt about his appreciation of both the varying quality of impressions of prints and the current market for them. Aside from his profession as a printer of books – including a recent experiment with the production of text editions containing engraved illustrations – by 1567 he had been dealing in prints for more than a decade. On at least one occasion, he even profited financially from such transactions. Nevertheless, the types of prints that he usually sold differed significantly from the preceding example. Indeed, we know of only a few other instances in which Plantin purchased prints by Dürer. For example, in 1569, he bought twenty-eight unspecified images by Dürer in addition to his engraved series of the Passion at

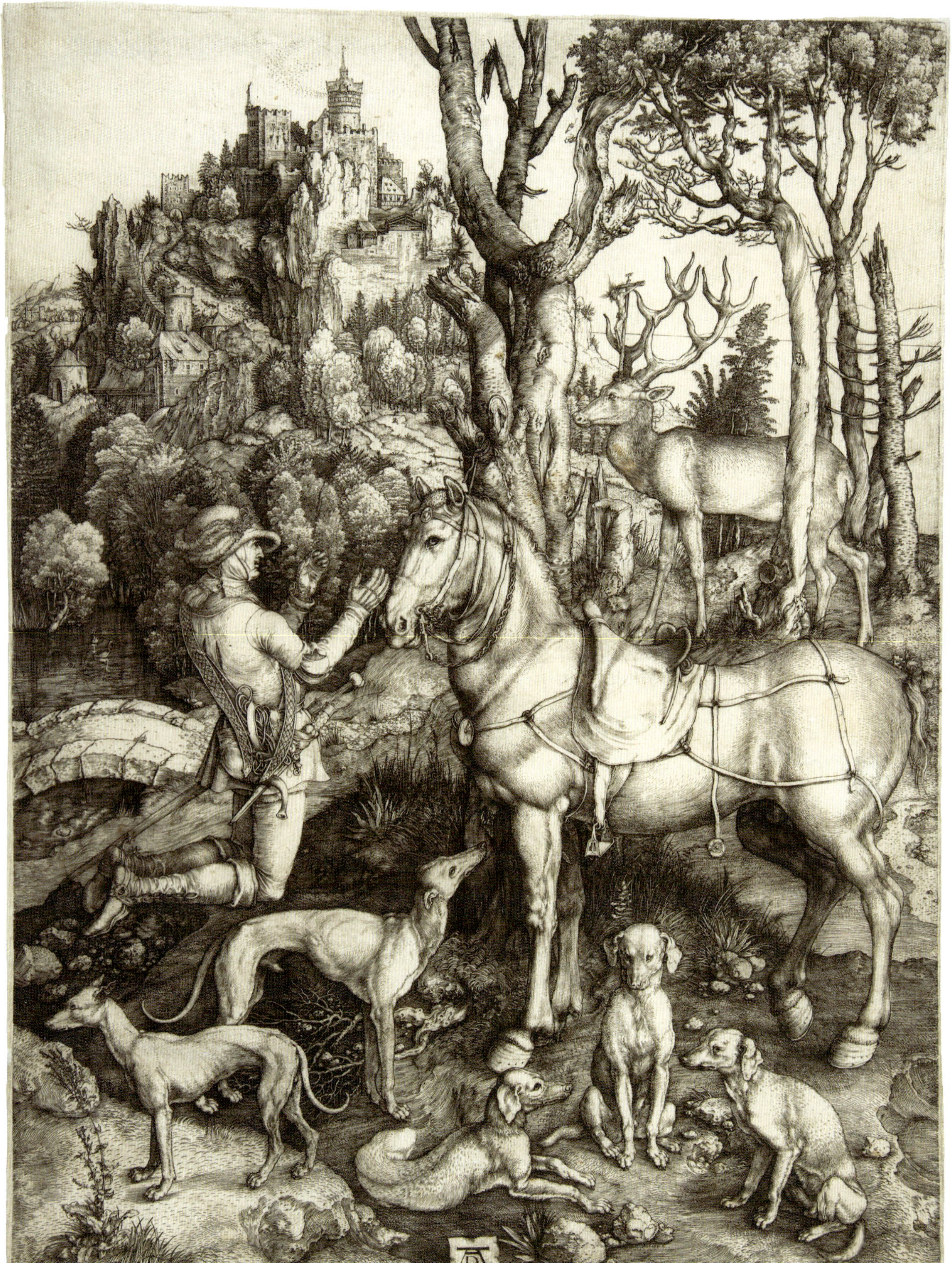

an auction near the Financial Exchange ("de Bourse") for Benito Arias Montano (or Benedictus Arias Montanus), a biblical scholar and chaplain to the Spanish king, Philip II.[6] In 1574, he provided the Italian bookseller Pedro Bocangelino (then living in Toledo) with nineteen unspecified engravings and one copy of Dürer's *Epitome in divae parthenices Mariae historiam* (1511).[7] Finally, in 1587, he purchased a selection of Dürer's woodcuts of the Passion and the Virgin in addition to a copy of his *De symmetria partium humanorum corporum* for Alexander Orsa, the secretary of Alexander Farnese who was then governor-general of the southern Netherlands.[8] Rather than these isolated acquisitions of renowned images, Plantin's dealings in prints are more accurately characterized by his procurement of diverse prints, often in bulk, primarily from contemporary Antwerp print publishers for a full spectrum of buyers and not just foreign collectors.

3.2 Albrecht Dürer, *Saint Hubert* (commonly identified as Saint Eustace), ca. 1501, engraving, 350 × 259 mm. New York, The Metropolitan Museum of Art: Fletcher Fund, 1919 (19.73.65). Image courtesy of the Metropolitan Museum of Art.

PLANTIN'S INITIAL DEALINGS IN PRINTS 1553–1565

Possibly born in or near Tours around 1520, details of Plantin's life prior to his arrival in Antwerp remain vague.[9] Essential here is the evidence that he had lived both in Paris and Caen, where he is assumed to have learned the trades of printing and bookbinding. Plantin also established both personal and professional contacts in Paris and would come to rely on these connections in the years to come. He eventually moved to Antwerp in 1548 or 1549, possibly attracted by the reputation of the city as one of the most important centers in sixteenth-century Europe for printing and for the international trade in art objects and other luxury goods: it was thus a place full of potential for entrepreneurs.[10] Hieronymus Cock similarly began his printmaking and publishing business called "Aux Quatre Vents" (At the Four Winds) in Antwerp in 1548; it soon became a model of international success within the print world and a landmark in the evolution of print publishing.[11] In 1550, Plantin was registered as a citizen of Antwerp and, on that occasion, identified himself as a bookbinder. He simultaneously sought admission to the city's Guild of St Luke as a printer, thereby keeping his options for employment open. Evidently, he initially decided to work as a bookbinder since he did not start his business as a printer until 1555. He and his wife also attempted to earn money via other means at this time, in particular through trade in lace and prints.[12]

The only independent confirmation of Plantin's dealings in prints before he started his business as a printer in 1555 is a contract from 14 March 1553 between Plantin (referred to as a bookbinder and merchant) and Lambert Suavius (referred to as an architect from Liège, but who was also known as an engraver and painter).[13] According to this agreement, Plantin paid Suavius for 100 sets of a series of the *Acts of the Apostles*, while Suavius agreed not to sell these prints himself in Antwerp or elsewhere in Charles V's empire for a year and to limit his sale of them in France to groups of one dozen or less.[14] In this way, Plantin endeavored to dominate the local distribution of the series for a year. Whether or not this agreement was typical of Plantin's dealings in prints during the early 1550s is impossible to say. Subsequent records indicate that it was not characteristic of his practices in the following decade. Indeed, while he purchased another fifty images of Sts Peter and John from Suavius on 16 October 1556, it was Hieronymus Cock and his widow Volcxken Diericx who appear to have gained control of the distribution of some of Suavius's prints by 1568, when Cock sold impressions of Suavius's series of *Christ and the Twelve Apostles* to Plantin.[15] Cock, a professional print publisher, may have gone one step further than Plantin and acquired the plates used to print the series – the ultimate means of controlling its distribution – as he did for other successful prints, such as Lambert Lombard's series of Apostles.[16] Most likely, Plantin was either experimenting with various options for dealing in prints or endeavoring to satisfy specific requests for these images from other individuals.

After Plantin began to work as a printer in 1555, there are more records of his dealings in prints, albeit neither methodically kept nor fully preserved. Many of these transactions demonstrate how Plantin periodically played an intermediary role, primarily in instances involving booksellers in Paris and print publishers in Antwerp. Among the Parisian booksellers, Martin Le Jeune and Lucas Breyer I are the most important. They were, perhaps not coincidentally, evidently on good terms with Plantin personally and also with a close friend of his in Paris, Pierre Porret.[17] Orders of books dominate their exchanges with Plantin, but they also occasionally traded in prints. For example, in 1556 and 1558 Plantin, sent Le Jeune several shipments of prints and maps, some of which were quite large. These consisted primarily of numerous prints from Cock and some "compartiments" (frames), most likely from Gerard de Jode, in addition to hundreds of unspecified prints. Indeed, a shipment from June 1558 amounted to more than 122 fl. (or 2440 st.), and many of the individual items cost just a few stuivers each.[18]

Le Jeune's orders were far larger than what Plantin is known to have sold to his other contacts. For example, in a shipment of 22 November 1559 to the Parisian bookseller Barthélemy Jourdain, the number of maps is substantially greater than the small selection of prints.[19] And, while a list of prints that Cock sold to Plantin in August 1561 (possibly intended for Breyer) amounted to more than 100 images, the total value of the order was still just 16 fl.[20]

Although Plantin's known transactions may not attest to any significant, systematic sale of prints to Paris, they still reveal the variety of his exchanges with Parisian book and print dealers. In particular, they document how he also relied on contacts in Paris to procure prints for several leading print sellers in Antwerp in a period when it was not uncommon for Parisian print and book dealers to distribute their wares via Antwerp. For example, in June 1559, a certain Hendrick Messagier supplied Plantin with various (potentially hundreds) of "portraictures … de Paris" (images from Paris).[21] While it is not clear for whom these prints were intended, some may have been included in Plantin's subsequent sale of 550 sheets of "protraictures coulorees de Paris" (colored images from Paris) to Hans Liefrinck I on 14 October 1559.[22]

Possibly as early as August 1559 and certainly in 1560, Plantin also sold various sets of prints by the then popular French architect and printmaker Jacques Androuet du Cerceau to Cock, Liefrinck, and De Jode. The most popular subjects were Androuet du Cerceau's series of round perspectives, "grotesques", arches, and books of architectural designs.[23] Prints by Jean Cousin, a French ornamental engraver, were also occasionally among the prints that Plantin supplied.[24] This trade was continued in 1564, following Plantin's self-imposed exile in Paris, while the printing of a heretical text at his Press in 1562 was investigated.[25] However, Breyer now supplied Plantin with the prints, a few of which may have been sold to De Jode immediately upon their arrival in Antwerp. In addition to many of the series cited above, Breyer's shipment may have comprised examples of Androuet du Cerceau's terms and caryatids, landscapes, ruins, and temples – subjects that De Jode and Cock also published in this period (compare figs. 3.3 and 3.4).[26]

Finally, Plantin also helped at least two of his Parisian contacts – Breyer and Le Jeune – obtain prints sold at the Frankfurt fair.[27] For example, there is a passing reference to "pourtraictures prinses a Francfort" (prints obtained in Frankfurt) that were charged to Breyer in March 1558, just when he might have been starting his own business in Paris.[28] Le Jeune was more explicit when he wrote to Plantin in August 1558 to ask that while he was in Frankfurt, he obtain and send him four to six impressions each of six specific subjects: Moses, the Red Sea, Lot, the city St Quentin, Patience, and Susanna.[29]

The timing of both of these requests is noteworthy because they coincide with the one known example of Plantin shipping hundreds of prints and maps (in addition to books) to the Frankfurt fair.[30] Significantly greater in quantity and value than even his sales to Le Jeune in Paris from the same period, this shipment (sent in March 1558) comprised prints from Paris as well as the local print publishers Cock and Hans Liefrinck, in addition to hundreds of prints characterized solely by their size. Nevertheless, this venture, like Plantin's large orders of prints for Paris, appears to have been more an anomaly than a recurring activity. Only one other shipment to Frankfurt (in August 1561), containing a comparatively modest allotment of ten 10 rolls "des hist.[oires]" (of stories) and seventy-seven individual prints from Cock is known from this period.[31] Consequently, Plantin's trade in prints via the Frankfurt fairs may well be yet another example of his testing the possibilities for such activities, but ultimately deciding against them.

During the first decade of his activities as a printer, and alongside his noteworthy exchanges with Parisian book and print sellers, Plantin sporadically traded prints with a few other individuals with whom he normally exchanged books or occasionally maps. For example, in 1558, he sold the Brussels bookseller Pierre de la Tombe twelve "Batailles" (battles) by Cock (possibly examples of Cock's *Siege of the Elephant*).[32] In 1561, Plantin sold a diverse assortment of prints – including copies of his and Cock's edition of the *Funeral Procession in Honor of Charles V* (often referred to as the *Pompe funèbre*), prints published by Androuet du Cerceau, and more than sixty-eight sheets of unspecified prints – to a certain Antoine de Ausburgh, who was a representative of the famous Fugger merchant family.[33]

Considered all together, what do these sundry glimpses of Plantin's earliest activities in the print trade reveal? As of 1553, Plantin was occasionally involved in the international distribution of both specific, individual images and groups of twenty-five, fifty, or even 100

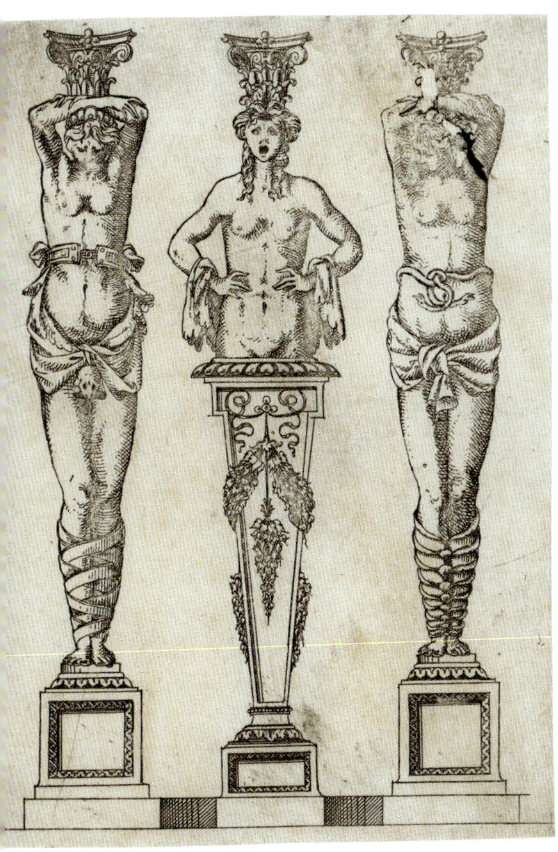

3.3 Jacques Androuet du Cerceau, *Designs for Two Caryatids and One Term.* from the series *Terms and Caryatids*, ca. 1546–1550, etching, 163 × 112 mm. New York, The Metropolitan Museum of Art: Harris Brisbane Dick Fund, 1932 (32.130.20). Image courtesy of the Metropolitan Museum of Art.

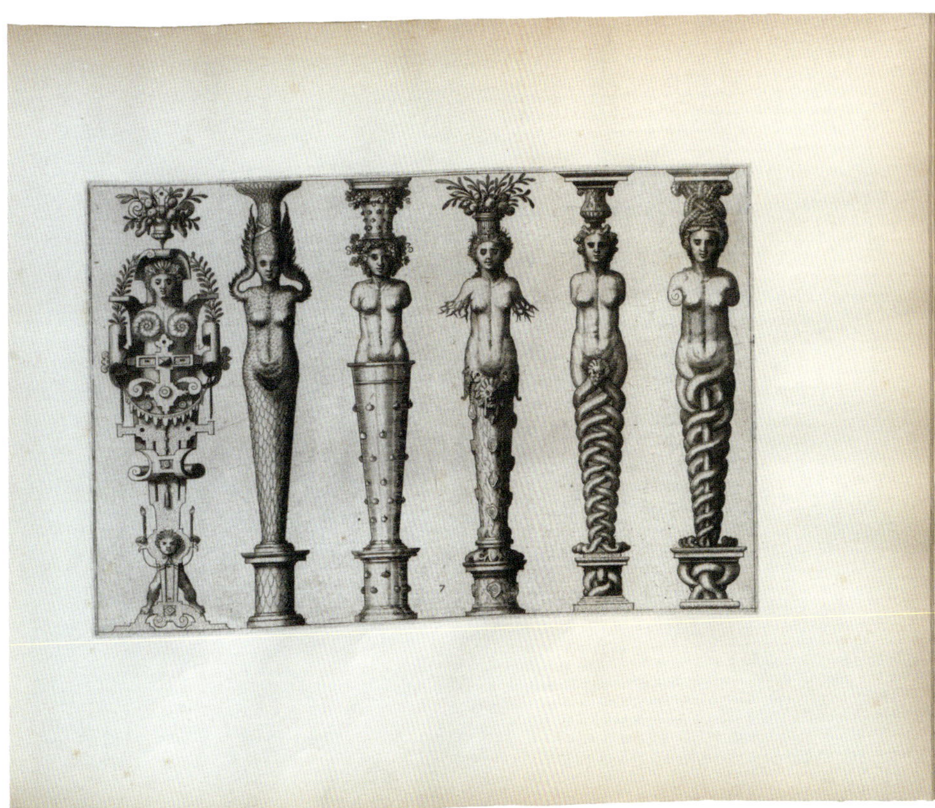

3.4 Joannes and Lucas van Doetecum after Hans Vredeman de Vries, *Caryatids and Terms*, print 7 from the series *Caryatidum*, ca. 1565, etching, ca. 160 × 236 mm. Antwerp, Museum Plantin-Moretus: PK. R 201. Appendix 1: GJ-6.

impressions sold in bulk. The subjects of these prints (when specified) ranged from more conventional mythological and religious subjects to perspective images and ornamental designs. Nonetheless, it remains impossible to gauge definitively the actual frequency with which Plantin engaged in these print-related transactions due to the incomplete survival and poor maintenance of the records of his transactions from this period.

Similarly unresolved is the important issue of the degree to which Plantin was simply responding to individual requests for prints, whereby his international contacts and his access to established transportation routes for shipping would have been significant advantages, and the degree to which he was actively endeavoring to work (at least part-time) as a print dealer. The former most likely prevailed. Plantin did not continue to trade in prints with these Parisian booksellers, despite maintaining contact with some (in particular, Breyer and Le Jeune) into the 1570s.[34] Likewise, there is no evidence of Plantin's overseeing any comparable, large-scale shipments of prints to Frankfurt in the following decades, when his transactions are otherwise well documented.[35]

Moreover, while Plantin may have possessed modest stocks of prints in 1562 and 1563, these do not appear to have been of significant value. Specifically, records of the sale of Plantin's possessions in 1562, when he was living temporarily in Paris, include five references to a "hoop consten" (a pile of art), possibly prints, the total value of which amounted to 92 schellingen and 15 deniers, or approximately 28 fl.[36] Similarly, soon after his return to Antwerp in September 1563, Plantin inventoried his possessions and noted under "pourtraictures" (images) fourteen groups of prints, ranging from a single copy of the *Pompe funèbre* and a few impressions of several other mythological and religious subjects to as many as 300 sheets of unspecified prints in bulk.[37] But once again, this diverse selection remained modest in comparison with the much larger shipment of prints to Frankfurt from 1558, for example, and would certainly not have supported an active trade in prints for long. The paucity of transactions in prints over the next few years (until 1568) suggests that while Plantin may have initially considered various ways in which he might participate in the local and international trade in prints, intensive involvement was no longer a priority in the mid-1560s.

This change may have been related to the new joint management of Plantin's resuscitated business, which had been prompted by Plantin's urgent need of funds.[38] While Plantin oversaw the revival of his Press, the merchant Cornelis van Bomberghen, who had invested the most in the business, kept detailed, methodically cross-referenced accounts. As the bulk of these records are still preserved today, the paucity of print-related transactions is all the more striking and most likely a conscious decision. However, in August 1567 Plantin's new partners were forced to flee Antwerp due to their Calvinist sympathies. Hereafter, Plantin continued his business with a simpler accounting system that featured interrelated entries between essential record books.[39] These reveal that within a year following the departure of his last Calvinist partner Plantin's involvement in the purchase, resale, and distribution of prints increased significantly. The main beneficiary, by far, of this shift was a new advisor and friend, the Spanish theologian and chaplain to Philip II, Benito Arias Montano.

Arias Montano

Philip II sent Arias Montano (fig. 3.5) to Antwerp in the spring of 1568 to oversee Plantin's work on a new, scholarly polyglot Bible, which Philip had agreed to subsidize; this became Plantin's famous *Biblia regia*.[40] Aside from being a trusted member of Philip II's entourage and a respected participant in the Council of Trent, Arias Montano's training in Oriental languages and biblical texts made him an excellent and logical choice for the task. He was also keenly interested in various branches of the arts and sciences. Indeed, as early as July 1568, just two months after his arrival in Antwerp, Arias Montano began to ask Plantin to buy prints on his behalf.[41] This relatively modest order, worth 3 fl. 13 st., consisted of two large, unspecified images, four print series, and thirty-six sheets of landscapes, all of which were supplied by Hieronymus Cock. The fact that Arias Montano bought single impressions of most of the prints listed suggests that he had most likely placed a personal order for individual enjoyment or use. This is in striking contrast to Arias Montano's subsequent orders for prints in December of that same year.

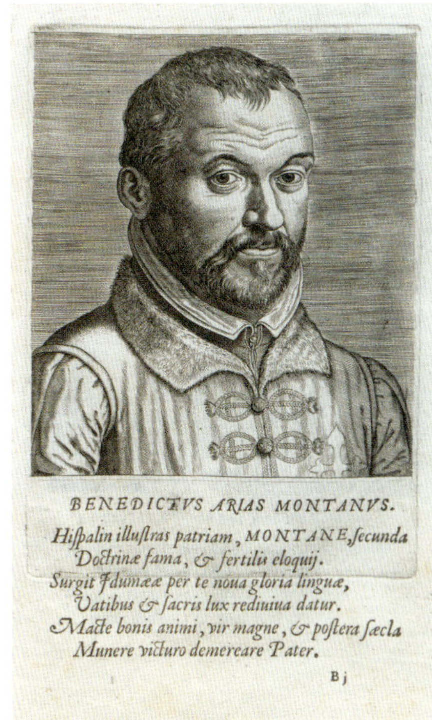

3.5 Philips Galle, *Benedictus Arias Montanus*, in the print book *Virorum docturum de disclipinis benemerentium effigies* XLIIII (Antwerp: Philips Galle, 1572), engraving, 175 × 121 mm. Antwerp, Museum Plantin-Moretus: 4–97, fol. B1r. Appendix 1: PG-123.

Specifically, on 18 December, Plantin noted the purchase of 1,668 sheets of "toutes differentes sortes" (all different types) "de fine taille" (of finely cut [images]), presumably engravings, from Hans Liefrinck, a book on the Golden Fleece, some "fines pieces de Paris" (skillfully executed pieces from Paris), and four long images of the city of Antwerp, for the sum of 71 fl. 5 st. for Arias Montano.[42] Aside from the last few items, no subjects are noted. Instead, different quantities of prints in different sizes for different prices are recorded:

2 × 10 "grandes doubles feilles" (large double sheets) at 4 st. per piece;
2 × 57 "pieces de doubles feilles" (pieces on double sheets) at 3 st. per sheet;
2 × 464 "pieces de feilles entieres" (pieces on full sheets) at 4 fl. (80 st.) per hundred, or .8 st. per piece;
2 × 112 "pieces doubles" (double pieces) at 2 fl. (40 st.) per hundred, or .4 st. per piece; and
2 × 191 "pieces simple" (single pieces) at 20 st. per hundred, or .2 st. per piece.

This list of prints most likely represented two large, identical orders, as each group of prints was noted twice and the quantities involved were far greater than what was necessary for a simple selection of a few prints for personal use.

Ten days later, on 29 December, numerous single prints, print series, and maps from Hieronymus Cock were bought for Arias Montano for a similarly large sum of 79 fl. 8 st. (fig. 3.6).[43] This purchase comprised copies of the *Pompe funèbre* and various print series – perspective images and decorative frame designs, tomb designs, sets of ruins and village houses, as well as Suavius's series of *Christ and the Twelve Apostles, with Saint Paul* – in addition to such single prints as the *Siege of the Elephant, Saint George's Kermis (Fair)*, the *Blue Cloak* (an image of forty-three Dutch proverbs), the *Naval Battle in the Strait of Messina* (fig. 3.7), and (most likely) Giorgio Ghisi's *Adoration of the Shepherds*. Nearly 1,000 unspecified sheets were also included in the purchase.[44] As Arias Montano usually bought at least two impressions of each subject, some portion of these (if not all of them) were most likely intended for someone else.

Immediately following these initial investments in thousands of prints, Arias Montano made only a few smaller print purchases via Plantin, such as the selection of prints after

Dürer in 1569 mentioned above and, in 1570, one copy each of Gerard de Jode's series of caryatids, grotesques, and fountains in perspective (fig. 3.4).[45] It was not until 1585, some fifteen years later and nearly a decade after his return to Spain, that Arias Montano asked to have numerous prints added to a large shipment of books that were to be sent to him. This time, the supplier was Philips Galle.[46]

Galle arrived in Antwerp a year or more after Arias Montano. Various sources attest to their decision to work together on the production of several print books soon thereafter, between 1572 and 1575, while Arias Montano was still in Antwerp, as well as their lasting friendship. Consequently, it is likely that Arias Montano usually bought prints directly from Galle, at least until his departure for Spain in May 1575, if not thereafter.[47] His subsequent acquisition of prints via Plantin's business in 1584–1585 may have been necessitated by Alexander Farnese's ongoing blockade of Antwerp. Begun in July 1584 as part of Farnese's effort to recapture Flemish towns for the Spanish crown during the Eighty Years' War, the blockade made all forms of commercial transport extremely difficult. Perhaps Arias Montano hoped that Plantin's sons-in-law, Jan Moretus I and Franciscus Raphelengius, who were managing the Press in Antwerp while Plantin was working in Leiden, would succeed in getting his purchases out of Antwerp.[48] Arias Montano's decision to turn to Plantin's business for this order may also have been motivated by the fact that the bulk of the shipment consisted of multiple copies of bound books, all with engraved or etched illustrations.[49] Additionally, Galle supplied multiple copies of several of their joint print books from the 1570s, as well as sundry print series, ranging in subject matter from "grotesques" and Galle's designs for pendants to hunts and other images of animals, series of portraits, and his popular series of the *Life and Passion of Christ*, designed by Johannes Stradanus (fig. 3.8).[50] Finally, 425 sheets of "diverses

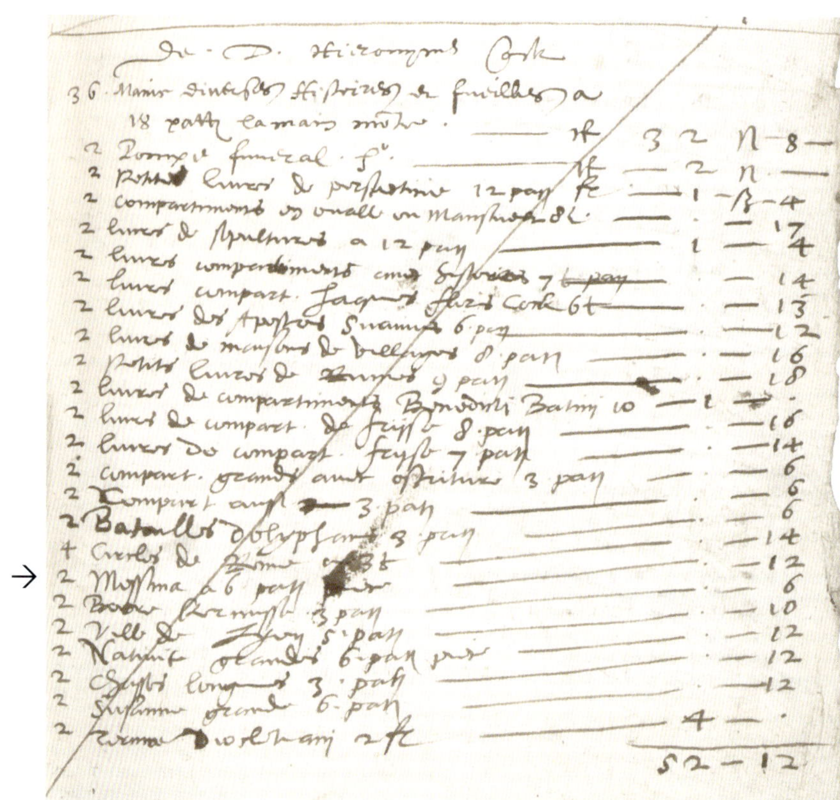

3.6 List of prints supplied by Hieronymus Cock for Benito Arias Montano on 29 December 1568; the seventh item from the bottom, "2 Messina a 6 patt." is reproduced in fig. 3.7. Antwerp, Museum Plantin-Moretus: Arch. 46, *Journal 1568*, fol. 242r.

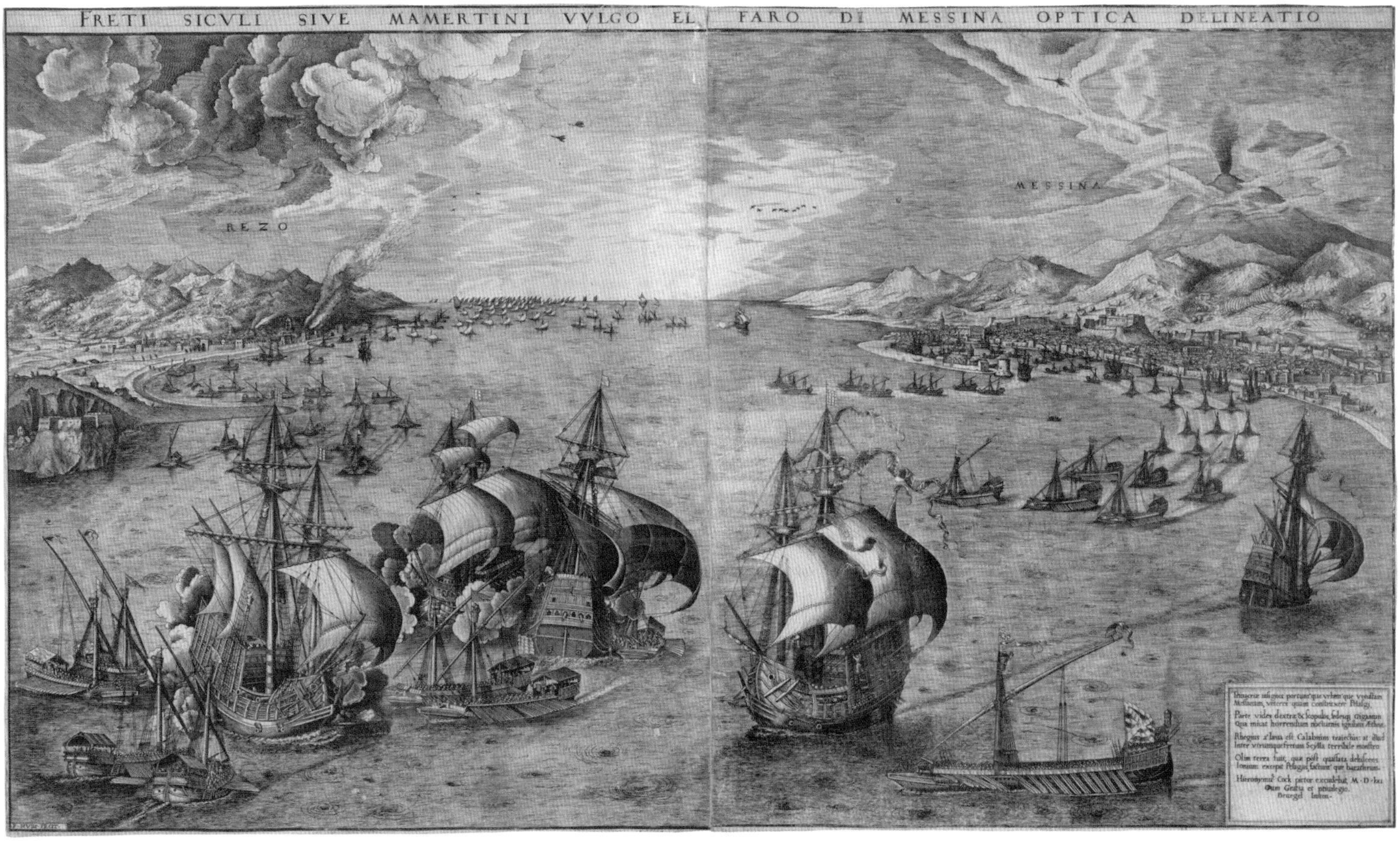

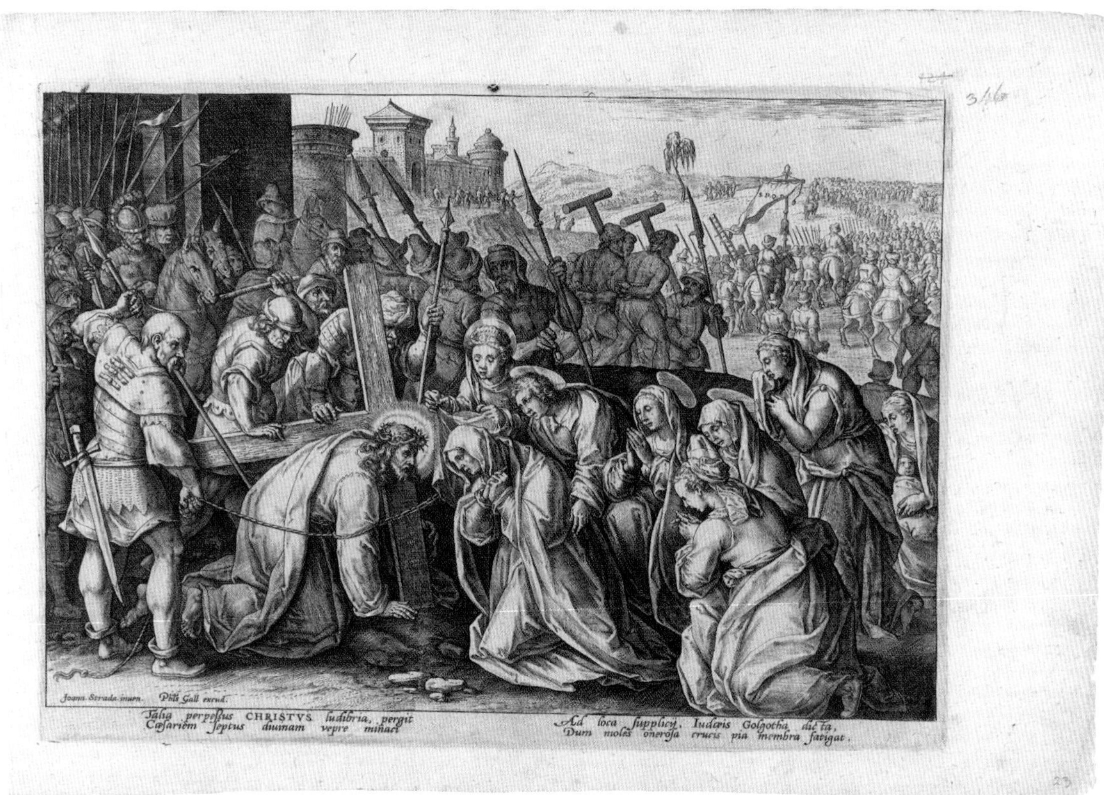

3.7 Frans Huys after Pieter Bruegel I, *Naval Battle in the Strait of Messina*, 1561, etching and engraving on two plates, measuring 426 × 717 mm in total. Amsterdam, Rijksmuseum: RP-P-1878-A-2729. Appendix 1: CD-15.

3.8 Jan Collaert II after Johannes Stradanus, *The Miraculous Cloth of Veronica*, from the series *The Passion, Death, and Resurrection of Christ*, ca. 1580–1586, engraving, ca. 193 × 262 mm. Amsterdam, Rijksmuseum: RP-P-1985-255. Appendix 1: PG-82.

sortes de pourtraittueres" (diverse types of images), sold at a bulk rate of 3 fl. 12 st. (or 72 st.) per one hundred sheets (which was the equivalent of 18 st. per quire of twenty-five sheets), were also included. This order is also noteworthy because Galle had evidently obtained two copies of Volcxken Diericx's *Portraits of Famous Painters from the Netherlands (Pictorum aliquot celebrium germaniae inferioris effigies)*, or so-called "schilderboek" or "livre des peinctres" (book of painters), and added them to his own list of what he had supplied (at her standard price of 12 st. per copy) (fig. 3.9). The inclusion of the two books demonstrates that he also traded in publications of contemporary print publishers.[51] Galle charged 48 fl. 8 st. for all of these works, which, while still a significant sum, was, nevertheless, notably less than either of Arias

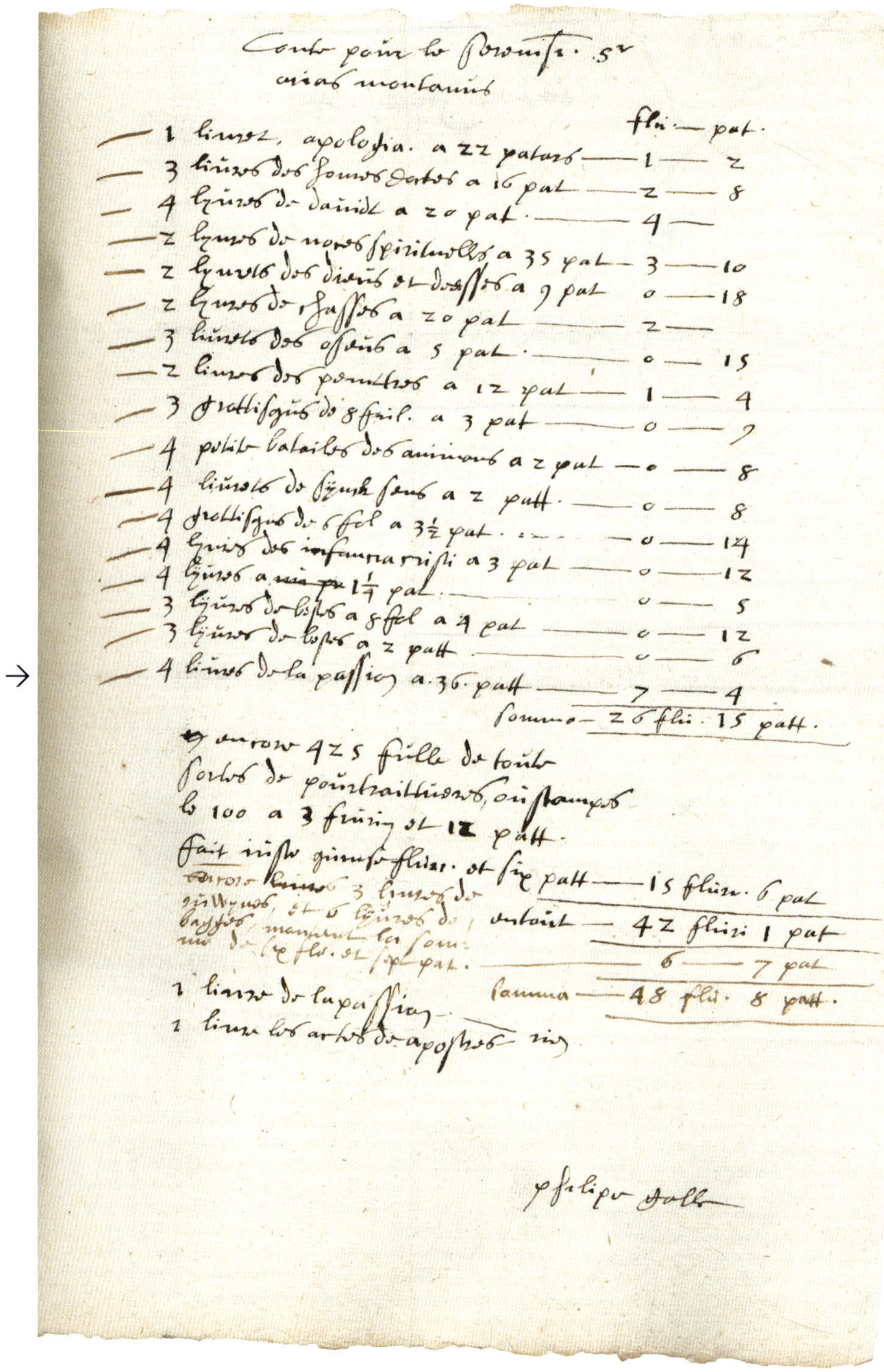

3.9 List of prints supplied by Philips Galle (and signed by him in the lower right) for Benito Arias Montano in 1585; fig. 3.8 is part of the last series, which is listed with a price: "4 livres de la passion a 36 patt. [= 36 st. / set] [fl.] 7 [st.] 4". Antwerp, Museum Plantin-Moretus: Arch. 20, *Grand livre 1582–1589*, between fols. 166 lft and 166 rht.

Montano's earlier purchases from Liefrinck and Cock. The fact that multiple copies of each item were sent indicates, once again, that this order was most likely not intended exclusively for Arias Montano himself. The question remains for whom the prints (or at least some of them) were intended.

The most obvious potential destination for Arias Montano's initial large orders, if not this last one, was Philip II's collection at the Escorial. The collection was formed between the mid-1560s and mid-1570s, and Arias Montano was its librarian from 1576 to 1586, as well as sporadically thereafter, until 1590.[52] However, a comparison of the print collection at the Escorial with what Arias Montano ordered via Plantin reveals striking incongruities.[53] For example, there are remarkably few prints by Liefrinck in the Escorial, despite the huge quantity (more than 1,600 sheets) Arias Montano purchased in December 1568. Likewise, not all of the prints he purchased from Cock that same month – *The Siege of the Elephant*, just to name one – are in the collection. Moreover, the Escorial has numerous images published by De Jode and Galle that are not listed in Arias Montano's orders from Plantin. Hence, while it remains likely that Arias Montano was involved in the acquisition of prints for the Escorial, they may well have been acquired and shipped via other means.[54] Plantin's business records provide exceptionally detailed evidence of how such transactions in prints took place, but he and his successors were certainly not the only individuals in Antwerp engaged in such practices.

Rather, Arias Montano's print purchases may be more readily linked to instances of his reliance on Plantin to manage the purchase and shipment of a variety of works of art, along with other objects of interest, ranging from seeds to furniture, for himself and various acquaintances.[55] One such individual was Philip II's head almoner, Luis Manrique, who approached Plantin directly in 1571 and 1581 for orders of hundreds of the newest prints from Galle and De Jode (among others).[56] One striking contrast betweeen Manrique's and Arias Montano's orders is that Plantin added a significant profit margin to each purchase Manrique made – nearly 4 fl. out of the 28 fl. 3 st. he charged in 1571 and approximately 2 fl. 12 st. out of the 10 fl. 3 st. he charged in 1581; no such profit margin was added to any of Arias Montano's purchases. Plantin's (as well as his successors') selective inclusion of variable profit margins recurs throughout their transactions.

Samuel Dilbaum

None of Plantin's other clients for prints from the 1560s onwards spent as much on their orders as Arias Montano: nearly 200 fl. for just the three large purchases detailed above. Only the exceptional sequence of print purchases made by Samuel Dilbaum while an assistant ("serviteur") to the Augsburg bookseller Georg Willer I approaches what Arias Montano paid. In just sixteen months between 21 August 1570 and 9 November 1571, Dilbaum spent nearly 150 fl.[57] While these purchases are the first known references to Dilbaum in the Plantin archives, Willer began to order books from Plantin in 1567 and would continue to do so into the 1580s.[58] Willer is perhaps best known for having initiated the publication of catalogues of, initially (in the spring of 1564), what he had purchased at the Frankfurt book fair, and, subsequently (as of the fall of 1573), what was for sale at the Frankfurt fairs more generally. By 1568, these catalogues also comprised sporadic references to prints and maps, as well as other special publications illustrated with a large number of engravings, such as Philips Galle's various print books.[59]

The print orders noted under Dilbaum's name were included in the barrels of books sent to Willer. The prints were routinely from Cock's widow Diericx and De Jode, and occasionally were supplied by Galle. Although the total value of the individual purchases, which mostly ranged in price from 7 to 20 fl., was generally far more modest than Arias Montano's huge orders, they often comprised hundreds of sheets of prints, sold in bulk, in addition to a few specific items, all of which Plantin usually sold to Dilbaum at cost, with no profit margin for himself as middleman.[60]

The obvious question is to what degree the prints sold to Dilbaum can be linked to those listed in Willer's catalogues. While it is impossible to answer for the hundreds of unspecified sheets of prints sent, the few itemized records suggest that there was no direct relationship to Dilbaum's orders from Plantin. Some of the prints Dilbaum bought do appear in Willer's lists, for example Lambert Lombard's and Suavius's series of the Apostles, but several, such as Pieter van der Heyden's portrait of Pius V and the Van Doetecums' series of vessels after Vredeman de Vries, do not.[61] The fact that Diericx sent Dilbaum at least eight sets of both Lombard's and Suavius's series of the Apostles in the span of twelve months underscores the enduring popularity of these series – even fifteen years following the publication of Suavius's – and their continued renown, which would have justified Willer's inclusion of these works in his catalogue. However, we cannot assume that all of the impressions of these series, much less the other images sent to Dilbaum, were intended for resale via Willer. Rather, as was the case with Plantin's shipments to Arias Montano, the surviving records document how Plantin served as the middleman for the acquisition and transportation of hundreds of prints sporadically, when the need arose, but not in a permanent, long-term, or systematic way. The fact that other prints, specfically publications by Galle, periodically appeared in Willer's catalogues from 1572 onwards, when Plantin's shipments of prints (but not books) to Dilbaum and Willer had ceased, indicates that they had found other ways to acquire the prints (or print books) they needed.

Altogether, the three cases detailed above – Arias Montano's and Dilbaum's exceptionally large purchases of prints at cost and Manrique's more moderate purchases with some profit margin for Plantin – reflect essential aspects of Plantin's trade in prints during the mid-1560s. In particular, the irregular occurrence of these transactions, the resale of prints at cost to fellow book dealers or good friends, and the rounding up of prices for prints sold to various other individuals – from merchants and nobles to local and distant Jesuits – were all common. The telling distinctions between all of the sales are found, rather, in the total number of purchases made over time, the relative quantities of prints bought, and preferences for works by certain publishers or even, on occasion, individual artists.

OTHER BOOKSELLERS

Let us now consider the sales of prints to other book dealers. In December 1573, Pedro Bocangelino, an Italian bookseller who had moved to Toledo, placed a particularly large order for books, worth nearly 600 fl., as well as a large selection of prints worth more than 34 fl.[62] Like the shipments to Dilbaum over the previous two years, the prints were supplied by Cock's widow, Diericx (for 18 fl. 12 ½ st.), Galle (for 8 fl. 11 st.), and De Jode (for 7 fl. 1 st.) and were all resold at cost, with no profit margin for Plantin.[63] In addition to the hundreds of unspecified sheets supplied in bulk by each printseller, Bocangelino also purchased single impressions of several specific images and print series. These included Cock's renowned Italianate prints from the early 1550s (*The Dispute about the Holy Sacrament* and *The Adoration of the*

Shepherds by Giorgio Ghisi, Pieter van der Heyden's *The Raising of the Brazen Serpent*, and the Van Doetecum brothers' *The Resurrection of Christ*), in addition to Cock's series of tomb designs, village houses, and the portraits of painters, which Diericx published in 1572. Bocangelino also purchased images of ruins from all three publishers, in addition to De Jode's series of caryatids and designs with grotesques and several of Galle's recently published print books, such as the *Deorum dearumque capita* and *Virorum doctorum … effigies* XLIIII (fig. 3.5).[64] The fact that just one copy of each of the prints listed by name was sent (as well as the frequency with which just one or two copies of each of the cited books was purchased), suggests that this order may have been placed for a specific client and not to stock a bookseller's shop. After his purchase of works by Dürer early in 1574, mentioned above, Bocangelino does not seem to have purchased prints from Plantin again, although he did place another large order for books in 1575.[65]

Bocangelino's purchase of prints by Dürer differs from the orders of prints placed by other booksellers in various ways. For example, in the early 1580s notably large consignments of prints were sold to the Antoni family of publishers and booksellers in Milan (fig. 3.10) and to Jan Poelman, a former shopkeeper for Plantin who was then working as his agent in Salamanca.[66] In both cases, the quantities of prints involved were significantly greater than those in Bocangelino's purchase: some 800 to 1,200 sheets of unidentified prints sold in bulk were complemented by often three, four, or six impressions of several specific print series. Not surprisingly, the total value of these sales was also substantially higher: approximately 69 fl. for Poelman and 58 fl. 7 st. for the Antoni family.[67] Both men were most likely stocking up for general resale and not simply satisfying the whim of a single client, although neither placed such a large order for prints again with Plantin, despite ordering books on other occasions.

These two purchases themselves diverge notably in terms of what exactly was sold. Presumably reflecting the distinct markets for which they were intended, the differences confirm that Plantin was not simply sending uniform, standardized lots of prints to various clients. Specifically, Poelman took only prints from Galle. In particular, in addition to 1,150 "feulles ordinaires" (ordinary sheets) and 36 "feulles grand" (large sheets), Poelman bought multiple copies of several of Galle's print books – such as his *De deis gentium imagines, Divinarum nuptiarum conventa et acta*, and *David, hoc est virtutis … spectaculum* – in addition to a few diverse print series, for instance, the Passion, sets of ruins, images of the five senses, and a set of pendant designs.[68] Galle also supplied the majority of the prints sent to the Antoni family (nearly 52 fl. worth), but this time, hundreds of prints of different sizes sold in bulk were combined with numerous specific print series, most of which were designed by Maarten van Heemskerck (such as *The Story of Judith and Holofernes* (fig. 3.11)) or Johannes Stradanus (such as his exceptionally popular imagery of hunts). This selection was then combined with multiple copies of a few print series supplied by Diericx (amounting to 6 fl. 10 st.), namely perspective prints designed by Vredeman de Vries, a set of the *Seven Liberal Arts*, the *Story of Daniel* designed by Van Heemskerck, and Stradanus's large series of hunts with frames. While the last may have been published in 1570, the year in which Cock died, the others were all clearly older prints that he had published in the 1560s, some fifteen years earlier.[69]

Another notable difference between these shipments is the fact that while all of the prints for Poelman were sold to him at cost, the prices of some of the prints sold to the Antoni family were rounded up. For example, prints that Galle had supplied in bulk at 1.75 st. per sheet were resold at 2 st. per sheet (while all of the prints supplied at 18 st. per quire, were resold at the same price). Likewise, although Cock's smaller perspective series dedicated to Cardinal Antoine Perrenot de Granvelle was resold at cost (at 12 st. per set), the price of the series

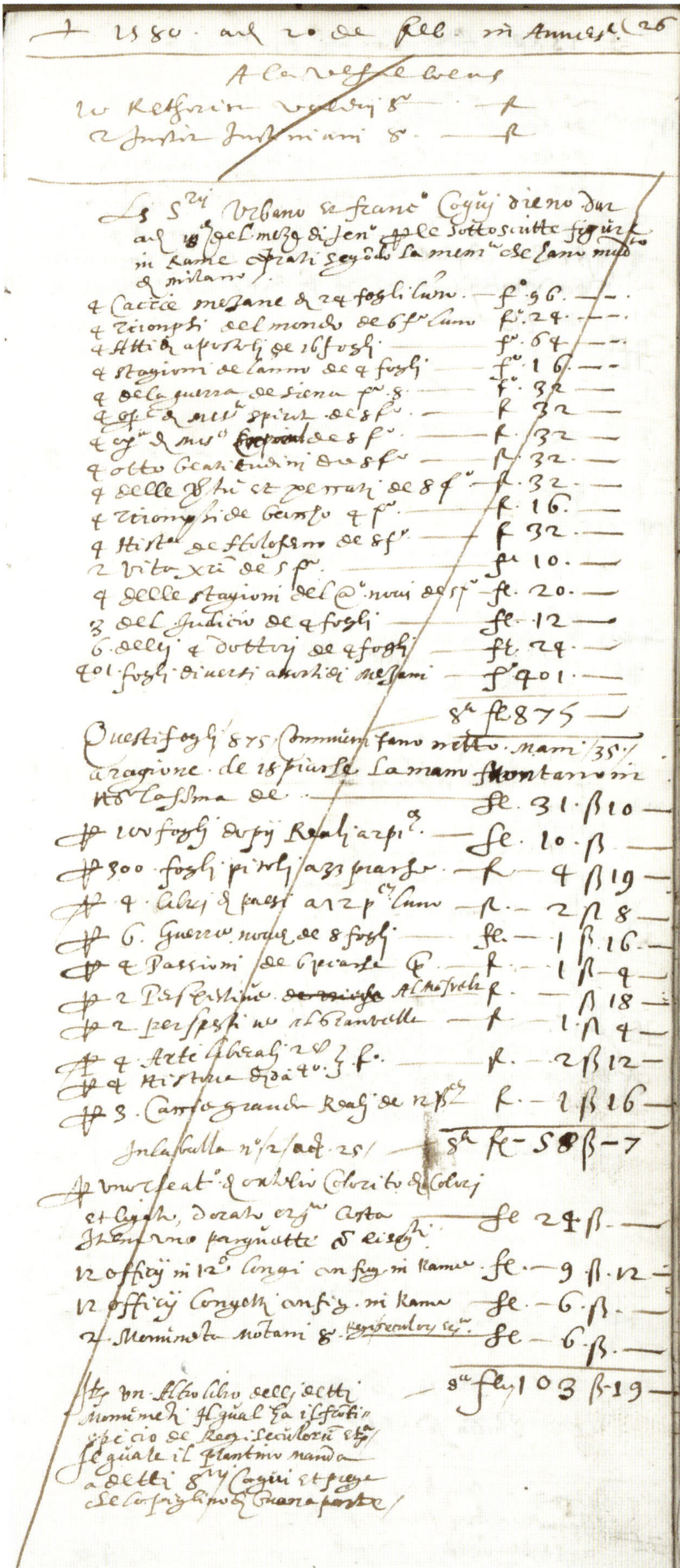

3.10 Record of shipment of prints to Giovanni Antonio degli Antoni of Milan via the merchants Urbano and Franc. Coqui; the eleventh item cited on this list: "Hist^{or} de Holoferno de 8 f°." is represented in fig. 3.11. Antwerp, Museum Plantin-Moretus: Arch. 58, *Journal 1580*, fol. 26r.

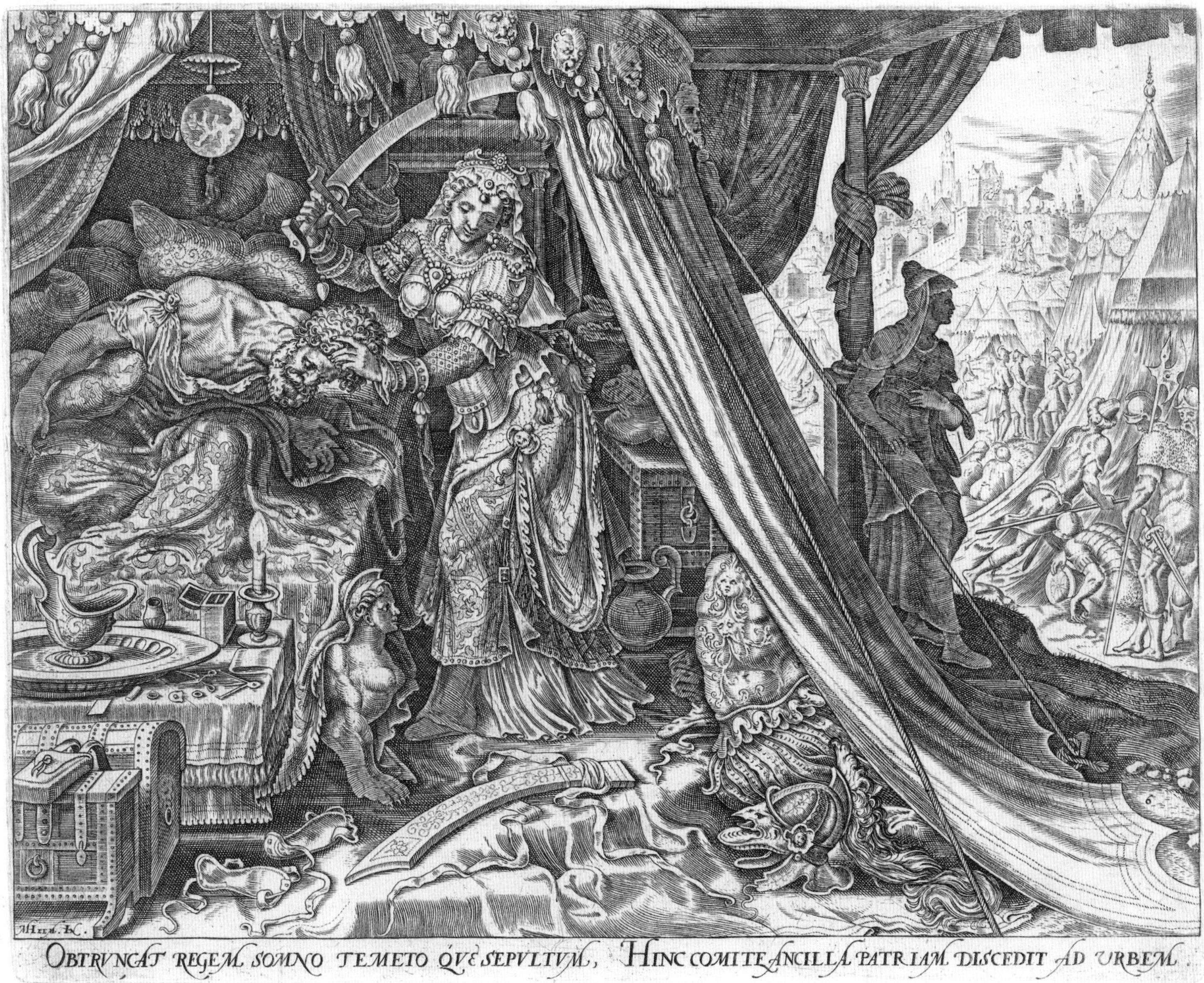

3.11 Philips Galle after Maarten van Heemskerck, *Judith Beheads Holofernes*, from the series *The Story of Judith and Holofernes*, 1564, engraving, 203 × 247 mm. Amsterdam, Rijksmuseum: RP-P-1904-3294. Appendix 1: PG-110.

dedicated to Peter Ernst von Mansfeld was rounded up from 8.5 st. per set to 9 st. per set. The reasons behind these small, occasional price increases are impossible to determine with certainty. Perhaps the ease of calculating sums with larger, simpler numbers played a role, or perhaps the fact that Plantin was dealing with a distant Italian bookseller instead of a familiar, former employee, like Poelman, was important. Whatever the reason, these small examples of price manipulation were the exception in Plantin's trade in prints with fellow booksellers.

Bocangelino's one-time order of approximately 34 fl. worth of prints in 1573 also differs significantly from the numerous smaller orders of prints placed between July 1586 and December 1588 by the bookseller François Boulet from Lille.[70] Comprising fourteen separate transactions, often for just a few florins each, together they amounted to approximately 33 fl. – nearly the same sum spent by Bocangelino. Boulet usually purchased batches of twenty-five or fifty sheets of prints in bulk; occasionally, he supplemented his orders with a few specific

3.12 Anonymous engraver after "D. Ste. Taborotius," *Allegory of Foolishness and Intoxication*, published by Adriaen Huberti in 1576, engraving, 168 mm diameter. Amsterdam, Rijksmuseum: RP-P-2004-45.

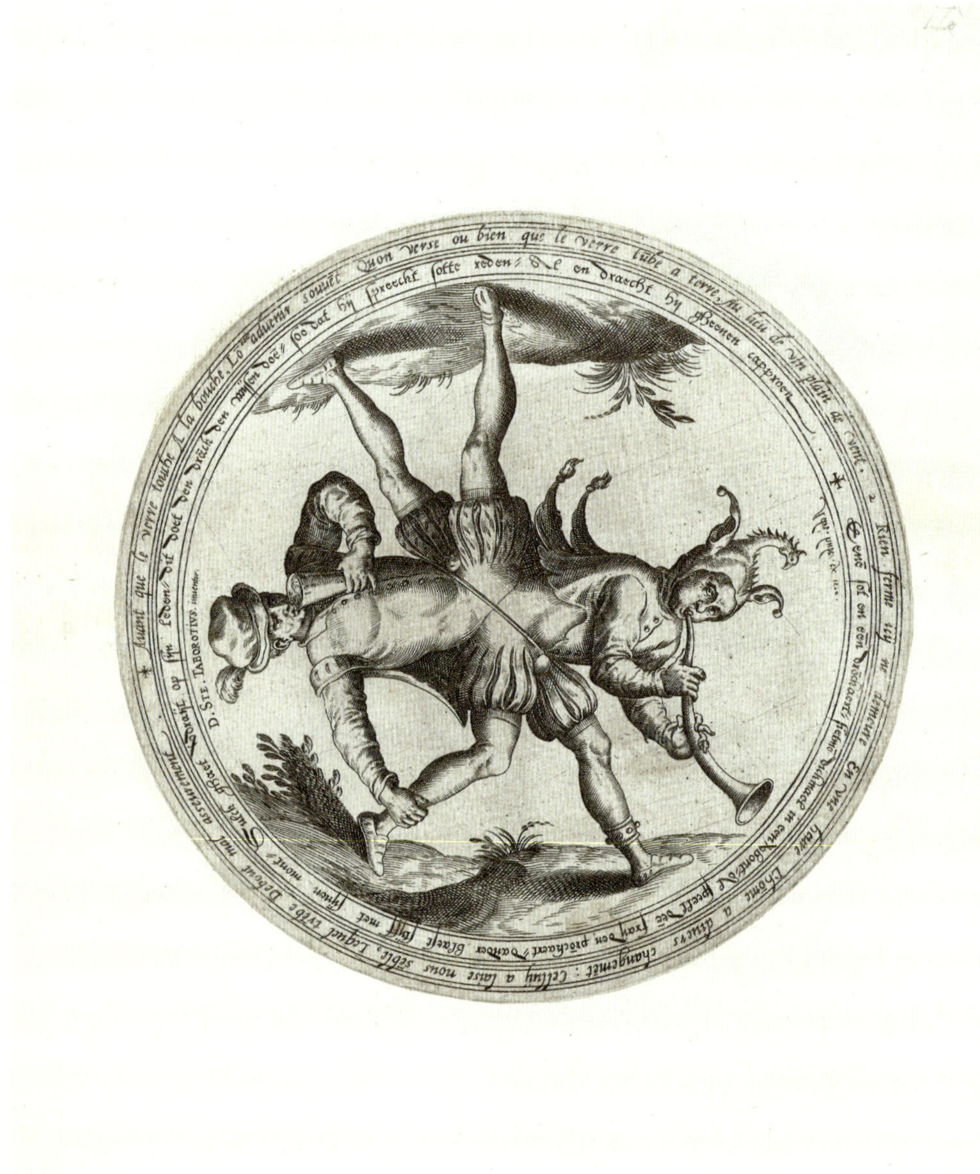

items, such as copies of Galle's *Virorum doctorum … effigies*, or "canons", which were decorative pieces (often bearing images) printed on one or three sheets that bore the essential parts of the text spoken during the celebration of mass.[71] Boulet's preferred supplier of prints in bulk was Adriaen Huberti (Huybrechts) I.[72] Several of these batches of prints were described as comprising "images rondes" (round images). Although known examples of Huberti's round prints suggest that they were for games or illusionistic tricks (fig. 3.12), the records of at least one such sale to Boulet suggests that this format was also used for a religious subject, namely the Lamb of God.[73] Though unusual for Plantin's print sales, the phenomenon of a relatively local bookseller making periodic purchases of often small quantities of prints would become more common under Plantin's successors, the Moretuses, who usually resold these prints at cost.

A few of Plantin's regular clients among booksellers also occasionally placed isolated orders for prints. For example, in 1581, Plantin sold copies of Abraham de Bruyn's brand-new edition of his *Omnium pene gentium imagines* (*Images of Nearly All Nations*) to both Cornelis

Claesz in Amsterdam and Jehan Aubri in Frankfurt, while in 1582, Dirk van Helmont from Middelburg bought approximately 200 prints from De Jode.[74] But these, as well as several other comparable examples, were all exceptional orders worth 5–7 fl. or less (sometimes just a few stuivers, even); they did not constitute a significant trade in prints, particularly when compared with their purchases of books. Instead, other individuals, in particular merchants and Jesuits, or members of the elite, like Philip II's almoner Manrique, turned to Plantin, on occasion, for their more noteworthy requests for prints.

MERCHANTS

Among such individuals, merchants spent the most on prints. Notably, most of these clients lived in Antwerp but were of Spanish, Portuguese, or Italian descent and often had business concerns in these countries. The most prominent was Ferdinand Ximenes, who spent more than 69 fl. on prints in just two purchases – one made in March 1587, the other in March 1588; the bulk of the prints that he ordered was supplied by Galle.[75] But, while the total value of his purchases was comparable to the largest sums spent by the professional booksellers discussed above, the selection of prints differed significantly. In particular, Ximenes ordered relatively few prints in bulk – only approximately 200 in 1587 – and, aside from seventeen copies of Galle's large Passion series designed by Stradanus, few other print series.[76] Rather, the majority of the images he bought were listed by subject and, notably, were all religious. Particularly in his 1588 order, exceptional attention was paid to recording which artists and publishers were responsible for which prints. A preference for images engraved by the Wierix brothers or designed by Stradanus is evident. Although such detail in the list would suggest the involvement of a particular collector, the quantities involved – most often six or eight impressions of each image – indicate that the images were intended for more than one specific individual. Finally, regardless of the supplier or print concerned, Plantin incorporated a profit margin for himself in the resale price, as he usually did when dealing with merchants.

A comparison of Ximenes's purchases with those made by fellow merchants reveals that his selection of single prints with assorted religious subjects was peculiar to him and not necessarily an interest shared by others, even among those with comparable ties to Spain or Portugal. For example, in 1588, Ferdinando de Sevilla purchased single impressions of a remarkably diverse array of Galle's print series, ranging from images of horses and the four seasons to the Ten Commandments; he also purchased 255 unidentified prints in bulk.[77] Similarly, in 1582, Martin de Varon, the son-in-law of Plantin's and Arias Montano's good friend Luis Perez, bought single impressions of disparate subjects, including a series of hunts published by Galle, his *Acts of the Apostles*, and De Jode's series of *The Seven Planets*, in addition to more than fifty other prints supplied by Galle that are simply described as "nuevas y curiosas" (new and curious).[78] Although Plantin did not incorporate any profit margin into his resale of prints to De Sevilla, he did round up the prices in his sale to De Varon. For example, De Jode supplied his series of *The Seven Planets*, which consisted of eight prints, for 6 st. (or .75 st. per print), and Galle had charged 18 st. per quire of twenty-five prints (or .72 st. per print) for all of the unspecified prints he supplied, along with his series of *The Acts of the Apostles*. Plantin then charged De Varon a simple 1 st. per print for all of these images, despite their distinct original values. Altogether, this amounted to a total of 1 fl. 14 ½ st. (or 34 ½ st.) profit for Plantin on a relatively modest sale

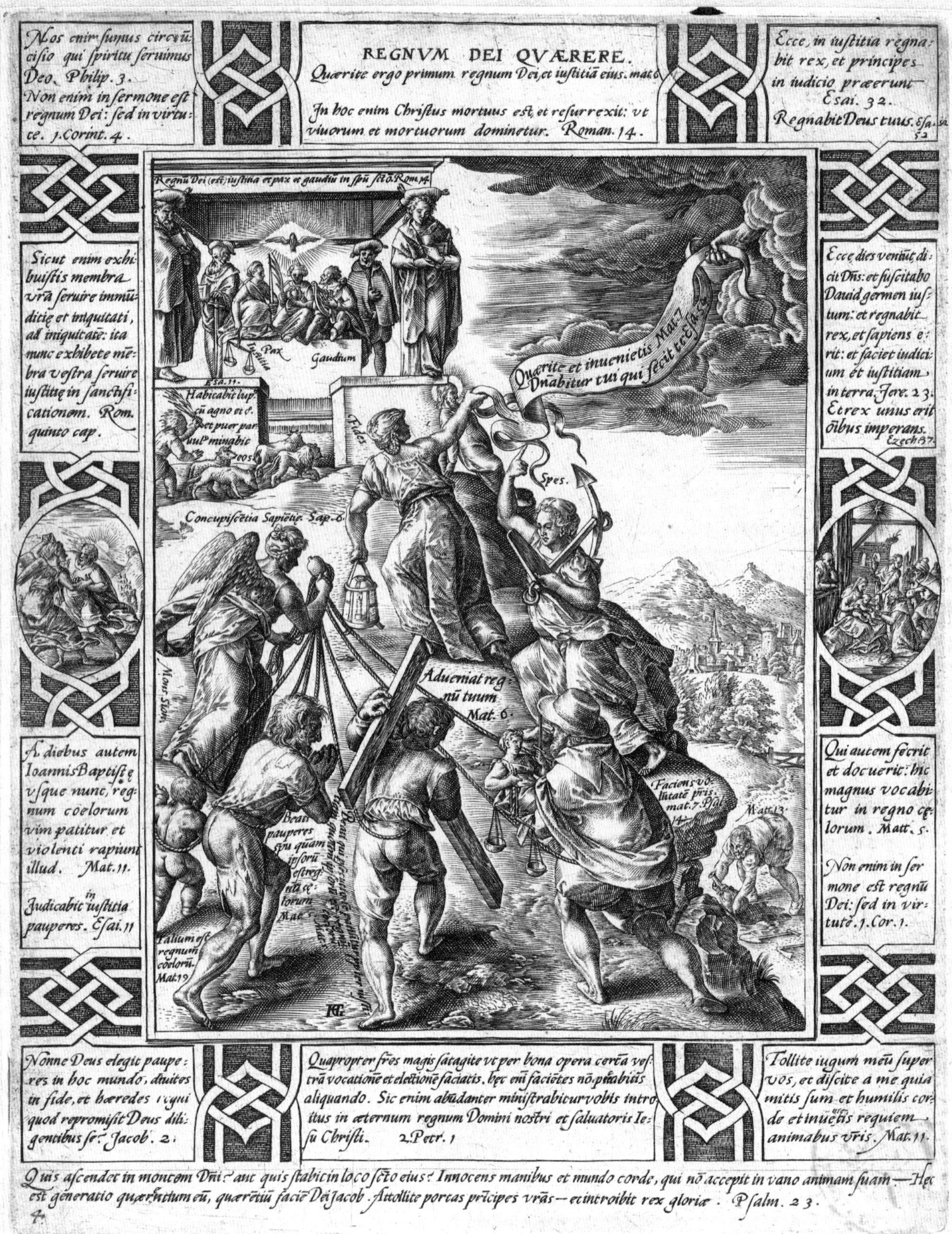
Nos enim sumus circu̅cisio qui spiritu seruimus Deo. Philip. 3. Non enim in sermone est regnum Dei: sed in virtute. 1. Corint. 4.
REGNVM DEI QVÆRERE.
Quærite ergo primum regnum Dei, et iustitiā eius. mat. 6.
In hoc enim Christus mortuus est, et resurrexit: vt viuorum et mortuorum dominetur. Roman. 14.
Ecce, in iustitia regnabit rex, et principes in iudicio præerunt. Esai. 32. Regnabit Deus tuus. Esa. 52
Regnu̅ Dei (est) iustitia et pax et gaudiu̅ in spu̅ sc̄to. Rom. 14
Iustitia
Pax
Gaudium
Esa. 11
Habitabit lupus cu̅ agno et ... puer paruul. minabit eos
Fides
Quærite et inuenietis Mat. 7
Dnabitur tui qui fecit te Esa. 54
Spes.
Concupiscētia Sapiētię. Sap. 6.
Mons Sion
Adueniat regnu̅ tuum Mat. 6.
Faciens voluntatē patris. mat. 7. Psal. 14
Mat. 13
Beati pauperes spu quoniam ipsoru̅ est regnu̅ cęlorum. Mat.
Talium est regnum coeloru̅. Mat. 19
Sicut enim exhibuistis membra vrā seruire immu̅ditię et iniquitati, ad iniquitatē: ita nunc exhibete me̅bra vestra seruire iustitię in sanctificationem. Rom. quinto cap.
Ecce dies veniu̅t, dicit Dn̄s: et suscitabo Dauid germen iustum: et regnabit rex, et sapiens erit: et faciet iudicium et iustitiam in terra. Jere. 23. Et rex vnus erit o̅ibus imperans. Ezech. 37.
A diebus autem Ioannis Baptistę vsque nunc, regnum coelorum vim patitur et violenti rapiunt illud. Mat. 11.
Judicabit in iustitia pauperes. Esai. 11
Qui autem fecerit et docuerit: hic magnus vocabitur in regno cęlorum. Matt. 5.
Non enim in sermone est regnu̅ Dei: sed in virtute. 1. Cor. 1.
Nonne Deus elegit pauperes in hoc mundo, diuites in fide, et hæredes regni quod repromisit Deus diligentibus se? Jacob. 2.
Quapropter frēs magis satagite vt per bona opera certā vestrā vocatione̅ et electione̅ faciatis. hęc eni̅ faciētes no̅ peccabitis aliquando. Sic enim abu̅danter ministrabitur vobis introitus in æternum regnum Domini nostri et saluatoris Iesu Christi. 2. Petr. 1
Tollite iugum meu̅ super vos, et discite a me quia mitis sum et humilis corde et inue̅etis requiem animabus vrīs. Mat. 11.
Quis ascendet in montem Dn̄i? aut quis stabit in loco sc̄to eius? Innocens manibus et mundo corde, qui no̅ accepit in vano animam suam — Hec est generatio quærentium eu̅, quærētiu̅ faciē Dei Jacob. Attollite portas principes vrās — et introibit rex gloriæ. Psalm. 23.
4.

of 6 fl. 7 st., or a profit margin of approximately 27%. As some of the following examples will make clear, this was a remarkably large and seemingly haphazard markup.

Purchases in the early 1580s by two merchants with possible ties to Italy or Spain, namely Simon de Tassis, then living in Antwerp, and Gabriel Langart, who worked for Santfort and Helman, similarly demonstrate that Ximenes's orders were exceptional, in terms of both the total sum spent and his preference for individual religious subjects.[79] For example, in 1581, Langart bought prints worth a total of 32 fl. 16 st., in which he favored series designed by Vredeman de Vries – several of his perspective views published by Cock and a series of fountains published by De Jode – in addition to landscape images. He also bought series of hunts and animals designed by Stradanus and supplied by Diericx and Galle; these images were then hand-colored for him.[80] While Tassis was similarly interested in a selection of Stradanus's images of hunts and animals, the bulk of the prints he purchased in 1580 (for a total of approximately 28 fl.) were published by Galle.[81] Tassis's order is noteworthy for the large number of engravings by Hendrick Goltzius, such as his *Story of Lucretia* and a selection of his series of *Allegories of the Christian Creed* (but *not* the entire series as a unit) (fig. 3.13).[82] In addition, Tassis bought sundry other devotional images published by Galle, many of which featured the Virgin and Christ and most of which had been published just a few years earlier. This was most likely not a coincidence, as the record of the sale to Tassis includes 191 prints, identified simply as "diversi altri novi" (diverse other new [prints]). Typically buying four or six impressions of each image noted, Tassis was most likely (in contrast to Langart) buying quantities of prints for general resale elsewhere. Regardless of the supplier or the ultimate destination of these prints, Plantin made a profit on the resale of all of them by, once again, rounding up the prices charged to the buyer, although, this time, his margin was closer to 11% of the total value, versus the significantly greater profit earned on the sale to De Varon.[83]

3.13 Hendrick Goltzius, *Man's Quest for the Kingdom of Heaven*, from the series *Allegories of the Christian Creed*, 1578, engraving, 259 × 186 mm. Amsterdam, Rijksmuseum: RP-P-OB-10.075. Appendix 1: PG-69.

JESUITS AND NOBLES

Alongside merchants, both local and distant Jesuits turned to Plantin on occasion when in need of prints. For example, several Jesuits active in northern Europe, above all in Stockholm and Vilnius, ordered both books and prints from Plantin between 1577 and 1583. Of particular importance were Joannes Herbest (confessor to Catharine Jagiellon, Queen of Sweden), as well as Stanislas Warszewicki and Laurentius Nicolai Norvegus, both of whom were similarly active in Sweden.[84] All three men were involved in the attempt to reinstate the Catholic faith in (then Protestant) Sweden. As part of this effort, they periodically ordered numerous books from Plantin, possibly for the new Jesuit Collegium Regium Stockholmense, and occasionally purchased selections of prints.[85] Although not all of the prints sent were specified, orders of several sets each of Galle's series of the *Our Father (Pater noster)*, *Seven Sacraments*, and *The Spiritual* [and] *Worldly Acts of Mercy* (fig. 3.14) were listed and may have been intended for visual instruction in the Catholic faith.[86]

When, in 1588, the local Jesuits Thomas Sailly and Vincentius Zeelander, who were at the Jesuit college in Bruges, bought more than 1,000 prints from diverse suppliers, these were most likely intended for diverse purposes.[87] For example, Sailly's purchases of 500 images of the Crucifixion supplied by the painter Maarten de Vos, as well as 100 small figures from Adriaen Huberti I and another 200 small images from an unspecified supplier, may all have been meant for use within the Jesuit order.[88] Similarly, Zeelander's purchases of fifteen copies of

3.14 Philips Galle, title plate for the series *The Seven Spiritual Acts of Mercy*, 1577, engraving, 260 × 190 mm. Amsterdam, Rijksmuseum: RP-P-2004-578. Appendix 1: PG-99.

canons, several of which were specially colored, in just three months between December 1587 and February 1588, may also have been intended for distribution within or through the Jesuit college in Bruges.[89] However, Sailly's smaller and more specific purchases of prints from Galle and by the Sadelers may have been for specific individuals rather than for general consumption. This was the case when he bought 306 small, diverse images of saints and devotions from Galle, Huberti, De Jode, and Hans van Luyck, who supplied the majority of prints. All of them were to be sent to the wife of Cosmo Masi, secretary to Alexander Farnese.[90]

In other instances, laity who cared for the libraries of distant nobles contacted Plantin to help build up not only their libraries, but also their print collections. For example, in 1579 and 1581, the Duke of Prussia in Königsberg (now Kaliningrad) authorized his librarian, Michael Scrinius, to purchase numerous books as well as several print series or print books, in addition to more than 100 unidentified prints in bulk; the total of the order was nearly 19 fl.[91] In striking contrast to the majority of the sales discussed above, Scrinius typically bought just one impression of each of the items listed – books or prints – thereby underscoring the likelihood that they were to be part of a personal collection. Perhaps indicative of some underlying methdology, Scrinius's two print orders were also neatly subdivided. In 1579, he bought two of Galle's print books (the *Divinarum nuptiarum conventa et acta* and *Deorum dearumque capita*), as well as his series of hunts after Stradanus. He also obtained two of De Bruyn's print series: *Omnium pene gentium imagines* (*Images of Nearly All Nations*) and a set of images of religious dress.[92] In 1581, Scrinius requested more than 100 unidentified prints from Cock's widow, Diericx, in addition to a selection of print series that Cock had first published some twenty years earlier, namely two series of perspective views and his sets of ruins and tomb designs. In addition, he acquired Cock's 1558 publication of *The Baths of Diocletian*.[93] As with nearly all of his sales to individual clients outside his familiar circle of friends or fellow booksellers, Plantin incorporated a small profit margin for himself in these transactions, namely: 13 st. of the 8 fl. 10 st. in the 1579 sale and 1 fl. 12 st. of the 10 fl. 6 st. in the 1581 sale.

Arranging all of Plantin's print sales from the mid-1560s onwards by the total amount charged to each client, rather than by the type of buyer, reveals several essential aspects of Plantin's dealings in prints. In particular, only two individuals purchased more than 100 fl. worth of prints from Plantin during his lifetime, namely his friend Arias Montano, who bought more than 215 fl. worth of prints, and his fellow bookseller Dilbaum from Augsburg, who purchased approximately 147 fl. worth of prints. Both men, in their own way, were investing intensively in remarkably large quantities of images. It is, then, all the more striking that Plantin did not add any profit margin to these sales. Plantin also sent exceptionally large quantities of Galle's print books to his own shop in Paris between September 1573 and March 1577. These shipments began soon after Galle's completion of several of these projects and ended shortly before Plantin sold his shop to the Parisian bookseller Michel Sonnius I in August 1577 to help compensate the significant financial losses he had suffered a year earlier during the pillaging of Antwerp by Spanish soldiers in November 1576. During this period, Plantin sent at least:[94]

- 18 copies of the *Virorum doctorum … effigies* from 1572, at 16 st. each, for a total of 14 fl. 8 st.
- 12 copies of the *Deorum dearumque capita* from 1573, at 12 st. each, for a total of 10 fl. 16 st.
- 30 copies of the Latin edition of the *Divinarum nuptiarum conventa et acta* and *Christi Jesu vitae* from 1573 and 4 of the French edition from 1573/1574, at 35 st. each (regardless of the language), for a total of 59 fl. 10 st.; and
- 24 copies of *David, hoc est virtutis … spectaculum* from 1575, at 1 fl. each, for a total of 24 fl.

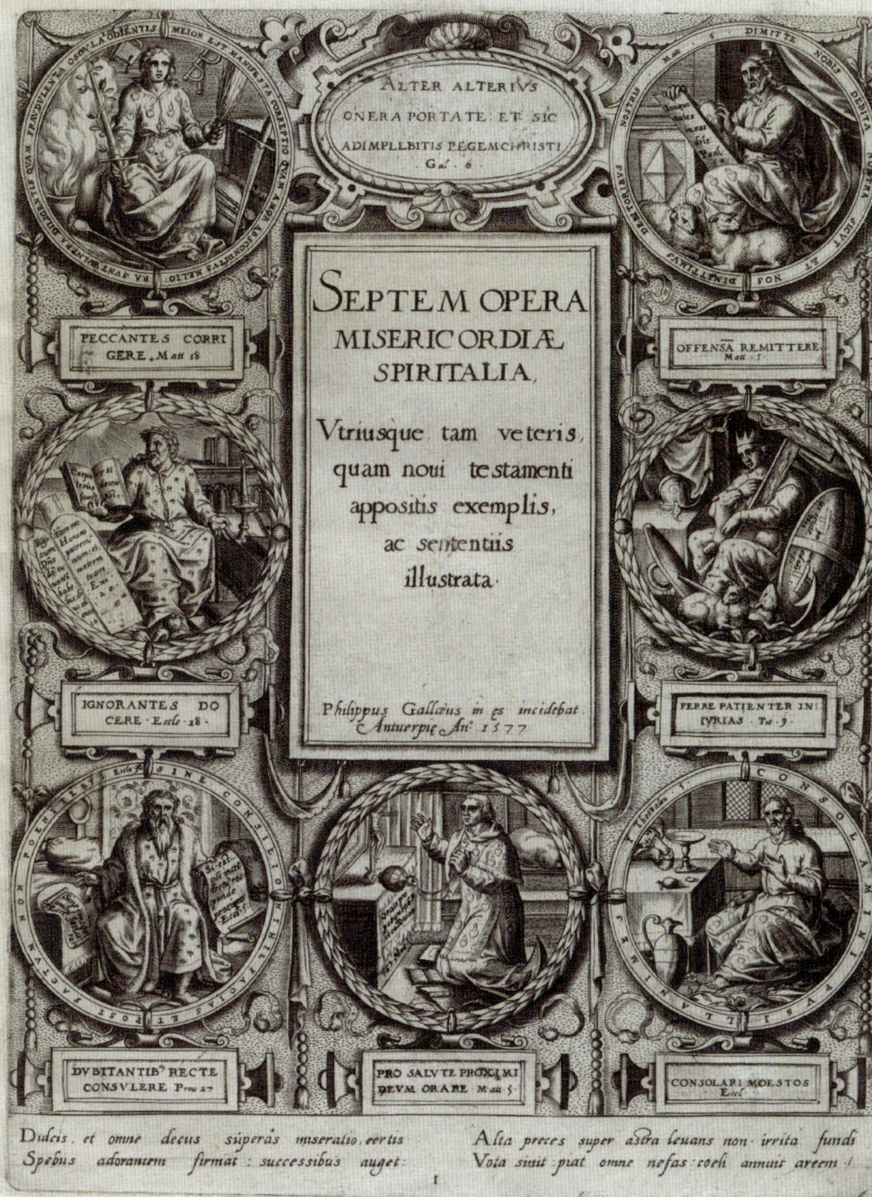
ALTER ALTERIVS
ONERA PORTATE: ET SIC
ADIMPLEBITIS LEGEM CHRISTI
Gal. 6
SEPTEM OPERA
MISERICORDIÆ
SPIRITALIA,
Vtriusque tam veteris,
quam noui testamenti
appositis exemplis,
ac sententiis
illustrata.
Philippus Gallæus in æs incidebat.
Antuerpiæ An. 1577
PECCANTES CORRIGERE. Matt 18
OFFENSA REMITTERE Matt 5
IGNORANTES DOCERE Eccle 18
FERRE PATIENTER INIVRIAS To. 9
DVBITANTIB. RECTE CONSVLERE Prov 27
PRO SALVTE PROXIMI DEVM ORARE Matt 5
CONSOLARI MOESTOS Eccl
Dulcis, et omne decus superas miseratio, certis
Spebus adorantem firmat: successibus auget.
Alta preces super astra leuans non irrita fundi
Vota sinit: piat omne nefas: coeli annuit aream.
1

Amounting to more than 112 fl. in total, these sales represented a significant outlet for Galle's print books at this time. It is, consequently, all the more noteworthy that Sonnius did not continue to import these works via Plantin once he had taken over Plantin's shop. Perhaps he placed his orders for them directly with Galle, or perhaps Galle had established his own contacts in Paris for their distribution.

Print purchases worth 40–100 fl. were likewise rare. The individuals involved in these purchases were merchants (such as Ximenes), members of the social and political elite (like Manrique), and booksellers (such as Poelman and the Antoni family in Milan). While the primary destination for these orders of hundreds, if not thousands, of prints remained southern Europe, in particular Italy, Spain, and Portugal, the exact mix of prints sent differed from one client to the next.

Sales of prints worth 10–40 fl. were more common. Although there is again a substantial number of merchants and book dealers linked to southern Europe, these sales are also characterized by a noticeable diversity in both the type of buyer and the destinations of the shipments. Encompassing not only more places in the Holy Roman Empire and in France (such as the booksellers Aubri in Frankfurt and Boulet in Lille), in addition to more local customers (like the Jesuits in Bruges), these examples are also noteworthy for the number of Jesuits and the members of nobility in distant cities – Stockholm, Vilnius, and Königsberg, for example – represented. Predictably, print purchases of less than 10 fl. are even more common; nearly half of such sales cost less than 2 ½ st. This last group comprises not only anonymous sales via Plantin's own shop in Antwerp, but also purchases by booksellers with whom he regularly did business (like Jan Bellerus in Antwerp and John Fowler's widow in Leuven) and by various other individuals, ranging from such notable figures as William Herle, the English ambassador-spy, to Pierre Hassaert, the local physician, astrologer and almanac author.[95]

Despite the disparate nature of Plantin's sales, particularly in terms of their total value, the type of client, and the final destination of the prints, the transactions suggest several important conclusions. The irregular, often isolated nature of the vast majority of the purchases indicates that Plantin was primarily responding to occasional requests for prints from individuals who usually dealt with him in other ways: primarily via his bookselling business, but also, as in the case of Arias Montano, on a more personal level. Whether or not Plantin made any profit on these transactions was, more often than not, determined on a case-by-case basis. As was common in Plantin's ordinary trade in books, prints bought by personal friends and fellow booksellers were usually sold at cost, while all other sales were often subject to an irregular rounding up of the prices for Plantin's own benefit.[96]

The varied content of Plantin's shipments reflects a wide-ranging demand for prints by distinct individuals. Although some subjects or particular publications were popular and recur – such as Stradanus's designs for hunts (published both by Diericx and Galle) or Galle's print books, like the *Virorum doctorum … effigies*, the majority of these sales also reveal the personal tastes of individual buyers. Recall, for example: Arias Montano's evident enjoyment of landscapes, prints after Van Heemskerck for the Antoni family of booksellers, prints engraved by Goltzius for Tassis, and De Bruyn's print series of people and their dress for the Duke of Prussia. Both renowned, older prints, like many of Cock's publications from the 1560s, which were still readily available via his widow Diericx, as well as new and curious images, were periodically requested. And yet, despite Plantin's ability to satisfy so many different requests for prints, one type of buyer is routinely absent, namely other independent print publishers. Only during the first decade of his activities in Antwerp did Plantin sporadically help such dealers in Antwerp procure prints from Paris. Similarly, Plantin does not appear to have endeavored to compete with print publishers at other major international markets, such as the Frankfurt fair. Thus, Plantin was not usually supplying the primary print salesmen, but more often selling to those on the periphery of this market. These clients included booksellers and merchants, who may have only occasionally participated in the print trade. Private collectors, often in distant places, also sent their requests to Plantin; his contacts with various well-known printmakers and publishers in Antwerp, as well as the ease of shipment because of his regular book transports, may have been his most important assets.

PLANTIN'S SOURCES FOR PRINTS 1566–1589

If Plantin's dealings in prints from the mid-1560s onwards were primarily responses to individual requests rather than an active endeavor on his part to seek clients for a sideline in the print trade, who, then, were the print publishers and printmakers most often sought by his contacts? When Plantin began to trade in prints in the first decade after his arrival in Antwerp, he obtained them from various sources. The most significant appear to have been booksellers in Paris, as well as several print publishers in Antwerp, in particular: Hans Liefrinck I, Gerard de Jode, and Hieronymus Cock, each of whom is named in Plantin's accounts by 1558.[97] When Plantin restarted his business in the mid-1560s, the last three were his primary suppliers of prints.

Of these, Liefrinck remained the least involved in Plantin's trade in prints, as his principal transactions all date to 1568. The most important of the transactions with Liefrinck was the large consignment of prints in bulk, worth 60 fl., that he provided for Arias Montano in November 1568. After 1568, Liefrinck no longer features in Plantin's accounts. He may have limited his activities due to poor health (he died in February 1573). However, since neither he nor his direct successors (his widow and son Hans II) provided Plantin with more prints, his publications may not have been of immediate interest to Plantin's clients and perhaps he preferred to distribute his prints via other channels. Liefrinck's independent activity in these years may be indicated by a transaction in which Plantin agreed to include two packages of Liefrinck's prints in one of his shipments to Paris in May 1568.[98] Even Liefrinck's sister, Mynken, who worked closely with Plantin on the production of the vast majority of his illustrated editions, among other activities, does not appear to have supplied Plantin with prints published by her brother or his heirs.[99] De Jode, Cock (and his successor, Volcxken Diericx), by contrast, continued to supply Plantin with prints for resale for the rest of his life.

Although the demand for De Jode's prints persisted throughout Plantin's lifetime, the quantities purchased were usually modest (fig. 3.15). Often amounting to just a few prints (or print series) of diverse subjects, ranging from series of the Passion to landscapes and designs for fountains, each purchase was worth no more than a few florins in total. De Jode's and Plantin's cartographic transactions were, however, far more significant in terms of the quantity and value of the items involved.[100] Even individuals who paid large sums for prints, such as the merchant Ximenes or the Jesuit Warszewicki, purchased just 12 or 9 st. worth of prints, respectively, from De Jode. Other sales often amounted to no more than approximately 7 fl. (140 st.) at most, as was the case with the booksellers Dirk van Helmont (from Middelburg) and Bocangelino (from Toledo), as well as Philip II's almoner, Manrique. Only Willer's assistant Dilbaum in Augsburg bought considerably more prints from De Jode, whose four separate purchases made between 22 November 1570 and 28 October 1571 amounted to a total of 24 fl. 13 ½ st..[101] Perhaps the international market for De Jode's prints (in addition to his maps) was satisfied primarily via other channels, as is suggested by the list of debtors to De Jode's estate, which comprised several other print and map dealers, ranging from Diericx and Jan Baptist Vrients in Antwerp to Cornelis Claesz of Amsterdam to both Balthasar and Cornelis Caymox of Nuremberg. Additionally, De Jode had contacts in Salamanca and London. Plantin's own records of when he received money on behalf of others attest to some of De Jode's contacts in London. For example, the London bookseller Robert Cambier paid him sums of 30 fl and 46 fl. 5 st. in 1579 and 1580, respectively, for De Jode.[102]

Remarkably, the exceptional amount spent by Dilbaum for hundreds of mostly unspecified images from De Jode is comparable to what De Jode charged in 1588 (24 fl. 16 st.) for two

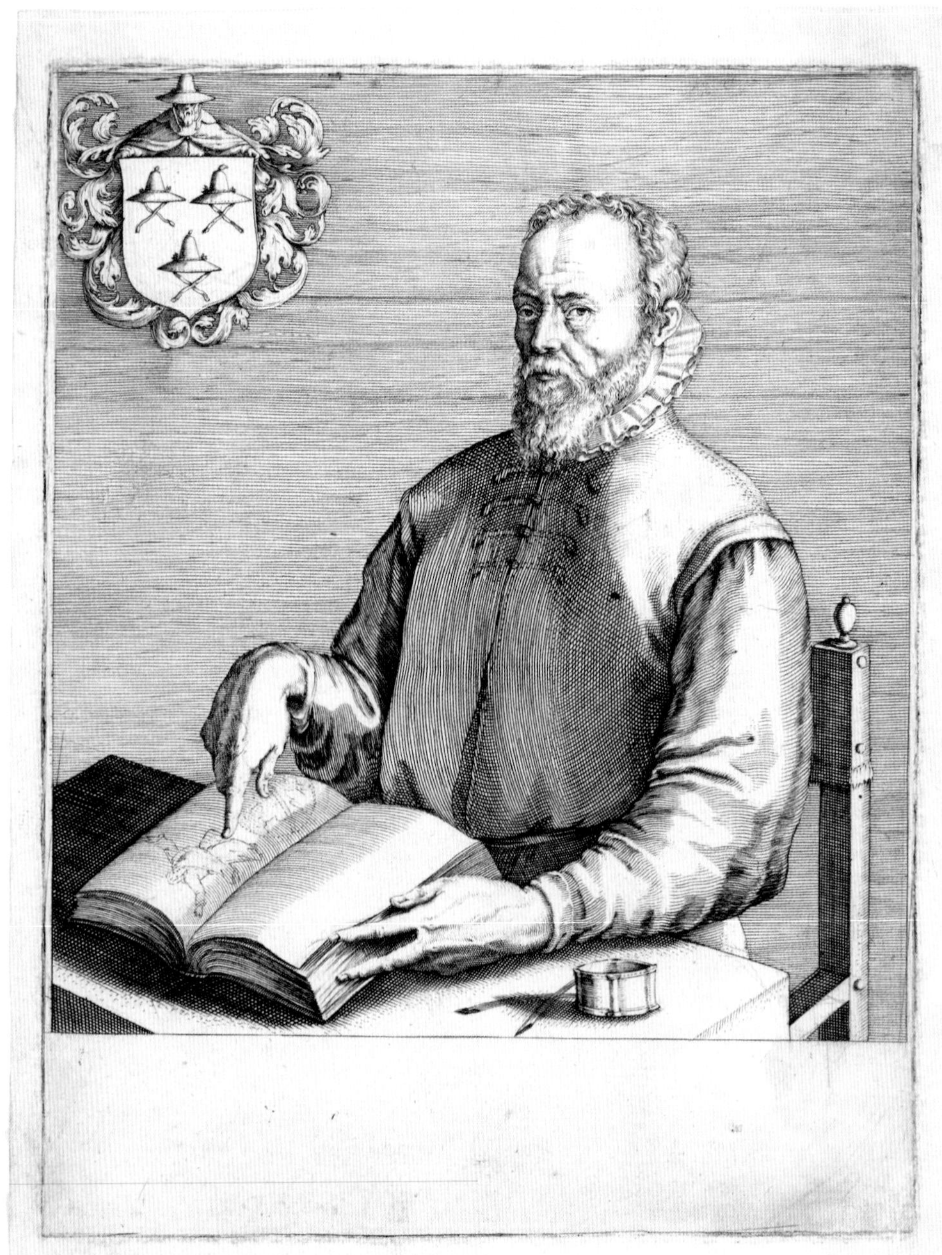

3.15 Gerard de Jode (attributed to) after Hendrick Goltzius, *Gerard de Jode*, ca. 1580, engraving, 203 × 150 mm. Princeton, NJ, Princeton University Art Museum: Bequest of Junius S. Morgan, Class of 1888.

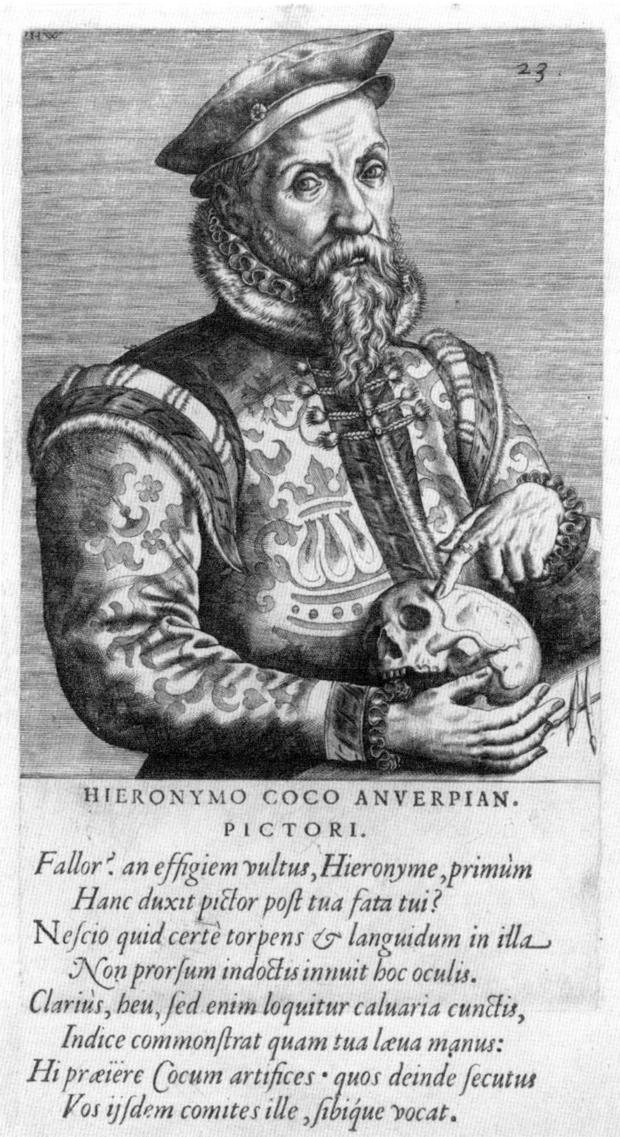

3.16 Jan Wierix, *Portrait of the Painter [and Print Seller] Hieronymus Cock*, print 23 from the series *Portraits of Famous Painters from the Low Countries*, ca. 1571, engraving, 115 × 119 mm. Amsterdam, Rijksmuseum: RP-P-OB-67.042. Appendix 1: CD-18.

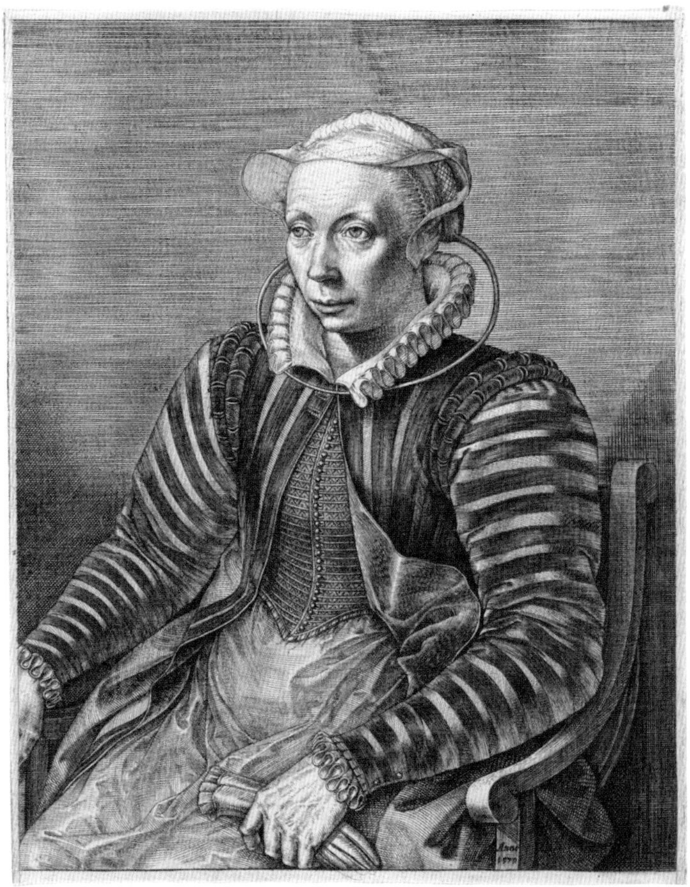

3.17 Jan Wierix (attributed to), *Portrait of the Print Seller Volcxken Diericx*, 1579, engraving, 159 × 124 mm. Amsterdam, Rijksmuseum: RP-P-OB-67.071.

copies of his *Thesaurus sacrarum historiarum* …, each of which contained 345 sheets (slightly less than the assumed standard length for this work). Plantin sold the copies a week later for 36 fl. (the significance price increase may have reflected the additional cost of having them bound) to the Antwerp merchant Diego Pardo for an unspecified third party.[103] The implied unit price (12 fl. 8 st.) for De Jode's famous print book may help identify another remarkably costly item that De Jode sold to Plantin in June 1580: a "livre des histoires du viel testament qu'il a imprime" (series of stories from the Old Testament that he printed). As the price he charged Plantin for this volume (6 fl. 13 st.) is essentially half of what he asked for his collection of images from both the Old and New Testament, it may have been the first part of the larger *Thesaurus*.[104] Because of these exceptional sales, the total value of what De Jode supplied to Plantin between 1569 and 1588 amounted to about 100 fl. While this sum is essentially twice what Liefrinck supplied (largely in one consignment for Arias Montano in 1568), it is nearly half the total value (approximately 230 fl.) of all the prints Cock and his widow, Diericx, provided for further sale via Plantin (figs. 3.16 and 3.17).

The relatively large quantity of prints supplied by Cock (worth about 100 fl.) went either, like Liefrinck's works, to Arias Montano in 1568 (approximately 74 fl. in total) or, like De Jode's, to Dilbaum (approximately 20 fl. 7 st.) in August 1570, shortly before Cock's death.[105] The most common subjects in these few large orders are prints with landscapes (primarily for Arias Montano), numerous sets of Lombard's and Suavius's series of Christ and his Apostles (for Dilbaum), various designs for compartments, Ghisi's *Adoration of the Shepherds*, and a selection of images of ruins, village houses, and tomb designs.[106]

Diericx continued to supply prints for Dilbaum from December 1570 until November 1571. In this short period, he was her biggest client via Plantin; there were four separate sales for thousands of prints (mostly unspecified and sold in bulk) worth more than 79 fl. When combined with Dilbaum's earlier purchase from Cock, these sales total more than four times what Dilbaum spent on Liefrinck's prints. After 1571, in notable contrast with the persistent, though limited, interest in De Jode's prints, the demand for prints from Diericx's "Aux Quatre Vents" (At the Four Winds) became more erratic and consisted primarily of isolated large purchases for distant clients. In particular, while the Toledo bookseller Bocangelino bought hundreds of prints in 1573 for 18 fl. 12½ st., more modest purchases (ranging from approximately 6 to 11 fl.) were made in 1580 and 1581 by the merchants Tassis and Langart, as well as by Scrinius, the librarian of the Duke of Prussia, and the Coqui merchants for the Antoni family of booksellers in Milan.[107] Bocangelino's, Langart's, and Scrinius's orders comprised hundreds of unspecified prints in bulk. However, all of the preceding orders also featured a select list of prints by subject, from which it is evident that perspective scenes by De Vries and images of hunts after Stradanus were the most widely sought. Aside from Stradanus's images of hunts and a few isolated sales of Diericx's 1572 *Portraits of Famous Painters from the Netherlands (Pictorum aliquot celebrium germaniae inferioris effigies)*, the vast majority of the prints that are recorded as having been sold via Plantin were older images, originally published by Cock, often some ten to twenty years earlier.[108]

Many of the prints Diericx sold via Plantin are also listed in her sales agreement with the local art dealer Bartolomeus de Mompere from 24 September 1582, a little more than a year after her last significant deliveries of prints to Plantin for resale in 1580–1581.[109] As is documented in greater detail in Appendix 1, the prices Diericx and De Mompere agreed upon are mostly (with only a few exceptions) comparable to the rates at which Diericx supplied the same prints to Plantin.[110] The primary difference between Diericx's agreement with De Mompere and her dealings with Plantin was the inclusion of an extra, fixed profit margin of 5% for De Mompere on all sales to other wholesalers and an even greater, flexible profit margin on sales to other individuals. Because Plantin did not usually add any profit margin when he resold prints to personal friends and other booksellers (like Arias Montano, Dilbaum, and Bocangelino) and because the profit margin that he added to his sales to other individuals was highly irregular, the majority of Plantin's sales of prints provided by Diericx should not have been to her disadvantage. Nevertheless, such arrangements were not continued into the latter 1580s. Either Plantin's clients were no longer interested in Diericx's stock of prints, or the prints were available elsewhere. Several sources indicate that the latter hypothesis was certainly possible. Not only had Diericx made the agreement with De Mompere in 1582, but, together with other local print publishers, she also initiated legal actions in 1582 and 1586 to gain compensation for unspecified works supplied to foreign art dealers in both Germany and France.[111] Moreover, Diericx's estate inventory, like De Jode's, also includes lists of debts and debtors. Aside from some local individuals, such as Hans Liefrinck – presumably the son of Hans I of Antwerp – and the bookseller, Cornelis Claesz of Amsterdam, two members of

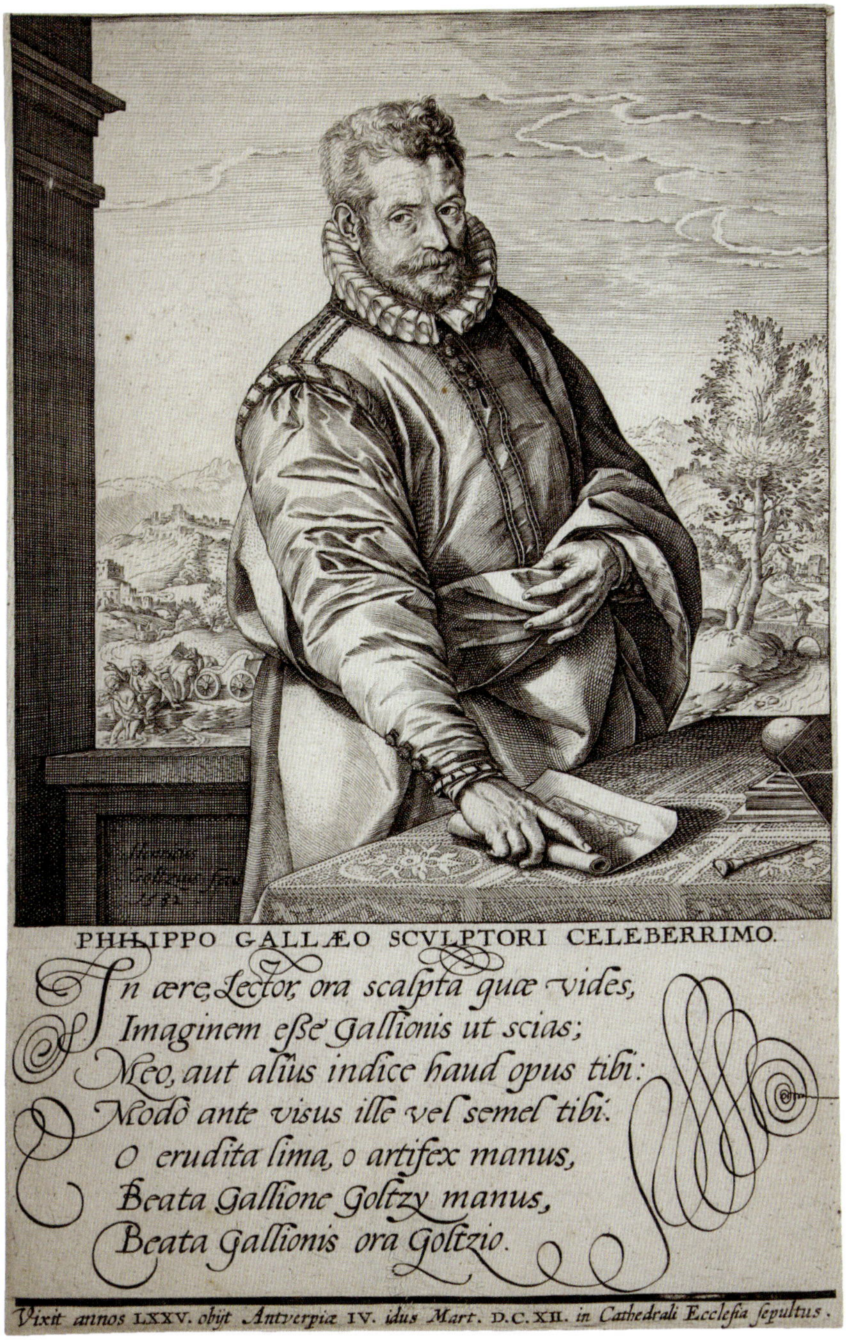

3.18 Hendrick Goltzius, *Philips Galle*, 1582, engraving, 152 × 135 mm. Antwerp, Museum Plantin-Moretus: PK.OP.07884.

the Caymox family – Balthasar (in Nuremberg) and Hans (in Frankfurt) – are also noted.[112] These references demonstrate that she had her own connections for the international distribution of her publications that comprised, notably, several of the individuals named in the inventory of De Jode's estate.

In addition to Plantin's original three primary suppliers of prints, Liefrinck, De Jode, and Cock, one other important print publisher in Antwerp regularly provided Plantin with prints for resale, namely Philips Galle (fig. 3.18). Galle began by satisfying one of Dilbaum's requests for prints in June 1571, a year and a half after his move to Antwerp.[113] By 1574, Galle had become Plantin's main supplier of prints. Indeed, the total value of all the prints (including print series and print books) that he sold to Plantin exceeded 665 fl., nearly three times the value of what Cock and Diericx provided, six times the value of De Jode's prints, and more than ten times the value of Liefrinck's isolated offerings. This staggering amount was the result of numerous factors. First, Galle's publications were sought far more often than those by any other printmaker or publisher who dealt with Plantin: there were some 270 separate requests for individual prints, print series, and print books, in addition to varying quantities of prints in bulk, versus approximately 100 such transactions for Cock and Diericx, and approximately seventy for De Jode. Second, when Galle supplied prints, he often sold them in notably greater quantities than did other print publishers. Thus, not only would he sell more unspecified prints in bulk, but he also sold multiple impressions of prints – often four or six sets at once – far more often than Cock, Diericx, or De Jode did. Third, because Galle not only dealt in print series (like De Jode, Cock, and Diericx), but also published several successful, large print books, the average price of what he had for sale was also significantly higher. Specifically, although each of these print publishers sold his or her individual prints for approximately ¾ st. to 2–3 st. per print, the cost of Galle's print books ranged from 16 to 35 st., while his large Passion series designed by Stradanus tops the list with its standard selling price of 36 st. De Jode, Cock, and Diericx also had some exceptionally costly items for sale, such as De Jode's *Thesaurus sacrarum historiarum*, which sold for 12 fl. 8 st. (or 248 st.) per copy, or Cock's *The Baths of Diocletian*, which he sold for 2 fl. (or 40 st.) in 1568 and Diericx sold for 2 fl. 10 st. (or 50 st.) in 1581. Nevertheless, these were uncommon items in their stocks; the bulk of their publications rarely exceeded 12 st. per series.[114]

Of all the works that Galle provided for resale via Plantin between 1571 and 1589, the most popular were several of his print books. In this context, it is important to recall that Plantin bought many of these copies himself for shipment to his own shop in Paris between September 1573 and March 1577. In particular, approximately one-third of all the copies Galle supplied of his *David, hoc est virtutis … spectaculum* from 1575 and his 1572 edition of the *Virorum doctorum … effigies*, (a minimum of sixty-six and fifty-six copies, respectively) were shipped to Paris. These shipments still left a considerable number of copies (at least forty-two and thirty-eight, respectively) for Plantin to distribute via other channels. Only in the case of Galle's 1573 Latin edition of the *Divinarum nuptiarum conventa et acta* and *Christi Jesu vitae Divinarum*, did Plantin's own purchases of thirty copies for his shop in Paris constitute the majority of what Galle supplied; only some twenty copies were left for Plantin to distribute via his business between 1573 and 1580 (when Galle published a new edition of this work). Remarkably, there is no trace of Plantin shipping copies of Galle's print books to the Frankfurt fairs during these years.[115] However, as has been argued here in connection with Dilbaum's print purchases, it is clear from Willer's catalogues that Galle's prints and print books were available for sale at the Frankfurt fairs. Evidently, they must have been distributed via someone other than Plantin. This underscores yet again the fact that while Plantin facilitated the resale of thousands of prints from diverse suppliers, he usually did not supply the primary markets or dealers. This serves, in turn, as a potent indication of the hitherto unimagined extent of the trade in prints.

Plantin also resold remarkable quantities of several of Galle's print series, in particular: the 1577 *Seven Sacraments* (twenty-six copies), the large Passion series after Stradanus (completed around 1584; twenty-four copies were sold just between 1586 and 1588), and his 1577 series of the *Seven Worldly* and *Seven Spiritual Acts of Mercy* (twenty copies of each series). Plantin sold fewer copies of other of Galle's print books, such as his *De deis gentium imagines* (thirteen copies), the 1573/74 French edition of the *Divinarum nuptiarum conventa et acta* and *Christi Jesu vitae Divinarum* and the 1580 reprint of the original Latin edition of the latter work; eight copies of each of these were sold. Similar amounts were sold of several other print series, like Galle's original, smaller Passion (fourteen copies), series of hunts and animals (twelve copies), pendant designs (twelve copies), and ruins (nine copies). In addition, there were isolated sales of numerous other subjects, ranging from sundry images of the Virgin to several series of Old Testament subjects by a range of designers, including Van Heemskerck and Stradanus, as well as thousands of sheets of unspecified prints.

These various prints and print books went to a broad spectrum of buyers – diverse in both occupation and location; the largest sales were not limited to individuals of one specific profession, but can more often be grouped by their final, often distant destination, namely: Spain (Arias Montano, for example), Portugal (the merchant Ximenes, for instance), and Italy (such as the Antoni family in Milan). Significant quantities of Galle's prints were also purchased by clients in Germany (in particular, Dilbaum in Augsburg), individuals further off in eastern or northern Europe (such as the bookseller Salomon Gisser in Danzig (Gdańsk)), and the Jesuits in Vilnius and Stockholm.[116] In several instances, the prints Galle supplied were explicitly described as being new and curious. Although the prints from Cock and his widow were never identified in this way, some of De Jode's were. Such was the case with 120 sheets of prints from De Jode that were sold to Philip II's almoner Manrique in 1571, as well as fifty sheets of prints sent to Hans Gundelach, a print dealer in Nuremberg, in 1580 – both of whom simultaneously acquired "new" prints from Galle. The sale to Gundelach is noteworthy for the striking number of prints De Jode sent that were designed by Jan Snellinck, like the series of *Famous Women and Men from Antiquity*. Nevertheless, in subsequent years, it was only Galle's engravings that were clearly sold as new and curious.[117] These remarks reveal why some prints may have been purchased and, consequently, why Galle, who was actively publishing new prints throughout this period, might have been such an appealing source for images.

Finally, as with all the print dealers mentioned thus far, it is important to recall that Plantin was certainly not Galle's only outlet for the distribution of his prints. Although no estate inventory for Galle is known, other records in the Plantin archives document that he also distributed his publications independently. For example, in 1579 and 1580, Plantin received money on behalf of Galle (sums of 21 fl. and 14 fl. 15 st.) from the London bookseller Robert Cambier, as he had done for De Jode.[118]

A much more revealing indication of Galle's own independent activity as a print seller is the number of packages that he had Plantin send to others on his behalf, where the most important destination by far was Paris. In 1579, three packages were sent to Pierre Jacquet, who is identified as a "marchant de poutraictures au palais etc." (dealer in images at the palace, etc.); in 1580 and 1586, Galle had several packages sent to Plantin's son-in-law, Gilles Beys, an independent bookseller in Paris; and in 1589, seven packages were sent to a certain Philippe Goudin.[119] Galle also occasionally exchanged packages with Frans Hogenberg and Peter Boons, both of whom dealt in prints in Cologne.[120] Although Galle dominated such transactions among the print dealers with whom Plantin dealt, new generations of printmakers and print dealers made far more extensive use of the transportation networks of Plantin's successors, the Moretuses, throughout the subsequent decades. These networks were an essential means of enabling assorted print sellers to maintain diverse, distant business contacts and, consequently, supported the burgeoning international trade in prints.

While Galle, Cock and Diericx, and De Jode were, without doubt, Plantin's primary sources for prints, Plantin also occasionally sold works by other local printmakers and print sellers, in particular, Abraham de Bruyn and Adriaen Huberti I. De Bruyn supplied prints for Plantin's clients primarily in 1581–1582, when he had returned to Antwerp after several years abroad. During this brief period, De Bruyn provided Plantin with at least fourteen copies of what was most likely his second edition of the *Omnium pene gentium imagines* (*Images of Nearly All Nations*) series at 2 fl. 5 st. or more per copy, for a total of approximately 47 fl. (fig. 3.19).[121] Plantin then sold this relatively costly print series to a remarkably diverse array of clients, ranging from unidentified buyers in Plantin's own shop in Antwerp and Plantin's friend Pierre Porret in Paris to the bookseller Jehan Aubri in Frankfurt and the bookseller and bookbinder Josias Specklin in Königsberg (most likely acting for the Duke of Prussia).[122] In comparison with most of the prints in which Plantin dealt, this series was notable on two counts. First, a relatively high percentage of copies were hand colored before they were resold (this was the case, for example, with the copies sold to Porret, Aubri, and Specklin). Only some canons and impressions of Stradanus's hunts were occasionally hand colored before being sold on via Plantin.[123] Second, De Bruyn's *Omnium pene gentium imagines* is a clear example of a print series that Plantin obtained from an individual who was not the original printmaker or publisher. While Philips Galle sold Plantin some copies of the first edition (published in Cologne), a certain Philips Moermans of Antwerp, also sold Plantin this and related series by De Bruyn in 1582.[124] Other, similar instances among Plantin's transactions are rare and often

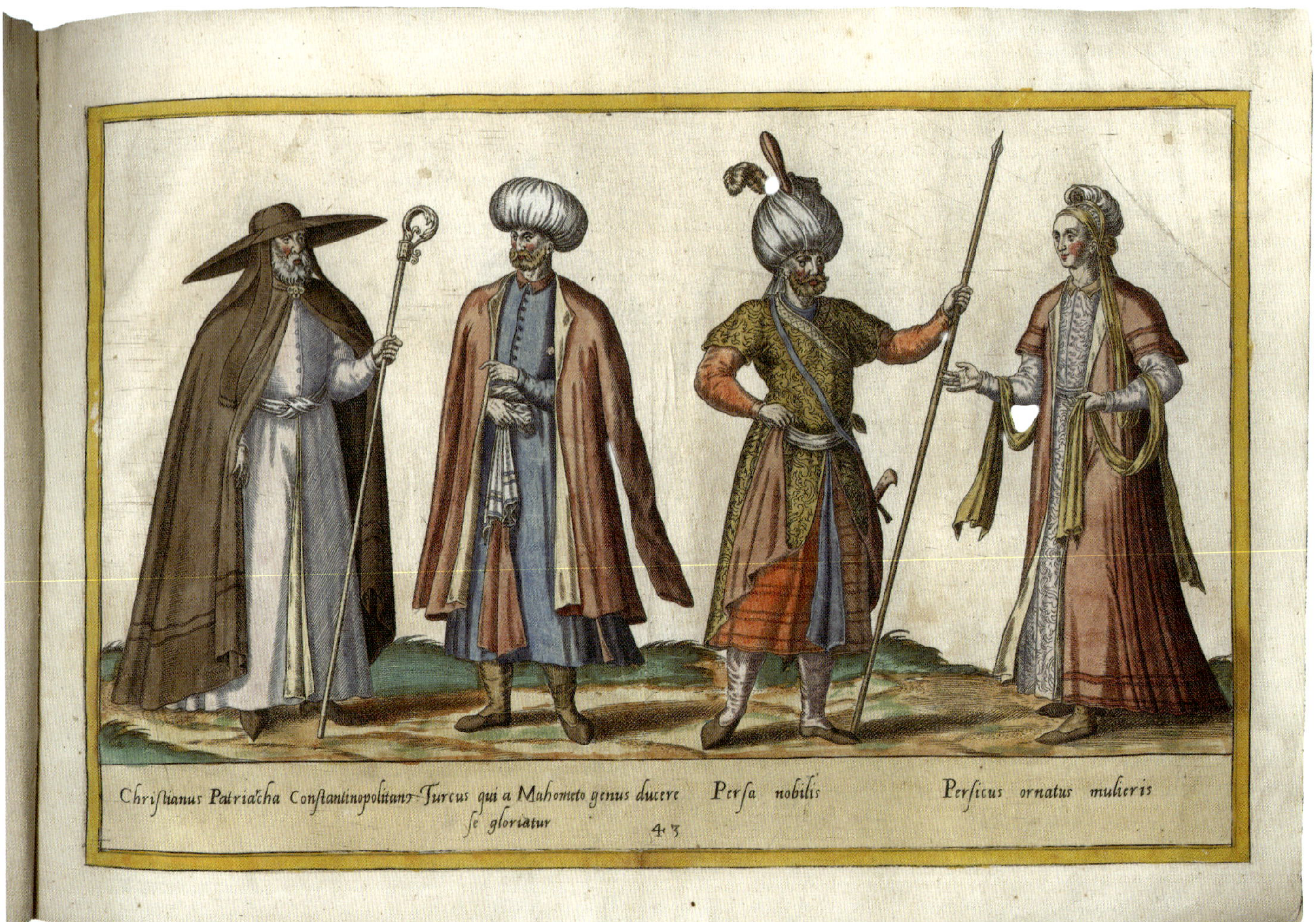

3.19 Abraham de Bruyn, *Christian Patriarch from Constantinople and Persian Nobles*, from the series *Omnium pene Europae, Asiae, Aphricae, atque Americae gentium habitus* (Antwerp, 1581), hand-colored engraving, 216 × 325 mm. Antwerp, Museum Plantin-Moretus: PK.OPB 176: print 43. Appendix 1: AB-1.

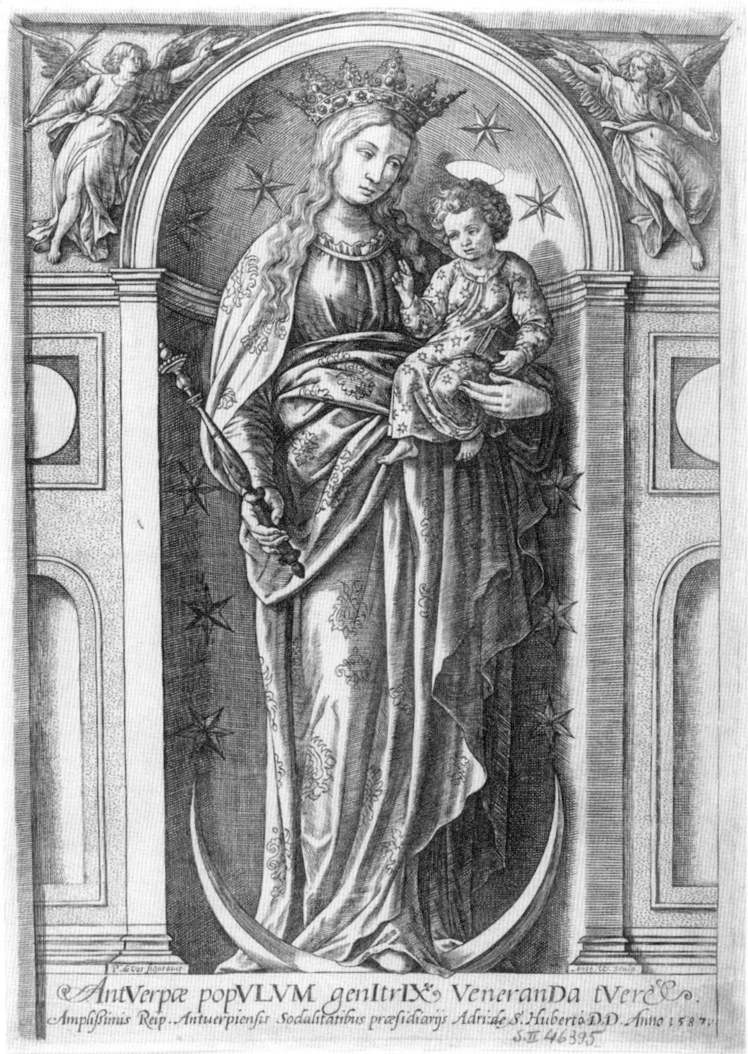

3.20 Anton Wierix II after the sculpture by Philip de Vos, *Virgin and Child on a Crescent from the Antwerp City Hall*, 1587, engraving, 281 × 194. Brussels, The Royal Library, Print Department: S.II 46395. Appendix 1: AH-10.

involved Philips Galle. Recall, for example, when he procured two copies of Diericx's *Portraits of Famous Painters from the Netherlands* for Arias Montano in 1585 and when he supplied prints by diverse artists, including works originally published by the Sadelers and Liefrincks, for Ferdinand Ximenes in 1588. It was, notably, Galle's son Theodore who would similarly assist the Moretuses with the acquisition of prints from other publishers in subsequent years.

Adriaen Huberti helped Plantin cater to yet another segment in the art market, namely individuals interested in small, inexpensive prints sold in bulk. Huberti began his transactions with Plantin in the spring of 1587 by supplying him with twelve impressions of his new print of the sculpture of the *Virgin and Child on a Crescent*, which had been installed at the Antwerp town hall earlier that year (fig. 3.20). However, in the two years thereafter, he provided Plantin primarily with unspecified images in bulk.[125] Plantin's two regular clients for Huberti's prints in bulk were the booksellers François Boulet, from Lille, and the family of Antonius de Tollenare, from Bruges.[126] In striking contrast to the typically isolated and often large orders for prints discussed above, both Boulet and the De Tollenare family tended to make small purchases of one to two quires of unspecified prints from Huberti at more regular intervals (every few months for Boulet and once a year for De Tollenare).[127] Thus, while the individual sales of these images were worth only 1, 2, or 3 fl. apiece, they amounted to approximately 15 fl. in just two years.

Plantin's dealings with Huberti and De Bruyn were, within the context of Plantin's total involvement in the print trade, relatively limited in time. Nevertheless, they remain significant as initial examples of practices that would become more important in the years to come when the Moretuses continued the Press's engagement in the distribution of prints from Antwerp. In particular, the interest in colored prints and the steady supply of prints in bulk would both continue to grow.

The only other supplier of prints who periodically appears in these records is Plantin himself, who sold primarily three distinct types of printed images: individual impressions of plates he had commissioned to illustrate editions of Arias Montano's *Humanae salutis monumenta*, impressions of his broadside with Arias Montano's description of Solomon's temple, and, above all, sundry canons.[128]

Arias Montano's original 8° edition of the *Monumenta* was published in 1571 and contained an exceptional number of engraved illustrations (seventy-one) for the time; many were by the impressive young printmakers Jan and Hieronymus Wierix.[129] New editions of this publication were printed in 1575 and 1581, while another edition in the larger 4° format and with a distinct series of plates appeared in 1583, although the vast majority of the illustrations had been engraved by 1576.[130] Plantin sold unspecified selections of the images from the first 8° editions to anonymous buyers via his own shop in 1572 and 1575. Additionally, in 1577, two Jesuits in Antwerp, Pedro Trigoso and Michael Fernandes, bought hundreds of impressions of these illustrations, as well as ninety-four leaves of "grandes fig. en 4°" (large figures in 4°), which may have been a selection of the new, but as yet unpublished, prints intended for the 4° edition of the *Monumenta*.[131]

It was highly unusual for Plantin to sell impressions of engravings he had ordered for the illustration of his books. Perhaps he made an exception in this case because he realized that the uncommonly high cost of the 8° editions – 3 fl. 10 st. with engraved borders, 3 fl. without – would keep many potential customers from buying them, while he could sell individual impressions of the images for much less.[132] Moreover, Plantin may also have reasoned that he would not need all of the plates used to illustrate the *Monumenta* for other editions and, consequently, could afford to wear down at least some of them a bit more by printing a few extra impressions. There is a clear difference between the numerous plates made after popular subjects that were used for both Plantin's liturgical editions and the *Monumenta* and those plates that were only engraved once for use in just this publication.[133]

Such sales of individual illustrations were rare under Plantin and his successors. The only publication related to his illustrated editions that Plantin did actively sell was a broadside featuring a large engraving (ca. 37.5 × 47.5 cm) of Solomon's temple that was based on a description of the structure provided by Arias Montano (fig. 3.21).[134] Although Plantin and Arias Montano may have originally intended to include this image in the final volume of Plantin's famous Polyglot Bible of 1568–1572, alongside other engravings made on the basis of Arias Montano's accounts, this did not occur. As the engraving was not completed until October 1575, it may simply not have been ready on time.[135] Plantin's distribution of it as an independent broadside began two months later, on 30 December 1575, when he sent Levinus Torrentius, who was then the Archdeacon of Liège, four copies as a gift. The broadside was so successful that Plantin had a new edition printed in 1578. Plantin sent the most copies (200) to his shop in Paris in 1577. He also sold thirty copies to Jan Poelman in Salamanca in

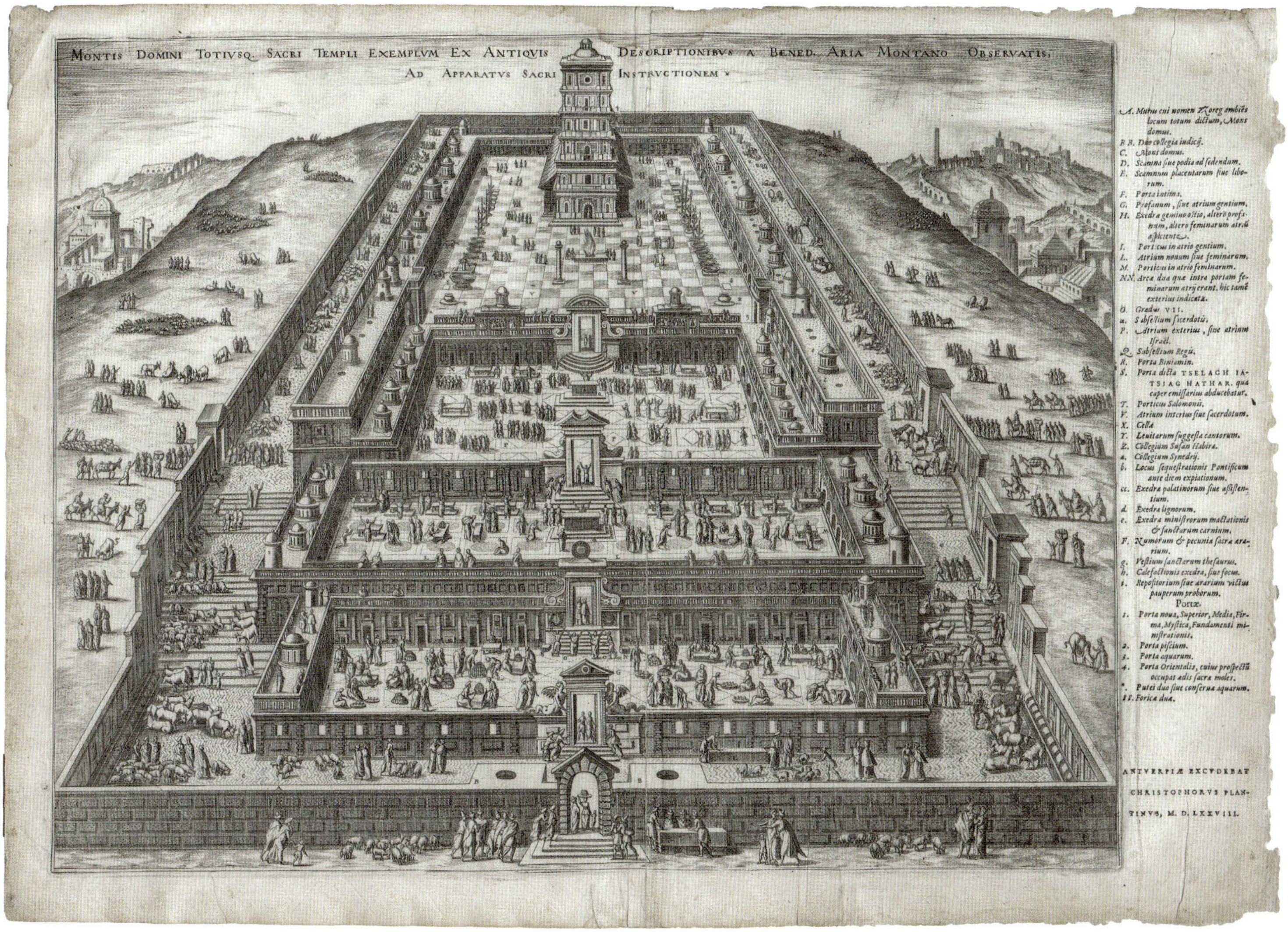

3.21 Anonymous engraver after Benito Arias Montano, *Temple of Solomon*, 1578, engraving, 415 × 570 mm. Antwerp, Museum Plantin-Moretus: 2–180. Appendix 1: CP-2.

1582, in addition to sending allotments of twenty-five copies to both of the Frankfurt fairs in 1577, as well as to those held in the fall of 1584 and the spring of 1587.[136] Moreover, in addition to all of these large consignments, as well as occasional sales to individual booksellers, for instance Antoine Maire in Valenciennes, and print dealers, for example Hubert Caymox of Nuremberg, this broadside was remarkably popular locally. Aside from two copies bought by Mynken Liefrinck, Plantin also sold numerous copies to unidentified buyers via his own shop in Antwerp.[137]

The prolonged success of Plantin's broadside was surpassed only by the even greater and more extensive interest in his canons – printed, and often illustrated, objects that are frequently overlooked due to a lack of documentation.[138] Plantin's production of canons is attested to by only a few disparate records. For example, around 1567–1568, he appears to have printed some in red and black ink, but the lack of reference to any illustrations and the relatively low price (½st.) per sheet suggests that they would at most have borne some woodcut embellishment set alongside the type.[139] Payments to one of his pressmen, Claes van Linschoten, on 9 July 1583 and 15 April 1589 similarly document Plantin's printing of canons in these years, although it is not known if these were illustrated editions or not.[140]

The potential scale of Plantin's production of canons containing intaglio illustrations is most clearly revealed in his accounts with Mynken Liefrinck, who, for example, was paid for adding intaglio illustrations to more than 500 sheets of canons in 1582, then to some 875 sheets of canons in 1583, and finally to 587 sheets of canons in 1586.[141] The sale of the 875 canons completed in 1583 to Jean Moflin, chaplain to Philip II in Madrid, is exceptional among Plantin's transactions. Previously, the single largest, known purchase of Plantin's illustrated canons was by Michel Sonnius I in Paris; he bought more than 100 canons in October 1578, at least sixty of which had engraved illustrations.[142] This transaction, like the payments to Liefrinck for printing illustrations in nearly 1,375 canons in 1582 and 1583, is noteworthy because it discloses Plantin's production of numerous copies of these visual reminders of the culmination of the mass while Antwerp was being ruled by a Calvinist government that was in open opposition to the Catholic sovereign of the Low Countries, Philip II. It is, then, perhaps not surprising that Plantin's flourishing, broad-based sale of these works is not fully evident until 1586, when Antwerp was definitively back under the control of Philip II's representatives, who reinstated the Catholic faith in the city and encouraged the departure of all Protestant sympathizers. Plantin's canons were now purchased by a wide range of booksellers, including not only Sonnius, but also François Boulet in Lille, Jan Scheffer in 's Hertogenbosch, and Jan Cordier in Antwerp.[143] Members of the clergy, in particular the Jesuits (like Vincentius Zeelander, who was discussed above) also purchased numerous canons in various forms, and Plantin had specially finished examples sent to important contacts, like Philip II's secretary in Madrid, Gabriel de Çayas.[144] Even more revealing, however, when considering the significance of these striking, often decorative objects under the openly Catholic rule of Antwerp, are the sales via Plantin's own shop. As of February 1586, purchases of canons appear regularly in these accounts, attesting to the interest in them among, most likely, local individuals – who were distinct from Plantin's professional, international clientele – responding to the official revival of Catholicism.[145] Consequently, canons became a standard component of not only Plantin's but also the Moretuses' stock for decades.

CONCLUSION

Between 1553, when Plantin signed his agreement with Lambert Suavius for the sale of 100 sets of his series of the Acts of the Apostles, and Plantin's death in 1589, his involvement in the print trade changed significantly. His early endeavors to procure and sell large quantities of prints locally and at important international print markets – as evidenced by his contract with Suavius and his 1558 shipment of prints to the Frankfurt fair – remained largely one-time initiatives. Even his periodic import of images from diverse sources in Paris had petered out by the time he turned his attention to resuscitating his business as a printer-publisher of texts in the mid-1560s.

Ultimately, Plantin favored the position of a middleman who facilitated transactions for a wide range of individuals who were often far removed from Antwerp and at the fringes of the print world: booksellers, merchants, private collectors, and members of the clergy (especially Jesuits). Many regularly purchased books from Plantin and only occasionally bought prints for themselves and others, resulting in an irregular ebb and flow of requests. Although some sought special antiquarian prints, in particular, the work of Albrecht Dürer, the vast majority of orders were for images sold by Antwerp's own eminent print publishers. Ranging in value from just a few stuivers (or less) to as much as 80 fl. (= 160 st.) per consignment, Plantin's profit margin on these sales was notably limited. Rather than imposing a consistent markup on all of his sales, Plantin usually only rounded up the resale prices for orders placed by merchants or distant collectors. When supplying fellow booksellers and personal friends with prints, Plantin tended to adhere to his standard practice when dealing in books: simply providing the item at cost. Why Plantin continued to assist his various contacts with their search for prints remains, consequently, an open question. Was he trying to keep his options open for a potential return to a more active engagement in the print trade? Or was he merely offering a courtesy or extra "service" to help friends, maintain good customer relations with existing clients, and possibly attract additional buyers?

Regardless of Plantin's reasons, his successors, the Moretuses, evidently approved of his involvement in the print trade. Not only did they continue Plantin's usual range of print-related activities, but they even amplified them. In addition to responding to requests for prints from their own growing network of personal and professional contacts, as Plantin had done, the Moretuses significantly augmented the assistance they offered to printmakers and print publishers (and their networks of customers and suppliers) for completing independent transactions of hitherto unimagined quantities of printed images in an international market. The stage was set for this expansion of the Press's print dealings by the diverse ways in which Philips Galle engaged Plantin to further his own sales of prints, in particular, Plantin's willingness to receive payments for Galle's publications and to serve as courier for Galle's shipments. Many among the next generation of Antwerp's printmakers and print publishers would make similar use of the Moretuses' business facilities. But, in order to fully appreciate the remarkable vitality of this international trade in printed images, including its explicit and implicit hierarchies, one must first consider the range of players involved and discern how the contributions and expertise of each supported the achievements of the Antwerp print industry as a whole.

1 MPM Arch. 7, fols. 33v-34r, letter from Christopher Plantin to Francesco Gentile, 19 July 1567; this citation is transcribed in Corr., vol. I, no. 59, p. 133, as follows: "Pour satisfaire donques à ce que demandés, j'ay cherché par toutes les boutiques de ceux qui vendent en ceste ville les pourtraictures que j'ay trouvées notées en l'autre page de vostre lettre … j'ay faict présentement trois feiles d'Albert Durer…."

2 In MPM Arch. 37, fol. 96 lft, a summary of these purchases is given, indicating that Stephano Gentile, a banker from Genoa, was the immediate contact person (see Willaert and Derde 1994, pp. 50–54, on Stefano Gentile). While the bulk of the prints went to Francesco Gentile in Padua, some were for another brother, Hieronymus (or Jeronimo) Gentile (specified in MPM Arch. 45, fol. 119v). Not only did Plantin obtain these prints locally, but some were also acquired in Paris and shipped to Antwerp for resale to the Gentiles and other unspecified clients (MPM Arch. 45, fols. 117v and 119v).

3 See, for example, Griffiths 2016, p. 20; Bury 1985, p. 17, for the former; and Van der Stock 1998, p. 114, for the latter.

4 Christopher Plantin to Francesco Gentile, 19 July 1567, MPM Arch. 7, fols. 33v-34r, transcribed in Corr., vol. I, no. 59, p. 134: "ce qui advient par le jugement ou affection de painctre[s] ou cognoisseurs de telles pourtraictures, qui prisent quelquefois l'une pièce (bien que d'une mesme main, planche, jour et heure imprimée) 2, 3 ou 4 fois au double plus que l'autre".

5 Although this image is traditionally identified as *Saint Eustace* (Bartsch 1808, vol. VII, pp. 73–74, no. 57), it is consistently referred to as an image of St Hubert in Plantin's records (see below); this agrees with the figure's dress as a hunter and not a knight. See the Note to the Reader for more on this currency and its relative value.

6 MPM Arch. 47, fol. 104r (for a total of 6 fl. 14 st.); not in Delen 1932. On Arias Montano, see, for example, Rekers 1972; Bécares Botas 1999; and Hänsel 1991 for his interest in art. On the art markets in Antwerp in this period, see Ewing 1990; and Vermeylen 2003.

7 MPM Arch. 52, fol. 29v (for a total of 7 fl. 15 st.); not in Delen 1932. According to this record, Plantin obtained these prints from a certain Vulcanius. He may have been Bonaventura Vulcanius, who had been in Toledo until at least 1570 and had dealings with Plantin in Frankfurt in 1574, the year of this transaction with Bocangelino (see MPM Arch. 18, fol. 367 lft).

8 MPM Arch. 64, fol. 126r (for a total of 12 fl. 10 st.); not in Delen 1932.

9 On Plantin's youth, see Davis 1957.

10 See Bowen and Imhof 2008, pp. 31–37.

11 See below and Appendix 1 for more on Cock and his widow, Volcxken Diericx, and also on the prints they sold via Plantin.

12 On Plantin's work as a bookbinder, see Colin and Nixon 1966. See Voet, GC, vol. I, p. 16, for his early trade in lace.

13 See Van der Stock 1998, pp. 374–75, for a full transcription of this document, which is discussed in numerous other sources and transcribed in part in Delen 1932, pp. 22–23.

14 See LS-1 in Appendix 1 for this series.

15 Appendix 1, LS-2, for the former, and CD-6 for the latter.

16 These plates are in Diericx's estate inventory (Duverger 1984–2009, vol. I, p. 35).

17 On Breyer and his connections with Plantin and Porret, see Renouard 1982, pp. 21–27; and Pallier 2016. On Le Jeune, see the online CERL Thesaurus, record no. cni00012050; Renouard 1965, pp. 261–262; and Corr., vol. I, nos. 2 and 3 (for Plantin's and Le Jeune's personal contact).

18 Partial transcriptions of most of these shipments are included in Delen 1932, pp. 8–11. What appears to be a single order on pp. 8–9 is actually a selection from two distinct shipments dating to 12 and 31 October 1556 (see MPM Arch. 34, pp. 5 and 8, for the original transactions). See MPM Arch. 34, p. 7, for the shipment of "deux sortes de compartiments de Guerard [de Jode?]" for 3 fl. 12 st. on 15 October 1556; not in Delen 1932. See below and Appendix 1 for more on De Jode and the prints he sold via Plantin.

19 See Delen 1932, pp. 11–12, for the identification of Jourdain and a partial transcription of his order; Delen overlooked, for example, a copy of Cock's *Baths of Diocletian* (Appendix 1, CD-3).

20 See Delen 1932, pp. 3–4, for a partial transcription of this record, which comes from MPM Arch. 35, fol. 152r (not Arch. 36, as indicated by Delen). It is possible that this was the group of prints alluded to in a separate, incomplete record of an unspecified consignment of prints from Cock that were to be sent to Lucas Breyer I, possibly in October 1561 (MPM Arch. 36, fol. 14r).

21 MPM Arch. 35, fols. 80v and 82v; not in Delen 1932. Messagier may have been related to the more famous print dealer Jean Messager, or the printer Thomas Messager (both active in Paris in the first quarter of the seventeenth century). See Lepape 2017, which includes references to Jean Messager (p. 224), and Renouard 1995, p. 315, for brief references to both Jean and Thomas Messager.

22 MPM Arch. 35, fol. 99r; not in Delen 1932. See below and Appendix 1 for more on Liefrinck and the prints he sold via Plantin.

23 On Androuet du Cerceau, see Du Cerceau 2010. For examples of these transactions, see MPM Arch. 35, fol. 89v (sale to Cock in August 1559; not in Delen 1932); MPM Arch. 35, fol. 183v (sale to Cock on 12 March 1560; see Delen 1932, p. 3); MPM Arch. 35, fol. 183v (sale to Liefrinck before 26 October 1560; not in Delen 1932); MPM Arch. 35, fol. 114v (sale to Liefrinck on 29 October 1560 to Liefrinck; not in Delen 1932); MPM Arch. 35, fol. 117v (sale to De Jode on 17 December 1560; not in Delen 1932, but discussed in Du Cerceau 2010, p. 51). For such subjects executed by Androuet du Cerceau, see Du Cerceau 2010, cat. VO or Vos (for round-perspective images), PG1 and PG2 (for series of "grotesques"), AM1 or A (for his arches), and LA1 for his book on architecture.

24 MPM Arch. 35, fol. 183v, under 7 November 1560 (not 1561, as noted in Delen 1932, p. 3).

25 See Voet, GC, vol. I, pp. 34–43, on this controversy.

26 See MPM Arch. 36, pp. 72 and 73 for Breyer's shipment of Androuet du Cerceau's prints to Plantin. Delen incorrectly states that Plantin sent these prints to Breyer (cf. Delen 1932, p. 4). See MPM Arch. 36, p. 71, for De Jode's purchase of Androuet du Cerceau's grotesques and round perspectives on 26 April 1564; not in Delen 1932. See Du Cerceau 2010, cat. TC, P or Ps, RM, and TL1 or TL2 T, respectively, for these subjects.

27 See Chapter 9 for an extensive discussion of the Moretuses' participation in the trade in prints at the Frankfurt fairs.

28 MPM Arch. 38, fol. 18 rht; not in Delen 1932.

29 Corr., vol. I, no. 3, pp. 11–12.

30 See Bowen 2019, pp. 70–71, for a more detailed analysis of this shipment, including the justification for dating it to 1558 instead of 1557, as is noted in Delen 1932, p. 12.

31 MPM Arch. 36, fol. 11v; see Delen 1932, p. 3.

32 MPM Arch. 35 fol. 36v; not in Delen 1932. See Appendix 1, CD-33, for this print. On De la Tombe, see Rouzet 1975, p. 119.

33 MPM Arch. 36, fol. 16v. In the index to this record book, Antoine is identified as: "Antoine ser. [viteur] [assistant of] des Fouck. a Ausburg". A few items from this order are included in Delen 1932, p. 4, but are incorrectly associated with an order for Porret and Le Jeune in Paris. For the *Pompe funebre*, see Appendix 1, CD-10. For the Androuet du Cerceau prints, see Du Cerceau 2010, p. 51, and nos. TC and VO or VOS 1–4.

34 For Breyer, see Renouard 1982; and for Le Jeune, see Pallier 2018, pp. 21–24.

35 See Bowen 2019.

36 MPM Arch. 27, fols. 36r and 38r.

37 MPM Arch. 36, p. 20; see Delen 1932, pp. 4–5, for a partial transcription (missing, for example, the "12 mains de feilles differentes" (12 quires of different sheets) alluded to here).

38 Voet, GC, vol. I, pp. 44–49.

39 See the Note to the Reader on the types of records consulted.

40 See Bowen and Imhof 2008, pp. 84–87, for an overview of this project and references to other discussions of it.

41 See Voet, GC, vol. I, p. 61, on the timing of Arias Montano's arrival in Antwerp; and MPM Arch. 46, fol. 151v, for his first order of prints (see Delen 1932, p. 5, for a partial transcription of this list of prints, but without the prices and also without a clear reference to Arias Montano as the intended recipient).

42 MPM Arch. 46, fol. 238r; not in Delen 1932.

43 MPM Arch. 46, fols. 242r–242v; most of the individual prints are transcribed, and many are identified in Delen 1932, pp. 5–6, but Delen omitted the maps and unspecified prints in bulk noted on fol. 242v.

44 Appendix 1, CD-6, CD-33, CD-24, CD-4, CD-15, and CD-1, respectively.

45 See MPM Arch. 48, fol. 134bis, for this record, transcribed in Delen 1932, p. 15, but with no reference to Arias Montano. 46 See Appendix 1 for more on Galle and the prints he sold via Plantin.

47 See Bowen and Imhof 2008, p. 286, for evidence of their continued friendship; and Hänsel 1991, pp. 90–127, for Arias Montano's contributions to various print books. One small exception is a shipment of several copies of two print books in July 1575, where the recent completion of one, *David, hoc est virtutis … spectaculum*, may clarify the timing of this shipment. See MPM Arch. 18, fol. 146r, for this shipment; and Bowen and Imhof 2008, p. 400, for the timing of the completion of this edition.

48 See Voet, GC, vol. I, pp. 105–113, for Plantin's sojourn in Leiden.

49 See MPM Arch. 62, fol. 119v, for the entire order, including a list of the prints Galle supplied, which is also transcribed in Delen 1932, pp. 20–21. A subsequent note indicates that the shipment was still in Antwerp in August 1586. The illustrated text editions included, for example, copies of Ludovicus Hillessemius's *Sacrarum antiquitatum monumenta* (1577) (Voet, PP, no. 1335) and Adrianus Barlandus's *Hollandiae comitum historia et icones* (1584) (Voet, PP, no. 625).

50 See, for example, Appendix 1, PG-42, PG-43, PG-21, PG-60, PG-122, and PG-82, respectively.

51 See Appendix 1, CD-18, for examples of Dierickx's sale of it to Plantin; and Sellink 1997, vol. I, p. 20, for related examples of Galle publishing prints while Diericx retained control of the plates used to print them.

52 McDonald 1998, pp. 17–18; and Rekers 1972, pp. 9 and 105–117. For additional examples of Arias Montano ordering books for others, see Dávila Pérez 2010.

53 For the Escorial's collection, we consulted González de Zárate 1992–1996.

54 Cf. McDonald 1998, pp. 18 and 21, where he admits that there is no concrete evidence to support the possible link between Arias Montano and Plantin and the supply of prints, but still maintains that it was highly likely.

55 See Imhof 2018b for examples of Arias Montano's purchases, including ones for Luis Manrique; and Hänsel 1991, pp. 170–196, on his various collections. See also Corr., vol. VII, no. 1011, p. 105, for Arias Montano's letter of 22 September 1583, in which he thanks Plantin for having sent him seeds, bulbs, and a piece of furniture.

56 On Manrique, see Bécares Botas 1999, pp. 248–52. See MPM Arch. 49, fol. 116v, for Manrique's purchase of new ("nouvelles") sheets from both De Jode and Galle; compare this record with that of the supply of these prints on fol. 102v. See MPM Arch. 59, fol. 175v, for his request in November 1581 for 203 diverse sheets that had been printed in the past year, and compare this request with the supply of these prints noted on the same folio. None of these records are mentioned in Delen 1932.

57 See, e.g., MPM Arch. 48, fol. 184r, for one such reference to Dilbaum. For more on Willer, see Gier and Janota 1997, pp. 31–36, and 1225–26; on Dilbaum, see Gier and Janota 1997, p. 1231. For these shipments and the related supply of prints from Cock's widow, Diericx, De Jode, and Galle, see MPM Arch. 48, fols. 136v, 139v, 177r, and 183v-184v; see also MPM Arch. 49, fols. 28v, 29v-30r, 86r, 87r, 88r, 142r, 143r, and 147r–147v. See Delen 1932, pp. 6, 7, and 15–17, for partial, occasionally faulty records of the supply of selected items; he does not mention any of the shipments to Dilbaum and Willer.

58 See MPM Arch. 45, fols. 23r–23v, for the first known reference from 11 February 1567; and MPM Arch. 58, fols. 162v-163r (9 December 1580), for one of his later purchases.

59 See Flood 2007, pp. 16–18, on these catalogues; Messkataloge 1972–2001 for reprints of them from 1564 to 1599; and Paisey 2006 for the latter topic.

60 In only one shipment (from 8 March 1571: MPM Arch. 49, fols. 28v, 29v–30r) was Dilbaum charged slightly more for an unspecified group of "folijs diversis" (diverse sheets) than the cost of the individual sheets supplied by De Jode and Diericx. However, this small price difference may also simply reflect the addition of some extra prints not included in the lists of what was supplied.

61 Appendix 1, CD-5, CD-6, CD-17, and CD-41, respectively. For Willer's references to Lombard's and Suavius's series, see his 1571 fall catalogue, fol. D3v (Messkataloge 1972–2001, vol. I, p. 400).

62 On Bocangelino, see Dadson 1983, pp. 1–17.

63 See MPM Arch. 51, fols. 199r and 199v (for the supply of prints from Galle and De Jode), fol. 200r (for the supply of prints from Diericx), and fols. 201r, 203r-204v, 207r–207v, and 209r (for the various parts of Bocangelino's order). Most of the prints supplied by Galle, De Jode, and Diericx are listed in Delen 1932, pp. 18, 16, and 7, respectively, but with no reference to Bocangelino.

64 Appendix 1, CD-9, CD-1, CD-20, CD-21, CD-29, CD-36, and CD-18, respectively, for Cock's and Diericx's publications, GJ-6 for an example of De Jode's work, and PG-19 and PG-122 for Galle's.

65 MPM Arch. 53, fol. 119r.

66 For the Antoni family, see Nuovo 2013, p. 383; for Poelman, see Robben 1993–1994.

67 For Poelman's transactions, see MPM Arch. 59, fol. 137r; and MPM Arch. 18, fol. 394 rht. These transactions are partially transcribed in Delen 1932, pp. 18–19. For the Antoni family's purchase (sent via the Italian merchant family, the brothers Urbano and Franc. Coqui, of Milan), see MPM Arch. 58, fols. 25v (for the supply) and 26r (for the purchase); and MPM Arch. 19, fol. 111 lft, for the link between Coqui and the Antoni family. Neither the purchase nor the link is noted in Delen 1932.

68 Appendix 1, PG-17, PG-28, PG-16, PG-82, PG-88, PG-38, and PG-21, respectively.

69 Appendix 1, PG-110, PG-60, CD-31, CD-37, and CD-11, respectively.

70 On Boulet, see Rouzet 1975, p. 25.

71 See MPM Arch. 63, fols. 65r-65v (Galle's *Effigies doctorum*), 69v, 84v, 117v, 127v; MPM Arch. 64, fol. 82v (for sales of canons); MPM Arch. 64, fols. 105v, 116r; and MPM Arch. 65, fols. 15r, 45v, 80r, 108r, 159v, and 178v, for Boulet's other purchases in 1587 and 1589, most of which are not in Delen 1932.

72 See Appendix 1 for more on Huberti and the prints he sold via Plantin.

73 See Griffiths 2016, pp. 207–08; and Rijksmuseum, Amsterdam, no. RP-P-2004–45, for mundane examples of these prints. For the sale of "50 Agnus dei" from Huberti to Boulet in December 1588, see MPM Arch. 65, fols. 177r and 178v; and MPM Arch. 20, fol. 259 rht. See also Delen 1932, p. 22, for an incomplete reference to this sale.

74 See MPM Arch. 59, fols. 154r and 190r–190v, respectively, for the sales to Claesz and Aubri, and Appendix 1, AB-1 for this series. On Claesz, see Burger 1931; on Aubri, see Benzing 1953. See MPM Arch. 60, fols. 24v–25r and 33v–34r, for the sales to Van Helmont. None of these is in Delen 1932. For this identification of Helmont, see MPM Arch. 110, fol. 82.

75 On Ximenes, see Pohl 1977, pp. 79–82. See MPM Arch. 64, fols. 29v and 34v, for Galle's supply and Ximenes's purchase in 1587; and MPM Arch. 65, fols. 13v, 30v, and 32r, for Galle's and De Jode's supply, and Ximenes's purchase in 1588. Of these, only De Jode's delivery of images noted on fol. 30v is also transcribed in Delen 1932 (p. 17).

76 Appendix 1, PG-82 for Stradanus's Passion series.

77 Appendix 1, PG-106, PG-50, and PG-116. MPM Arch. 65, fols. 125r-125v, for Galle's supply and De Sevilla's purchase; not in Delen 1932. On De Sevilla, see Bécares Botas 1999, pp. 164 and 261–63.

78 Appendix 1, PG-1 and GJ-35. See Bécares Botas 1999, p. 162 on De Varon. See MPM Arch. 60, fol. 134r, for De Jode's supply and De Varon's purchase; and MPM Arch. 20, fol. 57 rht, for Galle's supply. Only De Jode's record is transcribed in Delen 1932 (p. 16).

79 For the identification of Tassis and Langart, see MPM Arch. 18, fol. 133 (for Tassis) and fol. 434 (for Langart). For the Helman family and their links to Venice and Spain, see Crailsheim 2016, pp. 204–05.

80 Appendix 1, CD-2, CD-27, CD-34, and GJ-12, for example. See MPM Arch. 59, fol. 19r (for Diericx's and De Jode's supply of De Vries's prints and the landscapes for Langart) and fol. 20v (for his purchase of them). Only De Jode's entry is noted in Delen 1932 (p. 16). See MPM Arch. 59, fols. 109r (for Galle's and Diericx's supply of images of hunts; only Galle's is mentioned in Delen 1932 (p. 18)), and 128v and 129r (for the sale to Langart and the charge for having them colored, respectively).

81 MPM Arch. 58, fols. 19r–19v, for Diericx's and Galle's supply and Tassis's purchase; not in Delen 1932.

82 Appendix 1, PG-111 and PG-69, for example.

83 For example, Tassis's purchase in 1580 amounted to approximately 28 fl., which included a profit of roughly 3 fl. for Plantin.

84 On these individuals, see Garstein 1963, in particular, pp. 55–56 (Herbest), 51–53 and 82–85 (Warszewicki), and 40–47 (Nicolai Norvegus).

85 Garstein 1963, p. 151.

86 Appendix 1, PG-80, PG-97, PG-99, and PG-101. MPM Arch. 55, fols. 101r and 111r; MPM Arch. 56, fols. 52v and 58r; MPM Arch. 57, fol. 136v, for orders of multiple copies of several of Galle's print series; MPM Arch. 56, fol. 106v; MPM Arch. 57, fol. 44v; and MPM Arch. 59. fols. 47v–48r, for purchases of unspecified prints. None of these records is noted in Delen 1932.

87 On Sailly, see Imhof 2014b; on Zeelander, see Audenaert 2000, II, p. 464. None of the prints they purchased is noted in Delen 1932.

88 MPM Arch. 65, fols. 53r and 57v (de Vos), 102r (Huberti), and 107r (200 anonymous images).

89 MPM Arch. 64, fol. 162v; and MPM Arch. 65, fols. 3r and 21v.

90 MPM Arch. 65, fols. 103v (Galle's and Sadeler's prints) and 91v (prints purchased for Masi).

91 On Scrinius, see Cerl Thesaurus, no. cnp00439662; and Corr. vol. V, no. 653, p. 13.

92 Appendix 1, PG-26, PG-19, PG-60, and AB-1, respectively. MPM Arch. 57, fols. 40v, 41r, and 42r, for the supply and purchase of these prints; not in Delen 1932. The vaguely described collection of religious dress most likely refers to some selection of images catalogued in New Holl. De Bruijn, under nos. 457–58.

93 Appendix 1, CD-2, CD-34, CD-35, CD-29, and CD-3, for example. MPM Arch. 59, fols. 79v and 80r, for the purchase and supply of these prints; not in Delen 1932.

94 See Voet GC, vol. I, pp. 85–88, for this period of Plantin's business. See Appendix 1, PG-122, PG-19, PG-26, PG-27, and PG-16 for the cited print books MPM Arch. 51, fols. 134v and 155v; MPM Arch. 52, fols. 51v and 108v; MPM Arch. 53, fol. 126r; and MPM Arch. 55, fol. 14r, for these shipments.

95 See Rouzet 1975, pp. 8–10 (for Bellerus) and pp. 64–65 (for Fowler). For Herle, see the *Oxford Dictionary of National Biography* 2004, pp. 783–84; for Hassaert, see Voet, PP, vol. III, pp. 1086–87. For their purchases, see MPM Arch. 46, fol. 73v (Bellerus) and fol. 143r (Fowler's widow); MPM Arch. 60, fol. 77r (Herle); and MPM Arch. 51, fols. 59v and 159v (Hassaert).

96 Cf. MPM Arch. 58, fols. 31v and 32r-32v (for the resale of books bought from Bellerus for Ascanius de Renialme at cost); and fols. 15v and 18r (for the resale of a book bought from Sonnius, Jacques Cujas's *Paratitla* in folio, for the private individual Lamberto Herero, with a 10 st. profit margin).

97 See Appendix 1 for more on each of these individuals and the prints they sold via Plantin. For references to each publisher in 1558, see MPM Arch. 38, fols. 18 rht (de Jode; not in Delen 1932) and 100 rht (Liefrinck; cf. Delen 1932, pp. 13–14); and MPM Arch. 35, fols. 7v and 36v (Cock; not in Delen 1932).

98 MPM Arch. 46, fol. 104r.

99 On Liefrinck's various transactions with Plantin, see Imhof 2020a.

100 Denucé 1912–1913, vol. I, pp. 163–220.

101 See the discussion of these sales above.

102 See New Holl. De Jode, part I, pp. xxxiv and xxxvi–vii, for references to De Jode's contacts in Salamanca and ties to the Caymox family. See Antwerp, Felix Archives, WK 126, pp. 21, 31, 33, 34, and 47, for the examples of debtors from De Jode's estate that have been cited. See Chapter 9 for more on the Caymox family and their dealings in prints via the Moretuses. See MPM Arch. 57, fol. 96v; and MPM Arch. 58, fol. 24r, respectively, for De Jode's contacts in London.

103 Appendix 1, GJ-46 and GJ-47. See MPM Arch. 20, fol. 206 rht, for De Jode's supply of these volumes (cf. Delen 1932, p. 17); and MPM Arch. 65, fol. 107r, for Plantin's resale of them. De Jode supplied Plantin's successor, Jan Moretus I, with one more copy of this large publication by August 1590 at a slightly higher rate of 12 fl. 12 st. (MPM Arch. 21, fol. 59 rht). The subsequent amount noted in this account book on 30 August 1590 (75 fl. 2 st.) is just a general payment by De Jode on his account with Moretus and does not represent the purchase of additional copies of the *Thesaurus*, as is stated in New Holl. De Jode, part I, p. xlvi.

104 See MPM Arch. 18, fol. 66 rht, for this record; not in Delen 1932. We do not know who purchased it.

105 See the discussion of these sales above.

106 Appendix 1, CD-5, CD-6, CD-1, CD-35, CD-36, and CD-29, for example.

107 See the discussion of these sales above.

108 See, e.g., MPM Arch. 51, fols. 200r (partially transcribed in Delen 1932, p. 7) and 203r-204r (sale to Bocangelino); and MPM Arch. 261, fol. 6v (sale to an anonymous buyer via Plantin's own shop in Antwerp in August 1576). See Table 1 for several examples of the subsequent sale of Cock's prints.

109 Thereafter, Diericx provided Plantin with just one more copy of the *Portraits of Famous Painters from the Netherlands* in 1586 or 1587 (cf. MPM Arch. 20, fol. 2 rht).

[110] See Van der Stock 1998, pp. 406–08, for a transcription of this document; and De Pauw-De Veen 1975, pp. 225–33 and pp. 245–47, for her own transcription of this record, along with suggestions for the identification of the cited prints.

[111] Cock 2013, p. 18.

[112] See the Antwerp, Felix Archives, N 2860 (1600–1605), fols. 13v–14r. These records are not included in the transcription of Diericx's inventory in Duverger 1984–2009, vol. 1, doc. 7, pp. 17–37.

[113] MPM Arch. 49, fol. 86r, which is partly transcribed in Delen 1932, p. 17.

[114] See Tables 1–3 for these price comparisons.

[115] Records of shipments to Frankfurt between 1572 and 1574 are incomplete. In particular, with the exception of two shipments in February 1573, details of shipments from the summer of 1572 through the end of 1574 are missing. However, while the records for 1575–1577 are complete, not one of Galle's print books is mentioned. See Appendix 1, PG-16, PG-122, and PG-26, respectively, for these publications.

[116] For Gisser's purchase, see MPM Arch. 60, fols. 59r-60r; and MPM Arch. 110, fol. 87 lft, for his identification as a bookseller; the rest are all discussed in greater detail above.

[117] MPM Arch. 49, fol. 116v (Manrique); and MPM Arch. 58, fols. 39r-39v, for Gundelach's purchase and the supply of these prints. Only Galle's prints of the *Wars of the Medici* (sold to Gundelach) are noted in Delen 1932 (p. 18), but are listed incorrectly under 1576. See Appendix 1, GJ-13 and GJ-15 for these prints. For additional sales of Galle's new and curious prints, see, for example, MPM Arch. 58, fol. 19v (shipment to Tassis on 12 February 1580, with prints "novi"); and MPM Arch. 60, fol. 134r (shipment to De Varon on 22 August 1582: "con otras nuevas y curiosas" (with new and curious prints).

[118] MPM Arch. 57, fol. 96v; and MPM Arch. 58, fol. 24r, respectively.

[119] MPM Arch. 57, fol. 117v (Jacquet); MPM Arch. 58, fols. 17r and 45r (Beys); MPM Arch. 63, fol. 88r (Beys); and MPM Arch. 66, fol. 56r (Goudin).

[120] See, for example, MPM Arch. 64, fol. 95v (Hogenberg); and MPM Arch. 66, fol. 100r (Boons). Galle's dealings with both Boons and the Hogenberg family are discussed in greater detail in Chapter 9.

[121] Appendix 1, AB-1.

[122] For these sales, see MPM Arch. 491, fol. 38v (Plantin's shop in Antwerp); MPM Arch. 60, fols. 4r (Porret) and 116r (Specklin); and MPM Arch. 59, fols. 190r-190v (Aubri). None of these is discussed in Delen 1932.

[123] See, e.g., MPM Arch. 59, fol. 128v (for Gabriel Langart's purchase of colored hunts purchased from both Diericx and Galle); and MPM Arch. 64, fol. 82v (for François Boulet's purchase of painted canons). This excludes Plantin's distribution of hand-colored maps, atlases, and botanical editions, for example.

[124] See, e.g., MPM Arch. 57, fol. 117r (Galle); and MPM Arch. 60, fol. 73v (Moermans).

[125] See Appendix 1 for more on Huberti and the prints he supplied, especially AH-10 for the cited image of the Virgin. See MPM Arch. 64, fols. 50r, 54r, and 58v, for Huberti's sale of impressions of his print of the Virgin and Child in April and May 1587 and Plantin's shipment of them to the Brussels bookseller Philippe Zangre (see Rouzet 1975, p. 252, for more on Zangre). Huberti's supply of this print is noted in Delen 1932, p. 22, but with an incorrect identification of the subject.

[126] For the De Tollenare family, see Rouzet 1975, pp. 221–22.

[127] See, for example, MPM Arch. 65, fols. 14v, 15r, 80r–80v, 177r (for several sales to Boulet), and 18v (for the supply and sales of prints to the De Tollenare family). Only the sale recorded on fol. 177r is noted in Delen 1932, p. 22.

[128] We are not considering separate sales of sets of illustrations that were occasionally included in books, such as the De Valverde and Guicciardini illustrations, because it is usually unclear when these were sought as independent images and when they were requested to accompany an existing copy of the text. On these editions and their illustrations, see Bowen and Imhof 2008, pp. 67–84 and 196–200, respectively.

[129] See Bowen 2003 on the printing of Arias Montano's *Monumenta*; and Bowen and Imhof 2008, pp. 107–21, for the significance and success of these remarkably illustrated editions.

[130] See Bowen and Imhof 2008, pp. 179–87, for the production and illustration of this edition.

[131] MPM Arch. 43111, fols. 40r and 63v, for the sales via Plantin's shop; and MPM Arch. 55, fol. 45v, for the sales to Trigoso and Fernandes. For the identification of Fernandes as the secretary of the Antwerp Jesuits, see MPM Arch. 18, fol. 73. For Trigoso and Fernandes, see Dávila Pérez 2002, I, p. 270, nn. 8 and 9, in the context of a letter Plantin wrote to Arias Montano on 29 October 1575.

[132] See Bowen and Imhof 2008, pp. 115–19, for these prices and a discussion of the early sale of this work.

[133] Compare, for example, the descriptions of single plates of various prophets made for the *Monumenta* (e.g., M-H Wierix, 1978–1982, nos. 2179 and 2180) with the discussion of the image of the *Annunciation* (M-H Wierix, 1978–1982, no. 2181), all four versions of which are discussed and reproduced in Bowen and Imhof 2008, pp. 146–49.

[134] Appendix 1, CP-2.

[135] On the illustration of this Bible and Arias Montano's involvement in it, see Bowen and Imhof 2008, pp. 84–102. For the production and sale of this broadside, see Imhof 2015.

[136] MPM Arch. 53, fol. 229v (Torrentius); MPM Arch. 55, fol. 4v (Paris); MPM Arch. 60. fols. 137r-39r (Poelman); MPM Arch. 55, fols. 9r and 100v (Frankfurt in 1577); MPM Arch. 62, fol. 99r; and MPM Arch. 64, fol. 20v (Frankfurt fairs from 1584 and 1587, respectively).

[137] MPM Arch. 56, fols. 145r-146r (Maire); and MPM Arch. 57, fol. 26v (Caymox). For the identification of Maire, see MPM Arch. 110, fol. 69. See MPM Arch. 56, fol. 149r (Liefrinck); and MPM Arch. 43111, fol. 73v; MPM Arch. 261, fols. 7v, 30v, 47v, 58v, 61v, 79v, and 145v; and MPM Arch. 491, fol. 24v (sales via Plantin's shop in Antwerp).

[138] Griffiths 2016, p. 208, is one exception to this.

[139] See Voet PP, no. 904, for this record. Compare MPM Arch. 63, fol. 73v, where Plantin's sale on 7 August 1586 of twenty-five canons in folio "sans figure" (without illustrations) at 1 st. per piece to Jan Scheffer, is recorded.

[140] MPM Arch. 33, fols. 73 rht and 151 lft; not in Voet, PP.

[141] MPM Arch. 20, fols. 119 rht (1582), 186 rht (1583), and 237 rht (1586).

[142] See MPM Arch. 61, fol. 115r, for the sale to Moflin (worth 87 fl. 10 st.); MPM Arch. 57, fol. 138v, for that to Sonnius (worth 17 fl. 14 st.); and MPM Arch. 19, fol. 126 lft, for the identification of the latter as "canones missae en cuivre" (canons for the mass with copper-plate or intaglio illustrations). On Sonnius, see Renouard 1965, p. 400. Remarkably, Sonnius did not purchase other types of prints from Plantin.

[143] See, for example, MPM Arch. 65, fol. 82v (Sonnius); MPM Arch. 63, fols. 39v and 73v (Scheffer), and 117v (Boulet); and MPM Arch. 64, fol. 5v (Cordier). On Scheffer, see Van den Oord 1984, pp. 141–81; for Cordier, see Rouzet 1975, p. 47.

[144] MPM Arch. 64, fol. 19r (shipment to De Çayas).

[145] See MPM Arch. 491, fols. 119v, 120r, 121v, 127v, 128, 136r, 137r, 148r-148v, 150r, 158v, and 189r, for various examples of such purchases, all of which are by unidentified buyers.

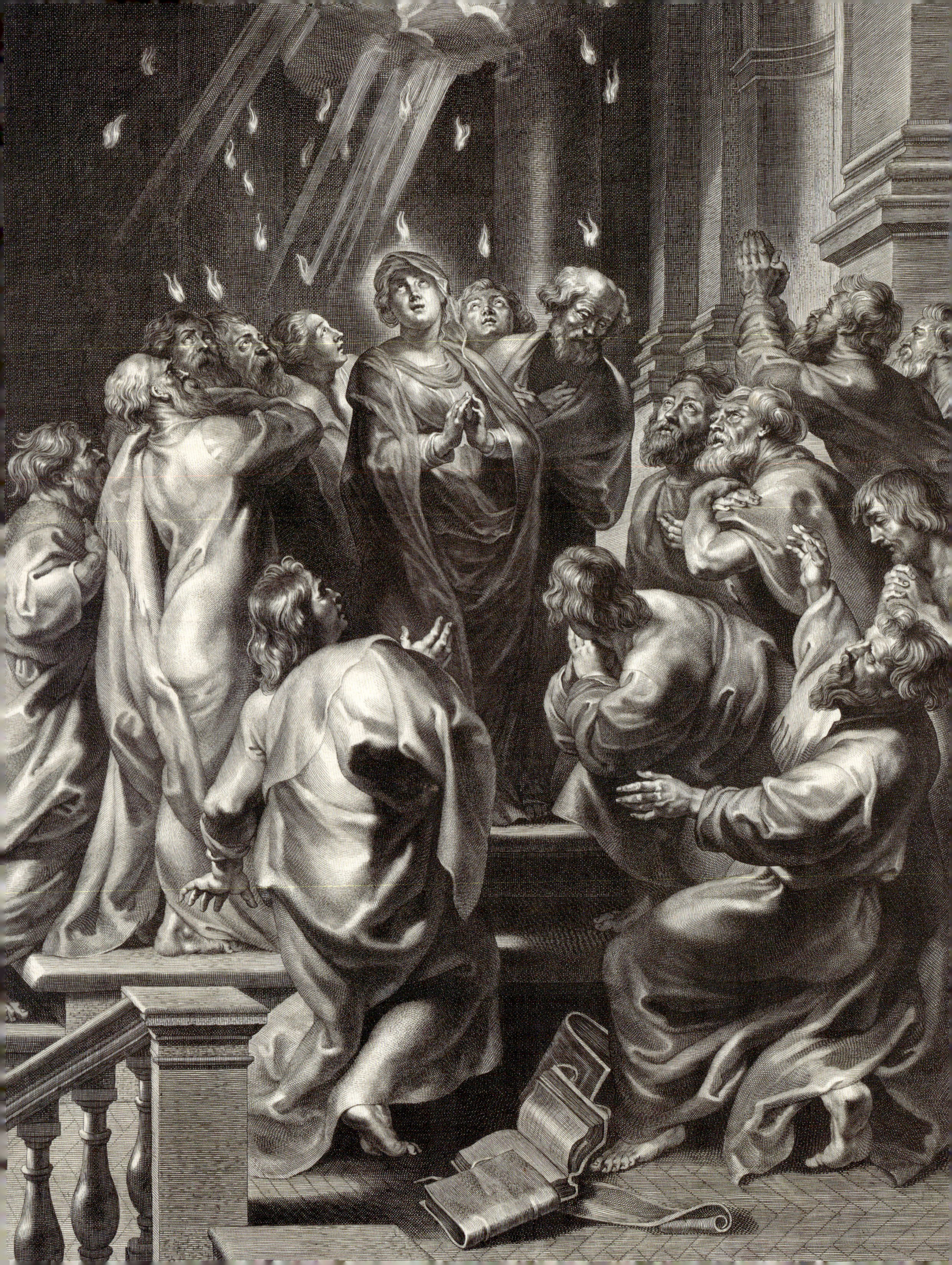

CHAPTER 4

THE MORETUSES

AND THE PRINT TRADE

> Although I do not earn my living by selling prints, I took your letter and visited some of the best who sell illuminated images and they provided me with the enclosed samples.[1]

Detail of fig. 4.12: Paulus Pontius after Peter Paul Rubens, *Pentecost*, 1627.

When Balthasar Moretus II thus described his participation in the trade in prints from Antwerp in May 1647, he was writing some ninety years after the earliest known ventures of his great-grandfather, Christopher Plantin, into the international print trade. Whether this was a polite disclaimer intended for one specific client or a maneuver to distance himself generally from any significant, personal engagement in the distribution of prints must still be determined. In order to evaluate Balthasar II's assertion accurately within the context of the family business, however, one must first consider the involvement of his immediate predecessors and Plantin's direct successors – Jan Moretus I and his sons Jan II and Balthasar I – in both the Antwerp art world and the broader European market for prints.

THE MORETUSES

Plantin's personally-selected successor was his son-in-law Jan Moerentorf (fig. 4.1), known professionally by the Latinized form of his surname: Moretus. Born in 1543, Moretus came from a family of merchants: his father, Jacques, was involved in the textile trade with England, while his mother, Adriana Gras, was the daughter of the Antwerp merchant Peeter Gras.[2] Moretus most likely began to work for Plantin around 1558, the year in which his father died, leaving him, as the eldest surviving son, with the burden of providing for his family. Plantin had himself begun to work as a printer just a few years before; the earliest known records of Plantin's regular involvement in the print trade similarly date from the late 1550s.[3] Initially assisting Plantin in his bookshop, Moretus stuck by Plantin through his early, turbulent years as a printer. He only left to work in Venice temporarily between the summer of 1562 and the spring of 1565, during which time the printing of a heretical pamphlet in Plantin's shop was investigated and Plantin subsequently had to revive his business with the help of new financial backers. Upon his return to Antwerp, Moretus's commitment to Plantin soon led to his amasssing ever more responsibilities – including, for example, representing the firm at the Frankfurt fairs from 1565 onwards – and winning the hand of Plantin's daughter Martine in 1570. Plantin's immense satisfaction with Moretus is attested to by both the spectacular

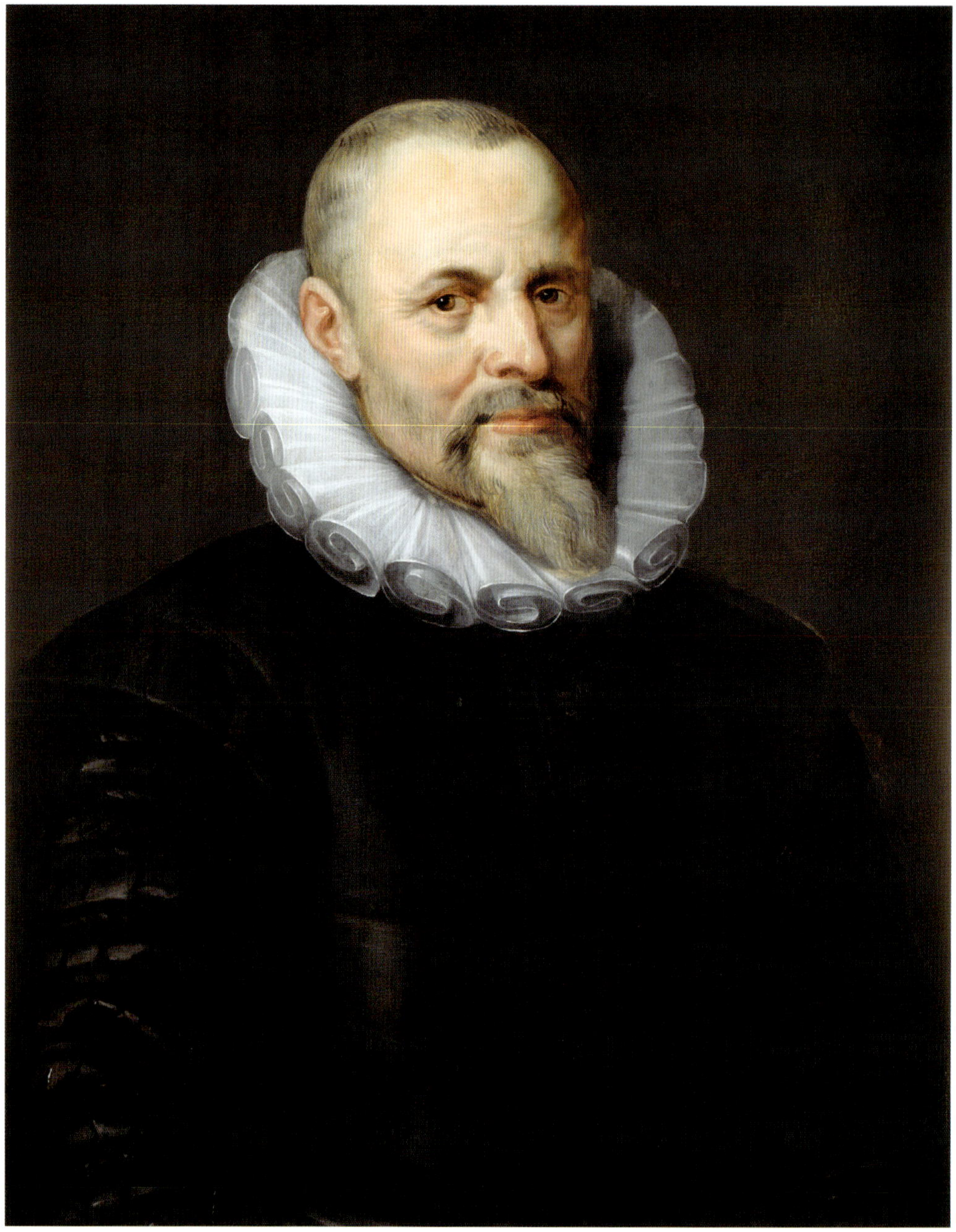

4.1 Workshop of Peter Paul Rubens, *Jan Moretus I*, 1612–1616, painting, 664 × 510 mm. Antwerp, Museum Plantin-Moretus: V.IV.051.

salary increases he awarded him and his efforts to secure Moretus's official recognition as a bookseller, which enabled Plantin and his wife to leave their business to him in its entirety. Although this decision was contested by Plantin's other four immediate heirs immediately following his death in 1589, Moretus persevered in striking a compromise with his relations that permitted him to retain full control of Plantin's business. Moretus's success in running the Press until his death in 1610 is indicated by the impressive estimated value of his wife's possessions in 1614: some 118,000 fl.[4]

Nevertheless, Moretus may not be allotted all the credit for such positive returns. By the early 1590s, his sons Jan II and Balthasar I (figs. 4.2 and 4.3) were already contributing to the management of the Press.[5] Born in 1574 and 1576, respectively, Balthasar's and Jan II's

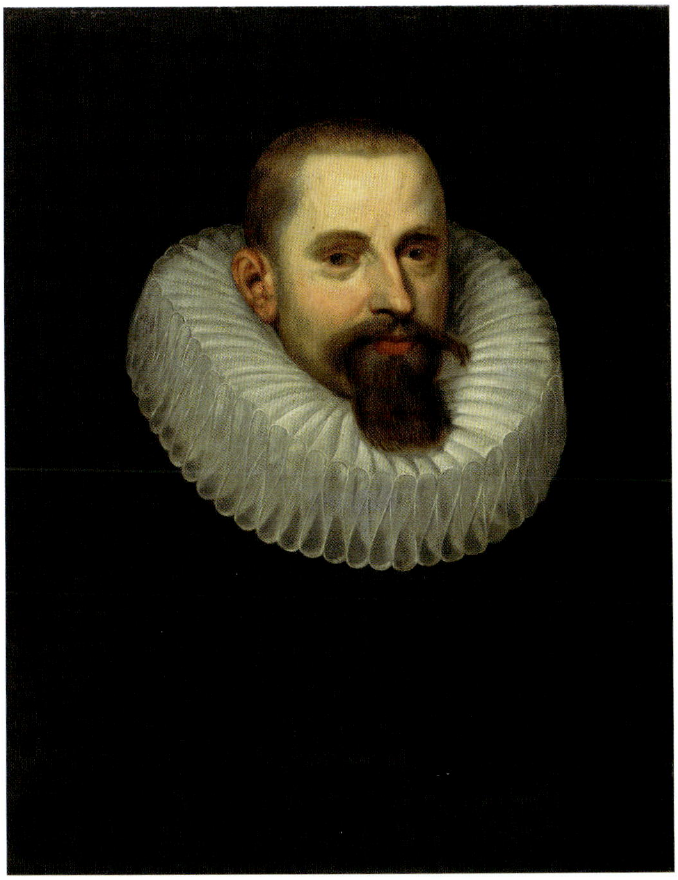 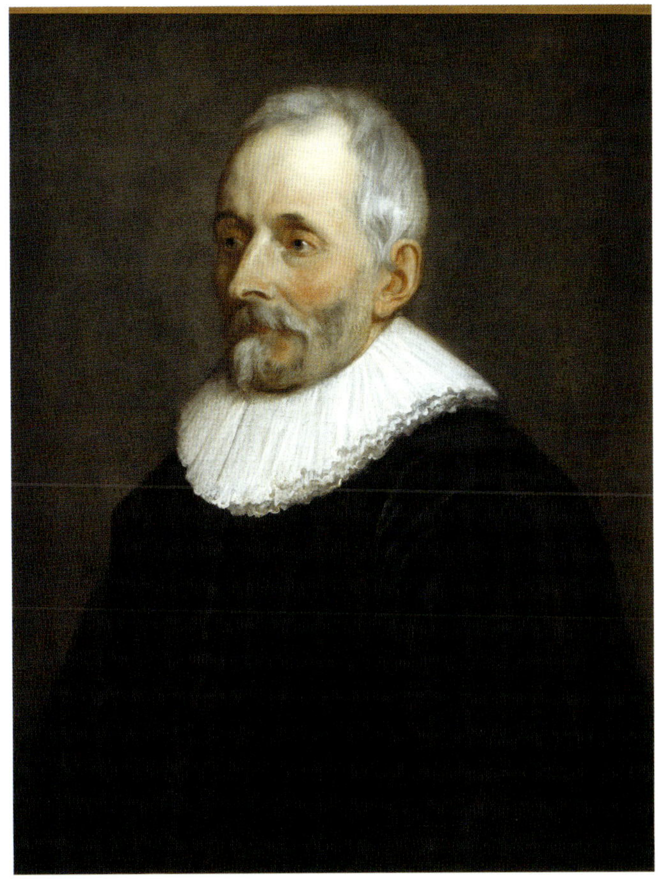

complementary skills and interests made them an ideal pair to assist in the assorted tasks associated with printing, publishing, and selling books.[6] A one-time student of the Latin scholar Justus Lipsius in Leuven, Balthasar was a highly skilled, exacting proofreader who also helped his father with business correspondence, particularly whatever needed to be written in Latin. Jan II, like his father, focused on their trade in books, including representing the Press at the Frankfurt fairs. Endowed with an affinity for bookkeeping and an astute judgment useful for turning a profit, Jan II also conducted a prosperous independent business as a bookseller.[7] When, in 1604, the two brothers asked their parents for a regular salary as compensation for their work, an official agreement was signed between them concerning the future management of the Press. In exchange for being granted their request to be paid, Jan II and Balthasar I promised to continue the Press as it was, under the name of the Officina Plantiniana, as Plantin had wished, and not to sell off parts of it when Jan I and his wife Martine passed away; instead, they were to find other means to compensate their fellow heirs financially for their share of the estimated value of the Press. Following the death of Jan I in September 1610, this agreement was put into effect, and Balthasar I assumed responsibility for the printing and publishing aspects of the business, while Jan II oversaw the sales.

Unfortunately, Jan II died in 1618, when he was merely forty-three years old. Balthasar initially formed a new partnership with Jan II's widow, Maria de Sweert, and her brother-in-law Jan van Meurs, but significant disagreements between Van Meurs and Balthasar resulted in the dissolution of this arrangement in early 1629.[8] Thereafter, several dependable, highly capable employees assisted Balthasar with the running the Press until the early 1630s, in

4.2 Erasmus Quellinus (attributed to), *Jan Moretus II*, 1642, painting, 659 × 510 mm. Antwerp, Museum Plantin-Moretus: V.IV.039.

4.3 Thomas Willeboirts Bosschaert, *Balthasar Moretus I*, after 1641, painting, 663 × 509 mm. Antwerp, Museum Plantin-Moretus: V.IV.003.

particular: Jan Ottens, Philips Collaert (the son of the engraver Adriaen Collaert, who was one of Philips Galle's sons-in-law), and Balthasar's cousin Louis Moerentorf.[9] However, when both Philips Collaert and Louis Moerentorf passed away in 1638, Balthasar, then sixty-four years old, had to rely increasingly on his nephew, Jan II's son Balthasar II (fig. 4.4). Born in 1615, shortly before the death of his father, Balthasar II's upbringing was supervised primarily by his mother and Balthasar I, who regarded him as his only possible successor and the "sole hope" of the Officina Plantiniana.[10] In 1632, when he was seventeen, Balthasar II began to work at the Press in order to learn about its management and the book trade. When Balthasar I died in 1641, he bequeathed his share of the Press, to Balthasar II. Becoming one of Antwerp's wealthiest citizens, Balthasar II maintained the family business and passed it on to his heirs, who kept it running with varying degrees of success until the mid-nineteenth century. In 1876, the printing house and all its accouterments were sold to the city of Antwerp, thereby establishing the museum and extraordinary historic resource that still exist today.

While numerous factors contributed to the prosperity and international renown of the Officina Plantiniana under the direction of Jan I and his sons Jan II and Balthasar I, the emphasis they placed on the quality of their publications, from the accuracy of the texts and their general layout to the choice of paper on which they were printed, was particularly important. Additionally, Jan I favored the production of more luxuriously crafted editions, which is evident in his preference for larger formats, selection of better quality paper for

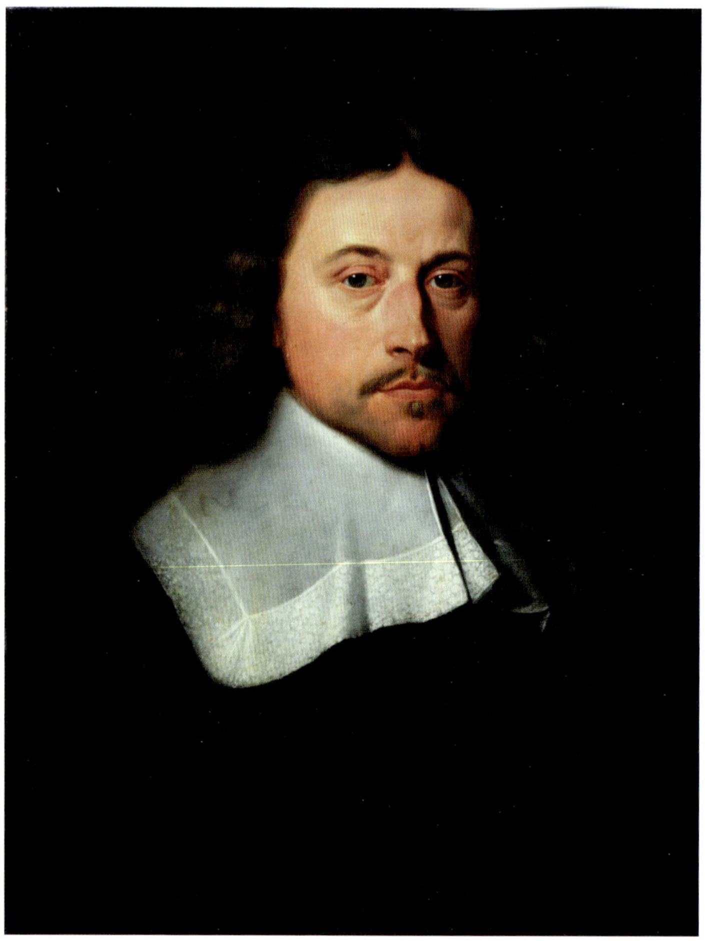

4.4 Jacob van Reesbroeck, *Balthasar Moretus II*, 1659, painting, 662 × 506 mm. Antwerp, Museum Plantin-Moretus: V.IV.043.

some copies, and increasing reliance on engravings for illustrations.[11] Balthasar I, in his turn, is credited with contributing to European-wide shifts in the visual aspects of books during the seventeenth century, primarily because of his periodic engagement of Peter Paul Rubens and his pupil Erasmus Quellin II for the design of numerous title pages and text illustrations. The impact of these editions was immense thanks to the extensive international reach of the Moretuses' professional networks.[12]

Although the Moretuses preferred to engage Rubens, Quellin, and the Galles for the production of most of their book illustrations, they dealt with other artists as well. Jan I, for example, regularly employed Peeter vander Borcht and also periodically Adam van Noort and Peeter de Jode I. Later on, Balthasar I engaged Abraham van Diepenbeeck and Nicolas van der Horst for new compositions, while Charles de Mallery and Andries Pauwels occasionally supplemented the engravings provided by the Galle workshop. Christoffel van Sichem and, above all, Christoffel Jegher executed new woodcuts for Balthasar I.[13]

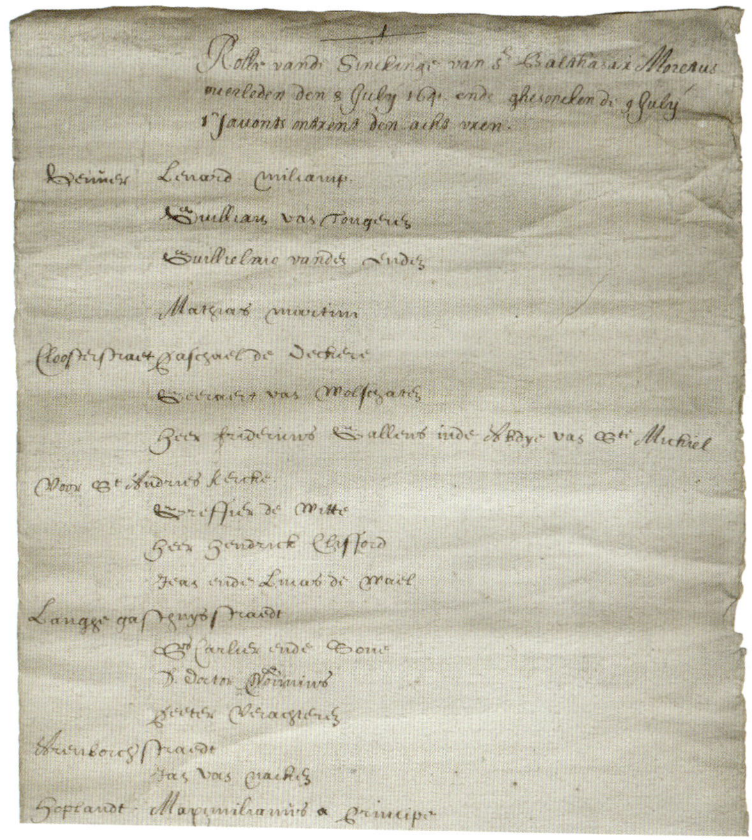
Rolle vande Sinckinge van Sr Balthasar Moretus overleden den 8 July 1641 ende ghesoncken den 9 July s'avonts ontrent den acht vren.

4.5 Excerpt from the list of invitations for the burial of Balthasar Moretus I, 1641, manuscript. Antwerp, Museum Plantin-Moretus: Arch. 1178, *Begrafenisrollen en Uitnoodigingen (1596–1710)*, roll 6.

Conversely, several local artists turned to the Moretuses for the purchase of books for personal and professional purposes. Although Rubens's extensive acquisitions for his library are well documented, other individuals, such as his fellow painters Hendrik van Balen and Jan Brueghel I, made isolated purchases of books either for their own personal collections or for a connection of theirs.[14] In some instances, the purchase of a larger number of copies of assorted editions indicates that some artists had most likely been commissioned to obtain volumes for someone else. For example, in 1617, Peeter de Jode I bought six copies each of fifteen different editions of classical authors, all in 24° and simply bound in parchment. In 1621, Crispijn de Passe I, then in Utrecht, acquired a few copies of Jan Moretus I's old publications of Ovid's *Metamorphoses* and Aesop's fables, both of which were extensively illustrated with etchings by Peeter vander Borcht. Perhaps most surprisingly of all, on 30 June 1631, Anthony van Dyck (then in Antwerp) bought more than 100 books of hours and diurnals in diverse formats, all illustrated with engravings and specially bound.[15]

The professional intermingling of artists and book publishers was also officially sanctioned in Antwerp by this time. As of 1558, all book printers (and also other individuals associated with the book trade) were required to join the Guild of St Luke's for artists, in part to facilitate the supervision of the activities of printers during the politically contentious decades of the sixteenth century.[16] Consequently, Jan I, Balthasar I, Jan II, and Balthasar II all joined the guild. However, Jan II appears to have participated the most actively in the guild, as he was both co-dean and dean of the guild between 1615 and 1617.[17] Consequently, the Moretuses would have known far more individuals involved in the production and sale of works of art than simply those who came to them as customers seeking books or those whom they employed for the illustration of their own publications.

Their broad network of contacts is poignantly attested to by the lists (arranged by street name) of who was invited to the funerals of members of the Plantin-Moretus family between 1596 (when Plantin's wife, Jeanne Rivière, died) and 1641 (when Balthasar Moretus I passed away) (fig. 4.5).[18] As with many weddings and funerals today, these lists comprise a mix of family members, valued personal acquaintances – including even common workmen, such as bricklayers, a woodworker, and a barber – business associates, and high-ranking governmental officials and ecclesiasts.[19] Scattered throughout the lists are the names of numerous artists. Of particular interest here are the clear distinctions made among the various individuals named. For example, although there is a general invitation to all the members of the Guild of St Luke at the end of Jan I's list from 1610, numerous artists are also mentioned individually. There are renowned painters like Rubens, Maarten de Vos, Otto van Veen, Jan Brueghel I, and Hendrik van Balen, as well as numerous printmakers. In addition to their relatives Catharina Moerentorf and her husband Theodore Galle, other members of the Galle family (Philips and Cornelis) and their relations, the Collaerts and Charles de Mallery, were similarly specified. Additionally, the list enumerates engravers and print publishers – in particular, Hieronymus Wierix, Peeter and Jacques de Jode, Adriaen Huberti, Jan-Baptist Vrients, and Abraham van Merlen – who were not related to the Moretuses or the Galles and who were most likely among their circle of friends or who were regarded as (potentially) significant professional associates. Such nuances are clearer in the list of those invited to Martine Plantin's funeral in 1616, for it has notes about who was invited to dine with the family (and who, by implication, was not). Although a few new figures appear on this list – David Teniers, François (or Frans) Snijders, Jan-Baptist Barbé, and Michael Snijders, for example – the artists cited are largely the same as those noted in 1610 – including, for example, Rubens, Brueghel, Wierix, De Mallery, Theodore and Cornelis Galle, the Collaerts, Van Merlen, and the De Jodes. Of this impressive group of highly successful painters and engravers, however, only a few were asked to dine with the family, namely: Theodore Galle, his wife (Catharina Moerentorf), and their daughter Catharina (whose godmother was the recently deceased Martine Plantin), Cornelis Galle, as well as Charles de Mallery and Adriaen Collaert, together with their wives, Catharina and Josine Galle, both daughters of Philips Galle and sisters to Theodore and Cornelis.[20] Demonstrating the priority given to family relations in the broadest sense, this group reveals in particular the importance the Moretuses placed on ties with *all* members of the extended Galle family of engravers and not just Theodore as their immediate relative.

Given the multifarious character of the Moretuses' interaction with sundry members of the Antwerp art world, it is all the more noteworthy that they appear to have prescribed their own involvement in the production and distribution of printed images more strictly than Plantin had done. Regardless of the form that this involvement took, they maintained a specific approach: they produced and distributed images as an intermittent sideline to their primary focus on maintaining their position as one of Europe's leading printing-publishing houses for books. As Balthasar II noted in the statement quoted at the beginning of this chapter, they did not intend to earn their living by selling prints. Nevertheless, their engagement with books did not preclude involvement with prints; rather, books and prints were routinely complementary for artists, booksellers, common consumers, and individual collectors alike. Moreover, the hundreds of thousands of prints sold by the Moretuses strikingly demonstrates the cumulative, pervasive significance of the transactions in which they (and many others like them) were involved and the extensive local and international audience both within and beyond the the Moretuses' book business.

THE MORETUSES' PRODUCTION OF PRINTED IMAGES

By far the most common way in which the Moretuses themselves contributed to the creation of images for the print market was their own, in-house production of thousands of woodcut images – occasionally with accompanying verses – at the request of diverse individuals or groups. Some commissions recurred regularly; others were exceptional. Together, these various orders constituted just one of a variety of small print jobs that were systematically completed (and often published anonymously) alongside their regular work of printing text for larger, ongoing projects that were the primary, official production of the Officina Plantiniana.

The images that are recorded the most frequently in assorted account books of the Plantin-Moretus Press are prints of the Virgin, many of which were commissioned by church wardens for chapels dedicated to the Virgin, including one in Antwerp Cathedral. For example, on 12 August 1604, Jan Moretus I had a ream (500 full sheets of paper) of images of the Assumption of the Virgin printed with accompanying verses for use in a chapel dedicated to the Virgin; the ream was to be delivered to an assistant at the chapel, Cornille Adriaenssens, via his servant Christiaen in time for the feast day three days later.[21] Similar records appear periodically throughout the following decades in the weekly summaries of the work completed by the pressmen working for the Press, confirming that the Moretuses' staff routinely produced such printed matter, in addition to a variety of other projects, some equally small, others more substantial. Orders were often limited to just one ream of images at a time, but larger quantities of up to five reams were printed occasionally in a single week.[22]

Although images of the Virgin were clearly the most popular of this type of printed matter produced at the Plantin-Moretus Press, they were not the only prints requested. For example, in 1606, the church warden Georgius Robyns was charged 3 fl. for the printing of two reams of images of St George (for which he had provided the paper). Once again, payments to the Moretuses' pressmen indicate that they occasionally printed such images in between their regular work.[23] Religious orders likewise supported the production and distribution of printed images. Although the Jesuits are best known in this regard, many other groups were similarly active, such as the Capuchins, for whom, on at least one occasion in 1640, Balthasar Moretus's staff printed some unspecified images.[24]

Thus, while the vast quantity of images that were thus commissioned from an assortment of printers active in Antwerp may be sparsely represented in the Moretuses' accounts, they evidently did not refuse to satisfy and profit from the immense, recurring demand for such work.[25] The most unexpected and prestigious of such commissions came from Peter Paul Rubens who, on multiple occasions in 1633 and possibly at other times as well, asked the Moretuses to print impressions of woodcuts made after his designs. For example, on 11 June 1633, Balthasar Moretus paid his pressmen for completing several small jobs, including printing three unspecified broadsides, a "Thesis" (which was usually a broadside composed in honor of the completion of an academic program), and two reams (1,000 full sheets of paper) of one "figure" by Rubens. Additionally, on 3 September 1633, he paid his staff for printing one ream of Christoffel Jegher's woodcut after Rubens's design of the *Temptation of Christ* (fig. 4.6), along with a ream of images of the Virgin. Although it is not clear from these records exactly how many woodcuts were printed for Rubens each time, Balthasar noted in April 1636 that Rubens owed him 72 fl. 3 st. for having printed 2,000 images (in addition to providing the paper on which they were printed) sometime prior to 31 March 1634.[26] Hence, Balthasar I was responsible for the production of 2,000 or more woodcut images after Rubens's designs

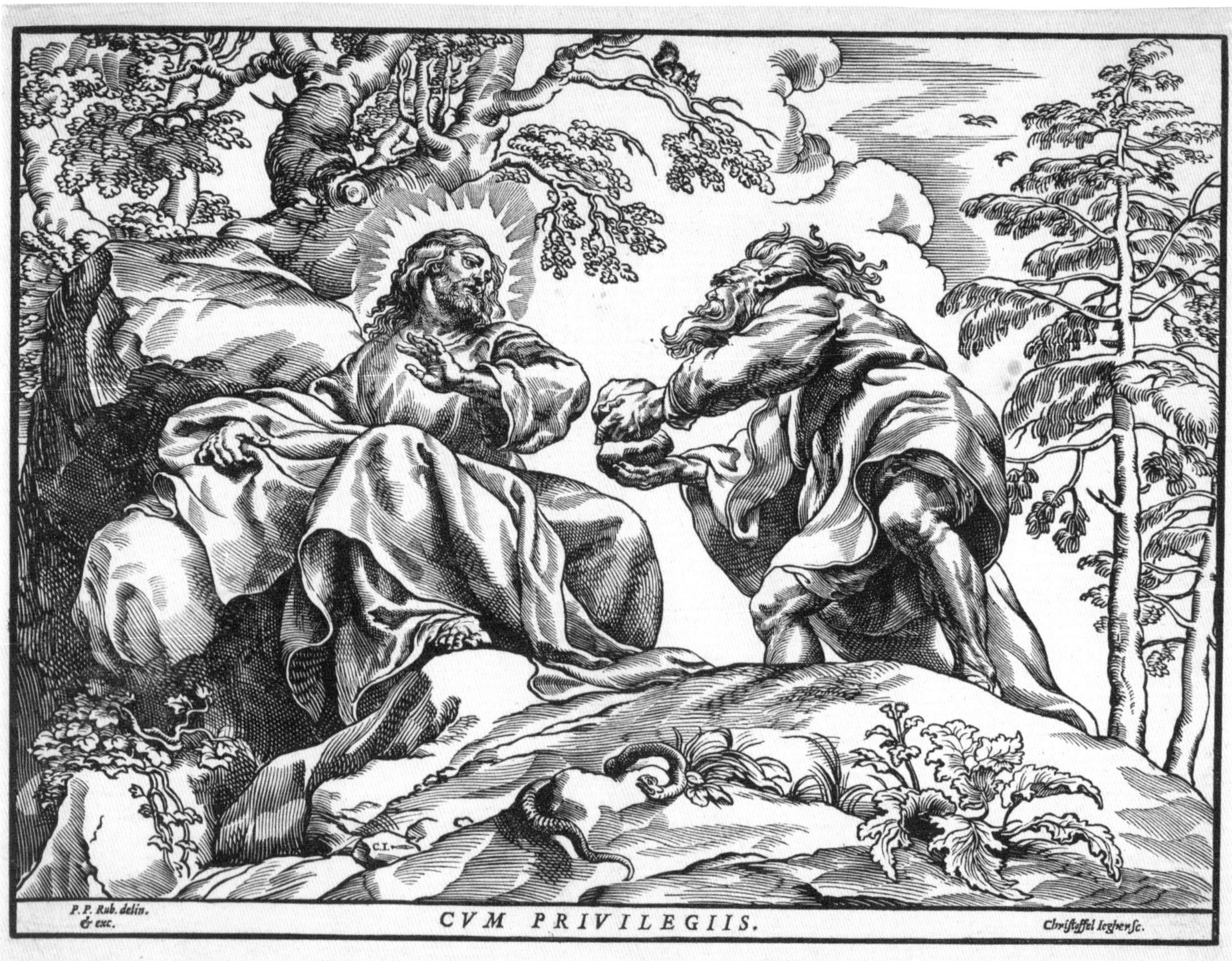

4.6 Christoffel Jegher after Peter Paul Rubens, *The Temptation of Christ*, by September 1633, woodcut, 334 × 441 mm. Amsterdam, Rijksmuseum: RP-P-OB-30.035

that Rubens himself would have subsequently distributed through his own networks of clients or agents. Balthasar's own involvement in the sale of engravings and woodcuts after Rubens was notably infrequent and more likely a reflection of exceptional circumstances. The record of his acquisition of unspecified images by Rubens for a sum of 30 fl. 10 st. by 4 January 1631 is worth citing in full here due to the unexpected use of the diminutive form of a Dutch word for images, namely "beldekens": "voor printe beldekens van P. P. Rubens" (for printed images by P. P. Rubens). It is important to note here that this phrase, commonly used in sixteenth- and seventeenth-century documents, was thus not applied strictly to small devotional images as is often assumed, but was also used to refer to potentially large images that were collected and prized.[27]

In striking contrast to these diverse, occasionally recurring instances of the Moretuses printing woodcut images for others, there is a relative paucity of records of their producing other forms of illustrated printed sheets – in particular, altar cards (commonly referred to as "canons" in these records) and *suffragia* (small, often illustrated leaves with interrelated religious and virtuous texts for self-improvement) – for resale to their own clients. Although

Plantin combined his own periodic production of canons with his purchase of them from other local suppliers, records of the Moretuses' printing of them are rare (fig. 2.6). Rather, the Moretuses appear to have relied primarily on external sources for these special renditions of the culmination of the Mass for public display and devotional practices, at least through the mid-seventeenth century.[28] Similarly, aside from an exceptional period in 1609 when Jan Moretus had *suffragia* printed in Dutch, Latin, and French on a weekly basis, the Moretuses routinely purchased them from Hendrik Aertssens, who specialized in their production.[29]

The Moretuses were also reluctant to sell loose impressions of the copper plates they had on hand for the illustrations of their own editions, despite the precedence of Plantin's occasional sale of the images made for Benito Arias Montano's editions of the *Humanae salutis monumenta* to various clients.[30] The few instances in which the Moretuses sold such loose sheets may well have been as special favors for an individual closely related to the given publication. For example, in May 1608, Jan I sent an extra twelve impressions of the engraving of St Thecla (fig. 4.7), which was printed opposite the dedication to the Spanish King Philip III in Basilius of Seleucia's *De vita ac miraculis D. Theclae* (1608) to the editor of the publication,

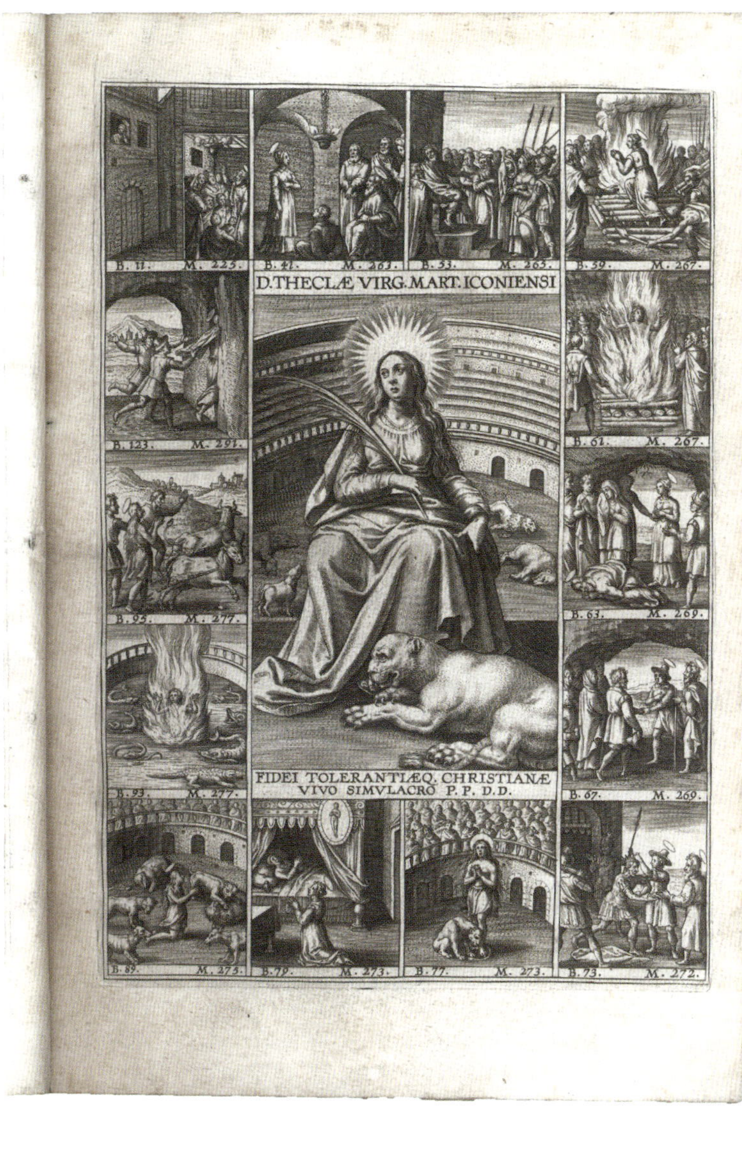

4.7 Jan II or Adriaen Collaert (attributed to), *Saint Thecla*, in: Basilius of Seleucia, *De vita ac miraculis D. Theclae* (Antwerp: Jan Moretus I, 1608), engraving, 215 × 147 mm. Antwerp, Museum Plantin-Moretus: A 1166, fol. *2r.

Petrus Pantinus.[31] Nearly three decades later, in 1634, Balthasar I sold four extra impressions of a portrait of Cardinal Petrus Aloysius Carafa printed on satin for the remarkable sum of 3 fl. 13 st. to Silvester Petrasancta, the author of *De symbolis heroicis libri IX* (Antwerp: Balthasar Moretus I, 1634), which was dedicated to the cardinal and which contained this portrait (fig. 4.8).[32] Balthasar I went to greater lengths to satisfy Bartholomeus de los Rios y Alarcon's desire for numerous extra impressions of several of the images commissioned for his *De hierarchia Mariana libri sex* (Antwerp: Balthasar Moretus I, 1641). In 1641 alone, Balthasar sold him initially twenty-four extra impressions of De los Rios's portrait (fig. 4.9) (which was ultimately not included in the final publication) and twelve of an image of the Virgin referred to as "Ave Maria". He subsequently sold De los Rios an extra twenty impressions of these same two images, as well as a representation of Our Lady of Good Success ("B. Maria de bono successu").[33] Nevertheless, even the relatively large orders for nearly 100 impressions of images commissioned for De los Rios's publication cannot compare with the more than 300 impressions of assorted images from the *Monumenta* that Plantin sold in the years immediately following its publication, nor the numerous copies of the two broadsides he produced with other engravings designed by Arias Montano.[34] The Moretuses favored a stricter distinction between the intaglio imagery they commissioned for their own textual publications and the loose prints produced by professional printmakers for independent sale.

A final, important example of how the Moretuses' engagement in the distribution of images diverged from Plantin's approach involves the acquisition of copper plates from prominent Antwerp engravers for third parties. Plantin received several requests to assist clients and acquaintances with such projects in the 1580s alone. Occasionally, he only served as the middleman for the final payment to the artist. This was the case in March 1583, when Jan Poelman, Plantin's agent in Salamanca, had commissioned two engravings (possibly for someone else), at least one of which was an image of the *Last Judgement* made by Jan Wierix.[35] A few years later, in 1586–1587, Plantin was more actively involved in negotiations with artists

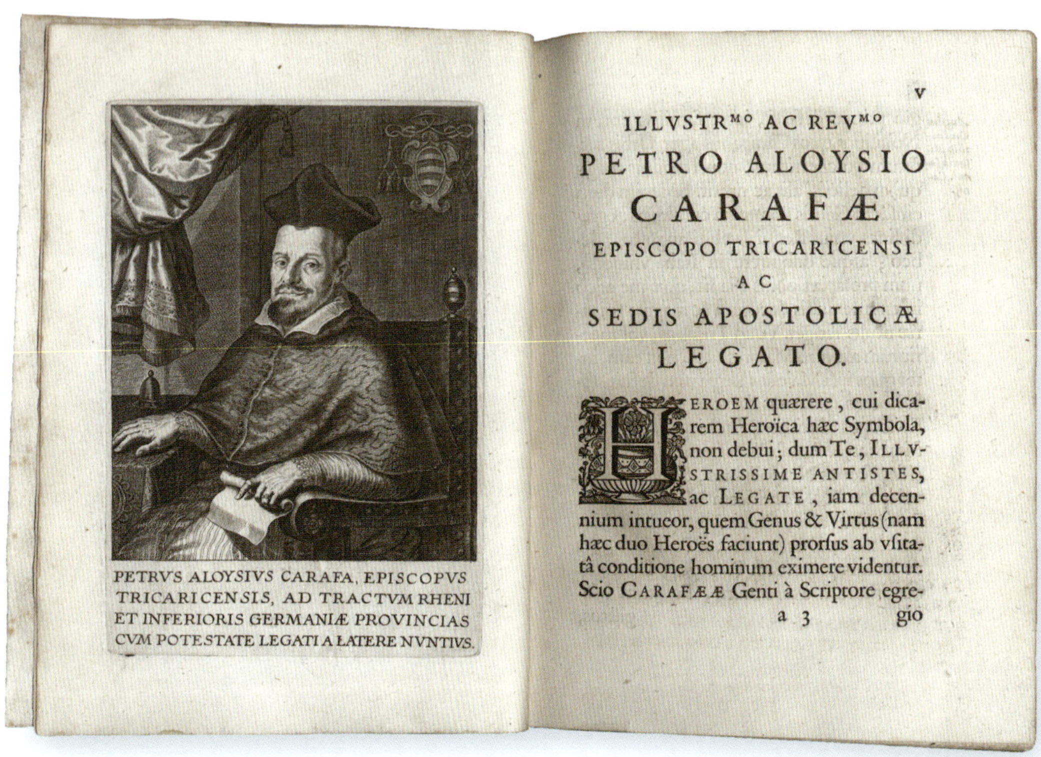

4.8 Cornelis Galle I, *Portrait of Cardinal Petrus Aloysius Carafa*, in: Silvester Petrasancta, *De symbolis heroicis libri IX* (Antwerp: Balthasar Moretus I, 1634), engraving, 165 × 114 mm. Antwerp, Museum Plantin-Moretus: R 56.18, fol. a2v.

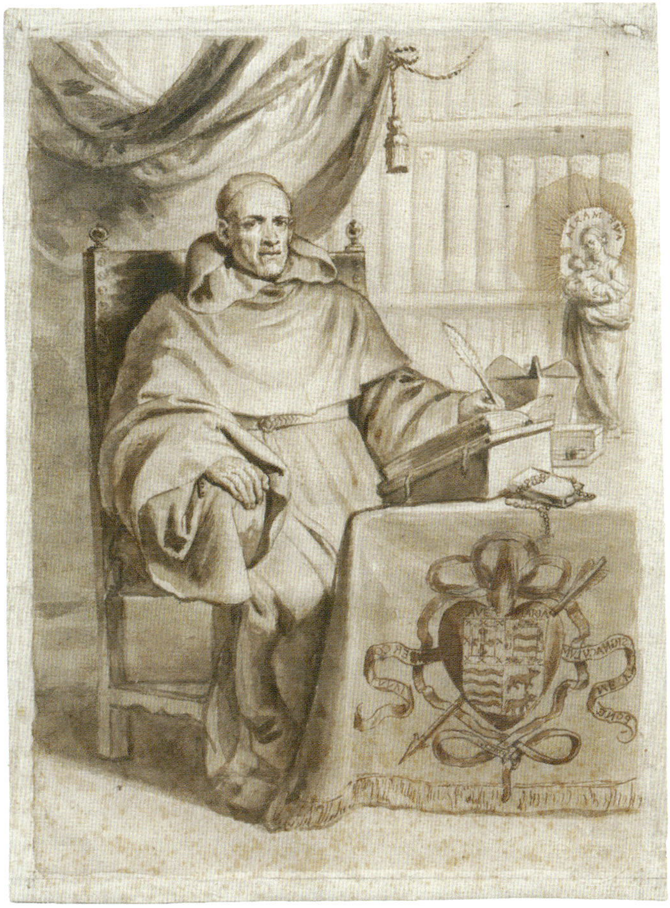

4.9 Erasmus Quellinus, *Portrait of Bartholomeus de los Rios y Alarcon*, 1640, drawing, 251 × 154 mm. Antwerp, Museum Plantin-Moretus: Tek. 410.

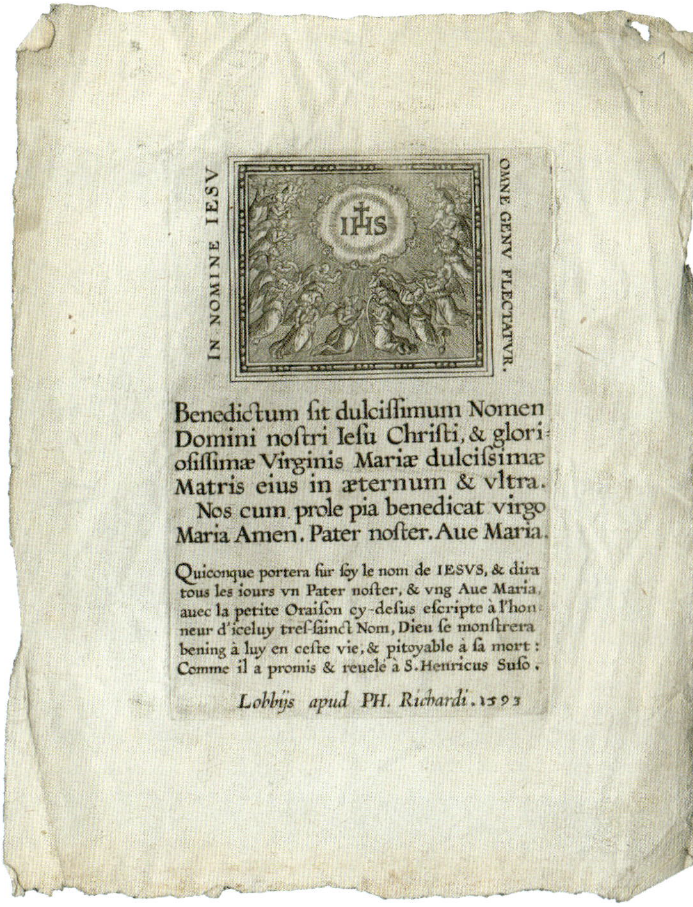

4.10 Anonymous, *Name of Jesus with an Accompanying Prayer*, 1593, engraving with some etching, 134 × 90 mm, published by Philippe Richard of Lobbes Abbey. Antwerp, Museum Plantin-Moretus: K 1026: 1.

on behalf of others for several different projects. For example, Hans Gundelach in Nuremberg asked to have an engraving of his "Monumentum" made and printed for him, which Plantin arranged to have done by Hubert Goltzius's son Jules.[36] Plantin also saw to a request from Jean Moflin, chaplain to Philip II and subsequently abbot of St Winoksbergen (now called Bergues), to have Hieronymus Wierix engrave an image of *The Seven Sorrows of the Virgin* after a design by Crispijn van den Broeck. Unfortunately, Moflin passed away before the plate was completed. Initially recorded in Plantin's inventory, it was acquired by Theodore Galle, who sold impressions of it to Jan Moretus I in 1602.[37]

Not all of Plantin's efforts were successful; for instance, he was unable to convince engravers to make the illustrations for Jerónimo Nadal's *Adnotationes et meditationes in evangelia*, which ultimately appeared in 1593, a few years following Nadal's death, under the title *Evangelicae historiae imagines*. Nevertheless, this intermediary role was one that Plantin was willing to assume.[38] However, under the Moretuses, such assistance with commissions for independent intaglio plates (versus exceptional instances when they helped arrange for the production of plates to embellish other publishers' books) soon came to an end.[39] One of the rare examples of their offering this service dates to 1593, just a few years after Plantin's death, when Jan Moretus I saw to the creation and printing of a plate that featured a small square image of angels adoring an IHS monogram, together with an accompanying prayer in Latin and a commentary in French (fig. 4.10). The image was produced at the request of Philippe Richard, a member of the

Benedictine abbey of Lobbes, near Mons, and Richard was charged for all of the related costs, including the copper used for the plate and the paper on which the 2075 images were printed.[40] However, by the time Arnold Havensius, a Carthusian monk in Ghent, sought Jan I's help in 1609 and 1610 to convince Theodore Galle to finish an engraving he had promised to make for a book Havensius was writing, there is no indication that Jan I, then near the end of his life, assisted him. As Havensius himself died in May 1610, the project was never completed.[41]

Consequently, while the Moretuses agreed to print assorted woodcut images by the hundreds, if not thousands, for diverse local clients on a regular basis amid their primary work of printing books, they did not maintain the breadth of Plantin's personal involvement in the production and distribution of loose, intaglio images. Rather, they favored a more limited selection of often passive forms of participation in the burgeoning international print market, each emanating, nevertheless, from Plantin's practices. The primary ways in which the Moretuses were involved in this market were shipping packages of prints along with their regular transport of books and processing payments from print dealers' independent contacts; both of these activities were natural extensions of their routine activities as booksellers. In addition, they fulfilled orders for prints placed with them directly – essentially, the work of a print seller that Balthasar II, at least, believed was not his primary occupation. Perhaps he and his predecessors regarded this assistance an extra service tendered to individuals within their own local and international networks or a favor to be completed for special clients as part of an effort to maintain good customer relations. Fulfilling such orders did not, in any event, provide regular, significant profit.[42] Regardless of the motivations behind these transactions, a consideration of the disparate requests for prints the Moretuses received and their responses to them give us a rare view of how those seeking prints defined what they sought and how such orders were attended to.

ORDERING PRINTS IN THE SIXTEENTH AND SEVENTEENTH CENTURIES

Numerous types of individuals, from artists to professional tradesmen of distinct backgrounds to itinerant peddlers, offered prints for sale. Locally, some individuals might have had stands or their own shops, while international transactions could be arranged, for example, via correspondence or through fairs (fig. 4.11). However, how did these various people obtain prints for resale that they did not make themselves or that were not readily available for purchase locally? Moreover, how did collectors procure particular prints by specific artists that they sought for their collections and how did they supplement what they may have purchased personally on a more casual basis? Logically, important suppliers would have been internationally oriented independent printmakers and print publishers such as Antonio Lafreri, Hieronymus Cock, and the Galles, or the Chéreau, De Poilly, and Mariette families, in addition to personal agents working for wealthy collectors.[43] However, one significant channel that is periodically acknowledged but has yet to be sufficiently explored is the book trade.[44] Thanks to the remarkable wealth of information preserved concerning numerous facets of Plantin's and the Moretuses' business, it is possible to gather and assess a range of examples of how requests for prints were placed, responded to, and fulfilled. Periodic overlaps between the Moretuses' practices and isolated records of other print dealers' and booksellers' participation in the print trade underscore that their approach was not unusual and, indeed, reflects some common standards of this period.

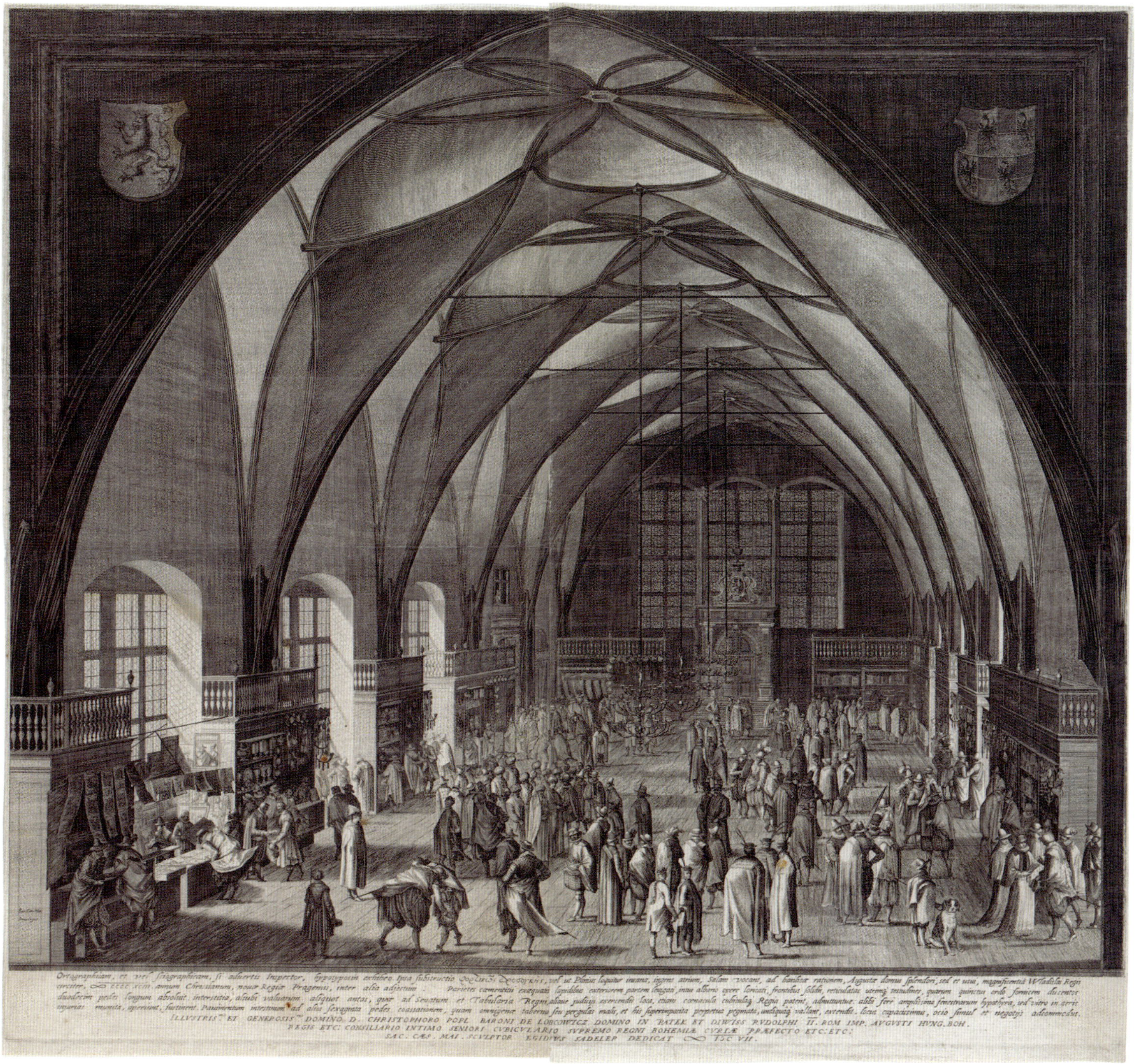

4.11 Aegidius Sadeler II, *Interior View of the Vladislav Hall at Prague Castle during the Annual Fair*, 1607, engraving, 562 × 616 mm. Amsterdam, Rijksmuseum: RPK RP-P-OB-70.089. See the lower left for a stall with prints for sale.

Predictably, when distant clients endeavored to obtain prints, they most often recorded their requests in letters or lists. The correspondence between the Jesuit Philippus de Peralta and Balthasar Moretus I between July 1614 and January 1616 provides a telling example of how such requests were made and addressed. These requests were often included alongside discussion of other topics. In this case, the context was work on a specially illustrated Office for use in the diocese of Toledo that De Peralta had commissioned. He initiated his request for prints in July 1614 by stating:

> I need 1,000 prints in folio, 4°, 8°, and 16° by the engraver Hieronymus Wierix, all of saints and of exquisite artistic quality; and see that there are four or five each of the best and most attractive. I have heard that the series of the apostles by this engraver has finally appeared. Let me know how much it costs before you send it to me and if it seems to be the best to you and not too highly priced, you can simply send it to me and I will expect no other answer.[45]

A note in the margin of this letter clarified that he wanted 100 prints in both folio and 4° and 400 each in 8° and 16°. In addition to stipulating the artist (Hieronymus Wierix) and the subject matter (saints in general and a new series of the Apostles about which he had heard), De Peralta stressed that he was interested in visually appealing works of superb artistic quality in a variety of sizes; a limited number of copies of the best prints (four or five of each) was acceptable. While he was concerned about the price, he was also willing to follow Moretus's judgement in that matter. When De Peralta wrote again a month later, he noted that he was still waiting for Wierix's prints – above all the series of the twelve Apostles – but that if it was not possible for Balthasar to meet his demands, he was also willing to receive a much smaller sampling of prints (just fifty or so) in the same variety of formats by other "proven artists" ("ex probatis artificibus"), remarking that if he liked them he would buy more.[46]

In Moretus's response to this last letter, he acknowledged that he could not satisfy De Peralta's initial request for prints by Hieronymus Wierix, as some were rather expensive – particularly those that Wierix engraved himself – and most of what Wierix had published was rather worn (and consequently not of the best quality). Instead, as De Peralta had suggested in his last letter, Balthasar had gathered together a selection of superior prints by both Hieronymus Wierix and Theodore Galle that he promised to send to him with the respective prices noted, so that De Peralta could decide how many of each he would like.[47] Hence, in his response, Balthasar demonstrated his knowledge of not only the current prices for specific prints, but also the range of quality of what was on the market – as his grandfather Plantin had when discussing the availability of prints by Albrecht Dürer in 1567, more than fifty years earlier.[48] Two weeks later, when Balthasar sent De Peralta a large order of books that he had ordered, he also included a selection of intaglio images published by Galle and Wierix worth 20 fl. 7.5 st. Remarkably, the record of the acquisition of these prints for De Peralta indicates that Galle had both provided his own assortment of prints (valued at just 5 fl. 18 st.) and chosen the ones from Wierix's stock (valued at 14 fl. 9.5 st.) for inclusion in the shipment to De Peralta. Thus, while Moretus served as De Peralta's primary point of contact for his print acquisitions, he was not necessarily the one who determined exactly which images were sent.[49] Although it is not known whether De Peralta ordered more prints from either Galle or Wierix at this time, the process had apparently taught him to adjust his expectations. When he wrote again to Balthasar more than a year later in January 1616, he appended a reminder that if Wierix had published any new prints, he would buy a hundred in a variety of formats. However, if only old images were available, he remarked that he would not take any.[50]

Although such exceptionally informative exchanges of letters concerning requests for prints are rarely preserved, other isolated examples of individuals asking for prints further elucidate the variety of approaches taken to buy them. Some middlemen hoped to obtain a specific work for one of their own clients. Such was the case when the Gdańsk bookseller Kaspar Förster wrote to Balthasar Moretus I in 1637, seeking a copy of Peter Paul Rubens's *Palazzi di Genova* on behalf of a high-ranking church official.[51] In other instances, the Moretuses' clients simply appended general requests for unspecified allotments of prints to itemized wish lists for books. While the Toulouse bookseller Pierre Jagourt categorized the images he sought by size, Förster focused on their physical appearance and asked for prints on parchment.[52] Other clients wrote because they, like De Peralta, had "heard" that a specific series of images in which they were interested had been published. For instance, Förster asked Balthasar I on 5 August 1638 about copies of the second part of Rubens's *Palazzi di Genova* because "it was said that it had certainly been published".[53] As with De Peralta's repeated assertions that he had heard that Hieronymus Wierix had recently published a new series of the Apostles, reports of what was available did not always guarantee that the specific items could be procured as desired. In Förster's case, Moretus did not send him copies of the second part of Rubens's publication until 1640.

A transcription of an extensive and detailed order for prints sent to Balthasar II by Kaspar Förster's son and successor Georg on 19 August 1644 reflects the fruits of the time Georg himself spent in Antwerp during the summer of 1643, when he evidently visited several print shops there.[54] Drawing upon his personal experience to formulate his requests, he relied upon Balthasar II to carry out the shopping he could not always do in person. His inquiry attests to his clear preference for the work of certain suppliers at specific shops, in addition to his firsthand knowledge of the full array of visual embellishments that might be added to prints and what the prices should be.[55] Naturally, other individuals who lived closer to Antwerp would have purchased their prints personally. For example, in 1615, the Lille bookseller Jean Morel had bought prints from Hieronymus Wierix while in Antwerp and left them with the Moretuses to be shipped along with numerous books that he had selected while there. Other records indicate that Morel did business personally with other Antwerp printmakers as well – in particular, Theodore Galle and Michael Snijders – and subsequently asked the Moretuses to help either with the transfer of funds or, once again, with the shipment of his independent acquisitions.[56]

Alternatively, if it was not possible to buy prints in person, there were various agents available aside from the Moretuses. Though there are numerous examples of professional print sellers assuming this role, other individuals could be engaged to provide the same service, in addition to friends or associates who might also agree to assist with such purchases. For example, between 1613 and 1615, the Antwerp merchant Diego Pardo Lopez was the intermediary for the Jesuit Pedro de Angulo in Seville when he wished to buy prints by Hieronymus Wierix, in addition to an occasional order from Charles de Mallery and Theodore Galle.[57] While these acquisitions may reflect a purely business arrangement, personal connections were sometimes enlisted to complete some print purchases. For example, in February 1616, the Capuchin Nathanael van Doornik (born as Nathanael de Barbigant-de la Haye), purchased prints from both Charles de Mallery and Hieronymus Wierix for the current guardian of the Capuchin order, Florianus van Antwerpen.[58] A month later, Nathanael also arranged for the purchase and shipment of unspecified packages of prints to both an abbey and the prior of St Martin in Tournai. While the abbey's order would most likely have been arranged within the Capuchin order, the latter intervention was managed in part (if not instigated by) Nathanael's brother Louis de Barbigant, who was a tax collector in Tournai.[59]

Although firsthand correspondence rarely survives, the Moretuses' accounts abound with records of what was sent in response to an array of requests for prints. Despite the immense diversity of clients and destinations for these images, the essential defining characteristics used to identify and distinguish the works sent are remarkably similar.

The most striking examples are the few instances when exceptional care was taken by those keeping the records to note not only the subject of the image, but also some combination of names of the designer and printmaker and the start of an inscription on the print so that there could be no doubt as to exactly which rendition of a specific subject was intended. Not surprisingly, such notation was most often applied to works by renowned artists that may have become collectors' items. Such details are noted, for example, in purchases made by the canon Hieronymus van Winghe in Tournai in 1637 and the London bookseller Humphrey Robinson in 1640. In several instances, the prints thus specified had been published a decade or more earlier (figs. 4.12 and 7.3).[60] Although neither Van Winghe's nor Robinson's written requests are preserved, presumably they had indicated that these specific prints were desired. While Van Winghe was most likely adding to his own private collection, Robinson was probably seeking to supplement his stock for assorted clients, as he ordered three impressions each of several images. Some records of Plantin's print sales, noted fifty years earlier or more, list similar elements to identify prints: names of printmakers and publishers or prominent inscriptions on the plates. For example, in a list of prints supplied by Philips Galle for the merchant Simon de Tassis in February 1580, citations from the inscriptions identify some of the images. In the record of a 1588 sale of engravings to the merchant Ferdinandus Ximenes, the subject of the work was occasionally combined with an identification of not only the publisher, but also the printmaker and designer.[61] Although the notation of inscriptions may have been the simplest means of identifying an unconventional allegorical subject among De Tassis's order, the extra attention paid to recording all of the figures responsible for the creation of the prints Ximenes purchased may reflect an art collector's interest in them. Nevertheless, despite the recurrence of these detailed records across decades, this approach to specifying individual prints remained exceptional in the accounts of the Officina Plantiniana.

Numerous other requests for certain subjects produced or published by specific print sellers often differ significantly from the precise orders discussed above; rather, they are reminiscent of De Peralta's inquiries after the new series of the Apostles by Hieronymus Wierix. For instance, a sampling of portrayals of St Hubert ordered for the Archduke and Archduchess of the Low Countries, Albrecht and Isabella, by their secretary Antonio Suarez in December 1617, is remarkable for the assortment of artists requested. Comprising two impressions each of this subject by Jan Sadeler I, Jan-Baptist Vrients, Charles de Mallery, Adriaen Collaert, and Hieronymus Wierix, the record for this group of prints was distinguished only by occasional indications of the general format of the image.[62] When the bookseller Pierre Geubels in St Omer requested books from the Moretuses in the spring of 1614, he had also evidently asked for twelve prints each of two specific subjects published by Theodore Galle, namely *Ecce homo* and *Christ at the Column*. The sale of these images was noted without any further specification.[63] The merchant Diego Pardo Lopez (most likely acting for a client) was also interested in specific subjects by just one artist: four distinct representations of Sts Ignatius and Xavier by Hieronymus Wierix, which he similarly purchased in groups of twelve or twenty-four impressions each.[64] With all of these examples, while the specification of the subjects and print publishers allow us to speculate about which images were actually sent, none can be identified with absolute certainty today.[65] The essential question remains: does this uncertainty simply reflect our currently imperfect knowledge of the oeuvre of these print publishers, or was the exact identification of specific prints unimportant to those purchasing these images? The prevalence of even more general descriptions of the types of subjects or visual qualities of prints sought by a variety of clients supports the latter hypothesis.

Notably, many of the qualities emphasized by De Peralta in his correspondence with Balthasar Moretus concerning prints recur in other contemporaneous orders for prints. In particular, the desire to obtain a variety of new, attractive, high-quality images is frequently repeated. Occurring in Plantin's dealings in prints during the 1570s and 1580s, requests for a sampling of new images continue into the seventeenth century. Diversity was sought in both subjects and formats, as was the case with De Peralta and Jagourt, for example. However, the Augsburg bookseller Johann Kruger was satisfied with just an "assortment" of the work of Charles de Mallery.[66] Recent publications were also often explicitly sought. When Philip II's head almoner, Luis Manrique, was sent a selection of 203 leaves of prints by Philips Galle in November 1581 that he had produced in 1580 or 1581, they were hot off the press. This practice is echoed in other records in Plantin's accounts where the prints supplied by Galle are periodically described as being new and curious. For other clients, such as the Kraków bookseller Christophorus Schedelius, requests for new prints were most likely made in order to avoid repetition of what he acquired. In De Peralta's case, new editions of the work of Hieronymus Wierix were most likely important as a means of quality control, helping him avoid the acquisition of impressions from older, worn plates. Alternatively, when the Flemish art dealer Jan Vlooitz, who was living in Vienna in 1636, requested new images, his goal was to avoid old-fashioned renditions of subjects.[67] Obtaining attractive, high-quality images was also a key concern for De Peralta and others, including Jagourt, Vlooitz, and Schedelius, as well as the Utrecht bookseller Jan van Doorn, who wrote to the Antwerp bookseller Hieronymus Verdussen and asked for an assortment of prints on parchment, stipulating that each had to be exceptional.[68]

Beyond these requirements concerning the general quality and appearance of the images sought, some buyers also occasionally specified which types of subjects they wanted. While De Peralta was interested in Wierix's images of saints, other customers, such as the bookseller Lambert Raesfeld in Münster, asked for devotional images in general. Still other clients, like Van Doorn or Jagourt, suggested more specific subjects, for instance images from the Passion of Christ.[69] The other general subject matter that periodically recurs in the Moretuses' records is landscapes. Already in the 1560s, Plantin had sold landscapes provided by Hieronymus Cock, and the Moretuses continued to provide various types of landscape images (some featuring figures or animals) that were supplied by succeeding generations of Antwerp print publishers, like the Galles and Adriaen Collaert.[70] The persistent interest in landscapes is confirmed by subsequent print orders, such as those from Jan Vlooitz in Vienna and Pieter de Haen in Amsterdam, who was an intermediary between Balthasar II and Schedelius for large shipments of prints destined for Kraków.[71] Though not as substantial as the interest in devotional images, the persistent, periodic sale of landscape images from the start of Plantin's trade in prints through the Moretuses' sales in the seventeenth century reveals that the demand for prints from Antwerp was

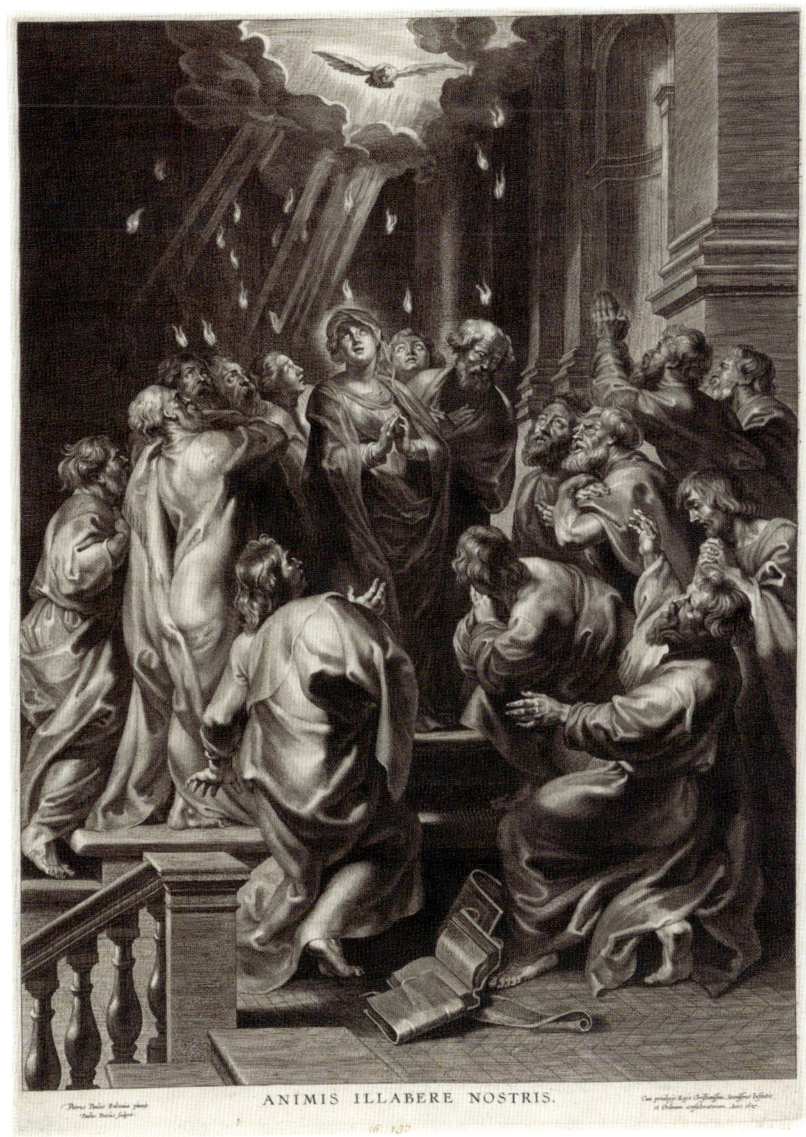

4.12 Paulus Pontius after Peter Paul Rubens, *Pentecost*, 1627, engraving, 596 × 421 mm. Amsterdam, Rijksmuseum: RP-P-OB-70.052.

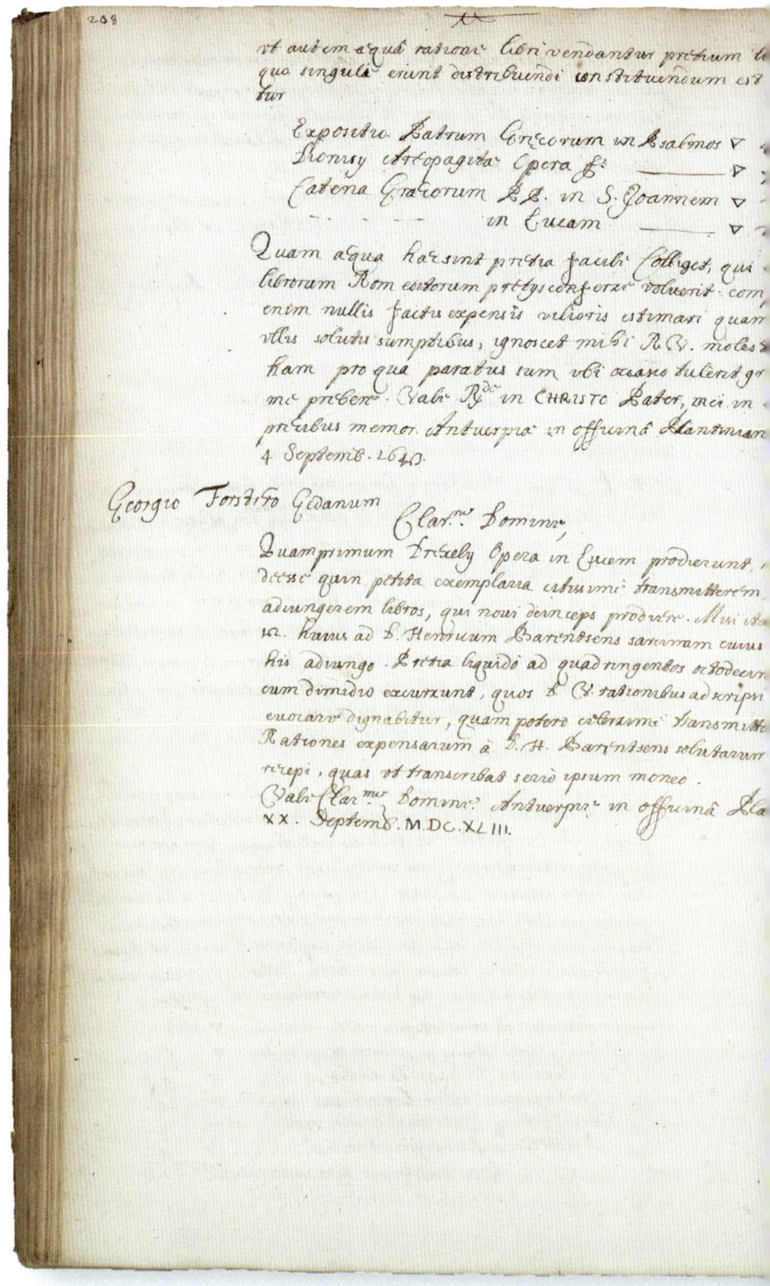

4.13 Letter from Balthasar Moretus II to Bernhard Raesfeld, 2 October 1643, with a sampling of print prices. Antwerp, Museum Plantin-Moretus: Arch. 150, *Copie de lettres 1640–1654*, p. 209.

not homogenous, despite the evidence of the mass export of devotional imagery. Moreover, even within the broad demand for religious subjects, some clients expressed preferences not only for which images they would like to receive, but also for which ones they did not want. Such was the case in Georg Förster's detailed instructions for a large order of prints that he placed with Balthasar II in 1644. After stipulating what he wanted from each of several print sellers in Antwerp, Förster also specified that he would not accept any profane subjects, images with captions in Dutch, or representations of Spanish or French monks and nuns that were not revered locally ("by us").[72]

Once the Moretuses received requests for prints, they had to determine what to send in reply. As Balthasar II made clear to Pieter de Haen in his letter of 1647, he needed to consult

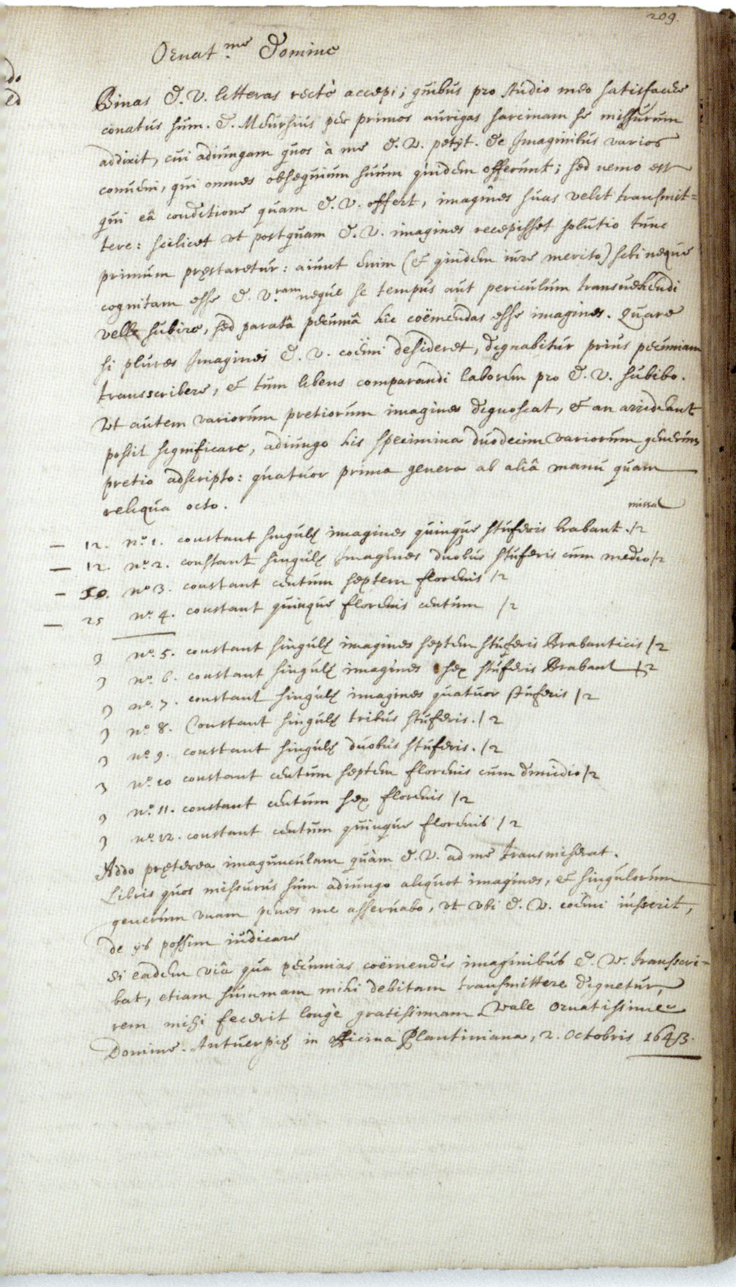

others better informed in such matters before he could respond because he was not a print seller by profession.[73] His uncle Balthasar I, who was more willing to express an opinion regarding the relative quality of images prepared by different print sellers in Antwerp, professed that he went personally in search of the desired prints when he responded to a request made for the Archduke and Archduchess of the Low Countries, Albrecht and Isabella.[74] Nevertheless, he also engaged other individuals to select prints for resale for him. Although he and his father Jan I often relied on the Galles to provide such assistance, for instance when Balthasar sent prints to De Peralta, they periodically also called upon other print dealers when fulfilling special requests. This was the approach used by Jan Moretus I when he sent two dozen of the best prints by Philips Galle and the Sadelers to Flaminio Garnier, the secretary to the king of Spain,

Philip II, in January 1590.[75] Matters may have changed by the end of Balthasar I's life. For example, on 20 October 1640, his nephew, the Jesuit Theodorus Moretus, wrote to the Antwerp Jesuit Joannes Bollandus that Balthasar had an unnamed employee choose prints for him and lamented that what was sent to him might then not be of the best quality.[76]

Balthasar II appears to have been more practical in such matters, attempting to ascertain what types of images his customers were looking for and what they were willing to pay before he purchased prints on their behalf. For instance, in 1643, he sent Georg Förster a "catalogus" (most likely a handwritten list) of engravings after Rubens that were available for purchase.[77] When he could not immediately satisfy a request from Schedelius for hand-colored prints at a reasonable price, he asked Schedelius to send him an example of the sort of print he was looking for and what he was willing to pay for it. Alternatively, when assisting the Münster bookseller Bernhard Raesfeld in 1643, Balthasar II sent Raesfeld a sampling of twelve different prints by two artists in a range of price categories and asked him to select the images he wanted (fig. 4.13).[78]

Essential to all of these transactions was negotiating the payment for the prints. As Balthasar II clearly stated in his 1643 letter, no one was willing to agree to Raesfeld's proposal that he would pay for the prints only after he had received them. Balthasar defended the print sellers' position, explaining that because they did not know Raesfeld, they understandably did not want to take any risks or wait for their payment. Consequently, all of their prints had to be paid for upfront in cash. Balthasar concluded by assuring Raesfeld that once he had transferred the necessary funds, Balthasar would be happy to help him acquire what he desired.[79] Balthasar II made similar demands for advance cash payment for prints ordered by distant customers when corresponding with Christophorus Schedelius in 1642.[80] While clearly advantageous for Balthasar as a means of minimizing his risk in such transactions, his insistence on upfront payments in cash for prints ordered by foreign customers was not new. Rather, it echoed sentiments expressed by Hieronymus Wierix nearly forty years earlier when involved in a legal dispute with Peeter de Jode I concerning whether or not he had agreed to pay in advance for a selection of Wierix's prints that he had sent to his sister in Gdańsk for resale there. Wierix defended his position by asserting that he only dealt with those whom he knew and did not engage in long-distance transactions that would require him to wait for the payment for his prints.[81] The possible negative consequences of sending prints on approval and waiting for one's payment, as Raesfeld had apparently suggested, are evident from an exchange of packages of prints between Charles de Mallery and a certain Nicolas de Bonta via the Frankfurt fair in 1614. Not only did De Mallery have to wait at least two months for his payment, but Bonta did not end up buying all of the prints De Mallery had sent. Consequently, the Moretuses charged De Mallery an extra fee for the return shipment of the rejected prints.[82]

Since most orders for prints were imprecise about exactly which images were desired, it is not surprising that some customers, like Bonta, were not always satisfied with the selection of prints they received. For example, the Utrecht bookseller Jan van Doorn, who had written to the Antwerp bookseller Hieronymus Verdussen in November and December 1629 to request some 120 prints, wrote again in January 1630 to complain about the selection of images he had been sent. Despite having asked for a variety of images, Van Doorn found that there were far too many of the same sort and that the friend for whom he had placed the order consequently would not be content. However, rather than indicating that he would return the undesired duplicates, Van Doorn simply asked for additional, different images.[83] Plantin also occasionally received complaints about the prints he sent to his own customers.

In a letter from 18 August 1558, the Parisian bookseller Martin Le Jeune noted that significant errors had occurred with his recent order and proceeded to list them, although it is not clear whether the specific images (or books) sent were wrong or just the quantities.[84] Periodically, a client did not simply complain, but, like Bonta, actually returned items that the Moretuses had already purchased in his or her name. When the canon Nicolas de Loos of Ypres returned a group of prints worth 12 fl.16 st. in 1604, the Moretuses sent the rejected images back to the supplier, Adriaen Collaert. Rather than ask to be refunded, they agreed to have Collaert engrave a plate for the illustration of a missal in folio for them instead.[85] Specific, well-documented examples of the purchase and possible return of particular prints are rare, but this was clearly part of the process throughout Plantin's and the Moretuses' involvement in the European print trade – just as it was in the book trade when they and other booksellers sent samplings of books to one another.

By endeavoring to satisfy their own clients' requests for prints, the Moretuses bolstered the existing, extensive international distribution of intaglio images produced by sundry local printmakers and print publishers. It is important to recall that as the Antwerp print industry and export trade expanded dramatically during the seventeenth century, the vast majority of the print sales managed by the Moretuses involved a myriad of images that were distinguished not by subject or printmaker, but rather by the supplier, the general size, the support on which they were printed (paper or parchment), and whether or not they were hand colored (or otherwise embellished with costly materials). Though the responses to such orders are best documented in Balthasar II's correspondence from the 1640s, the bulk sale of prints defined according to these criteria had been common for decades.[86] Thus, while historians often focus on transactions featuring identifiable subjects by renowned artists, the market for prints in Europe at large may be more aptly characterized by the immense traffic of hundreds of thousands of images in bulk.

However, the Moretuses' support of the international print trade was not limited to their own resale of prints. Like Plantin, they also served as intermediaries for print sellers and their clientele in the settlement of payments and as a transport company for the shipment of printed images to far-flung destinations at the request of third parties. Although these various means of assistance were available to all, the degree to which individual print dealers took advantage of them differs as much as one personality does from another. Consequently, an examination of each print distributor's transactions with the Moretuses reveals distinct approaches to managing the essential financial and practical concerns of in an international market and how each print seller defined his or her own business. The surprising diversity in this engagement in the print trade is compellingly evident from the Moretuses' accounts with Philips Galle's extended family. While it is natural to assume that the numerous, enduring professional and personal ties between these families would be similarly manifest in their dealings in prints, this was not always the case. Rather, as an examination of the Galle's and other Antwerp print publishers' trade in images via the Moretuses demonstrates, the range of their transactions and the value of the goods thus sold varied significantly and were, consequently, likely determined by other factors. Reflecting not only individual print sellers' aspirations, connections, and methods, these exchanges also provide a novel perspective on the allure of their work within the greater European print market.

1 MPM Arch. 151, p. 382, letter from Balthasar Moretus II to Pieter de Haen II, from 9 May 1647: “alsoo ick mij niet en geneire met beldekens te verkoopen, hebbe met u.l. brief geweest bij sommige persoonen die wel vande curieuste sijn vande gene die verlichte beldekens verkoopen, de welcke mij dese bijgaende monsters ghelevert hebben”.

2 This overview is drawn from Imhof 2014a, pp. ix-xxxv.

3 See, for example, MPM Arch. 38, fols. 18r and 84r.

4 MPM Arch. 102, p. 395.

5 On Balthasar I and Jan II, see Imhof 2014a, p. xxxii; and Imhof 2018c, pp. 10–28.

6 See Imhof 2023b on Balthasar I’s approach to correcting his publications.

7 For an example of his success in this regard, see Bowen and Imhof 2019.

8 See Voet, GC, vol. I, pp. 209–10, on this partnership.

9 See Diels 2010, pp. 265–66 on Philips Collaert; and Bowen 2020, p. 41, and Imhof 2025 on Louis Moerentorf.

10 Voet, GC, vol. I, p. 216 for this reference and pp. 216–27 for an overview of Balthasar II’s career at the Press. See also Imhof 2009 on Balthasar II.

11 Imhof 2014a, p. lxxxiv.

12 Imhof 2018c, pp. 10–28 and pp. 29–31, on Rubens’s contributions to the Press’s book illustrations, as well as additional sources on the topic.

13 Imhof 1996, in particular pp. 80–82; and Bowen and Imhof 2022, pp. 24–28, on Balthasar’s employment of De Mallery.

14 See Arents 2001 for Rubens’s collection of books. See also MPM Arch. 228, fol. 35v; MPM Arch. 233, fols. 178v and 187r (sampling of book purchases by Van Balen in 1621 and 1626, respectively); and MPM Arch. 221, fol. 53r (Bruegel’s purchase of a bound copy of Abraham Ortelius’s atlas in Dutch).

15 MPM Arch. 224, fol. 160r; MPM Arch. 228, fol. 50r; and MPM Arch. 239, fol. 91r, respectively. For the two cited editions by Jan Moretus, see Imhof 2014a, O-81 and A-2. See also Chapters 5 and 6 for additional examples of print sellers who traded their wares via the Moretuses.

16 Van der Stock 1998, pp. 27–58, in particular pp. 39–42.

17 Rombouts and Van Lerius 1872, vol. I, pp. 295, 317, and 342 (Jan I’s membership), 466 and 473 (Balthasar I), and 473, 573, and 524 (Jan II). Ibid., vol. II, p. 22 (Balthasar II). See also MPM Arch. 184, for a record book Jan II kept while he was dean; and Rooses 1878 for a publication thereof.

18 MPM Arch. 1178. In the following discussion, examples will be cited from roll 2 (Jan Moretus I, 22 September 1610), roll 3 (Martine Plantin, the widow of Jan I, 17 February 1616), roll 4 (Jan Moretus II, 11 March 1618), and roll 5 (Melchior Moretus, Jan I’s son, 4 June 1634). Additional lists, the last dating from 1710 (for Maria Catharina Moretus, the wife of Egidius Cornelis de Vlieghere) are also preserved.

19 See roll 3 for the citation of Hans and Baltasar Vel “metser” (bricklayer) and Wilm Bogard “timmerman” (woodworker) and roll 4 for that of Joos Claes “den barbier” (barber).

20 Génard 1859, p. 197, lists the godparents of Theodore’s and Catharina’s children.

21 MPM Arch. 176, fol. 107v: “La chapelle de Nre dame doibt pour l’impression d’une rame des images et vers de l’assumption de nre dame [no value noted for this work] Delivres a Cornille adriaenssens, knaep de la chappelle par son serviteur Christiaen”.

22 See, for example: MPM Arch. 785, fol. 4 lft (4 December 1610); MPM Arch. 785, fol. 95 rht (18 August 1617); MPM Arch. 773, p. 108 (8 July 1619); MPM Arch. 194, fol. 58 lft (5 and 6 August 1632, charged to the wardens of the chapel at Antwerp Cathedral); MPM Arch. 780, fol. 192 lft (15 July 1634, for five reams of images of the Virgin); and MPM Arch. 781, fol. 5 lft (21 and 28 July and 18 August 1640, for a total of eight reams of images).

23 For the former, see MPM Arch. 177, fol. 142v, under 31 August 1606: “Sr Georgius Robyns etc kerckmeesters de St George doibt pour Impression de deux Rames de l’image de St George desquelles avoyent apporte le papier fl. 3 st. __”. See also MPM Arch. 785, fol. 90 lft (23 April 1616).

24 MPM Arch. 781, fol. 5 lft, under 17 Nov 1640: “beldekens voor de Capucinen”.

25 See Thijs 1993, pp. 81–94, for an overview of such commissions.

26 These accounts are summarized in Bouchery and Van den Wijngaert 1941, pp. 100–01. For the payments to the pressmen cited here, see MPM Arch. 780, fol. 174 lft, under 11 June and 3 September 1633. For the charge to Rubens, see MPM Arch. 134, fol. 222 lft, where it is noted under 12 April 1636, as a reminder of an earlier charge that still needed to be paid.

27 MPM Arch. 185, fol. 20 lft, under 4 January 1631, for the cited text. See Bowen 2017 for an overview of the sale of prints after Rubens via the Plantin-Moretus Press, including older images sought by collectors. For an example of the assumption that "beldekens" only refers to small devotional images, see Thijs 1993.

28 For isolated examples of their own production, see Imhof 2014a, C-22; and MPM Arch. 785, fol. 5 lft, under 9 April 1611.

29 See MPM Arch. 786, fol. 219 lft, between 24 July and 17 October 1609, for the printing of suffragia by Moretus's pressmen; see Chapter 6 for Aertssens' production of them.

30 See Chapter 3 for examples of Plantin's sale of images from the Monumenta.

31 MPM Arch. 180, fol. 90v, for this shipment; and Imhof 2014a, B-23, on this edition.

32 MPM Arch. 242, fol. 80r, for this sale.

33 MPM Arch. 249, fols. 20r and 74v, for these shipments; and MPM Arch. 134, fol. 288 lft for the charges for them.

34 Appendix 1, CP-1 and CP-2.

35 MPM Arch. 61, fols. 28v and 30v, for the transactions involving Poelman. Only the transaction on fol. 28v is transcribed in M-H Wierix 1978–1982, vol. III.2, no. 36, but Poelman's name is erroneously recorded there as "Rutenas".

36 For Plantin's account of work on this project, see Corr., vol. VII, no. 1107. The final charge is noted in MPM Arch. 63, fol. 50r.

37 For the payments for this project, see MPM Arch. 64, fol. 40r; and MPM Arch. 21, fol. 19 lft. See also M-H Wierix 1978–1982, vol. III.2, no. 42, for an extract from a letter Plantin wrote to Moflin in this regard. For more on this transaction, including a reproduction of Van den Broeck's compositional drawing, see Imhof 2018b, p. 121. See also Appendix 1, TG-25 for this print.

38 For an overview of the production and distribution of Nadal's famous work, see Bowen and Imhof 2019.

39 See, for example, MPM Arch. 224, fol. 141r (plate engraved in 1617 by Cornelis Galle I for Hermann Mylius); and MPM Arch. 173, fols. 195r and 195v (devices of the bishop of St Omer for decorating bindings for François Bellet).

40 See MPM Arch. 21, fol. 194 lft, for the full cost accounting; and Imhof 2020a, p. 228, for a brief discussion of this image.

41 See, for example, Havensius's numerous letters to Jan I (MPM Arch. 85, pp. 222–38); and MPM Arch. 93, p. 267, a letter dated 19 August 1610 from Laurentius Serjans to Jan Moretus I, reporting Havensius's death.

42 Examples of profit margins – and the frequent lack thereof – are given throughout the following chapters.

43 Griffiths 2016, Part II (pp. 216–391), provides an overview of the various ways in which prints were bought and sold in the sixteenth to eighteenth centuries.

44 Ibid., pp. 223 and 337, for example.

45 MPM Arch. 90, p. 445, letter from Philippus de Peralta to Balthasar Moretus I, dated 22 July 1614: "Iconibus ad mille opus habeo, in folio, in 4°, in 8° in 16° sculptore Hieronymo Vierx, omnes de sanctis et exquisitissimi artificii atque pulcherrimae sint et optimae quaeque quadruplicatae et quintuplicatae. Apostoli hoc artifice nunc demum ut audivi in lucem prodire. Tu de pretio me monebis antequam ad me mittas et sane si optimae tibi videbuntur et non admodum carae poteris eas ad me mittere alio responte non expectabo".

46 MPM Arch. 90, p. 457, letter from Philippus de Peralta to Balthasar Moretus, dated 19 August 1614.

47 MPM Arch. 135, pp. 216–18, letter from Balthasar Moretus to Philippus de Peralta, dated 21 August 1614: "De imaginibus Hieronymi Wierkx vereor ut R.V. satisfaciam: quaedam satis carae sunt, praesertim quas ipse sculpsit, et pleraeque satis tritae [p. 216] … Icones meliores aliquot H. Wierckx et alterius artificis Theodori Gallaei comparavi, ex singulis unicam ut R.V. dispiciat quas, et quo numero malit. Pretia singularum in schedula ipsis imaginibus adiuncta aperte R.V. cognoscet" [pp. 217–18]. The first part of this text is also transcribed in M-H Wierix 1978–1982, vol. III.2, p. 566, under doc. 101.

48 See Chapter 3.

49 MPM Arch. 221, fols. 157r (shipment to De Peralta on 4 September 1614) and 176v (supply of prints by Galle and Wierix, where the record of Wierix's selection includes the note "pr Pr. [= pater] Philippus Peralta (choisies p[ar] Theodore Galle").

50 MPM Arch. 90, p. 514, letter from Philippus de Peralta to Balthasar Moretus, dated 15 January 1616: "Denique si Hieronymus Vierix novas aliquot edidit icones optimas ad me mitte, centum accipiam variae formae. Alioqui si novas non edidit nullam volo".

51 MPM Arch. 82, p. 73: "promisi enim Primati cuidam, qui me fore … suis obtundit".

52 MPM Arch. 521, fol. 355 (Jagourt); and MPM Arch. 82, p. 81 (Förster).

53 MPM Arch. 94, p. 517: "Inprimis rogo partem secundam Palatiorum Genuensium, quia certo prodiisse dicitur". See also Bowen 2017, p. 292, on this publication and for examples of Förster's purchase of it.

54 MPM Arch. 133, fol. 282 lft, for a reference to Georg's presence in Antwerp in 1643.

55 MPM Arch. 364, fols. 12v-13v (figs. 2.1–2.2). See, for example, his assertion that he had purchased gilded prints on parchment from a store at the sign of the black eagle on the Meir (in Antwerp) for 7 st. per print: "In foro vulgo dicto Meer penes nigram Aquilam 100 Imagines perg. maximae deauratae solvi quamlibet 7 stuferos".

56 For example: MPM Arch. 222, fol. 136r (transfer of 9 fl. to Galle on 9 August 1615); and MPM Arch. 233, fol. 148r (shipment of unspecified prints from Snijders on 17 October 1626).

57 For example: MPM Arch. 221, fols. 200r-200v (12 November 1614, where an order placed via letter by De Angulo that included prints from Wierix was sent to Pardo); and MPM Arch. 222, fol. 24r (6 February 1615, with deliveries of prints by Wierix, De Mallery, and Galle all recorded as being bought by Pardo at the request of De Angulo).

58 For the identification of both Capuchins, see Hildebrand 1945–1956, vol. I, p. 185, n. 3 and p. 317, n. 1 (Nathanael), and p. 237, vol. V, p. 225, and vol. VII, p. 279 (for Florianus). For Nathanael's role in these purchases, see MPM Arch. 128, fols. 219 rht and 108 rht; and MPM Arch. 223, fol. 20v, under 19 February 1616, for the sales record.

59 MPM Arch. 223, fol. 41v (26 March 1616). See Brussels, State Archives of Belgium, "Comptes de villes" (Stadsrekeningen), nos. 40,524–40,530, for example, for the identification of Louis de Barbigant.

60 See Bowen 2017 for an overview of such sales, and pp. 295 and 292, respectively, for the cited examples.

61 MPM Arch. 58, fol. 19r; and MPM Arch. 65, fol. 32r, respectively.

62 MPM Arch. 224, fol. 200v.

63 MPM Arch. 221, fol. 93r.

64 MPM Arch. 179, fol. 156r.

65 See, for example, the multiple options for the Wierix prints for Pardo noted in Appendix 1 under WX-12, WX-13, WX-14, and WX-16.

66 See above for De Peralta and Jagourt; and MPM Arch. 222, fol. 30v, for Kruger. See also Chapter 3 for Plantin's dealings with, for example, De Tassis and De Varon, as well as the print publishers P. Galle and G. de Jode.

67 MPM Arch. 49, fol. 175v (shipment to Manrique); MPM Arch. 364, fols. 15r and 30r (copies of Schedelius's orders from 1644 and 1645, respectively); and Thijs 1993, p. 37, for Vlooitz's request for prints that was sent to the Antwerp art dealer Guilliam Forchoudt in May 1636. Plantin's records of Galle's prints are discussed in Chapter 3.

68 Antwerp, Felix Archives, GF 160 (4), letter from 29 November 1629, in which Van Doorn states "maar elck beeldeken most bijzonder sijn".

69 For Raesfeld's request for "images de devotion petites", see MPM Arch. 219, fol. 161r. See above for the orders from Van Doorn and Jagourt.

70 See MPM Arch. 48, fol. 151v, for examples of Cock's supply of such images, among others, for Benito Arias Montano. See also Appendix 1, nos. AC-1, AC-3, AC-4, AC-5, PG-59, and PG-60 for examples of such images (with assorted staffage) from Collaert and Philips Galle; and MPM Arch. 223, fols. 204v and 227v, for Theodore Galle's supply of landscape images in diverse sizes.

71 MPM Arch. 151, p. 382, letter from Balthasar II to Pieter de Haen, dated 9 May 1647.

72 MPM Arch. 364, fol. 13v: "Si hae res apud unum inveniri non poterunt, enixe rogo ut apud alios conquirantur. Hoc monendum ne ullae profanae nec etiam cum subscriptione Belgica vel Monachorum vel Monacharum Hispaniae vel Galliae qui apud nos non coluntur accipiantur".

73 See the opening quotation for this chapter.

74 MPM Arch. 137, p. 51, letter from Balthasar Moretus I to their secretary, Antonio Suarez de Arguelo, dated 26 December 1617.

75 For the Galles' assistance with the supply of prints made elsewhere, see also Chapter 5. In a letter to Garnier dated 9 January 1590, Jan I states that the prints were selected by Sadeler (most likely Gillis I) and Galle ("les deux douzaines des figures des plus excellentes choisies par Galle et Sadeler"). Oddly, in the record of the shipment of these prints, Jan-Baptist Vrients is cited, along with Philips Galle, as the individuals whom Moretus paid for the supply of these same prints (MPM Arch. 67, fol. 3v).

76 MPM Arch. 89, p. 755: "Incidit autem incommode me haec fortassis D. Balthasari commendasse ut per aliquem famulorum eam procuraret electionem".

77 MPM Arch. 150, pp. 214–15, letter from Balthasar Moretus II to Georg Förster, dated 29 October 1643: "Catalogus tabularum aenearum Rubenii prima oportunitate transmittam".

78 MPM Arch. 150, p. 151, letter from Balthasar Moretus II to Christophorus Schedelius, dated 19 August 1642: "quare gratum mihi fuerit unam aut alteram imaginem primo cursore accipere, eius pretii et generis cuius sibi mitti D.V. desideret"; and MPM Arch. 150, p. 209, letter from Balthasar Moretus II to Bernhard Raesfeld, dated 2 October 1643.

79 MPM Arch. 150, p. 209, letter from Balthasar Moretus II to Bernhard Raesfeld, dated 2 October 1643:"De imaginibus varios conveni, qui omnes obsequium suum quidem offerunt, sed nemo est qui ea conditione quam D.V. offert, imagines suas velit transmittere, scilicet ut postquam D.V. imagines recepisset solutio tunc primum praestaretur. Aiunt enim (et quidem iure merito) sibi neque cognitam esse D.V.ram neque se tempus aut periculum transvehendi velle subire, sed parata pecunia hic coëmendas esse imagines. Quare si plures imagines D.V. coëmi desideret, dignabitur prius pecuniam transscribere et tum libens comparandi laborem pro D.V. subibo".

80 MPM Arch. 150, p. 120, letter from Balthasar Moretus II to Christophorus Schedelius, dated 14 March 1642: "verum quandoquidem imagines [aliude?] coemere et parata pecunia oportet, non inustem d.v. videbitur earum pretium parato transcribere".

81 Antwerp, Felix Archives, Processen supplement 288: no. 5284, a loose document dated 21 February 1608, point IX: "Ende wat apparentie heeft het dat den aenleggere die een werck man is, nyet gewoon synde op Dansick oft andere quartieren te negocieren, syn conste soude laten wech seynden naer Dansick, door den verweerdere, sonder dat hy kent den persoon aen de welcke dat de selve wort gesonden". This case is discussed in full in Chapter 6.

82 See Chapter 9 for this and other examples of charges for the shipment of prints.

83 Antwerp, Felix Archives, GF 160 (4), letter from Jan van Doorn to Hieronymus Verdussen, written between 10 and 20 January 1630: "oock die beeldekens door den bode gesonden mae ick hadde u.l. geschreven om verscheyden ende u.l. hebt gesonden … van een soo dat in die 125 beeldekens geen veertien of vyftien verscheyden soorten en waren soo dat den vriendt die se hebben soude dae mede niet tot syn contentement gedient en is".

84 Corr. vol. I, no. 2, pp. 4–11.

85 MPM Arch. 1104, fol. 8v (payment to Collaert for the prints for De Loos on 13 October 1604); MPM Arch. 176, fol. 139r (14 October 1604; De Loos's shipment, with the note that he had returned at least some part of it on 20 October) and fol. 145v (20 October 1604; note that the Moretuses had returned the prints to Collaert and that he now owed them 12 fl. 16 st.); and MPM Arch. 127, fol. 123 rht (note that Collaert had made an engraving in exchange for this sum).

86 Numerous examples of such sales will be discussed in the following chapters, and the rise in the popularity of hand-coloring is addressed in Chapter 2.

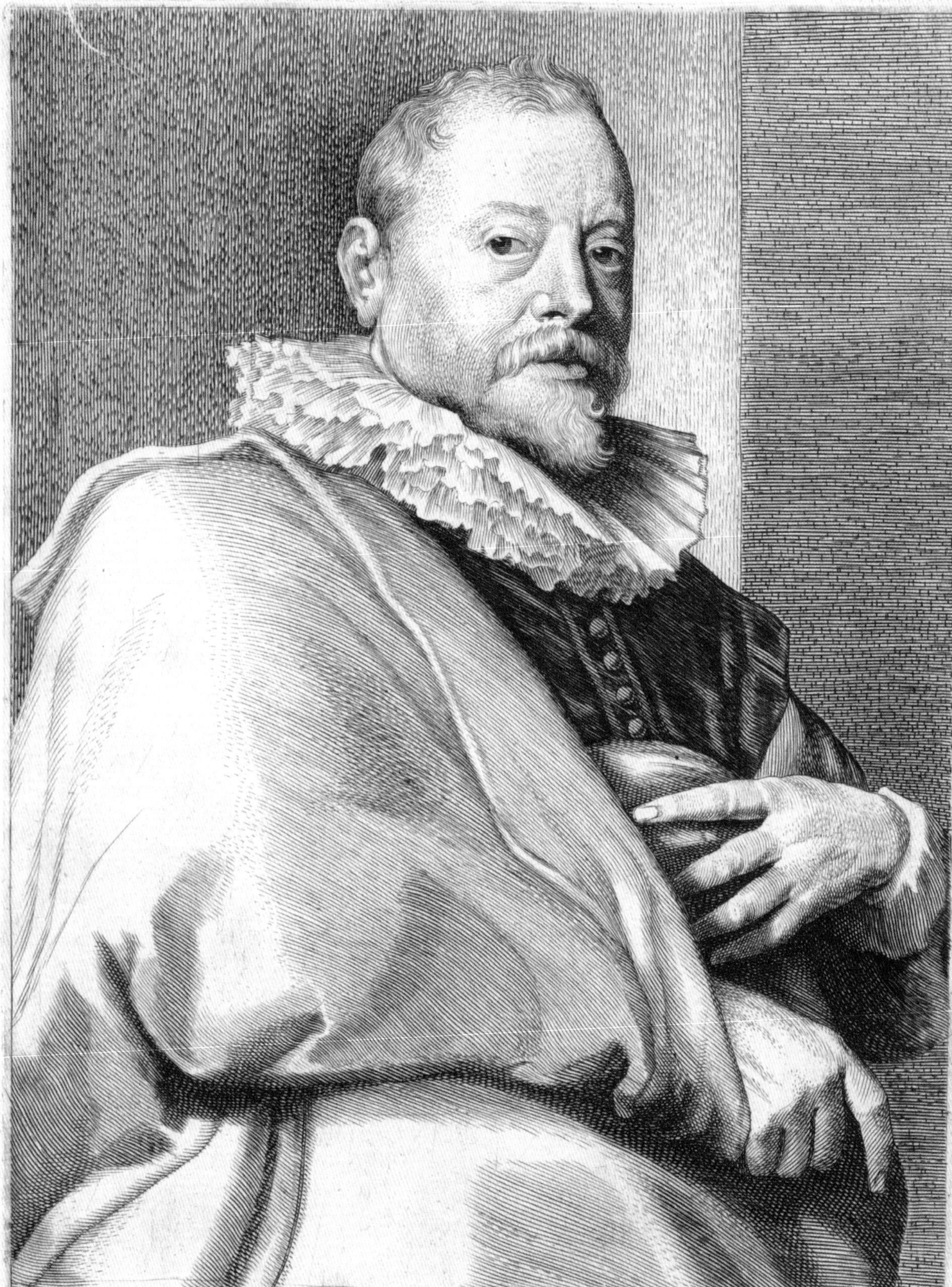

THEODORVS GALLE

Ant. van Dyck pinxit *Mart. vanden Enden excudit Cum priuilegio*

CHAPTER 5

FAMILY TIES AND THE PRINT TRADE

THE EXTENDED GALLE FAMILY

> I will have my brother-in-law Galle prepare 500 colored prints on parchment; they are far superior to what Cnobbaert has. There is a small difference in price, namely 8 st., but their greater elegance compensates that completely.[1]

5.1 Lucas Vorsterman after Anthony van Dyck, *Portrait of Theodore Galle*, 1630–1646, engraving, 236 × 157 mm. Amsterdam, Rijksmuseum: RPK RP-P-OB-33.113.

Thus wrote Balthasar Moretus I to the Münster bookseller Bernhard Raesfeld on 19 June 1631, advising him that colored prints on parchment supplied by Theodore Galle were superior to those sold by a fellow Antwerp bookseller, Jan Cnobbaert. Some two weeks later, on 4 July 1631, Moretus sent Raesfeld 500 such prints prepared by Galle. Moretus charged Raesfeld 50 fl., which was the equivalent of 2 st. per image, one of the cheaper rates Galle asked for illuminated prints on parchment.[2] Moretus hid neither his personal connection with Galle nor his preference (biased or not) for the prints Galle provided. Their mutually beneficial working relationship was the result of decades of professional interaction and personal contact between the two families.

Begun by Balthasar's grandfather Christopher Plantin and Galle's father, Philips, the personal links between the two families were solidified when Theodore Galle (fig. 5.1) married Moretus's sister Catharina on 2 August 1598. Catharina's parents, Jan Moretus I and Martine Plantin, marked the occasion by promising the newlyweds a generous dowry of 1,000 fl. and a furnished room (or an extra 400 fl.), in addition to allowing them (and any child who might be born) to live at their home free of charge for one year. Philips Galle and his wife, Catharina van Rollant, similarly promised to give the couple 1,000 fl., or the equivalent in other goods. Galle accepted 200 fl. immediately from Jan Moretus and allowed him to retain the rest temporarily, until he needed the extra funds (fig. 5.2).[3] The intimate, enduring nature of this official bond between the two families is evident from the regularity with which members of either branch were chosen as godparents for children born to the other side of the family tree.[4] Professionally, Theodore's and Catharina's marriage also most likely contributed to Jan Moretus's decision in 1600 to employ Theodore for the production and printing of the vast majority of the intaglio illustrations included in his numerous publications. This highly lucrative position was subsequently held by both Jan I's and Theodore's heirs until the mid-1670s.[5] The various ties between the two families may also account for another significant professional boost that Galle enjoyed from the sale of extraordinary quantities of his independent print publications via the Moretuses. Thus benefitting from far more than an occasional recommendation of his work by Balthasar Moretus, Theodore

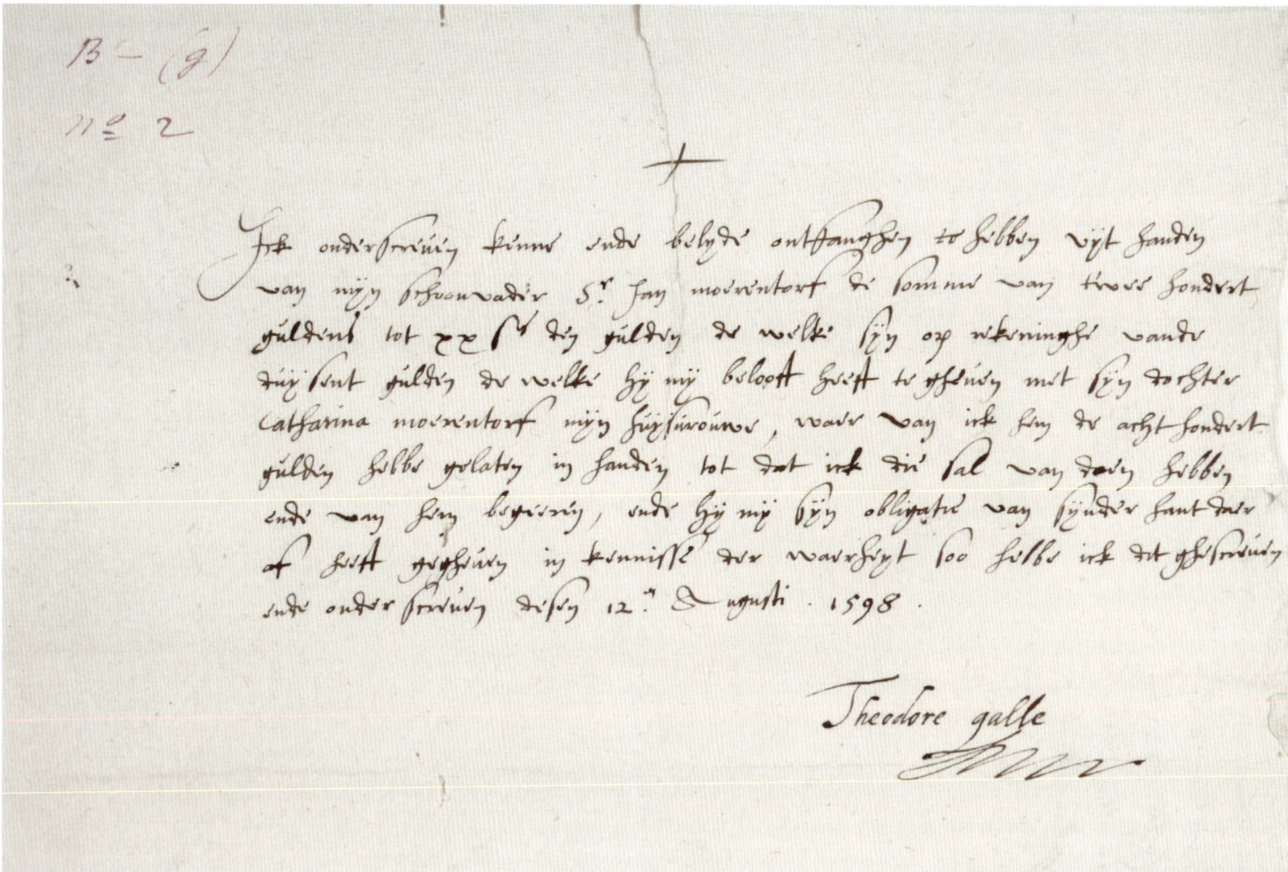

B-(9)

No 2

Ick onderschreven kenne ende belyde ontfanghen te hebben uyt handen van mijn schoonvader Sr Jan moerentorf de somme van twee hondert gulden tot xx st den gulden de welcke syn op rekeninghe vande duysent gulden de welcke hij mij belooft heeft te gheven met syn dochter Catharina moerentorf mijn huysvrouwe, waer van ick hem de acht hondert gulden hebbe gelaten in handen tot dat ick die sal van doen hebben ende van hem begeeren, ende hij mij syn obligatie van sijnder hant daer af heeft gegheven in kennisse der waerheyt soo hebbe ick dit gheschreven ende onderschreven desen 12en Augusti 1598.

Theodore galle

5.2 Theodore Galle's receipt of 200 florins from Jan Moretus I as part of Catharina Moerentorf's dowry, 12 August 1598. Antwerp, Museum Plantin-Moretus: Arch. 95bis, *Recueil de lettres Renette*, folder B-g-2.

5.3 Theodore Galle after Johannes Stradanus, *The Visitation*, 1586, engraving, 185 × 137 mm. Brussels, The Royal Library, Print Department: S.I 37891.

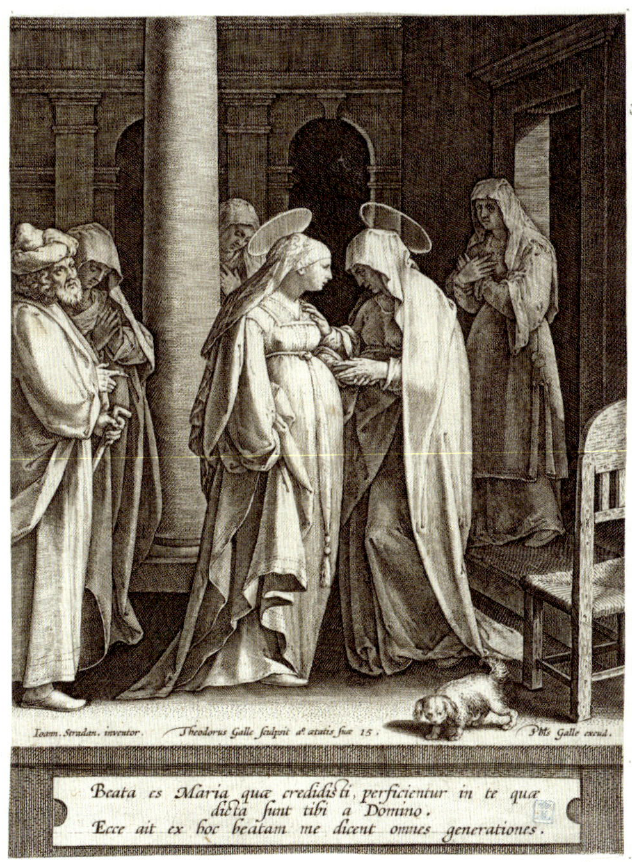

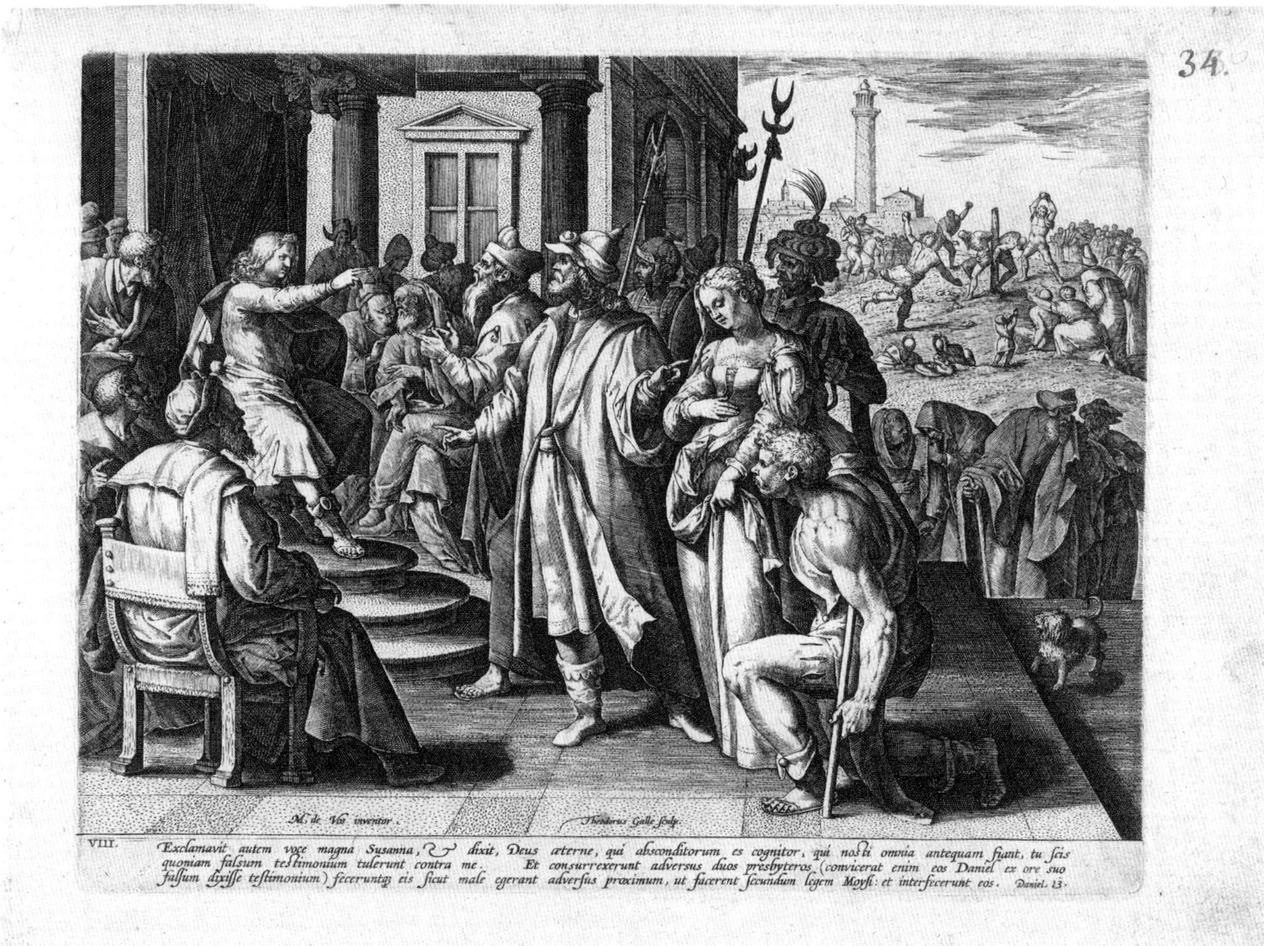

5.4 Theodore Galle after Maarten de Vos, *Thou Shalt not Bear False Witness against Thy Neighbor (Susanna and the Elders)*, from the series *The Ten Commandments*, after 1586, engraving, 193 × 244 mm. Amsterdam, Rijksmuseum: RPK RP-P-1981–162. Appendix 1: PG-116.

far outstripped all other Antwerp print publishers (including his own father) in the value of the work he sold in this fashion.

THEODORE GALLE

As Philips Galle's eldest son, the print publisher Volcxken Diericx's godchild, and Jan Moretus I's son-in-law, Theodore Galle enjoyed both a privileged position in the Antwerp art world and ready access to an array of international outlets for his work.[6] Trained in engraving from his youth, Theodore was already an accomplished practitioner of the craft by the time he was fifteen. He publicly asserted this fact by adding his age to his signature – "Theodorus Galle sculpsit a° aetatis suae 15" – on an engraving of the *Visitation* after Johannes Stradanus that he completed in 1586 (fig. 5.3).[7] Soon afterwards, Theodore was contributing engravings to a variety of his father's publications (fig. 5.4), alongside Jan Collaert II, his brother-in-law Adriaen Collaert, and his future brother-in-law Charles de Mallery. Following his return from Rome by 1595, Theodore was admitted to the Guild of St Luke in Antwerp and continued to complete engravings for his father (then nearly sixty years old). Nonetheless, shortly after his marriage to Jan Moretus I's daughter Catharina in 1598, he, like his brother and brothers-in-law, began to strike out on his own.

5.5 Theodore Galle, *Philistis*, print 108 in Galle's series *Illustrium imagines ex antiquis marmoribus*, 1598, engraving, ca. 140 × 100 mm. Antwerp, Museum Plantin-Moretus: A 832. Appendix 1: TG-7.

5.6 Theodore Galle, *Pythagoras*, print 124 in Galle's series *Illustrium imagines ex antiquis marmoribus*, 1598, engraving, ca. 140 × 100 mm. Antwerp, Museum Plantin-Moretus: A 832. Appendix 1: TG-7.

An important example of Theodore's early success as an independent engraver and print publisher is his *Illustrium imagines, ex antiquis marmoribus.* Completed in 1598, the series contained 151 finely engraved images of Greek and Roman busts from Fulvius Ursinus's collection of antique sculpture, gems, and coins, which Galle had consulted while in Rome several years earlier (figs. 5.5 and 5.6). Galle began to supply Jan Moretus with numerous copies of the series for resale in September, just one month after his marriage to Catharina. Moretus sent the first six of some thirty-six copies to another of his relatives, the bookseller Adriaen Perier in Paris.[8] Required to provide the Antwerp city government ("messieurs de la ville") with one copy of each of his new publications at the end of the year, Moretus also added Galle's work to his annual delivery at the end of 1598.[9] Whether this was simply an attempt to help advertise his son-in-law's publication or whether it was an indication that Moretus was actively involved in producing the series is not clear. However, the fact that Moretus duly continued to credit Galle for the full value of what he supplied (at the significant sum of 3 fl. per copy) suggests it was solely Galle's project.

In the following year, Moretus purchased more than 100 additional copies, just over half of which he sent to the Frankfurt fairs (forty-two in the spring and twelve in the fall).[10] Among those who bought the series in Frankfurt were the booksellers Georg Willer II from Augsburg (four copies), Giovanni Battista Giotti from Venice (two copies), Jacob Proos from Prague (three copies), and François le Fèvre from Geneva (one copy), as well as the art dealer Hubert Caymox from Nuremberg (two copies).[11] At home in Antwerp, Galle's publication was also remarkably popular. Moretus sold several copies each to such far-flung booksellers as Christophe Beys in Lille, Juan Boyer in Medina del Campo, and Ascanius de Renialme in London, in addition to sending another four copies to Perier in Paris, and one copy each to four booksellers in Gdańsk or Kraków, for whom Gerard de Jode's widow, Passchijnke

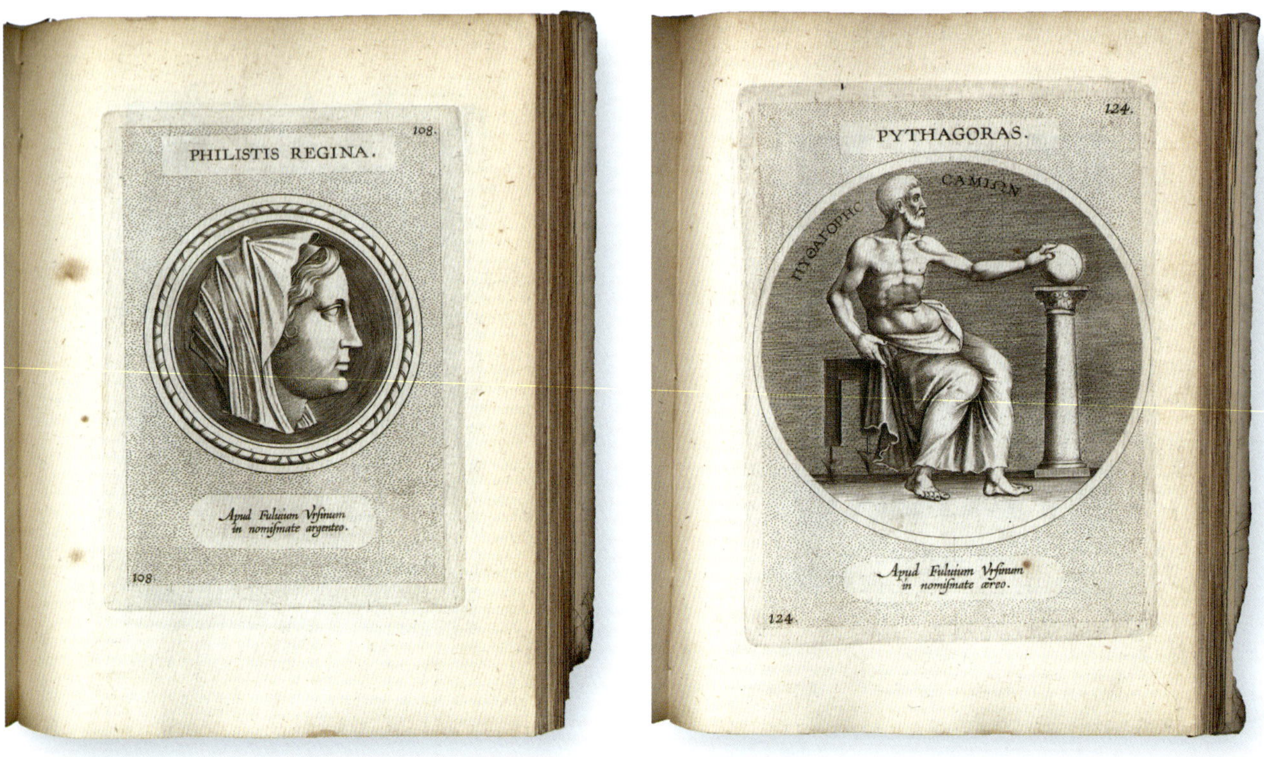

van Gelre, served as the intermediary.[12] Moretus also sold single copies of the series to an extraordinary array of private individuals, several of whom had some link to Italy. These included: Hendrik Halmale, the mayor of Antwerp; Carlo Lanfranchi, an Italian merchant in Antwerp; Louis d'Orleans, a political refugee from Paris; Lambert vander Burch, the dean of St Mary's Cathedral in Utrecht; Ottavio Mirto Frangipani, the papal nuncio in Brussels; and the Duke of Mantua.[13] Although Galle continued to supply Moretus with copies of this work through 1605 (the year before Moretus published an extensive commentary by Joannes Faber on these images, which was routinely combined with an expanded series of Galle's portraits), the interest in it among Moretus's clients, both in Antwerp and in Frankfurt, had waned considerably. Some forty copies were provided over a period of six years, and most were sent to either the Frankfurt fair or booksellers in Paris. Beyond these two primary outlets, De Renialme purchased two more copies, while only an occasional copy was sold to booksellers in the Low Countries, such as Germain vande Wervel in Mons and Hendrik Hompes in Roermond, to private individuals, for instance Jacques Charondelet in Liège, a member of the local clergy, and to the Jesuit college in Ghent.[14]

Galle's initial transactions with Jan Moretus simultaneously attests to Galle's own burgeoning independent work as a print dealer. Despite the numerous sales of this one intriguing series, it is evident that Galle also introduced a variety of imagery to his oeuvre and swiftly expanded his own network of clients within just five years of the first appearance of the *Illustrium imagines*. For example, he published large, impressive engravings, including his 1599 *Icones novem Graecorum*, a broadside with portraits of nine Greek scholars (Appendix 1, TG-19). Containing a dedication to the Jesuit Order in which Galle identifies himself as the engraver, this publication may have marked the start of a personal campaign to win the favor of this influential order. Jan Moretus promptly sent sixty of the seventy-five impressions that Galle sold him to the 1599 spring Frankfurt fair; fifty were soon sold, above all to Georg Willer II (ten copies), Balthasar Caymox from Nuremberg (twelve copies), Hubert Caymox (20 copies), and Jacob Proos (5 copies). Most of these individuals had also purchased copies of Galle's *Illustrium imagines*.[15] However, Galle's broadside does not appear to have been as popular among Moretus's other clients as was the *Illustrium imagines* since local sales were limited to one copy purchased by the bookseller Germain vander Wervel, who periodically bought works from Galle directly. Moretus's subsequent acquisition of twenty-five impressions on parchment for distribution via Frankfurt later that year suggests that the fair proved to be Moretus's most fruitful outlet.[16]

Regardless of the potentially mixed success of this broadside, Galle did establish profitable connections with a number of Jesuits and periodically supplied several Jesuit colleges with prints. The earliest and most striking examples of such ties are several print series he produced to accompany the theological emblem books written by Joannes David and printed by Jan Moretus I between 1601 and 1610.[17] But David was not Galle's only personal contact among the Jesuits. For example, Maximiliaan van Habbeke asked the Moretuses to pay money he owed Galle in 1614, and Galle paid Balthasar Moretus in 1621 for a specially bound breviary Habbeke had ordered, indicating that they were still in contact at that time. Similarly, in 1623, Balthasar Moretus was asked to settle debts that the Jesuit colleges in Halle and Maubeuge had with Galle and that amounted to some 97 fl. from Halle and 13 fl. 10 st. from Maubeuge.[18] Balthasar's occasional independent sales of Galle's prints to several Jesuit colleges suggest what prints might have been bought with these sums. For instance, in 1632, the college in Breda purchased nine large prints in folio at 4 st. each and sixteen prints in folio at 2.5 st. each, for a total of 3 fl. and 16 st. for all twenty-five prints from Galle. He provided

Balthasar Moretus with comparably priced prints for the Jesuit college in Halle in 1625 (in this case, six at 4 st. and eighteen at 2.5 st.), for a total of 3 fl. 9 st. (although Balthasar added a profit margin on the resale of these prints by charging the college at Halle 4 fl. 4 st. for all twenty-four images).[19] Consequently, when the college in Halle owed Galle 97 fl. in 1623, they may have been paying him for roughly 600 to 700 folio and large folio prints.

Even though the subjects of the images purchased by the Jesuits are not specified, other transactions indicate that Galle provided Jan Moretus with a diverse range of religious publications for further distribution soon after *Illustrium imagines* appeared. For instance, Moretus sold some prints identified as trees ("arbor") that were most likely genealogical trees, either of either religious orders, such as the Dominicans, or of Christ. Known examples of such images include Galle's large *Tree of Human Life* (*Arbor humanae vitae*) (456 × 329 mm), engraved anonymously after Nicolaus Christophorus Radzivilus and on the market by 1613 (fig. 7.14), and two independent, large renditions of a *Tree of the Franciscan Order*, printed from multiple plates, one published by Peeter de Jode I in 1626 (1,862 × 1,286 mm) and the other (548 × 400 mm) published by Jan Boel.[20] The variety of renditions of this general theme from different print publishers in this period reveals an unexpected interest in such imagery, which is poorly documented by the disparate, extant impressions.

Moretus also sold impressions of Galle's more conventional subject matter, including an assortment of representations of the Virgin and, in particular, the Sorrows of the Virgin, to the merchant Rocho di Gabrielli for export to Gdańsk in 1602. Although this sale may have represented an early breakthrough in a distant international print market for Galle, the fact that Di Gabrielli simultaneously spent far more on images published by Adriaen Collaert, Galle's brother-in-law, and the internationally renowned Hieronymus Wierix may reflect Galle's status as a newcomer.[21]

In addition, Galle was the intermediary in the sale of Philips Galle's 1603 publication of the *Life of Saint Catherine* during the first decade of the seventeenth century, before he began to distribute it himself after Philips Galle's death in 1612 (fig. 7.12). While Jan Moretus sold his first copy to Thomas Sailly at the Jesuit college in Brussels, subsequent copies went to booksellers in the Low Countries (Jan Scheffer II in 's Hertoghenbosch and Hendrik Barentsen in Amsterdam) and Cologne (Bernhard Wolters and Anton Hierat I).[22] Together, the sales of the *Life of Saint Catherine* disclose the wide variation in the profit margins that the Moretuses added to any given work. While Theodore consistently supplied the series to them at 1 fl. (or 20 st.) per copy, their resale of it ranged from the same, at-cost price (to Wolters in 1606 and Barentsen in 1618) to an elevated price with a profit margin of 4, 5, or 6 st. per copy for Hierat in 1611, Sailly in 1603, and Scheffer in 1610, respectively. It is not known whether the Galles were aware of these subjective variations in price, but the Moretuses' additional charges would explain why some buyers, such as the Jesuits in Halle, preferred to place their ongoing, potentially larger orders directly with Galle rather than with the Moretuses.

Though far from the immense initial success of Galle's *Illustrium imagines*, these early sales records attest to a burgeoning print publishing business that was supported by Galle's active commitment to building up a diverse stock of publications and by the appeal of such publications to a variety of buyers. Combined with what is already known of Galle's regular employment from 1600 by Jan Moretus for the production and printing of the vast majority of the intaglio book illustrations in his editions, these two factors clarify how Galle and his wife, Catharina, were able to purchase Philips Galle's home and workshop at the sign of "De Witte Lelie" (The White Lily) in the Huidevettersstraat on 5 March 1605 for an unspecified sum of money.[23]

Between 1608 and Galle's death in December 1633, sales of his publications via the Moretuses expanded significantly. While the remarkable array of individuals who purchased copies of Galle's *Illustrium imagines* in 1599 was never matched in his subsequent transactions involving the Moretuses, these transactions nevertheless demonstrate both the means by which prints reached distant destinations and the range of products Galle sold, often in unexpectedly large quantities. Consider, for example, the case of the Jesuit Pedro de Angulo in Seville, for whom the Antwerp merchant Diego Pardo Lopez regularly served as an intermediary. De Angulo initially wanted to order two book illustrations from Galle for Juan Sebastian's publication *De el bien excellencias y obligaciones de el estado clerical e sacerdotal* (Seville, 1615). In this instance, payments for Galle's work – encompassing the costs of purchasing the copper, engraving the plates, and printing the images – were made via the Moretuses.[24] However, De Angulo also asked to buy a selection of some 278 prints from Galle, in addition to 300 from Charles de Mallery and an unspecified quantity from Hieronymus Wierix, in 1615. For this order, Balthasar Moretus was the primary contact, and Pardo Lopez oversaw the finances. Similarities between this sale and one in 1607, involving Pardo Lopez's purchase of hundreds of images each from Galle, De Mallery, and Wierix, begs the question of whether this too was ultimately intended for De Angulo or someone else.[25]

Other merchants also occasionally feature in the Moretuses' records related to Galle and are often associated with isolated, exceptional orders of prints. For instance, the family of the Antwerp merchant Jacques de Braa purchased thousands of prints at a time in both 1625 and 1626.[26] Nevertheless, the vast majority of the Moretuses' clients interested in Galle's publications were other European booksellers from a number of different countries. One remarkable example is Giovanni Paolo Gelli in Rome, who, in 1608, placed a huge, one-time order with Jan Moretus for books, prints, and specially illustrated text editions worth more than 1,000 fl. Of this amount, more than 200 fl. were paid for prints provided by Charles de Mallery (25 fl.), Peeter de Jode I (26 fl. 8.75 st.), Adriaen Collaert (46 fl. 19 st.), Philips Galle (62 fl. 10.5 st.), and Theodore and Cornelis Galle (45 fl. 15.25 st.). Theodore Galle's contribution is noteworthy for the mix of items he could offer within a decade of when he began to manage his own print workshop. His prints ranged from genre images designed by Pieter Bruegel I and originally published by Hieronymus Cock (fig. 5.7; most likely purchased by Galle at the 1601 estate sale of Volcxken Diericx's property) to new devotional images from Galle's own assortment of publications (fig. 5.8) to 1250 unspecified images sold in bulk.[27]

Aside from Jan Moretus's initial sales of numerous copies of Galle's *Illustrium imagines* to his relations Adriaen Perier and Christophe Beys, there is a notable absence of transactions with other Parisian book or print dealers. Consequently, it is probable that Galle, like his father Philips, distributed his publications to this important market via his own connections. Nevertheless, the Moretuses sporadically sold impressions of his prints to booksellers beyond the capital, such as Jean Dassonleville in Hesdin in the Pas-de-Calais, who purchased hundreds of unspecified, plain prints on paper in bulk from Galle annually between 1624 and 1626.[28]

The Moretuses' relatively limited sale of Galle's prints to booksellers in the Low Countries and to those supporting the burgeoning print market in Cologne may likewise reflect Galle's preference to mange these markets on his own. Nevertheless, glimpses of the significant demand for his work in these regions can still be gleaned from the Moretuses' sporadic transactions. For example, in 1630 and 1631, Johann Kinckius, their former apprentice from Cologne, bought a selection of canons and hundreds of prints on parchment. These ranged from plain prints sold at 4 fl. per 100 to a selection of the best illuminated images Galle had at 12 fl. 10 st. per 100.[29] Purchases by Jean Valentin II of Namur reveal yet another aspect of

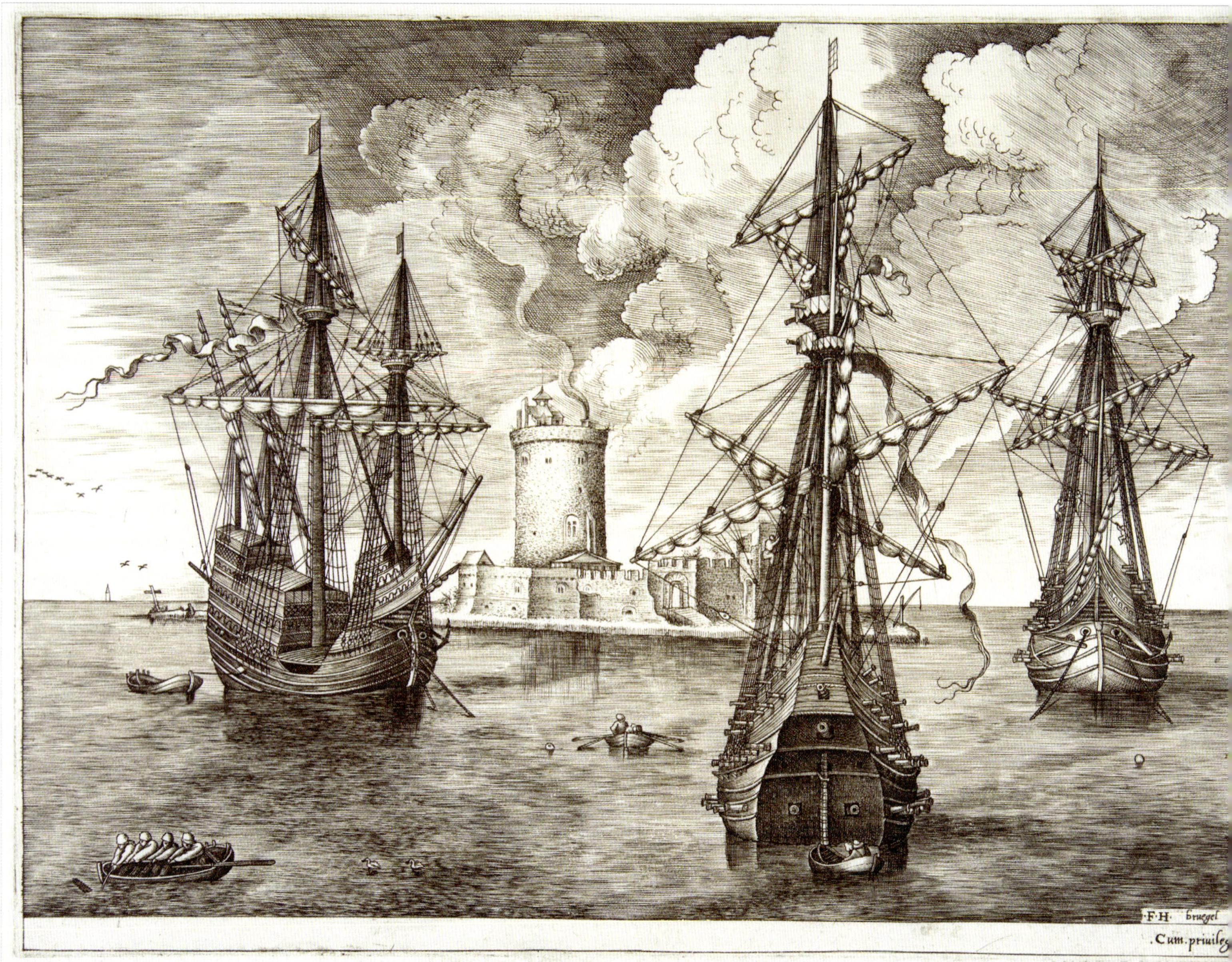

5.7 Frans Huys after Pieter Bruegel I, *Four-Master and Two Three-Masters Anchored near a Fortified Island*, from the series *The Sailing Vessels*, originally published by Hieronymus Cock ca. 1561–1565 and reissued by Theodore Galle by 1608, engraving, 225 × 294 mm. New York, The Metropolitan Museum of Art: Bequest of Alexandrine Sinsheimer, 1958 (59.534.23). Image courtesy of the Metropolitan Museum of Art. Appendix 1: TG-22.

5.8 Anonymous, *Donum pietatis*, print 2 from the series *Ave Maris Stella*, by 1608, engraving, ca. 131 × 81 mm. Antwerp, Museum Plantin-Moretus: PK: I/G.321. Appendix 1: TG-1.

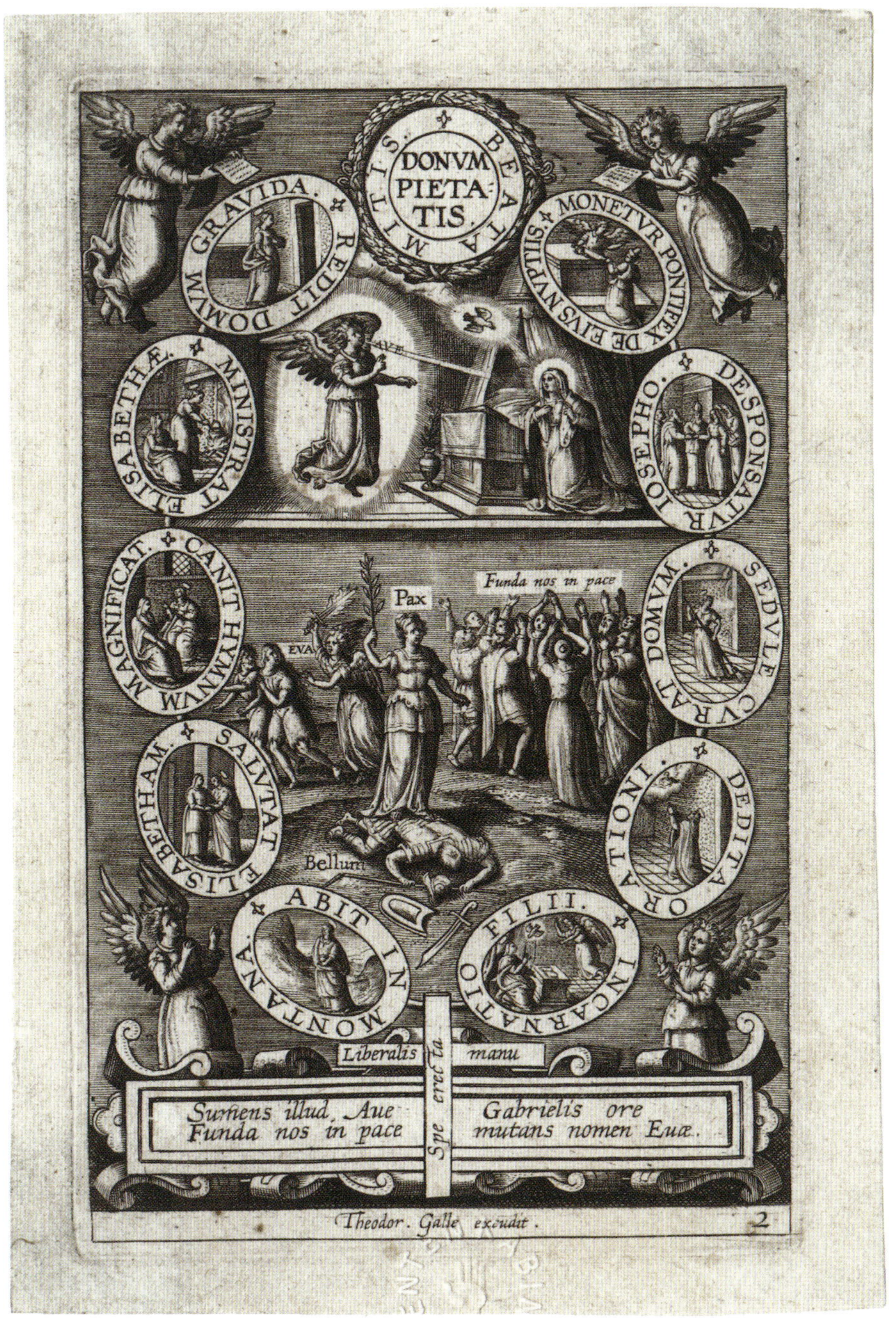

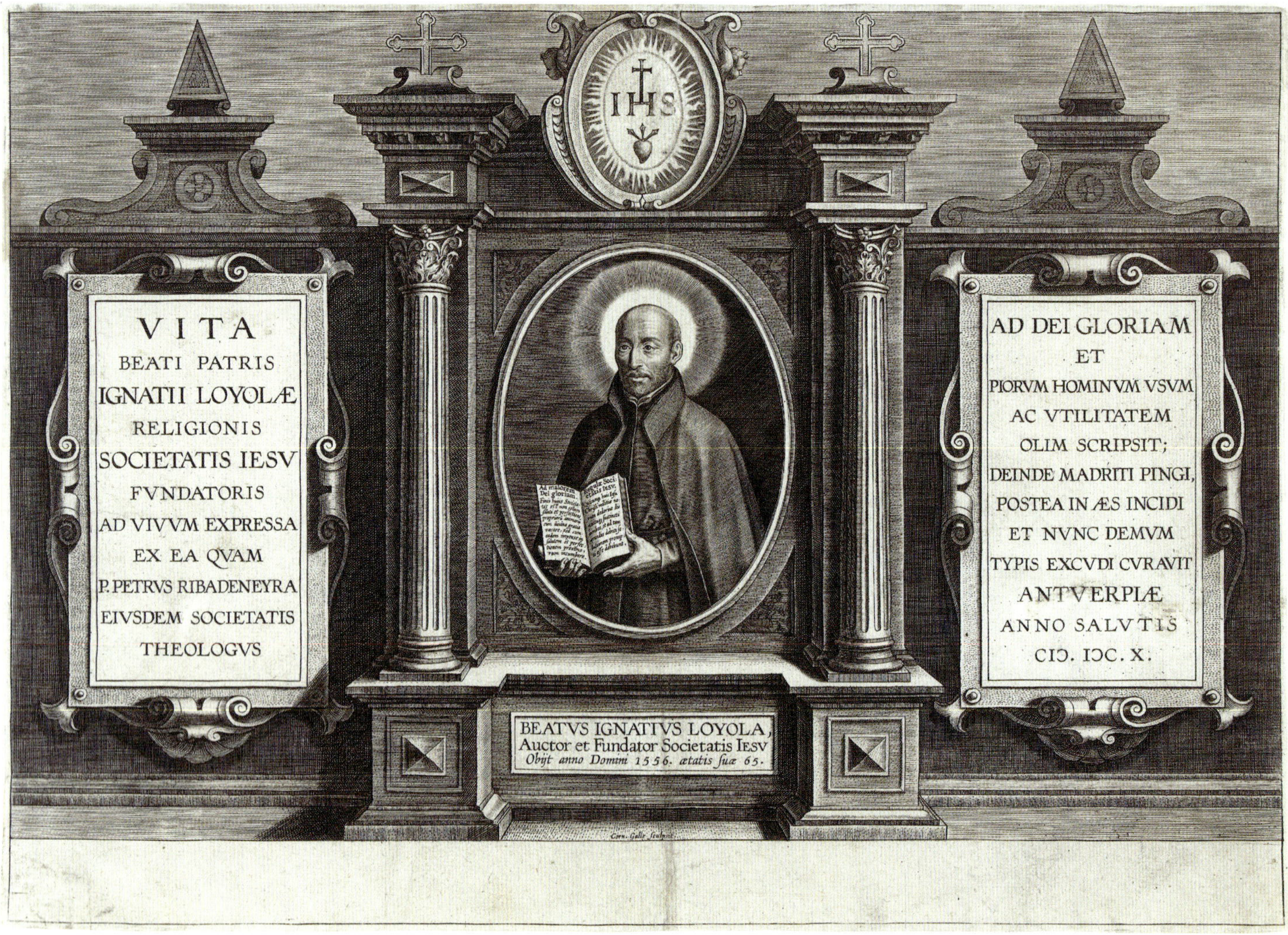

5.9 Cornelis Galle, title plate for *Life of Saint Ignatius*, 1610, engraving, 263 × 365 mm. Amsterdam, Rijksmuseum: RP-P-1963-281. Appendix 1: TG-10.

Galle's offerings because Valentin periodically bought large prints in folio individually rather than at bulk rates, as the Jesuit orders of Breda, Halle, and Oudenaarde also did on occasion. For example, in 1613 and 1618, Valentin acquired limited quantities (four to seventeen impressions each) of individual, but unspecified, prints priced from 1.5 st. (for a double leaf ["feulles doubles"]) to 2, 2.5, 3, or 4 st. (for works in folio) per piece. Valentin's 1613 purchase of two copies of Galle's *Tree of Human Life*, which measures 456 × 329 mm (Appendix 1, TG-29), for 3 st. offers an intriguing indication of the possible size of the folio prints Galle was selling at these rates, particularly when these prices are compared with Galle's bulk rates for smaller images, including the unspecified works in 8° that Valentin simultaneously purchased at the common 36 st. per-100-print rate, which amounted to just .36 st. per image.[30]

Nevertheless, the two most important outlets by far for the Moretuses' distribution of Galle's work were the Frankfurt book fair and Bernhard Raesfeld of Münster (in what is now the North Rhine-Westphalia state of Germany). Raesfeld's purchases are noteworthy because of the large sums he paid annually for hundreds of prints bought in bulk between 1630 and 1632, after which time the Thirty Years War may have made trade between Münster and Antwerp too risky to continue for the rest of the decade. When dealing with the Moretuses, Raesfeld appears to have taken Balthasar's advice to heart since he did not buy any prints from Jan Cnobbaert. Rather, he alternated his purchases of several distinct types of prints from Galle – ranging from plain prints on paper and plain prints on parchment to different grades of illuminated prints on parchment – with purchases of different (often more costly) categories of illuminated prints from Michael Snijders.[31]

Even though Raesfeld's purchases from Galle were remarkable, amounting to some 240 fl., they still fell short of the more than 350 fl. the Moretuses spent on buying up often astounding quantities of a few of Galle's newest print series for resale at the Frankfurt fairs. First deployed in 1599, when Jan I bought significant quantities of Galle's *Illustrium imagines* and portraits of Greek scholars, this practice peaked with the Moretuses' 1610 purchase of 110 copies of Galle's brand-new series of the *Life of Saint Ignatius* at 2 fl. per copy (fig. 5.9) for sale at the fall fair.[32] The new series met with immediate, widespread success among numerous German booksellers, as well as individuals from Prague, Kraków, and Paris. Georg Willer II from Augsburg, Balthasar Caymox from Nuremberg, and Bernhard Wolters from Cologne bought the most copies.[33] Jan Moretus II, in his guise as an independent bookseller, also purchased thirty-nine sets of Galle's *Portraits of Scholars from the Low Countries* (*Illustrium Galliae Belgicae scriptorum icones et elogia*) when it was published in 1608, at least thirty of which he sent to Frankfurt for sale at the fairs that year.[34] Balthasar I was much more restrained in this regard. His only dealings in Galle's prints at Frankfurt occurred some two decades later and were limited to a modest investment in just eighteen copies of Galle's 1630 publication, *Holy Founders of Religious Orders* (*Sancti fundatores religiosorum ordinum*) (fig. 7.2), which he sent to the 1631 spring fair.[35]

As with Galle's broadside featuring Greek scholars, the Moretuses' distribution of the same works via their Antwerp business was strikingly meager in comparison. For example, their sales of the St Ignatius series consisted primarily of one copy bought by the Brussels artist Michiel Verkoven in 1610, when he was in Antwerp, and the purchase of a few copies by the booksellers Hermann Mylius and Anton Hierat I in Cologne in 1611. Notably, in each case the Moretuses added a small profit margin.[36] Once again, this stark contrast between local and international sales may reflect their recognition of Galle's right to manage his own sales from Antwerp. Indeed, the Moretuses' sales of Galle's publications at the Frankfurt fairs stand out as the only instances of their dealing in prints by an Antwerp print seller at the fairs (versus their usual activities of transporting prints or accepting payments for print sellers). Perhaps the initial, immense success of Jan Moretus's sale of the *Illustrium imagines* convinced Galle that this was one place where it was advantageous to have his in-laws represent him.

When considered as a whole, Theodore Galle's regular supply of prints to the Moretuses for resale to sundry clients reveals shifting trends in the demand for his publications that, in turn, highlight evolutions changes in the market for prints. Until 1618, the Moretuses' records feature sales of numerous print series, ranging from the *Illustrium imagines* of 1598 to several highly successful religious series, including *Miracles of the Rosary* and *Life of Saint Ignatius*, both from 1610 (Appendix 1, TG-14 and TG-10). A variety of independent prints were also periodically requested (as in Gelli's order from 1608), and by 1607, the Moretuses began to sell Galle's prints in bulk by the hundreds, as is evident from their dealings with Pardo Lopez. In 1618, however, his work was more often distributed in bulk, defined simply by the price and quantity sold, rather than by specific subjects. While some larger images were sold for 2–4 st. each, most of the Moretuses' transactions featured hundreds to thousands of prints sold at the common rate of 36 st. per 100 prints (for instance, in the purchases by the heirs of the Antwerp merchant Jacques de Braa). By 1629, Galle had expanded his offerings to include a variety of sorts of illuminated prints, most of which were printed on parchment, such as the works ordered by Bernhard Raesfeld. These transactions were only occasionally interspersed with the sale of print series, like the *Holy founders of religious orders* from 1630 (fig. 7.2) and a few isolated prints, in particular canons and a game, commonly referred to as the *Goose Game*, which is still played in Belgium today.[37]

During the brief period between Galle's death in December 1633 and her own in 20 May 1636, Catharina Moerentorf was the official proprietor of the Galle workshop, and the Moretuses' sale of these publications declined significantly. While she still supplied some older, renowned print series, such as Cock's *Portraits of Famous Painters from the Low Countries* or some selection of Philips Galle's portraits of scholars, bulk print sales were now more often limited to smaller groups of twelve or twenty-four prints each.[38] Only once Jan Galle took over the management of the workshop, following the settlement of Catharina's estate in May 1636, were mass sales of Galle's prints resumed, in particular to the burgeoning market in Gdańsk. In just 1635 and 1639 alone, the Gdańsk bookseller Kaspar Förster purchased more than 3,000 prints in bulk, ranging from plain images on paper to illuminated ones on parchment, worth nearly 185 fl.[39] However, it is important to recall that when Jan Galle acquired his father's stock of plates in 1636, it contained some 3,260 plates, roughly one-third of which were smaller, unspecified plates that might have been used to fulfill these large orders for prints in bulk.[40] The remaining two-thirds of the stock consisted of assorted print series and individual, larger plates produced by Galle, in addition to the numerous older plates that he had acquired from others, in particular Philips Galle and Volcxken Diericx. Jan featured this last group of plates, in addition to others that he had purchased separately, in a stock list that he published around 1650. This document indicates that there was still a market for these larger plates, most of which dated from the late sixteenth to early seventeenth centuries; they could be sold alongside any smaller devotional images that Jan printed for sale en masse. While seemingly antiquated, their appeal may have extended beyond the basic subjects represented since they may have satisfied a collector's desire to own specific series by older, legendary artists.[41]

Though far less numerous, a variety of additional transactions involving Theodore Galle highlight other aspects of his own work as a print publisher. In particular, Galle occasionally asked the Moretuses to assist him with the transport of packages to his clients. While such requests were common for shipments to and from the Frankfurt fairs, Galle's engagement of the Moretuses for such deliveries to other locations remained minimal and infrequent, indicating that he may have preferred alternative means for supplying his clients. Galle also assisted the Moretuses with their trade in books and maps. In some instances, the Moretuses gave him items purchased by a third party, on the assumption that he would convey them to that client. In other cases, clients who owed the Moretuses money gave their payments to Galle, asking him to convey the funds to the Moretuses. In either case, the reliance upon Galle to complete such tasks suggests that he was a familiar, trusted figure with whom third parties dealt independently. Together, these additional activities reveal the types of contacts Galle established over the course of his career – from members of the clergy to various dealers in books, prints, and maps – and a sampling of the regions in which his work was sought.

For example, among professional tradesmen in prints, maps, and books, Galle served as a middleman for the transfer of payments between the Moretuses and both Jean du Puis in Lille and John Boswell in London, while Jean Morel in Lille asked the Moretuses to pay Galle in his name.[42] The Moretuses also gave Galle packages of maps to convey to Jean Leonard in Brussels, Willem Jansz Blaeu in Amsterdam, and Georg Meuting in Cologne.[43] Conversely, Galle asked the Moretuses to ship packages in his name to several of their mutual contacts. These included Du Puis, Blaeu, and the merchant-bookseller Paulus Claessens in Gdańsk, as well as several booksellers in Cologne – Bernhard Wolters, Hermann Mylius, and Cornelis van Egmont. Further, similar contacts were Claes Jansz Visscher in Amsterdam and a few print sellers with whom Galle also exchanged goods via the Moretuses' shop in Frankfurt, namely Crispijn de Passe, Justus Sadeler, and Abraham Hogenberg.[44]

Among the clergy, Galle's personal contacts extended beyond the Jesuits. For example, in 1611, Galle asked the Moretuses' assistance for the delivery of an exceptionally large allotment of four packages and two rolls of prints; the shipment was intended for the Antwerp Dominican Joannes Nys and was to be conveyed via his brother Gilles Nys, who was then living in the Zilversmidstraat in Antwerp.[45] Galle also corresponded with Dionysius Villerius, a canon at the cathedral of Tournai. Whereas Villerius took advantage of his own active contact with Jan Moretus I to ask him to settle debts involving Galle in both 1605 and 1607, Galle served as a middleman for a payment from Villerius for Balthasar Moretus in 1616.[46]

However, by far the best documented and telling of these connections were interactions with acquaintances of Villerius, namely the Van Winghe brothers: Abbot Anton van Winghe at the Benedictine abbey in Liessies and Hieronymus van Winghe, who was a canon at the cathedral of Tournai. Between March 1613 and July 1633 (some five months prior to Galle's death), both men routinely asked Galle to make payments to Balthasar Moretus on their behalf. These payments often ranged from 20–50 fl., but on one occasion, Galle even paid 215 fl. for Anton van Winghe. Conversely, Balthasar Moretus periodically gave Galle books to deliver to the Van Winghes.[47] Anton van Winghe's correspondence demonstrates that Galle likewise assisted him with the periodic payment of bills and conveyance of books that Van Winghe had ordered from other booksellers, independent of his dealings with the Moretuses. For example, on 14 May 1620, Van Winghe wrote to Galle's son-in-law Martinus Nutius III that Galle would pay him 370 fl. (an excessive amount, according to Van Winghe) to cover the costs of books that he had ordered from him. In a subsequent letter written to Galle on 27 October 1622, Van Winghe asked him to wait to send him some books until others that he was expecting from Frankfurt had arrived.[48] Galle may have been on even better personal terms with Hieronymus van Winghe. For example, Galle corresponded with Van Winghe to inform him of the latest news and to send him catalogues of the most recent publications available at the Frankfurt fairs, and Van Winghe composed a verse for Galle's *liber amicorum*.[49]

Although the evidence of Galle's dealings with the Van Winghes may be exceptional, the ways in which they engaged with one another were not necessarily unusual for how Galle (and other print publishers) interacted with acquaintances and potential clients. Comparable forms of exchanges are evident from Galle's contact with Villerius and various Jesuits and Jesuit orders, as well as from Galle's annual purchases of books from the Moretuses between 1601, at the start of his professional career, and 1632, a year before his death. Specifically, several of these annual purchases were listed as being intended for other individuals. In particular, copies of Abraham Ortelius's atlas were obtained for Georg Meuting at Cologne, a copy of the "Chronique des ducs de Brabant" was bought for one of the Sadelers, and one bound copy of the works of Demosthenes was procured for the Jesuit college in Maubeuge.[50] Presumably, Galle's occasional acquisition of large quantities of devotional works, such as six bound copies of litanies in Dutch (bought in April 1604), ten diurnals with engraved illustrations (purchased in May 1618), and twelve copies of Mathieu de Morgues's recent pamphlet in defense of Marie de Medici, entitled *Lettre de la Reyne Mere au Roy* and printed by Balthasar Moretus (acquired in January 1632), were similarly meant to be distributed among Galle's network of professional acquaintances.[51]

Naturally, Galle's offerings as a print publisher comprised a variety of printed images. The sales of his work via the Moretuses vividly documents which types of works were most popular among their clients. Furthermore, their records demonstrate that Theodore periodically dealt in prints produced by others. His sale of works made by his brother Cornelis Galle I is

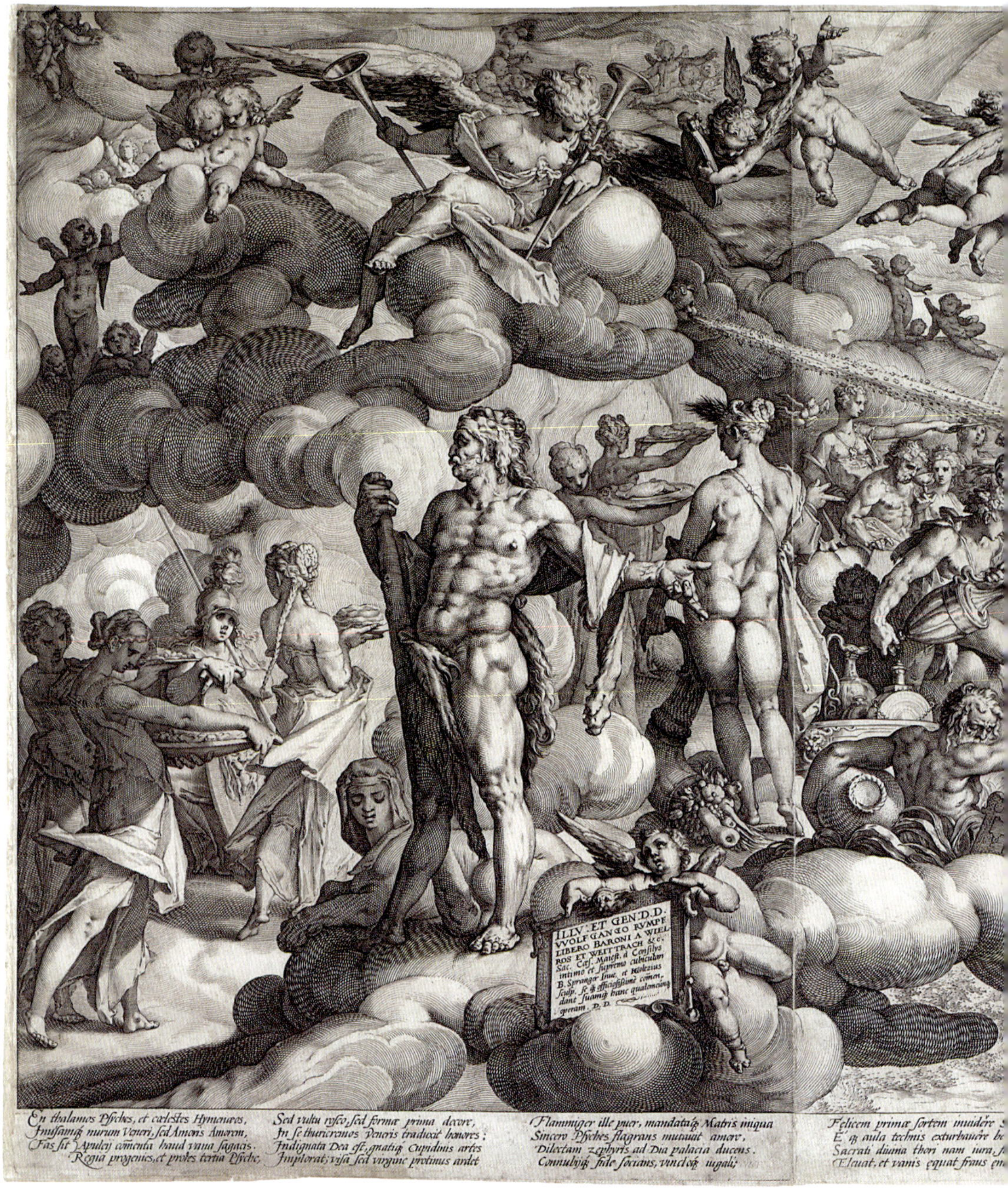

5.10 Hendrick Goltzius after Bartholomeus Spranger, *The Feast of the Gods at the Marriage of Cupid and Psyche*, 1587, engraving in three plates, 430 × 854 mm for the entire image. New York, The Metropolitan Museum of Art: Purchase, The Elisha Whittelsey Collection, The Elisha Whittelsey Fund, Martha Meltenstein Gift, A. Hyatt Mayor Purchase Fund, and Marjorie Phelps Staar Bequest, 2000 (2000.113). Image courtesy of the Metropolitan Museum of Art.

not surprising given Cornelis's participation in Theodore's workshop production through, for example, his engraving of numerous plates for the Moretuses' book illustrations. Theodore's trade in his brother's works suggests that Cornelis allowed Theodore to represent him, at least on occasion, in the distribution of his own engravings.[52] Theodore (and subsequently his son Jan) also supplied the Moretuses with prints originally published by his brother-in-law Charles de Mallery, with whom the Moretuses had regularly dealt directly until June 1626. This shift most likely occurred because De Mallery had sold his stock of plates to Galle in order to alleviate his own desperate financial situation following the death of his wife, Catharina Galle.[53]

In addition, Galle provided the Moretuses with prints by independent printmakers and publishers for resale to their clients, as his father Philips had done on several occasions in his dealings with Plantin. For example, Philips had assembled an important collection of his

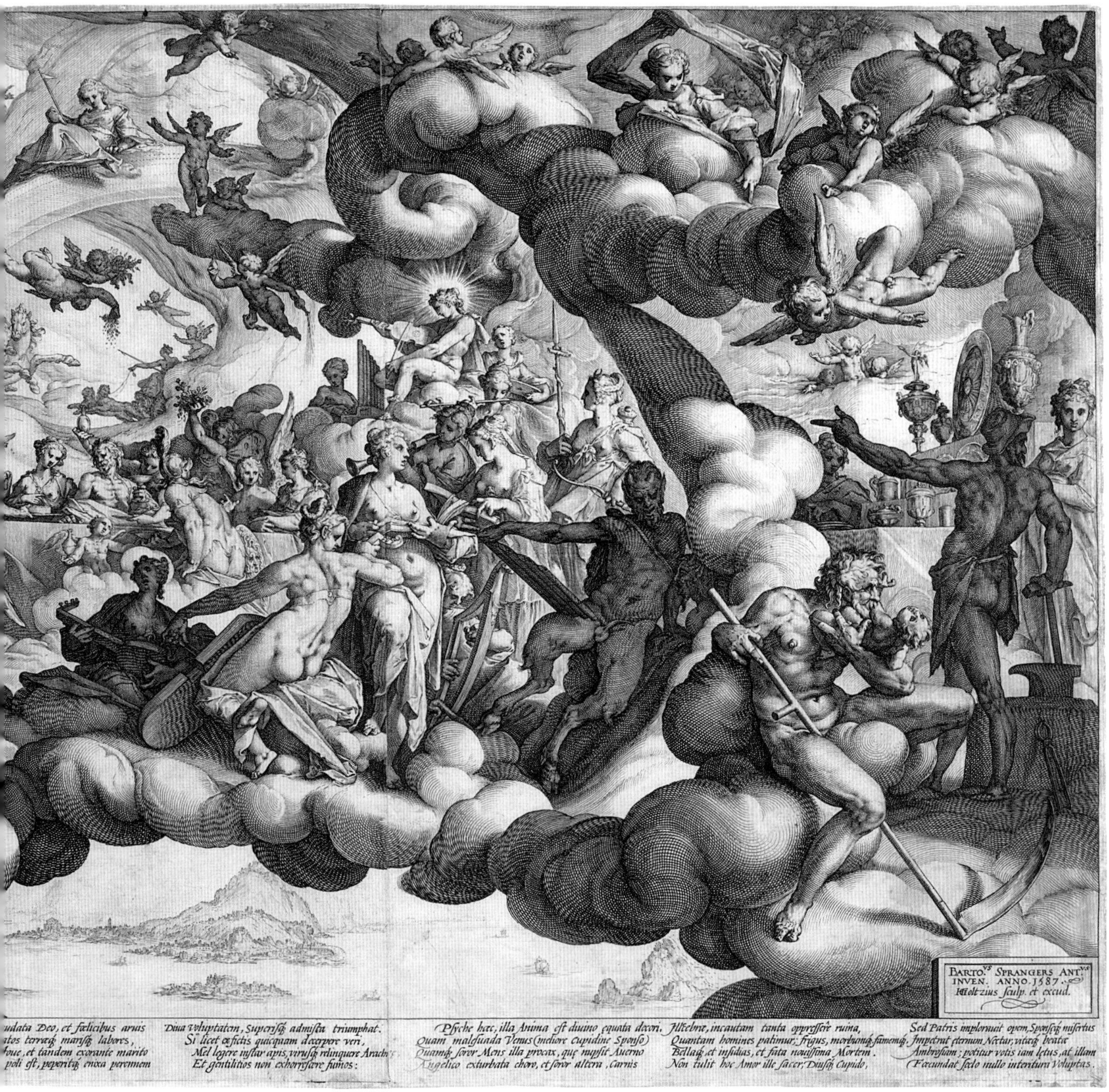

own works along with numerous prints by several contemporary Antwerp publishers for purchase by a wealthy collector, the merchant Ferdinandus Ximenes, in 1588.[54] Theodore followed this practice, as he selected prints by Hieronymus Wierix (while Wierix was still alive) for resale to the Jesuit Philippus de Peralta in 1614 and since he compiled an assortment of works by "diverse masters" that Balthasar Moretus then sold to Bernhard Raesfeld in 1632.[55] Moreover, Theodore occasionally supplied the Moretuses with specific, special images; for instance, in 1616, he sold them two impressions of Hendrick Goltzius's grand print of the *Feast of the Gods at the Marriage of Cupid and Psyche* (1587), after Bartholomeus Spranger and which extended across three plates, for 1 fl. 8 st. (or 28 st.) per impression (fig. 5.10). The trade in such prints was, once again, something Theodore would have known from his father, who had supplied Jan Moretus I with exceptional prints by Goltzius as well, offering his 1592 engraving, the *Triumph of Galatea* after Raphael, for 25 st. in 1596.[56] Presumably, Theodore would have likewise assisted other clients, such as the Van Winghes, and thus would have assumed the role of a print connoisseur and advisor for individual collectors' purchases.

Together, the Moretuses' transactions involving Theodore Galle, in particular their independent sales of his publications, underscore the extent of the interest in his work, revealing the international assortment of their clients who requested Galle's prints, as well as the quantities and types of images that were ordered. These sales most likely supplemented Galle's own distribution (and profits) significantly, through intermittent large sales at the Frankfurt fairs and the fulfillment of specific, and occasionally recurring, orders for his prints from booksellers, the clergy, and merchants, often in distant locales throughout Europe. Although Galle did not systematically ask the Moretuses to facilitate the exchange of funds and packages between himself and his network of clients, the records of when he did so highlight, nevertheless, a telling sampling of Galle's personal connections, for instance several dealers in printed images and texts in Amsterdam and Cologne, as well as isolated contacts in Gdańsk and several French cities. The relative infrequency of such records suggests that Galle preferred to manage the sale of his publications to his network of patrons independently, including to such important outlets as Paris. The glimpses of Galle's independent clients and the ways in which he interacted with them and the Moretuses contribute to a far richer and more nuanced understanding of Theodore Galle as a print publisher than one derived from a survey of his publication of religious prints. Clearly committed to maintaining personal contacts with sundry clients, in particular members of the clergy and professional associates, Galle served them in a variety of capacities and not simply as a publisher of his own plates. He was a connoisseur who selected prints from other publishers' stock or who located impressions of specific images to satisfy the wishes of individual clients, in addition to a reliable, trustworthy agent who conveyed money and other assorted items purchased elsewhere. Although Theodore may have learned many of these practices from his father, it does not appear that his son Jan was similarly engaged, at least through his interactions with the Moretuses.[57] Rather, as is demonstrated by the Moretuses' dealings with a variety of Antwerp print publishers, each had his or her own area of specialization and approach to managing their affairs. Fortunately, due to the consistent nature and unparalleled wealth of information in the Moretuses' accounts, it is possible to analyze their distinct approaches to the distribution and sale of their wares and to distinguish personal idiosyncrasies and individual market strategies within the broad realm of the international trade in prints.

ADRIAEN COLLAERT

Most likely trained independently by his father, Hans Collaert, Adriaen Collaert was making engravings for both Philips Galle and Gerard de Jode – an important patron of his father's – by the early 1580s (figs. 5.11 and 5.12).[58] Nevertheless, the appeal of working for Galle (in addition to the attraction of his daughter Josine, whom Collaert married in 1586), resulted in Collaert becoming a mainstay of Galle's workshop through the early 1590s. While in Galle's workshop, he completed diverse, often large engravings (figs. 5.13 and 5.14) and worked alongside Galle's own son Theodore and his contemporary Charles de Mallery (who also subsequently married another of Galle's daughters, Catharina). The strength of these ties with the extended Galle family is evident from whom Collaert and Josine chose to serve as godparents for their children. They asked not only Philips twice, but also Theodore Galle

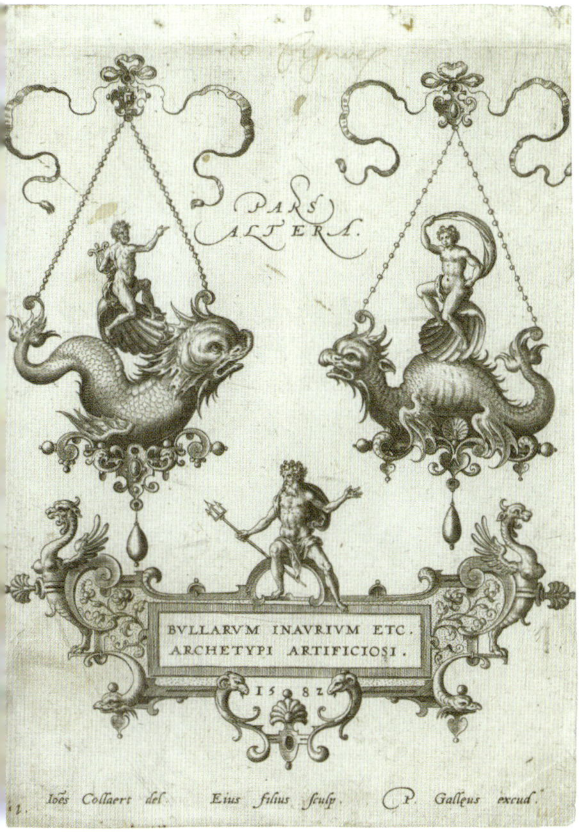

5.11 Adriaen Collaert after Hans Collaert I, title plate for the series *Designs for Pendants*, 1582, engraving, 170 × 125 mm. Amsterdam, Rijksmuseum: RP-P-OB-6050. Appendix 1: PG-22.

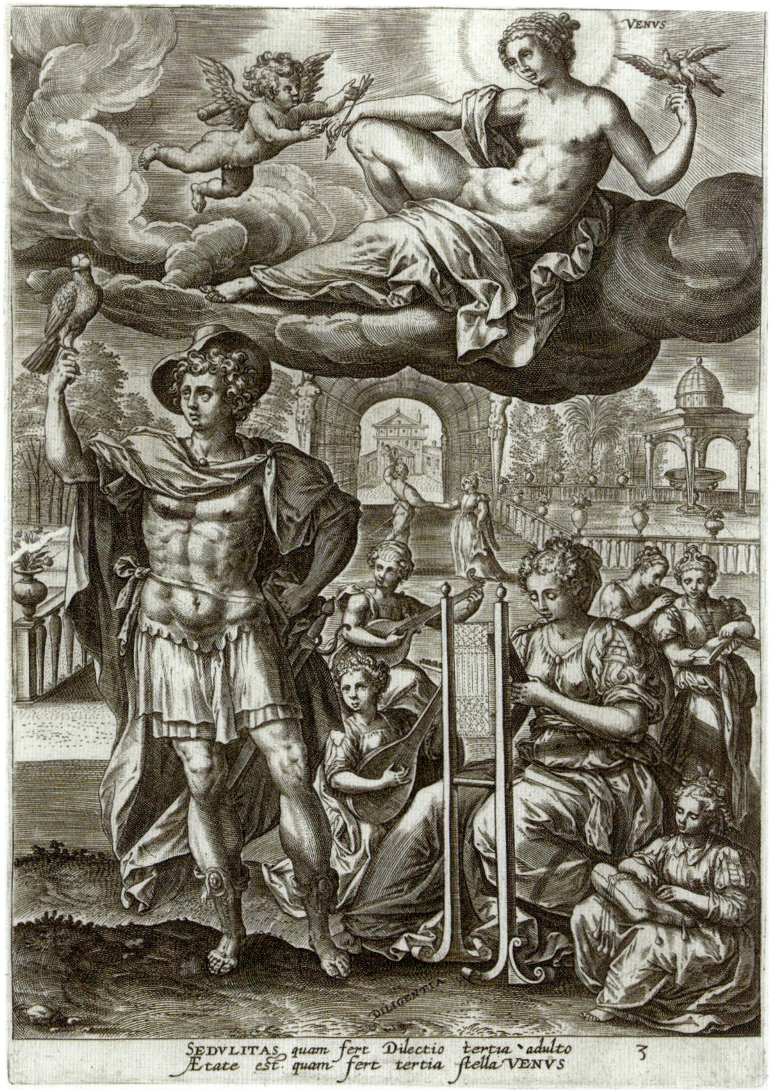

5.12 Adriaen Collaert after Maarten de Vos, *Venus*, from the series *The Seven Planets*, 1581, engraving, 311 × 222 mm. Amsterdam, Rijksmuseum: RP-P-1981-66. Appendix 1: GJ-35.

and his wife, Catharina Moerentorf, Theodore's brother and fellow-engraver Cornelis, as well as Charles de Mallery and his wife, Catharina Galle. Moreover, Jan Moretus I and Volcxken Diericx were witnesses for the baptism of Collaert's son Adriaen in 1594, thereby attesting to his personal connection with both of these families as well.[59]

Collaert benefited from his close ties to this assortment of prominent engravers once he started his own business in the mid-1590s. In addition to taking on several apprentices in this period, including Abraham van Merlen in 1597,[60] Collaert also engaged other established engravers, in particular his brother Jan II and brother-in-law Cornelis Galle I, to assist him with the completion of large series, such as the *Life, Passion, and Resurrection of Christ* (fig. 5.15).

In striking contrast to the work of his brother-in-law Theodore, though, Collaert's publications were not immediately sold via the Moretuses. Furthermore, only twice did such sales match or exceed what the Moretuses sold of Galle's works to the same clients. Specifically, when Giovanni Paolo Gelli bought thousands of prints from several Antwerp printmakers in 1608, the total value of what Collaert supplied (nearly 47 fl.) was nearly identical to the value of what Galle provided, but the assortment of prints purchased differed significantly. Among

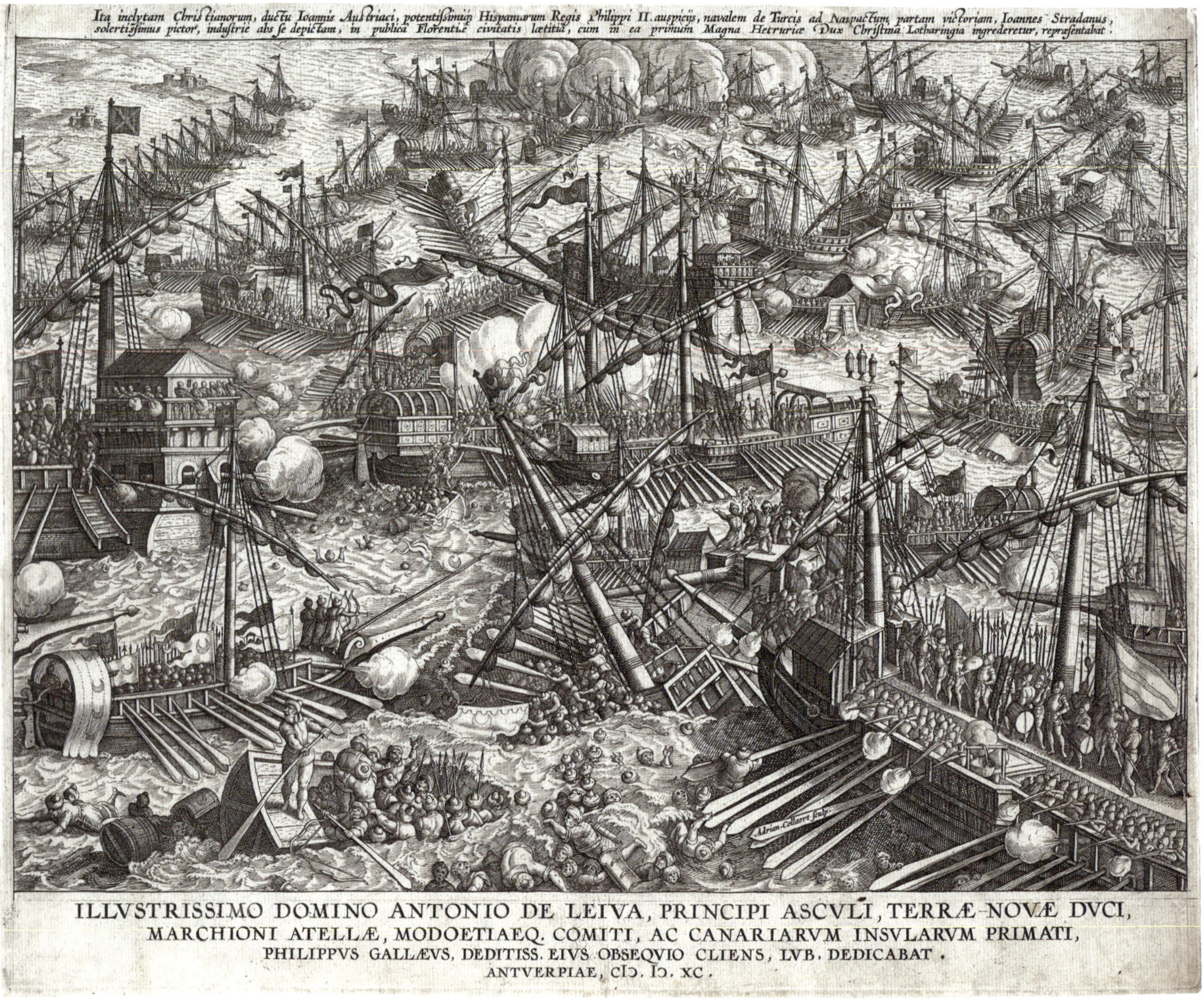

5.13 Adriaen Collaert after Johannes Stradanus, *The Naval Battle against the Turks at Lepanto*, 1590, engraving, 240 × 316 mm. Antwerp, Museum Plantin-Moretus: OP.11946. Appendix 1: PG-124.

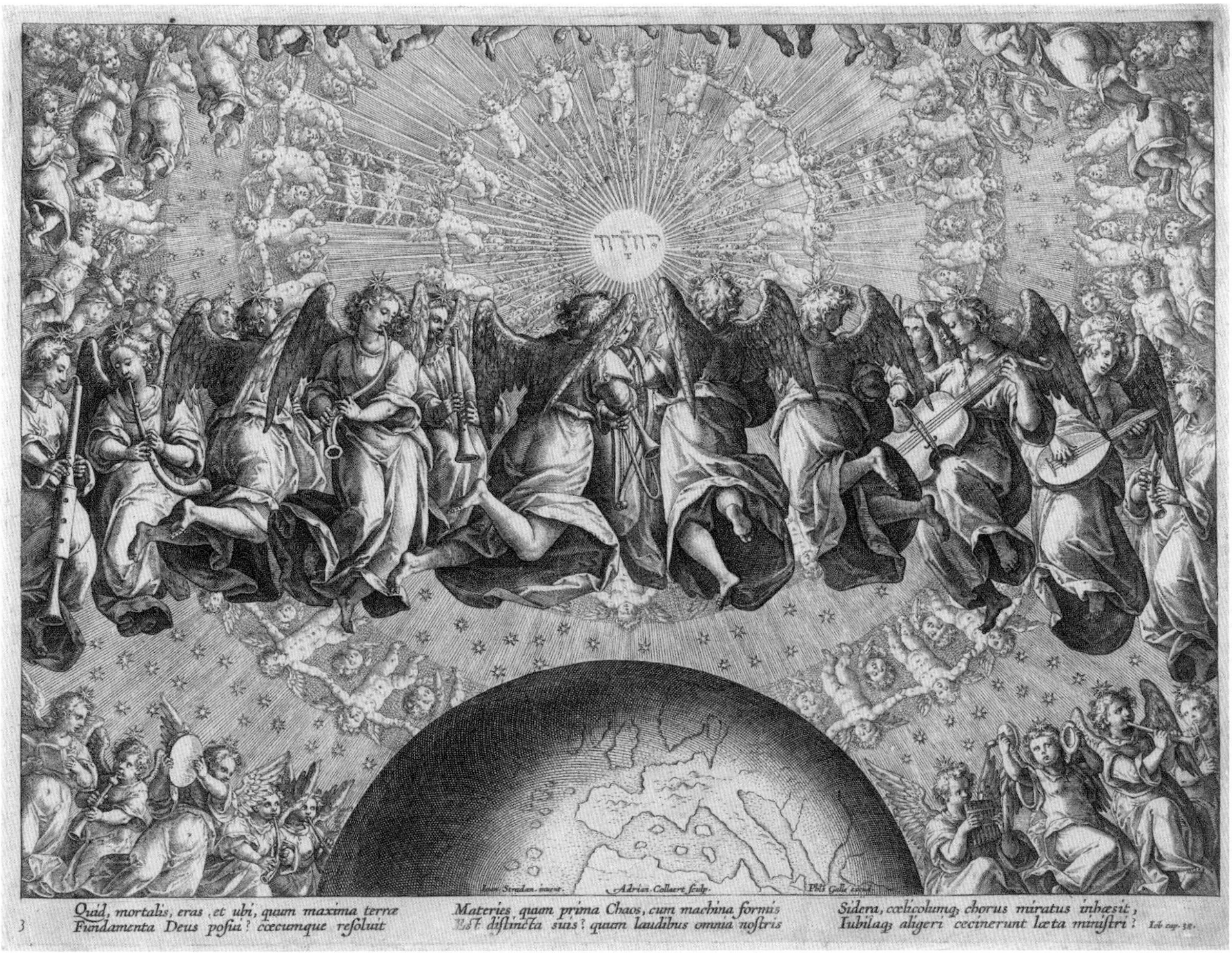

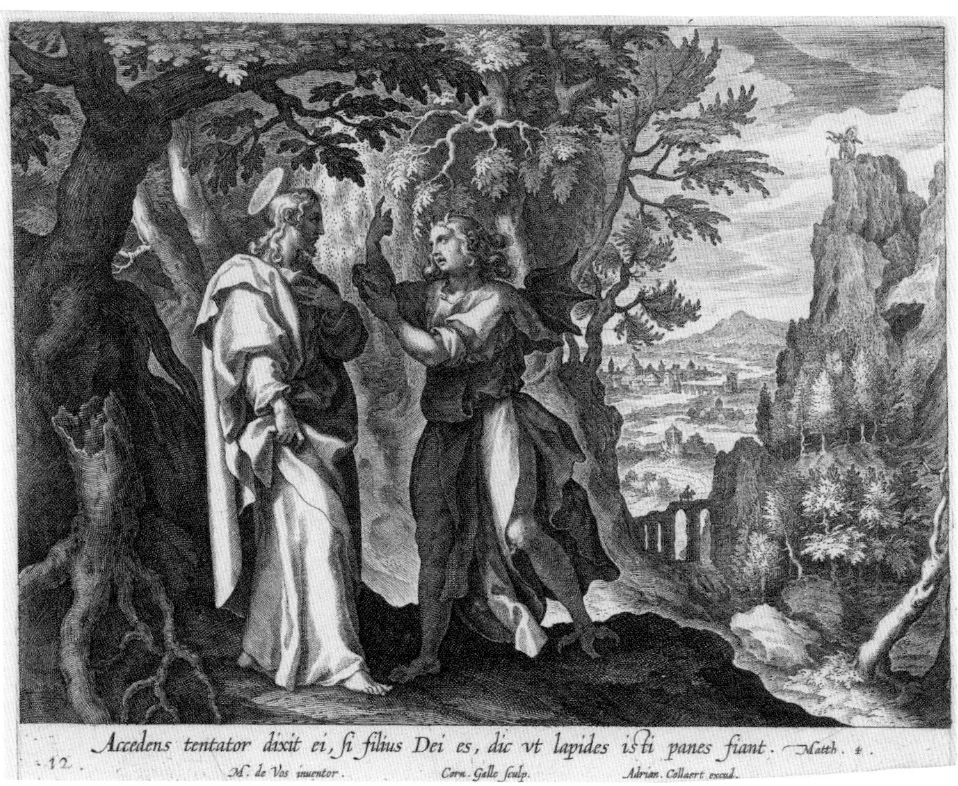

5.14 Adriaen Collaert after Johannes Stradanus, *God's Response to Job*, from the series *The Eulogy of Music*, 1591, engraving, 222 × 290 mm. Amsterdam, Rijksmuseum: RP-P-1938–1831. Appendix 1: PG-33.

5.15 Cornelis Galle I after Maarten de Vos, *Temptation of Christ*, print 12 from the series *The Life, Passion, and Resurrection of Christ*, 1598, engraving, 182 × 215 mm. Amsterdam, Rijksmuseum: RP-P-1885-A-9634. Appendix 1: AC-9.

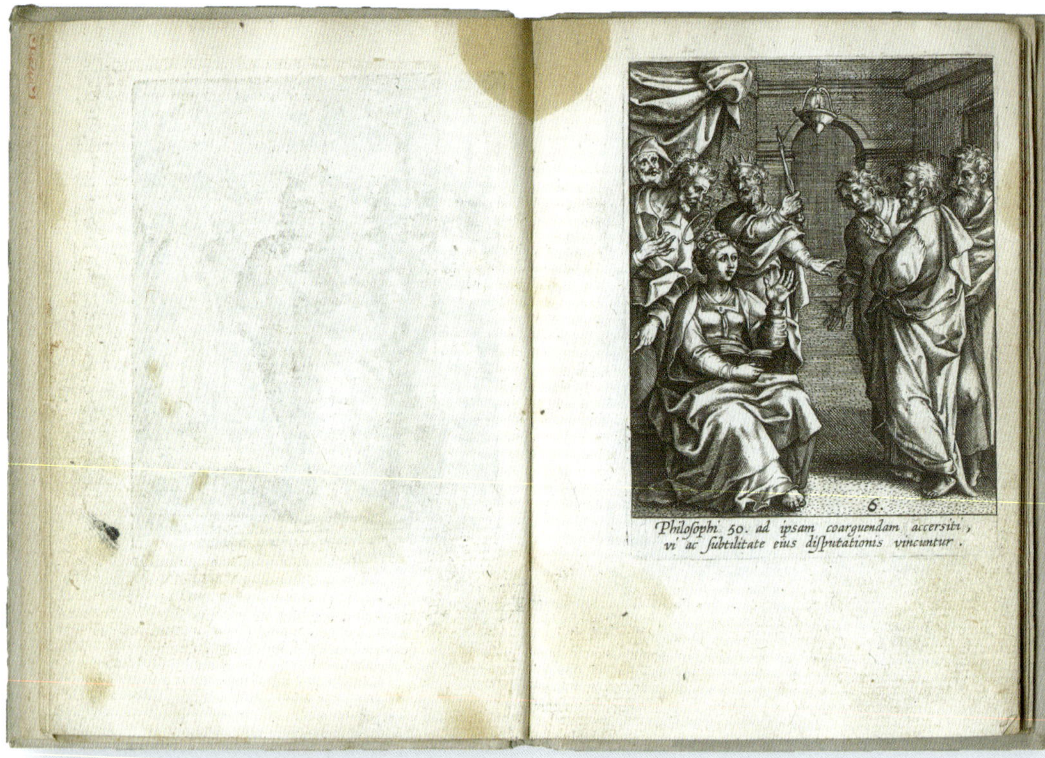

5.16 Adriaen Collaert, *Saint Catherine of Alexandria with the Philosophers*, print 6 from the series *The Life of Saint Catherine of Alexandria*, by 1608, engraving, 94 × 71 mm. Antwerp, Museum Plantin-Moretus: PK: OPB.0014–007. Appendix 1: AC-11.

Collaert's publications, Gelli purchased a large number of his small-scale series of the life of the Virgin, Christ, and an assortment of saints, in addition to four sets each of his series of birds, fish, and four-footed animals (figs. 5.16 and 5.17).[61] When the Gdańsk merchant Rocho di Gabrielli placed his order for prints with the Moretuses in 1602, the differences between the selections of Collaert's and Galle's print were much starker. Galle's offerings comprised some twenty-four images of the Virgin in 8°, two images in folio, and three print series. Collaert, by contrast, supplied sixty images of saints (Sts Peter, Antony, and Mary Magdalene), sixty images of crucifixions, fifty leaves with four images printed per leaf, 400 leaves with eight images per leaf, and 150 leaves with twelve prints per leaf, which amounted to 5,320 prints in total. As Collaert's images were generally much smaller than Galle's (and, consequently, less expensive on average), the difference in value of their offerings – just 1 fl. 6 st. for Galle's versus 20 fl. 15 st. for Collaert's – is all the more significant.[62] However, these two orders were exceptionally large for the Moretuses' trade in Collaert's prints. Concentrated primarily in the relatively brief period between August 1601 and Gelli's transaction in September 1608, the Moretuses' sales of Collaert's work often consisted of isolated acquisitions of 1.5 fl. or less with clients in the Low Countries, such as the bookseller Hendrik Hompes in Roermond and the Franciscan Antoine Bergaigne in Brussels.[63]

Similarly, Collaert used the Moretuses' other services far less extensively than his brother-in-law Theodore. Nevertheless, his sporadic transactions reveal something of the extent and nature of his own personal dealings in prints. For example, aside from Collaert's dealings at the Frankfurt fairs, his long-distance exchanges were rare. In 1602, the London bookseller Hans Woutneel had the Moretuses pay Collaert 35 fl., while in 1616, the Moretuses shipped a package of prints from Collaert to the merchant Paulus Claessens in Gdańsk.[64] Rather, the bulk of what Collaert arranged through the Moretuses involved individuals in the Low Countries and France. For example, Collaert had several packages sent to Paris – first to his

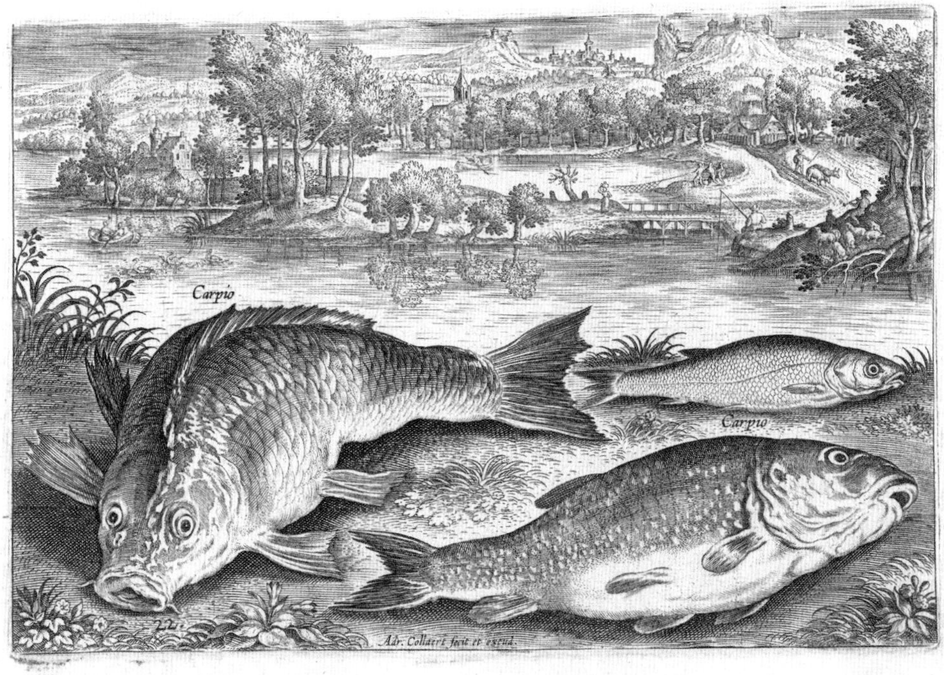

5.17 Adriaen Collaert, *Three Carp*, print 22 from his series of fish, by 1608, engraving, 130 × 188 mm. Amsterdam, Rijksmuseum: RP-P-OB-31.553 Appendix 1: AC-4.

brother-in-law Charles de Mallery in 1603, and, subsequently, in 1608 and 1609, to two Parisian print dealers with Netherlandish roots, namely Gabriel Tavernier I and Pierre Firens.[65] Collaert occasionally had comparable exchanges with local clients. For instance, the Moretuses sent solitary packages to the booksellers Jan Hompes (son of Hendrik) in Roermond and Alexander Sersanders in Ghent in 1612 and 1616, respectively, on Collaert's behalf.[66] He also most likely had clients in Ypres since Jan Moretus I gave him books to deliver to his own customers there on at least two separate occasions.[67]

While each of the examples above attests to the geographical scope of Collaert's trade via the Moretuses, the few figures who recur in these records reflect a stronger, lasting interest in his work among both individual collectors and professional sellers of books and prints. Consider, for example, the Jesuit Aegidius Schondonch, who was the rector of the Jesuit college at St Omer from 1601 to 1617. During these years, he purchased an unspecified group of prints from Collaert in December 1605, valued at 6 fl. 12 st., and had Collaert send him an additional package of prints shortly thereafter.[68] Of far greater significance, in terms of the frequency of the interactions as well as the sums of money involved, were Collaert's exchanges with the bookseller Jean du Puis in Lille. From 1607, midway through Collaert's career and shortly after Du Puis's accounts with the Moretuses began, they dealt regularly with one another via the Moretuses through 1616, just two years prior to Collaert's death. Hereafter, Du Puis and the Moretuses continued to do business into 1634.[69] The diversity and range of Collaert's and Du Puis's transactions indicate the intensity of their professional (and possibly personal) ties. There are numerous instances of the Moretuses giving Collaert books that Du Puis had ordered (and paid for), and on one occasion, the Moretuses even asked Collaert to deliver a package of prints from Hieronymus Wierix to Du Puis on their behalf.[70] Conversely, the Moretuses periodically sent Du Puis packages from Collaert.[71] Above all, between 1607 and 1616, Du Puis regularly used his accounts with the Moretuses to complete payments to

Collaert. Amounting to more than 200 fl. in total, they include one exceptional transaction of 100 fl. in 1607, while the majority range from 15 to 25 fl.[72]

The Moretuses' accounts document one other important professional and personal connection for Collaert, namely the Sadeler family of print publishers, whom Collaert would have known in the 1570s-1580s as successful, contemporary engravers in Antwerp. In addition to shipping numerous packages to the Sadelers among the Moretuses' transports to the Frankfurt book fairs, Collaert regularly received books from the Moretuses that Justus Sadeler (then in Venice) had purchased from them. Justus was also the only individual to whom Collaert sent multiple packages by way of the Moretuses' business in Antwerp. The infrequency with which the Sadelers asked the Moretuses to make payments to Collaert for them suggests that they had other means for settling their accounts, such as the Sadelers' agent (and relative) in Antwerp, Philips Liesaert III, who was a successful dealer in paintings.[73]

Following Adriaen Collaert's death in 1618, his relatives were even less inclined to participate in the print trade through the Moretuses. Limited to the 1630s, the records of such transactions are remarkable for the predominance of shipments of packages to the Cologne print seller Abraham Hogenberg (the son of Frans Hogenberg, who had emigrated from the Low Countries) from several members of the Collaert family: Collaert's widow, Josine Galle, his son Carel, and his nephew Willem. Even though some nine packages in total were sent, no money exchanged hands via the Moretuses, suggesting that they settled their accounts through other channels.[74] Only once, in 1638, did the Moretuses sell prints provided by the next generation of Collaerts, namely an allotment of 500 illuminated prints on parchment supplied by Carel Collaert for one of their clients, the bookseller Kaspar Förster in Gdańsk.[75]

The Moretuses' records primarily document Adriaen Collaert's dealings with individuals in assorted cities in the Low Countries, as well as in Paris and Lille, in addition to his ongoing interactions with the Sadelers. The international clients whom the Moretuses helped him serve often had links to the Low Countries. Whether this selection of clients is representative of the majority of Collaert's own network of customers is impossible to say, particularly because his involvement in the print trade via the Moretuses is remarkably limited when compared with that of other Antwerp print publishers. The relative paucity of his exchanges through the Moretuses is all the more poignant since each of Adriaen's relatives among the extended Galle family – from his father-in-law Philips Galle, to his brothers-in-law Theodore Galle and Charles de Mallery, and even his nephew Jan Galle – all sold hundreds to a thousand florins more in prints via the Moretuses. The personal nature of Collaert's apparent decision to focus on local contacts in these transactions is underscored by the striking contrast with De Mallery's extensive reliance upon the Moretuses' essential services and far-reaching international networks to support his own highly successful, extensive participation in the European print market.

CHARLES DE MALLERY

Though De Mallery was not born into a family of artists, his aptitude for engraving was recognized by Philips Galle, who agreed to engage him as an apprentice in 1586, precisely when his own son Theodore, similarly born in 1571, was training under him (fig. 5.18).[76] By the early 1590s, De Mallery was accomplished enough to contribute sizable engravings to assorted

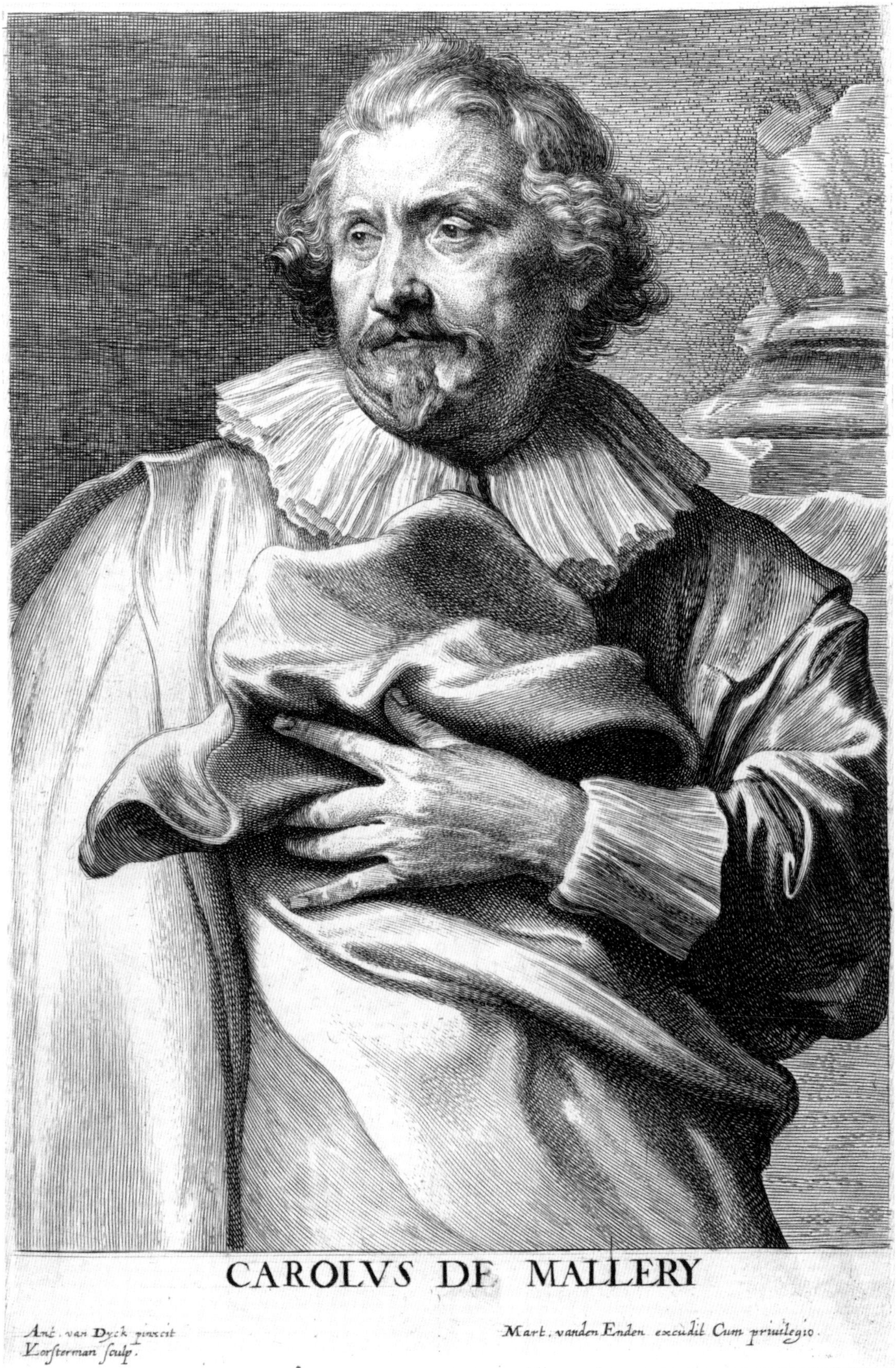

5.18 Lucas Vorsterman after Anthony van Dyck, *Portrait of Charles de Mallery*, 1630–1645, etching and engraving, 239 × 156 mm. Amsterdam, Rijksmuseum: RP-P-OB-33141.

print series published by Galle (fig. 5.19), in addition to completing prints for other major projects, including the *Evangelicae historiae imagines* series, which was first published in 1593 by the Antwerp Jesuits to accompany the *Adnotationes et meditationes in evangelia* by Jerónimo Nadal (Hieronymus Natalis).[77] De Mallery was also evidently sufficiently acquainted with Jan Moretus I to ask for his assistance in exchanging 100 fl. for an equivalent sum in other currencies at the Frankfurt fair in April 1594, when De Mallery was en route to Italy (fig. 9.5).[78] Within three years, De Mallery had returned to Antwerp. He promptly established himself professionally, gaining acceptance as a master engraver in the Guild of St Luke in 1597. He simultaneously solidified his connection with the Galle family by marrying Galle's daughter Catharina on 10 January 1598 and by resuming his work for Galle, alongside his brothers-in-law Theodore, Cornelis Galle I, and Adriaen Collaert. That the personal link between De Mallery's and Collaert's families was particularly strong is suggested by reciprocal requests to serve as godparents when their children were baptized in 1598, 1607, and 1624.[79]

Rather than rise in the Antwerp print world as part of the extended Galle family, however, De Mallery chose to move to Paris by the summer of 1599 to work there as an independent engraver and print seller. Once there, his connections with the Moretuses proved mutually advantageous. On the one hand, Jan Moretus I was able to call upon De Mallery to assist him with financial transactions to facilitate his son Melchior's stay in Paris and Bordeaux in

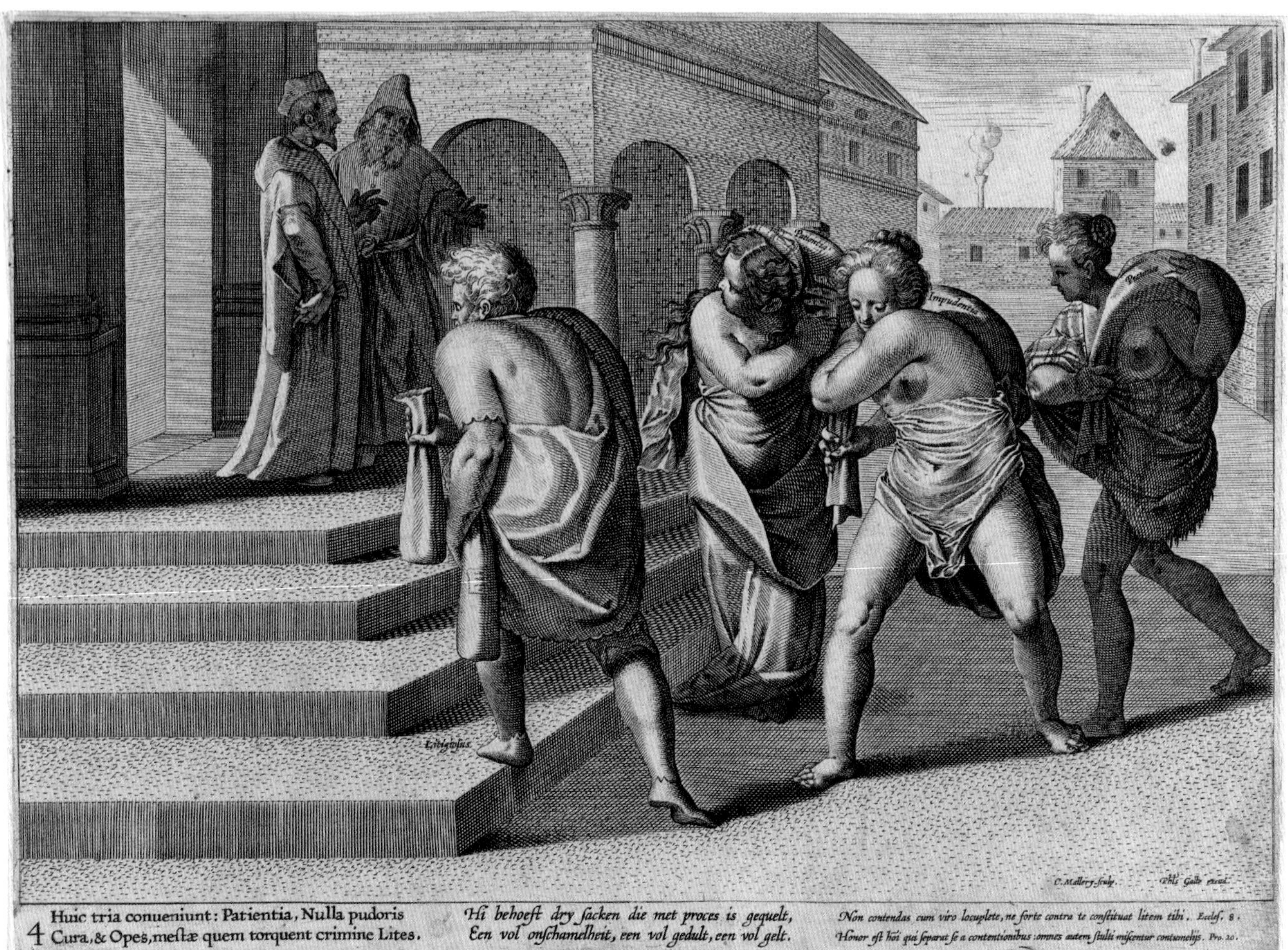

5.19 Charles de Mallery after Philips Galle, after Hendrick Goltzius, *Abuse of Jurisprudence*, print 4 from the series *Abuses of Process (Litis abusus)*, ca. 1590, engraving, 204 × 275 mm. Amsterdam, Rijksmuseum: RP-P-1963-164.

January 1602. Eighteen months later, in July 1603, his son Balthasar (De Mallery's contemporary) visited De Mallery and planned to tour Fontainebleau with him while there.[80] On the other hand, Moretus assisted De Mallery by occasionally including packages prepared for him by other Antwerp printmakers – Jan Baptist Vrients, in addition to his relations Theodore and Philips Galle and Adriaen Collaert – in his shipments to Parisian booksellers.[81] Thus, as his brother-in-law Theodore had done (and in striking contrast to his brother-in-law Adriaen), De Mallery benefited from Jan Moretus's transportation network to further his own business as a print seller from the start.

When De Mallery decided to return to Antwerp in the fall of 1605, Jan Moretus was among his professional visits, as De Mallery had some books printed by the Parisian bookseller Eustace Foucault for him.[82] De Mallery's subsequent transactions with Moretus that year and the next were limited to the purchase of six copies of small (8° or 24°), bound liturgical books – missals, breviaries, a litany, a diurnal, and a copy of Petrus Canisius's Catholic handbook – and a few small print sales.[83] By March 1607, however, the Moretuses' trade in De Mallery's prints began in earnest and continued virtually unabated through the spring of 1626.

Like his brothers-in-law, Adriaen, Theodore, and Cornelis, an impressive quantity of De Mallery's prints (1,000 unspecified images) were included in the Moretuses' exceptional 1608 sale of prints and books to the Roman bookseller Giovanni Paolo Gelli. De Mallery's place among the new generation of Antwerp print sellers was thus confirmed.[84] This sale is also significant as an early example of De Mallery's standard offerings for the international print market served by the Moretuses, namely unspecified prints on paper sold at the bulk rate of 50 st. per 100 images. Already evident in the Moretuses' records as early as March 1607, this practice would remain De Mallery's norm through his last known deliveries of prints for resale in the spring of 1626. A similar approach was used in the subsequent trade in De Mallery's prints that the Moretuses arranged via Theodore and Jan Galle during the 1630s and 1640s.[85] Little detail is recorded about the prints De Mallery distributed internationally through these channels; at most, they were identified as "fine devotional images" ("images fines de devotion") or simply as an assortment of his prints ("images de son assortiment").[86] Given the uniform pricing, it is likely that these shipments comprised a selection of comparably sized prints, such as the numerous small devotional images that he engraved and published and that were often based on the widely revered images produced by the Wierix brothers (figs. 5.20 and 5.21). In this regard, De Mallery periodically replicated prints published by Theodore Galle and other printmakers in Antwerp and elsewhere who likewise imitated the Wierixes' engravings (figs. 6.17–6.20). Adriaen Collaert, by contrast, generally did not and De Mallery rarely imitated Collaert's output.[87]

Thus, far more than either of his brothers-in-law, De Mallery opted for a simple marketing strategy, most likely relying on the small devotional images for which he is generally known, even though he published a broader range of prints.[88] He likewise did not expand his offerings to include batches of hand-colored prints or images printed on parchment, as did Theodore Galle and other contemporary print publishers. On the rare occasions that individuals procured his prints with such special finishings, this was arranged for on a piece-by-piece basis. For example, in February 1608, Jan Moretus I sold the Leuven canon Guillaume Wargnirius a total of seventy images of St Teresa, twenty-five of which were supplied by Jan Baptist Vrients, while De Mallery provided the rest, including one such image that was painted in gold and silver.[89] This last print may have resembled an extraordinary impression of a portrait of Carolus Borromeus engraved by De Mallery and now in the collection of the Counts of Waldburg-Wolfegg in the castle at Wolfegg, although it is not known when or

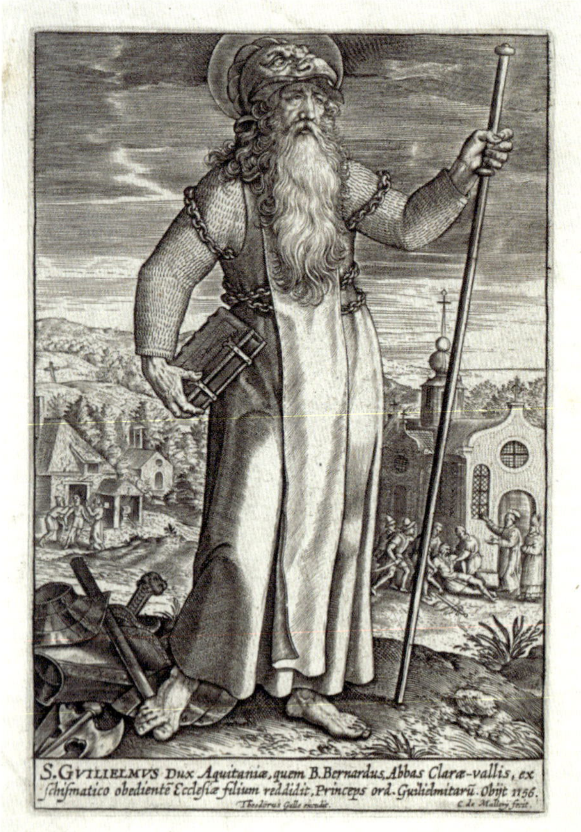

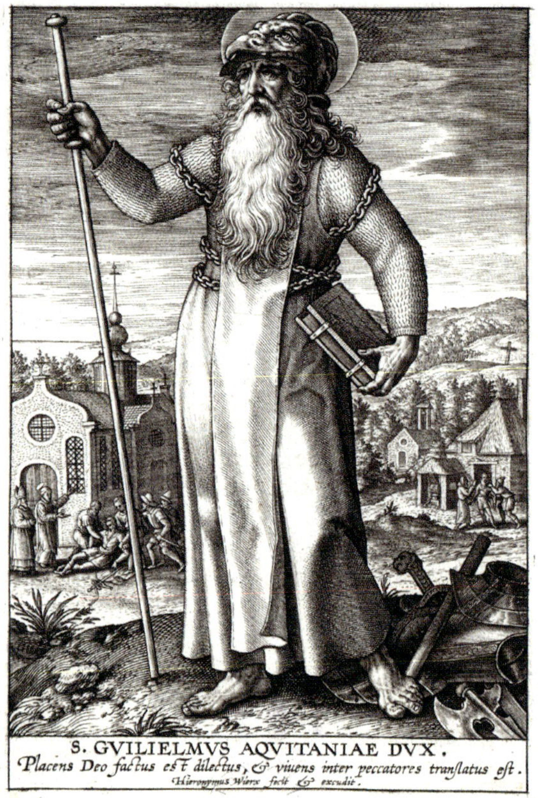

5.20 Charles de Mallery, *Saint William of Aquitaine*, s.a., engraving, 135 × 89 mm, published by Theodore Galle. Brussels, The Royal Library, Print Department: S.I 24148.

5.21 Hieronymus Wierix, *Saint William of Aquitaine*, s.a., engraving, 140 × 91 mm. Antwerp, Museum Plantin-Moretus: PK: OP-04205.

where that specific print was illuminated (fig. 5.22). The primary exception to this pattern were isolated sales of his 1614 series of images of men and women from the Franciscan order (fig. 7.7). This series was supplied at least once by De Mallery for resale via the Moretuses. Both Theodore Galle, who had acquired the plates for this series by the 1630s, and his son Jan resold impressions of it to the Moretuses in the 1630s, albeit at significantly elevated prices of 24 st. per series, in contrast to the 18 st. that De Mallery most likely charged.[90]

What did vary significantly in the Moretuses' trade in De Mallery's prints were the profit margins added to these transactions. One stunning example is the sale of some 3,000 unspecified prints in bulk and four sets of De Mallery's series of Franciscans to the bookseller Antonio de Toro at Seville. While De Mallery provided Balthasar Moretus with 3,000 prints at his standard rate of 50 st. per 100 prints, Moretus sold them to De Toro with a rare 50% markup; the final price was 75 st. per 100 prints.[91] Why De Toro was charged so much is not clear. In most of the Moretuses' exchanges with booksellers elsewhere in Europe, they made little or no profit on the resale of De Mallery's prints, as was the case even with Gelli's remarkable purchase discussed above.

Regardless of whether or not the Moretuses profited directly from the resale of De Mallery's prints, he, like Theodore Galle, benefited regularly from their international distribution of his publications. In addition to the exceptional transactions with Gelli in Rome and De Torro in Seville, the Moretuses also occasionally sold De Mallery's prints in bulk to distant booksellers in France, such as Charles de Gouy in Amiens in 1618 and Jean Dassonleville in the Pas-de-Calais in 1624 and 1626.[92] By far the most significant transactions, however, were the Moretuses' sales to booksellers in the Holy Roman Empire, especially in Augsburg,

Cologne, and Münster. While thousands of prints were sold to Georg Willer II and his former employee Johann Krüger in Augsburg between 1613 and 1615, orders from the Raesfeld family in Münster reflect the most prolonged interest in his work; beginning in 1612, they continued sporadically into the 1630s.[93]

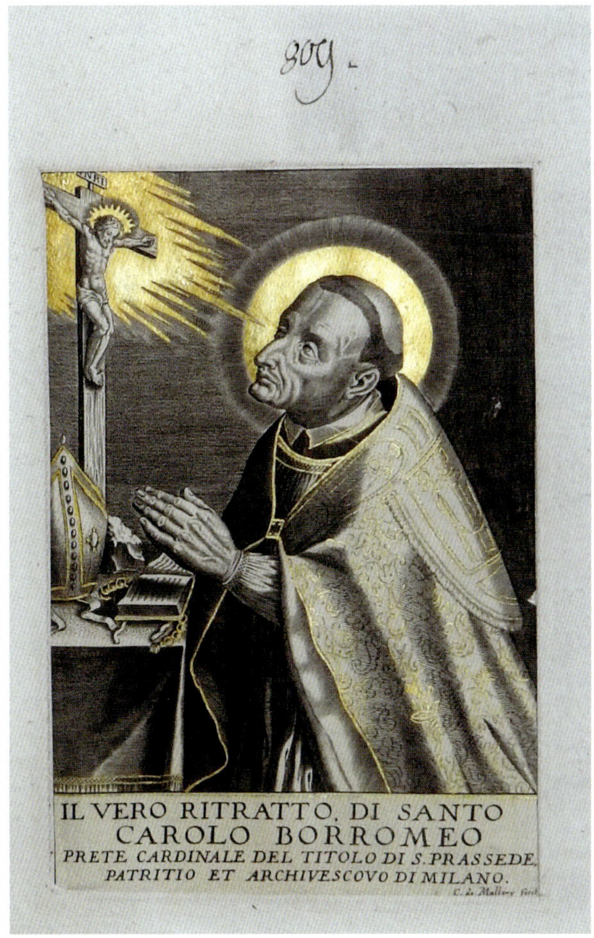

5.22 Charles de Mallery, *Portrait of Saint Carolus Borromeus*, s.a., engraving, 120 × 80 mm. Wolfegg, Fürstlich zu Waldburg-Wolfegg'sche Kunstsammlungen: vol. 208, print 809.

Although De Mallery does not appear to have maintained independent contact with any of these buyers accessible through the Moretuses, the Moretuses' sales and his clearly overlapped in Cologne, which may well have rivaled the Parisian market in terms of the sheer volume of the demand for his prints. In particular, both De Mallery and the Moretuses periodically supplied some of the same booksellers in the city, namely, two of the Moretuses' former apprentices, Bernhard Wolters and Johann Kinckius. Because the contents and value of De Mallery's packages are not always specified, it is impossible to compare specific transactions. What can be surmised is that between De Mallery and the Moretuses, these booksellers procured De Mallery's prints regularly for numerous years.[94] De Mallery does not appear to have competed with the Moretuses' trade in prints involving the bookseller Anton Hierat I of Cologne, for whom, in notable contrast to the bulk of their transactions with other Cologne booksellers, the Moretuses often included a profit margin for themselves.[95] In the case of Cornelis van Egmont, a distant relative of the Moretuses and yet another former apprentice, the Moretuses left the sale of De Mallery's prints to De Mallery and assisted only in organizing financial matters and the transport of his prints. The remarkable potential scale of De Mallery's personal transactions is suggested by a shipment of 3,000 prints in three packages that the Moretuses included in a bale of books sent to the bookseller Hermann Mylius in Cologne in August 1619. The payment for these prints may have been completed several months earlier in April via the same network of individuals. Mylius sent Moretus a letter of credit and asked him to pay De Mallery 75 fl. in Van Egmont's name, where 75 fl. was the equivalent of buying 3,000 prints at De Mallery's standard rate of 50 st. per 100 prints.[96]

The overlap between the Moretuses and De Mallery in the traffic in his prints in Cologne was exceptional, however. Sales or shipments to dealers in prints and books in the Low Countries are, for example, remarkably limited both via the Moretuses' own sales of his work and through De Mallery's reliance on their financial or transport networks. This is notably different from Collaert's use of the Moretuses' services and may well reflect a preference by De Mallery (possibly like Theodore Galle) to satisfy local demand for his work himself. In contrast, the notable absence of sales to the Moretuses' contacts in Paris can be readily accounted for by evidence of De Mallery's own dealings with several individuals there. In particular, just as Theodore Galle and Adriaen Collaert clearly maintained special relations with some of their clients, De Mallery did so with the Parisian bookseller Eustace Foucault. Foucault had employed De Mallery at least once while the latter was in Paris. Within two years of De Mallery's return to Antwerp, they began an intense exchange of packages and payments through the Moretuses that extended from December 1607 to March 1615. As Galle and Collaert had done for particular clients, De Mallery provided Foucault with both prints and books. Of the thirty-six packages that he is known to have sent Foucault between December 1607 and June 1614, at least two comprised books, while sixteen contained engravings ("fines images"). Although the types of prints De Mallery sent and the total quantities involved remain unknown, Foucault's payments were unprecedented among the Moretuses' accounts with any Antwerp artist. For example, between 31 January 1612 and 29 March 1615, the Moretuses paid De Mallery a total of 714 fl. on Foucault's behalf.[97] Averaging 200 fl. *per year* (possibly for some quantity of books in addition to prints), this sum was only slightly less than what Du Puis had the Moretuses pay Collaert *in the course of a decade* and far exceeded the value of what the Moretuses sold of De Mallery's prints to any client. Only their 1610 purchase of 110 copies of Galle's series of the *Life of Saint Ignatius* at 2 fl. per copy is comparable, but that remained an exceptional, one-time occurrence and not an ongoing exchange for several years. Rather, the best comparison for the sums Foucault paid De Mallery, are what the Moretuses received at the Frankfurt fairs for De Mallery from the Cologne print dealer Peter Overadt.[98]

Although De Mallery's exchanges with Foucault are the most impressive of his Parisian dealings, his contacts in Paris were far more extensive. The Moretuses' records alone document his periodic shipment of packages to the print publisher Jean Messager (eleven in total between 1610 and 1617). In addition, from 1608 to 1614, the Moretuses conveyed isolated shipments to other print sellers, like Jean Leclerc IV and a certain Jacques Bartrand – possibly the merchant Jacques Bertrant from Dauphiné, who was linked to the trade in prints between France and Spain, or perhaps a member of the Parisian Bertrand family of print and booksellers – as well as the book printer-publisher Abel L'Angelier (who had also engaged De Mallery to engrave plates for the illustration of his publications).[99] De Mallery similarly made sporadic use of the Moretuses' transportation network to reach such far-flung clients as Jan Baptist Vrients' brother-in-law Gaspar Vivario when he was in Rome, Justus Sadeler in Venice, and the merchant-bookseller Paulus Claessens in Gdańsk.[100]

De Mallery's use of the various services the Moretuses offered to support his traffic in prints and the Moretuses' own sales of his works demonstrate a remarkably extensive, international demand for his prints that resulted in the dissemination of hundreds of thousands of impressions of his publications. This is all the more impressive if one considers that the total value of all the prints he supplied to the Moretuses for further distribution – among the highest following Philips and Theodore Galle's – reflects the sales of just small images on paper sold at the bulk rate of 50 st. per 100. What De Mallery offered did not include the large and often costly print series sold by the Galles or the hand-colored prints often printed on parchment that Theodore Galle and, above all, Michael Snijders provided at notably high rates and that readily accounted for the exceptionally large sums associated with their works. The profitability of De Mallery's business as a print publisher is tellingly evident from his and his wife's investment in a number of houses in Antwerp between 1608 and 1622.[101] De Mallery's subsequent fall into poverty is thus all the more dramatic, as it forced him not only to sell off his property, but to barter for work and loans from both his brother-in-law Theodore and Balthasar Moretus I. One such request, in a letter from 13 March 1638 to Balthasar I (fig. 5.23), met only with pity, rather than the hoped-for funds.[102] Nevertheless, De Mallery's unfortunate decline does not diminish his stunning accomplishments as a print publisher; his work not only was actively sought in such important markets as Paris, but also helped meet the immense, ever-increasing demand for printed images in Cologne.

This evidence of the international commerce in prints engaged in by the extended Galle family documents the remarkable extent of this trade and the diverse approaches employed by print publishers at the turn of the seventeenth century. While one might argue that the Galles' dealings are exceptionally represented here due to their close personal connections with the Moretuses – as Balthasar Moretus's correspondence with Bernhard Raesfeld suggests – they had internationally recognized competitors within the Antwerp print world. Despite the lack of intimate ties to the Moretuses, these rival print publishers also had access to the Moretuses' varied services and benefited from them. Examining the diversity of their approaches and the range of involvement possible in the print trade through the single outlet offered by the Moretuses provides unprecedented insight into both the depth and breadth of Antwerp print publishers' participation in the vast international trade in prints, which went far beyond the reach of any one family business, no matter how well known today.

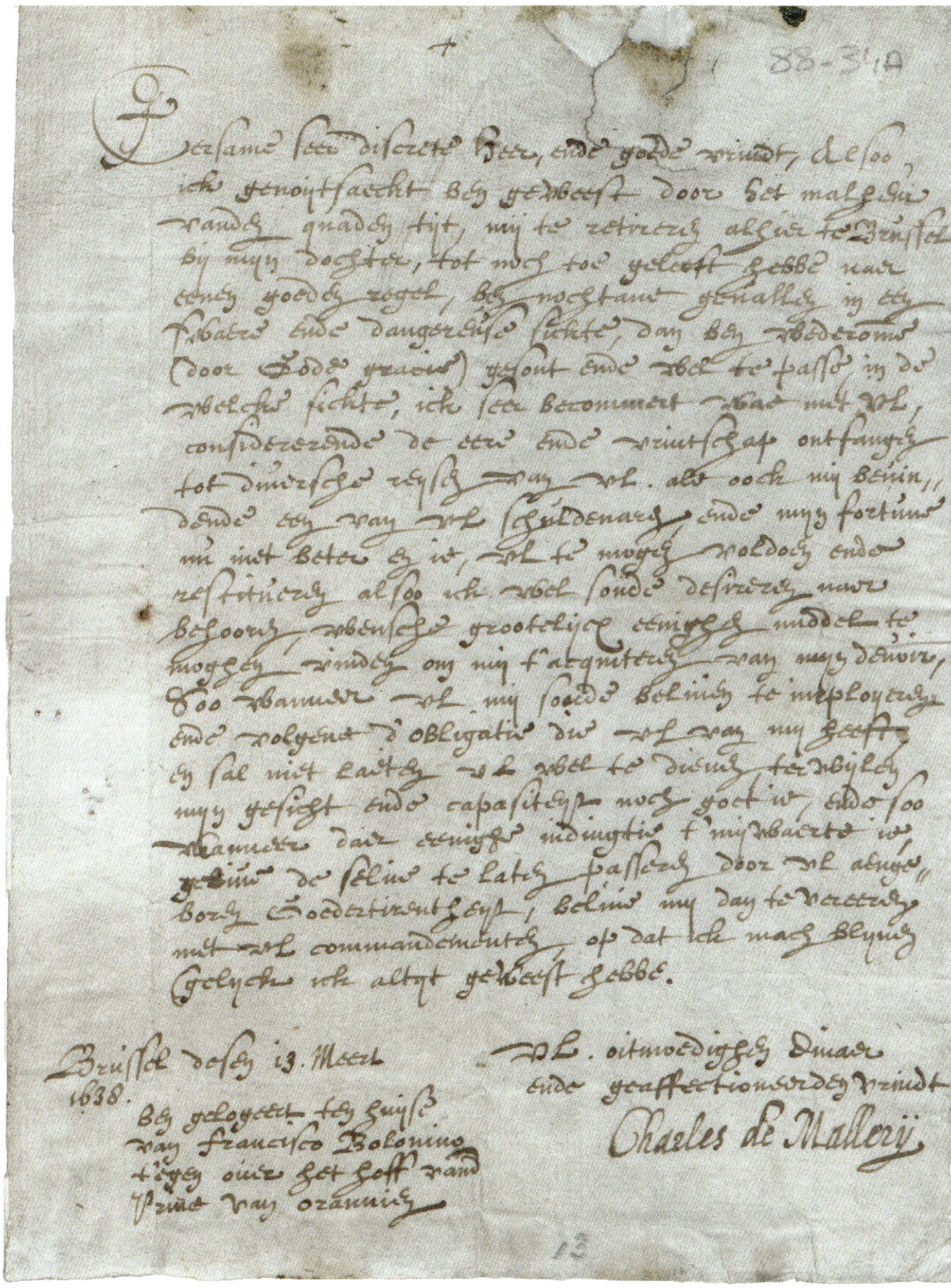

5.23 Letter from Charles de Mallery to Balthasar Moretus I, 13 March 1638. Antwerp, Museum Plantin-Moretus: Arch. 88, *Recueils de lettres Maccius-Montmorency*, document 34a.

1 MPM Arch. 144, fol. 203: "Quingentas imagines pictas in pergameno per sororium Gallaeum parari curabo; multo praestantiores prae iis quas Cnobbart habet. In pretio exiguum discrimen, octo scilicet asses, quos maior elegantia abunde compensat".

2 See MPM Arch. 239, fol. 93v for this shipment; and Appendix 1, under Theodore Galle's bulk print sales, for the rates he charged.

3 MPM Arch. 100, p. 55 (contract dated 11 July 1598 and signed by both Jan Moretus and Philips Galle); and MPM Arch. 95bis, folder B-g-2 (T. Galle's receipt of the first 200 fl.).

4 For numerous examples of this practice, see Génard 1859, p. 197 in particular; and Van der Straelen 1858, pp. 29, 35, 274, and D 34, D 35, and D 38.

5 Bowen 2009, pp. 129–41.

6 See also the discussion of Theodore Galle in Appendix 1.

7 Sellink 1997, vol. I, p. 105.

8 MPM Arch. 21, fol. 341 rht; and MPM Arch. 75, fol. 161r.

9 MPM Arch. 75, fol. 227r.

10 MPM Arch. 171, fols. 32v, 27v, 42r, and 104v.

11 MPM Arch. 987, fols. 1 rht, 61 rht, 56 rht, 20 lft, and 54 lft.

12 MPM Arch. 171, fols. 174, 90r-91r, 30v, and 138v, respectively (for Moretus's contacts), and fols. 130v-135v (for the sales via the widow of G. de Jode to Franciscus Affel, Michiel Beyer, Valentin Berisch, and Melchior Bericht in Danzig and Petrus Peresina in Kraków).

13 MPM Arch. 171, fols. 96r, 45r, 37r, 35v, 179r, and 116v, respectively.

14 MPM Arch. 172, fols. 37v (De Renialme), 98v (Frankfurt), 117r (Paris), and 180v (Jesuits); MPM Arch. 173, fol. 37v (Vande Wervel); MPM Arch. 174, fols. 56r, 93r, and 96v (all to Paris); MPM Arch. 175, fols. 28r and 155r (Paris), and 115v (Frankfurt); MPM Arch. 176, fol. 34r (Hompes); and MPM Arch. 177, fols. 18r (Frankfurt) and 174r (Charondelet).

15 MPM Arch. 987, fols. 2 lft, 33 rht, 54 lft, and 56 rht.

16 MPM Arch. 171, fols. 42r and 104v (copies for Frankfurt), and 46v (sale to Vander Wervel). For examples of Moretus sending packages to Vander Wervel at Galle's request, see also MPM Arch. 178, fol. 38r; and MPM Arch. 179, fol. 51v.

17 For David's and Galle's working relationship, see Imhof 2020b.

18 MPM Arch. 221, fol. 162v; MPM Arch. 228, fol. 47r (Habbeke's transactions); and MPM Arch. 230, fols. 29v and 210r (debts from Halle and Maubeuge, respectively).

19 MPM Arch. 240, fols. 124r and 127v (Breda); and MPM Arch. 232, fol. 16v (Halle).

20 See Appendix 1, TG-27, TG-28, and TG-29 for the three "Trees" Galle published, PJ-2 for De Jode's. See Chapter 7 for a discussion of the Tree of the Franciscan Order sold by the Moretuses in 1626 to the merchant Jan van Vucht. See also Holl. Dutch & Flemish, vol. III, p. 56; and Wolfegg, Fürstlich zu Waldburg-Wolfegg'sche Kunstsammlungen, vol. 9, no. 172, for Boel's print. The Moretuses also sold an anonymously supplied "Arbor S. Norberti" (a "Tree" image featuring St Norbert) for 5 st. in 1631 (MPM Arch. 239, fol. 141r).

21 MPM Arch. 174, fols. 11v (Galle's supply of prints) and 29r (Di Gabrielli's total purchase).

22 MPM Arch. 175, fol. 78r (Sailly); MPM Arch. 178, fol. 78r (Wolters); MPM Arch. 217, fol. 227r (Scheffer); MPM Arch. 218, fol. 207r (Hierat); and MPM Arch. 225, fol. 126r (Barentsen). For the series, see Appendix 1, PG-66 and TG-9.

23 Antwerp, Felix Archives, SR 457, 1605 KB II, fol. 397v.

24 MPM Arch. 221, fols. 100v (under Pardo Lopez), 200v and 224r; and MPM Arch. 222, fol. 104r.

25 MPM Arch. 222, fols. 24r and 59r (De Angulo's 1615 print purchase); MPM Arch. 179, fols. 38v and 47v; MPM Arch. 1104, fols. 45v and 46r (for supply and purchase of prints by Pardo Lopez in 1607).

26 MPM Arch. 232, fols. 97v and 104r; and MPM Arch. 233, fols. 44v and 45v, respectively.

27 See Bowen 2020 on Gelli's purchase; and MPM Arch. 180, fol. 155v, for the complete list of what Galle provided.

28 MPM Arch. 231, fols. 167r-167v (1624); MPM Arch. 232, fol. 16r (1625); and MPM Arch. 233, fols. 30v and 31r (1626).

29 MPM Arch. 238, fols. 85r and 86r (canons), and 108v and 113v (illuminated images on parchment); and MPM Arch. 239, fols. 18r and 23r (for plain and better-illuminated prints on parchment), and 132v (additional illuminated images on parchment).

30 MPM Arch. 220, fols. 154r and 155r (1613); and MPM Arch. 225, fols. 146v and 147r (Valentine's 1618 purchases of folio prints per piece).

31 See MPM Arch. 238, fol. 27r, for an example of his varied purchases from Galle; and Chapter 5 for his purchases from Snijders.

32 MPM Arch. 217, fol. 156r; and Appendix 1, TG-10.

33 MPM Arch. 217, fol. 156r (23 August 1610; shipment of the St Ignatius print series); and MPM Arch. 1009 (fall 1610), fols. 61 lft (Prague), 59 rht (Kraków), 39 lft (Paris), 13 lft (Willer), 28 rht (Caymox), and 26 lft (Wolters), for example.

34 MPM Arch. 1075, fol. 69r, for the total number of copies bought by Jan II; and MPM Arch. 180, fols. 29r and 134r, for the shipments to Frankfurt. See also Appendix 1, TG-21.

35 MPM Arch. 239, fol. 48r; and Appendix 1, TG-6.

36 MPM Arch. 217, fol. 174r (Verkoven); and MPM Arch. 218, fols. 27r and 207r (Mylius and Hierat, respectively).

37 Appendix 1, TG-6 and TG-5 for the Holy Founders series and the Goose Game, respectively; and MPM Arch. 238, fols. 85r and 86r, for an example of the resale of canons supplied by Galle. For a discussion of a rare example of the Goose Game produced by Galle's contemporary, Peeter de Jode I, see Leesberg 2015.

38 Appendix 1, TG-17 and TG-20 for these series; and MPM Arch. 242, fol. 161r, for examples of Catharina's supply of them at sixteenth-century prices. See MPM Arch. 242, fols. 161r and 170r, for the sale of small batches of illuminated prints on parchment to the Capuchin Jan van Gouda in Amsterdam.

39 MPM Arch. 245, fols. 70r and 73r (1637); and MPM Arch. 247, fols. 107r-107v (1639).

40 See Denucé 1927 and Duverger 1984–2009, vol. IV, no. 893, pp. 18–34, for this inventory.

41 Fuhring 2017, on Jan Galle's stock list.

42 MPM Arch. 178, fol. 194r; MPM Arch. 180, fol. 106r; and MPM Arch. 222, fol. 136r, respectively.

43 MPM Arch. 241, fol. 156r; MPM Arch. 222, fol. 136v; and MPM Arch. 220, fol. 44r, respectively.

44 MPM Arch. 222, fol. 19v (Du Puis); MPM Arch. 237, fol. 110v (Blaeu); MPM Arch. 222, fol. 172r, and MPM Arch. 223, fols. 111r and 123v (Claessens); MPM Arch. 217, fol. 230v, and MPM Arch. 218, fol. 187r (Wolters); MPM Arch. 219, fol. 23r (Mylius); MPM Arch. 238, fol. 161v (Van Egmont); MPM Arch. 239, fol. 94v (Visscher); MPM Arch. 179, fol. 41r, and MPM Arch. 217, fol. 230v (De Passe); MPM Arch. 222, fol. 170v, MPM Arch. 225, fol. 8r, and MPM Arch. 226, fol. 193v (Sadeler); and MPM Arch. 234, fol. 194r, and MPM Arch. 239, fol. 195r (Hogenberg).

45 MPM Arch. 218, fol. 71r; and MPM Arch. 128, fol. 137 lft.

46 Bowen 2022a, p. 39 and n. 13, for their correspondence; MPM Arch. 177, fol. 180v, and MPM Arch. 179, fol. 113r, for payments of 2 fl. 15 st. and 7 fl. 10 st. in 1605 and 1607, respectively; and MPM Arch. 128, fol. 94 rht, on Galle's assistance with a payment in 1616.

47 MPM Arch. 220, fol. 50v (38 fl. paid for H. van Winghe on 29 March 1613); MPM Arch. 241, fol. 110r (11 fl. paid for H. van Winghe on 12 July 1633); and MPM Arch. 224, fol. 137v (215 fl. paid on 9 February 1617 for A. van Winghe). For examples of conveying books, see MPM Arch. 223, fol. 211v (for H. van Winghe); and MPM Arch. 234, fol. 157v (for A. van Winghe).

48 Lille, Archives départementales du Nord, 9 H 61, for both of the cited letters.

49 On H. van Winghe, his interest in art and books, and his relations with Balthasar and Theodore Galle in particular, see Bowen 2022a, and pp. 41 and 40, respectively, for the cited examples.

50 MPM Arch. 127, fol. 48 lft, under 13 July 1601; MPM Arch. 131, fol. 80 lft, under 19 October 1618; and MPM Arch. 230, fol. 210r, under 15 November 1623, respectively.

51 MPM Arch. 127, fol. 211 lft (litanies); MPM Arch. 128, fol. 241 lft (diurnals); and MPM Arch. 134, fol. 85 lft (De Morgues).

52 On Cornelis I's involvement in Theodore's workshop, see Bowen 2009, pp. 128–31. See MPM Arch. 180, fols. 155v and 157r, for Theodore's supply of prints by Cornelis for Giovanni Paolo Gelli.

53 Bowen and Imhof 2022, pp. 22–23.

54 See Chapter 3.

55 MPM Arch. 221, fol. 176v; and MPM Arch. 240, fol. 24r, respectively.

56 MPM Arch. 223, fol. 204v; and MPM Arch. 21, fol. 248 rht, under 3 February 1596, respectively.

57 Cf. Jan Galle's apparently unsuccessful continuation of his father's assistance to Hieronymus van Winghe (Bowen 2022a, p. 41).

58 See also the discussion of Collaert in Appendix 1.

59 New Holl. Collaert, part 1, pp. xvi-xvii.

60 Rombouts and Van Lerius, vol. 1, pp. 380 (for three pupils in 1593–1594) and 398 (for Van Merlen in 1597)

61 MPM Arch. 180, fol. 155r. See Appendix 1, e.g., AC-1–7 and AC-11–13 for a sampling of these prints.

62 MPM Arch. 174, fols. 11v and 14r, for Galle's and Collaert's prints, respectively.

63 MPM Arch. 1104, fol. 6r, and MPM Arch. 176, fol. 108v (Hompes); and MPM Arch. 174, fols. 39r and 40r (Bergaigne).

64 MPM Arch. 174, fol. 165r, and MPM Arch. 111, fol. 138 rht (Woutneel); and MPM Arch. 223, fols. 11r and 123v (Claessens). See Chapter 9 for Collaert's dealings in Frankfurt.

65 MPM Arch. 175, fol. 155r; MPM Arch. 180, fol. 202v; and MPM Arch. 216, fol. 42r, respectively.

66 MPM Arch. 219, fol. 19v; and MPM Arch. 223, fol. 5v, respectively. See MPM Arch. 111, fol. 183 lft, for the confirmation of the family relationship between the Hompes.

67 See, for example, MPM Arch. 70, fol. 161v; and MPM Arch. 174, fol. 29v.

68 MPM Arch. 177, fol. 203v; MPM Arch. 1104, fol. 26r (for the print purchase and the corresponding payment via the merchant Gabriel Colphord at Douai); and MPM Arch. 178, fol. 1v (package of prints).

69 For summaries of Du Puis's and the Moretuses' initial and final transactions, see MPM Arch. 111, fol. 28; and MPM Arch. 133, fol. 46.

70 For example, MPM Arch. 217, fol. 27r (1610); MPM Arch. 221, fol. 148v (1614: books and a package of prints from Wierix); and MPM Arch. 129, fol. 158 lft (1616).

71 For example: MPM Arch. 216, fol. 54r (1609); MPM Arch. 220, fol. 104r (1613); and MPM Arch. 223, fol. 112r (1616).

72 For example: MPM Arch. 179, fols. 45v (17 fl.) and 147r (100 fl.) (both in 1607); MPM Arch. 219, fol. 147v (25 fl. in 1612); and MPM Arch. 220, fol. 104r (15 fl. in 1613).

73 See Chapter 9 for Collaert's dealings with the Sadelers via the Frankfurt fairs. See MPM Arch. 221, fol. 209r, and MPM Arch. 223, fol. 186r, for examples of Collaert's receipt of books for Justus; and MPM Arch. 222, fol. 170v, MPM Arch. 238, fol. 85r, and MPM Arch. 225, fol. 8r, for Collaert's shipment of packages to him in 1615, 1616, and 1618, respectively. See Appendix 1 for an overview of the Sadeler family; and Bowen 2022b for the Sadelers' activities as booksellers, and p. 380 on Liesaert.

74 For example: MPM Arch. 239, fol. 69v; MPM Arch. 246, fol. 200r; and MPM Arch. 245, fol. 41v, respectively.

75 MPM Arch. 246, fol. 64r; and MPM Arch. 1107, fol. 91r.

76 See also the discussion of De Mallery in Appendix 1.

77 For the production, publication, and distribution of this work, see Bowen and Imhof 2019.

78 Bowen and Imhof 2022, p. 4.

79 Ibid., pp. 29–30.

80 Ibid., pp. 8–9.

81 MPM Arch. 176, fol. 20r (Vrients); MPM Arch. 173, fol. 171v (T. Galle); and MPM Arch. 175, fol. 155r (P. Galle and Collaert).

82 MPM Arch. 127, fol. 8 rht, under 24 October 1605: "[Charles de Mallery] estant revenu de Paris donnoit quelques livres de l'impression d'Eustace Facault … fl. 5 st. 5".

83 MPM Arch. 177, fol. 189r (De Mallery's book purchase); and MPM Arch. 178, fols. 122v and 187v (J. Moretus's first sales of De Mallery's prints).

84 MPM Arch. 180, fols. 156r and 157r.

85 MPM Arch. 1104, fol. 46r (De Mallery's supply of prints at this rate on 13 March 1607); MPM Arch. 233, fols. 30v (sales to Dassonleville and the De Braa family in 1626); MPM Arch. 238, fol. 27r (T. Galle's sale of De Mallery's prints to B. Raesfeld in 1630); and MPM Arch. 252, fol. 58r (J. Galle's supply of De Mallery's prints at this rate for Abbot Philippe Chifflet in 1644).

86 MPM Arch. 128, fol. 108 rht (1611 sale of 400 images to Bernhard Wolters at Cologne); and MPM Arch. 222, fol. 30v (1615 sale of 1,000 prints to Johann Kruger at Augsburg), respectively.

87 Bowen and Imhof 2022, pp. 16–17.

88 Ibid., pp. 16–20.

89 MPM Arch. 1104, fol. 59r, for the payment to De Mallery for his supply of these prints, including one painted image; and MPM Arch. 180, fol. 23r, for Moretus's resale of them (with a profit margin) to Wargnirius, including the specification that one had been painted "avec or et argent" (with gold and silver).

90 For these sales, see Appendix 1, CM-1, TG-13, and JG-1.

91 MPM Arch. 230, fols. 4r and 26v, for records of De Toro's purchase and De Mallery's supply, respectively.

92 MPM Arch. 225, fol. 5r (De Gouy); and MPM Arch. 231, fol. 167r, and MPM Arch. 233, fol. 30v (Dassonleville).

93 Bowen and Imhof 2022, pp. 14–16; MPM Arch. 219, fol. 161r (1612 purchase by L. Raesfeld); and MPM Arch. 240, fol. 24v (1630 purchase of prints by B. Raesfeld, supplied by T. Galle).

94 For Wolters, see, for example, MPM Arch. 178, fol. 122v (his purchase of just thirty-six prints by De Mallery for 24 st. from Jan Moretus in 1606); and MPM Arch. 218, fols. 104v (a last purchase from the Moretuses in 1611) and fols. 110v and 187r (two separate shipments of packages with images sent to him that year from De Mallery, the first of which contained 400 prints). For Kinckius, see, for example, MPM Arch. 180, fol. 223v; MPM Arch. 221, fol. 18r (De Mallery's shipments of packages to Kinckius in 1608 and 1614; the second contained 200 prints); and MPM Arch. 227, fol. 205v (his purchase of 400 prints by De Mallery from Balthasar Moretus for 10 fl. in 1620).

[95] Compare MPM Arch. 218, fols. 207r and 208r, as well as MPM Arch. 230, fols. 143r and 143v, for De Mallery's supply of prints and the Moretuses' resale of them (and others) at higher prices. See also Chapter 5.

[96] MPM Arch. 226, fols. 53r and 185v, for the payment and shipping records, respectively.

[97] Bowen and Imhof 2022, p. 10.

[98] See Chapter 9.

[99] On Bertrant/Bertrand, see Fleury 1969, pp. 778–79, and Grivel 1986, pp. 280–81. See also Balsamo and Simonin 2022 on L'Angelier, including references to De Mallery (e.g., pp. 121–22).

[100] Bowen and Imhof 2022, pp. 11–12.

[101] Ibid., p. 30.

[102] Ibid., pp. 25–26.

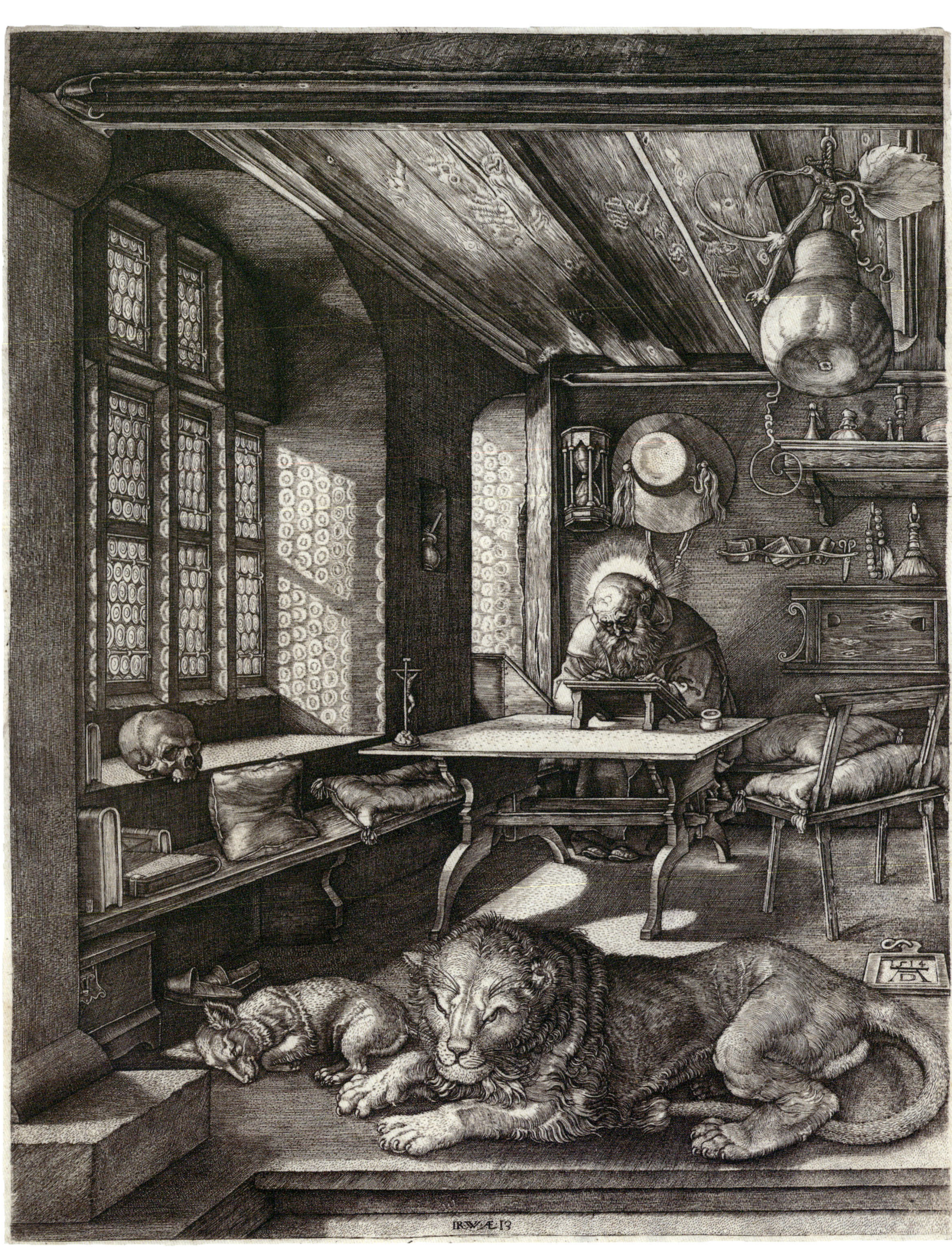

CHAPTER 6

A SPECTRUM OF PRINT DEALERS

IN ANTWERP

> I will see that the engraver Hieronymus Wierix is informed that he should prepare his prints. However, because he is an old man, he rarely works now and the prints that he made earlier are somewhat worn out. But there are others here who engrave beautifully and are recognized by those knowledgeable in the arts, although the fineness of the engraving is not the same.[1]

6.1 Hieronymus Wierix after Albrecht Dürer, *Saint Jerome in His Study*, ca. 1566, engraving, 243 × 188 mm. Antwerp, Museum Plantin-Moretus: PK.OP.17634.

THE WIERIX BROTHERS

Balthasar Moretus I was polite but cautious when he responded on 21 July 1614 to the request from the Jesuit Philippus de Peralta for engravings by Hieronymus Wierix, then sixty-one years old. Alluding to the current state of affairs, in which the engravings Hieronymus Wierix sold were mostly impressions from his stock of often worn-out plates, Moretus also acknowledged that Wierix's refined skill still surpassed that of even the best of Antwerp's new generation of engravers – including, by implication, his relatives the Galles and their brothers-in-law. Plantin, Moretus's grandfather, was less generous in his comments about Hieronymus Wierix and his brother Jan in several of his letters from the 1580s, when they were in their thirties. Of primary concern to him was how their lewd, disreputable, and irresponsible behavior rendered them extremely unreliable for the completion of commissions for engravings. Nevertheless, Plantin, like Moretus, acknowledged that the Wierixes were among the best engravers from the Low Countries, on a par with Philips Galle, the Sadeler brothers, and Hendrick Goltzius.[2]

Both Hieronymus and Jan Wierix demonstrated their superb, refined engraving style while just teenagers, when they completed remarkable copies of some of Albrecht Dürer's prints (fig. 6.1). Several Antwerp publishers, in particular Plantin, Cock, and Diericx, were quick to recognize the Wierix brothers' talent and soon employed them to execute engravings, even before they were registered as master engravers in Antwerp's Guild of St Luke. Hieronymus and Jan were ultimately accepted into the guild in 1572/73, when they were in their early twenties (figs. 6.2 and 3.17). During the last decades of the sixteenth century, they and their younger brother, Anton II, were regularly hired to complete engravings for prominent Antwerp print publishers, in particular Philips Galle, Gerard de Jode, Hans van Luyck, and

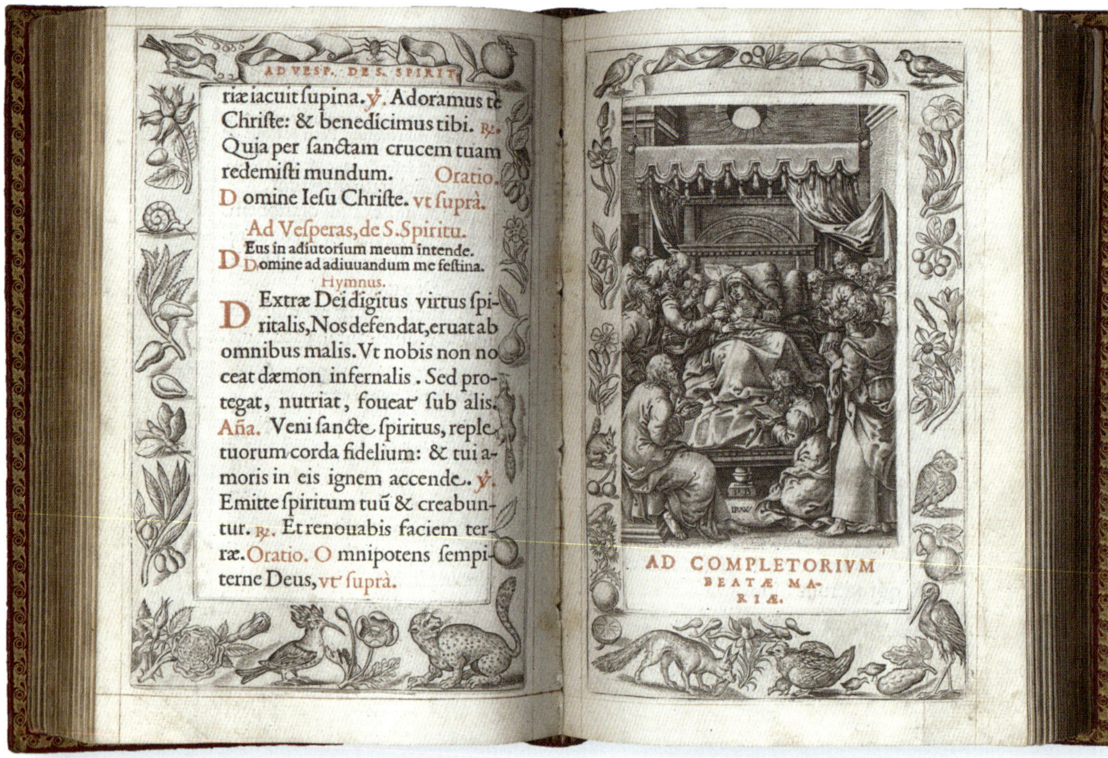

6.2 Hieronymus Wierix after Peeter van der Borcht, *The Death of the Virgin*, in: *Horae beatissimae Virginis Mariae* (Antwerp: C. Plantin, 1570), engraving, 116 × 74 mm. Antwerp, Museum-Plantin Moretus: 8–595, fol. F7r, together with fol. F6v.

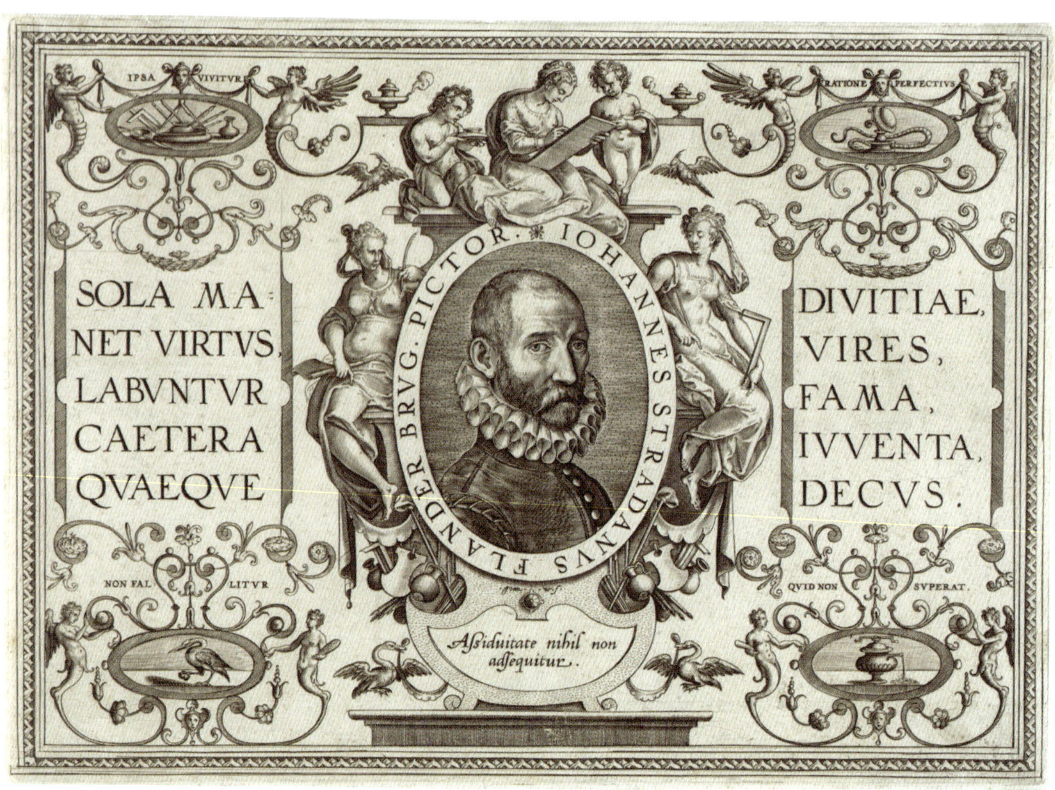

6.3 Jan Wierix after Johannes Stradanus, *Portrait of Johannes Stradanus*, ca. 1580, engraving, 193 × 264 mm. Amsterdam, Rijksmuseum: RP-P-1939-308. Appendix 1: PG-82.

Jan Baptist Vrients (fig. 6.3). Nonetheless, their most famous works from this period are the 131 large, delicately detailed engravings commissioned by the Jesuits for the highly influential *Evangelicae historiae imagines* series, which was designed to accompany the Jesuit Jerónimo Nadal's (Hieronymus Natalis) *Adnotationes et meditationes in evangelia* (fig. 6.4).[3] By the turn of the seventeenth century, however, all three Wierix brothers were pursuing independent careers. While Jan moved to Brussels, where he produced superb, finished drawings, Anton II and Hieronymus remained in Antwerp, focusing on their own extremely successful output and distribution of predominantly smaller prints of popular religious subjects. Plantin's and the Moretuses' records reveal an ongoing, especially strong preference for the Wierix brothers' work from assorted individuals with Spanish connections, ranging from Plantin's early projects featuring engravings that were designed to gain the support of King Philip II of Spain, to De Peralta's persistent endeavors to obtain engravings by Hieronymus decades later.[4]

By the start of the seventeenth century, when Hieronymus and Anton II, approximately fifty and forty-five, respectively, were both past their youthful prime, they were more inclined to enter into new types of transactions with the Moretuses by offering their own prints for resale. The first record of such a transaction dates from 1 February 1602, when Anton II provided twenty-five impressions each of several conventional devotional images, as well as

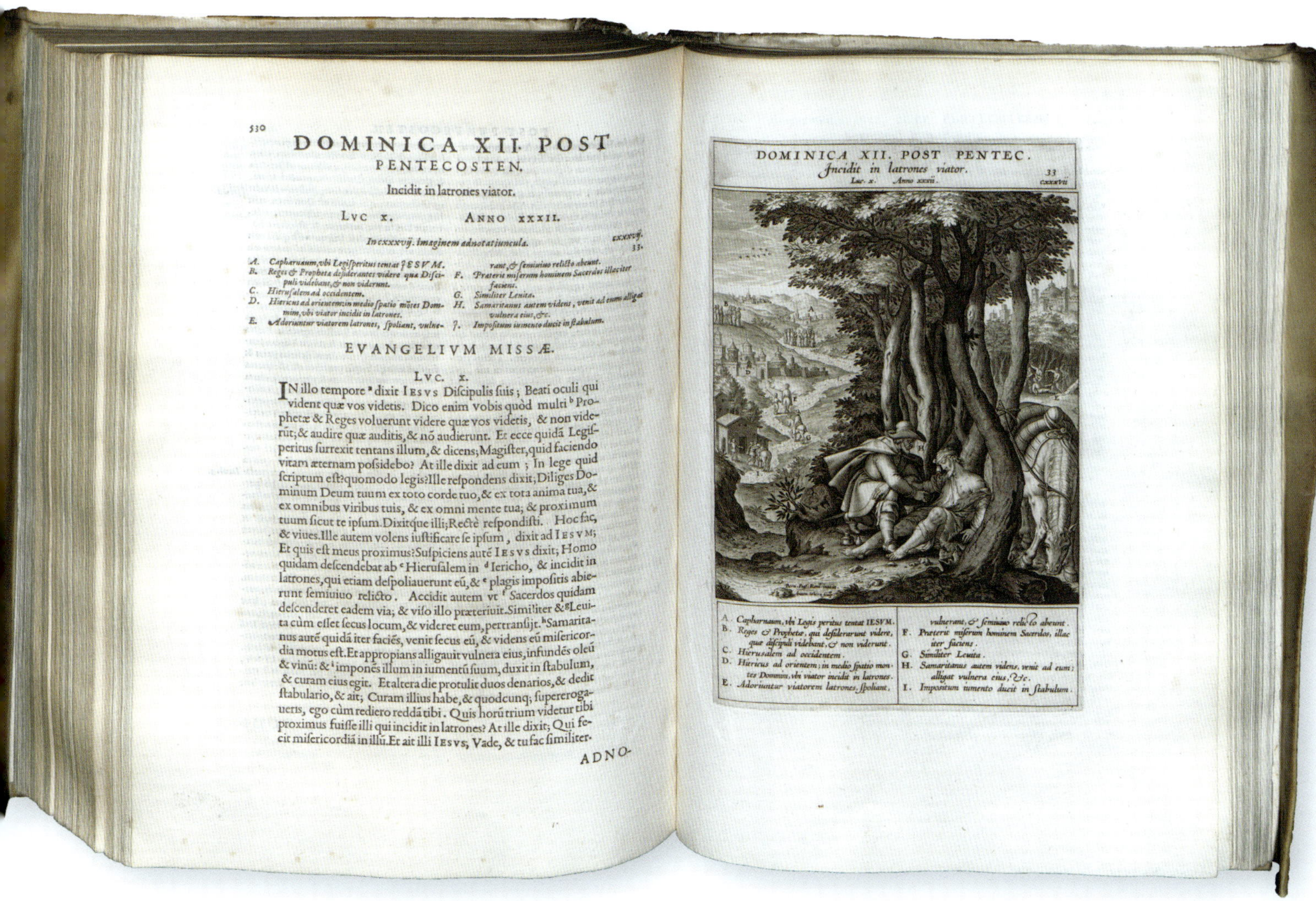

6.4 Anton Wierix II after Bernardino Passeri, *The Samaritan Taking Care of the Wounds of the Traveler*, in: *Evangelicae historiae imagines* (Antwerp: Jesuit order, 1593), engraving, 232 × 147 mm. Antwerp, Museum Plantin-Moretus: A 2682, plate 33 and p. cxxxvii, included following p. 530.

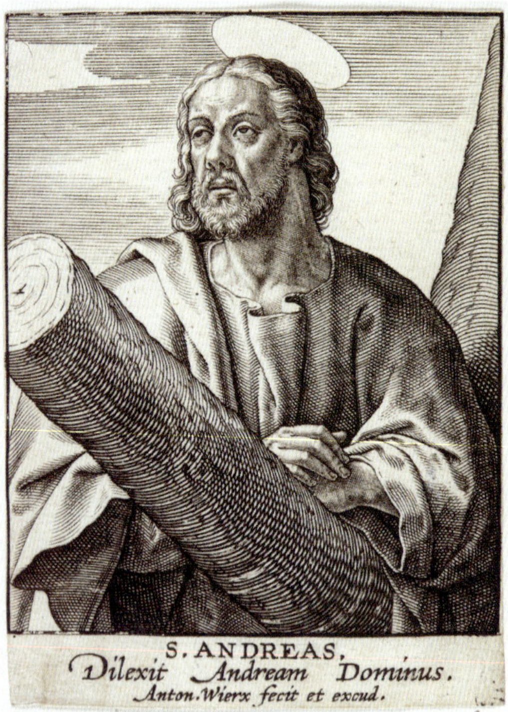

6.5 Anton Wierix II, *Saint Andrew*, from the series *Twelve Apostles*, published by Anton Wierix II by 1602, engraving, ca. 81 × 60 mm. Brussels, The Royal Library, Print Department: S.IV 16869. Appendix 1: WX-18.

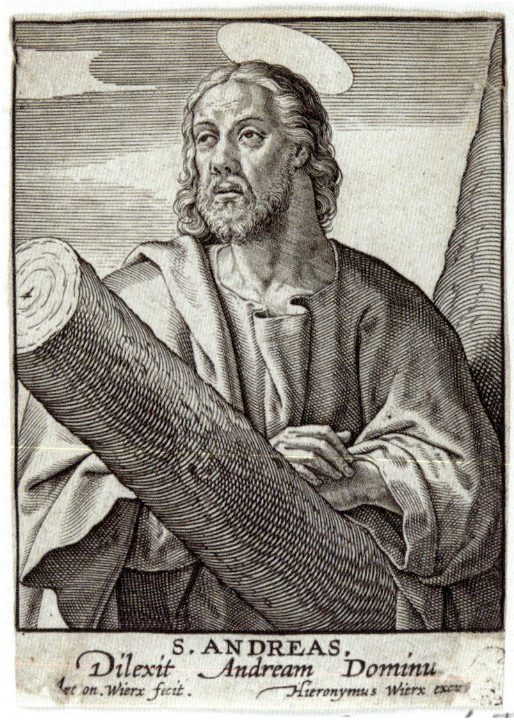

6.6 Anton Wierix II, *Saint Andrew*, from the series *Twelve Apostles*, published by Hieronymus Wierix by 1607, engraving, ca. 81 × 60 mm. Brussels, The Royal Library, Print Department: S.IV 16868. Appendix 1: WX-18.

twenty-five impressions of an allegorical portrayal of the *Triumph of Truth* (fig. 7.20), copied after a print by his brother Jan, for purchase by the merchant Rocho di Gabrielli, who would then export the prints to Gdańsk. Charging 1 st. per image for the majority of these engravings and 4 st. each for twelve prints of the Crucifixion, the total price for Anton II's selection of 112 prints amounted to 7 fl. 8 st.[5] Both the cost of the prints and the quantities in which most of the individual images were sold were typical of the Wierixes' sales of prints via the Moretuses and often stood in striking contrast to the offerings of their fellow Antwerp print dealers. For example, Di Gabrielli's purchase also included more than 5,000 small images provided by Adriaen Collaert, many of which were multiple prints – four, eight, or twelve – printed on a single leaf of paper, and sixty works with the lives of a few saints.[6] The price for all of these engravings was not calculated by the individual image, as Anton II's were, but rather by the piece of paper on which the images were printed. Anton II's price of 1 st. for most of his single engravings in this sale, bought one and a half sheets with multiple prints from Collaert. This difference in valuation is all the more notable when one considers that the actual size of some of the single images Anton II sold at 1 st., including the *Triumph of Truth*, suggests that four or more could have been printed on a single leaf of paper.

Anton II's supply of prints for resale to Di Gabrielli, coincided with a smaller consignment of engravings (worth just 2 fl. 6 st.) for the Rouen bookseller Mathieu Doom (fig. 6.5).[7] Both of these sales may reflect Anton II's attempt to generate new sources of income. Several lawsuits from the previous decade indicate that Anton II had multiple unpaid debts, forcing him to pawn some of his own copper plates, one group of which, a series with Christ and the twelve apostles, was valued at 400 fl.[8] The sale of a family interest in some property on 28 July 1601 may have alleviated his financial concerns. However, Anton II also evidently had decided to actively pursue professional, international contacts. This new approach is apparent from a legal case that he instigated on 24 November 1601 against his sister Sara, whom he had engaged to look after his household affairs and printshop while he was traveling for four to six months on business.[9] According to Anton II, Sara had not only profited excessively from the sale of his prints, but, even worse, she had supposedly taken some impressions home with her for resale for her own profit. Anton II was seeking a percentage of whatever extra profits she might thus have earned.

Although Anton II's death soon hereafter in March 1604, brought an early end to the possible expansion of his distribution network, his brother Hieronymus continued this practice. Together with Anton II, Hieronymus had provided a sampling of his prints for resale to Mathieu Doom in February 1602. However, he did not agree to sell prints through the Moretuses again until August 1605, when he provided 230 unspecified prints, valued at 1–2 st. apiece, in response to a request from the Jesuit Aegidius Schondonch in St Omer.[10] A package of prints that Hieronymus had Jan Moretus I send to St Omer in May 1604, as part of a shipment of books for Moretus's relative François Bellet, may have been intended for Schondonch as well.[11] From 1606 to 1618, a year prior to his death, Hieronymus supplied the Moretuses with prints for their clients on an annual basis.

Unlike his brother Anton II, Hieronymus periodically sold considerable quantities of prints in a single order, as he did for Schondonch. In addition to an exceptionally large sale of an unspecified group of 400 engravings to Father Juan de San Pedro of the Discalced Carmelites (possibly in Seville),[12] Hieronymus's largest consignments were a group of 500 prints sold to the bookseller Giovanni Ruardo in Naples in 1609 and a selection of nearly 400 prints sold to the Cologne bookseller Anton Hierat I in 1611. In these two cases, he supplied prints in the four different price categories that he regularly used in his transactions with the Moretuses, namely .75 st., 1 st., 1.5 st. and 2 st. per print. The Moretuses then rounded up the individual rates – slightly when reselling the prints to Ruardo and more so when dealing with Hierat – thereby garnering a small profit margin of some 3–5 fl. for themselves on each transaction.[13]

In only two instances were the subjects of the engravings Wierix sold in such quantities specified. In 1606, the Jesuit Thomas Sailly purchased 100 impressions of Wierix's portrayal of the *Death of Saint Cecilia* (fig. 6.7) at the notably high rate of 4 st. per print. The purpose behind this order is unclear. As the head of the Spanish military chaplaincy, Sailly may have intended these prints for some subsection of the Spanish troops in the Low Countries; his publication *Guidon, et practique spirituelle du soldat chrestien* of 1590 was directed to this audience. The prints may also have been purchased for the new Jesuit college in Brussels, which Sailly had helped to establish in 1604.[14] A similar ambiguity surrounds the 1610 sale of 100 impressions of an image of "four fathers", which most likely alludes to Wierix's engraving of *Christ on the Cross Venerated by Four Jesuit Saints (Ignatius of Loyola, Francis Xavier, Aloysius Gonzaga, and Stanislaus Kostka)*. Bought by the Cologne bookseller Bernhard Wolters at 2 st. per image, these prints may have been meant for export elsewhere in Cologne or for use in one of the city's numerous, burgeoning religious organizations, in particular the important Jesuit college, which owned one such image by the mid-eighteenth century (fig. 8.20).[15] In striking contrast to the sales of Wierix's prints to Ruardo and Hierat, the Moretuses resold all of these images at cost, with no profit margin for themselves. Perhaps this was due to the value they placed on their relationship with each client: Sailly was an important figure because of his ties to the Habsburg court in Brussels, while Wolters was on good personal terms with the Moretuses, following his apprenticeship under them during the 1590s.[16]

Other than these few examples of bulk sales, the Moretuses' clients usually purchased Hieronymus Wierix's prints in batches of twenty-five to seventy-five engravings, at 1–2 st. per print. When specific subjects were noted, individual images of Sts Ignatius or Xavier were

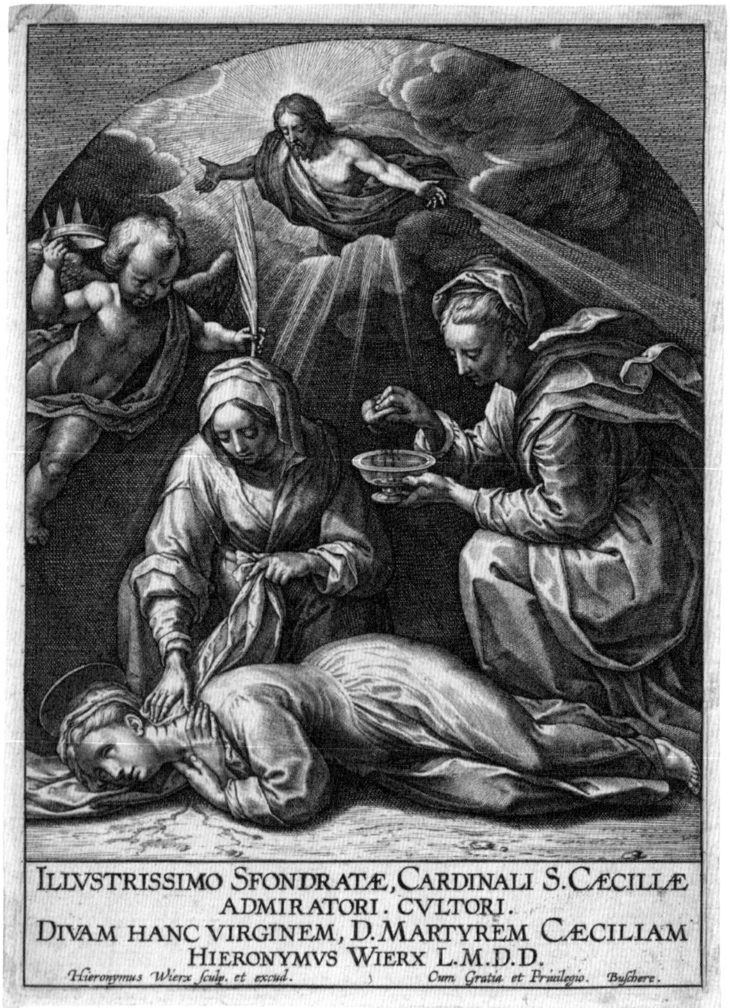

6.7 Hieronymus Wierix after Francesco Vanni, *The Death of Saint Cecilia*, between 1599 and 1605, engraving, 152 × 108 mm. New York, The Metropolitan Museum of Art: Bequest of Phyllis Massar, 2011 (2012.136.700). Image courtesy of the Metropolitan Museum of Art. Appendix 1: WX-2.

6.8 Hieronymus Wierix, title plate for the series *Life of the Infant*, by 1615, engraving, 99 × 65 mm. Amsterdam, Rijksmuseum: RP-P-1898-A-19903. Appendix 1: WX-7.

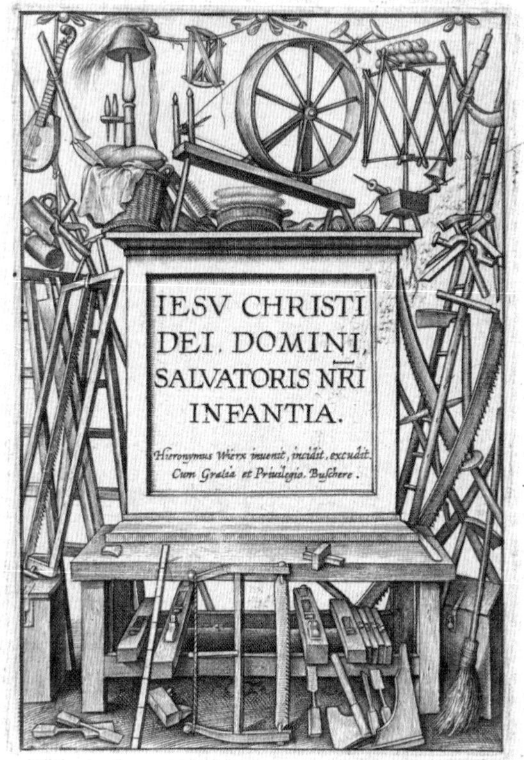

most common, while the *Life of the Infant* (*Iesu Christi … Infantia*) (fig. 6.8) was the most popular series, with a minimum of seven sets sold in 1615 and 1616 at 22 st. each.[17] Regardl ess of the quantities involved, and whether the subjects of the individual images were specified, it is essential to recall that, despite the relatively small scale of these engravings, Wierix always priced his images per print (or per series), but never per leaf, quire, or hundred, as did most other contemporary print sellers in Antwerp, particularly when selling images in bulk. Additionally, Wierix's work was often the costliest among comparably sized engravings printed simply on paper (rather than parchment), and without any added coloring or other forms of special finishing, but just the exquisitely fine rendering of tone and compositional details to recommend it.

The Moretuses sold Wierix's prints to a wide range of individuals, from members of the local elite (the Archduke and Archduchess of the Southern Netherlands, Albrecht and Isabella, and Anne de Croy, the Duchess of Arschot) to clerics of diverse denominations (Jesuits, Capuchins, and Carmelites) as well as foreign merchants and booksellers.[18] Geographically, the Moretuses' broad distribution of Wierix's prints stretched from Seville and Naples to Amsterdam and Cologne. The clients in Cologne and, above all, in Spain, were the most significant. In Cologne, all shipments went to fellow booksellers. Alongside Hierat and Wolters, Hermann Mylius, the manager of the internationally-oriented Birckman dynasty of booksellers, also engaged the Moretuses to make periodic purchases of unspecified prints from Wierix, amounting to some 30 fl. between 1608 and 1612.[19] However, these sales appear modest when compared with the avid requests for Wierix's prints placed by the Jesuit Pedro De Angulo in Seville; between 1613 and 1616, he purchased approximately 70 fl. worth of Wierix's prints via the Moretuses, all at cost. Though the majority of these sales consisted of large quantities of unspecified images sold in bulk, De Angulo also bought several of Wierix's series, including the *Life of the Infant* and the *Mirror of Virginity* (*Speculum virginitatis*).[20] Merchants in Antwerp with Spanish roots also periodically purchased Wierix's prints from the Moretuses. For example, Diego Pardo Lopez bought assorted images of Sts Ignatius and Xavier in August 1607, while Martin Fernando Carillo ordered a total of 100 prints at Wierix's bulk rates of 1, 1.5, and 2 st. per print.[21]

By contrast, sales to individuals in Italy, France, and the Low Countries are remarkably rare. In some instances, other agents may have been involved. For example, in 1606 and 1612, Jan Baptist Vrients' brother-in-law Gaspar Vivario, who was active as a print dealer in Rome, bought engravings from Hieronymus Wierix amounting to approximately 170 fl.[22] This also appears to have been the situation in France. While the Moretuses were not intermediaries for the actual sale of engravings there, Wierix did occasionally ask them to transport packages of prints for him, presumably to satisfy other independently arranged transactions. No shipment, notably, went to Paris, where Wierix may well have had his own established connections. Rather, prints were sent to the booksellers Charles de Gouy in Amiens and Jean Morel and Jean du Puis in Lille (then part of the Low Countries).[23] Although each may have been acting as an intermediary in turn, Jean du Puis's periodic exchanges with Adriaen Collaert suggest that he may have had a more active interest in the sale of prints from Antwerp.

This subdivision between markets that Wierix continued to manage on his own and sales that he was willing to complete via others is outlined at length in his testimony for a legal dispute involving him and Peeter de Jode I in 1608. The origins of the dispute dated back to 1606, when Wierix had just begun to sell his prints via the Moretuses. The essence of the dispute is whether or not De Jode had agreed to pay personally and within six months for a group of prints that he had selected from Wierix's stock for his sister to sell in Danzig (Gdańsk). In Wierix's reply to De Jode's defense, he begins by asserting that he does not know De Jode's sister, nor has he dealt with her before. Moreover, he argues, he generally did not do business in Germany or Gdańsk, but only with individuals in Antwerp or those who paid in cash. Wierix subsequently elaborates on this statement, claiming that he is a "worker" ("werckman") who is not familiar with trade in Gdańsk or other foreign places. Hence, he only deals with those whom he knows and does not engage in long-distance transactions where he must wait for payments.[24] Wierix's fundamental assertions that he restricted his business dealings to known, local individuals who paid upfront in cash align fully with his involvement in the international print trade through the Moretuses; they saw to the immediate payment for clients in distant places or for individuals whom Wierix did not know, and they assisted him by transporting his prints to clients in his personal network.

Over the course of fourteen years of transactions (1605–1618), Wierix supplied the Moretuses with engravings for resale that amounted to a minimum of nearly 250 fl.[25] Significantly less than what was provided by the Galles or Charles de Mallery, Wierix's offerings were comparable to what Hieronymus Cock and Volcxken Diericx had sold to the Moretuses' over the much longer timespan of nearly thirty-four years and were three times what Adriaen Collaert had supplied in the same period. Nevertheless, the relative value of Wierix's individual prints remained high despite their small scale. Consequently, when these sales were

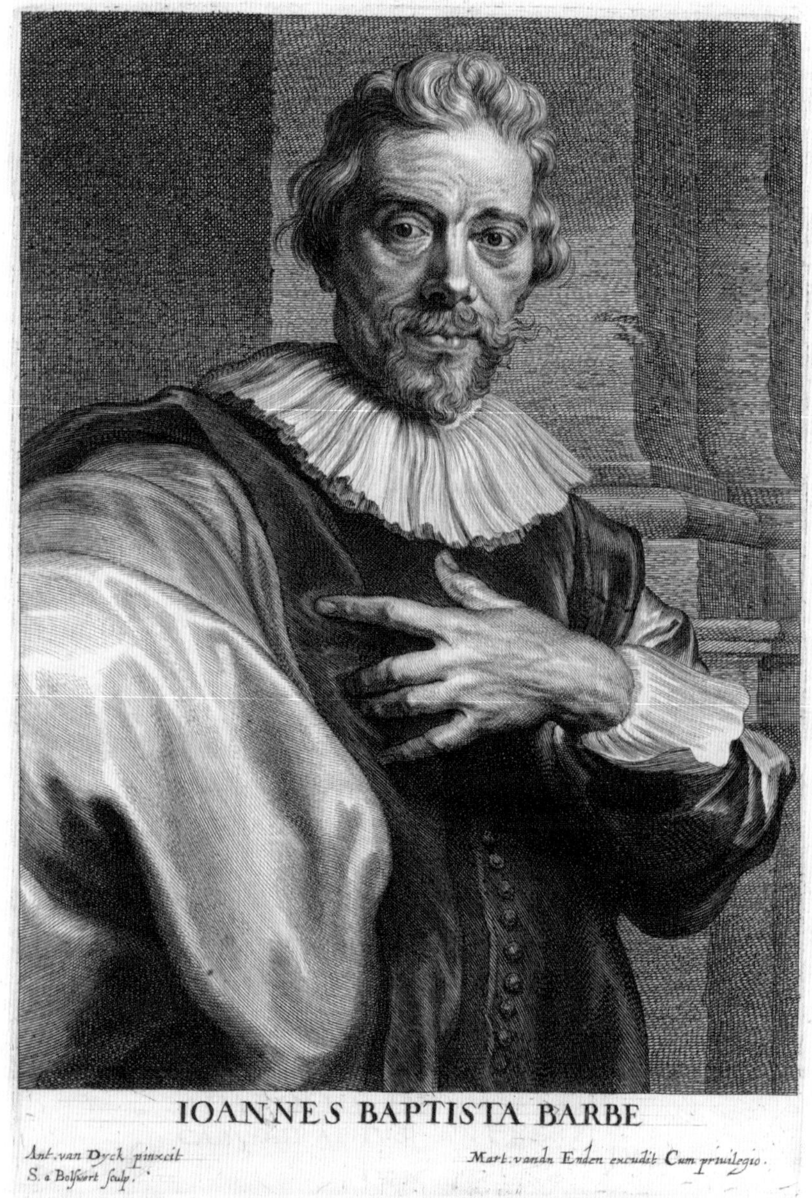

6.9 Schelte à Bolswert after Anthony van Dyck, *Jan-Baptist Barbé*, 1645–1646, engraving, 244 × 160 mm. Amsterdam, Rijksmuseum: RP-P-2010-327-44.

combined with his own personal transactions, they evidently generated substantial funds since he was able to buy shares in several houses in Antwerp during 1613 and 1615.[26] Indeed, the market for Hieronymus Wierix's print was such that on 11 December 1619, a little more than one month following his death, his children, Hieronymus II, Cecilia, and Catharina, obtained permission from the Council of Brabant "to profit from" their father's plates (namely, to sell impressions pulled from them) for a period of six years.[27] This was but the first of numerous legal proceedings concerning the ownership of Wierix's plates and the posthumous trade in his engravings and copies thereof. It is significant that the majority of these proceedings involved not simply Wierix's immediate heirs, but also the Antwerp engraver-print publisher Jan Baptist Barbé (fig. 6.9).

JAN-BAPTIST BARBÉ

Baptized in July 1578 and apprenticed to Philips Galle in 1594–1595, Barbé is listed as a master engraver in Antwerp's Guild of St Luke in 1610–1611 and served as a dean of the guild in 1627–1628.[28] His initial association with the Galle workshop may account for the fact that he, Cornelis Galle I, and another of Philips Galle's former pupils, Peeter Backeerel, were responsible for approving the inventory of the plates owned by Theodore Galle's widow, Catharina Moerentorf, at her death in 1636.[29] Like the Wierixes, Barbé initially executed many of his larger engravings in response to commissions from other publishers, in particular Philips Galle's sons-in-law Adriaen Collaert and Charles de Mallery. While these engravings often reproduced designs by Maarten de Vos and Peeter de Jode I (fig. 6.10), Barbé subsequently worked after other artists, such as Abraham van Diepenbeeck.[30] Nevertheless, he is known above all for his own smaller, finely engraved images of a range of religious subjects that are reminiscent of Hieronymus Wierix's publications (figs. 6.11 and 6.12). Barbé officially connected himself with the Wierix family by marrying Hieronymus's daughter Christina in March 1620, four months after Hieronymus's death and when Barbé was himself nearly forty-two years old.[31] Consequently, he was able to benefit from ties to two prominent families in the Antwerp print world. In November 1620, several months following his marriage, Barbé, along with his wife and his sister-in-law Cecilia, began a series of lawsuits that ultimately resulted in Hieronymus Wierix II selling his share of his father's estate to Christina and Cecilia on 31 January 1622. Barbé's active role in these proceedings is apparent from the surviving documents,

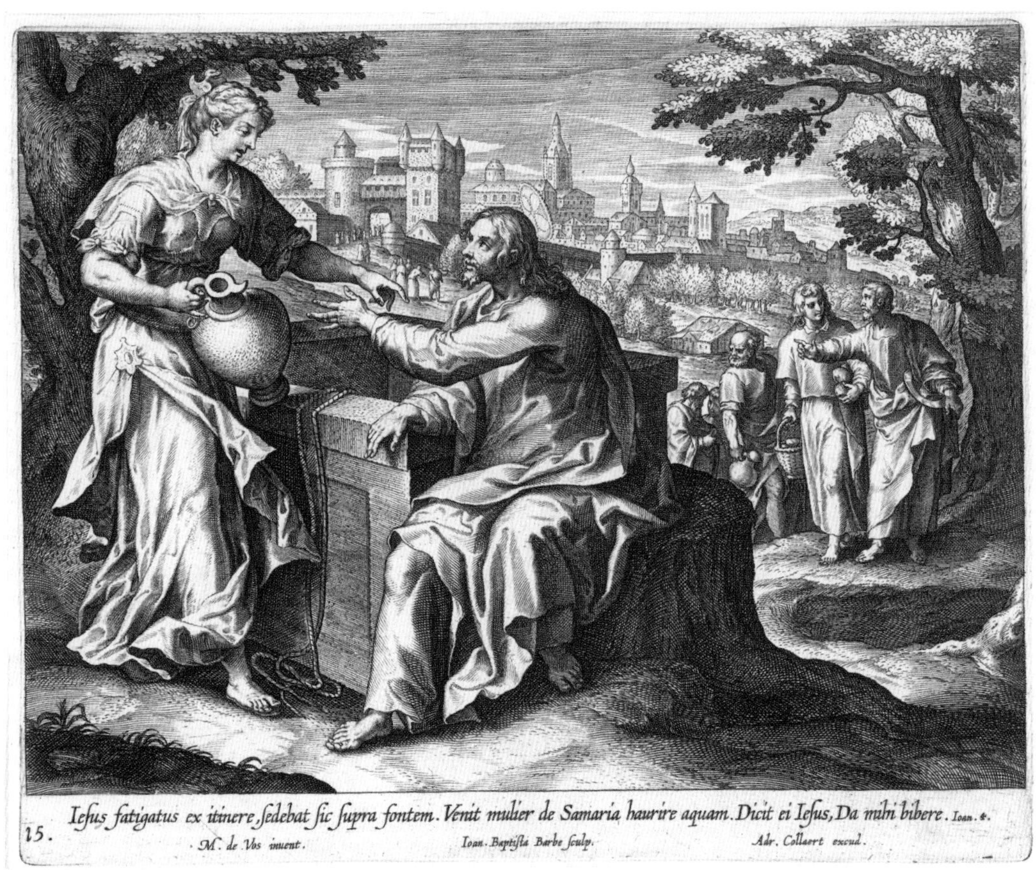

6.10 Jan-Baptist Barbé after Maarten de Vos, *Christ and the Woman of Samaria*, print 15 from the series *The Life, Passion and Resurrection of Christ*, 1598, engraving, 179 × 216 mm. Amsterdam, Rijksmuseum: RP-P-1885-A-9637. Appendix 1: AC-9.

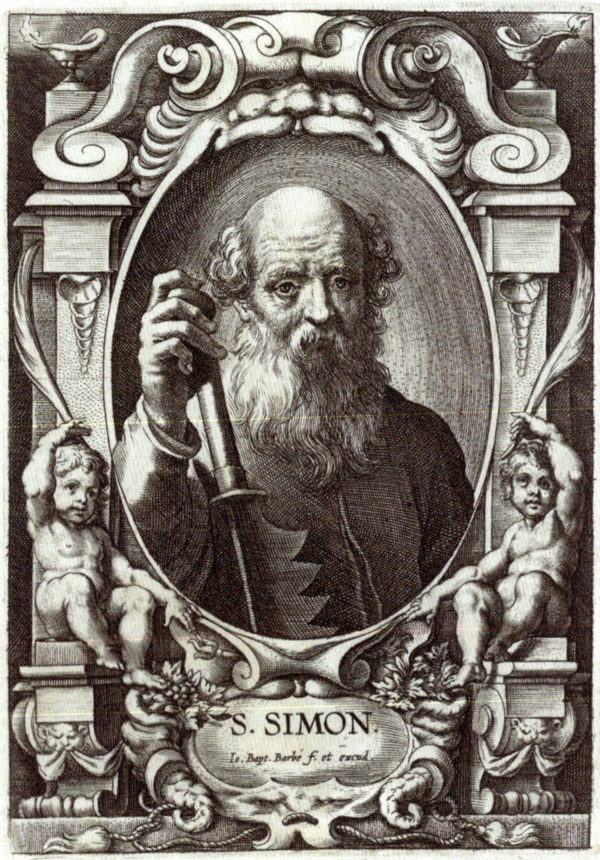

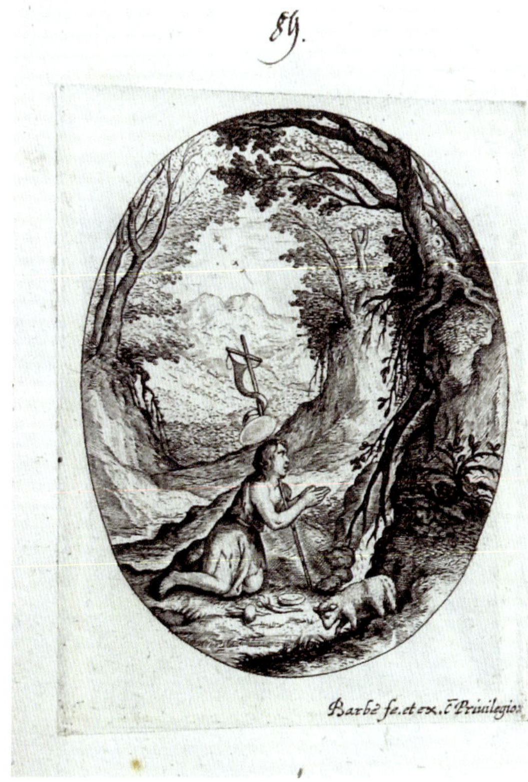

6.11 Jan-Baptist Barbé after Theodore van Loon, *Apostle Simon the Zealot*, from the series *SS. Apostolorum et Evangelistarum icones*, ca. 1610–1640, engraving, 129 × 94 mm. Amsterdam, Rijksmuseum: RP-P-1904-228.

6.12 Jan-Baptist Barbé, *Saint John the Baptist*, s.a., engraving, 85 × 64 mm. Wolfegg, Fürstlich zu Waldburg-Wolfegg'sche Kunstsammlungen: vol. 52, print 89.

where he is periodically cited as the one who instigated the case or the one to whom Hieronymus II felt obligated to respond in his own defense.[32]

Barbé subsequently endeavored to safeguard his own work from being pirated by requesting privileges to protect his engravings. The production of copies was rampant in Antwerp (and elsewhere), particularly among the popular devotional images in which both Hieronymus Wierix I and Barbé specialized.[33] While Barbé obtained one such privilege on 5 August 1624, he is best known for the controversy he instigated a decade later. In this instance, he sought to use a very broadly worded privilege he had requested to protect his financial and personal interests within the Dutchy of Brabant by prohibiting the sale of copies both of works that he had engraved, designed, or might produce in the future and also of the engravings made or designed by Hieronymus Wierix, his deceased father-in-law.[34] Although Barbé had directed his case against Nicolaus Lauwers, several Antwerp artists joined the fray. Barbé's rights, the importance of maintaining certain quality standards in the engravings produced, and, above all, the system of privileges were supported by Gerard Seghers, Theodore Rombouts, Theodore and Jan Galle, Lucas Vorsterman, Paulus Pontius, Willem van Haecht, Theodoor Jan van Merlen (a nephew of Abraham van Merlen), Willem Collaert, and Rubens (who had won a lawsuit against the plagiarism of his work in France), many of whom were major players in the Antwerp print market.[35] Several other artists were implicated alongside Lauwers, namely Philips de Mallery, Jan Boel, Jan Cnobbaert, Alexander Voet, Hans Witdoeck, Cornelis van Tienen, and Michael Snijders, while Maarten van den

Enden also backed Lauwers. Arguing that engraving was a free art form like painting, they asserted that Barbé's privilege was, consequently, an unjust limitation on their own activities and an inappropriate form of monopoly. Tensions over who sided with whom are evident from Abraham van Merlen's decision to declare himself officially a neutral party and from requests that the defendants comment on whom they had tried to convince to support them. Of greatest importance were the Galles, Boetius and Schelte à Bolswert, and unspecified members of the Collaert and Van Merlen families; the last two (in the opinion of the defendants) also sold similar prints.[36] This opinion is of particular significance. Although it is impossible to evaluate the veracity of Barbé's claims that his own work had been plagiarized, due to the currently imperfect knowledge of his production and that of the defendants, the application of his privilege to copies after Hieronymus Wierix's work was clearly not justified. While relatively few copies of Wierix's prints are known among the oeuvres of most of the accused, Charles de Mallery and Theodore Galle (who, by this time, may well have owned many of De Mallery's plates) had produced numerous such replicas (compare figs. 6.18 and 6.20), even though Galle officially supported Barbé in this case.[37] Barbé himself had even, on

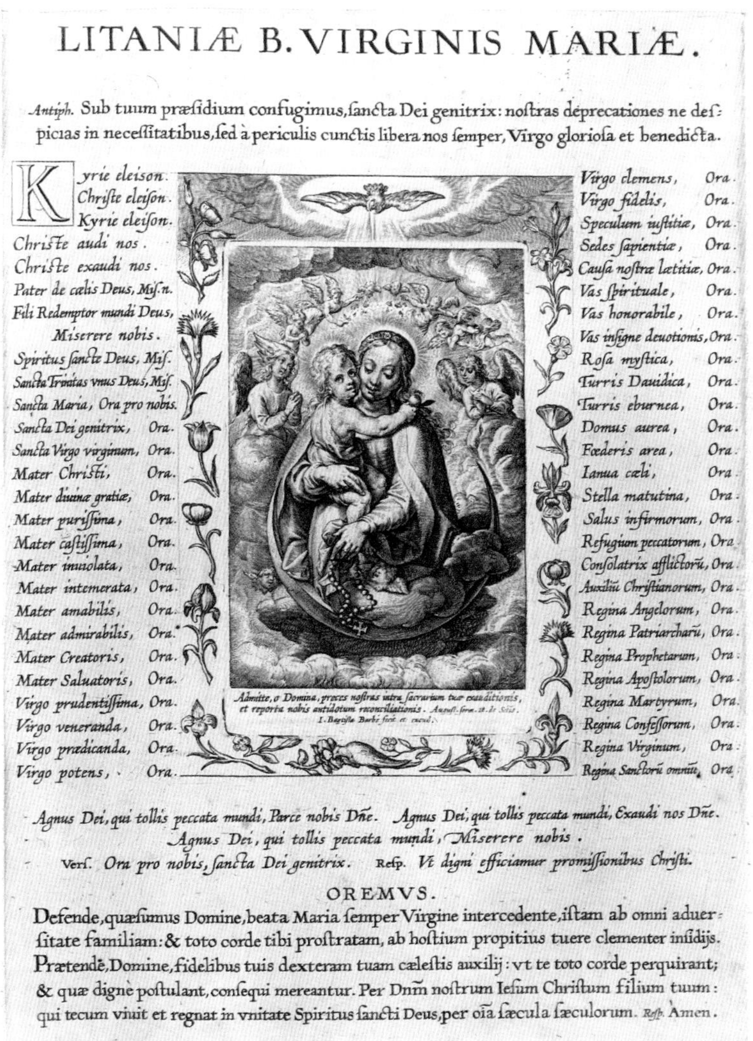

6.13 Jan-Baptist Barbé, *Litany with the Virgin and Child on a Crescent*, s.a., engraving, 110 × 68 mm. Wolfegg, Fürstlich zu Waldburg-Wolfegg'sche Kunstsammlungen: vol. 221, print 57.

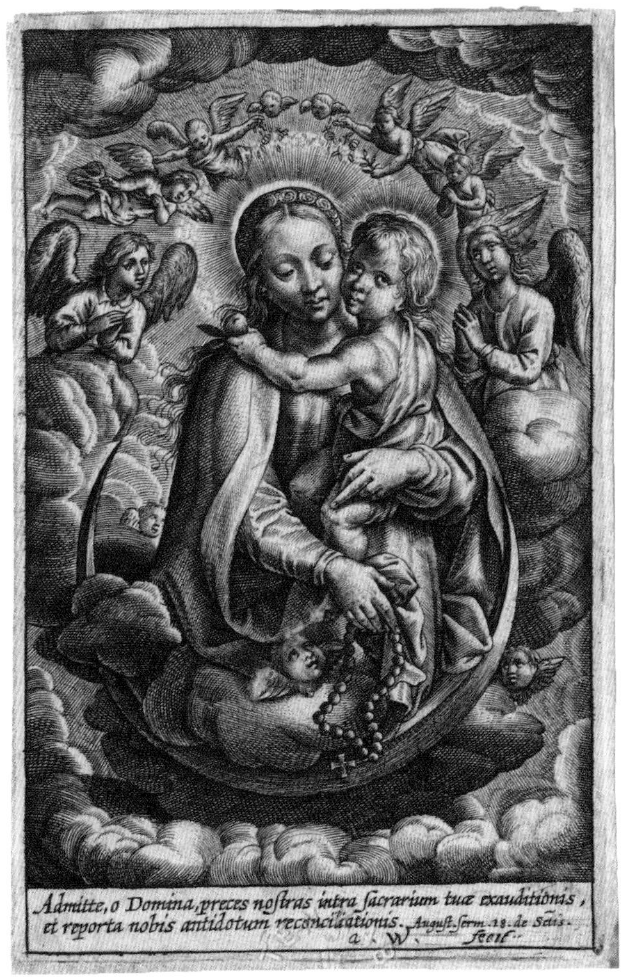

6.14 Anton Wierix II, *Virgin and Child on a Crescent*, s.a., engraving, 108 × 67 mm. Antwerp, Museum Plantin-Moretus: PK: OP-03605.

occasion, made and published copies of the Wierixes' engravings (figs. 6.13 and 6.14). Despite this potential irregularity in terms of who was liable to charges of plagiarism and who was not, the case was ultimately decided in Barbé's favor and resulted in the confiscation of the forbidden copies that were then in the possession of the cited defendants in October 1633. However, the stocks of copper plates owned by the Collaerts, Abraham van Merlen, and Theodore Galle were not touched.

The full significance of Barbé having his privilege confirmed for both his own and his father-in-law's engravings may be deduced from another case dated 22 August 1635, which concerned the ownership and use of Wierix's plates inherited by Barbé's sister-in-law Cecilia. Initiating the lawsuit in her defense against Barbé, Cecilia argued that she had agreed to move into her sister's and Barbé's home two years earlier due to her own serious ill health. Among the possessions she brought with her were numerous valuable plates from her father, which Barbé had convinced her could be used to print impressions for resale in Spain and elsewhere to generate funds for both of them. However, two years later, when Cecilia had recovered sufficiently from her illness and wished to return to her own home with her possessions, including her share of Wierix's copper plates, Barbé refused to let her take them and had her declared insane and, consequently, incompetent. Upon further investigation, it was determined that there was no basis for this claim. Instead, according to the notary Dirk Fabri, the author of the petition in Cecilia's defense, the real source of the problem was Barbé's own greed and his difficult, improper nature, which had already been evident on several previous occasions. Regrettably, it remains unclear whether Cecilia was able to retrieve her full share of Wierix's plates.[38] Nevertheless, when Cecilia completed a will on 14 March 1637, she owned at least enough copies of Hieronymus Wierix's plates (in addition to copies of other "masters") to hope to raise the significant sum of 400 fl. by allowing the chapel wardens to sell them to fund the purchase of a silver lamp for the chapel with the Holy Cross altar in St James's church in Antwerp. The remaining impressions of prints that were still in her possession were to be divided among several local monasteries and the Jesuit residence in Antwerp (the "Professiehuis"). By contrast, she left her sister Christina, Barbé's wife, just 6 fl. and one painting by Jan Francquaert.[39]

While Barbé's character and the motivations behind his interactions with various members of the Wierix family are suspect, his desire to protect and maximize his own profits from the resale of Hieronymus Wierix's engravings, alongside his own, is clear. When Balthasar Moretus II wrote to Philippe Chifflet on 16 July 1644 concerning who should engrave the frontispiece for a book, he observed that Barbé's skill as an engraver was comparable to Cornelis Galle II's, but that Barbé routinely asked twice or three times as much for his work.[40] Regrettably, the Moretuses' transactions with Barbé do not reveal what he charged for specific prints, as there is only one purchase from him and it was merely of an unspecified allotment of images ("beldekens") for just 7 fl. 4 st.[41] Barbé's other dealings with the Moretuses, primarily the export of packages – periodically identified as containing images – at his request, however, attest to some of the markets and individual clients interested in the prints in Barbé's possession – be they his own or posthumously printed impressions of plates from the Wierix family.

The first such shipments took place in 1616 and 1618, when Barbé had been working as an independent engraver in Antwerp for several years. These consisted of single packages that were sent to Justus Sadeler in Venice, along with packages from other Antwerp engravers and numerous books that Sadeler had ordered from the Moretuses.[42] Who instigated these exchanges – Barbé, Sadeler, or possibly even Adriaen Collaert, Sadeler's personal contact in Antwerp, who was often involved in these arrangements – is not known. Although such exchanges were just one of a series of contemporaneous transactions between the Moretuses and either Sadeler or Collaert, Barbé did not engage the Moretuses again until 1622. Then, on two separate occasions, the Moretuses sent an unspecified package from Barbé to the bookseller Andrea Brugiotti in Rome for the Antwerp painter Jacob de Hase, who had settled in Rome by 1601, joining a thriving community of artists from Flanders. Though a similar shipment occurred again in 1625, Barbé then sent no more packages to Italy via the Moretuses.[43]

The Moretuses contributed to a far more sustained trade in Barbé's wares with various individuals in France between 1630 and 1634, precisely when Barbé was engaged in protecting his rights locally for the production and distribution of his prints and those of Hieronymus Wierix. The single most important recipient was the Parisian print dealer Jean Messager, to whom Charles de Mallery had sent numerous packages two decades earlier. While Messager received a total of eleven packages from Barbé during these years, he also served as the point of exchange for packages from Barbé that were intended for the art dealer Jean Marin, who was active in Nancy.[44] Another important, albeit more limited, destination for Barbé's publications in Paris was the German-born engraver and print publisher Jacques Honervogt I, to whom Barbé sent six packages between 26 February 1633 and 14 October 1634.[45] Finally, in 1632, Barbé had the Moretuses send single packages to Carolus du Mere de Dieu, a Discalced Carmelite, and André Duchesne, a historian and geographer, via the Parisian bookseller Eustache Foucault.[46] Though occurring within a narrow timeframe, these accounts reveal not only how Barbé's network of contacts included important French print dealers, but also how he dealt directly with individual collectors. His reliance on the Moretuses for assistance with his transactions (at least in these four year) with these clients in Paris is in striking contrast to the practices of his father-in-law, who only employed the Moretuses for occasional shipments elsewhere in France.

From 1635, the focus of Barbé's international shipments via the Moretuses shifted to Cologne. In 1635–1636, Johann Kinckius, a bookseller and former apprentice of the Moretuses, received a minimum of five packages (most noted to contain prints) from Barbé. Kinckius simultaneously was the point of exchange for four additional, single packages that were sent between 1636 and 1638 for the print publisher Abraham Hogenberg, the son of Frans Hogenberg, an émigré from the Low Countries.[47] These examples highlight, once again, the multifaceted involvement of booksellers in the print trade.

Notably absent from the Moretuses' accounts are shipments of Barbé's publications to Spain, despite his sister-in-law Cecilia's claim that Barbé had asserted that they could benefit from the posthumous sale of prints by Hieronymus Wierix there, and in other lands, during the early 1630s. Perhaps the reference to Spain – a country where Hieronymus Wierix's prints were eagerly sought in his lifetime – was just a ruse to convince Cecilia to allow Barbé to print impressions from her collection of Wierix's plates that Barbé may actually have intended for various customers in France with whom he was trading actively at this time. The irregular but intense concentration of Barbé's shipments of prints to distinct destinations by way of the Moretuses may also indicate that he had a range of international clients for his prints (including individuals in Spain), whom he served through diverse means, just one of which was the Moretuses' own transport network. Regardless of this uncertainty, when Barbé passed away in 1649, his intimate association with the Wierixes' engravings, both in terms of the character of much of his own work and his control over many of Hieronymus's plates through his marriage, was enduring. When a box of copper plates executed by members of the Wierix family was discovered amid the possessions of the Jesuit order in Amsterdam in 2000, it also contained plates produced by Barbé.[48]

What of the other printmakers and publishers involved in the controversy concerning privileges instigated by Barbé's lawsuit? Not everyone who was named actively interacted with the Moretuses. Those who did, represented different standpoints, from the accused, to those who endeavored to remain neutral, and those who decided to side with Barbé. Already distinct in their output and the apparent scale of their activities, their varying opinions in this matter underscore underlying distinctions in their attitudes towards how to respond to the demand for prints from Antwerp and how the local market might function. Consequently, they constitute a diverse sampling of important figures in the debate over privileges and in the burgeoning Antwerp print market as a whole.

Several of those who challenged Barbé's privilege, such as Hans Witdoeck and Cornelis van Tienen, did not rely much, if at all, on the Moretuses between 1590 and 1641. Registered as a pupil of Lucas Vorsterman I in 1630–1631, Witdoeck engraved numerous prints after Rubens and Cornelis Schut, whose work was clearly influenced by the former. Registered in the Guild of St Luke as a master engraver in 1620–1621, Van Tienen appears to have lived much longer (to ca. 1678) and may have turned to the Moretuses for assistance with his ongoing trade in prints and paintings in the 1640s.[49]

Similarly, both Nicolaes Lauwers (the leading defendant in Barbé's suit) and Alexander Voet I appear to have had successful careers after Barbé's case was concluded and to have managed their business largely independently of the Moretuses. Admitted into the Guild of St Luke as a master engraver in 1619–1620, Lauwers was named a dean of the guild in 1635–1636 and took on at least five apprentices between 1635–1636 and 1652–1653.[50] Although he evidently maintained a workshop, Lauwers asked the Moretuses to help him with a shipment of prints only once, namely in December 1638, when he had them send a solitary package to the Cologne map and print seller Abraham Hogenberg.[51] However, the Moretuses never sold prints of his to third parties. Voet, who was not named a master engraver in the Guild of St Luke until 1628–1629, shortly before the start of Barbé's lawsuit, also took on several pupils in the years thereafter.[52] The timing of these apprenticeships presumably went hand-in-hand with the success of his business selling prints. The Moretuses' accounts provide an interesting glimpse of his initial activities; in November 1632, he had them send two packages to Jean Messager in Paris, which were ultimately destined for the print seller Jean Marin in Nancy.[53] As this shipment also included three packages from Barbé that were similarly intended for Marin, it may reflect a potential competition between the young, new printmaker and the aging Barbé and so may have contributed to Barbé's decision several months later to take legal action. The subsequent success of Voet's business (despite Barbé's case) is apparent from his dealings with the well-connected art dealers Lucas and Cornelis de Wael (who were firmly established in Italy by 1630), as well as from the sheer volume of his publications.[54]

Perhaps the most striking lacunae in the Moretuses' involvement in the print trade are dealings with Philips de Mallery. While the Moretuses actively participated in the international distribution of thousands of Charles de Mallery's prints for two decades, Philips was remarkably independent. Only once, in January 1629, did he provide a small allotment of thirty-one unspecified images, which the Moretuses resold to the Utrecht bookseller Jan van Doorn for just 1 fl. 5 st.[55] Philips de Mallery had certainly, on occasion, made engravings reminiscent of Hieronymus Wierix's work, including ones for the Parisian print seller Jean Messager, with whom Barbé also dealt. However, the extent of De Mallery's production remains too poorly documented to evaluate either Barbé's charges against him or his place in the European print market.[56] Of all the figures named in Barbé's complaint, only two repeatedly dealt with or via the Moretuses: the engraver and print publisher Jan Boel and Jan Cnobbaert, who, though officially working as a bookseller, also sold loose engravings.

ꕥ JAN BOEL AND THE CNOBBAERT FAMILY

Born in 1592, Boel was admitted into Antwerp's Guild of St Luke as a master engraver in 1610. His registrations of apprentices – one in 1621–1622 and one in 1624–1625 – coincide with other evidence that his business was flourishing at this time. In particular, between 1621–1622 and 1631–1632, he was able to afford the annual membership fees for the guild's rhetoric chamber ("Violiere") and similarly participated in the guild's annual banquet from 1621–1622 through 1630–1631, with the exception of the year 1629–1630, when he declared himself ill due to the plague.[57] Records of the baptisms of his nine children (between 25 January 1620 and 21 August 1629) indicate that he was also on good terms with the Galle family, as Theodore was named the godfather of his son Jan (baptized on 11 January 1624) and Jan Galle was godfather to Boel's daughter Claire (baptized on 14 March 1628).[58]

This was also the period (December 1620 through February 1631), when Boel made regular use of the Moretuses to further his participation in the print trade. He supplied them with prints for resale only twice: once in 1621, when he provided them with 100 unspecified prints at the frequently applied rate of 36 st. per 100 images (resold at cost to the Brussels bookseller Jean Leonard); and once in 1627, when he provided prints worth the remarkable sum of 100 fl. If the first rate of 36 st. per 100 images was used for this later sale, approximately 5,500 prints would have been exchanged. Such an astounding amount is possible, for the Moretuses sold the Cologne booksellers Anton II and Arnold Hierat a total of 6,300 prints in February 1627, where the images were recorded as having been supplied by [Theodore] Galle and others ("Imagines Gallei et aliorum").[59]

While these sales are intriguing for the insight they offer into the scale of Boel's activities, Boel more often simply asked the Moretuses to assist him with the transport of individual packages for clients in Germany between 1620 and 1626, when he had apprentices assisting him. The majority were sent to individuals in Cologne, in particular: the booksellers (and former apprentices of the Moretuses) Johann Kinckius and Cornelis van Egmont, as well as the print seller Abraham Hogenberg. The Flemish bookseller Michiel van Dale, who had married Lambert Raesfeld's widow, Anna Dörhoff, in Münster but who still had family in Antwerp, also received a few packages from Boel, often via Kinckius.[60] Recalling Hieronymus Wierix's assertion that he only did business with people he knew (or who paid upfront in cash), the predominance of individuals with current or past connections to Antwerp (or neighboring towns, in the case of Hogenberg) in these personal transactions is striking. Furthermore, these connections are in stark contrast to the individuals to whom the Moretuses sold Boel's prints. Two additional transactions, in which the Liège bookseller Jan Ouwerx asked the Moretuses to make payments of 25 fl. to Boel on his behalf in both 1628 and 1631, attest to another member of Boel's networks.[61]

Regrettably, no single, specific print is cited in any of these transactions, and the diversity of Boel's publications makes it difficult to speculate with any certainty about what types of prints he distributed via these channels. Though Boel was trained as an engraver, relatively few prints by Boel himself are known (fig. 6.15). Rather, his stock appears to have comprised numerous older plates originally owned and published by others, in particular Philips Galle (fig. 6.16), as well as new engravings that he himself had commissioned. Many of these images were smaller in format and included some copies after works by the Wierixes (compare figs. 6.17 and 6.20). However, he also published some exceptionally large prints, such as the *Tree of the Franciscan Order*.[62]

By 1632, just one year prior to Barbé's legal action, Boel's concentrated professional and

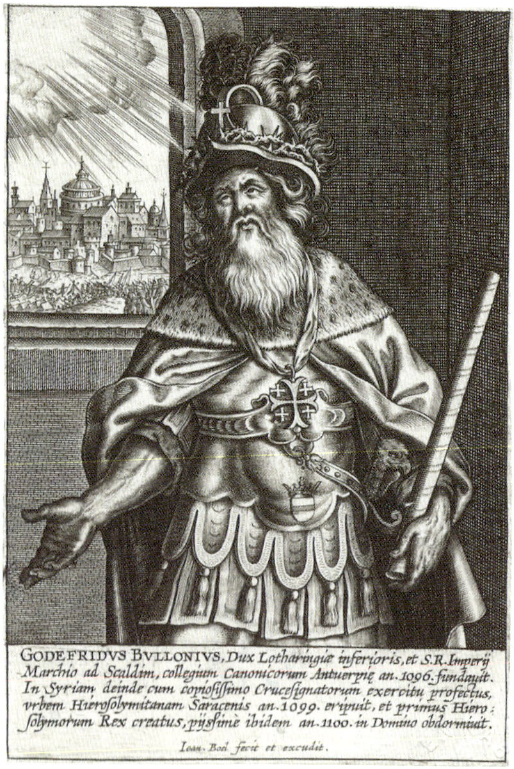

6.15 Jan Boel, *Godfrey of Bouillon*, s.a., engraving, 115 × 76 mm. Antwerp, Museum Plantin-Moretus: PK.OP.00065.

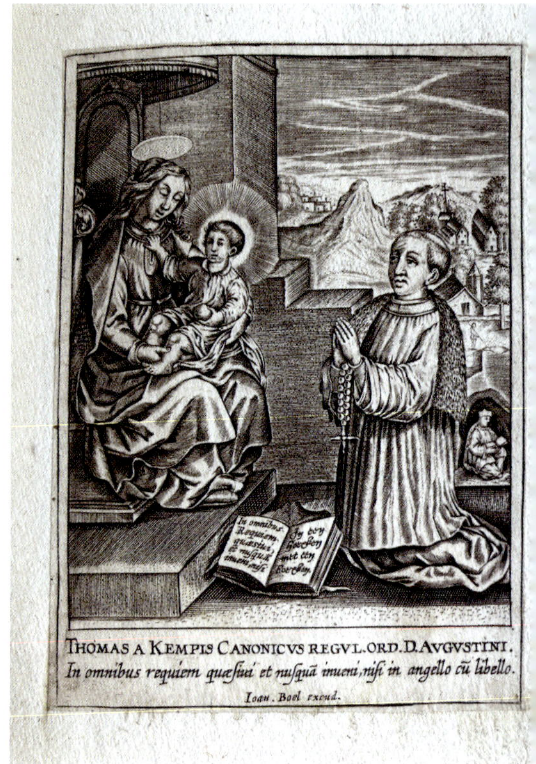

6.17 Anonymous engraver after Hieronymus Wierix, *Thomas à Kempis Adoring the Virgin and Child*, s.a., engraving, 96 × 68 mm, published by Jan Boel. Wolfegg, Fürstlich zu Waldburg-Wolfegg'sche Kunstsammlungen: vol. 155, print 172.

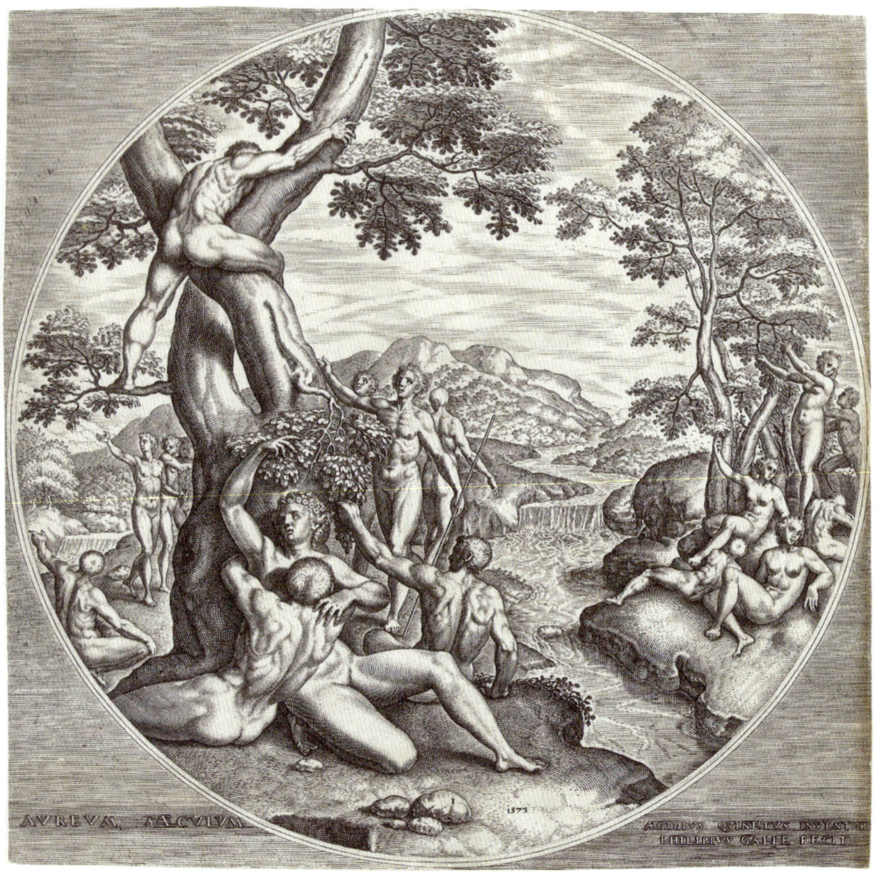

6.16 Philips Galle after Gilles Coignet, *The Golden Age*, from the series *The Four Ages*, 1573, engraving, 248 × 249 mm. Amsterdam, Rijksmuseum: RP-P-1926-415. Appendix 1: PG-40.

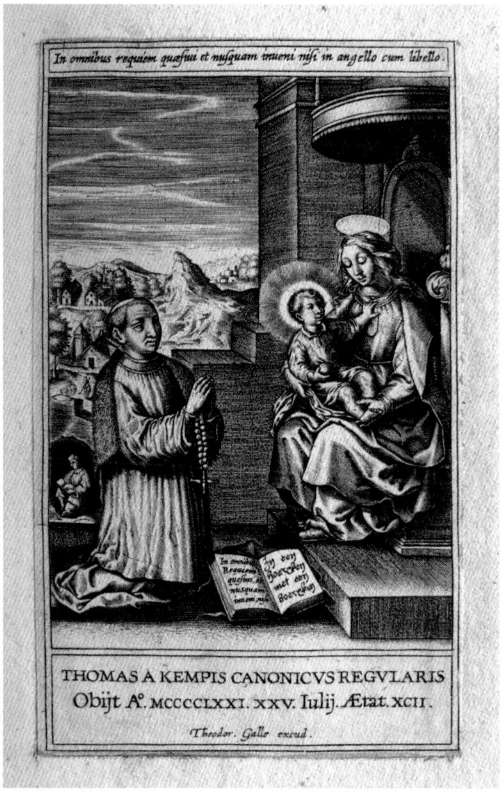

6.18 Anonymous engraver after Hieronymus Wierix, *Thomas à Kempis Adoring the Virgin and Child*, s.a., engraving, 119 × 68 mm, published by Theodore Galle. Wolfegg, Fürstlich zu Waldburg-Wolfegg'sche Kunstsammlungen: vol. 155, print 170.

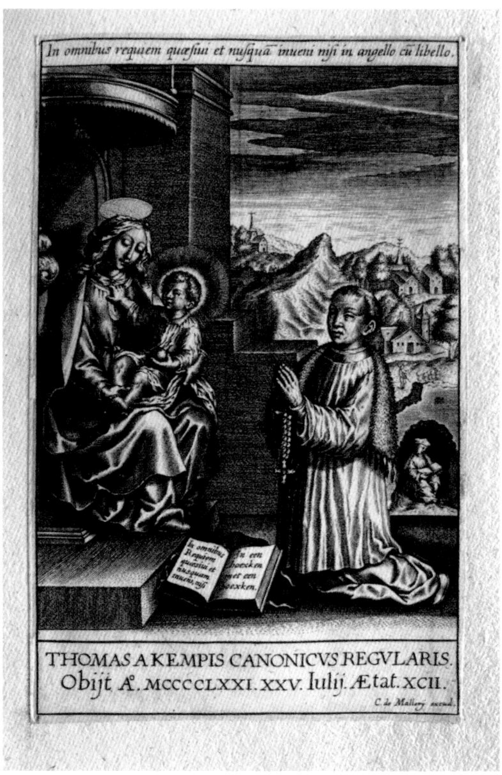

6.19 Anonymous engraver after Hieronymus Wierix, *Thomas à Kempis Adoring the Virgin and Child*, s.a., engraving, 110 × 68 mm, published by Charles de Mallery. Wolfegg, Fürstlich zu Waldburg-Wolfegg'sche Kunstsammlungen: vol. 155, print 171.

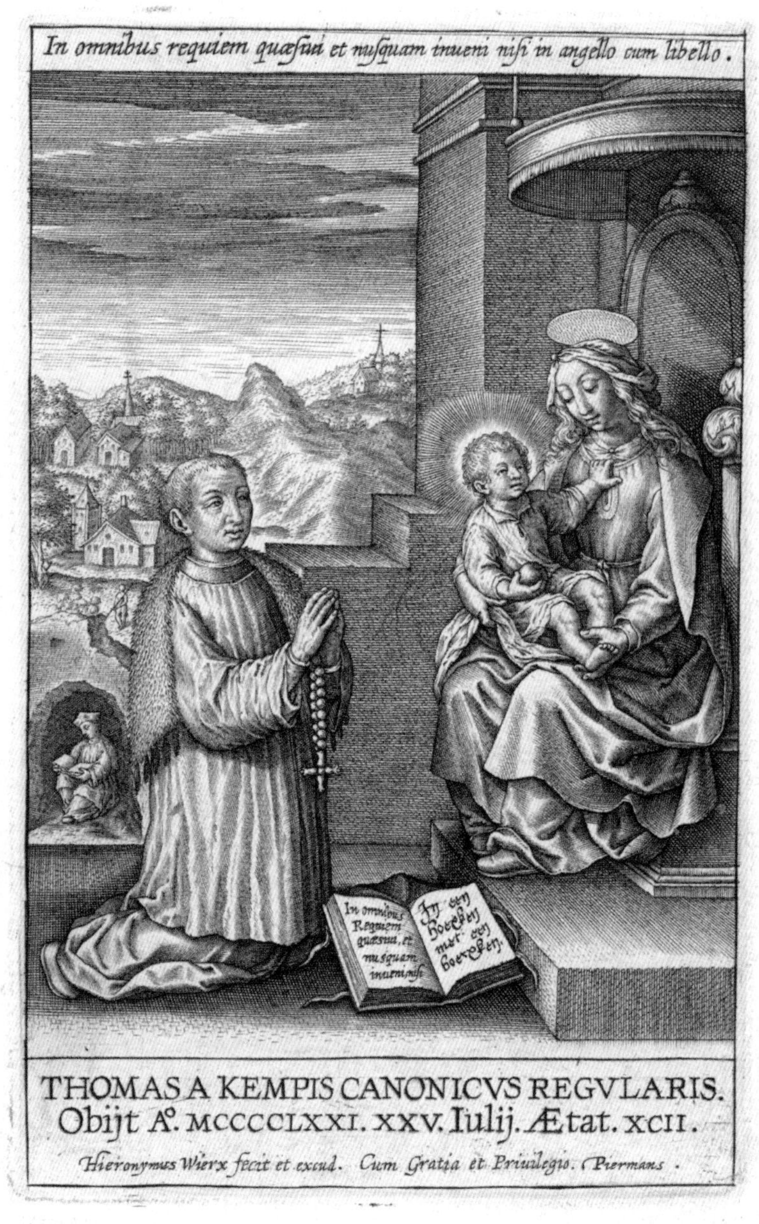

6.20 Hieronymus Wierix, *Thomas à Kempis Adoring the Virgin and Child*, by 1618, engraving, 111 × 69 mm. Amsterdam, Rijksmuseum: RP-P-1898-A-20088.

6.21 Paulus Pontius, *Saint Rosalia*, s.a., engraving, 132 × 84 mm, published by Jan Cnobbaert. Antwerp, Museum Plantin-Moretus: PK.OP.02739.

6.22 Cornelis Galle II after Abraham van Diepenbeeck, *Vision of the Virgin and Child, before a Cleric (Saint Ignatius?)*, s.a., engraving, 256 × 145 mm, published by Marie de Man, the widow of Jan Cnobbaert. Amsterdam, Rijksmuseum: RP-P-OB-7081.

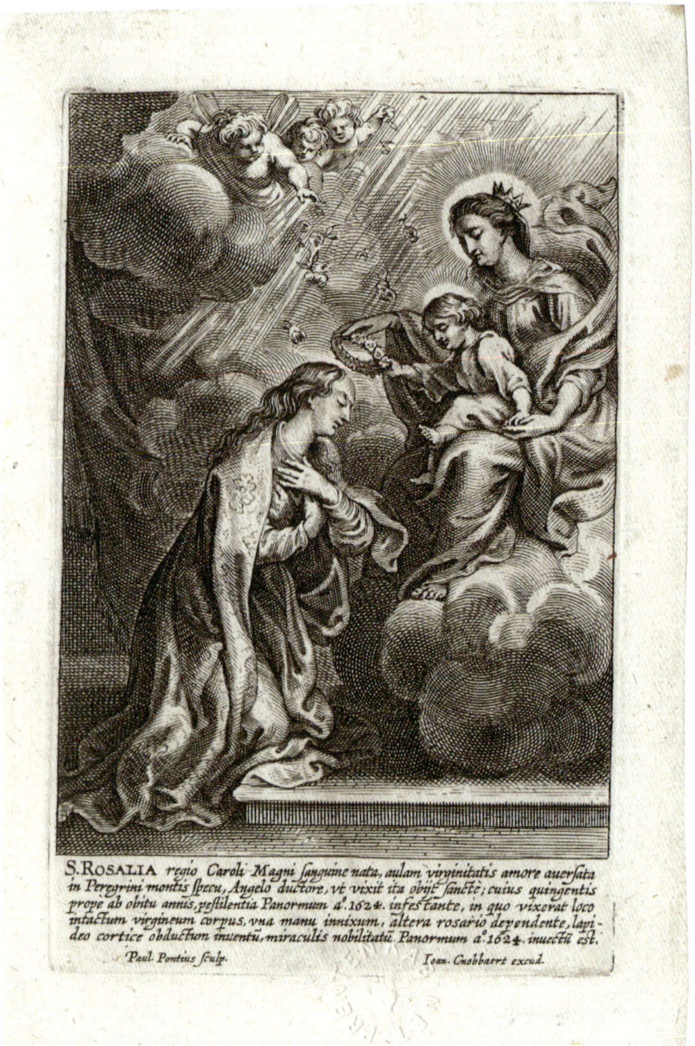

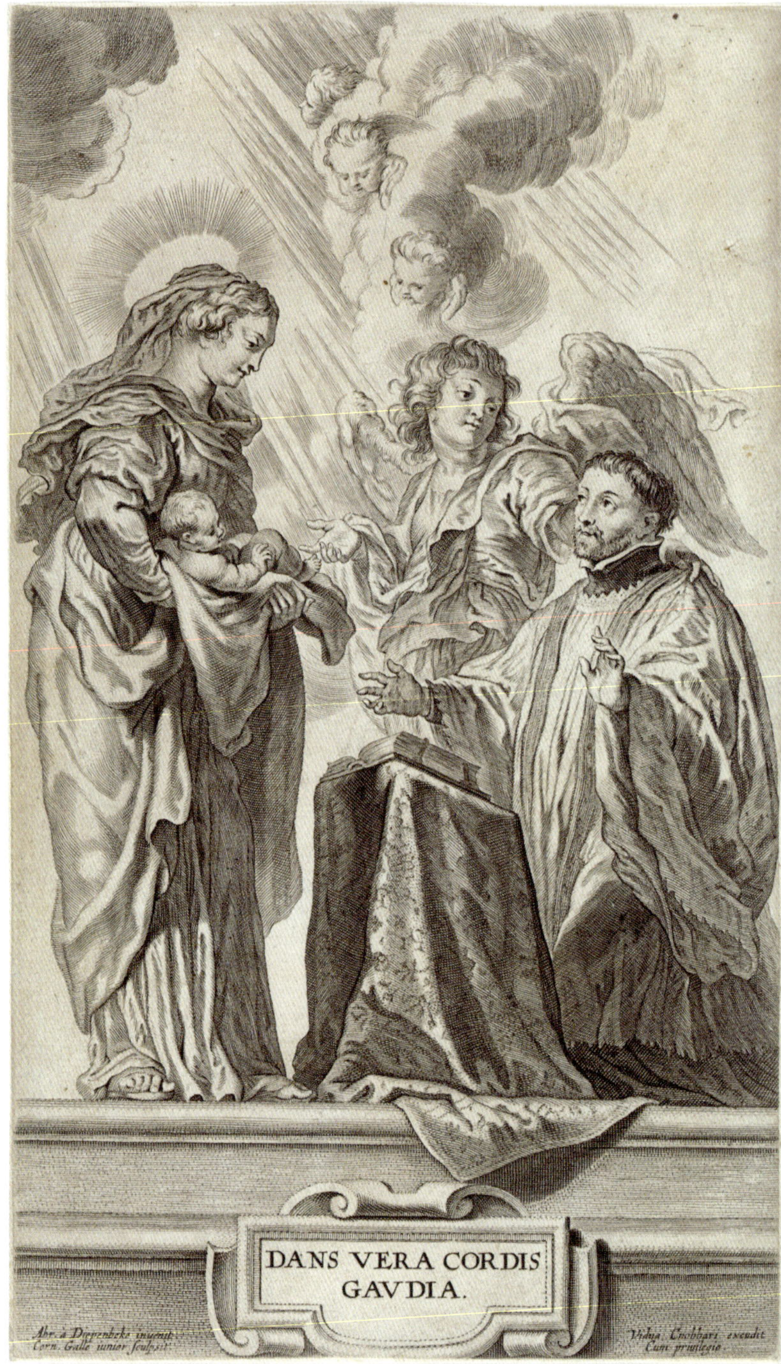

personal flurry of activity via the Guild of St Luke appears to have come to an abrupt halt. The only remaining, known document pertaining to Jan Boel is the inventory of his estate, compiled on 19 March 1640. Although he is identified as a dealer in paintings, few are listed among his possessions; instead, the majority of the art objects cited are copper plates. The presence of a printing press indicates that Boel could have continued to print and sell images during the 1630s, despite the lack of other evidence of any further engagement by him in the print trade.[63]

Perhaps the most surprising name among those charged alongside Lauwers was that of Jan

Cnobbaert, who is currently best known for his work as a printer and bookseller.[64] Although Cnobbaert was certainly engaged in both of these activities by 1620, he soon acquired enough copper plates and an intaglio printing press so that he could participate in the Antwerp market for loose images as well. In 1625 the local painter Jan van Mechelen, who not only traded in paintings, but also periodically purchased copper plates and sold thousands of engravings internationally, visited Cnobbaert's shop and discussed the possible purchase of some of his plates and printed images. However, he subsequently disagreed with Cnobbaert as to whether they had actually struck a deal. Additionally, in 1627, Van Mechelen attempted to prohibit Cnobbaert from selling prints engraved by Abraham van Merlen's nephew Theodore van Merlen. Regrettably, it is not known how either of these cases was resolved.[65]

That Cnobbaert was known as a supplier of engraved images is documented in correspondence between the Utrecht bookseller Jan van Doorn and the Antwerp bookseller Hieronymus Verdussen from 29 November 1629. Specifically, in his letter to Verdussen, Van Doorn asked him to send 100 to 130 small images by Philips de Mallery, including the complete Passion of Christ; these images were to be printed on plain parchment by Jan Cnobbaert. Van Doorn wanted each image be "special", but not colored. From a letter that Van Doorn wrote to Verdussen soon thereafter, in January 1630, it appears that he was dissatisfied with what Verdussen had sent; he complained that the shipment contained too many impressions (125) of a single image and not an assortment of subjects. Van Doorn's (or his clients') preference for the work of Philips de Mallery may account for the only instance in which De Mallery supplied the Moretuses with prints for resale.[66] Van Doorn's request that the images *not* be colored was pertinent, because by 1628, Cnobbaert evidently had enough requests for hand-colored prints to justify engaging Mynken Liefrinck's great granddaughter Catharina van Lanckvelt, who was approximately twenty years old at the time, to color prints for him on a full-time basis for a period of two years.[67] While the work of both Philips de Mallery and Theodore van Merlen may well have been regarded as close enough to Barbé's or Hieronymus Wierix's to warrant Cnobbaert's inclusion among the accused, Cnobbaert also employed Paulus Pontius to engrave a number of smaller prints that were inspired by Rubens's work (fig. 6.21). As Pontius is better known for his large-format prints produced after Rubens's designs, these images constitute an unexpected addition to what might otherwise be associated with both his and Cnobbaert's output.[68] Cnobbaert's widow, Marie de Man, similarly published images of this type (fig. 6.22).

Furthermore, the Moretuses' independent sales of works published by Cnobbaert and his widow document Cnobbaert's initial participation in the market for prints and reveal the general types and quantities of images that they offered for sale, as well as the greater, potential audience of their publications. Occurring between 1628 and 1634, Cnobbaert's transactions (in contrast to Boel's) comprise a number of individual sales of his prints (all at cost) to the Moretuses' contacts that are remarkably diverse both in terms of the type and location of the clients involved. In particular, the buyers ranged from the booksellers Nicolas Hecart in Reims and Hendrik Barentsen in Amsterdam to the merchant Jan van Vucht in Madrid and members of the Capuchin order in Namur.[69] Only for the last sale was one item specified: a canon for the mass in the form of a triptych, framed in leather and illuminated with gold leaf around the edges. In the records of all the other sales, the prints are described generally in terms of the support on which they were printed (paper or parchment) and whether or not they were illuminated. While the "plain" prints on paper or parchment were sold by the hundred, the illuminated images were priced per piece. Two individual packages – at least one of which was recorded as containing "images" – that Cnobbaert asked Balthasar Moretus I to send to the bookseller Jean Dassonleville in Hesdin in the Pas-de-Calais in 1630 and 1631 indicate that Cnobbaert simultaneously maintained his own network of contacts for the sale of his prints.[70]

It was not until 1640, several years after Cnobbaert's death, that his widow, Marie de Man, agreed to supply Balthasar Moretus I with a consignment of prints for resale. Nevertheless, this single transaction – 75 fl. worth of prints sold to the bookseller Kaspar Förster in Gdańsk – far outweighed the combined value of all of the sales to which her husband had agreed more than a decade earlier.[71] The significant difference in monetary value is due to the large quantities of images purchased – 1,400 in total. In addition, hand-colored prints on parchment dominated the order now and were sold by the hundreds and no longer by piece. A more subtle distinction between Cnobbaert's and De Man's offerings is the wider range of prices charged by De Man. Specifically, the lowest price category at which she offered plain prints on parchment for resale was 3 fl. per 100 (vs. the 4 fl. per 100 charged by Cnobbaert), while the highest rates that she asked for illuminated images on parchment were 6 and 10 fl. per 100, or 1.2 and 2 st. per image (vs. Cnobbaert's highest rates of 2.25 to 3 st. per image).[72] These differences can be explained in a variety of ways, from variations in both the quality of the works sold and the relative cost of the materials to economies of scale in production or discounts for large orders. Regardless of the reason, the astounding quantities of prints that De Man offered for sale continued to increase in subsequent decades. For example, in November 1647, the merchant Peeter de Haen II in Amsterdam purchased some 6,600 prints supplied by De Man for a total of 320 fl. 8 st., while in 1648, the Munich bookseller Johann Wagner bought 9,600 images from her press in February, and an additional 14,400 in September, for a total of 475 fl.[73]

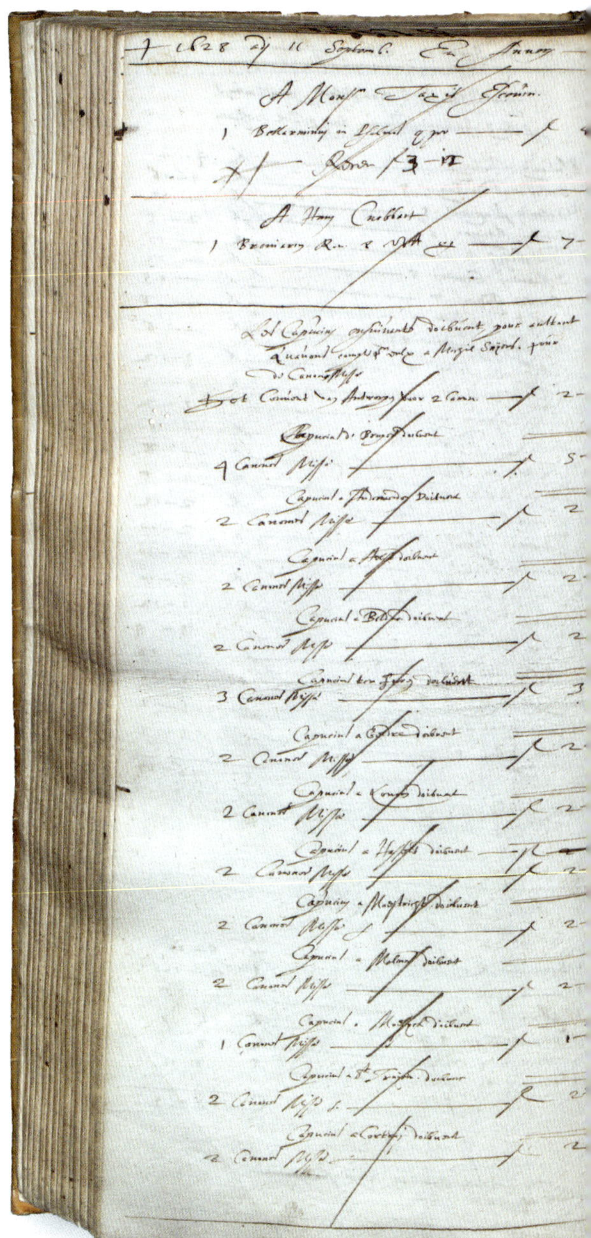

6.23 Order for canons from Michael Snijders for assorted Capuchin orders in the Low Countries. Antwerp, Museum Plantin-Moretus: Arch. 235, *Journal 1628*, fols. 129v-130r.

MICHAEL SNIJDERS

However remarkable these few examples of Marie de Man's trade in prints are, a consideration of Michael Snijders's transactions via the Moretuses demonstrates that the Cnobbaerts' international distribution of prints through the Moretuses was meager in comparison with what was possible. Indeed, of all of those indicted by Barbé, Snijders relied on the Moretuses by far the most and to such an extent that he alone, of all of the Moretuses' various contacts in the Antwerp print world, rivaled the Galles in terms of the total value of his transactions via the Moretuses' far-reaching networks.

Snijders's trade by way of the Moretuses began in 1616, six years after his admittance to Antwerp's Guild of St Luke as a master engraver and shortly after he had taken on an apprentice.[74] Snijders dealt with the Moretuses on a nearly annual basis through 1636 in at least one of three ways: he supplied them with prints for resale to their own clients, packages of his publications were transported along with their shipments of books, and he benefited from the secure transfer of payment for his own, independently arranged transactions via their accounts with distant merchants and booksellers. Of these various modes of interaction, the Moretuses' sale of Snijders's prints was the most common. The total value of the majority of the prints Snijders supplied from 1618 to 1634 amounts to nearly 484 fl. – that is, slightly more than what Charles de Mallery provided, though still distant third in comparison with what either Philips or Theodore Galle supplied.[75]

The lion's share of these transactions were sales to the Raesfeld family of booksellers in Münster (located in what is now the North Rhine-Westphalia province in Germany). Amounting to approximately 400 fl. of the 484 fl. total estimate, the bulk of these purchases were made between 1629 and 1632 and often featured hundreds of illuminated prints on parchment.[76] Indicative of the evolving taste in prints in the first half of the seventeenth century, earlier purchases by the same family usually featured relatively inexpensive plain prints on paper at Snijders's cheapest rate of 36 st. per 100 images.[77] Throughout, the Moretuses resold his prints at cost to the Raesfeld family.

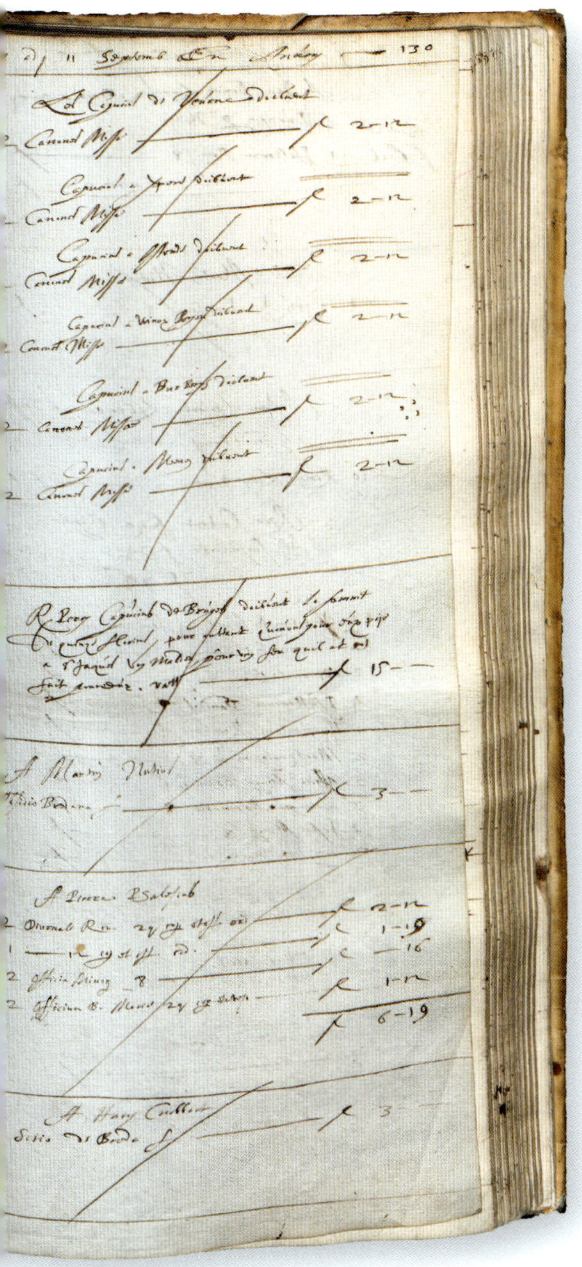

Matters were notably different with the Moretuses' other primary clients for Snijders's prints, namely the successors of the Antwerp merchant Jacques de Braa. Although Snijders supplied a significant quantity of prints worth at least 77 fl. in 1625 and 1626 alone, the De Braas preferred plain engravings on paper, rather than the illuminated images on parchment that dominated Raesfeld's orders. For example, in 1625, De Braa's successors purchased 1,000 plain prints from Snijders (in addition to several thousands of prints from other Antwerp artists), but only 100 of Snijders's illuminated and gilded images on parchment and eight of his illuminated canons.[78] Another important difference between the Moretuses' transactions with the Raesfeld family and the De Braas is the significant profit margin that the Moretuses added for themselves when they resold Snijders's prints (and those of other artists) to De Braa's heirs. This contrast is typical of the Moretuses' approach; friends, family, and most fellow booksellers were able to buy prints from them at cost, while distant, infrequent customers and merchants often had to pay extra.

Although the interest in Snijders's individual prints among the Moretuses' clients was primarily limited to these two families, there were more widespread, albeit still sporadic, requests for his canons for the altar (or altar cards). Several of the Moretuses' regular contacts among booksellers – Hendrik Barentsen in Amsterdam, Johann Kinckius, and Anton II and Arnold Hierat – all bought a number of examples of Snijders's canons between 1629 and 1634. The Hierats, in particular, evidently wanted to have a sampling of such items in stock, for they purchased canons in different sizes, some plain, some illuminated, and others both illuminated and gilded. The prices ranged from just 4 st. per piece for a plain, large canon to 16 st. for a large canon that was both illuminated and gilded.[79] However, the largest order for Snijders's canons was not placed by a bookseller, but by the Capuchin order, which, in 1628, requested an average of two canons for each of twenty different monasteries in the Low Countries, between Winoksbergen (now Bergues) in the south and 's-Hertogenbosch in the north, and between Oostende in the west and Maastricht in the east (fig. 6.23).[80] At 26 st. per piece – notably more than what Hierat was charged for the large, illuminated, and gilded canon that he purchased – this transaction amounted to 54 fl. 12 st. in total. There is only one other instance in the Moretuses' accounts of a religious institution purchasing prints supplied by Snijders, namely, when the Capuchin order in Geldre (which also acquired two of his canons in 1628) bought an unspecified selection of prints after Rubens for 18 fl. 18 st. that Snijders had provided in 1627.[81] The remarkable scarcity of orders from other religious institutions is all the more noteworthy given the significant number of Jesuits and Jesuit orders represented in the Moretuses' accounts. Snijders's desire to win the favor of this influential order is attested to by two exceptionally large prints that he made in 1616 and 1618, which were dedicated to the Jesuit order in Antwerp and the Jesuit Marian brotherhood of Antwerp, respectively.[82] Perhaps he was thus able to secure their esteem locally and supply them with prints directly.

Snijders supplemented the Moretuses' sales of his publications with the export of prints to his own network of clients. This is indicated in the Moretuses' records by both the numerous packages that they sent to distant individuals in Snijders's name, as well as their receipt of payments from the same for Snijders. Comprising some sixty packages, many of which were listed as containing images, these shipments primarily went to Gdańsk, Münster, Liège, and St Omer. Nearly half (twenty-eight) were sent to the merchant Paulus Claessens, who had married into the De Jode family and was able to succeed Gerard de Jode's son Jacques in the family's trade between Antwerp and Gdańsk as of 1606.[83] Concentrated mostly in just four shipments, the exceptionally large number of packages – nine each in 1624 and 1632, six in 1628, and three in 1627 – conjures up a tantalizing picture of the vast market for prints in the Baltic region, where Gdańsk was the principal port of entry. These evocative records gain in substance when they are combined with the payments Claessens sent Snijders in return, which amounted to more than 811 fl. just between 1623 and 1629. This sum may have been equivalent to nearly twice the value of all of Snijders's prints that the Moretuses sold between 1618 and 1634.[84] Nearly half (thirteen or more) of the remaining packages that Snijders asked the Moretuses to ship went to the Münster bookseller Michiel van Dale, a member of the Raesfeld family. Although Van Dale represented the Raesfelds between 1618 and 1628, Snijders's shipments to him occurred mainly in the years 1623–1626 (with a remarkable eleven sent in 1624 alone).[85] They follow the few requests for Snijders's prints that Van Dale sent directly with the Moretuses in 1619–1620 and precede the large orders placed by Bernhard Raesfeld.

Finally, Snijders also turned to the Moretuses to help him supply several customers, who were all booksellers, in the Low Countries. Shipments were made to several individuals, such as Hendrik Barentsen in Amsterdam, Jean Leonard in Brussels, Jean Morel in Lille, and the widow of Nicolas Laurent in Tournai. Two clients stand out, however, namely Jean Ouwerx in Liège and Pierre Geubels in St Omer. Snijders's trade with Ouwerx through the Moretuses was exceptional, as it consisted of a single shipment of seven packages in 1625. The interaction with Geubels was more prolonged, as Snijders sent him single packages in 1624, 1628, 1633, and 1636.[86] Of these booksellers, only Ouwerx and Geubels made use of their own accounts with the Moretuses to transfer money to Snijders – just 20 fl. from Ouwerx in 1628 and a total of 150 fl. sent by Geubels in 1625 and 1626.[87] Nevertheless, the lack of any systematic overlap between the years in which these payments were made and the years in which Snijders sent both booksellers packages suggests that the payments and shipments were not necessarily directly related to the other, as they most likely were in his dealings with Claessens. Consequently, rather than documenting a regular exchange between Snijders, on the one hand, and Ouwerx or Geubels on the other, these records highlight a significant traffic in prints that was probably primarily conducted via other channels.

The various ways in which the Moretuses supported Snijders's trade in prints with local and far-flung clients – primarily booksellers and merchants – thus reveal what was most likely an immense distribution of his works. Although customers in Gdańsk and Münster dominated the demand for his work, there was also a range of other sporadic transactions, including sales that may reflect Snijders's personal, and often more local, networks. The

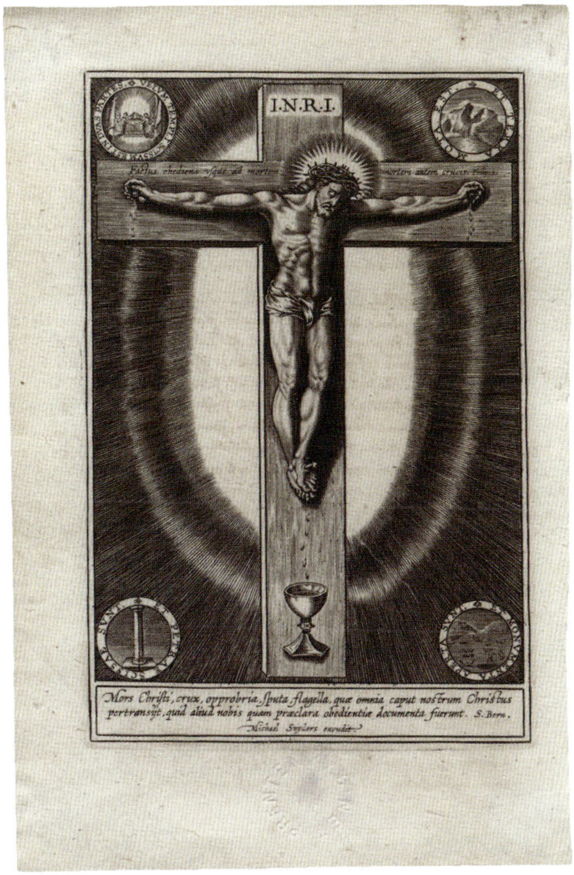

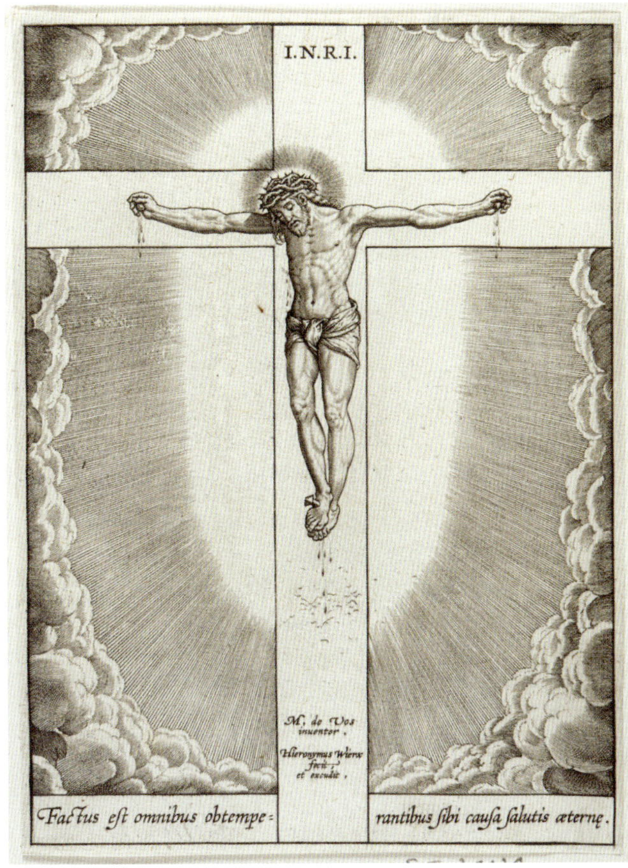

peak in all of these activities – from the shipment of Snijders's packages and the receipt of payments to the Moretuses' independent sales of Snijders products – stretched from 1623 to 1629. The importance of the mid-1620s for Snijders's extensive export of prints is underscored, moreover, by shipments to Spain in 1626 and 1627 of thousands of his works, along with paintings and prints by other Antwerp masters, under the auspices of the art dealer Crisostomo van Immerseel.[88]

Regrettably, no single print from all of these transactions can be identified with certainty. Given Snijders's inclusion in the group charged with infringing on Barbé's privilege, some subset of his publications must have been associated with images made by Barbé or the Wierixes, though not all were simple copies, but rather imitations or adaptations of these prints (compare figs. 6.24 and 6.25).[89] Nevertheless, Snijders's total stock of engravings was far more extensive and diverse in terms of the source of the image, its subject, and the range of works he could offer. For example, like most of his fellow print publishers, Snijders acquired and reissued plates from other publishers, in particular, Philips Galle and Gerard de Jode (fig. 6.26). His own publications also included a number of surprisingly large compositions, such as the prints he published with dedications to Jesuits and his *Tree of the Origin of the French Kings*, which measures 507 × 357 mm, and which might be linked to any of several references to "folio"-scaled copper plates in his estate inventory (fig. 6.27). Some of the plates listed as "quarto" in his inventory may, in turn, be connected to the hundreds of prints in 4° that were printed two to a leaf and sent to the Raesfeld family in both 1620 and 1629.[90]

Given the varied and extensive evidence of the immense demand for Snijders's work

6.24 Anonymous, *Christ on the Cross*, s.a., engraving, 126 × 83 mm, published by Michael Snijders. Antwerp, Antwerp, Museum Plantin-Moretus: PK.OP.03788.

6.25 Hieronymus Wierix after Maarten de Vos, *Christ on the Cross*, s.a., engraving, 146 × 106 mm. Brussels, The Royal Library, Print Department: S.I 39138.

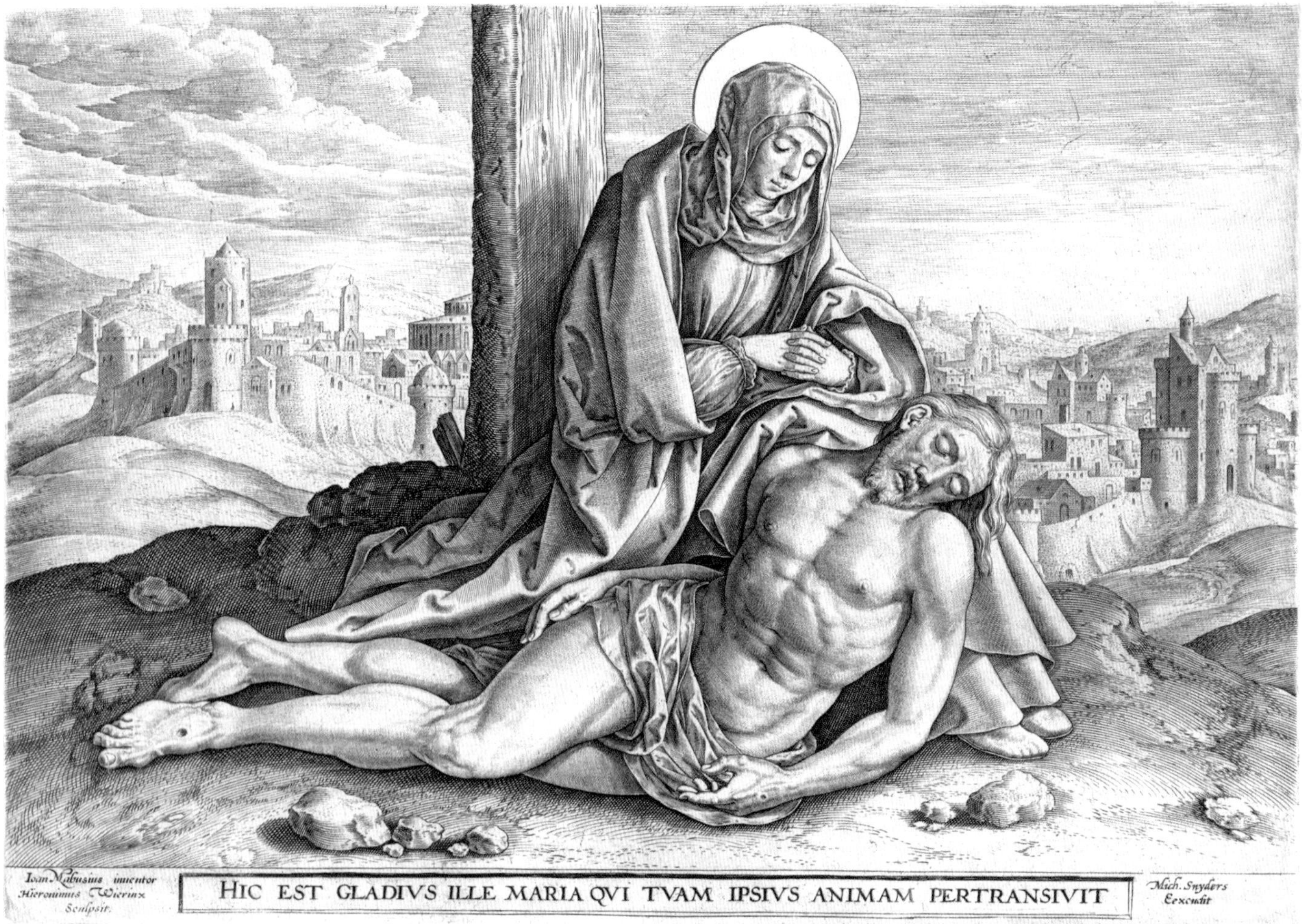

6.26 Hieronymus Wierix after Jan Gossaert (or Mabuse), *Pietà*, by 1591, engraving, 206 × 289 mm, originally published by Gerard de Jode. This state bears Michael Snijders's name as the publisher. Amsterdam, Rijksmuseum: RP-P-1907-3884.

until 1632, the subsequent, precipitous decline of his business is all the more surprising. Several factors may have contributed to this. In particular, Barbé's success with his lawsuit would have caused Snijders to lose some of his copper plates, although he clearly still had hundreds in his possession soon thereafter. He offered more than 220 as collateral for loans of more than 800 fl. that he was awarded in 1637 and 1638 from a certain Jeremias van Pelleken, in addition to the numerous plates that remained in his estate upon his death.[91] Snijders's most important client in the trade he conducted via the Moretuses, Paulus Claessens, also went bankrupt in 1634, just two years after Snijders's final, large shipment of nine packages of prints to him in April 1632. If Claessens did not compensate Snijders for these images, Snijders may have had a significant deficit in his accounts.[92] Moreover, despite the huge sums for which Snijders's works were bought and sold, Snijders may simply not have been very good at his own money management. This hypothesis is supported by the numerous records of outstanding debts that he had with his family, in addition to his loans from Van Pelleken. Ultimately, neither his successful brother Frans nor his sister Maria (Frans's sole heir) was willing to provide for Michael in their wills.[93]

Regardless of the exact cause of the decline in Snijders's prosperity, the ebb and flow of his transactions via the Moretuses follows remarkably closely what is known of his career from other sources. While Snijders enjoyed an initial period of widespread success, particularly in

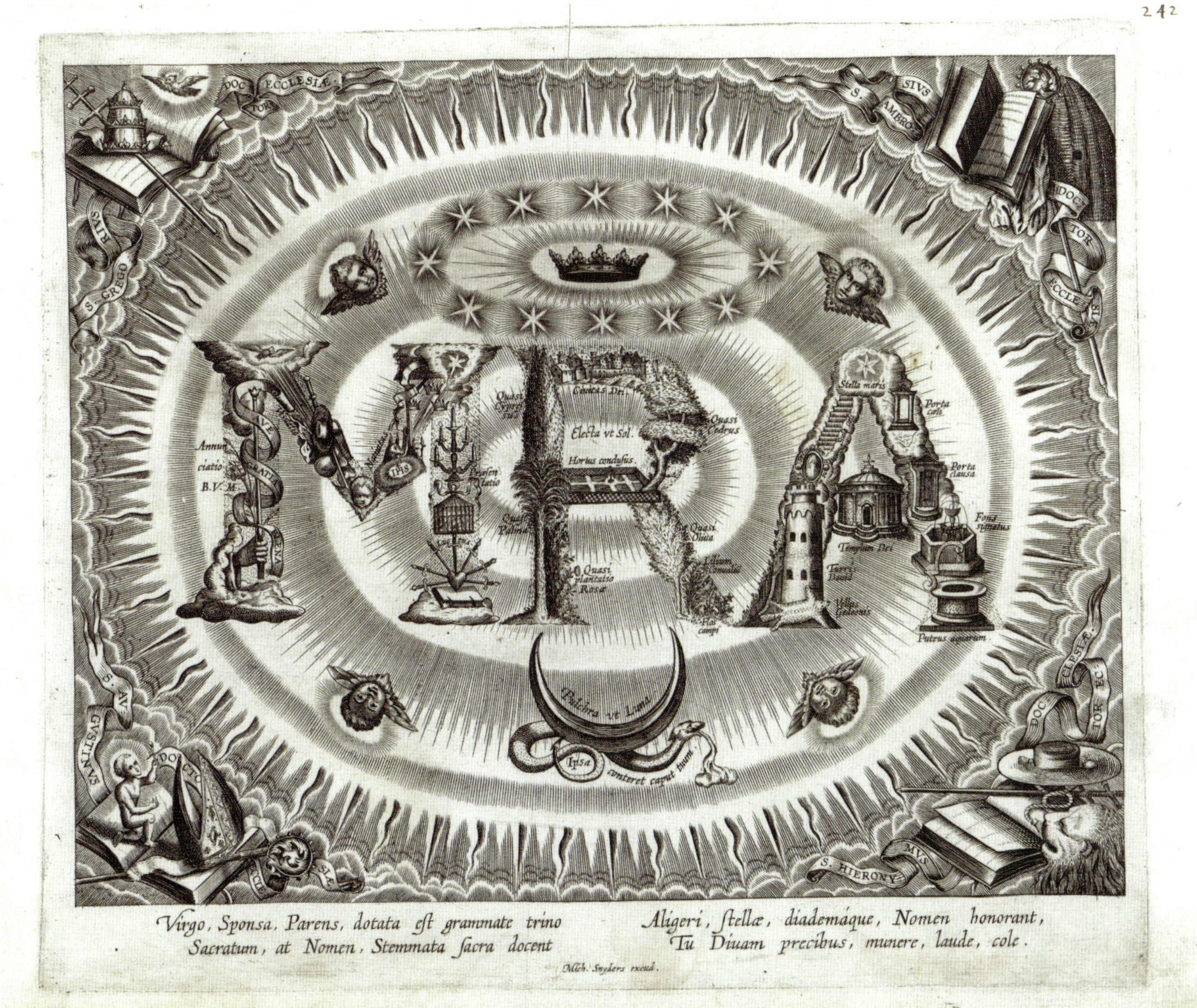

6.27 Anonymous, *MRA monogram*, s.a., engraving, 221 × 254 mm, published by Michael Snijders. Amsterdam, Rijksmuseum: RP-P-2000-25.

the 1620s, this was interrupted around 1631, when Snijders took out his first loan from Van Pelleken and when his dealings with the Moretuses were strikingly sparse. His prospects took a decided turn for the worse by 1636, at which point, after he had conducted no trade via the Moretuses in 1635, he sent one last package to Geubels. A veritable financial crisis evidently broke in 1637–1638, and he borrowed large sums from Van Pelleken; Snijders does not seem ever to have recovered from this crisis. His only known source of income following the heyday of his transactions via the Moretuses was his annual supply of hundreds of images of St Martin to the wine-tavern guild of Antwerp between 1632 and 1652. These images were presumably intended to be distributed among the guild's members on the saint's feast day on 11 November. Often amounting to as many as 500 prints per year, Snijders usually charged just 30 st. per 100 images. Although this rate may simply reflect the relatively small scale of the images, it remains notably less than the standard 36 st.-per-100-print rate that had been the lowest price at which the prints he sold via the Moretuses were offered.[94]

Consequently, among those figures accused by Barbé, the Moretuses were regularly called upon to assist these printmaker-publishers with their trade in prints in only two instances. Although Boel's transactions were particularly limited, Snijders's were very extensive and involved exceptionally large sums of money. This difference arose in part because of Snijders's involvement in the upper end of the market for specially printed and hand-colored devotional images, and in part because of the sheer number – thousands, if not tens of thousands – of prints sold. Nevertheless, while the Moretuses' records do not convey the full range of either Boel's or Snijders's activities, they do provide a poignant portrayal of both men's distinctive involvement in the print trade, as they did for the Moretuses' more intimate connections, the extended Galle family.

ABRAHAM VAN MERLEN AND HENDRIK AERTSSENS

The only remaining figures in the Antwerp print world who regularly engaged the Moretuses for assistance with their transactions are Abraham van Merlen, who sought to declare himself a neutral party in the debate engendered by Barbé's suit, and the bookseller Hendrik Aertssens.

Born around 1579, Van Merlen was registered as an apprentice under Adriaen Collaert in 1597, and just three years later, he was accepted as a master engraver in Antwerp's Guild of St Luke.[95] The 1610s were prosperous years for Van Merlen personally and professionally. Between 1610 and 1613, he was able to expand his business by taking on two pupils, one of whom was Michiel van Lochum (or Lochom), the son of a relative. Van Merlen was simultaneously selling via Gaspar Vivario, the brother-in-law of the local print and map publisher Jan Baptist Vrients, hundreds of prints for export to Rome.[96] Additionally, in June of 1617, Van Merlen and his wife, Constantia Alewyns (or Alowyns), purchased a sizable property ("den Draeck") in the Lombardenvest, the old, established center for printing and the graphic arts in Antwerp; the property became their home as well as Van Merlen's workshop and storefront. Whether this purchase reflects Van Merlen's early financial success as an engraver and print publisher or was made possible (at least in part) by personal funds and inheritance is not known. Regardless, Van Merlen appears to have enjoyed a stable life there until his children sold the house in his name shortly before his death in 1660.[97]

Most of Van Merlen's dealings with the Moretuses are concentrated between 1615 and 1620. The majority of these transactions consist of sales of his prints by the Moretuses to a small selection of booksellers in Germany; all of the sales occurred at cost. Once again, the Raesfeld family in Münster made significant purchases. For example, in 1619, Michiel van Dale bought 600 of Van Merlen's prints in 4° and five quires (or 125 leaves) with his prints in 8°, which may have amounted to as many as 500 additional images (if four prints in 8° were printed per leaf).[98] Johann Kinckius in Cologne also periodically bought groups of 100, 200, or 400 prints between 1617 and 1620, all at the same base rate of 36 st. per 100 prints.[99] Finally, Everhard Wessel in Emmerich made more limited purchases in 1615 and 1616.[100]

Van Merlen also took advantage of the Moretuses' regular transport of books to send packages to his own contacts. Individual shipments were sent to Jean Ouwerx in Liège, Gilles van Zwevenseel in Maastricht, and Alexander Sersanders in Ghent, but only Ouwerx is known to have actively acquired prints by Van Merlen and may actually have been the intended recipient of Van Merlen's work[101] The other men may simply have served as intermediaries or local "pickup points" for unspecified clients of Van Merlen. Given that all of these packages were sent within a few months of one another, between 19 September 1617 and 12 January 1618, they most likely represent a temporary alternative for Van Merlen's usual mode of distributing his prints, rather than a regular means of conducting his business. Nevertheless, these records provide a useful indication of the relatively local demand for Van Merlen's work beyond the German market that the Moretuses served. Van Merlen's earlier dealings with Vivario demonstrate a similar willingness to allow others to sell his publications in foreign markets. However, the simplest outlet for his prints (and any others he acquired for resale) may ultimately have been Paris, where Van Lochum, his relative and former apprentice, settled in 1625. Both men clearly appreciated the mutually beneficial possibilities of trading together from the start, for Van Merlen provided Van Lochum with several consignments of printed images between 1625 and 1626, including one worth a significant 76 fl. 12 st., that was noted as comprising "a large quantity of small images by all masters" and as having come from Van Merlen's shop.[102]

Van Merlen's initial support of Van Lochum's business in Paris coincided with his last known transactions via the Moretuses. In both 1625 and 1626, the Moretuses sold the heirs of the merchant Jacques de Braa an allotment of 1,000 prints from Van Merlen (with a significant profit margin for themselves included in the final selling price). In the course of July 1626, the Moretuses also sent the Gdańsk merchant Paulus Claessens two packages for Van Merlen and subsequently, in May 1628, received a payment from Claessens of 33 fl. 10 st. for Van Merlen, possibly in exchange for his shipment.[103] Like Van Merlen's earlier reliance on the Moretuses for the transport of packages in 1616–1617, these last transactions were isolated instances rather than a recurring practice (at least in Van Merlen's use of the Moretuses). Nevertheless, when considered together, these various examples reveal the remarkable, geographically extensive distribution of his work: from Rome to Gdańsk, with outlets in Paris and local demand in between.

Unfortunately, exactly which images Van Merlen sold remains unclear. Like De Mallery, he only offered plain prints on paper for resale through the Moretuses, all priced at common, modest rates of either 36 st. per 100 images or 18 st. per quire of twenty-five leaves with prints.[104] His own prints include finely crafted engravings, such as an early and unusually large work that he completed in 1610, which is dedicated to a Marian devotion located in a church dedicated to St Nicholas in Seville (fig. 6.28). However, the majority of his engravings – many of which are signed by him as the engraver and publisher – are smaller in scale and not always as extensively detailed. Some are especially intriguing given Van Merlen's official decision to remain neutral in the debate Barbé instigated on privileges and plagiarism in the early 1630s. While he did not necessarily copy individual prints exactly when creating his own images, he often blended elements from multiple engravings in circulation, including, for example, some of the Wierixes' own highly successful publications (figs. 6.29–6.31). Consequently, his work highlights the significant potential for subjective interpretations of notions of plagiarism, copying, imitation, emulation, and borrowing, as well as quality standards for execution and composition, all of which were associated with the protection of privileges in this dispute. Regardless of where Van Merlen fell within this spectrum of concepts, he appears to have held his own in the Antwerp art market. Even though Van Merlen did not attempt to compete at the upper end of costly finished products, his publications were sought internationally (along with, potentially, the works of any other "masters" that he had on hand in his shop). How long Van Merlen remained active as a print seller is uncertain. Aside from allusions to him in the Barbé debate from the early 1630s, there are no other

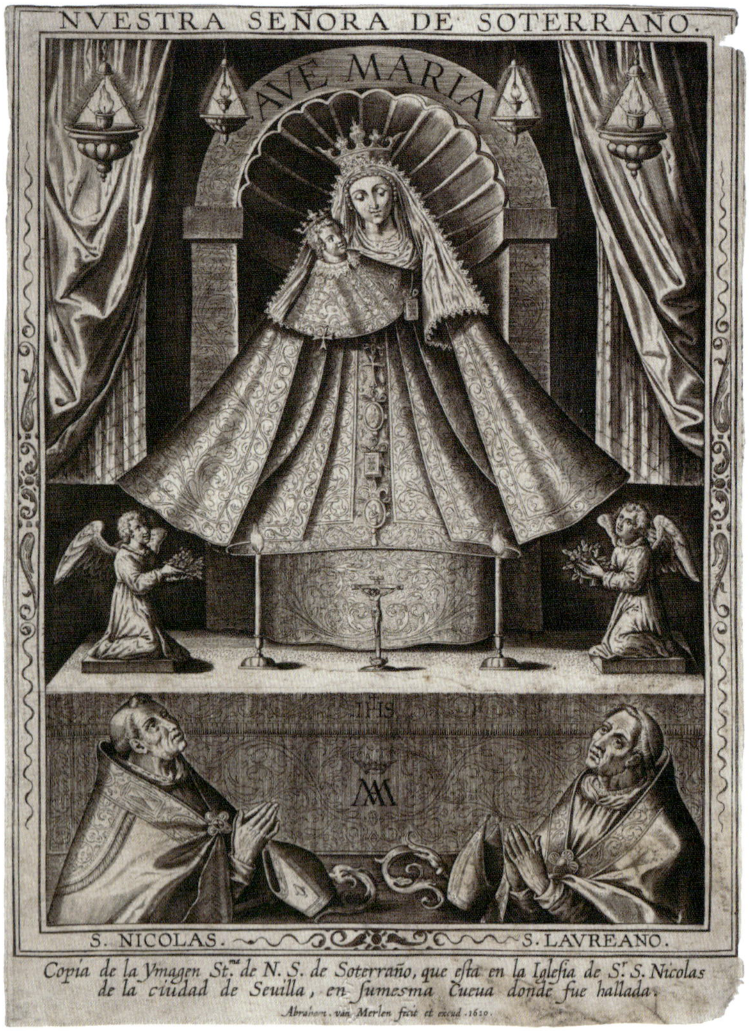

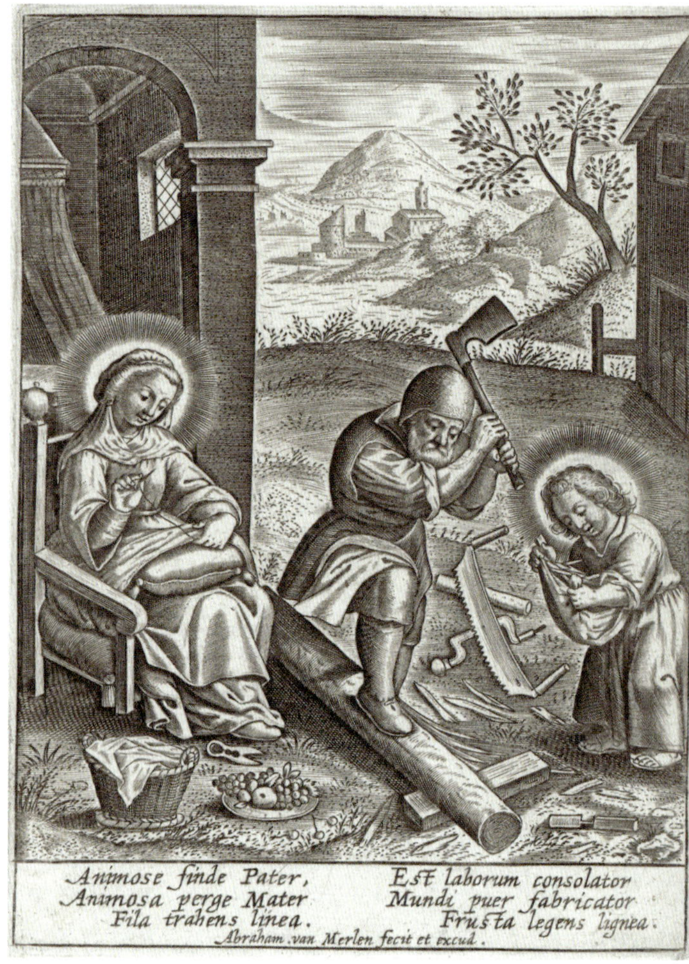

6.28 Abraham van Merlen, *Saints Nicolas and Laureano of Seville Adoring Our Lady of Soterraña*, 1610, engraving, 226 × 163 mm (trimmed). Antwerp, Museum Plantin-Moretus: PK.OP.09038.

6.29 Abraham van Merlen, *Infant Jesus Helps Joseph with His Woodwork*, s.a., engraving, 101 × 73 mm. Amsterdam, Rijksmuseum: RP-P-OB-48.101

references to sales of prints by him in this period. His eldest son, Theodoor II, who had just been admitted as a master engraver to the Guild of St Luke in 1631–1632, may have begun to assist with or take over his father's business.[105] Two decades later, in 1658, when Van Merlen composed a will shortly before his death in 1660, he referred to himself as a former ("eertijds") engraver, indicating that he had stopped working as such well before then, although his business would ultimately be continued for more than a century by his descendants.[106]

The one figure who frequently sold printed images via the Moretuses but remained completely free of Barbé's legal actions was Hendrik Aertssens, a fellow bookseller. Like Jan Cnobbaert, Aertssens was originally a printer and publisher of books. While he initially printed texts for other publishers, including that of Henricus Sedulius' *Historia seraphica vitae bmi. p. Francisci Assisiatis*, which was published in Antwerp by the heirs of Martinus Nutius II in 1613 and copies of which often contained Charles de Mallery's print series illustrating men and women of the Franciscan Order (Appendix 1: CM-1), Aertssens was publishing his own books by the mid-1610s. His earliest transactions with the Moretuses include the 1617 sale of a remarkably large number of copies (450) of Flaminio della Croce's *Theatro militare*, which he had published that year.[107] From this moment onwards, Aertssens and subsequently his son, Hendrik II, traded regularly with the Moretuses throughout their careers. Nevertheless, in contrast to Cnobbaert, who began to compete in the distribution of loose sheets of printed

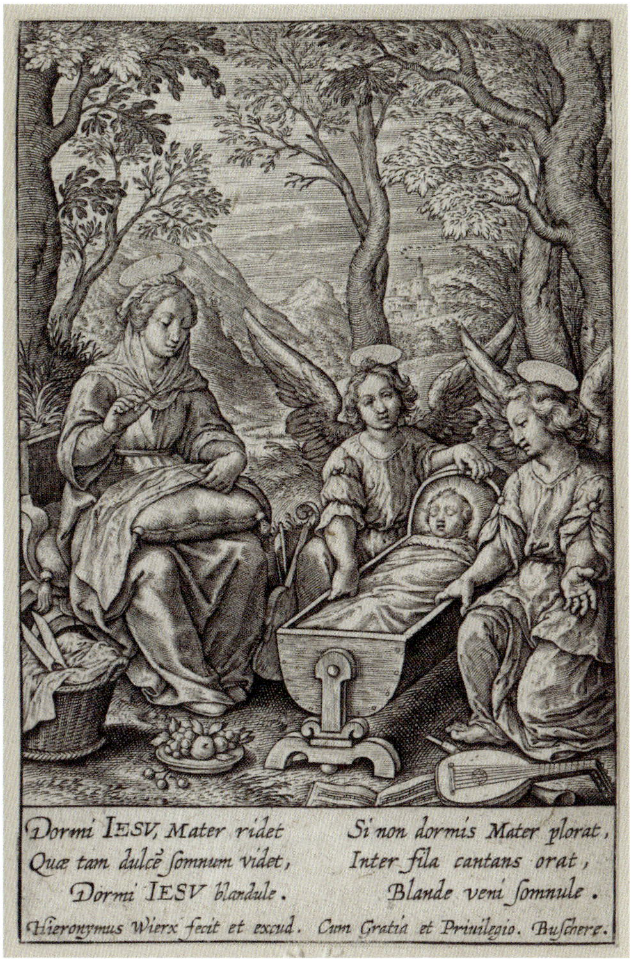

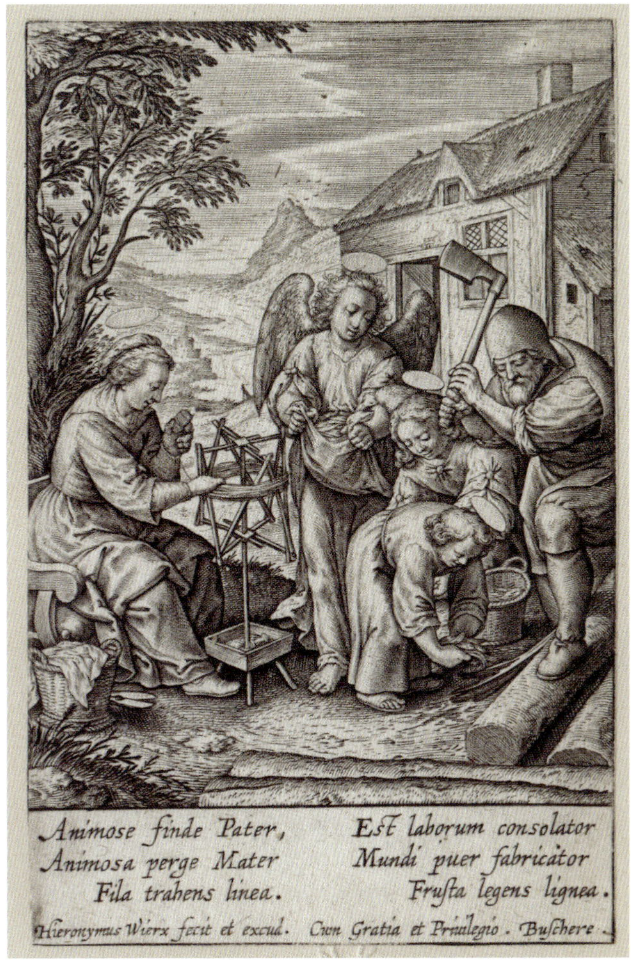

6.30 Hieronymus Wierix, *The Infant Sleeping (with the Virgin Sewing)*, from the series, *Life of the Infant*, by 1615, engraving, 98 × 64 mm. Antwerp, Museum Plantin-Moretus: PK: OPB.0012, print 002. Appendix 1: WX-7.

6.31 Hieronymus Wierix, *The Infant Collecting Wood Shavings with Joseph Chopping Wood*, from the series, *Life of the Infant*, by 1615, engraving, 99 × 63 mm. Antwerp, Museum Plantin-Moretus: PK: OPB.0012, print 004. Appendix 1: WX-7.

images within a few years of establishing his business in Antwerp, Aertssens waited nearly a decade before he entered the fray. Even then, his contributions were hundreds of sheets of *suffragia*, interspersed with periodic sales of Herman Hugo's *Pia desideria* and assorted works by Antonius Sucquet and Joannes Bourghesius (Jean Bourgeois), and were thus clearly distinct from the independent engravings produced by the other print publishers with whom the Moretuses dealt.[108]

Suffragia is the term commonly applied to slips of paper that usually bear the following interrelated elements: the name of a saint or an event in the life of Jesus or the Virgin and the associated feast day; a pertinent virtue, maxim, and prayer; and a space for the addition of the name of a fellow worshipper for whom one might pray.[109] Figures and events were grouped together by month so that exemplary patron saints, events, or virtues could be distributed each month to the faithful for them to study and revere (hence the term in Dutch: "maandbriefjes", or "the monthly small leaves").[110] Originally written out by hand, *suffragia* began to be printed en masse because of the growing demand for them in the later sixteenth century; this practice had the added benefit of allowing for the easy inclusion of images, as in fig. 6.32. In some cases (but not in fig. 6.32, for example), extra information on the featured figure or event was printed on the back. *Suffragia* were initially promoted in the sixteenth century by the Jesuits to encourage group prayer, self-improvement, and the study of selected saints and events within family groups, religious communities, and, above all, sodalities (groups of laymen and clerics who met to further their own devotional practices). However, the use of *suffragia* was soon taken up by other orders during the first half of the seventeenth century.[111] In March 1627, Aertssens, alert to the burgeoning market for these sheets which were distributed monthly among thousands of worshipers, applied to the provincial of the Jesuits in the Low Countries for permission to print *suffragia* in Dutch, French, and Latin for their order. Once this permission was granted for a period of sixteen years, Aertssens obtained a general patent from the king of Spain to prevent other printers from imitating his *suffragia* for the same period (until 1643), citing the wider interest in them among the Dominican and Augustinian orders.[112]

An examination of Aertssens's distribution of *suffragia* via the Moretuses reveals that he was already involved in the production of such sheets a year and a half earlier. In September 1625, they sold the bookseller Jean Ouwerx in Liège sixty unspecified sheets of Aertssens's *suffragia* at 1 st. per sheet.[113] Extending through February 1639 – when the Moretuses sold another bookseller in Liège, Marie Hovius, seven quires of Aertssens's *suffragia* in Latin at 2 fl. per quire – these records of transactions involving Aertssen's *suffragia* document much of what Aertssens asserted when justifying his need for a patent to safeguard his production of these devotional aides.

Printed in Latin, French, and Dutch (identified as "duyts" or "flandrice"), Aertssens's *suffragia* were usually sold either by quire or by a certain number of sheets per month; sometimes, specific months are cited, and sometimes sheets were purchased for an entire year. The frequent mentions of both one ream and twenty quires suggests that full sheets of paper printed with *suffragia* were traded, rather than leaves in smaller formats, as was common for individually printed images.[114]

The Moretuses sold the majority of Aertssens's *suffragia* at cost to fellow booksellers in distant cities across the Low Countries; presumably Aertssens satisfied the local demand for *suffragia* himself. By far the most avid purchaser of *suffragia* was Ouwerx, who bought as many as six to twenty quires on an annual basis between 1625 and 1631, in addition to one large, final purchase in 1635.[115] Clients from the northern Low Countries, such as Jacob Erasmus in Gouda and Hendrik Barentsen in Amsterdam, occasionally placed more modest orders.[116] A single sale of six quires of *suffragia* in 1630 to Johann Kinckius in Cologne was, in comparison, highly unusual. Not only was he the only individual beyond the Low Countries to buy Aertssens's *suffragia*, but the Moretuses also increased the prices to include a significant profit margin for themselves on all of the items in that shipment, which they normally did not do in their transactions with him.[117] Perhaps Kinckius was only serving as the intermediary for an exceptional order that was ultimately intended for someone else.

Additionally, an intriguing variety of representatives of several religious institutions also bought Aertssens's *suffragia* through the Moretuses. Purchases by the Jesuit college of Brussels in 1631 and by the Jesuits Philippe Bourgoys in Maubeuge and Petrus Franciscus Chifflet in Lille in 1630 and 1632, respectively, are not surprising given the Jesuit order's active encouragement of the use of *suffragia*. However, isolated requests for *suffragia* placed, for example, in 1635 by the Norbertine Gothofredus van Elshout for the abbey in Ninove, where he resided, and in 1640 for the Dominican order indicate how widespread the use of these objects was in the second quarter of the seventeenth century.[118] A relative of the Moretuses, the shipper Levinus wtten Eeckhaut from Dunkirk, also bought four quires of Aertssens's *suffragia* on two separate occasions in the early 1630s, most likely for customers of his own.[119]

Regardless of both the language in which the *suffragia* were printed and the specific client, Aertssens consistently supplied his *suffragia* at one of two rates. From 1625 to 1630, he charged 1 st. per sheet or 25 st. per quire, but between 1630 and 1639, he significantly increased his

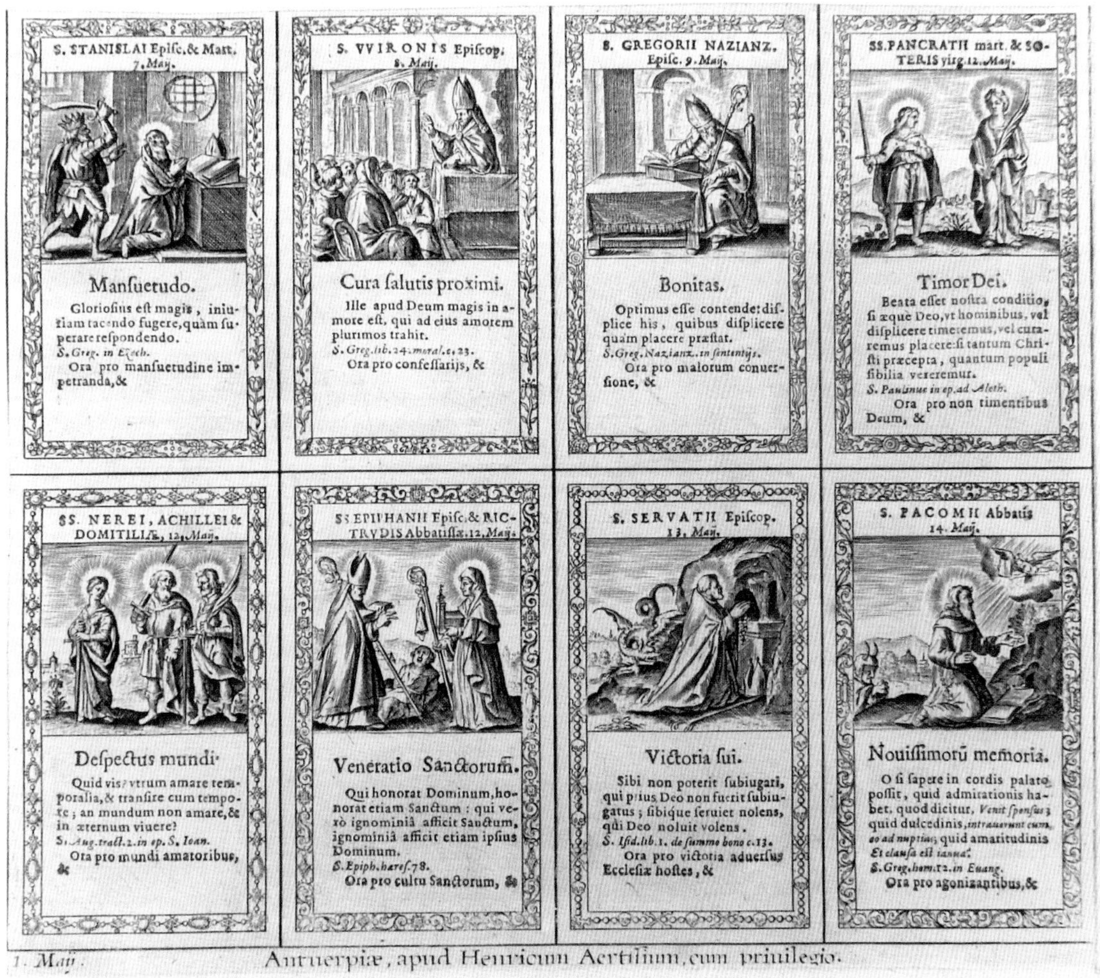

6.32 Anonymous, *Suffragia for May*, s.a., letterpress with engraving, 188 × 210 mm, published by Hendrik Aertssens I or II. Wolfegg, Fürstlich zu Waldburg-Wolfegg'sche Kunstsammlungen, vol. 240, print 462.

fees to 2 fl. (or 40 st.) per quire. This new price was notably more than the two usual base rates for selling loose prints, namely 18 st. per quire of twenty-five leaves with prints (used most often, but not exclusively, in the sixteenth century), and 36 st. per 100 images (common in the seventeenth century). However, the size of the sheets of paper Aertssens used for his *suffragia* may have been significantly larger than those bearing individually printed images for resale. Nothing in the Moretus's sales records clarifies the remarkable price increase in 1630, although it may have coincided with a switch from woodcuts to copper plates for the images. In only two instances – the unusual 1630 sale to Kinckius and Wtten Eeckhaut's first purchase in 1631 – did the Moretuses add any profit margin for themselves when reselling these prints.[120] Even so, Aertssens's supply of *suffragia* for resale via the Moretuses had a total value of some 346 fl., or approximately 23 fl. per year. This sum is comparable to the value of what the Moretuses sold of the work of several major print publishers with whom they dealt. While Snijders, Charles de Mallery, and the Galles clearly supplied more items for resale, Hieronymus Cock and Volcxken Diericx, Adriaen Huberti, Gerard de Jode, Adriaen Collaert, Hieronymus Wierix, Jan Boel, and Abraham van Merlen each provided far less. Such results vividly demonstrate how effectively the regular sale of simple, fundamental imagery for devotional use can contribute to business revenues.

CONCLUSION

That the Moretuses' records do not reflect the full extent of the burgeoning Antwerp print world is understandable. Some individuals, such as the Liefrinck family, conducted their business entirely independently of the Moretuses, while references to several others are rare. Consider, for example, Gerard de Jode's son Peeter. Given the long-established, international network of contacts associated with his family's prosperous print publishing business, Peeter de Jode did not need to call upon the Moretuses for assistance. Rather, the sporadic transactions in which they were involved between 1608 and 1631 most likely reflect exceptional circumstances.[121] For example, despite Plantin's periodic sale of Gerard de Jode's publications, Peeter agreed to supply the Moretuses with prints only once, namely in 1608, when he provided copies of Crispijn de Passe I's series of Ovid's *Metamorphoses*, as well as several hundreds of leaves of unspecified prints for resale to the Roman bookseller Giovanni Paolo Gelli. Similarly, he employed the Moretuses' transport network to complete some of his independent orders on just a few occasions. In 1615, he had a package of prints sent to Justus Sadeler in Venice and paid to have a package from Gaspar Vivario in Rome shipped back to him in Antwerp, while in 1617, he asked the Moretuses to send the Parisian engraver and print seller Jean Messager one package.[122] De Jode's involvement with the Moretuses ended nearly fifteen years later, in December 1631; the last transaction was their receipt of 36 fl. in his name from the Amsterdam bookseller Willem Jansz. Blaeu.[123] Thus, even though De Jode had no persistent need to conduct his business via the Moretuses, he was nevertheless aware of the full gamut of means by which the Moretuses could facilitate international trade.

Among the newcomers in the Antwerp print market, a number of successful engravers also refrained from engaging the Moretuses routinely. Paulus Pontius and Lucas Vorsterman I, for instance, appear only once in the Moretuses' records. The former sold a quantity of books valued at 48 fl. to Balthasar Moretus I in February 1641, and the latter provided Balthasar with images worth just 1 fl. 8 st. for the Capuchin Constantinus van Utrecht in Amsterdam in 1637.[124] The Moretuses also infrequently prevailed upon the engravers Boëtius and Schelte à Bolswert to supply them with prints for resale. The primary exception here was when they arranged for the purchase of 500 prints from the Bolswerts in 1627 and 1628 for the Liège bookseller Jean Ouwerx.[125] The lack of other types of transactions between such figures and the Moretuses underscores their preference to manage their professional affairs via other means and simultaneously highlights potential subdivisions within the Antwerp art market.

Within the new generation of print publishers, some, like Martinus van den Enden, were equally restrained in their dealings with the Moretuses. Born in 1605, Van den Enden was admitted to Antwerp's Guild of St Luke as an art dealer in 1630–1631 and soon became a prominent print publisher in the city, active up until the mid-seventeenth century.[126] He is known for being the first publisher of Anthony van Dyck's *Iconography* and for publishing plates acquired from a variety of sources, including many images inspired by Rubens and his followers. Nevertheless, Van den Enden expressed his support for the defendants in Barbé's suit, against whom Rubens himself had testified.[127] Between 1635 and 1639, Van den Enden also occasionally engaged the Moretuses to help him with the transport of packages and the receipt of payments on his behalf. The records of these few transactions demonstrate that even at this early stage of his career, Van den Enden's contacts were extensive and diverse; they included the engraver and print publisher Jean Messager in Paris, the bookseller Johann Kinckius in Cologne, as well as local clerics, like the Capuchin Winnocus van Winoksbergen in Nijmegen, and religious institutions, such as the Abbey of Loo in Ypres.[128] Of these clients, Kinckius was by far the most important, at least in terms of the sums (nearly 80 fl. in 1639 alone) that he asked the Moretuses to pay Van den Enden.[129] Nevertheless, these isolated transactions were ultimately just temporary solutions for matters that Van den Enden must have routinely resolved in other ways for the day-to-day management of his affairs.

Despite these lacunae in their circle of partners in the print trade, it is still evident that the Moretuses' network of contacts extended beyond those they knew from their own commissions for illustrations for their books and from their relatives, the successful Galle family of engravers and print publishers. Moreover, this assortment of print dealers was remarkably heterogeneous. It comprised exceptionally talented engravers like Hieronymus Wierix and more modest ones like Abraham van Merlen, both of whom were content to have the Moretuses sell their prints to distant, foreign clients. The Moretuses were simultaneously engaged by a range of print publishers. Some, for instance Jan Boel and Jan Baptist Barbé, occasionally sought support for the distribution of their prints, while Michael Snijders relied heavily on several facets of the Moretuses' business for his extensive sale of costly finished images. Even booksellers like Jan Cnobbaert, Marie de Man, and Hendrik Aertssens, who were involved in some segments of the print market, turned to the Moretuses to supplement their trade. This component of the Moretuses' business is often overlooked and underestimated due to insufficient information. When considered alongside the even more abundant transactions of Philips and Theodore Galle and their relatives Charles de Mallery and Adriaen Collaert, the Moretuses' records reveal the rich variety of offerings and opportunities for artists with a range of skills and products who were active during the first half of the seventeenth century, when the market for Antwerp prints was booming.

Thus, the various ways in which the Moretuses were able to further artists' and print dealers' participation in the thriving international print market were accessible to a range of individuals, regardless of their positions in the Antwerp art world and personal ties with the Moretuses. The specific nature of each interaction likely reflected the personal qualities and ambitions of the individuals concerned and thereby highlights a hitherto unimagined diversity in approaches to the publication and distribution of prints. Though not the only means by which an array of works could be distributed, the Moretuses' network, as conveyed through their records, demonstrate the types of transactions in which they and their contacts were engaged, how the transactions were brought to fruition, and how they compared with the activities of rival print sellers. Moreover, it is also important to recognize that what individual print sellers had to offer and what diverse customers sought were not necessarily homogenous, interchangeable items, regardless of the means by which they were sold or the quantities in which they were purchased. Rather, different artists and dealers featured their own specific styles and types of products, just as sundry clients endeavored to satisfy distinct preferences prevalent in their local markets. Hence, in order to fully appreciate the immense international traffic in prints in which assorted clients – booksellers, merchants, laymen, and clerics – participated, it is time to consider the business from their perspective.

1 MPM Arch. 135, p. 211, letter from Balthasar Moretus to Philippus de Peralta, dated 21 July 1614: "Hieronymum Wierickx sculptorem admonitum curabo ut imagines suas paret. Quamquam iam senior parum operetur et quas olim sculpsit, nonnihil sint attritae. Sed et alii hic sunt qui eleganter sculptant, quorum maiorem artem peritus aliquis agnoscat, etsi non eadem sit incisionis subtilitas".

2 Consider the letters transcribed in M-H Wierix, 1978–1982, vol. III.2, nos. 37, 39–41, and 43–44, as well as Corr., vol. VII, no. 1044, p. 207, and vols. VIII-IX, no. 1160, p. 71, no. 1182, pp. 107–08, no. 1188, p. 114, no. 1193, pp. 121–22, and no. 1194, pp. 123–24. See also the discussion of the Wierixes in Appendix 1.

3 For examples of prints executed by the Wierixes and published by these and other print publishers, see Holl. Dutch & Flemish, vol. LXIX, pp. lxxxv-lxxxiv. The Wierixes' engravings for the Jesuits' project are reproduced in full in Holl. Dutch & Flemish, vol. LXXI, nos. 56 and 58.

4 On the Wierixes' early contributions to Plantin's publications designed for Philip II and the Spanish market, see Bowen and Imhof 2008, pp. 84–118 and 352–56.

5 MPM Arch. 174, fol. 17v. See Holl. Dutch & Flemish, vol. LXVI, no. 1837 for Jan's engraving.

6 MPM Arch. 174, fol. 14r.

7 MPM Arch. 174, fol. 19v.

8 M-H Wierix, 1978–1982, vol. III.2, nos. 69–73, 75, 81, 83 (with the account of the pawned plates worth 400 fl.), and 87–93.

9 Ibid., nos. 94 (28 July 1601) and 95 (24 November 1601).

10 MPM Arch. 177, fol. 131v.

11 MPM Arch. 176, fol. 64r.

12 MPM Arch. 225, fol. 207v.

13 Compare MPM Arch. 216, fol. 232r (Ruardo purchase) with MPM Arch. 110r, fol. 86r (Wierix supply), and MPM Arch. 218, fols. 207r (Hierat purchase) with 208r (Wierix supply). See Appendix 1, under Wierix, for a sampling of his use of these rates for the supply of his prints in bulk.

14 Appendix 1, WX-2 for the print. Imhof 2014b, pp. 208–13, on the Guidon, and BN, vol. 21, cols. 46–51 on Sailly.

15 Appendix 1, WX-3. See Chapter 8 for the significance of the market for prints in Cologne and the Jesuit collection in particular.

16 Imhof 2016, pp. 5–10.

17 Appendix 1, WX-7 (Life of the Infant), and WX-12, WX-13, WX-14, and WX-16 for images of Sts Ignatius and Xavier.

18 MPM Arch. 216, fol. 172v (forty-eight prints each of guardian angels and possibly an image of Jesus walking between the Virgin and Joseph (see, for example, Appendix 1, WX-4 and WX-6) as well as two other publications for the Archduke and Archduchess); MPM Arch. 224, fol. 142r (unspecified prints worth 19 fl. 12 st. for Arenberg); and MPM Arch. 223, fol. 20v (unspecified, assorted images selected by the Guardian of the Antwerp Capuchins). Examples of sales to Jesuits, Carmelites, merchants, and booksellers appear above.

19 MPM Arch. 178, fol. 39r, MPM Arch. 178, fol. 78r, MPM Arch. 216, fol. 211r, and MPM Arch. 217, fol. 8v (for Wolters' additional purchases); and MPM Arch. 180, fol. 218v, MPM Arch. 217, fol. 229r, MPM Arch. 218, fol. 27r, and MPM Arch. 219, fol. 23r (for Mylius's purchases).

20 Appendix 1, WX-7 (Life of the Infant) and WX-8 (Mirror of Virginity); and MPM Arch. 220, fol. 190r, MPM Arch. 221, fol. 200r, MPM Arch. 222, fols. 59r and 97v, and MPM Arch. 223, fol. 86v, for these and other purchases by De Angulo.

21 Appendix 1, WX-12, WX-13, WX-14, and WX-16 (Pardo), and MPM Arch. 219, fol. 194v (Carillo).

22 Antwerp, Felix Archives, IB 2937, fols. 11v (under 1 April and 14 October 1606) and 17v (under 16 March 1612). For the association of this document with Vivario and a discussion of his range of activities, selling prints, maps, and books, see Chapter 7.

23 MPM Arch. 222, fols. 19v (Du Puis) and 70r (Morel); and MPM Arch. 225, fol. 5r (De Gouy).

24 Antwerp, Felix Archives, Processen supplement 288: no. 5284, a loose document dated 21 February 1608, points II and IX (transcribed in Chapter 2, n. 80).

25 As with all of the figures cited here, this is less than the total value of what the Moretuses sold of his prints; however, records documenting his supply of prints are not known for every transaction, and this total excludes the Moretuses' occasional profit margin on such transactions.

26 M-H Wierix, 1978–1982, vol. III.2, nos. 98–99 and 102.

27 Thijs 1993, p. 97: "om hun vaders copere platen te mogen beneficieren met interdictie van ses jaeren" and n. 67, with reference to Brussels, State Archives of Belgium, R.20800, 1618–1619, fols. 121r-121v.

28 BN, vol. I, cols. 706–08; and Rombouts and Van Lerius 1872, vol. I, pp. 383, 471, and 643, respectively.

29 Denucé 1927, p. 150; and Duverger 1984–2009, vol. IV, no. 893, pp. 23–24.

30 Diels 2009, pp. 126 and 168.

31 Given the dates when Wierix married (1587) and when his other children were born (1588, 1590, 1592, and 1594), Christina would most likely have been either a first, illegitimate child or his last, some twenty years younger than Barbé (M-H Wierix, 1978–1982, vol. III.2, p. 521).

32 Ibid., nos. 107, 109–14, pp. 568–70.

33 Thijs 1993, p. 130. The numerous copies after Wierix are discussed briefly in Holl. Dutch & Flemish, vol. LXIX, pp. xxxiii-xxxiv, and many are documented in vols. LIX-LXIX.

34 Thijs 1993, pp. 97–98 and n. 67, with reference to Brussels, State Archives of Belgium, R.20801, fol. 81v, for the first example. The second, frequently cited case, is summarized in Diels 2009, pp. 56–57, which is based in turn on testimonials transcribed in Génard 1867. See Antwerp, Felix Archives, N 736, fols. 302r-303v, for some of the original texts cited in Génard; and Duverger 1984–2009, vol. III, nos. 805 and 845 for additional documents pertaining to this case. On copyrights, privileges, and licenses to publish prints generally, see Griffiths 2016, pp. 97–107.

35 For examples of challenges to Rubens's privileges, see Grivel 1986, pp. 109–10; and Diels 2009, p. 57.

36 For Van Merlen's statement, see Génard 1867, p. 465; and Antwerp, Felix Archives, N 736, fol. 303v. See Duverger 1984–2009, vol. III, no. 845, p. 418, for the latter topic.

37 For this general discrepancy in terms of imitations of Wierix's work, see the indexes for engravers and publishers in Holl. Dutch & Flemish, vol. LXIX, pp. lxxvii-lxxxi and lxxxiv-lxxxix, respectively, and pp. lxxx and lxxxvi for examples produced by De Mallery and Galle, specifically. Thijs 1993, p. 98, argues that the percentage of such copies in Galle's stock of plates upon his death was relatively small.

38 Duverger 1984–2009, vol. III, no. 869, pp. 447–48, from Antwerp, Felix Archives, PK 736 (1635–1636), fols. 101r-101v. Fabri wrote regarding Barbé: "dat den oorspronck van alle dese moijelycheden eygentlyck procedeert vuytte giericheyt van den voors. Barbé, die in differente andere occasiën hem selven desaengaende te seer leelyck heeft laten kennen, ghelyck hem in tyden ende wylen by den advocaet dese onderteeckent hebbende ad oculum sal worden gedemonstreertt". This case is also mentioned in Thijs 1993, pp. 102 and 134.

39 Antwerp, Felix Archives, Notary H. van Cantelbeck, N 3391 (14 March 1637), transcribed in part in Duverger 1984–2009, vol. IV, no. 931, pp. 71–72.

40 MPM Arch. 151, p. 163.

41 MPM Arch. 1106, fol. 76v, under 21 February 1629.

42 MPM Arch. 223, fol. 85r; and MPM Arch. 225, fol. 8r. See also Bowen 2022b, pp. 380–83, on Justus's transactions with the Moretuses.

43 MPM Arch. 229, fols. 101r and 171r (1622); and MPM Arch. 232, fol. 30v (1625). On the abundance of Flemish artists in Rome around 1600, see, for example, Fiamminghi a Roma 1995.

44 MPM Arch. 238, fols. 72r and 149v (Messager, 1630); MPM Arch. 239, fol. 13r (Messager, 1631); MPM Arch. 240, fols. 159r (Messager, 1632), and 159r and 166r (Marin, 1632); MPM Arch. 241, fols. 30v, 87r, and 158r (Messager 1633); and MPM Arch. 242, fol. 127v (Messager, 1634).

45 MPM Arch. 241, fols. 30v, 64v, and 158r (1633); and MPM Arch. 242, fols. 89v, 127v, and 185v (1634).

46 MPM Arch. 240, fol. 159r.

47 MPM Arch. 243, fols. 148r, 156v, and 190r (Kinckius, 1635); MPM Arch. 244, fols. 2v and possibly 80v (Kinckius, 1636), and 92r (Hogenberg, 1636); MPM Arch. 145, fol. 249v (a draft of a letter from Louis Moretus to Kinckius regarding a shipment of prints from Barbé in December 1636); MPM Arch. 245, fol. 25v (Hogenberg, 1637); and MPM Arch. 246, fols. 89r and 200r (Hogenberg, 1638).

48 Begheyn 2001.

49 https://rkd.nl/explore/artists/85128 (Witdoeck) and https://rkd.nl/explore/artists/318394 (Van Tienen); and Rombouts and Van Lerius 1872, vol. II, p. 18 (Witdoeck as pupil of Vorsterman); and Ibid., vol. I, p. 567 (Van Tienen as a master in the Guild of St Luke). See, for example, MPM Arch. 187, fol. 87v, for a reference to approximately 2,000 prints from Van Tienen left in four packages in the Moretuses' shop in Frankfurt in 1644; and MPM Arch. 1107, fol. 130v, and MPM Arch. 252, fol. 143r, for examples of paintings that he traded via the Moretuses in 1642 and 1644, respectively.

50 https://rkd.nl/explore/artists/112969; Rombouts and Van Lerius, vol. I, pp. 560–61 (as master engraver); and Ibid., 1872, vol. II, pp. 74, 76, 164, 229, and 240 (his registration as a dean and that of his pupils).

51 MPM Arch. 246, fol. 200r.

52 Rombouts and Van Lerius 1872, vol. I, p. 664 (Voet's registration as a master engraver); and Ibid., vol. II, pp. 105, 133, 218, and 350 (the registration of five pupils between 1638–1639 and 1663–1664).

53 MPM Arch. 240, fol. 166r.

54 Stoesser 2018 and pp. 46–50 (Cornelis de Wael's establishment in Italy), 611–14 (engravings Voet published after Cornelis de Wael), and 330 (references to prints supplied by Voet in Cornelis de Wael's inventory from 2 May 1667). See also the sources cited in https://rkd.nl/explore/artists/81549, in particular Thijs 1993; Verheggen 2006; and Holl. Dutch & Flemish, vol. XLII, pp. 7–48.

55 MPM Arch. 236, fol. 4r.

56 See https://rkd.nl/explore/artists/318388 for basic information on Philips de Mallery; and Bowen and Imhof 2022, p. 10, for an example of his work for Messager.

57 These activities are summarized in Van Lerius 1880, pp. 86–88, including references to Rombouts and Van Lerius for the relevant payments to the Guild of St Luke.

58 Van Lerius 1880, p. 87; and Antwerp, Felix Archives, PR 14, fol. 38r.

59 MPM Arch. 228, fol. 127v, and MPM Arch. 1106, fol. 19r (Leonard); MPM Arch. 234, fol. 27v; and MPM Arch. 1106, fol. 64v (Hierats).

60 MPM Arch. 227, fol. 205v, and MPM Arch. 228, fols. 15v and 104v (Kinckius); MPM Arch. 233, fol. 9v (Van Egmont); MPM Arch. 228, fol. 15v (Hogenberg); and MPM Arch. 230, fol. 144v, and MPM Arch. 233, fols. 83v and 182v (Van Dale).

61 MPM Arch. 235, fol. 85v; and MPM Arch. 239, fol. 25v, respectively.

62 Holl. Dutch & Flemish, vol. III, p. 56; and Wolfegg, Fürstlich zu Waldburg-Wolfegg'sche Kunstsammlungen, vol. 9, no. 172, for an impression of it.

63 Boel's inventory is discussed in Van Lerius 1880, pp. 89–90, and is transcribed in part in Duverger 1984–2009, vol. IV, no. 1097.

64 See Appendix 1 for a brief overview of Cnobbaert's activities and the rates he and his widow charged for the prints they sold via the Moretuses.

65 For Van Mechelen and examples of his trade in copper plates and images (including the 1627 case), see Lemmens and Thijs 2006, pp. 99–100; and Imhof 2023a, pp. 119–21. For testimonials concerning the 1625 case, see Antwerp, Felix Archives, N 3457 (1625), fols. 147v and 382v.

66 Antwerp, Felix Archives, GF 160 (4) (Van Doorn to Verdussen on 29 November 1629 and between 10 and 20 January 1630, respectively).

67 This contract is discussed at greater length in Chapter 2 within a broader discussion of hand-colored prints.

68 For an overview of Pontius's work, see https://rkd.nl/explore/artists/64223; and Diels 2009, pp. 176–77.

69 MPM Arch. 235, fols. 26r and 28v (Hecart); MPM Arch. 236, fol. 2r (Barentsen); MPM Arch. 235, fol. 89r (Van Vucht); and MPM Arch. 242, fols. 101r and 102v (Capuchins).

70 MPM Arch. 238, fol. 140r; and MPM Arch. 239, fol. 112r.

71 MPM Arch. 248, fols. 33v and 41r, for the supply and resale, respectively.

72 See the discussion of the Cnobbaerts in Appendix 1 for a full overview of the rates they charged for their prints.

73 MPM Arch. 255, fols. 92v and 93r, for the supply and purchase, respectively, of her prints in 1647; and MPM Arch. 256, fols. 19r and 83v, for the sales to Wagner. See Thijs 1993 for numerous additional examples of the immense volume of prints printed in Antwerp and distributed both locally and internationally during the seventeenth and eighteenth centuries.

74 See Appendix 1 for a brief overview of Snijders's career and the prices he charged for the prints he sold through the Moretuses.

75 These figures are all minimal indications of these values because not all records of what a given print publisher supplied are known.

76 For examples of such sales from 1629 and 1632, see MPM Arch. 1107, fols. 5v and 29v (supply); and MPM Arch. 237, fol. 50r, and MPM Arch. 240, fol. 155r (Raesfeld's purchases), respectively.

77 For an example from 1619, see MPM Arch. 1105, fol. 85v (supply); and MPM Arch. 226, fol. 183r (purchase). See Chapter 7 for an overview of the Raesfeld family's acquisition of prints.

78 MPM Arch. 232, fols. 97v and 104r, for the purchase and supply, respectively, of these prints.

79 MPM Arch. 1107, fol. 1r (supply); and MPM Arch. 237, fol. 3v (purchase). See also Chapter 2 for examples of what it cost Snijders to have his canons hand colored and Chapter 3 for examples of Plantin's earlier production and sale of canons.

80 MPM Arch. 235, fols. 129v-130r.

81 MPM Arch. 234, fol. 142v.

82 See Wolfegg, Fürstlich zu Waldburg-Wolfegg'sche Kunstsammlungen, vol. 4, no. 265, for the former (an image of the Virgin with portraits of the four preeminent Jesuits of the time, Sts Ignatius of Loyola, Francis Xavier, Aloysius Gonzaga, and Stanislaus Kostka), and vol. 7, no. 141, for the latter (an image of the Virgin and Child within a rosary); both are roughly 310 × 440 mm.

83 MPM Arch. 179, fol. 111v, where it is noted that his wife, the daughter of De Jode's widow, was then in Antwerp: "sa femme la fille de la vefve de Jode presente en Anvers"; and MPM Arch. 127, fol. 245, for evidence of Claessens following Jacques de Jode in their accounts.

84 MPM Arch. 231, fol. 58r, MPM Arch. 240, fol. 59r, MPM Arch. 235, fol. 51v, and MPM Arch. 234, fol. 49r, respectively, for the packages sent; and MPM Arch. 230, fol. 170r, MPM Arch. 233, fol. 165v, MPM Arch. 234, fol. 58v, MPM Arch. 235, fol. 52v, and MPM Arch. 236, fol. 6r, for these payments. The print trade between Antwerp and Gdańsk is discussed in greater detail in Chapter 7.

85 MPM Arch. 230, fol. 38r (1623); MPM Arch. 231, fol. 195v (1624); and MPM Arch. 233, fol. 83v (1626).

86 MPM Arch. 232, fol. 33v (Ouwerx). See MPM Arch. 231, fol. 163r; MPM Arch. 235, fol. 165v; MPM Arch. 241, fol. 23r; and MPM Arch. 244, fol. 48r, respectively, for the shipments to Geubels.

87 MPM Arch. 235, fol. 3v (Ouwerx); and MPM Arch. 232, fol. 126r, and MPM Arch. 233, fol. 57r (Geubels).

88 Denucé 1934, pp. 52, 54–55, and 57–58.

89 See Holl. Dutch & Flemish, vol. LXIX, p. lxxxix, for more examples.

90 MPM Arch. 227, fol. 205v (1620 sale to Van Dale); and MPM Arch. 237, fol. 109v (1629 sale to B. Raesfeld). For a transcription of the list of copper plates in Snijders's estate, see Duverger 1984–2009, vol. IX, no. 2984. See Holl. Dutch & Flemish, vol. XXVII, p. 95, no. 17, for the genealogical tree.

91 Duverger 1984–2009, vol. IV, no. 1012, pp. 176–77, for a transcription of the records of these transactions.

92 For Claessens's bankruptcy, see MPM Arch. 134, fol. 23 rht.

93 Duverger 1990–1991, pp. 96–97.

94 SAA GA 4591, fols. 23v-79r, for these records, which are also discussed in Duverger 1990–1991, p. 101, although he incorrectly states that Snijders received just 30 deniers (instead of stuivers) per 100 prints.

95 Rombouts and Van Lerius 1872, vol. I, pp. 398 and 411, respectively. See also the discussion of Van Merlen in Appendix 1.

96 Rombouts and Van Lerius 1872, vol. I, pp. 466 and 470 (1610: a certain Hans Schorkens), and 498 and 501 (1613: Van Lochum). On Van Merlen and his descendants, see Lemmens and Thijs 2006, and pp. 94–95 for his sales via Vivario, which are discussed in greater detail in Chapter 7.

97 Lemmens and Thijs 2006, pp. 93 (Van Merlen's financial situation when he married in 1608 and a description of his house) and 95 (the sale of his house). On the Lombardenvest and its surroundings, see Van der Stock 1998, pp. 60–69.

98 MPM Arch. 1105, fol. 82r (supply); and MPM Arch. 226, fol. 103v (purchase).

99 MPM Arch. 224, fols. 171v-172r (1617); MPM Arch. 225, fols. 13v and 87r (purchase), and 137r (supply in 1618); and MPM Arch. 227, fol. 205v (1620).

100 MPM Arch. 1105, fol. 40r (supply), and MPM Arch. 222, fol. 83v (purchase in 1615); and MPM Arch. 1105, fol. 48r (supply) and MPM Arch. 223, fol. 6v (purchase in 1616).

101 MPM Arch. 224, fols. 144v (Van Zwevenseel), 164r (Ouwerx), 196v (Sersanders); and MPM Arch. 225, fol. 7r (Ouwerx).

102 Lemmens and Thijs 2006, p. 97 and n. 38, citing: SAA, N. 3496 (23 March 1626): "zeker groote quantiteyt cleyn beeldekens van alle meesters".

103 MPM Arch. 232, fols. 97v and 104r, MPM Arch. 233, fol. 45v, and MPM Arch. 1106, fol. 54v (De Braa); and MPM Arch. 233, fol. 99r, and MPM Arch. 235, fol. 52v (Claessens).

104 See under Van Merlen in Appendix 1 for examples of both.

105 On Theodoor II, see Rombouts and Van Lerius 1872, vol. II, p. 26; and Lemmens and Thijs 2006, pp. 106–09.

106 Lemmens and Thijs 2006, and p. 95 for this citation.

107 MPM Arch. 224, fol. 22r.

108 See, for example, MPM Arch. 115, fol. 131 rht. As discussed in Chapter 1, we are not tracing the distribution of these other illustrated publications supplied by Aertssens.

109 Thijs 1985, pp. 561–62 and 577.

110 Ibid., pp. 570–76.

111 Ibid., pp. 562–64, 573–74, and 578.

112 Ibid., pp. 579–80 and n. 79, with reference to Brussels, State Archives of Belgium, Conseil Privé espagnol, 1277, no. 107.

113 MPM Arch. 232, fol. 126r.

114 MPM Arch. 242, fol. 204v (suffragia in "duyts"); MPM Arch. 238, fol. 38v ("suffragia van elcke maendt [of each month] flandrice"); MPM Arch. 233, fol. 54v ("suffragia feuillies du mois Juing, Julliet, Augoust, novemb. Decemb. de chaque mois 24 feuillies (sheets for the months June, July, August, November, and December, 24 sheets of each (for Ouwerx)), MPM Arch. 243, fol. 188v ("1 Main des Suffrages pour un An" (1 quire of suffragia for one year)); MPM Arch. 238, fol. 21v (Aertssens's supply of twenty quires each of suffragia in Latin and French), and 13v (Ouwerx's purchase of the same, but identified as one ream of each), all at the price of 2 fl. per quire. See the Note to the Reader for a discussion of these terms and the relative formats of independent prints sold via the Moretuses.

115 See MPM Arch. 243, fol. 5v, for that from 1635, and the preceding note for other examples.

116 MPM Arch. 245, fols. 117v and 178r-178v (Erasmus); MPM Arch. 238, fols. 38v (supply) and 40r (purchase); MPM Arch. 246, fol. 154v (Barentsen).

117 MPM Arch. 238, fol. 86r (purchase); and MPM Arch. 738, fol. 136r (supply).

118 MPM Arch. 239, fol. 29v (Jesuit college, Brussels); MPM Arch. 238, fols. 26v (supply) and 27v (purchase by Bourgoys); MPM Arch. 240, fols. 59v (supply) and 60r (purchase by Chifflet); MPM Arch. 243, fol. 188v (Van Elshout); and MPM Arch. 248, fol. 53v (suffragia for Dominicans from an unknown source).

119 MPM Arch. 239, fols. 175r (supply) and 176v (purchase) (1631); and MPM Arch. 242, fols. 204r (supply) and 204v (purchase) (1634).

120 Unclear recordkeeping pertaining to a 1632 sale of just ten leaves of suffragia to the bookseller Jean de Rache of Lille makes it difficult to determine whether a profit margin was added here as well or not (MPM Arch. 240, fol. 151r; and MPM Arch. 738, fol. 144 rht).

121 On Peeter de Jode, see also Appendix 1.

122 MPM Arch. 180, fol. 152r (Gelli); MPM Arch. 222, fols. 170v (Sadeler), and 170v and 195r (Vivario); and MPM Arch. 224, fol. 20v (Messager). For De Passe's publication, see Veldman 2001a.

123 MPM Arch. 239, fol. 195v.

124 MPM Arch. 249, fol. 17r; and MPM Arch. 245, fol. 24v, respectively.

125 MPM Arch. 1106, fols. 66r and 70v (supply from an unspecified Bolswert); and MPM Arch. 234, fol. 165v, and MPM Arch. 235, fol. 31r (respective sales).

126 Rombouts and Van Lerius, vol. II, pp. 15 and 18 (his registration in the Guild of St Luke); and Stoesser 2018, Diels 2009, and Duverger and Maufort 1999, pp. 370–71 (Van den Enden as a print publisher).

127 Duverger 1984–2009, vol. III, no. 845, pp. 417–20.

128 MPM Arch. 243, fol. 10v (Messager); MPM Arch. 245, fol. 25v (Kinckius); and MPM Arch. 247, fols. 161r (Van Winoksbergen) and 171v (Abbey of Loo).

129 MPM Arch. 247, fols. 18r and 108v.

Eigentliche Abbildung deß ganzen Gewerbs der löblichen Kaufmannschafft/ samt etlich der nahmhafft- und fürnehmsten Handelstädt Signatur und Wappen/ darinnen zum Theil fürnehmlich die Märckt und Messen begriffen seyn/ so deß Jahrs über in jedem Monath einfallen/ auch hin und wider in Europa zu unterschidlichen Zeiten gehalten/ und von fürnehmen und geringen Gewerbs- und Handelsleuthen/ aus allerley Nationen besucht und gebauet werden; wie durch derselben mancherley Schild und Wappen hie unten und zum Eingang bey dem *Mercurio* angezeigt ist. Samt der löblichen schönen uralten Kunst deß Buchhaltens/ dardurch alle Kaufmanns-Gewerb schleunig und richtig unterhalten werden; Neben andern wolgemeinten Erinnerungen/ welche den Handelsleuthen nothwendig zu wissen und zu beobachten sind.

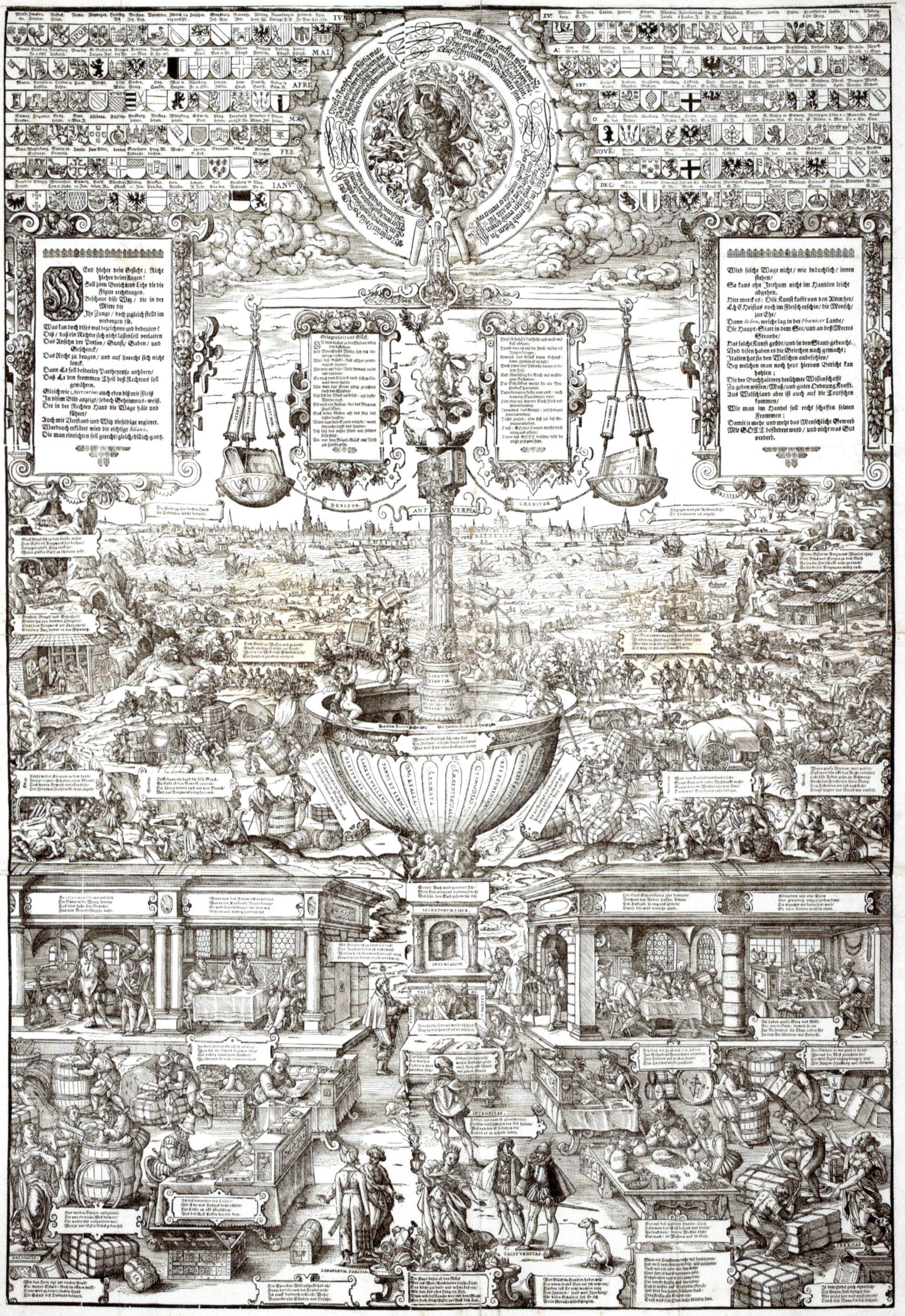

CHAPTER 7

THE DEMAND FOR PRINTS FROM ANTWERP

FAR AND NEAR

> The beginning [of the print trade] in 1550 is marked by the establishment of the first big publishers of intaglio plates in Rome and Antwerp, who realized that prints could be sold internationally and that to do so could be extremely profitable.[1]

7.1 Jost Amman, *Allegory of Trade with a View of Antwerp*, 1585, woodcut, 950 × 640 mm. Antwerp, Museum Plantin-Moretus, Print Department: PK.OP.21317.

In his introductory discussion of the European print trade, Antony Griffiths underscores the importance of Flemish printmakers and publishers, stating that by the 1580s, they were "supplying most of the engravings to the French and German markets and almost the entire market in Britain, Spain, Portugal and America".[2] Antwerp's significance and far-reaching potential as a center for international trade was similarly acknowledged in the sixteenth century. In Joost Amman's *Allegory of Trade* from 1585 (fig. 7.1), a large pair of scales, on which credits and debts are balanced, is held up in the center by a robust figure of Mercury, below whom is a view of the Antwerp skyline from the Schelde river, the city's thriving artery for traffic in diverse merchandise from sundry locations. That Antwerp is the only city to be depicted in this print indicates its immense significance in northern Europe for international trade among a slew of cities that are simply represented by the inclusion of their coats of arms in strips; one coat of arms is depicted for each month in which their local trade fairs were held. Many of these fairs are commonly associated with the production of prints – Rome (under June), Venice (under May), Paris (under January), and Amsterdam (under August). There are also cities where the substantial interest in prints is evident through the Moretuses' accounts, in particular: Frankfurt am Main (under both March and September), Danzig (now Gdańsk) (under January), and Cologne (under October). Below, some of the practical, day-to-day aspects of the trade in goods are portrayed. These range from meetings between merchants to the packing of barrels and bales of goods, several of which are marked by the initials or monograms of the intended recipients. Notably, similar marks appear in the shipping records of the Plantin-Moretus Press (see, for example, fig. 2.3). Finally, the transport of goods by horse and cart is juxtaposed with images of marauding soldiers and a warning about the detrimental effects of war on trade. This last allusion would certainly have resonated with all who saw the print when it was published in 1585; during that year, Antwerp finally capitulated to the general of the Spanish army, Alexander Farnese, following a siege that had included a blockade on the Schelde, the lifeline for international trade featured here. Nevertheless, although the wars of religion in the Low Countries and around Antwerp, in particular in the second half of the sixteenth century, certainly complicated the traffic in goods, they did not stop this traffic. Not only did businesses, like that of the Plantin-Moretus Press, rebound in the subsequent decades, but the accompanying emigration of individuals of all walks of life from the area facilitated the revival and expansion of trade throughout Europe via enlarged networks of countrymen and business associates. The accounts of the Plantin-Moretus Press cannot be expected to document the vast traffic in prints from Antwerp, which also intensified rapidly during the seventeenth century, in its entirety. Nevertheless, alongside other records, they provide key examples of the extent of the demand for images from Antwerp and the ways in which the international sale of prints prospered through a variety of channels. Consequently, while the story of the European market for prints may not yet be complete, the following glimpses of the magnitude of this trade will better enable us to fathom what has yet to be documented in full.

INDICATIONS OF THE PRINT TRADE IN ENGLAND, ITALY, AND SPAIN

Although requests for prints from individuals based in England were rare, the handful that the Moretuses did receive were diverse, reflecting some of the distinct aspects of the print market there.[3] For example, in 1635, the London bookseller Richard Whitacker, with whom the Moretuses traded between 1631 and 1646, placed an order for a few impressions of works in the possession of Theodore Galle's widow, Catharina Moerentorf.[4] Aside from a small portrait of the "Cardinal Infante", Ferdinand of Austria, he was also interested in images of apostles and saints, including Theodore Galle's 1630 series *Holy Founders of Religious Orders…* (*Sancti fundatores religiosorum ordinum*), which featured forty engravings by his brother Cornelius I

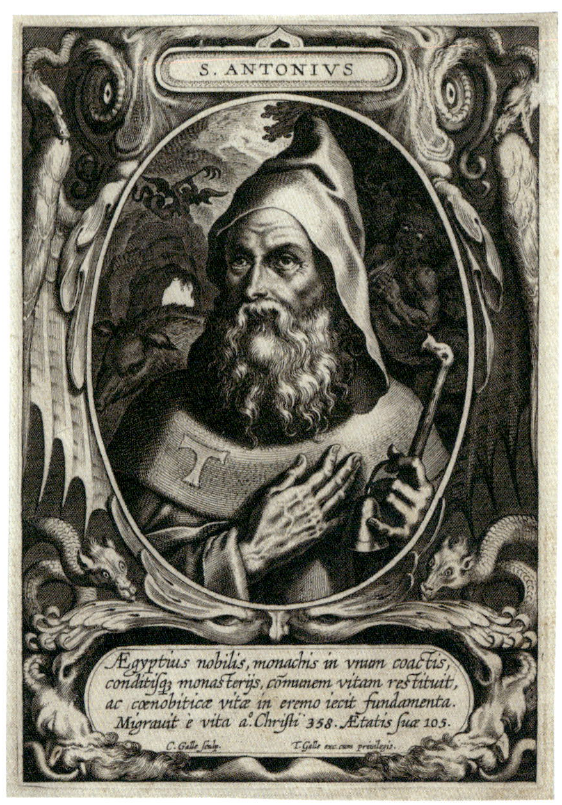

7.2 Cornelis Galle I, *Saint Antonius*, from the series *Holy Founders of Religious Orders*, 1630, engraving, 151 × 104 mm. Antwerp, Museum Plantin-Moretus: PK: OPB: 0098.007 Appendix 1: TG-6.

(fig. 7.2). The relatively few copies requested of these prints suggest that they may have been ordered for individual collectors. A noteworthy twelve images of the Crucifixion, all hand colored and printed on parchment, may well have been acquired for another purpose.[5] Noted at the end of a very large order of books, Balthasar Moretus I did not include a profit margin for himself on this isolated group of prints order. Circumstances were notably different when he dealt with another London bookseller, Humphrey Robinson.

Active as a bookseller in London for nearly fifty years (1624–1670), Robinson was an important figure in the London book world. Nevertheless, his contact with the Moretuses was limited to just one decade, from 1631 to 1640.[6] During these years, he ordered prints from them twice. In 1638, he requested fifty sets of a series of Christ with the twelve apostles in small 8° – the same subject, if not the exact same series, Whitacker had ordered just four sets of three years earlier – along with six sets of a set of prints that had been engraved to accompany an unspecified text by Jean Bourgeois (Joannes Bourgesius) and that were supplied by Hendrik Aertssens. While Jan Galle offered the series of Christ and the apostles at 5 st. per series, Aertssens provided the six sets at 3 fl. (60 st.) per series. As he had done for Whitacker, Balthasar I resold them all to Robinson at cost.[7] The significant difference in the number of sets of the series of the apostles purchased by Whitacker and by Robinson may reflect both the size of each business and the role of the sales of prints within it. The likelihood that Robinson was catering to a larger audience of print buyers, including potentially wealthier collectors, is reinforced by his second order of prints from the Moretuses in 1640. This order comprised not only three additional sets of the prints for Bourgesius's publication (still at 3 fl. per set), but also three impressions each of three different engravings after Rubens, namely images of fighting tigers, the *Adoration of the Magi*, and the *Raising of Lazarus* (fig. 7.3). For the fighting tigers, which were most likely smaller prints, Robinson paid 1 fl. 5 st. per impression, while the other two images cost 1 fl. 14 st. per impression; the total cost of the order was 13 fl. 19 st.[8] In notable contrast to all the other prints Balthasar sold to Robinson, Balthasar charged him more than he himself had paid for the images after Rubens and consequently earned a profit of 1 fl. 7 st. (27 st.) on their resale, or an average of 3 st. per print. The exceptional treatment of this one group of engravings, sold some five months following Rubens's death, underscores the speed with which Balthasar entered the lucrative traffic in Rubens's prints once Rubens could no longer control it.[9]

While these sales are valuable as concrete examples of specifically which prints were being purchased by whom and at what price, a more vivid picture of the potential for trade between print dealers in England and print sellers from Antwerp is provided by Plantin's and Jan Moretus I's accounts with the London-based bookseller Hans Woutneel. Best known for his involvement in the publication and sale of work by the engraver Crispijn de Passe I, who was in Antwerp in the mid-1580s, Woutneel's connections with Antwerp-based dealers in prints, maps, and books was far more extensive.[10] Already by July 1581, soon after his admission to the London Stationers' Company in 1579–1580, Woutneel was making nearly annual purchases of books from Plantin and Moretus, and continued to do so until 1600. The surviving records also reveal the frequency with which he was in Antwerp – indicated by the phrase "estant present" (present (in Antwerp)) – which recurs often in these years. His periodic trips to the city are understandable if the assumptions that he had emigrated from the Low Countries, and possibly Antwerp in particular, are true.[11] These visits would have provided him with ample opportunities for dealing directly with numerous local print dealers. That he was thus able to establish secure business relationships with several such figures is evident from the number of times Antwerp print sellers are named as the individuals

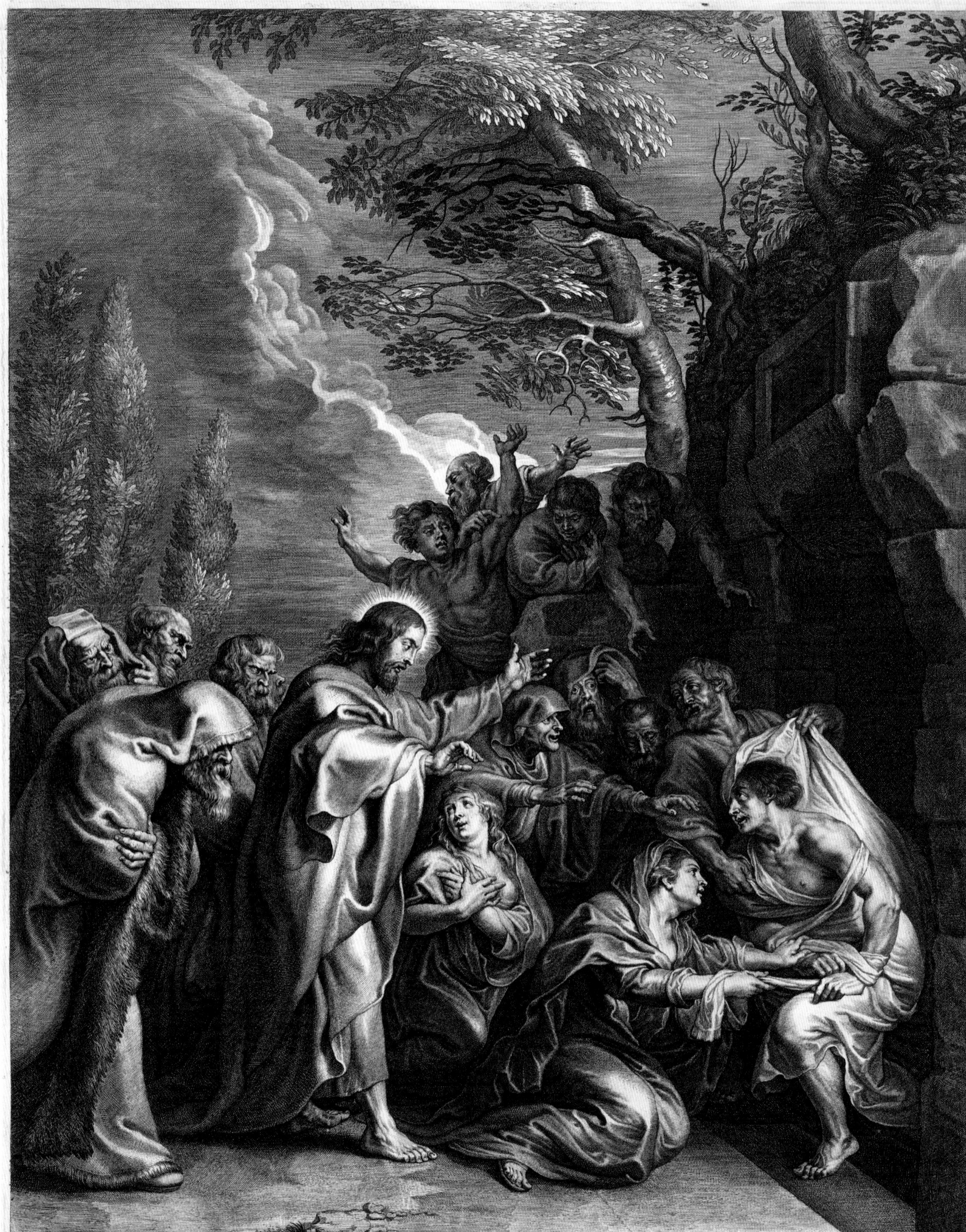

Petrus Paulus Rubens pinxit. LAZARE, VENI FORAS. Ioan. 11. Boetius à Bolswert sculp. et excud.

Cum Priuilegijs Regis Christianissimi, Serenissimæ Infantis, et Ordinum Confœderatorum.

7.3 Boëtius Adamsz. Bolswert after Peter Paul Rubens, *Raising of Lazarus*, 1620–1633, engraving, 655 × 506 mm. Amsterdam, Rijksmuseum: RP-P-PB-67.484.

who paid some of Woutneel's bills with Plantin and Moretus. Records from 1587 to 1592, for example, suggest that Woutneel dealt regularly with the De Jode family, as various members – Gerard de Jode, his daughter Tanneken van Hoeswinkel, and his widow, Passchijnke van Gelre – all transferred funds to Plantin and Moretus on Woutneel's behalf. Jan-Baptist Vrients is similarly cited as a financial middleman for Woutneel in 1591.[12] While references to these individuals continued in later years – in particular, Passchijnke and, subsequently, her son Jacques de Jode, as well as Vrients – by 1596, Woutneel had expanded his trusted contacts to include Philips Galle, who regularly paid off his debts with Moretus between 1596 and 1599.[13] Finally, Adriaen Collaert was added to Woutneel's group of contacts in 1602, shortly before Woutneel's death in 1604. A *datum ante quem* for Woutneel's passing is provided by a reference to Jacques de Jode paying Moretus 56 fl. in the name of Woutneel's widow sometime between 19 June and 7 August 1604 (fig. 7.4).[14]

Though the surviving records do not include further information about Woutneel's exchanges with these print sellers, the amounts they paid in his name to Plantin and Moretus were significant, often ranging from 50 to 100 fl. and even amounting to as much as 200 fl. on one occasion (as in fig. 7.4). Presumably, if Woutneel's debts with these print dealers were far less, the financial arrangements would have been reversed. Such was the case, for example,

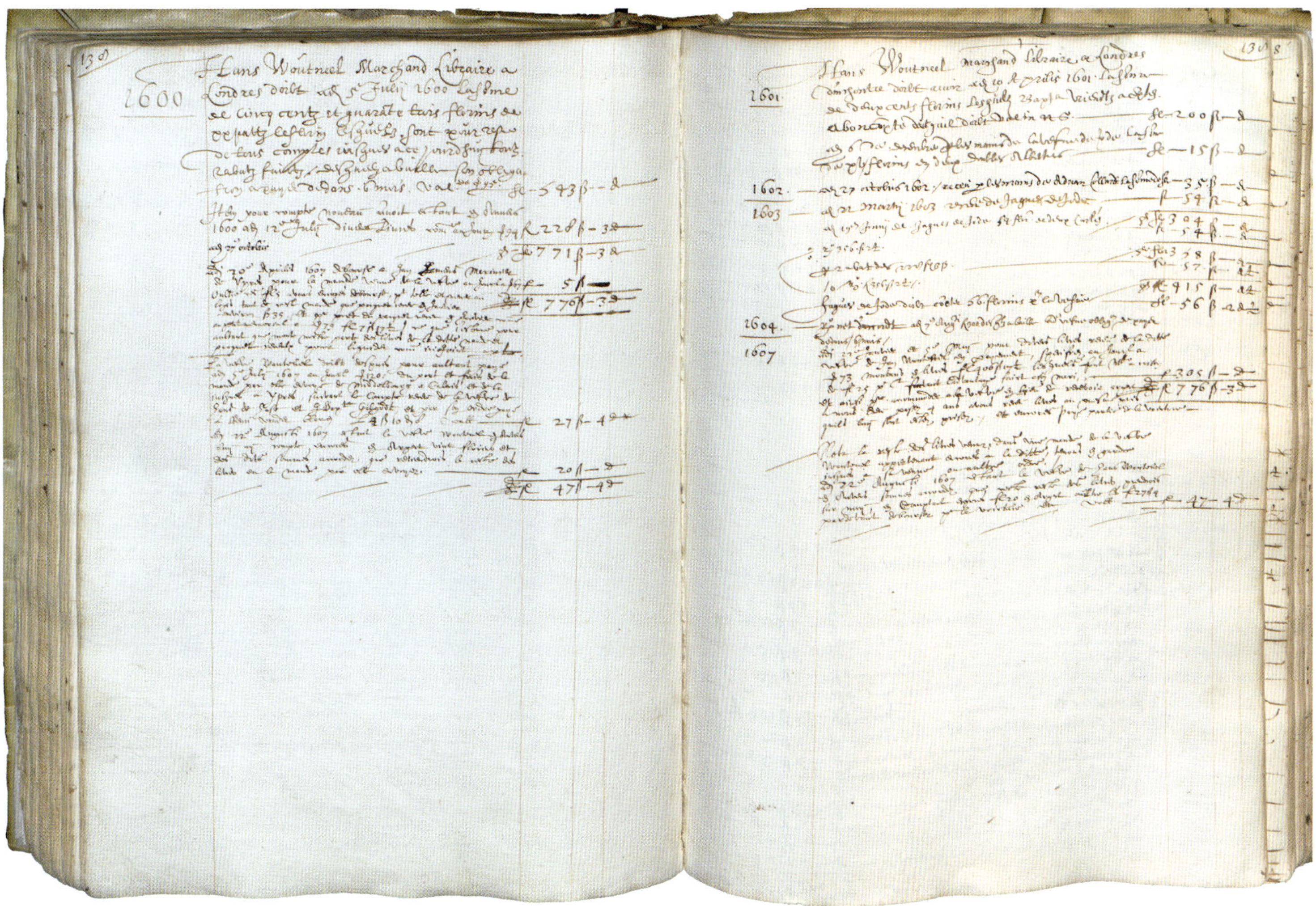

7.4 Accounts with Hans Woutneel from 1601 through his death in 1604. Antwerp, Museum Plantin-Moretus: Arch. 111, *Libraires étrangers. Grand livre F. 1594–1609*, fol. 138 rht.

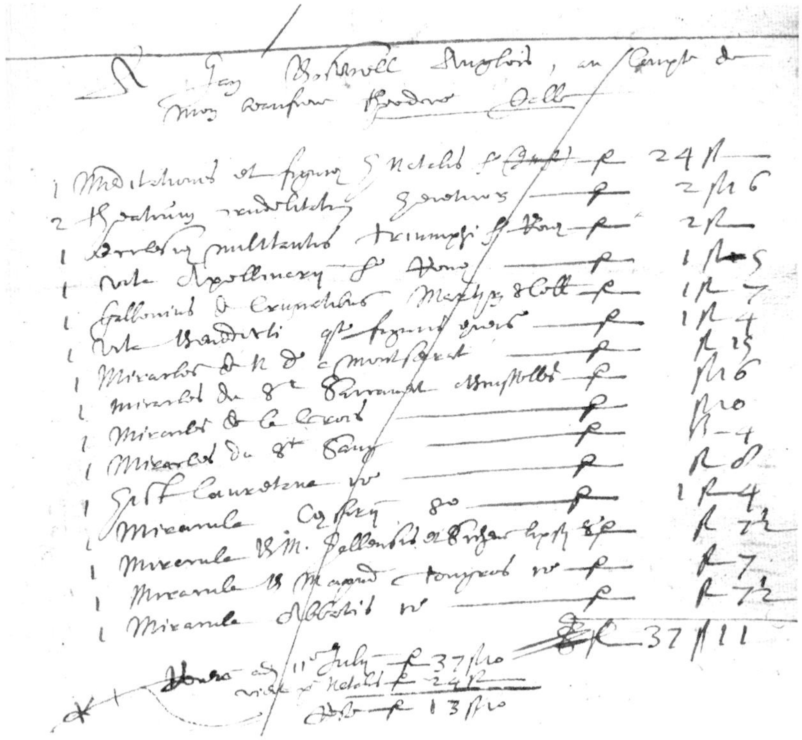

7.5 Order of books and prints for John Boswell of London, 28 June 1608. Antwerp, Museum Plantin-Moretus: Arch. 180, *Journal 1608*, fol. 106r.

when the London-based bookseller Ascanius de Renialme sent Jan Moretus I 522 fl. in August 1599, with the request that he use some of it to pay off debts De Renialme had, including 22 fl. for the Antwerp bookseller Petrus Bellerus and 83 fl. for Philips Galle. The remaining sum of 417 fl. was then applied to De Renialme's running account with Moretus.[15] Woutneel's practices were not exceptional. In 1608, Theodore Galle served as the financial intermediary between Jan Moretus and another London dealer in prints, maps, and books, John Boswell, who placed a remarkable order (paid for by Galle) for both prints and illustrated books that included older editions published in Rome during the mid-1580s (such as Bartholomaeus Grassi's 1586 *Beati Apollinaris martyris … res gestae*), a new edition of Nadal's *Evangelicae historiae imagines* together with the accompanying *Adnotationes et meditationes in evangelia*, and sundry print series portraying miracles (fig. 7.5).[16] Aside from two copies of Richard Verstegen's *Theatrum crudelitatum haereticorum* (the edition sent was not specified), Boswell ordered just one of each item listed, suggesting that this was a special request for one particular client. These diverse transactions attest to an active, direct trade between a number of Antwerp's print dealers and their personal contacts in London, who were responding in turn to the ongoing demand there for prints from Flanders.

Although the direct sale of prints to individuals in Italy was also sporadic, the remarkable volume of these sales leaves no doubt about the significant demand for images from Antwerp in Italian cities, above all Milan, Rome, and Venice. Exceptional orders placed with Plantin by the Degli Antoni family of booksellers in Milan between 1576 and 1580, like that placed by the Roman bookseller Giovanni Paolo Gelli with Jan Moretus I in 1608, document the informed demand for hundreds to thousands of prints by assorted Antwerp print publishers. Not only was the supplier of these images noted, but numerous works were listed so precisely that it is often possible to identify exactly which prints were sent (see, for example, figs. 3.11 and 3.12). The importance of the selection of those specific images is underscored by their juxtaposition with hundreds of sheets of unspecified images that were charged at bulk rates and that were bought simultaneously by the same individuals.[17] Though also comprising very focused requests for prints, both Robinson's and Boswell's orders were far more limited in scope and quantity.

In Venice, the Sadeler family supported the interest in Antwerp prints. Between 1614 and his untimely death in 1620, Jan Sadeler I's son Justus regularly received packages of prints from assorted print dealers in Antwerp – Charles de Mallery, Peeter de Jode I, Jan-Baptist Barbé, and, above all, Theodore Galle and Adriaen Collaert; these packages were shipped to his business in Venice, along with numerous, finely illustrated texts that he purchased from the Moretuses. Adriaen Collaert's willingness to serve periodically as a middleman for Sadeler's transactions, suggests that he and Justus were on good personal terms. Consequently, Justus would most likely have received a selection of prints from him, if not his associates in Antwerp. These unspecified allotments of images were small in comparison with the vast exchange of prints from 1591 to 1621 between some of these same artists and Justus's uncles Gillis Sadeler I and Raphael Sadeler I, both of whom, like his father Jan I, had grown up and were trained in Antwerp. Conveyed systematically via the Frankfurt fairs, many of these works may have been sent to the Sadelers' shop in Venice.[18]

Other records in the Moretuses' accounts provide glimpses of the concurrent, persistent demand in Italy for prints from Antwerp in bulk. For instance, on 21 August 1625, a group of five packages of unspecified prints supplied by Theodore Galle and worth the unusually high sum of 147 fl. was shipped to a certain Giovanni Battista Massanio.[19] Additionally, in the early 1630s, Balthasar Moretus I sold illuminated prints on parchment by the hundreds to the Milan bookseller Carlo Ferrandi.[20] An interest in special, illuminated works on parchment and canons (or altar cards) from Antwerp is also evident from several records involving members of the Annoni family of Italian merchants. In addition to assisting once with a shipment of books and prints for Justus Sadeler in Venice in 1616, they were involved in several individual purchases of canons ordered, for example, by Italian monks or priests. On at least one occasion, exceptionally costly illuminated canons were sent.[21]

However, a far better picture of the nature and immense potential scope of the exchange of images between Antwerp and Italy emerges from a sampling of records dating to 1606 and 1612–1615 and involving the Flemish bookseller, as well as print and map dealer, Gaspar Van de Wouwer (or Vivario in its Italianate form), who specialized in this trade, and his sister Clara van de Wouwer, the wife of Jan-Baptist Vrients, who occasionally assisted him.[22] Like Plantin and the Moretuses, Vivario worked with clients from a range of professional backgrounds – in particular print, map, and booksellers – to sustain his niche in the exchange of works of art and books between Italy and the Low Countries (and Antwerp in particular). Consequently, his prolific dealings within this extensive network underscore, once again, that these individuals were not isolated professionals, but instead had frequently intertwined business concerns. For example, in 1606, Van de Wouwer supplied a certain "Gio. Spiers" in Rome with a selection of maps, books, and watercolors on canvas ("waterverve doecken") – fourteen from Peeter de Jode I and seventy-four from a certain Maria Cosiers. Simultaneously, he sent the printmaker Guilliam van Nieulandt I (then in Rome) an assortment of prints from De Jode and Vrients, as well as from some unspecified members of the Galle, Collaert, and Wierix families (most likely, Philips Galle, Adriaen Collaert, and Hieronymus Wierix, who all supplied Vivario with prints in March and April 1606).[23] Between 1612 and 1615, Vivario supplemented purchases of prints from Hieronymus Wierix with images provided by Theodore Galle, Abraham van Merlen, Michael Snijders, and Charles de Mallery. In one instance at least, De Mallery was selling his prints to Vivario at the same 50 st.-per-100-print rate that he applied to the vast majority of his transactions with the Moretuses.[24] Across all of these accounts, no specific image is cited; the surviving records simply note payments for hundreds of leaves of prints or "diverse" "art" in bulk. Nevertheless, Vivario's accounts demonstrate that the print sellers who participated the most actively in the international print market via the Moretuses also featured in numerous shipments of prints and other works of art sent to Rome by way of Vivario. The thriving demand for their work in a burgeoning art market to which, on one occasion, Vivario sent an astounding quantity of more than 40,000 leaves of "art" ["fol. cunst"] is thus evident.[25]

Vivario also bought books from other booksellers in Antwerp – Hieronymus Verdussen and Martinus Nutius, for example – in addition to trading with print and map dealers in the

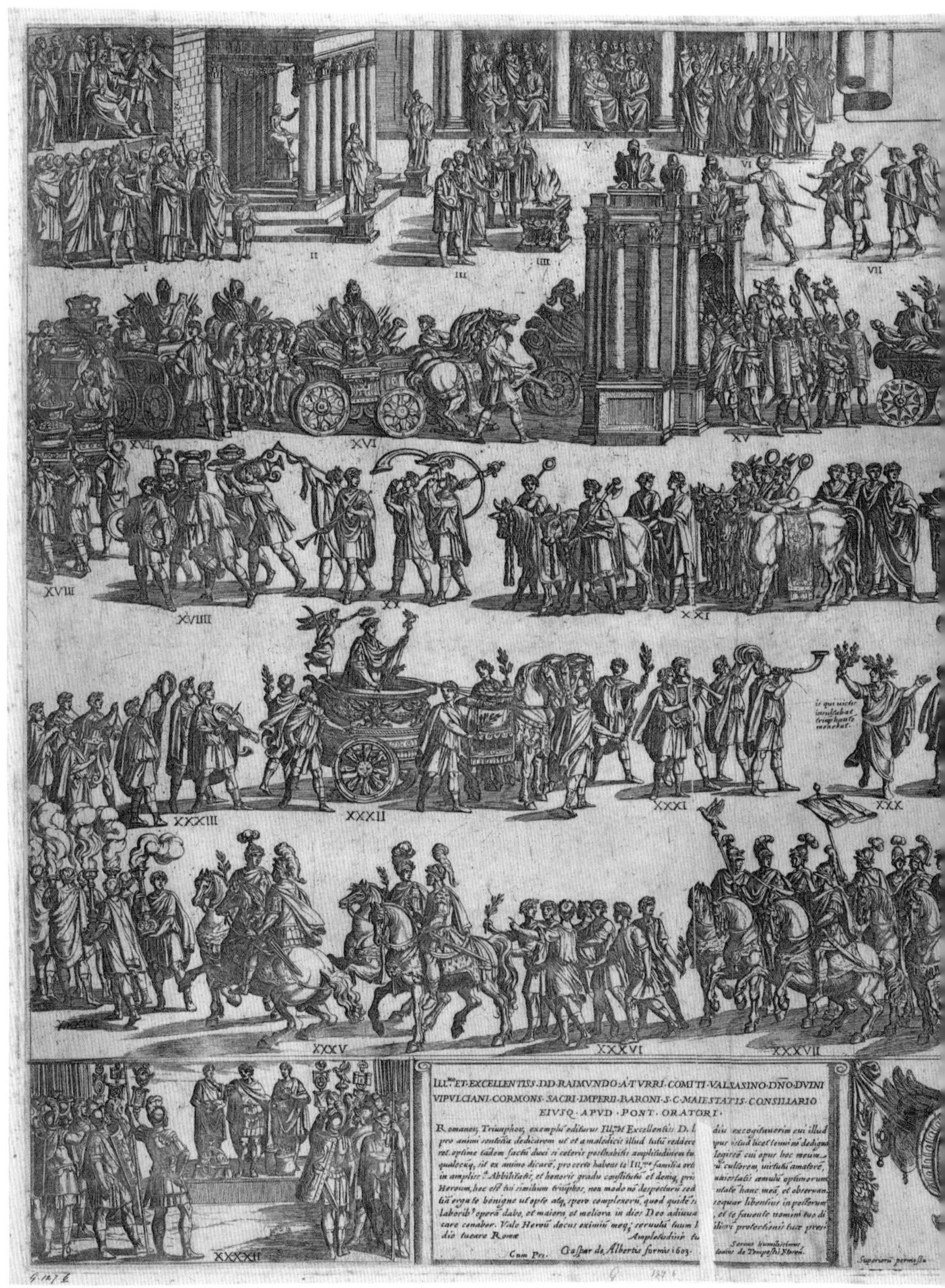

7.6 Anonymous etcher after Antonio Tempesta, *Triumphal Procession of a Roman Emperor*, published by Gasparo Alberti in 1603, etching, 480 × 746 mm. Amsterdam, Rijksmuseum: RP-P-H-OB-207.807.

northern Low Countries, such as Hendrick Hondius in The Hague, and above all in Amsterdam: Willem Blaeu and Cornelis Claesz, for example.[26] Occasionally, Jodocus Hondius supplied Vivario with works, including images by Goltzius and Jan Saenredam, while in other instances, Vivario provided his northern contactse and Antwerp print dealers with works from Italy.[27] Although one shipment sent to Blaeu in 1612 was simply described as "a package with Italian art" ("een paxken met Italiaensche cunst"), accounts recording Vivario's transactions with others are more detailed. Cornelis Claesz purchased unspecified works after Antonio Tempesta, while both De Jode and Vrients sought impressions of his "Triumphen", most likely his rendering of a procession of the triumph of a Roman emperor, which was published

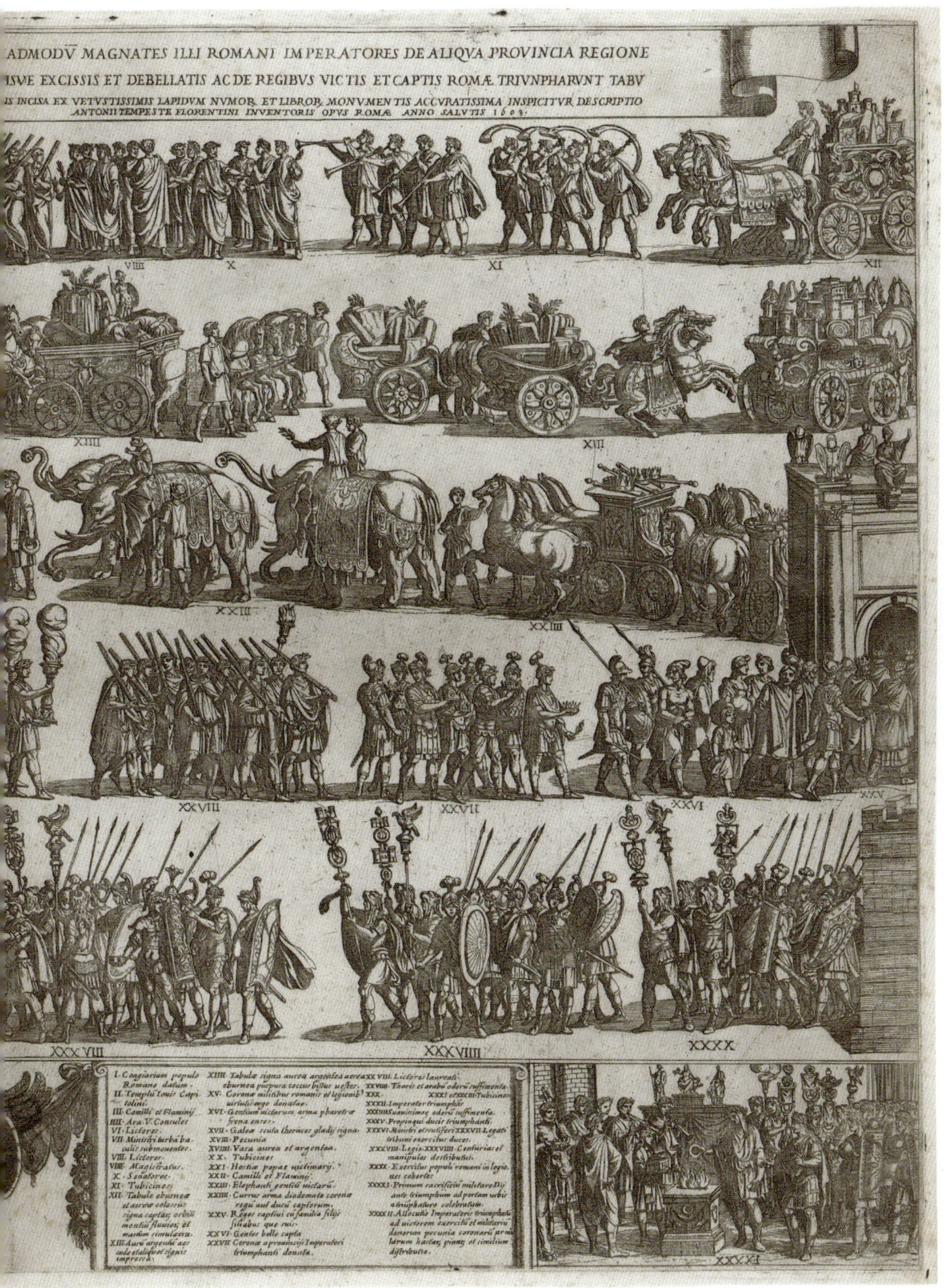

by Gasparo Alberti in 1603 (fig. 7.6). On one occasion, Vrients also acquired 53 leaves of "chiaroscure" and 17 assorted leaves of prints by Cornelis Cort.[28]

Vivario was occasionally assisted by his sister Clara. Most of these transactions are recorded in a document headed "Bills for my brother Gaspar Vivario, concerning what we have done since our last bill in the year 1612" (a year after the death of Clara's husband, Vrients).[29] Predictably, the list of "bills" includes the payment of local charges and the arrangements for the transport of packages to her brother in Rome. For instance, Clara sent parcels from Hieronymus Wierix, Charles de Mallery, Adriaen Collaert, Theodore Galle, and Abraham van Merlen via Hieronymus Verdussen in April 1615. She likewise asked the Moretuses to ship nine packages and some rolls to her brother in 1614. Additionally, in March 1614, she traveled specially to Amsterdam to pay bills in his name to, among others, the widow of Jodocus Hondius and Willem Janssen (Willem Bleau).[30]

These various records of Vivario's activities trading books, prints, maps, and other works of art between primarily Rome and Antwerp offer a telling complement to the Moretuses' own extensive accounts. Invaluable for the insight they provide into a part of the international market for prints that is not amply documented in the Moretuses' records, they simultaneously underscore the pervasiveness of what is evident from the Moretuses' transactions: the existence of a core group of print sellers who played an important role in the export of prints from Antwerp and the immense volume of that trade. Similarly, for the Spanish market, while the Moretuses' own accounts indicate the variety of clients seeking Antwerp prints, other records offer fundamental evidence of the enormous scale of the export of prints to this region.

Until the mid-1610s, the Moretuses had difficulties establishing reliable, trustworthy contacts among booksellers in Spain. They periodically tried working with their own personal contacts there (as when Plantin turned to a former employee, Jan Poelman), with fellow Antwerp booksellers or with personal relations who had emigrated to Spain. Such was the case when Jan Moretus II's brother-in-law, the merchant Nicolaas de Sweert, occasionally oversaw the transport of books and prints to clients in Seville. For example, in 1618, he helped arrange for the shipment of an order of books (including some 300 prayer books) and 400 unspecified prints by Hieronymus Wierix; the order was valued at 36 fl. and was for the Carmelite Joan de San Pedro. The shipment was delivered locally to Juan de Bellero, who was related to the Bellerus family of booksellers in Antwerp but was then working in Seville.[31] However, the sales of prints via such routes remained highly infrequent, idiosyncratic transactions. In 1623, De Sweert oversaw the transport of a huge consignment of books that was worth more than 4,470 fl. and that was destined for two booksellers in Seville, Hernando Mexia and Antonio de Toro. In one crate, 3,200 prints by Charles de Mallery, along with four sets of his series depicting members of the Franciscan order (fig. 7.7), were added for a total of 126 fl. – nearly 50 fl. more than what De Mallery had charged when he provided the same four series and 3,000 images for resale to De Toro. The remarkable markup in price of the prints was exceptional, and such print sales to De Toro were not repeated, despite his periodic purchase of books from the Moretuses into the 1640s.[32]

More often, the Moretuses were involved in selling prints to members of the clergy in Spain via a assorted Antwerp merchants. Not only did De Sweert undertake the 1618 transaction, but the Antwerp-based merchant Diego Pardo Lopez regularly assisted the Jesuit Pedro de Angulo in Seville with purchases of hundreds of unspecified prints by Theodore Galle, Charles de Mallery, and, above all, Hieronymus Wierix between 1613 and 1616.[33] Another merchant, Jan van Vucht from Brabant who was then based in Madrid, appears to have specialized in the exceptional export of prints, books, and other luxury items from Antwerp.

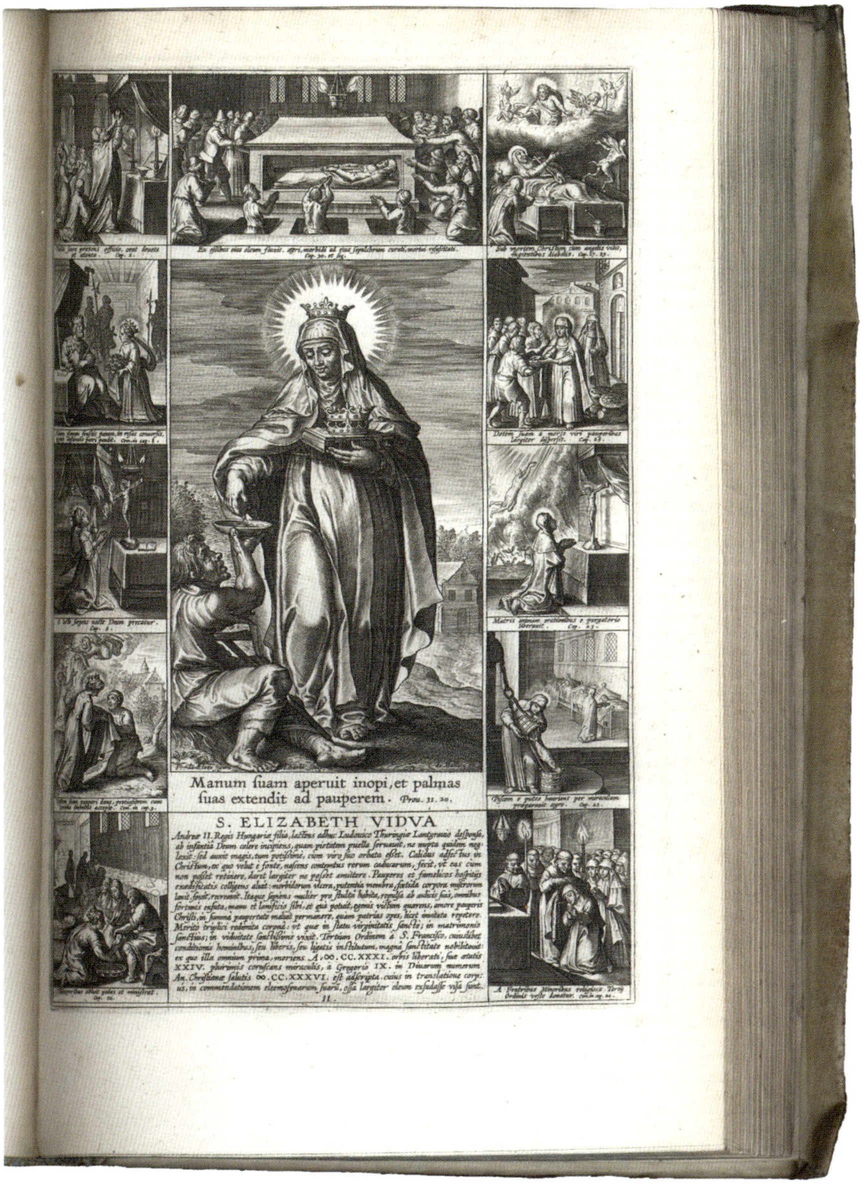

7.7 Anonymous engraver after Peeter de Jode I, *Saint Elizabeth*, print 11 from the series *Men and Women of the Franciscan Order*, originally published by Charles de Mallery in 1614, engraving, 253 × 165 mm. Antwerp, Museum Plantin-Moretus: A 1857. Appendix 1: CM-1, TG-13, and JG-1.

In October 1626, the Moretuses sold Van Vucht fifty-eight impressions of a representation of a "Tree" of the Franciscan order. Three were painted and affixed to canvas, and at least thirty others were intended for the Capuchin Francisco de Arvallo.[34] Between 1628 and 1630, Van Vucht's purchases of prints featured other costly items, namely illuminated prints on parchment. Following an initial, modest acquisition of just twenty-four such images from Jan Cnobbaert in 1628 (which the Moretuses resold to him with a small profit margin for themselves), Van Vucht proceeded to purchase several hundreds of such images, which Theodore Galle offered at three different rates. While most prints were priced similarly to Cnobbaert's work (just 2 or 3 st. per image), a few were significantly more expensive, costing 10 st. apiece. Regardless of the price, the Moretuses did not mark them up, but resold all of the images to Van Vucht at cost. Although it is not known for whom Van Vucht bought these prints, at least one group was intended for a Capuchin.[35] These transactions, combined with the Jesuit Philippus de Peralta's endeavors to acquire prints by Hieronymus Wierix, highlight the ongoing interest in prints from Antwerp by various members of the Spanish clergy.[36]

Van Vucht was not the only one involved in the export of finely finished prints from Antwerp to the Iberian Peninsula. In 1626, the Antwerp merchant Crisostomo van Immerseel, who traded in costly images from assorted Antwerp print dealers, including Michael Snijders, also purchased thousands of prints on parchment and paper from the art dealer Jan van Mechelen.[37] Likewise, in the early 1630s, the merchant Paul du Jon focused on the shipment of luxury products from Antwerp – diamonds and paintings from Rubens and Seghers – as well as thousands of prints, many by one of the Bolswerts, for the art market in Lisbon.[38]

The Spanish market for prints was also served by numerous dealers elsewhere. By far the most striking transactions involve the tens to hundreds of thousands of images some seventy French dealers in and around Paris exported to Spain and Portugal between 1603 and 1622. Destined for such cities as Madrid, Seville, Lisbon, Valladolid, San Sebastian, and Santiago de Compostela, the works sent were usually identified in general terms, most often as: "devotional", but occasionally as portraits, costume studies, or amusing images ("drôleries"). Though the specific clients for whom these images were intended is not known, it is often assumed that the prints were largely cheap items for common consumption and not collectors' items.[39]

The export of remarkably large quantities of prints in bulk – 6,000–7,000, or even as many as 17,000 at any one time – from France to the Iberian Peninsula may indeed support such assertions. However, numerous specially finished prints, in addition to other luxury items, were also regularly sent, indicating that the potential customers were expected to be much more diverse and well-off than the designation of a "popular" viewership might suggest. Consider, for example, a record from 26 November 1605 of purchases made by the French merchant Thomas Gauvin, then recorded as living in Neufchâteau in Lorraine, for shipment to Spain. Comprising a remarkable array of goods acquired from sundry tradesmen, ranging from scissors and knives to rosaries, silks, precious metals, and jewelry, Gauvin also bought a variety range of images, including varnished maps and dozens of narrative subjects – both illuminated and not – from Michel de Mathonière. In addition to dozens of illuminated devotional subjects, assorted canons (some also illuminated) and maps, there were also more than 9,000 engravings (2,000 of which bore devotional subjects) and 400 other large images depicting the life of St Francis, all supplied by Jean Leclerc IV.[40] Although these records of the trade between France and Spain are limited in time to primarily 1605, with a smattering from 1606–1609 and a few brief references from 1622, this general assortment of objects and range of prints in particular recurs throughout the first decade of the seventeenth century. It provides staggering traces of an immense exchange of goods that few would otherwise suspect.[41] These tantalizing records are also significant because several of the individuals involved in the traffic in prints destined for Spain and Portugal also had some contact with print sellers in Antwerp, above all Charles de Mallery, who may well have become acquainted with them while in Paris. Aside from Leclerc and the print seller Jean Messager, who provided one merchant, Clément Caillet, said to be from Neufchâtel in Lorraine, with seven packages of images printed on paper for export in April 1622, the merchant Jacques Bertrant from Dauphiné similarly facilitated the mass distribution of a range of printed images. For example, on 19 February 1607, he, together with another merchant, Jean Rambaud, purchased a variety of varnished images from both Michel de Mathonière and Nicolas Lalouette, in addition to a total of 9,000 engravings from Leclerc.[42] Evidence that he, along with established print sellers in Paris, also dealt directly with Antwerp print publishers underscores, once again, the fluidity and expanse of the European print trade, in which thousands of images of a range of qualities were traded via a variety of channels.

PACKAGES UPON PACKAGES FOR FRANCE

In striking contrast with the countries discussed above, France was home to a multitude of active trading partners for the managers of the Plantin-Moretus Press. Not only was Plantin French, but he and the Moretuses also had numerous personal and professional contacts there. Although their contacts were concentrated in Paris, they traded with various individuals beyond the capital as well. Because the burgeoning market for prints in Paris was strongly influenced by Flemish engravers – either directly via immigrants or indirectly through the import of their prints – it is not surprising that the Plantin-Moretus Press also frequently shipped prints to a variety of dealers there.[43] Nevertheless, they themselves sold relatively few prints to their own circle of clients. For example, the booksellers Simon de St. Martel in Toul in the northeast of France and Jean Dassonleville in Hesdin in the Pas-de-Calais both made modest purchases of a few hundred unspecified prints at base, bulk prices, but only for a few years running. While De St. Martel bought prints supplied by Philips Galle between 1589 and 1591, Dassonleville favored works published by Charles de Mallery and Theodore Galle, which he purchased between 1624 and 1626. Similarly, the Parisian bookseller Adriaen Perier, the second husband of Plantin's daughter Madeleine, relied on Jan Moretus I for his acquisition of a number of copies of Theodore Galle's 1598 series, the *Illustrium imagines, ex antiquis marmoribus*; this series contained 151 finely engraved images of Greek and Roman busts from Fulvius Ursinus's collection of antique sculpture, gems, and coins (figs. 5.5 and 5.6).[44]

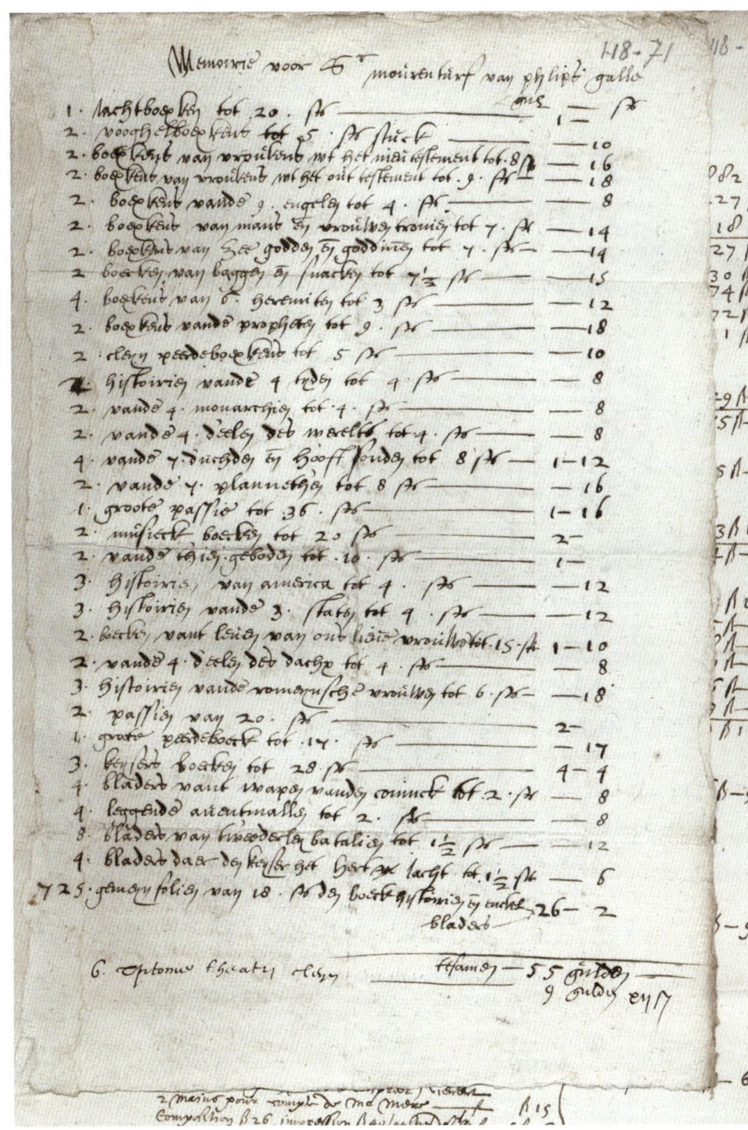

7.8 List of prints supplied by Philips Galle in 1594 for Théodore Rinsart. Antwerp, Museum Plantin-Moretus: Arch. 118, *Imprimerie 1600–1625*, p. 71.

However, of all the Moretuses' professional contacts in France, the most remarkable print purchases were made by the itinerant bookseller Théodore Rinsart. Belonging to the family of Gilles Beys, Madeleine Plantin's first husband, Rinsart was a distant relative of the Moretuses, although that did not earn him any special privileges. During the 1590s, Rinsart traveled along the west coast of France, between Normandy and Bordeaux. From 1591 to 1596, he ordered books from Jan Moretus I, asking that they be delivered to locations where he could collect them for resale during his travels.[45] In 1593 and 1594, Rinsart's also spent large sums (108 fl. 7 st. and 55 fl.) on works supplied by Philips Galle.[46] Although the precise prints that Rinsart bought in 1593 remain unknown, an indication of what this order may have contained is provided by detailed records of his smaller 1594 order for large quantities of diverse images (fig. 7.8). In addition to 725 leaves of unspecified, common ("ghemein") prints sold at Galle's standard bulk rate of 18 st. per quire of twenty-five leaves and a few special, individual prints, such as the *Deer Hunt of Emperor Frederick I* (fig. 7.9), Rinsart purchased nearly thirty different print series that reflected a significant range of what Galle published. Alongside traditional religious imagery, Rinsart's order also included series of horses and birds, as well as, perhaps, Galle's recent series of bust-length portrayals of men and women with fashionably coiffed hair and several allegorical prints, some of which had been made decades earlier (figs. 7.10

7.9 Adriaen Collaert after Johannes Stradanus, *The Deer Hunt of Emperor Frederick I Barbarossa and Ubaldino Ubaldini*, 1589, engraving, 249 × 271 mm (sheet). New York, The Metropolitan Museum of Art: The Elisha Whittelsey Collection, The Elisha Whittelsey Fund, 1949 (49.95.994). Image courtesy of the Metropolitan Museum of Art. Appendix 1: PG-18.

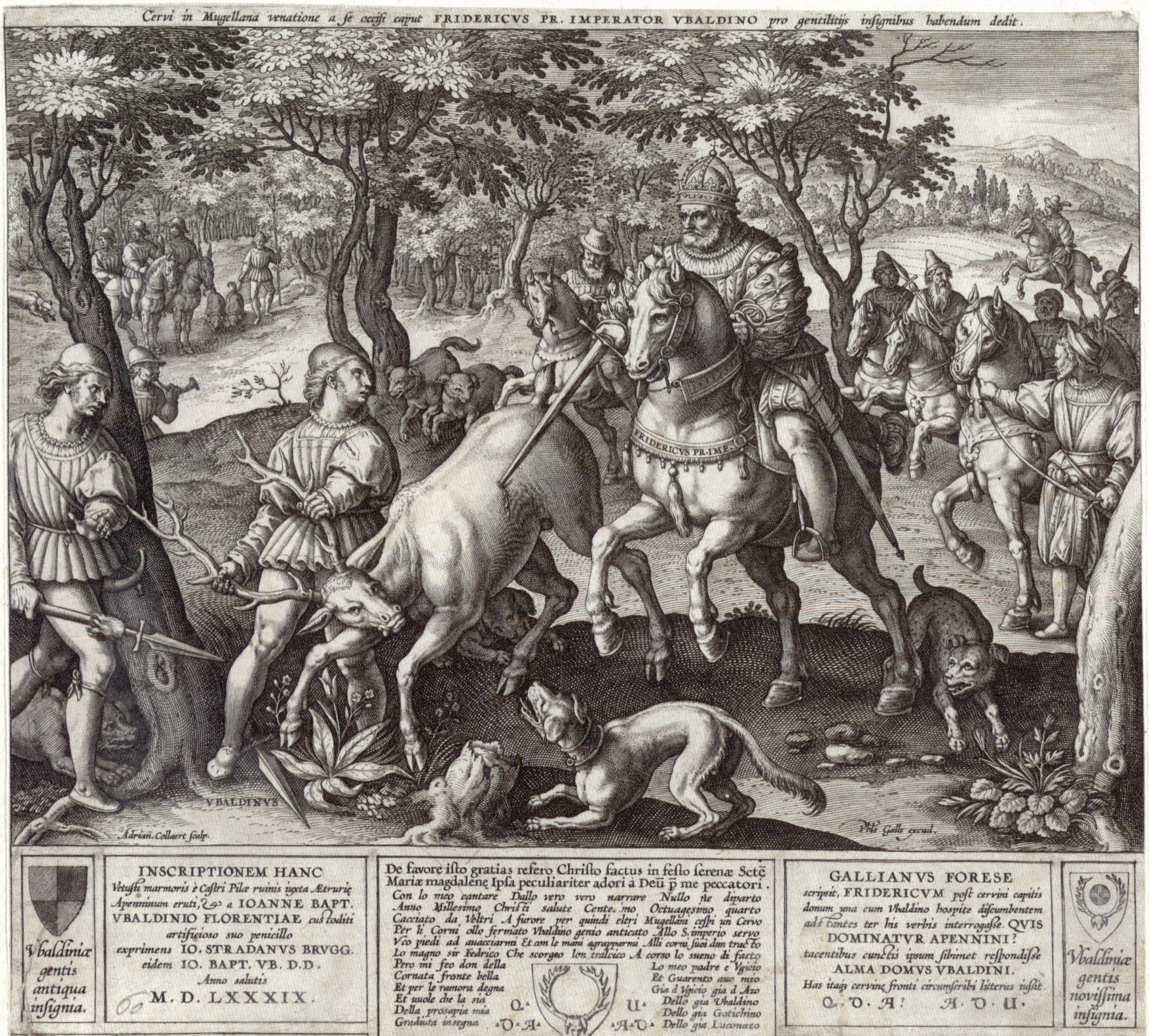

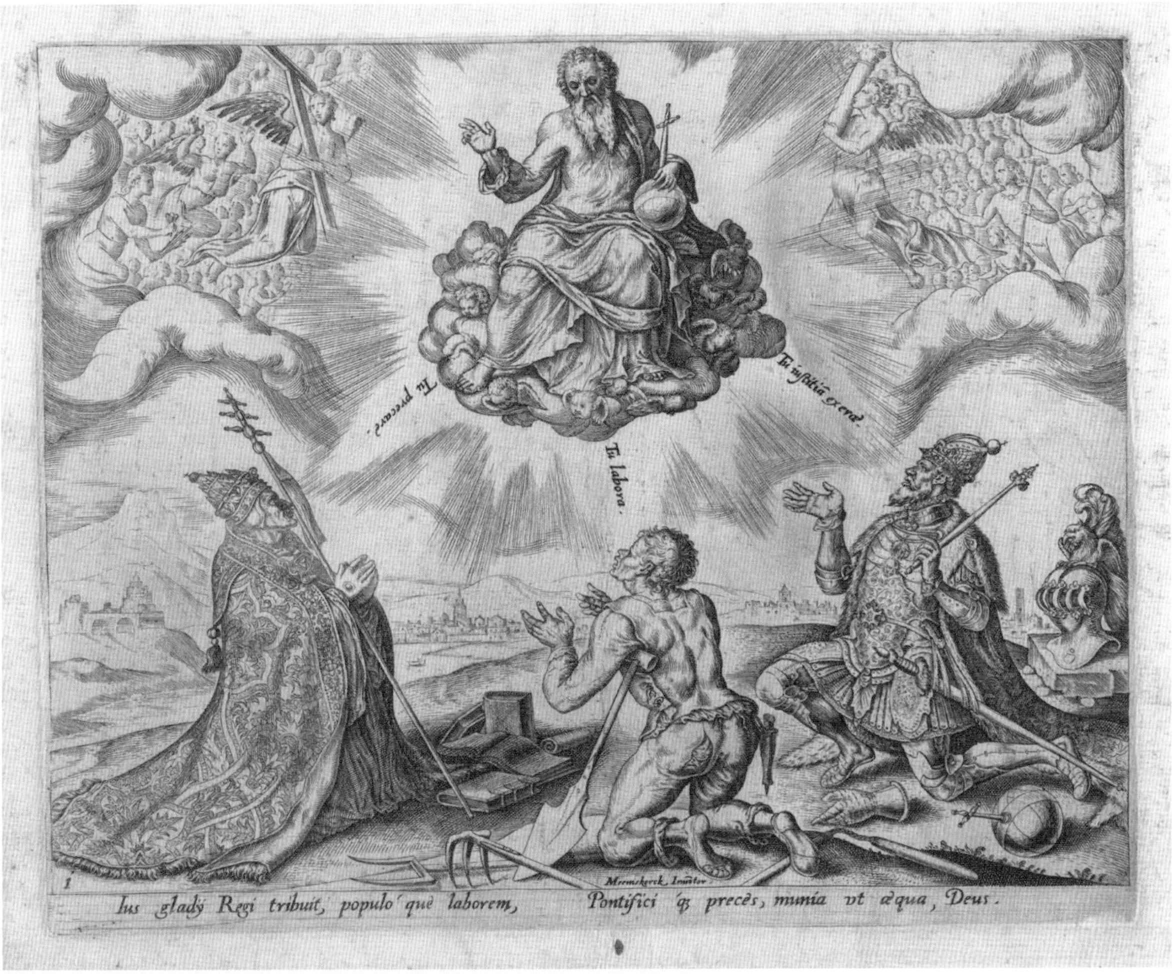

7.11 Philips Galle after Maarten van Heemskerck, *Divine Charge to the Three Estates*, 1565–1568, engraving, 204 × 248 mm. Amsterdam, Rijksmuseum: RP-P-1988-297-170. Appendix 1: PG-29.

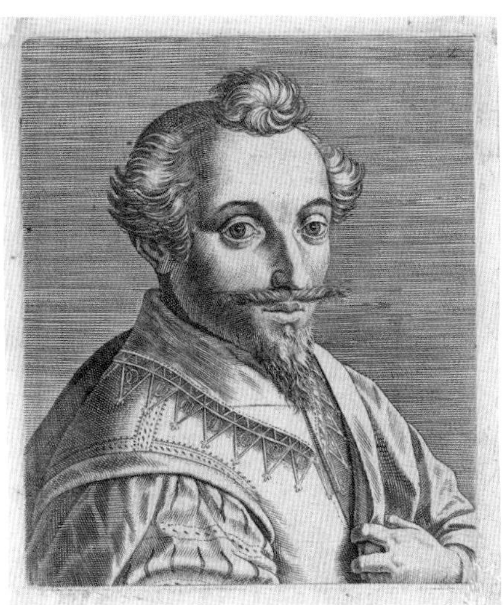

7.10 Philips Galle, *Man with Moustache and Pointed Beard*, print 2 from the series *Various Examples of Hair Styles and Beards*, ca. 1590–1594, engraving, 130 × 108 mm. Antwerp, Museum Plantin-Moretus: PK: OP.01244. Appendix 1: PG-54.

and 7.11). Nonetheless, like the orders placed by De St. Martel, Dassonleville, and Perier, these transactions remained isolated purchases and were not part of a regular chain of supply.

Far more significant for the international trade in prints was the Moretuses' assistance with the transport of packages between Antwerp print sellers and their own network of clients. The degree to which such transactions dominated the Moretuses' engagement with the traffic in prints in France in comparison with other regions underscores the strength of the ties between Flemish artists and French print dealers during the early seventeenth century. Dating back to 1578, when Plantin arranged for the transport of two packages of prints to the French artist and print seller Jean Rabel via the French bookseller Michel Sonnius I, this service was continued under the Moretuses through 1635.[47] Although they made arrangements primarily at the request of members of the extended Galle family – Philips Galle, Adriaen Collaert, and, above all, Charles de Mallery – in addition to Jan-Baptist Barbé, the recipients of the packages were remarkably diverse. Individual packages were sometimes sent directly to private individuals, such as Barbé's shipments to the Discalced Carmelite Carolus du Mere de Dieu and the historian and geographer André Duchesne in 1632. Numerous packages were also conveyed to several bookdealers, primarily at the request of De Mallery. Although some shipments contained books, sixteen packages that De Mallery had sent to Eustace Foucault were recorded as including prints, and thereby attest to his potential involvement in the print trade.[48] Nevertheless, the majority of the packages the Moretuses transported to France were destined for assorted print sellers in Paris.

While Collaert sent a few packages to some dealers with longstanding ties to Antwerp, especially Pierre Firens I and Gabriel Tavernier I, contact with such figures via the Moretuses remained limited.[49] Gabriel Tavernier and his son Melchior may have arranged for the import of works from Antwerp themselves. At least from 1613 to 1614, Melchior was periodically in Antwerp, lodging with Cornelis Galle. Once, in November 1613, he purchased (in his father's name) more than 900 maps (the majority had been made for Abraham Ortelius's atlas), in addition to several copies of Ortelius's *Parergon* and two studies of perspective and architecture by Giacomo Barozzi da Vignola; he then asked the Moretuses to send all of these items to Paris for him. During another visit to Antwerp in May 1614, Melchior personally settled a small debt his father had with the Moretuses.[50]

Primarily, the Moretuses assisted De Mallery and Barbé with their numerous shipments to several print dealers. Both men traded intermittently with a variety of individuals. De Mallery, for example, sent packages of prints to Jacques Bartrand (possibly the J. Bertrant cited above) and Jean Leclerc IV, who were likely involved in the trade in images to Spain, while Barbé dealt with Jacques Honervogt I. De Mallery's and Barbé's most frequent contact by far was the Parisian print seller Jean Messager.[51] Active as a print seller in Paris during the first half of the seventeenth century, Messager received a total of twenty-eight packages (none with any specified contents) via diverse clients of the Moretuses, in particular the booksellers Foucault, Michel Sonnius II, and Sébastien Cramoisy. De Mallery's significant contribution to these shipments (some thirteen packages sent between 1610 and 1617) is not surprising, as Messager occasionally engaged him and his son Philips to make engravings that he then published. Barbé may have shipped his remarkable supply of eleven packages to Messager between 1630 and 1634 because of Messager's predilection for Flemish engravings, evident from the copies he produced of them.[52] Finally, Messager also received one package from Peeter de Jode I in 1617 and one from Maarten van den Enden in 1635.[53] Together, these shipments underscore both the longevity of Messager's (and his clients') interest in works provided by Flemish print publishers and the relatively high concentration of some of his purchases with specific publishers. Since Messager evidently traded in large quantities of Flemish prints, he may have similarly acquired comparable works from other artists via alternative routes at other times. His willingness to assist other print sellers with their own transactions is evident from two instances in 1632, when the Moretuses sent him packages prepared by Barbé and Alexander Voet for the print and book dealer Jean Marin in Nancy.[54]

Amounting to more than one hundred packages in total, these shipments to diverse individuals in France from a variety of print sellers in Antwerp document just one part of what was most likely an immense, regular exchange of printed images between these two regions. It is, then, all the more regrettable that so little is known about what was sent. One could be tempted to generalize from common perceptions of the work published by the two most important exporters to France among the print sellers who employed the Moretuses – Charles de Mallery and Jan-Baptist Barbé – and the preferences of the most frequent recipient of these shipments, Jean Messager. However, this would not necessarily constitute a complete, accurate assessment of the French market for images from Antwerp. Jan Moretus I's sporadic sales of prints published by the Galles – both Perier's purchase of Theodore Galle's series based on Ursini's collection of ancient portraits and Rinsart's acquisition of diverse series published by Philips Galle – are clearly distinct in subject matter, design, and execution from the prints conventionally associated with De Mallery and Barbé. As Plantin's early success with the export of numerous copies of several of Philips Galle's extensive print series in the mid-1570s suggests, there was also a market for these works in France that the Galles may well have continued to supply subsequently via other channels.[55] More difficult to explain is the striking lack of references to the transport of goods to France for Michael Snijders, particularly given his constant reliance on the Moretuses for the shipment of his work elsewhere. Also regrettably poorly represented in the accounts discussed thus far are the primary consumers of these works whom the various local intermediaries – merchants, booksellers, and print dealers – served by providing essential links within the international supply chain of printed images. The Moretuses' abundant, wide-ranging transactions that supported the broad-based demand for prints in the Low Countries, by contrast, reveal both institutional and individual preferences that may, in turn, reflect types of requests elsewhere.

THE LOCAL MARKET IN THE LOW COUNTRIES: FROM BOOKSELLERS TO INDIVIDUAL COLLECTORS AND RELIGIOUS ORDERS

At the turn of the seventeenth century, the southern Netherlands encompassed the Prince-Bishopric of Liège and extended further to the east and the south than the present-day borders of Belgium. Plantin's and the Moretuses' network of fellow booksellers permeated this territory and included many who sporadically participated in the print trade when placing their regular orders for an assortment of books from the Officina Plantiniana.

To the east, in Maastricht and 's-Hertogenbosch, some booksellers periodically turned to Plantin and the Moretuses for illustrated altar cards (commonly referred to as "canon missae" in these records) and, less frequently, for special requests for specific prints. Both Gilles van Zwevenseel in Maastricht, who traded with the Officina Plantiniana between 1588 and 1631, and Jan Scheffer II in 's-Hertogenbosch, who dealt with Plantin and subsequently the Moretuses from 1574 to 1613, engaged in such acquisistions.[56] While Van Zwevenseel bought a couple of altar cards at 4–6 st. each several times in the first decade of the seventeenth century, Scheffer's early requests for numerous different types of canons in 1586, including ones featuring engravings at 4 st. per piece, diminished in the coming decades. Instead, he made isolated purchases of thirteen images of Archduke Ernest in 1594, in addition to one copy of Theodore Galle's series of the *Life of Saint Catherine of Siena* in 1610 (fig. 7.12).[57] Since Scheffer also asked Jan Moretus I to pay Philips Galle 20 fl. in his name in 1597, he may also have simultaneously ordered works from Galle directly.[58]

In contrast, to the west, in Bruges, Antonius de Tollenare II, who traded with the Officina Plantiniana between 1588 and 1595, routinely bought quires of twenty-five leaves of unspecified prints (some of which were identified as "taille douce", or engravings) supplied by Adriaen Huberti. Throughout, Huberti charged his standard bulk rate of 18 st. per quire, and the Moretuses resold the sheets at cost.[59] Notably, when De Tollenare's widow assumed the management of his business following his death in 1595, she no longer placed such orders with the Moretuses (although she might have dealt directly with Huberti). Only in 1616 did she buy any prints from them, namely, six copies of Theodore Galle's series of the *Miracles of the Rosary*, which were sold together with Vincent Hensbergh's accompanying text, *Wonderlijcke schoone gratien ende mirakelen* (Antwerp: Jan Moretus I, 1610) (fig. 7.13), at a strikingly high price of 18 st. per set, instead of the original 12 st.[60]

Purchase requests similar to those of Maastricht and Bruges were received from important cities to the east and south of Bruges, especially Ghent and Kortrijk. In Ghent, the bookseller Jan van Salenson, who traded with the Officina Plantiniana between 1577 and 1629,

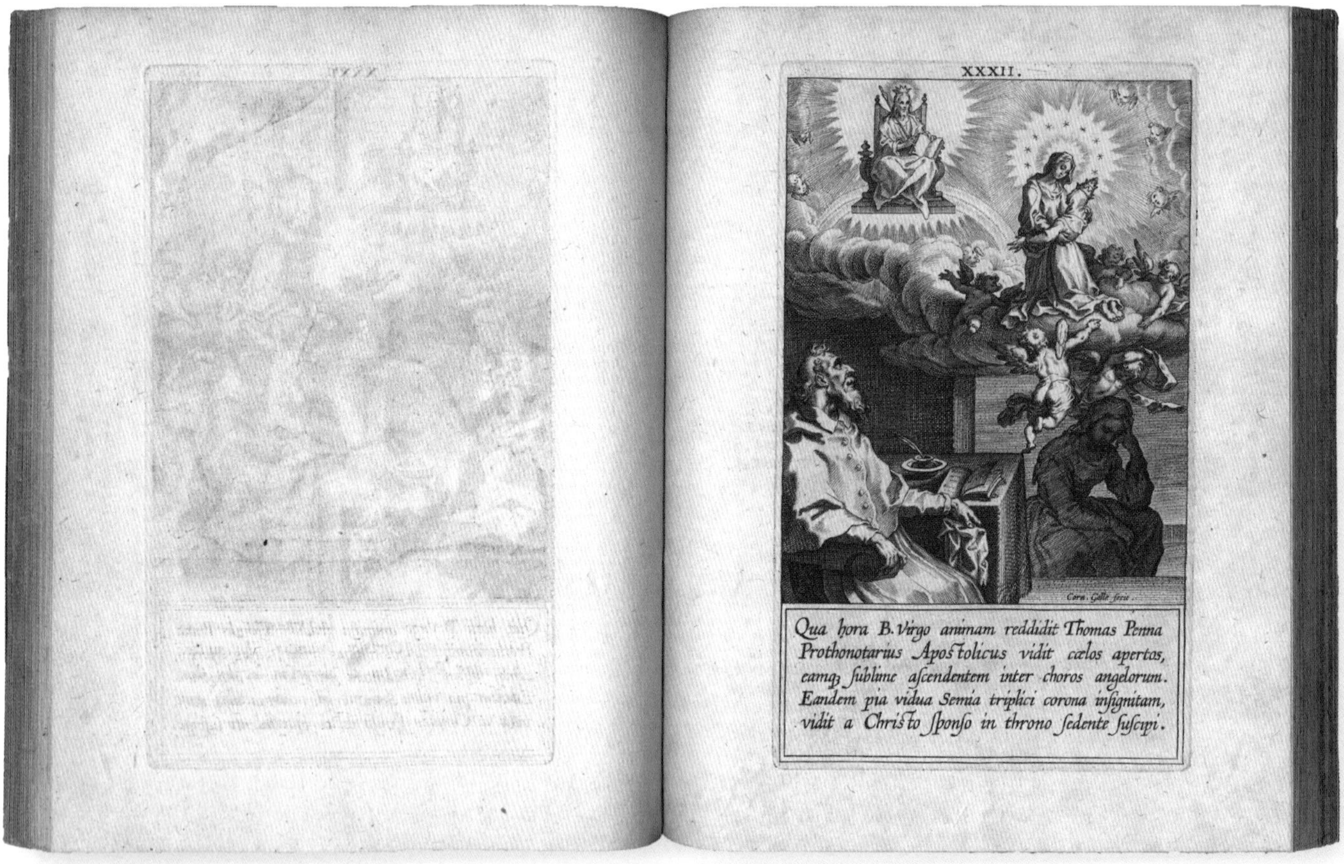

7.12 Cornelis Galle I after Francesco Vanni, *Thomas Penna's Vision of Saint Catherine*, print 32 from the series *The Life of Saint Catherine of Siena*, 1603, engraving, 154 × 91 mm. Antwerp, Museum Plantin-Moretus: R 72. Appendix 1: PG-66 and TG-9.

made isolated requests for individual altar cards beginning in 1588 and up until 1605.[61] Usually identified as folio in format and occasionally as comprising one or three sheets, these cards cost 4–8 st. each; the prices were thus on a par with what Van Zwevenseel and Scheffer paid for similarly sized altar cards.[62] The limited number and narrow scope of these orders suggests that Van Salenson was buying them on commission for specific clients. The Kortrijk bookseller Joos van der Straeten, who traded with the Moretuses from 1592 to 1606 (after which point he moved to Ghent), only purchased prints from them between 1592 and 1598.[63] Like De Tollenare in Bruges, Van der Straeten routinely bought one to two quires of twenty-five leaves of unspecified prints, the majority of which (if not all) were supplied by Huberti at his standard 18 st.-per-quire rate. The primary difference from De Tollenare's acquisitions is that Van der Straeten also occasionally requested quires of illuminated prints. In 1597, Huberti supplied Jan Moretus I with one quire of such prints in 4° and 8° formats for 2 fl. 10 st. (or 50 st.), while the plain prints that Van der Straeten purchased simultaneously (supplied at the standard rate of 18 st. per quire) were the smaller, 16° size.[64] Unusually, Jan Moretus I added a small profit margin for himself when reselling these prints, perhaps due to the inclusion of illuminated images in the order. Soon thereafter, however, Van der Straeten ceased to order prints from Moretus, even though he continued to purchase books. As Van der Straeten's steady acquisition of such prints suggests a persistent interest them in Kortrijk, it seems likely that he either decided to buy them directly from Huberti or via other suppliers.

Near the southern border in Lille (which was then still part of the southern Netherlands) and to the east in Liège, Plantin and the Moretuses supported a far more active trade in images from assorted Antwerp print publishers. In Lille, they helped three booksellers – François

Boulet, Jean du Puis, and Jean Morel – obtain prints across a forty-year period between 1586 and 1626. Boulet, who traded with the Officina Plantiniana between 1568 and 1605, did not start to buy prints in earnest from Plantin until 1586–1588, when he acquired an astounding assortment of works, including: four bound copies of Philips Galle's new, 1586 edition of his *Virorum doctorum … effigies* XLIIII (fig. 3.5), a selection of altar cards (several of which were illuminated), three quires of unspecified images in a full range of sizes (32°, 24°, 16°, and 8°) sold in bulk by Huberti, unspecified images sold by piece by Galle and Hans van Luyck, and series of the Passion supplied by both Galle and Gerard de Jode.[65] Nevertheless, despite his initial dabbling in various types of images, Boulet, like other booksellers from the southern Netherlands active in this period, most often acquired prints in bulk from Huberti. During the 1590s, Boulet's purchases declined to just a couple of quires of images that he bought at the common bulk rate of 18 st. per quire once every few years.[66]

In 1606, just one year after Boulet's death, Jean du Puis began not only to trade in books with the Moretuses, but also to seek their assistance for his own independent transactions with Antwerp print publishers, which he evidently had established prior to any prolonged

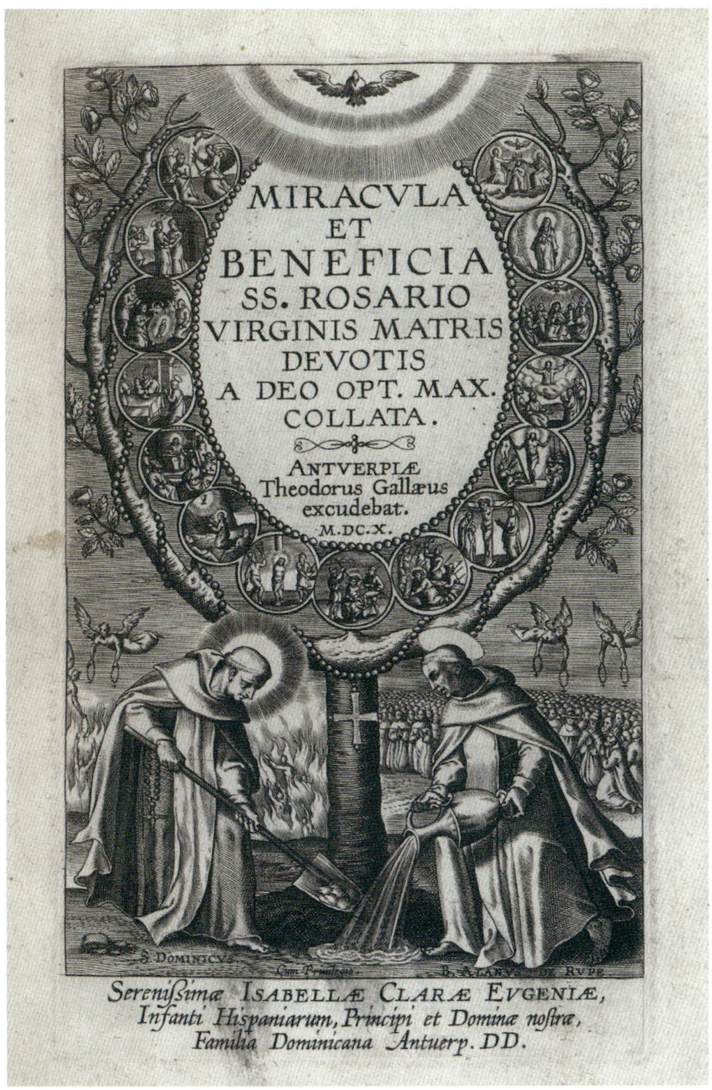

7.13 Anonymous, title plate for the series *Miracles of the Rosary*, 1610, engraving, 155 × 92 mm. Antwerp, Museum Plantin-Moretus: 8–612. Appendix 1: TG-14.

interaction with the Moretuses. Although Du Puis's earliest known request was to have Jan Moretus pay Theodore Galle 12 fl. in his name, his accounts are dominated by a variety of transactions involving Adriaen Collaert.[67] The exceptionally large sums involved and the Moretuses' occasional reliance on Collaert to convey items Du Puis had bought from them, reveal both the significance of Du Puis's purchases from Collaert and the likelihood that the two men would have, on occasion, seen one another in person, either in Lille or Antwerp. Du Puis continued to buy prints directly from other Antwerp print publishers. The Moretuses sporadically shipped his acquisitions from Hieronymus Wierix and Theodore Galle together with his orders of books.[68] Their involvement in Du Puis's print purchases came to an end in 1616, even though Du Puis maintained his trade in books with the Moretuses for another twenty years. The last few transactions involving Collaert were recorded just two years prior to his death.[69]

However, before Du Puis's dealings in prints via the Moretuses drew to a close, another bookseller in Lille, Jean Morel, had begun to procure prints from Antwerp publishers. He even traveled to Antwerp personally to choose the prints he wanted. In April 1615 for instance, Morel left a package of prints he had selected from Hieronymus Wierix's stock with the Moretuses, asking that it be sent to him in Lille, along with the books he had bought from them at that time. Morel's personal involvement in the acquisition process may account for his relatively infrequent reliance on the Moretuses for assistance with his print transactions throughout the period in which he purchased books from them (1612–1628).[70] Morel and Du Puis were both aware that they participated alongside each other in the traffic in prints from Antwerp; in July 1616, the Moretuses sent a package supplied by Collaert for Du Puis as part of a general shipment to Morel. Whether or not this awareness of their simultaneous involvement in the Antwerp print trade influenced Morel's and Du Puis's selection of which prints to sell is not known. Nevertheless, the few instances when the Moretuses assisted Morel with his print purchases document his contact with other Antwerp print publishers – Theodore Galle, Michael Snijders, and Wierix – and not the Collaert family.[71]

As with Du Puis and Morel, when the Liège bookseller Jean Ouwerx began to trade in books with the Moretuses in 1616, the Moretuses soon became involved in his independent transactions with Antwerp print publishers. They initially assisted him by shipping packages from Abraham van Merlen in both 1617 and 1618.[72] Although Ouwerx, like Morel, occasionally purchased prints from Snijders – including one astounding shipment of seven packages in March 1625 – the bulk of his transactions featured other print publishers. In addition to his initial acquisition of Van Merlen's prints, Ouwerx also periodically dealt with Jan Boel between March 1626 and February 1631 and received at least one package of prints from Gerard van Wolsschaten, an Antwerp typefounder who became a bookseller, in 1624.[73] Above all, however, Ouwerx ordered hundreds of sheets of *suffragia* printed by Hendrik Aertssens on a nearly annual basis between 1626 and 1631.[74] The only other artist(s) whose work Ouwerx obtained via the Moretuses was one or both of the Bolswerts. This is evident from two remarkable acquisitions of first 100 and then 400 unspecified prints in 1627 and 1628, respectively.[75] Ouwerx's final print purchase through the Moretuses in September 1636 consequently appears all the more exceptional. Instead of buying unspecified prints in bulk or receiving packages prepared by his suppliers, he requested a single impression of an image of the *Crucifixion* after Anthony van Dyck.[76] Regardless of the types of prints and suppliers preferred by these individual booksellers in Lille and Liège, their various transactions reveal thriving markets for prints that were supported by local booksellers whose networks comprised diverse Antwerp print publishers, along with the Moretuses. Thus, the intertwining of mutual acquaintances and business partners furthered the traffic in images.

The Moretuses' trade in prints with booksellers in Namur and Brussels, both of which were more centrally located in the southern Netherlands and closer to Antwerp, involved individuals who appear to have served primarily as agents for requests placed by others. This was also most likely the case for Scheffer and Van Zwevenseel in 's-Hertogenbosch and Maastricht, but the requests from Namur and Brussels were on a larger scale. Transactions originating in Namur are found predominantly among the Moretuses' dealings with three generations of the Valentin family of booksellers, who traded with them between 1590 and 1644.[77] During the 1590s, when the business was run by Jean Valentin I, he made only a few sporadic purchases in 1590 and 1595; initially, he bought three sheets with meditations on the Virgin, supplied by Huberti, and then subsequently acquired altar cards in folio for 4.5 or 5 st. each.[78] Although his son Jean II – who ran the family business between 1600 and 1632 – similarly began his acquisitions of prints in 1604 by buying a single altar card in folio for 4 st., his requests for prints gradually shifted. Following an isolated purchase in 1607 of one quire of unspecified images from Adriaen Collaert, which was sold at the common bulk rate of 18 st., Jean II's orders consisted of periodic requests for modest quantities of prints from Theodore Galle sold at piece rates and only an occasional request for works that Galle sold in bulk by the hundred. For example, a sale in September 1613 included:[79]

100 images in 8° sold at 1 fl. 16 st. (= 36 st.) per hundred, for a total of 1 fl. 16 st.
17 double leaves at 1.5 st. per piece, for a total of 1 fl. 5.5 st.
6 prints at 2.5 st. per piece, for a total of 15 st.
2 "Arbor vitae humanae" (*Tree of Human Life*) at 3 st. per piece, for a total of 6 st.

Containing the types of prints that Jean Valentin II often obtained through the Moretuses between 1613 and 1621, this order reflects the wide range of images Galle had to offer, as it encompases smaller prints in 8° sold at a common, low-end bulk rate, much larger images printed on full sheets of paper sold individually, and two impressions of one of Galle's exceptionally large prints (the *Tree of Human Life*, which measures some 456 × 329 mm) (fig. 7.14). However, Valentin's other orders of similarly priced prints from Galle were made just every two years, on average, and ranged from only six images in folio at 2 st. each in 1619 to as many as 225 prints sold in bulk in 1621.[80] Such variation in Valentin's orders suggests that he was not relying on the Moretuses to stock his own shop routinely with a selection of these prints. Perhaps he was acting as the intermediary for a specific client, such as a local Jesuit college or another religious institution or sodality that periodically needed to refresh its stock of prints or supplement purchases made via other channels. Moreover, following his 1621 purchase (which included an exceptional, small profit margin for the Moretuses in the resale price), Valentin's orders for prints ceased, although he continued to purchase books from them for more than a decade. It was not until 1637, when his son Jean III took over the management of the family business from his mother, that the Valentins asked the Moretuses for assistance in buying prints again. But the requests – isolated purchases of *suffragia* from Aertssens, thirty-six images of saints on paper, and a few illuminated images on parchment spread out between 1637 and 1641 – were even more limited.[81]

Although the Moretuses maintained contact with a number of booksellers in Brussels, only one, Jean Leonard, was periodically involved in the sale and distribution of prints. A long-term client of the Moretuses, with exchanges extending from 1619 through 1655, Leonard was involved in the print trade for most of these years. Nonetheless, the highly irregular and idiosyncratic nature of his requests vividly underscores his role as an intermediary for

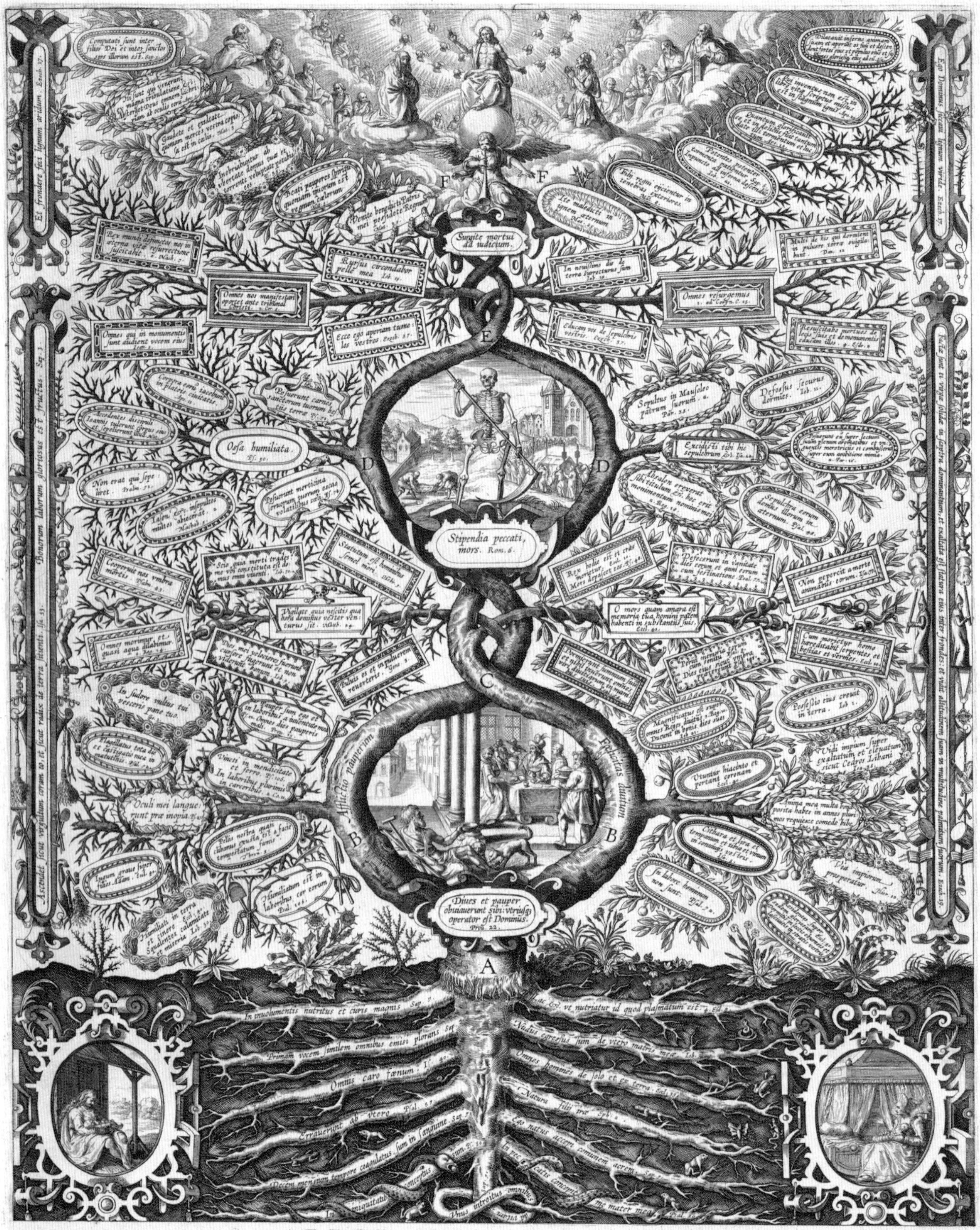

ARBOR HVMANÆ VITÆ.

A. *Nascimur pares, primaque iuuenta vbere contenta viuit.*
B. *Viuimus impares: et à lacte nos regna non capiunt; nec iam opum ac delitiarum finis.*
C. *Morimur pares, nullâ prerogatiuâ sceptri, aut pauperis casæ.*
D. *Integimur licet impares purpura aut vili lacerna, vermium tamen pabulo pares.*
E. *Resurgimus pares, omnibus exuti fortunæ mendacijs.*
F. *Præmiamur impares, è Lazari aut Epulonis tabulâ felici aut infelici æternitate donandi.*

Quisquis exitum cogitas, vitam intuere. neque ab Epulonis mensâ remuneratio Lazari, neque a Lazari palea Epulonius venit ignis.

Illust. Princeps Nicolaus Christophorus Radziuilus inuenit. *Theodorus Galleus excudit.*

7.14 Anonymous engraver after Nicolaus Christophorus Radzivilus, *Tree of Human Life*, by 1613, engraving, 456 × 329 mm. Amsterdam, Rijksmuseum: RP-P-OB-68.040. Appendix 1: TG-29.

7.15 Lucas Vorsterman I after Peter Paul Rubens, *The Battle of the Amazons*, engraving in six plates, 423 × 364 to 428 × 420 mm per plate, 856 × 1208 mm combined. Amsterdam, Rijksmuseum: RP-P-OB-33.047A. Appendix 1: PPR-1.

what was most likely a far more diverse range of clients than those for whom the Valentin family's orders were intended. Leonard acquired: prints in bulk from Charles de Mallery and Jan Boel (November 1621), 600 images of St Clement (August 1630), and twenty-five impressions of a *Goose Game* published by Theodore Galle (December 1632), portraits of Ferdinand of Austria (1635). In addition, he purchased an assortment of prints after Rubens between February 1632 and March 1633; these sheets ranged from an unspecified selection of images to two impressions of Rubens's *Battle of the Amazons* (fig. 7.15) and one copy of what was most likely the first part of his *Palazzi di Genova* (fig. 7.21).[82]

Moreover, the longstanding, good rapport between Balthasar Moretus I and Leonard made Leonard his preferred middleman for the transfer of a variety of packages from Antwerp print sellers, as well as for Balthasar's personal shipments of packages and payments for Cornelis Galle and his son when they were in Brussels.[83] As was the case when Leonard bought prints through the Moretuses, the dealers represented among the various packages sent to Leonard were diverse and the shipments were similarly scattered across the years between 1622 and 1641. The shipments comprised work from Jan Boel, Michael Snijders, Jan Cnobbaert, Peeter van Lanckvelt (who, while known as a painter, also had at least one package of prints sent to

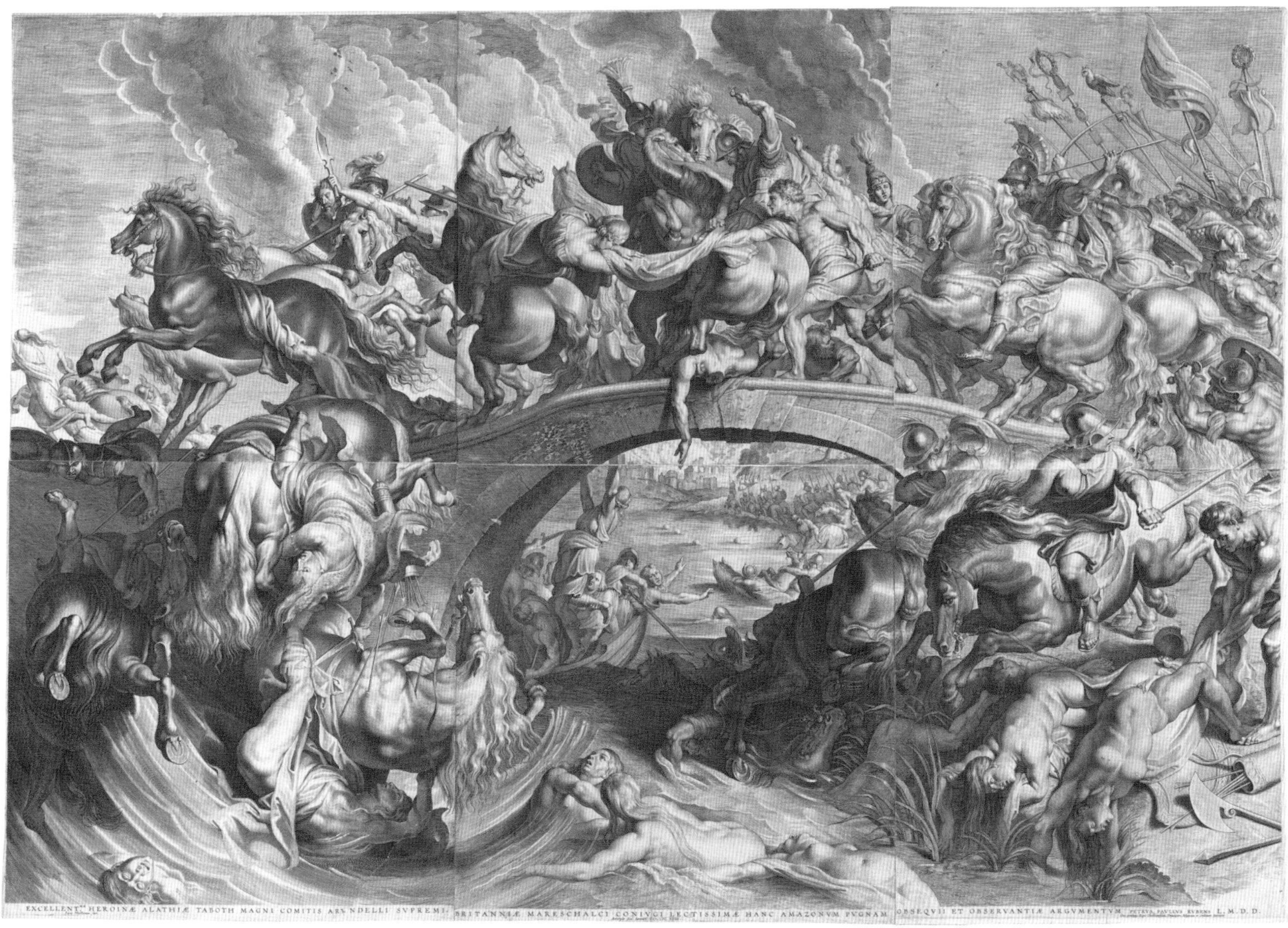

Brussels via Leonard), Theodore and Jan Galle, Jan-Baptist Barbé, Alexander Voet, and Hendrik Aertssens.[84] Aertssens sent the most sets of images – four packages in 1628 alone – and also the only consignment (in 1637), for which it was explicitly noted that Leonard was the intended recipient of the package. This note is significant because the predominance of sporadic shipments from diverse individuals and the lack of any monetary transfers between Leonard and these individuals suggests that such transactions may not have been a regular part of Leonard's own business – as was clearly the case with Du Puis's dealings with Collaert, for example. Rather, more often than not, Leonard may simply have been the preferred pickup point for packages prepared by various Antwerp artists for their own, independent clients in Brussels.

The evidence of the Moretuses' transactions with sundry booksellers in the southern Netherlands document that from the late 1580s to early 1590s, many sellers relied on the Moretuses for the procurement of quires of leaves with prints in assorted sizes that were sold in bulk by Adriaen Huberti. However, by the first decade of the seventeenth century, new print publishers had entered the field, and individual booksellers in the southern Netherlands began to carve out their own niches in the market for prints from Antwerp by favoring the publications of specific print sellers. Such scenarios ranged from Du Puis's close ties with Adriaen Collaert to Ouwerx's regular purchases of *suffragia* from Hendrik Aertssens and Jean Valentin's intermittent acquisition of a variety of prints from Theodore Galle. Several booksellers ordered directly from these three and other Antwerp print publishers and turned to the Moretuses for periodic assistance with transport and payments. Ultimately, the Moretuses were involved in only some of the myriad transactions that facilitated the exchange of prints in the Low Countries; there was a much broader spectrum of customers and suppliers than what is recorded in the Moretuses' accounts. Nevertheless, their records attest to the extent to which the networks of independent print dealers included an assortment of booksellers in disparate locations and the variety of ways in which these contacts contributed to

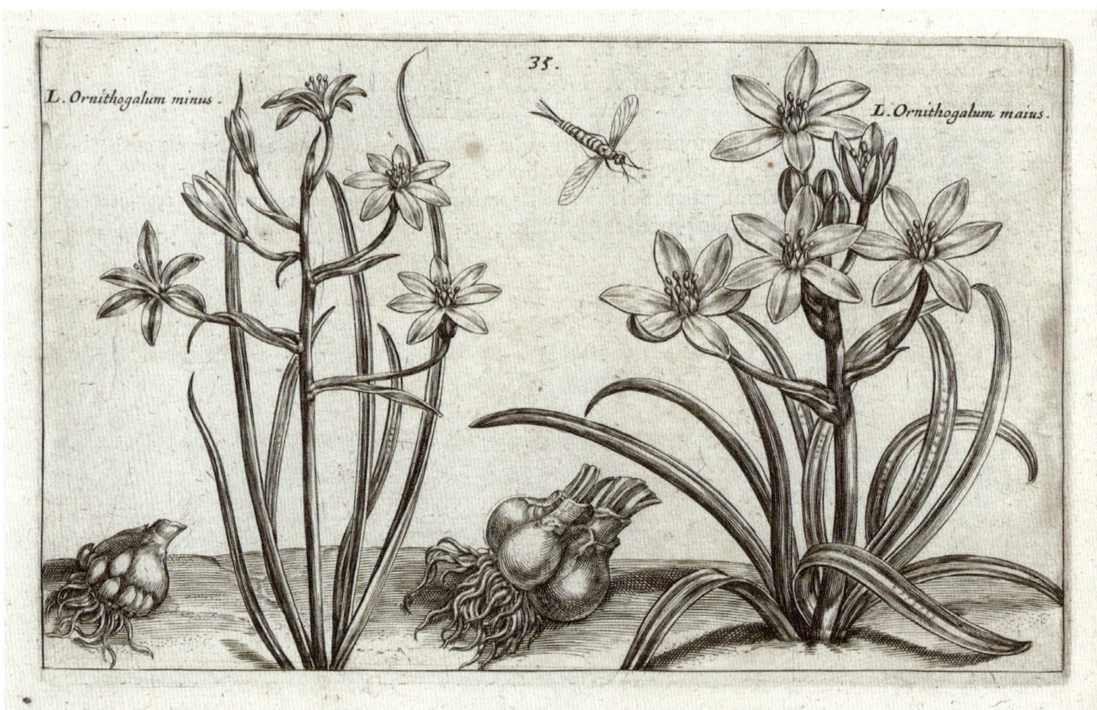

7.16 Crispijn de Passe I, *Star of Bethlehem (Ornithogalum)*, print 35 from the 1617 edition of his *Hortus floridus* series, engraving, 140 × 222 mm. Amsterdam, Rijksmuseum: RP-P-2020-3424-37.

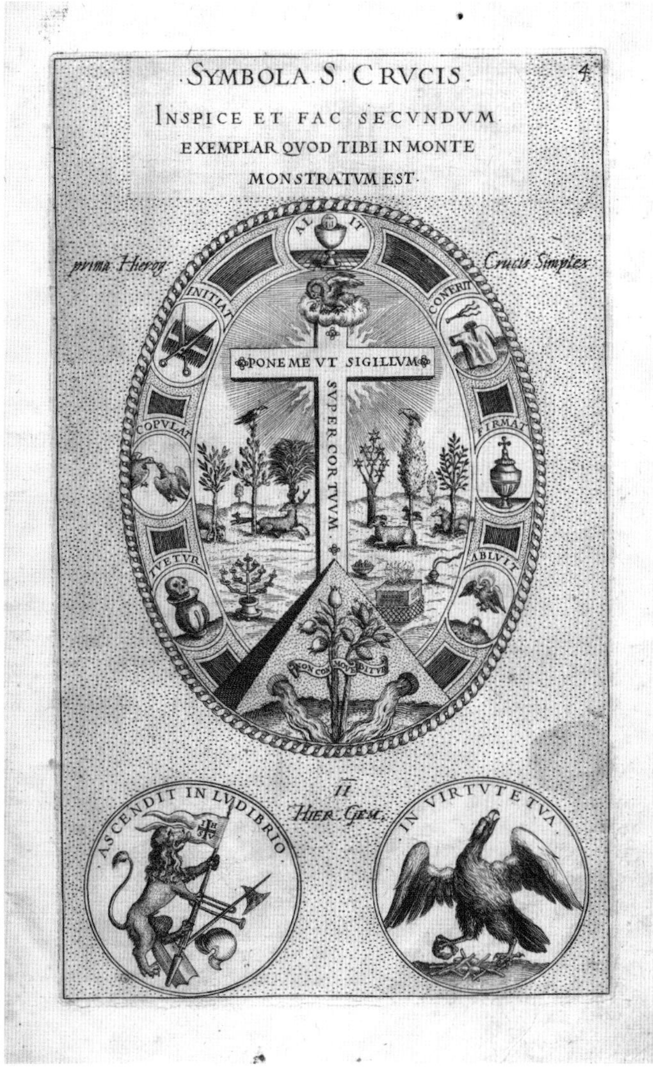

7.17 Aegidius Sadeler II, *Symbol of the Holy Cross*, print 4 from the print book *Symbola divina & humana pontificum imperatorum regum* (Prague, 1600), engraving, 236 × 138 mm. Antwerp, Museum Plantin-Moretus: B 1099. Appendix 1: SD-2.

the print trade at large. In addition to supporting those who routinely acquired prints for resale, middlemen like the Moretuses also served other agents who may not have consistently sold prints in their daily businesses, such as Leonard and the Valentin family; specifically, the Moretuses helped with the fulfillment of special orders, most likely requested by specific clients. Who these clients were remains largely unknown. Nonetheless, the Moretuses' sales and shipments of prints provide a glimpse into this often poorly documented realm, particularly among their wide base of customers in the Low Countries. Although our knowledge is limited by the only partial survival of the Moretuses' records of their local bookshop sales, orders placed by correspondence reveal diverse interests in prints among people of distinct occupations and backgrounds, as they acquired images to serve their discrete needs.

In 1612, for example, the Delft pharmacist Pierre vander Heyden, who regularly purchased books from the Officina Plantiniana, also ordered an image of Carolus Borromeus and scenes from his life.[85] Similarly unexpected are the occasional requests for prints that the Moretuses received from distant family members. In April 1624, Balthasar I sent Elisabeth van Hoinssem, a cousin of his father, Jan I, a selection of images supplied by Theodore Galle, along with some gingerbread, while in February 1630, he sent his own cousin Michelle Moerentorf 200 prints that were similarly provided by Galle.[86] Though the cost of Elisabeth's images is not known, Balthasar paid Galle just 1 fl. 16 st. for those he sent to Michelle, or 18 st. per one hundred prints, which is the lowest rate Galle is known to have charged for his publications.[87] Although an assortment of a few images may readily have been for personal enjoyment or use, a group of 200 was most likely intended for some other purpose.

A few purchases of extensive print books of flowers by academically trained professionals are notably different from the preceding examples in content and price. In 1614, the cosmographer Ottavio Pisani bought a two-volume set of Crispijn de Passe I's *Florilegium* for 6 fl., and then acquired Jan Theodore de Bry's *Florilegium* for 3 fl. 10 st. the following year. When the Brussels doctor Bartholomaeus Simonetti bought an enlarged, three-volume set of De Passe's *Florilegium* in 1617 (fig. 7.16), he was charged 7 fl. 10 st. for the work, which constituted a notable mark-up from the 5 fl. Adriaen Collaert asked when he provided this copy to the Moretuses for resale.[88] Already a costly addition to anyone's collection, the Moretuses' exceptional addition of such a significant profit margin on the resale of the last work may reflect the exceptional status this last publication had accrued among collectors.

A striking range of public officials also occasionally purchased prints from the Moretuses. Among those who served as mayors of Antwerp at the turn of the seventeenth century, Edouard vander Dilft, for example, bought an illuminated canon, or altar card, for the relatively high price of 9 st., while Hendrick Halmale I purchased disparate, extensive new print series, such as Theodore Galle's *Illustrium imagines* for 3 fl. 10 st. and Aegidius Sadeler II's *Symbola divina & humana pontificum imperatorum regum* for 3 fl. 15 st. (fig. 7.17).[89] In Brussels, Flaminio Garnier, the secretary of the king of Spain, Philip II, purchased two dozen "fine prints" by the Sadelers and Philips Galle, and Charles Tisnacq II, captain of the Spanish guard associated with the court of Archduke Albrecht and Archduchess Isabella, purchased three copies of an image of the garden of Hainaut (Henegouwen) that was supplied by Adriaen Huberti.[90] Remarkably, while Jan Moretus resold Garnier's specially selected prints at cost

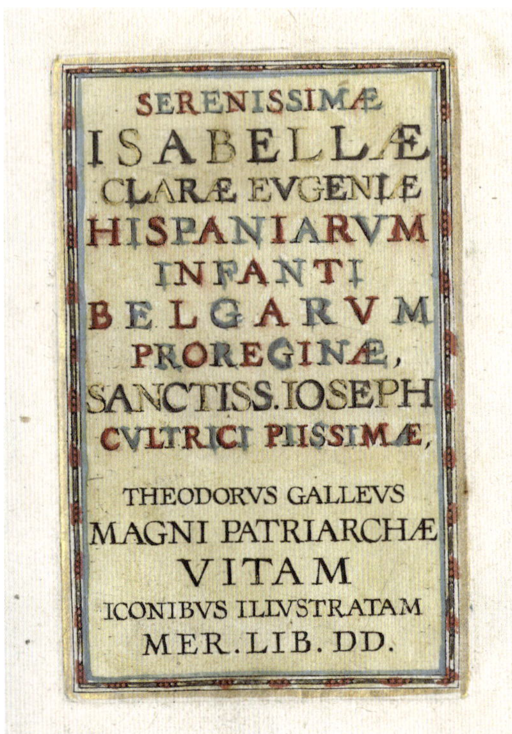

7.18 Anonymous, *Dedication to Archduchess Isabella*, from the series *The Life of Saint Joseph, Husband of the Virgin and Patriarch*, published by Theodore Galle by 1625, engraving, 93 × 59 mm. Antwerp, Museum Plantin-Moretus: PK.OPB.0023.036. Appendix 1: TG-11.

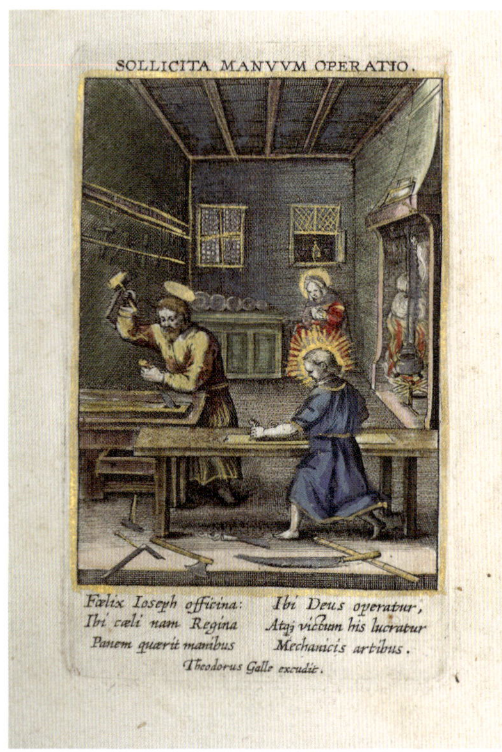

7.19 Anonymous, *Jesus and Joseph in the Woodworking Shop*, from the series *The Life of Saint Joseph, Husband of the Virgin and Patriarch*, published by Theodore Galle by 1625, engraving, 88 × 53 mm. Antwerp, Museum Plantin-Moretus: PK.OPB.0023.046. Appendix 1: TG-11.

for 1 fl. 16 st., he added a significant profit margin to the smaller sale to Tisnacq, charging him 9 st. for prints that had cost him just 7.5 st. Members of Albrecht and Isabella's court also sometimes placed personal orders with the Moretuses. For instance, their treasurer, Antonio de Rovelasca, purchased a specially bound copy of the Sadelers' complete series of hermits in 1610 for the large sum of 14 fl..[91]

The prints ordered for Albrecht and Isabella themselves are particularly intriguing, not only in terms of how these acquisitions were arranged, but also for the distinct quantities and uses to which the images bought may have been put. Some purchases were professionally motivated, as when Balthasar I was the intermediary between Theodore Galle and Archduchess Isabella in April 1625. In a letter written to Isabella's secretary, Antonio Suarez de Arguello, Balthasar remarked that he was sending her two presentation copies of a finely engraved print series that portrayed the life of St Joseph as the husband of the Virgin and an important patriarch and that Galle had dedicated to Isabella (figs. 7.18 and 7.19).[92] This overt attempt by Galle to make a favorable impression on Isabella was understandable, particularly since his work had rarely been selected in earlier orders for the Archduke and Archduchess.

The potentially personal nature of one of Albrecht's and Isabella's purchases in December 1617 is suggested by both the relatively limited number of prints sent and the effort that went into selecting them. On 26 December 1617, Balthasar I wrote to Suarez and related how, in response to a letter from Suarez, he had gone to all the shops of fine engravings in search of images of St Hubert and was consequently able to send ten examples to him for Albrecht and Isabella for a total of 11 st. In this group of images, there were two prints in folio by Jan Sadeler, one in folio and one in 4° by Jan-Baptist Vrients, and two in 8° by each of the following: Charles de Mallery, Hieronymus Wierix, and Adriaen Collaert; images by Theodore Galle were notably absent.[93] Although the exact purpose of this order is not clear, it remains distinct in scale and focus from Albrecht's and Isabella's other purchases in which numerous copies of just one or two renditions of a subject were bought simultaneously. For example, an order from October 1609 included forty-eight impressions of two different portrayals of a guardian angel, as well as forty-eight impressions of two other prints, which may have represented the Holy Family.[94] Both the quantities involved and the selection of two different types of each subject are echoed in another, less detailed print purchase from June 1619. Although this order was summarily recorded as ninety-eight images in 8° and was valued at 2 fl. 10 st. (or an average of .5 st. per print) in the Moretuses' running accounts, Balthasar I noted in the letter accompanying the shipment that he had sent eight dozen prints of two types for the "servicio" (service) of the Archduchess.[95] What exactly was meant by "servicio" cannot be deduced from this letter, but it may have been a recurring event for which Isabella periodically bought prints from the Moretuses. In addition to the earlier purchase of ninety-six prints of two different subjects in 1609, Balthasar also sent Isabella sixty impressions of one particular image of the Crucifixion in September 1619.[96]

As these examples suggest, the printed images that the Moretuses sold served multiple functions. They could be special renditions of a subject that were meant to attract the attention of a particular individual or group, practical and collectable images for personal use, or prints intended to accompany a particular event or religious service attended by a group. Although our focus thus far has been on laymen who bought prints, many individuals of diverse ranks within the church – including papal nuncios, abbots, and canons – made similar purchases, ranging from finely engraved prints like Galle's *Illustrium imagines* series to assorted altar cards or numerous impressions of one devotional image.[97] The Moretuses' accounts concerning members of the clergy are remarkable because they reveal the variety of religious orders whose members dealt directly with an assortment of Antwerp print sellers and the striking importance of printed images for the Franciscans, Jesuits, and Capuchins.

Of the various orders and their representatives who were among the Moretuses' clientele, the Augustine abbey of Van Loo in Ypres, the Cistercian abbeys of Nizelles and Orval, as well as representatives of the Benedictine abbey of Liessies (Anton van Winghe) and the Dominican order in Antwerp (Joannes Nys), all had personal contacts with diverse Antwerp print dealers. Attesting to this phenomenon are such transactions as a request that Balthasar I pay Maarten van den Enden 20 fl. in the name of the abbey of Van Loo and Balthasar's decision to give books ordered by the Abbess of Nivelles to Jan-Baptist Barbé, indicating that he was a trusted contact for the Moretuses.[98] Similarly, Balthasar I was asked to convey a package of prints from Theodore Galle to the Dominicans in Antwerp, while Galle frequently was an intermediary for transactions between Balthasar I and Abbot Anton van Winghe in Liessies. Galle also dealt extensively with the abbot's brother, the canon Hieronymus van Winghe, in addition to other individuals in their circle.[99]

In only a few instances, however, is it possible to determine the scope of the demand for prints at these disparate religious institutions. For example, in August 1622, the Moretuses helped convey not only an order of books for the Cistercian Abbey of Orval, but also ten packages of illuminated images that had been collected for the abbey by the Italian merchant Octavio Michaeli, who was then living in Antwerp and often assisted with payments between the Moretuses and the abbey.[100] Only Michael Snijders – by far the most frequent exporter of packages via the Moretuses – is known to have prepared more packages for a single shipment: eleven for the Münster bookseller Michel van Dale in November 1624.[101]

Though perhaps not generating the same volume of shipments, Antoine Bergaigne, the Guardian of the Franciscan order in Brussels, oversaw and funded orders of assorted images. Between 1601 and 1606 alone, he assisted with purchases not only by his fellow Franciscans, but also by members of affiliated orders of nuns, namely, the Poor Clares and the Order of the Annunciation of the Blessed Virgin Mary (the "Clarisses" and the "Annunciaten" in the Moretuses' records). These acquisitions comprised assorted prints obtained by fellow Franciscans from Philips Galle – including the *Life of Saint Francis* and Johannes Stradanus's series of the *Passion of Christ* – in addition to series of the *Life and Passion of Christ* and the *Life of the Virgin*, purchased from Adriaen Collaert. Periodically, quires of images (some illuminated) from the Huberti family were included, as were other quires of prints from unspecified suppliers and even a few paintings.[102]

The Moretuses' accounts also provide novel insights into the Jesuit order's role in the distribution of printed images. The order was well known for its active embrace of the use of printed images to support sundry goals within its extensive educational programs, missionary work, and local outreach. It is thus not surprising that various members of this order, in addition to several Jesuit colleges, appear in the Moretuses' accounts. Among the numerous, discrete print purchases, the single most noteworthy is Thomas Sailly's acquisition of 100 impressions of Hieronymus Wierix's portrayal of the *Death of Saint Cecilia* (fig. 6.7). However, it is the lack of any regular involvement of the Officina Plantiniana in their procurement of prints that truly stands out.[103] Presumably, like the various orders already mentioned, the Jesuits dealt directly with assorted print dealers to obtain images. The prefect of the Antwerp Jesuit college, Heribertus Rosweydus, for example, periodically sent packages of images to Jesuits abroad via the Moretuses' shipments to the Frankfurt fairs. Similarly, the college's rector, Carolus Scribani, took advantage of the transport of books to the rector of the Jesuit college in Lille, to send him some images as well.[104] More remarkable are the few times when the Moretuses purchased prints from Scribani that they then passed on to others: in 1595, they sent prints to Jesuits in or near Pont-à-Mousson (in France), and in 1604 to a favorite apprentice, Bernhard Wolters, who had recently established himself as an independent bookseller in Cologne.[105]

These 1595 and 1604 shipments may reflect instances when the Jesuits (like other religious institutions) commissioned engravings from local artists that they then had printed and distributed.[106] The English Jesuit college at St Omer (in addition to the booksellers there) similarly appears to have supported the printing of copper plates. In May 1614, when ink for printing engravings seems to have been difficult to obtain in the southern Netherlands, Theodore Galle sold the Jesuit John Wilson at St Omer eight pounds of ink for printing engraved images. During September 1614, Galle sent just two and a half pounds of ink to the bookseller Charles Boscard in St Omer, although it is not known whether this was ultimately intended for the Jesuit college or not.[107] Simultaneously, between August 1614 and October 1615, another St Omer bookseller, Pierre Geubels, purchased a remarkable 1,200 prints from the Moretuses that Galle supplied at his low-end bulk rates of 36 st. and 18 st. per 100 images.[108] Geubels's unusual purchase of this significant quantity of images in a little more than a year most likely reflects some exceptional request for prints to which he was responding. The conspicuous overlap in timing with Galle's equally unprecedented supply of ink and prints to individuals in St Omer in 1614–1615 and the lack of similar transactions beyond this sixteen-month period together suggest that the Jesuits in St Omer were experiencing difficulties obtaining prints via their regular sources and were seeking solutions to the problem. Their likely reliance on personal networks, including direct contact with Antwerp artists, at other times is evident in Geubels's subsequent transactions with the Moretuses. Despite his regular acquisition of books from the Moretuses between 1612 and 1642, Geubels did not ask them for assistance in obtaining images again until nearly a decade later, in 1624.[109] While no longer buying prints from the Moretuses directly, Geubels and his contacts among Antwerp print dealers – Michael Snijders and Jan-Baptist Barbé – occasionally needed assistance in settling their accounts and in shipping prints that Geubels had ordered independently. The transactions with Snijders were more extensive than those with Barbé, both in terms of the sums the Moretuses paid on Geubels's behalf – some 150 fl. in total – and his sporadic shipment of packages between 1624 and 1636.[110] The lack of connection in timing between the payments the Moretuses made and their shipment of packages between Snijders and Geubels suggests that the trade in images by the two men was more frequent than what is documented in the Moretuses' accounts.

Finally, in notable contrast to the Jesuits, the Capuchins in the Low Countries regularly turned to the Moretuses for help in acquiring the images they sought. As with the other orders discussed thus far, the Moretuses' accounts attest to the frequency of the Capuchins' approaches to artists of all ranks to satisfy their needs for visual imagery. For example, in February 1612, the Capuchin orders in Oudenaarde and Antwerp both had the painter Jan Bruegel I pay off their debts with the Moretuses, while in June 1626, the Guardian of the Capuchins, Cyprianus, requested that the Moretuses pay the painter Abraham Mathijs 60 fl. in the name of the Antwerp order.[111] The Moretuses were also periodically asked to ship packages of prints that others (often members of the Antwerp Capuchin order) brought to them for transport to monasteries elsewhere. In this way, the Capuchins in Geldre (most likely the former duchy of Guelders in the eastern Low Countries) were supplied with framed altar cards in 1628, while those in Oudenaarde and Tervuren were sent packages of images in 1630 and 1639, respectively.[112] Occasionally, Capuchins in diverse locations in the southern Netherlands approached the Moretuses with requests for specific prints. These ranged from series of subjects pertinent to religious orders, such as Charles de Mallery's series on Franciscan men and women (fig. 7.7) for the monastery in Charleville and Theodore Galle's *Holy Founders of Religious Orders* (fig. 7.2) for that in Antwerp, to unspecified prints after Rubens for the Capuchins in Geldre.[113] Above all, however, the Capuchins turned to the Moretuses for purchases of altar cards. Aside from their noteworthy request for multiple altar cards supplied by Michael Snijders for twenty different monasteries in the Low Countries, that in Namur ordered an exceptional altar card to be prepared by Jan Cnobbaert that consisted of three illuminated leaves in a gilded leather frame.[114]

Matters were significantly different when Franciscus Van Gouda began his missionary work in Amsterdam as the Provincial of the Capuchins in the northern Netherlands around 1628. Initially, he made a modest purchase of 6 fl. worth of unspecified images in October 1628 that was approved by the Antwerp Capuchin Thaddaeus. Subsequently, between 1630 and 1636, Van Gouda periodically turned to Balthasar Moretus I for the procurement of dozens of illuminated prints on paper and parchment that were supplied by Theodore Galle and his widow and that presumably could not be as readily obtained in the Calvinist north.[115] Thereafter, he and his successor in the northern Netherlands, Constantin le Roy (or Constantinus van Utrecht), occasionally had packages of images obtained for them by others shipped with books that they had ordered from the Officina Plantiniana. The main exception here was an image of the *Genealogical Tree of the Franciscan Order* from Peeter de Jode that Le Roy purchased via Balthasar for 8 fl. in 1639 and that was subsequently shipped to him in a roll.[116] The reasons for this shift in acquisition strategy are not clear, but ultimately – possibly due (in part) to the increasingly contentious position of the representatives of the Capuchins in the northern Netherlands – the Moretuses' involvement in this supply route petered out in 1640. Once again, like all the preceding instances in which sundry religious institutions procured printed images, recourse to the order's internal network, where personal, direct contact with an assortment of artists was possible, most likely prevailed. Only the occasional need for assistance with matters of transport and payment and isolated requests for specific images and canons necessitated the involvement of external middlemen, such as the Moretuses.

Beyond booksellers working in towns along the perpetually contested borders between the southern and northern Netherlands, such as 's-Hertogenbosch and Maastricht, the Moretuses had one additional, important contact for the trade in prints in the northern Netherlands, namely the Catholic bookseller Hendrik Barentsen in Amsterdam. Having established business ties with Balthasar I by 1612, Barentsen became a long-term partner in trade and a trusted personal contact; his significance extended far beyond his own periodic purchases of Catholic imagery.[117] Most of Barentsen's sporadic print purchases were highly diverse, ranging from two copies of Theodore Galle's series of the *Life of Saint Catherine of Siena* (fig. 7.12), bought in 1618, to 200 illuminated prints on parchment supplied by Jan Cnobbaert in 1629 and three quires of Hendrik Aertssens's *suffragia* with Dutch or German accompanying texts, which were purchased in 1638 (fig. 6.32).[118] The variety of his purchases suggests that he was commissioned to buy them for someone else. The one type of item that Barentsen purchased more regularly in significant quantities – thirty-six in 1629 and twelve in 1634, for example – were illuminated canons or altar cards, which he may have endeavored to keep in stock.[119]

However, Barentsen's significance for Balthasar Moretus's trade to the north, including exchanges involving prints, was far greater than the sum of these periodic purchases, as he was also an essential, trustworthy middleman for the Moretuses' far more extensive dealings with, above all, the Förster family of booksellers in Danzig (Gdańsk). In the spring of 1636, Balthasar I responded positively to Kaspar Förster's request to trade with one another, remarking that he had no reliable contact at that time for the distribution of his books to eastern Europe (in particular, Poland). After Balthasar had prepared his first shipment for Förster in April 1636, he wrote to inform him that he had sent the bale of books to Barentsen, who would oversee the further transport by boat to Förster in Gdańsk because Balthasar knew no better means of conveying merchandise or exchanging payments than trustworthy individuals in Amsterdam.[120] Though Balthasar focused on the benefit of these transactions for his own business as a bookseller, this link with Förster also served as an important channel for the international sale of prints to Gdańsk and beyond.

GDAŃSK: GATEWAY TO EASTERN EUROPE

Throughout the late sixteenth and seventeenth centuries, trade between the Low Countries and various Baltic ports was supported by an assortment of merchants, the majority of whom were based in Amsterdam. The primary, recurring destination was Gdańsk, which was an important port of entry for the distribution of goods throughout the Polish kingdom, in addition to serving as a point of exchange for exports and payments between that region and western Europe.[121] Consequently, the volume of shipments to Gdańsk was far greater than that for other cities in the area and appears to have reached record highs between 1632 and 1651.[122] The merchandise sent to Gdańsk was intended for consumption not simply in that city, but also for export to other destinations in Poland and beyond. Although books and prints are not listed among the primary goods that were transported, the regular use of these trade routes for the traffic in such staples as salt and grain also facilitated the international distribution of texts and images. This is vividly documented by the Moretuses' accounts. For example, the booksellers Kaspar and Georg Förster in Gdańsk, as well as Christophorus Schedelius in Kraków, spent exceptionally large sums on prints purchased via the Moretuses in just five years between 1637 and 1641. Previously, Paulus Claessens, a merchant in Gdańsk who was active in the book trade, received some ninety packages from Antwerp print dealers via the Moretuses between 1612 and 1632 – approximately three times the number of packages sent by Antwerp print sellers to other important participants in the print trade – the Parisian bookseller Eustache Foucault and print dealer Jean Messager, for example. In addition, this total exceeded the sum of packages sent by any one Antwerp print publisher – including Charles de Mallery and Michael Snijders, who distributed the most packages by way of the Moretuses.[123] However, periodic attempts to obtain works sold by the Officina Plantiniana and local Antwerp printmakers for resale in the Baltic and Polish markets date back even further, to the last quarter of the sixteenth century. When combined with the remarkably large investments in this trade route during the following decades, these shipments not only document the spectacular increase in the volume of demand for prints in the region, but also reveal how the taste in prints there evolved over a period of more than fifty years.

The two earliest known requests for prints for export to Gdańsk via the Officina Plantiniana were made in 1582 and 1596 and consisted exclusively of hundreds of images supplied by Philips Galle. The 1582 request was part of an isolated purchase by the Gdańsk bookseller Salomon Gisser that also included a large assortment of books, some writing paper, and 500 unspecified engravings supplied by Galle at his common bulk rate of 18 st. per quire of twenty-five leaves of prints.[124] The 1596 print order was the first placed by the merchant Rocho di Gabrielli. Comprising 350 prints provided by Galle, the actual engraver responsible for these images remains unclear. Attributed to one of the Wierixes in the sales record, the prints are listed in four distinct price categories, ranging from .5 st. to 2 st. per print, although no other records document that the Wierixes supplied prints in bulk for .5 st. per image.[125] In Gabrielli's subsequent purchases from 29 December 1601 and 22 January-1 February 1602, he initially bought a small sampling of four to eighteen prints from each of four different Antwerp print sellers – Philips Galle, Adriaen Collaert, Jan-Baptist Vrients, and Anton Wierix – at prices ranging from approximately .5 st. to 4 st. for Galle's prints, .75 st. for Collaert's and Vrients, and 1 st. per print for Wierix's work. Gabrielli subsequently ordered dozens of images from Theodore Galle, more than 100 from Anton Wierix, and some 5,320 prints from Collaert. This indicates a strong preference for Collaert's publications in bulk among his clientele, alongside a more limited interest in the (generally) more costly prints offered by Galle and Wierix.[126] Of all of the works identified by subject or some accompanying inscription, the vast majority were religious: images of saints, the Virgin and the Holy Family, and assorted portrayals of the Crucifixion. The one notable exception was an allegorical image of the *Triumph of Truth* by Anton Wierix, which was an imitation in reverse of a larger image by his older brother Jan Wierix, after Maarten de Vos (fig. 7.20).[127]

When we consider these early sales, it is also important to recall that as of 1592, Gerard de Jode's widow, Passchijnke van Gelre, was also actively engaged in the export of books purchased from Jan Moretus I for various booksellers and private individuals in Gdańsk and Kraków.[128] Naturally, she may well have simultaneously shipped assorted prints made from her husband's stock of plates, in addition to works provided by other Antwerp print sellers. Both of her sons, the print and map dealer Cornelis and the merchant Jacques, were similarly involved in this trade until about 1600 and 1606, respectively. Consequently, Jan Moretus's contribution was limited primarily to the sale and shipment of large quantities of books.[129] The Moretuses' involvement in the traffic in prints destined for Gdańsk (and beyond) changed dramatically when the merchant Paulus Claessens (most likely from the northern Netherlands but living at least part-time in Gdańsk) married into the De Jode family and succeeded Jacques in the family's dealings in Gdańsk.[130]

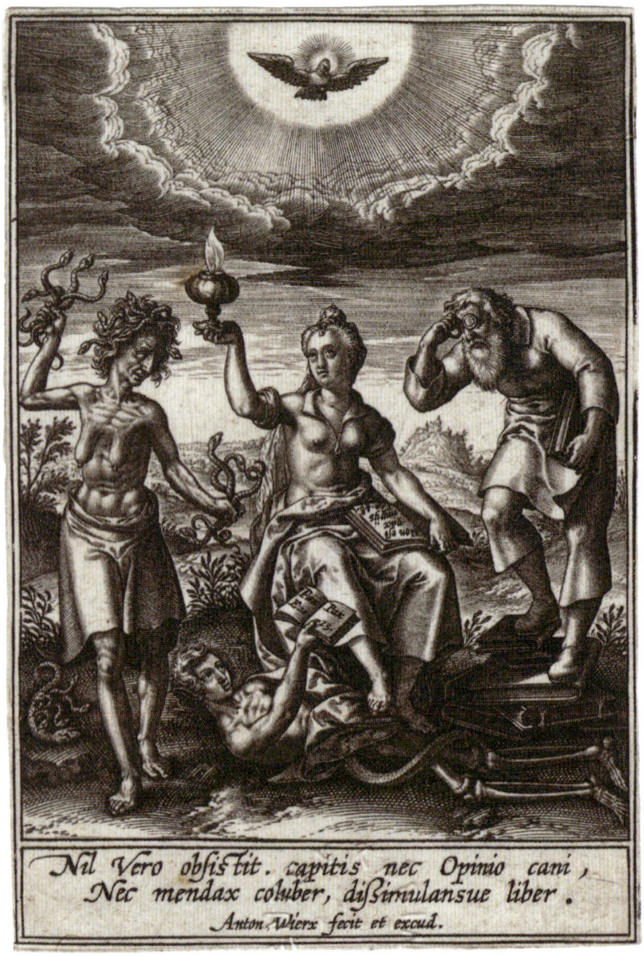

7.20 Anton Wierix II, *Triumph of Truth*, by 1602, engraving, 96 × 65 mm. Antwerp, Museum Plantin-Moretus: PK-OP-03652. Appendix 1: WX-17.

While Claessens's initial transactions with the Moretuses in 1606 consisted primarily of large orders of books, in 1607, he also began to import works of art – first a painting in March, and then packages of prints and other merchandise from unknown suppliers in June.[131] Though these 1607 transactions remained isolated acquisitions, as of 1612 packages of printed images were included in shipments of books for him on nearly an annual basis through 1632. Beginning modestly in October 1612 with just one package of "canon missae" (presumably altar cards) and one of "images", in the following year, a total of eleven packages of "finnes images" or "finnes figures" were sent to him.[132] Though the suppliers of these packages are not specified, another large shipment of packages of prints from July 1616 reveals the range of prints Claessens was importing at that time. Specifically, in addition to receiving sporadic packages of prints from several leading Antwerp print publishers – Theodore Galle, Charles de Mallery, Adriaen Collaert, and Michael Snijders – Claessens also obtained three packages prepared for him by the Antwerp merchant Christoffel Olimaerts (or Olimaers), who was married to Gerard de Jode's daughter Susanna; both Olimaerts and Susanna periodically served as intermediaries for Claessens's payments to the Moretuses. Thus, while some Antwerp print sellers had begun to supply Claessens with prints directly, this record also attests to the De Jode family's ongoing involvement in the export of prints to the Baltics.[133] Because the suppliers of the majority of the packages of prints sent to Claessens during the latter 1610s are not identified, it is impossible to determine whose work (if any) was preferred among Claessens's clients. However, during the final decade of Claessens's trade with the Moretuses (1623–1632), one print dealer clearly dominates the transactions, namely, Michael Snijders, who sent Claessens remarkably large numbers of packages of prints on multiple occasions: nine each in 1624 and 1632, six in 1628, and three in 1627. Although it is impossible to estimate the number of prints that might have been included in these parcels, some indication of their exceptional value is suggested by the sums Claessens asked the Moretuses to pay Snijders in his name: some 811 fl. in just five payments made between 1623 and 1629, which ranged from 14 fl. 11 st. in 1626 to 400 fl. in 1629.[134] No other individual who bought prints from the Officina Plantiniana spent as much, and only the values of *all* the prints supplied by the publishers Philips and Theodore Galle to *all* of the Moretuses' clients throughout Europe (more than 1,000 fl. and 1,780 fl., respectively) exceed Claessens' total payment. Just isolated shipments of one or two packages of prints to Claessens from the Antwerp merchant Ferdinand van den Eynde and from Abraham van Merlen in 1623 and 1626, respectively, deviate from this pattern.[135]

Balthasar Moretus I ended his substantial shipment of books and prints to Claessens in 1632 and demanded that he satisfy his sizable debts before placing any new orders.[136] During the 1620s, when he evidently no longer could rely on relatives or others in Antwerp to serve as intermediaries to pay off his debts, Claessens periodically sent allotments of feathers and leather to Antwerp, in the hope that the sale of these goods would help cover his expenditures, including some payments that he asked Balthasar to make in his name to both Snijders and Van Merlen in 1628.[137] The matter was never resolved in Balthasar I's lifetime. Despite Claessens's shipment of talc powder to Balthasar II in 1643 for resale to compensate for his debt, Balthasar ultimately decided to cancel the remaining sum of more than 1,834 fl. that Claessens owed in 1644 (or sometime thereafter), noting that he was bankrupt.[138]

In 1636, a few years after Balthasar I's refusal to sell Claessens more books, Balthasar received a request from Kaspar Förster, a long-established bookseller with good connections to the Polish court, to establish a trading alliance between them. Balthasar responded positively, observing that Claessens was no longer active in that sector and that another bookseller, Ernst Kruse, would only serve the market in Gdańsk; Balthasar was looking for someone who would distribute his books throughout the Polish kingdom.[139] Consequently, on 22 April 1636, the first of many large shipments of books from the Officina Plantiniana was sent to Förster via Barentsen in Amsterdam. Förster's son Georg, who had just begun to assist his father with their business, also occasionally traveled to Antwerp to see to these arrangements personally and subsequently (as of 1643) took over his father's business, including his transactions with the Moretuses.[140] As early as May 1637, the Försters began to buy prints by the thousands via the Moretuses. For their first order, the images were supplied by Theodore Galle's son Jan, who was now managing his father's workshop.[141] This choice may have been one of convenience; by this time, all of the print publishers from whom Claessens had ordered prints were no longer trading via the Moretuses or, like Jan's father, had passed away. While the Försters purchased 1,000 prints on paper, sold at cost at the basic bulk rate of 36 st.

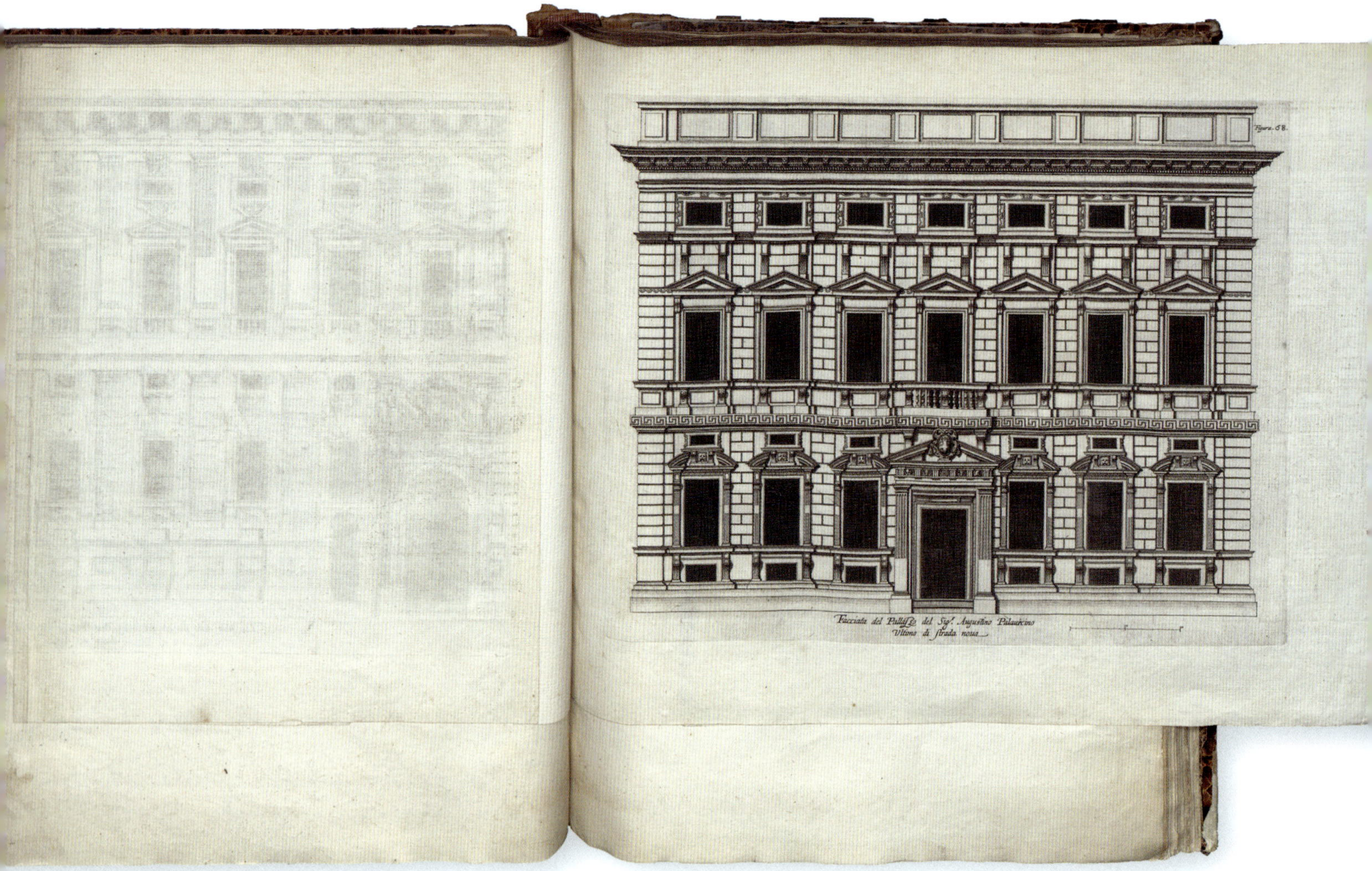

7.21 Nicolaes Ryckermans (attributed to) after Peter Paul Rubens, *Façade of the Palace of Agostino Pallavicino*, print 68 from the series *Palazzi antichi*, first part of the *Palazzi di Genova*, published by Rubens by 1622, engraving, 283 × 360 mm. Antwerp, Erfgoedbibliotheek Hendrik Conscience: H 20624. Appendix 1: PPR-2.

per 100 images, the majority of the images (1,600) were printed on parchment. and 1,000 of these were illuminated. In subsequent years, the Försters' preference for prints on parchment, which were often illuminated, prevailed, although the supplier of the images varied from year to year. In 1638, Carel Collaert provided 500 illuminated prints on parchment at 10 fl. per 100 pieces, while in 1639, Jan Galle supplied an additional 500 illuminated images on parchment at 9 fl. per 100. Then, in 1640, Jan Cnobbaert's widow, Marie de Man, provided 1,400 prints on parchment, the majority of which were hand colored; these fell into four different price categories, ranging from 3 fl. per 100 prints (for plain images without coloring) to 5, 6, or 10. fl. per 100 colored images.[142] Remarkably, all of these expensive, specially finished prints were resold to the Försters at cost, with no profit margin for Balthasar Moretus. Intermittently, the Försters also bought isolated copies of Rubens's *Palazzi di Genova* and exceptional print series, such as Jan Galle's *Speculum diversarum imaginum speculativum* (figs. 7.21 and 7.22). For these requests, in notable contrast to the bulk print orders, Balthasar I and II regularly included a profit margin for themselves, approximately 5 to 10 percent of the selling price.[143]

That there was significant demand for specially finished prints from Antwerp (at least among wealthier circles) in the Polish kingdom at this time is confirmed by similar sales of thousands of illuminated prints on parchment to the Kraków bookseller Christophorus Schedelius. Specifically, in October 1641, as part of his very first order of hundreds of books, Schedelius also requested 3,000 illuminated prints on parchment at 5 fl. per 100 images, another 300 at 9 fl. per 100, and two volumes of Rubens's *Palazzi di Genova* series.[144] Although neither the supplier nor the original selling price of the prints sold in bulk is known, the Moretuses bought Rubens's series from the art dealer Jacques Moermans and resold it to Schedelius with the same approximate 5 percent profit margin (amounting to 1 fl.) that they added to the Försters' contemporaneous purchases of the same work. When Balthasar II confirmed the terms of their trading agreement, including what discounts Schedelius might expect on certain types of books, he informed Schedelius that prints had to be paid for in cash, which suggests that Schedelius had inquired about buying prints from the start.[145] Also reminiscent of the Moretuses' transactions with the Försters was the fact that the transport of Schedelius's purchases of books (and prints), as well as Schedelius's payments, were arranged via a middleman in Amsterdam, a certain Peter de Haen II. Unfortunately for the Moretuses,

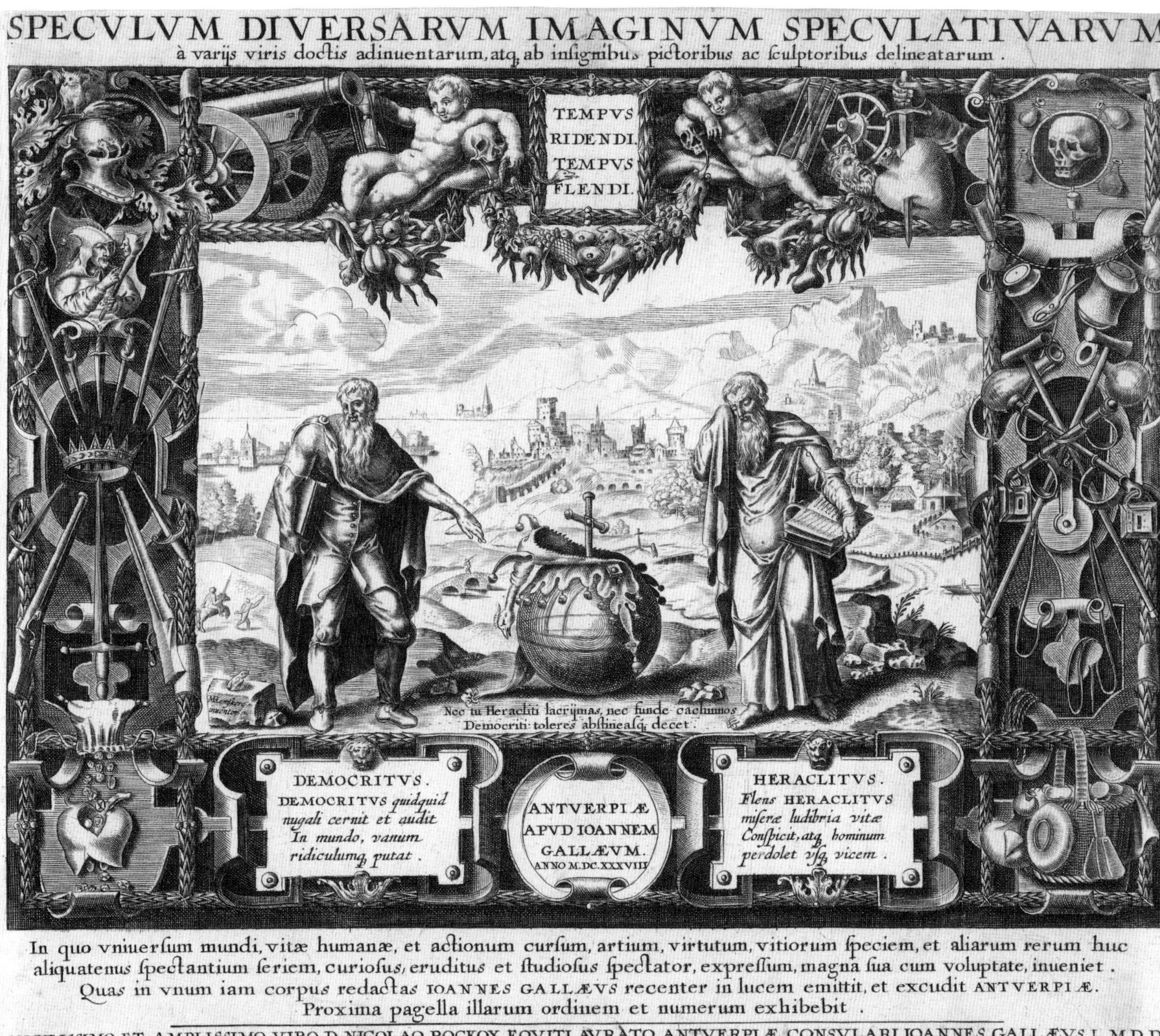

7.22 Anonymous, title plate for the series *Mirror of Assorted Images to Admire* (which includes the phrase "Tempus ridendi", which was regularly used to identify this series in the Moretuses' sales records), 1638, engraving, 227 × 253 mm. Amsterdam, Rijksmuseum: RP-P-1963-258. Appendix 1: JG-2.

their dealings with Schedelius ultimately resulted in a financial loss for them, as did their trade with Claessens, and led to Balthasar II's refusal to ship Schedelius any more books (or prints) until he had paid off his existing debts.[146]

Together, the Moretuses' sales to diverse booksellers and merchants reveal the evolving demand for prints in the Baltics. While Antwerp prints were nearly always purchased in remarkably large quantities at cost and at bulk rates from the Moretuses, the specific items ordered changed. Following an initial sampling of the wares provided by Philips Galle and subsequently his successors, prints by Collaert were sometimes favored above not only the work of Galle's own son Theodore, but even that of the Wierixes. The simultaneous lack of evidence of any significant export of prints by Hieronymus Wierix, Charles de Mallery, or Jan-Baptist Barbé to the Baltic regions is similarly striking, particularly given the contemporaneous strong demand for their publications in Spain and Paris. Whether this was due to stylistic and formal considerations or financial concerns, for example, is not clear. However, the former seems more likely, for among those with whom the Moretuses dealt, the individual who exported the most by far to the Baltics was Michael Snijders; he catered to the growing desire to possess costly, finely finished, and illuminated prints on parchment. Although the interest in such prints existed throughout Europe, the sellers serving the demand in the Baltics and Poland were exceptionally voracious in their acquisition of them. Purchasing prints by the hundreds, if not by the thousands, regardless of the specific supplier – be it Snijders or others who produced similar work – these booksellers and merchants were presumably responding to an ever-growing demand for such imagery. It was no longer a matter of engraving finesse or style that determined these later sales, but the physical quality of what was produced – parchment supports rather than paper, hand coloring and special finishing – that counted. Attested to by the export of prints to eastern Europe in the 1630s-1640s via the Moretuses, such criteria are also listed explicitly in Georg Förster's detailed 1644 request for assorted prints.[147] However, as demonstrated by the Moretuses' transactions with the Münster bookseller, Bernhard Raesfeld, the Försters and Schedelius were not the only ones to invest remarkably large sums in the acquisition of such works from Antwerp print sellers.

THE PERSISTENT DEMAND FOR PRINTS IN MÜNSTER

The Moretuses' contacts in the Holy Roman Empire, which was located primarily in those areas where Catholicism had won out following the religious conflicts of the sixteenth and seventeenth centuries, extended from Emmerich in the northwest, near the border with the northern Netherlands, to Vienna (then part of the Empire) in the southeast.[148] Predictably, much of their trade in books with German booksellers took place via the biannual Frankfurt fairs. Although they themselves did not trade in prints at the fairs, they played a vital, but significantly underestimated, role in facilitating the international exchange of prints between artists and their own extensive network of clients who attended the fairs.[149] Remarkably, the Moretuses' sales of prints were concentrated in just two cities: Münster and Cologne.

Located in the North Rhine-Westphalia state of Germany, Münster was an important and prosperous episcopal administrative center; by the year 1000, a cathedral, library, and accompanying school were all well established. A brief Anabaptist rebellion begun in 1534 was firmly repressed, and the Catholic faith was soon reinstated and officially reaffirmed during the signing of the Peace of Westphalia in 1648, following the Thirty Years' War. Consequently,

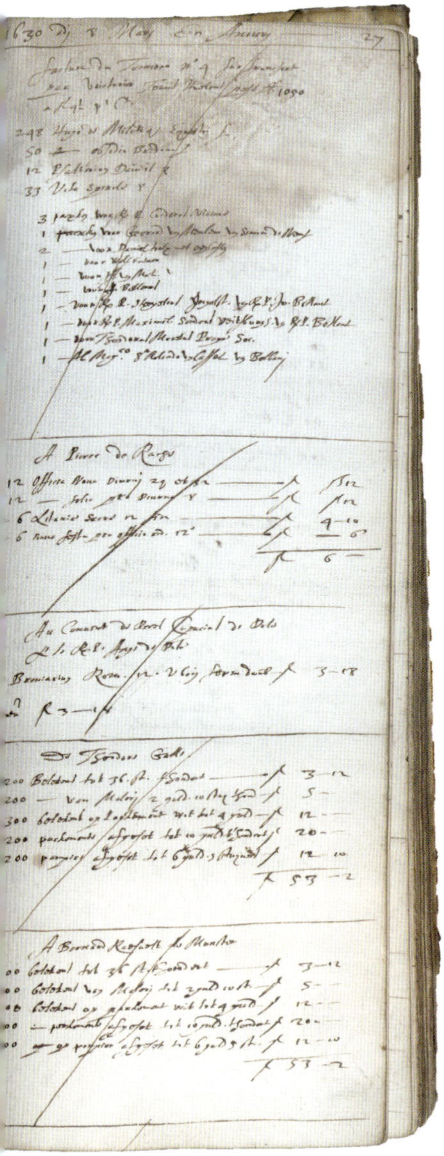

7.23 List of prints supplied by Theodore Galle and record of Balthasar Moretus I's resale of them to Bernhard Raesfeld on 8 March 1630. Antwerp, Museum Plantin-Moretus: Arch. 238, *Journal 1630*, fol. 27r.

when the prince-bishop asked Lambert Raesfeld to move to Münster from Cologne, where he had trained under Johann Gymnich III, and to establish himself as a printer and bookseller under the auspices of the cathedral in Münster, Raesfeld must have found the offer appealing. Arriving in 1589, Raesfeld established contact with the Officina Plantiniana at the Frankfurt fair the following year and began a modest trade in books.[150] It was not until October 1612, however, that Raesfeld began to order prints via the Moretuses. His desire to support local Catholic devotional practices with these purchases was clear from the start, for not only were the prints (supplied by Charles de Mallery) identified as 200 small devotional images ("2 cents images de devotion petites"), but Raesfeld had also asked for six dozen rosaries in diverse colors and materials, which were provided by Jacques de Jode.[151] Evidently, Raesfeld's initial purchase was well received by his clients; he ordered another 100 prints from De Mallery in December of that year, and at least 800 more between 1615 and 1617, the year of his death, in addition to occasional acquisitions of more rosaries from De Jode.[152] Consistently supplied by De Mallery with prints at his standard rate of 50 st. per 100 images, the Moretuses only added a small profit margin for themselves in their first transaction with Raesfeld in 1612. For all subsequent orders, they resold prints to Raesfeld and his heirs at cost.

Following Raesfeld's death, his widow, Anna Dörhoff, took over the business, but soon employed the bookseller Michael van Dale to manage it and married him shortly thereafter, in 1619. Van Dale's active involvement in the firm is first apparent from the Moretuses' accounts of May 1618 and continued until the business passed to Raesfeld's son Bernhard in 1628.[153] Initially, Dörhoff continued her husband's purchasing practices, simply buying 400 prints in bulk from De Mallery in January 1618. However, in May of that year, Van Dale decided to invest in a sampling of 400 prints by three other Antwerp print publishers – 100 prints from Theodore Galle and Michael Snijders each and 200 from Abraham van Merlen – in addition to another 100 from De Mallery.[154] While De Mallery's prints still cost 50 st. per 100 images, the other artists supplied their work at the common bulk rate of 36 st. per 100. As Van Dale was born and trained in Antwerp and still had family there, it is likely that he could rely on current, firsthand knowledge of the Antwerp art market.[155] Throughout his management of the Raesfeld business, Van Dale sought to diversify his print purchases. Following an order of an additional 400 prints from De Mallery in July 1619, Van Dale proceeded to buy more prints from Van Merlen, Snijders, and (as of 1623) Jan Boel. Among these purchases, those supplied by Snijders dominate these records In November 1624 alone, Snijders prepared eleven packages for Van Dale; this was the most sent at any one time by any print dealer via the Moretuses.[156] By contrast, orders from Theodore Galle are notably absent after his initial delivery of 100 prints in 1618. Additionally, during the 1620s, Van Dale took advantage of the relative proximity of the Moretuses to his family in Antwerp to periodically transfer both large sums of money, as much as 240 fl., and smaller sums to his two sisters, Janneken (or Tanneken) and Digna (or Dimphna), who occasionally sent him paintings in return within the Moretuses' shipments.[157] How much Van Dale spent on prints is difficult to assess, for as of 1622, he stopped ordering prints from the Moretuses and placed his orders directly with assorted Antwerp print sellers (presumably through his family in Antwerp); he simply relied on the Moretuses for transport. Nonetheless, the sheer volume of his transactions clearly exceeded Lambert Raesfeld's initial, steady acquisition of prints from De Mallery, while the total value of what his successor, Lambert Raesfeld's son Bernhard, bought in just four years (1628–1632), surpassed all of the recorded purchases by any of the Moretuses' other clients, including Kaspar Förster in Gdańsk.

Bernhard Raesfeld took over the management of his father's business in the fall of 1628, and by the spring of 1629, he was ordering large quantities of books via Balthasar Moretus I's shop at the Frankfurt fair and hundreds of specially finished images via his business in Antwerp.[158] Although the types of prints that Raesfeld sought for his customers were generally costly – often hand colored and printed on parchment – he clearly endeavored to procure an assortment in different price categories from two suppliers: Michael Snijders and Theodore Galle. For example, in March 1630, Raesfeld bought the following range of prints supplied by Galle and all resold to him by Balthasar at cost (fig. 7.23):[159]

200 images at 36 st. per 100 [images]	fl. 3 st. 12
200 [images] from [Charles de] Mallery at 2 fl. 10 st. (= 50 st.) per 100	fl. 5 st. __
300 images on parchment, white, at 4 fl. (= 80 st.) [per 100]	fl. 12 st. __
200 parchment [images] hand colored at 10 fl. (= 200 st.) [per 100]	fl. 20 st. __
200 paper [images] hand colored at 6 fl. 5 st. (= 125 st.) [per 100]	fl. 12 st. 10

The prices charged per print in this order range from .36 st. per plain print on paper published by Galle himself and .5 st. per plain print on paper originally published by De Mallery (but sold by Galle) to .8 st. per plain print printed on parchment, 1.25 st. per colored print on paper, and 2 st. per illuminated image printed on parchment. When Raesfeld ordered prints from Snijders, he often bought different types in different price categories simultaneously, as in July 1629, when he purchased 500 illuminated images on parchment at 33 st. per dozen (for a total of 68 fl. 5 st.) and 200 illuminated images on paper at 10 fl. per 100 (for a total of 20 fl.).[160] Snijders's price range, however, was notably higher; his hand-colored prints on paper cost 2 st. per image, and his illuminated prints on parchment were 2.75 st. per image. Consequently, while Galle charged 2 st. per image for his most expensive colored prints on parchment in the 1630 order, Snijders charged the same amount for his colored images on paper. Regrettably, nothing is known about the sizes of these images or the qualities of the parchment or the pigments used to color them.

Thus, by obtaining a variety of types of illuminated prints on parchment and paper – in addition to some plain prints on paper, including ones made by his father's favorite supplier, Charles de Mallery – Raesfeld was not limiting his offerings to one price category. Moreover, his acquisition of hundreds of such prints multiple times per year indicate that he was responding to a persistent, thriving, and diverse demand for these images. Who his clients were is not known. However, the original sponsorship of his father's business by the church, combined with his stepfather's and his own endeavors to print books for the local Jesuit order and Lower Rhine Jesuit province, suggest that all three men would most likely have been catering to Jesuit audiences and the local worshipers they served.[161] When considered together, the Raesfeld family's purchases demonstrate how a local market for prints, originally offered the limited supply of one print publisher's standard, basic offerings, could expand exponentially in response to the influx of works created by a variety of artists and offered at a range of prices. The distinctive mix of suppliers favored across this region, in contrast to other regions in Europe, underscores, once again, the fact that while the international print trade was pan-European, the characteristics of the local demand for prints was not.

And what of Cologne, the other important destination for Antwerp prints in Catholic Germany? A city with longstanding ties with Antwerp, a burgeoning center for the printing and distribution of books as well as for numerous independent print dealers, many of whom had ties to the Low Countries, it also hosted one of the oldest Jesuit communities in Germany, along with several other religious orders. The traffic in prints from Antwerp could not help but thrive on numerous, often interrelated levels.

1 Griffiths 2016, pp. 9–10.

2 Ibid., p. 216.

3 See Jones 2010 on the English print market.

4 For other transactions between Whitacker and the Moretuses, see Imhof 2001.

5 MPM Arch. 243, fols. 80v-81r (purchase), and 82v (supply).

6 On Robinson and his dealings with the Moretuses, see Bowen 2017, p. 283.

7 MPM Arch. 246, fol. 49v, for both the supply and resale of these prints. When Jan Galle's mother, Catharina Moerentorf, supplied the series of the twelve apostles for Whitacker, she charged 6 st. per series.

8 For Robinson's purchase of the Rubens prints and the identification of the prints concerned, see Bowen 2016, pp. 292–94.

9 See MPM Arch. 1107, fol. 121r (10 November 1640): "Voor 9 figuere van Rubbens voor Robinson fl. 12 st. 12" (Balthasar's purchase of these prints); and Wuestman 1998, for examples of prices charged for Rubens prints in the seventeenth century.

10 See Gerard 1996, pp. 366–68, for a considered account of the diverse forms of Woutneel's name and early references to him in secondary literature. Regrettably, as the author evidently did not make use of certain records in the Plantin archives (in particular, MPM Arch. 110, fol. 76, and MPM Arch. 111, fols. 41, 95, and 138), his account lacks some essential facts concerning Woutneel's dealings with other print publishers and the year of Woutneel's death (1604). On De Passe's publications for England, see Veldman 2001b.

11 Gerard 1996, pp. 366–67. For references to his presence in Antwerp, see, for example, MPM Arch. 110, fol. 76 lft, under 1581, 1586–1591; and MPM Arch. 111, fols. 41 lft (under 1595) and 95 lft (under 1598).

12 MPM Arch. 110, fol. 76 rht, under 1587 (Hoeswinkel), 1589 (G. de Jode), 1590 and 1592 (the widow of De Jode), and 1591 (Vrients).

13 MPM Arch. 111, fols. 95 rht (numerous references to Galle, in addition to ones to P. van Gelre under 1599–1600) and 138 rht (under 1601 (Vrients) and 1602–1603 (J. de Jode)). See also fig. 7.4.

14 MPM Arch. 111, fol. 138 rht: "Jaques de Jode doibt compter 56 florins pr la vefue [of Woutneel]".

15 MPM Arch. 171, fol. 120v. See also MPM Arch. 73, fol. 10r, for a similar transaction in January 1596, when De Renialme had Moretus pay Galle 52 fl. 10 st. in his name.

16 MPM Arch. 180, fol. 106r.

17 See Chapter 3 for a discussion of the Degli Antoni family purchases. For Gelli's acquisitions, Bowen 2020, as well as Chapter 5.

18 On Justus Sadeler's trade in books, in addition to these shipments of prints, see Bowen 2022b, pp. 380–83. On the Sadelers' exchange of packages via the Frankfurt fairs, see Chapter 9.

19 MPM Arch. 232, fol. 118r.

20 MPM Arch. 239, fol. 10v; MPM Arch. 240, fol. 195v; and MPM Arch. 241, fol. 178v.

21 MPM Arch. 223, fol. 85r (shipment to Sadeler); MPM Arch. 179, fol. 35v (canons bought for the father of the order of St Antonio of Malta in 1607); MPM Arch. 218, fol. 65v (canons for another Italian chaplain); and MPM Arch. 228, fol. 88v (twelve illuminated canons sold for 9 fl.).

22 Antwerp, Felix Archives, IB 2937 (Journal Gaspar Vivario = Van de Wouwer), and loose sheets at the back of this document. Information from these documents was first published in Diels 2000, but her account lacks many of the details presented here, including the identification of Vivario as the author of the bulk of these documents. This attribution can be confirmed by comparing references in these documents to his transactions with Jan Moretus II. For example, compare IB 2937, fol. 13v, with MPM Arch. 219, fol. 33r.

23 Antwerp, Felix Archives, IB 2937, fols. 7r-8v (Spiers) and 7v (watercolors), 5v (Nieulandt), and 11v-12v (prints from P. Galle, H. Wierix, A. Collaert, and P. de Jode).

24 Antwerp, Felix Archives, IB 2937, fols. 16v (T. Galle) and 17v (Van Merlen), and the verso of a separate account at the back of this document, headed "Rekeninghe voor mynen broeder Gaspar Vivario …" (bill for my brother Gaspar Vivario …), for H. Wierix, Van Merlen, Snijders, and De Mallery. See also Bowen and Imhof 2022, pp. 11–12, for a summary of De Mallery's transactions with Vivario.

25 Antwerp, Felix Archives, IB 2937, loose sheet: "Rekeninghe voor mynen broeder Gaspar Vivario …", verso: "[February 1614] noch voor 40180 fol. cunst" from an unspecified source.

26 For example: Antwerp, Felix Archives, IB 2937, fols. 14v-15v (purchases in 1612 from Verdussen and Nutius and references to Hondius and Blaeu (listed as Willem Janssen [Blaeu])) and 10v (Claessens).

27 Antwerp, Felix Archives, IB 2937, loose sheet.

28 Antwerp, Felix Archives, IB 2937, fols. 10v (Claessens in 1606), 12v (De Jode, 1606), and 13r (Vrients, 1606?).

29 Antwerp, Felix Archives, IB 2937, loose sheet: "Rekeninghe voor mynen broeder Gaspar Vivario vant gene wy gehandelt hebben sedert onse leste rekeninghe welck was int jaer 1612". Clara van der Wouwer's identity as the author of these records is confirmed when payments made to the Moretuses are compared with their own accounts, in which the "widow Vrients" is named (see, e.g., MPM Arch. 129, fol. 80 rht, under 21 January 1614).

30 Antwerp, Felix Archives, IB 2937, loose sheet, verso (Verdussen and a series of transactions under the heading: "In meerte [1614] hebbe ick [Clara] voor mijn broeder naer Amsterdam geweest ende hebbe aldaer voor hem betaelt …); and MPM Arch. 221, fols. 32r (nine packages), 110r (one "rolet"), and 125r (one "roulleau").

31 MPM Arch. 225, fol. 207v. See Chapter 3 for Poelman.

32 MPM Arch. 230, fols. 4r (shipment) and 26v (supply). See also MPM Arch. 140, fol. 72v, for a letter from Jan van Meurs of 24 January 1623 concerning this sale. For examples of De Toro's subsequent book orders, see MPM Arch. 142, p. 128 (1630); and MPM Arch. 147, p. 469 (1642).

33 These sales are discussed in Chapters 5 and 6.

34 See Imhof 2021, pp. 337–41, on Van Vucht's association with luxury exports. See MPM Arch. 1106, fol. 58r, and MPM Arch. 233, fol. 143v, for the purchase and sale, respectively, of these "Trees" ("Arbor S. Francisci") (the supplier of them is not known); and MPM Arch. 141, fol. 64v, for a letter of 29 April 1628 from Jan van Meurs to Van Vucht concerning this purchase.

35 MPM Arch. 235, fol. 89r (Cnobbaert); MPM Arch. 237, fol. 91v, and MPM Arch. 238, fols. 43r and 43v (Galle); and MPM Arch. 142, p. 324 (letter of 18 January 1633 from Balthasar Moretus I to Van Vucht regarding the shipment to a Capuchin).

36 De Peralta's interest in prints is discussed in Chapter 4.

37 Lemmens and Thijs 2006, pp. 99–100; and Denucé 1934, pp. 52, 54–55, and 57–58.

38 Stols 1971, vol. II, pp. 200–201, for a partial transcription of this record; and Antwerp, Felix Archives, IB 734 (formerly IB 458) and IB 736.

39 Grivel 1986, p. 218, and Griffiths 2016, p. 389, both of which are based on information from Fleury 1969, pp. 763–84, in particular.

40 Fleury 1969, pp. 774–76.

41 Ibid., pp. 766 (9 May 1605), 771–73 (19 October 1605), 780 (12 October 1607), 782 (5 May 1608), and 783 (17 May 1608, when François Gouault purchased 17,000 unspecified engravings, 7,000 small prints, and eight dozen paintings on canvas from Leclerc).

42 Ibid., pp. 784 (Messager) and 778–79 (Bartrand). See Bowen and Imhof 2022, p. 12, for an overview of De Mallery's trade with them, as well as Chapters 5 and 6 and the discussion below for additional references to their dealings with Antwerp print publishers.

43 On the Parisian print market in the seventeenth century, including the influence of Flemish dealers and prints, see Grivel 1986; and Griffiths 2016, pp. 218–19. See Appendix 2 for an overview of the Moretuses' contacts in France who were linked to the print trade.

44 For De St Martel's transactions, see MPM Arch. 66, fols. 158v-159v; MPM Arch. 67, fols. 99v-100r and 101r; and MPM Arch. 68, fols. 66v-66r. See Chapter 5 for Dassonleville's and Perier's purchases.

45 See Pallier 1985 for Rinsart's transactions with the Moretuses.

46 For a separate record of what Galle supplied, see MPM Arch. 70, fols. 88v and 91r (1594); MPM Arch. 71, fols. 60v and 61r-61v; and MPM Arch. 118, p. 71 (cf. fig. 7.8).

47 MPM Arch. 56, fol. 19r; and MPM Arch. 243, fol. 10v, respectively.

48 MPM Arch. 240, fol. 159r (Barbé's shipments); and Bowen and Imhof 2022, pp. 7–8 and 10–12, for De Mallery's contacts with French booksellers and print dealers.

49 MPM Arch. 216, fol. 42r (one package sent to Firens in 1609); MPM Arch. 180, fol. 202v, and MPM Arch. 217, fol. 57v (one package sent to Tavernier both in 1608 and in 1610, respectively). See Préaud et al. 1987 for basic information on Parisian print publishers active during the Ancien Régime.

50 MPM Arch. 220, fol. 209v; and MPM Arch. 221, fol. 83r, respectively. In both cases, Tavernier is noted as staying with Galle.

51 See Bowen and Imhof 2022, pp. 10 and 12; and Chapter 6 for these transactions.

52 New Holl. De Jode, part V, p. xlviii.

53 MPM Arch. 224, fol. 20v; and MPM Arch. 243, fol. 10v, respectively.

54 See MPM Arch. 240, fols. 159r and 166r, for these examples; and MPM Arch. 237, fol. 66v, for when the Moretuses sent Marin three packages of prints in 1629 via the Nancy bookseller Jacques Harpin. In other instances, Marin purchased assorted liturgical editions from the Moretuses (as Justus Sadeler had). See, for example, MPM Arch. 235, fol. 131r, and MPM Arch. 236, fol. 15r, for Marin's purchases; and Bowen 2022b, pp. 380–83, for Sadeler's.

55 See Chapter 3 for Plantin's shipment of some seventy-five of Galle's print series (valued at more than 112 fl.) to his own shop in Paris between 1573 and 1577.

56 For Van Zwevenseel, see MPM Arch. 110, fol. 15 (the start of their trade); and MPM Arch. 133, fol. 6 (the end of their trade). For Scheffer, see MPM Arch. 40, fol. 80 (the start of their trade); and MPM Arch. 101, fol. 41 (the end of their trade).

57 For example: MPM Arch. 172, fol. 185r, and MPM Arch. 217, fol. 144r (Van Zwevenseel); MPM Arch. 63, fols. 39v and 73v (canons for Scheffer); and MPM Arch. 71, fol. 14r, and MPM Arch. 217, fol. 227r (Scheffer's specific print purchases in 1594 and 1610, respectively).

58 MPM Arch. 74, fol. 86r.

59 See, for example, MPM Arch. 69, fol. 12v (1592); and MPM Arch. 71, fol. 1v (1594), where the prints are identified as "taille douce".

60 See MPM Arch. 111, fol. 25, for the transition in the management of De Tollenaer's business; and MPM Arch. 129, fol. 26, for the end of the widow's transactions in 1617. See Appendix 1, TG-14 for this and earlier examples of the sale of this series.

61 See MPM Arch. 17, fol. 406 (the start of their trade); and MPM Arch. 132, fol. 125 (the end of their trade).

62 MPM Arch. 73, fol. 105v (1596); and MPM Arch. 177, fol. 106v (1605), for example.

63 See MPM Arch. 110, fol. 178 (the start of their trade in Kortrijk); and MPM Arch. 111, fol. 120 (the end of their trade in Ghent).

64 MPM Arch. 70, fols. 13r-13v, for an example of a standard purchase (1593); MPM Arch. 74, fol. 9v, for a purchase of colored and plain prints in 1597; and MPM Arch. 21, fol. 182 rht, for the relative size of the plain prints.

65 For the start and end of Boulet's transactions, see MPM Arch. 17, fol. 83; and MPM Arch. 111, fol. 146. For this sampling of his print purchases, see MPM Arch. 63, fols. 65r-65v (Virorum series), and 69v and 84v (canons); MPM Arch. 64, fols. 105v (Huberti), 116r (twenty-five prints from Galle and fifty from Van Luyck); and MPM Arch. 65, fol. 45v (Galle and De Jode).

66 MPM Arch. 72, fol. 195v, for example.

67 MPM Arch. 178, fol. 194r (payment to Galle); and Chapter 5 on Collaert and Du Puis.

68 MPM Arch. 221, fol. 148v (1614: package from H. Wierix); and MPM Arch. 222, fol. 19v (packages from H. Wierix and T. Galle).

69 For the beginning and end of Du Puis's transactions with the Moretuses, see MPM Arch. 111, fol. 28; and MPM Arch. 133, fol. 46. For the Moretuses' last transactions involving Collaert, see MPM Arch. 223, fol. 112r.

70 MPM Arch. 222, fol. 70r (Wierix package). For the beginning and end of Morel's trade with the Moretuses, see MPM Arch. 129, fol. 85; and MPM Arch. 132, fol. 159.

71 MPM Arch. 223, fol. 112r (1616 shipment to Du Puis via Morel); MPM Arch. 222, fol. 136r (request from Morel to Moretuses to pay Galle 9 fl. in his name in 1615); and MPM Arch. 230, fol. 203r, and MPM Arch. 233, fol. 143v (shipments of packages of prints from Snijders to Morel in 1623 and 1626, respectively).

72 For the start and end of his trade (in 1643) with the Moretuses, see MPM Arch. 129, fol. 9; and MPM Arch. 133, fol. 296. For the shipment of isolated packages from Van Merlen, see MPM Arch. 224, fol. 164r; and MPM Arch. 225, fol. 7r.

73 MPM Arch. 232, fol. 33v (packages from Snijders), and MPM Arch. 235, fol. 3v (payment from Moretuses to Snijders of 20 fl. for Ouwerx); MPM Arch. 224, fol. 164r, and MPM Arch. 225, fol. 7r (Van Merlen); MPM Arch. 233, fol. 26v (shipment to Ouwerx of books from Balthasar Moretus I via Boel in 1626), MPM Arch. 235, fol. 85v, and MPM Arch. 239, fol. 25v (payment by Balthasar Moretus to Boel of 25 fl. in Ouwerx's name in both 1628 and 1631); and MPM Arch. 231, fol. 212v (Van Wolsschaten package of prints).

74 See, for example, MPM Arch. 233, fols. 54r-54v (1626); and MPM Arch. 239, fols. 12v and 13r (1631).

75 MPM Arch. 234, fol. 165v (purchase), and MPM Arch. 1106, fol. 66r (supply) (both in 1627); and MPM Arch. 235, fol. 31r (1628 purchase).

76 MPM Arch. 244, fol. 129v. This purchase is discussed in Bowen 2017.

77 MPM Arch. 110, fol. 162 (the start of trade between Jean Valentin I and Jan Moretus I); and MPM Arch. 133, fol. 286 (the end of Jean III's trade with Balthasar II).

78 MPM Arch. 67, fol. 127r (1590); and MPM Arch. 72, fols. 101v and 154v (1595).

79 MPM Arch. 176, fol. 180v (1604 canon purchase); MPM Arch. 179, fol. 160r, and MPM Arch. 1104, fol. 53r (purchase and supply of Collaert's prints); and MPM Arch. 220, fols. 154r and 155r (purchase and supply of Galle's prints). See Appendix 1, TG-29 for the Tree of Human Life.

80 MPM Arch. 226, fols. 135r-135v; and MPM Arch. 220, fols. 154r and 155r, respectively, where the Moretuses added an exceptional, small markup on the larger sale of prints in bulk.

81 See, for example, MPM Arch. 245, fol. 47v; and MPM Arch. 248, fol. 68r.

82 MPM Arch. 228, fol. 157v (1621); MPM Arch. 238, fol. 107v (1630); MPM Arch. 240, fol. 176r (1632); MPM Arch. 243, fols. 40v and 114r (1635 purchases); MPM Arch. 1107, fols. 55v and 60r (1635 supply); MPM Arch. 240, fol. 29r, and MPM Arch. 1107, fol. 23r (1632 purchase and supply of assorted prints after Rubens); MPM Arch. 240, fols. 157v and 162v (1632 purchase of the Battle of the Amazons); and MPM Arch. 241, fol. 32r, and MPM Arch. 1107, fol. 33r (purchase and supply of the Palazzi di Genova in 1633). See also Bowen 2017 for more on purchases of prints after Rubens, including by Leonard, and p. 292, in particular, for other sales of the Palazzi di Genova series to Kaspar Förster, with prices that indicate which volume Leonard bought. See also Appendix 1, TG-5 and Chapter 5 for more on the Goose Game.

83 For exchanges between Balthasar and the Galles, see, for example, MPM Arch. 247, fols. 4r, 47r, 57v, 158v, 159v, 166v, and 183r; and Bowen and Imhof 2010.

84 See MPM Arch. 229, fol. 206r (Boel); MPM Arch. 232, fol. 49v (Snijders); MPM Arch. 235, fol. 130v (Cnobbaert); MPM Arch. 238, fol. 41v, and MPM Arch. 241, fol. 24v (Van Lanckvelt); MPM Arch. 239, fol. 194r, and MPM Arch. 249, fol. 61r (T. and J. Galle, respectively); MPM Arch. 243, fol. 197v (Barbé); MPM Arch. 246, fol. 43v (Voet); and MPM Arch. 235, fol. 130v (1628) and MPM Arch. 245, fol. 118v (1637) (Aertssens).

85 MPM Arch. 219, fol. 105r, for this sale; and Appendix 1, PJ-3 for the print.

86 MPM Arch. 139, fol. 155 ("eenighe beldenkens en peperkoek" for Elisabeth); and MPM Arch. 166, fol. 101v (Michelle's prints).

87 For the rates Galle charged for his prints in bulk, see Appendix 1.

88 MPM Arch. 128, fol. 208 lft (Pisani's purchases); MPM Arch. 222, fol. 18r (T. Galle's supply of De Bry's work, which was resold at cost); and MPM Arch. 224, fols. 139r-139v (Collaert's supply and Simonetti's purchase).

89 MPM Arch. 172, fol. 183v (Vander Dilft); and MPM Arch. 171, fol. 96r (Galle's series: Appendix 1, TG-7), and MPM Arch. 172, fol. 153r (Sadeler's series: Appendix 1, SD-2), both for Halmale.

90 MPM Arch. 67, fols. 3v and 13v (supply and purchase for Garnier in 1590, discussed in Chapter 4); and MPM Arch. 70, fol. 16v (Tisnacq in 1593).

91 MPM Arch. 217, fol. 11v. See Appendix 1, SD-1 for this series.

92 MPM Arch. 142, p. 2. See Appendix 1, TG-11 for this series.

93 MPM Arch. 137, p. 51, for Balthasar's letter; and MPM Arch. 224, fol. 200v, for the list of prints sent, along with their individual prices.

94 MPM Arch. 216, fol. 170v, where the identification of one subject as "Jesus matris delicie" by Anton Wierix may refer to an image of the Holy Family by Anton Wierix that is similarly identified by this phrase in an earlier record (cf. Appendix 1, WX-6).

95 MPM Arch. 226, fol. 95v (18 June 1619 sales record); and MPM Arch. 137, p. 128 (letter from Balthasar Moretus I of 18 June 1619 to Isabella's secretary, Suarez).

96 MPM Arch. 226, fol. 134v (3 September 1619 sales record); MPM Arch. 137, p. 134 (letter from Balthasar Moretus I of 28 August 1619 to Isabella's secretary, Suarez).

97 MPM Arch. 171, fol. 179r, and MPM Arch. 71, fol. 169r (purchase by papal nuncios Ottavio Mirto Frangipani and Innocentius Malvasia of Galle's Illustrium series and altar cards, respectively); MPM Arch. 75, fol. 128r, and MPM Arch. 171, fol. 3v (purchase by Abbot Vaast de Grenet at St Bertin of an altar card and unspecified prints from T. Galle, respectively); and MPM Arch. 180, fol. 23r (purchase by Canon Guillaume Wargnirius in Leuven of seventy prints of St Theresa). See also Bowen 2022a for examples of print purchases by Canon Hieronymus van Winghe.

98 MPM Arch. 247, fol. 171v; and MPM Arch. 246, fols. 35v and 47v, respectively. Numerous other examples can be found in Appendix 2, among the clergy listed under the southern Netherlands.

99 For an overview of Galle's dealings with the Van Winghes and their associates, see MPM Arch. 218, fol. 71r (Dominicans); and Chapter 5.

100 MPM Arch. 229, fol. 126r, and MPM Arch. 131, fol. 138, for this and other transactions involving the Abbey of Orval and Michaeli.

101 MPM Arch. 231, fol. 195v. Snijders' dealings with the Raesfeld-Van Dale family of booksellers is discussed in greater detail in Chapter 6 and below.

102 See Appendix 1, PG-67, PG-82, and AC-9 for the first three series mentioned. The last cannot be identified with certainty. MPM Arch. 173, fol. 100r, and MPM Arch. 175, fol. 15r (purchases of prints by P. Galle for fellow Franciscans, as well as some paintings); MPM Arch. 174, fol. 39r (supply) and fols. 40r, 140r, and 152r (purchases of Collaert's series for others); MPM Arch. 174, fol. 186v (prints from Huberti for the nun Peryne des Derderen); MPM Arch. 174, fol. 180v, and MPM Arch. 175, fol. 93v (exchanges of prints involving a nun, Anne Groevens, affiliated with the Poor Clares); and MPM Arch. 178, fol. 128r (purchase of a woodcut image of St Joanna for the Order of the Annunciation).

103 See Chapter 6 for this purchase; and Chapter 8 for a more detailed examination of the Jesuit's use of printed images.

104 MPM Arch. 223, fol. 33v, and MPM Arch. 232, fol. 36v (Rosweydus, 1616 and 1625, respectively); and MPM Arch. 71, fol. 57r (Scribani, 1594).

105 MPM Arch. 72, fol. 158v (1595); and MPM Arch. 1104, fol. 5r (1604).

106 See Thijs 1993, pp. 81–95, for other examples.

107 MPM Arch. 221, fols. 93r and 161v, respectively. See Chapter 9 for the purchase of ink in Frankfurt and potential shortages in Antwerp.

108 MPM Arch. 221, fols. 93r-93v; and MPM Arch. 221, fols. 143v and 182v. See Appendix 1 under Galle for his bulk print prices.

109 MPM Arch. 129, fol. 79 (the start of their trade); and MPM Arch. 133, fol. 245 (the end of their trade).

110 For example: MPM Arch. 232, fol. 126r (payments of 30 fl. to Barbé and 60 fl. to Snijders in 1625); MPM Arch. 233, fol. 57r (payment of 90 fl. to Snijders in 1626); MPM Arch. 231, fol. 163r, and MPM Arch. 244, fol. 48r (shipments of packages from Snijders to Geubels in 1624 and 1636, respectively).

111 MPM Arch. 219, fol. 24r, and MPM Arch. 128, fols. 85 and 86 (Bruegel's payments); and MPM Arch. 233, fol. 67v (Mathijs).

112 MPM Arch. 235, fol. 165v (1628); MPM Arch. 238, fol. 155v (1630); and MPM Arch. 247, fol. 179v (1639).

113 MPM Arch. 239, fols. 124v and 126v (Charleville); and MPM Arch. 243, fols. 69v (Antwerp) and 142v (Geldre). See Appendix 1, TG-13 and TG-6 for these series.

114 See Chapter 6 for the former; and MPM Arch. 242, fols. 101r and 102v for the latter.

115 On the Capuchins in the Low Countries and their work in the northern Netherlands in particular, see Hildebrand 1945–1956, vol. VI, pp. 13–274 ("De Hollandse missie"). For examples of these purchases, see MPM Arch. 235, fol. 140r (initial order in 1628); MPM Arch. 238, fol. 18r (1630); and MPM Arch. 244, fol. 31r (1636).

116 On Le Roy and Van Gouda, see Hildebrand 1945–1956, vol. VII, pp. 197 and 288, respectively; and Ibid., vol. VI, pp. 135–57. For examples of shipments of packages of images to Van Gouda and Le Roy, see MPM Arch. 246, fol. 87v (supplied anonymously); and MPM Arch. 245, fol. 57r (supplied by a certain Sr de Nef), respectively. See MPM Arch. 1107, fol. 104r (supply), and MPM Arch. 247, fol. 53v (purchase) of De Jode's Tree (see Appendix 1, PJ-2).

117 MPM Arch. 129, fol. 91 (the start of their trade), which continued into the 1650s (see, e.g., MPM Arch. 133, fol. 324).

118 MPM Arch. 225, fol. 126r (1618); MPM Arch. 236, fol. 2r; MPM Arch. 115, fol. 62 rht (1629); and MPM Arch. 246, fol. 154v (1638).

119 MPM Arch. 236, fol. 2r, and MPM Arch. 237, fol. 69v (1629); and MPM Arch. 242, fols. 78r-78v, and MPM Arch. 1107, fol. 44v, for the purchase and supply of six canons from both Theodore Galle and Michael Snijders in 1634.

120 MPM Arch. 146, pp. 227–28, and 241–42, letters from Balthasar Moretus I to Förster, dated 17 February 1636 and 15 May 1636, respectively.

121 See Bogucka 1973 on this topic, and pp. 434–40 on the trade with Gdańsk (Danzig) in particular. See the correspondence between Jan Moretus I and Thomas Sailly in 1603 concerning the transfer of funds from Kraków to Gdańsk, Gdańsk to Hamburg, and Hamburg to Antwerp (MPM Arch. 12, pp. 220–23).

122 Bogucka 1973, pp. 434–37.

123 Förster's, Schedelius's, and Claessens's acquisitions are all discussed in greater detail below, while the export of De Mallery's and Snijders's work is discussed in Chapters 5 and 6, respectively.

124 See MPM Arch. 60, fols. 59r-60r, for Gisser's purchase; and MPM Arch. 110, fol. 87 lft, for his identification as a bookseller.

125 MPM Arch. 73, fol. 159v, for Gabrielli's purchase and Galle's supply of the same. Galle's supply of these prints is also confirmed in MPM Arch. 21, fol. 248 rht. See Appendix 1 under Wierix for a sampling of their bulk print prices, which usually ranged from .75 st. to 2 st. per print.

126 MPM Arch. 173, fol. 204r (1601); and MPM Arch. 174, fols. 11v, 14r, and 17v (supply by Galle, Collaert, and Wierix, respectively), and 29r (purchase by Gabrielli). See also Chapters 5 and 6 for more on Gabrielli's 1602 purchase.

127 Compare Holl. Dutch & Flemish, vol. LXVI, nos. 1837 and 1838.

128 MPM Arch. 69, fols. 36v-38v, for her first such shipment in 1592; and MPM Arch. 171, fols. 129v-136r, for a similar transaction in 1599, which included several copies of Theodore Galle's Illustrium imagines ex antiquis marmoribus series (discussed in Chapter 5).

129 The main exception here is Jan Moretus I's shipment of a package of books and a selection of impressions of prints that he had commissioned for the illustration of an exceptional book of hours in 4° to Adamus Steynhalen, a chaplain for the king of Poland, in Kraków within a bale marked for Jacques de Jode (MPM Arch. 176, fols. 88r and 90v).

130 MPM Arch. 179, fol. 111v, where it is noted that Claessens's wife, the daughter of De Jode's widow, was then in Antwerp: "sa femme la fille de la vefve de Jode presente en Anvers"; and MPM Arch. 127, fol. 245, for Claessens' succession of Jacques de Jode in their accounts. For Claessens' identification as a Gdańsk merchant with a father, Nicolas Pauwelsen, in Haarlem, see MPM Arch. 127, fol. 248 rht; and MPM Arch. 759, fol. 97 lft.

131 MPM Arch. 759, fol. 97 (the start of Claessens' transactions with the Moretuses); MPM Arch. 179, fol. 55v ("tableau de toille"); and fol. 111v ("3 pacquets de figures et aultres marchandises"), respectively.

132 MPM Arch. 219, fol. 172v (1612); and MPM Arch. 220, fols. 42r, 142r, and 191r, where the shipment of August 1613 (fol. 142r) is recorded as also containing one unspecified package prepared by the Antwerp Jesuit Rosweydus Heribertus for his fellow Jesuit Laurentius Nicolai Norvegus.

133 MPM Arch. 223, fols. 111r and 123v (shipment to Claessens); MPM Arch. 128, fol. 258, for the identification of Olimaerts; and MPM Arch. 128, fol. 198 rht, for examples of Olimaerts (or his widow) making payments in Claessens's name.

134 MPM Arch. 231, fol. 58r, MPM Arch. 240, fol. 59r, MPM Arch. 235, fol. 51v, and MPM Arch. 234, fol. 49r, respectively, for the packages sent; and MPM Arch. 230, fol. 170r, MPM Arch. 233, fol. 165v, MPM Arch. 234, fol. 58v, MPM Arch. 235, fol. 52v, and MPM Arch. 236, fol. 6r, for these payments.

135 MPM Arch. 230, fol. 70v; and MPM Arch. 233, fol. 99r, respectively. For several years starting in 1621–1622, Van den Eynde was listed among the "liefhebbers" (art enthusiasts) of Antwerp's Guild of St Luke (Rombouts and Van Lerius 1872, vol. I, p. 580 (for the guild year 1621–1622)).

136 See MPM Arch. 240, fol. 59r, for Balthasar's last shipment of books to Claessens; and MPM Arch. 142, p. 337, for the first letter (dated 21 March 1633) of several Balthasar wrote to Claessens concerning his debt.

137 See MPM Arch. 131, fol. 64 lft, for one early example of their trade in feathers from 7 September 1621; and MPM Arch. 142, pp. 134 and 136, for correspondence from June 1630 concerning the sale of leather in Claessens's name. See MPM Arch. 235, fols. 17v and 52v, for an example of the sale of seven packages of feathers via the merchant Michiel van Trist, the proceeds of which were used to pay 219 fl. 17 st. to Snijders and 33 fl. 10 st. to Van Merlen.

138 MPM Arch. 151, p. 72 (Balthasar II's response on 18 April 1643 to Claessens's offer of powder); and MPM Arch. 134, fol. 23 rht (declaration of Claessens's bankruptcy, sometime after 13 May 1644).

139 MPM Arch. 146, pp. 227–28, letter from Balthasar Moretus I to Kaspar Förster, dated 17 February 1636: "Mihi antehac isthic negotium cum D. Paulo Classens, qui iampridem negotiationem librorum mecum intermisit; deinde cum D. Ernesto Kruse negotiari incepi, at is solis fere Reip. Dantiscano finibus se continet, nec in variis amplissimi Poloniae regni ditionis libris dispergit".

140 On the Förster family of booksellers, see Heitjan 1975. For a reference to Georg Förster being in Antwerp, see, for example, MPM Arch 133, fol. 209 lft, under 13 September 1636; and MPM Arch. 133, fols. 307 (the start of Georg's accounts in July 1643, when he was in Antwerp), and 282 (the end of Kaspar's accounts in May 1643).

141 MPM Arch. 245, fols. 70r (supply) and 73r (purchase).

142 MPM Arch. 246, fol. 64r; MPM Arch. 247, fols. 107r-107v; and MPM Arch. 248, fols. 33v (supply) and 41v (purchase), respectively.

[143] See, for example, MPM Arch. 249, fols. 165v (supply, along with MPM Arch. 1107, fol. 129v) and 167r (purchase). Both works are described in Appendix 1, PPR-2 and JG-2. See also Bowen 2017, and p. 292 in particular, for the Försters' purchases of the Palazzi di Genova series.

[144] MPM Arch. 249, fols. 134v (supply) and 136v (purchase).

[145] MPM Arch. 150, p. 92, letter from Balthasar II to Schedelius, dated 20 October 1641.

[146] MPM Arch. 150, p. 329, letter from Balthasar II to Schedelius, dated 29 April 1651.

[147] MPM Arch. 364, fols. 12v-13v. This order is discussed in greater detail in Chapter 2.

[148] See Appendix 2 for assorted examples.

[149] These transactions are discussed in detail in Chapter 9.

[150] See Reske 2015, p. 635, on Raesfeld; and MPM Arch. 43I, fol. 145, for his initial contact with the Moretuses.

[151] MPM Arch. 219, fols. 160v (supply) and 161r (purchase).

[152] MPM Arch. 219, fol. 203v; MPM Arch. 759, fol. 114 lft (supply and purchase in December 1612); MPM Arch. 222, fols. 44v-45r (purchase and supply in 1615); MPM Arch. 223, fol. 215v (purchase in 1616); and MPM Arch. 224, fols. 66r and 67r (purchase and supply in 1617, including assorted rosaries).

[153] Reske 2015, pp. 636–37, on Van Dale and B. Raesfeld. See MPM Arch. 760, fol. 40 rht (the first reference to Van Dale in the Moretuses' accounts with the Raesfelds in May 1618) and 159 lft (the transition to Bernhard Raesfeld in the fall of 1628).

[154] MPM Arch. 225, fols. 13r (January 1618), and 83r-84r (supply and purchase of prints in May 1618).

[155] See Reske 2015, p. 636, on Van Dale's origins; and the discussion below for transactions involving his sisters in Antwerp.

[156] See, for example, MPM Arch. 226, fol. 103v, for purchases from De Mallery, Van Merlen, and Snijders in July 1619, when Van Dale bought more prints from Van Merlen than De Mallery. See MPM Arch. 230, fol. 144v, and MPM Arch. 233, fol. 83v, for the shipment of single packages from Boel for Van Dale in 1623 and 1626, respectively. See MPM Arch. 231, fol. 195v, for Snijders' eleven packages for Van Dale, in addition to the general discussion of Snijders in Chapter 6.

[157] See, for example, MPM Arch. 760, fol. 109 rht, where Van Dale is recorded as having used his account with the Moretuses to loan his sister Janneken 240 fl., in addition to making subsequent payments to both Digna and Janneken. See also MPM Arch. 232, fol. 174r, for a shipment of books for Van Dale via the Cologne bookseller Peter Henning, including a package of one or more paintings supplied by Van Dale's sister Digna.

[158] MPM Arch. 753, fol. 22 lft (book purchases via Frankfurt); and MPM Arch. 237, fol. 24v ("200 belekens afgeset op perkement heel scoon" (200 illuminated images on parchment, highly attractive), noted in the Antwerp accounts).

[159] MPM Arch. 238, fol. 27r.

[160] MPM Arch. 237, fol. 50r.

[161] Reske 2015, pp. 636–37, on agreements with the Jesuits.

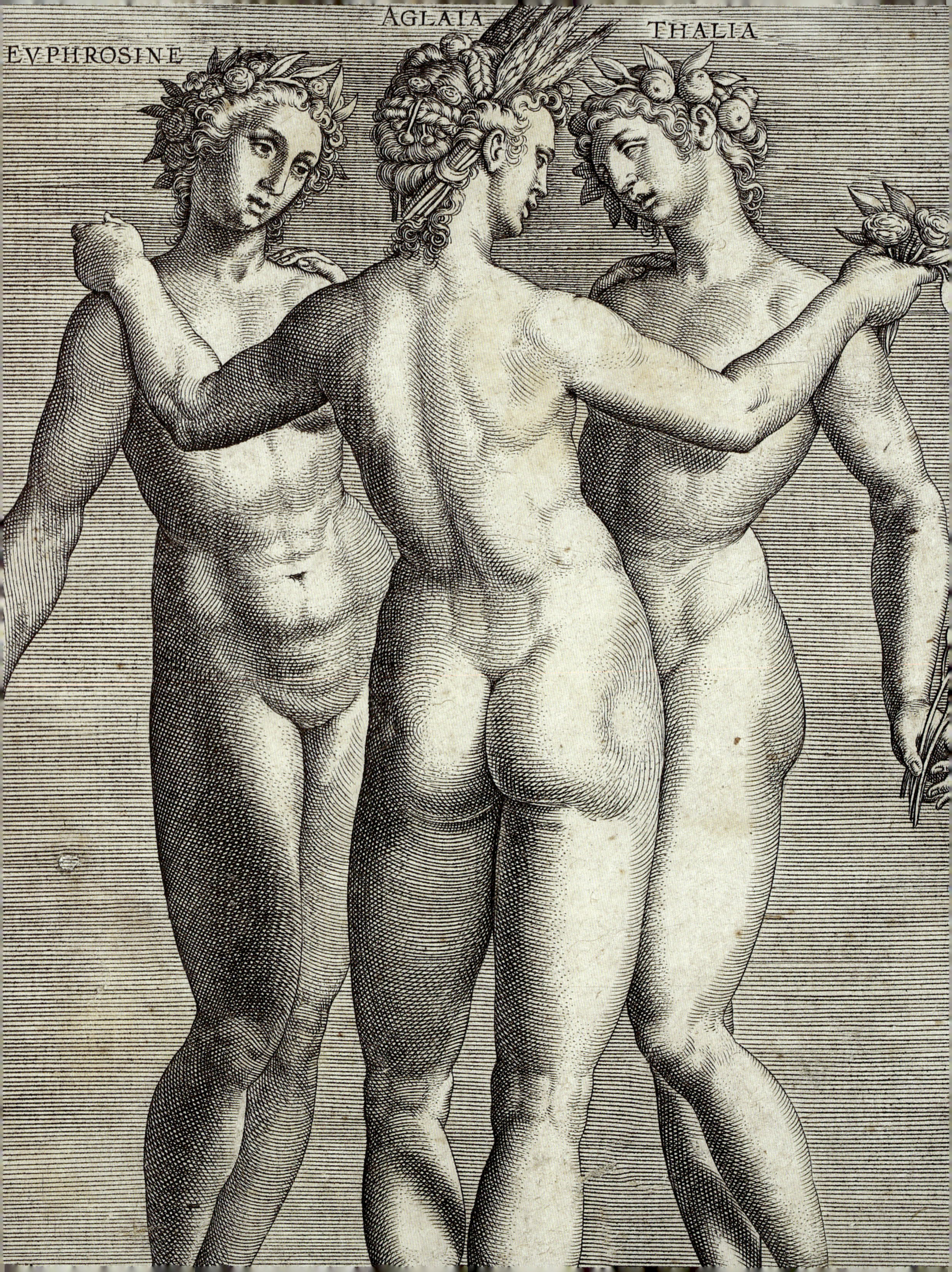
EVPHROSINE
AGLAIA
THALIA

CHAPTER 8

THE PROSPERING PRINT TRADE IN COLOGNE

> The remarkable book trade in Cologne, where countless beautiful books and pictures are conceived and printed, with which the Catholic faith has been and is still being greatly promoted throughout Germany.[1]

Detail of fig. 8.3:
Anonymous, *The Three Graces*, s.a., engraving.

This contemporary assertion of the immense importance of Cologne's trade in Catholic books and imagery in the early seventeenth century was no idle boast. Ulrich Zell's establishment of the first printing business in Cologne by 1466 was soon imitated by several other printing/publishing entrepreneurs. In the early sixteenth century, Cologne had become the most important city for printing texts throughout the entire Holy Roman Empire, in addition to prospering on an international scale. Cologne subsequently fell behind a few other German cities in the total production of texts by the end of the sixteenth century – Frankfurt am Main, Leipzig, Strasbourg, and Basel, for example. However, the Protestant orientation of these cities assured that Cologne remained the preeminent leader in the production and distribution of books (and prints) in support of the Catholic faith for the critical decades of the confessional battles in Germany, which continued through the mid-seventeenth century.[2] That this supremacy was recognized at the time is suggested by its inclusion in the text accompanying this view of Cologne (fig. 8.1), where it appears as a standard, common-place observation for anyone describing Cologne's essential attributes.

Absent from these self-promoting remarks, however, is Cologne's simultaneous significance at the turn of the seventeenth century as a vital market for both books and prints from the Catholic, Spanish Netherlands (the southern Low Countries), where Antwerp still reigned as the leading center of production. One unexpected but striking aspect of this trade is the participation of sundry Cologne booksellers, as well as many print publishers there, in the acquisition of remarkable quantities of prints from assorted Antwerp printmakers in the first half of the seventeenth century. The result was an active procurement of images from Antwerp print dealers as of 1588 that, as of 1606, was supplemented by regular purchases of prints from the Moretuses in Antwerp by various agents in Cologne. Combined, these transactions rivalled Plantin's and the Moretuses' involvement in the market for prints in Paris; the essential difference was the greater variety of individuals who were thus engaged in the print trade in Cologne. But in order to appreciate this phenomenon fully, one must understand both why the export of prints from Antwerp to Cologne was, at this time, a ready option and why the demand for prints in Cologne by the early seventeenth century would have encouraged their import on such a stunning scale.

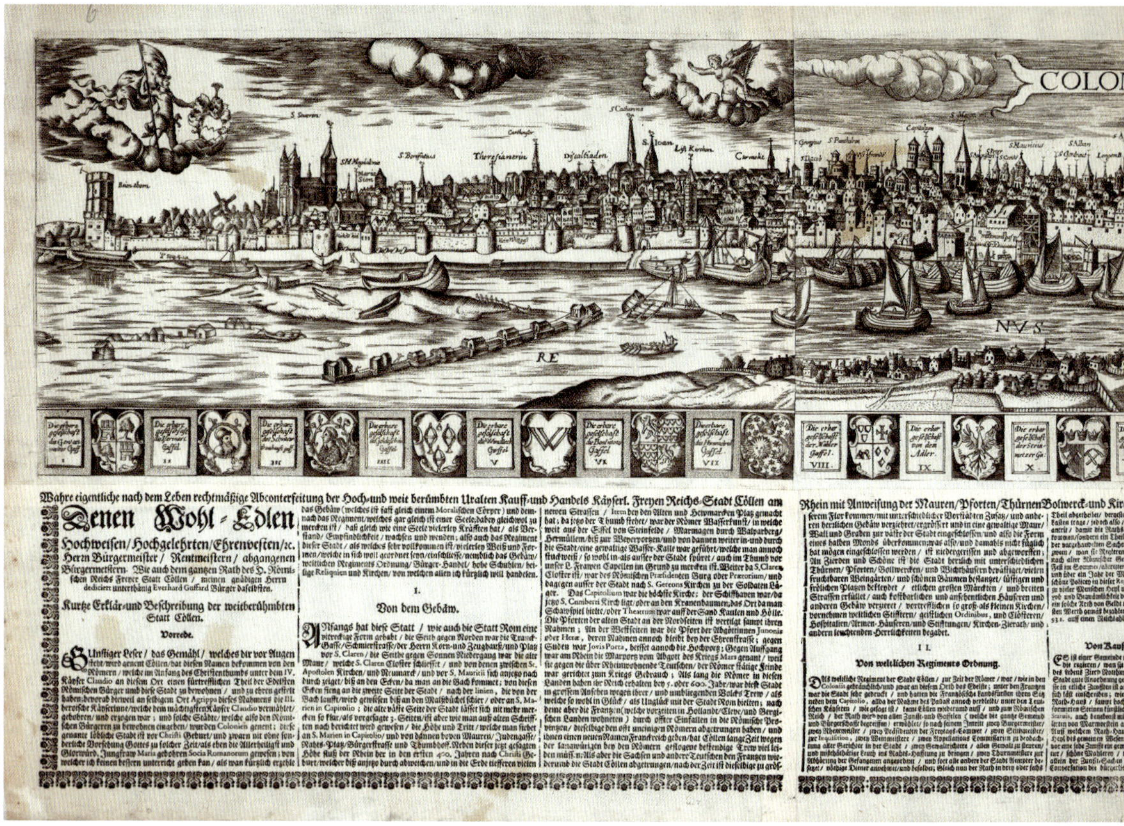

8.1 Anonymous, *View of Cologne*, published by Henricus Rieger in 1619, letterpress with an engraving on six sheets, 350 × 1090 mm (all six sheets). Darmstadt, Universitäts- und Landesbibliothek Darmstadt: his Ansichten 3949/90.

LONG-ESTABLISHED CONNECTIONS BETWEEN ANTWERP AND COLOGNE

The noteworthy prominence of Cologne among German cities as an exceptional market for prints from Antwerp is a logical result of a mix of economic, political, and cultural factors. The foundations for this flourishing trade between Antwerp and Cologne extend back to the thirteenth century, well before the traffic in printed texts and images began.

Because of a combination of favorable locations along major waterways and prudent economic policies of local governments, a mutually advantageous economic exchange between Cologne and Antwerp was established in the Middle Ages. On the one hand, Cologne was the gateway for the distribution of goods within Germany and beyond via ship and barge as well as via several important land routes. On the other hand, Antwerp was an important link for German merchants dealing in goods originating not only from the Low Countries, but also from out of London, Spain, and Portugal. During the Middle Ages, the essential products traded were Rhine wine alongside dry goods from the area around Cologne, and fish, leather products, pelts, salt, and butter from Antwerp. Over the course of the fifteenth century, Antwerp became an active transit point and finishing center for cloth, which resulted in an increase in the export of these wares to Cologne, from where they would have been distributed elsewhere in Germany. By the end of the fifteenth century, most of Antwerp's exports to cities in Germany went to Cologne, while merchants from Cologne routinely traveled to Antwerp and were generally the best-represented subgroup of German merchants in the city into the sixteenth century.[3] This preponderance of Cologne merchants in Antwerp is telling because in the course of the sixteenth century, the range of cities within Germany receiving goods from Antwerp expanded, and the relative values of goods shipped shifted so that Cologne was no longer the single most important market. Nevertheless, the

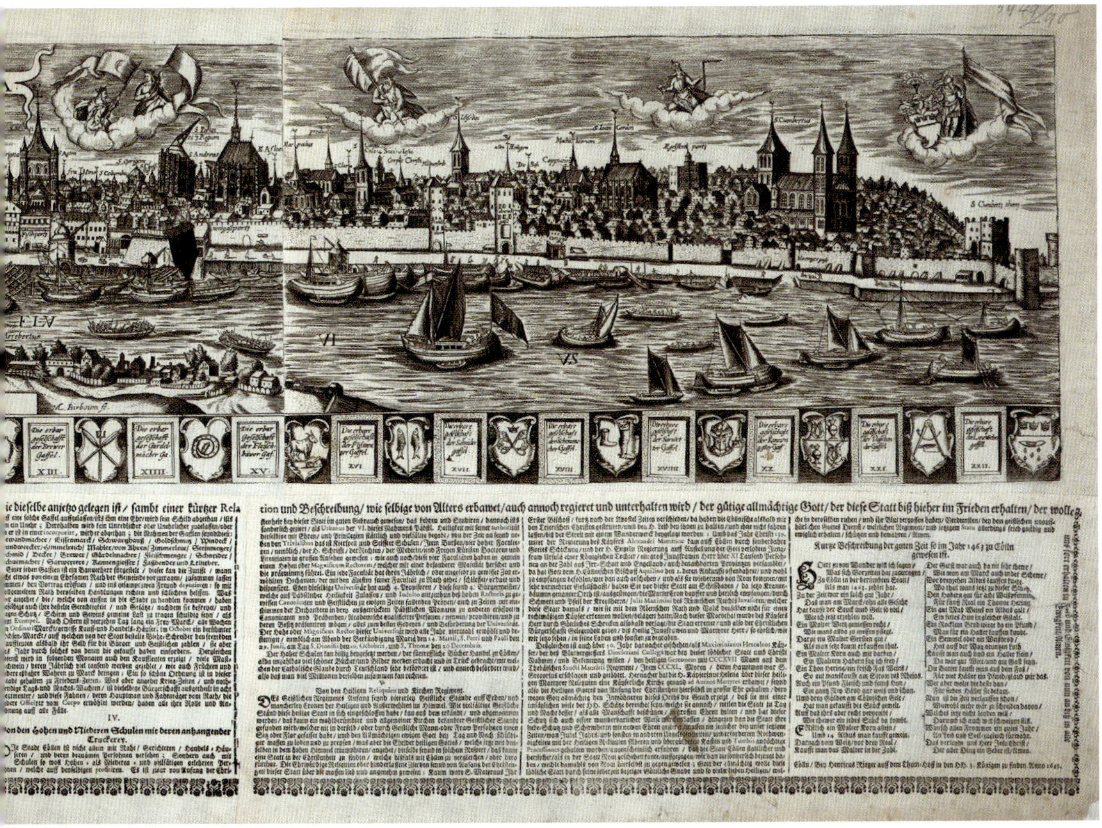

overland route to Cologne (the "Keulse baan") remained the most frequently traveled route between Antwerp and Germany. Consequently, Cologne now served both as a useful "transshipment center" and as a final destination. Moreover, Antwerp remained an important link in Cologne's international distribution network for much of the sixteenth century, and the bond of long-established mercantile ties was likewise still strong.[4]

Though often omitted in discussions of the quantifiable exchange of goods between Antwerp and Cologne, the significance of the trade in books and prints is attested to in other ways. Within decades of Johann Gutenberg's successful printing of books with movable type, book printers and booksellers from Cologne were establishing branch offices in Antwerp, while books printed in Antwerp were simultaneously being sold in Cologne and other German cities. Cologne's publishers would have benefited from the long-established trade routes between Antwerp and Cologne, including the opportunity to ship heavy loads of books via the waterways connecting the two cities. The desire to maintain good relations among those involved in the book trade was logical. While the importance of printing businesses grew in other German cities during the later sixteenth and seventeenth centuries, Cologne continued to dominate the production and distribution of texts supporting the Catholic faith for the Holy Roman Empire as a whole. Antwerp enjoyed a similarly prominent position in northern Europe. In the late sixteenth century, this was due in particular to the fame of the Plantin-Moretus Press, which was renowned, along with several other publishers in the Low Countries, for the publication of a variety of essential Catholic texts..[5] For example, one of the most prominent of these Cologne-Antwerp business establishments was founded by Franz Birckman, who originally dealt in books, spices, and herbs in Antwerp in 1513 and whose printing and bookselling activities developed into a successful international business with offices in Cologne, Antwerp, and London. Arnold Mylius, who managed the Birckman family office in Antwerp from 1565 to 1577, maintained regular business relations with the

Plantin-Moretus Press and other local businesses. After his move to Cologne, he became not only a prominent figure in the book trade there, but also in the city government. Active, and often personal, business connections between the two cities continued into the seventeenth century, when, for instance, new generations of printers and booksellers in Cologne found an apprenticeship in Antwerp a worthwhile means of learning the trade.[6] Moreover, while Antwerp may have lost some ground to other burgeoning centers of printing in seventeenth-century Europe, such as Amsterdam, texts supporting the Catholic Counter-Reformation that were published in Antwerp remained sought-after commodities in Cologne. Cologne was not only Germany's center of production for such books, including assorted works by authors from the Spanish-Habsburg Low Countries, but it simultaneously served as the focal point for the distribution of Catholic literature to the rest of Germany.[7]

Just as many individuals involved in the book trade in Cologne found connections with businesses in Antwerp advantageous, artists from the Low Countries periodically traveled to Cologne. For some, Cologne was a convenient stop on routes leading through Germany to Italy. Furthermore, when the Eighty Years' War began in the Low Countries in the mid-sixteenth century, sundry individuals, including several artists, fled to Cologne – a readily accessible destination due to the well-established transportation routes. During the second half of the sixteenth century, Cologne's reception of these artist-émigrés was ambivalent. On the one hand, the government of this Catholic city was wary of Calvinists who might disrupt, and ultimately corrupt, the local citizens in this precarious period of religious affiliation. On the other hand, some members of the city council favored the integration of skilled tradesmen, particularly in sectors where there was little local talent, as was the case among intaglio printmakers. By the end of the sixteenth century, despite the waves of stricter control and repression of non-Catholic immigrants, the vast majority of engravers and art dealers in Cologne had come from the Low Countries.[8] Consequently, it is not surprising that when the Dutch antiquarian Arnold van Buchell purchased numerous prints in Cologne at the end of 1599, his records reveal that prints by artists and print publishers from the Low Countries were commonly available. Moreover, several of the émigrés had important professional connections in Antwerp, for instance the Hogenberg family and Crispijn de Passe.[9] Hence, around the turn of the seventeenth century, anyone who was in Cologne and who was interested in printed images – for personal use, as collector's items, or as commodities for resale – would most likely have come to appreciate the work of Netherlandish printmakers and publishing houses generally and the wealth of Antwerp's exports in particular. At the end of the sixteenth century, Antwerp had recently been reincorporated into the Spanish, Catholic Netherlands and had become a vital protagonist supporting the propagation of the Catholic Counter-Reformation via various means, including a broad range of artistic and literary products.

REVITALIZING THE CATHOLIC FAITH IN COLOGNE AND THE DEMAND FOR PRINTS

Towards the end of the sixteenth century, the revival of the Catholic faith in Cologne became stronger in both conviction and daily practice. In 1595, Ferdinand of Bavaria was named the coadjutor of his uncle Ernest of Bavaria. Trained at the Jesuit college in Ingolstadt and already a canon in several German cities, Ferdinand committed himself to reviving Catholicism in Germany, with a special focus on the archbishopric of Cologne. Already home to the papal nuncio and also the base of operations for the Jesuits in central and northern Germany, Cologne would become the center for the dissemination of the Catholic faith throughout Germany. Over the next two decades, Cologne's government assiduously repressed and evicted any remaining Protestants. Consequently, the ambiguous, semi-tolerant atmosphere of the late sixteenth century was definitively replaced with a fervent, multifaceted program of embedding the teachings of the Catholic church in Cologne's society and of intensifying citizens' engagement with it in a range of ways.[10]

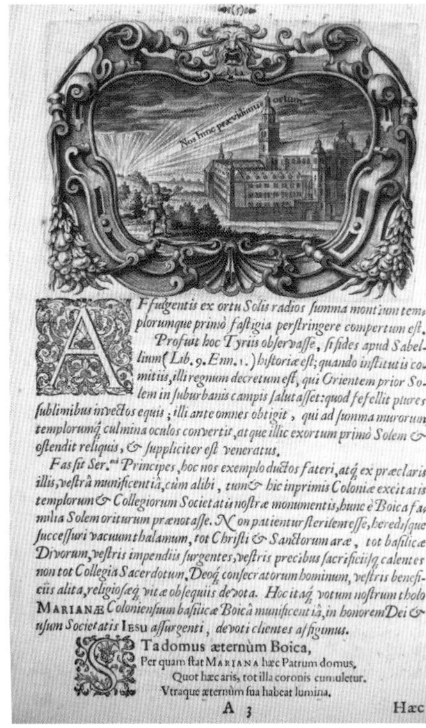
Affulgentis ex ortu Solis radios summa montium templorumque primò fastigia perstringere compertum est.
Profuit hoc Tyriis observasse, si fides apud Sabellium (Lib. 9. Enn. 1.) historiæ est; quando institutis comitiis, illi regnum decretum est, qui Orientem prior Solem in suburbanis campis salutasset: quod fefellit plures sublimibus invectos equis; illi ante omnes obtigit, qui ad summa murorum templorumq; culmina oculos convertit, atque illic exortum primò Solem & ostendit reliquis, & suppliciter est veneratus.
Fas sit Ser.mi Principes, hoc nos exemplo ductos fateri, atq; ex præclaris illis, vestrâ munificentiâ, cùm alibi, tum & hic inprimis Coloniæ excitatis templorum & Collegiorum Societatis nostræ monumentis, hunc è Boica familia Solem oriturum prænotasse. Non patientur sterilem esse, heredisque successuri vacuum thalamum, tot Christi & Sanctorum aræ, tot basilicæ Divorum, vestris impendiis surgentes, vestris precibus sacrificiisq; calentes non tot Collegia Sacerdotum, Deoq; consecratorum hominum, vestris beneficiis alita, religiosæq; vitæ obsequiis devota. Hoc itaq; votum nostrum tholo MARIANÆ Coloniensium basilicæ Boicâ munificentiâ, in honorem Dei & usum Societatis IESU assurgenti, devoti clientes affigimus.
STa domus æternùm Boica,
Per quam stat MARIANA hæc Patrum domus,
Quot hæc aris, tot illa coronis cumuletur.
Vtraque æternùm sua habeat lumina.
A 3 Hæc

8.2 Anonymous, *Jesuit College in Cologne*, intaglio in: *Dies Natalis Serenissimi Infantis et Principis Boiorum, Maximiliani Em[m]anuelis Favoribus Sanctorum, heroum crepundiis, et votis Patrum S.I. coronatus, In solennibus baptismalibus* (Cologne, s.n., 1662). Munich, Bayerische Staatsbibliothek: 2 P.o.germ. 29 f#Beibd.2; VD17 12:653188T.

Although assorted individuals and government bodies contributed to the Catholic revival in Cologne as part of the broader confessional battle within Germany, the activities of the Jesuit college there were fundamental and pervasive. While the Jesuits arrived in Cologne in 1544, they did not exert much influence in the city until 1557, when the supervision of the lower municipal schools came under their control. Even then, the Jesuits did not gain official permission to establish an order in the city until 1582 and did not begin construction of their own church and college until 1618 (fig. 8.2).[11] Nevertheless, the Jesuits vigilantly increased their presence and authority within Cologne in the interim. For example, their educational method was commonly applied to both secondary and higher schools in Cologne, and they actively supported instruction in the catechism for all levels of society. The Jesuits also led the way in the establishment of lay brotherhoods or sodalities with a didactic emphasis, encouraging personal immersion in and study of the Catholic faith, thus attracting hundreds of members in Cologne alone. Such endeavors, along with the organization of processions and pilgrimages, unified different subgroups of the society in the expression of the Catholic faith, both in intimate, personal settings and in the public sphere. Simultaneously, the Jesuits in Cologne routinely sent members to work in other cities in order to support their order's contribution to a far-reaching Catholic revival across Germany.[12]

The development of a library for instruction and as a resource with the most recent publications of an international array of Jesuits was essential and can be traced back to the Jesuits' original settlement in Cologne during the mid-sixteenth century.[13] This project most likely went hand in hand with the purchase of prints that both served the Jesuits' didactic, devotional, and pastoral goals and promoted their order and the reassertion of Catholicism in Germany more generally. The Jesuits' multifaceted interest in imagery from a variety of artists throughout Europe is evident from their substantial collection of prints and drawings that, by the mid-eighteenth century, comprised approximately 27,000 prints and at least 5,000 drawings. Although the majority of the drawings were probably collected during the first half of the eighteenth century, it is commonly believed that most of the prints were purchased earlier. Regrettably, because the Jesuits' collection was confiscated by French troops and sent to Paris in 1794, where nearly 90 percent of the drawings and 80 percent of the prints still remain, it is impossible to reconstruct fully the original contents of the collection.[14] Nevertheless, a catalogue of the entire collection that was compiled in 1778 offers an informative overview, while an online catalogue of nearly 6,000 prints and drawings that were returned to Cologne in 1815 supplies telling examples of individual works that the Jesuits acquired. Together, these resources present an exceptionally well-documented, detailed view of the works on paper amassed by the Jesuit college of Cologne and, by extension, of what other similar institutions might have owned. A consideration of the objects that the Jesuits in Cologne collected and of the potential uses to which their prints may have been put is particularly informative in this context due to the remarkably large number of prints made or published by several seventeenth-century Antwerp print publishers that remain in the collection today. In particular, it comprises some 700 works by Charles de Mallery, Hieronymus

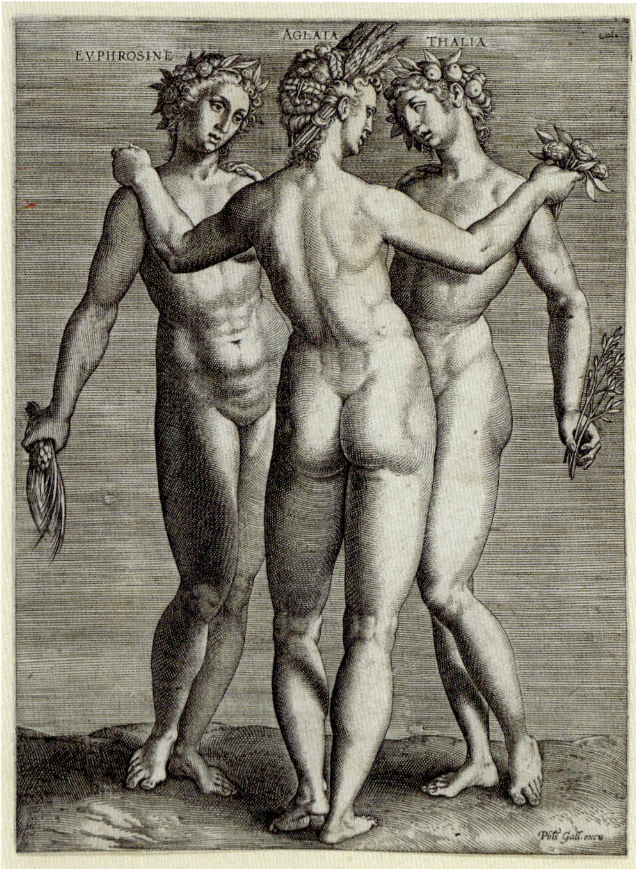

8.3 Anonymous, *The Three Graces*, s.a., engraving, ca. 191 × 142 mm, published by Philips Galle. Cologne, Wallraf-Richartz-Museum & Fondation Corboud, Graphische Sammlung, no. 30155. © Photo: Stanislaw Rusch.

Wierix, Philips and Theodore Galle, Adriaen Collaert, Abraham van Merlen, and Michael Snijders, all of whom exported their work via the Moretuses. Not only does such an analysis reveal the Jesuits' specific interest in Antwerp prints, but it also helps clarify the extraordinarily extensive and persistent demand for prints from Antwerp in Cologne more generally.

During the eighteenth century, the Jesuits' print collection was diverse and well regarded; it contained enough works designed or made by various internationally prominent artists – for instance, Albrecht Dürer, Anthony van Dyck, Peter Paul Rubens, Jacques Callot, Nicolas Poussin, Michelangelo, and Annibale Carracci – to satisfy many collectors. These works also covered a broad spectrum of topics, ranging from landscapes and geographical works, as well as detailed images of the natural world, to historical themes (with examples of scenes from antiquity and laudatory depictions of past rulers), architectural and ornamental designs, and both worldly and spiritual allegories.

While this great variety most likely reflected the wide array of interests of those who acquired the images and the Jesuits' evolving didactic needs, an even more extensive selection of religious subjects reveals the extent to which such imagery was valued within the order itself and the myriad ways in which prints served and supported the Jesuits' sundry activities. The numerous prints produced in Antwerp offered many appealing options for the Jesuits in Cologne; there were models for abstract concepts and designs, possibly derived from works published by Philips Galle (fig. 8.3), as well as word play, as found in works distributed by Hieronymus Cock and Volcxken Diericx (fig. 8.4), and a wide assortment of religious themes (figs. 8.5–8.16).[15]

For example, the plethora of images of St Ignatius, his life, and his visions, along with portrayals of his contemporary St Francis Xavier and the younger novices Aloysius Gonzaga and Stanislas Kostka, all of which were produced by different artists, were essential for the legitimization and promotion of the relatively new Jesuit order and were common in the work of several Antwerp print publishers (figs. 8.5 and 8.6).[16] Concurrently, many prints provided step-by-step aids and mnemonic devices for forms of personal devotion inspired

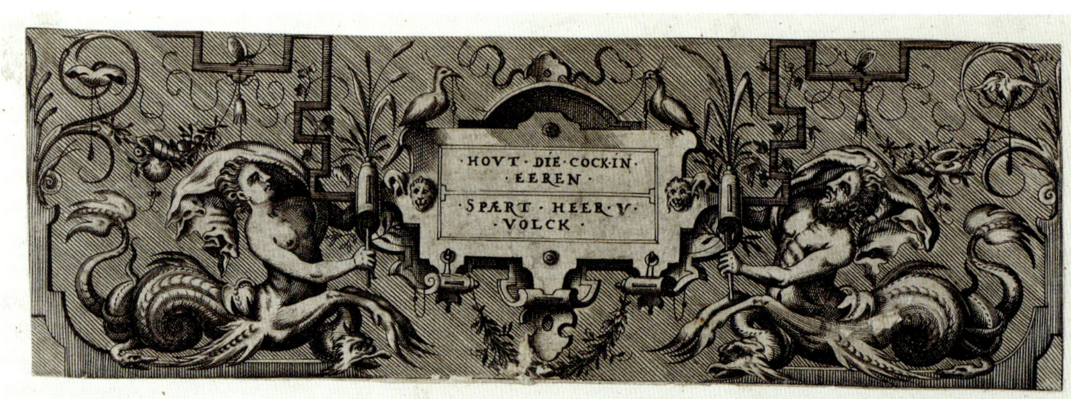

8.4 Pieter van der Heyden after Jacob Floris, *Cartouche Held by a Mermaid and Merman, with References to Hieronymus Cock and Volcxken Diericx*, the lower half of the second print of the series, *Compertimenta pictoriis flosculis manubiisque bellicis variegata*, published by Cock in 1567, engraving, 67 × 200 mm. Cologne, Wallraf-Richartz-Museum & Fondation Corboud, Graphische Sammlung, no. 30165. © Photo: Stanislaw Rusch.

8.5 Hieronymus Wierix, *Saint Ignatius of Loyola*, s.a., engraving, 109 × 72 mm. Cologne, Wallraf-Richartz-Museum & Fondation Corboud, Graphische Sammlung, no. 16471. © Photo: Stanislaw Rusch.

8.6 Anonymous, *Four Jesuits (Ignatius, Francis Xavier, Aloysius Gonzaga, and Stanislas Kostka) in Ovals on Either side of the Christ Child*, s.a., engraving, 155 × 100 mm, published by Michael Snijders. Cologne, Wallraf-Richartz-Museum & Fondation Corboud, Graphische Sammlung, no. 33445. © Photo: Stanislaw Rusch.

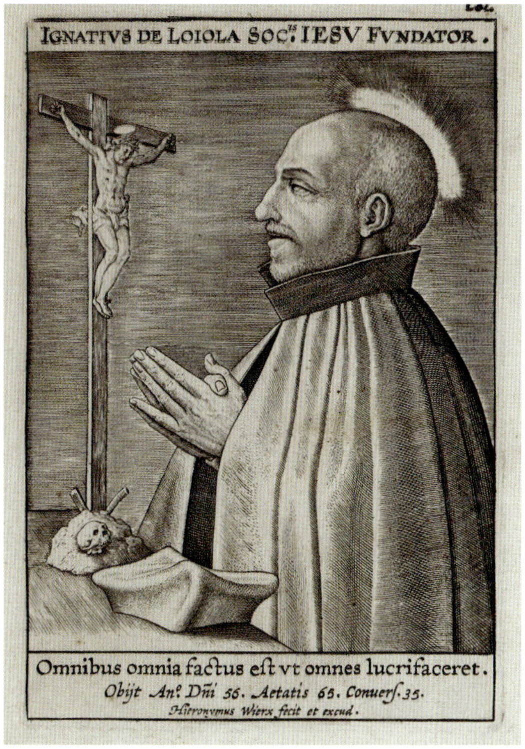

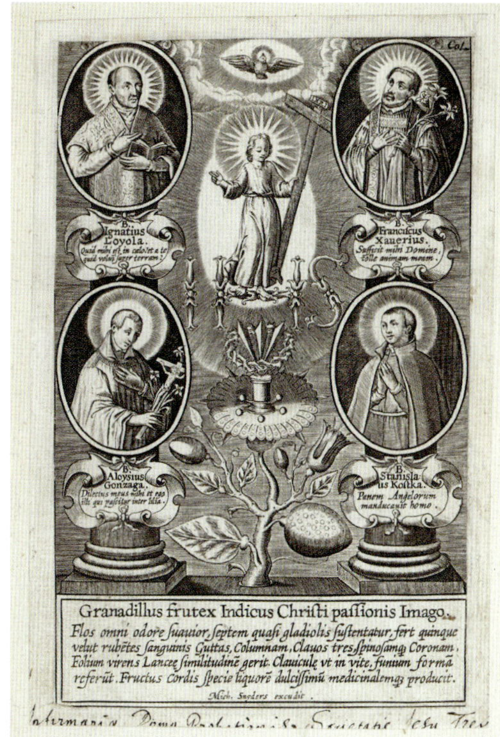

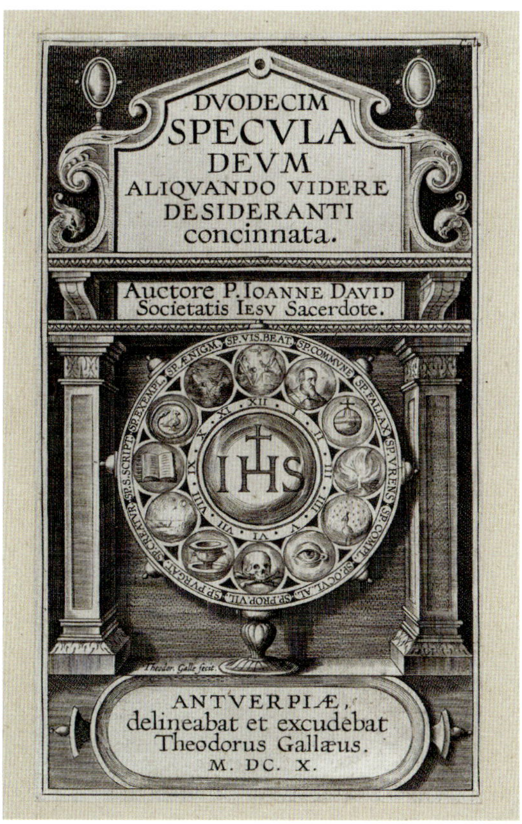

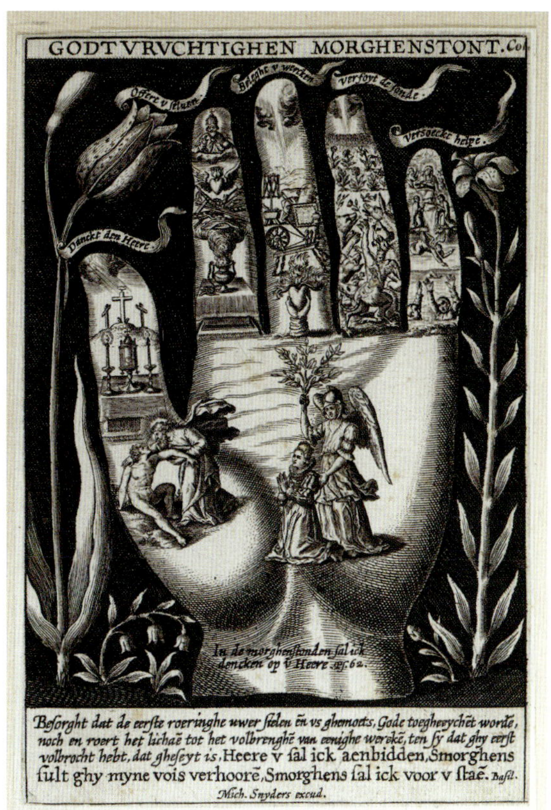

8.7 Theodore Galle, title plate for the independent print series, *Duodecim specula deum aliquando videre desideranti concinnata*, published by Theodore Galle in 1610, engraving, 159 × 92 mm. Cologne, Wallraf-Richartz-Museum & Fondation Corboud, Graphische Sammlung, no. 16526. © Photo: Stanislaw Rusch.

8.8 Anonymous, *Godtvruchtighen Morghenstont*, s.a., engraving, 135 × 88 mm, published by Michael Snijders. Cologne, Wallraf-Richartz-Museum & Fondation Corboud, Graphische Sammlung, no. 22332. © Photo: Stanislaw Rusch.

8.9 Adriaen Collaert after Hans Bol, *The Parable of the Sower* (illustrating March), from the series *Emblemata evangelica ad XII signa coelestia*, published by Jan Sadeler I in 1585, engraving, 151 × 207 mm. Cologne, Wallraf-Richartz-Museum & Fondation Corboud, Graphische Sammlung, no. 33394. © Photo: Stanislaw Rusch.

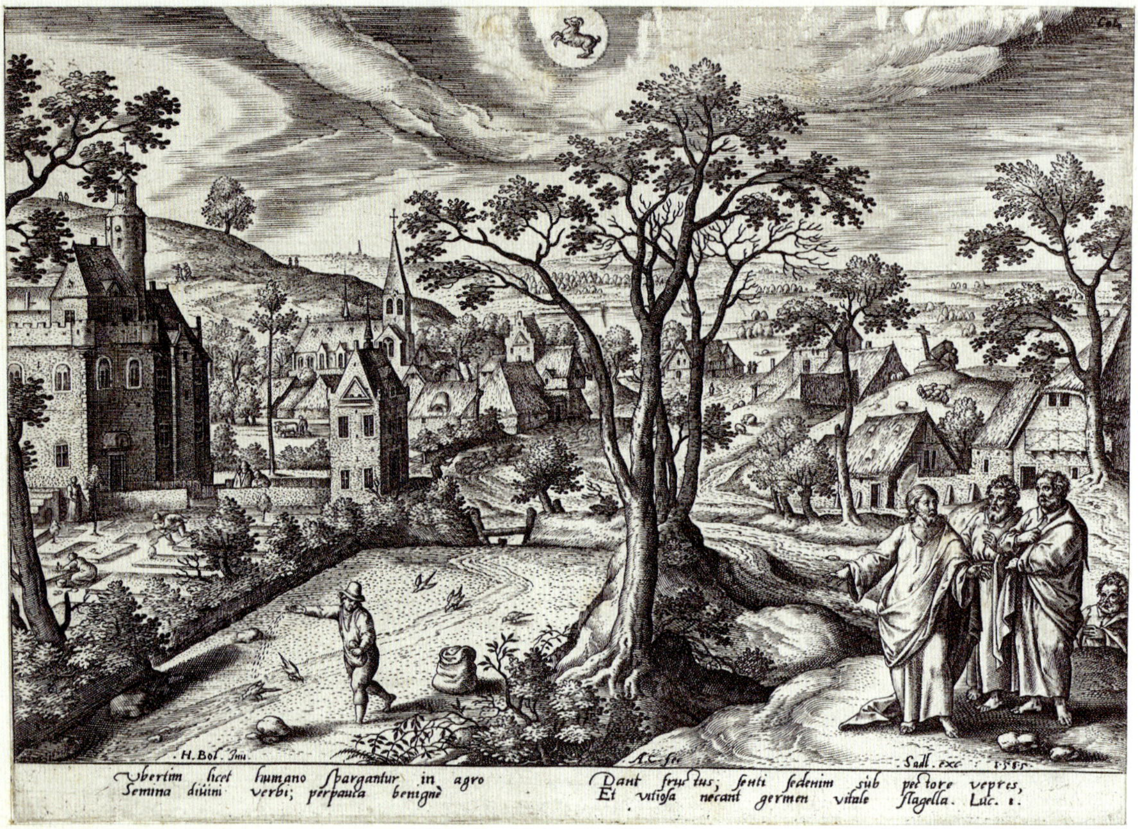

8.10 Charles de Mallery, reduced copy in reverse of Hieronymus Wierix after Bernardino Passeri, *Christ on the Mount of Olives*, s.a., engraving, 121 × 80 mm. Cologne, Wallraf-Richartz-Museum & Fondation Corboud, Graphische Sammlung, no. 15264. © Photo: Stanislaw Rusch.

8.11 Charles de Mallery, *The Devout Soul in a Valley of Misery, with a Vision of the Christ Child in a Flaming Heart*, s.a., engraving, 115 × 77 mm. Cologne, Wallraf-Richartz-Museum & Fondation Corboud, Graphische Sammlung, no. 15289. © Photo: Stanislaw Rusch.

8.12 Anonymous, *Saint Matthew*, from a series of the *Four Evangelists*, s.a., engraving, 110 × 65 mm, published by Theodore Galle. Cologne, Wallraf-Richartz-Museum & Fondation Corboud, Graphische Sammlung, no. 16556. © Photo: Stanislaw Rusch.

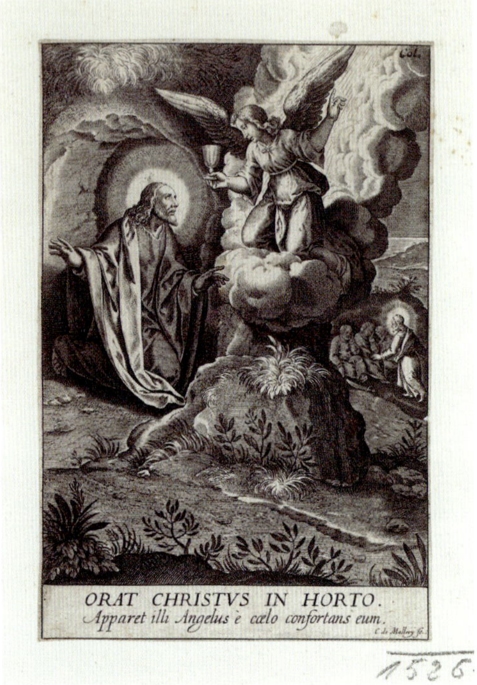

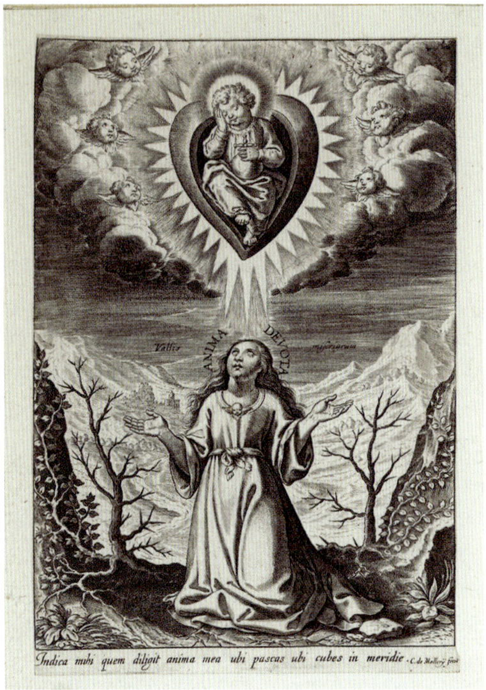

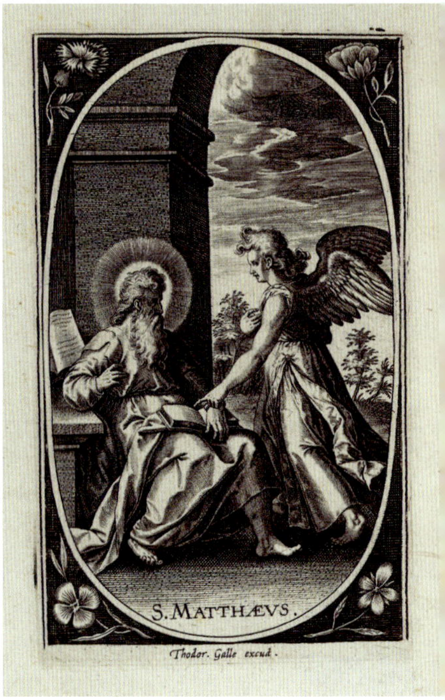

by St Ignatius's teachings. Some images, such as Theodore Galle's print series entitled *Duodecim specula deum aliquando videre desideranti concinnata*, which he published independently in 1610 (fig. 8.7) and also offered as sets of prints for insertion in the book of the same title by the Jesuit Joannes David, were clearly designed to serve an educated audience. Other prints, like Michael Snijders's symbolic hand (fig. 8.8), vividly render the essential components of meditation, as described in Petrus Canisius's popular catechism, for a broader spectrum of the faithful.[17] More general principles, such as links between the heavenly and earthly domains and the ability to discover God in all things, were embedded in what otherwise might appear to be attractive landscapes from a series of the twelve months, as engraved by Adriaen Collaert after Hans Bol (fig. 8.9).

The print collection of the Cologne Jesuits also attests to the immense value they placed on smaller images in which essential narratives and components of the catechism or portrayals of saints and the Christian soul were rendered in a readily comprehensible, appealing manner. Charles de Mallery specialized in this imagery, and it was also commonly published by Theodore Galle and other Antwerp print sellers (figs. 8.10–8.12). Useful as reminders of subjects important in services, lessons, feast days, or other church rituals, such works were well suited to the Jesuits' practice of giving prints as gifts (along with other, more practical items) that would be a form of praise to bolster their broader, instructive mission. Thus, in addition to supporting personal devotion via immediately accessible and appealing imagery, these prints also reinforced public Catholic piety among the general populace.[18]

Other, more specific links between public activities supported by the Cologne Jesuits and the prints in their collection include, for example, Philips Galle's series of the *Seven Churches of Rome*, engraved by Adriaen or Jan Collaert II (fig. 8.13). This may have functioned as a striking visual reminder of the inspiration for the Jesuits' "Roman procession", which featured the seven main churches of Cologne. Begun by 1613, if not earlier, it had become so popular by 1628 that it was held twice a year, in addition to being organized for special occasions.[19] Of even greater importance on a day-to-day basis were the sodalities supported by the Jesuits, as well as those affiliated with other religious orders and independent institutions in Cologne. Marian sodalities, actively promoted by Canisius and other Jesuit authors, were especially successful and resulted in a flood of imagery portraying the Immaculate Conception of the Virgin, her sorrows, joys, and miracles, or cherished devotional practices associated with her, such as the rosary, as in works published by both Michael Snijders and Abraham van Merlen, among others (figs. 8.14 and 8.15).

Finally, the Jesuits' collection of prints also included numerous images from saints' lives and the tragedies of martyrs that would have been applicable to other aspects of the lives of the faithful. In some instances, such works might have served as sources for the dramatic portrayals of various events that the Jesuits and sodalities organized in a range of contexts. These images would also have been linked to recent incidents in Germany and the Low Countries, where confessional

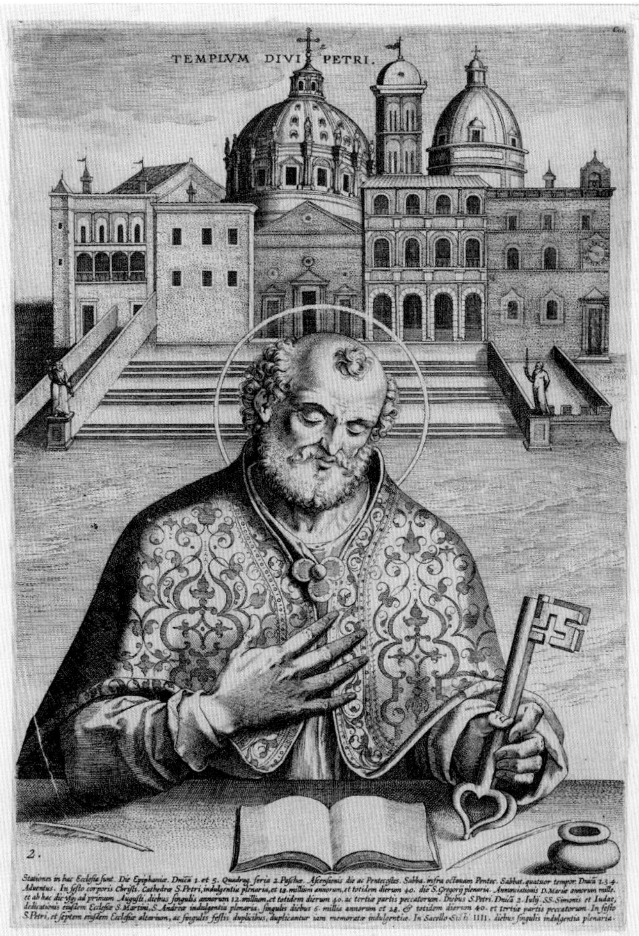

8.13 Adriaen or Jan Collaert II (attributed to), *The Church of Saint Peter*, print 2 from the series *The Seven Churches of Rome*, published by Philips Galle ca. 1598, engraving, 299 × 205 mm. Cologne, Wallraf-Richartz-Museum & Fondation Corboud, Graphische Sammlung, no. 14038. © Photo: Stanislaw Rusch. Appendix 1: PG-93.

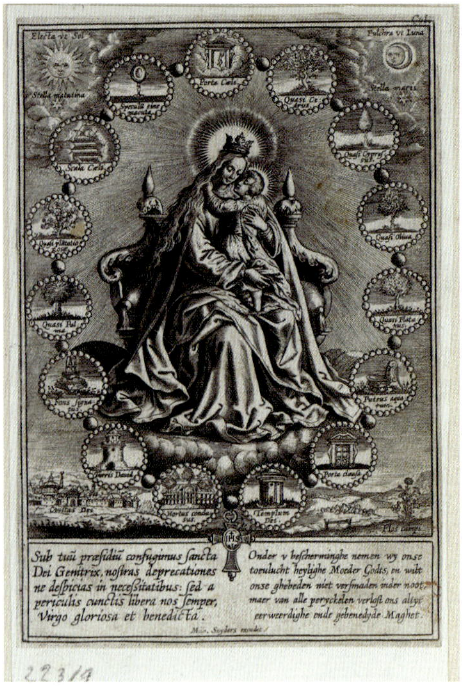

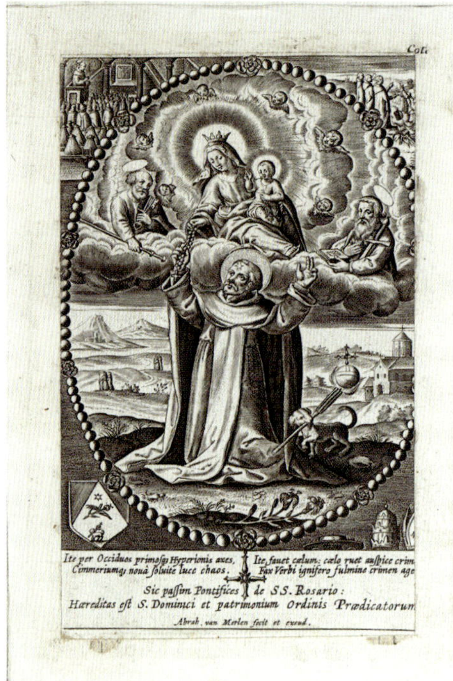

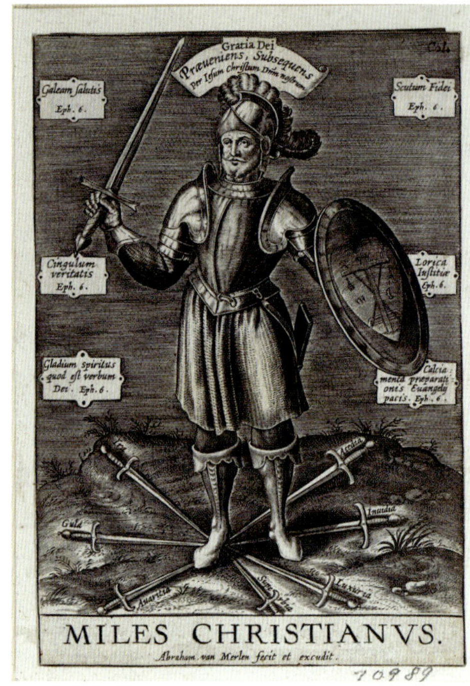

8.14 Anonymous, *Virgin, with Child Enthroned, within a Representation of the Fifteen Mysteries of the Rosary*, s.a., engraving, 141 × 94 mm, published by Michael Snijders. Cologne, Wallraf-Richartz-Museum & Fondation Corboud, Graphische Sammlung, no. 22319. © Photo: Stanislaw Rusch.

8.15 Abraham van Merlen, *Saint Dominicus with the Virgin and Child and Saints Peter and Paul, all within a Rosary*, s.a., engraving, 123 × 76 mm. Cologne, Wallraf-Richartz-Museum & Fondation Corboud, Graphische Sammlung, no. 11006. © Photo: Stanislaw Rusch.

8.16 Abraham van Merlen, *Miles Christianus*, s.a., engraving, 121 × 81 mm. Cologne, Wallraf-Richartz-Museum & Fondation Corboud, Graphische Sammlung, no. 10989. © Photo: Stanislaw Rusch.

battles were ongoing and often took a violent, military form. The implications of following in Christ's footsteps were real and one could either endure them, as did the model saints, or engage in them, echoing the frequently reiterated concept of the "Miles Christianus" (Christian soldier), who was considered to be an exemplar of a true follower of Christ and defender of Catholicism and who was depicted by numerous printmakers (fig. 8.16).[20]

The above sampling of prints from the Jesuits' collection is by no means exhaustive. Nor, given the relatively small percentage of the original collection that was found in Paris and returned to Cologne in the early nineteenth century, can it be regarded as fully representative of what the Jesuits originally collected, used, and distributed among the general populace in Cologne during the sixteenth and seventeenth centuries. Nevertheless, the pervasive reliance on prints for personal edification, devotion, extensive pastoral duties, and diverse forms of public engagement, all of which were part of the active reassertion of Catholicism in Cologne by the Jesuits and other religious institutions, would have had an immense impact on the local market for prints. Moreover, strong bonds between Catholic rulers in Germany and those in the Spanish, Habsburg-ruled Low Countries encouraged the import of religious practices and associated products, including texts and images. Although other cities in the Low Countries, like Leuven and Douai, were known for their Catholic publications, Antwerp remained the undisputed center of production for such texts and images and was, thanks to century-old trade routes, an obvious place to start.[21] Together, these factors help clarify the remarkably substantial export of prints from Antwerp to diverse individuals in Cologne via the Officina Plantiniana, which in turn provides an exceptional insights into the ways in which individuals in Cologne, as well as larger religious institutions like the Jesuits, could have acquired the distinct types of prints they sought.

Some Jesuits, in addition to individuals associated with other religious orders, occasionally benefited from the Moretuses' connections when acquiring their individual orders of prints. For example, in 1634, the nun Magdalena Hellebrand received a package of images from an unspecified supplier that Balthasar Moretus I had sent to the Cologne bookseller Peter Eller. Subsequently, in 1638 and 1639, respectively, the Jesuits Joachim Greuter and Johann Alting, the rector of the Jesuit college in Osnabrück, near Cologne, both obtained works with the help of the Moretuses' former apprentice, Johann Kinckius. While Greuter's two packages came from Jan-Baptist Barbé, Balthasar himself arranged for the images sent to Alting.[22] Notably absent in the Moretuses' records are transactions involving the Antwerp Jesuits, who periodically made use of the Moretuses' routine transport of barrels to the Frankfurt fairs (usually via Cologne) to ship assorted items to Jesuit colleges elsewhere. These packages ranged from sporadic shipments destined for Mainz, Würzburg, and Dillingen to the regular acquisitions by the Jesuits in Augsburg, where Jakobus Mair and subsequently Melchior Stör were the local contacts, between 1615 and 1627.[23]

The Jesuits (like other residents in Cologne) would most likely have approached local dealers first for their immediate print purchases. According to Dietmar Spengler, the records of several librarians of the Jesuit college indicate that a number of local booksellers gave books to the college between 1621 and 1703, and may have donated prints as well.[24] Of the businesses he names – those run by the Cholinus, Chrithius (Crith), Gymnich, Hierat, Kinckius, and Mylius families – all but the Gymnichs (who did trade with the Officina Plantiniana from 1579 (or earlier) to 1648) were involved to varying degrees in the distribution of prints via the Moretuses. The Cholinus and Crith families generally remained at the periphery of the print trade that was facilitated by the Moretuses. They only sporadically served as a pickup point for isolated packages from Antwerp print sellers included in the Moretuses' book shipments to them. However, the other three families participated more frequently in the print trade facilitated by the Moretuses.[25]

Not only was the Mylius family renowned for overseeing one of the long-established and internationally active printing houses in Cologne, but Arnold and his son Hermann Mylius were also prominent locally as political figures who had close ties to the economic and academic elite of the city, including the Cologne Jesuits.[26] Consequently, it is not surprising that they appeared in the Jesuits' accounts. In the Moretuses' records, aside from the family's ongoing trade in books, Arnold features as Jan Moretus I's preferred middleman for the transfer of numerous packages exchanged between Antwerp and Cologne from 1585 to 1592. When the purveyor of these consignments in Antwerp is identified, Philips Galle is the only one named. The bulk of what Jan Moretus sent was destined for the print and map dealers Peter Boons and Frans Hogenberg, or Hogenberg's heirs.[27] Mylius himself did not order prints directly from the Moretuses and, on only a few occasions, did Philips Galle prepare a package for him personally.[28] Unfortunately, neither the contents of these orders nor of any of the other packages sent along with book shipments to Mylius between 1585 and 1592, are specified; they may or may not have contained printed images (as distinct from, for example, atlases or other cartographic works). In 1601, Mylius received two parcels with printed images (and two months later some copper plates), but they were from the Antwerp bookseller Jan van Keerberghen.[29] Nonetheless, the question remains open as to whether Mylius was acquiring plates for producing independent images for further distribution or plates for printing images to embellish his own books. Thus, while he was familiar with important figures in the print trade in both Antwerp and Cologne, the Moretuses' records do not reveal any active involvement on his part. This situation changed when his son Hermann was managing the family business during the first half of the seventeenth century.[30]

Differences between Arnold's and Hermann's interactions with the Moretuses and the traffic in prints between Antwerp and Cologne are evident in several ways. For example, despite trading regularly with Hermann Mylius until 1650, the Moretuses rarely included packages from Antwerp print dealers in their shipments of books to him. Unusually, in 1610 and 1612, he was sent packages prepared by Hieronymus Wierix and Theodore Galle, while he served simply as a pickup point for parcels intended for others in 1619 and 1634.[31] This general lack of assistance with the exchange of packages is all the more striking because Hermann also deviated from his father's practices by periodically buying prints through the Moretuses: above all, the work of Hieronymus Wierix, and, to a far lesser degree, that of Theodore Galle. The contrast between his recurring purchases of Wierix's prints in bulk between 1608 and 1612 and his isolated acquisitions of only a couple of copies of specific print series published by Theodore Galle is demonstrated by an order that he placed in 1611, when he bought groups of 50, 75, and 100 prints by Wierix in four distinct price categories, ranging from 2.25 to 1 st. per image, but just two copies of Galle's series of the *Life of Saint Ignatius* (fig. 5.9). A comparison with the record of Wierix's supply of these prints and what Galle had previously charged for his series indicates that the Moretuses added a notable profit margin for themselves on this transaction.[32] Hermann's acquisitions of prints in bulk via the Moretuses – either by purchase through them or directly via the artists themselves – soon came to an end. After 1612, he placed only one order, namely, for two sets of another of Galle's series, his *Holy Founders of Religious Orders* (fig. 7.2), to which Balthasar once again added a significant profit margin of 3 fl. for himself.[33] Hermann may have been more actively involved in the print trade through other channels. At the very least, his sporadic purchases of Galle's series indicate that he most likely, on occasion, bought prints on commission for specific clients. However, his concentrated acquisitions of Wierix's prints in bulk may well reflect an endeavor to satisfy a more pervasive, general demand for such images in Cologne during the first half of the seventeenth century, for similar purchases were made simultaneously by other booksellers in the city.

One such figure was Anton Hierat I. Trained under Johann Gymnich III, who ran another of Cologne's important printing-publishing houses, Hierat went on to establish a new successful business of his own in Cologne that he and his successors managed through the middle of the seventeenth century.[34] Although Hierat and his sons, like Mylius and his son, did not deal in prints routinely with the Moretuses, the remarkable volume of the Hierats' purchases vividly attests to their involvement in the large-scale traffic in printed images in Cologne, which may well justify Spengler's reference to them as one possible source of images for the Jesuit college.

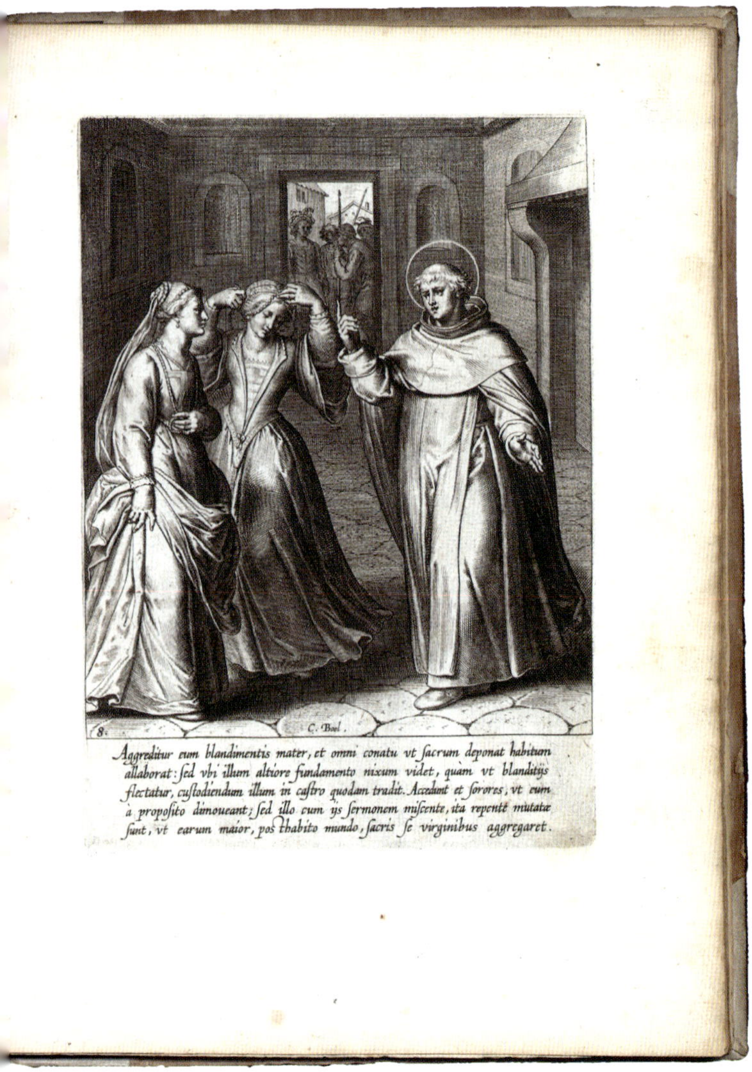

8.17 Cornelis Boel after Otto van Veen, *Thomas of Aquinas with His Sisters*, print 8 from the series *Life of Saint Thomas of Aquinas*, 1610, engraving, 210 × 147 mm. Antwerp, Museum Plantin-Moretus: PK.OPB.0075. Appendix 1: OV-1.

Specifically, Anton I is known to have bought prints from the Moretuses on just two occasions, in December of 1611 and August of 1623. Nevertheless, both of his purchases amounted to 1,000 prints or more. In 1611, Hierat, as Hermann Mylius had done earlier that year, acquired unspecified prints in bulk from Hieronymus Wierix at rates ranging from 2.25 to 1 st. per image. However, Hierat not only ordered more prints from Wierix (nearly 400, in contrast to the 300 requested by Mylius), but he supplemented them with hundreds of additional images, while Mylius had simply added just two copies of Galle's series of the *Life of Saint Ignatius*. In particular, along with four copies of Galle's St Ignatius series, Hierat bought six impressions each of two other series published by Galle – the *Life of Saint Dominic* and that of *Saint Catherine of Siena* (fig. 7.12). He also acquired six copies of Otto Venius's *Life of Saint Thomas* (fig. 8.17), two copies of De Mallery's series of the *Sins and Penance of Man* (fig. 8.18), and an additional 600 unspecified prints in bulk from De Mallery. Again, as when they sold prints to Hermann Mylius, the Moretuses added a significant profit margin for themselves on each

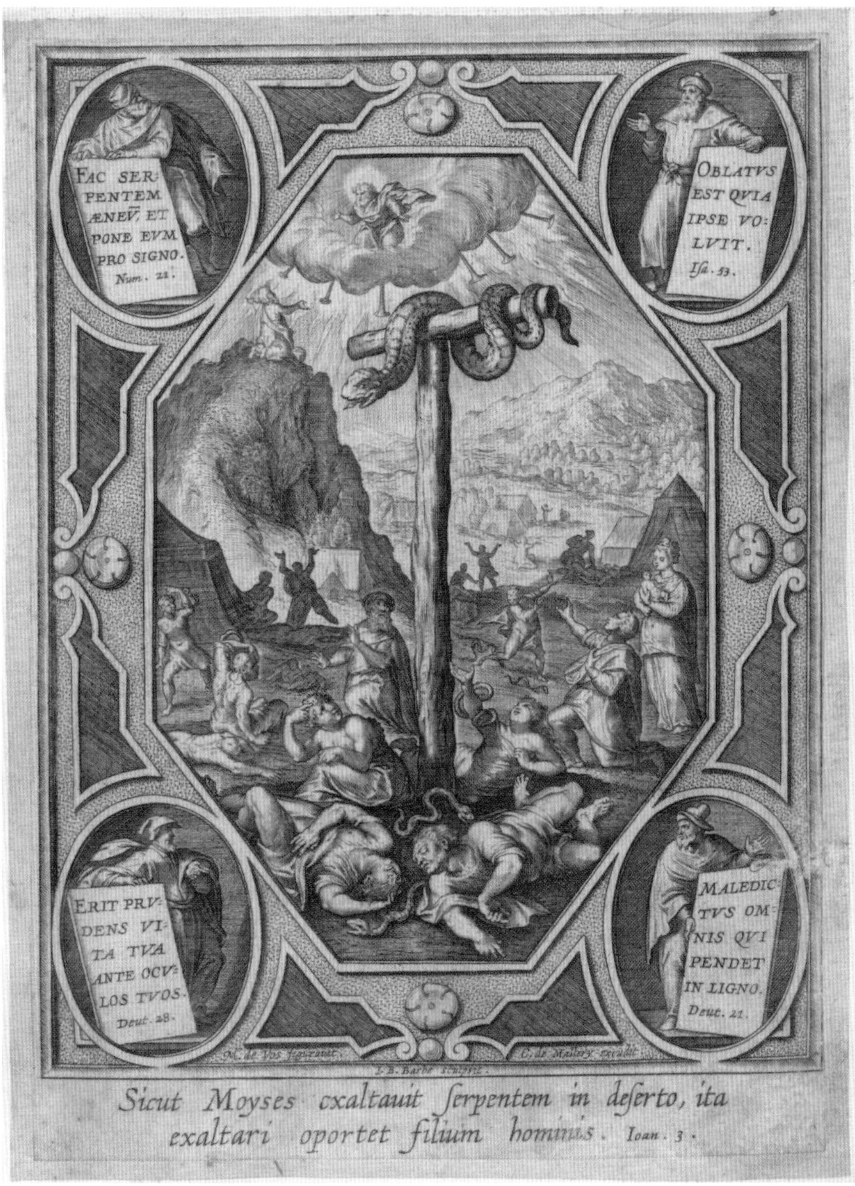

8.18 Jan-Baptist Barbé, *Adoration of the Brazen Serpent*, print 3 from the series *The Sins and Penance of Man*, published by Charles de Mallery ca. 1610, engraving, 161 × 115 mm, Antwerp, Museum Plantin-Moretus: PK.OPB.0085.004. Appendix 1: CM-4.

item sold, regardless of the supplier.[35] In 1623, Hierat's order was much simpler, "just" 1,000 unspecified prints in bulk from De Mallery that were sold at the high price of 60 st. per 100 images, instead of the 50 st.-per-100 rate at which De Mallery supplied them.[36]

Between 1627 and 1629, Hierat's sons Anton II and Arnold, who had recently taken over the management of the family business following Hierat's death in 1627, also placed two remarkable orders for printed images with the Moretuses. In February 1627, they acquired 1,000 unspecified images from Theodore Galle and 3,000 more from other print publishers, including Jan Boel. In striking contrast to their father's earlier transactions, these prints were sold to them at the basic rate of 36 st. per 100 images, without any price markup by Balthasar Moretus. They simultaneously requested an additional 2,300 images, at least 200 of which were hand-colored works printed on parchment. Two years later, instead of buying prints in bulk by the thousands, Anton II and Arnold requested sixteen altar cards from Galle and Michael Snijders executed with a variety of finishings while some were left plain, half were specially painted or gilded, and two had leather frames.[37] Together, the Hierats' exceptional purchases document very specific items – either particular print series by diverse print publishers or a selection of altar cards – that may well have been requested on commission for individual clients. At the same time, however, the Hierats placed sporadic but substantial orders for prints in bulk that either could have been intended to stock their own shop or could have been requested by an institution that required them for their own purposes, in particular the Jesuits' various activities involving printed images. Although the Moretuses did not supply images for such acquisitions frequently, this does not imply that the general demand in Cologne for such imagery was as irregular. The Hierats (like the Mylius family) may simply have relied on other suppliers elsewhere to satisfy additional requests for a plethora of prints.

Of all the booksellers associated with the donation of books and possibly prints to the Jesuit college in Cologne, the Kinckius family had the strongest connection by far to the Moretuses. Dating back to Johann Kinckius's apprenticeship under Jan Moretus I between 1600 and 1608, the close personal and professional ties linking these two families lasted into the mid-seventeenth century. Following his apprenticeship, Kinckius soon established himself among Cologne's booksellers by marrying a daughter of Anton Hierat I and beginning his own productive, successful business as both a publisher and a bookseller. Catering to the needs of the Counter-Reformation, he was in especially frequent contact with the Jesuits and Benedictines.[38]

During the first decade of his independent activities in Cologne, Kinckius was only sporadically involved in the import of prints to Cologne through the Moretuses, primarily by serving as the local middleman for the transfer of prints sent by a few Antwerp print dealers: Hieronymus Wierix, Charles de Mallery, and Theodore Galle. While some of these packages were clearly marked for other individuals – the publisher Georg Meuting and bookseller Bernhard Wolters – even those addressed to Kinckius may ultimately have been intended for someone else.[39] However, in addition to becoming the Moretuses' preferred pickup point for packages sent by Antwerp print dealers throughout the subsequent decades, Kinckius began to supplement this activity with his own periodic acquisition of prints. Between 1617 and 1620, Kinckius primarily ordered unspecified prints in bulk by the hundreds from De Mallery, Abraham van Merlen, and occasionally Michael Snijders. In striking contrast to the Moretuses' sales of prints to both Mylius and the Hierats, these purchases did not routinely include a profit margin for the Moretuses.[40] In 1630–1631, Kinckius turned to the Moretuses again, but now for an assortment of works, the majority of which were printed on parchment or were illuminated. Alongside some 500 prints on parchment (all but 100 of which were colored) that Kinckius acquired at cost from Theodore Galle, he bought seven canons, four of which were specially colored, and six quires of *suffragia* supplied by Hendrik Aertssens. Remarkably, when the Moretuses sold Kinckius the canons and the *suffragia*, they added a significant markup – more than doubling the prices for the canons and raising the price of the *suffragia* by 5 percent.[41] This stark contrast to Kinckius's other purchases suggests that the Moretuses knew that his special order of canons and *suffragia* was for an exceptional client.

The only other notable, later transactions consisted of a concentrated exchange of packages and payments that the Moretuses facilitated between Kinckius and Maarten van den Enden between 1637 and 1639. In total, nine packages prepared by Van den Enden (eight of which were noted to contain prints) were sent by the Moretuses to Kinckius in 1637 and 1638, while Kinckius paid some 80 fl. to Van den Enden in 1639 via a series of middlemen. Regrettably, the client behind these requests for Van den Enden's publications remains unknown. Given the broad array of individuals – booksellers, print publishers, and members of the clergy – who had packages sent to them in care of Kinckius, it seems most likely that Kinckius did not initiate these orders himself, but was, once again, fulfilling his primary role of the preferred point of exchange in Cologne for shipments from Antwerp artists arranged by the Moretuses.[42]

Among the Moretuses' trading partners in Cologne, the one who appears to have been most routinely engaged in the acquisition of prints was another former apprentice, Bernhard Wolters (or Gualterus). Apprenticed under Jan Moretus I from 1594 to 1598, Wolters settled in Cologne and remained on good personal and professional terms with the Moretuses during the decades to come. By the spring of 1599, Wolters had married a daughter of the Cologne book publisher Martinus Cholinus, Caecilia Cholinus. Caecilia's former husband, another Cologne book publisher, Heinrich Falckenburg, had recently passed away, leaving her (and then Wolters) with an established business to run.[43] Wolters's print acquisitions began modestly in the next two years with, initially, seven canons bought in 1600 and a series of the Passion purchased in 1601.[44] Between 1604 and 1611, however, he frequently obtained prints from a variety of sources. Starting with an unusual purchase of images worth 11 fl. from the rector of the Antwerp Jesuit college, Carolus Scribani, in June 1604, Wolters simultaneously ordered prints directly from Adriaen Huberti and had them shipped to him by the Moretuses.[45]

However, between 1605 and 1611, Wolters primarily imported images published by Hieronymus Wierix and Charles de Mallery via the Moretuses. As was the case with his earlier purchases from Huberti, Wolters acquired the work of these print publishers through the Moretuses before all of their other contacts in Cologne. Perhaps Wolters enjoyed the advantage of having met these print dealers in person when he was in Antwerp. Usually, the Moretuses purchased prints for him and offered them to him at cost. Like many other booksellers in Cologne, Wolters occasionally requested a selection of prints from Wierix, distinguished only by price – which in his case ranged from 1 to 2 st. per print.[46] Although these specific purchases suggest that Wolters was more modest than other Cologne booksellers in terms of the quantities of Wierix's prints he bought – some 20 to 50 or 70 prints in any one price category – the total value of other purchases, amounting to 16 fl. 15 st. in one instance, indicate that he nevertheless repeatedly bought notable quantities of prints.[47] The prices that the Moretuses asked for De Mallery's prints, which were always sold in bulk, occasionally varied. For a purchase of 350 prints, they charged Wolters the same, slightly higher 60 st.-per-hundred print rate that they had applied to Mylius's and Hierat's orders, but, in most other instances, including two allotments of 200 prints, they resold the prints at De Mallery's usual base rate of 50 st. per hundred prints.[48]

The two significant deviations from this pattern among Wolters's purchases were his orders for 100 impressions of two specific images: De Mallery's *The Virgin and Holy Trinity*

Appear to the First Ten Jesuits and Hieronymus Wierix's *Christ on the Cross Venerated by Four Jesuit Saints*, which he requested in 1609 and 1610, respectively.[49] Not only do these acquisitions stand out among all the Moretuses' sales of prints to booksellers in Cologne because the image sold in bulk quantities (in contrast to the sales of a few copies of specific print series published by Theodore Galle) is identified precisely, but both works were also part of the local Jesuit college's print collection (figs. 8.19 and 8.20). Although it is impossible to determine whether Wolters sold some or all of these particular prints to the Jesuit college, he may certainly have done so.

Remarkably, Wolters's regular reliance on the Moretuses for his print orders ended soon thereafter with a series of shipments of packages of prints from Theodore Galle, De Mallery, and Wierix during 1611.[50] Their subsequent dealings in prints were all isolated, sporadic transactions. Aside from two packages of prints prepared by a certain Martinus Rijndorff, which the Moretuses sent to him in 1621 and which may ultimately have been intended for someone else, Wolters's last print purchases were dominated by orders that were placed specially for third parties, just as his two specific print purchases from 1609 and 1610 may have been commissioned by the Jesuits. In 1635, for example, he requested that five altar cards be shipped to a former employee ("famulus") of his, Joannes Brouwers, who was then working as a bookseller in Kraków.[51] In 1628, he received most items (193) of an even more astounding order for 244 altar cards. Made expressly at his request, each card consisted of six leaves and was embellished with four engravings. According to Balthasar Moretus I's accounts, these cards would normally have cost 20.5 st. apiece, or 250 fl. 2 st. for the group. However, he agreed

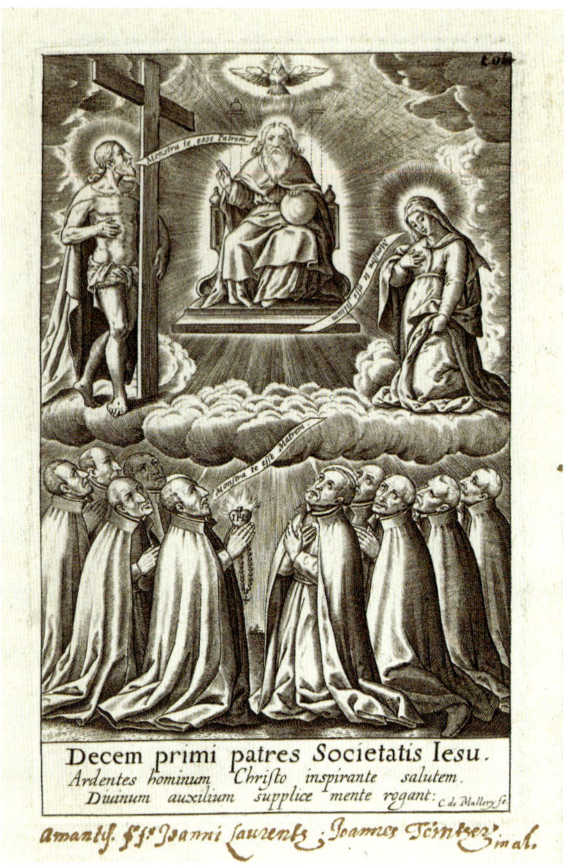

8.19 Charles de Mallery, *The Virgin and Holy Trinity Appear to the First Ten Jesuits*, by 1609, engraving, 105 × 66 mm. Cologne, Wallraf-Richartz-Museum & Fondation Corboud, Graphische Sammlung, no. 15222. © Photo: Stanislaw Rusch. Appendix 1: CM-5.

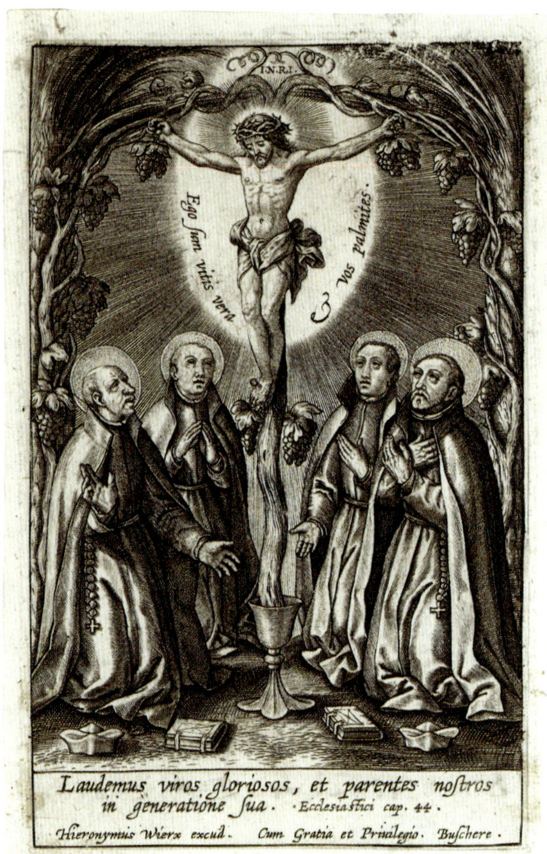

8.20 Hieronymus Wierix, *Christ on the Cross Venerated by Four Jesuit Saints (Ignatius of Loyola, Francis Xavier, Aloysius Gonzaga, and Stanislaus Kostka)*, by 1610, engraving, 109 × 66 mm. Cologne, Wallraf-Richartz-Museum & Fondation Corboud, Graphische Sammlung, no. 16630. © Photo: Stanislaw Rusch. Appendix 1: WX-3.

to deduct one-third of the price, as he had for the contemporaneous consignment of large folio missals that had been produced for use in Cologne (at the request of the prince-elector and archbishop of Cologne, Ferdinand of Bavaria). These missals were sold exclusively to Wolters and Petrus Cholinus, a relative of his and of Joannes Cholinus, who was Ferdinand's *Domherr (praepositus)*.[52] Although it is tempting to associate Wolters's order of the altar cards with his allotment of missals for use in Cologne, no known records document such a link. Nevertheless, these two late orders, together with Wolters's exceptional purchases of very specific Jesuit imagery in 1609 and 1610, demonstrate how he used his Antwerp connections to assist others with the acquisition of printed images from Antwerp. This in turn raises the question of whether Wolters's other print purchases in the first decades of the seventeenth century were similarly made on consignment – as seems to have been the case with the other Cologne booksellers with whom the Moretuses dealt – or if he (temporarily) attempted to combine the sale of books with the occasional sale of images in his own shop. Regardless of the answer, Wolters remains a significant figure among Cologne booksellers for the traffic in prints from Antwerp.

SUPPLYING COLOGNE'S PRINT DEALERS WITH IMAGES FROM ANTWERP

The relative lack of evidence that Cologne booksellers themselves systematically dealt in prints – as other booksellers did throughout Europe, including the Raesfeld family in Münster – may also be explained by the active community of print dealers in the city, many of whom had their own personal connections with the Low Countries and Antwerp in particular. Local residents and members of religious institutions could readily turn to these dealers to acquire prints from Antwerp. Consider, for example, the records kept by Arnold van Buchell when he was required to stay in Cologne to settle a legal matter during the second half of 1599. According to his diary, his recurring visits to a number of print shops across the city resulted in approximately 170 purchases of prints from primarily three dealers and may have amounted to some 300–400 sheets of prints in just six months.[53] Though acquainted with two important, local German dealers, Johann Bussemacher and Peter Overadt, Van Buchell bought the vast majority of his prints at the shops run by Maximilian de la Court, Johannes Boons, and Crispijn de Passe I and his wife. Each shop appears to have had its own area of specialization: De la Court's offerings in Italianate images enabled Van Buchell to acquire works by the Sadelers, as well as Cornelis Cort's prints after revered Italian artists, while Van Buchell preferred Boons for selections of Flemish prints and De Passe for assorted portraits. In contrast, Van Buchell purchased only a few prints from Bussemacher and Overadt, whose known publications suggest that they produced numerous imitations of Flemish didactic and religious imagery.[54]

The representation of the print market in Cologne that emerges from Van Buchell's diary is both supported and amplified by the Moretuses' accounts. Although Johannes Boons is not mentioned in the records of the Officina Plantiniana, a certain Peter Boons (or Buon), from whom Van Buchell also occasionally purchased prints in Cologne, appears. Notably, Van Buchell describes both men as coming from the Brabant region of the Low Countries, suggesting that they may have been related.[55] The shipments to Peter Boons are noteworthy for the exceptionally large number of packages – twelve in total – that he received in just four years, between 1588 and 1591. While these shipments were sent primarily in care of Arnold Mylius, at least eight more were left for Peter Boons at the Officina Plantiniana's shop in the Frankfurt fairs between 1588 and 1595. In both cases, when the origin of the packages was noted, Philips Galle was cited most often; in one instance, Abraham Ortelius was identified, most likely reflecting Boons's interest in cartographic works in addition to prints.[56] Although the content of a package was never specified, the regularity with which Boons was sent multiple packages per year suggests that he was actively engaged in the trade of prints and maps from Antwerp. Since Van Buchell acquired prints from both Johannes and Peter Boons in Cologne in 1599, Boons clearly continued to participate in the print trade for a number of years after the end of Jan Moretus I's involvement in the transport of his orders. Given the remarkable volume of his imports via Moretus in the preceding decade, Boons may simply have opted for a more direct or specialized means of obtaining the works he sought for resale in Cologne.

De Passe also occasionally benefited from the various services the Moretuses offered for facilitating the trade in prints. He had strong ties to the Antwerp art world. Registered in Antwerp's Guild of St Luke in the guild year 1584–1585 as an engraver, he subsequently married a niece of the wife of the prominent local painter and designer, Maarten de Vos. De Passe also completed at least one engraving for Plantin just when he was forced to emigrate from the city in 1588 due to his religious beliefs.[57] De Passe settled in Cologne in 1589, and, shortly thereafter, in November 1590, Jan Moretus sent him a single, unspecified package by way of the Cologne bookseller Arnold Quentel.[58] However, De Passe evidently relied primarily on other means (via his relations in Antwerp, perhaps) to obtain goods from the city during his first fifteen years in Cologne, including when he became acquainted with Van Buchell. Notably, once De Vos passed away in December 1603, the situation changed, and the Moretuses were periodically engaged for the transport of packages or the transfer of funds between De Passe and, above all, Philips and Theodore Galle and Adriaen Collaert. Dating from 1604 to 1612, the bulk of these transactions were concentrated between 1607 and 1612, during which time De Passe, like Boons before him, often received multiple packages annually, in addition to sending payments back to the Galles and Collaert via the Moretuses. Not once did De Passe send a package of his own to Antwerp via the Moretuses. Although the majority of these shipments were received at the Moretuses' shop in the Frankfurt book fairs, a few were negotiated through booksellers and merchants in Cologne. In 1607, for example, De Passe received four packages – one each from Thedore Galle and Adriaen Collaert, and two from an unspecified source – and also arranged for the payment of the significant sum of 100 fl. to Philips Galle through Nicolas van Egmont, a relative of the Moretuses who oversaw most of their financial transactions between Cologne and Frankfurt.[59] Following De Passe's eviction from Cologne in the summer of 1611 due to his adherence to the Mennonite faith, he settled in Utrecht, and his transactions via the Moretuses petered out in the 1610s. Occurring nearly exclusively at the Frankfurt fairs, these comprised just one last payment to Adriaan Collaert in the spring of 1612 and De Passe's receipt of two packages sent by Justus Sadeler in the spring of 1617. Finally, in 1621, De Passe made an exceptional, single purchase directly from the Moretuses of a few copies of Jan Moretus I's old publications of Ovid's *Metamorphoses* and Aesop's fables (along with two other undetermined books), which were, in essence, picture books filled with etchings by Peeter vander Borcht.[60]

Despite the importance of the records of Boons's and De Passe's acquisitions of printed images via the managers of the Officina Plantiniana, particularly for the documentation of the potential volume and value of this trade, it was the Hogenberg family who employed the Moretuses the most to further their independent dealings with Antwerp print publishers.

The founder of this business, Frans Hogenberg, was born in Mechelen, but established connections with print publishers in Antwerp early on, as Hieronymus Cock had published several of his etched, moralizing genre scenes by the late 1550s, including *The Blue Cloak* (Appendix I, CD-4). Soon thereafter, Hogenberg appears to have traveled between Antwerp and several German cities until he settled in Cologne by 1570, where he specialized in the publication of maps and city views, in addition to images of contemporary history. Most famous among these works are his *Civitates orbis terrarum* (the first volume of which was published jointly with Philips Galle in 1572 and his images of the Eighty Years' War (in which the Low Countries feature prominently). The latter are known in particular through their publication from 1583 in multiple editions of *De Leone Belgico, eiusque topographica atque historica descriptione* by Michael Eytzinger (or Aitsingerus).[61] Because of these and other publications, it is not surprising that Hogenberg stayed in contact with colleagues in Antwerp, especially Philips Galle, who had similarly been employed by Cock in the late 1550s and who is said to have traveled with Hogenberg, as well as Abraham Ortelius, Jan Sadeler I, and Gerard Mercator, to Poitiers in 1560 to see the then famous "Pierre Levée", a large stone on which they are reputed to have carved their names, as did many others.[62] Indeed, a periodic exchange between Hogenberg and Galle is evident in Plantin's accounts between 1580 and 1589, just prior to Hogenberg's death. The details of what Galle and Hogenberg sent to one another are never recorded, although on one occasion, in December 1580, Hogenberg sent letters (along with other unspecified items) for Gerard de Jode in an independent shipment to Galle, and Galle then asked Plantin to convey the shipment to De Jode.[63]

Following Frans Hogenberg's death around 1590, his second wife, Agnes Lomar, continued his business of publishing maps and other printed images for several years. Initially, she may have worked with one of Frans's sons from his first marriage, Johann (or Hans) Hogenberg, who was trained in engraving; as of 1594, he was making prints periodically for other local print publishers, like Johann Bussemacher. Some authors assert that Agnes bought out two of Frans's children from his first marriage (including Johann) by 1594 in order to manage the family business on her own. While the bookseller Georg Meuting, whom she married by the spring of 1604, first assisted her in the business, her son Abraham Hogenberg had taken over its management by the spring of 1615.[64]

Whether the initial, postulated subdivision of the Hogenberg business in 1594 is related to the timing of Johann Hogenberg's work for others is not clear. However, the records of the Moretuses' shipments to the Hogenberg family support arguments that some change in management occurred in 1594 and that Philips Galle, at least, continued to support Johann Hogenberg's activities. Specifically, between 1590 and 1593, the packages Jan Moretus I sent to the Hogenberg family in Cologne were either addressed to Hogenberg's widow (Agnes Lomar) or to the Hogenbergs generally, without further specification. Additionally, in November 1593, a large shipment to Moretus with works provided by various booksellers in Cologne also contained three unspecified packages from Lomar for Galle (possibly including copies of the *Civitates*, for example).[65] In February 1594, however, Galle asked Jan Moretus to convey a package to Cologne that was marked as explicitly for Hans (Johann) Hogenberg. This was the last package the Moretuses would send to any of the Hogenbergs via Cologne until November 1617, when a shipment destined for Abraham Hogenberg was included in a transport to Kinckius. One of the Hogenbergs (occasionally identified as Hans (Johann)), though, periodically received packages via the Moretuses' shop at the Frankfurt fair between 1594 and 1603. If the source of the package was noted, it had come from Philips Galle.[66] Hence, in the years immediately Frans Hogenberg's death, his widow, Agnes, continued to publish his work, possibly in conjunction with Meuting, while his elder son Johann appears to have branched out on his own, working independently as an engraver and as a print seller.

When Frans Hogenberg's and Agnes Lomar's son Abraham entered the fray in the mid-1610s, he evidently decided to combine the sale of some of his father's publications, in particular the *Civitates*, with trade in the prints published by several contemporary Antwerp print dealers. Initially, between 1616 and 1628, the bulk of his transactions in which the Moretuses were involved took place at the Frankfurt book fairs. In addition to receiving a number of packages prepared for him by Theodore Galle in the 1610s, Abraham also took advantage of the fairs to request that the Moretuses convey money he owed to Charles de Mallery – suggesting that he was obtaining prints from De Mallery by other means during the 1620s.[67] Since the Moretuses asked Galle to transport a copy of an Italian edition of Abraham Ortelius's atlas that Hogenberg had ordered from them in July 1620, Hogenberg must have been acquiring more works (and not necessarily just prints) than what the Moretuses sporadically sent him in the 1620s.[68] It was not until 1631 that the situation changed, due (at least in part) to the increasing dangers of travel and the transport of goods to the Frankfurt fairs in the 1630s because of the Thirty Years' War.[69] Hogenberg's flurry of trade via Balthasar Moretus I in this decade reveals the assortment of Antwerp artists whom he approached for prints. Alongside consignments from his former primary supplier, Theodore Galle (and subsequently his son Jan), Hogenberg also received packages prepared by Nicolas Lauwers (one in 1638), Michael Snijders (two in 1632), Jan-Baptist Barbé (four between 1636 and 1638), and, above all, various members of the Collaert family, who provided him with a total of nine packages between 1631 and 1639. In only a few instances were the general contents of these packages noted: unspecified images. Hogenberg also never sent packages or other forms of remuneration back – underscoring, once again, how the transport of goods and the payments for them were often two distinct operations.

When compared with what is known about Cologne booksellers' purchases of prints from the Moretuses and the shipment of packages to other Cologne print sellers, Hogenberg's dealings reveal both the breadth and potential areas of specialization in his traffic in Antwerp prints. While there are intermittent indications of his interest in the work of De Mallery and subsequently Jan-Baptist Barbé, his acquisitions via the Moretuses – like those of De Passe – centered around shipments from the Galle and Collaert families. This emphasis is in striking contrast to the orders placed by the Moretuses' contacts among Cologne's booksellers, which reveal their preference for large quantities of prints by the Wierixes and De Mallery. The primary exception was Johann Kinckius. Not only did he occasionally buy basic prints on paper in bulk from both Abraham van Merlen and Michael Snijders, but he also requested several hundreds of prints on parchment, many of which were colored, from Theodore Galle in 1630–1631. Although nothing is known about the type of imagery that Snijders, the Galles, or the Collaerts sent to Abraham Hogenberg, the purchase of specially illuminated images on parchment remained notably exceptional among the orders by Moretuses' clients in Cologne. Only isolated sales of specially embellished altar cards periodically recur. This general distinction, combined with Kinckius's apparent lack of interest in Snijders's illuminated prints on parchment, stands out all the more in the context of the Moretuses' routine sale of hundreds to thousands of such images from the Galles, Cnobbaerts, and Snijders to booksellers in Münster and the Baltics between the 1630s and 1641.

The emphasis in the quotation at the beginning of this chapter on the importance of the book trade in Cologne for the support of the Catholic faith throughout Germany – which was thought to go hand in hand with the large-scale production of attractive books and images – is understandable from a local perspective. Nevertheless, the statement ignores the immense significance of the import of prints to satisfy the burgeoning demand for them in Cologne and, potentially, one of the distinguishing features of the imagery sought to foster indoctrination in the Catholic faith. In Cologne, the need for plain engravings on paper in bulk quantities appears to have prevailed over trends favoring the costly finishing of prints. Despite the city's consequence for the distribution of printed matter across Catholic Germany, the print market in Cologne paled in comparison with the even more extensive exchanges occurring at the biannual Frankfurt fairs between individuals of diverse national origins. An essential destination for most internationally oriented booksellers, including those active in Cologne, the Frankfurt fairs were attended routinely by many of Cologne's print dealers, who often picked up more packages of works from Antwerp print sellers at the Moretuses' shop there than they received through the shipments the Moretuses sent directly to Cologne. Even individual collectors, such as Arnold van Buchell, attended the fairs on occasion.[70] Additionally, the Frankfurt fairs were advantageous for the settlement of debts from international transactions, including those involving prints acquired by a variety of Cologne's print dealers who did not otherwise tend to operate through the Moretuses, for instance Johann Bussemacher and, above all, Peter Overadt. Attesting to the traffic in astounding quantities of prints that go far beyond the extent of most print collections today, a better understanding of the magnitude of the trade in prints in Frankfurt is essential to comprehending the immense and vibrant international market for prints in early modern Europe.

1 "Der fürtreffeliche Bücher handel zu Cöllen, alda unzahlbar viel schöner Bücher, und Bilder werden erdacht und in Trück gebracht, mit welchen der Catholische Glaube durch Teutschland sehr befördert ist, und annoch befördert wird." Excerpt from the text accompanying Henricus Rieger's 1619 publication of a map of Cologne (fig. 8.1).

2 Corsten 1985; Enderle 2000, pp. 168–69 and 179; and Chaix 2021, pp. 164–75, 362, and 369–71, on Cologne as a center for Catholic texts. See Schöller 1992 on the simultaneous production of prints.

3 Corsten 1985, p. 189; Harreld 2004, pp. 29–31 and 165–67; and Chaix 2021, pp. 47–51 (on trade generally). See also Harreld 2004, pp. 129, 159, and 160 on Cologne merchants in Antwerp.

4 Harreld 2004, pp. 105–06, 129, 157, and 170 on exports from Antwerp; Schöller 1992, p. 18, on exports from Cologne; and Chaix 2021, pp. 217–19, for a general overview of the ties between Antwerp and Cologne at the end of the sixteenth century.

5 Chaix 2021, pp. 362–78; Schöller 1992, p. 27; and Bergerhausen 2010, pp. 252–61, on the status of Cologne's printing industry. See also Bowen and Imhof 2008, p. 35, for an overview of Antwerp's importance in the printing of Catholic texts.

6 Corsten 1985, pp. 195–98; Reske 2015, pp. 470–71; and Rouzet 1975, pp. 19–20 on Birckman. See Rouzet 1975, pp. 157–58; and Reske 2015, p. 492, on Mylius. See also Imhof 2016, on apprentices from Cologne at the Officina Plantiniana.

7 Bergerhausen 2010, p. 254; Enderle 2000, p. 169; and Schöller 1992, pp. 27–28.

8 Veldman 1993, pp. 35–37 and 45.

9 Schöller 1999, on Van Buchell's purchases; New Holl. Hogenberg, part 1, pp. xxii–xxvi, and Saur 2012, pp. 178–183, on the Hogenberg family; and Veldman 2001a on De Passe.

10 Bergerhausen 2010, pp. 177–93; and Spengler 2003, pp. 17 and 22.

11 For an overview of the Jesuits' activities in Cologne and sources on them, see Bergerfurth 2010. We are grateful to Henrike Stein of the University of Cologne for her reference to this article. The establishment of the Jesuit order in Cologne is also discussed in detail in Spengler 2003, pp. 13–22; and Schmitz 2000, p. 84.

12 Spengler 2003, p. 18; and Bergerhausen 2010, pp. 180–89 and 199.

13 Schmitz 2000, p. 84.

14 Spengler 2003, pp. 11–12, 30–44, 49, and 369–377, and Schwaighofer 2010 provide overviews of the collection and of what remained in Paris, as well as references to other Jesuit collections with important print collections. The works that were returned are now catalogued as a long-term loan to the Wallraf-Richartz Museum & Fondation Corboud, Graphische Sammlung, of Cologne, where the origin of individual prints from the former Jesuit collection is noted under their provenances (see www.kulturelles-erbe-koeln.de).

15 For the identification of the preserved section (fig. 3) of a larger ornamental print, see De Jong and De Groot 1988, p. 73, no. 82.2; and MPM PK.OP.08078 for a complete impression of it (reproduced and discussed in Grotesken 2019, pp. 70–71).

16 Spengler 2003, pp. 341–45.

17 Ibid., pp. 121–22.

18 Bergerhausen 2010, p. 180; and Spengler 2003, pp. 157–58, 164–65, 178, and 292.

19 Bergerhausen 2010, p. 186.

20 Spengler 2003, pp. 165–80 and 345–46.

21 Bergerhausen 2010, pp. 197, 199, and 254; and Schöller 1992, p. 27.

22 MPM Arch. 242, fol. 144v (Hellebrand); MPM Arch. 246, fol. 14r (Greuter); and MPM Arch. 148, fol. 199r (Alting).

23 MPM Arch. 218, fol. 150r (a roll sent to Mainz in 1611); MPM Arch. 1051 (fall 1631), fol. [111] lft (a package with plates (possibly copper plates), sent by Joannes Bollandus to Joachim Joannes in Würzburg in 1631); MPM Arch. 221, fol. 61r (two packages of "images" sent by the procurator of the Antwerp Jesuits, Antoine du Carne, to Petrus Bacherius in Dillingen in 1614); MPM Arch. 222, fol. 49r (shipment of "images" to Mair in 1615); and MPM Arch. 234, fol. 28r (an unspecified package sent by the prefect of the Antwerp Jesuit college, Heribertus Rosweydus, to Stör in 1627). Our thanks to Dr. Clemens Brodkorb of the Archiv der Deutscher Provinz der Jesuiten for his help in identifying Mair and Stör.

24 Spengler 2003, pp. 49–50, but without any clear source for these remarks.

25 See MPM Arch. 962, fol. 35, for a reference to contact with Johann Gymnich III at the 1579 spring Frankfurt fair; and MPM Arch. 754, fol. 41, for the end of Balthasar Moretus II's trade with the widow of Johann Gymnich IV in 1648. See MPM Arch. 71, fol. 22v, for an example of a package from Philips Galle intended for Hans Hogenberg that was sent to Goswinus Cholinus in 1594; and MPM Arch. 239, fols. 69v and 195r, for packages prepared by a member of the Collaert family and Theodore Galle, respectively, for Abraham Hogenberg that were sent to Heinrich Crith in 1631.

26 Reske 2015, pp. 492 and 500–01; and Enderle 2000, pp. 172 and 178 in particular, on the importance of the Mylius family.

27 See, for example, MPM Arch. 62, fol. 134r (1585); and MPM Arch. 67, fol. 57v (1590). Boons and Hogenberg are discussed in greater detail below.

28 See MPM Arch. 67, fol. 57v, for a shipment to Mylius in May 1590 that comprised not only a large quantity of books, but also three packages for the Hogenberg family, two for Boons, and one for Mylius from Philips Galle.

29 MPM Arch. 173, fols. 34v and 73v.

30 See Reske 2015, pp. 500–01, on Hermann Mylius and his management of the Mylius firm, initially with his brother Arnold II until his death in 1605, and then alone until 1657.

31 See MPM Arch. 759, fol. 48, and MPM Arch. 492, fol. 22, for the start and end of their trade with Hermann in 1607 and 1662, respectively; and MPM Arch. 217, fol. 230v (1610: Wierix), MPM Arch. 219, fol. 23r (1612: Galle), MPM Arch. 226, fol. 185v (1619), and MPM Arch. 242, fol. 77r (1634), for packages sent to him.

32 MPM Arch. 1104, fol. 102v, for Wierix's supply of his prints for 18 fl. 2.5 st.; and MPM Arch. 218, fol. 102v, for Mylius's purchase of them for 21 fl. 17 st., in addition to Galle's series for 2 fl. 5 st. per copy, which Galle had previously supplied to Balthasar Moretus for just 2 fl. (see Appendix 1, TG-10).

33 MPM Arch. 238, fols. 133v-134r (purchase and supply, respectively).

34 Reske 2015, pp. 497 and 504–05. Enderle 2000, pp. 172–73, erroneously identifies Anton Hierat II as Gymnich's apprentice and the founder of the family business.

35 MPM Arch. 218, fols. 207r (purchase) and 208r-208v (supply). For the named print series, see Appendix 1, TG-6-TG-9, OV-1, and CM-4.

36 MPM Arch. 230, fols. 143r-143v (purchase and supply, respectively).

37 MPM Arch. 234, fols. 27v (1627 purchase) and 30v (supply by Galle); MPM Arch. 1106, fol. 64v (supply by Boel); and MPM Arch. 237, fol. 3v (1629 purchase).

38 Imhof 2016, pp. 10–16 on Kinckius's apprenticeship, including p. 14 on his marriage and p. 16 on the enduring positive personal relationship between his family and the Moretuses. See Enderle 2000, p. 172, on Kinckius's relative importance in Cologne; and Reske 2015, p. 501, on his local ties. Both Enderle (p. 173) and Reske assert that Kinckius trained under Johann Gymnich III and married his daughter Elisabeth.

39 For shipments of packages from both Wierix and Galle, see, for example, MPM Arch. 177, fol. 79v (1605; specified as comprising prints); and MPM Arch. 218, fol. 81v (Galle).

40 For examples for De Mallery and Van Merlen, see MPM Arch. 224, fols. 171v and 172r (supply and purchase); and MPM Arch. 225, fols. 13v (purchase) and 13r and 137r (supply). For a purchase of 200 prints from Snijders at the common, low-end rate of 36 st. per hundred prints, see MPM Arch. 226, fol. 87r.

41 Compare MPM Arch. 238, fols. 108v and 113v, and MPM Arch. 239, fols. 18r, 23r, and 132v (all examples of the resale of bulk images on parchment at cost) with MPM Arch. 238, fols. 85r and 86r (supply and purchase of canons and suffragia with profit).

42 See MPM Arch. 245, fols. 25v and 182v, and MPM Arch. 246, fol. 14r, for Van den Enden's packages; and MPM Arch. 247, fols. 18r and 108v, for payments to him. Recall the packages sent to the Jesuits Greuter and Alting via Kinckius, for example. See below for examples among print dealers in Cologne. In addition to serving as an important transit point for packages from Snijders and Jan Boel destined for Michiel van Dale in Münster (e.g., MPM Arch. 233, fol. 83v (1626)), Kinckius also assisted with packages for other booksellers in Cologne, including Georg Meuting in 1614 (MPM Arch. 221, fol. 123r), Hermann Mylius in 1620 (MPM Arch. 227, fol. 206r), and Cornelis van Egmont in 1630 (MPM Arch. 238, fol. 161v).

43 Imhof 2016, pp. 5–10 (Wolters' apprenticeship) and 6–7 (his marriage). See also Reske 2015, pp. 498–99.

44 MPM Arch. 172, fol. 18v; and MPM Arch. 173, fol. 185v, respectively.

45 MPM Arch. 1104, fol. 5r (Scribani); MPM Arch. 176, fol. 176r; and MPM Arch. 177, fol. 79v, all regarding three packages from Huberti.

46 MPM Arch. 216, fols. 130v and 211r, for example.

47 MPM Arch. 759, fol. 41 rht.

48 See MPM Arch. 216, fol. 211r, for the former; and MPM Arch. 218, fols. 104v, 108v, and 110v (shipment), and MPM Arch. 128, fol. 108 rht (prices charged), for the latter.

49 For De Mallery's print, compare MPM Arch. 1104, fol. 79v (supply) and MPM Arch. 216, fol. 130v (purchase), which indicate that while De Mallery originally charged 3 fl. for these prints, the Moretuses sold them to Wolters for just 2 fl. 10 st. (the equivalent of De Mallery's usual 50 st.-per-hundred-print rage). For Wierix's print, see MPM Arch. 217, fols. 8r-8v (supply and purchase at 2 st. per print). See also Appendix 1, CM-5 and WX-3 for these images.

50 MPM Arch. 218, fol. 187r.

51 MPM Arch. 243, fols. 121r-121v (supply by Theodore Galle's widow, Catharina Moerentorf, and resale at cost).

52 Imhof 2016, pp. 7–10, for the Cologne missal project; MPM Arch. 144, p. 6, for Balthasar's summary of the costs for the canons; and MPM Arch. 235, fol. 57v, for the shipment of the canons, along with the last of the missals for Cologne that Wolters was to receive.

53 Schöller 1999 on Van Buchell's purchases generally and p. 381 for this summary.

54 Ibid., pp. 383 (Van Buchell's primary purchases) and 387–88 (his minimal purchases from Bussemacher and Overadt). See also Schöller 1992, pp. 32–37 in particular, for a more detailed examination of Bussemacher's publications.

55 Schöller 1999, pp. 381 and 383, for Van Buchell's references to both Boons; and Keussen 1908, p. 109, for a transcription of Van Buchell's original Latin text, which reads: "Petro Bons Brabanto".

56 For at least four packages sent by Galle to Boons in Cologne, see MPM Arch. 66, fol. 100r; and MPM Arch. 68, fol. 60r. See Chapter 9 for Boons's dealings in Frankfurt, including exchanges with the Moretuses in cartographic publications there; and MPM Arch. 65, fol. 107v, for a package from Ortelius for him that was shipped to Frankfurt.

57 Veldman 2001a, pp. 19–31, on De Vos's Antwerp period; Rombouts and Van Lerius 1872, vol. I, p. 291, for his registration in the guild; and MPM Arch. 65, fol. 73r, for a payment to De Vos for an engraving of St Bruno by De Passe.

58 Veldman 2001a, p. 38–41, on De Passe's move to Cologne; and MPM Arch. 67, fol. 124v, for this one shipment.

59 For the Antwerp transactions, see MPM Arch. 179, fols. 414 and 153r (packages from Galle and Collaert, and subsequently an unspecified source) and 218r (payment for Galle).

60 Veldman 2001a, pp. 172–75, on De Passe's eviction from Cologne; Chapter 9 for his transactions there; and MPM Arch. 1012 (spring 1612), fol. 4 lft, and MPM Arch. 219, fol. 112r, for his payment of some 30 fl. to Collaert (in German currencies) in 1612. For the two cited Jan Moretus editions, see MPM Arch. 228, fol. 50r; and Imhof 2014a, O-81 and A-2.

61 On the Hogenberg family, see Saur 2012, pp. 178–83. On the editions of the Civitates, including the first one published jointly by Galle and Hogenberg, see Van der Krogt 2010, vol. IV.1, pp. 35–261, and p. 39 in particular for Galle as a co-publisher of the first volume. On this volume, see also Meurer 1988, p. 31. See Bowen 2016 on Hogenberg's images of the Eighty Years' War. The Hogenbergs' trade in these and other publications is also discussed in Denucé 1912–1913, vol. I, pp. 260–98.

62 See Van den Broecke, Van der Krogt, and Meurer 1998, pp. 35 and 53–54, for this legendary excursion to Poitiers. Joris Hoefnagel's portrayal of people cutting into this stone, was even included in the 1598 edition of the Civitates (vol. V, pl. 18 by Poitiers). Ursula Mielke asserts that Joris Hoefnagel carved the above names on the stone in 1561, implying that Hogenberg, Galle, Sadeler, and Mercator had never made the trip together (New Holl. Hogenberg, part I, p. xxiii).

63 MPM Arch. 58, fol. 166r: "Receu par les mains de Philippus Galle ung pacquet venant de Coulogne de Francois Hogenberghe ... ung petit pacquet de deux lettres etc. cachetees pour Gerard de Jode que ie luy ay delivre entre ses mains propres" (Received from the hands of Philips Galle, a package from Cologne from Frans Hogenberg ... [including] a small package with two letters, etc., sealed, for Gerard de Jode that I delivered to him personally). For examples of Galle sending an unspecified package to Hogenberg via shipments to Arnold Mylius in 1585 and 1587, respectively, see MPM Arch. 62, fol. 134r; and MPM Arch. 64, fol. 95v.

64 On Johann Hogenberg and his work for Bussemacher and others, see Schöller 1992, p. 30; and Merlo 1966, cols. 377–80. For Agnes Lomar's possible arrangements with Johann Hogenberg, see Meurer 2001, p. 29. Saur 2012, p. 180, provides a brief summary of these claims, but often without clear support. See MPM Arch. 759, fol. 71 rht, for the following reference in the spring of 1604 to Lomar's and Meuting's marriage: "Georgius Muytinx ayant espouse la vefve de Hoghenberg". On Abraham Hogenberg, see Saur 2012, p. 178. For the transition from Meuting's to Abraham Hogenberg's involvement in the sales of Frans Hogenberg's publications, in particular the Civitates, compare MPM Arch. 221, fol. 152r (Meuting in August 1614), and MPM Arch. 760, fol. 27 (A. Hogenberg in 1615).

65 For example, MPM Arch. 67, fol. 124v, and MPM Arch. 68, fol. 24v, for the Moretuses' shipments; and MPM Arch. 70, fol. 151v, for the shipment from Lomar.

66 MPM Arch. 71, fols. 22v and 109v (packages to Johann (Hans) in 1594 in Cologne and Frankfurt, respectively); and MPM Arch. 224, fol. 172r (1617 unspecified package for Abraham in Cologne). For examples of Galle's shipments to Johann at Frankfurt during this period, see, for example, MPM Arch. 72, fol. 108r (August 1595); and MPM Arch. 173, fol. 126v (August 1601). See also Chapter 9.

67 See Chapter 9.

68 MPM Arch. 227, fol. 111v (1620 atlas); and MPM Arch. 228, fol. 15v, and MPM Arch. 234, fol. 194r, for single, unspecified packages from Jan Boel and Theodore Galle, sent in 1621 and 1627, respectively.

69 See Chapter 9 for this topic.

70 Schöller 1999, p. 390, with reference to Keussen 1907, p. 93.

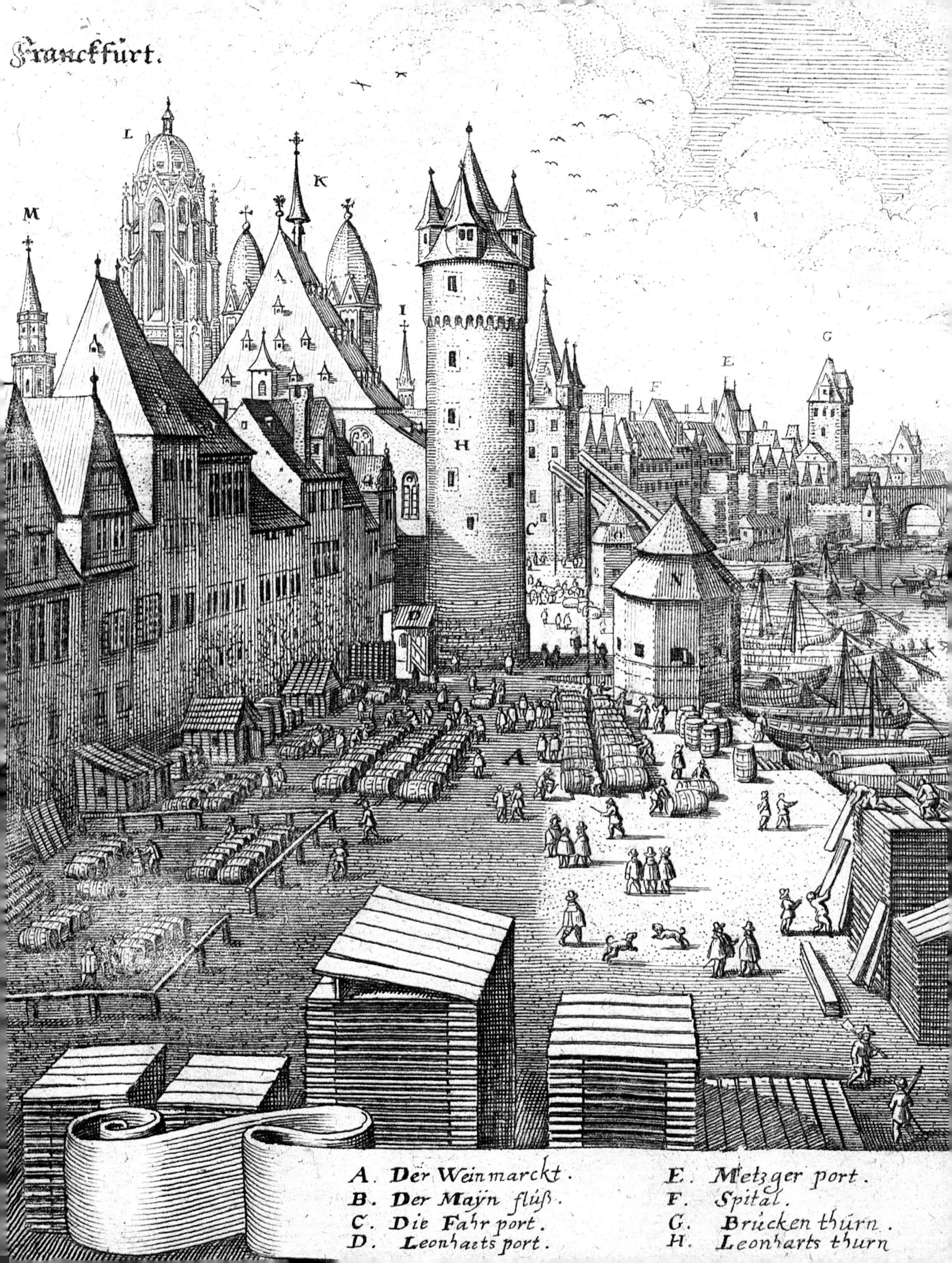
Franckfurt.
A. Der Weinmarckt.
B. Der Mayn fluß.
C. Die Fahr port.
D. Leonharts port.
E. Metzger port.
F. Spital.
G. Brucken thurn.
H. Leonharts thurn

CHAPTER 9

THE IMPORTANCE OF THE FRANKFURT FAIRS

FOR THE PRINT TRADE IN SEVENTEENTH-CENTURY EUROPE

> [The Frankfurt fair] was an institution known to almost everyone, visited by so many, its benefits numerous and great, from which many became richer and not a few went from poor to rich.[1]

Detail of fig. 9.2:
Matthäus Merian I,
View of Frankfurt, 1655.

When, in 1574, Henri Estienne II published his eulogy of the biannual fairs held at Frankfurt-am-Main (fig. 9.1) and the book fair in particular, he was most likely motivated by diverse concerns. Potentially in need of financial backing and, therefore, of increasing interest in his own publications, he offered an appealing account of a flourishing event attended by many of his associates that would have brought him welcome attention. At the very least, his dedication of the work to the Frankfurt consuls inspired them to give him a gold and silver goblet. Other accounts of drunken brawls and theft reveal that the Frankfurt fairs were not always as idyllic as Estienne would have had his audience believe.[2] Nevertheless, their international fame for trade in a dazzling array of luxury goods, as well as their significance for professional interactions, cannot be denied. While the majority of those attending the fairs came from the Holy Roman Empire, Frankfurt's fortuitously central location on a number of important trade routes simultaneously enhanced its advantages to foreigners. Not only was it feasible to ship heavy loads of various goods to and from the fairs (fig. 9.2), but Frankfurt was a mutually convenient place to meet for individuals from Italy, France, the Low Countries, and even more remote locations in England, Scandinavia, and territories along the Baltic Sea. Moreover, booksellers routinely settled outstanding debts there: either from the current or past fairs, or from shipments sent to distant clients in between fairs. Consequently, Frankfurt's importance as a place for financial exchange during the fairs was also essential to its success.[3] Whether or not it was possible to become rich from participating in the fairs is difficult to determine and probably would have been due primarily to one's own business skills. Nonetheless, through the early seventeenth century, despite civil unrest and war across Europe that hindered travel and the shipment of goods, the Frankfurt fairs continued to attract people as valuable and bountiful opportunities for obtaining rare items and for promoting one's newest creations, including printed images.

Already by 1520, people interested in scarce, renowned prints, such as the works of Albrecht Dürer, sought them at the Frankfurt fairs. This practice would continue into the seventeenth century – as long as the fairs remained viable. For example, in 1608, Jan Moretus I observed to Antonio de Rovelasca, the treasurer for Archduke Albrecht and Archduchess

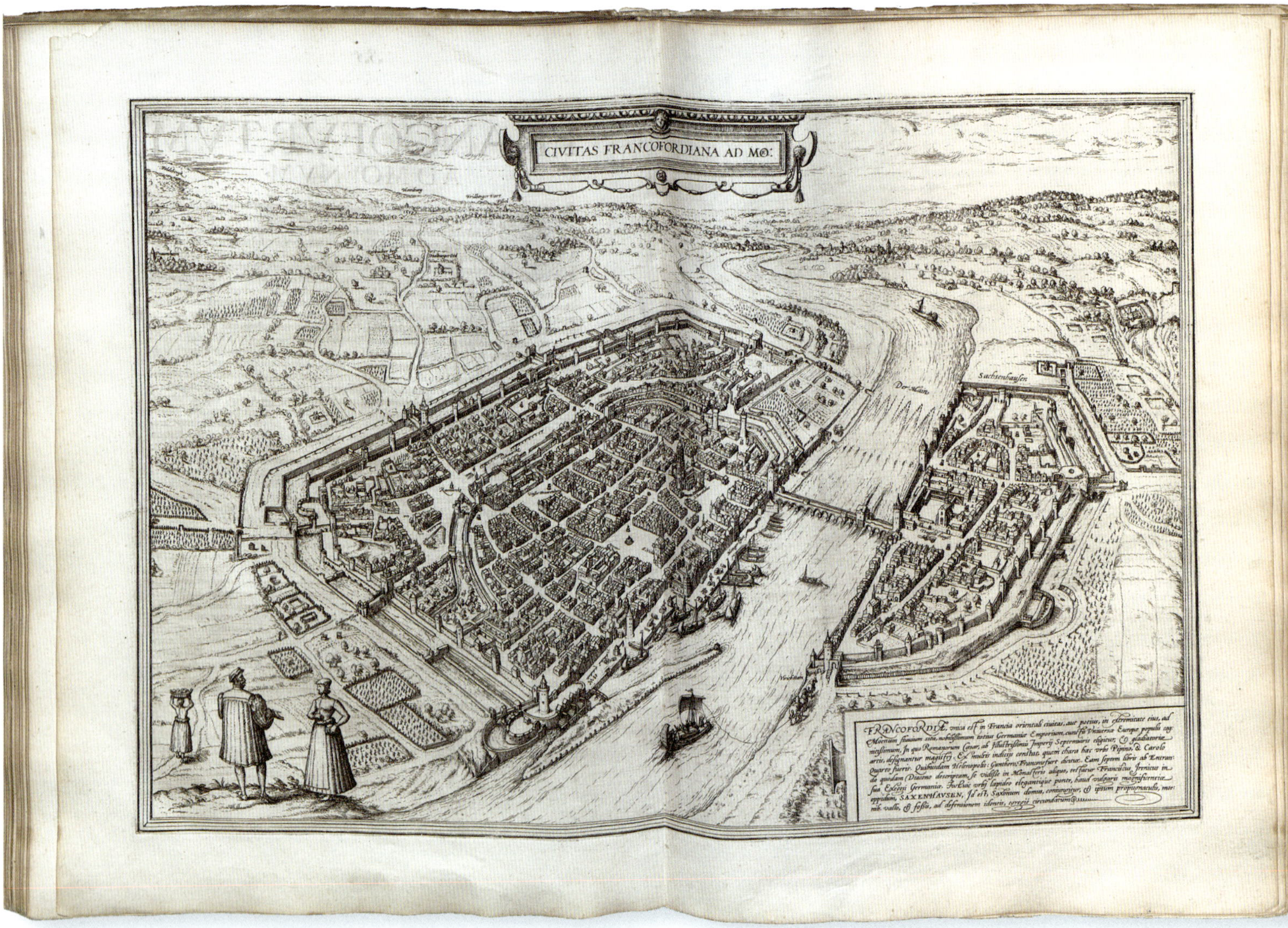

9.1 Frans Hogenberg, *View of Frankfurt*, in: Georg Braun, *Civitates orbis terrarum* (Cologne: G. Braun and F. Hogenberg; and Antwerp: P. Galle, 1572), etching and engraving, 337 × 480 mm. Antwerp, Museum Plantin-Moretus: 2–36, map 35.

Isabella, that while Dürer's prints were not easy to find in Antwerp, they could be obtained at the fairs in Frankfurt.[4] Moreover, throughout the sixteenth century, contemporary artists marketed their wares (often through agents) at both regional and international fairs, including those held in Frankfurt. With his brother Conrad based nearby in Cologne, it is not surprising that Hendrick Goltzius had his latest stunning prints sold at Frankfurt. Indeed, when attending one fair, Abraham Ortelius purchased impressions of Goltzius's newest, spectacular tour de force, his engraving of *The Feast of the Gods at the Marriage of Cupid and Psyche* after Bartholomeus Spranger (fig. 5.10), the very year it was published. News of Ortelius's acquisitions spread and caused Dominicus Lampsonius to write to him on 2 November 1587, asking him to sell him an impression.[5] The strong allure of the immense potential of the Frankfurt fairs for trade in sundry goods is evident not only from the Moretuses' own dealings at the fairs, but also from the unexpected frequency with which they facilitated transactions there for a multitude of contacts, including numerous individuals engaged in the trade of hundreds of thousands of prints.

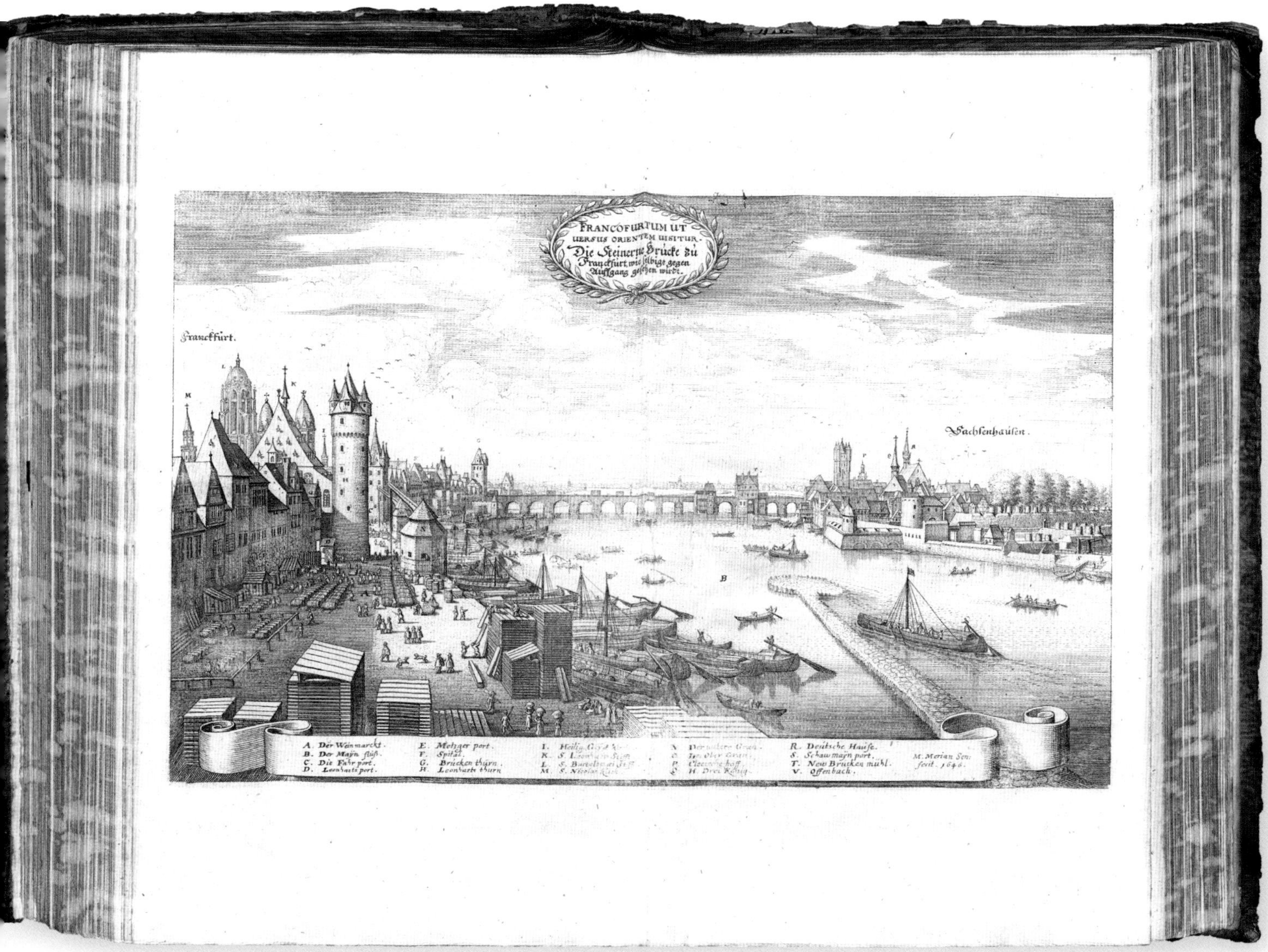

9.2 Matthäus Merian I, *View of Frankfurt*, in: Martin Zeiller, *Topographia Hassiae, et regionum vicinarum: das ist: Beschreibung und eigentliche Abbildung der vornehmsten Städte und Plätze in Hessen, und denen benachbarten Landschafften* (Frankfurt: Heirs of Merian, 1655), engraving, 210 × 340 mm. Heidelberg, Universitätsbibliothek: A 1939 G Folio RES, inserted between pp. 52 and 53.

THE MORETUSES' PRESENCE AT THE FRANKFURT FAIRS

Although Estienne begins by highlighting the busy spectacle of an abundance of finely made products, inventions, animals, and food stuffs at the Frankfurt fairs, his account culminates with his glorification of the book fair. Having developed into a separate, but simultaneously held, event by the end of the fifteenth century, the Frankfurt book fair remained the most important opportunity of its kind in all of Europe through the early seventeenth century.[6] Attracting people from assorted related fields, including paper merchants, type founders, bookbinders, printers, authors, scholars, and librarians, it is not surprising that Plantin and the Moretuses regularly attended these fairs from Plantin's first years as a printer-publisher.[7] As the Press's fame and production grew, its abundant offerings at the fairs attracted a broad range of potential clients and made their shop a routine stop for many attending the fairs. For example, in addition to sundry booksellers and others involved in the book trade, several librarians purchased works from them. Among these were Janus Gruterus, the librarian of the Bibliotheca Palatina in Heidelberg, and Marcantonio Palazzolo, the librarian for the Duke of Mantua, Vincenzo Gonzaga I, as well as Adrianus Romanus, a doctor and mathematician who periodically bought books for the archbishop of Würzburg, Julius Echter von Mespelbrunn. Other contacts included the Frankfurt goldsmith Guillaume Leenwaert, the cartographer Gerard Mercator from Duisburg, and the artist Joris Hoefnagel from Prague.[8] Often as many as eighty to a hundred people (primarily, but not exclusively, living in German towns) bought works from the Moretuses when they attended the fairs between 1590 and 1631.[9] As these were often not just one-time transactions, it was clearly worth some effort to attend the fairs, not only to maintain such contacts but also to collect payment on these and other accounts. While some charges were reconciled via an exchange of merchandise of equal value, a letter of credit, or by a credit/debit accounting system that was settled at a later time, the Moretuses frequently sought to conclude a significant part of their dealings at the fairs with some form of cash payment.[10] Indeed, while attending the Frankfurt fairs, the Moretuses regularly amassed cash in various currencies worth thousands of florins, which they subsequently took back to Antwerp. This money was then used to pay some of the Moretuses' exceptionally large bills, such as the hundreds of florins that they regularly owed Theodore Galle for adding engraved illustrations to many of their books.[11] But what, exactly, did participating in the Frankfurt fairs entail in practical terms?

In the sixteenth and seventeenth centuries, the Frankfurt fairs took place in the spring (generally during the three weeks before Easter) and in the fall (for three weeks starting on the Monday between 6 and 12 September). These general timespans are also indicated in Jost Amman's *Allegory of Trade* (fig. 7.1) under March and September. Although the official start and end of transactions was marked with the ringing of bells and raising of flags, in reality, the booksellers traded when they could, depending on when their barrels of books arrived and when their fellow booksellers were present. On the basis of the Moretuses' records from Frankfurt, it appears that they were often selling books for approximately two weeks per fair.[12]

The Moretuses frequently sent four to six barrels of books to each fair, typically between December and the following February for the spring fair and from July through August for the fall fair. In some instances, they sent as many as nine barrels.[13] Remarkably, when the weight of the barrels was recorded between 1586 and 1631, most weighed approximately 1,000 Antwerp pounds, or roughly 470 kilograms today.[14] This suggests that there was no significant decrease in the quantity (at least in terms of weight) of what the Moretuses shipped to Frankfurt between 1589, when Jan Moretus I took over his father-in-law's business, and the Moretuses' temporary cessation of activities in Frankfurt in the early 1630s due to the intensification of the Thirty Years' War in that region.[15] Usually, the barrels were shipped first via waterways from Antwerp to Cologne. Not only was Cologne significant for the book trade in Germany and a common, important destination for shipments from the Plantin-Moretus Press, but it was also a logical stop en route to Frankfurt. While the Moretuses employed a variety of individuals who specialized in this type of transport each year, they routinely directed their shipments to a preferred contact person in Cologne, who then supervised the subsequent transport to Frankfurt. The contact was usually a member of the Van Egmont family of merchants (first Nicolas, who was related by marriage to one of Jan Moretus I's uncles, and then his son Jan). The Van Egmonts also helped by advancing funds to pay for additional charges.[16] When ground transport ("par terre") was used, the routes were occasionally specified, frequently as either the straight road ("droit chemin") or the high road ("hoog chemin").[17]

Despite this wealth of information about shipping, it remains difficult to calculate exactly what it cost to send the barrels to Frankfurt. It is not always evident whether the rate recorded covered just travel to Cologne or encompassed the entire route to Frankfurt. The complexity of such transportation is revealed in an exceptionally detailed receipt of all the costs incurred by one shipper, a certain Nicolaes Tserraerts, for conveying two barrels from Cologne to Antwerp in the spring of 1592 (fig. 9.3). One had to stop to pay tolls, city taxes, and dues for passports, in addition to periodically having to pay others to unload and reload the freight. Consequently, these various extra charges could easily outweigh the basic cost of floating the barrels down a river.[18] For the brief overview presented below and the subsequent comparisons with the costs charged for sending smaller packages of goods together with the barrels of books, we will be using the median of the few clear examples of what the Moretuses paid to ship barrels directly between Antwerp and Frankfurt, namely 5 fl. (or 100 st.) per 100 Antwerp pounds.[19]

Once the books arrived in Frankfurt, they would have been taken to the shop the Moretuses rented there, or perhaps to their warehouse, where what was not sold at a given fair was stored until the next one.[20] The person who managed the shop and oversaw the Moretuses' transactions at Frankfurt traveled separately from the books.[21] This was typically a relative. Jan II, Jan I's son, attended the fairs by 1597 and continued to do so up to his death in 1618. Thereafter, Balthasar I's new business partner, Jan van Meurs (another relative), assumed this role until he left the family business in 1629, after which point Balthasar I's nephew Louis Moerentorf went to the fairs whenever possible through 1631. Finally, when trade at Frankfurt was revived in the later 1630s, Balthasar I decided to employ Michael Demen, a bookseller based in Cologne, to represent the Press there.

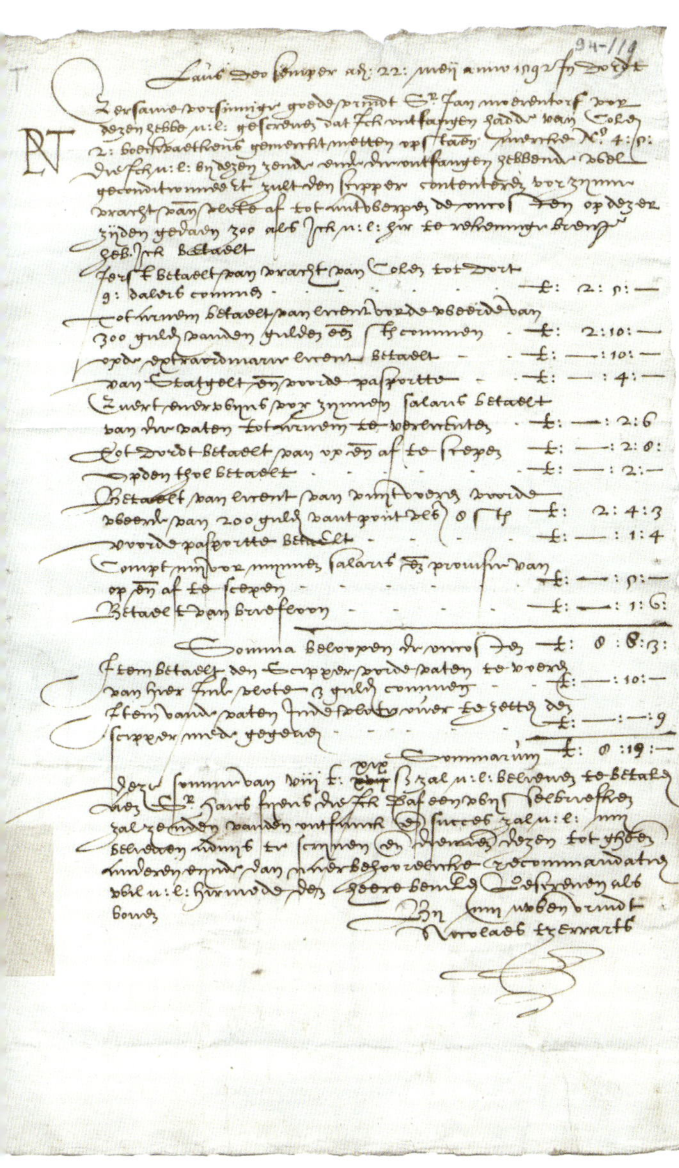

9.3 List of costs for conveying two barrels from Cologne to Antwerp in the spring of 1592 by the shipper Nicolaes Tserraerts. Antwerp, Museum Plantin-Moretus: Arch. 94, *Recueils de lettres Tavernier - Litterae incognitae*, p. 119.

Participation in the Frankfurt fairs brought with it significant logistical challenges that required the involvement of numerous individuals and a multitude of financial outlays by the Moretuses, regardless of whether they profited from their trade there. In addition, there was the risk that a shipment might be waylaid en route by robbers and roving bands of militia.[22] This would undoubtedly have been a concern for the transport of all the money the Moretuses collected during the fairs. However, they do not seem to have had a standard system for safeguarding the transport of this money. Sometimes it was simply packed with the books in the barrels that were shipped back to Antwerp. In other instances, the Van Egmont family (and others) assumed the risk of conveying the money back to Cologne, at which point sums were exchanged via their accounts with the Moretuses.[23] The fact that the Moretuses persisted in maintaining a presence at Frankfurt despite all of these concerns underscores, once again, the remarkably strong appeal of the fairs and the perceived, considerable potential of sustaining contacts and earning large profits there. The cumbersome and risky nature of both personal travel and the transport of goods and money to and from Frankfurt would have been commonly known and most likely regarded as a significant obstacle to engaging in business and settling other personal matters there. It is, then, not surprising that numerous people engaged the Moretuses to assist them with their business at the fairs. The Moretuses' records reveal that they helped a wide range of personal and professional connections beyond the ranks of their fellow booksellers, including sundry merchants, members of the clergy and nobility, as well as many individuals involved in the print trade. The evidence of how such long-distance transactions were completed in practice documents the array of networks involved as various people strove to achieve a similar goal: the distribution of thousands of prints through the multitude of opportunities provided by the Frankfurt fairs.

ARRANGING MATTERS FOR OTHERS

The three primary ways in which the Moretuses assisted others with their personal business at the Frankfurt fairs are: the receipt, exchange, and transport of money; the purchase of items at Frankfurt in someone else's name; and the shipment of a variety of packages at another person's request.

Taking payments in foreign currencies from assorted booksellers and diverse private individuals was an essential part of the Moretuses' business at the Frankfurt fairs. Between 1600 and 1631, they helped professional and personal acquaintances with their financial transactions at the fairs on a regular basis. For example, in 1607, a certain Jan Gryn, identified as an English comedian ("comediant anglois"), asked the Moretuses to take money back to his wife in Antwerp. Later on, in 1627 and 1628, the Antwerp merchant Michiel van Triest asked them to transport packages or bags of money to a certain Daniel le Veau in Frankfurt. Similarly, at the spring fair of 1628, the Antwerp-born but Münster-based bookseller Michiel van Dale requested that the Moretuses transfer money to both the Antwerp bookseller Jan Cnobbaert and Van Dale's sister in Antwerp. During the spring fair of 1631, the Moretuses' representative at Frankfurt accepted a bag of money from someone in Salzburg for delivery to the noble "Jonghe Heere Van Marduyn" in Leuven or Douai.[24] Nevertheless, financial transfers for merchants, booksellers, and other private individuals via the Frankfurt fairs were unusual and most likely reflect exceptional circumstances, such as the temporary interruption of their regular means of transport or concerns about conveying money safely during periods of civil unrest. For many Antwerp print publishers and far-flung art dealers, however, the Moretuses' presence at Frankfurt provided a useful alternative for making payments.

As early as the fall fair of 1601, Balthasar Caymox and the widow of Hubert Caymox – both of whom were members of a family of art dealers based in Nuremberg – made payments in Philippstalers and Reichsthalers, respectively, for Philips Galle and Adriaen Collaert. On 4 December 1601, Jan Moretus I recorded the transfer of the equivalent amount of Brabant florins to Galle and Collaert.[25] These were significant sums of money, as Galle received 159 fl. 10 st. from the widow of Hubert Caymox and 112 fl. 10 st. from Balthasar, while Collaert was given 124 fl. 5 st. and 75 fl. from each, respectively. Similarly, at the fall fair in 1611, the Cologne print seller Peter Overadt made a payment for Charles de Mallery with six different types of currency, which were recorded as having a total value of 80 Brabant florins (fig. 9.4).[26] When Charles de Mallery planned to travel to Italy in the spring of 1594, he paid Jan Moretus I 100 Brabant florins in March in Antwerp, with the understanding that he would be repaid an equivalent sum (in other currencies) once he arrived in Frankfurt. A month later, Moretus's representative in Frankfurt, Gommer van Sulsen, completed the transaction and had De Mallery sign a statement acknowledging the receipt of his money (fig. 9.5).[27] It was obviously safer and more convenient for De Mallery to receive the sum in local currencies in Frankfurt, rather than travel with it all the way from Antwerp. Sometimes the Moretuses did not have to convert any money at all, but were simply given an unspecified sum to be taken back to Antwerp. For instance, at the spring fair in 1618, the Cologne print and map dealer

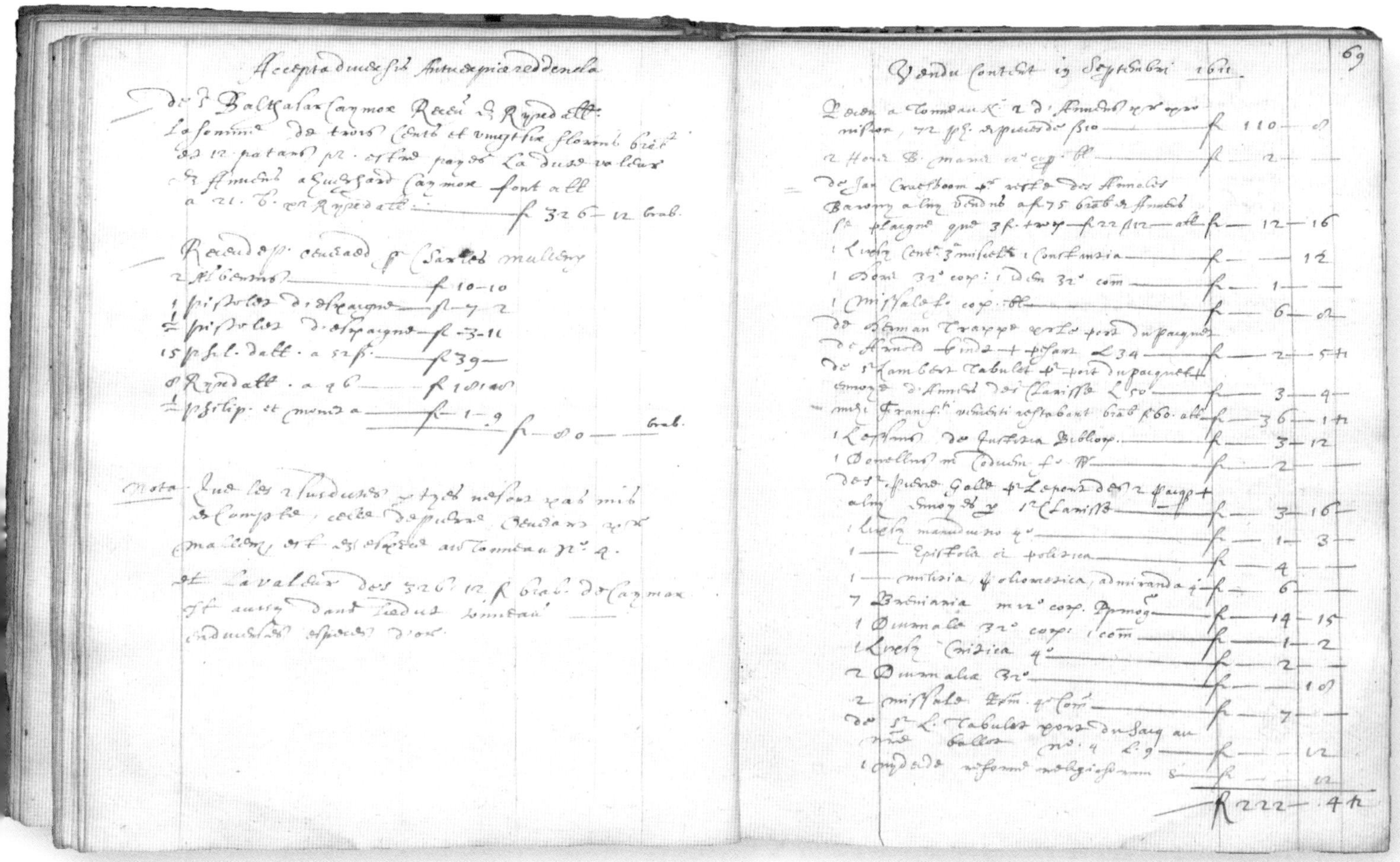

9.4 Payment of 80 florins (Brabant guilders) from the Cologne print dealer Peter Overadt for Charles de Mallery, made at the fall Frankfurt fair of 1611 in six different currencies. Antwerp, Museum Plantin-Moretus: Arch. 1011, *Cahier de Francfort* (fall 1611), fol. 69 lft.

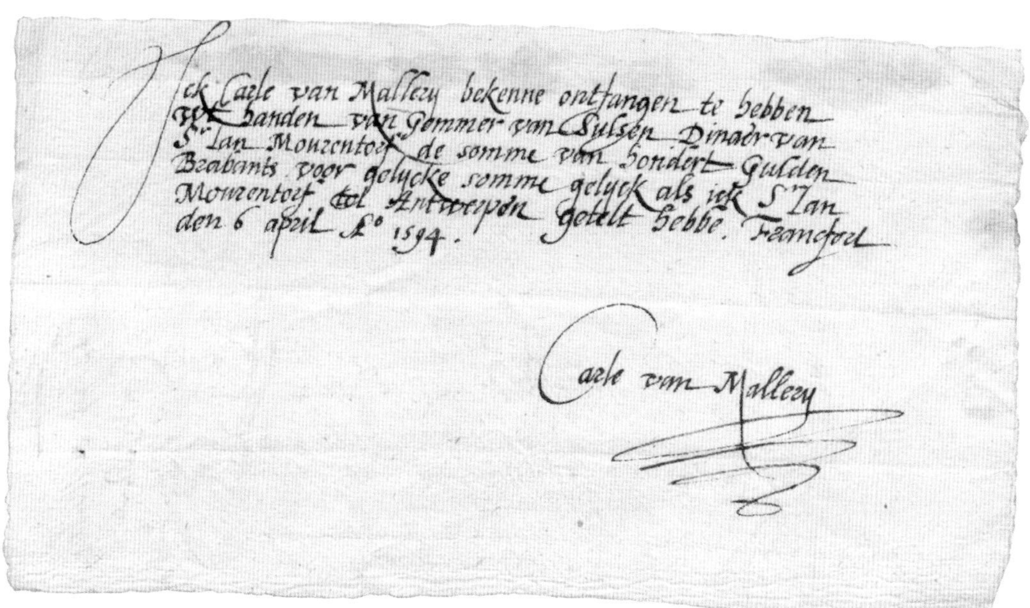

Ick Carle van Mallery bekenne ontfangen te hebben
Wt handen van Gommer van Sulsen Dinaer van
Sr Ian Moerentorf de somme van hondert Gulden
Brabants voor gelycke somme gelyck als ick Sr Ian
Moerentorf tot Antwerpen getelt hebbe. Francfort
den 6 april Ao 1594.

Carle van Mallery

9.5 Signed declaration by Charles de Mallery, acknowledging the receipt of 100 florins (Brabant guilders) from Jan Moretus I's representative at the Frankfurt fair, Gommer van Sulsen, on 6 April 1594. Antwerp, Museum Plantin-Moretus: Arch. 88, *Recueils de lettres Maccius – Montmorency*, p. 37.

Georg Meuting requested that a sealed envelope ("eenen gesloten brieff") with money for De Mallery be transported to Antwerp for him. During the spring fair of 1631, the Cologne print publisher Abraham Hogenberg asked to have a small bag ("een klyn saxken") of money taken to Jan-Baptist Barbé.[28] As will be discussed in greater detail below, the extent to which a given print dealer availed himself of this option varied from one individual to another.

Remarkably, among all of these transactions, there is never any indication that the Moretuses charged a fee either for the exchange of currency or for the transport of it. As most of these payments involved third parties who would also have wanted to confirm that the correct amounts were recorded, it is doubtful that a profit margin was embedded in the exchange rate without being noted explicitly. A more likely (but not documented) possibility is that something may have been charged for transport, at least if a significantly heavy packet of money was involved.

A more exceptional service that the Moretuses performed for various individuals was the purchase of specific items for them at the Frankfurt fairs. The assortment of objects bought confirms Estienne's emphasis on the immense variety of special, high-quality goods that could be found there, including: a chandelier ("coronne de cuivre") for Jan II's aunt Catherine Jansens, a gilded cup ("vergult copken") for a certain Hendric den Packer, and boxes for diamonds for Jan I's brother Peter Moerentorf. The Moretuses were also occasionally asked to purchase paintings at Frankfurt, such as a work by Hendrick van Balen for the canon Jakob von Wiltberg of Mainz.[29] Only Philips Galle may have been surprised by the unexpected bill for a piece of clothing that his son Cornelis I (then twenty-two years old) had obtained from the Cologne bookseller (and former apprentice to Jan Moretus I) Bernhard Wolters at the fall fair of 1598, when Cornelis was on his way to Italy.[30] Of all the examples of what the Moretuses bought for someone else, only their purchases of ink (discussed in greater detail below) recurred a number of years in a row.

Regardless of what was purchased, the Moretuses usually charged for the transport of what they shipped for third parties. Although such fees were regularly noted between 1590 and 1618, it is difficult to establish whether or not the Moretuses had a prescribed system for calculating these costs. Nevertheless, despite the significant potential variation in what they paid for the transport of their own goods, the rates the Moretuses charged others for the transport of their property routinely ranged from 1 to 3 st. per pound, where 2 st. per pound was by far the most common price. This amount was significantly less than the official rates charged by the local postal service; in 1613, for example, a single letter sent just from Frankfurt to Cologne would have cost a minimum of 3 st. per ounce (or 48 st. per pound).[31] The Moretuses applied their 2 st.-per-pound rate to a variety of clients throughout the period under consideration, including: the cartographer Abraham Ortelius in 1595; Jan I's brother, the merchant Peter Moerentorf, in 1603; the Jesuit Andreas Schottus in 1607; a Polish noble, Stanislaus Zukowski, in 1615; and the bookseller Anton Hierat in 1627. The Moretuses also periodically shipped packages for others at a slightly lower rate of 1.5 st. per pound, but this price seems to have been reserved primarily for local artists and booksellers, several of whom had close personal ties with the Moretuses, such as the Galles or the Nutius family of booksellers, who were related by marriage to the Galles.[32]

Naturally, in order to calculate the total shipping cost, one needed to know how much the object to be sent weighed. Predictably, the barrels of ink were the heaviest items recorded (other than the books). These typically weighed some 50 to 100 pounds apiece and exceptionally as much as 200 pounds.[33] The lightest known item recorded was a package of letters weighing just 1 pound that was brought back from Frankfurt for the bookseller Nicolas

Laurent of Tournai by 20 April 1612. Just two lighter packages, for which the contents were not specified, were noted.[34] Individual packages containing "images", or prints, weighed approximately 5 to 38 pounds each, while 44 to 62 pounds was recorded for pairs of packages.[35] The median weight was approximately 20 pounds (or 9.5 kilograms) per package of images, according to the exceptional surviving accounts containing such details. Since the Moretuses most often paid approximately 5 fl. (or 100 st.) per 100 pounds for the direct transport of their barrels between Antwerp and Frankfurt, they probably made some profit on their shipments for others. For example, an average package of 20 pounds of prints shipped at their most common rate of 2 st. per pound would have resulted in a small profit of 20 st. per shipment.

It is important to note that the person asked to pay for the transportation costs was normally the one who received the package, rather than the one who sent it. This was the standard practice for transactions with the Plantin-Moretus Press, as they consistently charged their clients for all costs pertaining to the shipment of whatever was ordered.[36] In terms of shipments going to and from Frankfurt, this practice is best illustrated by an exchange of packages of prints in 1614 between Charles de Mallery and a certain Nicolas Bonta. In March 1614, De Mallery sent Bonta three packages of prints, two of which were recorded as having a combined weight of 44 pounds. At the spring fair, Bonta paid the Moretuses for the transport of 40 pounds of prints, in addition to giving them a sum of money (in diverse currencies) that was to be paid out to De Mallery in Antwerp. When the Moretuses' barrels of merchandise from the fair arrived in Antwerp in May, De Mallery was then charged (at the 2 st.-per-pound rate) for the return of a package of 9 pounds of prints that Bonta did not want.[37]

Although the Moretuses may not have earned much per shipment with these fees, the regularity of their transports of objects for others indicates that it was a service worth offering, particularly if they were simply using space in their barrels that would otherwise be empty. Indeed, of all the means by which the Moretuses facilitated other individuals' transactions at Frankfurt, the shipment of goods to and from the fairs was by far the most common. These packages are described in a variety of ways in the Moretuses' records, most often simply as a "package" ("pacquet" or "pacxken"). However, sacks ("sac"), boxes ("boitte" or "doos(ken)"), caskets ("cassette" or "kasken"), crates ("kisten"), rolls ("rolleau" or "roll(eken)"), and small barrels ("tonnelets") were also occasionally sent. The contents of these extra, personal items are indicated in only approximately one-third of the records of these shipments. While barrels were routinely used for transporting ink and crates were deployed for paintings, the remaining, occasional references to the contents of shipments not only demonstrate the unexpected range of what was sent, but also warn against drawing conclusions as to the content of a shipment simply on the basis of the form in which it was transported. For example, a sack might contain either money (as observed above) or basil.[38]

The extra items that the Moretuses sent for themselves reflect what they needed for their business in Frankfurt beyond their books. These included prints, sets of book illustrations, and maps (which will be discussed in greater detail below), as well as numerous packages of imperfect sheets ("imperfections") and hundreds of title pages. Some of the title pages are simply described as "various new titles" ("diverse niue tijtels") and were most likely intended as advertisements. Others, such as those for Emanuel Sa's *Scholia in quatuor evangelia* or a new folio breviary, were sent in such large quantities that they were presumably necessary, last-minute additions to sheets of publications that had already been sent.[39] The Moretuses also regularly shipped packages with clothes – especially shoes, shirts, and undergarments ("linge") – for those managing the shop in Frankfurt. In one instance, the Moretuses even used these ordinary items to help conceal a quantity of pearls sent on behalf of their relative

Henri de Clerck, which they wrapped up in a shirt intended for Cornelis van Egmont.[40] Finally, despite Estienne's emphasis on the bountiful supply of assorted food stuffs (notably wine) at the Frankfurt fairs, there were evidently some favorite items from home that could not be found there. Not only the Moretuses' own employees (like Cornelis van Egmont), but also other acquaintances whom they met at the fairs, such as a member of the Verspreet family of merchants and the Ingolstadt bookseller Johann Hertsroy, who was related to the Nutius family of booksellers in Antwerp, were apparently fond of a type of sugar bread ("suiker brood") that the Moretuses also periodically sent to Frankfurt for them.[41]

Not surprisingly, when the Moretuses transported items to and from Frankfurt for others, these consignments (when identified) often contained books. Some booksellers who would have visited the Moretuses' shop in Frankfurt asked to have books for some of their own clients in the Antwerp area sent back in the Moretuses' barrels. For example, the Mylius family of booksellers from Cologne had books shipped to the Jesuit Andreas Schottus and the merchant Emmanuel Ximenes in Antwerp, as well as to the Jesuit Franciscus Costerus in Brussels. The Antwerp Jesuits similarly used the Moretuses to convey books to fellow Jesuits elsewhere in Europe.[42] The Moretuses' shipments also regularly contained letters for others. The botanist Carolus Clusius periodically received correspondence in this fashion, while the Parisian bookseller Sébastien Cramoisy occasionally exchanged items with his brother via the Moretuses at Frankfurt. Even some Polish nobles (a number of whom were based in Leuven) evidently found the Moretuses' transports to and from Frankfurt a convenient means of staying in touch with distant contacts.[43] All of these examples underscore, once again, the importance of the Frankfurt fairs as opportunities for otherwise far-flung individuals not only to do business, but also simply to meet and make personal exchanges.

EXCHANGES OF WORKS OF ART VIA THE FRANKFURT FAIRS

Many of the packages that the Moretuses conveyed contained works of art sent by an unexpected assortment of individuals. Numerous such requests came from sundry members of the clergy who had links to Antwerp, especially the Jesuits. For example, a certain N. Pugelrave had a painting sent to Frankfurt in 1617 for the Franciscan Jacobus Farsin, who was traveling from Antwerp to Prague via Cologne that year.[44] In 1631, the Antwerp Jesuit Joannes Bollandus first asked the Moretuses to help transfer money via the spring fair to the Jesuit Petrus Franciscus Chifflet for the purchase of some copper plates. Bollandus then asked to have the plates sent to the Jesuit Joachimus Joannis in Würzburg via the fall fair that same year. The Jesuits also had several packages of unspecified "figures", "images", or "beldekens" transported to fellow Jesuits in Prague, Augsburg, Dillingen, and Rome via the Frankfurt fairs.[45] Although the Moretuses' records do not indicate which images were included in these various shipments, a request for prints placed at the fall fair of 1631 reveals how one such shipment was initiated and what it might have contained. In this case, the Jesuit Joannes Baptist de Borges of Mainz asked the Moretuses to bring him a selection of small prints on white ground (implying they were not colored) from Jan-Baptist Barbé, Abraham van Merlen, Michael Snijders, and one of the Galles, with representations of the Virgin Mary, the Crucifixion, Holy Virgins, etc., worth a total of 2 or 3 Reichsthalers. They were also to convey two small knitted black caps to wear under a hat, as the Jesuits did.[46] Important here (aside from learning how Jesuits kept their heads warm) was the selection of artists, a general indication of the types of common subjects that were of interest, and the degree of finishing of the images (whether they were colored or not) – all of which would also have significantly affected the price.

Some merchants who were intermediaries in the distribution of works of art via the Frankfurt fair also occasionally shipped packages via the Moretuses. For example, Jan Peborgh of Antwerp asked them to transport numerous packages of prints between 1598 and 1603. His transactions are noteworthy for the quantities involved; for instance, twelve packages were sent to a certain Abraham and Adriaen vander Voort in 1598 alone (see fig. 9.6 for a selection of these).[47] However, these were not systematic requests. Rather, like Peborgh's, most were concentrated in brief periods of time, suggesting either the occasional importance of the distribution of prints in these merchants' businesses or their preference for different means of transporting such goods at other points in time.

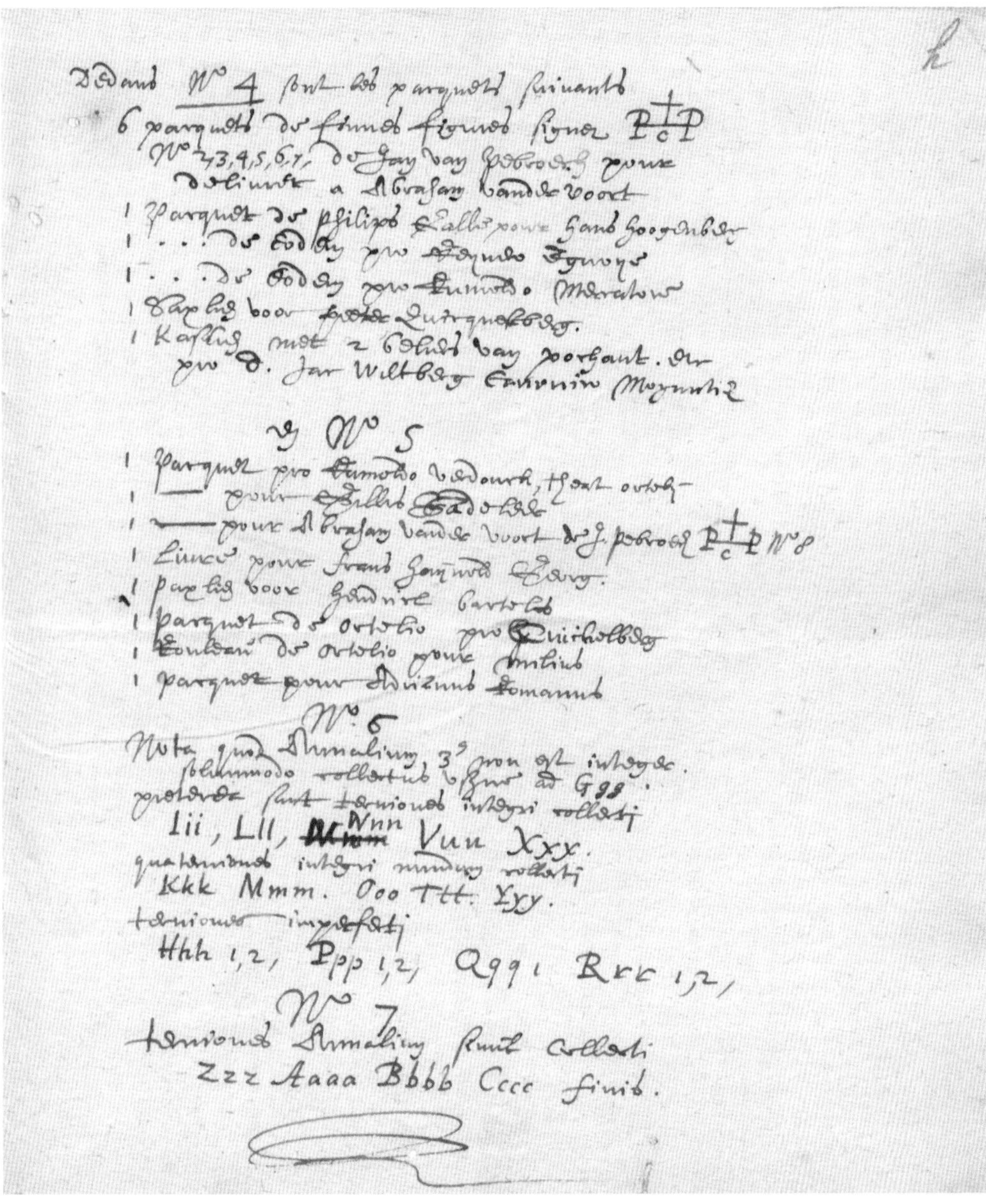

9.6 List of contents of barrels 4–7, shipped on 2 March 1598 or soon thereafter. This list includes: in barrel 4, six packages of "finnes figures" sent by Jan Peborgh for Abraham vander Voort and three packages sent by Philips Galle, one each for Hans Hogenberg, the Jesuit Reinerus Egnoy, and Rumold Mercator; and in barrel 5, a package for Gillis Sadeler, as well as a package and a roll sent by Abraham Ortelius to Peeter Quickelberg and Arnold Mylius, respectively. Antwerp, Museum Plantin-Moretus: Arch. 985, *Cahier de Frankfurt* (spring 1598), fol. 8r.

Others involved in the book trade also occasionally participated in the distribution of prints. Despite their professional proximity to those engaged in the print trade, their participation in this market, at least via the Moretuses and the Frankfurt fairs, remained just as irregular as that of the members of the clergy and merchants discussed above.[48] For example, Cornelis van Egmont, who helped Jan II manage the Moretuses' shop at Frankfurt between 1609 and 1618, occasionally had packages of prints sent to him there. Consisting of just a few packages in 1614 and 1616, these shipments climaxed and ended in 1617 and 1618, with seven and four packages, respectively.[49]

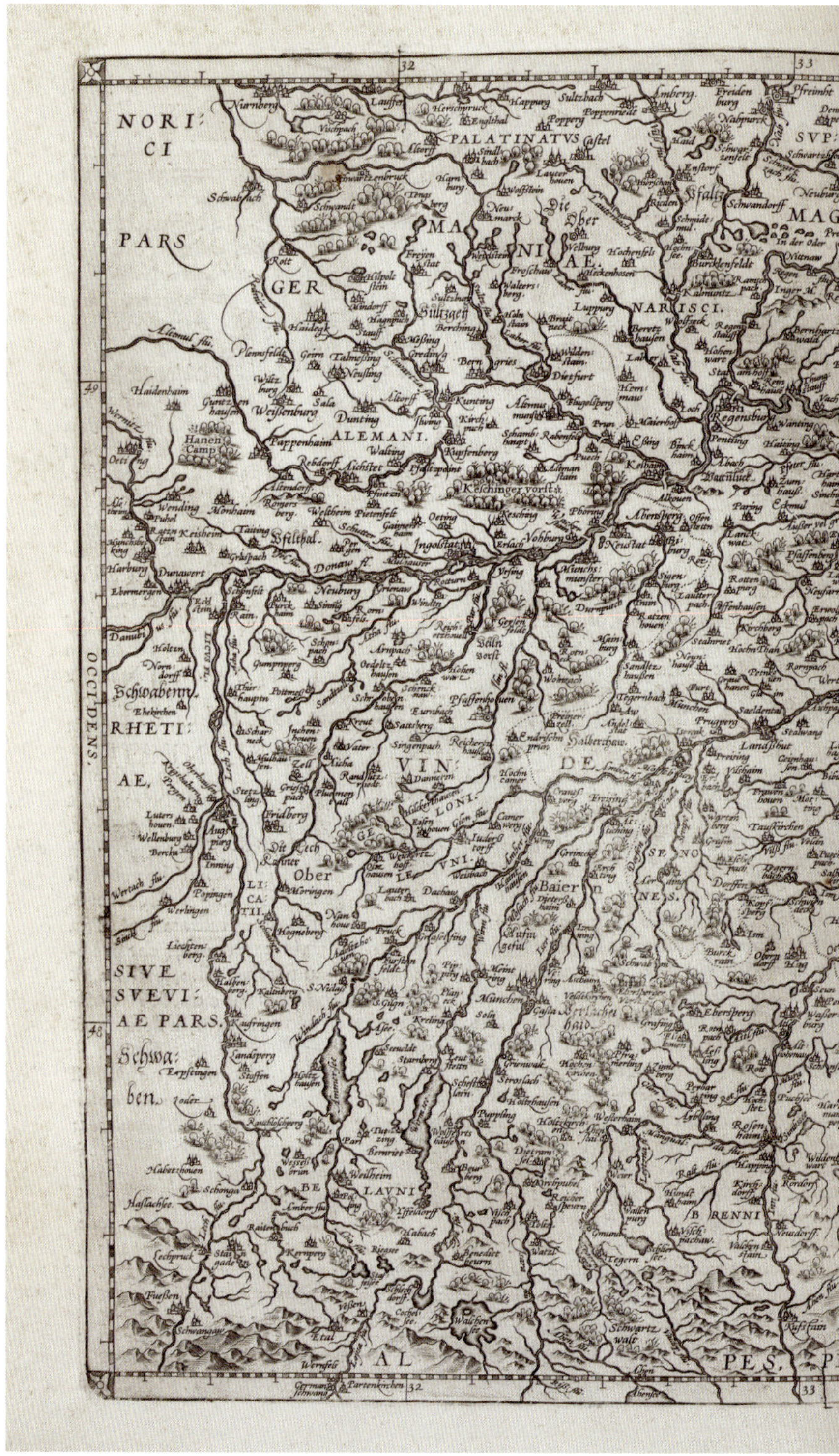

9.7 Anonymous, *Map of Bavaria*, from Abraham Ortelius's *Theatro del mondo* (Antwerp: Widow and sons of Jan Moretus I, 1612), etching and engraving, ca. 384 × 487 mm. Antwerp, Museum Plantin-Moretus: A 935, map no. 68.

Even the Moretuses' shipment of printed images for their own shop at Frankfurt is characterized by exceptional transactions involving works with some family connection that were then sold in discrete periods of time; they were not seeking to acquire prints for general, ongoing sales. Specifically, in 1594 and 1597, Jan I sent sixteen and twenty-five copies, respectively, of Plantin's broadside of Solomon's temple, which had been popular among Plantin's clients during the 1570s. In 1599 and 1610, the Moretuses featured hundreds of copies of a few of Theodore Galle's new print series and broadsides among their wares in Frankfurt. These unusual, but generally successful, decisions were clearly taken with Galle's approval and were

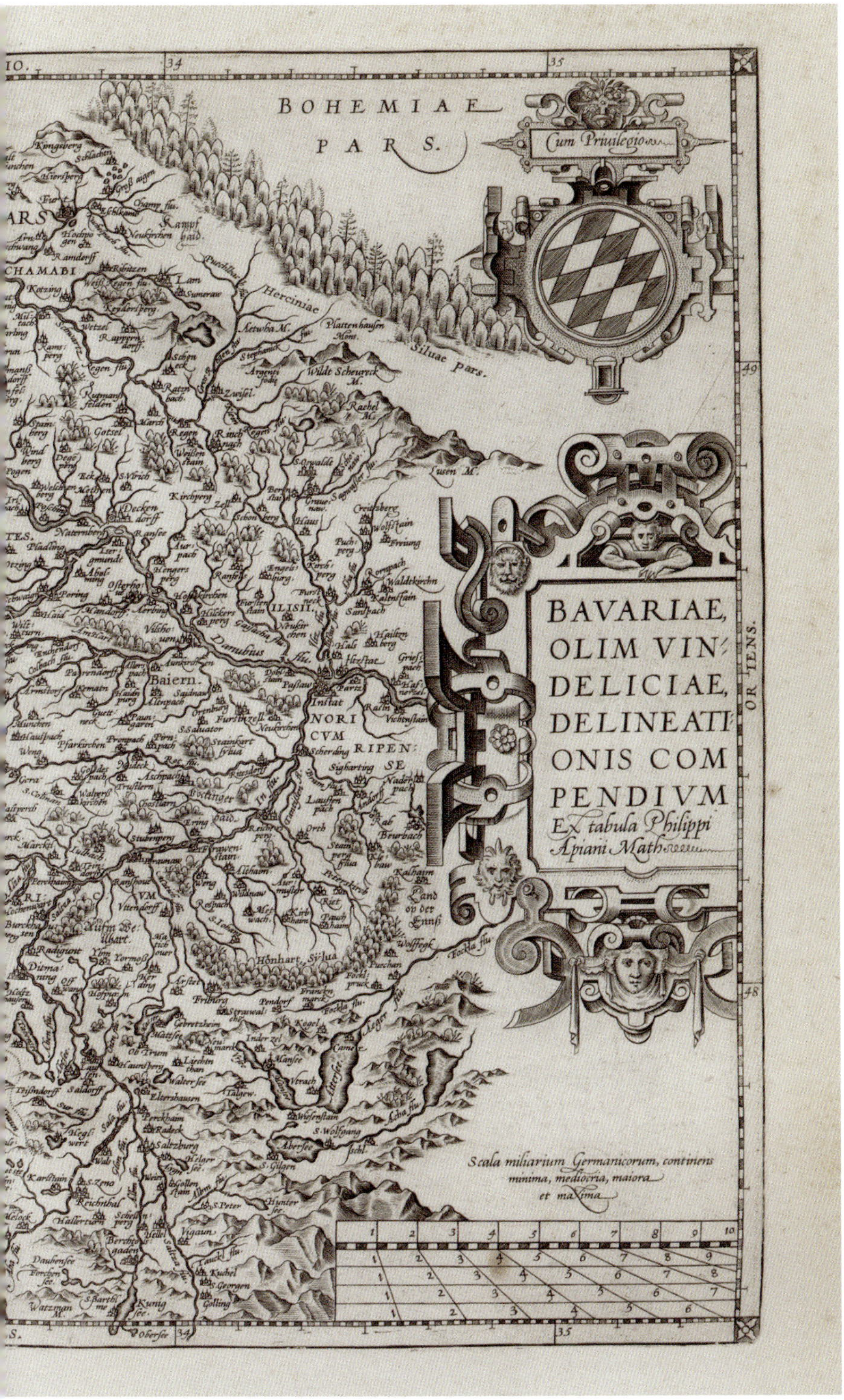

most likely made possible by Galle's intimate connection with their family. Consequently, the Moretuses' sale of such items would not have been considered to be in competition with the business of an independent Antwerp print publisher.[50] Finally, a few years later, in 1614 and 1615, they sent more than 500 impressions of maps from Abraham Ortelius's renowned atlas for the Nuremberg-based Caymox family of art dealers (fig. 9.7).[51] The only items that the Moretuses appear to have kept in stock at Frankfurt in reasonable quantities, at least between 1599 and 1604, were illustrated canons in assorted formats. An exceptional, significantly later shipment of fifty canons in 1624 may have been inspired by a request from the bookseller Michiel van Dale, who bought ten of them at the fair immediately thereafter.[52]

The Moretuses are known to have sent prints in bulk to Frankfurt for sale to a specific client only once. In March 1614, they purchased 1,600 prints from Charles de Mallery at the request of the Augsburg bookseller Georg Willer II, who then paid the Moretuses for them along with the books that he bought at the spring fair.[53] Perhaps there was an understanding that the Moretuses would not compete openly with Antwerp printmakers by selling their works via the Frankfurt fair since they clearly did not endeavor to satisfy a regular clientele in this niche of the print market.

Despite the irregular, idiosyncratic qualities of these various examples, one cannot ignore the participation of this broad spectrum of people – above all, members of the clergy, booksellers, and merchants – in the distribution of images via the Frankfurt fairs. In particular, their various activities reveal how many distinct networks of individuals were engaged in the exchange of unknown quantities of prints (and other objects) beyond the more conventional trade that occurred via art dealers.

The abundant references in the Moretuses' records to transactions at the Frankfurt fairs involving a number of Antwerp printmakers and publishers document how they, too, sought to benefit from the multitudes attracted to these fairs by the opportunity to exchange merchandise, settle debts, and maintain distant contacts in an extensive and burgeoning international market for prints. Indeed, Antwerp artists and print publishers were by far the largest group of individuals who asked the Moretuses to assist them with transactions at the Frankfurt fairs. Because the contents of many of the packages and rolls sent were not recorded, the nature of these shipments must be evaluated with caution. For example, title pages, sheets making up entire books (or booklets), imperfect sheets, unspecified images, and maps, were all sent in rolls, while print publishers also provided each other with books and not just prints.[54] Nevertheless, the following analysis of several print sellers' dealings via the Frankfurt fairs conveys an astounding amount of information about what the trade in prints during the early seventeenth century entailed, from diverse networks and personal approaches to this business to the hitherto unimagined quantities of prints involved.

PHILIPS GALLE

In 1588, during the last year of Plantin's life and when Galle was himself more than fifty years old, he made his first request: to have a single package sent to the fall fair for the Cologne-based print and map dealer Peter Boons.[55] Thereafter, he routinely asked the Moretuses to send on average at least one package annually to the fairs for the next twenty-two years. In some years (1589, 1592, 1595, 1598, and 1600–1606), he shipped as many as three or four packages annually. Galle concluded his transactions via the Moretuses a year and a half before he died, with two small packages weighing just 6 pounds combined that he had sent to the fall fair of 1610 for a fellow print publisher, Crispijn de Passe I, who was then based in Cologne.[56] In stark contrast to his regular shipment of packages to Frankfurt, Galle only occasionally received something in return. Most often, this is simply documented by a charge to his account for the transport of an unspecified package for him from Frankfurt in the early 1590s. In just two instances were the contents recorded: when Galle received eight plates (most likely, copper plates) in 1588 and when he was sent a package weighing 19.5 pounds with copies of a "costume book" (identified generally as "habitus gentium") in 1590.[57] Only once was the origin of the shipment indicated, namely, when the Duisburg bookseller Rumold Mercator (the son of the cartographer Gerard Mercator) arranged to send Galle a package at the spring fair of 1599.[58]

As Galle's print series and print books were available for sale at the Frankfurt fairs by 1572, Galle most likely had his publications distributed there via other means during the initial expansion of his business.[59] Why, once he was established as one of the leading print publishers in Antwerp and had built up his own network of clients, he was prepared to supply his customers with works via the Moretuses' shop at the fairs, is not known.

Who were Galle's primary clients at this point? A few were print and map dealers based in Cologne. While Galle began by periodically sending packages to Boons between 1588 and 1595, he subsequently shipped even more to the Hogenberg family (between 1595 and 1600) and, thereafter, at least four to De Passe (in 1604 and 1610).[60] All of these shipments supplemented similar transactions arranged between Jan Moretus and booksellers in Cologne. Galle may well have known – or have been familiar with – most, if not all, of these individuals. Several of Galle's packages were addressed to Johann (Hans) Hogenberg, Frans Hogenberg's son (see, for example, fig. 9.6), whom Galle would most likely have known, at least by report, due to his longstanding ties with Frans.[61] Galle also knew De Passe, for he published prints by him as of 1586, soon after De Passe's registration in the Antwerp Guild of St Luke guild.[62] Only the source of Boons's connection with Galle is unclear. It is possible that Boons initiated his contact with Galle via the Moretuses since Boons and the Moretuses were trading at the Frankfurt fairs (primarily in cartographic works) by 1585, a few years prior to Galle's first known shipment to him. The Dutch antiquarian Arnold van Buchell referred to Boons as someone from the Brabant region of the Low Countries.[63] Consequently, even if Galle and Boons did not know one another personally, they would have shared a common national origin. Galle occasionally supplemented his transactions involving his clients in Cologne with packages the Moretuses sent directly to Cologne for him between the fairs; these packages were included in their shipments to Cologne booksellers. In this way, both Boons and the Hogenbergs received a few extra packages, although notably the majority were packed into the Moretuses' shipments to Frankfurt.[64]

Other individuals who had Antwerp connections and to whom Galle periodically sent packages via the Frankfurt fairs were Jacob de Kempener and the Caymox family. De Kempener was originally a painter and copper plate printer from Brussels; he was in Antwerp in September of 1586, when Gillis Sadeler I, together with the painter Guillaume Flocquet, attested to his good character. That same year, De Kempener traveled with Jan Sadeler I to Frankfurt, where he initially worked for him. Following De Kempener's death in 1612, his sons remained in Frankfurt, passing away themselves in the mid-1620s.[65] De Kempener's and his heirs' sales of ink both to Theodore Galle between 1612 and 1616 and to the Vrients family in Antwerp indicate that they continued to work as copper plate printers following Jan Sadeler's departure from Frankfurt. De Kempener, who designed some prints, may also have dealt in them, for Galle shipped him four packages in 1605 and 1606, while Galle's son Theodore and his son-in-law Adriaen Collaert both sent solitary packages as well, one of which contained "images".[66]

Cornelis Caymox I, possibly originally from Antwerp, had trained under Gerard de Jode in Antwerp around 1562 and subsequently settled in Nuremberg by 1564.[67] Other family members, including Hubert and Balthasar, as well as Hubert's son-in-law Peter Knabenhouwer, who was a brother-in-law of the Antwerp painter Jan Snellinck, were similarly active as art dealers in Nuremberg, trading in a variety of luxury goods, from paintings to maps and atlases to prints and richly illustrated books.[68] While Cornelis I was Gerard de Jode's representative at the Frankfurt fairs during the 1560s, Hubert and, especially, Balthasar Caymox regularly bought works from the Moretuses there. The family was also active elsewhere, including at the Leipzig fairs (where Cornelis I died in 1588).[69] Although there are only records of Galle sending a total of four packages to Balthasar Caymox (two in 1589 and one each in 1601 and 1608), in addition to one to Knabenhouwer in 1606, he received several payments from not only Balthasar, but also Hubert Caymox and, thereafter, his widow and Knabenhouwer. It is striking how the timing of these payments does not always follow Galle's shipments.[70] It is always possible that the payments were meant to settle debts or make advance payments, but the recurring imbalance of when payments were made versus when packages were sent suggests that Galle's trade with these clients was more extensive than what is documented by the Moretuses' records of what they shipped for him. This possibility is supported by the significant sums involved – often 90 to 110 fl. or more – unless Galle routinely provided particularly costly merchandise, such as his print books or hand-colored maps.[71] Thus, the records indicate that the Moretuses were employed more often for the receipt and safe conveyance of often large cash payments back to Antwerp than for the transport of merchandise to the fairs. This hypothesis is supported even more clearly by the transactions between Adriaen Collaert and the Caymox family, as well as between Charles de Mallery and the Cologne print dealer Peter Overadt, all of which are discussed below. Consequently, their transactions simultaneously underscore how the Moretuses were not the only ones assisting with the international transport of prints.

Despite the noteworthy monetary value of Galle's transactions with the Caymoxes, Galle had the Moretuses send the most packages – more packages, in fact, than he conveyed to all the other print dealers combined – to yet another Antwerp family, namely the Sadelers. Galle dealt primarily with Gillis Sadeler I, Raphael I's and Jan I's brother. Identified as a "cunstdrucker" (printer of art, presumably prints) living in Antwerp when he attested to the good character of Jacob de Kempener in 1586, Gillis was officially registered as a citizen of Frankfurt in 1598, although the Moretuses had been bringing packages to the fairs for him from Galle at least by 1592. When he died in Frankfurt in October 1609, soon after the conclusion of the fall fair, he was listed in the local records as an engraver, printer of art (engravings), and an art dealer.[72] Between 1592 and October 1609, Galle's exchanges with Gillis I dominated both men's transactions via the Moretuses.

Because the people associated with the shipment of packages (either the one for whom it was intended or the one sending it) are not always noted in the Moretuses' accounts, it is impossible to state exactly how many packages were sent to the Sadelers. Nevertheless, the relative significance of these various shipments is indisputable, as Galle sent Gillis Sadeler at least twenty-five packages between 1592 and 1608, while a minimum of six packages from him were transported to Johann Hogenberg and four each were conveyed to Boons, De Kempener, Balthasar Caymox, and De Passe, in the course of Galle's dealings with them.

Between the fairs in the spring of 1606 and the fall of 1609, Sadeler also regularly sent Galle money via the Moretuses. In contrast to Galle's dealings with the Caymoxes, these payments alternate regularly with Galle's shipment of packages to Sadeler, resulting in Sadeler sending money more often than any single member of the Caymox family. The individual sums concerned were often smaller, ranging from 30 fl. to nearly 90 fl., but if one considers the totals of what Sadeler sent per year, they were ultimately comparable to the Caymox family's larger but more irregular payments; for instance, in 1606 and 1607, Sadeler's payments amounted to 134 fl. and 117 fl. 15 st., respectively.[73]

Because the Sadeler brothers are usually regarded as a model of an international family business focused on the distribution of the Sadelers' own prints, one must also consider the extent to which the works Galle sent to Gillis I were intended for his local Frankfurt business or for sale via his brothers Raphael I (in Munich and Venice) and Jan I and his successors (mostly in Venice).[74] When Galle first shipped packages to the Sadelers via the Moretuses, he seemingly differentiated between Gillis I and Raphael I, as he sent four packages explicitly addressed to Gillis in the spring of 1592 and two marked for Raphael in the spring of 1593.[75] The latter, however, is the exception, since the overwhelming majority of the packages (regardless of who provided them) that the Moretuses conveyed to the Frankfurt fairs for the Sadelers during Gillis's lifetime were marked with his name. He was evidently the local contact for the entire Sadeler family and presumably would have passed on what was meant for other family members via their own preferred means. Gillis I's widow was, in fact, asked to do just this in 1611, when Theodore Galle had the Moretuses convey two packages for a Sadeler in Venice (most likely, Jan I's son Justus).[76] The timing of this shipment may well have been intended to coincide with a well-known episode: when Raphael I, his son Johann II, and Jan I's son Justus, stopped at the 1611 spring fair in Frankfurt prior to traveling to Augsburg in order to discuss the sale of drawings and paintings with Philipp Hainofer, the agent of Philipp II von Pommern-Stettin.[77] Consequently, it is difficult to know with certainty for which branch of the Sadeler family's operations (and, hence, which international market) Galle's packages were destined. Galle may not even have known himself. Nevertheless, the trade between Theodore Galle and Raphael Sadeler I (discussed below) indicates that despite the easily constructed, uniform appearance of one large international Sadeler business, each family member managed his affairs separately, presumably in accordance with his personal needs and practical concerns.

The transactions the Moretuses arranged at the Frankfurt fairs in Philips Galle's name illuminate several key facets of his business during the final decades of his life. Although family members, such as his son-in-law Adriaen Collaert and his own son Theodore were ready to manage businesses of their own or to take over his, Galle maintained a remarkably active distribution of packages to other art dealers. Antwerp émigrés (or their families), in particular De Kempener, De Passe, the Hogenbergs, the Caymoxes, and, above all, the Sadelers, were the usual recipients. Galle's solitary shipments to Theodore de Bry in the spring of 1595 and Gerard Mercator's son Rumold in the spring of 1598 stand out all the more in contrast.[78] The vast majority of Galle's transactions involved either the export of merchandise or receipt of payment. Only rarely (primarily in the early 1590s) did he pay to receive packages from someone else. While Galle may have sent the most packages to the Sadelers, the Moretuses received the most money for Galle from the Caymox family. Regrettably, it is impossible to determine whether this discrepancy arose because of the type or quantity of goods that Galle sent the Sadelers and Caymoxes respectively. It was not uncommon for Galle to receive approximately 100 fl. per year via the Moretuses at the Frankfurt fairs, and even this sum is an incomplete, minimal estimate of his total annual earnings from international sales. Such amounts are all the more remarkable if one remembers that Galle continued to export prints through the first decade of the seventeenth century, until a year and half before his death at approximately seventy-five years of age. His son Theodore had most likely taken over the practical management of his workshop nearly a decade earlier, around 1600. Soon thereafter, the Moretuses stopped keeping separate accounts for their exchanges with Philips Galle and switched to recording jointly their dealings with him and with Theodore.[79] However, from the records of both Philips's and Theodore's shipments to Frankfurt via the Moretuses, it appears as if the actual shift to Theodore in this aspect of the Galle print publishing business did not take place until 1608, when Theodore's shipments of packages to Frankfurt via the Moretuses began in earnest and Philips's were coming to an end.[80] Nevertheless, Theodore's transactions reveal that while his base of operations and his collection of copper plates may have overlapped with his father's, his contacts and approach to dealing in prints did not.

THEODORE GALLE

Theodore Galle began to make regular use of the Moretuses' transport of goods to and from the Frankfurt fairs in the spring of 1608. He was then nearly thirty-seven years old and had been managing a print workshop and oversaw the production and inclusion of intaglio book illustrations in the majority of the Moretuses' editions for some eight years.[81] Thus, in striking contrast to his father, he was in the process of building up his career as a print publisher instead of simply benefiting from an established reputation. Although Theodore was not as regular with his shipments as his father had been, the Moretuses conveyed something to Frankfurt for him in most years until 1621. While he employed them the least between 1612 and 1615, sending perhaps just three packages, he compensated for this dip in trade immediately thereafter with his most intense period of activity, when he engaged the Moretuses to take a minimum of twenty packages to Frankfurt between 1616 and 1618.[82]

Because Theodore's shipments began just when his father's were tapering off, it is tempting to imagine that Theodore was simply picking up where Philips had left off. This logical assumption is justified in terms of the clients with whom he traded the most, namely the Hogenberg family in Cologne and, above all, the Sadelers. However, Theodore Galle's contacts were mostly the successors of those with whom his father Philips had originally dealt, especially, Frans Hogenberg's son Abraham, to whom he sent eight packages weighing some 228 pounds in just 1616 and 1617, and Gillis Sadeler I's brother Raphael I (see, for example, fig. 9.8).[83] Moreover, rather than maintaining a seemingly uniform continuation of the family business, he pursued a different course from his father in more ways than one.

In particular, Theodore developed a distinct pool of clients. For example, his transactions with the Caymox family appear to have been more limited, as Balthasar Caymox made just one relatively modest payment of 57 fl. for Theodore.[84] Similarly, Theodore had far fewer important clients in Cologne. Of Philips' former contacts there, some, like Peter Boons, were most likely no longer active in the field; even Philips Galle's shipments to Boons had stopped in the 1590s, and Jacob de Kempener passed away soon after Theodore sent him the single package of images in 1612 mentioned above. Although Theodore initially shipped four packages to Crispijn de Passe in the spring of 1609 (weighing a total of 57 pounds) and a smaller package weighing 13 pounds in the spring of 1611, De Passe moved to Utrecht later in 1611, after which any subsequent shipments may have been sent via other routes. Finally, while

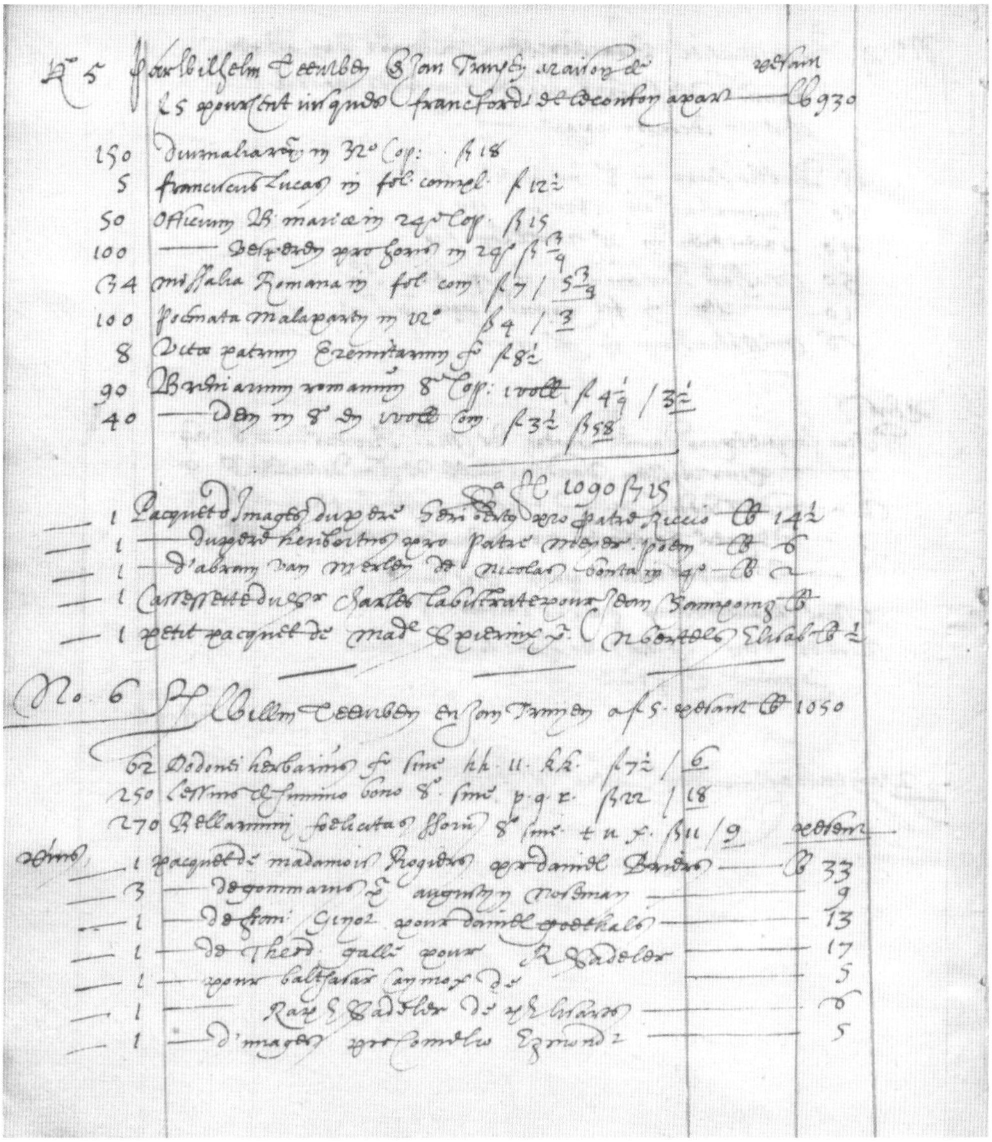

9.8 List of contents of barrels 5–6, recorded on 17 March 1616. This list includes: in barrel 5, one package of "images" from the Jesuit Heribertus Rosweydus of Antwerp for a certain Father Ricci and one package from Abraham van Merlen for Nicolas Bonta; and in barrel 6, one package from Theodore Galle for Raphael Sadeler, a package for Balthasar Caymox, one package for Raphael Sadeler from Philips Liesaert, and a package with "images" for Cornelius van Egmont. Antwerp, Museum Plantin-Moretus: Arch. 1020, *Cahier de Francfort* (spring, 1616), fol. 3v.

Theodore also sent the Cologne print seller Peter Overadt two packages weighing 40 pounds in 1611, the Moretuses' records indicate, as will be discussed below, that Overadt preferred to deal with Charles de Mallery.[85] Additionally, Galle occasionally supplied other individuals who were better known for their trade in books and cartographic works. They included Johann Craesboom from Augsburg, Jan Jansonius II from Amsterdam, and Cornelius Leysser from Munich, each of whom received a single package from Galle.[86]

Theodore Galle was also sent much less money through the Moretuses than his father. Not only were far fewer payments made in his name than in his father's, but the average amount paid was also less. For example, while the 57 fl. from Balthasar Caymox was one of the largest sums Theodore was given, such an amount was on the lower end of what his father had received via the Moretuses at Frankfurt. As the exact contents of the various packages sent to Frankfurt are not specified, it is impossible to determine the degree to which this discrepancy was due to the types of works sent, the quantities involved, or an incalculable valuation of the relative fame and skill of one artist versus another. Furthermore, Raphael Sadeler

I may have sent Theodore prints or other publications in exchange for his shipments instead of payments in cash, as Gillis I did for Philips Galle. For example, between 1614 and 1618, Raphael sent Theodore packages each spring, three of which were said to contain "images", "figures", or "tailles doulces" (engravings).[87]

A final significant aspect of how Theodore's transactions at the Frankfurt fairs differed from his father's was his decision to use the Moretuses to help him acquire ink there between 1612 and 1616. In his discussion of the ink used for printing copper plates, Antony Griffiths observes that in the seventeenth century, ink from Germany, referred to as "Frankfurt black" in Britain, was considered to be the best ink for printing plates and was twice as expensive as the ordinary ink that was then made in Paris.[88] Thus, internationally renowned printmakers and print publishers might have elected to use such ink even if it were more costly than what was available locally. It is also logical that ink could be purchased at the Frankfurt fairs given the importance of the book fair and the crafts related to it. However, all of the Moretuses' purchases and shipments of barrels of ink for others (in addition to one large barrel for themselves in the fall of 1615) are notably concentrated in a relatively brief span of time: between the spring fair of 1612 and the fall fair of 1616. Specifically, at the fall fair of 1612, the Moretuses agreed to transport barrels of ink supplied by a member of the Caymox family back to Antwerp for both Hieronymus Wierix and, most likely, Adriaen Collaert, while the heirs of Jacob de Kempener simultaneously sent a barrel of ink weighing an exceptional 100 pounds to Theodore Galle. Charles de Mallery similarly had the Moretuses bring him a barrel of ink weighing 58 pounds from the next fair. These are the only known instances when the Moretuses brought back ink for Wierix or Collaert, while De Mallery was sent ink just once more (this time by Balthasar Caymox), after the fall fair of 1615.[89] Such rare instances of ink purchases suggest that there may have been a temporary shortage in the local supply of ink for Antwerp copper plate printers and that there was not a sudden, simultaneous switch in the preference of several individuals for ink from Frankfurt. This hypothesis may be supported by the fact that, from the fall of 1612 through all of 1613, not one Antwerp print seller sent anything to Frankfurt via the Moretuses.[90] How can one produce sufficient quantities of prints for export if one does not have a ready supply of ink with which to print them?

Only Theodore Galle, who had started to import ink from Frankfurt via the Moretuses a season earlier (in the spring of 1612), continued to do so regularly through the fall of 1616. Galle may have been motivated to make these extra purchases because, in addition to guaranteeing his own print production, he also had to print the thousands of intaglio book illustrations that the Moretuses required annually. Galle was also involved in the sale of ink to the Jesuit order in St Omer, as well as to one bookseller there.[91] His independence in these transactions is underscored by his preference for obtaining ink from the family of Jacob de Kempener, instead of, for example, acquiring it via the Caymoxes, who provided the ink that was sent to his fellow Antwerp printmakers. Galle's focus on the De Kempeners was explicitly stated following the spring fair of 1616, where the Moretuses had purchased ink for Galle from a certain Hans Eckenthaller, who is identified in the Moretuses' accounts as Theodore de Bry's printer. The Moretuses subsequently returned the ink for Galle, noting that it was not as good as the De Kempener family's ink. Galle paid for one more shipment of ink from the De Kempener family at the fall fair in 1616, even though it was slightly more expensive than Eckenthaller's.[92] This is the last known transaction involving ink in the Moretuses' Frankfurt accounts. As the De Kempeners' representative in the Moretuses' records appears to have changed from one fair to the next, the management of their business may no longer have been reliable. Or, perhaps Galle simply decided (as Wierix, Collaert, and De Mallery had before him) that he could obtain sufficient, suitable ink via other means.

Together, these records document Theodore Galle's trade in various goods with sundry individuals via the Frankfurt fairs. Consequently, one might argue that he was taking fuller advantage of the opportunities there, both to purchase items and to exchange merchandise with a more diverse range of customers, than had his father, Philips. Nevertheless, this stronger focus on the fairs does not necessarily mean that Theodore was more successful financially than Philips, who could benefit from the fame his publications had accrued over time and simply respond to the incoming demand for them. Theodore had opted for a different type of business in Antwerp – one that included regular work for the Moretuses, printing their intaglio book illustrations. As his trade in prints via the Moretuses' shop in Antwerp reveals, Theodore simultaneously distributed an assortment of prints that comprised numerous devotional images, in addition to offering his services as a print dealer who would procure images by other artists that his and the Moretuses' clients sought. His import of works from Raphael Sadeler I through the Frankfurt fairs may have contributed to this last aspect of his business. Although it is impossible to determine why Theodore chose a different path than his father, the Moretuses' assistance with the Sadelers' affairs at the Frankfurt fairs confirms that such variation among family members was not unusual. It was, rather, the logical result of distinct individuals endeavoring to find a personally effective means of participating in the ever evolving and burgeoning market for images in seventeenth-century Europe.

THE SADELERS

Of all the print dealers discussed here, the Sadelers' movements and activities attest most to the powerful appeal of being in Frankfurt, where, particularly during the fairs, one could maintain contact with an array of individuals, in addition to exchanging merchandise with far-flung clients. Jan I and Raphael I had tried working intermittently in Cologne for several years around 1580, when it was a receptive center for the production and sale of prints by artists from the Low Countries. However, after their return to Antwerp in 1585–1586, during which time their father died and his estate had to be settled, they decided to move to Frankfurt. Although Jan I soon left to work elsewhere, Raphael I stayed in Frankfurt until 1591, by which time his brother Gillis I had joined him. Raphael I then followed in Jan I's footsteps by working in Munich and Venice, while Gillis I remained in Frankfurt until his own death in 1609. Thus, the Sadeler family was represented in Frankfurt continuously for more than two decades.[93] Gillis I's own limited dealings with the Moretuses reveals how he served as the international point of contact for his brothers Jan I and Raphael I in Munich and Venice, as well as for his cousin, Aegidius (or Gillis) II in Prague. For example, he occasionally provided the Moretuses with prints after Jacopo Bassano, which were often made in Italy under or by Jan I, in addition to numerous copies of the *Symbola divina et humana*, which was published by Aegidius II in Prague.[94] Given the Sadelers' Antwerp origins, it is not surprising that they made use of the Moretuses' participation in the Frankfurt fairs to facilitate their own dealings with both distant relations and business connections back in Antwerp. The importance of Gillis I in this regard is suggested by the striking dominance of his name in the Moretuses'

Frankfurt accounts until his death in October 1609, even though his brothers (and their relatives) were also simultaneously active in the print trade.[95]

After Gillis I's death, Jan I's son Justus (who had taken over the management of the family's business in Venice) was initially (in 1610 and 1611) the sole recipient of packages sent via the Moretuses. However, following a brief break in such transactions in 1612–1613, it was Raphael I (fig. 9.9) who recommenced trade via the Moretuses at Frankfurt by sending Theodore Galle a package of prints during the spring of 1614. Subsequently,

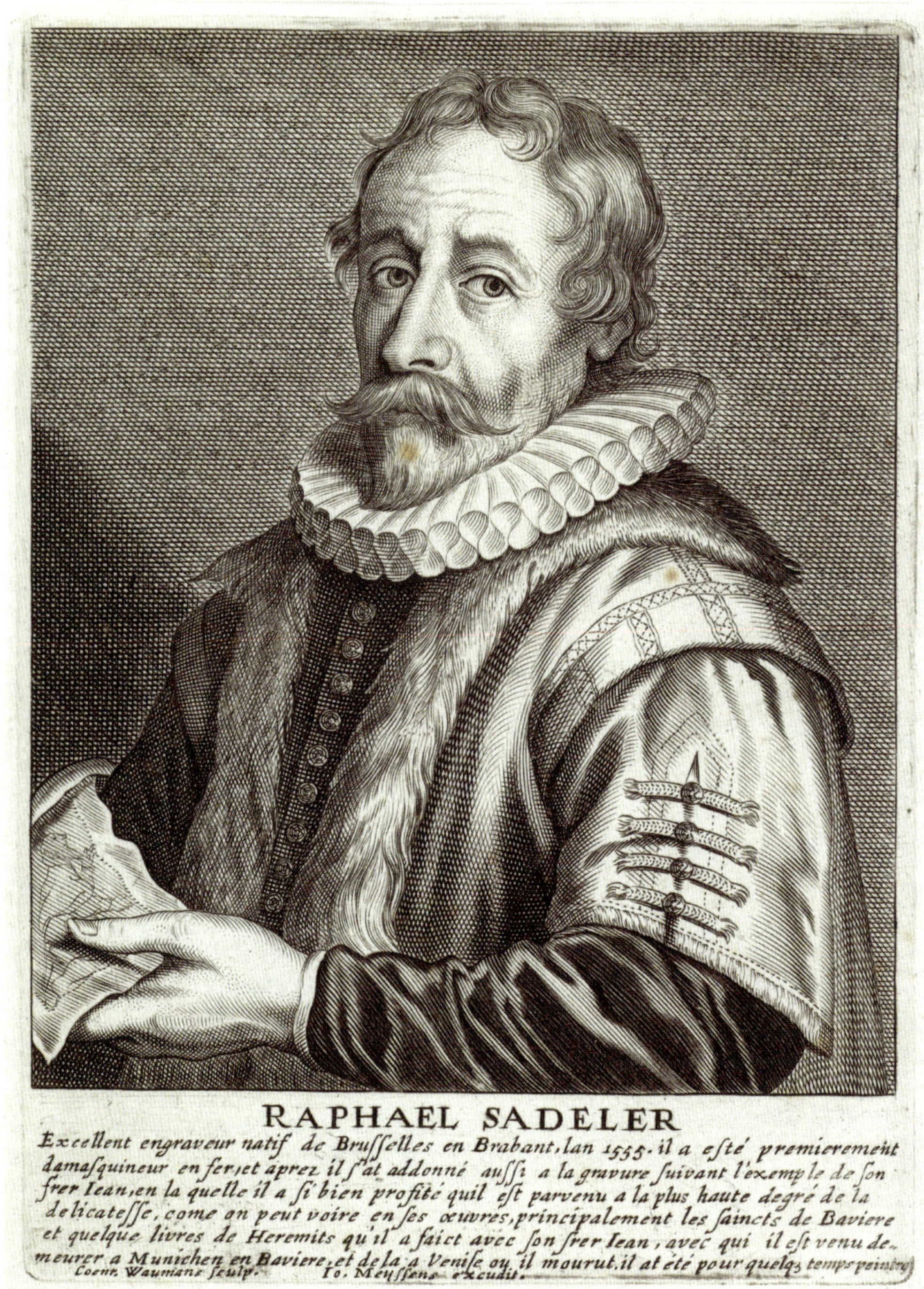

9.9 Coenraet Waumans, *Raphael Sadeler I*, in: *Image de divers hommes* (Antwerp: Joannes Meyssens, 1649), engraving, 166 × 117 mm. Amsterdam, Rijksmuseum: RP-P-OB-61.269.

packages were generally sent either to an unspecified "Sadeler" or, more often, explicitly to Raphael, until these shipments essentially came to an end in 1621, when Raphael was sixty years old and may have suffered a crippling illness, such as a stroke.[96] Although Justus continued to run the family business in Venice up to his death in 1620, his name is noticeably absent from the Moretuses' records. Only once, in 1617, did he arrange to have two packages of prints for Crispijn de Passe left at the Moretuses' shop in Frankfurt. Justus may well have been acquiring prints from Antwerp via other means. By 1615, he had expanded his operations to include trade in the Moretuses' illustrated devotional and liturgical editions and occasionally imported prints along with these shipments, which were not usually sent via Frankfurt.[97]

Justus's independent transactions with the Moretuses raise the question of whether Raphael I was acting as a general family representative at Frankfurt or whether he was pursuing his own business needs. Given the distinct ways in which packages were traded under Gillis and Raphael, the latter seems more likely. While Gillis received packages at the Frankfurt fairs each year (primarily from Philips Galle, but also occasionally from Adriaen Collaert and Theodore Galle), he did not send packages back in return. However, as of 1604, he regularly gave the Moretuses money for print sellers in Antwerp instead.[98] Raphael, by contrast, never made payments via the Moretuses, but often sent packages of his own in exchange. He traded packages with Theodore Galle on a nearly annual basis between 1614 and 1618, but a similar, though far more limited, form of exchange may also have taken place between him and Adriaen Collaert in 1615 and 1618.[99] Although it is possible that some of the packages shipped between Justus and Theodore Galle represented the return of unwanted merchandise, the regularity with which one shipment from Antwerp was matched by one from Munich and the corresponding lack of cash payments support the hypothesis that Raphael preferred a reciprocal trade in goods. The main potential exceptions to this pattern are two packages that Raphael sent to Theodore's brother Cornelis seemingly without having received a shipment from him in return.[100] However, Cornelis may have sent something via Theodore Galle. Raphael Sadeler may also not have been able to represent the family at Frankfurt readily, as he did not always go in person himself. Rather, there are numerous references to his transactions at Frankfurt being handled by the Ingolstadt bookseller Johann Hertsroy.[101]

In addition to their trade with Antwerp print sellers, the settlement of some of the Sadelers' personal affairs was facilitated by the Moretuses' presence in Frankfurt. Following Jan I's death in 1600, Gillis I, Raphael I, and Justus agreed in August 1601 to appoint Raphael's brother-in-law, the painter and art dealer Philips Liesaert III, to manage their concerns in Antwerp. While this decision would explain the packages that Liesaert sent to Gillis and Raphael via the Frankfurt fairs between 1601 and 1603, subsequent shipments sent to Justus in 1606 and Raphael in 1616 (see fig. 9.8) may have simply been related to their mutual trade in works of art.[102] Regardless of the content or purpose of these shipments, all of them were clearly addressed to one specific member of the Sadeler family. Consequently, the transactions suggest that while the Sadelers worked together effectively on the publication and distribution of numerous successful print series, each family member simultaneously maintained his own business and mode of interacting with other international connections. In particular, following the death of their primary point of contact in Frankfurt, Gillis I, the remaining family members may have decided to act independently and pursue the type of business that suited each one of them best.

ADRIAEN COLLAERT

Two of Philips Galle's sons-in-law, Adriaen Collaert (approximately ten years older than Theodore) and Charles de Mallery (the same age as Theodore) also engaged the Moretuses on occasion to assist them with their business concerns via the Frankfurt fairs. Collaert first asked the Moretuses to ship a package in 1600 (it was addressed to Gillis Sadeler I), more than a decade later than Philips Galle's initial shipment. Never sending more than one package at a time to a given individual, the bulk of Collaert's transactions were concentrated in a relatively brief period, from 1600 to 1608. Thereafter, he sent just six packages to other individuals via the Moretuses across the following decade, before he died in June 1618. As with Philips and Theodore Galle, the vast majority of the packages that the Moretuses conveyed for Collaert were directed to various members of the Sadeler family. Otherwise, his shipments were limited to just a few packages for diverse individuals, including Crispijn de Passe and Peter Overadt in Cologne, and Jacob de Kempener in Frankfurt, each of whom had similarly minimal dealings with Theodore.[103] Remarkably, there is no evidence of contact between Collaert and the Hogenberg family, who were important clients for both Philips and Theodore Galle during these years, although Abraham Hogenberg received a number of packages from Collaert's successors in the 1630s via Balthasar Moretus's shipments to booksellers in Cologne.[104]

Because the volume of Collaert's exports by way of the Moretuses was relatively modest, the amount of money that he received from them is all the more noteworthy, especially in the case of the Caymox family. Ranging from 75 fl. to approximately 127 fl., these sums are similar to what they paid Philips Galle through the Moretuses and are consistently greater than what Theodore Galle received from any of his contacts via the Frankfurt fairs.[105] However, while the payments to Philips Galle may have, on occasion, been matched by works that Galle sent to the Caymoxes via the Moretuses, the money received by Collaert was not. All of the Caymoxes' payments to him were made between 1600 and 1604, several years prior to Collaert's one known shipment of a package to a member of the family via the Moretuses in 1608.[106] Given the Caymoxes' local connections, in particular to the De Jode family of print and map publishers, they may have relied on personal connections other than the Moretuses for the transport of merchandise. Indeed, as the recipients of shipments usually had to pay the transport costs, they could have stipulated how they would prefer to have their orders sent. Collaert may also have sent merchandise to Frankfurt via other Antwerp booksellers, such as the Verdussen and Van Keerbergen families, for whom his relatives occasionally made book illustrations.[107] Whatever the arrangements, the above details demonstrate unequivocally that the Moretuses' shipments to Frankfurt were not the only means available to Antwerp print publishers who wished to distribute their wares internationally.

Moreover, the intense concentration of the Caymox family's payments between 1600 and 1604 for Collaert, as well as for Jan Brueghel I on one occasion, and above all for Philips Galle, suggests that exceptional circumstances had prompted them to rely on the Moretuses for financial exchanges at this specific point in time. Thereafter, such payments were rare and relatively small in comparison with the sums that had previously been sent.[108] In contrast to the Caymoxes' decisions about how to conduct their business, clients of other Antwerp print publishers continued to make use of the Moretuses' willingness to accept a variety of currencies at the Frankfurt fairs and to transfer large sums back to Antwerp for decades, as is evident from De Mallery's exchanges with Peter Overadt in Cologne.

CHARLES DE MALLERY

Charles de Mallery's transactions at the Frankfurt fairs via the Moretuses stand out from all the Moretuses' other dealings with Antwerp print publishers due to the predominance of financial matters. Following De Mallery's loan of 100 fl. from the Moretuses in 1594, when he was en route to Italy (fig. 9.5), the next reference to him in the Moretuses' Frankfurt accounts dates to the fall fair of 1607, when they accepted a payment in his name from Peter Overadt of Cologne. Most likely a native of the city, Overadt maintained an active print-publishing business throughout the first half of the seventeenth century that was known for assorted maps and town views and, above all, for numerous images designed to satisfy the various needs of the flourishing Catholic community. The fact that he was commissioned to print the official court calendar for the archbishopric of Cologne in 1608 suggests that local officials approved of his work.[109] De Mallery's first known shipments to the Frankfurt fair occurred that same yearr, at the fall fair of 1608, just when his brother-in-law and contemporary Theodore Galle had begun to send packages via the Moretuses on a regular basis and when Adriaen Collaert's and Philips Galle's transactions were tapering off.[110] Resettled in Antwerp after having worked in Paris during the early 1600s, De Mallery was similarly exploring the options for participating in the international print market via the fairs.

Nevertheless, the destinations of De Mallery's packages were remarkably distinct. In striking contrast to Collaert and the Galles, De Mallery did not routinely trade with the Sadelers or the Caymoxes.[111] Rather, aside from four packages sent to a certain Nicolas Bonta in 1614 and 1615, De Mallery dealt nearly exclusively with Overadt. Following De Mallery's initial shipment of a package weighing 19.5 pounds to him in 1608, he sent Overadt several packages simultaneously, weighing between 26 and 69 pounds in total, at each of the next five fairs (from the spring of 1609 through the spring of 1611), along with an additional three packages that were shipped to the fall fair of 1617.[112] Overadt appears to have been similarly exclusive in his preference for works from De Mallery, as he only occasionally received isolated shipments from four other Antwerp print publishers: Theodore Galle, Adriaen Collaert, Abraham van Merlen, and Michael Snijders.[113] Although these print sellers were popular internationally, their transactions via the Moretuses suggest that they did not suit Overadt's (or his customers') preferences as well as De Mallery did.

Between 1607 and 1618, De Mallery's shipments to Overadt alternated regularly with payments that Overadt made to the Moretuses in De Mallery's name (as in fig. 9.4). However, during the 1620s, Overadt continued to give the Moretuses money periodically for De Mallery, even though he had not received a package from him via the Frankfurt fairs since 1617. While this pattern is reminiscent of Philips Galle's and Adriaen Collaert's transactions with various members of the Caymox family, the Caymoxes' payments were concentrated in a relatively brief period of just four years, between 1600 and 1604. In De Mallery's case, though, not only was Overadt making one-sided payments over a longer period (from 1621 through 1627), but two other print dealers from Cologne, Johann Bussemacher and Abraham Hogenberg, also simultaneously gave the Moretuses money for De Mallery at a number of the fairs in the 1620s and there is no record of De Mallery sending them packages in exchange.[114] The relative lack of packages from Antwerp print publishers among the Moretuses' shipments to the Frankfurt fairs in the 1620s was pervasive and not just idiosyncratic to De Mallery. For example, the last packages that Theodore Galle sent to the Sadelers were shipped in 1620 and 1621. Just Jan Jansonius II, an Amsterdam dealer in books and maps, received any packages at Frankfurt from Antwerp print publishers in this decade.[115] The Jesuits' continued reliance on the Moretuses for the transport of packages to and from the fairs during the 1620s demonstrates that the Moretuses were still offering this service.[116] Most likely, Antwerp print publishers had begun to turn to other options for the transport of their merchandise to art dealers elsewhere. It is, then, all the more significant that, despite these alternatives, the Moretuses' business at Frankfurt continued to be favored by many print sellers as a means of making payments in foreign currencies that could then be transferred back to Antwerp.

OTHER ANTWERP PRINT PUBLISHERS

The remarkable extent to which the Moretuses facilitated sundry transactions at the Frankfurt fairs for the Galles, Adriaen Collaert, and Charles de Mallery, in addition to the extended Sadeler and Caymox families, as well as for an assortment of their other clients, is irrefutable. These transactions attest to the applicability of Henri Estienne's portrayal of the fairs as profitable places to meet and do business to those engaged in the print trade as well. Nevertheless, not all Antwerp-based print publishers similarly availed themselves of the Moretuses' services. For example, the Moretuses' accounts for their business in Antwerp reveal a significant interest in the work of both Abraham van Merlen and Michael Snijders in several northern European cities. Not only did they have the Moretuses distribute numerous packages for them to distant contacts, but the Moretuses themselves also sold thousands of impressions of Van Merlen's and Snijders's prints to their own clientele, including the Raesfelt family from Münster and other booksellers whom they encountered at the Frankfurt fairs. Nevertheless, neither Van Merlen nor Snijders made as much use of the opportunities provided by the Moretuses' presence at the Frankfurt fairs as they did of similar services available through the Moretuses' business in Antwerp. Aside from both publishers' shipment of packages to Overadt in 1618, only Van Merlen is known to have sent one other package to the Frankfurt fairs (for Nicolas Bonta in the spring of 1616). Thereafter, in the 1620s, Van Merlen, like Snijders, just received an occasional payment that was given to the Moretuses' representative at Frankfurt.[117]

One can only speculate why Van Merlen and Snijders rarely employed the Moretuses to further their trade in prints at Frankfurt. Regardless of the reason, however, their dealings with the Moretuses support the logical observation that there were other means available to Antwerp-based print publishers for doing business with far-flung individuals who, on occasion, visited the Frankfurt fairs. This was undoubtedly the case for Hieronymus Wierix. While his work, like his brothers', enjoyed international acclaim and was actively sought during his lifetime, his only known transaction at Frankfurt in which the Moretuses were involved was that cited above, when one of the Caymoxes had the Moretuses bring him a barrel of ink upon their return from the fall fair of 1612. The fact that the Caymoxes were willing to arrange this transaction for Wierix suggests that they did business in other contexts. Similarly, Wierix's son-in-law, the print publisher Jan-Baptist Barbé, rarely asked the Moretuses to assist him with transactions at the Frankfurt fairs, despite his evident concern for the distribution of his father-in-law's prints in addition to his own. In particular, he sent packages to Frankfurt via the Moretuses on just three occasions: in 1614 to Balthasar Caymox and to a certain Nicolas Barbé, and in 1630 to the Sadeler family in Munich. Finally, at the spring fair of 1631, Abraham Hogenberg gave the Moretuses money for Barbé.[118] The Moretuses' limited interventions at Frankfurt on behalf of other Antwerp print publishers active at the turn of the seventeenth century – the Huberti and De Jode families, for example – similarly support these observations as well.[119]

Although the Plantin-Moretus Press maintained an important presence at the Frankfurt fairs throughout the early seventeenth century and rendered diverse services for others there, the Moretuses were not the only ones to whom people could turn for such transactions. Some print publishers kept their own shops at the fairs and had, like the De Jodes, longstanding ties to other international art dealers, such as the Caymoxes, who frequented these and fairs elsewhere. Other publishers, like Van Merlen and Snijders, may have simply worked with clients who had their own preferred means of conducting their business or may have engaged different Antwerp booksellers or merchants who also attended the fairs. These observations do not diminish the significance of all that the Moretuses' records reveal concerning the multitude of transactions that took place at the Frankfurt fairs. Rather, they amplify it by confirming that the Moretuses ran just one of sundry businesses that supported the international trade in prints in a variety of ways at this exceptional venue. That said, one tantalizing topic remains, namely: how many prints might have been involved?

RELATIVE QUANTITIES OF PRINTS TRADED AT FRANKFURT

However much one would like to quantify the traffic in prints at the Frankfurt fairs, this remains an extremely difficult task. The frequent, generic references to rolls and packages without any specification of the contents is itself problematic due to the assortment of items in which many of the individuals featured in the Moretuses' records traded. Philips Galle, the Hogenbergs, and the Caymoxes, for example, dealt in maps, atlases, and similar publications, as well as individual prints, while other print sellers, for instance Theodore Galle, Raphael I and Justus Sadeler, also offered illustrated books. Moreover, even if a package was recorded as containing prints, often the number of prints was not noted. In particular, since packages with prints or images weighed some 5 to 38 pounds, the quantity of paper sent in a package could vary significantly, not to mention the number of images printed per sheet. For example, in February 1602, the Moretuses sent the merchant Rocho di Gabrielli in Danzig numerous books along with one package of fine images ("1 pacquet avec finnes images") provided by Adriaen Collaert, Theodore Galle, and Anton Wierix II.[120] Among the prints supplied by Collaert were fifty sheets with four images per sheet, 150 sheets with twelve images per sheet, and 400 sheets with eight images per sheet. This amounted to 600 sheets of paper bearing a total of 5,200 images, alongside all of the other prints provided by Collaert, Wierix, and Galle that were included in the same package. By contrast, in 1615, the Moretuses sent Pierre Geubels, a bookseller in St Omer, a single package comprising just 800 prints from Theodore Galle.[121] Thus, one cannot estimate the relative quantity of prints that might have been bought and sold at the Frankfurt fairs simply on the basis of how many packages were sent.

Rather, the payments made by Peter Overadt for Charles de Mallery provide a better means of gauging the quantities of prints that might have been involved in such transactions. Of all the print publishers discussed here, De Mallery was the most consistent in what he distributed internationally (at least via the Moretuses), namely: plain prints on paper, sold in bulk at 50 st. (or 2.5 fl.) per 100 images. While this rate was slightly more than what Adriaen Collaert and Theodore Galle typically charged for their plain prints on paper, it was less than Philips Galle's standard prices or what other artists such as the Wierixes and Peeter de Jode often asked. Consequently, De Mallery's fees would not have represented an extreme among contemporary print prices.[122] Assuming that De Mallery charged Overadt the same rates that he routinely applied to the prints he supplied to the Moretuses and other international clients, it is possible to calculate the number of prints De Mallery might have sent to Overadt in exchange for his payments. If De Mallery had given Overadt an exceptional discount in recognition of his evident preference for his work, then the total quantity of prints sold would only be greater.

Specifically, from the fall of 1608 through the spring of 1618, a decade in which the Moretuses helped complete numerous transactions at the Frankfurt fairs for disparate individuals involved in the print trade, Overadt made regular, nearly biannual payments for De Mallery. Ranging from 32 fl. 10 st. (in the fall of 1608) to 182 fl. 15 st. (in the spring of 1611), these payments amounted to a total of 1,446 fl. 13 st..[123] Paired with De Mallery's standard rate of 50 st. per 100 images, this sum would imply that he alone sold Overadt as many as 57,860 prints in just one decade, or approximately 5,800 prints per year on average. Such a figure is notably, but not impossibly, larger than the Moretuses' contemporaneous sale of 1,600 prints from De Mallery (supplied at his usual rate of 50 st. per 100 prints) to the Augsburg book dealer Georg Willer II in 1614.[124] For example, the difference in quantity may reflect the fact that print sales were a sideline to Willer's primary business as a bookseller, while for Overadt and all the other print dealers like him at the Frankfurt fairs, the print trade was the focus of their activities. If this estimate of Overadt's purchases from De Mallery is reasonably accurate, the total quantity of prints that might have been exchanged at the Frankfurt fairs by all those engaged in the print trade could have amounted to hundreds of thousands annually – quantities that go far beyond what one might imagine on the basis of extant impressions of prints in any collection known today.

CONCLUSION

It is difficult for us today to fully appreciate the extent to which the Frankfurt fairs remained enticing realms of opportunity into the early seventeenth century, decades after the publication of Estienne's glorification of them. In addition to the primary participants, who were from the Holy Roman Empire, a wide range of individuals of diverse international origins and of varying professions, from craftsmen to merchants, scholars, and nobles, attended the fairs. People came to meet each other, as well as to observe and trade in the rich profusion of merchandise available and settle various matters of business between otherwise distant clients and relations. The records of the Moretuses' dealings at the Frankfurt fairs attest to this immense potential and reveal how sundry individuals with distinct aspirations and needs partook of the plethora of opportunities offered by the fairs via the Moretuses. The remarkable mix of transactions that the Moretuses facilitated included: Gillis Sadeler's steady import of goods from Antwerp, Philips Galle's export of works to a number of familiar contacts abroad, the exchange of merchandise that Raphael Sadeler seems to have preferred, and Justus Sadeler's occasional use of the Moretuses' shop as a pickup point for his own international shipments. In addition, the Moretuses assisted with more personal requests, from transferring money for De Mallery and purchasing clothes for Cornelis Galle when both were en route to Italy to shipping ink to several Antwerp printmakers and facilitating the settlement of matters between the Sadelers and their representative in Antwerp, Philips Liesaert III. Consistently, the Moretuses' ability to receive payments in foreign currencies and transport large sums of cash back to Antwerp was clearly valued by many, even those who may have relied on other means to convey their merchandise to international clients.

This abundant evidence of the wealth of possibilities furnished by the Frankfurt fairs emanates from a single, prominent business that was a committed, prominent participant in the fairs at the turn of the seventeenth century. Nevertheless, the Moretuses' records do not simply document the myriad means by which the print trade was fostered at the fairs by an array of individuals; they also shed light on a far more extended period of time. Contemporary remarks concerning the availability of works by successful printmakers at the fairs in the early sixteenth century, as well as suppositions about the importance of booksellers and merchants in the distribution of prints at that time, are now vividly supported. Similarly, subsequent accounts of collectors' acquisitions of prints via the fairs gain in significance. For example, Count Max Willibald von Waldburg-Wolfegg asked both his personal agent and an Antwerp textile merchant to help him purchase prints at the fairs in 1645. Some 150 years later, in 1807, Count W. von Witzleben, asked the printmaker Jean-Jacques de Boissieu in Lyon to arrange for a local merchant of his own choosing to take Witzleben's order of prints to the Frankfurt fair so that he could avoid costly postal fees and simply pick up his prints and pay for them there.[125] These intriguing excerpts from isolated letters resonate all the more now due to the striking parallels with the Moretuses' transactions and demonstrate how common such dealings were beyond the Moretuses' own sphere of influence. Together, the examples discussed in this chapter illuminate the enduring trade in prints at the Frankfurt fairs, which, at their height, supported traffic in thousands of images from a wide assortment of dealers annually, alongside the bountiful variety of merchandise for which they are better known.

1 Kammerer 2017, p. 94, as translated by Paul White. See Henricus Stephanus, Francofordiense emporium, sive Francofordienses nundinae (Geneva: Henricus Stephanus, 1574), p. 3, for the original text, which reads: "Francofordiense emporium … à plurimis frequentetur, multi ex eo multa magnáque commoda consequantur: plerique ex eo ditiores, non pauci è pauperibus divites reddantur".

2 Kammerer 2017, p. LXXVIII (on the consuls' gift), p. LXXXIX (on contemporary complaints about inebriation and fights), and LXXXIX-XCI for a spoof of Estienne's text. Jan Moretus II also recounts, for example, how the bookseller Simon Martel was robbed while buying cloth there (MPM Arch. 84, p. 337, letter dated 23 September 1606). Among the various studies of the Frankfurt fairs, Flood 2007 offers an excellent and informative overview based on various sources, while Dietz 1910–1921 (in particular vol. III (1921)) and Kapp 1886 remain useful, detailed works.

3 Dietz 1910–1921, vol. III (1921), pp. 179–238, discusses Frankfurt's early financial exchange. See Flood 2007, pp. 11–12, as well as examples below from the Moretuses, for the settlement of accounts there.

4 Landau and Parshall 1994, p. 349, for the former; and MPM Arch. 13, fol. 154r, for the latter.

5 Hessels 1887, no. 154, on Lampsonius and Ortelius's purchase; and Griffiths 2016, pp. 288–89, for other examples of the distribution of prints at fairs.

6 Flood 2007, pp. 11 and 24–28; Laeven 1992, pp. 186–87; and Nuovo 2013, pp. 282–83.

7 On Plantin's dealings at the Frankfurt fair, see Bowen 2019 and Lauwaert 1972–1973. For a case study of the Moretuses' transactions at the fairs, see Breuls 2005.

8 See MPM Arch. 70, fol. 121r (28 August 1593); MPM Arch. 177, fol. 36r (11 March 1605); and MPM Arch. 217, fol. 165r (5 September 1610) for examples of Gruterus receiving packages via the Moretuses' shop in Frankfurt. See MPM Arch. 1001 (spring 1606), fol. 76 lft (Palazzolo); MPM Arch. 981 (spring 1596), fol. 62; MPM Arch. 983 (spring 1597), fol. 41 (Romanus); MPM Arch. 762, fol. 94; and MPM Arch. 759, fol. 40, for Leenwaerts' accounts with the Moretuses, which often include charges for weights for measuring the carats of precious metals that the Moretuses sent him. On 18 February 1615, he was also shipped a roll of images ("rolleau images"; MPM Arch. 222, fol. 31r). See MPM Arch. 68, fol. 20v (= fol. 30v) (8 March 1591), for a roll sent to Mercator; and MPM Arch. 70, fols. 41r (20 March 1593) and 121r (28 August 1593), for examples of packages sent to Hoefnagel via the Moretuses.

9 Lauwaert 1972–1973, vol. 50, pp. 135–36 and 137–78, provides a detailed account of those with whom Plantin and Jan Moretus I traded at the Frankfurt fairs during the sixteenth century. Breuls 2005, pp. 97–109, provides an overview (within the selected periods of his study) of those with whom the Moretuses dealt between 1589 and 1631, including the countries of origin of these clients. The individuals with whom the Moretuses dealt are also recorded in their Cahiers. Only around 1620–21 does there seem to be a slight dip in the number of people with whom the Moretuses traded at Frankfurt in this period. As is noted by Lauwaert and documented in Laeven 1992, Table 1, p. 192, offerings at Frankfurt by the German booksellers still far outweighed those from other countries.

10 For an example of the even exchange of goods, see MPM Arch. 989 (spring 1600), fol. 60 lft and rht. This practice is discussed in Maclean 2012, pp. 181–86. For a payment via a letter of credit ("lettre de change"), see MPM Arch. 1018 (spring 1615), fol. 52r. For debit/credit accounts kept with numerous individuals, most of which were ultimately settled with a cash payment, see the Frankfurt Grand livres (MPM Arch. nos. 43I, 498, 753–54, and 759–62). In addition to the examples of cash transactions in various currencies cited in this chapter, numerous cash payments are also noted after the lists of specific purchases in each Cahier. On the Moretuses' preference for payments in cash, see MPM Arch. 89, p. 379 (letter from Jan Moretus II to his parents following his arrival at the Frankfurt fair, dated 29 September 1598).

11 For examples of the return of large sums in diverse currencies, see MPM Arch. 180, fol. 68r (29 April 1608), for some 1,985 fl.; MPM Arch. 226, fol. 59r (18 April 1619), for 3,750 fl. 13 st.; and MPM Arch. 234, fol. 64r (15 May 1627), for some 4,737 fl. On 17 January 1613, for example, it was noted that the Moretuses would pay Galle their remaining debt of 360 fl. following the Frankfurt fairs, as usual ("Pour reste de ce compte vienent pr reste a mon beaufrere Theodore Galle trois cents et soisante florins a payer comme dordinaire appres les deux foires de francfort"; MPM Arch. 128, fol. 90 lft). See MPM Arch. 220, fols. 85v (21 May 1613) and 179r (22 October 1613), for the agreed payments of 180 fl. each (to pay off the 360 fl. owed), following the spring and fall fairs.

12 Flood 2007, pp. 4–7 and 12, on the general practice. In his letters, Jan Moretus II noted that he was still waiting for a shipment of books and periodically recorded when certain booksellers arrived and departed (for example, MPM Arch. 89, pp. 377 (letter dated 26 September 1598) and 379 (letter dated 29 September 1598)). The concluding lists of cash receipts at the fairs in the Frankfurt Cahiers (listed in the Bibliography) reveal when such transactions occurred.

13 Bowen 2019, pp. 68–70, discusses Plantin's arrangements for shipping his books to the fairs. For an overview of how the books might have been packed, see Voet, GC, vol. II, pp. 427–28. For examples of larger shipments, see MPM Arch. 174, fols. 38r-38v (9–11 March 1602); and MPM Arch. 221, fols. 60v-61r (5 April 1614).

14 See the Note to the Reader on weight equivalencies. For examples of barrels weighing approximately 1,000 Antwerp pounds, see MPM Arch. 65, fols. 107v and 144r (1588); MPM Arch. 175, fols. 5v and 11r (1603); MPM Arch. 222, fol. 49r (1615); MPM Arch. 230, fol. 163v (1623); and MPM Arch 238, fols. 27r-27v (1630).

15 On the implications of the Thirty Years' War for the Moretuses' trade in Frankfurt, see, for example, MPM Arch. 144, p. 259 (letter from Balthasar Moretus I to the bookseller Johann Kinckius, dated 1 March 1632); and MPM Arch. 146, p. 75 (letter from Balthasar I to Jean-Jacques Chifflet, Archduchess Isabella's doctor, dated 11 May 1634). On 6 August 1637, Balthasar I wrote to Philippe Chifflet, vicar-general for the archbishop of Besançon, that hardly any booksellers had attended the Frankfurt fairs in the past several years (MPM Arch. 146, pp. 314–15).

16 For example: MPM Arch. 217, fol. 200r (5 November 1610), concerning a return shipment from Frankfurt to Antwerp. On the Van Egmont family and their connection to the Moretuses, see Imhof 2016, p. 17.

17 For example: MPM Arch 223, fol. 34r (17 March 1616), for the former; and MPM Arch. 71, fol. 29r (12 March 1594), for the latter. See Dietz 1910–1921, vol. III (1921), pp. 287–315 (transport to Frankfurt via waterways) 313–15 (the connection between Frankfurt and Cologne), and 316–60 (various options for transport over land, including routes such as those alluded to here (e.g., 325–26)).

18 MPM Arch. 94, pp. 119–20. See Flood 2007, p. 3, for similar remarks concerning the large number of tolls that had to be paid within the Holy Roman Empire.

19 There are one-time charges of 4.5 fl. per 100 pounds (MPM Arch. 221, fols. 60v-61r (5 April 1614)), and 6.5 fl. per 100 pounds (MPM Arch. 178, fol. 47r (30 March 1606)). However, there are several instances of a rate of 5 fl. per 100 pounds (MPM Arch. 221, fol. 158v (6 September 1614); and MPM Arch. 222, fols. 49r (24 March 1615) and 154v (9 September 1615)).

20 Inventories of what was left in storage ("in het packhuys") at Frankfurt were usually included in the Cahiers, as were references to the costs of renting the shop (the "boutique"). See, for example, MPM Arch. 995 (spring 1603), fol. 71 rht ff., various expenses, and loose sheets with lists of which books were left where; and MPM Arch. 1011 (fall 1611), fols. 66–68 (various expenditures) and 72 ff. (lists of the books left in Frankfurt).

21 The costs for traveling to and from Frankfurt were noted separately; see, for example, a bill prepared by Gommer van Sulsen for his return from the spring fair in 1594 (MPM Arch. 117, p. 567). The day-to-day costs incurred in Frankfurt were noted in the Cahiers (see the examples in the preceding note).

22 In March 1586, Jan Dresseler, who represented Plantin at the Frankfurt fairs, was abducted, together with other booksellers, and Plantin had to pay a ransom to free him (Voet, GC, vol. I, p. 117). Similarly, in a letter dated 9 August 1600, Balthasar I described how their shipment from Frankfurt was ravaged by thieves (MPM Arch. 12, p. 114).

23 For example, MPM Arch. 989 (spring 1600), fol. [70] lft, details how money was taken back to Cologne by both a former apprentice, the bookseller Bernhard Wolters (see Chapter 8), and the Van Egmonts, while additional sums in various currencies were also included in barrels 1 and 3, which were being sent back to Antwerp.

24 MPM Arch. 1003 (spring 1607), fol. 79 rht (Gryn); MPM Arch. 234, fol. 129r (20 August 1627), and MPM Arch. 235, fols. 26v (29 February 1628) and 125v (4 September 1628) (Van Triest); MPM Arch. 1044 (spring 1628), fol. [87] rht (Van Dale); and MPM Arch. 1050 (spring 1631), fol. [94] lft and rht (Van Marduyn).

25 MPM Arch. 992 (fall 1601), fol. 81 rht, for the payment in Frankfurt; and MPM Arch. 173, fol. 194r, for the payment in Antwerp.

26 MPM Arch. 1011 (fall 1611), fol. 69 lft.

27 MPM Arch. 71, fol. 29r, for De Mallery's advance; and MPM Arch. 88, p. 37, for the receipt. See Bowen and Imhof 2021 for De Mallery's time in Italy.

28 MPM Arch. 1024 (spring 1618), fol. 77 lft; and MPM Arch. 1050 (spring 1631), fol. [110] lft, respectively. Although neither De Mallery nor Barbé are known to have had works sent to either Meuting or Hogenberg via the Frankfurt fairs, the Moretuses occasionally did send packages from them to Cologne. See MPM Arch. 220, fol. 211r, and MPM Arch. 221, fol. 123r, for individual packages sent from De Mallery to Meuting in 1613 and 1614, respectively. See also Chapter 8 on Barbé's exchanges with Hogenberg.

29 MPM Arch. 1003 (spring 1607), fol. 76 lft, and MPM Arch. 179, fol. 85r (17 May 1607) (the chandelier); MPM Arch. 234, fol. 172r (13 November 1627) (the cup); MPM Arch. 180, fol. 77r (10 May 1608) (the boxes); and MPM Arch. 985 (spring 1598), fol. 55 rht (the painting). For the identification of Von Wiltberg, see MPM Arch. 762, fol. 66.

30 MPM Arch. 986 (fall 1598), fol. 27 lft.

31 For examples of the Moretuses' 1 and 3 st. rates (both applied to Philips Galle), see MPM Arch. 21, fol. 203 lft (17 May 1594); and MPM Arch. 67, fol. 60r (6 June 1590), respectively. For a decree from the Antwerp government from 20 September 1613 with the official postal rates, see MPM L 636.

32 For examples of the 2 st. rate, see MPM Arch. 72, fol. 107v (20 August 1595, A. Ortelius); MPM Arch. 175, fol. 83r (2 June 1603, P. Moerentorf); MPM Arch. 179, fol. 189r (24 October 1607, A. Schottus); MPM Arch. 222, fol. 45r (14 March 1615, S. Zukowski); and MPM Arch. 234, fol. 142r (11 September 1627, Hierat). For examples of their 1.5 st. rate, see MPM Arch. 175, fol. 76v (24 May 1603, M. Nutius II); and MPM Arch. 225, fol. 171r (19 October 1619, T. Galle). For the marriage between Theodore Galle's daughter Catherina and Martinus Nutius III, see Van der Straelen 1858, p. 232.

33 MPM Arch. 1015 (fall 1613), fol. 63 lft (52 pounds); MPM Arch. 1013 (fall 1612), fol. 50 rht (100 pounds); and MPM Arch. 1018 (spring 1615), fols. 40 lft, 51 lft, and 53 rht (210 pounds). Each of these was purchased by Theodore Galle from the family of Jacob de Kempener.

34 MPM Arch. 219, fol. 61v (letters); and MPM Arch. 223, fols. 33r-33v (unspecified).

35 MPM Arch. 223, fol. 33v ("images" weighing 5 pounds and sent to the Moretuses' agent in Frankfurt, Cornelis van Egmont, on 17 March 1616); MPM Arch. 225, fol. 42r (prints weighing 38 pounds and sent by Theodore Galle to Raphael Sadeler I on 23 March 1618); and MPM Arch. 1022 (spring 1617), fol. 50 lft (prints weighing 62 pounds and sent by Justus Sadeler for Crispijn de Passe I in May 1617).

36 Voet, GC, vol. II, p. 426.

37 MPM Arch. 221, fols. 56v and 61r (De Mallery's shipment to Bonta); MPM Arch. 1016 (spring 1614), fol. 65 rht (Bonta's payment for transport under 26 April 1614), and fol. 64 rht (his payment for De Mallery); and MPM Arch. 221, fol. 86r (23 May 1614: transport charges to De Mallery).

38 MPM Arch. 171, fol. 32v (26 February 1599): "1 Sac de Verspreet avec semen basilicum [basil seeds]".

39 MPM Arch. 177, fol. 129r (17 August 1605: shipment of imperfect sheets for their shop ("taberna")); MPM Arch. 239, fol. 48r (26 March 1631: new titles), and MPM Arch. 221, fol. 158v (6 September 1614: 100 title pages for the folio breviary); and MPM Arch. 72, fol. 108r (22 August 1595: 270 title pages for the work by Sa).

40 For example: MPM Arch. 177, fol. 33v (8 March 1605: most likely, items for Jan Moretus II); MPM Arch. 222, fol. 49r (24 March 1615: items for Cornelis van Egmont); and MPM Arch. 222, fol. 150r (20 August 1615); and MPM Arch. 1019 (fall 1615), introductory list (contents of barrel 3, including: "bezaeltien peerlen de cousin H. de Clercq dans la chemise de Corneille Egmont")).

41 MPM Arch. 221, fol. 158v (6 September 1614) and MPM Arch. 224, fol. 44r (15 March 1617), both for Van Egmont; MPM Arch. 172, fol. 19v (26 February 1600, for Verspreet); and MPM Arch. 179, fol. 46r (17 March 1607) and MPM Arch. 227, fol. 44r (28 March 1620), both for Hertsroy. On the Verspreet family of paper merchants in Antwerp in this period, see MPM Arch. 126, fol. 183 (for Jan in 1605). For the merchant Jacques Verspreet, see Gelderblom 2000, pp. 229 and 316. See MPM Arch. 180, fol. 100v, for a reference to Hertsroy as Martin Nutius II's "cousin".

42 MPM Arch. 174, fol. 66r (8 May 1602: Schottus and Ximenes); MPM Arch 180, fol. 74v (8 May 1608: Costerus); and MPM Arch. 1041 (fall 1626), fol. 60 lft (shipments between Jesuits).

43 MPM Arch. 69, fol. 101v (28–31 August 1592: Clusius); MPM Arch. 231, fol. 60v (19 April 1624) and MPM Arch. 232, fol. 52v (17 April 1625: the Cramoisy family); MPM Arch. 219, fol. 61v (20 April 1612: correspondence from Antwerp to a certain Polish noble, Alexandre Tryebinski); and MPM Arch. 221, fol. 77r (letters brought back from Frankfurt on 4 May 1614 for the Polish noble Stanislaus Zukowski, then living in Leuven).

44 MPM Arch. 224, fol. 141r (7 September 1617); and MPM Arch. 1023 (fall 1617), at the end of the list of objects left in the Moretuses' shop in Frankfurt. For the identification of Farsin, see MPM Arch. 128, fol. 286 lft.

45 MPM Arch. 1050 (spring 1631), fol. 33 lft, for Bollandus's financial transfer; and MPM Arch. 1051 (fall 1631), fol. [111] lft, for details of the shipment, which involved yet another Jesuit intermediary, Joannes Schne of Würzburg. See MPM Arch. 175, fol. 45r (28 March 1603), for a shipment from the Antwerp Jesuits for those in Prague; and MPM Arch. 995 (spring 1603), fol. 75 lft, for the payment for the transport of "le pacquet des figures" by a certain Baptista van Hollant (from Prague). For the shipment of unspecified "images", see MPM Arch. 222, fol. 49r (24 March 1615, for Augsburg); MPM Arch. 221, fol. 61r (29 March 1614, for Dillingen); and MPM Arch. 223, fol. 33v (17 March 1616, for Rome).

46 MPM Arch. 1051 (fall 1631), fol. [111] lft: "voor Rvd. P. Jo Bap. de Borges Soc. Jesu Moyant te coopen: 2 gebreyde swerte mutsen om onder den hoot te dragen gelyc de Jesuiten doen … Item voor twee oft dry Rexdallers belekens te weten klyn witte gronden van Barbe Snyers Merle, Galle, B. Virgo Maria, Crucifixen, Stae Virgines etc.".

47 MPM Arch. 75, fols. 29r, 40v, and 155r (2 and 21 March and 1 September 1598, respectively).

48 It is important to remember that artists and booksellers in Antwerp were all members of the Guild of St Luke and, like the printmakers and booksellers in Paris, often lived in the same areas. For this last point, see, for example, Van der Stock 1998, pp. 60–71; and Grivel 1986, pp. 57–69.

49 On Van Egmont's involvement in the Moretuses' affairs at Frankfurt, see Imhof 2016, pp. 17–18. For the shipments of prints, see MPM Arch. 221, fol. 158v (1614); MPM Arch. 223, fols. 33v and 158r (1616); MPM Arch. 224, fol. 53r (1617); and MPM Arch. 225, fol. 145v (1618).

50 See Appendix 1, CP-2 for an overview of the sales of Solomon's temple, and Chapter 5 on Galle's publications.

51 For maps for Balthasar Caymox and his relative Peter Knabenhouwer, see MPM Arch. 221, fols. 52r and 61r (22 and 29 March 1614); and MPM Arch. 222, fol. 49r (24 March 1615). See Imhof 2018a, pp. 53 and 59–60, for the Moretuses' purchase of the plates used to illustrate Ortelius's atlas and this transaction. See Meurer 1993 on the Caymoxes' dealings in maps in general.

52 For various shipments of canons between 1599 and 1604, see MPM Arch. 171, fol. 104v; MPM Arch. 174, fol. 31v; MPM Arch. 176, fol. 26r; and MPM Arch. 178, fol. 44r. See MPM Arch. 231, fol. 155v (4 September 1624), for the 1624 shipment; and MPM Arch. 1037 (fall 1624), fol. 36 lft, for Van Dale's purchase.

53 See MPM Arch. 13, p. 219 (Jan II's acknowledgement of Willer's request for the prints); MPM Arch. 128, fol. 108 rht (the Moretuses' purchase of the prints from De Mallery); and MPM Arch. 1016 (spring 1614), fol. 23 rht (Willer's payment).

54 For the variety of items shipped in rolls, see MPM Arch. 73, fols. 124v (2 September 1596: title pages), and 10v (21 January 1596: imperfect sheets); MPM Arch. 247, fol. 182r (14 December 1639: sheets with a Litany in 24°); and MPM Arch. 222, fol. 31r (18 February 1615: "images"). Many, if not all, of the various rolls shipped at the request of the cartographer Abraham Ortelius most likely contained maps (see, e.g., MPM Arch. 72, fol. 34r (15 March 1595)). Finally, Theodore Galle sent two books to Raphael Sadeler I: Adrianus Barlandus' Chroniques des ducs de Brabant, most likely the Moretuses' edition from 1612, and a copy of Epictetus's Enchridion in 16°, which may have been the Plantin edition from 1585 (Voet, PP, nos. 1123–24; MPM Arch. 1024 (spring 1618), fol. 44 lft). Sadeler was also active as a bookseller as of 1613 (Bowen 2022b).

55 MPM Arch. 65, fol. 107v (12 August 1588). See also Chapter 8 on Boons.

56 MPM Arch. 217, fol. 165r (6 September 1610).

57 See Bowen 2019, p. 74, for the former; and MPM Arch. 67, fol. 60r (6 June 1590), for the latter. The remaining unspecified charges are noted in MPM Arch. 21, fols. 22 lft, 104 lft, and 203 lft.

58 MPM Arch. 171, fol. 68v (15 May 1599).

59 See Paisey 2006, p. 57 ff, and Chapter 3.

60 In addition to the sample shipments to Boons and De Passe cited above, see MPM Arch. 72, fol. 108r (22 August 1595, for one to Hans Hogenberg.

61 See Chapter 8 on the Hogenbergs and Galle's dealings with them, including Frans Hogenberg, in Frankfurt.

62 Rombouts and Van Lerius 1872, vol. I, p. 291; and Veldman 2001a, p. 19.

63 MPM Arch. 43I, fol. 107 lft and rht, for Boons's initial accounts with the Moretuses. On Boons, see Meurer 1988, p. 200, n. 27; and Chapter 8 on Van Buchell and his dealings with print sellers in Cologne.

64 See MPM Arch. 68, fol. 60r (31 May 1591; Boons via Mylius); and MPM Arch. 71, fol. 22v (26 February 1594; Hogenberg via the bookseller Goswinus Cholinus in Cologne).

65 Antwerp, Felix Archives, CERT 47, fol. 186r, for the 1586 document. For the De Kempener family and their establishment in Frankfurt, see Zülch 1935, pp. 408–10 (Jacob I), 447 (his son Anthoni), and 454 (his son Jakob II).

66 See below for the ink sales to T. Galle; and Antwerp, Felix Archives, IB 2938, bundle L, undated list of debts of J.B. Vrients's brother Gerard, fol. 3v, which contains the following reference to "Jacques" de Kempener (I or II), as the one who had always supplied the De Kempeners with ink for printing and who had recently died: "Jacques de Kempener is den man die ons altyt besorgt heeft ons druckswert ende alsoo hy is coemen te sterven". Bury 2001, pp. 201–02, gives two examples of prints after De Kempener's designs. For examples of packages sent to De Kempener, see MPM Arch. 177, fol. 136v (2 September 1605: two unspecified packages from Philips Galle); MPM Arch. 178, fol. 144v (2 September 1606: one unspecified package from Collaert); and MPM Arch. 219, fol. 42v (23 March 1612: one package of "images" from Theodore Galle).

67 On the connections between the Caymox and De Jode families, see New Holl. De Jode, part I, p. xxxiv; and Meurer 1993, pp. 26–28. On Cornelis's move to Nuremberg, see Wagner 2019, p. 110.

68 On Balthasar Caymox, see Meurer 1993, pp. 28–43. See Wagner 2019 on the family's trade in paintings. Although she states (p. 110) that a Hubert Caymox was active in Speyer and Frankfurt, the Hubert Caymox with whom the Moretuses traded was based in Nuremberg (see MPM Arch. 431, fol. 113 lft and rht; and MPM Arch. 762, fol. 47 lft). For the connection between Hubert Caymox and Knabenhouwer, see MPM Arch. 762, fol. 97 lft; see MPM Arch. 1003 (spring 1607), fol. 79 rht for the link between Knabenhouwer and Snellinck. See Kirchhoff 1889 for examples of the prints and illustrated books that Cornelis I had on hand at the Leipzig fair in October 1588. Balthasar also had a son Cornelis in Antwerp (possibly the painter mentioned above), to whom he sent a sword (MPM Arch. 1018 (spring 1615), fol. 54 lft).

69 On Cornelis Caymox's representation of Gerard de Jode, see New Holl. De Jode, part 1, p. xxxiv. The Caymoxes' purchases from the Moretuses are summarized in MPM Arch. 431, fol. 113, MPM Arch. 762, fols. 38 and 47; MPM Arch. 759, fols. 51 and 74; and MPM Arch. 760, fols. 29 and 49. For evidence of the Caymoxes' presence at the Leipzig fairs, see Kirchhoff 1889, pp. 190–92.

70 For Galle's shipments to Balthasar Caymox, see MPM Arch. 66, fol. 108r; MPM Arch. 173, fol. 127r' and MPM Arch. 180, fol. 148v. See MPM Arch. 997 (spring 1604), fol. 69 rht, for an example of one of Balthasar Caymox's payments for Galle, although Galle did not send him anything within several years of that date. Hubert Caymox or his widow gave the Moretuses money for Galle on three occasions between the fall of 1600 and fall of 1601 (including the exceptionally large sum of 159 fl. 10 st. at the fall fair of 1601, discussed above), even though Galle never sent them a package directly. Similarly, while Galle's one known shipment to Knabenhouwer was sent to the fall fair in 1606 (MPM Arch. 178, fol. 144v), Knabenhouwer gave the Moretuses money for Galle at the spring fair in 1603 and the fall fair in 1604 (MPM Arch. 995, fol. 75 lft; and MPM Arch. 998, fol. 71 lft, respectively).

71 For example, in December 1601, Galle received 159 fl. 10 st. from Hubert Caymox (MPM Arch. 173, fol. 194r); in June 1604, he received 111 fl. from Balthasar Caymox (MPM Arch. 176, fol. 72v); and in November 1604, he was given the largest sum of all, more than 181 fl., by Peter Knabenhouwer (MPM Arch. 176, fol. 156r). See Chapter 2 and Appendix 1 for an overview of what Galle and others charged for their prints. These shipments may also have contained either cartographic works or Galle's print books, which would have been more costly, on average, than individual prints.

72 See above for the Sadelers' association with De Kempener; and Zülch 1935, pp. 416–17, for Gillis I's registration as a citizen of Frankfurt and his death in 1609. See MPM Arch. 69, fol. 27r (15 February 1592), for Galle's first known shipment to him.

73 MPM Arch. 178, fols. 87r and 172r (payments from 1606); and MPM Arch. 179, fols. 82v and 218r (payments from 1607).

74 For an example of this perspective on the Sadelers, see Griffiths 2016, pp. 179 and 218.

75 MPM Arch. 69, fol. 27r (29 February 1592); and MPM Arch. 7, fol. 28r (6 March 1593), respectively.

76 MPM Arch. 218, fol. 40r (5 March 1611): "2 [packages] pr le vefve de gillis Sadeler pr Sadeler a Venise pr addresser Th G".

77 Sénéchal 1990, p. 26.

78 MPM Arch. 72, fol. 30r (8 March 1595, to De Bry); and MPM Arch. 75, fol. 29r (2 March 1598, to Mercator).

79 For example, see MPM Arch. 127, fol. 211 rht (Theodore Galle's accounts with the Moretuses; for prints that Philips Galle sold to the Moretuses in March and October 1604) and 211 lft (a book that Philips bought from the Moretuses on 20 October 1605). On the timing of Theodore's management of the Galle workshop, see Bowen 2009, pp. 127–28.

80 MPM Arch. 180, fol. 22r (27 February 1608; Theodore Galle's first two packages (to Gillis Sadeler)).

81 Strictly speaking, the Moretuses first recorded Theodore Galle's name in their Frankfurt account books for the spring fair of 1603, when they made a payment in Theodore Galle's name to Georg Meuting (MPM Arch. 995, fol. 71 rht), who had married Frans Hogenberg's widow, Agnes Lomar, by the spring of 1604 (MPM Arch. 759, fol. 71 rht). The fact that there is no evidence of any contact between Theodore Galle and the Hogenbergs or Meuting at this time, while Philips Galle was still in contact with them (see, for example, MPM Arch. 175, fol. 45r (28 March 1603), for Philips's contemporaneous shipment of a package to the Hogenberg family), suggests that this payment may actually have been made for Philips Galle and that, like the Moretuses' own transactions with the Galles in this decade (see above), the record keeping was simply done in Theodore's name.

82 For the sparse shipments between 1612 and 1615, see MPM Arch. 219, fol. 42v (23 March 1612, package of "images" to Jacob de Kempener); MPM Arch. 1018, fol. 52 lft and 53 lft (13 April 1615, unspecified number of packages for Raphael Sadeler via Johann Hertsroy); and MPM Arch. 222, fol. 154r (7 September 1615, a package to one of the Sadelers). For examples of the large shipments that followed, see MPM Arch. 223, fol. 30v (12 March 1616, two packages sent to Abraham Hogenberg, weighing 55 pounds); MPM Arch. 1022 (spring 1617), introductory list of the contents of barrel 5 (three packages sent to Abraham Hogenberg, weighing 77 pounds); and MPM Arch. 225, fols. 145v-46r (7 September 1618, four packages for Raphael Sadeler for a total of 81 pounds).

83 MPM Arch. 223, fols. 30v and 158r; and MPM Arch. 224, fols. 53r and 137v, respectively. Galle's trade with the Sadelers is discussed below.

84 MPM Arch. 1024 (spring 1618), fol. 63 rht.

85 MPM Arch. 216, fol. 46v (24 March 1609), and MPM Arch. 218, fol. 40r (5 March 1611) (both for De Passe); and MPM Arch. 218, fol. 40r (5 March 1611; Overadt).

86 See MPM Arch. 217, fol. 41v (20 March 1610); MPM Arch. 227, fol. 50r (6 April 1620); and MPM Arch. 1049, fol. [114] lft (October 1630), respectively.

87 MPM Arch. 221, fol. 82r (15 May 1614, for a package of "figures" weighing 26 pounds); MPM Arch. 223, fol. 58v (21 April 1616, for a packages of "images", weighing 27 pounds); and MPM Arch. 1024 (spring 1618), fol. 76 rht (for a package of "tailles doulces").

88 Griffiths 2016, pp. 32–33.

89 MPM Arch. 1019 (fall 1615), fol. 45 lft (ink for the Moretuses); MPM Arch. 1013 (fall 1612), fol. 50 rht (ink for Wierix, Collaert, and Galle in 1612); MPM Arch. 1014 (spring 1613), fol. 64 rht and the back flyleaf (ink shipment), and MPM Arch. 220, fol. 83r (18 May 1613), for the shipping charges for De Mallery; and MPM Arch. 1019 (fall 1615), fol. 45 lft (ink for De Mallery).

90 Both De Mallery and Jan-Baptist Barbé exported packages of "images" again in 1614 (see, for example, MPM Arch. 221, fol. 61r, 29 March 1614), while Collaert and Galle shipped single packages again in 1615 (MPM Arch. 222, fol. 154r, 7 September 1615).

91 See Chapter 7.

92 MPM Arch. 1012 (spring 1612), fol. 1 rht, for Galle's first known purchase; and MPM Arch. 1021 (fall 1616), fol. 54 rht, for his last. See MPM Arch. 1020 (spring 1616), fol. 24 rht, for the poorer quality of Eckenthaller's ink: "Notes que iay rendu a Hans Eckenthaller imprimeur de Theod. de Bry le tonnelet de noir pour tailles doulces lequel en foire de Sept: 1615 de luy avois achapte a la parolle du de Bry susdict; pour fort bon noir; et a condition de le rapporter en cas qu'il ne fust aussy bon comme Kempeners". Finally, while Eckenthaller's ink cost 4 batz per pound, the De Kempeners' cost 5 batz per pound (MPM Arch. 1020 (spring 1616), fols. 24 rht and 48 lft, respectively).

93 De Ramaix 1989 documents the Sadelers' movements generally, while Zülch 1935, pp. 397–401 and 416–17, provides more details concerning the Sadelers' residence in Frankfurt.

94 For the former, see, for example, De Ramaix 1992, p. 12 and cat. nos. 1, 31, and 32. For the latter, see Appendix 1, SD-2; and Bowen 2022b.

95 For example, while Gillis I received packages most years between 1592 and 1609, only a few were marked expressly for Raphael, namely: in the fall of 1592 (MPM Arch. 69, fol. 102v), the spring of 1593 (MPM Arch. 70, fol. 28r, from Philips Galle), the spring of 1602 (MPM Arch. 174, fol. 38r, from Philips Liesaert III), and the fall of 1607 (MPM Arch. 179, fol. 155r). Jan I's son Justus received just one package in this same period, namely in the spring of 1606 (MPM Arch. 178, fol. 47r, from Philips Liesaert III).

96 See, for example, MPM Arch. 217, fol. 41v (20 March 1610); MPM Arch. 218, fol. 40r (5 March 1611); and MPM Arch. 221, fol. 82r (15 May 1614). See Mayerhofer 2011, pp. 38–39 and 59–62 on Raphael's ill health in this period. After 1621, only Jan-Baptist Barbé sent a package to one of the Sadelers – most likely, Raphael I or one of his sons (MPM Arch. 1049 (fall 1630), fol. [114] lft).

97 For Justus's trade with the Moretuses via Antwerp, see MPM Arch. 1022 (spring 1617), fol. 50 lft (for De Passe); and Bowen 2022b. See MPM Arch. 1024 (spring 1618), fol. 76 lft, for the only known example of the Moretuses sending an order for Justus via the representative (Huberto Faber) of another bookseller (Roberto Meietti of Venice) at the Frankfurt fair.

98 See above for examples of his and Philips Galle's transactions, as well as MPM Arch. 176, fol. 34r (18 March 1604, shipment of one package from Collaert to Sadeler), and MPM Arch. 176, fol. 72r (5 June 1604, payment from Sadeler for Collaert).

99 Compare, for example, MPM Arch. 225, fol. 42v (23 March 1618: package from Collaert for Sadeler); and MPM Arch. 1024 (spring 1618), fol. 76 rht (package from Sadeler for Collaert); both of these occurred via the spring fair of 1618.

100 MPM Arch. 1018 (spring 1615), fol. 54 lft; and MPM Arch. 1020 (spring 1616), fol. 51 rht.

101 See, for example, MPM Arch. 1011 (fall 1611), introductory list for barrel 4; MPM Arch. 222, fol. 49r (24 March 1615); MPM Arch. 1022 (spring 1617), fol. 52 rht (26 April); and MPM Arch. 1024 (spring 1618), fol. 76 lft.

102 For a transcription of this agreement, see De Ramaix 1989, p. 41 (Appendix 6). For a discussion of the Liesaert family of painters, see Van Roey 1967. On Raphael's marriage to Katelyne Liesaert, see De Ramaix 1989, pp. 12 and 38. Sénéchal also refers to this agreement, but incorrectly identifies Liesaert as Raphael's father-in-law (Sénéchal 1990, p. 25). For these shipments, see MPM Arch. 173, fols. 34r and 126v (shipment of four packages to Gillis in 1601); MPM Arch. 174, fol. 38r (shipment of two packages to Raphael in 1602); MPM Arch. 175, fol. 135r (shipment of one package to Gillis in 1603); MPM Arch. 178, fol. 47r (shipment of four packages to Justus in 1606); and MPM Arch. 1020 (spring 1616), introductory list of the contents of barrel 6 (small package weighing 6 pounds sent to Raphael in 1616).

103 On Collaert's apprentices, see New Holl. Collaert, part I, p. lix. For the cited shipments see MPM Arch. 172, fol. 19v (26 February 1600); MPM Arch. 218, fol. 40r (5 March 1611), for small, single packages weighing just 17 and 9 pounds, respectively, sent to Justus Sadeler in Venice and Peter Overadt in Cologne; MPM Arch. 1024 (spring 1618), fol. 76 lft, (a final package of prints sent to Raphael Sadeler) and n. 66 above (a package sent to De Kempener); MPM Arch. 176, fol. 110r (14 August 1604, to "C. Passeo").

104 See Chapter 8.

105 See, for example, MPM Arch. 173, fol. 194r (4 December 1601), for payments of 75 fl. and some 124 fl. by Balthasar and Hubert Caymox, respectively; and MPM Arch. 995 (spring 1603), fol. 75 lft, for a payment of nearly 127 fl. by Peter Knabenhouwer.

106 MPM Arch. 180, fol. 148v (5 September 1608, a 12-pound package for Balthasar Caymox).

107 New Holl. Collaert, part VII.

108 See MPM Arch. 995 (spring 1603), fol. 75 lft, for a notably large payment of 150 Reichsthalers and 21 batz, worth 210 fl., from Balthasar Caymox for Brueghel; MPM Arch. 179, fol. 218r (10 December 1607), for a payment from Knabenhouwer for Philips Galle; MPM Arch. 1016, fol. 64 rht (spring 1614), for a payment from Balthasar Caymox for Brueghel; and MPM Arch. 1024 (spring 1618), fol. 63 rht, for a payment from Balthasar Caymox for Theodore Galle.

109 MPM Arch. 1004 (fall 1607), fols. 12 lft and 80 rht. In his discussion of Overadt's publishing of maps and town views, Meurer asserts that there is no evidence that Overadt printed books (Meurer 2001, p. 32). Overadt's appointment to print the calendar is mentioned in both Meurer 2001, p. 32 (as the "Hofkalender"); and Schöller 1992, p. 37 (as the "Wappenkalenders").

110 MPM Arch. 180. fol. 148v (5 September 1608: shipment of single packages to Overadt and Balthasar Caymox, weighting 19.5 and 14 pounds, respectively).

111 For an example of an isolated shipment to the Sadeler family via Frankfurt, see MPM Arch. 222, fol. 49r (24 March 1615: delivered to Hertsroy for Raphael Sadeler in Munich). Similarly, De Mallery sent Balthasar Caymox only one small roll via Anton Hierat in Cologne in 1613 (MPM Arch. 220, fol. 221r) and Justus Sadeler one package of prints via the Moretuses in Antwerp in 1615 (MPM Arch. 222, fol. 170v).

112 See, for example, n. 37 above for his trade with Bonta; MPM Arch. 218, fol. 40r (two packages sent on 5 March 1611, weighing 26 pounds); MPM Arch. 217, fol. 41v (four packages sent on 20 March 1610, weighing 69 pounds); and MPM Arch. 224, fol. 53r (5 April 1617; the last known shipment).

113 MPM Arch. 218, fol. 40r (5 March 1611; packages from Collaert and Galle, weighing 9 and 40 pounds, respectively); and MPM Arch. 225, fol. 42r (23 March 1618; a shipment of two packages from Snijders, weighing 17 pounds total, and two packages from Van Merlen weighing 9 pounds).

114 MPM Arch. 1035 (fall 1623), fol. 72 rht, and MPM Arch. 1036 (spring 1624), fol. 67 rht, for payments from both Bussemacher and Hogenberg; and MPM Arch. 1040 (spring 1626), fol. [88] lft, for a payment from Bussemacher.

115 See MPM Arch. 227, fol. 44r (28 March 1620), and MPM Arch. 228, fol. 124v (4 September 1621) for the Sadelers; and MPM Arch. 227, fol. 50r (6 April 1620, from Galle and De Mallery), and MPM Arch. 231, fol. 39r (10 March 1624, from Jan Boel), all for Jansonius.

[116] For examples of shipments arranged for the rector of the Antwerp Jesuits, Heribertus Rosweydus, see MPM Arch. 229, fols. 38r-38v (23 March 1622); and MPM Arch. 1041 (fall 1626), fol. 60 lft.

[117] See MPM Arch. 1020 (spring 1616), introductory list of contents for barrel 5 (Van Merlen's shipment), and fol. 42 lft (money that Bonta gave the Moretuses for Van Merlen at the same fair). For payments for Van Merlen made by a certain Baptist or Jan Baptist Colpyn, see MPM Arch. 1040 (spring 1626), fol. [88] lft; and MPM Arch. 1044 (spring 1628), fol. [90] lft. For the two known payments for Snijders made at the fairs, see MPM Arch. 1030 (spring 1621), fol. 60 rht (from Overadt); and MPM Arch. 1044 (spring 1628), fol. 94 rht (from Michael van Dale).

[118] For Barbé's shipments to Frankfurt, see MPM Arch. 1016, introductory list of contents for barrel 8 (sent to the spring fair of 1614; "images fines" for Caymox); MPM Arch. 221, fol. 158v (a book for N. Barbé); and MPM Arch. 1049 (fall 1630), fol. [114] lft (Sadelers). See MPM Arch. 1050 (spring 1631), fol. [110] lft, for Hogenberg's payment.

[119] For examples involving the Hubertis, see MPM Arch. 218, fol. 40r (a shipment to the Cologne bookseller Johann Kinckius on 5 March 1611); and MPM Arch. 177, fol. 62r (22 April 1605: a payment for Adrian Huberti II (perhaps) from a certain Hans van Loo). For a package from the Caymoxes for Hans de Jode, see MPM Arch. 1023 (fall 1617), fol. 56 lft.

[120] MPM Arch. 174, fol. 29r (the reference to the package) and 14r (the list of what Collaert supplied).

[121] MPM Arch. 222, fol. 182v.

[122] Chapter 2 contains a detailed discussion of the prices Antwerp print sellers charged for their works.

[123] For these two payments, see MPM Arch. 180, fol. 192r; and MPM Arch. 218, fol. 70r, respectively.

[124] See n. 53 above for this sale.

[125] Landau and Parshall 1994, pp. 348–49; Eitel 1996, p. 27; and Perez 1981, p. 11, respectively.

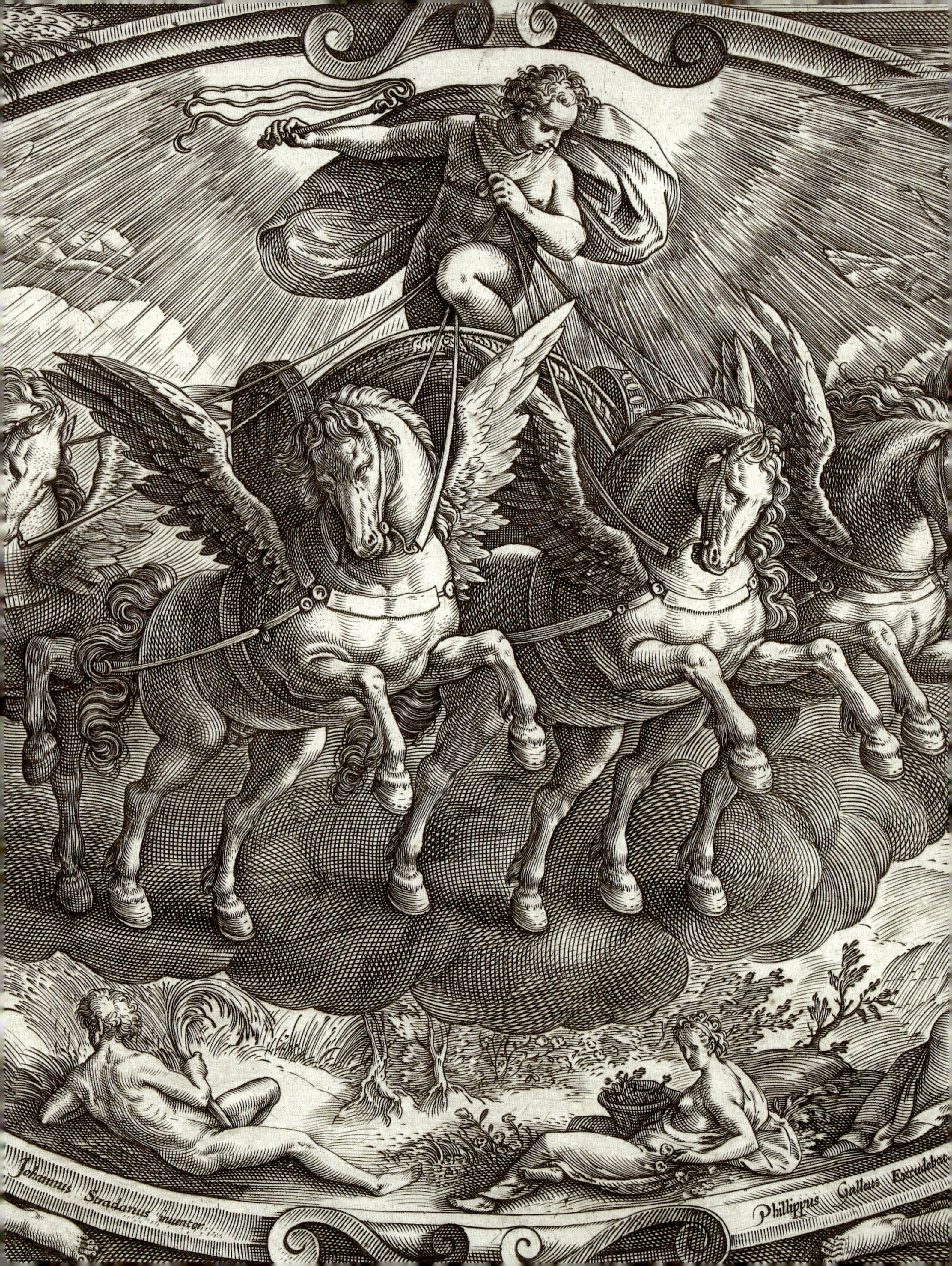
Johannus Stradanus inventor
Phillippus Galleus Excudebat

CHAPTER 10

EPILOGUE

ONWARDS INTO THE SECOND HALF OF THE SEVENTEENTH CENTURY

Detail of fig. 10.3:
Philips Galle after Johannes Stradanus, *Apollo in His Chariot*, engraving, in or before 1580.

> It is true that in the past Mr. Mallery was able to engrave letters as well as anyone, but I believe that his skill has declined significantly due to his old age.[1]

In January 1642, Balthasar II thus assessed Charles de Mallery's capabilities as an engraver (De Mallery was then seventy years old) when he responded to an inquiry from Frederick de Marselaer, the mayor of Brussels. De Marselaer wished to have a print made to commemorate Prince Baltasar Carlos's slaying of a bull and wild boar at the age of nine and evidently had asked if De Mallery might engrave the text on the plate.[2] Thus, despite De Mallery's limitations as a printmaker at this time, he still enjoyed a reputation for executing fine engravings, regardless of the decades that had passed since his active and successful practice of the craft. The lasting interest in his work is also reflected, for example, in purchases two years later, in 1644, by Philippe Chifflet, abbot of Balerne, who bought some 500 unspecified prints produced by De Mallery. Remarkably, when Jan Galle provided these images for Chifflet, he still charged De Mallery's old rate of 50 st. per 100 prints, which De Mallery himself had applied when he supplied the Moretuses with prints for resale between 1607 and 1626.[3]

De Mallery was not the only print seller among Plantin's and the Moretuses' original suppliers whose wares continued to be bought and sold in the mid-seventeenth century. Engravings originally published by Philips and Theodore Galle were also still available from Theodore's son Jan. In March 1646, for example, the Polish noble Jan Sobiepan Zamoyski, who was an advisor to the king of Poland during the 1650s, ordered single copies of several print series, most of which were supplied by Jan Galle, along with some 1,500 fl. worth of books. The predominance of single copies of both the books and print series suggests that these works were intended for a personal collection. Although not all of the subjects of the prints can be linked definitively to specific works, they clearly comprised a mix of Jan Galle's own publications, in particular, his *Speculum diversarum imaginum speculativum* – itself a compendium of several older print series – in addition to other popular series originally conceived of by his grandfather Philips, such as his extensive selection of hunting scenes.[4] Jan Galle's supply of images for Zamoyski is especially interesting because of the range of prices he charged. While he offered his own *Speculum* series at the same price that he had requested during the previous five years (9 fl.), he asked notably more for the series he had obtained from his parents' stock of plates. In the case of Philips Galle's large series of hunts, the 5 fl. Jan sought was a modest increase from the 4 fl. 10 st. that Philips had charged Jan Moretus I for potentially 104 such prints in 1608. Likewise, the 2 fl. recorded for Jan's supply of a series of the *Acts of the Apostles* was notably more than the 1 fl. 5.2 st. Philips was credited in 1608 for his expanded suite of

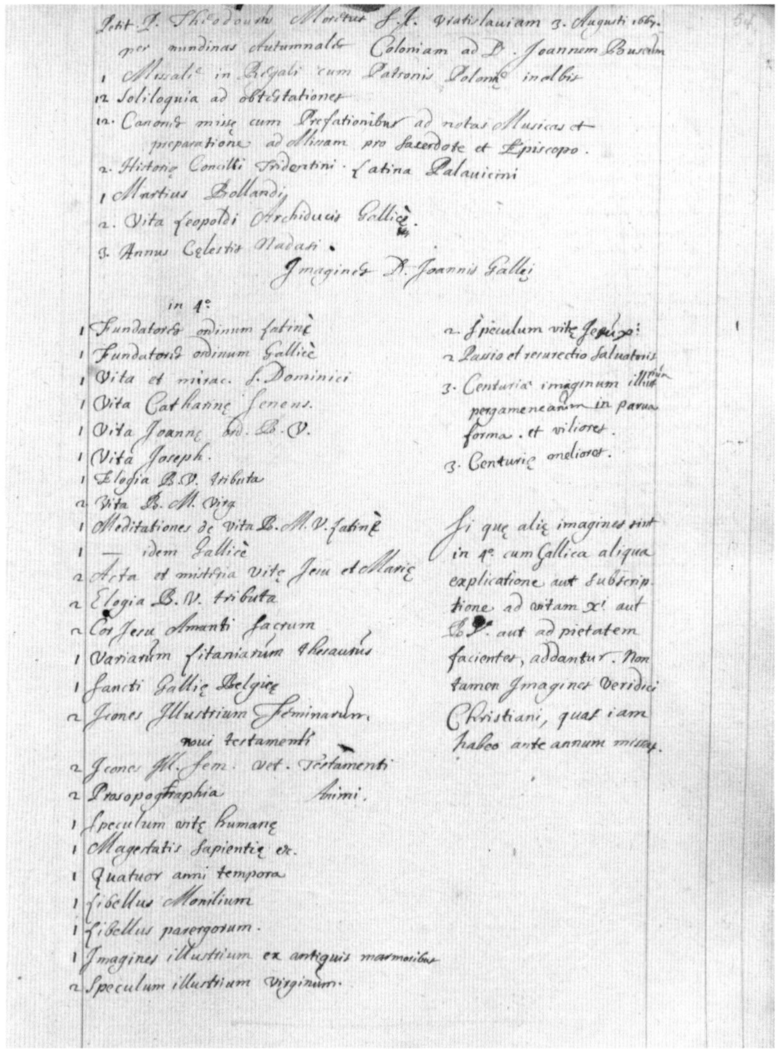

Ibit P. Theodoro Moreto S.J. Vratislaviam 3. Augusti 1667.
per nundinas Autumnales Coloniam ad D. Joannem Buseum
1 Missale in Regali cum Patronis Polonic. in albis
12 Soliloquia ad obtestationes
12 Canones missae cum Praefationibus ad notas Musicas et praeparatione ad Missam pro Sacerdote et Episcopo.
2 Historiae Concilii Tridentini Latina Palauicini
1 Martius Bollandi
2 Vita Leopoldi Archiducis Gallice.
3 Annus Caelestis Nadasi.
Imagines D. Joannis Gallei

in 4°
1 Fundatores ordinum Latine
1 Fundatores ordinum Gallice
1 Vita et mirac. S. Dominici
1 Vita Catharinae Senens.
1 Vita Joannae [illegible] B.V.
1 Vita Joseph.
1 Elogia B.V. tributa
2 Vita B.M. Virg.
1 Meditationes de vita B.M.V. Latine
1 — idem Gallice
2 Acta et mysteria vitae Jesu et Mariae
2 Elogia B.V. tributa
2 Cor Jesu Amanti Sacrum
1 Variarum Litaniarum thesaurus
1 Sancti Galliae Belgicae
2 Icones Illustrium Feminarum novi testamenti
2 Icones Ill. Fem. vet. Testamenti
2 Prosopographia Animi.
1 Speculum vitae humanae
1 Magestatis Sapientiae etc.
1 Quatuor anni tempora
1 Libellus Monitium
1 Libellus parergorum.
1 Imagines illustrium ex antiquis marmoribus
2 Speculum illustrium Virginum.

2 Speculum vitae Jesu:
2 Passio et resurrectio Salvatoris
3 Centuriae imaginum illustrium pergamenearum in parua forma. et viliores.
3 Centuriae meliores.

Si quae aliae imagines sint in 4° cum Gallica aliqua explicatione aut subscriptione ad vitam Xi aut B.V. aut ad pietatem facientes, addantur. Non tamen Imagines Veridici Christiani, quas iam habeo ante annum missas.

10.1 List of print series requested by Theodorus Moretus on 3 August 1667. MPM Arch. 351, *Libraires étrangers, 1665–1718*, fol. 54r.

thirty-five images of this subject. The inclination to gain a profit from the resale of these older print series was even stronger for Balthasar II, who not only convinced Jan Galle to give him a 10 percent discount on what Jan had asked for these works, but also marked up Jan's pre-discount prices significantly – by some 25–30 percent – when he resold the prints to Zamoyski, generating a total profit for himself of more than 20 fl. on the resale of just eight older print series, most likely represented by impressions of indeterminate quality.[5]

Zamoyski was not alone among the Moretuses' clients in his desire for old series published by the Galles. Unusually well-documented instances of this interest are the orders placed by Balthasar II's cousin, the Jesuit Theodorus Moretus, when he was working in various cities in Bohemia. Theodorus's sporadic commissions for prints date back to at least 1640, when he regretted that Balthasar Moretus I had not personally selected the images he desired.[6] Despite this earlier disappointment, he persisted in asking his relatives to send him prints in subsequent decades. Occasionally, these shipments were packages of unidentified images prepared by others, in particular Jan Galle or the Jesuit Franciscus de Smidt. However, for the purchases Theodorus made through the Moretuses between 1662 and 1667, both the print publisher and the subject of the works are often noted. While Theodorus obtained one large allotment of

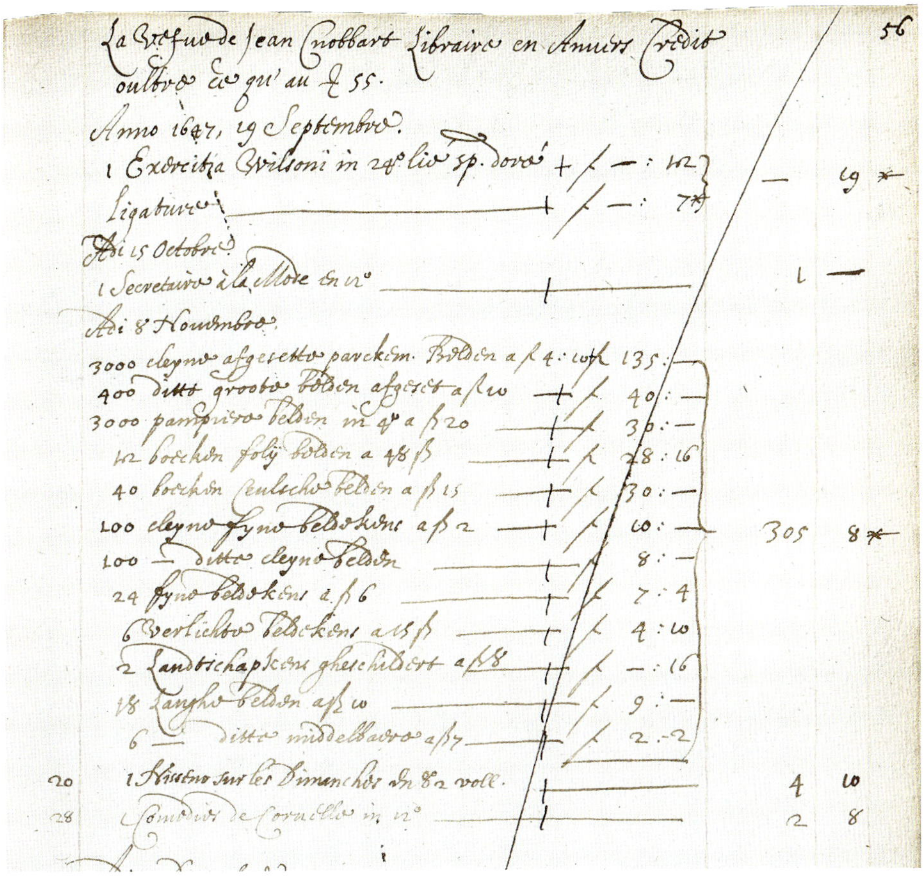

10.4 List of prints supplied by Marie de Man, the widow of Jan Cnobbaert, on 8 November 1647 for the Amsterdam merchant Peter de Haen II. MPM Arch. 740, *Libraires d'Anvers* KK, *1644–1655*, fol. 56 rht.

example, after buying 3,000 illuminated prints on parchment in 1642 and another 1,000 in 1643 (all supplied by Nicolas Lauwers), Schedelius appears to have concluded his purchases of prints via the Moretuses in 1644 with an order of just 500 illuminated prints on parchment supplied by a widow in the Huberti (Huybrechts) family, in addition to thirty canons (altar cards) in folio provided by Marie de Man, the widow of Jan Cnobbaert.[12] Both Bernhard Raesfeld's and the Försters' last known purchases date from the following year. While Raesfeld bought only 450 illuminated prints on parchment from the widow of Adriaen Huberti II in March 1645, Georg Förster acquired 2,000 prints on paper in June 1646, similarly offered by a widow of the Huberti family. The last differed significantly from Förster's detailed request for more than 7,000 prints, mostly illuminated images on parchment, the year before.[13]

Only Peter de Haen, a merchant and not a bookseller like the three preceding clients, concluded his procurement of prints through the Moretuses in a spectacular fashion; he bought more than 19,000 images, mostly illuminated and printed on parchment, over the course of 1647. While the widow of Paulus Huberti satisfied De Haen's first purchase of 4,500 illuminated images on parchment in May, Marie de Man supplied nearly half (more than 2,500) of the prints he bought in June and all of the more than 7,500 images he was sent in November (fig. 10.4).[14] There is no indication of the ultimate destination for the prints De Haen sought. However, the reference in the record of his November purchase to forty quires of "Cologne images" ("40 boecken keulsche papiere belden" or "Ceulsche belden"), which were sold at the notably low rate of just 15 st. per quire (instead of the 18 st. that was usually charged for a quire of prints in Antwerp), suggests that at least this group may have been commissioned for a German or Eastern European market. Remarkably, amid all of the instances in which both the supply and purchase prices are known for De Haen's transactions, Balthasar II added a profit margin to just one category of images: the small, illuminated prints on parchment that De Man provided at 4.5 fl. per hundred and that Balthasar resold to De Haen at 5 fl. per hundred. Applied to 4,000 images in De Haen's May and November orders, this rate generated a profit of 17 fl. 10 st., which remained significantly less than the profit that Balthasar had dared to arrange for himself on his resale of eight older print series from the Galles to the Polish noble Jan Sobiepan Zamoyski the previous year.

There is no single explanation for why each of these clients ceased to seek prints from the Moretuses. Some, like Raesfeld, may have reached the end of their careers, while others, like Förster, had to pay off large debts before making new requests. Furthermore, Förster and other individuals who had likewise traveled to Antwerp personally to buy prints there directly may have ultimately decided to draw on their independent contacts with Antwerp print sellers. Nevertheless, the demand for prints from Antwerp not only continued, but grew. It was satisfied, at least in part, by other intermediaries who periodically engaged the Moretuses as their local agent for assistance with these transactions. For example, the Antwerp merchants Nicolas and Deodatus Gaultier periodically conveyed large shipments of books, along with, on occasion, packages of images, to individuals in Poland during the 1650s. In March 1651, a Jesuit college in Poland thus received seventeen packages of images from the Gaultiers, together with an allotment of books. A year later, the Gaultiers, sent an additional thirteen packages of images along with numerous books.[15] Similarly, the Prague merchant Diederick de France oversaw the transport of considerable quantities of books, in addition to paintings and packages of prints, between Antwerp and Prague. In 1654 alone, he shipped nineteen packages of prints in March and another twenty in September to the Prague bookseller Jan Kraus.[16] The exact assortment of images and who provided them is not known, but these transactions may well have included more than 10,000 prints since a single package could contain hundreds of prints, if not a thousand prints or more.[17]

Indeed, Förster's request for prints from August 1644 and De Haen's from November 1647 reveal that it was not exceptional to buy some 7,000 prints at one time. For instance, the Amsterdam bookseller Abraham Wolfgang purchased nearly 6,000 prints in October 1678 and 8,650 more in April 1679 (fig. 10.5), in addition to 500 canons.[18] In both cases, he asked for a mix of illuminated images on parchment and plain images on paper in diverse formats. Although the quantities are comparable to those sold some thirty years earlier, a new generation of suppliers satisfied these commissions. While Cornelis Galle II provided the prints for Wolfgang's 1678 order (it is not known who supplied the prints in 1679), Michiel Cnobbaert, the son of Marie de Man and Jan Cnobbaert, offered the plain canons, and Balthasar Moretus III had impressions of his own edition of canons specially illuminated, in compliance with Wolfgang's guidelines concerning what he was willing to pay for that service.[19]

However incredible Wolfgang's acquisition of some 14,600 prints and 500 canons in just six months, may seem now, purchases of nearly 28,600 prints by the Munich bookseller Johann Wagner between July 1647 and September 1648 demonstrate that such concentrated investments in tens of thousands of prints cannot be dismissed as idiosyncratic, isolated events. Rather, they were common to the seventeenth-century European print trade.[20] Like Wolfgang, Wagner asked for a more modest assortment of images when he first inquired after them in July 1647.[21] However, the selection of some 975 prints on paper, 2,400 plain prints on parchment, and 1,200 illuminated images on parchment indicated a preference for plain images on paper or parchment as opposed to the illuminated prints favored by most of the Moretuses' other important buyers during the mid-seventeenth century, like Raesfeld,

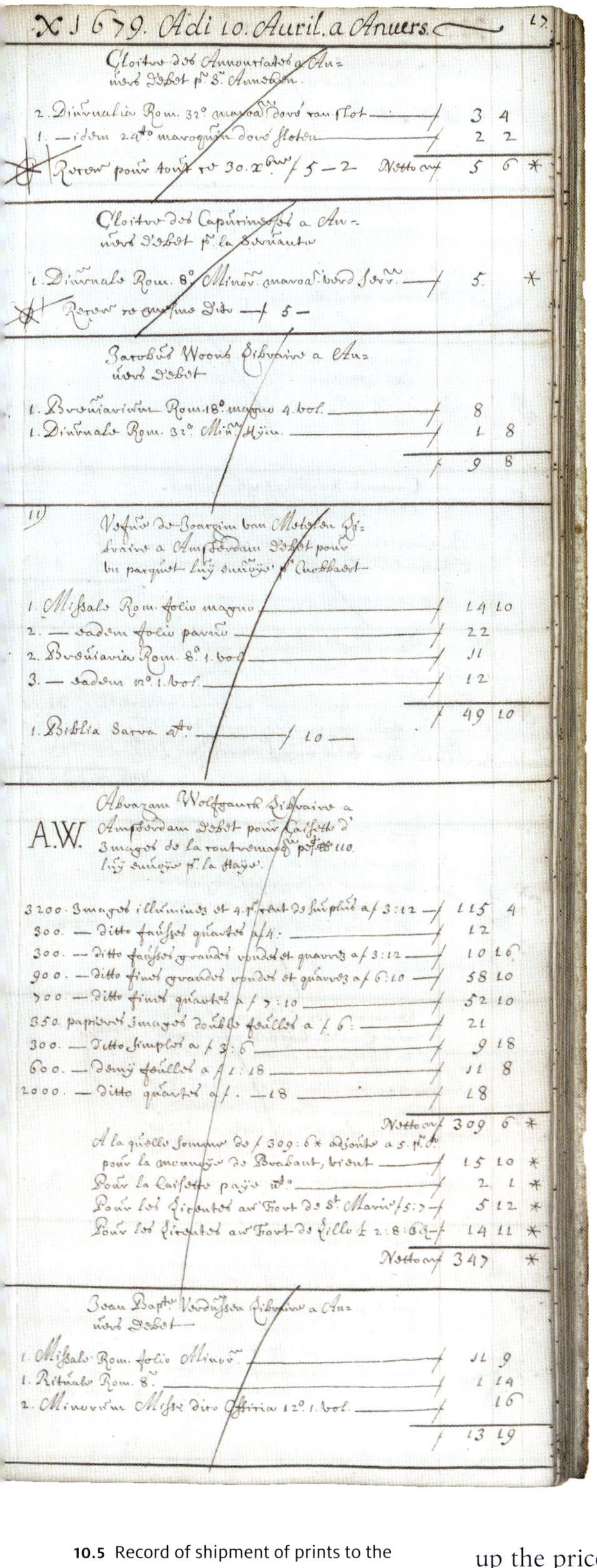
X 1679. Adi 10. Auril. a Anuers.

10.5 Record of shipment of prints to the bookseller Abraham Wolfgang in Amsterdam on 10 April 1679. MPM Arch. 394, *Journal 1679*, fol. 17r.

Förster, Schedelius, De Haen, and (subsequently) Wolfgang. Hence, Wagner's commission may have been intended as an initial sampling to test a local, potentially distinctive market. The response among his clients was evidently positive, for less than a year later, Wagner commissioned 9,400 prints by February 1648 and an additional 14,400 in August.[22] These two requests are remarkable not simply because of the immense quantities involved, but also because of the complete lack of illuminated images. In total, Wagner acquired: 10,000 small images and 800 in 4°, all printed on parchment and left plain; 10,000 prints on paper of unspecified format; 3,000 images in 4°; and 200 in a large folio format. As with Wagner's initial purchase in 1647, these items were all supplied by Marie de Man. While the quantities involved reveal the enormous potential volume of her trade, the brief three weeks that transpired between Balthasar II's receipt of Wagner's last order – 16 August – and the date when De Man provided him with the 10,000 images on paper and 4,400 images on parchment that Wagner sought – 7 September – underscores how her business may have evolved into one that featured the mass production of such works by the mid-seventeenth century.[23] Such a transformation would concur with Alfons Thijs's observations that by this time, the quality of the devotional engravings produced in Antwerp had begun to decline due to ever fewer engravers producing new images and ever more impressions being pulled from existing, worn, and reworked plates.[24]

Although Wagner did not specify for whom he was making these purchases in his correspondence, he stipulated which subjects should be portrayed on the works sent. In particular, the 200 large folio format prints that he asked for in February were to bear images appropriate for the Jesuits and Carmelites, as well as representations of the Virgin and Christ. For his request in August, he similarly sought images of iconic Jesuits, the Virgin and Christ, and male and female saints.[25] The repeated references to religious orders, above all the Jesuits, and the emphasis on standard devotional subjects are strongly reminiscent of the market for prints in Cologne, where most sales concerned plain prints on paper, in striking contrast to contemporary shipments of numerous colored images on parchment to Münster and Gdańsk, for example. The connection to the Jesuits and the potential similarities with the demand for prints in Cologne are also underscored by the only printmakers named in these commissions: the Wierixes, Charles de Mallery, or one of the Bolswerts. Specifically, in the two records of De Man's delivery of the 10,000 prints on paper, Wierix and Bolswert are identified as the engravers in one, while Wierix and De Mallery are recorded as the engravers of the images in the other.[26] Although it is impossible to determine whether De Mallery or one of the Bolswerts was actually represented in the shipment, the fact remains that this sizable group of prints by renowned, past engravers was the only one on which Balthasar II made a profit in his transactions with Wagner. All of the remaining prints, including the thousands printed on parchment, were resold to Wagner at cost. Moreover, it was not simply a case of rounding up the price, as Plantin and the Moretuses had done periodically in the past. These prints were supplied at just .25 st. per print, or 125 fl. for all 10,000 images, and Balthasar II doubled the price, charging Wagner 250 fl. for the group. This increased fee resulted in the equivalent of selling 10,000 engravings at De Mallery's old rate of 50 st. per 100 prints, or just .5 st. per image, which was itself still notably less than the Wierixes' former standard rates of .75 to 2 st. per print for the majority of the engravings they sold in bulk (see Table 7).

The sampling discussed above of the various orders for prints that the Moretuses continued to receive in the second half of the seventeenth century reveals several important facets of the international market for prints from Antwerp during these years. Significantly, the demand for prints persisted throughout many of the same regions that had been served by the previous managers of the Officina Plantiniana, despite the ongoing shifts in the management of their business and the succession of intermediaries facilitating this trade. Indeed, the quantities of prints requested grew, on average, resulting in the production and sale of astonishing numbers of images. Predictably, just as the specific individuals who generated this demand and saw to the practical matters of payment and transport changed, so did those who provided the desired images. Amid this fluctuating, though flourishing, group of suppliers, there is a notable increase in the number of women who were either managing print shops originally run by their husbands – Marie de Man, and the wives of several members of the Huberti family, for example – or who, like Constantia van Merlen, worked independently in a field with which they would have been familiar due to the professional activities of other family members.[27] The Galle family also continued to provide the Moretuses with prints for resale. Though this task was originally supervised by a single individual – first Philips Galle and then his son Theodore – it was subsequently split between Theodore's son Jan and Cornelis Galle I's son Cornelis II (Jan's cousin). Jan's transactions came to be dominated by the reprinting of numerous works originally published by his father and grandfather (among others) decades earlier. By contrast, Cornelis II remained active as an engraver, in addition to distributing colored images, not only through the Moretuses, but also independently to international clients. Evident from the large sums that Balthasar II and his agents received in Galle's name at the revived Frankfurt fairs during the mid-1650s, these transactions recall the services the Moretuses had offered to assorted Antwerp print sellers at the fairs in the early seventeenth century.[28] Remarkably, despite the relative paucity of references to specific works sought by the Moretuses' clients, the consistent recurrence of a few names among the sundry orders that they received attests to a continuing interest in a select group of Antwerp's famed artists within certain circles. Occurring alongside occasional purchases of Rubens's *Palazzi di Genova* series and other prints after his designs, as well as series by the Galles, requests for prints by the Wierixes and Charles de Mallery provide concrete reminders of how preferences for their engravings endured into the later seventeenth century.[29]

Against the backdrop of these various trends, many of which reflected the continuation of practices and the perpetuation of practitioners from previous decades, the emergence of one new market for prints from Antwerp stands out, namely Latin America. An early example of such a shipment, from 18 January 1650, typifies Balthasar Moretus II's involvement in this trade (fig. 10.6).[30] Sent to the merchant Lorenço de Veles, who is identified as serving Mexico, Peru, and other lands in the "Indes Occidentales" (the name at that time for Latin America), the consignment consisted primarily of thousands of books (primarily liturgical texts in assorted formats) in ten crates ("caisse"). Packages of 1,000 or 1,500 images were added to crates 4–7 in the shipment, according to a note at the bottom of the list of contents of crates 4 and 5, which appears in fig. 10.6. There is no indication of the value, subject matter, or source of the images. The export of these images was also not Balthasar's II's principal concern. Rather, as his correspondence from this period indicates, he was considering the advisability of assisting with the shipments of books (including his own editions) to the Americas. Having received a letter

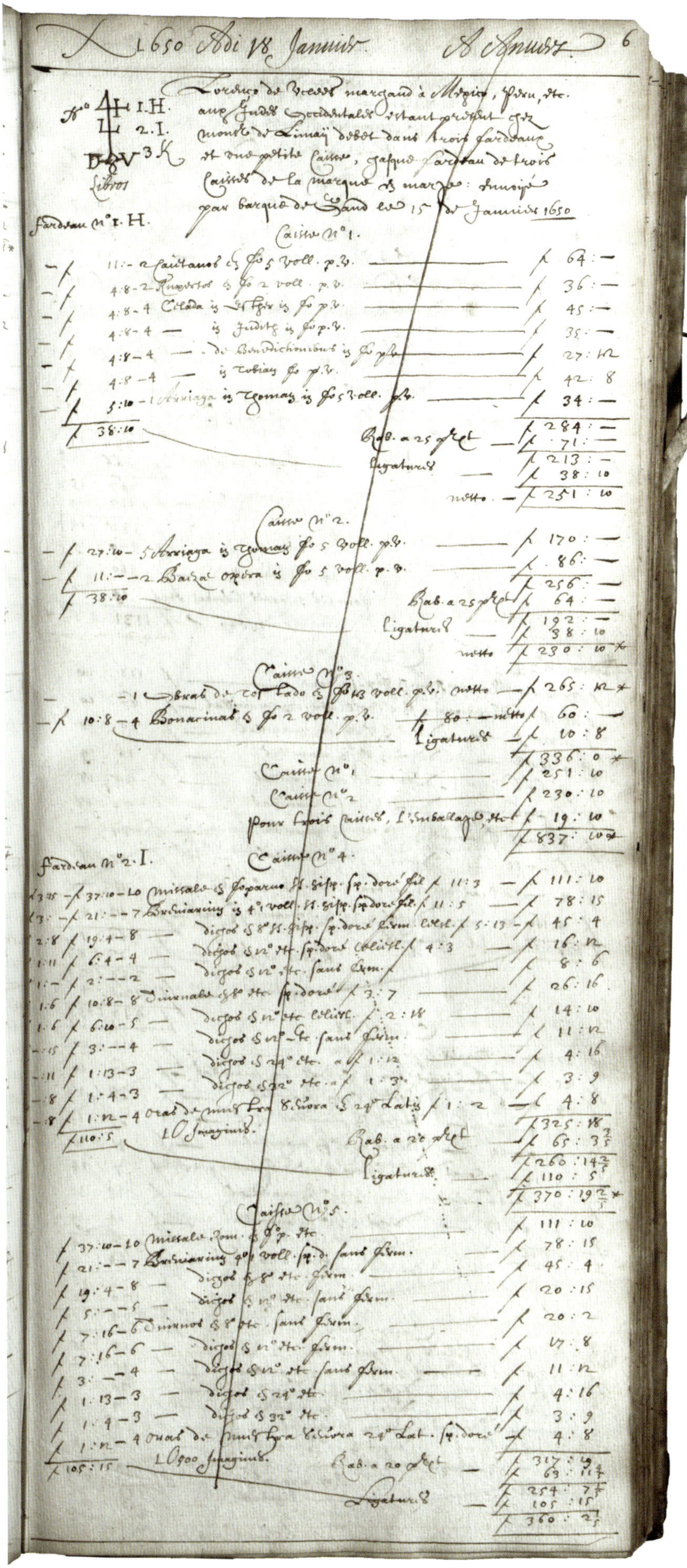

10.6 Record of shipment of books and prints to the merchant Lorenço de Veles, serving Latin America, from 18 January 1650. MPM Arch. 258, *Journal 1650*, fol. 6r.

in the spring of 1650 from Ludovicus Peres in Seville, a procurator for the Jesuit mission in "las Indias" (Latin America), raising this question, Balthasar consulted others whom he trusted, in particular the Jesuits Godefridus Henschenius and Joannes Bollandus, as well as the merchants Carlos de Licht and Jorge de Coninck, to determine if he should become involved in trade involving the Americas and if Peres was to be trusted financially. By May 1650, Balthasar II had decided to assist Peres with this export, and an initial shipment of books (but no images) was sent to him in July 1650.[31] The merchant De Veles also continued to oversee periodic shipments to the "Indes", but again, most of the items sent were books, while packages of 500–1,000 unspecified prints were added only occasionally.[32]

As with other transactions involving the Moretuses, these shipments provide just a glimpse – the proverbial tip of the iceberg – of a trade that was also pursued more systematically elsewhere via other agents in Antwerp and abroad. Nevertheless, while perhaps not reflecting the entirety of the market in the Americas, the examples in the Moretuses' records underscore the range of possibilities open to entrepreneurs in previous centuries that scholars today can pursue when investigating the traffic in prints. Furthermore, when considered together, these multifarious instances of both the desires of individual collectors or agents and the purchase of prints en masse by diverse middlemen coalesce and create a substantial basis for an improved understanding of the internal mechanisms of the European print trade and its remarkable extent. Despite the focus on just one transit venue for prints from Antwerp, the abundance of diverse transactions described here provides a wealth of information about a much broader international framework. Moreover, these results will nourish future studies exploring the tantalizing, hitherto unimagined scope of the immense traffic in prints in other times and places.

1 MPM Arch. 147, p. 421: "Het is waer dat Sr. Malleri eertyts de letteren soo wel plachte te snyden als iemant soude konnen, maer gheloove door den ouderdom syne conste seer verloren te hebben."

2 Dated 1642, this print was engraved by Cornelis Galle I in Brussels. Impressions of it were subsequently added to a later edition of De Marselaer's text, Legatus … ad Philippus IV Hispaniarum regem (Antwerp: B. Moretus II, 1666); see, for example, MPM A 940.

3 MPM Arch. 252, fols. 58r, 60v, and 66v, for Galle's supply and Chifflet's purchases; and Table 7 for the rates De Mallery charged for prints sold in bulk.

4 MPM Arch. 254, fols. 26r (purchase) and 22v and 30v (supply).

5 MPM Arch. 254, compare fols. 26r and 30v for Balthasar's markups and his discount from Galle. For earlier examples of the sales of this series, see Appendix 1, JG-2, PG-60, and PG-2, respectively.

6 See Chapter 4.

7 For examples of the packages sent, see MPM Arch. 405, fol. 28r (prepared by Smidt); MPM Arch. 415, fol. 72v (a gift from Jan Galle); and MPM Arch. 416, fol. 27r (three packages of prints prepared by Jan Galle, valued at 214 fl. 8 st.). The last group of packages may have contained the images that were created more than sixty years earlier in conjunction with Johannes David's Veridicus Christianus (see Imhof 2020b on this publication), to which Theodorus refers at the end of an order placed the following year (MPM Arch. 351, fol. 54r). For his orders of prints by the Wierixes, see MPM Arch. 412, fol. 144r (print series identified as "Passio, Vita Ignatii, Specul. Salve"); and MPM Arch. 415, fol. 72v (110 unspecified prints).

8 MPM Arch. 351, fol. 54r.

9 Ibid., "Si quae aliae imagines sint in 4° cum Gallica aliqua explicatione aut subscriptione ad vitam Xri. aut B.V. aut ad pietatem facientes, addantur".

10 Since neither the artists nor the number of sheets in the series of the Four Seasons ("Quatuor anni tempora") are specified, it is impossible to link the series definitively to one of Philips Galle's depictions of this subject (Appendix 1, PG-49 (four sheets designed by M. van Heemskerck) or PG-50 (five sheets designed by J. Stradanus)). However, given that the phrase used to identify the series is exactly the same as that used in a 1580 sales record of Stradanus's series, we are favoring the connection to Stradanus's version here.

11 See Chapter 7.

12 MPM Arch. 250, fols. 36v (supply) and 37v (purchase); MPM Arch. 251, fols. 62r (purchase) and 64r (supply); and MPM Arch. 252, fol. 150r (purchase) and 150v (supply), respectively.

13 MPM Arch. 253, fols. 26r (supply) and 27r (purchase by Raesfeld), and 76r (supply and purchase by Förster); and Chapter 2 for Förster's exceptional 1644 purchase.

14 MPM Arch. 255, fols. 44r (May purchase), 46v (June supply) and 50r (June purchase), and 92v (November supply) and 93r (November purchase); and MPM Arch. 740, fol. 56 rht (another record of the November supply).

15 For a summary of the Gaultier brothers' transactions, see MPM Arch. 134, fols. 218 and 394. For the cited examples, see MPM Arch. 401, fol. 21v (3 March 1651 shipment to Jesuits in Poland); and MPM Arch. 402, fol. 30v (1652 shipment).

16 MPM Arch. 404, fols. 24v and 92v, respectively.

17 Compare with MPM Arch. 222, fol. 182v (800 prints from Theodore Galle in one package sent in 1615), and MPM Arch. 226, fol. 185v (3,000 prints from Charles de Mallery in three packages sent in 1619). See also Chapter 9 for more examples of the shipment of numerous packages, including their weights.

18 MPM Arch. 393 (1678), fols. 22r (supply by C. Galle II) and 23r (shipment); and MPM Arch. 394 (1679), fols. 17r (print purchase), 38v (supply of canons by M. Cnobbaert), and 39r (purchase of canons).

19 MPM Arch. 297, fol. 121r, letter from Balthasar Moretus III to Wolfgang, dated 23 July 1679, in which he wrote that he had sent a sample of the type of canons they had on hand and requested that Wolfgang reply, stating how much he was willing to spend on having the canons colored.

20 Thijs 1993, p. 15, postulates that a selection of the Antwerp sodalities (excluding those associated with the Jesuit college) would have needed even more prints – some 45,600 impressions of suffragia – annually to satisfy just the rudimentary needs of their members.

21 MPM Arch. 255, fol. 59v.

22 MPM Arch. 256, fols. 14r (supply on 21 February), 19r (extra supply and purchase on 5 March), 83v (purchase on 4 September), and 86v (supply on 7 September).

23 See MPM Arch. 364, fol. 48r, and the introductory remarks to Balthasar II's record of what Wagner had requested on 4 August 1648.

24 Thijs 1993, pp. 44–46.

25 MPM Arch. 364, fols. 45r and 48r, respectively.

26 Compare MPM Arch. 256, fol. 86v; and MPM Arch. 740, fol. 57 rht.

27 Constantia van Merlen is discussed in greater detail in Chapter 2.

28 See MPM Arch. 130, fols. 188 rht and 192 rht, for an overview of these initial transactions.

29 See Bowen 2017 on the sale of Rubens' works; and MPM Arch. 411, fols. 25v and 26r, for another late sale of his Palazzi di Genova (supplied by Jacques Moermans and sent to the bookseller Johann Busäus in Cologne in March 1661).

30 MPM Arch. 258, fols. 6r-7r, for the entire order.

31 MPM Arch. 150, p. 318 (letter to Henschenius, dated 30 April 1650); MPM Arch. 299, pp. 13–14 (letter to Peres, dated 12 May), 15 (letters to Carlos de Licht and Jorge de Coninck, dated 12 May); and MPM Arch. 258, fols. 68v-69v (the July shipment).

32 See, for example, MPM Arch. 404, fols. 133v-135v (a sale from 26 December 1654, which included ten packages of 500 prints each, one of 1,000, and another of 600 illuminated images). For other examples of the export of books or works of art from Antwerp to Latin America, see Manrique Figueroa 2019 (for books), Van Ginhoven 2017 (for paintings), and Thijs 1993, pp. 24–31 (for prints). Our thanks to Carme Lopez Calderon for her perspective on the current research concerning the export of images to the Americas.

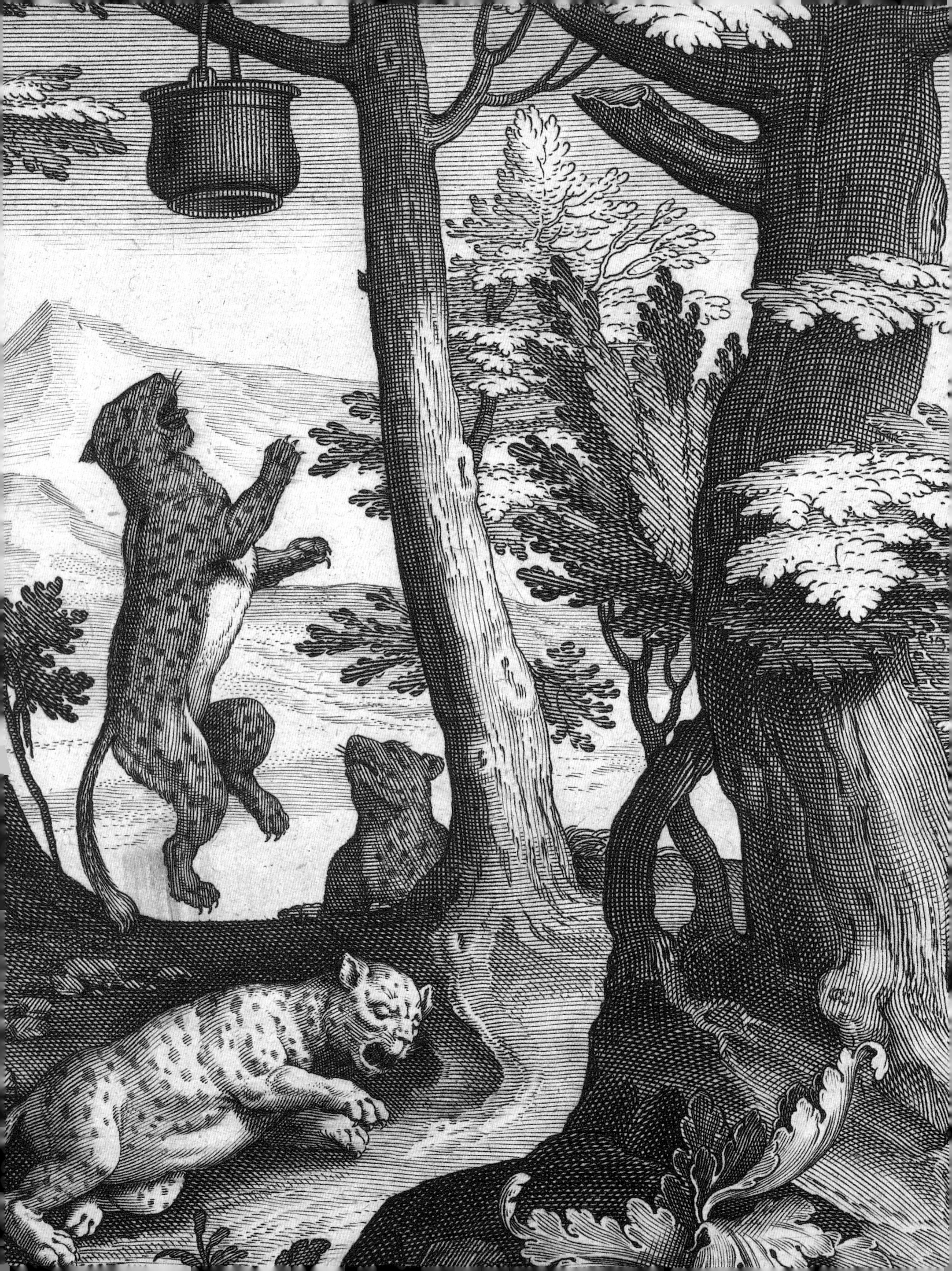

APPENDIX 1

Print Publishers and the Prints They Sold via the Officina Plantiniana

All of the print publishers or artists who supplied Plantin or the Moretuses with prints are presented here alphabetically by last name. In each case, a brief account of the individual(s) concerned is followed by a list of all the prints (or print series or print books) supplied by the publisher that can be identified with reasonable certainty; these are arranged alphabetically by title. Generally, the common title in English is noted first, then the original title, if given in an accompanying title page or title plate. Only when the work is better known by its original title (as is often the case with print books) does this appear before an English title. Hereafter, the following are listed: the names of the designers and printmakers (if known); the print technique; the number of prints in a series; the approximate size in millimeters of the image(s); a recent, standard secondary source for the print(s); the price Plantin or the Moretuses paid – whenever possible, according to the record of supply by the print publisher; and the year in which the purchase was made, in order to document any possible change in price over time. Each item is numbered and prefaced by an abbreviation derived from the name of the given publisher(s). We have focused on the prices at which the prints were offered to Plantin and the Moretuses by the print publisher in order to avoid any occasional, often unsystematic, markup of the prices that might occur when the prints were sold via other intermediaries, as this would confuse and complicate an analysis of what the given publisher charged for his or her prints. Plantin's and the Moretuses' resale of these prints is discussed throughout the main text. The identification of the dedicatees or the authors of accompanying texts or captions is not noted here, unless such information is necessary for the identification of the image. More extensive discussions of the publishers and specific examples of the sales of these prints are given in the relevant chapters. For each of the works listed here, examples of the citation(s) of the image(s) in the Plantin-Moretus archives are included in the accompanying notes. While citations are often abbreviated references to the subjects of the images, occasionally with the names of the artist(s) and/or the number of images in a series, they may also consist of an excerpt from a title or caption included in the image. For example, Hendrick Goltzius's engraving, *The Atonement of Christ*, published by Philips Galle in 1578 (see PG-8), is referred to in the surviving records as "Satisfactio Christi" because that phrase appears in the border at the top of the print. It was not possible to link each citation of an image to a specific print. However, if the description of the work is detailed enough to enable someone else to identify it at another point in time, we have listed it among the other known works. We have not included generic references to common subjects, such as the Passion, the Crucifixion, images of the Virgin, or landscapes, since the possible images are too numerous to permit a reasonable, unique identification of the print concerned. As a result, such an identification would adversely dilute the otherwise extensive and concrete documentation of print prices provided here. The itemized list of prints supplied by a given publisher is followed by another list of the rates the same publisher charged when selling unspecified prints in bulk. First, entries on these lists are grouped according to the basic unit by which the prints were sold, namely: by print, by leaf, by the dozen, by quires, or by the hundred. Within each subgroup, individual entries are arranged by price, from high to low, and any exceptional, distinguishing features of the prints sold at the given rate are provided – in particular, its general size, whether it was colored, and whether it was printed on parchment. Unless noted otherwise, one should assume that the images cited below were plain (not colored) prints on paper. Print formats and the units by which prints were sold to Plantin and the Moretuses are discussed more extensively in the Note to the Reader and in Chapter 2. Finally, when a publisher provided a significant number of identifiable works for resale via the Officina Plantiniana, we have summarized the prices at which he or she sold specific images in Tables 1–6. The prices at which publishers sold prints in bulk are summarized in Tables 7 and 8. Across all of these tables, we focused on arranging the prints by price, from high to low. We have not offered a chronological arrangement for several reasons, the most important being: (1) the dating of many of the prints recorded here is uncertain; (2) a chronological arrangement would result in a random mix of formats and numbers of prints – for instance, an intermingling of images and series – that would make comparisons among the prints more difficult; and (3) a chronological arrangement would not highlight any general trends in pricing. Despite the nearly ninety-year period considered here, most of the prices at which the prints were supplied appear to have remained fairly stable and not to have changed over time (for example, PG-82 and CD-29). When changes occurred, there was no consistent trend of price increases (for example, CD-18 and TG-17). Occasionally, the price asked for a given work rose (as with CD-3), and occasionally, it fell (as with PG-28). All such price fluctuations (or lack thereof) for specific images or series are also documented in the descriptions of them.

Jan Collaert II after Johannes Stradanus, *Hunting Leopards with Human Excrement* (detail), after 1594–1598, engravinG from the series Hunts and Animal Scenes, published by Philips Galle (PG-60).

The following individuals are discussed here:

- Abraham de Bruyn: AB-1
- Jan Cnobbaert and Marie de Man: see also Tables 7 and 8
- Hieronymus Cock and Volcxken Diericx: CD-1 to CD-41; see also Tables 1 and 7
- Adriaen Collaert: AC-1 to AC-18; see also Tables 2 and 7
- Jan Galle: JG-1 and JG-2; see also Table 8
- Philips Galle: PG-1 to PG-124; see also Tables 3 and 7
- Theodore Galle and Catharina Moerentorf: TG-1 to TG-32; see also Tables 4, 7, and 8
- Adriaen Huberti (Huybrechts): AH-1 to AH-10; see also Table 7
- Gerard de Jode and Passchijnke van Gelre: GJ-1 to GJ-48; see also Tables 5 and 7
- Peeter de Jode I and Peeter de Jode II: PJ-1 to PJ-3; see also Table 7
- Hans Liefrinck I: see also Table 7
- Charles de Mallery: CM-1 to CM-5; see also Table 7
- Abraham van Merlen: see also Table 7
- Christopher Plantin: CP-1 and CP-2
- Peter Paul Rubens: PPR-1 and PPR-2
- The Sadeler family: SD-1 to SD-3
- Michael Snijders: see also Tables 7 and 8
- Lambert Suavius: LS-1 and LS-2
- Otto van Veen: OV-1
- Anton II and Hieronymus Wierix: WX-1 to WX-20; see also Tables 6 and 7

ABRAHAM DE BRUYN Antwerp? 1538/1540?–1587 Cologne?

The place and date of De Bruyn's birth, as well as for his early training, are uncertain. Several series of etchings bear either his name or monogram, while others are attributed to him. Many of these may be early works from the 1560s, although some date to the 1580s. However, De Bruyn is better known for his engravings. Regardless of the medium, the subjects of his prints range from conventional religious imagery to portrayals of animals and contemporary figures. Due to the ongoing military conflict in the Low Countries during the third quarter of the sixteenth century, De Bruyn fled Antwerp for Breda in 1570 and subsequently moved to Cologne by 1577, where he, together with fellow refugees, was able to work on his own illustrated publications. Around 1580, he returned to Antwerp; he then took on some pupils and published new editions of his successful depictions of the dress of various classes of individuals. De Bruyn most likely decided to return to Cologne once Alexander Farnese began his siege of the city in 1584.

Plantin employed De Bruyn to execute the engravings for several of his publications before and after De Bruyn's first sojourn in Cologne (ca. 1576–1578). These included images for devotional works, diagrams, and title pages. However, De Bruyn was usually just one of several engravers who completed selected engravings for a project, rather than serving as the primary engraver. Moreover, despite their periodic contact, De Bruyn rarely supplied Plantin with print series for resale. Plantin's clients were primarily interested in copies of De Bruyn's series of different types of dress of various professions (see below), which De Bruyn provided only in 1581–1582, during his brief return to Antwerp.

LIT.: Bowen and Imhof 2008, pp. 330–31; New Holl. De Bruijn, part I, pp. xix–xxiv.

Identifiable prints sold by title

AB-1 *Omnium pene gentium imagines (Images of Nearly All Nations)*, often referred to as "Habitus gentium" in the Plantin archives: Abraham de Bruyn, variable number of plates in a mix of etching and engraving, in diverse sizes, 1581 (Antwerp). LIT.: New Holl. De Bruijn, nos. 381–431, 2nd edition. See fig. 3.19.

De Bruyn supplied Plantin with copies of this series at notably diverse prices in 1581 and 1582; the prices were largely dependent upon whether the prints were colored or not, but also may have reflected some variation in the number of images included. While De Bruyn sold plain copies to Plantin for 2 fl. 5 st. (= 45 st.) or 2 fl. 10 st. (= 50 st.) per series,[1] he sold him colored copies for either 4 fl. 10 st. (= 90 st.) or 5 fl. 10 st. (= 110 st.) per series.[2]

JAN CNOBBAERT I Antwerp 1590–1637 Antwerp
MARIE DE MAN ?–1671 Antwerp[3]

Jan Cnobbaert was the son of the Antwerp alderman Michiel Cnobbaert, who is now known primarily as a publisher and printer of books in Antwerp during the early seventeenth century. When he officially started to print and publish books is not known, but by May 1619, he was purchasing books from the Moretuses, and by 1620 he had begun to print his own publications, such as an account of the current situation in Bohemia (*Informatio fundamentalis super hodierno Bohemiae statu*).[4] In 1621, he married Marie de Man, who continued her husband's business through the 1650s. Although she initially published books on her own, as of the mid-1640s, she also printed works in collaboration with Jan Cnobbaert's "heirs" (presumably their son Michiel). Her production petered out during the last decade of her life, just when Michiel Cnobbaert began to publish more actively under his own name. By the mid-1620s, Cnobbaert's activities also comprised printing and publishing individual engravings. While the full extent of his and his widow's activities in this regard have yet to be documented, several of the prints published by Jan Cnobbaert were engraved by Paulus Pontius, and several of those published by Marie de Man bear the signatures of Abraham van Diepenbeek and Cornelis Galle II.

LIT.: Lemmens and Thijs 2006, p. 100; Rombouts and Van Lerius 1872, vol. II, pp. 89 and 407; Thijs 1993, pp. 112–13; Van Heurck 1930, p. 53; De Vlieger-De Wilde 2004, pp. 30–32.

Unspecified prints sold in bulk

See also the Note to the Reader and Chapter 2.

- per *print on parchment, colored*: sold to Balthasar Moretus I at 3.5 st. per image, in 1628.[5]
- per *print on parchment, colored*: sold to Balthasar Moretus I at 3 st. per image, in 1628.[6]
- per *print on parchment, colored*: sold to Balthasar Moretus I at 2.25 st. per image, in 1628.[7]
- per *100 images on parchment, colored*: sold to Balthasar Moretus I at 10 fl. (= 200 st.) per hundred (= 2 st. per image) in 1640.[8]
- per *100 images on parchment, colored*: sold to Balthasar Moretus I at 6 fl. (= 120 st.) per hundred (= 1.2 st. per image) in 1640.[9]
- per *100 images on parchment, colored*: sold to Balthasar Moretus I at 5 fl. (= 100 st.) per hundred (= 1 st. per image) in 1640.[10]
- per *100 images on parchment (plain)*: sold to Balthasar Moretus I at 4 fl. (= 80 st.) per hundred (= .8 st. per image) in 1628.[11]
- per *100 images on parchment (plain)*: sold to Balthasar Moretus I at 3 fl. (= 60 st.) per hundred (= .6 st. per image) in 1640.[12]
- per *100 images on paper (plain)*: sold to Balthasar Moretus I at 1 fl. (= 20 st.) per hundred (= .20 st. per image) in 1628.[13]

HIERONYMUS COCK Antwerp ca. 1517/1518–1570 Antwerp
VOLCXKEN DIERICX ? ca. 1522–1600 Antwerp

Hieronymus Cock was the son of the Antwerp-based artist Jan Wellens de Cock and the brother of the painter Matthijs Cock. After traveling in Italy during the late 1540s, where he might have observed the practices of contemporary Italian print publishers, such as Antonio Lafreri, Cock returned to Antwerp and began his own print publishing business, "Aux Quatre Vents" (At the Four Winds) in 1548.[14] Antwerp was then already home to several printmakers and print publishers, like Hans Liefrinck I (see below), in addition to hosting an active art market.[15] Within this context, Cock endeavored to produce a diverse selection of technically well-executed prints after both Italian and local artists. These ranged from prints after paintings by Raphael, Agnolo Bronzino, and Hieronymus Bosch to new images designed by Pieter Bruegel I, Frans and Cornelis Floris, Maarten van Heemskerck, and Hans Vredeman de Vries. Following his initial success in convincing the Mantuan engraver Giorgio Ghisi to move to Antwerp and work for him, Cock also managed to engage other proficient local printmakers, such as Cornelis Cort, Pieter van der Heyden, Joannes and Lucas van Doetecum, and Philips Galle. After Cock's death in 1570, his widow, Volcxken Diericx, continued to add to Cock's stock of plates with, for example, images designed by Johannes Stradanus and Maarten de Vos and engraved by the Wierix brothers and Hendrick Goltzius. Together, Cock and Diericx published a diverse array of subjects, encompassing both numerous Italianate figural compositions and landscapes (containing Italian ruins, as well as Netherlandish villages) and traditional Netherlandish subjects, like images of proverbs, architectural and ornamental designs, as well as maps.

Plantin dealt in prints published by Cock almost immediately from the beginning of his career as a bookseller in Antwerp in the mid-1550s. Cock's widow continued to supply Plantin with prints for resale through 1581, and then again in late 1586 or early 1587. At Diericx's death, she owned more than 1,600 copper plates, at least 1,400 of which had been commissioned or purchased by Cock between 1549 and 1570.[16] These were then auctioned off and dispersed among numerous other print publishers – including Adriaen Collaert, as well as Philips and Theodore Galle (see below) – who continued to sell impressions from the plates in the decades to come.

LIT.: Bassens and Van Grieken 2019; Cock 2013; Denucé 1912–1913, vol. I, pp. 118–39 and 135–39; De Pauw-De Veen 1975; Duverger 1984–2009, vol. I, pp. 17–37 (document no. 7, which is a partial transcription of the 1601 estate inventory for Diericx); Simiolus 2017; Wouk 2015–2016.

Identifiable prints sold by title

Below, the prices of prints sold to the Antwerp art dealer Bartholomeus de Mompere are taken from the 1582 contract signed between Diericx and De Mompere. See Van der Stock 1998, pp. 406–08, for a transcription of this document, and De Pauw-De Veen 1975, pp. 225–33 and pp. 245–47, for another transcription of this record, along with suggestions for the identification of the cited prints.

CD-1 *The Adoration of the Shepherds*: **Giorgio Ghisi after Agnolo Bronzino.** Engraving, printed from two plates, total dimensions 662 × 452, 1553. LIT.: Cock 2013, cat. 23.

Sold to Plantin at: 6 st. per print in 1568, and 8 st. per print in 1573.[17] Most likely sold to De Mompere in 1582 as "Kersnachten" (*Nativity*) at 6 st. per print.

CD-2 *Architectural Perspective Views in Oval Frames*: **Joannes and Lucas van Doetecum after Hans Vredeman de Vries.** Twenty etchings and one engraved plate by an anonymous artist with a dedication to Peter Ernst von Mansfeld, ca. 162 × 212 or 212 × 162, 1560–1562. LIT.: Cock 2013, cat. 84. See back cover.

Sold to Plantin at: 8 ½ st. per series, with two images printed per leaf, in 1568, 1580, and 1581.[18]
Possibly sold to Jan Moretus I in 1594, with all of the images printed on just eight leaves. The selling price was not noted.[19]

CD-3 *The Baths of Diocletian (Thermae Diocletiani imp. …)*: **Joannes and Lucas van Doetecum after Sebastiaan van Noyen.** Thirty-two etchings of varying sizes, with two introductory pages in letterpress, 1558. LIT.: Cock 2013, cat. 19.

Sold to Plantin at: 2 fl. (= 40 st.) per series in 1568, and at 2 fl. 10 st. (= 50 st.) per series in 1581.[20]
Sold to De Mompere in 1582 at: 2 fl. 10 st. per series.

CD-4 *The Blue Cloak (Die blau huicke …)*: **Frans Hogenberg.** Etching, printed from two plates, total dimensions 373 × 460, 1558. LIT.: Cock 2013, p. 24; New Holl. Hogenberg, no. 18.

Sold to Plantin at: 1 ½ st. per print in 1568.[21]

CD-5 *Christ and the Twelve Apostles*: **anonymous engraver after Lambert Lombard.** Thirteen engravings, ca. 200 × 118, 1560–1570. LIT.: Cock 2013, p. 24.

Sold to Plantin at: 5 st. per series in 1570 and 1571.[22]
Sold to De Mompere in 1582 at: 5 st. per series.

CD-6 *Christ and the Twelve Apostles, with Saint Paul*: **Lambert SuaviusF.** Fourteen engravings, ca. 198 × 90, ca. 1545. LIT.: Cock 2013, p. 24 and figs. 11–12; Holl. Dutch & Flemish, vol. XXVIII, pp. 169–74, nos. 9–22. This is distinct from the series of *The Acts of the Apostles* (LS-1), which Suavius sold to Plantin in 1553.

Sold to Plantin at: 6 st. per series in 1568, 1570, and 1571.[23]
Sold to De Mompere in 1582 at: 5 st. per series.

CD-7 *Circus Maximus* **[and]** *Circus Flaminius* **(no impression known).** Most likely completed by June 1558, when Plantin appears to have sold four impressions of each image at 5 ½ st. apiece to the French bookseller Martin le Jeune.[24] LIT.: Duverger 1984–2009, vol. I, p. 28: "Twee lange coperen plaeten van Circus Maximus ende van Circus Flaminio".

Sold to Plantin at: 3 ½ st. per print in 1568.[25]

CD-8 *Compartments by Battini*: **attributed to Pieter van der Heyden after Benedictus Battini.** Twenty-eight engravings of varying sizes, 1553. LIT.: Cock 2013, cat. 77.

Sold to Plantin at: 10 st. per series in 1568.[26]
Sold to De Mompere in 1582 at: 10 st. per series.

CD-9 *Dispute about the Holy Sacrament*: **Giorgio Ghisi after Raphael.** Engraving printed from two plates, total dimensions 510 × 850, 1552. LIT.: Cock 2013, cat. 21.

Sold to Plantin at: 12 st. per print in 1573.[27]
Sold to De Mompere in 1582 at: 8 st. per print.

CD-10 *Funeral Procession in Honor of Charles V (La magnifique et sumptueuse pompe funèbre …)*: **Joannes and Lucas van Doetecum after Hieronymus Cock.** Thirty-four etched and engraved plates of varying dimensions, occasionally accompanied by a text in letterpress in either French, Italian, Dutch, German, or Spanish, 1559. LIT.: Cock 2013, cat. 89.

Sold to Plantin at: 1 fl. (= 20 st.) per series in 1568.[28]

CD-11 *Hunts* **(within ornamental frames): Harmen Jansz. Muller and an anonymous engraver after Johannes Stradanus.** Six engravings, ca. 327 × 448, 1570. LIT.: Cock 2013, cat. 45.

Possibly sold to Plantin at: 12 st. per series (2 st. per print) in August 1571.[29]
Sold to Plantin at: 10 ½ st. per series (1.75 st. per print) in 1580 and 1581.[30]
Possibly sold to De Mompere in 1582 as the "groote jachten" (large hunts) with six prints at: 2 "blanks" = 1 ½ st. per print.

CD-12 *Hunts* **(without frames): anonymous engraver after Johannes Stradanus.** Six engravings, ca. 220 × 300, 1570 or 1574. LIT.: New Holl. Stradanus, nos. 409–14 or 415–20.

Sold to Plantin at: 18 st. per quire of 25 leaves in 1580.[31]
= .72 st. per leaf; each print was the equivalent of one leaf, amounting to 4.32 st. per series.

CD-13 *Landscape with Balaam and an Angel*: **Dirck Volckertsz. Coornhert after Maarten van Heemskerck.** Engraving, 295 × 850, 1554. LIT.: New Holl. Heemskerck, no. 77. See fig. 2.7.

Sold to Plantin at: 4 st. per print in 1568.[32]

• *Landscape with the Temptation of Christ* (Bassens and Van Grieken 2019, cat. 1): see CD-14: *Large Landscapes after Bruegel.*
• *Large Alpine Landscape* (Bassens and Van Grieken 2019, cat. 3): see CD-14: *Large Landscapes after Bruegel.*
• *The Large Landscapes* (Bassens and Van Grieken 2019, cat. 2): see CD-14: *Large Landscapes after Bruegel.*

CD-14 *Large Landscapes after Bruegel*
This group of landscapes most likely comprised the following images that are conventionally described separately in literature on Pieter Bruegel I:
• *Landscape with the Temptation of Christ*: Hieronymus Cock after Pieter Bruegel I, etching and engraving, 319 × 439, ca. 1554. LIT.: Bassens and Van Grieken 2019, cat. 1.
• *Large Alpine Landscape*: Joannes and Lucas van Doetecum after Pieter Bruegel I, etching and engraving, 368 × 468, ca. 1555–1556. LIT.: Bassens and Van Grieken 2019, cat. 3.
• *The Large Landscapes*: Joannes and Lucas van Doetecum after Pieter Bruegel I, twelve etchings with engraving of varying dimensions, ranging from 320 × 420 to 396 × 428, ca. 1555–1556. LIT.: Bassens and Van Grieken 2019, cat. 2.

In Bassens and Van Grieken, all of the above plates are associated with the single reference to fourteen copper plates with landscapes after Bruegel ("Veertien coperen plaeten van Lantschappen van Bruegel") in Diericx's estate inventory.[33] Cock's etching of *The Rabbit Hunt* (CD-19) is distinctly smaller. The fact that Diericx sold a group of fourteen large landscapes after Bruegel to Plantin in 1581 (which Plantin immediately resold as a group) indicates that she and prospective clients regarded them as a single larger set of images and not necessarily as the single prints and independent series of twelve landscapes traditionally discussed in literature on Bruegel and Cock's publications.

Sold to Plantin at: 1.5 st. per leaf (print), or 18 st. for the series of twelve large landscapes, or 21 st. per group of fourteen, in 1581.[34]

CD-15 *Naval Battle in the Strait of Messina*: **Frans Huys after Pieter Bruegel I.** Engraving and etching, printed from two plates, total dimensions 428 × 717, 1561. LIT.: Bassens and Van Grieken 2019, cat. 5. See fig. 3.7.

Sold to Plantin at: 6 st. per print in 1568.[35]
Sold to De Mompere in 1582 at: 4 st. per print.

CD-16 *Ornamental Compartments*: **Pieter van der Heyden after Jacob Floris.** Twelve engravings, ca. 135 × 204, 1567. LIT.: Riggs 1972, cat. 102.

Sold to Plantin at: 6.5 st. per series in 1568 and 1570.[36]

CD-17 *Pope Pius V*: **Pieter van der Heyden.** Engraving, 198 × 158, 1550s?. LIT.: Holl. Dutch & Flemish, vol. IX, p. 32, no. 155.

Sold to Plantin in 1571, but with no clear price for this specific print.[37]

CD-18 *Portraits of Famous Painters from the Low Countries (Pictorum aliquot celebrium Germaniae inferioris effigies)*: **Cornelis Cort, Jan Wierix, and an anonymous engraver.** Twenty-three engravings of varying dimensions, ca. 198/225 × 121/130, 1572. See TG-17 for a later edition of this work published by Theodore Galle, but still sold at the same 12 st. price. LIT.: Cock 2013, cat. 5 and 73. See fig. 3.16.

Sold to Plantin at: 12 st. per series in 1573 and 1586/1587; and at 15 st. per series in 1576.[38]
Sold to De Mompere in 1582 at: 12 st. per series.

CD-19 *The Rabbit Hunt*: **Pieter Bruegel I.** Etching, 223 × 292, 1560. LIT.: Bassens and Van Grieken 2019, cat. 4.

Sold to Plantin at: 20 st. per quire of 25 leaves in 1561.[39]
= .80 st. per leaf or individual print.

CD-20 *The Raising of the Brazen Serpent*: **Pieter van der Heyden after Frans Floris.** Engraving, printed from two plates: left: 583 × 449, right: 582 × 452, 1555. LIT.: Cock 2013, cat. 42.

Sold to Plantin at: 12 st. per print in 1573.[40]
Sold to De Mompere in 1582 at: 8 st. per print.

CD-21 *The Resurrection of Christ*: **Joannes and Lucas van Doetecum after Frans Floris.** Etching and engraving, printed from two plates, total dimensions 638 × 445, 1557. LIT.: Cock 2013, cat. 33.

Sold to Plantin at: 5 st. per print in 1573.[41]
Sold to De Mompere in 1582 at: 4 st. per print.

CD-22 *The Resurrection of Christ*: **Philips Galle after Pieter Bruegel I.** Engraving, 451 × 330, ca. 1561. LIT.: Bassens and Van Grieken 2019, cat. 29.

Sold to Plantin at: 2.5 st. per print in 1561.[42]

CD-23 *Sailing Vessels*: **Frans Huys and Cornelis Cort (?) after Pieter Bruegel I.** Ten engravings, with some etching, ca. 225 × 290 or 290 × 220, ca. 1561–1565. LIT.: Bassens and Van Grieken 2019, cat. 6. See also TG-22.

Sold to Plantin at: 18 st. per quire of 25 leaves in 1568.[43]
= .72 st. per leaf; each print of this size was most likely the equivalent of one leaf, amounting to 7.2 st. per series.

CD-24 *Saint George's Kermis (Fair)*: **Joannes or Lucas van Doetecum after Pieter Bruegel I.** Etching and engraving, 332 × 523, ca. 1558. LIT.: Bassens and Van Grieken 2019, cat. 24.

Sold to Plantin at: 3 st. per print in 1568.[44]
Sold to De Mompere in 1582 at: 3 st. per print.

CD-25 *Saint Jerome*: **Philips Galle.**Engraving, 193 × 150, 1561. LIT.: New Holl. Galle, no. 230.

Sold to Plantin at: 20 st. per quire of 25 leaves in 1561.[45]
= .80 st. per leaf or individual print.

CD-26 *Salome with the Head of John the Baptist*: **anonymous artist after Andrea del Sarto.** Engraving, 278 × 342, by 1561. LIT.: Riggs 1972, p. 358, no. 187.

Sold to Plantin at: 20 st. per quire of 25 leaves in 1561.[46]
= .80 st. per leaf or individual print.

CD-27 *Scenographiae sive perspectivae … pulcherrimae viginti selectissimaru fabricarum … (Large Perspective Book)*: **Joannes and Lucas van Doetecum after Hans Vredeman de Vries.** Twenty etchings (preceded by a title page in letterpress and an anonymous engraved plate with a dedication to Antoine Perrenot de Granvelle), ca. 205 × 260, 1560. LIT.: Cock 2013, cat. 81. See also TG-24.

Plantin resold this in 1581 at: 21 st. per series (the price Plantin paid for it is not known).[47]

CD-28 *Scrollwork Compartments with Mythological and Old Testament Scenes*: **Pieter van der Heyden after Jacob Floris.** Seventeen engravings, ca. 135 × 204, 1566. LIT.: Cock 2013, cat. 79.

Sold to Plantin at: 7 st. per series in 1568; and at 7 ½ st. per series in 1570.[48]
Possibly sold to De Mompere in 1582 at: 7 st. per series.

CD-29 *Sepulchral and Tomb Designs and Funeral Monuments (Pictores, statuarii, architecti, latomi, et quicunque principum magnificorum … adeste … coenotaphiorum, tumulorum & mortuorum monumentorum formas … inspicitote …)*: **Joannes and Lucas van Doetecum after Hans Vredeman de Vries.** Twenty-seven etchings, variable dimensions, including ca. 166 × 210, 1563. LIT.: New Holl. Van Doetecum, nos. 300–26.

Sold to Plantin at: 12 st. per series in 1568, 1573, and 1581.[49]
Possibly sold to De Mompere in 1582 at: 12 st. per series.

CD-30 *The Seven Deadly Sins and the Last Judgment*: **Pieter van der Heyden after Pieter Bruegel I.** Eight engravings, ca. 226 × 295, 1558. LIT.: Bassens and Van Grieken 2019, cat. 11 and 12a.

Sold to Plantin at: 18 st. per quire of 25 leaves in 1580.[50]
= .72 st. per leaf; each print was the equivalent of one leaf, amounting to 5.76 st. per series.

CD-31 *The Seven Liberal Arts*: **possibly Cornelis Cort after Frans Floris.** Seven engravings, ca. 229 × 281, 1565. LIT.: Cock 2013, cat. 44 (see New Holl. Floris, nos. 130–36, for a series of etchings of the same subject after Floris that Cock published in 1551, but that does not appear to have been listed in Diericx's 1601 estate, nor to have been republished by others).

Sold to Plantin in 1580, but with no clear price for this series.[51]

CD-32 *The Seven Virtues*: **Philips Galle after Pieter Bruegel I.** Seven engravings, ca. 226 × 294, ca. 1559–1560. LIT.: Bassens and Van Grieken 2019, cat. 13.

Sold to Plantin at: 20 st. per quire of 25 leaves in 1561.[52]
= .80 st. per leaf; each print was the equivalent of one leaf, amounting to 5.60 st. per series.

CD-33 *The Siege of the Elephant*: **Joannes and Lucas van Doetecum after a print by Alart du Hameel.** Engraving, 402 × 538, ca. 1563. LIT.: Cock 2013, cat. 61.

Sold to Plantin at: 3 st. per print in 1568.[53]

CD-34 *Small Architectural Perspective Views*: **Joannes and Lucas van Doetecum after Hans Vredeman de Vries.** Twenty-eight etchings and one anonymous engraved plate with a dedication to Antoine Perrenot de Granvelle, ca. 150/155 × 210, 1562. LIT.: Cock 2013, cat. 82.

Sold to Plantin at: 12 st. per series in 1568, 1580, and 1581.[54]
Possibly sold to Jan Moretus I in 1594, with all of the images printed on just fifteen leaves. The selling price was not noted.[55]

CD-35 *Small Book of Roman Ruins and Buildings (Operum antiquorum Romanorum hinc inde per diversas Europae regiones extructorum reliquias ac ruinas …)*: **Joannes and Lucas van Doetecum.** Twenty etchings and engravings (ca. 155 × 213), and a title plate (210 × 150), 1562. LIT.: Cock 2013, cat. 12.

Sold to Plantin at: 9 st. per series in 1568, 1573, and 1581.[56]
Possibly sold to De Mompere in 1582 at: 9 st. per series.

CD-36 *Small Landscapes with Views of Villages, Farms, Gates, and Castles (Multifariarum casularum ruriumque lineamenta curiose ad vivum expressa* [and] *Praediorum villarum et rusticarum casularum icones elegantissimae ad vivum in aere defomatae)*: **Joannes and Lucas van Doetecum after the Master of the Small Landscapes.** Two groups of etchings of landscapes printed in pairs, one with nine and one with thirteen plates, for a total of forty-four landscapes; each of the original plates measured ca. 320 × 205, with one image above the other; the plates were subsequently cut in half and reduced in size, making it possible to print each image independently, 1559–1561. LIT.: Cock 2013, cat. 97b.

Some part of these were most likely the series of village houses that Plantin purchased at 8 st. per copy in July and December 1568 and December 1573, but with no indication of the number of images (see below).

Sold to Plantin at: 8 st. per series in 1568 and 1573.[57]

CD-37 *The Story of Daniel, Bel, and the Dragon*: **Philips Galle after Maarten van Heemskerck.** Ten engravings, ca. 204 × 246, 1565. LIT.: New Holl. Galle, nos. 93–102.

Sold to Plantin in 1580, but with no clear price for this series.[58]

CD-38 *The Story of Tobias*: **Dirck Volckertsz. Coornhert after Maarten van Heemskerck.** Six engravings, ca. 239/243 × 186/191, ca. 1548. LIT.: New Holl. Van Heemskerck, nos. 183–88.

Sold to Plantin at: 18 st. per quire of 25 leaves in 1568.[59]
= .72 st. per leaf; each print may have been the equivalent of one leaf, amounting to 4.32 st. per series.

CD-39 *The Temptation of Saint Christopher*: **Joannes and Lucas van Doetecum, after an imitator of Hieronymus Bosch.** Etching and engraving, 336 × 430, 1561. LIT.: Cock 2013, cat. 64.

Sold to Plantin at: 2.5 st. per print in 1561.[60]

CD-40 *The Three Fates (Shown Spinning)*: **Cornelis Cort after Giulio Romano.** Engraving, 220 × 264, 1561. LIT.: Cock 2013, cat. 27.

Sold to Plantin at: 20 st. per quire of 25 leaves in 1561.[61]
= .80 st. per leaf or individual print.

CD-41 *Vessels*: **Joannes and Lucas van Doetecum after Hans Vredeman de Vries.** Eleven etchings and one engraving, ca. 200 × 140, 1563. LIT.: New Holl. Van Doetecum, nos. 327–38.

Sold to Plantin at: 5 st. per series in 1570.[62]
Sold to De Mompere in 1582 at: 5 st. per series.

Unspecified prints sold in bulk
See also the Note to the Reader and Chapter 2.

- per *large ("double double" leaf or "grandes pieces")*: sold to Plantin at: 4 st. per leaf in 1568 and 1573.[63]
- per *double* leaves: sold to Plantin at: 2 st. per leaf in 1568, 1571, and 1573.[64]
- per *medium* leaves: sold to Plantin at: 1.5 st. per leaf in 1568, 1571, and 1573.[65]
- per *quire* of 25 leaves: sold to Plantin at: 18 st. per quire (= .72 st. per leaf) between 1568, 1571, and 1581.[66]

ADRIAEN COLLAERT Antwerp ca. 1560–June 1618 Antwerp

Adriaen Collaert was the son of the versatile artist Hans Collaert. Though most likely trained as a painter, Hans Collaert was primarily active as an engraver. Both his prints and his independently commissioned designs were used for the production of tapestries, metalwork, and glass windowpanes.[67] Adriaen Collaert, who was registered as a master's son in Antwerp's Guild of St Luke in 1580, was most likely taught to engrave by his father.[68] Within a year, Adriaen began to produce engravings for several important Antwerp print publishers, in particular Gerard de Jode, who had commissioned numerous engravings from Adriaen's father and who also served as one of the guardians for Hans Collaert's children following his and his wife's death in October 1580.[69] By 1582, Adriaen was also making engravings for Philips Galle. In this initial stage of his career, he completed numerous works after designs by Hans Bol, as well as images after Maarten de Vos. After his marriage to Galle's daughter Josine in 1586, Collaert began to contribute more to Galle's various publications, often in conjunction with other engravers, for instance his brother Jan Collaert II, Charles de Mallery, and Galle's own sons, Theodore and Cornelis. He often engraved larger prints with a variety of subjects after primarily De Vos and Johannes Stradanus. However, by 1590, Collaert reduced the amount of work he did for Galle and began to publish his own prints. His acceptance of three apprentices in the guild year 1593–1594, and then three others in the years 1597, 1602, and 1605, suggests that he was endeavoring to bolster his own business as a print publisher. Since he was also assistant dean and, subsequently, dean of the Guild of St Luke between 1596 and 1598, he must have achieved some measure of success by this time that was recognized by his peers.[70] Although Collaert is best known for small religious images, often featuring saints, his series of birds, fish, and four-legged animals were also extremely popular, as is evident from the frequency with which they were reissued (by him and his brother-in-law Theodore Galle) and imitated.[71] Collaert also purchased plates previously published by others, including a variety of prints made for Hieronymus Cock and Volcxken Diericx, including the images of hunts that they had commissioned from Stradanus (CD-11 and CD-12), thus adding both prestige and diversity to his stock.[72] Furthermore, Collaert occasionally agreed to execute or rework book illustrations. By far the most impressive are the eleven engravings he made for the 1593 publication of the *Evangelicae historiae imagines*, a work that was created in conjunction with Jerónimo Nadal's *Adnotationes et meditationes in evangelia* and that featured primarily prints by the renowned Wierix brothers. However, he also completed smaller, isolated commissions from other publishers; his works for the Moretuses are the best documented examples.[73] His brother Jan II, who engraved just one print for the *Evangelicae historiae imagines*, was more frequently employed by other book publishers. Because of these various activities, Collaert became the most productive engraver and print publisher of his family. Following his death in 1618, his son Carel (1598–1654) reprinted numerous plates from his stock, including ones he had most likely acquired from Diericx's and Philips Galle's estate sales.[74]

LIT.: Diels 2010, pp. 150–245; New Holl. Collaert.

Identifiable prints sold by title

AC-1 *Birds (Avium vivae icones)*: **Adriaen Collaert.** Thirty-two engravings, including a title plate, ca. 131 × 188, ca. 1600. LIT.: New Holl. Collaert, nos. 1404–35.

Sold to Jan Moretus I at: 8 st. per series in 1608.[75]

AC-2 *Christ, the Virgin, the Twelve Apostles with the Creed, and Saint Paul*: **Adriaen Collaert.** Fifteen engravings of varying dimensions, including a title plate, ca. 169 × 114/122, between 1592 and 1608?. LIT.: New Holl. Collaert, nos. 693–708.

Sold to Jan Moretus I at: 3.5 st. per series in 1608.[76]

AC-3 *Female Hermits in Landscapes (Solitudo, sive vitae foeminarium anachoritarum …)*: **Adriaen Collaert, Jan Collaert II, and Cornelis Galle I after Maarten de Vos.** Twenty-four engravings of various sizes (ca. 172/179 × 219/226), and a title plate (185 × 222), by 1608. LIT.: New Holl. Collaert, nos. 766–90.

Sold to Jan Moretus I at: 1 fl. (= 20 st.) per series in 1608.[77]

AC-4 *Fish (Piscium vivae icones)*: **Adriaen Collaert.** Twenty-five engravings of various sizes (ca. 122/130 × 188) and a title plate (135 × 184), between 1598 and 1608. LIT.: New Holl. Collaert, nos. 1436–61. See fig. 5.17.

Sold to Jan Moretus I at: 16 st. per series in 1608.[78]

AC-5 *Four-Legged Animals (Animalium quadrupedum omnis generis verae et artificiosissimae delineationes …)*: **Adriaen Collaert.** Nineteen engravings of various sizes (ca. 124 × ca. 190) and a title plate (137 × 192), ca. 1597. LIT.: New Holl. Collaert, nos. 1462–81.

Sold to Jan Moretus I at: 12 st. per series in 1608.[79]

AC-6 *Infancy or Youth of Jesus*: in twelve prints (not yet linked to a known series).

Sold to Jan Moretus I at: 4.5 st. per series in 1608.[80]

AC-7 The Lamb of God: most likely: ***Christ as the Sacrificial Lamb on Mount Zion*, Hans Collaert I after Crispijn van den Broeck.** Engraving, 258 × 203, by 1608, originally published by Hans van Luyck. The words "Agnus dei" (used to identify this print in the sales record) appear clearly on a tablet on the left of the image. LIT.: New Holl. Collaert, no. 1132.

Sold to Jan Moretus I at: .75 st. per print in 1608.[81]

AC-8 *Life of Mary Magdalene*: possibly the single engraving of the repentant Mary Magdalene, surrounded by scenes from her life, with the subtitle: "Vita Sanctae Mariae Magdalenae", attributed to Jan II or Adriaen Collaert, 270 × 200. LIT.: New Holl. Collaert, no. 996.

Sold to Jan Moretus I in 1602, together with more than 600 sheets (or leaves) of paper at the rate of 30 full sheets of paper per 1 fl. (= 20 st.), or 2/3 st. per sheet of paper. Because the identification of this image and the size of the sheets (or leaves) of paper referred to in the sale are not certain, it is impossible to determine how much each individual print cost.[82]

AC-9 *The Life, Passion and Resurrection of Christ (Vita, passio, et resurrectio Iesu Christi …)*: **Jan Baptist Barbé, Jacques de Bie, Adriaen Collaert, Jan Collaert II, and Cornelis Galle I after Maarten de Vos.** Fifty engravings (ca. 180 × 219) and a title plate (168 × 218), 1598. LIT.: New Holl. Collaert, nos. 174–224. See figs. 5.15 and 6.10.

Sold to Jan Moretus I at: 22 st. in 1602; and at 17 st. per series in 1608.[83]

AC-10 *Life of Saint Antony* (not yet linked to a known print).

Sold to Jan Moretus I in 1602, together with more than 600 sheets (or leaves) of paper at the rate of 30 full sheets of paper per 1 fl. (= 20 st.), or 2/3 st. per sheet of paper. Because the identification of this image and the size of the sheets (or leaves) of paper referred to in the sale are not certain, it is impossible to determine how much each individual print cost.[84]

AC-11 *The Life of Saint Catherine of Alexandria (Vita S. Catharinae virg. et martyris …)*: **attributed to Adriaen or Jan Collaert II.** Fifteen engravings (ca. 90 × 67) and a title plate (93 × 70), by 1608. LIT.: New Holl. Collaert, nos. 884–99. See fig. 5.16.

Sold to Jan Moretus I at: 4 st. per series in 1608.[85]

AC-12 *The Life of Saint John the Baptist (Vita S. Ioannis Baptistae)*: **Adriaen Collaert.** Sixteen engravings, including a title plate, ca. 91 × 66, by 1608. LIT.: New Holl. Collaert, nos. 265–80.

Sold to Jan Moretus I at: 4 st. per series in 1608.[86]

AC-13 *The Life of Saint John the Evangelist (Vita S. Ioannis apostoli et evangelistae …)*: **attributed to Adriaen Collaert.** Fifteen engravings (ca. 91 × 66), and a title plate (96 × 64), by 1608. LIT.: New Holl. Collaert, nos. 665–80.

Sold to Jan Moretus I at: 4 st. per series in 1608.[87]

AC-14 *Life of Saint Peter* (not yet linked to a known series).

Sold to Jan Moretus I in 1602, together with more than 600 sheets (or leaves) of paper at the rate of 30 full sheets of paper per 1 fl. (= 20 st.), or 2/3 st. per sheet of paper. Because the identification of this image and the size of the sheets (or leaves) of paper referred to in the sale are not certain, it is impossible to determine how much each individual print cost.[88]

AC-15 *The Life of the Virgin* **(in sixteen leaves): anonymous engraver after Jan Wierix.** Sixteen engravings, 125 × 85, by 1608, currently known only in an edition published by Carel Collaert. LIT.: New Holl. Collaert, nos. 566–81.

Sold to Jan Moretus I at: 6 st. per series in 1608.[89]

AC-16 *The Life of the Virgin* **("small"), possibly: Adriaen Collaert.** Twenty engravings, including a title plate, ca. 87 × 66, by 1608. LIT.: New Holl. Collaert, nos. 528–47.

Sold to Jan Moretus I at: 5 st. per series in 1608.[90]

AC-17 *The Seven Churches of Rome*: **attributed to Adriaen Collaert.** Seven engravings, one ca. 100 × 66, the rest ca. 107 × 74, ca. 1600. LIT.: New Holl. Collaert, nos. 1214–20.

Sold to Jan Moretus I at: 2.5 st. per series in 1608.[91]

AC-18 *The Seven Gifts of the Holy Spirit*: **Adriaen Collaert after Johannes Stradanus.** Seven engravings, ca. 210 × 274, ca. 1595. LIT.: New Holl. Stradanus, nos. 256–62.

Sold to Jan Moretus I at: 8 st. per series in 1608.[92]

Unspecified prints sold in bulk

See also the Note to the Reader and Chapter 2.

- per *full sheet of paper*: sold to Jan Moretus I at 30 sheets per 20 st. (or 1 fl.) in 1602, which is 2/3 (= .67) st. per sheet.[93] This rate was applied to both individual prints (presumably printed with multiple images per sheet), as well as to multiple, unspecified images printed together on one sheet (either 4, or 8, or 12 to a sheet). Thus, evidently the amount of paper involved was more important than the number of images sold.
- per *single image*: sold to Jan Moretus I at .75 st. per image in 1601.[94]
- per *leaf* (with 2 images on each leaf): sold to Jan Moretus I at .75 st. in 1608.[95]
- per *quire* of 25 leaves: sold to Jan Moretus I at: 18 st. per quire (= .72 st. per leaf) in 1607 and 1608.[96]
- per *100 images*: sold to Jan Moretus I at 20 st. per hundred (= .2 st. per image) in 1608.[97]

JAN GALLE Antwerp 1600–1676 Antwerp

Although Jan Galle was registered as an engraver in Antwerp's Guild of St Luke by the time that he turned twenty-eight, he is not known to have worked actively as an engraver.[98] Rather, in contrast to his father and grandfather, Jan Galle focused almost exclusively on printing plates. While printing the engravings used to embellish the books published by the Moretus family was one mainstay of his business, Galle also worked as an independent print publisher and printseller. He consequently remained a prominent figure in the Antwerp print world and even served as dean of the Guild of St Luke in 1638–1639.[99] Though a large portion of his stock of plates depicted religious subjects, he reissued a variety of famous secular images that had been commissioned by earlier print publishers, such as allegories designed by Maarten van Heemskerck, genre scenes by Pieter Bruegel I, hunts by Stradanus, and architectural and ornamental prints by Hans Vredeman de Vries. Not only did Galle inherit more than 3,200 plates from his parents, but he also purchased plates from other print publishers, in addition to commissioning new ones. By the time an inventory of his stock was compiled in 1677, soon after his death, the number of plates that he owned had more than doubled since the mid 1630s.[100] However, Galle's sons Norbertus and Guilliam decided to sell his plates, as advertised in the *Amsterdam Courant* of 4 February 1677.[101] Although the exact means by which the plates were sold remains unclear, the subsequent publication of numerous items from Galle's collection by various print publishers from the Low Countries confirms the dispersal of the Galle family's stock of plates, which reflected three generations of collecting and publishing a cherished assortment of renowned prints from Antwerp.

LIT.: Bowen 2004; Bowen 2009, pp. 134–41; Fuhring 2017.

Identifiable prints sold by title

JG-1 *Men and Women of the Franciscan Order (Imagines seraphicae S.mi p. Francisci Assisiatis illustriumque virorum et feminarum)*: **Charles de Mallery after Peeter de Jode I.** Fourteen engravings ca. 255 × 165, and a title plate (267 × 176), originally published in 1614 by Charles de Mallery (CM-1) and reissued by Thedore Galle by 1631 (TG-13). This series was often included in: Henricus Sedulius, *Historia seraphica vitae bmi. p. Francisci Assisiatis* (Antwerp: Heirs of M. Nutius, 1613). LIT.: New Holl. De Jode, part VII, nos. 572–86. See fig. 7.7.

Sold to Balthasar Moretus I at: 24 st. per series in 1638.[102]

JG-2 *Mirror of Assorted Images to Admire (Speculum diversarum imaginum speculativum)*: a compendium of thirty distinct older series by various artists that Jan Galle published in 1638, with a new title plate featuring a cartouche at the top with the phrase "*Tempus ridendi, tempus flendi*" (A time to laugh, a time to cry), and an introductory list of the featured series in letterpress. LIT.: Fuhring 2017, figs. 5–7, pp. 229–30, 238, and nos. 149, 150, 152, 153, 155–62, and 164–78. See fig. 7.22.

Sold to Balthasar Moretus I at: 9 fl. (or 180 st.) per copy with 186 leaves in 1641, amounting to nearly 1 st. per leaf.[103]

Unspecified prints sold in bulk

See also the Note to the Reader and Chapter 2.

- per *single image, illuminated on parchment*: sold to Balthasar Moretus I at 2 st. in 1637.[104]
- per *100 images, illuminated on parchment*: sold to Balthasar Moretus I at 9 fl. (= 180 st.) per hundred (= 1.8 st. per image) in 1639.[105]
- per *100 images on parchment*: sold to Balthasar Moretus I at 3 fl. 12 st. (= 72 st.) per hundred (= .72 st. per image) in 1637.[106]
- per *100 images*: sold to Balthasar Moretus I at 36 st. per hundred (= .36 st. per image) in 1637.[107]

PHILIPS GALLE Haarlem ca. 1537–1612 Antwerp

Born in Haarlem around 1537, Galle trained as an engraver there under Dirck Volckertsz. Coornhert. In 1557, he was making engravings for others, in particular Cock, primarily after designs by Pieter Bruegel I, Frans Floris, and especially Maarten van Heemskerck, who was also from Haarlem. Six years later, in 1563, Galle began to publish his own prints, many of which he engraved himself either after his own designs or ones by Van Heemskerck. Clearly aware of the potential of Antwerp as a center for print production and distribution, Galle moved there either late in 1569 or early in 1570, a few months before Cock died. By 1570, he was registered in Antwerp's Guild of St Luke as a master engraver and started to publish prints after a new group of designers, including Hans Vredeman de Vries, Gerard van Groeningen, Maarten de Vos, and Johannes Stradanus. Although Galle still occasionally made his own engravings, he worked increasingly with other engravers. At first, he engaged local independent printmakers, for instance the Van Doetecum brothers, Hieronymus Wierix, and Jan Sadeler I, in addition to Hendrick Goltzius in Haarlem. However, Galle also began to train new engravers in his own workshop; several of his students went on to produce engravings for his later publications. Particularly important in this regard were his sons Theodore and Cornelis, as well as his apprentices Adriaen Collaert and Charles de Mallery, each of whom married one of his daughters. In the course of his career, Galle oversaw the creation of an extensive and diverse range of publications, including didactic and allegorical imagery, common religious subjects, several series of portraits, and emblematic and cartographic publications. While the timing of Galle's move to Antwerp may suggest that he hoped to replace Cock as the leading publisher of engravings there, he appears to have remained on good terms with Cock's widow, Volcxken Diericx.[108] Galle acquired some plates from Diericx's stock, most likely following her death in 1600.

Once in Antwerp, Galle also soon became close friends with Plantin. Although Galle and the members of his workshop made engravings for just a few of Plantin's own publications, he ended up supplying Plantin with far more prints for resale than any other publisher in Antwerp. Indeed, despite having sold his primary residence, the "Witte Lelie", in 1605 to his son Theodore (who had begun to work as an independent print publisher by 1600), Philips Galle continued to provide Plantin's successors, the Moretuses, with prints for resale through 1608, a few years before his own death.[109] Regrettably, nothing is known about any arrangements for the transfer or sale of his stock of plates, which may have amounted to approximately 2,500 images.[110] Subsequent editions of several sets of plates reveal that the plates were not simply transferred to Theodore, but that others, in particular various relatives like the Collaerts and Charles de Mallery, had acquired some. Nevertheless, many, if not all of these plates, were in the possession of Theodore's widow, Catharina Moerentorf, at her death in 1636.[111]

LIT.: Bowen 2009, pp. 125–27; Bowen and Imhof 2008, in particular pp. 248–86 and 333–35; New Holl. Galle 2001, 4 parts, in particular the introductory remarks in part 1, pp. xxxiii-lxxxi; Sellink 1997.

Identifiable prints sold by title

PG-1 ***The Acts of the Apostles*: Philips Galle after Maarten van Heemskerck.** Sixteen engravings, ca. 213 × 274, 1575. LIT.: New Holl. Heemskerck, nos. 395–410.

Sold to Plantin at: 18 st. per quire of 25 leaves in 1580.[112] = .72 st. per leaf; each print was the equivalent of one leaf, amounting to 11.52 st. per series.

PG-2 ***The Acts of the Apostles (Acta apostolorum …)*: Adriaen Collaert, Philips Galle, and Hendrick Goltzius after Johannes Stradanus.** Eighteen engravings, including a title plate, ca. 200 × 266, 1582. LIT.: New Holl. Stradanus, nos. 209–26.

This series was combined with seventeen other engravings designed by Maarten van Heemskerck and engraved by Philips Galle to form a new, enlarged series of thirty-five plates, including a title plate. For the earlier series, see PG-1 and New Holl. Heemskerck, no. 411 (*The Burial of Saint Stephen*, 209 × 270). LIT.: New Holl. Galle, nos. 187–219.

Sold to Jan Moretus I at: 18 st. per quire of 25 leaves in 1608. = .72 st. per leaf; each print was the equivalent of one leaf, amounting to 25.2 st. (= 1 fl. 5.2 st.) per series of thirty-five prints.[113]

PG-3 ***Adoration of the Holy Vernicle*: anonymous artist after Johannes Stradanus.** Engraving, 251 × 181, by 1588. LIT.: New Holl. Stradanus, no. 175.

Sold to Plantin at: .72 or 1 st. per print in 1588.[114]

PG-4 ***Adoration of the Name of Jesus*: Philips Galle.** Engraving, 248 diameter, ca. 1569. LIT.: New Holl. Galle, no. 225.

Sold to Plantin at: 18 st. per quire of 25 leaves in 1580.[115] = .72 st. per leaf; each print was the equivalent of one leaf.

PG-5 ***Adoration of the Virgin by Saints Antony and Francis*: Adriaen Collaert (attributed to) after Johannes Stradanus.** Engraving, 248 × 180, by 1588. LIT.: New Holl. Stradanus no. 186.

Sold to Plantin at: .72 or 1 st. per print in 1588.[116]

• *Allegories of the Christian Creed*, Hendrick Goltzius, ten engravings, ca. 244 × 190, 1578. LIT.: New Holl. Goltzius, nos. 59–68. Not sold as a series, but as individual prints; see under the titles: *The Atonement of Christ* (PG-8), *Disagreement in the Church* (PG-23), *The Forgiveness of Transgressions* (PG-39), *The House Built on Sand* (PG-57), *The House Built on the Rock* (PG-58), *Man's Quest for the Kingdom of Heaven* (PG-69), *The Relief of Suffering* (PG-85), and *The Solicitude of the Lord* (PG-105).
• *The Apostles' Creed*: See *The Twelve Articles of Faith*

PG-6 ***The Annunciation*: Philips Galle after Anthonie Blocklandt van Montfoort.** Engraving, 288 × 201, ca. 1577–1578. LIT.: New Holl. Galle, no. 139.

Sold to Plantin at: 18 st. per quire of 25 leaves in 1580.[117] = .72 st. per leaf; each print was the equivalent of one leaf.

PG-7 ***Archangels*: Crispijn de Passe I after Maarten de Vos.** Nine engravings, ca. 162 × 92, ca. 1584–1585. LIT.: Holl. Dutch & Flemish, vol. XLIV, nos. 756–64.

Sold to Jan Moretus I at: 4 st. per series in 1594.[118]

PG-8 ***The Atonement of Christ*: Hendrick Goltzius.** Engraving, 244 × 190, 1578. LIT.: New Holl. Goltzius, no. 61, part of the series *Allegories of the Christian Creed* (nos. 59–68), but sold individually by Plantin.

Sold to Plantin at: 18.25 st. per quire of 25 sheets in 1579.[119] = .73 st. per leaf; each print was the equivalent of one leaf.

PG-9 ***Book of Birds (Avium vivae icones)*: possibly Philips Galle after Marcus Gheeraerts I or** II. Twelve engravings, ca. 78 × 209, by 1594. LIT.: Holl. Dutch & Flemish, vol. VII, p. 103, nos. 33–44.

Sold to Jan Moretus I at: 5 st. in 1594.[120]

PG-10 ***The Casting out of Evil*: Hendrick Goltzius.** Engraving, 251 × 187, [1578]. LIT.: New Holl. Goltzius, no. 69.

Sold to Plantin at: 18 st. per quire of 25 leaves in 1580.[121] = .72 st. per leaf; each print was the equivalent of one leaf.

PG-11 ***Celebrated Women of the New Testament (Icones illustrium feminarum novi testamenti)*: Adriaen Collaert, Jan Collaert** II**, and Charles de Mallery after Maarten de Vos.** Sixteen engravings, including a title plate, ca. 156 × 92, by 1594. LIT.: Holl. Dutch & Flemish, vol. XLIV, nos. 508–22.

Sold to Jan Moretus I at: 8 st. per series in 1594.[122]

PG-12 ***Celebrated Women of the Old Testament (Icones illustrium feminarum veteris testamenti)*: Jan Collaert** II **after Maarten de Vos.** Twenty-one engravings, including a title plate, ca. 156 × 92, by 1594. LIT.: New Hollstein Collaert, nos. 86–105. See fig. 10.2.

Sold to Jan Moretus I at: 9 st. per series in 1594.[123]

PG-13 ***Christ at the Column*: anonymous artist after Johannes Stradanus.** Engraving, 200 × 144, by 1588. LIT.: New Holl. Stradanus, no. 165.

Sold to Plantin at: .72 or 1 st. per print in 1588.[124]

PG-14 *Christ on the Cross with Angels*: **Adriaen Collaert after Johannes Stradanus.** Engraving, 247 × 181, by 1588. LIT.: New Holl. Stradanus, no. 170.

Sold to Plantin at: .72 or 1 st. per print in 1588.[125]

PG-15 *Coat of Arms of the King*: possibly an earlier state of the following print (or one similar to it), featuring Philip III, by 1594. Compare: Adriaen Collaert after Johannes Stradanus, *Allegory of the Power of Philip III of Spain*, engraving, 327 × 216, 1598. LIT.: New Holl. Stradanus, no. 402.

Sold to Jan Moretus I at: 2 st. in 1594.[126]

PG-16 *David, hoc est virtutis exercitatissimae probatum Deo spectaculum (David or the Spectacle of the most Skilled Virtue Sanctioned by God)*: **Jan Sadeler I (attributed to) after Gerard van Groeningen and Crispijn van den Broeck (attributed to).** Forty-eight engravings (ca. 107 × 140) and an engraved title plate (103 × 147), with an introductory text in letterpress, 1575. LIT.: Bowen and Imhof 2008, pp. 400–01.

Sold to Plantin at: 20 st. (= 1 fl.) per series numerous times between 1575 and 1589;[127] and at just 18 st. per series in 1581 and 1583.[128]

PG-17 *De deis gentium imagines … (Images of Pagan Gods)*: **Philips Galle.** Twenty-nine engravings (ca. 131 × 81) and an engraved title plate (ca. 143 × 92), as well as a dedication in letterpress, 1581. LIT.: New Holl. Galle, nos. 448–77.

Sold to Plantin at: 10 st. per series in 1581; and at 9 st. per series in 1583 and 1585.[129]

PG-18 *The Deer Hunt of Emperor Frederick I Barbarossa and Ubaldino Ubaldini*: **Adriaen Collaert after Johannes Stradanus.** Engraving, 251 × 272, 1589. LIT.: New Holl. Stradanus, no. 377. See fig. 7.9.

Sold to Jan Moretus I at: 1 ½ st. in 1594.[130]

PG-19 *Deorum dearumque capita … (Heads of Gods and Goddesses …)*: **attributed to Joannes and Lucas van Doetecum after Gerard van Groeningen and Hans Vredeman de Vries.** Fifty-five plates, etching and engraving, ca. 120 × 84, with introductory texts and an index in letterpress, 1573. LIT.: Holl. Dutch & Flemish, vol. XLVIII, nos. 353–83; New Holl. Van Groeningen, nos. 25–36 and 406–17; New Holl. Van Doetecum, nos. 657–702; BT 2285; Adams O-325. See Bowen and Imhof 2008, p. 407, for a discussion of the 1582 edition of this publication.

Sold to Plantin at: 16 st. per series in 1573, 1577, and 1579;[131] and at 18 st. per series in 1574.[132]

PG-20 *Designs for Furniture (Differents pourtraicts de menuiserie)*: **Peeter van der Borcht after Hans Vredeman de Vries.** Title plate and sixteen etchings, ca. 258 × 191 or ca. 188 × 258, ca. 1583. LIT.: New Holl. Van der Borcht, nos. 218–34.

Jan Moretus I resold this in 1594 at: 1 fl. per series (the price at which Galle supplied this series is not specified).[133]

PG-21 *Designs for Pendants (with Deities and Strapwork)*: **anonymous artist after Hans Collaert I.** Ten engravings, ca. 173 × 120/125, 1581. Lit.: New Holl. Collaert, nos. 1644–53.[134]

Sold to Plantin at: 9 st. per series once in 1581;[135] and at 8 st. per series twice in 1581.[136] The latter price is repeated for the 1581 edition of this series in Plantin's list of publications by his contemporaries.[137]

PG-22 *Designs for Pendants (with Sea Monsters)*: **Adriaen Collaert after Hans Collaert I.** Ten engravings, ca. 172 × 127, 1582. LIT.: New Holl. Collaert, nos. 1654–63. See fig. 5.11.

This or the preceding series of pendants was sold to Jan Moretus I at: 7 ½ st. per series in 1594.[138]

PG-23 *Disagreement in the Church*: **Hendrick Goltzius.** Engraving, 256 × 187, 1578. LIT.: New Holl. Goltzius, no. 66, part of the series *Allegories of the Christian Creed* (nos. 59–68), but sold individually by Plantin.

Sold to Plantin at: 18 st. per quire of 25 leaves in 1580.[139]
= .72 st. per leaf; each print was the equivalent of one leaf.

PG-24 *Disasters of the Jewish People*: **Philips Galle after Maarten van Heemskerck.** Twenty-two engravings, ca. 150 × 220, 1569. LIT.: New Holl. Galle, nos. 103–24.

Plantin sent four sets of this series to his shop in Paris in 1573, with a price of 9 st. per series.[140]
Plantin resold this series in 1582 at: 28 st. (= 1 fl. 8 st.) per series (the price Plantin paid for it is not known).[141]

PG-25 *The Discovery of America*: **Adriaen Collaert after Johannes Stradanus.** Four engravings, ca. 212 × 282, by 1588. LIT.: New Holl. Stradanus, nos. 342–45.

Sold to Plantin at: 5 st. per series in 1588.[142]
Sold to Jan Moretus I at: 4 st. per series in 1594.[143]

PG-26 *Divinarum nuptiarum conventa et acta* [and] *Christi Jesu vitae admirabiliumque actionum speculum (Agreements and Acts of Divine Mariages [and] The Mirror of the Life of Jesus Christ and his Miraculous Acts)*: **Jan Wierix (and possibly other engravers) after Gerard van Groeningen (and possibly others).** Twenty-eight engravings for the first part and fifty-one for the second, ca. 99 × 140, with a brief, introductory Latin text in letterpress, 1573. LIT.: Bowen and Imhof 2008, pp. 406–07; BT 1207; Holl. Dutch & Flemish, vol. LXX, book no. 13; New Holl. Van Groeningen, nos. 286–313; M-H Wierix 1978–1982, nos. 1978–82.

Sold to Plantin at: 35 st. (= 1 fl. 15 st.) per series numerous times between 1573 and 1579 and once in 1585.[144]

PG-27 *Divinarum nuptiarum conventa et acta* [and] *Christi Jesu vitae admirabiliumque actionum speculum speculum (Agreements and Acts of Divine Mariages [and] The Mirror of the Life of Jesus Christ and his Miraculous Acts)*: as above, but now with a French translation of the introductory text, printed in letterpress in 1573/1574. LIT.: BT 1208.

Sold to Plantin at: 35 st. (= 1 fl. 15 st.) per series in 1574 and 1575.[145]

PG-28 *Divinarum nuptiarum conventa et acta* [and] *Christi Jesu vitae admirabiliumque actionum speculum speculum (Agreements and Acts of Divine Mariages [and] The Mirror of the Life of Jesus Christ and his Miraculous Acts)*: as above, but now with a reprint of the introductory Latin text in letterpress, 1580. LIT.: BT 1209.

Sold to Plantin at: 35 st. (= 1 fl. 15 st.) per series in 1579 and 1581; and at 32 st. per series in 1587.[146]

PG-29 *The Divine Charge to the Three Estates*: **Philips Galle after Maarten van Heemskerck.** Four engravings, ca. 204 × 251, ca. 1565–1568?. LIT.: New Holl. Galle, nos. 299–302. See fig. 7.11.

Sold to Plantin at: 5 st. per series in 1588.[147]
Sold to Jan Moretus I at: 4 st. per series in 1594.[148]

PG-30 *The Eight Beatitudes*: **Harmen Jansz. Muller after Maarten van Heemskerck.** Eight engravings, ca. 210 × 250, ca. 1566. LIT.: New Holl. Van Heemskerck, nos. 313–20.

Sold to Plantin at: 18 st. per quire of 25 leaves in 1580.[149]
= .72 st. per leaf; each print was the equivalent of one leaf, amounting to 5.76 st. per series.
This same series appears to have been sold much earlier; in November 1567, the Florentine branch of the Giunti booksellers offered it to Vincenzio Borghini for the more significant sum of 5 lire 6 soldi and 8 denari.[150]

PG-31 *The Eight Beatitudes*: **Hendrick Goltzius.** Engraving, 257 × 187, 1578. LIT.: New Holl. Goltzius, no. 71.

Sold to Plantin at: 18.25 st. per quire of 25 leaves in 1579.[151]
= .73 st. per leaf; each print was the equivalent of one leaf.

PG-32 *The Eight Wonders of the World*: **Philips Galle after Maarten van Heemskerck.** Eight engravings, ca. 213 × 264, 1572. LIT.: New Holl. Galle, nos. 478–85. This may well be the series referred to in Plantin's accounts as the "Pyramides"; the first image features a pyramid.

Sold to Plantin at: 6 st. per series in 1582.[152]

PG-33 *The Eulogy of Music (Encomium musices)*: **Adriaen Collaert and Theodore Galle after Johannes Stradanus.** Seventeen engravings, including a title plate, ca. 210 × 285, with a dedication in letterpress, 1591. LIT.: New Holl. Stradanus, nos. 135–51; Imhof 2014a, no. G-3. See fig. 5.14.

Sold to Jan Moretus I at: 20 st. per series in 1594.[153]
Sold to Jan Moretus I at: 17 st. per series in 1608.[154]

PG-34 *Examples of Repentant Sinners from the Old and New Testament (Typus divinae indulgentiae atq. misericordiae …)*: **anonymous engraver(s) after Maarten de Vos.** Ten engravings, including a title plate, ca. 200 × 228, by 1608. LIT.: Holl. Dutch & Flemish, vol. XLIV, nos. 1137–46.

Sold to Jan Moretus I at: 18 st. per quire of 25 leaves in 1608.
= .72 st. per leaf; each print was the equivalent of one leaf, amounting to 7.2 st. per series of ten prints.[155]

PG-35 *The Fall of Babylon*: **Philips Galle after Maarten van Heemskerck.** Engraving, 256 × 411, 1569. LIT.: New Holl. Galle, no. 220.

Sold to Plantin at: 2.5 st. per print in 1571.[156]

PG-36 *Famous Roman Women*: **Theodore Galle after Johannes Stradanus.** Six engravings, ca. 224 × 289, by 1594. LIT.: New Holl Stradanus, nos. 301–06.

Sold to Jan Moretus I at: 6 st. per series in 1594 and 1608.[157]

PG-37 *The Fifteen Mysteries of the Rosary*: possibly an anonymous engraving after Johannes Stradanus, 436 × 298, 1577. LIT.: New Holl. Stradanus, no. 180.

Sold to Plantin at: 2 st. per print in 1577.[158]

PG-38 *The Five Senses*: **Hendrick Goltzius.** Five engravings, ca. 160 × 91, 1578. LIT.: New Holl. Goltzius, nos. 194–98.

Sold to Plantin at: 1.75 st. and 2 st. per series in 1581.[159]

PG-39 *The Forgiveness of Transgressions*: **Hendrick Goltzius.** Engraving, 254 × 189, 1578. LIT.: New Holl. Goltzius, no. 60, part of the series *Allegories of the Christian Creed* (nos. 59–68), but sold individually by Plantin.

Sold to Plantin at: 18 st. per quire of 25 leaves in 1580.[160]
= .72 st. per leaf; each print was the equivalent of one leaf.

PG-40 *The Four Ages: Golden, Silver, Bronze, and Iron*: **Philips Galle after Gilles Coignet.** Four engravings, ca. 247 × 248, 1573. LIT.: New Holl. Galle, nos. 378–81. See fig. 6.16.

Sold to Plantin at: 3 st. per series in 1573.[161]
Possibly sold to Plantin at: 5 st. per series in 1588.[162]
Sold to Jan Moretus I at: 4 st. per series in 1594.[163]

PG-41 *The Four Continents*: **Adriaan Collaert after Maarten de Vos.** Four engravings, ca. 212 × 259, ca. 1588–1589(?). LIT.: New Holl. Collaert, nos. 1314–17.

Sold to Jan Moretus I at: 4 st. in 1594.[164]
Sold to Jan Moretus I at: 18 st. per quire of 25 leaves in 1608.
= .72 st. per leaf; each print was the equivalent of one leaf, amounting to 2.88 st. per series.[165]

PG-42 ***The Four Continents*: anonymous engraver after Marcus Gheeraerts I.** Four engravings, ca. 197 × 132, by 1585. LIT.: Holl. Dutch & Flemish, vol. VII, nos. 44–47.
[and]
PG-43 ***The Four Elements*: anonymous engraver after Marcus Gheeraerts I.** Four engravings, ca. 198 × 132, by 1585. LIT.: Holl. Dutch & Flemish, vol. VII, nos. 48–51.

Sold to Plantin at: 3 st. per set of eight images in 1585.[166]
Sold to Jan Moretus I at: 18 st. per quire of 25 leaves in 1608.
= .72 st. per leaf; each print was the equivalent of one leaf, amounting to 5.76 st. per series of eight prints.[167]

PG-44 ***The Four Doctors* [*of the Church*] in four leaves** (not yet linked to a specific series).

Sold to Plantin in 1580 and to Jan Moretus I in 1608 at: 18 st. per quire of 25 leaves.[168]
= .72 st. per leaf; each print was the equivalent of one leaf, amounting to 2.88 st. per series of four prints.

PG-45 ***The Four Evangelists*: Philips Galle after Anthonie Blocklandt van Montfoort.** Four engravings, ca. 217 × 280, ca. 1575. LIT.: New Holl. Galle, no. 238.

Sold to Plantin at: 18 st. per quire of 25 leaves in 1576.[169]
= .72 st. per leaf; each print was the equivalent one leaf, amounting to 2.88 st. per series.

PG-46 ***The Four Last Things*: Philips Galle after Maarten van Heemskerck.** Four engravings, ca. 230 diameter, 1569. LIT.: New Holl. Galle, nos. 277–80.

Sold to Plantin at: 4 st. per series in 1575.[170]

PG-47 ***The Four Last Things*: Hendrick Goltzius after Johannes Stradanus.** Four engravings, ca. 260 diameter. ca. 1578. LIT.: New Holl. Goltzius nos. 342–45.

Sold to Plantin at: 18 st. per quire of 25 leaves in 1580.[171]
= .72 st. per leaf; each print was the equivalent of one leaf, amounting to 2.88 st. per series.

PG-48 ***The Four Parts of the Day*: probably the series engraved by Adriaen Collaert after Maarten de Vos: *The Four Times of the Day and the Four Ages of Man*.** Four engravings, ca. 206 × 260, by 1594. LIT.: New Holl. Collaert, nos. 1363–66.

Sold to Jan Moretus I at: 4 st. per series in 1594.[172]

PG-49 ***The Four Seasons*: Philips Galle after Maarten van Heemskerck.** Four engravings, ca. 210 × 250, 1563. LIT.: New Holl. Galle, nos. 369–72.

Sold to Plantin at: 18 st. per quire of 25 leaves in 1580.[173]
= .72 st. per leaf; each print was the equivalent of one leaf, amounting to 2.88 st. per series.

PG-50 ***The Four Seasons with the Sun*: Philips Galle after Johannes Stradanus.** Five engravings, ca. 219 × 303, by 1580. LIT.: New Holl. Stradanus, nos. 385–89. See fig. 10.3.

Sold to Plantin at: 18 st. per quire of 25 leaves in 1580.[174]
= .72 st. per leaf; each print was the equivalent of one leaf, amounting to 3.6 st. per series.

PG-51 ***The Four Strongest Powers*: Philips Galle after Gerard van Groeningen.** Four engravings, ca. 191 × 266, ca. 1574(?). LIT.: New Holl. Galle, nos. 273–76. This may well be the series referred to in Plantin's accounts as the "Triumph of Bacchus"; the first image ("The Power of Wine") features a triumphant Bacchus.

Sold to Plantin at: 18 st. per quire of 25 leaves in 1580.[175]
= .72 st. per leaf or 2.88 st. per series; each print was the equivalent of one leaf.

PG-52 ***The Four Ways of Living on Earth*: Philips Galle's workshop (attributed to) after Gerard van Groeningen.** Four engravings, ca. 209 × 255, by 1573. LIT.: New Holl. Van Groeningen, nos. 150–53.

Sold to Plantin at: 3 st. per series in 1573.[176]

PG-53 ***Gardens*.** For an overview of these series, see Fuhring 2017, p. 272. The sale by Philips Galle in 1608 of each of the series listed below as individual sets calls into question the ca. 1601 dating of Theodore Galle's first edition of them; this date was proposed in Holl. Dutch & Flemish, vol. XLVIII, pp. 122 and 156, and New Holl. Van der Borcht, part I, p. 167.

• Series of six prints of gardens with lovers: Peeter van der Borcht Etchings, ca. 187 × 248, ca. 1587?. LIT.: New Holl. Van der Borcht, nos. 161–66.

Sold to Jan Moretus I at: 18 st. per quire of 25 leaves in 1608.
= .72 st. per leaf; each print was the equivalent of one leaf, amounting to 4.32 st. per series of six prints.[177]

• Series of eight prints of gardens: anonymous artist after Hans Vredeman de Vries. Eight etchings, 185 × 247, 1587?. LIT.: Holl. Dutch & Flemish, vol. XLVIII, nos. 508–15.

Sold to Jan Moretus I at: 18 st. per quire of 25 leaves in 1608.
= .72 st. per leaf; each print was the equivalent of one leaf, amounting to 5.76 st. per series of eight prints.[178]

• Series of twenty-one prints of gardens: *Hortorum viridariorumque elegantis & multiplicis formae …*: anonymous artist after Hans Vredeman de Vries. Twenty-one etchings, including a title plate, ca. 194 × 246, 1583. LIT.: Holl. Dutch & Flemish, vol. XLVIII, nos. 470–90.

Sold to Jan Moretus I at: 18 st. per quire of 25 leaves in 1608.
= .72 st. per leaf; each print the equivalent of one leaf, amounting to 15.12 st. per series of twenty-one prints.[179]

PG-54 *Heads of Men and Women*: **possibly the series** ***Various Examples of Hair Styles and Beards (Variae comarum et barbarum formae)*****: Philips Galle.** Eighteen engravings, including a title plate, ca. 120 × 100, ca. 1590–1594. LIT.: New Holl. Galle, nos. 564–81. See fig. 7.10.

Sold to Jan Moretus I at: 7 st. in 1594.[180]

PG-55 *The History of the Medici (Mediceae familiae rerum felicter gestarum victoriae et triumphi)*: **Philips Galle and Hendrick Goltzius after Johannes Stradanus.** Twenty-one engravings, including a title plate, ca. 208 × 281, 1577–1583. LIT.: New Holl. Stradanus, nos. 352–72.

There is no clear evidence of the sale of this entire series as a single unit; rather, groups of eight leaves were sold in 1580 under the headings of "Historia Medices 8 f°" (History of the Medicis, 8 leaves), "Expeditiones Caroli V Siene etc. Jo. Strad. 8 f°" (Expeditions of Charles V in Siena by Johannes Stradanus, 8 leaves), "de la guerra de Siena f. 8 Stradan." (of the Battle of Siena, 8 leaves, Stradanus),[181] "Guerre novae de 8 fogli f° … de … Medicis" (8 leaves of new battles of the Medicis), and eight leaves of "oorloghen van medicis" (battles of the Medicis). As these prints are of similar size to (or are slightly larger than) others that were sold at the same rate (see, for example, *The Annunciation* (PG-6) or *The Acts of the Apostles* (PG-1 and PG-2) above), most likely each leaf bore a single image. Since all of the following examples of sales can be dated to 1580, as can the one reference to Charles V, the eight leaves concerned are most likely the series of eight numbered prints engraved by Philips Galle by 1577 (nos. 361–68). The other subsections of this series are dated 1582 (nos. 369–72) and 1583 (nos. 352–60).

In 1580, several groups of eight leaves, most likely all the first group of eight plates from this series, despite their distinct titles, were sold to Plantin at 18 st. per quire of 25 leaves (= .72 st. per leaf), or simply the total of 5.75 st. per group of eight.[182]
In 1580, Galle also sold Plantin what were presumably the same eight leaves from this series for a slightly higher price of 6 st; this sum reflects a rounding up of the initial price.[183]
The complete series of twenty-one engravings was sold to Jan Moretus I at: 18 st. per quire of 25 leaves in 1608.
= .72 st. per leaf; each print was the equivalent of one leaf, amounting to 15.12 st. per series of twenty-one prints.[184]

PG-56 *The History of the Silkworm (Vermis sericus)*: **Charles de Mallery after Johannes Stradanus.** Six engravings, including a title plate, ca. 200 × 270, 1590–1600?. LIT.: New Holl. Stradanus, nos. 346–51.

Sold to Jan Moretus I at: 6 st. per series in 1608.[185]

PG-57 *The House Built on Sand*: **Hendrick Goltzius.** Engraving, 256 × 186, 1578. LIT.: New Holl. Goltzius, no. 65, part of the series *Allegories of the Christian Creed* (nos. 59–68), but sold individually by Plantin.

Sold to Plantin at: 18 st. per quire of 25 leaves in 1580.[186]
= .72 st. per leaf; each print was the equivalent of one leaf.

PG-58 *The House Built on the Rock*: **Hendrick Goltzius.** Engraving, 259 × 186, 1578. New Holl. Goltzius, no. 64, part of the series *Allegories of the Christian Creed* (nos. 59–68), but sold individually by Plantin.

Sold to Plantin at: 18 st. per quire of 25 leaves in 1580.[187]
= .72 st. per leaf; each print was the equivalent of one leaf.

PG-59 *Hunts (Venationis, piscationis, et aucupii typi)*: **attributed to Adriaen Collaert and anonymous engravers after Hans Bol.** Forty-eight engravings, including a title plate, ca. 80 × 215, 1582. LIT.: New Holl. Bol, nos. 277–324.

Sold to Plantin at: 20 st. in 1585.[188]
Sold to Jan Moretus I at: 20 st. in 1608.[189]

PG-60 *Hunts and Animal Scenes (Venationes ferarum, avium, piscium, pugnae bestiariorum & mutuae bestiarum …)*: **Philips Galle and possibly Anton Wierix II after Johannes Stradanus.** Forty-four engravings, ca. 205/216 × 275/295, 1578–1580 (for the first and second states). LIT.: New Holl. Stradanus, nos. 421–64. See front cover.

Plantin never sold this series in its entirety as it is described in New Holl. Stradanus. Rather, he periodically sold groups of twenty-four leaves with hunts. Because these prints are of similar size to (or are slightly larger than) others that were sold at the same rate (see, for example, *The Annunciation* (PG-6) or *The Acts of the Apostles* (PG-1 and PG-2) above), most likely each leaf bore a single image. Galle also supplied Plantin with smaller sets of images of animals, some containing just eight leaves.[190]
Galle sold Plantin groups of twenty-four leaves of hunts at 18 st. per quire of 25 leaves in 1580 = .72 st. per leaf, amounting to 17.28 st. per group of twenty-four leaves.[191]

Galle also sold groups of twenty-four leaves of hunts at the slightly higher price of 18 st. per group in both 1579 and 1581; this sum reflects a rounding up of the initial price.[192]
Sold to Jan Moretus I at: for 1 fl. (20 st.) in 1594.[193]
Since the number of leaves included was not recorded, it is not possible to determine the number of images included in this sale.

Around 1596–1597, Galle published a new series of thirty-two similarly sized images of hunts after Stradanus, with a new title plate. He subsequently added another twenty-nine plates to the series. The sixty-one engravings were engraved by various artists, including Adriaen Collaert, Jan Collaert II, Charles de Mallery, Theodore Galle, and Cornelis Galle I. Philips Galle also sold these later prints together with his original series of hunts described above or with a group of close copies of his original series; the copies included the same signatures and addresses (presumably because the original plates were becoming too worn to be combined with the newer ones), thus creating an extensive series of 104 images of hunting scenes (prefaced by the ca. 1596 title plate). LIT.: New Holl. Stradanus, nos. 465–562, editions 1 and 2, for the additional prints Galle added to this series around 1596.

Sold to Jan Moretus I at: 4 fl. 10 st. (= 90 st.) in 1608.[194]
The significantly higher price and the identification of the series as the "large" book of hunts suggest that this was the full, expanded series of 104 prints.

PG-61 *Imagines L. doctorum virorum … (Images of Fifty Famous Men)*: **attributed to Philips Galle.** Fifty engravings, ca. 168 × 119, with introductory texts in letterpress, 1587. LIT.: Bowen and Imhof 2008, pp. 412–13; New Holl. Galle, part IV, pp. 27–29, and the portraits listed there. For an overview of this series, see Sellink 1997, vol. II, pp. 228–30. See also PG-123.

Sold to Plantin at: 20 st. (= 1 fl.) per series in 1588.[195]

PG-62 *Imagines L. doctorum virorum … (Images of Fifty Famous Men)*: **Philips Galle (attributed to), Theodoor Galle, and Gijsbert van Veen.** Fifty engravings, ca. 168 × 119, with introductory texts in letterpress, 1595. LIT.: New Holl. Galle, part IV, pp. 27–29, and the portraits listed there. For an overview of this series, see Sellink 1997, vol. II, pp. 228–30. See also PG-123 and TG-20.

Sold to Jan Moretus I in 1597 at: 1 fl. 16 st. (= 36 st.) per series (in two volumes, which most likely included PG-123).[196]

PG-63 *The Immaculate Conception of the Virgin*: **Hieronymus Wierix after Johannes Stradanus.** Engraving, 196 × 134, by 1588. LIT.: New Holl. Stradanus, no. 179.

Sold to Plantin at: .72 or 1 st. per print in 1588.[197]

PG-64 *The Lamentation with Two Angels*: **Adriaen Collaert after Johannes Stradanus.** Engraving, 196 × 140, by 1588. LIT.: New Holl. Stradanus, no. 172.

Sold to Plantin at: .72 or 1 st. per print in 1588.[198]

PG-65 *The Last Supper*: **anonymous engraver after Johannes Stradanus.** Engraving, 236 × 301, by 1594. LIT.: New Holl. Stradanus, no. 111.

Sold to Jan Moretus I at: 2 st. per print in 1594.[199]

PG-66 *The Life of Saint Catherine of Siena (D. Catharinae Senensis … vita ac miracula)*: **Cornelis Galle I after Francesco Vanni.** Thirty-four engravings, including a title plate and portrait ("vera effigies") of St Catherine of Siena, ca. 151 × 91, published in 1603 by Philips Galle and subsequently sold to the Moretuses by Theodore Galle (see TG-9). LIT.: Imhof 2014a, O-55–56; New Holl. Galle, R 12; New Holl. De Jode, part V, nos. 52–63, copy a (p. 87). See fig. 7.12.

Sold to Jan Moretus I at: 1 fl. (= 20 st.) in 1603, 1606, and 1608.[200]

PG-67 *The Life of Saint Francis (D. Seraphici Francisci totius evangelicae perfectionis exemplaris, admiranda historia)*: **anonymous artists.** Eighteen etchings and engravings (ca. 155 × 236), in addition to an engraved frontispiece (166 × 236), with introductory texts in letterpress, 1582 or earlier. LIT.: Bowen and Imhof 2008, pp. 413–14.

Sold to Plantin at: 12 st. per series in 1582 and 1583.[201]
This or a later edition of the same series was sold to Jan Moretus I at:
15 st. in 1601 and 1604;[202]
20 st. per series in 1603; [203] and
18 st. per quire of 25 leaves in 1608
= .72 st. per leaf; each print was the equivalent of one leaf, amounting to 14.4 st. per series of eighteen prints.[204]

PG-68 *The Life of Saint John the Baptist*: **Cornelis Galle I after Johannes Stradanus.** Ten engravings ca. 225 × 285, ca. 1595–1604. LIT.: New Holl. Stradanus, nos. 124–33.

Sold to Jan Moretus I at: 18 st. per quire of 25 leaves in 1608.
= .72 st. per leaf; each print was the equivalent of one leaf, amounting to 7.2 st. per series.[205]

PG-69 *Man's Quest for the Kingdom of Heaven*: **Hendrick Goltzius.** Engraving, 259 × 186, 1578. LIT.: New Holl. Goltzius, no. 62, part of the series *Allegories of the Christian Creed* (nos. 59–68), but sold individually by Plantin. See fig. 3.13.

Sold to Plantin at: 18 st. per quire of 25 leaves in 1580.[206]
= .72 st. per leaf; each print was the equivalent of one leaf.

PG-70 *The Martyrdom of Saint Barbara*: **Jan Wierix after Johannes Stradanus.** Engraving, 240 × 176, by 1588. LIT: New Holl. Stradanus, no. 232.

Sold to Plantin at: .72 or 1 st. per print in 1588.[207]

PG-71 *The Martyrdom of Saint Lawrence*: **Adriaen Collaert after Johannes Stradanus.** Engraving, 202 × 140, by 1588. LIT: New Holl. Stradanus, no. 246.

Sold to Plantin at: .72 or 1 st. per print in 1588.[208]

PG-72 *The Martyrdom of Saint Lucy*: **Jan Wierix after Johannes Stradanus.** Engraving, 243 × 182, by 1588. LIT: New Holl. Stradanus, no. 247.

Sold to Plantin at: .72 or 1 st. per print in 1588.[209]

PG-73 *Misericordia Dei (Mercy of God)*: **Hendrick Goltzius.** Engraving, 254 × 184, ca. 1577. LIT.: New Holl. Goltzius, no. 72.

Sold to Plantin at: 18 st. per quire of 25 leaves in 1580.[210]
= .72 st. per leaf; each print was the equivalent of one leaf.

PG-74 *Monkey Antics*: **Peeter van der Borcht.** Sixteen etchings of varying dimensions, ca. 204/225 × 288/294, s.a. LIT.: New Holl. Van der Borcht, nos. 183–99.

Sold to Jan Moretus I at: 18 st. per quire of 25 leaves in 1608.
= .72 st. per leaf; each print was the equivalent of one leaf, amounting to 11.52 st. per series.[211]

PG-75 *Mysteries of the Childhood of Christ*, on five leaves (not yet linked to a known series), completed by October 1579.

Sold to Plantin at: 18.25 st. per quire of 25 leaves in 1579.[212]
= .73 st. per leaf; each print was the equivalent of one leaf, amounting to 3.65 st. per series.
Sold to Plantin at: 18 st. per quire of 25 leaves in 1580.[213]
= .72 st. per leaf; each print was the equivalent of one leaf, amounting to 3.6 st. per series.
Possibly subsequently sold to Plantin at: 3 st. per series in 1585.[214]

PG-76 *(Fifteen?) Mysteries of the Virgin (or Rosary): The Joyful, Sorrowful, and Triumphant*, each group of mysteries within circles on one leaf, creating a series with three leaves.

Although this is not yet linked to a known series, it may be related to (or the same as) the group of three plates representing the Virgin nursing her baby, the Pietà, and the Virgin within a rosary in a rose bush. In the latter group, each plate has five circular scenes by an anonymous artist; the plates are cited in New Holl. Stradanus, under no. 180, copy b, of the engraving: *The Fifteen Mysteries of the Rosary*, by an anonymous engraver after Johannes Stradanus and published by Philips Galle in 1577.[215] LIT.: New Holl. Stradanus, no. 180b. A similar group of three plates was listed in the inventory of Theodore Galle's widow, Catharina Moerentorf as: "de vijftien misterien in drij platen".[216]

Sold to Plantin at: 18 st. per quire of 25 leaves in 1580.[217]
= .72 st. per leaf; each print was the equivalent of one leaf, amounting to 2.16 st per series.
Sold to Jan Moretus I at: 2.25 st. per series of three prints in 1592.[218]

PG-77 *The Nativity, Crucifixion, and Resurrection*: **anonymous artists.** Engraving, 190 × 298, 1578. See The British Museum, no. 1937,0915.154.

Sold to Plantin at: 18 st. per quire of 25 leaves in 1580.[219]
= .72 st. per leaf; each print was the equivalent of one leaf.

PG-78 *Nova reperta (New Inventions of Modern Times)*: **Jan Collaert II, Theodore Galle, and anonymous engravers after Johannes Stradanus.** Twenty engravings, including a title plate, ca. 203 × 270, ca. 1591. New Holl. Stradanus, nos. 322–41.

Sold to Jan Moretus I at: 20 st. in 1608.[220]

PG-79 *Old Testament Prophets (Icones prophetarum maiorum et minorum)*: **Jan Collaert II, Charles de Mallery, Petrus Perret, and an anonymous engraver after Nicolaes de Hoey.** Seventeen engravings, ca. 150 × 89, 1594. LIT.: New Holl. Collaert, part I, p. 100.

Sold to Jan Moretus I at: 9 st. per series in 1594.[221]

PG-80 *Our Father (Pater noster)*: **Jan Wierix after Maarten van Heemskerck.** Eight engravings, ca. 204 × 248, ca. 1571. LIT.: Holl. Dutch & Flemish, vol. LXIII, nos. 1037–44.

Sold to Plantin at: 6 st. per series in 1582.[222]
Possibly sold to Jan Moretus I at: 18 st. per quire of 25 leaves in 1608.
= .72 st. per leaf; each print was the equivalent of one leaf, amounting to 5.76 st. per series.[223]

PG-81 *The Passion of Christ* **in 21 leaves** (not yet linked to a known series).

Sold to Jan Moretus I at: 18 st. per quire of 25 leaves in 1608.
= .72 st. per leaf; each print was the equivalent of one leaf, amounting to 15.12 st. per series.[224]

PG-82 *The Passion, Death, and Resurrection of Christ (Passio, mors, et resurrectio dn. nostri Iesu Christi)*: **Philips Galle, Adriaen Collaert, Jan Collaert II, and possibly others, after Johannes Stradanus.** Forty-one engravings, including a title plate, dedication, and portrait of Johannes Stradanus by Jan Wierix, ca. 193 × 262, 1580–1586. LIT.: New Holl. Stradanus, nos. 48–88; Baroni-Sellink 2012, pp. 137–145 and nos. 55–80. See figs. 3.8 and 6.3.

Sold to Plantin at: 36 st. (= 1 fl. 16 st.) per series several times between 1585 and 1588.[225]
Sold to Jan Moretus I at: 36 st. (= 1 fl. 16 st.) per series in 1594 and 1608.[226]
Sold to Jan Moretus I at: 40 st. (= 2 fl.) per series in 1603.[227]

PG-83 *Portraits of Popes (Pontificum maximorum XXVII effigies)*: **Philips Galle after Philippe Soye.** Twenty-nine engravings (ca. 161/181 × 118/121) and an engraved title plate (ca. 176 × 127), with introductory texts in letterpress, 1572. Galle and Gerard de Jode published this work jointly, and both sold copies to Plantin at the same price (see GJ-28). LIT.: BT 1214; New Holl. Galle, nos. 692–719; New Holl. De Jode, part III, nos. 681–710 and part I, p. lix.

Sold to Plantin at: 12 st. per series in 1572 and 1573.[228]
Sold to Jan Moretus I at: 16 st. per series in 1595.[229]

PG-84 *The Power of Women (Famous Women)*: **Philips Galle.** Six engravings, ca. 239 diameter, ca. 1569. LIT.: New Holl. Galle, nos. 125–30.

Sold to Jan Moretus I at: 3 st. per series in 1608.[230]

PG-85 *The Relief of Suffering*: **Hendrick Goltzius.** Engraving, 247 × 186, 1578. LIT.: New Holl. Goltzius, no. 59, part of the series *Allegories of the Christian Creed* (nos. 59–68), but sold individually by Plantin.

Sold to Plantin at: 18 st. per quire of 25 leaves in 1580.[231]
= .72 st. per leaf; each print was the equivalent of one leaf.

PG-86 ***The Resurrection of Christ*****: Hendrick Goltzius after Anthonie Blocklandt van Montfoort.** Engraving, 262 × 200, 1577–1578. LIT.: New Holl. Goltzius, no. 313.

Sold to Plantin at: 18 st. per quire of 25 leaves in 1580.[232]
= .72 st. per leaf; each print was the equivalent of one leaf.

PG-87 ***Roman Emperors on Horseback (Imperatorum XII. a Suetonio descriptorum effigies resque gestae …)*****: Adriaen Collaert after Johannes Stradanus.** Thirteen engravings, including a title plate, ca. 328 × 227, ca. 1587–1589. LIT.: New Holl. Stradanus, nos. 308–20.

Sold to Jan Moretus I at: 26 st. in 1594.[233]
Possibly sold to Jan Moretus I at: 28 st. per series in 1595.[234]

PG-88 ***Ruins***: a series with eleven leaves completed by 1571 (not yet linked to a known series). Given the dating, this series must be distinct from Adriaen Collaert's ten engravings after Hendrick van Cleve III of *Landscapes with Ruins (Regionum, rurium, fundorumque, varii at ove amoeni prospectus)*, dated 1587 (see New Holl. Collaert, nos. 1265–74).

Sold to Plantin at: 9 st. per series in 1571, 1573, and possibly 1581.[235]

PG-89 ***Ruins (Ruinarum varii prospectus, ruriumq. aliquot delineationes)*****: anonymous artists after Hendrik van Cleve.** Thirty-eight engravings, ca. 175 × 245, by 1608. LIT.: New Holl. Galle, no. R 18.

Sold to Jan Moretus I at: 18 st. per quire of 25 leaves in 1608.
= .72 st. per leaf; each print was the equivalent of one leaf, amounting to 27.36 st. (= 1 fl. 7.36 st.) per series of 38 prints.[236]

PG-90 ***Saint Catherine*****: Theodore Galle after Johannes Stradanus.** Engraving 248 × 187, by 1590. LIT.: New Holl. Stradanus, no. 234.

Possibly sold to Jan Moretus I at: 1 st. per print in 1590.[237]

PG-91 ***The Sea Gods and Goddesses***: most likely the following two series: *Sea and River Gods* (*Semideorum marinorum …*) and *Nymphs of the Ocean* (*Nimpharum oceanitidum …*), Philips Galle, two series of engravings, each comprising eighteen plates, including individual title plates, ca. 164 × 100, 1587. Jan Galle published the two series jointly, with the images intermingled. LIT.: New Holl. Galle, nos. 412–29 and 430–47.

Sold to Jan Moretus I at: 7 st. for the two series together in 1594.[238]

PG-92 ***The Seven Christian Virtues and Seven Deadly Sins (Vices)*****: Hieronymus Wierix after Johannes Stradanus and Philips Galle, respectively.** Two companion series of eight engravings each, ca. 186 × 133, by 1594. LIT.: Holl. Dutch & Flemish, vol. LXVI, nos. 1677–84 (the *Virtues*, after Stradanus) and 1758–65 (the *Vices* after Galle).

Sold to Jan Moretus I at: 8 st. for the two series together in 1594.[239]

PG-93 ***The Seven Churches of Rome (Septem urbis ecclesiae primariae …)*****: attributed to Adriaen Collaert and Jan Collaert II.** Seven engravings of varying dimensions (ca. 285/297 × 192/205) and a title plate (291 × 208), ca. 1598. LIT.: New Holl. Collaert, nos. 1221–28. See fig. 8.13.

Sold to Jan Moretus I at: 18 st. per quire of 25 leaves in 1608.
= .72 st. per leaf; each print was the equivalent of one leaf, amounting to 5.76 st. per series.[240]

PG-94 ***Seven Effusions of Christ's Blood*****, in circles on one leaf, completed by 1580 (not yet linked to a known print).[241]**

Sold to Plantin at: 18 st. per quire of 25 leaves in 1580.[242]
= .72 st. per leaf; each print was the equivalent of one leaf.

PG-95 ***Seven Joys of the Virgin*****, in circles on one leaf, completed by 1580 (not yet linked to a known print.[243]**

Sold to Plantin at: 18 st. per quire of 25 leaves in 1580.[244]
= .72 st. per leaf; each print was the equivalent of one leaf.

PG-96 ***The Seven Planets***:
• **Philips Galle after Jacques Jonghelinck,** ***Statues of Bacchus and the Seven Planets.*** Eight engravings, ca. 248 × 162, 1585. LIT.: New Holl. Galle, nos. 404–11.
or:
• **Jan Collaert II after Stradanus.** Eight engravings, ca. 197 × 137, 1587 or later. LIT.: New Holl. Stradanus, nos. 390–97.

It is possible that either of the above series was sold to Jan Moretus I in 1594 and 1608. The significantly different price noted in the two sales below may reflect one series being sold in one year and the other in the other year.
Sold to Jan Moretus I at: 8 st. per series in 1594.[245]
Sold to Jan Moretus I at: 18 st. per quire of 25 leaves in 1608.
= .72 st. per leaf; each print was the equivalent of one leaf, amounting to 5.76 st. per series.[246]

PG-97 ***The Seven Sacraments*****: Philips Galle.**
Eight engravings, ca. 256 × 190, 1576. LIT.: New Holl. Galle, nos. 265–72.
Usually sold to Plantin at: 6 st. per series in 1576–1578.[247]

Sold to Plantin at: 18 st. per quire of 25 leaves in 1580.
= .72 st. per leaf; each print was the equivalent of one leaf, amounting to 5.76 st. per series.[248]

PG-98 ***Seven Sorrows of the Virgin***, in circles on one leaf, completed prior to February 1580 (not yet linked to a known print).

Sold to Plantin at: 18 st. per quire of 25 leaves in 1580.[249]
= .72 st. per leaf; each print was the equivalent of one leaf.

PG-99 *The Seven Spiritual Acts of Mercy*: **Philips Galle.** Eight engravings, ca. 259 × 190, 1577. LIT.: New Holl. Galle, nos. 249–56. See fig. 3.14.

Usually sold to Plantin at: 6 st. per series from 1577 through 1583. Galle also offered this series at slightly reduced rates for those buying in bulk.[250] Specifically, in 1577 and 1580, he sold this series to Plantin in bulk at 18 st. per quire of 25 leaves (= .72 st. per leaf; each print was the equivalent of one leaf, amounting to 5.76 st. per series.).[251]

PG-100 *The Seven Spiritual Acts of Mercy with Christ as Salvator Mundi.* Most likely an anonymous engraving, 247 × 186, by 1580. It would have been paired with PG-102, *The Seven Worldly Acts of Mercy with the Last Judgement*, on one leaf. These two prints are bound adjacent to one another, along with other similar works published by Philips Galle, in: Fürstlich zu Waldburg-Wolfegg'sche Kunstsammlungen at Wolfegg, vol. 211, print numbers 36 and 37, respectively.

Sold to Plantin at: 18 st. per quire of 25 leaves in 1580.[252]
= .72 st. per leaf; each print was the equivalent of one leaf.

PG-101 *The Seven Worldly Acts of Mercy*: **Philips Galle.** Eight engravings, ca. 253 × 190, 1577. LIT.: New Holl. Galle, nos. 257–64.

Usually sold to Plantin at: 6 st. per series from 1577 through 1583. Galle also offered this series at slightly reduced rates for those buying in bulk.[253] Specifically, in 1577 and 1580, he sold this series to Plantin in bulk at 18 st. per quire of 25 leaves (= .72 st. per leaf; each print was the equivalent of one leaf, amounting to 5.76 st. per series.).[254]

PG-102 *The Seven Worldly Acts of Mercy with the Last Judgment*: anonymous engraving that includes a copy after a Hendrick Goltzius engraving of the *Last Judgment*, 255 × 190, by 1580. It would have been paired with PG-100, the *Seven Spiritual Acts of Mercy with Christ as Salvator Mundi*, on one leaf. LIT.: New Holl. Goltzius, part I, p. 165, no. 111 (impressions in the collection of The Metropolitan Museum of Art, New York, no. 53.601.14, and Wolfegg, Fürstlich zu Waldburg-Wolfegg'sche Kunstsammlungen, vol. 211, print number 37); Sellink 1997, vol. III, fig. 58 to Chapter 4.

Sold to Plantin at: 18 st. per quire of 25 leaves in 1580.[255]
= .72 st. per leaf; each print was the equivalent of one leaf.

PG-103 *Six Hermits*: **completed prior to May 1594 (not yet linked to a known print).**

Sold to Jan Moretus I at: 3 st. per series in 1594.[256]

PG-104 *Small Wells*: **Joannes and Lucas van Doetecum after Hans Vredeman de Vries.** Twenty-four etchings, ca. 203 × 145, ca. 1574. LIT.: New Holl. Van Doetecum, nos. 703–26.

Plantin resold this in 1582 at: 28 st. (= 1 fl. 8 st.) per series (the price Plantin paid for it is not known).[257]
Possibly sold to Jan Moretus I in 1594, with two images printed per leaf. The selling price was not recorded.[258]

PG-105 *The Solicitude of the Lord*: **Hendrick Goltzius.** Engraving, 255 × 181, 1578. LIT.: New Holl. Goltzius, no. 63, part of the series *Allegories of the Christian Creed* (nos. 59–68), but sold individually by Plantin.

Sold to Plantin at: 18 st. per quire of 25 leaves in 1580.[259]
= .72 st. per leaf; each print was the equivalent of one leaf.

PG-106 *The Stable of Don Juan of Austria* (*Equile Ioannis Austriaci …*): **Adriaen Collaert, Hendrick Goltzius, Hieronymus Wierix, and possibly Hans Collaert I after Johannes Stradanus.** Forty engravings, in four groups, ca. 200 × 261, ca. 1580–1585. The first group contains the title plate and fifteen images engraved largely by Hieronymus Wierix, while each of the subsequent groups has eight images apiece, most of which were engraved by Hendrick Goltzius and possibly Hans Collaert I. LIT.: New Holl. Stradanus, nos. 527–66, which also lists two sets of copies of a selection of these images (reduced and in reverse) that were similarly published by Philips Galle; one set consisted of a title and twelve plates, and the other had just eight numbered plates. Despite the subdivisions of these plates in New Holl. Stradanus, mentions of Philips Galle's supply of series of images of horses consistently state that the series comprised either seventeen or eight images. There is similarly a reference to a series of horses with seventeen plates in the estate inventory of Theodore Galle's widow, Catharina Moerentorf.[260] See fig. 1.2.

Galle sold Plantin a group of seventeen leaves with images of horses that may have been part of this series at: 17 st. (or 1 st. per image) in 1588.[261]
Galle sold Jan Moretus I a "small" series of prints with horses at: 5 st. per series in 1594.[262]
Galle also sold Jan Moretus I a "large" series of prints with horses at: 17 st. per series in 1594.[263]
Galle sold Jan Moretus I two sets of seventeen prints of horses at: 18 st. per quire of 25 leaves in 1608.
= .72 st. per leaf; each print was the equivalent of one leaf, amounting to 12.24 st. per series of seventeen prints.[264]

PG-107 *The Story of Adam and Eve*: **Crispijn de Passe I after Maarten de Vos.** Six engravings, ca. 94 diameter on rectangular plates (ca. 101 × 94), 1580–1600. LIT.: Holl. Dutch & Flemish, vol. XLIV, nos. 19–24.

Sold to Jan Moretus I at: 3 st. per series in 1608.[265]

PG-108 *The Story of Adonis*: **Philips Galle after Anthonie Blocklandt van Montfoort.** Four engravings, ca. 220 × 305, ca. 1579. LIT.: New Holl. Galle, nos. 400–03.

Sold to Plantin at: 18 st. per quire of 25 leaves in 1580.[266]
= .72 st. per leaf; each print was the equivalent of one leaf, amounting to 2.88 st. per series.

PG-109 ***The Story of Esther and Xerxes*: Philips Galle after Maarten van Heemskerck.** Eight engravings, ca. 205 × 248, 1564. LIT.: New Holl. Galle, nos. 49–56.

Sold to Plantin at: 6 st. per series in 1575.[267]
Sold to Jan Moretus I at: 18 st. per quire of 25 leaves in 1608.
= .72 st. per leaf; each print was the equivalent of one leaf, amounting to 5.76 st. per series of eight prints.[268]

PG-110 ***The Story of Judith and Holofernes*: Philips Galle after Maarten van Heemskerck.** Eight engravings, ca. 204 × 248, 1564. LIT.: New Holl. Galle, nos. 79–86. See fig. 3.11.

Sold to Plantin at: 18 st. per quire of 25 leaves in 1580.[269]
= .72 st. per leaf; each print was the equivalent of one leaf, amounting to 5.76 st. per series.

PG-111 ***The Story of Lucretia*: Hendrick Goltzius.** Four engravings, ca. 210 × 248, 1578–1579. LIT.: New Holl. Goltzius, nos. 159–62.

Sold to Plantin at: 18 st. per quire of 25 leaves in 1580.[270]
= .72 st. per leaf; each print was the equivalent of one leaf, amounting to 2.88 st. per series.

PG-112 ***The Story of Mars and Venus*: Jan Collaert II after Philips Galle.** Four engravings, ca. 186 × 229, by 1608. LIT.: New Holl. Collaert, nos. 1164–67.

Sold to Jan Moretus I at: 18 st. per quire of 25 leaves in 1608.
= .72 st . per leaf; each print was the equivalent of one leaf, amounting to 2.88 st. per series of four prints.[271]

PG-113 ***Story of Susanna* in six leaves: possibly Philips Galle after Maarten van Heemskerck.** Six engravings, ca. 205 × 246/251, originally published by Hieronymus Cock in 1563 and possibly reissued by Galle by 1608. Carel Collaert subsequently published this series. LIT.: New Holl. Galle, nos. 87–92.

Sold to Jan Moretus I at: 18 st. per quire of 25 leaves in 1608.
= .72 st. per leaf; each print was the equivalent of one leaf, amounting to 4.32 st. per series of six prints.[272]

PG-114 ***The Story of the Miller, His Son, and the Donkey* (*Animae incuria ob nimiam corporis curam*): anonymous artists.** Four engravings, ca. 224 × 154 (based on an edition of this series published by Jan Galle and preserved in the Rijksmuseum, Amsterdam: RP-P-1938–1499-RP-P-1938–1502), by 1576. LIT.: Luijten 1996, pp. 158–60.

Sold to Plantin at: 18 st. per quire of 25 leaves in 1576.[273]
= .72 st. per leaf; each print was the equivalent of one leaf, amounting to 2.88 st. per series.

PG-115 ***The Story of the Miller, His Son, and the Donkey*: Charles de Mallery after Ambrosius Francken.** Six engravings, including a title plate, ca. 195 × 247, by 1608. LIT.: Holl. Dutch & Flemish, vol. VII, p. 8, nos. 6–11. For a complete set of the series as published by Philips Galle, see the Rijksmuseum, Amsterdam, nos. RP-P-1969–124–29.

Sold to Jan Moretus I at: 18 st. per quire of 25 leaves in 1608.
= .72 st. per leaf; each print was the equivalent of one leaf, amounting to 4.32 st. per series of six prints.[274]

PG-116 ***The Ten Commandments* (*Decalogus cum acerbissimis praevaricatorum poenis*): Adriaen Collaert, Jan Collaert II, Theodore Galle, and Crispijn de Passe I after Maarten de Vos.** Eleven engravings, including a title plate, ca. 200 × 244, ca. 1587. LIT.: See Holl. Dutch & Flemish, vol. XLIV, nos. 72–82, for the entire series; New Holl. Collaert, nos. 30–38, and. New Holl. Galle, R-3 for subsequent references to it. See fig. 5.4.

Sold to Plantin at: 10 st. per series in 1588.[275]
Sold to Jan Moretus I at: 10 st. per series in 1594.[276]
Sold to Jan Moretus I at: 18 st. per quire of 25 leaves in 1608.
= .72 st. per leaf; each print was the equivalent of one leaf, amounting to 7.92 st. per series.[277]

PG-117 ***The Triumphs of Petrarch*: Philips Galle after Maarten van Heemskerck.** Six engravings, ca. 194 × 263, ca. 1565. LIT.: New Holl. Galle, nos. 293–98.

Sold to Plantin at: 18 st. per quire of 25 leaves in 1580.[278]
= .72 st. per leaf; each print was the equivalent of one leaf, amounting to 4.32 st. per series.
This same series appears to have been sold much earlier, in November 1567; the Florentine branch of the Giunti booksellers offered it to Vincenzio Borghini for the more significant sum of 4 lire.[279]

PG-118 ***Twelve Articles of Faith (The Apostles' Creed)*, on one leaf, completed prior to October 1579 (not yet linked to a known print).**

Sold to Plantin at: 18.25 st. per quire of 25 leaves in 1579; and at 18 st. per quire of 25 leaves in 1580.[280]
= .73 and .72 st. per leaf, respectively; each print was the equivalent of one leaf.

PG-119 ***The Twelve Months* (*Menses* XII. *anni solaris*): Adriaen Collaert and Jan Collaert II after Joos de Momper.** Thirteen engravings, including a title plate, 206 × 260, ca. 1600–1608. LIT.: New Holl. Collaert, nos. 1350–62.

Sold to Jan Moretus I at: 18 st. per quire of 25 leaves in 1608.
= .72 st. per leaf; each print was the equivalent of one leaf, amounting to 9.36 st. per series.[281]

PG-120 ***Virgil*: by 1596 (not yet linked to a known series).**

Sold to Jan Moretus I at: 3 fl. (= 60 st.) in 1596.[282]

PG-121 *Virgin and Child, Crowned by Two Angels (Nuestra Señora de l'Antigua)*: **Hieronymus Wierix.** Engraving, 237 × 172, by 1588. LIT.: Holl. Dutch & Flemish, vol. LXIII, no. 1004.

Sold to Plantin at: .72 or 1 st. per print in 1588.[283]

PG-122 *Virorum doctorum … effigies XLIIII (Forty-four Portraits of Learned Men)*: **Philips Galle.** Forty-four engravings, ca. 176 × 122, with introductory texts in letterpress, 1572. LIT.: Bowen and Imhof 2008, pp. 258–61 and 410–11; New Holl. Galle, part IV, pp. 25–27, and the portraits listed there.

Sold to Plantin at: 16 st. per series numerous times between 1572 and 1585.[284]

PG-123 *Virorum doctorum … effigies XLIIII (Forty-four Portraits of Learned Men)*: **Philips Galle.** Forty-four engravings, ca. 176 × 122, with introductory texts in letterpress, 1586. LIT.: Bowen and Imhof 2008, pp. 410–11; New Holl. Galle, part IV, pp. 25–27, and the portraits listed there. See also PG-61, PG-62, TG-20, and fig. 3.5.

Sold to Plantin at: 16 st. per series in 1586; and at 18 st. per series in 1588, 1599 and 1600.[285]

PG-124 *The War against the Turks*: **Adriaen Collaert after Johannes Stradanus.** A pair of engravings: *The Naval Battle against the Turks at Lepanto*, 240 × 316, and *The Siege of Vienna by the Turks*, 232 × 309, 1590. LIT.: New Holl. Stradanus, nos. 375–76. See fig. 5.13.

Sold to Jan Moretus I at: 1 ½ st. per set of two engravings in 1594.[286]

Unspecified prints sold in bulk

See also the Note to the Reader and Chapter 2.

- per *single image*: sold to Jan Moretus I at 4 st. per image in 1601.[287]
- per *single image*: sold to Jan Moretus I at 2 st. per image in 1596.[288]
- per *single image*: sold to Jan Moretus I at 1 st. per image in 1596.[289]
- per *single image*: sold to Jan Moretus I at .75 st. (= 1 "blanc") per image in 1596.[290]
- per *single image*: sold to Jan Moretus I at .5 st. per image in 1596.[291]
- per *single image*: sold to Jan Moretus I at .375 st. per image in 1601.[292]
- per *single image*: sold to Plantin I at .25 st. per image in 1587.[293]
- per *single leaf with 5 small images*: sold to Plantin at 4.5 st. per leaf in 1578.[294]
- per *double "royal" or "reali" or "grande" leaves*: sold to Plantin at 1.75 st. per leaf in 1580 and 1581.[295]
- per *single leaf*: sold to Jan Moretus I at 1.25 st. per leaf in 1592.[296]
- per *single leaf*: sold to Plantin and Jan Moretus I at 1 st. per leaf in 1587, 1588, 1592, and 1608.[297]
- per *single leaf*: sold to Plantin and Jan Moretus I at .75 st. (= 1 "blanc") per leaf in 1579, 1588, and 1592.[298]
- per *quire* of 25 leaves: sold to Plantin at: 20 st. per quire (= .8 st. per leaf) in 1579.[299]
- per *quire* of 25 leaves of *colored* prints: sold to Plantin at 19.5 st. per quire (= .78 st. per leaf) in 1586.[300]
- per *quire* of 25 leaves: sold to Plantin at: 19 st. per quire (= .76 st. per leaf) in 1578.[301]
- per *quire* of 25 leaves: sold to Plantin at: 18.25 st. per quire (= .73 st. per leaf) in 1579.[302]
- per *quire* of 25 leaves: sold to Plantin and Jan Moretus I at: 18 st. per quire (= .72 st. per leaf) between 1571 and 1608, with the majority of such sales occurring between 1580 and 1594.[303]
- per *100 leaves*: sold to Plantin at 3 fl. 12 st. (= 72 st.) per hundred (= .72 st. per leaf) in 1585.[304]
- per *100 leaves*: sold to Plantin at 32 st. per hundred (= .32 st. per leaf) in 1580.[305]
- per *100 images*: sold to Jan Moretus I at 30 st. per hundred (= .33 st. per image) in 1592.[306]

THEODORE GALLE Antwerp 1571–1633 Antwerp
CATHARINA MOERENTORF Antwerp 1580–1636 Antwerp

Born in 1571, Theodore Galle was the eldest son of the successful engraver and print publisher Philips Galle. Trained by his father, Theodore was contributing engravings to print series Philips published by the early 1590s, including such projects as *The Ten Commandments* after Maarten de Vos (PG-116). and Galle's renowned *Nova reperta (New Inventions of Modern Times)* after Johannes Stradanus (PG-78). Like many Netherlandish artists of his generation, Theodore also traveled to Rome to complement his schooling at home. Known to have visited the Catacombs of Domitilla in 1594 (where he, like many others, cut his name into the walls), he must have left soon thereafter, for he was registered as a master's son in Antwerp's Guild of St Luke in the guild year 1595–1596.[307] After his return to Antwerp, Theodore continued to assist his father with his publications, for instance Philips Galle's series entitled XII *Cardinalium pietate doctrina … imagines et elogia*, from 1598.[308] However, soon after his marriage to Catharina Moerentorf, Jan Moretus I's daughter, in that same year, Theodore began his own print workshop, which, as of 1600, supported not only the publication of his own engravings, but also the production and printing of numerous engraved book illustrations for his father-in-law. The need for assistance with the ever-increasing workload may be reflected in the timing of Galle's registration of apprentices (in 1600, 1613, 1616–1617, 1619–1620, and 1620–1621). His brother Cornelis I is also regularly noted as one of the engravers who assisted him with the new engravings that the Moretuses requested for their book illustrations between 1625 and Theodore's death in 1633.[309] Despite these demands, Theodore simultaneously maintained his activities as an independent print publisher; his appointment as co-dean and dean of the Guild of St Luke between 1609 and 1611 attests to his professional recognition.[310] Galle's publications were notably diverse. His own engravings, most of which date to the 1600s and 1610s, range in subject matter from portraits of Greek and Roman figures to images of saints and complex religious allegories composed in collaboration with the Jesuit Joannes David.[311] Alongside this work, Galle published both large-scale religious subjects, several of which were dedicated to prominent local figures, and numerous smaller, common devotional images by anonymous engravers.[312] Galle also republished several series created by his brother-in-law, Adriaen Collaert. In addition, he reissued various plates that he had acquired from prominent sixteenth-century Antwerp print publishers – Volcxken Diericx, Gerard de Jode, Hans Liefrinck I, and above all, his father Philips.[313] Consequently, his stock, which comprised a minimum of 3,260 plates when it was inventoried in 1636 following the death of his wife, Catharina, boasted a great variety of subjects in a broad range of formats; this variety and breadth are also revealed in the works Galle sold via the Moretuses. Designs by Maarten van Heemskerck, Maarten de Vos, Stradanus, and Philips Galle are particularly well represented in the Moretuses' records related to Theodore, largely due to the selection of plates that he acquired from others. Various printmakers, most of whom were active in Antwerp during the later sixteenth and early seventeenth centuries, likewise appear frequently. Galle appears to have been particularly interested in acquiring plates that Anton II and, above all, Hieronymus Wierix had made for other publishers, such as Liefrinck and Vrients, in addition to some of their work for Philips Galle (e.g., PG26–28, PG-60, and PG-106). Theodore's appreciation of the immense popularity of the Wierixes' engravings is similarly evident from the numerous copies of their work that he commissioned and published himself.[314] Although it is impossible to determine the extent to which Galle's mix of activities generated personal and financial success, the settlement of his wife's estate in 1636, more than three years after Galle's death, contained a careful record of what remained in his former workshop. Aside from those vying to inherit this property – his son, Jan Galle, and his son-in-law, the printer and book publisher Martinus Nutius III (the husband of Jan's sister Catharina Galle) – the estate settlement was witnessed by Balthasar Moretus I, Cornelis Galle I, Jan Baptist Barbé, and Peter Baquereel, a one-time pupil of Philips Galle.[315] Of these, the last three were jointly responsible for compiling a list of copper plates. According to the agreement that was created, Jan Galle had to pay Nutius 3,600 fl. in order to retain the copper plates (of which there were more than 4,000), an unspecified number of printing presses, and all other related materials, as well as an additional 600 fl. for the printed images that numbered more than 2,000 and that were found in the workshop.[316] For the sum paid for the copper plates alone, Balthasar Moretus I could have purchased some eight-two newly engraved plates from Cornelis Galle, measuring ca. 194 × 135 mm each.[317] Such an investment in Theodore's stock of mostly old and used plates, in addition to the related materials needed to continue to print impressions of them, suited Jan's needs, as he, like Theodore before him, chose to realign the activities of the print workshop inherited from his father.

LIT.: Bowen 2004, pp. 73–81; Bowen 2009, pp. 127–34; Denucé 1927; Duverger 1984–2009, vol. IV, no. 893, pp. 18–24.

Identifiable prints sold by title

TG-1 *Ave Maris Stella* (*Hail Star of the Sea*): **anonymous artist after Peeter vander Borcht.** Seven engravings, ca. 132 × 79, published by Theodore Galle by 1608. For a copy of this series, see, e.g., Herzog August Bibliothek, Graph. A1:784q-v, which is reproduced, at least in part, on www.virtuelles-kupferstichkabinett.de. See fig. 5.8.

Sold to Jan Moretus I at: 4 st. per series in 1608.[318]

TG-2 *Caesar Baronius* **(portrait in folio), by 1605.** This anonymous engraving (attributed to Philips Galle's workshop by Manfred Sellinck) is most likely the folio portrait of Baronius that was in the possession of Theodore Galle in 1603, when Jan Moretus I was permitted to borrow the plate and print impressions of it for the tenth volume of Baronius's *Annales ecclesiastici*, which Moretus published that year. In that case, the present work would measure 320 × 190. LIT.: Imhof 2014a, B-11.

Sold to Jan Moretus I at: 1 st. per print in 1605.[319]

TG-3 ***The Cycle of the Vicissitudes of Human Affairs*: Cornelis Cort after Maarten van Heemskerck.** Nine engravings, ca. 224 × 297, originally published by Hieronymus Cock in 1564 and reissued by Theodore Galle by 1608. LIT.: New Holl. Heemskerck, nos. 482–90.

Sold to Jan Moretus I at: 18 st. per quire of 25 leaves in 1608. = .72 st. per leaf; each print was the equivalent of one leaf, amounting to 6.48 st. per series of nine prints.[320]

TG-4 *Divine Love (Typus amoris)*: two leaves per series, 1605. These images were designed to accompany a text composed by Henricus Sommalius, identified as "Divini amoris typus" in Jan Moretus I's records. This was most likely a broadside in which images were combined with some text in letterpress. Moretus charged Galle 6 fl. on 28 February 1605 for printing 1,000 copies of this text. LIT.: Imhof 2014a, no. G-15.

Sold to Jan Moretus I at: 4 st. per series (= 2 st. per leaf) in 1608.[321]

TG-5 ***The Goose Game*: anonymous artists, in folio, by 1632.** LIT.: Leesberg 2015.

Sold to Balthasar Moretus I at: 1.5 st. in 1632.[322]

TG-6 ***Holy Founders of Religious Orders… (Sancti fundatores religiosorum ordinum …)*: Cornelis Galle.** Forty engravings (ca. 150 × 104) and a title plate (165 × 107), 1630. LIT.: New Holl. De Jode, part VII, no. 606; Fuhring 2017, pp. 248–49.

This series was based on a group of paintings that hung in the choir of the Abbey of Liessies when Anton van Winghe was abbot there. In 1634, the Jesuit Estienne Binet composed a commentary to accompany these images; his text was published in Antwerp by Martinus Nutius III under the title *Abregé des vies des principaux fondateurs des religions des l'eglise* …. See fig. 7.2.

Sold to Balthasar Moretus I at: 2 fl. (= 40 st.) per series in 1630, 1631, and 1635.[323]

In an undated letter concerning the shipment of six presentation copies of Galle's publication to an unspecified recipient, Abbot Anton van Winghe remarked that he was not sending many copies because Galle (either Theodore or Jan) was selling them at 3 fl. per unbound copy (the equivalent of 1.5 sol per image). Van Winghe observed that this price seemed expensive to him, but that the series appeared to be selling well anyway.[324]

TG-7 ***Illustrium imagines ex antiquis marmoribus (Portraits of Famous Individuals from Ancient Sculptures)*: Theodore Galle.** An engraved title plate (163 × 105) and 151 engravings (ca. 140 × 100) of Greek and Roman figures, after sketches Galle made in Rome from antique busts, gems, and coins in the collection of Fulvius Ursinus, with dedication and index in letterpress, 1598.

The sale of the 1606 edition of this work is not included here because, alongside the addition of eighteen images, the prints were paired with an extensive commentary by Joannes Faber; the publication thus became more akin to an illustrated book than a print series. LIT.: Imhof 2014a: no. G-13.[325] See figs. 5.5 and 5.6.

Sold to Jan Moretus I at: 3 fl. (60 st.). per series from 1598 through 1605.[326]

TG-8 ***The Life and Miracles of Saint Dominic (Vita et miracula S.P. Dominici …)*: Theodore Galle and workshop after Peeter de Jode I after compositions by Joannes Nys, a Dominican in Antwerp.** Thirty-four engravings, including a title plate, ca. 156 × 92, 1611. LIT.: New Holl. De Jode, part VI, nos. 332–65.

Sold to Balthasar Moretus I at: 1 fl. (= 20 st.) per series in 1611.[327]

TG-9 ***The Life of Saint Catherine of Siena (Vita, mors, gesta, et miracula quaedam selecta B. Cahterinae Senensis …)*: Cornelis Galle I after Francesco Vanni.** Thirty-four engravings, including a title plate and portrait ("vera effigies") of St Catherine of Siena, ca. 151 × 91, with introductory and concluding texts in letterpress; originally published in 1603 by Philips Galle (PG-66) and subsequently sold to the Moretuses by Theodore Galle. LIT.: Imhof 2014a, O-55–56; New Holl. Galle, R 12; New Holl. De Jode, part V, nos. 52–63, copy a (p. 87). See fig. 7.12.

Sold to Jan II and Balthasar Moretus I at: 1 fl. (= 20 st.) per series in 1610, 1611, and 1618.[328]

TG-10 ***The Life of Saint Ignatius of Loyola (Vita beati patris Ignatii Loyolae …)*: Adriaen Collaert, Jan Collaert II, Cornelis Galle I, Theodore Galle, Charles de Mallery, and an unspecified engraver after Juan de Mesa.** Sixteen engravings including a title plate, ca. 264 × 366, 1610. LIT.: New Holl. Collaert, part IV, p. 176 and nos. 967–71. See fig. 5.9.

Sold to Jan II and Balthasar Moretus I at: 2 fl. (= 40 st.) per series in 1610 and 1611.[329]

TG-11 ***The Life of Saint Joseph, Husband of the Virgin and Patriarch (Vita S. Joseph, B.mae Virginis sponsi patriarcharum maximi …)*: anonymous artists.** About twenty to thirty engravings, including an engraved dedication to Archduchess Isabella, ca. 90 × 53, by 1625. LIT.: Melion 2022. See figs. 7.18 and 7.19.

In April 1625, Balthasar Moretus I sent Archduchess Isabella two presentation copies of this series on Theodore Galle's behalf.[330]

TG-12 ***The Life of Saint Teresa of Avila (Vita B. virginis Teresiae a Iesu …)*: Adriaen Collaert and Cornelis Galle I after Peeter de Jode I.** Twenty-five engravings, including a title plate, ca. 183 × 218, published jointly by Adriaen Collaert and Cornelis Galle in 1613 and thereafter by Adriaen Collaert and Theodore Galle. LIT.: New Holl. De Jode, part VI, nos. 429–53.

Sold to Balthasar Moretus I at: 1 fl. 5 st. (= 25 st.) per series in 1616.[331]

TG-13 *Men and Women of the Franciscan Order* (*Imagines seraphicae S.mi p. Francisci Assisiatis illustriumque virorum et feminarum*): **Charles de Mallery after Peeter de Jode I.** Fourteen engravings (ca. 255 × 165) and a title plate (267 × 176), 1614 (when originally published by Charles de Mallery). This series was often included in an earlier publication by Henricus Sedulius: *Historia seraphica vitae bmi. p. Francisci Assisiatis* (Antwerp: heirs of M. Nutius, 1613). It was re-issued by Theodore Galle by 1631. LIT.: New Holl. De Jode, part VII, nos. 572–86. See also CM-1 and JG-1 for other editions of this series distributed via the Moretuses. See fig. 7.7.

Sold to Balthasar Moretus I at: 24 st. per series in 1631.[332]

TG-14 *Miracles of the Rosary* (*Miracula et beneficia SS. Rosario Virginis Matris devotis a Deo opt. Max. Collata*): **anonymous artists.** Fifteen engravings (ca. 149 × 89) and a title plate (155 × 92), 1610. This series was occasionally sold together with Vincent Hensbergh's text, *Wonderlijcke schoone gratien ende mirakelen …* (Antwerp, Jan Moretus I, 1610). LIT.: Imhof 2014a, no. H-3. See fig. 7.13.

Sold to Balthasar Moretus I at: 12 st. per series with the introductory text in 1610 and 1611; and at 18 st. per series with the introductory text in 1616.[333]
Sold to Balthasar Moretus I at: 10 st. per series without the introductory text in 1611 and 1612.[334]

TG-15 *The Nine Worthies*: **Harmen Jansz. Muller after Maarten van Heemskerck.** Three engravings, ca. 216 × 250, originally published by Hieronymus Cock ca. 1567 and reissued by Theodore Galle by 1608. LIT.: New Holl. Muller, nos. 92–94.

Sold to Jan Moretus I at: 18 st. per quire of 25 leaves in 1608.
= .72 st. per leaf; each print was the equivalent of one leaf, amounting to 2.16 st. per series of three prints.[335]

TG-16 *Pastoral Goddesses and Nymphs*: **Cornelis Cort after Frans Floris.** Eight engravings, ca. 270 × 192, originally published by Hieronymus Cock in 1564 and reissued by Theodore Galle by 1608. LIT.: New Holl. Floris, nos. 102–09.

Sold to Jan Moretus I at: 18 st. per quire of 25 leaves in 1608.
= .72 st. per leaf; each print was the equivalent of one leaf, amounting to 5.76 st. per series of eight prints.[336]

TG-17 *Portraits of Famous Painters from the Low Countries* (*Illustrium quos Belgium habuit pictorum effigies …*). Twenty-two engraved portraits (that of Hieronymus Cock was omitted in Galle's edition) by Cornelis Cort, Jan Wierix, and an anonymous engraver, varying dimensions (ca. 198/225 × 121/130), and a title plate (204 × 136, etching with some engraving), originally published by Volcxken Diericx in 1572 and reissued by Theodore Galle by 1634. LIT.: Cock 2013, cat. 5 and 73; Holl. Dutch & Flemish, vol. LXVII, nos. 2023–35. See also CD-18.

Sold to Balthasar Moretus I at: 12 st. per series in 1634. This was the same price at which Diericx sold the publication to Plantin and De Mompere some fifty to sixty years earlier (see CD-18).[337]

TG-18 *Portraits of Italian Scholars* (*Italorum doctrina illustrium imagines*): **Philips Galle and anonymous engravers after various designers.** Twenty-five engravings of varying dimensions (ca. 167/179 × 117/123), with title page and index in letterpress, 1599/1600. LIT.: New Holl. Galle, part IV, pp. 32–33; Sellink 1997, vol. II, pp. 310–16.

Sold to Jan Moretus I at: 10 st. per series in 1599 and 1600.[338]

TG-19 *Portraits of Nine Greek* [*Scholars*] (*Icones novem Graecorum*): **Theodore Galle.** Engraving, 305 × 190, printed together with letterpress in the form of a broadside (550 × 420), with a dedication to the Jesuit Order by Theodore Galle, in which he identifies himself as the engraver, 1599. LIT.: Imhof 2014a, no. G-12.

Sold to Jan Moretus I at: 5 st. in 1599.[339]
Copies printed on parchment and shipped to the Frankfurt fair in 1599 were valued at: 6 st. each.[340]

TG-20 *Portraits of Scholars* (*Effigies doctorum*) **in folio.** It is not clear exactly which edition of this work was sold, nor the number of engravings it comprised. Most likely, it consisted of some assortment of portraits from Philips Galle's earlier editions of the *Imagines L. doctorum virorum* (PG-61 and PG-62) and *Virorum doctorum* (PG-122 and PG-123). LIT.: Imhof 2014a, no. G-6; New Holl. Galle, part IV, pp. 24–29 and 35–197.

Sold to Balthasar Moretus I at: 1 fl. 10 st. (= 30 st.) in 1634.[341]

TG-21 *Portraits of Scholars from the Low Countries* (*Illustrium Galliae Belgicae scriptorum icones et elogia*): **Philips Galle and anonymous engravers after various designers.** Sixty-four engravings of varying dimensions, ca. 167/179 × 103/123, with a dedication and index printed in letterpress, 1608. This is a revised and enlarged edition of Philips Galle's 1604 publication with the same title that Sellink associates with Aubertus Miraeus's *Elogia illustrium Belgii scriptorum*, originally published without illustrations in 1602 (Antwerp: Widow and heirs of Joannes Bellerus). Subsequently, Miraeus's text was published together with this series of images in 1609 (Antwerp: David Martinius). LIT.: Imhof 2014a, no. G-4; New Holl. Galle, part IV, pp. 29–31.

Sold to Jan Moretus II at: 30 st. (= 1 fl. 10 st.) per series in 1608.[342]

TG-22 *Sailing Ships*: **Frans Huys and Cornelis Cort (attributed to) after Pieter Bruegel I.** Ten engravings, with some etching, ca. 225 × 290 or 290 × 220, originally published by Hieronymus Cock ca. 1561–1565 and reissued by Theodore Galle by 1608, together with one extra image, possibly *Sixteen Ships at Sea*, by an anonymous engraver (214 × 297) which had likewise originally been published by Cock.[343] LIT.: Bassens and Van Grieken 2019, cat. 6. See also CD-23 and fig. 5.7.

Sold to Jan Moretus I at: 18 st. per quire of 25 leaves in 1608.
= .72 st. per leaf; each print was the equivalent of one leaf, amounting to 7.92 st. per series of eleven prints.[344]

TG-23 *Saint Dominic.* Possibly an engraving (ca. 270 × 200) of the saint in a landscape, with twelve rondels of scenes from his life, forming a frame around him, engraved and published by Theodore Galle by 1608. See Wolfegg, Fürstlich zu Waldburg-Wolfegg'sche Kunstsammlungen, vol. 211, print number 152.

Sold to Jan Moretus I at: 1.5 st. per print in 1608.[345]

TG-24 ***Scenographiae sive perspectivae ... pulcherrimae viginti selectissimarum fabricarum ... (Large Perspective Book)*: Joannes and Lucas van Doetecum after Hans Vredeman de Vries.** Twenty etchings (preceded by a title page in letterpress and an anonymous engraved plate with a dedication to Antoine Perrenot de Granvelle), ca. 205 × 260, originally published by Hieronymus Cock in 1560 and reissued by Theodore Galle by 1608. LIT.: Cock 2013, cat. 81. See also CD-27.

Sold to Jan Moretus I at: 18 st. per quire of 25 leaves in 1608. = .72 st. per leaf; each print was the equivalent of one leaf, amounting to 15.12 st. per series of twenty-one plates.[346]

TG-25 ***Seven Sorrows of the Virgin*: Hieronymus Wierix after Crispijn van den Broeck.** Engraving, 446 × 300, originally made in 1587 for Jean Moflin and reissued by Theodore Galle in 1601. LIT.: Holl. Dutch & Flemish, vol. LXII, no. 895, Imhof 2018b, p. 121. See fig. 2.8.

Sold to Jan Moretus I at: 4 st. per print in 1602.[347]

TG-26 *Seven Sorrows of the Virgin.* A print series comprising eight images, not yet associated with a known series, by 1602.

Sold to Jan Moretus I at: 3 st. per series of eight prints in 1602 and possibly 1608.[348]

TG-27 *Tree of the Dominicans.* Possibly an engraving published by Theodore Galle by 1601.

Sold to François Bellet for an unspecified sum in 1601.[349]

TG-28 ***Tree of the Genealogy of Christ*, in folio.** Possibly sold together with a 1602 publication by Georg Meuting, *Genealogia Christi ...* (published both in Latin and German); the text and image may have been intended to clarify each other.

Sold to Jan Moretus I, together with another publication, for 18 st. in 1603.[350]

TG-29 ***Tree of Human Life (Arbor humanae vitae)*: anonymous artist after Nicolaus Christophorus Radzivilus.** Engraving, 456 × 329, by 1613. See Amsterdam, Rijksmuseum, RP-P-OB-68.040, and Wolfegg, Fürstlich zu Waldburg-Wolfegg'sche Kunstsammlungen, vol. 9, no. 171. See also fig. 7.14.

Sold to Balthasar Moretus I at: 3 st. per print in 1613.[351]

TG-30 ***Virgin* "in planctu": possibly an image of the Virgin with the word "planctu" (sorrow) in an accompanying text.**

Sold to Jan Moretus I at: 4 st. per print in 1608.[352]

TG-31 ***Virgin* "quae est ista".** Possibly an anonymous engraving featuring the Virgin and Christ in the center, with the Coronation of the Virgin above and the apostles and other saints below, and with an accompanying caption beginning "Quae est ista ...", 184 × 140 (trimmed), by 1602. For an example of this image, see the British Museum, no. 1858,0417.1317.

Sold to Jan Moretus I at: 3/8 (= .375) st. per print in 1602.[353]

TG-32 ***Virgin* "ventura."** Possibly an image of the Virgin with the word "ventura" in an accompanying text.

Sold to Jan Moretus I at: 1.5 st. per print in 1608.[354]

Unspecified prints sold in bulk

See also the Note to the Reader and Chapter 2.

- per *single image on parchment, colored*: sold to Balthasar Moretus I at 10 st. in 1630.[355]
- per *single image on satin, colored*: sold to Balthasar Moretus I at 7 st. in 1633.[356]
- per *single image on parchment, colored*: sold to Balthasar Moretus I at 5 st. in 1634 and 1636.[357]
- per *single image in folio*: sold to Balthasar Moretus I at 4 st. in 1618, 1625, and 1632.[358]
- per *single image in folio*: sold to Balthasar Moretus I at 3 st. in 1618 and 1633.[359]
- per *single image in 8° on parchment, colored*: sold to Balthasar Moretus I at 3 st. in 1629.[360]
- per *single image on parchment, colored* (no format specified): sold to Balthasar Moretus I at 3 st. in 1633 and 1636.[361]
- per *single image on parchment, colored*: sold to Balthasar Moretus I at 2.5 st. in 1634.[362]
- per *single image, large or in folio*: sold to Jan Moretus I and Balthasar Moretus I at 2.5 st. sporadically between 1608 and 1632.[363]
- per *single image on parchment, colored*: sold to Balthasar Moretus I at 2 st. in 1636.[364]
- per *single image in folio*: sold to Balthasar Moretus I at 2 st. in 1618 and 1619.[365]
- per *single image in 8°, on parchment, colored*: sold to Balthasar Moretus I at 2 st. in 1629.[366]
- per *single image* (often identified as: double folios [or] leaves): sold to Balthasar Moretus I at 1.5 st. in 1613 and 1616.[367]
- per *single image*: sold to Jan Moretus I at 1 st. in 1608.[368]
- per *single image in large, common folio*: sold to Balthasar Moretus I at .75 st. in 1624.[369]
- per *single image*: sold to Jan Moretus I at .5 st. in 1607 and 1631.[370]
- per *single image*: sold to Jan Moretus I at .25 st. in 1607.[371]

• per *dozen images on parchment, colored*: sold to Balthasar Moretus I at 30 st. (= 2.5 st per image) in 1630 and 1631.[372]
• per *dozen images on paper, colored*: sold to Balthasar Moretus I at 15 st. (= 1.25 st per image) in 1630.[373]
• per *quire* of 25 leaves: sold to Jan Moretus I at: 18 st. per quire (= .72 st. per leaf) in 1608 and 1621.[374]
• per *100 images on parchment, colored*: sold to Balthasar Moretus I at 12 fl. 10 st. (= 250 st.) per hundred (= 2.5 st. per image) in 1631 and 1632.[375]
• per *100 images on parchment, colored*: sold to Balthasar Moretus I at 10 fl. (= 200 st.) per hundred (= 2 st. per image) periodically between 1630 and 1633.[376]
• per *100 images on paper, colored*: sold to Balthasar Moretus I at 6 fl. 5 st. (= 125 st.) per hundred (= 1.25 st. per image), in 1630 and 1631.[377]
• per *100 images on parchment*: sold to Balthasar Moretus I at 4 fl. (= 80 st.) per hundred (= .80 st. per image) periodically between 1630 and 1633.[378]
• per *100 images in f°*: sold to Balthasar Moretus I at 3 fl. 12 st (= 72 st.) per hundred (= .72 st. per image) in 1633.[379]
• per *100 images in f°*: sold to Balthasar Moretus I at 70 st. per hundred (= .70 st. per image) in 1626.[380]
• per *100 images*: sold to Jan Moretus I and Balthasar Moretus I at 36 st. per hundred (= .36 st. per image) periodically between 1608 and 1633. In 1613, one such order was noted as including images in 8°, while in 1633, the images were said to be in 4°.[381]
• per *100 images in 8°*: sold to Balthasar Moretus I at 35 st. per hundred (= .35 st. per image) in 1626.[382]
• per *100 images*: sold to Jan Moretus I at 20 st. per hundred (= .20 st. per image) in 1608.[383]
• per *100 images*: sold to Balthasar Moretus I at 18 st. per hundred (= .18 st. per image) in 1615 and 1630.[384]

ADRIAEN HUBERTI I (Huybrechts) Antwerp? ca. 1550–1614 Antwerp

Adriaen Huybrechts I was the first of an extensive family who worked as engravers, print publishers, or colorers of printed images in Antwerp into the early eighteenth century. While the contemporary records of the family's activities usually feature the name "Huybrechts", their publications (particularly if accompanied by some text in Latin) often bear the Latinized form of their name, "Huberti", which is, consequently, commonly found in modern catalogs of their work.

Huberti's exact date of birth is not known, but is usually estimated on the basis of other records. In particular, in the guild year 1573–1574, he was registered in Antwerp's Guild of St Luke as both an engraver and art dealer. By 1577, he had married Mynken Liefrinck's daughter Marguerite, who was Hans Liefrinck I's niece. Their son, Adriaen II, was registered as an apprentice to his father in the guild year 1611–1612 and subsequently as a colorer of images (an "afzetter"), a role that indicates another important aspect of Adriaen I's activities. However, Huberti is known above all as a publisher of maps and prints, especially images engraved by the Wierix brothers (often after designs by Maarten de Vos) and by Hans Collaert I, as well as of some illustrated texts. Indeed, Huberti occasionally employed Plantin (and then Jan Moretus I) for the printing of texts that would accompany several of his publications, ranging from simple indulgences to both Latin and French editions of his best-known publication, Richard Verstegen's *Theatrum crudelitatum haereticorum nostri temporis (Theatre of the Cruelties of Heretics of Our Time*"). Between 1587–1597 and 1601–1605, Plantin and Moretus turned to Huberti for individual images, prints in bulk, and canons in various sizes. Only occasionally did they employ him for small, specialized engraving work, such as adding the lettering to copper plates engraved by others, in addition to the coloring of some images.[385]

LIT.: Bowen and Imhof 2008, in particular pp. 300–303, 341–42, and 416–18; Diels 2010, pp. 113–31; Rouzet 1975, pp. 100–101.

Identifiable prints sold by title

AH-1 *Four Doctors [of the Church?]*: in 8°, completed by 1594 (not yet linked to a known print). LIT.: Delen 1932, p. 22.

Most likely sold to Jan Moretus I at: .75 st. per leaf (or group of four prints) in 1594.[386]

AH-2 *Four Evangelists*: in 8°, completed by 1594 (not yet linked to a known print). LIT.: Delen 1932, p. 22.

Most likely sold to Jan Moretus I at: .75 st. per leaf (or group of four prints) in 1594.[387]

AH-3 *Garden of Hainaut (Henegouwen)*: completed by 1593 (not yet linked to a known print).

Sold to Jan Moretus I at: 2 ½ st. per print in 1593.[388]

AH-4 *Lamb of God*: a small, circular image, completed by 1588 (not yet linked to a known print). LIT.: Delen 1932, p. 22.

Sold to Plantin at: 1 st. per print or leaf in 1588.[389]

AH-5 *Meditation on the Virgin*: on one leaf, completed by 1590 (not yet linked to a known print).

Sold to Jan Moretus I at: 2 ½ st. per print in 1590.[390]

AH-6 *Name of Jesus*: on one leaf, completed by 1590 (not yet linked to a known print).

Sold to Jan Moretus I at: 3 st. per print in 1590.[391]

AH-7 *Queen of Scotland, Mary Stuart*: completed by 1587 (not yet linked to a known print). LIT.: Delen 1932, p. 22.

Sold to Plantin at: 6 st. per print in 1587.[392]

AH-8 *Rosary of the Virgin*: completed by December 1589 (not yet linked to a known print).

Sold to Jan Moretus I at: 3 fl. per quire (= 2.4 st. per print) in 1589; and at 2 ½ st. per print in 1590.[393]

AH-9 *Speculum pro Christianis seductis (Mirror for Christians who have been led astray)*: broadside with four engravings and text by Richard Versteghen, published either in Latin or in French in 1590. LIT.: Imhof 2014a, nos. V-60 and V-62, and V-61 for a later edition in Latin from 1609.

Sold by Versteghen to Jan Moretus I at: 8 st. per print in 1590 and 1591.[394]
Sold by Versteghen to Jan Moretus I at: 6 or 7 st. per print between 1592 and 1599.[395]
Sold by Huberti to Jan Moretus I at: 6 st. per print in 1609 and 1610.[396]

AH-10 *Virgin and Child on a Crescent*: Anton Wierix II after the sculpture by Philip de Vos on the Antwerp city hall, engraving, 281 × 194, 1587. LIT.: Holl. Dutch & Flemish, vol. LXIII, no. 955; Thijs 1993, pp. 9–10. See fig. 3.20.

Sold to Plantin at: 2.5 st. per print in 1587 and possibly 1590.[397]

Unspecified prints sold in bulk

See also the Note to the Reader and Chapter 2.

• per *single leaf*: sold to Jan Moretus I at .75 st. (= 1 "blanc") per leaf in 1596.[398]
• per *quire* of 25 leaves colored images in 4° and 8°: sold to Jan Moretus I at: 2 fl. 10 st. per quire = 1.2 st. per leaf in 1597.[399]
• per *quire* of 25 leaves: sold to Plantin at: 20 st. per quire (= .8 st. per leaf) in 1587 and 1588.[400]
• per *quire* of 25 leaves: sold to Plantin and Jan Moretus I at: 18 st. per quire (= .72 st. per leaf) regularly between 1588 and 1597.[401]

GERARD DE JODE Nijmegen ca. 1516/1517–1591 Antwerp
PASSCHIJNKE VAN GELRE ?–1601 Antwerp

Although Gerard de Jode was trained as an engraver, he is better known as a publisher and seller of maps and prints. Indeed, in the first reference to him in the records of Antwerp's Guild of St Luke from 1547–1548, he is identified as a print seller. In subsequent records, he is variously identified as a merchant, art dealer, bookseller, painter, engraver, and printer of copper plates (among other occupations). While revealing the breadth of his business dealings, the relative importance of these activities remains unclear. Like his contemporary Hieronymus Cock, De Jode appears to have focused more on managing the production and distribution of prints and maps than on making them himself. From 1555, De Jode began to publish prints and maps, and by 1570, he was well-known among Antwerp printmakers and publishers; his prosperous business even included international sales, in particular via the Frankfurt fairs. De Jode published prints by a variety of designers, for instance Hans Vredeman de Vries, Maarten de Vos, Gerard van Groeningen, and Jan (Hans) Snellinck (who married one of De Jode's daughters). Like Cock, he also worked with many of the best local printmakers, in particular Lucas and Johannes van Doetecum, Hans I and his son Adriaen Collaert, Jan Sadeler I, and the Wierix brothers. While De Jode was the first to publish Vredeman de Vries's ornamental prints, as well as (later on) De Vries's popular *Architectura* series, he also published numerous religious subjects and allegories, as well as images of ancient history and mythology. However, he is perhaps best known now for his various maps, his atlas (the *Speculum orbis terrarum*), and his *Thesaurus veteris et novi testamenti*, an exceptionally large collection of prints of Old and New Testament subjects. When De Jode died in 1591, he had amassed a stock of some 1,200 prints and maps, approximately 400 of which were used for his *Thesaurus*.[402] His business was continued under the direction of his widow Passchijnke van Gelre, who was assisted by their son Cornelis de Jode. Following Van Gelre's and Cornelis's deaths in 1601 and 1600, respectively, De Jode's stock of plates was sold – most likely to facilitate the division of De Jode's and Van Gelre's estate among their numerous heirs and to pay off outstanding debts. Consequently, the vast majority of the plates ended up in the hands of various other publishers, including Charles de Mallery, Theodore Galle, and above all, Jan Baptist Vrients.

Plantin's (and his successors') transactions with De Jode, while varied, were generally infrequent. For his part, De Jode employed Plantin and his sons-in-law to print texts to accompany some of his illustrated publications on just a few occasions. Plantin, in turn, dealt only occasionally in De Jode's cartographic works, and Plantin's contact with other map publishers, like Gerard Mercator and Abraham Ortelius, was far more extensive. Similarly, Plantin's and Jan Moretus I's resale of De Jode's prints was highly irregular and limited, at least in comparison with that of the other major Antwerp print publishing houses in the period, namely those run by Philips and Theodore Galle, as well as Cock and his widow Diericx.

LIT.: Bowen and Imhof 2008, in particular pp. 300–06, and 419–21; Denucé 1912–1913, vol. I, pp. 163–220; New Holl. De Jode, parts I–IV, in particular the introductory remarks in part I, pp. xxix–lxv.

Identifiable prints sold by title[403]

GJ-1 *The Agony in the Garden*: **Jan Wierix, possibly after Crispijn van den Broeck.** Engraving, 168 × 125, 1572. LIT.: New Holl. De Jode, part II, no. 335, part of the series *The Passion of Christ* (GJ-25).

Plantin resold this print, together with an image of *The Flagellation* (GJ-11), most likely from the same series of the Passion at: 2 st. for the 2 prints (= 1 st. per print on average) in 1575.[404]

GJ-2 *Allegory of Temperance and Vice*: **anonymous engraver after Jan Snellinck (attributed to).** Engraving, 213 × 289, ca. 1574–1580. LIT.: New Holl. De Jode, part II, no. 538 (in New Holl. De Jode, this image is paired with GJ-3: *Allegory of Temperance and Virtue* under *Allegories of the Golden Mean*).

Sold to Plantin at: 18 st. per quire of 25 leaves in 1580.[405]
= .72 st. per leaf; each print was the equivalent of one leaf.

GJ-3 *Allegory of Temperance and Virtue*: **anonymous engraver after Jan Snellinck (attributed to).** Engraving, 217 × 292, ca. 1574–1580. LIT.: New Holl. De Jode, part II, no. 537 (in New Holl. De Jode, this image is paired with GJ-2: *Allegory of Temperance and Vice*, under *Allegories of the Golden Mean*).

Sold to Plantin at: 18 st. per quire of 25 leaves in 1580.[406]
= .72 st. per leaf; each print was the equivalent of one leaf.

GJ-4 *Bird's Eye View of Ancient Jerusalem with the Crucifixion*: **Anton Wierix II after a description by the cartographer Pieter Lacksteyn.** Engraving, 219 × 271, by 1587. LIT.: New Holl. De Jode, part IV, no. 1068 (companion piece to GJ-21: *Map of Modern Jerusalem*).

Sold to Plantin at: 1 st. per print in 1587.[407]

GJ-5 *Calendar of Saints (Calendarium sanctorum)*: in folio, published by 12 July 1595 by the widow of Gerard de Jode (not yet linked to a known print).

Sold to Jan Moretus I at: 10 st. in 1595.[408]

GJ-6 *Caryatids and Terms* (*Caryatidum (vulgus termas vocat) …*): **Joannes and Lucas van Doetecum after Hans Vredeman de Vries.** Sixteen etchings (ca. 160 × 235) and an etched title plate (173 × 235), ca. 1565. LIT.: New Holl. De Jode, part III, nos. 853–69. See fig. 3.4.

Sold to Plantin at: 9.5 st. per series in 1570; and at 7.5 st. per series in 1573.[409]

GJ-7 *Christ's Sermon on the Last Days*: **anonymous engraver after Jan Snellinck (attributed to).** Engraving, 227 × 311, ca. 1580. LIT.: New Holl. De Jode, part II, no. 438.

Sold to Plantin at: 18 st. per quire of 25 leaves in 1580.[410]
= .72 st. per leaf; each print was the equivalent of one leaf.

GJ-8 *The Conversion of Saul*: **Petrus Jalhea Furnius (attributed to) after Gerard van Groeningen (attributed to)**
engraving, 202 × 320, by 1571. LIT.: New Holl. De Jode, part II, no. 508.

Sold to Plantin in 1571, but with no clear price for this specific print.[411]

GJ-9 *Ecce Homo*: **Petrus Jalhea Furnius (attributed to)**
engraving, 298 × 221, by 1588. LIT.: New Holl. De Jode, part II, no. 450.

Sold to Plantin at: 2 st. per print in 1588.[412]

GJ-10 *The Five Orders of Architecture* (*Architectura*): **Joannes and Lucas van Doetecum after Hans Vredeman de Vries.**
Twenty-three etched and engraved plates (ca. 340/352 × 256) and an etched and engraved title plate (320 × 234), alternated with brief explanatory texts printed in letterpress, first published by Gerard de Jode in 1577, with accompanying texts in German and French and reissued by him with texts in Dutch and German in 1581. Subsequent editions in French were published by his heirs in 1597 (Cornelis de Jode), as well as in 1615 and 1619 (Peeter de Jode I), and another edition in Dutch appeared in 1598 (Cornelis de Jode). LIT.: New Holl. De Jode, part III, nos. 888–911.

Sold to Plantin at: 1 fl. 4 st. (= 24 st.) per series in 1582; and at 1 fl. 7 st. (= 27 st.) per series in 1588.[413]

GJ-11 *The Flagellation*: **Jan Wierix, possibly after Crispijn van den Broeck.** Engraving 166 × 128, 1572. LIT.: New Holl. De Jode, part II, no. 340, part of the series *The Passion of Christ* (GJ-25).

Plantin resold this print together with an image of *The Agony in the Garden* (GJ-1), most likely from the same series of the Passion at: 2 st. for the 2 prints (= 1 st. per print on average) in 1575.[414]

GJ-12 *Fountains and Wells with Architectural Background* (*Artis perspectivae*): **Joannes and Lucas van Doetecum after Hans Vredeman de Vries.** Seventeen etched and engraved plates (ca. 174 × 240 or 240 × 174) and an etched and engraved title plate (182 × 249), 1568. LIT.: New Holl. De Jode, part III, nos. 870–87.

Sold to Plantin at: 10.75 st. per series in 1570; and at 13.5 st. per series in 1581.[415]

GJ-13 *Four Famous Women from Antiquity (Lucretia, Virgina, Cleopatra, and Sophonisba)*: **attributed to Hans Collaert I after Jan Snellinck.** Engraving, 220 × 284, ca. 1574–1580. LIT.: New Holl. De Jode, part II, no. 626 (in New Holl. De Jode, this image is paired with *Four Roman Heroes*, under *Heroes and Heroines from Ancient History*).

Sold to Plantin at: 18 st. per quire of 25 leaves in 1580.[416]
= .72 st. per leaf; each print was the equivalent of one leaf.

GJ-14 ***The Four Kingdoms*: Jan Wierix after Gerard van Groeningen.** Four engravings, ca. 197 × 287, by 1573. LIT.: New Holl. De Jode, part III, nos. 596–99.

Sold to Plantin at: 3 st. per series in 1573.[417]
Possibly sold to Jan Moretus I by Philips Galle at: 4 st. in 1594.[418]

GJ-15 ***Four Roman Heroes (Mutius Scaevola, Horatius Cocles, Cincinnatus, and Marcus Curtius)*: attributed to Hans Collaert I after Jan Snellinck.** Engraving, 220 × 285, ca. 1574–1580. LIT.: New Holl. De Jode, part II, no. 627 (in New Holl. De Jode, this image is paired with *Four Famous Women from Antiquity*, under *Heroes and Heroines from Ancient History*, although this series is not mentioned in Plantin's accounts).

Sold to Plantin at: 18 st. per quire of 25 leaves in 1580.[419]
= .72 st. per leaf; each print was the equivalent of one leaf.

GJ-16 ***The Four Seasons*: Hans Collaert I (attributed to) after Jan Snellinck (attributed to).** Engraving, 218 × 282, ca. 1574–1580. LIT.: New Holl. De Jode, part II, no. 628.

Sold to Plantin at: 18 st. per quire of 25 leaves in 1580.[420]
= .72 st. per leaf; each print was the equivalent of one leaf.

GJ-17 ***The Kings of Judah*: anonymous engraver after Jan Snellinck.** Nine engravings, ca. 220 × 287, ca. 1579. LIT.: New Holl. De Jode, part I, nos. 208–16.

Eight leaves of this series (not nine, as described in New Holl. De Jode) were sold to Plantin at: 18 st. per quire of 25 leaves in 1580.[421]
= .72 st. per leaf; each print was the equivalent of one leaf, amounting to 5.76 st. per eight prints.

GJ-18 ***Lessons from Ecclesiastes and the Wisdom of Sirach*: Hans Collaert I (attributed to) after Jan Snellinck (attributed to).** Engraving, 277 × 218, ca. 1574–1580. LIT.: New Holl. De Jode, part II, no. 549 (in New Holl. De Jode, this image is paired with GJ-19: *Lessons from Proverbs*, under *Lessons from Ecclesiastes and Proverbs*).

Sold to Plantin at: 18 st. per quire of 25 leaves in 1580.[422]
= .72 st. per leaf; each print was the equivalent of one leaf.

GJ-19 ***Lessons from Proverbs*: Hans Collaert I (attributed to) after Jan Snellinck (attributed to).** Engraving, 287 × 221, ca. 1574–1580. LIT.: New Holl. De Jode, part II, no. 550 (in New Holl. De Jode, this image is paired with GJ-18: *Lessons from Ecclesiastes and the Wisdom of Sirach*, under *Lessons from Ecclesiastes and Proverbs*).

Sold to Plantin at: 18 st. per quire of 25 leaves in 1580.[423]
= .72 st. per leaf; each print was the equivalent of one leaf.

GJ-20 ***Man between the Old and New Covenant*: Pieter Nagel after Gerard van Groeningen.** Engraving, 220 × 325, ca. 1567. LIT.: New Holl. De Jode, part II, no. 552.

Sold to Plantin in 1571, but with no clear price for this specific print.[424]

GJ-21 ***Map of Modern Jerusalem*: anonymous artist after a description by the cartographer Pieter Lacksteyn.** Engraving, 214 × 280, by 1587. LIT.: New Holl. De Jode, part IV, no. 1069 (companion piece to GJ-4: *Bird's Eye View of Ancient Jerusalem with the Crucifixion*).

Sold to Plantin at: 1 st. per print in 1587.[425]

GJ-22 ***Moses and Aaron with the Tables of the Law*: Frans Huys after Lambert van Noort.** Engraving and woodcut: three plates, 320 × 740 for all three plates together, 1556. The two side plates are engraved images of Moses (left) and Aaron (right), while the central image with the Tables of the Law is a woodcut with letterpress text in the middle. LIT.: New Holl. De Jode, part II, no. 393.

Sold to Plantin at: 2.25 st. per set of three plates in 1558.[426]

GJ-23 ***Panels with Grotesques (Grottesco: in diversche manieren …)*: Joannes and Lucas van Doetecum after Hans Vredeman de Vries.** Seventeen etchings, including a title plate, 158 × 208 or ca. 208 × 158, ca. 1565–1571. LIT.: New Holl. De Jode, part III, nos. 819–35.

Sold to Plantin at: 9.5 st. per series in 1570; and at 7.5 st. per series in 1573.[427]

GJ-24 ***The Parable of the Prodigal Son*: Hans Collaert I after Crispijn van den Broeck.** Four engravings, ca. 195 × 270, by 1571. LIT.: New Holl. De Jode, part II, nos. 298–301.

Sold to Plantin at: 2 st. per series in 1571.[428]

GJ-25 ***The Passion of Christ (Mnimata dominicae passionis …)*: Jan Wierix, possibly after Crispijn van den Broeck.** Sixteen engravings, including a title plate, ca. 167 × 126, 1572. LIT.: New Holl. De Jode, part II, nos. 333–48. See GJ-1 and GJ-11 for two prints from this series, *The Agony in the Garden* and *The Flagellation*, which Plantin may have sold independently in 1575.

Sold to Plantin at: 12 st. per series in 1576 and 1583.[429]

GJ-26 ***Plans for Fortifications (Form und weis zu bauwen …)*: Joannes and Lucas van Doetecum after Hans van Schille.** Fourteen etched and engraved plates (ca. 267 × 230) and an etched and engraved title plate (ca. 306 × 204), 1580. LIT.: New Holl. De Jode, part III, nos. 912–26.

Sold to Plantin at: 11.25 st. per series in 1588.[430]

GJ-27 ***Portraits of Emperors (Icones duodecim caesarum Roma[norum] …)*: Joannes and Lucas van Doetecum after Hans Vredeman de Vries.** Twelve etched and engraved plates (ca. 129 × 83) and an etched and engraved title plate (116 × 86), ca. 1565–1569. LIT.: New Holl. De Jode, part III, nos. 711–23.

Sold to Plantin at: 5 st. per series in 1572 or 1573.[431]

GJ-28 *Portraits of Popes* (*Pontificum maximorum XXVII effigies*): **Philips Galle after Philippe Soye.** Twenty-nine engravings (ca. 161/181 × 118/121) and an engraved title plate (ca. 176 × 127), with introductory texts in letterpress, 1572. LIT.: BT 1214; New Holl. Galle, nos. 692–719; New Holl. De Jode, part III, nos. 681–710 and vol. I, p. lix. De Jode and Philips Galle published this work jointly, and both sold copies to Plantin at the same price (see PG-83).

Sold to Plantin at: 12 st. per series in 1572 and 1573.[432]

GJ-29 *The Prodigal Son in Luxury*: **anonymous engraver after Maarten van Cleve.** Engraving, 200 × 280, by 1571. LIT.: New Holl. De Jode, part II, no. 437 (possible attribution).

Sold to Plantin in 1571, but with no clear price for this specific print.[433]

GJ-30 *Ruins and Fantastical Buildings* (*Ruinarum variarum fabricarum*): **Lambert Suavius.** Thirty-three etchings of various dimensions, 1554. LIT.: New Holl. De Jode, part III, nos. 927–59.

Sold to Plantin at: 5 st. per series in 1558; and at 6 st. per series in 1573.[434]

GJ-31 *The Seven Acts of Mercy*: **Pieter Nagel after Gerard van Groeningen.** Seven engravings, ca. 200 × 250, ca. 1571. LIT.: New Holl. De Jode, part II, nos. 439–45.

Probably sold to Plantin at: 18 st. per quire of 25 leaves in 1573.[435] = .72 st. per leaf; each print was the equivalent of one leaf, amounting to 5.04 st. per series.

GJ-32 *The Seven Deadly Sins* (*Septem peccata mortalia …*): **attributed to Hans Collaert I after Jan Snellinck.** Five engravings, 144 × 109 (title plate), 154 × 112 (*Envy*), and ca. 153 × 229 (pairs of remaining images), ca. 1574–1580. LIT.: New Holl. De Jode, part II, nos. 526–30.

Sold to Plantin in 1581, but with no clear price for this series.[436]

GJ-33 *The Seven Liberal Arts* (*Chorus septem liberalium artium*): **Hans Collaert I (attributed to) after Jan Snellinck (attributed to).** Seven engravings (ca. 141 × 107) and an engraved title plate (ca. 152 × 108), ca. 1574–1580. LIT.: New Holl. De Jode, part III, nos. 647–54.

Sold to Plantin in 1581, but with no clear price for this series.[437]

GJ-34 *The Seven Planets*: **Hans Collaert I (attributed to) after Jan Snellinck (attributed to).** Six engravings, comprising seven representations of planets and a title plate, ca. 152 × 110 or ca. 152 × 229, ca. 1574–1580. LIT.: New Holl. De Jode, part III, nos. 642–46.

Sold to Plantin in 1581, but with no clear price for this series.[438]

GJ-35 *The Seven Planets* (*Septem planetae …*): **Adriaen Collaert after Maarten de Vos.** Seven engravings (ca. 300 × 215) and an engraved title plate (ca. 289 × 211), 1581. LIT.: New Holl. De Jode, part III, nos. 634–41. See fig. 5.12.

Sold to Plantin at: 6 st. per series in 1582.[439]

GJ-36 *Small Passion*, **with four plates: possibly a series with an image of *Christ Sitting on a Cold Stone* on the title plate** engraving 62 × 50 (trimmed), ca. 1570?. LIT.: Van der Coelen and Leesberg, p. 38.

Sold to Plantin at: 5 st. per group of four images in 1570 and 1571.[440]

GJ-37 *The Story of Daniel*: **Joannes and Lucas van Doetecum after Hans Vredeman de Vries.** Six etched and engraved plates, ca. 242 × 327, 1576–1579. LIT.: New Holl. De Jode, part I, nos. 202–07.

Sold to Plantin at: 4.5 st. per series in 1582.[441]

GJ-38 *The Story of Joseph*: **several engravers, including possibly Hans Collaert I and Jan Sadeler I, after Michiel Coxie.** Seven engravings, ca. 210 × 260, 1579. LIT.: New Holl. De Jode, part I, nos. 50–56.

Sold to Plantin at: 4.5 st. per series in 1584.[442]

GJ-39 *The Story of Samson*: **Anton Wierix II after Jan Snellinck.** Three engravings, ca. 213 × 293, 1579. LIT.: New Holl. De Jode, part I, nos. 99–101.

Sold to Plantin at: 18 st. per quire of 25 leaves in 1580.[443] = .72 st. per leaf; each print was the equivalent of one leaf, amounting to 2.16 st. per series.

GJ-40 *The Story of Solomon*: **Hans Collaert I (attributed to) after Jan Snellinck.** Four engravings, ca. 187 × 243, ca. 1574. LIT.: New Holl. De Jode, part I, nos. 127–30.

Sold to Plantin in 1575, but with no clear price for this series.[444]

GJ-41 *The Story of Susanna*: **possibly the series engraved by Hans Collaert I after Gillis Coignet.** Four engravings, ca. 195 × 263, by 1571. LIT.: New Holl. De Jode, part I, nos. 198–201.

Sold to Plantin at: 3.5 st. per series in 1571.[445]

GJ-42 *The Story of Tobias*: **most likely Joannes and Lucas van Doetecum after Hans Bol.** Six etched and engraved plates, ca. 237 × 323, by 1576. LIT.: New Holl. De Jode, part II, nos. 177–82. This was sold together with the series of *The Story of Daniel* (GJ-37), which comprises similarly sized engravings by the Van Doetecums.[446]

Sold to Plantin at: 4.5 st. per series in 1582.[447]

GJ-43 *Strapwork Cartouches with Biblical Texts* (*Multarum variarumque protractionum*): **Frans Huys after Hans Vredeman de Vries.** Twelve plates, etching and engraving, 180/190 × 135/140 or 136/144 × 187/205, and a title plate (175 × 142), 1555. LIT.: New Holl. De Jode, part III, nos. 728–40.

Sold to Plantin at: 5 st. per series in 1558.[448]

GJ-44 ***Strapwork Cartouches with Classical Texts (Variarum protractionum)*****: Frans Huys after Hans Vredeman de Vries.** Twelve plates, etching and engraving, 170/188 × 133/140 ca. or 132/144 × 180/185, and a title plate (170 × 139), 1555. LIT.: New Holl. De Jode, part III, nos. 741–53.

Sold to Plantin at: 5 st. per series in 1558.[449]

GJ-45 ***The Temple Book (Events in and around the Temple) (Memorabilium Novi Testamenti in templo gestorum)*****: Lucas (and Joannes?) van Doetecum after Gerard van Groeningen.** Fourteen etched and engraved plates, including a title plate, ca. 203 × 289, ca. 1572. LIT.: New Holl. De Jode, part II, nos. 250–54 and 316–24, where the original publication is discussed in two subsections, as it was included in De Jode's subsequent *Thesaurus novi testamenti* (see below).

Sold to Plantin in 1576, but with no clear price for this series.[450]

GJ-46 ***Thesaurus sacrarum historiarum veteris testamenti*** **(Old Testament images).** 165 leaves of engravings of diverse dimensions by various artists, 1579. LIT.: New Holl. De Jode, part I, nos. 1–232 and pp. xxxviii-xliv.

Sold to Plantin in 1580 at: 6 fl. 13 st. (= 133 st.).[451]

GJ-47 ***Thesaurus novi testamenti*** **(New Testament images).** 183 leaves of engravings of diverse dimensions by various artists, 1585. LIT.: New Holl. De Jode, II, nos. 233–392; New Holl. De Jode, part I, pp. xxxviii–liii.

Two copies of the Old and New Testament images, each comprising 345 leaves (slightly less than the 348 leaves discussed in New Holl. De Jode, p. xliv) were sold to Plantin in 1588 at: 12 fl. 8 st. (= 248 st.) apiece.[452]
One copy of the Old and New Testament images (number of leaves not specified) was sold to Jan Moretus I in 1590 at: 12 fl. 12 st. (252 st.).[453]
A "figures Bibliorum" sold to Jan Moretus I on 17 January 1600 by Cornelis de Jode for 15 fl. may similarly refer to this publication, or an enlarged version thereof.[454]

GJ-48 ***Twelve Parables from the New Testament*****: anonymous engraver after Ambrosius Francken.** Twelve engravings, ca. 217 × 283, 1580–1585. LIT.: New Holl. De Jode, part II, nos. 282–93.

Sold to Plantin as two groups of six leaves of parables at: 18 st. per quire of 25 leaves in 1580.[455]
= .72 st. per leaf; each print was the equivalent of one leaf, amounting to 4.32 st. per group of six prints, or 8.64 st. per group of twelve.

Unspecified prints sold in bulk

See also the Note to the Reader and Chapter 2.

- per *quire* of 25 leaves: sold to Plantin intermittently between 1570 and 1590 at: 18 st. per quire (= .72 st. per leaf).[456]

PEETER DE JODE I Antwerp 1573–1634 Antwerp
PEETER DE JODE II Antwerp 1606–1670 or later, Antwerp

The son of Gerard de Jode and Passchijnke van Gelre, Peeter de Jode I presumably received his initial training as an engraver in his father's workshop in Antwerp while still in his early teens.[457] However, when Gerard de Jode died in 1591, Peeter de Jode (then just seventeen years old) was already working as an apprentice in Hendrick Goltzius's workshop in Haarlem. He most likely returned to Antwerp soon thereafter and engraved a number of prints that his mother subsequently published. However, within a few years, he left for Italy, where he worked in Venice, Siena, and Rome and was influenced particularly by the work of Francesco Vanni and Antonio Tempesta. Most likely the death of his brother Cornelis in 1600 prompted his return to Antwerp in 1601; he was registered as an engraver in the Guild of St Luke toward the end of the 1600–1601 guild year. Due to the sale of his father's stock of plates, Peeter de Jode had to build up his own business essentially from scratch. In addition to engraving works for others, De Jode also started his own publishing enterprise with both a few of his father's series, such as the plates for *The Five Orders of Architecture* (GJ-10), and a small selection of plates that he had brought back from Italy. Additionally, De Jode continued to acquire plates from other sources. Of the roughly 460 plates that bear his name as the publisher, the majority are of Italian origin, including a series of 150 images illustrating Ovid's *Metamorphoses* by Tempesta, in addition to some fifty other works by him.[458] De Jode also published a small number of works that he had engraved himself. Far more often, he designed images that were engraved by someone else; most of these images were then published by others, in particular Theodore Galle. For instance, De Jode created a number of book illustrations throughout his career, most of which were commissioned by the Moretuses or Galle.[459] Remarkably, De Jode began to sell off some of his stock of plates during his lifetime, and it is unclear what happened to most of what remained following his death. His son Peeter II, who enjoyed a successful career as a reproductive engraver in Antwerp and, above all, as an engraver of portraits, is only known to have reissued two images by his father: portraits of the king and queen of Scotland and England.[460] Since Peeter II also sold Balthasar Moretus I an impression of his father's *Genealogical Tree of the Franciscan Order* in 1639, he had evidently retained impressions of this exceptional work, if not the plates used to print it.

LIT.: New Holl. De Jode, parts V-X, in particular the introductory remarks in part V, pp. xiii-lvii, and part VIII, pp. 133–54; Van der Coelen and Leesberg 2021.

Identifiable prints sold by title

PJ-1 ***Book of Pleasures*****:** possibly Peeter de Jode I's copy of Agostino Carracci's series *The Love of the Gods*, in twenty plates from ca. 1602, currently known only via a later copy of it by Jacques Joseph Coiny, published in 1798. LIT.: New Holl. de Jode, part VIII, nos. 904–23.[461]

Sold to Jan Moretus I by Peeter de Jode I at: 14 st. per series in 1608.[462]

PJ-2 ***Genealogical Tree of the Franciscan Order*: Peeter de Jode I after his own drawings after an initial compositional design by Vital d'Algésiras.** Twelve engravings amounting to a total measurement of 1,862 × 1,286, originally published by Peeter de Jode I in 1626. De Jode (or his son Peeter II) sold the plates for this image (among others) to Peter Goetkindt II in 1632, when Goetkindt was active as an art dealer in Paris. LIT.: Duverger 1984–2009, vol. IV, p. 139; New Holl. de Jode, part V, p. xlvii and no. 68.

Sold to Balthasar Moretus I by Peeter de Jode II at: 8 fl. (= 160 st.) in 1639.[463]

PJ-3 ***Saint Carolus Borromeus* (surrounded by twenty-two scenes from his life): Peeter de Jode I.** Engraving, 515 × 404, by 1612. LIT.: New Holl. de Jode, part V, no. 51.

Sold to Balthasar Moretus I by Peeter de Jode I at: 7 st. per print in 1612.[464]

Unspecified prints sold in bulk

See also the Note to the Reader and Chapter 2.

- per *single leaf*: sold to Jan Moretus I at: 2 st. per leaf in 1608.[465]
- per *single leaf*: sold to Jan Moretus I at: 1 st. per leaf in 1608.[466]
- per *quire* of 25 leaves: sold to Jan Moretus at: 18 st. per quire (= .72 st. per leaf) in 1608.[467]

HANS LIEFRINCK I Augsburg or Antwerp 1514/15–1573 Antwerp

It is often assumed that Hans Liefrinck I was born in Augsburg because his father, the woodcutter and print publisher Willem Liefrinck, worked there for Emperor Maximilian I from 1516 to 1518. However, Willem had roots in Brabant and may have worked in Antwerp early in his career, which may account for his decision to settle there in the 1520s. In the guild year 1538–1539, Hans Liefrinck is listed as a master in Antwerp's Guild of St Luke. The guild's accounts indicate that he took on at least two apprentices over the course of the following decade and was even appointed dean of the guild in 1558–1559. Like his father, Liefrinck began as a woodcutter, but he soon expanded his operations to include publishing woodcuts and, as of the 1550s, intaglios executed by (among others) Pieter van der Heyden, Pieter and Frans Huys; he also published a few works that he etched himself. Although Liefrinck is perhaps best known for his woodcut portraits of European nobles, his offerings were more diverse and included: maps; architectural, ornamental, and perspective images; renditions of animals; religious and allegorical subjects; and works after Italianate and antique models. Many of his prints are known in colored impressions that may well have been handmade with stencils in his own workshop. Several of Liefrinck's relatives likewise worked in the print business. Following Hans I's death, his son Hans II continued to publish intaglios (in particular, engraved religious subjects) and run an art shop in Antwerp, together with Hans I's widow Catherine Cordier. Hans I's sister Mynken is known in particular for her work coloring maps, in addition to printing intaglio book illustrations and broadsides for Plantin.[468]

LIT.: New Holl. Liefrinck, part I, pp. xxxvi-xli; Van der Stock 1998, pp. 61–66 in particular.

Unspecified prints sold in bulk

See also the Note to the Reader and Chapter 2.
The accounts of the individual prints Liefrinck supplied to Plantin are too imprecise to support the identification of specific images here. See, for example, Delen 1932, pp. 13–14, for his own conflicting attributions of some prints.

- per *grand double double leaf*: sold to Plantin at: 4 st. per leaf in 1568.[469]
- per *double leaf*: sold to Plantin at: 3 st. per leaf in 1568.[470]
- per *double leaf*: sold to Plantin at: 2 st. per leaf in 1558.[471]
- per *double leaf*: sold to Plantin at: 1.5 st. per leaf in 1558.[472]
- per *quire* of 25 leaves: sold to Plantin at: 18 st. per quire (= .72 st. per leaf) in 1558.[473]
- per *100 leaves*: sold to Plantin at: 4 fl. per 100 in 1568.[474]
- per 100 *"pièces"*: sold to Plantin at: 2 fl. per 100 in 1568.[475]
- per 100 *"pièces"*: sold to Plantin at: 1 fl. per 100 in 1568.[476]

CHARLES DE MALLERY Antwerp 1571–after January 1642 Brussels

The son of the lawyer Philips de Mallery, Charles de Mallery was apprenticed to Philips Galle in 1586, when he was fifteen years old. He would most likely have worked alongside Galle's own son Theodore, who was also born in 1571 and was already an accomplished engraver.[477] By the early 1590s, De Mallery was completing isolated engravings for some of Philips Galle's series, together with Galle's son Theodore, as well as Adriaen and Jan Collaert II. One clear indication of the recognition of De Mallery's skill during these years was his employment to complete nine engravings for the 1593 publication of the *Evangelicae historiae imagines*, which featured primarily prints by the renowned Wierix brothers.[478] Shortly thereafter, De Mallery traveled to Rome, stopping at the Frankfurt fair en route in April 1594. Following his return to Antwerp, he was swiftly accepted as a master engraver in the Guild of St Luke in 1597 and began to make engravings for Philips Galle. Nevertheless, De Mallery was evidently not satisfied with this arrangement, for within twenty months of his marriage to Philips' daughter Catharina on 10 January 1598, De Mallery's young family was settled in Paris, where he proceeded to execute engravings for both Parisian printsellers – Jean Messagier, for example – and an assortment of Parisian book printers, who engaged him to make title plates, portraits, and some text illustrations for their editions. In the fall of 1605, however, De Mallery decided to return to Antwerp, where he soon established a profitable business as an engraver and print publisher. Although De Mallery's oeuvre has yet to be documented in detail, a consideration of online print collections and references to his prints in various catalogues indicate that he specialized in the publication of small religious images, many of which were derived from or were close copies of work by the Wierix brothers, who were revered internationally. This production of new images – either engravings he made himself or anonymous works that he published – took priority over reissuing the work of earlier Antwerp print publishers, as several contemporary Antwerp print publishers were doing. Even the work of De Mallery's father-in-law, Philips Galle, is sparsely represented among his later publications and consequently forms an idiosyncratic component of his stock marked by the disparate subjects he acquired by a remarkably diverse assortment of artists.[479]

The remarkable success De Mallery enjoyed is evident not simply from his appointment as a dean of the Guild of St Luke for 1621–1622 year, but also from De Mallery's and Catharina Galle's spending spree in Antwerp real estate; they purchased four houses and shares in a fifth between 1608 and 1622.[480] However, significant testamentary obligations after Catharina Galle's death in 1624 resulted in De Mallery's tumultuous financial demise. Forced to sell his real estate piecemeal over the next several years, he was also forced to sell some, if not all, of his valuable stock of copper plates. Ultimately, between 1628 and 1636, when he was approximately sixty years old, De Mallery was back to where he started, namely working as a hired hand for others, engraving and reworking plates for book illustrations. Only now, were his employers – initially, his brother-in-law Theodore Galle and, following his death, Balthasar Moretus I – motivated by old ties and obligations rather than De Mallery's skill. While De Mallery's talent for engraving fine letters was still recognized, his inability to engrave deeply enough to satisfy a book publisher's demands for engraved text illustrations was also acknowledged and contributed to a lackluster end to an otherwise talented artist's career.

LIT.: Bowen and Imhof 2022.

Identifiable prints sold by title

CM-1 *Men and Women of the Franciscan Order (Imagines seraphicae S.mi p. Francisci Assisiatis illustriumque virorum et feminarum)*: **Charles de Mallery after Peeter de Jode I.** Fourteen engravings (ca. 255 × 165) and a title plate (267 × 176), 1614. This series was often included in an earlier publication by Henricus Sedulius: *Historia seraphica vitae bmi. p. Francisci Assisiatis* (Antwerp: Heirs of M. Nutius, 1613). LIT.: New Holl. De Jode, part VII, nos. 572–86. See also TG-13 and JG-1 for subsequent editions of this series traded by the Moretuses. See fig. 7.7.

Sold to Balthasar Moretus I at: 18 st. (possibly) per series in 1623.[481]

CM-2 *Saint John the Baptist in the Wilderness*: **Charles de Mallery.** Engraving, 117 × 79, by 1614. For this image, see, e.g., the Philadelphia Museum of Art, acc. no. 1985–52–29966; Cologne, Wallraf-Richartz-Museum & Fondation Corboud, Graphische Sammlung, no. 15252.

Sold to Balthasar Moretus I at: ½ st. per print in 1614.[482]

CM-3 *Saint Ursula*: possibly an engraving by Charles de Mallery, ca. 105 × 70, by 1626. For an example of this image, see Wolfegg, Fürstlich zu Waldburg-Wolfegg'sche Kunstsammlungen, vol. 186, no. 390.

Sold by Balthasar Moretus I to Jean Leonard at: ½ st. per print in 1626.[483] Since this is the rate that De Mallery usually charged for the prints he sold in bulk, it is most likely what he would have charged Moretus when supplying this image.

CM-4 *The Sins and Penance of Man (Peccati, fomes, vincula, poena, medela)*: **Jan-Baptist Barbé, Cornelis Galle, and Charles de Mallery after Maarten de Vos.** Eleven engravings, including a title plate, ca. 161 × 113, ca. 1610. LIT.: Holl. Dutch & Flemish, vol. XLIV, nos. 1225–35. See fig. 8.18.

Sold to Balthasar Moretus I at: 12 st. per series in 1611.[484]

CM-5 *The Trinity and the Virgin Appear to the First Ten Jesuits*: **Charles de Mallery.** Engraving, 105 × 66, by 1609. For an example of this print, see Cologne, Wallraf-Richartz-Museum & Fondation Corboud, Graphische Sammlung, no. 15222. See fig. 8.19.

Sold to Balthasar Moretus I at: ½ st. per print in 1609.[485]

Unspecified prints sold in bulk
See also the Note to the Reader and Chapter 2.

• per *single image*: sold to Jan Moretus I at .75 st. per image in 1608.[486]
• per *100 images*: sold to Balthasar Moretus I at 3 fl. (= 60 st.) per hundred (= .60 st. per image) in 1609.[487]
• per *100 images* (occasionally identified as prints in 8°): sold by De Mallery to the Moretuses at 50 st. per hundred (= .50 st. per image) nearly annually between 1607 and 1626. Theodore Galle also applied this rate when selling De Mallery's prints to Balthasar Moretus I between 1630 and 1633.[488]

ABRAHAM VAN MERLEN Antwerp 1579–1660 Antwerp

Van Merlen's date of birth (ca. 1579) is estimated on the basis of later documents in which his age is given. While his apprenticeship to Adriaen Collaert in 1597 and subsequent acceptance as a master engraver in 1610 are duly noted in the accounts of Antwerp's Guild of St Luke, there are no records documenting that he was also a pupil of Hieronymus Wierix, as some older biographers, for instance A. Goovaerts, have asserted.[489] Van Merlen, who engraved and published far more prints than those currently noted in the Hollstein Dutch & Flemish catalogue, appears to have specialized in small (ca. 120 × 80 mm or less) religious images and enjoyed a long, successful career without financial or legal crises. Many of his descendants continued to work as engravers or print publishers into the eighteenth century, in particular his son Theodoor II (followed by his widow Mari Wiggers) and Theodoor's son Cornelius (followed by his widow Sara-Maria Huybrechts and her daughters).

LIT.: Holl. Dutch & Flemish, vol. XIV, pp. 10–11, Lemmens and Thijs 2006.

Unspecified prints sold in bulk
See also the Note to the Reader and Chapter 2.

• per *quire* of 25 leaves: sold to Balthasar Moretus I in 1619 at: 18 st. per quire (= .72 st. per leaf), possibly used for images in 8°, with multiple images (possibly as many as four) printed per leaf.[490]
• per *100 images*: sold to Balthasar Moretus I at 36 st. per hundred (= .36 st. per image) between 1615 and 1619 and again in 1625.[491]
• per *100 images*: sold to Balthasar Moretus I at 32 st. per hundred (= .32 st. per image) in 1626.[492]

CHRISTOPHER PLANTIN Tours? ca. 1520–1589 Antwerp

Christopher Plantin is rightly known as a leading – if not, the foremost – publisher in Europe during the second half of the sixteenth century. He began his printing-publishing business in 1555 and initially also worked as a bookbinder and occasionally traded in prints (as is discussed in full in Chapter 3). He soon decided to focus on printing and publishing books and successfully kept his business going despite the difficult years of war across the southern Netherlands in the later sixteenth century. At the height of his career in 1575, Plantin employed enough staff to man sixteen printing presses, a remarkable number for this period. He is currently credited with publishing nearly 2,000 works, although this total omits some of his lesser-known, often ephemeral publications. While he regularly was a middleman in the distribution and sale of prints, he rarely published individual images; usually, he commissioned the production of prints for the embellishment of the books he published. Notable exceptions to this practice are the broadsides listed below, which were originally meant to be book illustrations, but appeared independently first.

LIT.: Bowen and Imhof 2008; Voet, GC; Voet, PP; and the various publications cited in these works.

Identifiable prints sold by title

CP-1 *Roman Calendar (Antiquarum rerum studiosis omnibus …* **(To All Students of Roman Antiquity …))**. Engraving, 245 × 386, 1575. Plantin published this reproduction of an old Roman calendar as a broadside; the explanatory remarks around the image were composed, at least in part, by Benito Arias Montano. LIT.: PP 863. Sold by Plantin at: 2 ½ st. per leaf in 1575 and 1576.[493]

Sold by Jan Moretus II and Balthasar Moretus I at: 1 st. per leaf in 1619.[494]

CP-2 *Temple of Solomon*: **anonymous engraver after Benito Arias Montano.** Engraving, 415 × 570, 1576 and reissued in 1578. LIT.: Imhof 2015. See fig. 3.21.

Between 1576 and 1587, Plantin's standard price for this broadside (usually referred to as the "Templum Salomonis" in his records) was 3 st.[495]
Plantin also occasionally sold it for slightly less: 2.5 st. in 1577 and 1578, via his own shop in Antwerp, or 2.75 st. per copy when sent in bulk to his shop in Paris in 1575.[496]
In a few transactions from 1576, 1577, and 1579, he asked slightly more (3 ½ st. per copy).[497]

PETER PAUL RUBENS Siegen, Westphalia, 1577–Antwerp 1640

Peter Paul Rubens was the son of a Protestant lawyer who had fled Antwerp and settled in Cologne in 1568. Following a temporary residence in Siegen, Rubens's family returned to Cologne, where he lived until his father died when he was eleven years old. Rubens's mother subsequently moved the family back to Antwerp, where they converted to Catholicism. After attending the Latin school of Rombout Verdonck – where he met Balthasar Moretus I – Rubens worked as a page for Marguerite de Lalaing d'Arenberg, Comtesse de Ligne, prior to studying painting under several masters, including Adam van Noort and Otto van Veen. He was registered as a master painter in Antwerp's Guild of St Luke in the guild year 1598–1599.[498] Consequently, by the time he was twenty, Rubens was able to combine a standard education in classical literature and contemporary European languages with an understanding of court life and a thorough training received from prominent, well-connected local painters. In the years to come, he deployed these skills and networks to solidify his career as an educated painter sought out by the elite throughout Europe, as a diplomat, and as a draughtsman who not only created paintings, but also completed designs for works in a full range of media, for instance tapestries, small works in metal, sculptures, pageant decorations, book illustrations, and even his own home in Antwerp. Rubens was also actively engaged in the controlled dissemination of his work in printed form, beginning in the 1610s – most often as engravings, but also periodically as woodcuts during the 1630s; he simultaneously endeavored to protect his designs from unauthorized replication.[499] The subjects of these prints included not only his better-known religious imagery, but also portraits and, as documented below, classical subjects and architectural designs. Although numerous engravers made prints after Rubens's work, those with whom Rubens appears to have worked the most were Schelte à Bolswert, Paulus Pontius, and Lucas Vorsterman I. For woodcut renditions of his compositions, Rubens engaged only Christoffel Jegher. Following Rubens's death in May 1640, the market for printed reproductions of his work – authorized and plagiarized – in various media exploded. This makes the few examples provided here of his own sale of printed images after his designs all the more valuable in comparison.

LIT.: Bowen 2017; Diels 2009, p. 165; Dutuit 1885 / 1972; Schneevoogt 1873; Van Hout 2004; Vlieghe 1996.

Identifiable prints sold by title

PPR-1 *The Battle of the Amazons*: **Lucas Vorsterman I after Pieter Paul Rubens.** Printed from six engraved plates, measuring 423 × 364 to 428 × 420 per plate and ca. 856 × 1208 combined, 1623. LIT.: Bowen 2017; Holl. Dutch & Flemish, vol. XLIII, pp. 96–97, no. 100. See fig. 7.15.

Sold to Balthasar Moretus I at 3 fl. 10 st. (= 70 st.) in 1632.[500]

PPR-2 *Palazzi di Genova*: **after drawings by Pieter Paul Rubens.** Part I: *Palazzi antichi*, comprising seventy-two plates of varying dimensions with plans and elevations attributed to the engraver Nicolaes Ryckemans, after various drawings collected by Rubens of villas and palaces built during the later sixteenth century in or near Genoa; with introductory texts in letterpress, published in 1622. Part II: *Palazzi moderni*, comprising sixty-seven plates with plans and elevations of an additional selection of buildings constructed between 1540 and 1620; possibly not completed until 1640. LIT.: Bowen 2017; Lombaerde 2002; Rott 2002, pp. 17–20. See fig. 7.21.

When Rubens sold four copies of this series to Balthasar Moretus I in 1632, they were simply identified in Moretus's account book as "diverse belden van Rubbens voor Borraj" (diverse images from Rubens for "Borraj"). It is only when the prints were resold to the bookbinder Pierre Bouray at cost that the actual subjects were specified, namely: "2 Palazzi di Genova f groot met [?] [and] 2 [Palazzi] di Genova f klyn" (two *Palazzi di Genova* in folio large with [?] and two small).[501] The difference in size could indicate either the size of the paper used to print the engravings or the number of images included in the series. Both the timing of the sale to Bouray and the price at which Balthasar Moretus sold copies of this series to Kaspar Förster in 1637 and 1640 suggest that the "large" series cited here was Part I. The prices Moretus charged for the second part in 1640 vary from ca. 80 or 90 st. to 115 st. and consequently cannot be related with certainty to the "small" series sold to Bouray in 1632.[502]

THE SADELERS

The following family members are featured in this study:
- Gillis (Aegidius) I (Brussels? ?–1609 Frankfurt am Main)
- Jan (Johannes) I (Brussels 1550–1600 Venice)
- Raphael I (Antwerp 1560/1561–1632 Munich)
- Justus (Antwerp 1583–1620 Leiden)

Gillis I, Jan I, and Raphael I were all sons of Jan de Saeyeleer, who was trained in the inlay of metals and most likely moved from Brussels to Antwerp in the early 1550s. His brother Emmanuel likewise moved to Antwerp by 1561 and was the father of Aegidius (Gillis) Sadeler II (Antwerp, ca. 1570–1629, Prague), who is known for becoming a court artist for Emperor Rudolf II in Prague. Each of the aforementioned brothers trained in Antwerp and was registered in the Guild of St Luke there. Both Jan I and Raphael I were listed as engravers (in 1572 and 1582, respectively) and soon gained international renown for their work. Gillis I was registered as an art dealer in 1580, although he may well have been active by 1571; in 1586, he was also identified as a "constdrukker" ("printer of art", presumably intaglio prints). These seem to have remained his primary occupations throughout his life.[503] During the later 1570s, Jan I and Raphael I left Antwerp for Germany, and by 1580, they were in Cologne. Several artists from Antwerp – such as Abraham de Bruyn – and other parts of the Low Countries – Frans Hogenberg, for example – had similarly emigrated there in the same period. Both Jan I and Raphael I returned to Antwerp in 1585 and remained there into 1586, by which time their father had passed away and his estate was settled. This was also when Antwerp fell to Alexander Farnese, and residents were forced to declare themselves faithful to the Catholic church or leave the city. Consequently, between July and September 1586, each of the three brothers was cited in official statements for the Antwerp government that attested to their good character and to the moral conduct of individuals known to them.[504] Jan I and Raphael I must have left for Frankfurt soon thereafter; both were registered there in 1586 and became citizens of the city in 1587. However, Jan I left for Munich the following year, and subsequently traveled between Cologne, Munich, Prague, Rome, and Venice, until he ultimately settled in Venice around 1595 and established a print publishing business there. Raphael I was based in Frankfurt until 1591, by which time his brother Gillis I had joined him there. Gillis I became a citizen of Frankfurt in 1598 and remained in the city until his death in 1609.[505] Meanwhile, Raphael I worked temporarily in Cologne and Munich prior to joining his brother Jan in Venice in the late 1590s. Following Jan's death in 1600, the family business there was initially continued by Raphael I and then by his son Justus, once Raphael and his family had moved back to Munich in 1604 to work for the Duke of Bavaria, Maximilian I. Justus continued to work as a print publisher, bookseller, and art dealer in Venice until his early death in 1620. Raphael I remained in Munich, where he and his three sons worked on the *Bavaria sancta* series for Maximilian I, as well as on numerous book illustrations, including ones for several illustrated texts that Raphael I published during the 1620s. Both Raphael I and his eldest son, Raphael II, died in Munich in 1632. Raphael's remaining sons appear to have occupied themselves primarily by engraving images for other publishers' books.

The Sadelers are well known for their numerous individual prints (especially those designed by Maarten de Vos and Jacopo Bassano), copies of prints by Cornelis Cort after renowned Italian painters, and several extensive print series (such as those of hermits or Mathaeus Rader's *Bavaria sancta*). According to Jan I's will, his stock of copper plates was to be divided between Raphael I and Justus (but not Gillis I). Justus's stock was soon dispersed after his death, and the Sadeler family's plates remained a sought-after commodity into the early eighteenth century and may have been reprinted in the Veneto into the mid-nineteenth century, reflecting the immense, prolonged fame their prints enjoyed.[506]

Despite the fact that Plantin employed Jan I around 1570 and between 1575–1576 for the production of engraved borders and illustrations for some of his books, there is no evidence that Jan I subsequently supplied Plantin or the Moretuses with impressions of his own print publications. Rather, other print dealers in Antwerp (most often Philips Galle) appear to have acted as intermediaries for such sales. Galle performed this role in early 1588, when the Antwerp merchant Ferdinandus Ximenes ordered a selection of images, including some published by Jan Sadeler.[507] Among the Sadelers, Gillis I appears to have been the primary point of contact for international sales of prints published by diverse family members. Remarkably, even he does not seem to have provided either Plantin or Jan Moretus I with prints often. Aside from a few isolated examples of Gillis I supplying the Moretuses with prints via the Frankfurt fairs in 1601–1603, there is only one known instance of a Sadeler providing Plantin with prints, namely in August 1588, when Gillis I was the only one of the three brothers who was still in Antwerp. Nevertheless, these rare sales document how Gillis I provided images originally published by Jan I, Aegidius II, and Raphael I, in addition to unspecified leaves with prints after Jacopo Bassano that were most likely supplied by Justus. Among the other few instances when Plantin sold prints by the Sadelers to some of his clients, the source of these prints is not noted, while the Moretuses, on occasion, obtained some of the Sadelers' works via other, unrelated individuals.[508]

LIT.: Bowen 2022b; Holl. Dutch & Flemish, vols. XXI and XXII; De Ramaix 1989; De Ramaix 1992; De Ramaix 1997–2014 (for the best family tree); Sénéchal 1990 (for Justus); Vignau-Wilberg 2005, pp. 435–36; Zülch 1935, pp. 416–17 (for Gillis I).

Identifiable prints sold by title

SD-1 ***Hermits (Solitudo sive vitae patrum eremicolarum (1585–1586), Sylvae sacrae monumenta … anachoretarum* (1593–1594), *Trophaeum vitae solitariae* (1598), and *Oraculum anachoreticum* (1595–1600): Jan Sadeler I and Raphael Sadeler I after Maarten de Vos.** 110 engravings, including four title plates, ca. 166/188 × 203, published in four volumes between 1585 and 1600 by Jan I and Raphael I in Munich and then in Venice. LIT.: Holl. Dutch & Flemish, vol. XXI, nos. 377–450, under Jan I, and nos. 118–57, under Raphael I; Holl. Dutch & Flemish, vol. XLIV, nos. 964–1075.

Sold to Jan Moretus I at: 3 _ 18 ½ Rhenish guilders for all four volumes in the spring of 1605.[509]

SD-2 ***Symbola divina et humana* [vol. I], *Symbola varia* … [vols. II and III] *(Divine and Human Symbols)*: Aegidius Sadeler II.** 150 engraved text illustrations (ca. 238 × 135) and an engraved title plate (263 × 158), published by Aegidius Sadeler in Prague in three volumes between 1601 and 1603, with commentary by Jacobus Typotius (vols. 1 and 2) and Anselmus de Boodt (vol. 3). LIT.: Holl. Dutch & Flemish, vols. XXI and XXII, no. 392 (p. 81, under Aegidius Sadeler); Bowen 2022b, pp. 379–80.

Sold to Jan Moretus I as individual volumes of the "Simbola" or "Simbolorum" at:

- 18 batz for vol. 1, possibly without the text, in the fall of 1600 and the spring of 1601.[510]
- 1 Rhenish guilder in the spring of 1602 for three copies of the text for vol. 1.[511]
- 1 fl. 15 st. for vol. 1 with text in the spring of 1603.[512]
- 2 fl. for vol. 2 in the spring of 1602 (without reference to the text).[513]
- 2 fl. 5 st. for vol. 3 in the spring of 1603 (without reference to the text).[514]

These sales are discussed in greater detail in Bowen 2023.

SD-3 ***Virtues of Christ*: Jan Sadeler I after Maarten de Vos.** Nine engravings, including a title plate, ca. 194 × 133, 1585–1588. LIT.: Holl. Dutch & Flemish, vol. XLIV, nos. 1152–60.

Sold to Plantin at: 13 ½ st. per series in 1588.[515]

MICHAEL SNIJDERS Antwerp 1586–1672 Antwerp

Although there are no records of where or when Snijders trained as an engraver, he was admitted as a master engraver in Antwerp's Guild of St Luke in 1610, eight years after the acceptance of his elder brother François (Frans) Snijders (1579–1657), who soon became a highly respected and wealthy painter, primarily of animals and still-life elements. In 1614, Michael Snijders was already endeavoring to expand his business in various ways. When he registered his one known apprentice with the Guild of St Luke, he was identified as both an art dealer and an engraver. This shift in the focus of his activities is also evident from the fact that examples of Snijders's work in collections today are primarily prints that he published rather than engraved; the extent of his publications is far greater than what is noted in the Hollstein Dutch & Flemish print catalogs.[516] While the majority of these images are anonymous devotional prints in small formats, Snijders also produced some exceptionally large prints, such as the representation of the origin of the kings of France in the form of a tree (Holl. no. 17), and reissued several engravings originally published by other Antwerp print publishers, in particular Gerard de Jode and Philips Galle. Furthermore, he published a couple of emblem books, of which *Amoris divini et humani antipathia* (1629) is best known.[517] Nevertheless, despite his various endeavors, Snijders spent the last decades of his life in ill health and poverty.

LIT.: Duverger 1990–1991; Holl. Dutch & Flemish, vol. XXVII, pp. 91–96; Rombouts and Van Lerius, vol. I, pp. 462, 472, and 507–08.

Unspecified prints sold in bulk

See also the Note to the Reader and Chapter 2.

- per *print, on paper, colored*: sold to Balthasar Moretus I at 2 st. per print (in 4°), in 1629.[518]
- per *print, "large", plain (support not specified)*: sold to Balthasar Moretus I at 2 st. per print in 1632.[519]
- per *12 images on parchment, colored*: sold to Balthasar Moretus I at 33 st. per dozen (= 2.75 st. per image) in 1629 and 1632.[520]
- per *100 images on parchment, colored*: sold to Balthasar Moretus I at 13 fl 15 st (= 275 st.) per hundred (= 2.75 st. per image) in 1632.[521]
- per *100 images on parchment (plain)*: sold to Balthasar Moretus I at 4 fl. 10 st. (= 90 st.) per hundred (= .9 st. per image) in 1629.[522]
- per *100 images on parchment (plain)*: sold to Balthasar Moretus I at 4 fl. (= 80 st.) per hundred (= .8 st. per image) in 1632.[523]
- per *100 images on paper (plain)*: sold to Balthasar Moretus I at 36 st. per hundred (= .36 st. per image) occasionally between 1618 and 1626.[524]

LAMBERT SUAVIUS Liège ca. 1510–1567 Frankfurt am Main?

Suavius was the son of a goldsmith and the brother-in-law of Lambert Lombard, who was his teacher and exerted a significant influence on his work. Like Lombard, Suavius pursued a broad range of activities; however, he was primarily known for his work as an engraver and architect. By the mid-1550s, Suavius held the position of city architect in Liège. He was still engaged in the distribution of his own prints at this time, for in 1553, he supplied Plantin with the substantial quantity of 100 sets of a series of the *Acts of the Apostles*, which he is believed to have engraved himself. In the early 1560s, Suavius traveled to Frankfurt am Main via Antwerp and Cologne. Having arrived by 1562, he most likely died there in 1567.

LIT.: Holl. Dutch & Flemish, vol. XXVIII, p. 165.

Identifiable prints sold by title

LS-1 *The Acts of the Apostles*: **attributed to Lambert Suavius.** Nineteen or twenty engravings, ca. 107 × 153, completed by 1553. LIT.: Holl. Dutch & Flemish, vol. XXVIII, p. 195, no. 127. See The British Museum, nos. 1925,1117.51–68 for the prints associated with this series; see also the comment on no. 1925,1117.19.

Sold to Plantin at: 10 st. per series in 1553.[525]
As observed by Van der Stock, this series is distinct from that of *Christ, the Twelve Apostles, and Saint Paul* (CD-6), which Cock and Diericx consistently sold to Plantin for 6 st. per series in 1568, 1570, and 1571.[526]

LS-2 *Apostles Peter and John Healing the Paralytic*: **Lambert Suavius.** Engraving, 305 × 420, 1553. LIT.: Holl. Dutch & Flemish, vol. XXVIII, p. 174, no. 23.

Sold to Plantin at: 5 st. per print in 1556.[527]

OTTO VAN VEEN Leiden ca. 1556–Brussels 1629

Born to a Catholic, patrician family in Leiden, Otto van Veen attended the local Latin school and trained as a painter under Isaac Claesz. van Swanenburgh. However, in 1572, his father decided to leave Leiden, in part due to the family's faith and in part due to his political career. Soon thereafter, Van Veen traveled independently to Rome to pursue his artistic career. He left the city around 1580 and ultimately settled in Brussels, where he served Alexander Farnese, who was then governor of the southern Netherlands. Following Farnese's death in 1592, Van Veen moved to Antwerp, where he was registered as a member of the Guild of St Luke in the guild year of 1593–1594.[528] The success of his workshop, which was well regarded locally and abroad, may account for Rubens's desire to work under him. Regarded as a learned artist with assorted contacts among Netherlandish scholars, Van Veen increased his output of illustrated books, in particular emblem books, while also producing some print series and personal writings on theoretical topics, during the first decade of the seventeenth century, when his activities as a painter were in decline.

LIT.: Holl. Dutch & Flemish, vol. XXXII, pp. 159–84. Van de Velde 1996.

Identifiable prints sold by title

OV-1 *Life of Saint Thomas Aquinas (Vita d. Thomae Aquinatis)*: **Cornelius Boel, Cornelis Galle, Egbert van Panderen, and Willem van Swanenburg after Otto van Veen.** Thirty engravings (ca. 210 × 149) and an engraved title plate (216 × 155), with introductory texts in letterpress, 1610. LIT.: Imhof 2014a, no. V-1. See fig. 8.17. Sold to Balthasar Moretus I at: 2 fl. (= 40 st.) per series in 1611.[529]

THE WIERIXES

The following family members are featured in this study:

- Hieronymus Wierix I (Antwerp 1553–1619 Antwerp)
- Anton Wierix II (Antwerp ca. 1557–1604 Antwerp)

The Wierix brothers – Jan I (Antwerp 1549–ca. 1620 or later Brussels), Hieronymus I, and Anton II – are justifiably renowned as remarkable engravers who regularly produced exceptionally fine engravings, while periodically (during moments of leisure) exhibiting their disreputable and unreliable characters. All three brothers were sons of the painter and cabinetmaker Anton I. However, only Jan and Hieronymus are assumed to have been trained in engraving by a local goldsmith. Although their teacher remains unknown, their stunning adolescent "exercises" in copying prints by former master engravers – in particular, Albrecht Dürer – are understandably famous. Around 1570, before either Jan or Hieronymus had officially registered with Antwerp's Guild of St Luke, as would occur in 1572–1573, Plantin began to employ both Hieronymus and Jan to make book illustrations, while Cock and Diericx hired Jan to work on their famous series of portraits of painters from the Low Countries (*Pictorum aliquot celebrium Germaniae inferioris effigies* (CD-18)). Anton II, who may have learned to engrave under Hieronymus, did not join the Guild of St Luke until 1590/91. Once they became officially master engravers, however, all three brothers focused on completing work for prominent local print publishers or for their own profit during the last quarter of the sixteenth century. Creating prints for Philips Galle, Hans van Luyck, Gerard de Jode, Jan Baptist Vrients, and Willem van Haecht, the brothers worked primarily after compositions by Maarten de Vos, but also engraved numerous, diverse subjects designed by Johannes Stradanus, Crispijn van den Broeck, Gerard van Groeningen, and Ambrosius Francken; all of these images were often in a larger format than the Wierixes' personal work. By the start of the seventeenth century, each brother began to pursue a more independent career. Jan, who had already tried working in Delft between roughly 1575 and 1579, settled in Brussels by 1609 and focused increasingly on producing highly finished pen drawings on vellum as independent works of art. Hieronymus came to specialize in small, high-quality devotional images. The immense, immediate success of Hieronymus's images is evident from the numerous copies or variations of them that were produced – both by Hieronymus himself and by fellow, competing engravers. Anton II was less fortunate. Periodically in debt during the 1590s, he died early, in 1604, cutting short his attempt to benefit from the sale of his own prints. His engravings are often confused with those of his son Anton III (1596–1624), who also worked in the family style, imitating, in particular, Hieronymus's small devotional prints; Anton III did not distinguish his signature on plates from his father's. Consequently, when one envisions the legacy of the Wierix brothers, one must consider diverse, often large images produced by one of the three brothers for other publishers, exquisite drawings from Jan that were sought by the elite, and hundreds of popular engravings made or published by Hieronymus or his brother and nephew, Anton II and

III. The impact of the Wierixes' work was enormous, instantaneous, and widespread. Not only were innumerable copies and variants made of their engravings, but their prints were also used as models and patterns for various other art objects, ranging from needlework to stained glass and a variety of metal objects.[530] Additionally, the copper plates used to print Hieronymus's devotional images were immediately recognized as valuable commodities; they were coveted and fought over in the decades immediately following his death, and impressions continued to be printed from them into the nineteenth century. While the prolonged reuse of Hieronymus's plates attests to the lasting admiration for his work, early impressions of his engravings, along with those of his brothers, clarify why they were so eagerly sought by collectors throughout Europe from the start.

LIT.: Bowen and Imhof 2008, passim, and pp. 352–56 for Hieronymus I's and Jan Wierix's work for Plantin; Holl. Dutch & Flemish, vol. LXIX, pp. xi-xlv; M-H Wierix 1978–1982, in particular Carl Van de Velde's transcriptions of documents pertaining to the family in vol. III.2, pp. 529–71.

Identifiable prints sold by title

WX-1 *Annunciation and Nativity*: in 16°, by 1602 (not yet linked to a known print). See, for example, Holl. Dutch & Flemish, vol. LIX, no. 123, for an example of an appropriately small image of the Annunciation published by Anton Wierix II.

Sold to Jan Moretus I by Anton Wierix at: .5 st. per pair of images in 1602.[531]

WX-2 *The Death of Saint Cecilia*: **Hieronymus Wierix after Francesco Vanni.** Engraving, 152 × 117, between 1599 and 1605. LIT.: Holl. Dutch & Flemish, vol. LXV, no. 1413. See fig. 6.7.

Sold to Jan Moretus I by Hieronymus Wierix at: 4 st. per print in 1606.[532]

WX-3 *Four "Fathers"*, **possibly:** ***Christ on the Cross Venerated by Four Jesuit Saints (Ignatius of Loyola, Francis Xavier, Aloysius Gonzaga, and Stanislaus Kostka).*** Given the selling price, this was most likely not a series of four separate images of the four fathers of the church, but an impression of one of Hieronymus Wierix's engravings of four prominent sixteenth-century Jesuits, each of which is ca. 110 × 67, by 1610. LIT.: Holl. Dutch & Flemish, vol. LXIV, nos. 1279–82. See fig. 8.20.

Sold to Jan Moretus I by Hieronymus Wierix at: 2 st. per print in 1610.[533]

WX-4 *Guardian Angel*: **Hieronymus Wierix.** Engraving, 147 × 103, by 1602. LIT.: Holl. Dutch & Flemish, vol. LXIII, no. 1088.

Sold to Jan Moretus I by Hieronymus Wierix at: 3 st. per print in 1602.[534]

WX-5 *Jesus and Joseph* **(booklet)**: by 1613. Possibly the same as Hieronymus Wierix's *Life of the Infant* series (WX-7), which was sold for the same price.

Sold to Balthasar Moretus I by Hieronymus Wierix at: 22 st. per series in 1613.[535]

WX-6 *Jesus Walking between the Virgin and Joseph with the Trinity above*: **Anton Wierix** II. Engraving, 97 × 65, by 1602. LIT.: Holl. Dutch & Flemish, vol. LXII, no. 769.

Sold to Jan Moretus I by Anton Wierix II at: 1 st. per print in 1602.[536]

WX-7 *Life of the Infant (Iesu Christi ... Infantia)*: **Hieronymus Wierix.** Thirteen plates, including a title plate, ca. 99 × 64, by 1615. LIT.: Holl. Dutch & Flemish, vol. LXI, nos. 484–96 and nos. 497–509 (two sets of engravings of this same series by Hieronymus Wierix). This may well be the same series as that referred to in the Moretuses' accounts as a booklet with Jesus and Joseph (WX-5), which was sold for the same price. See figs. 6.8, 6.30, and 6.31.

Sold to Balthasar Moretus I by Hieronymus Wierix at: 22 st. per series in 1615 and 1616.[537]

WX-8 *Mirror of Virginity (Speculum virginitatis)*: **Hieronymus Wierix.** Seven engravings, including a title plate, ca. 93 × 54, by 1616. LIT.: Holl. Dutch & Flemish, vol. LXVI, nos. 1743–49.

Sold to Balthasar Moretus I by Hieronymus Wierix at: 14 st. per series in 1616.[538]

WX-9 *Novus Jesus*: most likely a series given the price, completed by 1616 (not yet linked to a specific series).

Sold to Balthasar Moretus I by Hieronymus Wierix at: 18 st. per series in 1616.[539]

WX-10 *Saint Anna*: in 4°, completed by 1602 (not yet linked to a known print).

Sold to Jan Moretus I by Hieronymus Wierix at: 3 st. per print in 1602.[540]

WX-11 *Saint Francis of Assisi Receiving the Girdle from the Virgin*: **Anton Wierix** II. Engraving, 102 × 67, by 1602. LIT.: Holl. Dutch & Flemish, vol. LXV, no. 1450.

Sold to Jan Moretus I by Anton Wierix at: 1 st. per print in 1602.[541]

WX-12 *Saint Francis Xavier*: most likely an impression of one of the prints Hieronymus Wierix published of this subject (not all are signed by him as engraver) that are comparable in size to the individual images of St Ignatius listed below here (namely, ca. 110 × 70), due to the similarity in price, by 1607. LIT.: Holl. Dutch & Flemish, vol. LXV, nos. 1460–62.

Sold to Jan Moretus I by Hieronymus Wierix at: 1 st. per print in 1607.[542]

WX-13 ***Saint Ignatius of Loyola with a Book***: most likely an impression of one of Hieronymus Wierix's engravings of this subject, each of which is ca. 109 × 66, by 1607. LIT.: Holl. Dutch & Flemish, vol. LXV, nos. 1522–24.

Sold to Jan Moretus I by Hieronymus Wierix at: 2 st. per print in 1607.[543]

WX-14 ***Saint Ignatius of Loyola with a Cross***: most likely an impression of one of Hieronymus Wierix's engravings of this subject, each of which is ca. 108/112 × 68/73, by 1607. LIT.: Holl. Dutch & Flemish, vol. LXV, nos. 1525–28.

Sold to Jan Moretus I by Hieronymus Wierix at: 1 st. per print in 1607.[544]

WX-15 ***Saints Agnes and Margaret of Antioch***: possibly two similarly sized prints, ca. 82 × 58, Anton Wierix II, by 1602. LIT.: Holl. Dutch & Flemish, vols. LXIV and LXV, nos. 1317 and 1584, respectively.

Sold to Jan Moretus I by Anton Wierix at: .75 st. per image(s) of the two saints together in 1602.[545]

WX-16 ***Saints Ignatius of Loyola and Francis Xavier***: most likely one of the pairs of companion prints of these saints engraved by Hieronymus Wierix after Diego da Garça, ca. 81 × 61 (each individual print), by 1607. LIT.: Holl. Dutch & Flemish, vol. LXV, nos. 1517–18 and 1520–21.

Sold to Jan Moretus I by Hieronymus Wierix at: 2 st. per pair in 1607.[546]

WX-17 ***Triumph of Truth*: Anton Wierix II after an engraving by Jan Wierix after Maarten de Vos.** Engraving, 96 × 65, by 1602. LIT.: Holl. Dutch & Flemish, vol. LXVI, no. 1838. See fig. 7.20.

Sold to Jan Moretus I by Anton Wierix at: 1 st. per print in 1602.[547]

WX-18 ***Twelve Apostles*: Anton Wierix** II. Twelve engravings, ca. 81 × 60, by 1602. LIT.: Holl. Dutch & Flemish, vol. LXIV, nos. 1124–35. See figs. 6.5 and 6.6.

Sold to Jan Moretus I at: 6 st. by Anton Wierix in 1602 and by Hieronymus Wierix in 1607.[548]

WX-19 ***Virgin and the Sleeping Child*: Anton Wierix** II. Engraving, 85 × 60, by 1602. LIT.: Holl. Dutch & Flemish, vol. LXII, no. 784.

Sold to Jan Moretus I by Anton Wierix II at: 1 st. per print in 1602.[549]

WX-20 ***Virgin and Child on a Crescent Moon*: Hieronymus Wierix.** Engraving, 147 × 103, by 1602. LIT.: Holl. Dutch & Flemish, vol. lxiii, no. 1030.

Sold to Jan Moretus I by Hieronymus Wierix at: 4 st. per print in 1602.[550]

Unspecified prints sold in bulk
See also the Note to the Reader and Chapter 2.

- per *single image*: sold to Jan Moretus I and Balthasar Moretus I by Hieronymus at 2 st. per image in between 1609 and 1616.[551]
- per *single image*: sold to Jan Moretus I and Balthasar Moretus I by Hieronymus at 1.5 st. per image between 1609 and 1616.[552]
- per *single image* (occasionally identified as an image in 8°): sold at 1 st. per image to Jan Moretus I by Anton II in 1601 and to Balthasar Moretus I by Hieronymus in 1602 and periodically between 1609 and 1616.[553]
- per *single image*: sold to Balthasar Moretus I by Hieronymus at .75 st. per image in 1611.[554]

1 MPM Arch. 20, fol. 87 rht (for the lower price); and MPM Arch. 59, fol. 173r, and MPM Arch. 18, fol. 436 rht (for the higher price).

2 MPM Arch. 60, fol. 113v; and MPM Arch. 59, fol. 185v, respectively.

3 Although her name is often given as "Marie Le Man", we are using the form of her name as she signed it herself on her will and other notarial documents (see Antwerp, Felix Archives, N 3082, will from 27 June 1631, and N 1195, fol. 1r (15 January 1642)).

4 MPM Arch. 114, fol. 160, for his initial contact with the Moretuses; and the Universal Short Title Catalogue (https://www.ustc.ac.uk/), no. 1003743, for the cited book.

5 MPM Arch. 235, fol. 26r.

6 MPM Arch. 235, fol. 89r.

7 MPM Arch. 235, fols. 26r and 89r.

8 MPM Arch. 248, fol. 33v.

9 MPM Arch. 248, fol. 33v.

10 MPM Arch. 248, fol. 33v.

11 MPM Arch. 235, fol. 26r.

12 MPM Arch. 248, fol. 33v.

13 MPM Arch. 235, fol. 26r.

14 On print publishing in sixteenth-century Italy, see Bury 2001, pp. 68–74; and Witcombe 2008.

15 Ewing 1990; and Van der Stock 1998.

16 Cock 2013, pp. 25–26.

17 MPM Arch. 46, fol. 221r: "Nativitas Georgii Gizi Mantuani"; and MPM Arch. 51, fol. 200r: "kersnacht 2 bladeren dobbel", respectively.

18 For such sales, see MPM Arch. 46, fol. 242r: "compartements en ovalle ou Mansfelt"; MPM Arch. 58, fol. 25v: "Perspective di Vrise dedicate comiti di Mansvelt f° 11 a 2 figures sur chaque fueille"; and MPM Arch. 59, fol. 80r: "pros. mansvelt". See also MPM M 296 (= MPM Arch. 1227; Plantin's list of publications by his contemporaries), fol. 388v, for the same price, with a note similar to that in Arch. 58, recording how it was sold with two images per leaf: "Perspectives de Vries Corn. Mansvelt a 2 fig. sur fueille st. 8 ½".

19 MPM Arch. 71, fols. 64r (for the resale of this series, printed on eight leaves) and 64v (for the supply of: "bastiment mansvelt").

20 MPM Arch. 46, fol. 242r: "Termae Diocletiani"; and MPM Arch. 59, fol. 80r: "Thermae f°".

21 MPM Arch. 46, fol. 242v: "Blaw huickes".

22 MPM Arch. 48, fol. 177r: "apostelen Lombardi"; and MPM Arch. 49, fol. 143r: "apostel boeck L", respectively.

23 MPM Arch. 46, fol. 242r: "Apostres Suavius"; MPM Arch. 48, fol. 177r: "apostelen Suavii"; and MPM Arch. 49, fol. 143r: "apostelboek suavius", respectively.

24 MPM Arch. 34, p. 26: "Cercles de Rome".

25 MPM Arch. 46, fol. 242r: "4 circles de Rome". We would like to thank Joris Van Grieken for his advice on the attribution of these prints.

26 MPM Arch. 46, fol. 242r: "compartiments Benedicti Batini".

27 MPM Arch. 51, fol. 200r: "consilium 2 groote dobbel bladeren".

28 MPM Arch. 46, fol. 242r: "Pompe funeral f°".

29 MPM Arch. 49, fol. 102v: "doubles f° grandes de Jachten".

30 For such sales, see MPM Arch. 58, fol. 19r: "jacht groot Jo: Stradani in f° real met compartimenten van 6 bladeren"; and MPM Arch. 59, fol. 19r: "cachie gra[nd] stradanj". See also MPM M 296 (= MPM Arch. 1227), fol. 388v, for the same price in Plantin's general list of prices of publications by his contemporaries.

31 MPM Arch. 58, fol. 19r: "jachten van 6 folien Stradani".

32 MPM Arch. 46, fol. 151v: "lanck landtschap van balam".

33 Duverger 1984–2009, vol. 1, p. 28.

34 MPM Arch. 59, fol. 19r: "paesages breugel", and fol. 20v: "Paesi grandi folii depii 14 f°".

35 MPM Arch. 46, fol. 242r: "Messina".

36 MPM Arch. 46, fol. 242r: "compart. Jaques Floris Cock"; and MPM Arch. 48, fol. 177r: "comp[ar]timenten Floris", respectively.

37 MPM Arch. 49, fol. 28v: "pius v. cok".

38 MPM Arch. 51, fol. 200r: "Schilders boek"; MPM Arch. 20, fol. 2 rht: "Pictorum effigies"; and MPM Arch. 54, fol. 138v: "Effigies Pictorum f°", respectively.

39 MPM Arch. 35, fol. 152r: "lantscap brueghel". Although Delen links this reference to the series of twelve "Large Landscapes" by the Van Doetecums after P. Bruegel I, which Cock published ca. 1555–1556, we believe that this may simply refer to Bruegel's own landscape, for the number "12" that precedes this reference reflects the number of copies of the image that Cock provided and not the number of prints in a possible series (see Delen 1932, p. 4).

40 MPM Arch. 51, fol. 200r: "serpent van 2 bladeren dobbel dubbel".

41 MPM Arch. 51, fol. 200r: "v[er]rysenis 2 bladeren dobbel".

42 MPM Arch. 35, fol. 152r: "Verrysenissen".

43 MPM Arch. 46, fol. 151v: "Alle de schepen".

44 MPM Arch. 46, fol. 242r: "boere kermisse".

45 MPM Arch. 35, fol. 152r: "Hieronimus Galle".

46 MPM Arch. 35, fol. 152r: "S. Jans onthoofding".

47 MPM Arch. 59, fol. 20v: "Scenographia Jo: vreedmanni frisij 21 f° Cock 1560 Granvelle".

48 MPM Arch. 46, fol. 242r: "compartiments avec histoires"; and MPM Arch. 48, fol. 177r: "comp[ar]timentken historial", respectively.

49 MPM Arch. 46, fol. 242r: "livres de sepultures"; MPM Arch. 51, fol. 200r: "Sepultur boek"; and MPM Arch. 59, fol. 80r: "Sepultura boek", respectively.

50 MPM Arch. 58, fol. 19r: "7 doot sonden 8 f° Breughel".

51 MPM Arch. 58, fol. 25v: "Arti liberali 7 f° … floris".

52 MPM Arch. 35, fol. 152r: "seven vrouwen". We have linked the reference to seven women to this series because each image features a female figure at its center.

53 MPM Arch. 46, fol. 242r: "Batailles dolyphanes".

54 For such sales, see MPM Arch. 46, fol. 242r: "petites livres de perspective"; MPM Arch. 58, fol. 25v: "Perspective de Vriese … Granvellano f°16"; and MPM Arch. 59, fol. 80r: "prospect Granvelle". See also MPM M 296 (= MPM Arch. 1227), fol. 388v, for the same price in Plantin's list of publications by his contemporaries, with the note, as in Arch. 58, that this series was printed on sixteen leaves: "Perspect. De Vriese Granvell. f° 16 st. 12".

55 MPM Arch. 71, fols. 64r (for the resale of this series, printed on fifteen leaves) and 64v (for the supply of "bastimen dedie Card.").

56 MPM Arch. 46, fol. 242r: "petits livres de ruines"; MPM Arch. 51, fol. 200r: "Ruyn boek"; and MPM Arch. 59, fol. 80r: "Ruyn Boek", respectively.

57 MPM Arch. 46, fols. 151v: "dorp huis boexken" and 242r: "livres de maisons de villages"; and MPM Arch. 51, fol. 200r: "dorp huyskens boek", respectively.

58 MPM Arch. 58, fol. 25v: "Historie di Daniel Heem.".

59 MPM Arch. 46, fol. 151v: "Thobias Hist.".

60 MPM Arch. 35, fol. 152r: "Christoffel".

61 MPM Arch. 35, fol. 152r: "spinsters". In Cock 2013, no. 27, this image is similarly linked to a reference to "Een coperen plaete van de Spinsters" (a copper plate of the spinners) in the 1601 inventory of Diericx's possessions.

62 MPM Arch. 48, fol. 177r: "Vasa".

63 MPM Arch. 46, fol. 242v (1568: Cock); and MPM Arch. 51, fol. 200r (1573: Diericx).

64 MPM Arch. 46, fols. 151v and 242v (1568: Cock); MPM Arch. 49, fol. 143r (1571: Diericx); and MPM Arch. 51, fol. 200r (1573: Diericx).

65 MPM Arch. 46, fol. 242v (1568: Cock); MPM Arch. 49, fol. 143r (1571: Diericx); and MPM Arch. 51, fol. 200r (1573: Diericx).

66 MPM Arch. 48, fol. 139v (1568: Cock); MPM Arch. 49, fol. 143r (1571: Diericx); and MPM Arch. 59, fol. 19r (1581: Diericx).

67 Diels 2010, pp. 76–106.

68 Rombouts and Van Lerius, vol. I, p. 273.

69 Ibid. p. 76 and n. 209, with reference to Antwerp, Felix Archives, WK 27, document bundle 31, for Hans Collaert's estate from 21 February 1581.

70 Rombouts and Van Lerius, vol. I, pp. 380, 398, 420, and 432 (for the pupils registered under Collaert, including Abraham van Merlen in 1597), and 389 and 396 (for his terms as dean).

71 Diels 2010, pp. 215–23.

72 Ibid., p. 168, Diels estimates that Collaert may have bought as many as seventy-three plates from the sale of Diericx's stock.

73 On the production and distribution of Nadal's work, see Bowen and Imhof 2019. For Adriaen Collaert's engravings, see New Holl. Collaert, nos. 1713–14 and 1716–24.

74 Diels 2010, pp. 261–63; and also New Holl. Collaert, part VIII.

75 MPM Arch. 180, fol. 155r: "Voghelboecken".

76 MPM Arch. 180, fol. 155r: "Apostelen tot 3 ½ in 15 stucxkens".

77 MPM Arch. 180, fol. 155r: "Heremiten Boecken".

78 MPM Arch. 180, fol. 155r: "Vischboecxkens".

79 MPM Arch. 180, fol. 155r: "Beestboeckens".

80 MPM Arch. 180, fol. 155r: "Jonckheyt Christi in 12° stuxkens".

81 MPM Arch. 180, fol. 155r: "Agnus Dei".

82 MPM Arch. 174, fol. 14r: "Vita Magdalenae". See the Note to the Reader and Chapter 2 on the sizes of images and sheets of paper.

83 MPM Arch. 174, fol. 39r: "Vita Iesu passio B. Mariae figures" (1602); and MPM Arch. 180, fol. 155r: "Vita Christi mette passie" (1608).

84 MPM Arch. 174, fol. 14r: "[Vita] Sti Antoni". See the Note to the Reader and Chapter 2 on the sizes of images and sheets of paper.

85 MPM Arch. 180, fol. 155r: "[Vita] Catharine".

86 MPM Arch. 180, fol. 155r: "[Vita] St Joannes Baptae".

87 MPM Arch. 180, fol. 155r: "[Vita] St Joannes Evangelistae".

88 MPM Arch. 174, fol. 14r: "Vita S^ti^ Petri". See the Note to the Reader and Chapter 2 on the sizes of images and sheets of paper.

89 MPM Arch. 180, fol. 155r: "Vita Mariae in 16 folien".

90 MPM Arch. 180, fol. 155r: "[Vita] B. Mariae cleyn".

91 MPM Arch. 180, fol. 155r: "7 kercken".

92 MPM Arch. 180, fol. 155r: "de seven gaven des H. Geestes".

93 MPM Arch. 174, fol. 14r (1602).

94 MPM Arch. 173, fol. 204r.

95 MPM Arch. 180, fol. 155r.

96 MPM Arch. 1104, fol. 53r (1607); and MPM Arch. 180, fol. 155r (1608).

97 MPM Arch. 180, fol. 155r.

98 Rombouts and Van Lerius 1872, vol. I, p. 651.

99 Ibid., vol. II, pp. 98 and 104.

100 See Fuhring 2017, p. 234, for estimates ranging from 6,870 plates to more than 10,000.

101 Fuhring 2017, p. 235; and Dudok van Heel 1975, p. 154, no. 4.

102 MPM Arch. 246, fols. 10v: "Leven der Heyligen van de ordre van St. Franciscus p. Malerj", and 118r.

103 MPM Arch. 249, fol. 165v (with possible reference to the number of leaves); and MPM Arch. 134, fol. 241 rht: "Tempus ridendi etc. in magno 4°".

104 MPM Arch. 245, fol. 70r.

105 MPM Arch. 247, fol. 107r.

106 MPM Arch. 245, fol. 70r.

107 MPM Arch. 245, fol. 70r.

108 Sellink 1997, vol. I, p. 20.

109 For the deed of sale (March 1605) for this house, see Antwerp, Felix Archives, SR 457, 1605 KB II, fol. 397v. See Chapter 3 for more on Theodore Galle's work as a publisher and supply of prints to the Moretuses.

110 Sellink 1997, vol. I, p. 11.

111 See, for example, New Holl. Collaert, nos. 2242–59; and New Holl. Stradanus, nos. 322–41.

112 MPM Arch. 58, fol. 25v: "Atti di apostoli de 16 foli Heemsk.".

113 MPM Arch. 180, fol. 155r: "wercken der apostelen in 35 [leaves]".

114 MPM Arch. 65, fol. 32r: "Imago vultus Salvatoris cum 2 bus [= duobus] angelis unum a dext. et alterum a sin. et uno inferius. Strad. Galle". See MPM Arch. 65, fol. 13v, for Galle's supply of this print.

115 MPM Arch. 58, fols. 19r: "Nomen Jesu en ovalle".

116 MPM Arch. 65, fol. 32r: "Imago B. Virg. cum duobus angelis et 2-obus [=duobus?] Stis Ant° et Franc° Galle excud.". See MPM Arch. 65, fol. 13v, for Galle's supply of this print.

117 MPM Arch. 58, fols. 19r: "B. Virgo Maria Ant. Bloclandt".

118 MPM Arch. 71, fol. 60v: "9 Engeln".

119 MPM Arch. 18, fol. 321 rht, for the total value of what Galle supplied; and MPM Arch. 57, fol. 136v, for the itemized list of specifically which prints Galle supplied, including: "Satisfactio Christi 8°".

120 MPM Arch. 71, fol. 60v: "vooghelboexkens".

121 MPM Arch. 58, fols. 19r: "Ablatio malorum".

122 MPM Arch. 71, fol. 60v; and MPM Arch. 18, p. 71: "vroukens vant het nieu testament".

123 MPM Arch. 71, fol. 60v; and MPM Arch. 18, p. 71: "vroukens vant het out testament".

124 MPM Arch. 65, fol. 32r: "Imago Dni. ad Columnam. Strad.; Galle". We are favoring this attribution (instead of New Holl. Stradanus, no. 114, which is a conventional image of the Flagellation), due to the lack of reference to the act of flagellating Christ and the focus, as in this image, on Christ tied to the column. See MPM Arch. 65, fol. 13v, for Galle's supply of this print.

125 MPM Arch. 65, fol. 32r: "Imago crucifixi cum duobus angelis, cum B. Virg^e. St^o Joan Evangta, Sta Maria Magd^na etc Strad. Collart Galle". See, for example, MPM Arch. 18, fol. 64 rht (1575): "David Montani etc. 4°"; and MPM Arch. 66, fol. 14v (1589): "hist. davidis in 4°". See also MPM M 296 (= MPM Arch. 1227), fol. 388r, for the same price in Plantin's list of publications by his contemporaries, under "Speculum Davidis" and possibly "Davidis hist.a". See MPM Arch. 59, fol. 137r: "Davidis hist."; and MPM Arch. 65, fol. 13v, for Galle's supply of this print.

126 MPM Arch. 71, fol. 60v; and MPM Arch. 118, p. 71: "vanden wapen vande coninck".

127 See, for example, MPM Arch. 18, fol. 64 rht (1575): "David Montani etc. 4°"; and MPM Arch. 66, fol. 14v (1589): "hist. davidis in 4°". See also MPM M 296 (= MPM Arch. 1227), fol. 388r, for the same price in Plantin's list of publications by his contemporaries, under "Speculum Davidis" and possibly "Davidis hist.a".

128 See MPM Arch. 59, fol. 137r: "Davidis hist."; and MPM Arch. 20, fol. 57 rht: "David", respectively.

129 For the price of 10 st., see MPM Arch. 59, fols. 121r: "De deis gentium Favolii" and 137r: "De deis gentium"; and also MPM M 296, fol. 388r, for the same price in Plantin's list of publications by his contemporaries. For the price of 9 st., see MPM Arch. 61, fol. 16r: "de dys gentium favo[lii]" (1583); MPM Arch. 62, fol. 119v "Imagines deorum"; and MPM Arch. 20, fol. 166 rht (1585).

130 MPM Arch. 71, fol. 60v; and MPM Arch. 118, p. 71: "den Keyser het hert iacht".

131 MPM Arch. 51, fol. 199r (1573): "livre des dieux capita deorum"; MPM Arch. 55, fol. 97v (1577): "deorum capita"; and MPM Arch. 57, fol. 40v (1579): "Capita deorum".

132 MPM Arch. 52, fol. 30v: "capita deorum dearumque". Both the original price of 16 st. and the later price of 18 st. are noted for the 1573 edition in Plantin's list of publications by his contemporaries (MPM M 296 (= MPM Arch. 1227), fol. 388r, under "Capita deorum et Dearum").

133 MPM Arch. 71, fol. 64r: "portraictes de Menuserie de Galleus". For Galle's supply of the series, see MPM Arch. 21, fol. 203 rht.

134 Given the 1581 dating of this series, it seems unlikely that they were engraved by Hans Collaert, who died in 1580.

135 MPM Arch. 59, fol. 121r: "bagboexken" ("bag" or "bagge" is an old Dutch word for jewel).

136 MPM Arch. 59, fol. 137r: "Baggas"; and MPM Arch. 18, fol. 394 rht: "Baghe boeckxen".

137 MPM M 296 (= MPM Arch. 1227), fol. 388r, under "Baggheboeckxen".

138 MPM Arch. 71, fol. 60v: "van Bagghen en smecken".

139 MPM Arch. 58, fols. 19r: "Dissidium in ecclesia".

140 MPM Arch. 51, fol. 134v: "Clades gentis Iudeae".

141 MPM Arch. 60, fol. 96r: "Clades Iudei".

142 MPM Arch. 65, fol. 125r: "historie van America".

143 MPM Arch. 71, fol. 60v: "historia van America".

144 See, for example, MPM Arch. 51, fol. 128v (1573): "Acta nuptiarum"; MPM Arch. 57, fol. 40v (1579): "Nuptiae"; and MPM Arch. 20, fol. 166 rht: "livres de noces spirituelles" (1585). See also MPM M 296 (= MPM Arch. 1227), fol. 388r, for the same price in Plantin's list of publications by his contemporaries, under "Nuptiae Sacrae".

145 See, for example, MPM Arch. 52, fol. 109r (1574): "divinarum nuptiarum conventa et acta fr."; and MPM Arch. 53, fol. 35v (1575): "nuptiae francois".

146 See, for example, MPM Arch. 57, fol. 114v: "Nuptiae sacrae 8°" (1579); MPM Arch. 59, fol. 190v (1581): "Nuptiae divinae et vita Christi 4°"; and MPM Arch. 64, fol. 16r (1587): "Vita Christi cum sponsa 4°".

147 MPM Arch. 65, fol. 125r: "van de 3 staten". See also Duverger 1984–2009, vol. IV, no. 893, p. 18, for a similar reference to "De Dry Staten van Hemskerck in vier platen".

148 MPM Arch. 71, fol. 60v; and MPM Arch. 118, p. 71: "historien vande 3 staten".

149 MPM Arch. 58, fol. 25v: "otto beatitudine de 8 f. Heemsk.".

150 Carrara and Gregory 2000, p. 11, fol. 17r, and p. 13, print no. 16.

151 MPM Arch. 18, fol. 321 rht, for the total value of what Galle supplied; and MPM Arch. 57, fol. 136v, for the itemized list of specifically which prints Galle supplied, including: "Octo beatitudines de 1 f°".

152 MPM Arch. 60, fol. 101v: "Pyramides 4°".

153 MPM Arch. 71, fol. 60v: "Musiek boecken".

154 MPM Arch. 180, fol. 155v: "musycq Boeck".

155 MPM Arch. 180, fol. 155r: "vanden 9 Penitencie 10 [leaves]".

156 MPM Arch. 49, fol. 86r: "grande p[iece] de babilon".

157 MPM Arch. 71, fol. 60v: "Historie vande Romeynsche vrou[wen]" (1594); and MPM Arch. 180, fol. 155v: "historien vande Romeynsche vrouwen" (1608).

158 MPM Arch. 55, fol. 114v: "B. Virginis 15 mysteria misteria rosarii".

159 MPM Arch. 59, fols. 137r: "5 sens", and 121r: "vijf sinnen", respectively.

160 MPM Arch. 58, fol. 19r: "Remissio peccatorum".

161 MPM Arch. 51, fol. 51v: "Quatuor Tempora".

162 MPM Arch. 65, fol. 125r: "vande vier tijen".

163 MPM Arch. 71, fol. 60v: "Histoire vande 4 tyden".

164 MPM Arch. 71, fol. 60v: "4 deelen des Werelts".

165 MPM Arch. 180, fol. 155r: "de 4 werelden in 4 f°".

166 MPM Arch. 20, leaf inserted at fol. 166: "Grottisques de 8 fuil.". See MPM Arch. 62, fol. 119v, for the 1585 dating of this transaction. Marjolein Leesberg has suggested that the group of prints referred to here are these two series by Gheeraerts on the basis of a reference to "Grotissen acht platen van Marcus Geraerts" (eight plates with grotesques by Marcus Gheeraerts I) in the inventory of Theodore Galle's stock of plates following the death of his widow, Catharine Moerentorf, in 1636 (Duverger 1984–2009, vol. IV, no. 893, p. 20).

167 MPM Arch. 180, fol. 155r: "de 4 delen 1 de 4 elementen grotis.".

168 MPM Arch. 58, fol. 19v: "4 Doctores ecclesiae 4 f.[olia]" (1580); and MPM Arch. 180, fol. 155r: "de vier doctrien in 4 [leaves]" (1608).

169 MPM Arch. 18, fol. 321 rht, for the total value of what Galle supplied; and MPM Arch. 54, fol. 135v, for the itemized list of specifically which prints Galle supplied, including: "quatuor evangelistae".

170 MPM Arch. 53, fol. 141v: "de vier uterste / vier figuren 4 folia".

171 MPM Arch. 58, fols. 19v: "Iudicium Stradani in ronden 4 f", and 25v: "Iudicio de 4 fogli Stradani".

172 MPM Arch. 71, fol. 60v: "4 deelen des dachs".

173 MPM Arch. 58, fol. 25v: "Stagioni de lanno de 4 f. Heemsk.".

174 MPM Arch. 58, fols. 19v: "Quatuor anni tempora 5 f. J. Stradanus", and 25v: "dlle stagioni de lanno novi Stradani de 5 f°".

175 MPM Arch. 58, fol. 26r: "Trionphi di Baccho". Our thanks to Marjolein Leesberg for the identification of this series.

176 MPM Arch. 16, fol. 172 rht: "Culturae Mundi 4 f°".

177 MPM Arch. 180, fol. 155r: "hoven in 6 [leaves]".

178 MPM Arch. 180, fol. 155r: "hoven in 8 [leaves]".

179 MPM Arch. 180, fol. 155r: "boeck van hoven 21 [leaves]".

180 MPM Arch. 71, fol. 60v; and MPM Arch. 118, p. 71: "van mans en vrouwen tronien".

181 See also MPM M 296 (= MPM Arch. 1227), fol. 388r, for the following reference (without a price), which underscores the link between these subjects: "Guerre de Siennes de 8 f° de Jo: Medicis".

182 See MPM Arch. 58, fols. 19v: "Expeditiones Caroli V Siene …" and "Historia Medices …", and 25v: "de la guerra de Siena …" and "Guerre novae …".

183 MPM Arch. 18, fol. 321 rht: "oorlogen van Medicis f°".

184 MPM Arch. 180, fol. 155r: "Oorlogen medices 21 [leaves]".

185 MPM Arch. 180, fol. 155v: "Sywormen".

186 MPM Arch. 58, fol. 19r: "Edificatio s. arenam".

187 MPM Arch. 58, fol. 19r: "Edificatio S. terram".

188 MPM Arch. 20, leaf inserted at fol. 166: "lyvres de chasses". When this series was resold to Benito Arias Montano in 1585, it was identified as "Venationum libelli" (MPM Arch. 62, fol. 119v).

189 MPM Arch. 180, fol. 155v: "Lanck jaght boexken".

190 See MPM Arch. 20, leaf inserted at fol. 166, for "lijvres des bestes a 8 fol", as well as another set of images of animals ("lijvres de bestes"), sold for just 2 st. for an unspecified number of images. See MPM Arch. 62, fol. 119v, for the 1585 date of this transaction.

191 MPM Arch. 58, fols. 19v: "Jachten van Stradanus van Florentien 24 f.", and 25v: "Caccie mezane de 24 fogli".

192 MPM Arch. 57, fol. 41r (1579): "venatio 24 foliorum"; and MPM Arch. 18, fol. 394 rht (1581): "groote Jachten". See also MPM M 296 (= MPM Arch. 1227), fol. 388r, for the same price for twenty-four leaves of hunts in Plantin's list of publications by his contemporaries, under "Chasse grande" and "Chasses de stradanus".

193 MPM Arch. 71, fol. 60v, "jachtboexken".

194 MPM Arch. 180, fol. 155v: "groote jaghtboecken".

195 MPM Arch. 65, fol. 8v: "Effigies doctorum f° … idem novi".

196 MPM Arch. 74, fol. 5r: "1 Imagines doctorum 2 voll.".

197 MPM Arch. 65, fol. 32r: "Imago conceptionis B. Virg. Jo. Strad.[anus] Hier. Wirx. Phil. Galle". See MPM Arch. 65, fol. 13v, for Galle's supply of this print.

198 MPM Arch. 65, fol. 32r: "Imago salvatoris mortui et depositi in sindone cum duobus angelis habentibus faculas accensas etc. Strad. Col. Gal.". See MPM Arch. 65, fol. 13v, for Galle's supply of this print.

199 MPM Arch. 71, fol. 60v: "Leggenden aventmael".

200 MPM Arch. 175, fol. 78r (1603): "Vita S^tae^ Catherinae Senensis"; MPM Arch. 178. fol. 78r (1606): "Vita Catharine Sienensis 4°"; and MPM Arch. 180, fol. 155v (1608): "Leven van St Catherine van Siene".

201 See, for example, MPM Arch. 60, fol. 83v (1582): "Vita Francisci cobre 4°"; and MPM Arch. 20, fol. 57 rht (1583): "vita S. Francisci".

202 MPM Arch. 173, fol. 7v: "Vita S^ti^ Francisci f° coper f. 20" (1601); and MPM Arch. 176, fol. 139v: "Vita S^ti^ Francisci fig. aeneis" (1604).

203 MPM Arch. 175, fol. 15r: "Vitae Francisci".

204 MPM Arch. 180, fol. 155r: "Leven van St. Franciscus in 20 folien".

205 MPM Arch. 180, fol. 155r: "levens Sti Joannis 10 f°".

206 MPM Arch. 58, fol. 19r: "Regnum Dei quaerere".

207 MPM Arch. 65, fol. 32r: "Imago Ste Barbarae Strad. Galle". See MPM Arch. 65, fol. 13v, for Galle's supply of this print.

208 MPM Arch. 65, fol. 32r: "Images Ste Laurentij Strad. Colart. Galle". See MPM Arch. 65, fol. 13v, for Galle's supply of this print.

209 MPM Arch. 65, fol. 32r: "Imago S^tae^ Lucie Strad. Wir. Galle". See MPM Arch. 65, fol. 13v, for Galle's supply of this print.

210 MPM Arch. 58, fol. 19v: "Misericordia Dei 1 f.".

211 MPM Arch. 180, fol. 155r: "vanden simmen in 16 [leaves]".

212 MPM Arch. 18, fol. 321 rht, for the total value of what Galle supplied; and MPM Arch. 57, fol. 136v, for the itemized list of specifically which prints Galle supplied, including: "Mysteria infantiae Chrisit etc. 5 f°".

213 MPM Arch. 58, fol. 19v: "Infantia Christi etc. 5 f°"; and MPM Arch. 18, fol. 321 rht, for the total value of what Galle supplied.

214 MPM Arch. 20, leaf inserted at fol. 166: "lyvries de infancia cristi". See MPM Arch. 62, fol. 119v, for the 1585 date of this transaction.

215 New Holl. Stradanus, no. 180.

216 Duverger 1984–2009, vol. IV, p. 19.

217 MPM Arch. 58, fol. 19v: "Mysteria laeta, luctuosa, gloriosa in rondekens elck op een blat 3 bladeren".

218 MPM Arch. 69, fol. 99r: "4 grote rosarie comptes pr 3 f°".

219 MPM Arch. 58, fol. 19r: "Nativitas passio resurrectio en ovale".

220 MPM Arch. 180, fol. 155v: "Nova reperta".

221 MPM Arch. 71, fol. 60v: "cleyn peerdeboexkens".

222 MPM Arch. 60, fol. 101v: "Explication de pr [= pater] n[oste]r".

223 MPM Arch. 180, fol. 155r: "historije vanden paternoster 8 [leaves]".

224 MPM Arch. 180, fol. 155r: "passien in 21 [leaves]".

225 See, for example, MPM Arch. 62, fol. 119v: "Passio Domini grandes" (1585); MPM Arch. 64, fol. 29v: "Passien"; and MPM Arch. 65, fol. 46v: "passien en 4°".

226 MPM Arch. 71, fol. 60v; MPM Arch. 118, p. 71 (1594): "Groote passie"; and MPM Arch. 180, fol. 155v: "passien" (1608).

227 MPM Arch. 175, fol. 154: "Passien Stradani".

228 MPM Arch. 50, fol. 48v: "Pontificum effigies"; and MPM Arch. 51, fol. 51v: "Pontificum effigies f".

229 MPM Arch. 72, fol. 111r: "effigies pontificum 4°".

230 MPM Arch. 180, fol. 155v: "Ronde Leven vrouwen".

231 MPM Arch. 58, fol. 19r: "Levamen onustorum".

232 MPM Arch. 58, fol. 19v: "Resurrectio Christi 1 f. A. Blocklandt".

233 MPM Arch. 71, fol. 60v: "Keijsersboecken".

234 MPM Arch. 72, fol. 111r: "effigies Caesarum f°".

235 MPM Arch. 49, fols. 86r: "ruin boeken", and 102v: "1 ruyn boek pr 9 st. 11 f°" (both from 1571); MPM Arch. 51, fols. 132r: "4 Ruine regionum", and 199r: "Ruyn boek" (both from 1573); and MPM Arch. 59, fol. 137r: "ruynes" (1581). Our thanks to Marjolein Leesberg for her advice regarding this series.

236 MPM Arch. 180, fol. 155r: "de 7 kercken in 8 [leaves]".

237 MPM Arch. 67, fol. 101r: "Sta Catherina".

238 MPM Arch. 71, fol. 60v; and MPM Arch. 118, p. 71: "zee godden en goddinen".

239 MPM Arch. 71, fol. 60v: "7 duchden en hooft sonden".

240 MPM Arch. 180, fol. 155r: "de 7 kercken in 8 [leaves]".

241 Possibly an earlier state of a print fitting this description that was published by both Theodore Galle (see Wolfegg, Fürstlich zu Waldburg-Wolfegg'sche Kunstsammlungen, vol. 185, print number 408, 138 × 90 mm) and Jan Galle (see Spengler 2003, p. 357 and fig. 129, ca. 141 × 92 mm; and Cologne, Wallraf-Richartz-Museum & Foundation Corboud Graphische Sammlung, no. 22685).

242 MPM Arch. 58, fol. 19r: "Septem effusiones sang[uinis] Christi rondeken".

243 Possibly related to a print of this subject published by Theodoor Galle (HAB [Herzog August Bibliothek, Wolfenbüttel]: Graph. A1: 7840, available online via the Virtuelles Kupferstichkabinett: http://diglib.hab.de?grafik=graph-a1–7840).

244 MPM Arch. 58, fol. 19r: "Septem gaudia Virginis Mariae 1 f° rond".

245 MPM Arch. 71, fol. 60v: "7 planeten".

246 MPM Arch. 180, fol. 155r: "7 planeten 8 [leaves]".

247 MPM Arch. 55, fol. 112v (1577): "Septem sacramenta f°"; MPM Arch. 56, fol. 52v (1578): "Septem Sacramenta f°"; and MPM Arch. 18, fol. 187 rht, for both a 6 st. rate in 1576 and the only known example of a slightly higher rate of 6.75 st. per series, also in 1576. See also MPM M 296 (= MPM Arch. 1227), fol. 388r, for the standard 6 st. price in Plantin's list of publications by his contemporaries, under "Septem Sacramenta f° 7 a° 77", but with just seven leaves and dated 1577.

248 MPM Arch. 58, fol. 19v: "Septem sacramenta en 8 f.".

249 MPM Arch. 58, fol. 19r: "Septem dolores B. Mariae in rondekens".

250 For the standard 6 st. price, see, for example, MPM Arch. 18, fol. 253 rht (1577): "opera misericordiae spirit. et corpor."; and MPM Arch. 61, fol. 143v (1583): "Septem Op[er]a misericordiae".

251 MPM Arch. 18, fol. 253 rht; and MPM Arch. 58, fols. 19r: "Septem opera miser. spirit. in 8 f.", and 25v: "Opere di misericordia spirituali de 8 f." (1580).

252 MPM Arch. 58, fol. 19v: "Septem opera misericordiae corporalia in rondekens … eadem spiritualia".

253 For the standard 6 st. price, see, for example, MPM Arch. 18, fol. 253 rht (1577): "opera misericordiae spirit et cooper"; and MPM Arch. 61, fol. 143v (1583).

254 MPM Arch. 18, fol. 253 rht; and MPM Arch. 58, fols. 19v: "Septem opera miser. corporalia 8 f.", and 25v: "Opere de misericordia corporali de 8 f." (1580).

255 MPM Arch. 58, fol. 19v: "Septem opera misericordiae corporalia in rondekens".

256 MPM Arch. 71, fol. 60v: "6 Heremiten".

257 MPM Arch. 60, fol. 96r: "Puteorum Gallei".

258 MPM Arch. 71, fol. 64v: "des puis 12 [leaves]".

259 MPM Arch. 58, fol. 19r: "Cura Dei pro suis".

260 Duverger 1984–2009, vol. IV, p. 22.

261 MPM Arch. 65, fol. 125r: "peertboeck vande 17 fol.".

262 MPM Arch. 71, fol. 60v: "cleyn peerdeboexkens".

263 MPM Arch. 71, fol. 60v: "groot peerdeboeck".

264 MPM Arch. 180, fol. 155r: "pierdeboecken in 17 [leaves per series]".

265 MPM Arch. 180, fol. 155v: "Adam en Eva".

266 MPM Arch. 58, fol. 19v: "Historia van Adonis 4 f. Ant. Blocland".

267 MPM Arch. 18, fol. 64 rht: "Historie van Assueres 8 f° oft Hestor".

268 MPM Arch. 180, fol. 155r: "historije hester 8 [leaves]".

269 MPM Arch. 58, fol. 25v: "Historia de Holoferno de 8 f. Heemsk.".

270 MPM Arch. 58, fol. 19v: "Historia Tarquinii de 4 f. Hen. Golsii".

271 MPM Arch. 180, fol. 155r: "hestorien meers en venus 4 [leaves]".

272 MPM Arch. 180, fol. 155r: "historien van Susanna 6 [leaves]".

273 MPM Arch. 18, fol. 321 rht, for the total value of what Galle supplied; and MPM Arch. 54, fol. 135v, for the itemized list of specifically which prints Galle supplied, including: "de asino". Our thanks to Marjolein Leesberg for her identification of this series and the reference to Luijten 1996.

274 MPM Arch. 180, fol. 155r: "vanden Esel 6 [leaves]".

275 MPM Arch. 65, fol. 125r: "de thien geboden".

276 MPM Arch. 71, fol. 60v: "10 gheboden".

277 MPM Arch. 180, fol. 155r: "de 10 geboden 11 [leaves]".

278 MPM Arch. 58, fol. 25v: "Triumphi del mondo de 6 f. luno Heemsk.".

279 Carrara and Gregory 2000, p. 11, fol. 17r, and p. 13, print no. 15.

280 MPM Arch. 18, fol. 321 rht, for the total value of what Galle supplied in 1579; and MPM Arch. 57, fol. 136v, for the itemized list of specifically which prints Galle supplied at that time, including: "Articuli fidei". See also MPM Arch. 58, fol. 19r: "Duodecim articuli symboli" (1580).

281 MPM Arch. 180, fol. 155r: "de 12 maanden 13 [leaves]".

282 MPM Arch. 73, fol. 157r: "Virgilij figurae".

283 MPM Arch. 65, fol. 32r: "Imago B. M. ornata stellis cum duobus angelis Hier. Wirickx. Phil. Galle". See MPM Arch. 65, fol. 13v, for Galle's supply of this print.

284 See, for example, MPM Arch. 50, fol. 48v (1572): "Effigies doctorum virorum Gallei"; MPM Arch. 60, fol. 198r (1582): "Effigies doctorum f°"; and MPM. Arch. 20, fol. 166 rht: "livres de hommes doctes" (1585). See also MPM M 296 (= MPM Arch. 1227), fol. 388r, for the same price in Plantin's list of publications by his contemporaries, under "Effigies Doctorum".

285 MPM Arch. 63, fol. 62v (1586): "Vies des hommes illustres f°"; MPM Arch. 65, fol. 8v: "Effigies doctorum f°" (1588); MPM Arch. 171, fol. 170v: "Effigies 44 Ph. Gallei" (1599); and MPM Arch. 172, fol. 85r: "Images 44 doctorum" (1600).

286 MPM Arch. 71, fol. 60v; and MPM Arch. 118, p. 71: "tweedeilen batalien".

287 MPM Arch. 173, fol. 204r.

288 MPM Arch. 73, fol. 157r.

289 MPM Arch. 73, fol. 157r.

290 MPM Arch. 73, fol. 157r.

291 MPM Arch. 73, fol. 157r.

292 MPM Arch. 173, fol. 204r.

293 MPM Arch. 64, fol. 29v.

294 MPM Arch. 18, fol. 282 rht: "folia a 5 figures". See also MPM Arch. 56, fol. 107r.

295 MPM Arch. 58, fol. 25v: "fogli dopii reali" (1580); and MPM Arch. 59, fol. 137r (1581).

296 MPM Arch. 69, fol. 99r: "groote bladeren".

297 MPM Arch. 64, fol. 29v (1587); MPM Arch. 20, fol. 307 rht (1588); MPM Arch. 69, fol. 99r (1592); and MPM Arch. 180, fol. 155v (1608).

298 MPM Arch. 57, fol. 70r (1579); MPM Arch. 65, fol. 103v (1588); and MPM Arch. 69, fol. 99r (1592).

299 MPM Arch. 57, fol. 70r.

300 MPM Arch. 63, fol. 125v: "feuilles de diverses peintures f° cobre".

301 MPM Arch. 18, fol. 282 rht.

302 MPM Arch. 18, fol. 321 rht.

303 For example: MPM Arch. 49, fol. 86r (1571); MPM Arch. 66, fol. 168v (1589); and MPM Arch. 180, fol. 155r (1608).

304 MPM Arch. 62, fol. 119v: "feuilles de diverses sortes de protraictures".

305 MPM Arch. 58, fol. 25v: "fogli picoli".

306 MPM Arch. 69, fol. 112v.

307 Hensen 1916, pp. 420 and 423, for the former; and Rombouts and Van Lerius 1872, vol. I, pp. 384–87, for the latter.

308 Imhof 2014a, no. G-9.

309 Rombouts and Van Lerius 1872, vol. I, pp. 415, 498 and 500, 528 and 558, and 565, for Galle's apprentices; and Bowen 2009, pp. 130–31, on Cornelis Galle.

310 Rombouts and Van Lerius 1872, vol. I, pp. 452 and 459.

311 See TG-7 and TG-8 for the first and second, respectively; and Imhof 2020b on Galle and David.

312 See, for example, TG-1 and Wolfegg, Fürstlich zu Waldburg-Wolfegg'sche Kunstsammlungen, vol. 7, no. 167 (*Repraesentatio imaginativa vitae Domini Iesu Christi*, dedicated by Galle to Chrysostomus van der Sterre), for the former, and TG-9 for the latter.

313 See, for example, AC-4, AC-9, TG-22, GJ-12, New Holl. Collaert nos. 1624–43 (Liefrinck), and the portrait series originated by Philips Galle.

314 Holl. Dutch & Flemish, vol. LXIX, p. lxxxvi. See also Chapter 6 and figs. 2.8 and 6.18.

315 Rombouts and Van Lerius 1872, vol. I, p. 432.

316 Denucé 1927, pp. 138 and 150; and Duverger 1984–2009, vol. IV, pp. 23–24.

317 MPM Arch. 123, fol. 77r, for a payment of 44 fl. for the title plate of Casimiri Sarbievius's *Lyricorum libri* IV, designed by Rubens and engraved by Cornelis in 1632.

318 MPM Arch. 180, fol. 155v: "Ave Maris Stella".

319 MPM Arch. 127, fol. 211 rht: "Baroni effigies"; and MPM Arch. 177, fol. 12v: "Imagines Baronij f°".

320 MPM Arch. 180, fol. 155v: "Loop des werelts".

321 MPM Arch. 180, fol. 155v: "Typus Amoris".

322 MPM Arch. 134, fol. 85 rht: "Gansespel f°".

323 MPM Arch. 238, fol. 115r: "fundatores ordinum 4 cop." (1630); MPM Arch. 239, fol. 48r: "Fundatores ordinum" (1631); and MPM Arch. 243, fol. 82v: "Fundatores Ord. sonder schrift".

324 Lille, Archives départementales du Nord, 9 H 61, undated letter from Anton van Winghe, probably intended for Estienne Binet: "J'en envoye peu, par ce que (pour vous le dire ingenuement) le pris est grand et beaucoup plus que i'avois opine, car Galle les mect a 3 flor. sans la ligature, qui est un sol et demi l'image, et ceneantmoins dict qu'elles se vendront bien".

325 By 1606 Galle had added eighteen engravings to this series. Jan Moretus I then published this expanded print series together with an extensive textual commentary, thereby creating an illustrated book, the sales of which are not traced here (see Imhof 2014a, no. G-14).

326 For example: MPM Arch. 75, fol. 169r (1598): "Imagines Illustrium"; MPM Arch. 177, fol. 82v; and MPM Arch. 127, fol. 211 rht (for the price): "Imagines Ursini 4°" (1605).

327 MPM Arch. 218, fol. 208r: "Vite d. Dominici 4°".

328 MPM Arch. 217, fol. 227r: "Leven van Catharina van Sienen" (1610); MPM Arch. 218, fol. 208r: "Vita de Catherine Senensis" (1611); and MPM Arch. 225, fol. 126r: "Leven van Ste. Catharina van Senen cop." (1618).

329 MPM Arch. 217, fol. 150r: "Vitae p. Ignatij fig^ras^"; MPM Arch. 128, fol. 90 rht, for the price (1610); and MPM Arch. 218, fol. 208r: "Vita Ignatii" (1611).

330 MPM Arch. 142, p. 2. See also Chapter 5.

331 MPM Arch. 223, fol. 204v: "Leven van Mater Teresa f°".

332 MPM Arch. 239, fol. 126v: "Imagines seraphicae f".

333 MPM Arch. 217, fol. 92v: "Miracule Rosarij 4to"; MPM Arch. 128, fol. 90 rht: "Mirakelen van het Roosenkransken" (1610); MPM Arch. 218, fol. 158r: "Miracule Rosarij 4° met het schrift"; MPM Arch. 128, fol. 90 rht, for the price (1611); and MPM Arch. 223, fol. 18r: "myrakelen van het roosencransken met schrift en figuren" (1616).

334 MPM Arch. 218, fol. 158r: "[Miracule Rosarij 4°] Item sonder schrift" (1611); and MPM Arch. 219, fol. 146v: "Mirakelen van het Roosenkransken met de figuren" (1612). See MPM Arch. 128, fol. 90 rht, for the prices.

335 MPM Arch. 180, fol. 155v: "de 9 Besten 3 [leaves]".

336 MPM Arch. 180, fol. 155v: "1 Landt Godinnen 8 [leaves]". The identification of this series is supported by the following reference to it in the estate inventory of Theodore Galle's widow, Catharina Moerentorf: "de lantgodinnen van Floris acht platen"; Duverger 1984–2009, vol. IV, p. 18.

337 MPM Arch. 242, fol. 161r: "[Effigies] Pictorum f".

338 MPM Arch. 171, fol. 170r: "Italorum doctrina illustrium imagines"; and MPM Arch. 172, fol. 85r: "Italorum doctorum imagines" (1600).

339 For example: MPM Arch. 21, fol. 341 rht: "Icones 9 Graecorum".

340 MPM Arch. 171, fol. 104v: "Imagines graecorum f° pchementi".

341 MPM Arch. 242, fol. 161r: "Effigies Doctorum f".

342 MPM Arch. 180, fol. 27v: "Icones Scriptorum Belgii".

343 Cock 2013, p. 368, n. 4; and Riggs 1972, p. 325, no. 54.

344 MPM Arch. 180, fol. 155v: "de Schepen in 11 [leaves]".

345 MPM Arch. 180, fol. 155v: "Sainct Dominicus".

346 MPM Arch. 180, fol. 155v: "Perspettiven in 21 folien".

347 MPM Arch. 174, fol. 11v: "L Vrouw 7 weeen f°".

348 MPM Arch. 174, fol. 11v: "boexkens van 7 weeen 8 blaykens" (1602); and MPM Arch. 180, fol. 155v: "Lieve vrowen mette 7 weeen" (1608).

349 MPM Arch. 173, fol. 149r: "arbor S. Dominici".

350 MPM Arch. 175, fols. 13v: "Genealogia Christi f° Coll. [and] Arbor Christi f° figur coper", and 94v: "arbor genealogica Christi f°".

351 MPM Arch. 220, fol. 155r "Arbor vitae humanae".

352 MPM Arch. 180, fol. 23r: "B. Mariae in planctu".

353 MPM Arch. 174, fol. 11v: "[L Vrauw] quae est ista 8°".

354 MPM Arch. 180, fol. 155v: "Lieve vrouen ventura".

355 MPM Arch. 238, fol. 43r.

356 MPM Arch. 241, fol. 26r.

357 MPM Arch. 242, fol. 161r (1634); and MPM Arch. 244, fols. 31r and 32r (1636).

358 MPM Arch. 225, fol. 146v (1618); MPM Arch. 232, fol. 126v (1625); and MPM Arch. 240, fol. 127v (1632).

359 MPM Arch. 225, fol. 146v (1618); and MPM Arch. 241, fol. 66v (1633).

360 MPM Arch. 237, fol. 91v: "item [images] illuminer 8° en perchemin a 3 p[att.]".

361 MPM Arch. 241, fol. 26r: "[Belden] op perkement afgeset a st. 3" (1633); and MPM Arch. 244, fols. 31r and 32r (1636).

362 MPM Arch. 242, fol. 161r (1634).

363 For example: MPM Arch. 180, fol. 23r (1608, large images ("imagies maiores") in folio); MPM Arch. 220, fol. 155r (1613, double folio leaves ("dubbel [f°]")); MPM Arch. 230, fol. 158r: "groote belden in f°" (1623); and MPM Arch. 240, fol. 127v (1632).

364 MPM Arch. 244, fols. 31r and 32r.

365 MPM Arch. 225, fol. 146v (1618); and MPM Arch. 226, fol. 135v (1619).

366 MPM Arch. 237, fol. 91v: "Images illuminer 8° en perchemin a 2 patt.".

367 MPM Arch. 220, fol. 155r (1613, double folio leaves ("dubbel f°")); and MPM Arch. 223, fol. 154v: "Images fines doubles feulles" (1616).

368 MPM Arch. 180, fol. 23r: "images in folio".

369 MPM Arch. 231, fol. 167v: "[Imagines] grote gemyn f°".

370 MPM Arch. 179, fol. 38v (1607); and MPM Arch. 239, fol. 34v (1631).

371 MPM Arch. 179, fol. 38v.

372 MPM Arch. 238, fol. 20r (1630); and MPM Arch. 239, fol. 34v (1631).

373 MPM Arch. 238, fol. 20r.

374 MPM Arch. 180, fol. 155v (1608); and MPM Arch. 228, fol. 121v.

375 For example: MPM Arch. 239, fol. 11v (1631); and MPM Arch. 240, fol. 195v (1632).

376 For example: MPM Arch. 238, fol. 27r (1630); and MPM Arch. 241, fol. 66v (1633).

377 MPM Arch. 238, fol. 27r (1630); and MPM Arch. 239, fols. 179r and 179v (1631).

378 For example: MPM Arch. 238, fol. 27r (1630); and MPM Arch. 241, fol. 66v (1633).

379 MPM Arch. 241, fol. 66v.

380 MPM Arch. 233, fol. 31r.

381 For example: MPM Arch. 180, fol. 155v (1608); MPM Arch. 220, fol. 155r (1613, in 8°); and MPM Arch. 241, fol. 66v (1633, in 4°).

382 MPM Arch. 233, fol. 31r.

383 MPM Arch. 180, fol. 155v.

384 MPM Arch. 222, fol. 182v (1615); and MPM Arch. 166, fol. 101v (1630).

385 MPM Arch. 66, fol. 92v (a payment for engraving letters on a title plate) and MPM Arch. 70, fol. 14r (a payment for coloring three canons).

386 MPM Arch. 21, fol. 182 rht (6 August 1594): "6 bladers vier evangelistes 8°. [en] 6 vande 4 doctores [is together] fl._ st. 9"; and MPM Arch. 71, fol. 101v, for a confirmation of the general size of the images.

387 MPM Arch. 21, fol. 182 rht (6 August 1594): "6 bladers vier evangelistes 8°. [en] 6 vande 4 doctores [is together] fl._ st. 9"; and MPM Arch. 71, fol. 101v, for a confirmation of the general size of the images.

388 MPM Arch. 21, fol. 182 rht (11 February 1593): "3 Jardin de Henault".

389 MPM Arch. 65, fol. 177r (12 December 1588): "2 mains d'Images petit rondes fl. 2 st. 10"; and MPM Arch. 20, fol. 259 rht (7 December 1588): "50 Agnus dei … tot 1 st. [amounts to] fl. 2 st. 10".

390 MPM Arch. 67, fol. 127r (7 November 1590): "Meditat de notre dame une fol.".

391 MPM Arch. 67, fol. 79v (29 July 1590): "Nomen Jesu".

392 MPM Arch. 20, fol. 259 rht (6 August 1587): "2 figurae Regine scotiae".

393 MPM Arch. 66, fol. 171v (22 December 1589): "main de Rosaria"; and MPM Arch. 67, fols. 75r (18 July 1590) and 79v (29 July 1590), both citing a "Rosarium B. Virginis".

394 MPM Arch. 21, fol. 33 rht: "Speculum pro xnis. seductis".

395 MPM Arch. 21, fol. 179 rht: "Speculum pro seductis".

396 MPM Arch. 127, fol. 229 rht; MPM Arch. 216, fol. 200v: "Speculum pro Christianis Seductis Latine" (for this identification of the subject and the date of sale in 1609); and MPM Arch. 217, fol. 90v, for the additional copies with a Latin text in 1610.

397 MPM Arch. 64, fols. 54r and 58v, both with references to: "Imagines b. maria bochij" (alluding to Joannes Bochius, Antwerp city clerk). See MPM Arch. 67, fol. 24v, for "figuren de Marie", which may refer to the same print.

398 MPM Arch. 21, fol. 182 rht.

399 MPM Arch. 74, fol. 9v.

400 MPM Arch. 64, fol. 105v (1587); and MPM Arch. 65, fol. 14v (1588).

401 For example: MPM Arch. 65, fol. 18v (1588); and MPM Arch. 74, fol. 9v (1597).

402 New Holl. De Jode, part I, p. lxxii.

403 We would like to thank Marjolein Leesberg for her help in identifying many of these prints.

404 MPM Arch. 53, fol. 114v: "1 Hofken …" (as supplied by De Jode) and "1 du jardinet …" (when resold to S. de Tassis).

405 MPM Arch. 58, fol. 39v: "Modus vitium etc.".

406 MPM Arch. 58, fol. 39v: "Virtutes connexiae foedere".

407 MPM Arch. 20, fol. 206 rht: "2 Hierusalem antiqua, 2 Nova. st. 4".

408 MPM Arch. 72, fol. 89r: "Calendarium sanctorum f°".

409 MPM Arch. 48, fol. 134bis v: "cariatides" (1570); and MPM Arch. 51, fol. 199v: "Termarum liber Carijatiden etc." (1573).

410 MPM Arch. 58, fol. 39v: "ruinae mundi".

411 MPM Arch. 49, fol. 28v: "Saulus".

412 MPM Arch. 65, fol. 30v: "ecce homo".

413 MPM Arch. 60, fol. 121v: "1 architectura de Vredeman f°" (1582); and MPM Arch. 65, fol. 119v: 1 architectura fig." (1588).

414 MPM Arch. 53, fol. 114v: "1 du jardinet 1 de la flagellation" (under the resale of these prints to S. de Tassis). In the record of De Jode's supply of these images, the identification of this subject is confused because the subject of the Flagellation ("Geseling van Christus") is combined with a reference to a temple (see also MPM Arch. 53, fol. 114v; and Delen 1932, p. 16).

415 MPM Arch. 48, fol. 134bis v:"1 fontes"; MPM Arch. 59, fol. 19r: "livre de perspectieve des fontaines p. Jo. Freidmannus frisius de 18 f°"; and MPM Arch. 18, fol. 66 rht, for the price.

416 MPM Arch. 58, fol. 39v: "Feminae illustres q[uae] violenta morte perierunt f° ovalle".

417 MPM Arch. 51, fol. 51r: "Monarchiae quatuor … 4 f°".

418 MPM Arch. 71, fol. 60v: "4 monarchien".

419 MPM Arch. 58, fol. 39v: "Quatuor Romani en ovalle".

420 MPM Arch. 58, fol. 39v: "Anni partes en ovalle".

421 MPM Arch. 58, fol. 39v: "Reges Israel 8°".

422 MPM Arch. 58, fol. 39v: "Sententiae ex Ecclesiastico".

423 MPM Arch. 58, fol. 39v: "Sententiae ex Proverbiis".

424 MPM Arch. 49, fol. 28v: "Lex per Nagel".

425 MPM Arch. 20, fol. 206 rht: "2 Hierusalem antiqua, 2 Nova. st. 4".

426 MPM Arch. 38, fol. 18 rht: "Moyses et Aaron".

427 MPM Arch. 48, fol. 134bis v: "Grotesque" (1570); and MPM Arch. 51, fol. 199v: "grotiscorum liber" (1573).

428 MPM Arch. 49, fol. 143r: "Hist. van v[er]loren sohn".

429 MPM Arch. 54, fol. 50v: "Mimanata passionis" (1576); and MPM Arch. 61, fol. 139r: "3 passies (?) 4° 48 f°" (1583).

430 MPM Arch. 65, fol. 119v: "fortificatie boech".

431 MPM Arch. 16, fol. 196 rht: "[Imagines] Caesars".

432 MPM Arch. 16, fol. 196 rht: "Imagines Pontif" (1572); and MPM Arch. 51, fol. 199v: "effigies pontificum" (1573).

433 MPM Arch. 49, fol. 28v: "verloren soon".

434 MPM Arch. 38, fol. 18 rht: "livres de ruines" (1558); and MPM Arch. 51, fol. 199v: "Ruinarum liber" (1573).

435 MPM Arch. 51, fol. 40r: "Oeuvres de misericorde f° 7".

436 MPM Arch. 59, fol. 121r: "7em p[ec]c[a]ta mortalia & 4".

437 MPM Arch. 59, fol. 121r: "Artes liberales & 4".

438 MPM Arch. 59, fol. 121r: "planete boecxken & 4", where "4" = 4°, indicating that this series comprised smaller images than De Jode's other series of *The Seven Planets* (see below).

439 MPM Arch. 60, fol. 134r: "Septem Planetae f° cobre", where "f°" = folio, indicating that this is the larger of the two known series of this subject published by de Jode (see above).

440 MPM Arch. 48, fol. 177r: "Passikens 4 stucken" (1570); and MPM Arch. 49, fol. 28v: "Passien p." (1571).

441 MPM Arch. 60, fols. 33v and 34r: "Histoire de Tobias et [2 de] Daniel cobre 4°".

442 MPM Arch. 20, fol. 206 rht: "histoire de Joseph fol. 7".

443 MPM Arch. 58, fol. 39v: "Sampson de 3 f°".

444 MPM Arch. 18, fol. 66 rht: "Hist. de Salomon".

445 MPM Arch. 49, fol. 143r: "Hist. van Susanna kleyn".

446 See New Holl. De Jode, part II, nos. 183–88, for another edition of this subject with six engravings (ca. 197 × 284) after Maarten de Vos.

447 MPM Arch. 60, fols. 33v and 34r: "Histoire de Tobias et [2 de] Daniel cobre 4°".

448 MPM Arch. 38, fol. 18 rht: "livres de compartiment de 2 sortes".

449 MPM Arch. 38, fol. 18 rht: "livres de compartiment de 2 sortes".

450 MPM Arch. 18, fol. 66 rht: "tempel boekxken 14 f°".

451 MPM Arch. 18, fol. 66 rht: "livre des histoires du viel testament".

452 MPM Arch. 20, fol. 206 rht: "Thesaurus Sacrarum Historiarum de 345 f°". See New Holl. De Jode, part I, p. xxxviii, for the authors' estimate of the total number of leaves in this publication.

453 MPM Arch. 21, fol. 59 rht: "ung figurae Bibliorum 4°".

454 MPM Arch. 172, fol. 7v: "1 figures Bibliorum".

455 MPM Arch. 58, fol. 39v: "Parabolae Christi de 6 f°".

456 For example: MPM Arch. 49, fol. 143r (1571); and MPM Arch. 60 fol. 25r (1582).

457 We favor this rendition of his name on the basis of how he signed several legal documents, such as Antwerp, Felix Archives, N 3841, 26 June 1632. For similar reasons, we also favor spelling his son's name as Peeter de Jode (II). See, for example, Antwerp, Felix Archives, N 587, document from 28 July 1659.

458 New Holl. De Jode, part V, p. xlii.

459 See New Holl. De Jode, part VII, nos. 515–61, 564–71, 607–42; and Van der Coelen and Leesberg 2021, nos. 9–12 and 17.

460 New Holl. De Jode, part VIII, p. 143.

461 Our thanks to Marjolein Leesberg for this possible attribution and for sharing her information on this subject.

462 MPM Arch. 180, fol. 152r: "Boexken deliciarum.".

463 MPM Arch. 1107, fol. 104r: "Aen een Arbor Ordinis S. Francisci".

464 MPM Arch. 219, fol. 105r: "D. Boromeij effigies cum myraculis Petri de Jode".

465 MPM Arch. 180, fol. 152r.

466 MPM Arch. 180, fol. 152r.

467 For example: MPM Arch. 180, fol. 152r.

468 Imhof 2020a.

469 MPM Arch. 46, fol. 238r: "grandes doubles feilles doubles".

470 MPM Arch. 46, fol. 238r: "doubles feilles".

471 MPM Arch. 38, fol. 100r: "doubles feilles".

472 MPM Arch. 38, fol. 100r: "doubles feilles".

473 MPM Arch. 38, fol. 100r.

474 MPM Arch. 46, fol. 238r.

475 MPM Arch. 46, fol. 238r: "pieces doubles de fine taille".

476 MPM Arch. 46, fol. 238r: "pieces simples de fine taille".

477 Rombouts and Van Lerius 1872, vol. I, p. 298, n. 4, and p. 310.

478 On the production and distribution of this monumental work, see Bowen and Imhof 2019.

479 For a representative sampling of De Mallery's limited acquisitions, see PG-22 (designs for pendants by Hans Collaert I), PG 40 (symbolic representations of the "Four Ages" designed by Gillis Coignet), PG-78 (Stradanus's *Nova reperta*), and CD-29 (Vredeman de Vries's designs for funeral monuments, which Galle had acquired from Diericx).

480 See Bowen and Imhof 2022, Appendix, p. 30, for an overview of these purchases; and Rombouts and Van Lerius 1872, vol. I, p. 571, for De Mallery's appointment as dean.

481 MPM Arch. 230, fol. 26v: "Hist. seraph imagines".

[482] MPM Arch. 221, fol. 187r: "D. Joanne … factum est verbum Domini(?)". See MPM Arch. 128, fol. 108 rht, for the selling price.

[483] MPM Arch. 233, fol. 55v: "Imago S. Ursule Malleri".

[484] MPM Arch. 218, fol. 208r: "peccatie, fomes libellus".

[485] MPM Arch. 216, fol. 130v: "Images avec les dix Jesuites".

[486] MPM Arch. 180, fol. 116r.

[487] MPM Arch. 216, fol. 211r.

[488] For example: MPM Arch. 1104, fol. 46r (1607), and MPM Arch. 233, fol. 44v (1626) for De Mallery; and MPM Arch. 238, fol. 27r (1630), and MPM Arch. 241, fol. 66v (1633) for Theodore Galle. See MPM Arch. 225, fols. 13v (1618), for the identification of such prints as 8° in format.

[489] BN, vol. XIV (1897), cols. 511–14 (as observed in Lemmens and Thijs 2006, p. 92, n. 7).

[490] MPM Arch. 226, fol. 103v.

[491] MPM Arch. 222, fol. 132r (1615); and MPM Arch. 232, fol. 104r (1625).

[492] MPM Arch. 1106, fol. 54r.

[493] See, for example, MPM Arch. 53, fol. 197v (1575): "Calendaria antiqua"; and MPM Arch. 54, fol. 67v (1576): "Calendaria antiqua".

[494] MPM Arch. 226, fol. 88r: "kalendarium Montani".

[495] See, for example, MPM Arch. 54, fol. 7v (1576); and MPM Arch. 64, fol. 20v (1587).

[496] See MPM Arch. 261, fols. 30v and 79v, for the sales in 1577 and 1578; and MPM Arch. 55, fol. 4v, for the shipment to Paris.

[497] See, for example, MPM Arch. 43III, fol. 73v (1576); and MPM Arch. 57, fol. 26v (1579).

[498] Rombouts and Van Lerius 1872, vol. I, p. 401.

[499] For examples of challenges to Rubens's privileges (as cited in Chapter 6) see Grivel 1986, pp. 109–110; and Diels 2009, p. 57.

[500] MPM Arch. 1107, fols. 30r and 30v: "een beldt vanden slag vande Amasones" and "la bataille des Amasones", respectively.

[501] MPM Arch. 1107, fol. 26v; and MPM Arch. 240, fol. 95v, respectively.

[502] Bowen 2017, p. 292.

[503] Rombouts and Van Lerius 1872, vol. I, pp. 247 (Jan I), 281 (Raphael I), and 272 (Gillis I), for connections to Antwerp's Guild of St Luke; De Ramaix 1989, pp. 10 and 19, on Gillis I's professions; and Antwerp, Felix Archives, CERT 47, fol. 186r, for the 1586 document.

[504] De Ramaix 1989, Appendices 4 and 5, pp. 38–39, for Raphael I and Jan I; and Antwerp, Felix Archives, CERT 47, fol. 186r, for Gillis I and others.

[505] Zülch 1935, pp. 416–17.

[506] Sénéchal 1990, pp. 34–35.

[507] MPM Arch. 65, fols. 13v (Galle's supply of the bulk of the prints Ximenes requested), and 32r (the details of what was sent to Ximenes, including, for example, Jan Sadeler's series of *The Twelve Articles of Faith (The Apostles' Creed)* (cf. Holl. Dutch & Flemish, vol. XXI, pp. 157–58, nos. 465–76; and Holl. Dutch & Flemish, vol. XLIV, nos. 871–82)).

[508] See the prints listed below; and Chapter 6 for Gillis's print sales. For an example of the purchase of two volumes of the Sadelers' *Symbola* series in 1605 from Levinus Hulsius, a Calvinist scholar-publisher who had roots in Ghent and who had emigrated first to Middelburg and thereafter to Nuremberg (by 1583), see MPM Arch. 999, fol. 45 rht.

[509] MPM Arch. 999 (spring 1605), fol. 43 rht, as the "Eremiten van Sadeler"; and MPM Arch. 189, fol. 57r.

[510] MPM Arch. 990 (fall 1600), fol. 19 lft; and MPM Arch. 991 (spring 1601), fol. 50 lft, respectively.

[511] MPM Arch. 993 (spring 1602), fol. 43 rht.

[512] MPM Arch. 189, fol. 57r, for the price and the clear reference to the inclusion of the accompanying text; and MPM Arch. 995 (spring 1603), fol. 20 rht, for the date of sale.

[513] MPM Arch. 189, fol. 57r for the price; and MPM Arch. 993 (spring 1602), fol. 43 rht, for the date of the sale in German currency.

[514] MPM Arch. 189, fol. 57r for the price; and MPM Arch. 995 (spring 1603), fol. 20 rht, for the date of the sale in German currency.

[515] MPM Arch. 65, fol. 103v, as the "virtutes filij dei" with nine leaves.

[516] See, for example, the collection of the Counts of Waldburg-Wolfegg in the castle at Wolfegg or what remains of the former Jesuit college collection of Cologne, which is now part of the Wallraf-Richartz-Museum & Foundation Corboud, Graphische Sammlung in Cologne.

[517] Snijders' reissues of prints are discussed in Chapter 6. For this emblem book, see Holl. Dutch & Flemish, vol. XXVII, p. 96, no. 18; and Porteman 1975.

[518] MPM Arch. 237, fol. 109v: "verlichte pampieren twee op een blat in 4to" (1629).

[519] MPM Arch. 1107, fol. 29v: "groote witte" (1632).

[520] MPM Arch. 237, fol. 26r (1629); and MPM Arch. 1107, fol. 29v (1632).

[521] MPM Arch. 240, fol. 155r.

[522] MPM Arch. 237, fol. 109v (1629).

[523] MPM Arch. 1107, fol. 29v (1632).

[524] MPM Arch. 225, fol. 84r (1618); and MPM Arch. 227, fol. 96v (1620).

[525] Van der Stock 1998, pp. 374–75.

[526] Ibid., p. 374, n. 56. These two series are discussed as one and the same in Cock 2013, p. 24.

[527] MPM Arch. 38, fol. 84r: "Pierre et Jan".

[528] Rombouts and Van Lerius 1872, vol. I, p. 375.

[529] MPM Arch. 218, fol. 208v: "Vita Ste Thomae f° Cop. [fols.] 30/35".

[530] See Holl. Dutch & Flemish, vol. LXIX, p. xl; and the examples cited in n. 83.

[531] MPM Arch. 174, fol. 19v: "Salutatio & kersnacht 16°".

[532] MPM Arch. 178, fol. 107v: "Images Secilae dedicata Cardinali Sfondrato p Hier. Wirx." (image of St. Cecilia, dedicated to Cardinal Sfondrato, by Hieronymus Wierix).

[533] MPM Arch. 217, fol. 8r: "Images des 4 peres".

[534] MPM Arch. 174, fol. 19v: "Angelus Custos 4°".

[535] MPM Arch. 220, fol. 190r: "Libelle de Jesu et Josepho".

[536] MPM Arch. 174, fol. 17v: "Jesus matris deliciae".

[537] MPM Arch. 222, fol. 213v: "Jesu christi Infantia" (1615); and MPM Arch. 223, fol. 78v: "Infantia Christi" (1616).

[538] MPM Arch. 223, fol. 78v: "Speculum virginitatis".

[539] MPM Arch. 223, fol. 78v: "novus Jesu".

[540] MPM Arch. 174, fol. 19v: "Sta Anna 4°".

[541] MPM Arch. 174, fol. 17v: "in funeculis adam … 8°".

[542] MPM Arch. 179, fol. 156r: "P Xaverius".

[543] MPM Arch. 179, fol. 156r: "P Ignatius cum libro".

[544] MPM Arch. 179, fol. 156r: "P Ignatius apt cum Cruce".

[545] MPM Arch. 174, fol. 19v: "Sta Margareta et Agnes 16°".

[546] MPM Arch. 179, fol. 156r: "P Ignatius et Xaverius".

[547] MPM Arch. 174, fol. 17v: "Nil vero obsistit 8°".

[548] MPM Arch. 174, fol. 19v: "Apostel boexken 16°" (1602); and MPM Arch. 1104, fol. 45v: "12 apostres" (1607).

[549] MPM Arch. 174, fol. 17v: "dilectus meus candidus".

[550] MPM Arch. 174, fol. 19v: "Ave Regina Celorum 4°".

[551] MPM Arch. 216, fol. 130v, and MPM Arch. 1104, fol. 79v (1609); and MPM Arch. 223, fol. 78v (1616).

[552] MPM Arch. 216, fol. 130v, and MPM Arch. 1104, fol. 79v (1609); and MPM Arch. 223, fol. 78v (1616).

[553] MPM Arch. 173, fol. 204r (1601, prints in 8°, supplied by Anton II); MPM Arch. 174, fol. 19v (1602, prints in 8°, supplied by Hieronymus); MPM Arch. 216, fol. 130v, and MPM Arch. 1104, fol. 79v (1609, supplied by Hieronymus); and MPM Arch. 223, fol. 78v (1616, supplied by Hieronymus).

[554] MPM Arch. 1104, fol. 102v; and MPM Arch. 218, fol. 27r (resold with .25 st. profit margin added to the price) (1611).

APPENDIX 2

Individuals Who Purchased Prints via the Officina Plantiniana

Below, we list all of the individuals who, according to the records of the Officina Plantiniana in Antwerp, either purchased prints or received packages through that business between 1556 and 1641. We only considered packages that were either explicitly noted as containing images or most likely contained them due to the people involved in the transaction (two print sellers, for example). We have omitted individuals who were simply intermediaries for other known recipients in these transactions, such as merchants who arranged for the transport of the requested items for someone else. The Officina Plantiniana's clients are listed alphabetically according to the place where they were living at the time that they acquired the prints. If they were residing temporarily in a different country, for instance when Cosmo Masi and his wife Laura were in the Low Countries during his appointment as secretary to Alexander Farnese, then the buyer is listed under his or her native residence (in their case, Padua). Place names are arranged alphabetically by country, then by city. As in the main text, we are listing cities under the country with which they were affiliated in the period under consideration. For example, St Omer and Lille are listed under The Low Countries and not France. At the end of the known places for each country, individuals from that country whom we could not localize are listed under "unknown location". Similarly, those for whom the country of origin is not known appear at the very end of this appendix under the general heading "Unknown location". The name of each person cited is followed by a general indication of their profession, if it is recorded. Then, there are at least one or two examples of the client's acquisition of prints, listed by date; each example has a reference to the source for the record of the purchase in MPM (Plantin-Moretus archives). There are numerous instances in which only one acquisition is known. If the individual purchased prints on multiple occasions, we have cited one of the earliest and one of the latest known transactions in which they were involved. Consequently, not all transactions involving the distribution of prints appear here. In many cases, a more detailed discussion of these or other purchases can be found by consulting the general index of our volume.

CHINA / FAR EAST

- Trigault, Nicolas: Jesuit, 1616 (Arch. 223, fol. 216v) and 1617 (Arch. 224, fol. 145r)

FRANCE

AMIENS

- Gouy, de, Charles: bookseller, 1618 (Arch. 225, fol. 5r)

CAEN

- Rinsart, Théodore: bookseller, 1593 (Arch. 70, fol. 91r) and 1594 (Arch. 71, fols. 61r-61v)

EPINAL

- Thouvenot, Nicolas: bookseller, 1633 (Arch. 241, fol. 66v)

HESDIN

- Dassonleville, Jean: bookseller, 1624 (Arch. 231, fol. 167r) – 1631 (Arch. 239, fol. 112r)

LA ROCHELLE

- Bourdigale, de, Louis: squire, 1578 (Arch. 56, fol. 21v)
- Pillet, du, Thomas: merchant, 1591 (Arch. 68, fols. 26v-27v)

LYON

- Chifflet, Petrus Franciscus: Jesuit, 1632 (Arch. 240, fol. 60r)
- Rouille, Guillaume: bookseller, 1576 (Arch. 54, fol. 67v)

MAUBEUGE

- Bourgoys, Philippe: Jesuit, 1630 (Arch. 238, fol. 27v)

NANCY

- Marin, Jean: print seller, 1629 (Arch. 237, fol. 66v) – 1632 (Arch. 240, fol. 166r)

PARIS

- Angelier, l', Abel: bookseller, 1556 (Arch. 34, p. 10)
- Bartrand, Jacques: unknown, 1614 (Arch. 221, fol. 102v)
- Beys, Adriaen: bookseller, 1602 (Arch. 174, fol. 93r) – 1603 (Arch. 175, fol. 155r)
- Beys, Christophe: bookseller, 1599 (Arch. 171, fol. 17r)
- Beys, Gilles: bookseller, 1580 (Arch. 58, fol. 17r)
- Boutique, Paris de (Plantin's): bookseller, 1573 (Arch. 51, fol. 134v) – 1577 (Arch. 55, fol. 41r)
- Breyer, Lucas: bookseller, 1561 (Arch. 36, fol. 14r)
- Duchesne, André: scholar, 1632 (Arch. 240, fol. 159r)

- Firens, Pierre I: print seller, 1609 (Arch. 216, fol. 42r)
- Foucault, Eustace: bookseller, 1607 (Arch. 179, fol. 227v) – 1614 (Arch. 221, fol. 102v)
- Gerard, Pierre: bookbinder, 1556 (Arch. 34, p. 5)
- Gourmont, de, Jean: unknown, 1560 (Arch. 35, fol. 110v)
- Honervogt, Jacques I: print seller, 1633 (Arch. 241, fol. 30v) – 1634 (Arch. 242, fol. 185v)
- Huybrecht, Pauwels II: colorer of prints, 1634 (Arch. 242, fol. 120v)
- Jacquet, Pierre: art dealer, 1579 (Arch. 57, fol. 117v)
- Jeune, le, Martin: bookseller, 1556 (Arch. 34, p. 7) – 1561 (Arch. 36, fol. 16r)
- Jourdain, Barthélemy: bookseller, 1559 (Arch. 34, fol. 34)
- Leclerc, Jean IV: print seller, 1613 (Arch. 220, fol. 55r)
- Mallery, de, Charles: print seller, 1601 (Arch. 173, fol. 171v) – 1604 (Arch. 176, fol. 20r)
- Marchand ?, Daniel: art dealer, 1630 (Arch. 238, fol. 72r)
- Mere du Dieu, du, Carolus: Discalced Carmelite, 1632 (Arch. 240, fol. 159r)
- Messager, Jean: print seller, 1610 (Arch. 217, fol. 209v) – 1635 (Arch. 243, fol. 10v)
- Orleans, d', Louis: lawyer, 1599 (Arch. 171, fol. 37r)
- Orleans, duc d', Gaston: noble, 1634 (Arch. 242, fol. 57r)
- Perier, Adriaen: bookseller, 1598 (Arch. 75, fol. 161r) – 1602 (Arch. 174, fol. 96v)
- Porret, Pierre: merchant, 1570 (Arch. 48, 66v) – 1582 (Arch. 60, fol. 4r)
- Rabel, Jean: print seller, 1578 (Arch. 56, fol. 19r)
- Rambouillet, de, monsieur: unknown, 1582 (Arch. 60, fol. 197r)
- Sonnius, Michel I: bookseller, 1579 (Arch. 57, fol. 138v) – 1588 (Arch. 65, fol. 82v)
- Tavernier, Gabriel I: print and map seller, 1608 (Arch. 180, fol. 202v) – 1613 (Arch. 220, fol. 209v)
- Tavernier, Melchior II: print and map seller, 1630 (Arch. 238, fol. 34r)

PONT-À-MOUSSON
- Jesuits, 1595 (Arch. 72, fol. 158v)

REIMS
- Hecart, Nicolas: bookseller, 1628 (Arch. 235, fol. 28v)

REMBERVILLE
- Berel, Hubert: bookseller, 1611 (Arch. 218, fol. 217v)

ROUEN
- Cousturier, le, Jean: bookseller, 1631 (Arch. 239, fol. 16r)
- Doom, Mathieu: bookseller, 1602 (Arch. 174, fol. 19v)

TOUL
- Martel, de St, Simon: bookseller, 1589 (Arch. 66, fol. 158v) – 1591 (Arch. 68, fols. 65v-66r)
- Trostot, Hierosme: bookseller, 1592 (Arch. 69, fol. 24v)

TOULOUSE
- Jagourt, Pierre: bookseller, 1592 (Arch. 69, fols. 100r-100v)

TOURS
- Patin, monsieur: gentleman, 1582 (Arch. 60, fol. 160v)

FRANCE, UNKNOWN LOCATION
- Chevallier, Jean: unknown, 1611 (Arch. 218, fol. 72v)
- Gaultier, Pierre: unknown, 1573 (Arch. 51, fol. 6r)
- Goudin, Philippe: unknown, 1589 (Arch. 66, fol. 56r)
- Sagin, Nicolas: laity, 1607 (Arch. 179, fol. 176r)

HOLY ROMAN EMPIRE

AACHEN
- Capuchins, 1614 (Arch. 221, fol. 183v)
- Radermacher, Johan: merchant, 1595 (Arch. 72, fol. 205r)

AUGSBURG
- Augsburg, van, Antoine: representative of the Fugger family, 1561 (Arch. 36, fol. 16v)
- Dilbaum, Samuel: bookseller, assistant to Georg Willer, 1570 (Arch. 48, fol. 136v) – 1571 (Arch. 49, fols. 147r-147v)
- Kruger, Johann: bookseller, 1613 (Arch. 220, fol. 218v) – 1615 (Arch. 222, fol. 30v)
- Liedel, Lenaert: unknown, 1560 (Arch. 35, fol. 183v)
- Willer, Georg I: bookseller, 1570 (Arch. 48, fol. 139v)
- Willer, Georg II: bookseller, 1614 (Arch. 221, fol. 56r)

COLOGNE
- Alting, Johann: Jesuit, 1639 (Arch. 148, fol. 199r)
- Boons / Buon, Peter: art dealer, 1589 (Arch. 66, fol. 100r) – 1591 (Arch. 68, fol. 60r)
- Bussemacher, Johann: print seller, 1588 (Arch. 65, fol. 165r)
- Cholinus, Maternus: bookseller, 1560 (Arch. 35, fol. 114v)
- Clerck, de, Hendrik: merchant, 1611 (Arch. 218, fol. 41r)
- Egmont, van, Cornelis: bookseller, 1619 (Arch. 226, fol. 185v) – 1630 (Arch. 238, fol. 161v)
- Egmont, van, Nicolas: merchant, 1612 (Arch. 219, fol. 23r)
- Greuter, Joachim: Jesuit, 1638 (Arch. 246, fol. 14r)
- Hellebrand, Magdalena: nun, 1634 (Arch. 242, fol. 144v)
- Hierat, Arnold and Anton II: bookseller, 1627 (Arch. 234, fol. 27v) – 1629 (Arch. 237, fol. 3v)
- Hierat, Anton I: bookseller, 1611 (Arch. 218, fol. 207r) – 1623 (Arch. 230, fol. 143r)
- Hogenberg, Abraham: print and map seller, 1617 (Arch. 224, fol. 172r) – 1639 (Arch. 247, fol. 185v)
- Hogenberg, Agnes Lomar: print and map seller, 1590 (Arch. 67, fol. 124v)
- Hogenberg, Frans: print and map seller, 1585 (62, fol. 134r) – 1589 (Arch. 66, fol. 2v)
- Hogenberg, Johann (Hans): print and map seller, 1594 (Arch. 71, fol. 22v)
- Hogenberg, Agnes Lomar and Hans: print and map sellers, 1590 (Arch. 67, fol. 57v) – 1593 (Arch. 67, fol. 57v)
- Kinckius, Johann: bookseller, 1603 (Arch. 175, fol. 91v) – 1637 (Arch. 245, fol. 25v)
- Meuting, Georg[ius]: bookseller, 1613 (Arch. 220, fol. 211r) – 1614 (Arch. 221, fol. 123r)

- Mylius, Arnold: bookseller, 1588 (Arch. 65, fol. 164bis r) – 1601 (Arch. 173, fol. 34v)
- Mylius, Hermann: bookseller, 1608 (Arch. 180, fol. 223v) – 1630 (Arch. 238, fol. 133v)
- Overadt, Peter: print and map seller, 1621 (Arch. 228, fol. 104v)
- Passe, de, Crispijn I: print seller, 1590 (Arch. 67, fol. 124v) – 1610 (Arch. 217, fol. 230v)
- Wolters, Bernhard: bookseller, 1600 (Arch. 172, fol. 18v) – 1635 (Arch. 243, fol. 121v)

EMMERICH

- Wessel, Everhard: bookseller, 1601 (173, fols. 116v-117r) – 1616 (Arch. 223, fol. 6v)

FRANKFURT

- Aubry, Johann I: bookseller, 1577 (Arch. 55, fol. 100r) and 1581 (Arch. 59, fols. 190r-190v)
- Bry, de, Theodore: print seller, 1592 (Arch. 69, fol. 148v)
- Joannis, Joachim: Jesuit, 1639 (Arch. 247, fol. 120r)

HAMBURG

- Vos, de, Willem: unknown, 1582 (Arch. 60, fol. 121v)

KONINGSBERG

- Specklin, Josias: bookbinder, 1582 (Arch. 60, fol. 116r)
- Scrinius, Michael: librarian, 1577 (Arch. 55, fol. 180r) – 1583 (Arch. 61, fols. 124r-124v)

MUNICH

- Segen, Melchior: bookseller, 1625 (Arch. 232, fol. 40v)

MÜNSTER

- Dale, van, Michiel: bookseller, 1619 (Arch. 226, fol. 103v) – 1626 (Arch. fol. 233, 182v)
- Raesfeld, Bernhard: bookseller, 1629 (Arch. 237, fol. 24v) – 1632 (Arch. 240, fol. 155r)
- Raesfeld, Lambert: bookseller, 1612 (Arch. 219, fol. 161r) – 1617 (Arch. 224, fol. 66r)
- Raesfeld, Lambert, Widow: bookseller, 1618 (Arch. 225, fol. 13r)

NUREMBERG

- Camerarius, Joachim: scholar, 1576 (Arch. 54, fol. 51v)
- Caymox, Balthasar: art dealer, 1613 (Arch. 220, fol. 211r)
- Caymox, Cornelis: art dealer, 1579 (Arch. 57, fol. 26v)
- Gundelach, Hans: bookseller, 1576 (Arch. 54, fol. 49v) – 1586 (Arch. 63, fol. 77v)

OLOMOUC

- Moretus, Theodore: Jesuit, 1631 (Arch. 239, fol. 35r)

XANTEN

- Pighius, Stephanus: canon, 1589 (Arch. 66, fol. 114v)

ITALY

BOLOGNA

- Malvasia, Innocentius: papal nuncio, 1594: see Brussels

FLORENCE

- Francheschi, Paolo: merchant, 1586 (Arch. 63, fol. 28v) and 1588 (Arch. 65, fol. 52r)

MANTUA

- Duke of Mantua (Vincenzo I Gonzaga): 1599 (Arch. 171, fol. 116v)

MILAN

- Antoni, degli, Giovanni Antonio: bookseller, 1576 (Arch. 54, fol. 147v) and 1578 (Arch. 56, fols. 24v-25v)
- Coqui brothers: merchants, 1580 (Arch. 58, fol. 26r)
- Ferrandi, Carlo: bookseller, 1631 (Arch. 239, fol. 10v) – 1633 (Arch. 241, fol. 178v)
- Martyre, Pietro: bookseller, 1599 (Arch. 171, fol. 87v)
- Sfondrate, Paolo: member of Oratorian order, 1640 (Arch. 248, fol. 166r)

NAPLES

- Everhardi, Pietro: unknown, 1610 (Arch. 217, fol. 224v)
- Ruardo, Giovanni: bookseller, 1609 (Arch. 216, fol. 232r)

PADUA

- Gentili brothers: merchants, 1567 (Arch. 45, fol. 69v) – 1568 (Arch. 46, fol. 57r)
- Masi, Cosmo: secretary to Alexander Farnese, 1593 (Arch. 70, fol. 129r)
- Masi, Laura: wife of Cosmo Masi, 1588 (Arch. 65, fol. 91v)

ROME

- Cope, Alan: priest, 1574 (Arch. 52, fol. 15r)
- Franzini, Ger. and Giovanni: booksellers, 1587 (Arch. 64, fol. 89r)
- Gelli, Giovanni Paolo: bookseller, 1608 (Arch. 180, fol. 157r)
- Hase, de, Jacob: painter, 1622 (Arch. 229, fol. 101r) – 1625 (Arch. 232, fol. 30v)
- Hulder, de, Raymuno: ecclesiastic, 1625 (Arch. 232, fol. 30v)
- Baronius, Caesar: cardinal, 1599 (Arch. 171, fol. 76r)
- Massanio, Giovanni Battista: unknown, 1625 (Arch. 232, fol. 118r)
- Petrasancta, Silvester: Jesuit, 1634 (Arch. 242, fol. 80r) - 1637 (Arch. 245, fol. 33r)
- Quaille, de, Jacobus: Jesuit, 1616 (Arch. 136, fol. 38)
- Ursinus, Fulvius: scholar, 1574 (Arch. 52, fol. 31v)
- Vivario, Gaspar: art dealer, 1614 (Arch. 221, fol. 32r) – 1615 (Arch. 222, fol. 200r)

VENICE

- Sadeler, Justus: print and bookseller, 1615 (Arch. 222, fol. 170v) – 1618 (Arch. 225, fol. 8r)

ITALY, UNKNOWN LOCATION

- Ansaldus, Bernardinus: Franciscan, 1575 (Arch. 53, fol. 141v)
- Bonomi (Bonomigni), Giovanni Francesco: papal nuncio, 1586 (Arch. 63, fol. 9r)

- Cini, Cesare: bookseller, 1587 (Arch. 64, fol. 31r)
- Cremona, di, Cesare: unknown, 1618 (Arch. 225, fol. 74v; Arch. 128, fol. 240)
- Judice, Giovanni Battista: merchant, 1596 (Arch. 73, fol. 17v)
- Julio (father): Dominican, 1605 (Arch. 177, fol. 60r)
- Trivulzio, conte de, chaplain of, 1611 (Arch. 218, fol. 65v)

LOW COUNTRIES

AALST
- Capuchins, 1628 (Arch. 235, fol. 129v)

AMSTERDAM
- Barentsen, Hendrik: bookseller, 1618 (Arch. 225, fol. 126r) – 1638 (Arch. 246, fol. 154v)
- Claesz, Cornelis: bookseller, 1579 (Arch. 57, fol. 131v) and 1581 (Arch. 59, fol. 154r)
- Gouda, van, Franciscus: Capuchin, 1628 (Arch. 235, fol. 140r) – 1638 (Arch. 1107, fol. 92v)
- Paets, Claes Jacobsz: bookseller, 1614 (Arch. 221, fol. 187r) – 1615 (Arch. 222, fol. 214r)
- Utrecht, van, Constantinus: Capuchin, 1637 (Arch. 245, fol. 24v) – 1640 (Arch. 248, fol. 25v)
- Visscher, Claes Janssoon: bookseller, 1631 (Arch. 239, fol. 94v)

ANTWERP
- Annoni (family): merchants, 1607 (Arch. 179, fol. 35v) – 1621 (Arch. 228, fol. 88v)
- Anthonis, Andries: merchant, 1583 (Arch. 61, fol. 138v) and 1584 (Arch. 62, fol. 6r)
- Antwerp, city government: 1598 (Arch. 75, fol. 227r)
- Antwerpen, van, Florentius: Capuchin, 1616 (Arch. 223, fol. 20v)
- Bellerus, Jan: bookseller, 1587 (Arch. 64, fol. 73v)
- Bontempo, Leonardo: noble, 1612 (Arch. 219, fol. 119v) and 1615 (Arch. 222, fols. 64v and 69r)
- Bourrai, Pierre: bookbinder, 1632 (Arch. 240, fol. 95v)
- Braa, de, heirs, Jacques: merchant, 1624 (Arch. 231, fol. 121r) – 1626 (Arch. 233, fol. 45v)
- Capuchins, 1628 (Arch. 235, fol. 129v) and 1635 (Arch. 243, fol. 69r)
- Carillo, Martin Fernando: merchant, 1612 (Arch. 219, fol. 194r)
- Clarisse, Louis and Rogier: merchants, 1621 (Arch. 228, fol. 34r)
- Cock, Hieronymus: print and map seller, 1559 (Arch. 35, fol. 89v) and 1560 (Arch. 35, fol. 183v)
- Cordier, Jan: bookseller, 1587 (Arch. 64, fol. 5v)
- Deegbroot, Gillis: merchant, 1611 (Arch. 218, fol. 38r)
- Dilft, vander, Edouard: mayor, 1600 (Arch. 172, fol. 183v)
- Dorcho, Jan Paulo: merchant, 1582 (Arch. 60, fol. 83v)
- Fernandes, Michael: Jesuit, 1577 (Arch. 55, fol. 45v)
- Fossa, Vincentio: merchant, 1592 (Arch. 69, fol. 144v)
- Ghysbrecht: intaglio printer, 1559 (Arch. 35, fol. 91r)
- Halmale, Hendrik I: mayor, 1599 (Arch. 171, fol. 96r)
- Homodei, Cesare: unknown, 1581 (Arch. 59, fol. 173v)
- Jesuits, 1593 (Arch. 70, fol. 125v) – 1613 (Arch. 220, fol. 185v)
- Jode, de, Cornelis: art dealer, 1597 (Arch. 74, fol. 93v)
- Jode, de, Gerard: print seller, 1560 (Arch. 35, fol. 117v) and 1564 (Arch. 36, 71)
- Lanfranchi, Carlo: merchant, 1599 (Arch. 171, fol. 45r)
- Langart, Gabriel: merchant, 1581 (Arch. 59, fol. 20v) – 1582 (Arch. 60, fol. 14r)
- Langhen, Mathieu: merchant?, 1599 (Arch. 171, fol. 20v)
- Lavello de Vergano, de, Antonio: merchant, 1608 (Arch. 180, fol. 116v)
- Lesteens, Guillaume: bookseller, 1640 (Arch. 248, fol. 52r)
- Liefrinck, Hans I: print seller, 1559 (Arch. 35, fol. 99r) – 1560 (Arch. 35, fol. 114v)
- Liefrinck, Mynken: map and print seller, copper-plate printer, 1576 (Arch. 54, fol. 149r)
- Liesaert, Philips III: art dealer and merchant, 1591 (Arch. 68, fol. 129v)
- Lumnius, Fredericus: priest in the beguinage, 1588 (Arch. 65, fol. 171v)
- Luyck, van, Hans: print seller, 1591 (Arch. 68, fol. 129v)
- Malvasia, Innocentius: papal nuncio, 1594 (Arch. 71, fol. 169r)
- Moerentorf, Michelle: member of the Moretus family, 1630 (Arch. 166, fol. 101v)
- Mol, van, Jacques: unknown, 1604 (Arch. 176, fol. 32v)
- Moretus, Melchior: priest and member of the Moretus family, 1602 (Arch. 174, fol. 96r)
- Nathaniel: Capuchin, 1616 (Arch. 223, fol. 41v)
- Nys, Joannes: Dominican, 1611 (Arch. 218, fol. 71r; Arch. 128, fol. 137 lft)
- Ortelius, Abraham: art and map dealer, 1575 (Arch. 53, fol. 197v) – 1585 (Arch. 62, fol. 112r)
- Pardo Lopez, Diego: merchant, 1606 (Arch. 178, fol. 51r) and 1607 (Arch. 179, fol. 47v)
- Perez, Luis: merchant, 1577 (Arch. 55, fol. 63r)
- Perez de Varon, Martin: merchant, 1577 (Arch. 55, fol. 68v) and 1582 (Arch. 60, fol. 134r)
- Petit, Jean: unknown, 1559 (Arch. 35, fol. 79r)
- Pisani, Ottavio: scholar, 1614 (Arch. 221, fol. 217v) and 1615 (Arch. 128, fol. 208 lft)
- Plantin, Christopher: bookseller, 1564 (Arch. 36, fol. 73)
- Ranst, van, Willem: canon, 1592 (Arch. 69, fol. 65r)
- Raphelengius, Franciscus I: bookseller, 1579 (Arch. 57, fol. 83v)
- Recanati, di, Cornelius: ecclesiastic, 1604 (Arch. 176, fol. 91r)
- Roosendael, Cornelis: merchant, 1581 (Arch. 59, fol. 133v)
- Rosco, Jan Paulo: cashier for the Italian merchant G.A.Vergano, 1596 (Arch. 73, fol. 101v)
- Rundtfleisch, Daniel I: merchant, 1578 (Arch. 56, fol. 133v) and 1588 (Arch. 65, fol. 119v)
- Schottus, Andreas: Jesuit, 1619 (Arch. 226, fol. 88r)
- Sevilla, de, Ferdinando: merchant, 1588 (Arch. 65, fol. 125v) – 1600 (Arch. 172, fol. 86v)
- Sohier, Hugues: merchant, 1583 (Arch. 61, fol. 133v)
- Spierinck, Hans: merchant, 1599 (Arch. 171, fol. 170r)

- Spinola and Cattaneo, company: merchants, 1592 (Arch. 69, fol. 113r)
- Sterre, van der, Chrysostomus: Norbertine, 1631 (Arch. 239, fol. 141r)
- Tassis, de, Carolus: government official, 1594 (Arch. 71, fol. 101r)
- Tassis, de, Simon: merchant, 1575 (Arch. 53, fol. 114v) and 1580 (Arch. 58, fol. 19v)
- Tongeren, van, Peter: bookseller, 1586 (Arch. 63, fol. 124r)
- Trigoso, Pedro: Jesuit, 1577 (Arch. 55, fol. 45v)
- Veltwyck, van, Melchior: unknown, 1599 (Arch. 171, fol. 166bis v) and 1600 (Arch. 172, fol. 29v)
- Vergano, Giovanni Angelo: merchant, 1596 (Arch. 73, fol. 156v) and 1599 (Arch. 171, fol. 82r)
- Verkoven, Michiel: painter, 1610 (Arch. 217, fol. 174r)
- Vianen, van, Willibrordus: Capuchin, 1638 (Arch. 246, fol. 87v)
- Woverius, Joannes: laity, 1609 (Arch. 216, fol. 36r)
- Ximenes, Ferdinandus: merchant, 1587 (Arch. 64, fol. 34v) – 1588 (Arch. 65, fol. 32r)
- Zinger, Hans: painter, 1561 (Arch. 36, fol. 11v)
- Zurich, van, François: merchant, 1577 (Arch. 55, fol. 17r)

ARMENTIÈRES

- Capuchins, 1605 (Arch. 177, fol. 83r)

ARRAS

- Bauduin, Gilles: bookseller, 1586 (Arch. 63, fol. 125r)
- Dacquin, Nicolas: bookseller, 1578 (Arch. 56, fol. 36v)

ATH

- Bosquier, Philippe: Recollect, 1597 (Arch. 74, fol. 9r)

BERGUES (WINOKSBERGEN)

- Capuchins, 1628 (Arch. 235, fol. 129v)
- Leen, vander, Jan, Widow: bookseller, 1632 (Arch. 240, fol. 36r)
- Nooman, Philippe: ecclesiastic, 1610 (Arch. 217, fol. 58r)

BOURBOURG

- Capuchins, 1628 (Arch. 235, fol. 129v)

BREDA

- Geldre, de, Peeter: bookseller, 1566 (Arch. 44, fol. 41r)
- Janssen van Kampen, Gerard: bookseller, 1568 (Arch. 46, fol. 1v) and 1575 (Arch. 53, fol. 56v)
- Jesuits, 1632 (Arch. 240, fol. 124r)

BRUGES

- Brugensis, Guardi[anus]: ecclesiastic, 1589 (Arch. 66, fol. 124v)
- Brussel, van, Charles: bookseller, 1615 (Arch. 222, fol. 132r) and 1618 (Arch. 225, fol. 103r)
- Capuchins, 1628 (Arch. 235, fol. 129v)
- Lucas, Franciscus: ecclesiastic, 1581 (Arch. 59, fol. 130r)
- Pamelius, Jacobus: canon, 1575 (Arch. 53, 209r)
- Tollenare, Antonius II: bookseller, 1588 (Arch. 65, fol. 18v) – 1595 (Arch. 72, fol. 57r)
- Tollenare, Antonius II, Widow: bookseller, 1616 (Arch. 223, fol. 18r)
- Vincx, Jan II: bookseller, 1587 (Arch. 64, fol. 112v) – 1603 (Arch. 175, fol. 74r)
- Zeelandre, Vincentius: Jesuit, 1587 (Arch. 64, 162r) – 1593 (Arch. 70, fol. 46v)

BRUSSELS

- Archduke and Archduchess, Albert and Isabella, nobles: 1609 (Arch. 216, fol. 172v) – 1619 (Arch. 226, fol. 134v) and 1625 (Arch. 142, p. 2)
- Arenberg, d', Contesse, duchess Aarschot: noble, 1617 (Arch. 224, fol. 142r)
- Arenberg, d', Charles: noble, 1594 (Arch. 71, fol. 113v)
- Assonleville, d', Christophe: noble, 1587 (Arch. 20, fol. 252 lft)
- Bergaigne, Antoine: Franciscan: 1587 (Arch. 64, fol. 26r) – 1606 (Arch. 178, fol. 128r)
- Cameren, vande, madame: unknown, 1590 (Arch. 67, fol. 85v)
- Carstijn, Guilielmus: Franciscan, 1601 (Arch. 173, fol. 100r)
- Chapelain de son exc, (Requesens): ecclesiastic, 1575 (Arch. 53, fol. 78r)
- Chifflet, Philippe: abbot, 1633 (Arch. 144, pp. 369 and 373; Arch. 166, fol. 141r)
- Egnoye, de, François: Jesuit, 1591 (Arch. 68, fol. 109v) – 1597 (Arch. 74, fol. 34v)
- Frangipani, Ottavio Mirto: papal nuncio, 1599 (Arch. 171, fol. 179r)
- Garnier, Flaminio: noble and secretary to Alexander Farnese, 1590 (Arch. 67, fol. 3v)
- Haius, Jo.: Jesuit, 1606 (Arch. 178, fol. 19r)
- Hartlieb, Joseph: treasurer for Albert and Isabella, 1602 (Arch. 174, fol. 197r)
- Hillen, Adriana: Poor Clares, 1590 (Arch. 67, fol. 79v)
- Hoetmaker, de, Ferdinand: bookseller, 1612 (Arch. 219, fol. 146v)
- Horick, van den, Jean: bookseller, 1638 (Arch. 246, fol. 118r)
- Jesuits, 1610 (Arch. 217, 116r) and 1631 (Arch. 239, fol. 29v)
- Jodevelt, de, Michault: unknown, 1600 (Arch. 172, fol. 22v)
- Landman, Michael: Franciscan, 1601 (Arch. 173, fol. 9r) – 1603 (Arch. 175, fol. 190v)
- Leonard, Jean: bookseller, 1621 (Arch. 228, fol. 157v) – 1637 (Arch. 245, fol. 118v)
- Mol, de, Philibert: Franciscan, 1605 (Arch. 177, fol. 55r)
- Mommaert, Jan I: bookseller, 1602 (Arch. 174, fol. 137r)
- Numan, Philips: government official, 1591 (Arch. 68, fol. 9r)
- Ovando, de, Mathias: Dominican, 1599 (Arch. 171, fol. 60v)
- Pantinus, Petrus: dean of St Goedele, 1608 (Arch. 180, fol. 90v) – 1611 (Arch. 218, fol. 53r)
- Paz, Francisco: laity, 1610 (Arch. 217, fol. 212v)
- Piens, Jan (Hans): merchant, 1628 (Arch. 235, fol. 171v) and 1629 (Arch. 236, fol. 23v)
- Rios, de los, Bartholomaeus: Augustine, 1639 (Arch. 247, fol. 87v) – 1641 (Arch. 249, fol. 74v)
- Rovelasca, de, Antonio: treasurer to Archduke Albrecht and Archduchess Isabella, 1609 (Arch. 1104, fol. 83r) and 1610 (Arch. 217, fol. 11v)
- Sailly, Thomas: Jesuit, 1588 (Arch. 65, fol. 18v) – 1606 (Arch. 178, fol. 117v)
- Salamanca, de, Miguel: noble and military advisor at the court in Brussels, 1635 (Arch. 243, fol. 177r)
- Simonetti, Bartholomaeus: doctor, 1617 (Arch. 224, fol. 139v)
- Soto, de, Andres: Franciscan, 1603 (Arch. 175, fol. 15r)

- Tisnacq, Charles II: commander of the army, associated with Albert and Isabella's court, 1593 (Arch. 70, fol. 16v)
- Tombe, de la, Pierre: bookseller, 1558 (Arch. 35, fol. 36v)
- Vierpont, Guillaume: bookseller, 1635 (Arch. 243, fol. 16v)
- Walter Zapata (Capata), Hieronymus: pagador general (a court official), 1599 (Arch. 171, fol. 91v)

CAMBRAI
- Duflos, Valeriaen: archdeacon, 1592 (Arch. 69, fol. 65v)

CHARLEVILLE
- Capuchins, 1615 (Arch. 222, fol. 62v) and 1631 (Arch. 239, fol. 124r)

DELFT
- Heyden, vander, Pierre: pharmacist, 1612 (Arch. 219, fol. 98r)

DEN BOSCH
- Capuchins, 1628 (Arch. 235, fol. 129v)
- Scheffer, Jan II: bookseller, 1586 (Arch. 63, fol. 39v) – 1611 (Arch. 218, fol. 59r)

DINANT
- Sommalius, Henricus: Jesuit, 1604 (Arch. 176, fol. 59v)
- Zandre, Albert: bookseller, 1634 (Arch. 242, fol. 20v)

DORDRECHT
- Janssens, Philips: bookseller, 1610 (Arch. 217, fol. 25r)

DOUAI
- Bogardus, Joannes I: bookseller, 1577 (Arch. 55, fol. 113r) and 1592 (Arch. 69, fol. 126v)
- Estius, Guillaume: theologian, 1590 (Arch. 67, fol. 103r)
- Fowler, Alice: bookseller, 1587 (Arch. 64, fol. 143r) and 1599 (Arch. 171, fol. 18v)
- Schipman, Jacobus: Jesuit, 1569 (Arch. 47, fol. 221v)

DUNKIRK
- Eeckhout, utten, Levinus: lawyer, 1631 (Arch. 239, fol. 176v) – 1634 (Arch. 242, fol. 204v)
- Verbeeck, Pedro: merchant, 1637 (Arch. 245, fol. 102v)

GELDRE
- Capuchins, 1627 (Arch. 234, fol. 142v) and 1628 (Arch. 235, fol. 129v)

GHENT
- Havensius, Arnoldus: Carthusian, 1601 (Arch. 85, fol. 219) and 1609 (Arch. 216, fol. 141v)
- Jesuits, 1600 (Arch. 172, fol. 180v)
- Kerckhove, vanden, Joos: bookseller, 1596 (Arch. 73, 144r)
- Manilius, Gislenius: bookseller, 1569 (Arch. 47, fol. 225r)
- Salenson, van, Jan: bookseller, 1588 (Arch. 65, fol. 104r) – 1605 (Arch. 177, fol. 106v)
- Sersanders, Alexander: bookseller, 1616 (Arch. 223, fol. 5v)
- Zeelandre, Jacobus: Jesuit, 1571 (Arch. 49, fol. 117v)

GOUDA
- Erasmus, Jacob: bookseller, 1637 (Arch. 245, fol. 117v)

HALLE
- Jesuits, 1625 (Arch. 232, fol. 126v)

HASSELT
- Capuchins, 1628 (Arch. 235, fol. 129v) and 1638 (Arch. 246, fol. 2r)

HERENTALS
- Knepkens, Franciscus: Franciscan, 1606 (Arch. 178, fol. 196r)

KORTRIJK
- Capuchins, 1628 (Arch. 235, fol. 129v)
- Mahieu, Jan: bookseller, 1592 (Arch. 69, fol. 93r) – 1594 (Arch. 71, fol. 88r)
- Simons, Peter: bookseller, 1591 (Arch. 68, 1 fol. 25v) and 1592 (Arch. 69, fol. 4r)
- Straeten, van der, Joos: bookseller, 1592 (Arch. 69, fol. 25v) – 1598 (Arch. 75, fol. 181r)
- Schondonch, Aegidius: Jesuit, 1593 (Arch. 70, fol. 30r) – 1607 (Arch. 179, fol. 181r)

LEIDEN
- Dousa, Janus: scholar, 1583 (Arch. 61, fol. 4v)
- Nessens, Jacobus: Franciscan, 1615 (Arch. 222, fol. 57v)
- Raphelengius, Franciscus II: bookseller. 1604 (Arch. 176, fol. 139v)

LEUVEN
- Capuchins, 1628 (Arch. 235, fol. 129v)
- Clemens, Caesar: ecclesiastic, 1590 (Arch. 67, fol. 101r)
- Faber, Joannes: Franciscan, 1600 (Arch. 172, fol. 135v)
- Fowler, John: bookseller, 1577 (Arch. 55, fol. 133r)
- Jesuits, 1613 (Arch. 220, fol. 114r)
- Sassenus, Andreas: bookseller, 1593 (Arch. 70, fol. 6r)
- Spierinck, Philippus: Jesuit, 1577 (Arch. 55, fol. 115v)
- Talbot, James: Franciscan at the Irish college, 1629 (Arch. 237, fol. 73r)
- Vacquerio, Antonio: Minims, 1603 (Arch. 175, fol. 33r)
- Wargnirius, Guillaume: canon, 1608 (Arch. 180, fol. 23r)
- Zangre, Philippe: bookseller, 1587 (Arch. 64, fol. 50r) – 1597 (Arch. 74, fol. 112v)

LIÈGE
- Charondelet, Jacques: ecclesiastic and chancellor of Liège, 1605 (Arch. 177, fol. 174r)
- Coste, de la, Lambert: bookseller, 1599 (Arch. 171, fol. 173r)
- Hassaert, Pierre: doctor, 1573 (Arch. 51, fol. 59v)
- Houthem, Libertus: Hieronymite, 1577 (Arch. 55, fol. 129v)
- Hovius, Marie: bookseller, 1639 (Arch. 247, fol. 32v)
- Ingelbert, Nicolas: bookseller, 1595 (Arch. 72, fol. 62v) and 1596 (Arch. 73, fol. 99r)
- Ouwerx, Jean: bookseller, 1625 (Arch. 232, fol. 126r) – 1636 (Arch. 244, fol. 129v)
- Torrentius, Laevinus: vicar general of the cathedral, 1575 (Arch. 53, fol. 229v)

LILLE

- Boulet, François: bookseller, 1586 (Arch. 63, fol. 65r-v) – 1602 (Arch. 174, fol. 105v)
- Hangouart, Guillaume: Jesuit, 1594 (Arch. 71, fol. 57r)
- Jesuits, 1614 (Arch. 221, fol. 184r)
- Meurchin, de, monsieur: government official, 1573 (Arch. 51, fol. 51v)
- Morel, Jean: bookseller, 1615 (Arch. 222, fol. 70r) and 1626 (Arch. 233, fol. 148r)
- Nielandt, Jan: unknown, 1609 (Arch. 216, fol. 54r) – 1616 (Arch. 223, fol. 112r)
- Puis, du, Jean: bookseller, 1609 (Arch. 216, fol. 54r) – 1616 (Arch. 223, fol. 112r)
- Rache, de, Jean: bookseller, 1632 (Arch. 240, fol. 151r)

LOBBES

- Richard, Philippe: Benedictine, 1593 (Arch. 70, fol. 71v) and 1594 (Arch. 21, fol. 194 lft)

MAASEIK

- Capuchins, 1628 (Arch. 235, fol. 129v)
- Oudewater, van, Zacharias: ecclesiastic, 1638 (Arch. 246, fol. 61v)

MAASTRICHT

- Bael, van, Petrus: ecclesiastic, 1602 (Arch. 174, fol. 198r)
- Capuchins, 1628 (Arch. 235, fol. 129v)
- messagier de Maastricht, Jacob: messenger for the postal system, 1600 (Arch. 172, fol. 147r)
- Zwevenseel, van, Gilles: bookseller, 1600 (Arch. 172, fol. 185r) – 1610 (Arch. 217, fol. 144r)

MECHELEN

- Campenhout, van, Hans: bookseller, 1587 (Arch. 64, fol. 148v) and 1597 (Arch. 74, fol. 162v)
- Capuchins, 1628 (Arch. 235, fol. 129v)
- Oudaert, Nicolas: secretary to the Archbishop of Mechelen, 1608 (Arch. 180, fol. 73r)

MENEN

- Capuchins, 1628 (Arch. 235, fol. 129v)

MIDDELBURG

- Helmont, van, Dirk: bookseller, 1582 (Arch. 60, fols. 24v-25r)

MONS

- Wervel, vande, Andre: bookseller, 1589 (Arch. 66, fol. 172r) – 1591 (Arch. 68, fol. 51r = 61r)
- Wervel, vande, Germain: bookseller, 1589 (Arch. 66, fol. 127v) – 1607 (Arch. 179, fol. 51v)
- Woudre, François, bookseller, 1633 (Arch. 241, fol. 196v)

NAMUR

- Capuchins, 1634 (Arch. 242, fol. 102v) and 1639 (Arch. 247, fol. 50v)
- Valentin, Jean I: bookseller, 1590 (Arch. 67, fol. 127r) – 1595 (Arch. 72, fol. 154v)
- Valentin, Jean II: bookseller, 1604 (Arch. 176, fol. 180v) – 1621 (Arch. 228, fol. 121v)
- Valentin, Jean III: bookseller, 1637 (Arch. 245, fol. 47v) – 1641 (Arch. 249, fol. 138r)
- Valentin, Jean II, Widow: bookseller, 1637 (Arch. 245, fol. 65v)

NIJMEGEN

- Winoksbergen, van, Winnocus: Capuchin, 1640 (Arch. 248, fol. 6r)

NINOVE

- Ninove Abbey, monks: Norbertines, 1635 (Arch. 243, fol. 188v)

OOSTENDE

- Capuchins, 1628 (Arch. 235, fol. 129v)

OOSTERWIJK

- Abenthouts, Arnold: ecclesiastic, 1588 (Arch. 65, fol. 13r)

ORVAL

- Montgaillard, de, Bernard: Cistercian, 1622 (Arch. 229, fol. 126r)

OUDENAARDE

- Capuchins, 1628 (Arch. 235, fol. 129v) and 1630 (Arch. 238, fol. 155v)
- Jesuits, 1623 (Arch. 230, fol. 158v) and 1624 (Arch. 231, fol. 147r)

ROERMOND

- Franciscans, 1605 (Arch. 177, fol. 85r)
- Hompes, Hendrik: bookseller, 1599 (Arch. 171, fol. 76v) – 1604 (Arch. 176, fol. 108v)
- Hompes, Jan: bookseller, 1609 (Arch. 216, fol. 39r) – 1618 (Arch. 225, fol. 85r)
- Lindanus, Willem: bishop, 1576 (Arch. 54, fol. 59v)

ST OMER

- Geubels, Pierre: bookseller, 1614 (Arch. 221, fol. 93r) – 1624 (Arch. 231, fol. 163r)
- Grenet, de, Vaast: abbot, 1598 (Arch. 75, fol. 128r) – 1599 (Arch. 171, fol. 3v)
- Bellet, François: bookseller, 1601 (Arch. 173, fol. 149r)

ST TRUIDEN

- Capuchins, 1628 (Arch. 235, fol. 129v) and 1634 (Arch. 242, fol. 215v)
- Ketel, de, Hans: messenger for the postal service, 1596 (Arch. 73, fol. 26v)

TERVUREN

- Capuchins, 1628 (Arch. 235, fol. 129v) and 1639 (Arch. 246, fol. 2r)

TOURNAI

- Laurent, Nicolas: bookseller, 1608 (Arch. 180, fol. 23r)
- Laurent, Nicolas, Widow: bookseller, 1619 (Arch. 226, fol. 64r)
- Vendeville, Jean: bishop, 1587 (Arch. 64, fol. 82r)
- Winghe, van, Hieronimus: canon, 1637 (Arch. 245, fol. 127v)

UTRECHT

- Borculo, van, Herman: bookseller, 1630 (Arch. 238, fol. 79r)
- Burch, vander, Lambert: dean of St Mary's Cathedral, 1599 (Arch. 171, fol. 35v)
- Canterus, Theodorus: mayor, 1584 (Arch. 62, fol. 89r)
- Doorn, van, Jan: bookseller, 1623 (Arch. 230, fol. 60r) – 1641 (Arch. 249, fol. 14r)
- Geeraertsen, Willem: bookseller, 1611 (Arch. 218, fol. 181r)
- Montis, Sigimundus: messenger, 1605 (Arch. 177, fol. 105v)

VALENCIENNES

- Maire, Antoine: bookseller 1576 (Arch. 54, fol. 146r)
- Oudot, François: canon, 1590 (Arch. 67, fol. 75v)
- Oultreman, d', Henri: secretary for the city government, 1595 (Arch. 72, fol. 43v) and 1603 (Arch. 175, fol. 144v)
- Poyvre, le, Antoine: unknown, 1587 (Arch. 65, fol. 84v)
- Robat, Adriaen: bookseller, 1592 (Arch. 69, fol. 64v) – 1595 (Arch. 72, fol. 13r)

VEURNE

- Capuchins, 1628 (Arch. 235, fol. 129v)

YPRES

- Capuchins, 1628 (Arch. 235, fol. 129v)
- Jesuits, 1609 (Arch. 216, fol. 29r)
- Loos, de, Nicolas: canon, 1598 (Arch. 75, fol. 189r)
- David, Joannes: Jesuit, 1607 (Arch. 179, fol. 14r) and 1609 (Arch. 216, fol. 55r)
- Mariaval, Michiel: bookseller, 1586 (Arch. 63, fol. 126r)
- Parmentier, Nicolas: bookseller, 1597 (Arch. 74, fol. 73v)
- Parmentier, Sebastiaan, Widow: bookseller, 1628 (Arch. 235, fol. 87v)

LOW COUNTRIES, UNKNOWN LOCATION

- Derderen, des, Peryne: nun or beguine, 1602 (Arch. 174, fol. 186v)
- Groevens, Anna: ecclesiastic, 1602 (Arch. 174, fol. 180v)
- Hoinssem, van, Elsabeth: laity, 1624 (Arch. 139, fol. 155)
- Opstal, van, Perine: nun, 1602 (Arch. 174, fol. 54r) – 1603 (Arch. 175, fol. 87r)

POLAND

KRAKÓW

- Mertzenich, de, Franciscus Jacobus: bookseller, 1613 (Arch. 220, fol. 4r)
- Peresina, Petrus: bookseller, 1599 (Arch. 171, fol. 131v)
- Schedelius, Christophorus: bookseller, 1641 (Arch. 249, fol. 136v)
- Steynhalen, Adamus: canon, 1604 (Arch. 1104, fol. 1v) – 1609 (Arch. 216, fol. 53r)

GDAŃSK

- Affel, Franciscus: bookseller, 1599 (Arch. 171, fol. 135v)
- Bericht, Melchior: bookseller, 1599 (Arch. 171, fol. 130v)
- Berisch, Valentin: bookseller, 1599 (Arch. 171, fol. 134r)
- Beyer, Michiel: bookseller, 1599 (Arch. 171, fol. 133r)
- Claessens, Paulus: merchant, 1612 (Arch. 219, fol. 172v)
- Förster, Kaspar: bookseller, 1637 (Arch. 245, fol. 73r) – 1641 (Arch. 249, fol. 167r)
- Gabrielli, di, Rocho: merchant, 1601 (Arch. 173, fol. 204r) – 1602 (Arch. 174, fol. 29v)
- Gisser, Salomon: bookseller, 1582 (Arch. 60, fols. 59r-60r)
- Kruse, Ernst: bookseller, 1635 (Arch. 243, fol. 86r)

VILNIUS

- Warszewicki, Stanislas: Jesuit, 1578 (Arch. 56, fol. 106v) – 1581 (Arch. 59, fol. 47v)

POLAND, UNKNOWN LOCATION

- Fabricus, Paulus: unknown, 1598 (Arch. 75, fol. 63r)
- Magnus Gothus, Laurentius: Jesuit, 1583 (Arch. 61, fol. 50r) and 1590 (Arch. 67, fol. 99r)
- Nicovius, Simon: Jesuit, 1583 (Arch. 61, fol. 49v)
- Rick, Goddart: bookseller, 1619 (Arch. 226, fol. 69r)

SCANDINAVIA

STOCKHOLM

- Herbest, Joannes: Jesuit, 1582 (Arch. 56, fol. 58r)
- Nicolai Norvegus, Laurentius: Jesuit, 1577 (Arch. 222, fol. 57v) – 1579 (Arch. 57, fol. 44v)

SPAIN AND PORTUGAL

LISBON

- Desselmans, Adriaen: bookseller, 1635 (Arch. 243, fol. 42r)
- Moerentorf, Peter II: bookseller, 1618 (Arch. 225, fol. 206v)
- Valvano, Hieronymo: ecclesiastic, 1618 (Arch. 225, fol. 38v)

MADRID AND THE ESCORIAL

- Çayas, de, Gabriel: secretary to King Philip II, 1587 (Arch. 64, fol. 19r)
- Hieronymites, Escorial: 1617 (Arch. 224, fol. 38r) and 1649 (Arch. 248, fol. 20r)
- Lanselius, Petrus: Jesuit, 1631 (Arch. 166, fol. 114v)
- Manriquez de Lara, Luis: chaplain to Philip II, 1571 (Arch. 49, fol. 116v) and 1581 (Arch. 59, fol. 175v)
- Moflin, Jean: chaplain to Philip II, 1583 (Arch. 61, fol. 115r; Arch. 20, fol. 186 rht)
- Peralta, de, Philippe: Jesuit, 1614 (Arch. 221, fol. 157r)
- Philip II: king, 1580 (Arch. 58, fol. 132v)
- Vilalva, de, Francesco: ecclesiastic, 1571 (Arch. 49, fol. 116v)
- Vucht, van, Jan: merchant, 1626 (Arch. 233, fol. 143v) – 1630 (Arch. 238, fol. 43r)

MEDINA DEL CAMPO

- Boyer, Juan: bookseller, 1599 (Arch. 171, fols. 90r-91r)

SALAMANCA

- Poelman, Jan: bookseller, 1581 (Arch. 18, fol. 394) – 1582 (Arch. 60, fol. 137r-v)

SEVILLE

- Angulo, de, Pedro: Jesuit, 1613 (Arch. 220, fol. 190r) – 1615 (Arch. 222, fol. 59r)
- Arias Montano, Benito: theologian and chaplain to Philip II, 1568 (Arch. 4, fols. 6, 151v) – 1594 (Arch. 71, fol. 64v)
- Lopez, Fabian: ecclesiastic, 1623 (Arch. 230, fol. 73r)
- Toro, de, Antonio: bookseller, 1623 (Arch. 230, fol. 4r)

TOLEDO

- Bocangel, Pietro: bookseller, 1573 (Arch. 51, fols. 203r-204v) – 1574 (Arch. 52, fol. 29v)

SPAIN, UNKNOWN LOCATION

- Alonso de Herrera, Hernando: merchant, 1609 (Arch. 216, fol. 38v) – 1610 (Arch. 217, fol. 12r)
- Alzenmora, Sr: unknown, 1559 (Arch. 35, fol. 80v)
- Capillas, Pater: prior of the Order of Santiago, 1582 (Arch. 60, fols. 147r-147v)
- Gomez, Diego: noble, 1588 (Arch. 65, fol. 40v)
- San Pedro, de, Joan: Discalced Carmelite, 1618 (Arch. 225, fol. 207r)

UNITED KINGDOM

DOVER

- Heemssen, David: merchant, 1639 (Arch. 247, fol. 159r)

IRELAND

- Black, John: merchant, 1611 (Arch. 218, fol. 65r)

LONDON

- Bonneval, Pierre: merchant, 1577 (Arch. 55, fols. 167v-174r)
- Boswell, John: print and map seller, 1608 (Arch. 180, fol. 106r)
- Gabelleone: ambassador, 1613 (Arch. 220, fol. 155r)
- Herle, William: ambassador, 1582 (Arch. 60, fol. 77r)
- Renialme, de, Ascanius: bookseller, 1599 (Arch. 171, fol. 30v) and 1600 (Arch. 172, fol. 37v)
- Robinson, Humphrey: bookseller, 1638 (Arch. 246, fol. 49v) and 1640 (Arch. 248, fol. 155r)
- Whitacker, Richard: bookseller, 1635 (Arch. 243, fol. 81r)
- Woutneel, Hans: bookseller, 1591 (Arch. 68, fol. 134v)

UNKNOWN LOCATION

- Alyn, van, N.: unknown, 1608 (Arch. 180, fol. 84r)
- Andreas, Balthasar: unknown, 1599 (Arch. 171, fol. 94r)
- Arteriga, Joanna Carlota: ecclesiastic, 1602 (Arch. 174, fol. 152r)
- Ballaer, van, Jacobus: ecclesiastic, 1640 (Arch. 248, fol. 75r)
- Bastida Pincera, de, Josephus: noble, 1576 (Arch. 54, fol. 58r)
- Baudaen, Andreas: unknown, 1579 (Arch. 57, fol. 65r)
- Boverus, Pater: Franciscan, 1640 (Arch. 248, fol. 53v)
- Brie?, Guillaume: unknown, 1576 (Arch. 54, fol. 82r)
- Burgos, de, Balthasar: unknown, 1592 (Arch. 69, fol. 65v)
- Butkens, Claude: bookseller, 1578 (Arch. 56, fol. 37r)
- Cassina, Hieronymo: merchant, 1598 (Arch. 75, fol. 151v)
- Castilla, de, Luis: unknown, 1599 (Arch. 171, fol. 59v)
- Detellair, Jan: ecclesiastic, Carthusian, 1606 (Arch. 178, fol. 187v)
- Diepenbeeck, van, Pierre: unknown, 1575 (Arch. 53, fol. 137r)
- Fabri, François: unknown, 1599 (Arch. 171, fol. 139v)
- Fortuin, Adriaen: unknown, 1590 (Arch. 67, fol. 122v)
- Granvelle, de, monsieur: unknown, 1596 (Arch. 73, fol. 50r)
- Grenier, Pierre: unknown, 1581 (Arch. 59, fol. 134r)
- Isonca, de, Jan: government official, 1577 (Arch. 55, fol. 19r)
- Laere, vande, François: unknown, 1625 (Arch. 232, fol. 116r)
- Matta, de la, Giovanni Gil.: unknown, 1591 (Arch. 68, fol. 40v = 50v)
- Moulin, Nicolas: unknown, 1595 (Arch. 72, fol. 111r)
- Orosio, Paolo: cashier for the Italian merchant G.A.Vergano, 1595 (Arch. 72, fol. 99v)
- Orsa, Alexander: secretary to Alexander Farnese, 1587 (Arch. 64, fol. 126r)
- Peniard d'Avrand, F.: unknown, 1593 (Arch. 70, fol. 4v)
- Pharisi, monsieur: unknown, 1582 (Arch. 60, fol. 96r)
- Pons, de, monsieur: unknown, 1575 (Arch. 53, fol. 31v)
- Putte, van de, Vincent: unknown, 1576 (Arch. 54, fol. 127r)
- Requesens, de, Alphonse: ecclesiastic, 1603 (Arch. 175, fol. 16r)
- Rigo, Jan: merchant, 1592 (Arch. 69, fol. 99r)
- Rodrigues, Simon: merchant, 1601 (Arch. 173, fol. 17v)
- Saltard, Joannes: ecclesiastic, 1635 (Arch. 243, fol. 182v)
- Schappelari, Sr: secretary to the Genoese Nation, 1593 (Arch. 70, fol. 91v)
- Succa, Guillaume: unknown, 1582 (Arch. 60, fol. 17r)
- Veluti et Cambi, Antonio: merchant, 1588 (Arch. 65, fol. 177r)
- Wassenberghe, Hans: bookseller, 1558 (Arch. 38, fol. 16v)
- Wens, Jacques: unknown, 1601 (Arch. 173, fol. 74r)

TABLES OF PRINT PRICES

TABLES 1–6 *Prices for Individual Prints, Identified by Subject*

Prints are arranged by price, from high to low, and then alphabetically for any given price. See Appendix 1, under the publisher and print number (given in each table immediately prior to the title of the image) for more information on any of the prints cited in the following tables. The list of prints in Appendix 1 also contains items that have not been included in these tables due to the lack of a clear unit price, such as Hieronymus Cock's *Scenographiae sive perspectivae ... pulcherrimae viginti selectissimarum fabricarum* (Large Perspective Book) from 1560 (CD-27).

TABLE 1 Prices of Prints as Supplied by Hieronymus Cock and Volcxken Diericx

Price in st.	Subject (date made)	Subject	Printmaker	Medium	Size in mm	Date sold
50	CD-3 *Baths of Diocletian* (1558)		J. & L. van Doetecum	etching	32 plates of varying sizes	1581
40	CD-3 *Baths of Diocletian* (1558)	S. van Noyen	J. & L. van Doetecum	etching	32 plates of varying sizes	1568
20	CD-10 *Funeral Procession for Charles V* (1559)	H. Cock	J. & L. van Doetecum	etching & engraving	34 plates of varying sizes	1568
18	CD-14 *Large Landscapes* (1555–1556)	P. Bruegel I	J. & L. van Doetecum	etching & engraving	12 plates ca. 320/96 × 420/28	1581
15	CD-18 *Portraits of Painters* (1572)	anonymous	C. Cort, J. Wierix, & others	engraving	23 plates ca. 210 × 125	1576
12	CD-9 *Dispute of the Holy Sacrament* (1552)	Raphael	G. Ghisi	engraving	2 plates together 510 × 850	1573
12	CD-11 *Hunts* (within frames) (1570)	J. Stradanus	H. J. Muller	engraving	6 plates ca. 327 × 448	1571
12	CD-18 *Portraits of Painters* (1572)	anonymous	C. Cort, J. Wierix, & others	engraving	23 plates ca. 210 × 125	1573 1586/1587
12	CD-20 *Raising of the Brazen Serpent* (1555)	F. Floris	P. van der Heyden	engraving	2 plates: 583 × 449 left 582 × 454 right	1573
12	CD-29 *Sepulchral and Tomb Designs* (1563)	H. Vredeman de Vries	J. & L. van Doetecum	etching	27 plates of varying sizes, e.g. 166 × 210	1568 1573 1581
12	CD-34 *Small Architectural Perspective Views* (Granvelle) (1562)	H. Vredeman de Vries	J. & L. van Doetecum	etching & engraved dedication	29 plates ca. 153 × 210	1568 1580 1581
10.50	CD-11 *Hunts* (within frames) (1570)	J. Stradanus	H. J. Muller	engraving	6 plates ca. 327 × 448	1580 1581
10	CD-8 *Compartments by Battini* (1553)	B. Battini	P. van der Heyden	engraving	28 plates of varying sizes	1568
9	CD-35 *Small Book of Ruins* (1562)	anonymous	J. & L. van Doetecum	etching & engraving	21 plates ca. 155 × 213	1568 1573 1581
8.50	CD-2 *Architectural Perspective Views* (Mansfeld) (1560–1562)	H. Vredeman de Vries	J. & L. van Doetecum	etching & engraved dedication	21 plates ca. 162 × 212 or 212 × 162	1568 1580 1581
8	CD-1 *Adoration of the Shepherds* (1553)	A. Bronzino	G. Ghisi	engraving	2 plates together 662 × 452	1573
8	CD-36 *Small Landscapes ... Villages ... Castles* (1559–1561)	Master of the Small Landscapes	J. & L. van Doetecum	etching	Uncertain no. of images and unknown sizes.	1568 1573
7.50	CD-28 *Scrollwork Compartments* (1566)	J. Floris	P. van der Heyden	engraving	17 plates ca. 13.5 × 20.4	1570
7.20	CD-23 *Sailing Vessels* (ca. 1561–1565)	P. Bruegel I	C. Cort? & F. Huys	etching & engraving	10 plates ca. 225 × 290 or 290 × 220	1568
7	CD-28 *Scrollwork Compartments* (1566)	J. Floris	P. van der Heyden	engraving	17 plates ca. 135 × 204	1568
6.50	CD-16 *Ornamental Compartments* (1567)	J. Floris	P. van der Heyden	engraving	12 plates ca. 135 × 204	1568 1570
6	CD-1 *Adoration of the Shepherds* (1553)	A. Bronzino	G. Ghisi	engraving	2 plates together 662 × 452	1568
6	CD-6 *Christ & Twelve Apostles & St Paul* (ca. 1543)	anonymous	L. Suavius	engraving	14 plates ca. 198 × 90	1568 1570 1571

Price in st.	Subject (date made)	Subject (date made)	Printmaker	Medium	Size in mm	Date sold
6	CD-15 *Naval Battle in the Strait of Messina* (1561)	P. Bruegel I	F. Huys	etching & engraving	2 plates together 428 × 717	1568
5.76	CD-30 *Seven Deadly Sins & Last Judgment* (1558)	P. Bruegel I	P. van der Heyden	engraving	8 plates ca. 226 × 295	1580
5.60	CD-32 *Seven Virtues* (ca. 1559–1560)	P. Bruegel I	P. Galle	engraving	7 plates ca. 226 × 294	1561
5	CD-5 *Christ & Twelve Apostles* (1560–1570)	L. Lombard	anonymous	engraving	13 plates ca. 200 × 118	1570 1571
5	CD-21 *Resurrection of Christ* (1557)	F. Floris	J. & L. van Doetecum	etching & engraving	2 plates together 638 × 445	1573
5	CD-41 *Vessels* (1563)	H. Vredeman de Vries	J. & L. van Doetecum	etching & engraving	12 plates ca. 200 × 140	1570
4.32	CD-12 *Hunts* (without frames) (1570 / 1574)	J. Stradanus	anonymous	engraving	6 plates ca. 220 × 300	1580
4.32	CD-38 *Story of Tobias* (ca. 1548)	M. van Heemskerck	D. V. Coornhert	engraving	6 plates ca. 241 × 188	1568
4	CD-13 *Landscape with Balaam & Angel* (1554)	M. van Heemskerck	D. V. Coornhert	engraving	2 plates together ca. 295 × 850	1568
3.50	CD-7 *Circus Maximus & Flaminius* (by 1558)	?	?	?	2 plates	1568
3	CD-24 *St George's Kermis* (ca. 1558)	P. Bruegel I	J. or L. van Doetecum	etching & engraving	1 plate 332 × 523	1568
3	CD-33 *Siege of the Elephant* (ca. 1563)	A. du Hameel	J. & L. van Doetecum	engraving	1 plate 402 × 538	1568
2.50	CD-22 *Resurrection of Christ* (1561)	P. Bruegel I	P. Galle	engraving	1 plate 451 × 330	1561
2.50	CD-39 *Temptation of St Christopher* (1561)	imitator of H. Bosch	J. & L. van Doetecum	etching & engraving	1 plate 336 × 430	1561
1.50	CD-4 *Blue Cloak* (1558)	anonymous	F. Hogenberg	etching	2 plates together 373 × 460	1568
1.50	CD-14 *Large Alpine Landscape* (ca. 1555)	P. Bruegel I	J. & L. van Doetecum	etching & engraving	1 plate 368 × 468	1581
1.50	CD-14 *Landscape with the Temptation of Christ* (ca. 1554)	P. Bruegel I	H. Cock	etching & engraving	1 plate 319 × 439	1581
.80	CD-19 *Rabbit Hunt* (1560)	P. Bruegel I	P. Bruegel I	etching & engraving	1 plate 223 × 292	1561
.80	CD-25 *St Jerome* (1561)	anonymous	P. Galle	engraving	1 plate 193 × 150	1561
.80	CD-26 *Salome with the Head of St John the Baptist* (by 1561)	A. del Sarto	anonymous	engraving	1 plate 278 × 342	1561
.80	CD-40 *Three Fates* (1561)	G. Romano	C. Cort	engraving	1 plate 220 × 264	1561

TABLE 2 Prices of Prints as Supplied by Adriaen Collaert

Price in st.	Subject	Designer	Printmaker	Medium	Size in mm	Date sold
22	AC-9 *Life, Passion, and Resurrection of Christ* (1598)	M. de Vos	various	engraving	50 plates ca.180 × 219 & title plate 168 × 218	1602
20	AC-3 *Female Hermits* (by 1608)	M. de Vos	A. Collaert J. Collaert II C. Galle I	engraving	24 plates ca. 175 × 222 & title plate 182 × 222	1608
17	AC-9 *Life, Passion, and Resurrection of Christ* (1598)	M. de Vos	various	engraving	50 plates ca.180 × 219 & title plate 168 × 218	1608
16	AC-4 *Fish* (1589–1608)	A. Collaert?	A. Collaert	engraving	25 plates ca.126 × 188 & title plate 135 × 184	1608
12	AC-5 *Four-Legged Animals* (ca. 1597)	A. Collaert?	A. Collaert	engraving	19 plates ca. 124 × 190 & title plate 137 × 192	1608
8	AC-1 *Birds* (ca. 1600)	A. Collaert?	A. Collaert	engraving	32 plates ca. 131 × 188	1608
8	AC-18 *Seven Gifts of the Holy Spirit* (ca. 1595)	J. Stradanus	A. Collaert	engraving	7 plates ca. 210 × 274	1608
6	AC-15 *Life of the Virgin* (by 1608)	J. Wierix	anonymous	engraving	16 plates ca. 125 × 85	1608
5	AC-16 *Life of the Virgin* (by 1608)	A. Collaert?	A. Collaert?	engraving	20 plates ca. 87 × 66	1608
4.50	AC-6 *Infancy or Youth of Jesus* (by 1608)	?	?	?	12 plates	1608
4	AC-11 *Life of St Catherine of Alexandria* (by 1608)	?	A. Collaert? or J. Collaert II?	engraving	15 plates ca. 90 × 67 & title plate 93 × 70	1608
4	AC-12 *Life of St John the Baptist* (by 1608)	A. Collaert	A. Collaert	engraving	16 plates ca. 91 × 66	1608
4	AC-13 *Life of St John the Evangelist* (by 1608)	A. Collaert?	A. Collaert?	engraving	15 plates ca. 91 × 66 & title plate 96 × 64	1608
3.50	AC-2 *Christ, the Virgin, the Twelve Apostles, and St Paul* (1592–1608)	A. Collaert?	A. Collaert	engraving	15 plates ca. 169 × 114/122	1608
2.50	AC-17 *Seven Churches of Rome* (ca. 1600)	A. Collaert?	A. Collaert	engraving	7 plates ca. 100/107 × 66/74	1608
.75	AC-7 *Lamb of God* (by 1608)	C. van den Broeck	H. Collaert I	engraving	1 plate 258 × 203	1608

TABLE 3 Prices of Prints as Supplied by Philips Galle

Price in st.	*Subject*	*Designer*	*Printmaker*	*Medium*	*Size in mm*	*Date sold*
90	PG-60 *Hunts and Animal Scenes* (1596/97)	J. Stradanus	various	engraving	104 plates ca. 205/216 × 275/295	1608
60	PG-120 *Virgil* (by 1596)	?	?	?	?	1596
40	PG-82 *Passion of Christ* (1580–1586)	J. Stradanus	various	engraving	41 plates ca. 193 × 262	1603
36	PG-62 *Imagines L. doctorum virorum* (1595)	Anonymous	P. Galle? T. Galle G. van Veen	engraving	50 plates ca. 168 × 119	1597
36	PG-82 *Passion of Christ* (1580–1586)	J. Stradanus	various	engraving	41 plates ca. 193 × 262	1585–1588 1594 1608
35	PG-26 *Divinarum nuptiarum & Christi Jesu speculum* (1573)	G. van Groeningen (and others?)	J. Wierix (& others?)	engraving	28 + 51 plates ca. 99 × 140	1573–1579 1585
35	PG-27 *Divinarum nuptiarum & Christi Jesu speculum* (1574)	G. van Groeningen (& others?)	J. Wierix (& others?)	engraving	28 + 51 plates ca. 99 × 140	1574 1575
35	PG-28 *Divinarum nuptiarum & Christi Jesu speculum* (1580)	G. van Groeningen (& others?)	J. Wierix (& others?)	engraving	28 + 51 plates ca. 99 × 140	1579 1581
32	PG-28 *Divinarum nuptiarum & Christi Jesu speculum* (1580)	G. van Groeningen (& others?)	J. Wierix (& others?)	engraving	28 + 51 plates ca. 99 × 140	1587
28	PG-87 *Roman Emperors on Horseback* (ca. 1587–1589)	J. Stradanus	A. Collaert	engraving	13 plates ca. 328 × 227	1595
27.36	PG-89 *Ruins* (by 1608)	H. van Cleve	anonymous	engraving	38 plates ca. 175 × 245	1608
26	PG-87 *Roman Emperors on Horseback* (ca. 1587–1589)	J. Stradanus	A. Collaert	engraving	13 plates ca. 328 × 227	1594
25.20	PG-2 *Acts of the Apostles* (1582)	J. Stradanus	A. Collaert P. Galle H. Goltzius	engraving	18 plates ca. 200 × 266	1608
25.20	PG-53 *Gardens* (1583 and 1587)	P. van der Borcht and H. Vredeman de Vries	P. van der Borcht & anonymous artists	etching & engraving	35 plates of varying sizes, ca. 190 × 248	1608
20	PG-16 *David hoc est ... Deo spectaculum* (1575)	G. van Groeningen & C. van den Broeck?	J. Sadeler I?	engraving	48 plates ca. 107 × 140 & title plate ca. 103 × 147	1575–1589
20	PG-33 *Eulogy of Music* (1591)	J. Stradanus	A. Collaert T. Galle	engraving	17 plates ca. 210 × 285	1594
20	PG-59 *Hunts* (1582)	H. Bol	A. Collaert? & anonymous artists	engraving	48 plates ca. 80 × 215	1585 1608
20	PG-60 *Hunts and Animal Scenes* (1578–1580)	J. Stradanus	P. Galle & possibly A. Wierix	engraving	24 plates ca. 205/216 × 275/295	1594
20	PG-61 *Imagines L. doctorum virorum* (1587)	anonymous	P. Galle?	engraving	50 plates ca. 168 × 119	1588
20	PG-66 *Life of St Catherine of Siena* (1603)	F. Vanni	C. Galle I	engraving	34 plates ca. 151 × 91 mm	1603 1606 1608
20	PG-67 *Life of St Francis* (1582 or earlier)	anonymous	anonymous	etching & engraving	18 plates ca. 155 × 236 & engraved title plate 166 × 236	1603

Price in st.	Subject	Designer	Printmaker	Medium	Size in mm	Date sold
20	PG-78 *Nova reperta* (ca. 1591)	J. Stradanus	J. Collaert II, T. Galle, & anonymous artists	engraving	22 plates ca. 203 × 270	1608
18	PG-16 *David hoc est ... Deo spectaculum* (1575)	G. van Groeningen & C. van den Broeck?	J. Sadeler I?	engraving	48 plates ca. 107 × 140 & title plate ca. 103 × 147	1581 1583
18	PG-19 *Deorum dearumque capita* (1573)	G. van Groeningen & H. Vredeman de Vries?	J. & L. van Doetecum?	etching & engraving	55 plates ca. 120 × 84	1574
18	PG-60 *Hunts and Animal Scenes* (1578–1580)	J. Stradanus	P. Galle & possibly A. Wierix	engraving	24 plates ca. 205/216 × 275/295	1579 1581
18	PG-123 *Virorum doctorum ... effigies XLIIII* (1586)	anonymous	P. Galle	engraving	44 plates ca. 176 × 122	1588 1599 1600
17.28	PG-60 *Hunts and Animal Scenes* (1578–1580)	J. Stradanus	P. Galle & possibly A. Wierix	engraving	24 plates ca. 205/216 × 275/295	1580
17	PG-33 *Eulogy of Music* (1591)	J. Stradanus	A. Collaert T. Galle	engraving	17 plates ca. 210 × 285	1608
17	PG-106 *Stable of Don Juan* (1591)	J. Stradanus	various	engraving	17 plates ca. 200 × 261	1588 1594
16	PG-19 *Deorum dearumque capita* (1573)	G. van Groeningen & H. Vredeman de Vries?	J. & L. van Doetecum?	etching & engraving	55 plates ca. 120 × 84	1573 1577 1579
16	PG-83 *Portraits of Popes* (1572)	P. Soye	P. Galle	engraving	29 plates ca. 170 × 120 & title plate 176 × 127	1595
16	PG-122 *Virorum doctorum ... effigies XLIIII* (1572)	anonymous	P. Galle	engraving	44 plates ca. 176 × 122	1572–1585
16	PG-123 *Virorum doctorum ... effigies XLIIII* (1586)	anonymous	P. Galle	engraving	44 plates ca. 176 × 122	1586
15	PG-67 *Life of St Francis* (1582 or earlier)	anonymous	anonymous	etching & engraving	18 plates ca. 155 × 236 & engraved frontispiece 166 × 236	1601 1604
15.12	PG-55 *History of the Medici* (1577–1583)	J. Stradanus	P. Galle H. Goltzius	engraving	21 plates ca. 208 × 281	1608
15.12	PG-81 *Passion of Christ* (by 1608)	?	?	?	21 plates	1608
14.40	PG-67 *Life of St Francis* (1582 or earlier)	anonymous	anonymous	etching & engraving	18 plates ca. 155 × 236 & engraved frontispiece 166 × 236	1608
17	PG-106 *Stable of Don Juan* (1591)	J. Stradanus	various	engraving	17 plates ca. 200 × 261	1608
12	PG-67 *Life of St Francis* (1582 or earlier)	anonymous	anonymous	etching & engraving	18 plates ca. 155 × 236 & engraved frontispiece 166 × 236	1582 1583
12	PG-83 *Portraits of Popes* (1572)	P. Soye	P. Galle	engraving	29 plates ca. 170 × 120 & title plate 176 × 127	1572 1573
11.52	PG-1 *Acts of the Apostles* (1575)	M. van Heemskerck	P. Galle	engraving	16 plates ca. 213 × 274	1580

Price in st.	*Subject*	*Designer*	*Printmaker*	*Medium*	*Size in mm*	*Date sold*
11.52	PG-74 *Monkey Antics* (by 1608)	P. van der Borcht	P. van der Borcht	etching	16 plates ca. 204/225 × 288/294	1608
10	PG-17 *De deis gentium imagines* (1581)	anonymous	P. Galle	engraving	29 plates ca. 131 × 81 & title plate ca. 143 × 92	1581
10	PG-116 *Ten Commandments* (ca. 1587)	M. de Vos	Various	engraving	11 plates ca. 200 × 243	1588 1594
9.36	PG-119 *Twelve Months* (ca. 1600–1608)	J. de Momper	A. Collaert J. Collaert II	engraving	13 plates ca. 206 × 260	1608
9	PG-12 *Celebrated Women of the Old Testament* (by 1594)	M. de Vos	J. Collaert II	engraving	21 plates ca. 156 × 92	1594
9	PG-17 *De deis gentium imagines* (1581)	anonymous	P. Galle	engraving	29 plates ca. 131 × 81 & title plate ca. 143 × 92	1583 1585
9	PG-21 *Designs for Pendants with Deities* (1581)	H. Collaert I	anonymous	engraving	10 plates ca. 173 × 123	1581
9	PG-79 *Old Testament Prophets* (1594)	N. de Hoey	J. Collaert II, C. de Mallery, P. de Perret, & anonymous artists	engraving	17 plates ca. 150 × 89	1594
9	PG-88 *Ruins* (by 1571)	?	?	?	11 leaves	1571 1573 1581?
8	PG-11 *Celebrated Women of the New Testament* (by 1594)	M. de Vos	A. Collaert J. Collaert II C. de Mallery	engraving	16 plates ca. 156 × 92	1594
8	PG-21 *Designs for Pendants with Deities* (1581)	H. Collaert I	anonymous	engraving	10 plates ca. 173 × 123	1581
8	PG-92 *Seven … Virtues & Seven Deadly Sins* (by 1594)	J. Stradanus P. Galle	H. Wierix	engraving	16 plates ca. 186 × 133	1594
8	PG-96 *Seven Planets* (by 1594)	?	?	engraving	8 plates?	1594
7.92	PG-116 *Ten Commandments* (ca. 1587)	M. de Vos	various	engraving	11 plates ca. 200 × 243	1608
7.50	PG-22 *Designs for Pendants with Sea Monsters* (1582)	H. Collaert I	A. Collaert	engraving	10 plates ca. 172 × 127	1594
7.20	PG-34 *Examples of Repentant Sinners* (by 1608)	M. de Vos	anonymous	engraving	10 plates ca. 200 × 228	1608
7.20	PG-68 *Life of St John the Baptist* (ca. 1595–1604)	J. Stradanus	C. Galle I	engraving	10 leaves ca. 225 × 285	1608
7	PG-54 *Heads of Men and Women* (ca. 1590–1594)	P. Galle	P. Galle	engraving	18 plates ca. 120 × 100	1594
7	PG-91 *Sea Gods and Goddesses* (1587)	P. Galle	P. Galle	engraving	36 plates ca. 164 × 100	1594
6	PG-32 *Eight Wonders of the World* (1572)	M. van Heemskerck	P. Galle	engraving	8 plates ca. 213 × 264	1582
6	PG-36 *Famous Roman Women* (by 1594)	J. Stradanus	T. Galle	engraving	6 plates ca. 224 × 289	1594 1608

Price in st.	Subject	Designer	Printmaker	Medium	Size in mm	Date sold
6	PG-55 *History of the Medici* (1577–1583)	J. Stradanus	P. Galle H. Goltzius	engraving	8 plates ca. 208 × 281	1580
6	PG-56 *History of the Silkworm* (1590–1600?)	J. Stradanus	C. de Mallery	engraving	6 plates ca. 200 × 270	1608
6	PG-80 *Our Father (Pater noster)* (ca. 1571)	M. van Heemskerck	J. Wierix	engraving	8 plates ca. 204 × 248	1582
6	PG-97 *Seven Sacraments* (1576)	anonymous	P. Galle	engraving	8 plates ca. 256 × 190	1576–1578
6	PG-99 *Seven Spiritual Acts of Mercy* (1577)	anonymous	P. Galle	engraving	8 plates ca. 259 × 190	1577–1583
6	PG-101 *Seven Worldly Acts of Mercy* (1577)	anonymous	P. Galle	engraving	8 plates ca. 253 × 190	1577–1583
6	PG-109 *Story of Esther* (1564)	M. van Heemskerck	P. Galle	engraving	8 plates ca. 205 × 248	1575
5.76	PG-30 *Eight Beatitudes* (ca. 1566)	M. van Heemskerck	H. J. Muller	engraving	8 plates ca. 210 × 250	1580
5.76	PG-42 & PG-43 *Four Continents & Four Elements* (by 1585)	M. Gheeraerts I	anonymous	engraving	8 plates ca. 197 × 132	1608
5.76	PG-80 *Our Father (Pater noster)* (ca. 1571)	M. van Heemskerck	J. Wierix	engraving	8 plates ca. 204 × 248	1608
5.76	PG-93 *Seven Churches of Rome* (ca. 1598)	?	J. Collaert? A. Collaert?	engraving	8 plates ca. 285/297 × 192/205	1608
5.76	PG-96 *Seven Planets* (by 1608)	?	?	engraving	8 plates?	1608
5.76	PG-97 *Seven Sacraments* (1576)	anonymous	P. Galle	engraving	8 plates ca. 256 × 190	1580
5.76	PG-109 *Story of Esther* (1564)	M. van Heemskerck	P. Galle	engraving	8 plates ca. 205 × 248	1608
5.76	PG-110 *Story of Judith & Holofernes* (1564)	M. van Heemskerck	P. Galle	engraving	8 plates ca. 204 × 248	1580
5.76- 5.75	PG-99 *Seven Spiritual Acts of Mercy* (1577)	anonymous	P. Galle	engraving	8 plates ca. 259 × 190	1577 1580
5.76- 5.75	PG-101 *Seven Worldly Acts of Mercy* (1577)	anonymous	P. Galle	engraving	8 plates ca. 253 × 190	1577 1580
5.75	PG-55 *History of the Medici* (1577–1583)	J. Stradanus	P. Galle H. Goltzius	engraving	8 plates ca. 208 × 281	1580
5	PG-9 *Book of Birds* (1594)	M. Gheeraerts I or II	P. Galle?	engraving	12 plates ca. 78 × 209	1594
5	PG-25 *Discovery of America* (by 1588)	J. Stradanus	A. Collaert	engraving	4 plates ca. 212 × 282	1588
5	PG-29 *Divine Charge to the Three Estates* (ca. 1565–1568?)	M. van Heemskerck	P. Galle	engraving	4 plates ca. 204 × 251	1588
5?	PG-40 *Four Ages: Golden ... and Iron* (1573)	G. Coignet	P. Galle	engraving	4 plates ca. 247 × 248	1588
4.32	PG-113 *Story of Susanna* (1563)	M. van Heemskerck	P. Galle?	engraving	6 plates ca. 205 × 246/251	1608
4.32	PG-115 *Story of the Miller* (by 1608)	A. Francken	C. de Mallery	engraving	6 plates ca. 195 × 247	1608

Price in st.	Subject	Designer	Printmaker	Medium	Size in mm	Date sold
4.32	PG-117 *Triumphs of Petrarch* (ca. 1565)	M. van Heemskerck	P. Galle	engraving	6 plates ca. 194 × 263	1580
4	PG-7 *Archangels* (ca. 1584–1585)	M. de Vos	C. de Passe I	engraving	9 plates ca. 162 × 92	1594
4	PG-25 *Discovery of America* (by 1588)	J. Stradanus	A. Collaert	engraving	4 plates ca. 212 × 282	1594
4	PG-29 *Divine Charge to the Three Estates* (ca. 1565–1568?)	M. van Heemskerck	P. Galle	engraving	4 plates ca. 204 × 251	1594
4	PG-40 *Four Ages: Golden … and Iron* (1573)	G. Coignet	P. Galle	engraving	4 plates ca. 247 × 248	1594
4	PG-41 *Four Continents* (ca. 1588–1589?)	M. de Vos	A. Collaert	engraving	4 plates ca. 212 × 259	1594
4	PG-46 *Four Last Things* (1569)	M. van Heemskerck	P. Galle	engraving	4 plates ca. 230 diameter	1575
4	PG-48 *Four Parts of the Day* (by 1594)	M. de Vos	A. Collaert	engraving	4 plates ca. 206 × 260	1594
3.65	PG-75 *Mysteries of the Childhood of Christ* (by 1579)	?	?	?	?	1579
3.60	PG-50 *Four Seasons with the Sun* (by 1580)	J. Stradanus	P. Galle	engraving	5 plates ca. 219 × 303	1580
3.60	PG-75 *Mysteries of the Childhood of Christ* (by 1579)	?	?	?	?	1580
3	PG-40 *Four Ages: Golden … and Iron* (1573)	G. Coignet	P. Galle	engraving	4 plates ca. 247 × 248	1573
3	PG-42 & PG-43 *Four Continents & Four Elements* (by 1585)	M. Gheeraerts I	anonymous	engraving	8 plates ca. 197 × 132	1585
3	PG-52 *Four Ways of Living on Earth* (by 1573)	G. van Groeningen	P. Galle's workshop?	engraving	4 plates ca. 209 × 255	1573
3	PG-84 *Power of Women* (ca. 1569)	P. Galle	P. Galle	engraving	6 plates ca. 239 diameter	1608
3	PG-103 *Six Hermits* (by 1594)	?	?	?	?	1594
3	PG-107 *Story of Adam and Eve* (1580–1600)	M. de Vos	C. de Passe I	engraving	6 plates ca. 101 × 94	1608
2.88	PG-41 *Four Continents* (ca. 1588–1589?)	M. de Vos	A. Collaert	engraving	4 plates ca. 212 × 259	1608
2.88	PG-44 *Four Doctors of the Church* (s.a.)	?	?	?	?	1580 1608
2.88	PG-45 *Four Evangelists* (ca. 1575)	A. Blocklandt van Montfoort	P. Galle	engraving	4 plates ca. 217 × 280	1576
2.88	PG-47 *Four Last Things* (ca. 1578)	J. Stradanus	H. Goltzius	engraving	4 plates ca. 260 diameter	1580
2.88	PG-49 *Four Seasons* (1563)	M. van Heemskerck	P. Galle	engraving	4 plates ca. 210 × 250	1580

Price in st.	*Subject*	*Designer*	*Printmaker*	*Medium*	*Size in mm*	*Date sold*
2.88	PG-51 *Four Strongest Powers* (ca. 1574?)	G. van Groeningen	P. Galle	engraving	4 plates ca. 191 × 266	1580
2.88	PG-108 *Story of Adonis* (ca. 1579)	A. Blocklandt van Montfoort	P. Galle	engraving	4 plates ca. 220 × 305	1580
2.88	PG-111 *Story of Lucretia* (1578–1579)	anonymous	H. Goltzius	engraving	4 plates ca. 210 × 248	1580
2.88	PG-112 *Story of Mars & Venus* (by 1608)	P. Galle	J. Collaert II	engraving	4 plates ca. 186 × 229	1608
2.88	PG-114 *Story of the Miller* (by 1576)	anonymous	anonymous	engraving	4 plates ca. 224 × 154	1576
2.50	PG-35 *Fall of Babylon* (1569)	M. van Heemskerck	P. Galle	engraving	1 plate ca. 256 × 411	1571
2.25	PG-76 *(Fifteen?) Mysteries of the Virgin (or Rosary)* (1577)	?	?	?	possibly 3 plates	1592
2.16	PG-76 *(Fifteen?) Mysteries of the Virgin (or Rosary)* (1577)	?	?	?	possibly 3 plates	1580
2	PG-15 *Coat of Arms of the King* (by 1594)	J. Stradanus	A. Collaert	engraving	1 plate ca. 327 × 216	1594
2	PG-37 *Fifteen Mysteries of the Rosary* (1577)	J. Stradanus	anonymous	engraving	1 plate 436 × 298	1577
2	PG-38 *Five Senses* (1578)	anonymous	H. Goltzius	engraving	5 plates ca. 160 × 91	1581
2	PG-65 *Last Supper* (by 1594)	J. Stradanus	anonymous	engraving	1 plate ca. 236 × 301	1594
1.75	PG-38 *Five Senses* (1578)	anonymous	H. Goltzius	engraving	5 plates ca. 160 × 91	1581
1.50	PG-18 *Deer Hunt of Emperor Barbarossa* (1589)	J. Stradanus	A. Collaert	engraving	1 plate ca. 251 × 272	1594
1.50	PG-124 *War against the Turks* (1590)	J. Stradanus	A. Collaert	engraving	2 plates ca. 240 × 316 & 232 × 309	1594
1	PG-90 *St Catherine* (by 1590)	J. Stradanus	T. Galle	engraving	1 plate ca. 248 × 187	1590
1 or .72	PG-3 *Adoration of the Holy Vernicle* (by 1588)	J. Stradanus	anonymous	engraving	1 plate ca. 251 × 181	1588
1 or .72	PG-5 *Adoration of the Virgin by Sts Antony & Francis* (by 1588)	J. Stradanus	A. Collaert?	engraving	1 plate ca. 248 × 180	1588
1 or .72	PG-13 *Christ at the Column* (by 1588)	J. Stradanus	anonymous	engraving	1 plate ca. 200 × 144	1588
1 or .72	PG-14 *Christ on the Cross with Angels* (by 1588)	J. Stradanus	A. Collaert	engraving	1 plate ca. 247 × 181	1588
1 or .72	PG-63 *Immaculate Conception of the Virgin* (by 1588)	J. Stradanus	H. Wierix	engraving	1 plate ca. 196 × 134	1588
1 or .72	PG-64 *Lamentation with Two Angels* (by 1588)	J. Stradanus	A. Collaert	engraving	1 plate ca. 196 × 140	1588
1 or .72	PG-70 *Martyrdom of St Barbara* (by 1588)	J. Stradanus	J. Wierix	engraving	1 plate ca. 240 × 176	1588

Price in st.	*Subject*	*Designer*	*Printmaker*	*Medium*	*Size in mm*	*Date sold*
1 or .72	PG-71 *Martyrdom of St Lawrence* (by 1588)	J. Stradanus	A. Collaert	engraving	1 plate ca. 202 × 140	1588
1 or .72	PG-72 *Martyrdom of St Lucy* (by 1588)	J. Stradanus	J. Wierix	engraving	1 plate ca. 243 × 182	1588
1 or .72	PG-121 *Nuestra Señora de l'Antigua* (by 1588)	H. Wierix?	H. Wierix	engraving	1 plate ca. 237 × 172	1588
.73	PG-8 *Atonement of Christ* (1578)	anonymous	H. Goltzius	engraving	1 plate ca. 244 × 190	1579
.73	PG-31 *Eight Beatitudes* (1578)	anonymous	H. Goltzius	engraving	1 plate ca. 257 × 187	1579
.73	PG-118 *Twelve Articles of Faith* (by 1579)	?	?	?	?	1580
.72	PG-4 *Adoration of the Name of Jesus* (ca. 1569)	anonymous	P. Galle	engraving	1 plate ca. 248 diameter	1580
.72	PG-6 *Annunciation* (ca. 1577–1578)	A. Blocklandt van Montfoort	P. Galle	engraving	1 plate ca. 288 × 201	1580
.72	PG-10 *Casting out of Evil* (1578)	anonymous	H. Goltzius	engraving	1 plate ca. 251 × 187	1580
.72	PG-23 *Disagreement in the Church* (1578)	anonymous	H. Goltzius	engraving	1 plate ca. 256 × 187	1580
.72	PG-39 *Forgiveness of Transgressions* (1578)	anonymous	H. Goltzius	engraving	1 plate ca. 254 × 189	1580
.72	PG-57 *House Built on Sand* (1578)	anonymous	H. Goltzius	engraving	1 plate ca. 256 × 186	1580
.72	PG-58 *House Built on the Rock* (1578)	anonymous	H. Goltzius	engraving	1 plate ca. 259 × 186	1580
.72	PG-69 *Man's Quest for ... Heaven* (1578)	anonymous	H. Goltzius	engraving	1 plate ca. 259 × 186	1580
.72	PG-73 *Misericordia Dei* (ca. 1577)	anonymous	H. Goltzius	engraving	1 plate ca. 254 × 184	1580
.72	PG-77 *Nativity, Crucifixion & Resurrection* (1578)	anonymous	anonymous	engraving	1 plate ca. 190 × 298	1580
.72	PG-85 *Relief of Suffering* (1578)	anonymous	H. Goltzius	engraving	1 plate ca. 247 × 186	1580
.72	PG-86 *Resurrection of Christ* (1577–1578)	A. Blocklandt van Montfoort	H. Goltzius	engraving	1 plate ca. 262 × 200	1580
.72	PG-94 *Seven Effusions of Christ's Blood* (by 1580)	?	?	?	?	1580
.72	PG-95 *Seven Joys of the Virgin* (by 1580)	?	?	?	In circles on one leaf	1580
.72	PG-98 *Seven Sorrows of the Virgin* (by 1580)	?	?	?	In circles on one leaf	1580
.72	PG-100 *Seven Spiritual Acts of Mercy* (by 1580)	anonymous	anonymous	engraving	1 plate ca. 247 × 186	1580
.72	PG-102 *Seven Worldly Acts of Mercy* (by 1580)	anonymous	anonymous	engraving	1 plate ca. 255 × 190	1580

Price in st.	*Subject*	*Designer*	*Printmaker*	*Medium*	*Size in mm*	*Date sold*
.72	PG-105 *Solicitude of the Lord* (1578)	anonymous	H. Goltzius	engraving	1 plate ca. 255 × 181	1580
.72	PG-118 *Twelve Articles of Faith* (by 1579)	?	?	?	?	1579

TABLE 4 Prices of Prints as Supplied by Theodore Galle and Catharina Moerentorf

Price in st.	*Subject*	*Designer*	*Printmaker*	*Medium*	*Size in mm*	*Date sold*
60	TG-7 *Illustrium imagines* (1598)	T. Galle	T. Galle	engraving	151 plates ca. 140 × 100 & title plate 163 × 105	1598–1605
40	TG-6 *Holy Founders of Religious Orders* (1630)	?	C. Galle I	engraving	40 plates ca. 150 × 104 & title-plate 165 × 107	1630 1631 1635
40	TG-10 *Life of St Ignatius* (1610)	J. de Mesa	various	engraving	16 plates ca. 264 × 366	1610 1611
30	TG-20 *Portraits of Scholars* (s.a.)	various	various	engraving	?	1634
30	TG-21 *Portraits of Scholars from the Low Countries* (1608)	various	anonymous	engraving	64 plates ca. 167/179 × 103/123	1608
25	TG-12 *Life of St Teresa of Avila* (1613)	P. de Jode I	A. Collaert C. Galle I	engraving	25 plates ca. 183 × 218	1616
24	TG-13 *Men and Women of the Franciscan Order* (1614)	P. de Jode I	C. de Mallery	engraving	14 plates ca. 255 × 165 & title plate 267 × 176	1631
20	TG-8 *Life and Miracles of St Dominic* (1611)	J. Nys and P. de Jode I	T. Galle and workshop	engraving	34 plates ca. 156 × 92	1611
20	TG-9 *Life of St Catherine of Siena* (1603)	F. Vanni	C. Galle I	engraving	34 plates ca. 151 × 91	1610 1611 1618
18	TG-14 *Miracles of the Rosary* (1610) with introductory text	anonymous	anonymous	engraving	15 plates ca. 149 × 89 & title plate 155 × 92	1616
15.12	TG-24 *Scenographiae sive perspectivae* (1560)	H. Vredeman de Vries	J. & L. van Doetecum	etching & engraving	20 plates ca. 205 × 260	1608
12	TG-14 *Miracles of the Rosary* (1610) with introductory text	anonymous	anonymous	engraving	15 plates ca. 149 × 89 & title plate 155 × 92	1610 1611
12	TG-17 *Portraits of Famous Painters* (1572)	anonymous	C. Cort, J. Wierix, & others	engraving	23 plates ca. 210 × 125	1634
10	TG-14 *Miracles of the Rosary* (1610) without the introductory text	anonymous	anonymous	engraving	15 plates ca. 149 × 89 & title plate 155 × 92	1611 1612
10	TG-18 *Portraits of Italian Scholars* (1599/1600)	various	P. Galle & anonymous artists	engraving	25 plates ca. 167/179 × 117/123	1599 1600
7.92	TG-22 *Sailing Ships* (ca. 1561–1565)	P. Bruegel I	F. Huys & C. Cort?	etching & engraving	10 plates ca. 225 × 290 or 290 × 220	1608
6.48	TG-3 *Cycle of Vicissitudes* (1564)	M. van Heemskerck	C. Cort	engraving	9 plates ca. 224 × 297	1608
5.76	TG-16 *Pastoral Goddesses and Nymphs* (1564)	F. Floris	C. Cort	engraving	8 plates ca. 270 × 192	1608
5	TG-19 *Portraits of Nine Greek Scholars* (1599)	anonymous	T. Galle	engraving	1 plate 305 × 190	1599
4	TG-1 *Ave Maris Stella* (by 1608)	P. van der Borcht	anonymous	engraving	7 plates ca. 132 × 79	1608
4	TG-4 *Divine Love* (1605)	?	?	?	2 leaves	1605
4	TG-25 *Seven Sorrows of the Virgin* (1587)	C. van den Broeck	H. Wierix	engraving	1 plate 446 × 300	1602

Price in st.	*Subject*	*Designer*	*Printmaker*	*Medium*	*Size in mm*	*Date sold*
4	TG-30 *Virgin "in planctu"* (by 1608)	?	?	?	?	1608
3	TG-26 *Seven Sorrows of the Virgin* (by 1602)	?	?	?	8 plates	1602
3	TG-29 *Tree of Human Life* (by 1613)	N. C. Radzivilus	anonymous	engraving	1 plate 456 × 329	1613
2.16	TG-15 *The Nine Worthies* (ca. 1567)	M. van Heemskerck	H. J. Muller	engraving	3 plates ca. 216 × 250	1608
1.50	TG-5 *The Goose Game* (by 1632)	anonymous	anonymous	?	?	1632
1.50	TG-23 *St Dominic* (by 1608)	anonymous	T. Galle	engraving	1 plate 270 × 200	1608
1.50	TG-32 *Virgin "ventura"* (by 1608)	?	?	?	?	1608
1	TG-2 *Caesar Baronius* (by 1605)	?	?	engraving	1 plate 320 × 190	1605
.375	TG-31 *Virgin "quae est ista"* (by 1602)	anonymous	anonymous	engraving	1 plate 184 × 140 (trimmed)	1602

TABLE 5 Prices of Prints as Supplied by Gerard de Jode and Passchijnke van Gelre

Price in st.	*Subject*	*Designer*	*Printmaker*	*Medium*	*Size in mm*	*Date sold*
252	GJ-47 *Thesaurus novi & veteris testamenti* (1585)	various	various	engraving	348? diverse sheets	1590
244	GJ-47 *Thesaurus novi & veteris testamenti* (1585)	various	various	engraving	345 diverse sheets	1588
133	GJ-46 *Thesaurus ... veteris testamenti* (1579)	various	various	engraving	165 diverse sheets	1580
27	GJ-10 *Five Orders of Architecture* (1577)	H. Vredeman de Vries	J. & L. van Doetecum	etching & engraving	23 plates ca. 340/52 × 256 title plate 320 × 234	1588
24	GJ-10 *Five Orders of Architecture* (1577)	H. Vredeman de Vries	J. & L. van Doetecum	etching & engraving	23 plates a. 340/52 × 256 title plate 320 × 234	1582
13.50	GJ-12 *Fountains & Wells* (1568)	H. Vredeman de Vries	J. & L. van Doetecum	etching & engraving	17 plates ca. 174 × 240 & title plate 182 × 249	1581
12	GJ-25 *Passion of Christ* (1572)	C. van den Broeck?	J. Wierix	engraving	16 plates ca. 167 × 126	1576 1583
12	GJ-28 *Portraits of Popes* (1572)	P. Soye	P. Galle	engraving	29 plates ca. 170 × 120 title plate 176 × 127	1572 1573
11.25	GJ-26 *Plans for Fortifications* (1580)	H. van Schille	J. & L. van Doetecum	etching & engraving	14 plates ca. 267 × 230 & title plate 306 × 204	1588
10.75	GJ-12 *Fountains & Wells* (1568)	H. Vredeman de Vries	J. & L. van Doetecum	etching & engraving	17 plates ca. 174 × 240 & title plate 182 × 249	1570
10	GJ-5 *Calendarium sanctorum* (by 1595)	?	?	?	?	1595
9.50	GJ-6 *Caryatids and Terms* (ca. 1565)	H. Vredeman de Vries	J. & L. van Doetecum	etching	16 plates ca. 160 × 235 & title plate 173 × 235	1570
9.50	GJ-23 *Panels with grotesques* (ca. 1565–1571)	H. Vredeman de Vries	J. & L. van Doetecum	etching	17 plates ca. 158 × 208 or 208 × 158	1570
8.64	GJ-48 *Twelve Parables* (1580–1585)	A. Francken	anonymous	engraving	12 plates ca. 217 × 283	1580
7.50	GJ-6 *Caryatids and Terms* (ca. 1565)	H. Vredeman de Vries	J. & L. van Doetecum	etching	16 plates ca. 160 × 235 & title plate 173 × 235	1573
7.50	GJ-23 *Panels with Grotesques* (ca. 1565–1571)	H. Vredeman de Vries	J. & L. van Doetecum	etching	17 plates ca. 158 × 208 or 208 × 158	1573
6	GJ-30 *Ruins & Fantastical Buildings* (1554)	L. Suavius	L. Suavius	etching	33 plates of varying sizes	1573
6	GJ-35 *Seven Planets* (1581)	M. de Vos	A. Collaert	engraving	7 plates ca. 300 × 215 & title plate ca. 289 × 211	1582
5.76	GJ-17 *Kings of Judah* (ca. 1579)	J. Snellinck	anonymous	engraving	8 plates ca. 220 × 287	1580
5.04	GJ-31 *Seven Acts of Mercy* (ca. 1571)	G. van Groeningen	P. Nagel	engraving	7 plates ca. 200 × 250	1573
5	GJ-27 *Portraits of Emperors* (ca. 1565–1569)	H. Vredeman de Vries	J. & L. van Doetecum	etching & engraving	12 plates ca. 129 × 83 & title plate 116 × 86	1572 or 1573
5	GJ-30 *Ruins & Fantastical Buildings* (1554)	L. Suavius	L. Suavius	etching	33 plates of varying sizes	1558
5	GJ-36 *Small Passion of Christ* (ca. 1570?)	?	?	?	?	1570 1571

Price in st.	*Subject*	*Designer*	*Printmaker*	*Medium*	*Size in mm*	*Date sold*
5	GJ-43 *Strapwork Cartouches with Biblical Texts* (1555)	H. Vredeman de Vries	F. Huys	etching & engraving	12 plates ca. 185 × 137 or 137 × 197 & title-plate 175 × 142	1558
5	GJ-44 *Strapwork Cartouches with Classical Texts* (1555)	H. Vredeman de Vries	F. Huys	etching & engraving	12 plates ca. 179 × 137 or 138 × 183 & title plate 170 × 139	1558
4.50	GJ-37 *Story of Daniel* (1576–1579)	H. Vredeman de Vries	J. & L. van Doetecum	etching & engraving	6 plates ca. 242 × 327	1582
4.50	GJ-38 *Story of Joseph* (1579)	M. Coxie	various	engraving	7 plates ca. 210 × 260	1584
4.50	GJ-42 *Story of Tobias* (by 1576)	H. Bol	J. & L. van Doetecum	engraving	6 plates ca. 237 × 323	1582
3.50	GJ-41 *Story of Susanna* (by 1571)	G. Coignet	H. Collaert I	engraving	4 plates ca. 195 × 263	1571
3	GJ-14 *Four Kingdoms* (by 1573)	G. van Groeningen	J. Wierix	engraving	4 plates ca. 197 × 287	1573
2.25	GJ-22 *Moses and Aaron* (1556)	L. van Noort	F. Huys	engraving	3 plates 320 × 740	1558
2.16	GJ-39 *Story of Samson* (1579)	J. Snellinck	A. Wierix II	engraving	3 plates ca. 213 × 293	1580
2	GJ-9 *Ecce Homo* (by 1588)	anonymous	P. J. Furnius?	engraving	1 plate 298 × 221	1588
2	GJ-24 *Parable of the Prodigal Son* (by 1571)	C. van den Broeck	H. Collaert I	engraving	4 plates ca. 195 × 270	1571
1	GJ-4 *Bird's Eye View of Ancient Jerusalem* (by 1587)	P. Lacksteyn	A. Wierix II	engraving	1 plate 219 × 271	1587
1	GJ-21 *Map of Modern Jerusalem* (by 1587)	P. Lacksteyn	anonymous	engraving	1 plate 214 × 280	1587
.72	GJ-2 *Allegory of Temperance and Vice* (ca. 1574–1580)	J. Snellinck?	anonymous	engraving	1 plate 213 × 289	1580
.72	GJ-3 *Allegory of Temperance and Virtue* (ca. 1574–1580)	J. Snellinck?	anonymous	engraving	1 plate 217 × 292	1580
.72	GJ-7 *Christ's Sermon on the Last Days* (by 1580)	J. Snellinck?	anonymous	engraving	1 plate 227 × 311	1580
.72	GJ-13 *Four Famous Women from Antiquity* (ca. 1574–1580)	J. Snellinck?	H. Collaert I?	engraving	1 plate 220 × 284	1580
.72	GJ-15 *Four Roman Heroes* (ca. 1574–1580)	J. Snellinck?	H. Collaert I?	engraving	1 plate 220 × 285	1580
.72	GJ-16 *Four Seasons* (ca. 1574–1580)	J. Snellinck?	H. Collaert I?	engraving	1 plate 218 × 282	1580
.72	GJ-18 *Lessons from Ecclesiastes* (ca. 1574–1580)	J. Snellinck?	H. Collaert I?	engraving	1 plate 277 × 218	1580
.72	GJ-19 *Lessons from Proverbs* (ca. 1574–1580)	J. Snellinck?	H. Collaert I?	engraving	1 plate 287 × 221	1580

TABLE 6 Prices of Prints as Supplied by Anton II and Hieronymus Wierix

Price in st.	Subject	Designer	Printmaker	Medium	Size in mm	Date sold
22	WX-5 *Jesus and Joseph* (by 1613)	?	?	?	?	1613
22	WX-7 *Life of the Infant* (by 1615)	H. Wierix	H. Wierix	engraving	13 plates ca. 99 × 64	1615 1616
18	WX-9 *"Novus Jesus"* (by 1616)	?	?	?	?	1616
14	WX-8 *Mirror of Virginity* (by 1616)	H. Wierix	H. Wierix	engraving	7 plates ca. 93 × 54	1616
6	WX-18 *Twelve Apostles* (by 1602)	A. Wierix II	A. Wierix II	engraving	12 plates ca. 81 × 60	1602 1607
4	WX-2 *Death of St Cecilia* (1599–1605)	F. Vanni	H. Wierix	engraving	1 plate 152 × 117	1606
4	WX-20 *Virgin and Child on a Crescent Moon* (by 1602)	H. Wierix	H. Wierix	engraving	1 plate 147 × 103	1602
3	WX-4 *Guardian Angel* (by 1602)	H. Wierix	H. Wierix	engraving	1 plate 147 × 103	1602
3	WX-10 *St Anna* (by 1602)	?	H. Wierix?	?	in 4°	1602
2	WX-3 *Four "Fathers"* (by 1610)	H. Wierix	H. Wierix	engraving	1 plate ca. 110 × 67	1610
2	WX-13 *St Ignatius with a Book* (by 1607)	?	H. Wierix?	engraving?	1 plate ca. 109 × 66	1607
2	WX-16 *Sts Ignatius and Xavier* (by 1607)	D. da Garça	H. Wierix	engraving	2 plates ca. 81 × 61 each	1607
1	WX-6 *Jesus Walking with the Virgin & Joseph* (by 1602)	A. Wierix II	A. Wierix II	engraving	1 plate ca. 97 × 65	1602
1	WX-11 *St Francis of Assisi with the Virgin* (by 1602)	A. Wierix II	A. Wierix II	engraving	1 plate ca. 102 × 67	1602
1	WX-12 *St Francis Xavier* (by 1607)	?	H. Wierix?	engraving?	1 plate ca. 110 × 70	1607
1	WX-14 *St Ignatius with a Cross* (by 1607)	?	H. Wierix?	engraving?	1 plate ca. 108/112 × 68/73	1607
1	WX-17 *Triumph of Truth* (by 1602)	M. de Vos	A. Wierix II	engraving	1 plate ca. 96 × 65	1602
1	WX-19 *Virgin and the Sleeping Child* (by 1602)	A. Wierix II	A. Wierix II	engraving	1 plate 85 × 60	1602
.75	WX-15 *Sts Agnes and Margaret* (by 1602)	A. Wierix II	A. Wierix II	engraving	2 plates? ca. 82 × 58 each	1602
.50	WX-1 *Annunciation and Nativity* (by 1602)	?	A. Wierix II?	?	?	1602

TABLES 7–8 *Prices for Unspecified Prints Sold in Bulk*

The rates are listed from high to low, and, within a given rate, the information is organized chronologically, from early to late examples. If a rate is usually recorded for groups of 12 or 100 images, then the equivalent price per print is also noted in the last column, preceded by "=" to distinguish it from instances in which a unit price per print was recorded. Please see Appendix 1, under each of the print publishers named, for examples of each of the rates given. The rates charged by Volcxken Diericx, Catharina Moerentorf, and Marie de Man are listed under their husbands' names (Widow H. Cock, Widow T. Galle, and Widow J. Cnobbaert, respectively) to underscore the evolution in prices within one family business.

TABLE 7 Prices Charged for Plain Prints on Paper Sold in Bulk Between 1558 and 1637

Supplier	*Dates*	*Rate per 100 prints*	*Rate per quire of 25 leaves*	*Rate per print*
H. Cock	1568			4 st.
P. Galle	1601			4 st.
T. Galle	1618, 1625			4 st.
T. Galle	1618, 1633			3 st.
T. Galle	1608, 1613, 1618, 1623, 1625, 1632			2.50 st.
P. Galle	1596			2 st.
H. Wierix	1609–1616			2 st.
T. Galle	1618, 1619			2 st.
H. Wierix	1609–1616			1.50 st.
T. Galle	1613, 1616			1.50 st.
P. Galle	1596			1 st.
A. Wierix II	1601			1 st.
H. Wierix	1602, 1609–1616			1 st.
T. Galle	1608			1 st.
P. Galle	1579		20 st. = .8 st. / leaf	
A. Huberti	1587, 1588		20 st. = .8 st. / leaf	
P. Galle	1578		19 st. = .76 st. / leaf	
P. Galle	1596			.75 st.
A. Collaert	1601			.75 st.
C. de Mallery	1608			.75 st.
H. Wierix	1611			.75 st.
T. Galle	1624			.75 st.
P. Galle	1579		18.25 st. = .73 st. / leaf	
H. Liefrinck	1558		18 st. = .72 st. / leaf	
H. Cock	1568		18 st. = .72 st. / leaf	
Widow H. Cock	1570–1571, 1573, 1581		18 st. = .72 st. / leaf	
G. de Jode	1570–1571, 1573, 1576, 1581–1582, 1590		18 st. = .72 st. / leaf	
P. Galle	1571, 1573, 1580–1594, 1601, 1608		18 st. = .72 st. / leaf	
A. Huberti	1588–1597		18 st. = .72 st. / leaf	
A. Collaert	1607–1608		18 st. = .72 st. / leaf	
P. de Jode I	1608		18 st. = .72 st. / leaf	
T. Galle	1608, 1621		18 st. = .72 st. / leaf	
A. van Merlen	1619		18 st. = .72 st. / leaf	
T. Galle	1633	72 st.		= .72 st.
T. Galle	1626	70 st.		= .70 st.

Supplier	*Dates*	*Rate per 100 prints*	*Rate per quire of 25 leaves*	*Rate per print*
C. de Mallery	1609	60 st.		= .60 st.
C. de Mallery	1607–1618, 1623–1626	50 st.		= .50 st.
P. Galle	1596			.50 st.
T. Galle	1607, 1631			.50 st.
P. Galle	1601			.375 st.
T. Galle	1608, 1613–1615, 1618, 1621, 1624–1627, 1630–1633	36 st.		= .36 st.
A. van Merlen	1615–1619, 1625	36 st.		= .36 st.
M. Snijders	1618–1620, 1625–1626	36 st.		= .36 st.
J. Boel[1]	1621, 1623	36 st.		= .36 st.
J. Galle	1637	36 st.		= .36 st.
T. Galle	1626	35 st.		= .35 st.
A. van Merlen	1626	32 st.		= .32 st.
P. Galle	1592	30 st.		= .30 st.
P. Galle	1587			.25 st.
T. Galle	1607			.25 st.
A. Collaert	1608	20 st.		= .20 st.
T. Galle	1608	20 st.		= .20 st.
J. Cnobbaert	1628	20 st.		= .20 st.
T. Galle	1615, 1630	18 st.		= .18 st.

1 MPM Arch. 228, fol. 157v; and MPM Arch. 1106, fol. 19r.

TABLE 8 Prices Charged for Colored Prints on Parchment Sold in Bulk Between 1628 and 1640

Supplier	*Dates*	*Rate per 100 prints*	*Rate per 12 prints*	*Rate per print*
T. Galle	1630			10.0 st.
Widow T. Galle	1634, 1636			5.0 st.
J. Cnobbaert	1628			3.50 st.
J. Cnobbaert	1628			3.0 st.
T. Galle	1629, 1633			3.0 st.
Widow T. Galle	1636			3.0 st.
M. Snijders	1629		33 st.	= 2.75 st.
M. Snijders	1632	13 fl. 15 st.		= 2.75 st.
J. Cnobbaert	1628			2.50 st.
T. Galle	1630		30 st.	= 2.50 st.
T. Galle	1631–1632	12 fl. 10 st.		= 2.50 st.
Widow T. Galle	1634			2.50 st.
T. Galle	1629			2.0 st.
T. Galle	1630–1633	10 fl.		= 2.0 st.
Widow T. Galle	1636			2.0 st.
Widow J. Cnobbaert	1640	10 fl.		= 2.0 st.
J. Galle	1637			2.0 st.
J. Galle	1639	9 fl.		= 1.80 st.
Widow J. Cnobbaert	1640	6 fl.		= 1.20 st.
Widow J. Cnobbaert	1640	5 fl.		= 1.0 st.

BIBLIOGRAPHY

Primary Sources

Antwerp, Plantin-Moretus Museum (MPM)

The titles given below for the archival documents from the Plantin-Moretus Museum are taken from Jan Denucé's *Inventaris op het Plantijnsch Archief / Inventaire des Archives Plantiniennes* (Antwerp: De Sikkel, 1926). See the Note to the Reader for a brief overview of the primary types of documents from the Plantin-Moretus Museum that we consulted, the various systems used in these documents for noting pages, and the abbreviations used in this book.

Arch. 7: *Copie de lettres de Christophe Plantin 1561–1572*
Arch. 12: *Copie de lettres de Jean Moretus I, 1598–1607*
Arch. 13: *Copie de lettres de Plantin-Moretus I, 1597–1617*
Arch. 16: *Grand livre 1568–1573*
Arch. 17: *Grand livre des libraires 1568–1578*
Arch. 18: *Grand livre + + 1571–1582*
Arch. 19: *Grand livre signé C. 1572–1589*
Arch. 20: *Grand livre 1582–1589*
Arch. 21: *Grand livre 1590–1599*
Arch. 27: *Verkoop van Plantijns goed, 1562*
Arch. 33: *Livre des ouvriers 1580–1590*
Arch. 34: *Livre de vente 1556–1559*
Arch. 35: *Journal 1558–1561*
Arch. 36: *Journal 1561–1574*
Arch. 37: *Débiteurs 1565–1569*
Arch. 38: *Libraires et autres 1555–1562*
Arch. 40: *Libraires A 1566–1569*
Arch. 43I: *Grand livre de Francfort, 1566–1596*
Arch. 43III: *Vente à la boutique 1569–1576*
Arch. 45: *Journal 1567*
Arch. 46: *Journal 1568*
Arch. 47: *Journal 1569*
Arch. 48: *Journal 1570*
Arch. 49: *Journal 1571*
Arch. 50: *Journal 1572*
Arch. 51: *Journal 1573*
Arch. 52: *Journal 1574*
Arch. 53: *Journal 1575*
Arch. 54: *Journal 1576*
Arch. 55: *Journal 1577*
Arch. 56: *Journal 1578*
Arch. 57: *Journal 1579*
Arch. 58: *Journal 1580*
Arch. 59: *Journal 1581*
Arch. 60: *Journal 1582*
Arch. 61: *Journal 1583*
Arch. 62: *Journal 1584–1585*
Arch. 63: *Journal 1586*
Arch. 64: *Journal 1587*
Arch. 65: *Journal 1588*
Arch. 66: *Journal 1589*
Arch. 67: *Journal 1590*
Arch. 68: *Journal 1591*
Arch. 69: *Journal 1592*
Arch. 70: *Journal 1593*
Arch. 71: *Journal 1594*
Arch. 72: *Journal 1595*
Arch. 73: *Journal 1596*
Arch. 74: *Journal 1597*
Arch. 75: *Journal 1598*
Arch. 82: *Recueils de lettres Fabianus-Gassen*
Arch. 84: *Recueils de lettres Gras*
Arch. 85: *Recueils de lettres Grimaldi-Huysten*
Arch. 88: *Recueils de lettres Maccius-Montmorency*
Arch. 89: *Recueils de lettres Moretus*
Arch. 90: *Recueils de lettres Moriconij-Périer*
Arch. 93: *Recueils de lettres Sabbetius-Symont*
Arch. 94: *Recueils de lettres Tavernier-Litterae incognitae*
Arch. 100: *Papiers de famille des Moretus 1597–1605*
Arch. 101: *Livre des affaires de famille 1605–1657*
Arch. 102: *Papiers de la famille Moretus 1606–1623*
Arch. 110: *Libraires étrangers. Grand livre E 1575–1593*
Arch. 111: *Libraires étrangers. Grand livre F. 1594–1609*
Arch. 114: *Libraires d'Anvers FF 1615–1629*
Arch. 115: *Libraires d'Anvers GG 1622–1625*
Arch. 117: *Imprimerie 1585–1599*
Arch. 118: *Imprimerie 1600–1625*
Arch. 123: *Graveurs I. Galle. 1600–1692*
Arch. 126: *Grand livre signé D. 1590–1614*
Arch. 127: *Grand livre du soleil 1600–1608*
Arch. 128: *Grand livre signé A. 1610–1618*
Arch. 129: *Grand livre des libraires G. 1610–1618*
Arch. 130: *Grand livre E. 1614–1661*
Arch. 131: *Grootboek B. 1618–1629*
Arch. 132: *Grootboek H. 1618–1629. Boekhandelaars*
Arch. 133: *Grand livre des libraires étrangers 1629–1655*
Arch. 134: *Grand livre 1624–1655*
Arch. 135: *Copie de Lettres 1607–1615*
Arch. 137: *Copie de Lettres 1616–1620*
Arch. 139: *Copie de Lettres 1620–1625*
Arch. 140: *Copie de Lettres de Meursius 1621–1625*
Arch. 141: *Copie de Lettres de Meursius 1625–1629*
Arch. 142: *Copie de Lettres 1625–1635*
Arch. 144: *Copie de Lettres 1628–1633*
Arch. 145: *Copie de Lettres 1633–1637*
Arch. 146: *Copie de Lettres, 1633–1640*
Arch. 147: *Copie de Lettres 1635–1642*
Arch. 148: *Copie de lettres 1637–1640*
Arch. 150: *Copie de lettres 1640–1654*
Arch. 151: *Copie de lettres 1642–1650*
Arch. 157: *Missale et Breviarium: Procès*
Arch. 166: *Dépenses spéciales 1620–1636*
Arch. 171: *Journal 1599*
Arch. 172: *Journal 1600*
Arch. 173: *Journal 1601*
Arch. 174: *Journal 1602*
Arch. 175: *Journal 1603*
Arch. 176: *Journal 1604*
Arch. 177: *Journal 1605*
Arch. 178: *Journal 1606*
Arch. 179: *Journal 1607*
Arch. 180: *Journal 1608*
Arch. 184: *Boek gehouden door Jan Moretus II, als deken der St. Lucasgilde (1616–1617)*
Arch. 185: *Kasboek 1629*
Arch. 187: *Foire de Francfort, 1644–47*
Arch. 189: *Libraires étrangers 1596–1605*
Arch. 194: *Grand livre 1629–1638*
Arch. 198: *Comptes du collège des Jésuites, 1634–1637*
Arch. 216: *Journal 1609*
Arch. 217: *Journal 1610*
Arch. 218: *Journal 1611*
Arch. 219: *Journal 1612*
Arch. 220: *Journal 1613*
Arch. 221: *Journal 1614*
Arch. 222: *Journal 1615*
Arch. 223: *Journal 1616*
Arch. 224: *Journal 1617*
Arch. 225: *Journal 1618*
Arch. 226: *Journal 1619*
Arch. 227: *Journal 1620*
Arch. 228: *Journal 1621*
Arch. 229: *Journal 1622*
Arch. 230: *Journal 1623*
Arch. 231: *Journal 1624*
Arch. 232: *Journal 1625*
Arch. 233: *Journal 1626*
Arch. 234: *Journal 1627*
Arch. 235: *Journal 1628*
Arch. 236: *Journal 1629 A*
Arch. 237: *Journal 1629 B*
Arch. 238: *Journal 1630*
Arch. 239: *Journal 1631*
Arch. 240: *Journal 1632*
Arch. 241: *Journal 1633*
Arch. 242: *Journal 1634*
Arch. 243: *Journal 1635*
Arch. 244: *Journal 1636*
Arch. 245: *Journal 1637*
Arch. 246: *Journal 1638*
Arch. 247: *Journal 1639*
Arch. 248: *Journal 1640*
Arch. 249: *Journal 1641*
Arch. 250: *Journal 1642*
Arch. 252: *Journal 1644*
Arch. 253: *Journal 1645*
Arch. 254: *Journal 1646*

Arch. 255: *Journal 1647*
Arch. 256: *Journal 1648*
Arch. 258: *Journal 1650*
Arch. 261: *Journal vente de livres 1576–1580*
Arch. 297: *Copie de lettres 1677–1683*
Arch. 299: *Copie de lettres 1650–1659*
Arch. 351: *Libraires étrangers, 1665–1718*
Arch. 364: *Comptes d'Espagne 1644–1665*
Arch. 393: *Journal 1678*
Arch. 394: *Journal 1679*
Arch. 401: *Journal 1651*
Arch. 402: *Journal 1652*
Arch. 404: *Journal 1654*
Arch. 405: *Journal 1655*
Arch. 411: *Journal 1662*
Arch. 412: *Journal 1661*
Arch. 415: *Journal 1665*
Arch. 416: *Journal 1666*
Arch. 491: *Journal 1581–1588 (librairie)*
Arch. 492: *Libraires étrangers 1619*
Arch. 498: *Libraires étrangers 1643–1656*
Arch. 521: *Varia, 16e-18e siècles*
Arch. 738: *Libraires d'Anvers* HH, *1629–1639*
Arch. 740: *Libraires d'Anvers* KK, *1644–1655*
Arch. 753: *Grand livre de Francfort, 1627–1638*
Arch. 754: *Grand livre de Francfort, 1630–1650*
Arch. 759: *Grand livre de Francfort, 1603–1614*
Arch. 760: *Grand livre de Francfort, 1615–1629*
Arch. 761: *Grand livre de Francfort, 1627–1638*
Arch. 762: *Grand livre de Francfort, 1596–1604*
Arch. 773: *Ouvriers 1617–1624*
Arch. 780: *Ouvriers 1622–1639*
Arch. 781: *Ouvriers 1640–1660*
Arch. 785: *Ouvriers 1610–1622*
Arch. 786: *Ouvriers 1590–1610*
Arch. 962: *Cahier de Francfort* (spring 1579)
Arch. 981: *Cahier de Francfort* (spring 1596)
Arch. 983: *Cahier de Francfort* (spring 1597)
Arch. 985: *Cahier de Francfort* (spring 1598)
Arch. 986: *Cahier de Francfort* (fall 1598)
Arch. 987: *Cahier de Francfort* (spring 1599)
Arch. 989: *Cahier de Francfort* (spring 1600)
Arch. 990: *Cahier de Francfort* (fall 1600)
Arch. 991: *Cahier de Francfort* (spring 1601)
Arch. 992: *Cahier de Francfort* (fall 1601)
Arch. 993: *Cahier de Francfort* (spring 1602)
Arch. 995: *Cahier de Francfort* (spring 1603)
Arch. 997: *Cahier de Francfort* (spring 1604)
Arch. 998: *Cahier de Francfort* (fall 1604)
Arch. 999: *Cahier de Francfort* (spring1605)
Arch. 1001: *Cahier de Francfort* (spring 1606)
Arch. 1003: *Cahier de Francfort* (spring 1607)
Arch. 1004: *Cahier de Francfort* (fall 1607)
Arch. 1009: *Cahier de Francfort* (fall 1610)
Arch. 1011: *Cahier de Francfort* (fall 1611)
Arch. 1012: *Cahier de Francfort* (spring 1612)
Arch. 1013: *Cahier de Francfort* (fall 1612)
Arch. 1014: *Cahier de Francfort* (spring 1613)
Arch. 1015: *Cahier de Francfort* (fall 1613)
Arch. 1016: *Cahier de Francfort* (spring 1614)
Arch. 1018: *Cahier de Francfort* (spring 1615)
Arch. 1019: *Cahier de Francfort* (fall 1615)
Arch. 1020: *Cahier de Francfort* (spring 1616)
Arch. 1021: *Cahier de Francfort* (fall 1616)
Arch. 1022: *Cahier de Francfort* (spring 1617)
Arch. 1023: *Cahier de Francfort* (fall 1617)
Arch. 1024: *Cahier de Francfort* (spring 1618)
Arch. 1030: *Cahier de Francfort* (spring 1621)
Arch. 1035: *Cahier de Francfort* (fall 1623)
Arch. 1036: *Cahier de Francfort* (spring 1624)
Arch. 1037: *Cahier de Francfort* (fall 1624)
Arch. 1040: *Cahier de Francfort* (spring 1626)
Arch. 1041: *Cahier de Francfort* (fall 1626)
Arch. 1044: *Cahier de Francfort* (spring 1628)
Arch. 1049: *Cahier de Francfort* (fall 1630)
Arch. 1050: *Cahier de Francfort* (spring 1631)
Arch. 1051: *Cahier de Francfort* (fall 1631)
Arch. 1052: *Cahier de Francfort* (spring 1639)
Arch. 1075: *Livre de caisse 1605–1617*
Arch. 1104: *Menues dépenses 1604–1713 1° 1604–1612*
Arch. 1105: *Menues dépenses 1604–1713 2° 1612–1621*
Arch. 1106: *Menues dépenses 1604–1713 3° 1621–1629*
Arch. 1107: *Menues dépenses 1604–1713 4° 1629–1643*
Arch. 1178: *Begrafenisrollen en Uitnoodigingen (1596–1710)*
L 636: *Gheboden … ende wt-gheroepen … der stadt van Antwerpen, opden xx. september 1613: Alsoo … verscheyden clachten zijn ghecomen … in't overheysschen van't port oft bode-loon vande brieven …* [Antwerp, heirs Jan Moretus I, 1613]
M 39: *Catalogue des éditions plantiniennes 1590–1651* (Denucé 1926, Arch. no. 1232)
M 296: *Catalogue d'éditions de Plantin et de ses contemporains, 1555–1593* (Denucé 1926, Arch. no. 1227)

Antwerp, Felix Archives (Municipal Archives)

CERT Certificatieboeken
GA Gilden en Ambachten
GF Genealogisch Fonds
IB Insolvente Boedelkamer
N Notariaat
PK Privilegiekamer – Rekwestboek Processen
PR Parochieregisters
SR Schepenregisters
WK Weeskamer

Secondary Sources

ADB
Allgemeine Deutsche Biographie, 56 vols. Berlin: Duncker und Humblot, 1875–1912.

Arents 2001
Arents, Prosper. *De bibliotheek van Pieter Pauwel Rubens: een reconstructie*, ed. by Alfons K.L.Thijs. Antwerp: Vereniging der Antwerpse Bibliofielen, 2001 (*De Gulden Passer*, 78–79).

Aspital 1980
Catalogue of the Pepys Library at Magdalene College Cambridge, vol. III, part 1: *Prints and Drawings*, compiled by A.W. Aspital, with an introduction by P.H. Hulton. Woodbridge, Suffolk: D.S. Brewer, and Totowa, NJ: Rowman and Littlefield, 1980.

Audenaert 2000
Audenaert, Willem. *Prosopographia Iesuitica Belgica Antiqua. A Biographical Dictionary of the Jesuits in the Low Countries 1542–1773*, 4 vols. Leuven-Heverlee: Filosofisch en Theologisch College, 2000.

Baroni-Sellink 2012
Baroni, Alessandra, and Manfred Sellink, eds. *Stradanus 1523–1605: Court Artist of the Medici*. Catalogue for the exhibition held at the Groeningemuseum, Bruges, 9 October 2008–4 January 2009. Turnhout: Brepols, 2012.

Bartsch 1808
Bartsch, Adam. *Le peintre graveur*, vol. VII. Vienna: De l'imprimerie de J. V. Degen, 1808.

Bassens and Van Grieken 2019
Bassens, Maarten, and Joris Van Grieken. *Bruegel in Black and White*. Catalogue for the exhibition held at the Royal Library, Brussels, 15 October 2019–16 February 2020. Brussels and Furnes: KBR and Hannibal Publishing, 2019.

Bécares Botas 1999
Bécares Botas, Vicente. *Arias Montano y Plantino. El libro flamenco en la España de Felipe II*. León: Universidad de León, Secretariado de Publicaciones, 1999.

Begheyn 2001
Begheyn, Paul. "The collection of copperplates by members of the Wierix family in the Jesuit church 'De Krijtberg' in Amsterdam", in: *Quaerendo*, 31 (2001), pp. 192–204.

Benzing 1953
Benzing, Josef. "Aubry, Johann", in: NDB, 1 (Berlin: Duncker und Humblot, 1953), p. 427.

Bergerfurth 2010
Bergerfurth, Yvonne. "Jesuitica im Historische Archiv der Stadt Köln", in: *Geschichte in Köln: Zeitschrift für Stadt- und Regionalgeschichte*, 57 (2010), pp. 39–56.

Bergerhausen 2010
Bergerhausen, Hans-Wolfgang. *Köln in einem eisernen Zeitalter, 1610–1686*. Cologne: Greven Verlag, 2010 (*Geschichte der Stadt Köln*, vol. 6, ed. by Werner Eck).

BN
Biographie nationale [de Belgique], 44 vols. Brussels: H. Thiry-Van Buggenhoudt, 1866–1986.

Boeheim 1888–1889
Boeheim, Wendelin. "Urkunden und Regesten aus der K. K. Hofbibliothek", in: *Jahrbuch der Kunsthistorischen Sammlungen des Allerhöchsten Kaiserhauses*, vol. 7 (Vienna, 1888), pp. ccxxvi–cccxii (no. 5556: "1596 Mai 30 Innsbruck. Inventari weilend der … erzherzog Ferdinanden zu Österreich etc."); and vol. 10 (Vienna, 1889), pp. i–x ("Biblioteca oder püecherkunstkammer").

Bogucka 1973
Bogucka, Maria. "Amsterdam and the Baltic in the First Half of the Seventeenth Century", in: *The Economic History Review* 26:3 (1973), pp. 433–447.

Booton, Nuovo, and Proot 2022
Booton, Diane E., Angela Nuovo, and Joran Proot, eds. *Competition in the European Book Market. Prices and privileges (fifteenth-seventeenth centuries)*, Antwerp: Vereniging der Antwerpse Bibliofielen, 2022 (*De Gulden Passer*, 100:2).

Bouchery and Van den Wijngaert 1941
Bouchery, Herman F., and Frans van den Wijngaert. *P.P. Rubens en het Plantijnsche huis*. Antwerp: De Sikkel and the Plantin-Moretus Museum, and Utrecht: Mij. W. de Haan N.V., 1941.

Bowen 1997
Bowen, Karen L. *Christopher Plantin's Books of Hours: Illustration and Production*. Nieuwkoop: De Graaf Publishers, 1997.

Bowen 2003
Bowen, Karen L. "Illustrating Books with Engravings: Plantin's Working Practices Revealed", in: *Print Quarterly*, 20:1 (2003), pp. 3–34.

Bowen 2004
Bowen, Karen L. "Declining wages for the printing of book illustrations: Arrangements between the Galle family of Printmakers and the Managers of the *Officina Plantiniana* in seventeenth-century Antwerp", in: *Doodgewoon: Mensen en hun dagelijks leven in de geschiedenis. Liber Amicorum Alfons K.L. Thijs*. Antwerp: Centrum voor Bedrijfsgeschiedenis, 2004 (*Bijdragen tot de Geschiedenis*, 87, nos. 1–2), pp. 63–85.

Bowen 2009
Bowen, Karen L., "Workshop Practices in Antwerp: The Galles", in: *Print Quarterly*, 26:2 (2009), pp. 123–42.

Bowen 2016
Bowen, Karen L. "Frans Hogenberg's Views of the Wars in the Low Countries", in: *Print Quarterly*, 33:2 (2016), pp. 156–59.

Bowen 2017
Bowen, Karen L. "Print Prices in Antwerp: Rubens and his Contemporaries", in: *Print Quarterly*, 34:3 (2017), pp. 282–97.

Bowen 2019
Bowen, Karen L. "Frankfurt in the Sixteenth Century. The Antwerp Plantin Press and the distribution of images", in: Kirch, Münch, and Stewart, 2019, pp. 66–77.

Bowen 2020
Bowen, Karen L. "Philips Galle's *Nova Reperta*: A Case Study in Print Prices and Distribution", in: *Renaissance Invention: Stradanus's Nova Reperta*, ed. by Lia Markey. Evanston: Northwestern University Press, 2020, pp. 41–54.

Bowen 2022a
Bowen, Karen L. "Hieronymus van Winghe and Collecting Prints from the Southern Netherlands in the Early Seventeenth Century", in: *Curieux d'estampes. Collections et collectionneurs de gravures en Europe (1500–1815)*, ed. by M. Grivel, V. Meyer, E. Leutrat, and P. Wachenheim. Rennes: Presses Universitaires de Rennes, 2022, pp. 35–48.

Bowen 2022b
Bowen, Karen L. "The Sadelers: From Printmakers to Booksellers", in: *Print Quarterly*, 39:4 (2022), pp. 3–19.

Bowen and Imhof 2008
Bowen, Karen L., and Dirk Imhof. *Christopher Plantin and Engraved Book Illustrations in Sixteenth-Century Europe*. Cambridge: Cambridge University Press, 2008.

Bowen and Imhof 2010
Bowen, Karen L., and Dirk Imhof. "Exchanges between friends and relatives, artists and their patrons: the Correspondence between Cornelis Galle I and II and Balthasar Moretus I", in: *In monte artium*, 3 (2010), pp. 89–113.

Bowen and Imhof 2019
Bowen, Karen L., and Dirk Imhof. "Publishing and Selling Jerónimo Nadal's Trend-Setting *Evangelicae historiae imagines* and *Adnotationes et meditationes in evangelia*: Dealings with the Moretuses, 1595–1645", in: *The Library*, 20 (September 2019), pp. 307–39.

Bowen and Imhof 2022
Bowen, Karen L., and Dirk Imhof. "The Rise and Fall of Charles de Mallery", in: *Print Quarterly*, 39:1 (2022), pp. 3–30.

Brakensiek 2003
Brakensiek, Stephan. *Vom "Theatrum mundi" zum "Cabinet des Estampes": das Sammeln von Druckgraphik in Deutschland 1565–1821*. Hildesheim: Olms, 2003.

Bruels 2005
Bruels, Erik. *Inpakken en wegwezen: de Officina Plantiniana op de Büchermesse van Frankfurt am Main (1589–1640)*, bachelor's thesis for the History Department of the University of Antwerp. Antwerp, 2005.

BT
Cockx-Indestege, Elly, and Geneviève Glorieux and Bart Op de Beeck. *Belgica typographica 1541–1600. Catalogus librorum impressorum ab anno MDXLI ad annum MDC in regionibus quae nunc regni Belgarum partes sunt*, 4 vols. Nieuwkoop: De Graaf, 1968–1994.

Burger 1931
Burger, C. P. Jr. "De Amsterdamsche uitgever Cornelis Claesz (1578–1609)", in: *De Gulden Passer*, 9 (1931), pp. 59–68.

Bury 1985
Bury, Michael. "The Taste for Prints in Italy to c. 1600", in: *Print Quarterly*, 2:1 (March 1985), pp. 12–26.

Bury 2001
Bury, Michael. *The Print in Italy 1550–1620*. London: The British Museum Press, 2001.

Bury 2005
Bury, Michael. "Infringing Privileges and Copying in Rome, c. 1600", in: *Print Quarterly*, 22:2 (June 2005), pp. 133–38.

Carrara and Gregory 2000
Carrara, Eliana, and Gregory Sharon. "Borghini's Print Purchases from Giunti", in: *Print Quarterly*, 17:1 (2000), pp. 3–17.

Chaix 2021
Chaix, Gérald. *Köln in Zeitalter von Reformation und katholischer Reform, 1512/13–1610*, trans. by Ursula Vones-Liebenstein. Cologne: Greven Verlag, 2021 (*Geschichte der Stadt Köln*, vol. 5, ed by Werner Eck).

Cock 2013
Van Grieken, Joris, and Ger Luijten and Jan Van der Stock, eds. *Hieronymus Cock. The Renaissance in Print*. Brussels: Mercatorfonds, 2013.

Colin and Nixon 1966
Colin, Georges, and Howard M. Nixon. "La question des reliures de Plantin", in: *Studia bibliographica in honorem Herman de la Fontaine Verwey*. Amsterdam: Menno Hertzberger, 1966, pp. 58–9.

Corr. and Corr. supplement
Rooses, Max, and Jan Denucé, eds. *Correspondance de Christophe Plantin*, 9 vols. Antwerp: De Groote Boekhandel and 's Gravenhage: Martinus Nijhoff, 1883–1918; and Van Durme, M., ed. *Supplément* à la correspondance de Christophe Plantin. Antwerp: De Nederlandsche Boekhandel, 1955 (reprint: Nendeln, Liechenstein: Kraus, 1968).

Corsten 1985
Corsten, Severin. "Kölner Drucker und Verleger in Antwerpen (15. und 16. Jahrhundert)", in: *Liber Amicorum Leon Voet*, ed. by Francine de Nave. Antwerp: Vereeniging der Antwerpsche Bibliophielen, 1985, pp. 189–204. (*De Gulden Passer*, nos. 61–63)

Crailsheim 2016
Crailsheim, Eberhard. *The Spanish Connection: French and Flemish Merchant Networks in Seville (1570–1650)*. Cologne: Böhlau Verlag, 2016 (*Wirtschafts- und Sozialhistorische Studien*, 19).

Dadson 1983
Dadson, Trevor J. *The Genoese in Spain: Gabriel Bocangel y Unzueta (1603–1658). A Biography*. London: Tamesis Books, 1983.

Dávila Pérez 2002
Dávila Pérez, Antonio, ed. *Benito Arias Montano Correspondencia conservada en el Museo Plantin-Moretus de Amberes*, 2 vols. Madrid: Alcañiz, 2002.

Dávila Pérez 2010
Dávila Pérez, Antonio. "Lezers, boeken en lectuur van een humanistenkring in de zestiende eeuw. Boekbestellingen door Arias Montano en zijn Sevilliaanse vrienden", in: *De Gulden Passer* 88:1 (2010), pp. 7–119.

Davis 1957
Davis, Natalie Zemon. "Christophe Plantin's Childhood at Saint Just", in: *De Gulden Passer* 35 (1957), pp. 107–20.

DBS
De Backer, A., and C. Sommervogel. *Bibliothèque de la Compagnie de Jésus*, 12 vols. Brussels: Oscar Schepens – Paris: Alphonse Picard, 1890–1932.

De Jong and De Groot 1988
De Jong, Marijnke, and Irene de Groot. *Ornamentprenten in het Rijksprentenkabinet, I: 15de & 16de eeuw*. The Hague: Staatsuitgeverij, 1988.

Delen 1924–35
Delen, A.J.J. *Histoire de la gravure dans les anciens Pays-Bas & dans les provinces belges des origines jusqu'à la fin du XVIIIe siècle*, 3 vols. Paris: Editions d'art et d'histoire, 1924–1935 (vol. I: *Des origines à 1500* (1924); vol. II.1: *Le XVIe siècle: Les graveurs-illustrateurs* (1934); vol. II.2: *Le XVIe siècle: Les graveurs d'estampes* (1935)) (reprint: Paris: F. de Nobele, 1969, 3 vols. in 1).

Delen 1932
Delen, A.J.J. "Christoffel Plantin als prenthandelaar", in: *De Gulden Passer*, 10 (1932), pp. 1–24, and, for essentially the same text in French: Delen, A.J.J. *Histoire de la gravure dans les anciens Pays-Bas et dans les provinces belges des origines jusqu'à la fin du XVIIIe siècle*, vol. II:2. Paris, Editions d'art et d'histoire, 1935, pp. 149–170.

Denucé 1912–1913
Denucé, Jan. *Oud-Nederlandsche kaartmakers in betrekking met Plantijn*, 2 vols. Antwerp: De Nederlandsche Boekhandel, and The Hague: Martinus Nijhoff, 1912–1913 (*Uitgaven der Antwerpsche bibliophielen*, nos. 27 and 28).

Denucé 1926
Denucé, Jan. *Inventaris op het Plantijnsch Archief. Inventaire des Archives Plantiniennes*. Antwerp: De Sikkel, 1926.

Denucé 1927
Denucé, Jan. "Prentenhandel Theodoor Galle en Catharina Moerentorf. Inventaris van 1636", in: *Antwerpsch archievenblad*, 2nd series, 2:2 (April 1927), pp. 1–16.

Denucé 1934
Denucé, Jan. *Brieven en documenten betreffend Jan Bruegel I en II, Bronnen voor de geschiedenis van de Vlaamsche Kunst*, III. Antwerp: De Sikkel, and The Hague: Martinus Nijhoff, 1934.

De Pauw-De Veen 1975
De Pauw-De Veen, Lydia. "Archivalische gegevens over Volcxken Diercx, weduwe van Hieronymus Cock", in: *Bijdragen tot de geschiedenis van de grafische kunst opgedragen aan Prof. Dr. Louis Lebeer ter gelegenheid van zijn tachtigste verjaardag*. Antwerp: Vereeniging der Antwerpsche Bibliophielen, 1975, pp. 215–47 (*De Gulden Passer*, 53).

De Ramaix 1989
De Ramaix, Isabelle. "Les Sadeler: de damasquineur à graveur et marchand d'estampes: quelques documents inédits", in: *Le livre et l'estampe*, 35 (1989), no. 131, pp. 7–46.

De Ramaix 1992
De Ramaix, Isabelle. *Graveurs en uitgevers Sadeler / Les Sadeler: graveurs et éditeurs*. Catalogue for the exhibition held at the Royal Library of Belgium, Brussels, 14 February-28 March 1992.

De Ramaix 1997–2014
De Ramaix, Isabelle. *The Illustrated Bartsch*, vols. 70–73. New York: Abaris Books, 1997–2014.

De Vlieger-De Wilde 2004
De Vlieger-De Wilde, Koen, ed. *Adresboek van zeventiende-eeuwse drukkers, uitgevers en boekverkopers in Vlaanderen / Directory of seventeenth-century Printers, Publishers and Booksellers in Flanders*. Antwerp: Antwerpse Bibliofielen, 2004.

Diels 2005
Diels, Ann. *'Wat d'yser can bemaelen': prenten van de Antwerpse graveursfamilie Collaert (1550–1630)*. Catalogue for the exhibition held at the Royal Library of Belgium, Brussels, 25 February-9 April 2005.

Diels 2009
Diels, Ann. *The Shadow of Rubens: Print Publishing in 17th-Century Antwerp. Prints by the history painters Abraham van Diepenbeeck, Cornelis Schut and Erasmus Quellinus* II, trans. by Irene Schaudies and Michael Hoyle. London and Turnhout: Harvey Miller Publishers, 2009

Diels 2010
Diels, Ann. *De familie Collaert (ca. 1555–1630) en de prentkunst in Antwerpen*. Brussels: Archief- en Bibliotheekwezen in België, 2010 (*Archives et bibliothèques de Belgique / Association des archivistes et bibliothécaires de Belgique*, 88).

Dietz, 1910–1921
Dietz, Alexander. *Frankfurter Handelsgeschichte*, 3 vols. Frankfurt am Main: Hermann Minjon, 1910–1921.

Du Cerceau 2010
Guillaume, Jean, and Peter Fuhring, eds. *Jacques Androuet du Cerceau: "un des plus grands architectes qui se soient jamais trouvés en France"*. Paris: Picard/Le Passage/Cité de l'architecture et du patrimoine, 2010.

Dudok van Heel 1975
Dudok van Heel, S.A.C. "Honderdvijftig advertenties van kunstverkopingen uit veertig jaargangen van de Amsterdamsche Courant 1672–1711", in: *Jaarboek Amstelodamum* 67 (1975), pp. 149–73.

Duroselle-Melish and Lines 2015
Duroselle-Melish, Caroline, and David A. Lines. "The Library of Ulisse Aldrovandi (†1605): Acquiring and Organizing Books in Sixteenth-Century Bologna", in: *The Library*, 7th series, 16:2 (June 2015), pp. 133–61.

Dutuit 1885 / 1972
Dutuit, Eugène. *Manuel de l'amateur d'estampes*, vol. VI: *Écoles flamande et hollandaise*, tome III. Paris : A. Lévy and London : Dulau, 1885 (reprint: Amsterdam: G.W. Hissink & Co., 1972, vol. IV).

Duverger 1984–2009
Duverger, Erik. *Antwerpse kunstinventarissen uit de zeventiende eeuw*, 14 vols. Brussels: Koninklijke Academie voor Wetenschappen, Letteren en Schone Kunsten van België, 1984–2009 (*Fontes historiae artis Neerlandicae. Bronnen voor de kunstgeschiedenis van de Nederlanden*, 1).

Duverger 1990–1991
Duverger, Erik. "Le graveur et marchand imagier anversois Michael Snyders (1586–1673)", in: *Gentse bijdragen tot de kunstgeschiedenis en oudheidkunde*, 29 (1990–1991), pp. 91–116.

Duverger and Maufort 1999
Duverger, Erik, and Danielle Maufort. "The cast for the production of Van Dyck prints", in: *Anthony van Dyck as a printmaker*, ed. by Carl Depauw and Ger Luijten. New York: Rizzoli, 1999, pp. 366–90 (Catalogue for the exhibition *Van Dyck – a gifted engraver* held at the Museum Plantin-Moretus – Stedelijk Prentenkabinet, Antwerp, 15 May–22 August 1999; and Rijksmuseum, Rijksprentenkabinet, Amsterdam, 9 October 1999–9 January 2000).

Eitel 1996
Eitel, Peter. "Truchsess Max Willibald, der Bergründer des Kupferstichkabinetts auf Schloss Wolfegg", in: *Von Schongauer zu Rembrandt: Meisterwerke der Druckgraphik aus der Sammlung der Fürsten zu Waldburg-Wolfegg*, ed. by Bernd W. Mayer. Ravensburg: Verlag Gerd Hatje, 1996, pp. 21–30.

Enderle 2000
Enderle, Wilfried. "Die Buchdrucker der Reichsstadt Köln und die katholische Publizistik zwischen 1555 und 1648", in: *Köln als Kommunicationszentrum*, ed. by Georg Mölich and Gerd Schwerhoff. Cologne: Dumont, 2000, pp. 167–82.

Ewing 1990
Ewing, Dan. "Marketing Art in Antwerp, 1460–1560: Our Lady's Pand", in: *The Art Bulletin*, 72:4 (December 1990), pp. 558–84.

Fiamminghi a Roma 1995
Fiamminghi a Roma, 1508–1608: artistes des Pays-Bas et de la principauté de Liège à Rome à la Renaissance, ed. by Anne-Claire de Liedekerke. Catalogue for the exhibition held at the Palais des beaux-arts, Brussels, 24 February–21 May 1995; and Palazzo delle esposizioni, Rome, 7 June–4 September 1995. Brussels: Société des expositions du Palais des beaux-arts, 1995.

Filedt Kok, Hinterding, and Van der Waals 1994
Filedt Kok, J.P., and Erik Hinterding and Jan van der Waals. "Jan Harmensz. Muller as Printmaker – II", in: *Print Quarterly*, 11:4 (1994), pp. 351–78.

Fletcher, Glinsman, and Oltrogge 2009
Fletcher, Shelley, and Lisha Glinsman and Doris Oltrogge. "The Pigmnets on Hand-Colored Fifteenth-Century Relief Prints from the Collections of the National Gallery of Art and the Germanisches Nationalmuseum", in: *The Woodcut in Fifteenth-Century Europe*, ed. by Peter Parshall New Haven and London: Yale University Press, 2009, pp. 277–97 (*Studies in the History of Art*, 75, Center for Advanced Study in the Visual Arts, Symposium Papers LII, held at the National Gallery of Art).

Fleury 1969
Fleury, Marie-Antoinette. *Documents du Minutier Central concernant les peintres, les sculpteurs et les graveurs au XVIIe siècle (1600–1650)*, vol. I. Paris: S.E.V.P.E.N., 1969.

Flood 2007
Flood, John L. "'Omnium totius orbis emporiorum compendium': the Frankfurt Fair in the Early Modern Period", in: *Fairs, Markets and the Itinerant Book Trade*, ed. by Robin Myers, Michael Harris, and Giles Mandelbrote. New Castle, Delaware: Oak Knoll Press, and London: The British Library, 2007, pp. 1–42.

Fuhring 2010
Fuhring, Peter. "Jean Nicolas de Tralage: la documentation d'un collectionneur d'estampes au XVIIe siècle", in: *L'Estampe au Grand Siècle. Études offertes à Maxime Préaud*. Paris: École nationale des chartes and Bibliothèque nationale de France, 2010, pp. 515–38 (*Matériaux pour l'histoire publiés par l'École des chartes*, 9).

Fuhring 2017
Fuhring, Peter. "The stocklist of Joannes Galle, print publisher of Antwerp, and print sales from old copperplates in the seventeenth century", in: *Simiolus: Netherlands quarterly for the history of art*, 39:3 (2017), pp. 225–309.

Garstein 1963
Garstein, Oskar. *Rome and the Counter-Reformation in Scandinavia until the establishment of the S. Congregatio de Propaganda Fide in 1622*. Oslo: Universitetsførlaget, 1963.

Gaskell 1972
Gaskell, Philip. *A New Introduction to Bibliography*. New York – Oxford: Oxford University Press, 1972 (reprint: New Castle, Delaware: Oak Knoll Press, 1995).

Gelderblom 2000
Gelderblom, Oscar. *Zuid-Nederlandse kooplieden en de opkomst van de Amsterdamse stapelmarkt (1578–1630)*. Hilversum: Verloren, 2000.

Génard 1859
Génard, P. "Les grandes familles artistiques d'Anvers", in: *Revue d'histoire et d'archéologie*, 1 (1859), Galles: pp. 194–201.

Gerard 1996
Gerard, Robert A. "Woutneel, de Passe and the Anglo-Netherlandish Print Trade", in: *Print Quarterly*, 13:4 (1996), pp. 363–76.

Gier and Janota 1997
Gier, Helmut, and Johannes Janota. *Augsburger Buchdruck und Verlagswesen: von den Anfängen bis zur Gegenwart*. Wiesbaden: Harrassowitz Verlag, 1997 (reissue).

González de Zárate 1992–1996
González de Zárate, Jesús María, ed. *Real colección de estampas de San Lorenzo de El Escorial*, 10 vols. Vitoria-Gasteiz: Instituto Municipal de Estudios Iconográficos Ephialte, 1992–1996.

Griffiths 1989
Griffiths, Antony. "The Print Collection of Cassiano dal Pozzo [1588–1657]", in: *Print Quarterly*, 6:1 (1989), pp. 2–10.

Griffiths 2016
Griffiths, Antony. *The Print before Photography: An Introduction to European Printmaking, 1550–1820*. London: The British Museum, 2016.

Grivel 1986
Grivel, Marianne. *Le commerce de l'estampe à Paris au 17e siècle*. Geneva: Droz, 1986 (*Histoire et civilisation du livre*, 16).

Grotesken 2019
Grotesken : een fascinerende fantasiewereld / Grotesques: fantasy portrayed. Catalogue for the exhibition held at the Museum Plantin-Moretus, Antwerp, 5 April-15 September 2019. Kontich : BAI, 2019.

Hänsel 1991
Hänsel, Sylvaine. *Der Spanische Humanist Benito Arias Montano (1572–1598) und die Kunst*. Münster: Aschendorffsche Verlagsbuchhandlung, 1991.

Harreld 2004
Harreld, Donald J. *High Germans in the Low Countries: German Merchants and Commerce in Golden Age Antwerp*. Leiden-Boston: Brill, 2004.

Hartig 1917
Hartig, Otto. *Die Gründung der Münchner Hofbibliothek durch Albrecht V. und Johann Jacob Fugger*. Munich: Verlag der Königlich Bayerischen Akademie der Wissenschaften, 1917 (*Abhandlung der Königlich Bayerischen Akademie der Wissenschaften Philosophisch-philologische und historische Klasse*, vol. XXVII, 3. Abhandlung).

Haskell and Griffiths 1993
The Paper Museum of Cassiano dal Pozzo, with introductory remarks by Francis Haskell and Antony Griffiths. London: The British Museum, 1993 (*Quaderni Puteani*, 4).

Heitjan 1975
Heitjan, Isabel. "Kaspar und Georg Förster, Buchhändler und Verleger zu Danzig im 17. Jahrhundert: ihre Geschäftsverbindung mit Antwerpen und Bibliographie ihrer Verlagswerke", in: *Archiv für Geschichte des Buchwesens*, 15:2 (1975), cols. 337–434.

Hensen 1916
Hensen, A.H.L. "Nederlanders op het eind der zestiende eeuw in de catacombe van Domitilla", in: *De katholiek: godsdienstig, geschied- en letterkundig maandschrift* 149 (1916), pp. 410–23.

Hernad 1990
Hernad, Béatrice. *Die Graphiksammlung des Humanisten Hartmann Schedel*, Catalogue for the exhibition held at the Bavarian State Library, Munich, June 20–Sept. 15, 1990. Munich: Prestel, 1990 (*Ausstellungskatalog*, 52).

Hessels 1887
Hessels, J.H. *Abrahami Ortelii (geographi Antverpiensis) et virorvm ervditorvm ad evndem et ad Jacobvm Colivm Ortelianvm (Abrahami Ortelii sororis filivm) epistvlae*. Cambridge: Typis Academiae, 1887.

Hildebrand, 1945–1956
Hildebrand, P. *De kapucijnen in de Nederlanden en het prinsbisdom Luik*, 10 vols. Antwerp: Archief der Kapucijnen, 1945–1956.

Holl. Dutch & Flemish
(see also under New Holl.)
F. W. Hollstein. *Dutch & Flemish Etchings, Engravings and Woodcuts, ca. 1450–1700*. Amsterdam: Menno Hertzberger, 1949–1964; Amsterdam: Van Gendt & Co., 1974–1987; Roosendaal: Koninklijke van Poll, 1988–1994; Rotterdam, Sound & Vision Publishers, 1995–2004; Ouderkerk aan den Ijssel: Sound & Vision Publishers, 2005–2010.
- vol. III (1957) (including Jan Boel).
- vol. VII (1952) (including Ambrosius Francken, Marcus Gheeraerts, and Nicolas van Hoey).
- vol. IX (1953) (including Pieter van der Heyden).
- vol. XIV (1956) (including Abraham van Merlen).
- vols. XXI–XXII (1980): Sadelers, compiled by Dieuwke de Hoop Scheffer, ed. by K.G. Boon.
- vol. XXVII (1983) (including Michael Snijders).
- vol. XXVIII (1984) (including Lambert Suavius).
- vol. XXXII (1988) (including Otto van Veen).
- vol. XLII (1993) (including Alexander Voet).
- vol. XLIII (1993) (including Lucas Vorsterman).
- vols. XLIV–XLVI (1995–1996): Maarten de Vos (1 vol. text, then plates in two "parts"), compiled by Christiaan Schuckman, ed. by D. De Hoop Scheffer.
- vols. XLVII and XLVIII (1997): Vredeman de Vries, compiled by Peter Fuhring, ed. by Ger Luijten.
- vols. LIX–LXIX (2003–2004): Wierix family. Independent prints, compiled by Zsuzsanna van Ruyven-Zemen, in collaboration with Marjolein Leesberg, ed. by Jan van der Stock and Marjolein Leesberg.
- vols. LXX–LXXI (2006–2007), Wierix family. Book illustrations, parts I and II, compiled by Harriet Stroomberg, ed. by Jan van der Stock.

Hommel 2012
Hommel, K. "'…die ohnehin mehr eingebildeten als reellen Preise der Kunstsachen…': ein Beitrag über die Frühgeschichte des Leipziger Kunsthandels", in: *Leipziger Stadtgeschichte: Jahrbuch*, ed. by M. Cottin et al., 2012, pp. 55–82.

Imhof 1996
Imhof, Dirk, ed. *The Illustration of Books Published by the Moretuses*. Catalogue for the exhibition held at the Plantin-Moretus Museum, Antwerp, 19 October 1996–17 January 1997. Antwerp: 1996.

Imhof 2001
Imhof, Dirk. "Return my woodblocks at one: dealings between the Antwerp publisher Balthasar Moretus and the London bookseller Richard Whitacker in the seventeenth century", in: *The Bookshop of the World. The role of the Low Countries in the book-trade 1473–1941*, ed. by Lotte Hellinga, Alastair Duke, Jacob Harskamp, and Theo Hermans. 't Goy-Houten: HES & De Graaf, 2001, pp. 179–90.

Imhof 2009
Imhof, Dirk. "De Plantijnse uitgeverij onder Balthasar II Moretus (1641–1674): een vergelijking met het uitgeversfonds van zijn grootvader Jan I Moretus (1589–1610)", in: *Jaarboek van de Nederlandse Vereniging voor Boekgeschiedenis*, 16 (2009), pp. 13–129.

Imhof 2014a
Imhof, Dirk. *Jan Moretus and the Continuation of the Plantin Press: A Bibliography of the Works published and printed by Jan Moretus I in Antwerp (1589–1610)*, 2 vols. Leiden: Brill, 2014.

Imhof 2014b
Imhof, Dirk. "An Author's Wishes versus a Publisher's Possibilities: The Illustration of Thomas Sailly's Prayer Books Printed by the Plantin Press in Antwerp c. 1600", in: *Illustrated Religious Texts in the North of Europe, 1500–1800*, ed. by Feike Dietz, Adam Morton, Lien Roggen et al. Farnham: Ashgate, 2014, pp. 205–20.

Imhof 2015
Imhof, Dirk. "Arias Montanus' voorstelling van de tempel in Jeruzalem: de aankoop van een zeldzame prent uitgegeven door Plantijn in 1576 en 1578", in: *De Gulden Passer*, 93:2 (2015), pp. 240–47.

Imhof 2016
Imhof, Dirk. "*Three Future Cologne Publishers as Apprentices in Antwerp: Bernhard Wolters, Johann Kinckius and Cornelis van Egmont", in: The Library*, seventh series, 17:1 (2016), pp. 3–27.

Imhof 2018a
Imhof, Dirk. "The Trade in Individual Maps from Ortelius's *Theatrum orbis terrarum* after 1612", in: *Imago mundi*, 70:1 (2018), pp. 52–64.

Imhof 2018b
Imhof, Dirk. "*The Plantin Book Trade and the Supply of Art Objects to the Spanish Elite", in: Netherlandish Art and Luxury Goods in Renaissance Spain*, ed. by Daan Van Heesch, Robrecht Janssen, and Jan Van der Stock. Turnhout: Brepols, 2018, pp. 107–21.

Imhof 2018c
Imhof, Dirk. "'Ex arte et decore typographica': Balthasar Moretus I, publisher of Baroque books", in: *Balthasar Moretus and the Passion of Publishing*, ed. by Dirk Imhof. Antwerp: Museum Plantin-Moretus, and Kontich: BAI, 2018, pp. 10–28.

Imhof 2020a
Imhof, Dirk. "The enterprising Mynken Liefrinck: coloring, printing and selling maps and prints in sixteenth-century Antwerp", in: *Simiolus: Netherlands quarterly for the history of art*, 42:3/4 (2020), pp. 220–40.

Imhof 2020b
Imhof, Dirk. "Joannes David's Emblem Books: Successful Co-operative Ventures between the Galle Print Workshop and the Moretus Press", in: *El Sol de Occidente. Sociedad, textos, imágenes simbólicas e interculturalidad*, ed. by Carme López Calderón and Juan Manuel Monterroso Montero. Santiago de Compostela: Andavira Editora and Universidade de Santiago de Compostela, 2020, pp. 580–600.

Imhof 2021
Imhof, Dirk. "The Problematic Sales of the Spanish Ortelius Atlas after 1612", in: *Quaerendo*, 51:4 (2021), pp. 331–47.

Imhof 2022
Imhof, Dirk. "Christoffel Plantijn en zijn handel in kaarten: van uitgever tot tussenpersoon", in: *Atlas amicorum Peter van der* Krogt, ed. by Paula Van Gestel-van het Schip. Leiden-Boston: Brill, 2022, pp. 376–83.

Imhof 2023a
Imhof, Dirk. "Petrus Biverus's Sacrum Oratorium and Sacrum Sanctuarium (Antwerp, 1634): Balthasar Moretus's Preference for Pearls over Glass", in: *The Library*, seventh series, 24:2 (June 2023), pp. 115–40.

Imhof 2023b
Imhof, Dirk. "Managing Misprints: Jan Moretus I's Diverse Approaches to Correcting Errors", in: *Printing and Misprinting. A Companion to Mistakes and In-House Corrections in Renaissance Europe (1450–1650)*, ed. by Geri Della Rocca de Candal, Anthony Grafton, and Paolo Sachet. Oxford: Oxford University Press, 2023, pp. 198–212.

Imhof 2025
Imhof, Dirk. "Advantages and Disadvantages of a Family Enterprise: The Plantin-Moretus Press in the First Half of the Seventeenth Century", forthcoming in 2025.

Jansen 1997
Jansen, Dirk Jacob. "Antiquarian Drawings and Prints as Collector's Items", in: *Journal of the History of Collections*, 6:2 (1994), pp. 181–88.

Jones 2010
Jones, Malcom. *The Print in Early Modern England: An Historical Oversight*. New Haven and London: Yale University Press, 2010.

Kamen 2019
Kamen, Henry. *The Escorial*. New Haven: Yale University Press, 2019.

Kammerer 2017
Estienne, Henri. *Nundinarum Francofordiensium encomium*, introduction and general ed. by Elsa Kammerer. Geneva: Droz, 2017.

Kapp 1886
Kapp, Friedrich. *Geschichte des Deutschen Buchhandels bis in das siebzehnte Jahrhundert*. Leipzig: Verlag des Börsenvereins der Deutschen Buchhändler, 1886.

Keussen 1907–1908
Keussen, Hermann. "Die drei Reisen des Utrechters Arnoldus Buchelius nach Deutschland, insbesondere sein Kölner Aufenthalt", in: *Annalen des Historischen Vereins für den Niederrhein*, 84 (1907), pp. 1-102; and 85 (1908), pp. 43–114.

Kirch, Münch, and Stewart, 2019
Hall Kirch, Miriam, Birgit Ulrike Münch, and Alison G. Stewart, eds. *Crossroads: Frankfurt am Main as Market for Northern Art 1500–1800*. Petersberg: Imhof Verlag, 2019.

Kirchhoff 1889
Kirchhoff, Albrecht. "Beitrag zur Geschichte des Kunsthandels auf der Leipziger Messe", in: *Archiv für Geschichte des Deutschen Buchhandels*, 12 (1889), pp. 178–200.

Koch 1991
Koch, Rainer, ed. *Brücke zwischen den Völkern: zur Geschichte der Frankfurter Messe*, 3 vols. Frankfurt am Main: Historisches Museum, 1991.

Laeven 1992
Laeven, A.H. "The Frankfurt and Leipzig Book Fairs and the History of the Dutch Trade in the Seventeenth and Eighteenth Centuries", in: *Le magasin de l'univers: The Dutch Republic as the Centre of the European Book Trade*, ed. by C. Berkvens-Stevelinck, H. Bots, P.G. Hoftijzer, and O.S. Lankhorst. Leiden: E. J. Brill, 1992, pp. 185–97 (*Brill's Studies in Intellectual History*, 31).

Landau and Parshall 1994
Landau, David, and Peter Parshall. *The Renaissance Print, 1470–1550*. New Haven and London: Yale University Press, 1994.

Lauwaert 1972–1973
Lauwaert, Raf. "De handelsbedrijvigheid van de Officina Plantiniana op de Büchermessen te Frankfurt am Main in de XVIe eeuw", in: *De Gulden Passer*, 50 (1972), pp. 124–80; and 51 (1973), pp. 70–105.

Leesberg 2015
Leesberg, Marjolein. "*El Juego Real de Cupido*: a Spanish board game published in Antwerp, c. 1620", in: *Delineavit et Sculpsit*, 39 (October 2015), pp. 23–44.

Lehmann 1956–1960
Lehmann, Paul. *Eine Geschichte der alten Fuggerbibliotheken*, 2 vols. Tübingen: J.C.B. Mohr, 1956 and 1960 (*Studien zur Fuggergeschichte*, 12).

Lemmens and Thijs 2006
Lemmens, Filip, and Alfons K.L. Thijs. "Van 'cunst' tot populair beeldmateriaal Van Merlen: Twee eeuwen prentenproductie te Antwerpen (1600-circa 1830)", in: *Liber memorialis Erik Duverger: Bijdragen tot de kunstgeschiedenis van de Nederlanden*, ed. by Henri Pauwels, André Van den Kerkhove, and Leo Wuyts. Wetteren: Universa, 2006, pp. 91–129.

Lepape 2017
Lepape, Séverine. "The production of prints in France at the time of Hieronymus Cock", in: *Simiolus: Netherlands quarterly for the history of art*, 39:3 (2017), pp. 215–24.

Lombaerde 2002
Lombaerde, Piet, ed., *The Reception of P.P. Rubens's Palazzi di Genova during the 17th Century in Europe: Questions and Problems*. Turnhout: Brepols, 2002 (*Architectura Moderna*, 1).

Luijten 1996
Luijten, Ger. "Frills and furbelows: satires on fashion and pride around 1600", in: *Simiolus: Netherlands quarterly for the history of art*, 24:2/3 (1996), pp. 140–60.

M-H Wierix 1978–1982
Mauquoy-Hendrickx, Marie. *Les estampes des Wierix*, 3 vols. in 4 parts. Brussels: The Royal Library, 1978–1982.

Maclean 2012
Maclean, Ian. *Scholarship, Commerce, Religion. The Learned Book in the Age of Confessions, 1560–1630*. Cambridge, MA: Harvard University Press, 2012.

Manrique Figueroa 2019
Manrique Figueroa, César. *El libro flamenco para lectores novohispanos: una historia internacional de comercio y consumo libresco*. Mexico City: Universidad Nacional Autónoma de México, 2019.

Marolles 1666
De Marolles, Michel. *Catalogue de livres d'estampes et de figures en taille douce, avec un dénombrement des pièces qui y sont contenues fait à Paris en l'année 1666 par M. de Marolles Abbé de Villeloin*. Paris: F. Léonard, 1666.

Martin 1988
Martin, Henri-Jean. *Histoire et pouvoirs de l'écrit*. Paris: Perrin, 1988.

Mayer and Falk 2003
Mayer, Bernd M., and Tilman Falk. *Europäische Meisterzeichnungen aus der Sammlung der Fürsten zu Waldburg-Wolfegg*. Münsterschwarzach, 2003.

Mayerhofer 2011
Mayerhofer, Matthias. *Kupferstiche im Dienst politischer Propaganda: die "Bavaria Sancta et Pia" des pater Matthäus Rader SJ*. Munich: Kommission für Bayerische Landesgeschichte, 2011.

McDonald 1998
McDonald, Mark P. "The Print Collection of Philip II at the Escorial", in: *Print Quarterly*, 15:1 (1998), pp. 15–35.

McDonald 2004
McDonald, Mark P. *The Print Collection of Ferdinand Columbus (1488–1539): A Renaissance Collector in Seville*. London, British Museum Press, 2004.

Meadow 2002
Meadow, Mark A. "Merchants and Marvels: Hans Jacob Fugger [active ca. 1550s-70s] and the Origins of the Wunderkammer", in: *Merchants and Marvels: Commerce, Science, and Art in Early Modern Europe*, ed. by Pamela H. Smith and Paula Findlen. London: Routledge, 2002, pp. 182–200.

Meadow and Robertson 2013
Meadow, Mark A., and Bruce Robertson, trans. and ed. *The First Treatise on Museums: Samuel Quiccheberg's Inscriptiones, 1565*. Los Angeles: Getty Research Institute Publications, 2013.

Meganck 2017
Meganck, Tine Luk. *Erudite Eyes: Friendship, Art and Erudition in the Network of Abraham Ortelius (1527–1598)*. Leiden and Boston: Brill, 2017 (*Studies in Netherlandish Art and Cultural History*, 14).

Melion 2022
Melion, Walter. "Jesus, Mary, and Joseph as Artisans of the Heart and Home in Manuscript MPM R 35 'Vita S. Joseph beatissimae Virginis sponsi' of ca. 1600", in: *Early Modern Privacy: Sources and Approaches*, ed. by Michaël Green, Lars Cyril Nørgaard, and Mette Birkedal Bruun. Leiden: Brill, 2022, pp. 317–63 (*Intersections*, 78).

Merlo 1966
Merlo, Johann Jacob. *Kölnische Künstler in alter und neuer Zeit*. Nieuwkoop: B. De Graaf, 1966. Reprint of: Johann Jacob Merlo, *Nachrichten von dem Leben und den Werken Kölnische Künstler*, ed. and expanded by Eduard Firmenich-Richartz and Hermann Keussen. Düsseldorf: L. Schwann, 1895.

Messkataloge 1972–2001
Fabian, Bernhard, ed. *Die Messkataloge des sechzehnten Jahrhunderts. Die Messkataloge Georg Willers*, 5 vols. Hildesheim: Georg Olms Verlag, 1972–2001.

Meurer 1988
Meurer, Peter H. *Atlantes Colonienses. Die Kölner Schule der Atlaskartographie 1570–1610*. Bad Neustadt a.d. Saale: Verlag Dietrich Pfaehler, 1988.

Meurer 1993
Meurer, Peter H. "Der Nürnberger Verlag Caymox und die Kartographie", in: *Quaerendo* 23 (1993), pp. 24–43.

Meurer 2001
Meurer, Peter H. "The Cologne map publisher Peter Overadt (fl. 1590–1652)", in: *Imago Mundi*, 53:1 (2001), pp. 28–45.

Meyer 2015
Meyer, Véronique. "Collectors and Collecting Prints", in: *A Kingdom of Images: French Prints in the Age of Louis XIV, 1660–1715*, ed. by Peter Fuhring, Louis Marchesano, Rémi Mathis, and Vanessa Selbach. Los Angeles: Getty Research Institute and Paris: Bibliothèque nationale de France, 2015, pp. 36–44.

NDB
Neue Deutsche Biographie, 27 vols., ed. by Fritz Wagner and Karl Otmar et al. Berlin: Duncker & Humblot, 1953– (2nd edition: 1971–).

New Holl.
(see also under Holl. Dutch & Flemish)
The New Hollstein Dutch & Flemish Etchings, Engravings, and Woodcuts, 1450–1700 (Roosendaal: Koninklijke van Poll, 1993–1994; Rotterdam: Sound & Vision Publishers, 1995–2004; Ouderkerk aan den Ijssel: Sound & Vision Publishers, 2005-).

New Holl. Van der Borcht
New. Holl., Peeter van der Borcht (2004), compiled by Hans and Ursula Mielke, ed. by Ger Luijten.

New Holl. de Bruijn
New Holl., Abraham de Bruijn (2017), 2 vols., compiled by Ursula Mielke, ed. by Ger Luijten.

New Holl. Collaert
New Holl., The Collaert Dynasty (2005–2006), 8 vols., compiled by Ann Diels and Marjolein Leesberg; vols. 1–6 ed. by M. Leesberg and Arnout Balis; vol. 7 ed. by M. Leesberg and Karen L. Bowen; vol. 8 ed. by M. Leesberg.

New Holl. Van Doetecum
New Holl., The Van Doetecum Family (1998), 4 vols., compiled by Henk Nalis, ed. by Ger Luijten and Christiaan Schuckman.

New Holl. Floris
New Holl., Frans Floris (2011), 2 vols., compiled by Edward H. Wouk, ed. by Ger Luijten.

New Holl. Galle
New Holl., Philips Galle (2001), 4 vols., compiled by Manfred Sellink and Marjolein Leesberg, ed. by Manfred Sellink.

New Holl. Goltzius
New Holl., Hendrick Goltzius (2012), 4 vols., compiled by Marjolein Leesberg, ed. by Huigen Leeflang.

New Holl. Heemskerck
New Holl., Maarten van Heemskerck (1994), 2 vols., compiled by Ilja M. Veldman, ed. by Ger Luijten.

New Holl. Hogenberg
New Holl., Remigius and Frans Hogenberg (2009), 3 vols., compiled by Ursula Mielke, ed. by Ger Luijten.

New Holl. De Jode
New Holl., The De Jode Dynasty (2018–2020), 10 vols., compiled by Marjolein Leesberg, ed. by Peter van der Coelen.

New Holl. Liefrinck
New Holl., The Liefrinck Dynasty (2021), 2 vols., compiled by Jeroen Luyckx, ed. by Huigen Leeflang.

New Holl. Muller
New Holl., The Muller Dynasty (1999), 3 vols., vols. 1–2 compiled by Jan Piet Filedt Kok, vol. 3 compiled by Harriet Stroomberg, all vols. ed. by Ger Luijten and Christiaan Schuckman.

New Holl. Stradanus
New Holl., Johannes Stradanus (2008), 3 vols., compiled by Marjolein Leesberg, ed. by Huigen Leeflang.

New Holl. Van Groeningen
New Holl., Gerard van Groeningen (1997), 2 vols., compiled by Christiaan Schuckman, ed. by Ger Luijten.

Nuovo 2013
Nuovo, Angela. *The Book Trade in the Italian Renaissance*, trans. by Lydia G. Cochrane. Leiden-Boston: Brill, 2013.

Olmi 1985
Olmi, Giuseppe. "Science – Honour – Metaphor: Italian Cabinets of the Sixteenth and Seventeench Centuries", in: *The Origins of Museums. The Cabinet of Curiosities in Sixteenth- and Seventeenth-Century Europe*, ed. by O. Impey and A. MacGregor. Oxford: Clarendon Press, 1985, pp. 5–16.

Oltrogge 2009
Oltrogge, Doris. "Illuminating the Print: The Use of Color in Fifteenth-Century Prints and Book Illumination", in: *The Woodcut in Fifteenth-Century Europe*, ed. by Peter Parshall. New Haven and London: Yale University Press, 2009, pp. 299–315 (*Studies in the History of Art*, 75, Center for Advanced Study in the Visual Arts, Symposium Papers LII, held at the National Gallery of Art).

Oxford Dictionary of National Biography 2004
Oxford Dictionary of National Biography, vol. 26, ed. by H. C. G. Matthew and Brian Harrison. Oxford: Oxford University Press, 2004.

Paas 2020
Paas, John Roger. *The Altzenbachs of Cologne: Early Modern German Print Publishers: Popular Prints of the Seventeenth Century*, 2 vols. Wiesbaden: Harrassowitz Verlag, 2020.

Paisey 2006
Paisey, David. "Prints at the Frankfurt Book Fairs; 1568–1600", in: *Print Quarterly*, 23:1 (2006), pp. 54–61.

Pallier 1985
Pallier, Denis. "La firme plantinienne et le marché français pendant la Ligue: les voyages du libraire Théodore Rinsart en France (1591–1596)", in: *Liber amicorum Leon Voet*, ed. by Francine de Nave. Antwerp: Vereeniging der Antwerpsche Bibliophielen, 1985, pp. 117–35 (*De Gulden Passer*, 61–63 (1983–1985).

Pallier 2016
Pallier, Denis. "L'apothicaire Pierre Porret, ami et agent de Plantin", in: *De Gulden Passer* 94:2 (2016), pp. 219–62.

Pallier 2018
Pallier, Denis. "Recherches sur le cercle plantinien en France: amis, appuis, familistes", in: *De Gulden Passer* 96:1 (2018), pp. 7–72.

Parshall 1982
Parshall, Peter. "The Print Collection of Ferdinand, Archduke of Tyrol", in: *Jahrbuch der kunsthistorischen Sammlungen in Wien* 42 (1982), pp. 139–84.

Parshall 1994
Parshall, Peter. "Art and the Theatre of Knowledge: The Origins of Print Collecting in Northern Europe", in: *Harvard Art Museums Bulletin*, Spring 1994, pp. 7–36.

Perez 1981
Perez, Marie-Félicie. "La diffusion en Allemagne des gravures de Jean-Jacques de Boissieu (1736–1810) d'après sa correspondence", in: *Nouvelles de l'Estampes*, no. 57 (May/June 1981), pp. 4–13.

Pérez Fernández and Wilson-Lee 2021
Pérez Fernández, José María, and Edward Wilson-Lee. *Hernando Cólon's New World of Books: Towards a Cartography of Knowledge*. New Haven and London: Yale University Press, 2021.

Pohl 1977
Pohl, Hans. *Die Portugiesen in Antwerpen (1567–1648): zur Geschichte einer Minderheit*. Wiesbaden: Steiner, 1977.

Porteman 1975
Porteman, Karel. "Nieuwe gegevens over de drukgeschiedenis: de bronnen en de auteur van de embleembundel 'Amoris divini et humani antipathia'", in: *Ons Geestelijk Erf*, 49:2 (1975), pp. 193–213.

Préaud et al 1987
Casselle, Pierre, and Marianne Grivel, Corinne Le Bitouzé, and Maxime Préaud. *Dictionnaire des éditeurs d'estampes à Paris sous l'Ancien Régime*. Paris: Promodis, Editions du Cercle de la Librairie, 1987.

Primeau 2002
Primeau, Thomas. "The Materials and Technology of Renaissance and Baroque Hand-Colored Prints", in: *Painted Prints: The Revelation of Color in Northern Renaissance and Baroque Engravings, Etchings, and Woodcuts*, ed. by Susan Dackerman. Baltimore: The Baltimore Museum of Art, 2002, pp. 49–78.

Rekers 1972
Rekers, B. *Benito Arias Montano (1527–1598)*. London: The Warburg Institute, 1972.

Renier 1878
Renier, J.S. *Catalogue de l'oeuvre de Lambert Suavius, graveur liègeois*. Liège: H. Vaillant-Carmanne, 1878.

Renouard 1965
Renouard, Philippe. *Répertoire des imprimeurs parisiens, libraires, fondeurs de caractères et correcteurs d'imprimerie depuis l'introduction de l'imprimerie à Paris, 1470, jusqu'à la fin du seizième siècle*. Paris: M.J. Minard, 1965.

Renouard 1982
Renouard, Philippe. *Imprimeurs & libraires parisiens du XVIe siècle*, fascicule "Breyer". Paris: Bibliothèque nationale de France, 1982.

Renouard 1995
Renouard, Philippe. *Répertoire des imprimeurs parisiens: libraires et fondeurs de caractères en exercice à Paris au 17e siècle: avec tables des adresses, des enseignes et des noms de personnes*. Paris: Jacques Laget, 1995.

Reske 2015
Reske, Christoph. *Die Buchdrucker des 16. und 17. Jahrhunderts im deutschen Sprachgebiet: auf der Grundlage des gleichnamigen Werkes von Josef Benzing*. Revised and expanded edition. Wiesbaden: Harrassowitz Verlag, 2015 (*Beiträge zum Buch- und Bibliothekswesen*, 51).

Riebesell 1989
Riebesell, Christina. *Die Sammlung des Kardinal Alessandro Farnese: ein "Studio" für Künstler und Gelehrte*. Weinheim: VCH, Acta Humaniora, 1989.

Riggs 1972
Riggs, Timothy A. *Hieronymus Cock. Printmaker and Publisher*. Ann Arbor: UMI microfilm, 1972. Also published: New York: Garland, 1977 (*Outstanding Dissertations in the Fine Arts*, 6).

Robben 1993–1994
Robben, Frans. "De boekhandel van Jan Poelman in Salamanca, 1579–1607", in: *De Gulden Passer*, 71–72 (1993–1994).

Robinson 1981
Robinson, William W. "'This Passion for Prints': Collecting and Connoisseurship in Northern Europe during the Seventeenth Century", in: *Printmaking in the Age of Rembrandt*, ed. by Clifford S. Ackley. Boston: Museum of Fine Arts, 1981, pp. xxvii-xlviii.

Rombouts and Van Lerius 1872
Rombouts, P., and T. van Lerius, eds. *De Liggeren en andere historische archieven der Antwerpsche Sint Lucasgilde / Les Liggeren et autres archives historiques de la gilde Anversoise de Saint Luc*, 2 vols. Antwerp: Baggerman, 1872.

Rooses 1878
Rooses, Max, ed. *Boek gehouden door Jan Moretus II als deken der St. Lucasgilde (1616–1617)*. Antwerp: Kockx, 1878 (*Uitgaven der Antwerpsche bibliophilen*, 1).

Rooses 1914
Rooses, Max. *Le Musée Plantin-Moretus. Contenant la vie et l'oeuvre de Christophe Plantin et ses successeurs, les Moretus, ainsi que la description du musée et des collections qu'il renferme*. Antwerp: G. Zazzarini & Co., 1914.

Rott 2002
Rott, Herbert W. *Palazzi di Genova: Architectural Drawings and Engravings*, trans. by Michael Robertson, 2 vols. London and Turnhout: Harvey Miller Publishers, 2002 (*Corpus Rubenianum Ludwig Burchard*, part XXII).

Rouzet 1975
Rouzet, Anne. *Dictionnaire des imprimeurs, libraires et éditeurs des XVe et XVIe siècles dans les limites géographiques de la Belgique actuelle*. Nieuwkoop: De Graaf Publishers, 1975.

Saur 2012
Mielke, Ursula. "Hogenberg", in: *Allgemeines Künstlerlexikon. Die bildenden Künstler aller Zeiten und Völker*, ed. by Andreas Beyer, Bénédicte Savoy, Wolf Tegethoff, vol. 74. Berlin: De Gruyter, 2012, pp. 178–83.

Savage and Stijnman 2015
Savage, Elizabeth, and Ad Stijnman, eds. *Printing Colour 1400–1700: History, Techniques, Functions and Receptions*. Leiden and Boston: Brill, 2015 (*Library of the Written Word*, 41; *The Handpress World*, 32).

Scheicher 1985
Scheicher, Elizabeth. "The Collection of Archduke Ferdinand II at Schloss Ambras: Its Purpose, Composition and Evolution", in: *The Origins of Museums: The Cabinet of Curiosities in Sixteenth- and Seventeenth-Century Europe*, ed. by Oliver Impey and Arthur MacGregor. Oxford: Clarendon Press, 1985 (reprint: 1987), pp. 29–38.

Schmitz 2000
Schmitz, Wolfgang. "Die Kölner Gymnasialbibliothek. Buchbestände und Handschriften aus sechs Jahrhunderten", in: *Bildung stiften. Kölner Gymnasial- und Stiftungsfonds*. Cologne: Kölner Gymnasial- und Stiftungsfonds, 2000, pp. 84–93.

Schnapper 1986
Schnapper, Antoine. "The King of France as Collector in the Seventeenth Century", in: *The Journal of Interdisciplinary History*, 17:1 (Summer 1986), pp. 185–202.

Schneevoogt 1873
Schneevoogt, C.G. Voorhelm. *Catalogue des estampes gravées d'après P. P. Rubens*. Haarlem: Les Héritiers Loosjes, 1873.

Schöller 1992
Schöller, Bernadette. *Kölner Druckgraphik der Gegenreformation. Ein Beitrag zur Geschichte religiöser Bildpropaganda zur Zeit der Glaubenskämpfe mit einem Katalog der Einblattdrucke des Verlages Johann Bussemacher*. Cologne: Kölnisches Stadtmuseum, 1992 (*Veröffentlichungen des kölnischen Stadtmuseums*, 9).

Schöller 1999
Schöller, Bernadette. "Der Kölner Graphikmarkt um 1600. Der Warenkorb des Arnoldus Buchelius", in: *Coellen eyn Croyn. Renaissance und Barock in Köln*, ed. by Werner Schäfke. Cologne: DuMont, 1999, pp. 379–91 (*Der Riss im Himmel. Clemens August und seine Epoche*, 1).

Scholliers 1976
Scholliers, Etienne. "De lagere klassen: een kwantitatieve benadering van levenswijze", in: *Antwerpen in de XVIde eeuw*. Antwerp: Genootschap voor Antwerpse Geschiedenis, 1976, pp. 161–80. Published in French as: "Le pouvoir d'achat dans les Pays-Bas au 16me siècle", in: *Album aangeboden aan Charles Verlinden ter gelegenheid van zijn dertig jaar professoraat. Album offert à Charles Verlinden à l'occasion de ses trente ans de professorat*. Ghent: Rijksuniversiteit, 1975 (*Studia historica Gandensia*, no. 192), pp. 305–30.

Scholliers 1989
Scholliers, Etienne. "Peilingen naar de conjunctuur en de koopkracht", in: *Antwerpen in de XVIIde eeuw*. Antwerp: Genootschap voor Antwerpse Geschiedenis, 1989, pp. 153–67.

Schwaighofer 2010
Schwaighofer, Claudia-Alexandra. "Die druckgraphische Sammlung des ehemaligen Kölner Jesuitenkollegs", in: *Druckgraphik. Zwischen Reproduktion und Invention*, ed. by Markus A. Castor et. al. Munich and Berlin: Deutscher Kunstverlag, 2010, pp. 393–402.

Seelig 1985
Seelig, Lorenz. "The Munich 'Kunstkammer', 1565–1807", in: *The Origins of Museums. The Cabinet of Curiosities in Sixteenth- and Seventeenth-Century Europe*, ed. by O. Impey and A. MacGregor. Oxford: Clarendon Press, 1985 (reprint: 1987), pp. 76–89.

Sellink 1997
Sellink, Manfred. *Philips Galle (1537–1612), Engraver and Print Publisher in Haarlem and Antwerp*, 3 vols., doctoral dissertation for the Vrije Universiteit of Amsterdam. Amsterdam, 1997.

Sénéchal 1990
Sénéchal, Philippe. "Justus Sadeler Print Publisher and Art Dealer in Early Seicento Venice", in: *Print Quarterly*, 7:1 (March 1990), pp. 22–35.

Simiolus 2017
Simiolus: Netherlands quarterly for the history of art, 39: 3 (2017): *Six studies on Hieronymus Cock and his print publishing business*.

Spengler 2003
Spengler, Dietmar. *Spiritualia et pictura. Die Graphische Sammlung des ehemaligen Jesuitenkollegs in Köln. Die Druckgraphik*. Cologne: SH-Verlag, 2003.

Stoesser 2018
Stoesser, Alison. *Van Dyck's Hosts in Genoa: Lucas and Cornelis de Wael's Lives, Business Activities and Works*, 2 vols. Turnhout: Brepols, 2018 (*Pictura Nova: Studies in 16th- and 17th-Century Flemish Painting and Drawing*, 19).

Stols 1971
Stols, Eddy. *De Spaanse Brabanders, of: De handelsbetrekkingen der Zuidelijke Nederlanden met de Iberische wereld, 1598–1648*, 2 vols. Brussels: Paleis der Academiën, 1971 (*Verhandelingen van de Koninklijke Vlaamse Academie voor Wetenschappen, Letteren en Schone Kunsten van België. Klasse der Letteren*, 70).

Thijs 1985
Thijs, Alfons K.L. "Notities voor een studie van de Antwerpse 17de-eeuwse *suffragia*", in: *Liber amicorum Leon Voet*, ed. by Francine de Nave. Antwerp: Vereeniging der Antwerpsche Bibliophielen, 1985, pp. 561–93 (*De Gulden Passer*, 1983–1985).

Thijs 1993
Thijs, Alfons K.L. *Antwerpen, internationaal uitgeverscentrum van devotieprenten, 17de-18de eeuw*. Leuven: Peeters, 1993 (*Miscellanea Neerlandica*, 7).

Tuin 2017
Tuin, B.P. "Hieronymus Cock's Volck: her family, wealth and anxieties", in: *Simiolus: Netherlands quarterly for the history of art*, 39:3 (2017), pp. 141–60.

Van den Broecke, Van der Krogt, and Meurer 1998
Van den Broecke, Marcel, and Peter Van der Krogt and Peter Meurer, eds. *Abraham Ortelius and the First Atlas. Essays Commemorating the Quadricentennial of his Death, 1598–1998*. 't Goy-Houten: Hes Publishers, 1998.

Vanden Bussche 1880
Vanden Bussche, Emile. "Un évêque bibliophile: notes sur la bibliothèque et le cabinet des gravures de Charles Vanden Bosch, neuvième évêque de Bruges; ses relations avec Elséviers, Meyssens, etc.", in: *La Flandre: revue des monuments d'histoire et d'antiquités*, Bruges, 1880, pp. 345–63.

Van den Oord 1984
Van den Oord, Cornelis J.A. *Twee eeuwen Bosch' boekbedrijf 1450–1650. Een onderzoek naar de betekenis van Bossche boekdrukkers, uitgevers en librariërs voor het regionale socio-culturele leven*. Tilburg: Stichting Zuidelijk historisch contact, 1984.

Van der Coelen and Leesberg 2021
Van der Coelen, Peter, and Marjolein Leesberg. "The De Jode Dynasty: additions to the work of Gerard de Jode, Pieter de Jode I, and Pieter de Jode II," in: *Delineavit et Sculpsit* 49 (2021), pp. 36–57.

Van der Krogt 2010
Van der Krogt, Peter. *Koeman's Atlantes Neerlandici, New Edition*, vol. IV-1. Houten: Hes & de Graaf, 2010.

Van der Stock 1998
Van der Stock, Jan. *Printing Images in Antwerp. The Introduction of Printmaking in a City: Fifteenth Century to 1585*, trans. by Beverley Jackson. Rotterdam: Sound and Vision Interactive, 1998.

Van der Straelen 1858
Van der Straelen, J.-B. *Geslagt-lyste der nakomelingen van den vermaerden Christoffel Plantin, koninklyken aerts-boekdrukker, binnen de stad Antwerpen; waer by gevoegd is eene geslagt-lyste der familie Mourentorff alias Moretus*. Antwerp: P.E. Janssens, 1858.

Van der Waals 1984
Van der Waals, Jan. "The Print Collection of Samuel Pepys", in: *Print Quarterly*, 1:4 (1984), pp. 236–57.

Van de Velde 1996
Van de Velde, Carl. "Veen, van, Otto", in: *The Dictionary of Art*, vol. 32, ed. by Jane Turner. London: Macmillan Publishers Limited, and New York: Grove Dictionaries Inc., 1996, pp. 114–16.

Vandewalle 1984
Vandewalle, Paul. *Oude maten, gewichten en muntstelsels in Vlaanderen, Brabant en Limburg*. Ghent: Belgisch Centrum voor Landelijke Geschiedenis, 1984.

Van Ginhoven 2017
Van Ginhoven, Sandra. *Connecting Art Markets: Guilliam Forchondt's Dealership in Antwerp (c.1632–78) and the Overseas Paintings Trade*. Leiden: Brill, 2017 (*Studies in the History of Collecting and Art Markets*, 1).

Van Hout 2004
Van Hout, Nico. *Rubens et l'art de la gravure*. Catalogue for the exhibition held at the Koninklijk Museum voor Schone Kunsten, Antwerp, 12 June-12 September 2004 and Musée national des beaux-arts du Québec, Quebec City, 14 October 2004–9 January 2005. Ghent: Ludion, 2004.

Van Lerius 1880
Van Lerius, Théodore. *Biographies d'artistes Anversois*, vol. 1. Antwerp: P. Kockx, 1880 (*Uitgaven der Antwerpsche bibliophilen*, 8).

Van Roey 1967
Van Roey, J. "Een Antwerpse schilderdynastie: de Liesaerts (XVIe-XVIIe eeuw)", in: *Jaarboek van het Koninklijk Museum voor Schone Kunsten Antwerpen*, 1967, pp. 83–116.

Van Selm 1987
Van Selm, Bert. *'Een menighte treffelijcke Boecken'. Nederlandse boekhandelscatalogi in het begin van de zeventiende eeuw*. Utrecht: Hes, 1987.

Veldman 1993
Veldman, Ilja M. "Keulen als toevluchtsoord voor Nederlandse kunstenaars (1567–1612)", in: *Oud Holland*, 107 (1993), pp. 34–58.

Veldman 2001a
Veldman, Ilja M. *Profit and Pleasure Print Books by Crispijn de Passe*, trans by Michael Hoyle. Rotterdam: Sound & Vision Publishers, 2001 (*Studies in Prints and Printmaking*, vol 4).

Veldman 2001b
Veldman, Ilja M. "Crispijn de Passe: his books and prints for the English market", in: *The Bookshop of the World. The role of the Low Countries in the book-trade 1473–1941*, ed. by Lotte Hellinga, Alastair Duke, Jacob Harskamp, and Theo Hermans. 't Goy-Houten: Hes & De Graaf, 2001, pp. 159–68.

Verheggen 2006
Verheggen, Evelyne M.F. *Beelden voor passie en hartstocht: bid- en devotieprenten in de Noordelijke Nederlanden, 17de en 18de eeuw*. Zutphen: Walburg Pers, 2006.

Verheggen 2024
Verheggen, Evelyne M.F. "Te versnijden devotieprenten in Keulen, Antwerpen en de Noord-Nederlandse Republiek, 1600–1800 – Een eerste verkenning", in: *Delineavit et Sculpsit* 54 (June 2024), pp. 15–38.

Verlinden 1959–1973
Verlinden, C. et al. *Dokumenten voor de geschiedenis van de prijzen en lonen in Vlaanderen en Brabant (XVe–XVIIIe eeuw). Documents pour l'histoire des prix et des salaires en Flandre et en Brabant (XVe–XVIIIe siècle)*. 4 vols. Bruges: "De Tempel", 1959–1973.

Vermeylen 2003
Vermeylen, Filip. *Painting for the Market: Commercialization of Art in Antwerp's Golden Age*. Turnhout: Brepols, 2003 (*Studies in Urban History (1100–1800)*, 2).

Veyrin-Forrer 1982
Veyrin-Forrer, Jeanne. "Fabriquer un livre au XVIe siècle", in: *Histoire de l'édition française, I: Le livre conquérant. Du Moyen Age au milieu du XVIIe siècle*, ed. by Henri-Jean Martin and Roger Chartier. Paris: Promodis, 1982, pp. 279–301.

Vignau-Wilberg 2005
Vignau-Wilberg, Thea. *In Europa zu Hause – Niederländer in München um 1600 / Citizens of Europe: Dutch and Flemish Artists in Munich c. 1600*. Catalogue for the exhibition held at the Staatlichen Graphischen Sammlung München, Neue Pinakothek, Munich, 12 October 2005–8 January 2006. Munich: Hirmer Verlag, 2005.

Vlieghe 1996
Vlieghe Hans. "Rubens, Peter Paul", in: *The Dictionary of Art*, vol. 27, ed. by Jane Turner. London: Macmillan Publishers Limited, and New York: Grove Dictionaries Inc., 1996, pp. 287–303.

Voet, GC
Voet, Leon. *The Golden Compasses. The History of the House of Plantin-Moretus*, 2 vols. Amsterdam: Vangendt & Co., London: Routledge & Kegan Paul, and New York: Abner Schram, 1969 and 1972.

Voet, PP
Voet, Leon. *The Plantin Press (1555–1589). A Bibliography of the Works Printed and Published by Christopher Plantin at Antwerp and Leiden*, 6 vols. Amsterdam: Van Hoeve, 1980–1983.

Wagner 2019
Wagner, Berit. "Flämische Kunst für deutsche Sammlungen: Cornelis Caymox d.Ä. (gest. 1588) und andere *schildervercoopere* im Frankfurter Kunsthandel", in: Kirch, Münch, and Stewart, 2019, pp. 104–27.

Willaert and Derde 1994
Willaert, Saskia and Katrien Derde. "Het mecenaat van de Genuese natie in Antwerpen in de tweede helft van de 16de eeuw", in: *Orlandus Lassus en Antwerpen, 1554–1556*. Catalogue for the exhibition held at the Museum Vleeshuis, Antwerp, 20 August–27 November 1994. Antwerp, 1994, pp. 47–56.

Witcombe 2008
Witcombe, Christopher L.C.E. *Print Publishing in Sixteenth-Century Rome: Growth and Expansion, Rivalry and Murder*. Turnhout: Brepols, and London: Harvey Miller Publishers, 2008.

Wouk 2015–2016
Wouk, Edward. "Antoine Perrenot de Granvelle, the Quatre Vents Press, and the patronage of Prints in Early Modern Europe", in: *Simiolus: Netherlands quarterly for the history of art*, 38 (2015–2016), pp. 31–61.

Wuestman 1998
Wuestman, Gerdien. "Prijzen van Rubensgrafiek in de zeventiende eeuw", in: *Delineavit et Sculpsit*, 19 (1998), pp. 1–7.

Wyffels 1959
Wyffels, A. "Maten en gewichten / Poids et mesures employés", in: Verlinden 1959–1973, vol. 1, pp. 1–15.

Zülch 1935
Zülch, Walther Karl. *Frankfurter Künstler: 1223–1700*. Frankfurt am Main: Diesterweg, 1935.

INDEX

References to page numbers are followed by, when appropriate, references to specific catalogue entries in Appendix 1 and then illustrations, preceded by "fig." See also the list of buyers in Appendix 2 and the titles of specific prints described in Appendix 1, listed here under their respective print publishers.